# Introducing
# Contemporary
# ECONOMICS

## Discover the Perfect Blend of Text and Technology

## New Text. Proven History.

- Written by an award-winning teacher, economist, and author with more than 30 years of experience

- Backed by South-Western's leadership in business and economics publishing

- Shaped by an advisory board of high school teachers

William A. McEachern was born in Portsmouth, NH, earned an undergraduate degree in the honors program from College of the Holy Cross, served three years as an Army officer, and earned an M.A. and Ph.D. in economics from the University of Virginia. He began teaching economic principles at the University of Connecticut in 1973. In 1980 he started offering teaching workshops around the country and, in 1990, created *The Teaching Economist*, a newsletter that focuses on making teaching more effective and more fun.

Professor McEachern has advised federal, state, and local governments on policy matters and has appeared in media such as the *New York Times, London Times, Wall Street Journal, Christian Science Monitor, Boston Globe, USA Today*, CBS Market-Watch.com, Voice of America, *Now with Bill Moyers*, and *Reader's Digest*.

## ▶ about South-Western

**Developing Lifelong Learning Solutions for All Students**

South-Western—a Thomson business—is the leading provider of business and economics learning materials worldwide. We offer the most extensive selection in business educational materials for the K–12, higher education, corporate, and professional markets. With innovative tools and resources that engage and enhance learning, South-Western leads the way to business success. Our rich spectrum of textbooks, simulations, online courses, web sites, and software products offers the best possible learning solutions that lead students to real careers and lifetime skills.

## from the Author

Hello, Colleagues,

Because there can be no real learning without student interest, my first priority in writing **Contemporary Economics** is to generate interest. How do I know what interests students? Decades of experience in the classroom have helped me figure out what works and what doesn't.

My approach in **Contemporary Economics** is to remind students how much they already know since they make economic decisions every day. Never has there been a better time to learn economic principles. As the world grows more competitive, your students need the market advantage that economic insight provides.

I use timely, relevant examples to stimulate student interest. My examples build bridges from what students know to what they need to learn—moving from the familiar to the new. Examples should be self-explanatory, conveying their meaning quickly and directly. Having to explain an example is like having to explain a joke. The point gets lost.

Interest also flows from variety—variety in the way material is presented. My explanations of economic theory, economic events, and economic institutions include not only examples but also anecdotes, analogies, parables, case studies, facts, statistics, photographs, web links, questions, graphs, exercises, and other vehicles that keep the presentation fresh and lively.

I show students how economic theory helps them understand a changing world. But the intuition behind the theory is introduced as something familiar, often reflected by common expressions. For example, the idea of diminishing marginal utility is captured by the expression "Been there. Done that."

Nor am I afraid to use graphs, but I use them judiciously. A graph should make things clearer, not become an obstacle to teaching and learning. Some textbooks use graphs the way a drunk uses a lamppost—more for support than for illumination.

I believe I can help you help your students learn more economics. I am new enough to the task to keep it fresh but experienced enough to get it right.

— **Will McEachern**

# TODAY'S TEACHING TOOLS

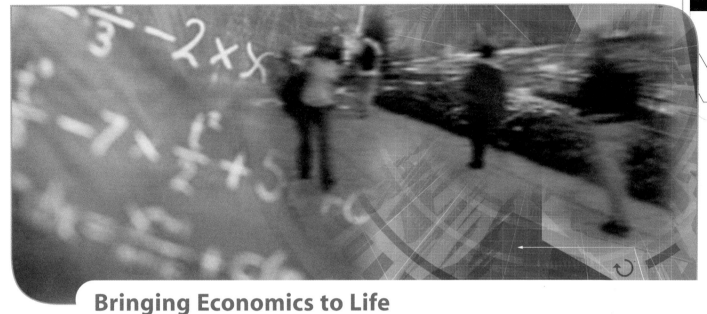

## Bringing Economics to Life

***Contemporary Economics***, a brand new text from South-Western, blends comprehensive economic content, sound instructional design, and extensive print and media teaching tools into the perfect combination of text and technology.

Students become involved in the classroom and the real world where supply and demand, capital and labor, and business and government have meaning. They discover how economic principles relate to their personal lives and the world around them, from the local movie theater to current international events.

Rich, practical examples make concepts clear and intriguing as author Will McEachern starts where students are and makes the connections with concrete illustrations. Each lesson is concise and appropriately paced for maximum learning.

A blend of economic expertise and educational insight helps students move from the basics to demand, supply, market equilibrium, decision making, market institutions, the national economy, government's role, public policy, and the international economy.

The book repeatedly covers all 20 of the NCEE Voluntary National Content Standards in Economics, with clear icons that identify these points for your convenience.

Students learn by experiencing economics, using integrated online learning resources that provide flexibility for various learning styles and links to current events.

> *Exceptional text! Very good use of events from the real world, which will engage students.*
>
> — *Jim Ragusa, Florida*

## Meeting Tomorrow's Challenges

A minute before the bell sounds, Sam slips into his desk, his mind still on his most recent cell call, the e-mail he needs to send, this afternoon's basketball game, and his upcoming job interview at the local computer store. He's a typical Generation Y student: tech-savvy, socially aware, surrounded by media pressures and limited time.

These are students looking for the practical, the immediate results, the relationships between the classroom and the world beyond. It's a new generation of education and teaching tools must reflect those changes.

Today's high school economics teachers deserve the tools to stay ahead. ***Contemporary Economics*** is ready to deliver, with a blend of practical text and applicable technology like no other product on the market today.

# The Power of Choice

## Using Supplements to Their Full Potential

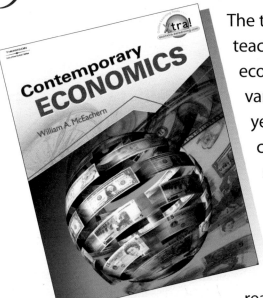

The tools you need to teach an effective economics class can vary from year to year, classroom to classroom, even student to student. With ***Contemporary Economics***, it's all there and ready for you. A wealth of student and teacher materials offer built-in flexibility and choice. Print, video, and electronic media make it easier to address varied learning styles, use formal and informal assessment, and integrate technology where it makes sense to you.

### Student Text
*ISBN 0-538-43700-6*
Get students involved in the classroom and the real world where supply and demand, capital and labor, and business and government have meaning. Rich examples, intriguing real world features, and solid economic insights demonstrate how economic principles relate to the world.

### Wraparound Teacher's Edition
*ISBN 0-538-43701-4*
Reduced student pages are surrounded with comprehensive teaching tools in the margins to help you create a dynamic learning environment with minimal preparation. Solutions, background info, and projects address different learning styles and abilities.

- **Complete Lesson Plans** are based on the teach, apply, assess, enrich, reteach, and close model to lead students from learning to applying to mastering the material.
- **Teaching Notes and Answers** are in the margins, at point of use.
- **Outside Resources** help connect content to current events.
- **Enrichment Activities** offer options for students who have mastered the basics.
- **Economic Headlines** demonstrate how to use current events to emphasize economic concepts in the world today.
- **Curriculum Connections** offer suggestions for integrating economics with geography, government, history, performing arts, literature, math, science, writing, and others.
- **Reteach** helps students needing additional assistance with lesson content.
- **Pacing Guide** helps you determine how long you'll need for each lesson.
- **Look Beyond the Classroom** provides suggestions for using community resources to enhance learning.

## Instructor's Resource CD
*ISBN 0-538-43702-2*
Discover a large selection of lesson plans in Word format, teaching materials, activity masters, projects, communication and ethics masters, Spanish resources, presentation software, and reference materials.

- The CD also offers electronic versions of the Teacher's Solutions Booklets for ready access to workbook and test answers.
- PowerPoint slides for every lesson are included.
- Six educational topics in a series of professional development titles are available electronically and include: Alternative Assessment, Diverse Population and Learning Styles, Using Technology and the Internet, Test Preparation and Study Skills, Strategies for Block Scheduling, and Involving Parents and the Community.

## Workbook
*ISBN 0-538-43703-0*
When students need additional review, this workbook provides a pen and paper method for classroom preparation or review.

## ExamView CD
*ISBN 0-538-43706-5*
Make testing a snap with this electronic testing method that allows you to edit, customize, and quickly evaluate professionally written tests.

## Chapter and Unit Tests
*ISBN 0-538-43704-9*
Printed chapter tests, unit tests, and a final exam are ready for classroom use.

## *Contemporary Economics* Video
*ISBN 0-538-43705-7*

## Xtra! Web Site
This free web site provides a wealth of online learning tools designed to help students experience economics using media, interactive technology, guided research, current events links, and graphing. A special instructor's section offers additional teaching and research tools to connect your classroom to current events. Visit econxtra.swlearning.com today.

## Teacher's Resource Box
*ISBN 0-538-43965-3*
Find all of the teaching materials and solutions in one handy location! The box includes:

- Teacher's Edition of the Workbook
- Teacher's Edition of Chapter and Unit Tests
- Activities and Projects Masters
- Lesson Plans
- Personal Finance Guide
- Communications and Ethics Activity Masters
- Social Studies Skills Review
- Reading Comprehension Booklet
- Spanish Resources
- Professional Development Materials: Alternative Assessment, Diverse Population and Learning Styles, Using Technology and the Internet, Test Preparation and Study Skills, Strategies for Block Scheduling, and Involving Parents and the Community
- Sampler with Demo CD

## Contemporary Economics

| | | | | |
|---|---|---|---|---|
| Student Text | 0-538-43700-6 | | Chapter and Unit Tests | 0-538-43704-9 |
| Wraparound Teacher's Edition | 0-538-43701-4 | | *Contemporary Economics* Video | 0-538-43705-7 |
| Instructor's Resource CD | 0-538-43702-2 | | Xtra! Web Site | econxtra.swlearning.com |
| Workbook | 0-538-43703-0 | | Teacher's Resource Box | 0-538-43965-3 |
| ExamView CD | 0-538-43706-5 | | | |

# Contemporary ECONOMICS

**Movers & Shakers** Students are introduced to individuals who have made significant impacts on economics with their entrepreneurial ideas.

**Sharpen Your Life Skills** Students learn skills, such as interpreting graphs, that demonstrate and reinforce their knowledge of economics. These skills are critical for standardized or proficiency tests.

**Team Work** offers in-class collaborative activities—students work in small groups while developing economic knowledge.

**In the News** links economic principles to current events.

**Reading It Right** examines excerpts from *The Wall Street Journal* to bring periodicals into the classroom.

**Ethics in Action** takes a close look at actual economic questions and encourages student input.

**Point Your Browser** highlights additional resources available on the web.

**Connect to History** This historical viewpoint explores how economic principles relate to American history for a strong cross-curricular emphasis.

**E-conomics** focuses on e-commerce with critical-thinking—challenges that question the economic principles at work.

**NETBookmark** encourages students to use the Internet for research. Xtra! Web Site provides a safe portal for students to gather real data for analysis.

**Investigate Your Local Economy** Students learn through concrete examples drawn from their local communities.

**Span the Globe** brings an international focus to economic principles as students look at global interactions and their impact on local, regional, and national economies.

**Chapter Opening Objectives** and **Key Terms** in the margin and glossary help improve student comprehension and clarify the economics vocabulary.

**Comprehensive Assessment** at the end of each lesson and at the end of each chapter help students evaluate their understanding of the principles presented.

- **Checkpoints** throughout the chapter provide opportunities for informal evaluations of learning.

- **Thinking Critically** links economics to other subjects such as government, math, history, or English.

- **Graphing Exercises**, **Key Concepts**, and **Online Study Tools** for every lesson are available on the Xtra! Web Site.

**Investing in Your Future** This ongoing unit project follows an entrepreneur from her high school years through adulthood, allowing students to analyze information and develop decision-making, research, and presentation skills along the way.

Today's teaching tools must be as diverse as today's students.
Flexible, ever ready to respond. Practical minded and intriguing.

# The Tip Sheet

## Delivering Lectures with Lasting Impressions

**By William A. McEachern**
Excerpt/edited from *The Teaching Economist, Issue 24,* Fall 2003

Active learning is timely and promising, but most teachers still find themselves lecturing much of the time. Here are a few tips to maximize the impact of lectures:

- **Provide an outline or handout** to show students the structure of the day's class. Students do better when they know where they are going. Leave enough room for students to take notes.

- **Write important material** on the blackboard, overhead, or medium you prefer. Say it and repeat it as you write, then say it again. (Repetition is the mother of mastery.)

- **Show students how** to construct graphs, labeling the axes. Students see a finished graph, but they don't know how to build it and can't on tests.

- **Pace your presentation**, so students can absorb and process information. Short breaks for students to summarize main ideas from the previous 15 minutes help.

- **Avoid information overload** with transparencies, slides, or other medium.

- **Tell students what tests will be like** and what you expect from them. Don't make it a scavenger hunt.

Some of these suggestions may seem obvious, but remember that success is a study of the obvious. Try a few and develop your own lectures with a lasting punch impact.

# How to Order

### Get the Perfect Blend of Text and Technology Tools

> **Call 800.354.9706**
> **Click econxtra.swlearning.com**

| | |
|---|---|
| Student Text | 0-538-43700-6 |
| Wraparound Teacher's Edition | 0-538-43701-4 |
| Instructor's Resource CD | 0-538-43702-2 |
| Workbook | 0-538-43703-0 |
| ExamView CD | 0-538-43706-5 |
| Chapter and Unit Tests | 0-538-43704-9 |
| *Contemporary Economics* Video | 0-538-43705-7 |
| Xtra! Web Site | econxtra.swlearning.com |
| Teacher's Resource Box | 0-538-43965-3 |

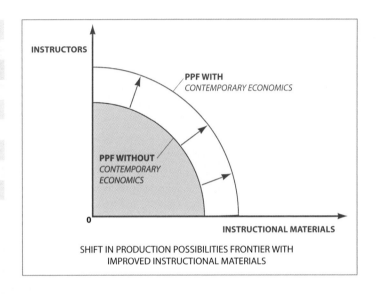

SHIFT IN PRODUCTION POSSIBILITIES FRONTIER WITH
IMPROVED INSTRUCTIONAL MATERIALS

# Also Available

## *Everyday Knowledge Everyone Needs*

More than ever before, students need practical skills to prosper in the financial world. *Banking and Financial Systems* provides an excellent text and media solution with everyday relevance for high school students. Practical activities reinforce math and language skills. It's the perfect supplement for the high school economics course. This full-color text bridges the gap from the classroom to the real world with hands-on activities and creative special features that enhance learning.

### *Banking and Financial Systems*

By Center for Financial Training
0-538-43241-1    $27

## *Real Life 101*

Students don't have to learn the hard way! *On Your Own: A Personal Budgeting Simulation* is a learn-by-doing simulation with serious financial literacy results. Students actually prepare budgets, create filing systems, learn comparative purchasing skills, and prepare for unexpected financial events. This all-in-one simulation teaches more in 20 hours than most programs teach in a semester. Definitely find a spot for this in your economics classroom!

### *On Your Own: A Personal Budgeting Simulation*

By Mary Queen Donnelly
0-538-43680-8    $25

# Contemporary ECONOMICS
# It All Clicks!

econxtra.swlearning.com

## The Fusion of Text and Technology

Ten years ago we laughed as six- and seven-year-olds outdistanced parents in programming the VCR or fixing computer glitches. Today these techno-savvy students are filling our classrooms. How do we meet their unique learning needs?

Technology is second-nature to this growing generation, immersed in our tech-driven society. To underutilize this avenue of education is to miss a great opportunity to connect.

But technology can be cumbersome if not integrated and purposeful. Technology tools must not be add-ons but an integrated part of the learning process to truly enhance educational success. The comprehensive *Contemporary Economics* package is a perfect blend of text and technology designed to help students learn by experiencing economics.

## Supplement Your Class with Power
### The Technology-Driven Differentiators

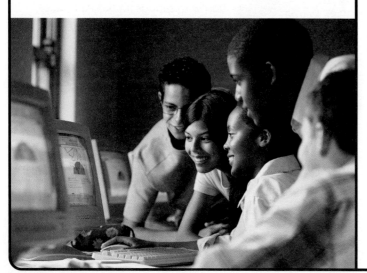

> ### Xtra! Web Site
> Tap into a wealth of online learning tools to help students experience economics using media, interactive technology, videos, guided research, current events links, and graphing tools. A special teacher's section offers additional teaching and research tools to connect your classroom to current events. Visit econxtra.swlearning.com today!

> ### Instructor's Resource CD
> Discover a large selection of lesson plans in Word format, teaching materials, activity masters, projects, communication and ethics masters, Spanish resources, lesson-by-lesson PowerPoint presentations, and reference materials.

> ### ExamView CD
> Make testing a snap with this electronic testing method that allows you to edit, customize, and quickly evaluate professionally written tests.

The free *Contemporary Economics* **Xtra! Web Site** contains a wealth of online learning tools designed to help students experience economics using media, interactive technology, guided research, and current events links. Students enrich their learning experience as they review, assess, analyze data, use primary documents, and develop economic graphing skills.

A separate, password-protected Teacher's Site contains all student activities, plus teacher's support materials. Teachers can also access *The Teaching Economist*, an online newsletter written by author William A. McEachern.

**The site is organized by chapter and activity for easy navigation and access to online resources and study tools.**

**The Graphing Workshop** includes *animated tutorials* that guide students through explanations of the economic concepts behind the graphs. Students then prepare their own graphs using *GraphIt*.

**This series of videos** feature an economist answering frequently asked economic questions. Economic concepts are presented to appeal to the visual and auditory learner.

**Xtra! STUDY TOOLS**

**Study Tools** provide interactive game-like reviews for every lesson, such as *Beat the Clock, Sort It Out, Scenario, First Things First*, and more.

**Xtra! Quiz Prep** provides students with online chapter review and immediate feedback to assess understanding.

**E-con @pps** offer a library of news summaries, policy debates, data, and links to economics web sites. Online resources deepen student understanding through hands-on exploration and analysis of the latest economic news stories, policy debates, and data.

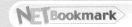

**Net Bookmark** encourages students to use the Internet for research by providing current web links for textbook activities.

# Does the Net Offer the Key to Hooking Students?

### Finding Common Ground on the Internet

Through timely examples teachers make teaching more relevant to students. But connecting with students is easier said than done. For example, we may reference current events, but what if students don't pay attention to current events? According to Peter Francese, founder of *American Demographics Magazine,* newspaper readership among young adults has dropped more than half in the last 15 years. Young people also watch less TV news than they used to. So how do you find common ground?

### Online Diaries Provide Insight into Today's Students

The Internet offers a promising tool. Online journals, or diaries, present daily snapshots of what young people think about their worries, hopes, relationships, studies, jobs, and the other stuff in their lives. Now, tens of thousands of online diaries exist.

As a start, find the member directory at www.diaryland.com and sample some entries. By searching through the profile of diarists, you can see what students write about day to day. You can learn about favorite authors (Stephen King, J.K. Rowling, and Anne Rice are the top three); favorite music (Linkin Park, Incubus, and Weezer); and favorite movies (Fight Club, The Matrix, and American Beauty). Online diarists are not necessarily representative of the population as a whole, but their ideas may help close the generation gap.

### Weblog: Your Connection to Culture of the Times

Another Internet development, the Weblog, offers an additional way to keep up with the zeitgeist, or culture of the times. A Weblog, or "blog" for short, is a site that usually provides the writer's daily observations along with constantly updated links to other sites, often with terse, sometimes sarcastic, commentary about the linked site. This guided tour of the Web frequently includes links to other blogs. Today, there are tens of thousands of blogs. Some are general; others deal with specific topics, such as politics or economics.

How can teachers use blogs to capture the pulse of the day? Find links to the more recently updated blogs at www.weblogs.com (the blogs monitored by this site are updated at a rate of about 300 per hour). After a major economic event, you can quickly see what, if anything, bloggers have to say about it.

> *We need teaching tools that help us better educate and keep us with the changing times…. **Contemporary Economics** delivers.*
>
> *– Brenda Grannan, Ohio*

# Standards Are the Foundation of Excellence

By Doug Haskell, Associate Director
Economic Center for Education & Research
University of Cincinnati

If I had to put together a high school economics course syllabus that would be usable in a large number of states and include the most critical concepts for basic economic literacy, finding a starting point would not be difficult. I would simply reach for a copy of the "Voluntary National Content Standards in Economics." The standards have become a very powerful influence on educators, curriculum directors, and textbook writers around the country. When South-Western asked me for advice about developing a new high school economics program, my first suggestion was to be as consistent with the standards as possible.

## Developing the Standards

In December of 1994, I was asked to speak at the annual meeting of the Board of Trustees of the National Council on Economic Education (NCEE). It was at this meeting that a representative confirmed that the U.S. Department of Education was recommending the funding of standards in economics as part of implementation of the *Goals 2000: Educate America Act*. Economic education supporters were elated. The work NCEE had done over the previous twenty years to develop and refine "A Framework for Teaching Basic Economic Concepts" would now have even more impact on the teaching of economics in the nation's schools.

Despite the rocky road the standards movement has taken, this document has risen to the top. National standards were authorized and written in arts, civics, history, and geography. Privately initiated projects had prepared standards documents in mathematics, social studies, physical education, and health. Criticism of the history standards, from a variety of groups, galvanized an anti-standards movement. Imagine trying to please every interest group and region with just a few examples of leaders and important events in each era. By comparison, the economic standards have received relatively little criticism.

This might have been the end of the story, had the leading economics organizations not believed so strongly in the need for national standards. A coalition, consisting of the National Council, the Foundation for Teaching Economics (FTE), the National Association of Economic Educators (NAEE), and the American Economic Association Committee on Economic Education, produced the "Voluntary Standards." The standards are "voluntary" because they do not have the force of law. There is no Department of Education mandate or strong incentive to use the standards. What exists is a widespread acceptance of these standards as the guidelines of what should be taught in grades K-12. I don't know of any state standards that are not already aligned or soon to be aligned with the national standards

## The National Standards and NAEP

The voluntary standards will get even more attention as they are essentially the content of the economics assessment on the National Assessment of Educational Progress (NAEP), to be administered for the first time in 2006. The NAEP economics exam is being developed by the American Institute for Research (AIR) and Educational Testing Service (ETS), with input from NCEE and other groups. The NAEP economics framework is essentially the voluntary standards with just a few minor changes.

## Instructor Support from the Centers for Economic Education

How will the states and schools work to be consistent with the standards and meet the challenge of the first NAEP assessment in 2006? That's where NCEE and its network of State Councils and Centers for Economic Education will play a critical role. The Centers will work directly with state standards committees, assist curriculum developers, and provide professional development for teachers. The economists and educators from the Centers will be well versed in the standards and familiar with the variety of resources available to schools. Center staff

> *South-Western's comprehensive coverage of the national standards is combined with many other great qualities of the package: web-based resources, history connections, activities and projects, personal finance topics, video, technology-based teaching tools, and much more.*

members from around the country participated in the process of developing the NAEP questions. In many cases, school districts and teachers can ask the Center professionals for their advice about content and textbooks.

### Contemporary Economics

It was critical to me that South-Western's *Contemporary Economics* be consistent with both the voluntary standards and the economic content covered by the NAEP assessment. Coverage of the standards will be the number one criterion for many high school economics textbook selection committees. South-Western's comprehensive coverage of the national standards is combined with many other great qualities of the package: web-based resources, history connections, activities and projects, personal finance topics, video, technology-based teaching tools, and much more.

### Web Resources

For more information about the standards, visit these sites:

National Council on Economic Education, "Welcome to NCEE Online."
www.ncee.net

National Center for Education Statistics, "The Nations Report Card" (NAEP Homepage).
nces.ed.gov/nationsreportcard/sitemap.asp

National Assessment Governing Board, "2006 National Assessment of Economics Progress in Economics, Assessment Framework."
www.nagb.org/pubs/econ_fw_06.pdf

## About NCEE

**NCEE**

National Council on Economic Education

The National Council on Economic Education (NCEE) is a nationwide network that leads in promoting economic literacy with students and their teachers. NCEE's mission is to help students develop the real-life skills they need to succeed: to be able to think and choose responsibly as consumers, savers, investors, citizens, members of the workforce, and effective participants in a global economy.

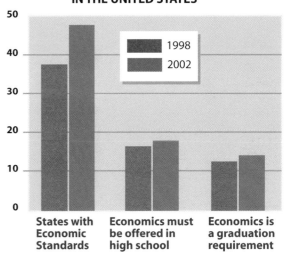

**STATE STANDARDS FOR ECONOMIC EDUCATION IN THE UNITED STATES**

Legend: 1998, 2002

Categories: States with Economic Standards; Economics must be offered in high school; Economics is a graduation requirement

## Charts and Figures

# Shifts of the Demand Curve

In Figure 6.2, demand curve $D$ and supply curve $S$ intersect at the equilibrium price of $9 and the initial equilibrium quantity of 20 million 12-inch pizzas per week. What happens to equilibrium price and quantity when the demand curve shifts? A shift of the demand curve means that quantity demanded changes at each price.

## What Could Shift the Demand Curve?

If one of the factors that determine the demand for pizza changes in a way that increases demand, this would shift the demand curve to the right from $D$ to $D'$. Any of the following could shift the demand for pizza rightward:

1. An increase in the money income of consumers (because pizza is a normal good)

2. An increase in the price of a substitute, such as tacos, or a decrease in the price of a complement, such as beverages

3. A change in expectations that encourages consumers to buy more pizza now

4. A growth in the population of pizza consumers

5. A change in consumer tastes in favor of pizza

## An Increase in Demand

Any one of those five changes could increase the demand for pizza. An **increase in demand** means that consumers are now more willing and able to buy the product at every price. Note that none of these changes will shift the supply curve.

After the demand curve shifts rightward to $D'$ in Figure 6.2, the amount demanded at the initial price of $9 increases to 30 million pizzas. Because producers supply only 20 million pizzas at that price, there is a shortage of 10 million pizzas. Many consumers are frustrated because they can't find pizza at that price. Producers realize that they could charge more for pizza. This shortage puts upward pressure on the price.

As the price increases, the quantity demanded decreases along the new demand curve, $D'$, and the quantity supplied increases along the existing supply curve, $S$, until the two quantities are once again equal. The new equilibrium price is $12, and the new equilib-

**increase in demand**
Consumers are more willing and able to buy the product at every price

**The Graphing Workshop**
econxtra.swlearning.com

**Effects of an Increase in Demand**

**Figure 6.2**

After an increase in demand shifts the demand curve from $D$ to $D'$, quantity demanded exceeds quantity supplied at the old price of $9 per pizza. As the price rises, quantity supplied increases along supply curve $S$, and quantity demanded falls along demand curve $D'$. When the new equilibrium price of $12 is reached, the quantity demanded once again equals the quantity supplied. Both price and quantity are higher following the increase in demand.

# Contemporary
# ECONOMICS

## William A. McEachern

### Teacher's Wraparound Edition

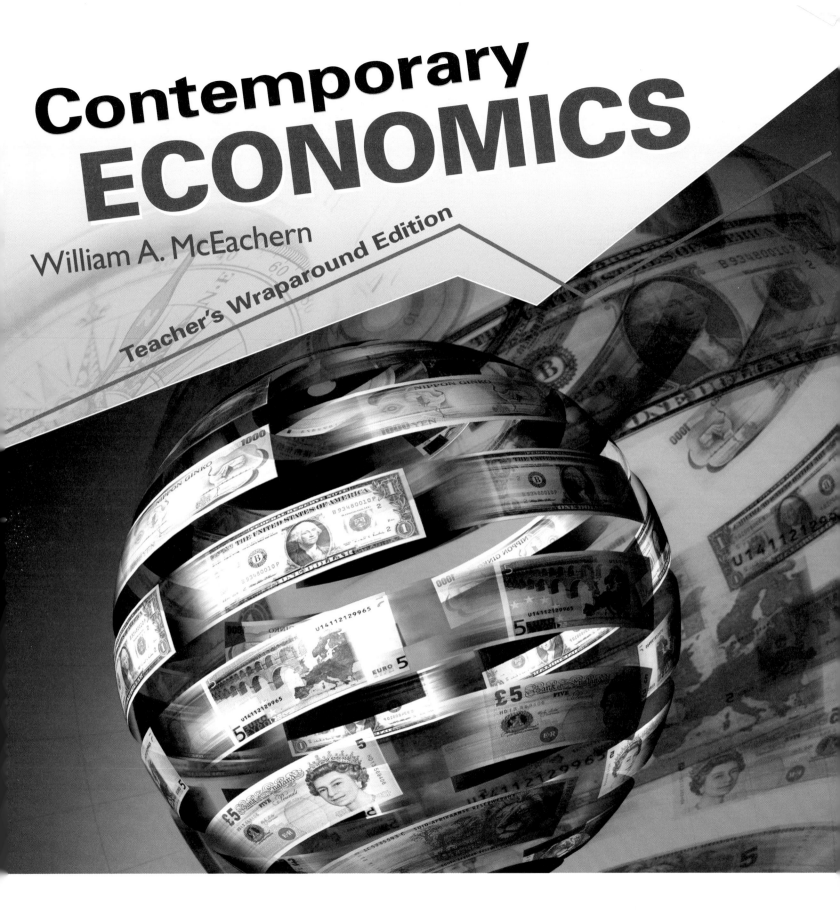

**THOMSON**

**SOUTH-WESTERN**

Australia · Canada · Mexico · Singapore · Spain · United Kingdom · United States

**THOMSON**

**SOUTH-WESTERN**

**Contemporary Economics Teacher's Wraparound Edition**

William A. McEachern

**VP/Editorial Director**
Jack W. Calhoun

**VP/Editor-in-Chief**
Dave Shaut

**Senior Publisher**
Karen Schmohe

**Executive Editor**
Eve Lewis

**Project Manager**
Carol Sturzenberger

**Consulting Editor**
Jeanne Busemeyer

**VP/Director Educational Marketing**
Carol Volz

**Senior Marketing Manager**
Nancy A. Long

**Marketing Coordinator**
Angela Russo

**Production Editor**
Darrell Frye

**Production Manager**
Patricia Matthews Boies

**Manufacturing Coordinator**
Kevin Kluck

**Media Developmental Editor**
Matthew McKinney

**Design Project Manager**
Stacy Jenkins Shirley

**Production House**
New England Typographic Service (NETS)

**Cover Designer**
Grannan Graphic Design, Ltd.

**Cover Images**
© David Muir/Masterfile and Ian McKinnell/Getty Images

**Internal Designer**
Grannan Graphic Design, Ltd.

**Printer**
RR Donnelley & Sons
Willard, OH

Username: **demand**
Password: **supply**

# William A. McEachern

William A. McEachern began teaching large classes of economic principles when he joined the University of Connecticut faculty in 1973. In 1980, he started offering teaching workshops around the country and, in 1990, created *The Teaching Economist*, a newsletter that focuses on making teaching more effective and more fun.

His research has appeared in a variety of journals, including *Economic Inquiry, National Tax Journal, Journal of Industrial Economics, Public Choice,* and *Quarterly Review of Economics and Business*. His books include *Managerial Control and Performance* and *Economics: A Contemporary Introduction*, a college textbook now in its sixth edition. That textbook has also appeared in an Australian edition, a Spanish edition, and an Indonesian edition. A Chinese edition will be published shortly.

Professor McEachern has advised federal, state, and local governments on policy matters and has appeared in media such as the *New York Times, London Times, Wall Street Journal, Christian Science Monitor, Boston Globe, USA Today*, CBS MarketWatch.com, Voice of America, *Now with Bill Moyers,* and *Reader's Digest*.

In 1984, Professor McEachern won the University of Connecticut Alumni Association's Faculty Award for Distinguished Public Service and in 2000 won the Association's Faculty Excellence in Teaching Award. He is the only person in University of Connecticut history to win both awards.

He was born in Portsmouth, New Hampshire, earned an undergraduate degree in the honors program from College of the Holy Cross, served three years as an Army officer, and earned an M.A. and Ph.D. in economics from the University of Virginia.

## ABOUT SOUTH-WESTERN—DEVELOPING LIFELONG LEARNING SOLUTIONS FOR ALL STUDENTS

South-Western—a Thomson business—is the leading provider of business and economics learning materials worldwide. We offer the most extensive selection in business educational materials for the K-12, higher education, corporate, and professional markets. With innovative tools and resources that engage and enhance learning, South-Western leads the way to business success. Our rich spectrum of textbooks, simulations, online courses, web sites, and software products offers the best possible learning solutions that lead students to real careers and lifetime skills.

## Program Consultants

Douglas Haskell
Associate Director, Center for Economic
Education & Research
University of Cincinnati
Cincinnati, Ohio

James Martin
Teacher, Social Studies Department
Walnut Hills High School
Cincinnati, Ohio

Michael O'Bryant
Social Studies Consultant
Mason City Schools
Mason, Ohio

Alice Temnick
Economics Teacher
Cactus Shadows High School
Cave Creek, Arizona

## Economics Advisory Board

James Bauer
Economics Teacher
Archbishop Moeller High School
Cincinnati, Ohio

Timothy L. Davish
Teacher, Social Studies Department
Lakota Local Schools
Liberty Township, Ohio

Dennis M. Dowling
Teacher, Social Studies Department
Lakota West High School
West Chester, Ohio

John Hamstra
Economics Teacher
Mason City Schools
Mason, Ohio

James L. Jurgens
Teacher, Social Studies Department
St. Xavier High School
Cincinnati, Ohio

Sandra L. Mangen
Teacher, Business Department
Beavercreek High School
Beavercreek, Ohio

# Reviewers

Fernando Arencibia, Jr.
Social Studies Teacher
Miami Coral Park Senior High
Miami, Florida

Matthew C. Ethen
History-Social Science Teacher
Edison High School
Fresno, California

Alan Fontenot
Teacher
Pineville High School
Pineville, Louisiana

Pete A. Martinez
Microeconomics Teacher
Danbury High School
Danbury, Connecticut

Sally Meek
Economics Teacher
Plano West Senior High School
Plano, Texas

Renee K. Metcalfe
Curriculum Specialist
Springfield School District 19
Springfield, Oregon

Patti Pair
Economics Teacher
Chattahoochee High School
Alpharetta, Georgia

John Papadonis
Social Studies Department Head
Lexington High School
Lexington, Massachusetts

Carol Penland
Teacher, Business Department
South Cobb High School
Austell, Georgia

James P. Rademacher
Teacher—Economics, Business
Mainland High School
Daytona Beach, Florida

James Ragusa
Teacher, Social Studies Department
Gulf Coast High School
Naples, Florida

Alan R. Ramos
Economics Teacher
Marjory Stoneman Douglas
High School
Parkland, Florida

Paul Spegele
Economics Teacher
Pine Ridge High School
Deltona, Florida

Gail A. Tamaribuchi
Director, Center for Economic
Education
University of Hawaii
at Manoa
Honolulu, Hawaii

Shawn Prewitt Woodham
Economics Teacher
Hoover High School
Hoover, Alabama

v

# Contents

## Features

## Ask the Xpert!

# CONNECT to History

# ⏴ E-CONOMICS

# Ethics in Action

# [ In the News ]

Investigate Your Local Economy

Main Idea

# movers & shakers

## NET Bookmark

## Sharpen Your Life Skills

## SPAN THE GLOBE

## TEAM WORK

# THE WALL STREET JOURNAL

## Styles of Learning and Teaching Approaches

Specific icons have been used within the text of the *Contemporary Economics* Wraparound Teacher's Edition to denote activities that are targeted to a variety of learning styles and teaching approaches.

 Denotes activities that appeal to *visual learners* (students who need to "see" a concept through mental visualization).

 Denotes activities of interest to *auditory learners* (students who learn best by hearing).

 Denotes activities that benefit *kinesthetic learners* (students who achieve best by taking an active part in the instruction).

 Denotes activities involving student research.

 Denotes activities that require original student writing.

# Charts and Figures

Chapter 17    **Money Creation, the Federal Reserve System, and Monetary Policy**

Chapter 18    **International Trade**

Chapter 19    **Economic Development**

# National Content Standards in Economics

NCEE
National Council on Economic Education

| Standard | Chapter Coverage in *Contemporary Economics* |
|---|---|
| **1. Scarcity.** Productive resources are limited. Therefore, people cannot have all the goods and services they want; as a result, they must choose some things and give up others. | Chapters 1, 2, 3, 4, 5, 8, 9, 12, 19 |
| **2. Marginal Cost/Benefit.** Effective decision making requires comparing the additional costs of alternatives with the additional benefits. Most choices involve doing a little more or a little less of something: few choices are "all or nothing" decisions. | Chapters 1, 2, 3, 4, 5, 6, 8, 9, 10, 12, 14 |
| **3. Allocation of Goods and Services.** Different methods can be used to allocate goods and services. People acting individually or collectively through government must choose which methods to use to allocate different kinds of goods and services. | Chapters 1, 2, 3, 19 |
| **4. Role of Incentives.** People respond predictably to positive and negative incentives. | Chapters 1, 2, 3, 4, 5, 6, 7, 8, 9, 10, 12, 13, 15, 16, 17, 18, 19 |
| **5. Gain from Trade.** Voluntary exchange occurs only when all participating parties expect to gain. This is true for trade among individuals or organizations within a nation, and usually among individuals or organizations in different nations. | Chapters 2, 3, 6, 10, 11, 16, 18, 19 |
| **6. Specialization and Trade.** When individuals, regions, and nations specialize in what they can produce at the lowest cost and then trade with others, both production and consumption increase. | Chapters 1, 2, 3, 5, 6, 7, 16, 18, 19 |
| **7. Markets—Price and Quantity Determination.** Markets exist when buyers and sellers interact. This interaction determines market prices and thereby allocates scarce goods and services. | Chapters 1, 2, 4, 5, 6, 7, 13, 18, 19 |
| **8. Role of Price in the Market System.** Prices send signals and provide incentives to buyers and sellers. When supply or demand changes, market prices adjust, affecting incentives. | Chapters 4, 5, 6, 9 |
| **9. Role of Competition.** Competition among sellers lowers costs and prices, and encourages producers to produce more of what consumers are willing and able to buy. Competition among buyers increases prices and allocates goods and services to those people who are willing and able to pay the most for them. | Chapters 3, 6, 7, 8, 12 |
| **10. Role of Economic Institutions.** Institutions evolve in market economies to help individuals and groups accomplish their goals. Banks, labor unions, corporations, legal systems, and not-for-profit organizations are examples of important institutions. A different kind of institution—clearly defined and enforced property rights—is essential to a market economy. | Chapters 2, 3, 7, 8, 9, 10, 11, 12, 13, 15, 16, 17, 18, 19 |

| | |
|---|---|
| **11. Role of Money.** Money makes it easier to trade, borrow, save, invest, and compare the value of goods and services. | Chapters 2, 3, 8, 10, 16, 17, 18 |
| **12. Role of Interest Rates.** Interest rates, adjusted for inflation, rise and fall to balance the amount saved with the amount borrowed, which affects the allocation of scarce resources between present and future uses. | Chapters 3, 10, 11, 13, 15, 16, 17 |
| **13. Role of Resources in Determining Income.** Income for most people is determined by the market value of the productive resources they sell. What workers earn depends, primarily, on the market value of what they produce and how productive they are. | Chapters 1, 3, 5, 9, 11, 12, 13, 15, 19 |
| **14. Profit and the Entrepreneur.** Entrepreneurs are people who take the risks of organizing productive resources to make goods and services. Profit is an important incentive that leads entrepreneurs to accept the risks of business failure. | Chapters 1, 3, 5, 8, 10, 12, 19 |
| **15. Growth.** Investment in factories, machinery, new technology, and in the health, education, and training of people can raise future standards of living. | Chapters 1, 2, 3, 8, 9, 10, 11, 12, 13, 15, 17, 19 |
| **16. Role of Government.** There is an economic role for government in a market economy whenever the benefits of a government policy outweigh its costs. Governments often provide for national defense, address environmental concerns, define and protect property rights, and attempt to make markets more competitive. Most government policies also redistribute income. | Chapters 2, 3, 6, 7, 8, 12, 13, 14, 15, 16, 17, 18, 19 |
| **17. Using Cost/Benefit Analysis to Evaluate Government Programs.** Costs of government policies sometimes exceed benefits. This may occur because of incentives facing voters, government officials, and government employees; because of actions by special interest groups that can impose costs on the general public; or because social goals other than economic efficiency are being pursued. | Chapters 3, 7, 13, 14, 18, 19 |
| **18. Macroeconomy—Income, Employment, Prices.** A nation's overall levels of income, employment, and prices are determined by the interaction of spending and production decisions made by all households, firms, government agencies, and others in the economy. | Chapters 1, 11, 13, 15, 19 |
| **19. Unemployment and Inflation.** Unemployment imposes costs on individuals and nations. Unexpected inflation imposes costs on many people and benefits some others because it arbitrarily redistributes purchasing power. Inflation can reduce the rate of growth of national living standards because individuals and organizations use resources to protect themselves against the uncertainty of future prices. | Chapters 11, 13, 15, 17, 19 |
| **20. Monetary and Fiscal Policy.** Federal government budgetary policy and the Federal Reserve System's monetary policy influence the overall levels of employment, output, and prices. | Chapters 3, 13, 14, 15, 16, 17, 18 |

## ANALYZING PRIMARY SOURCES

*Analyzing* something involves breaking down and looking at all of the parts of the item in order to better understand it. *Primary sources* are historical materials that were created by the people who actually participated in the historical events. Primary sources might include personal letters, diaries, memos, legal documents, photographs, artwork, or other artifacts. Some primary sources may be more valuable to one's research than others might be.

The process of analyzing primary sources can help us determine how helpful a primary source might be. For example, if someone was writing a history of an oil company that rose and fell in the 1920s, he or she might use primary sources such as diaries from the company's founders, internal company memos, or examples of advertisements for the company. The author also might come across primary sources that describe fashion trends in the 1920s, but an analysis of that information would show that it was not very useful to the study of the oil company. In analyzing primary sources, you should answer questions about it, such as what it is, who created it, when, where, how it relates to your research, and why it is important. Using a graphic organizer like the one below can help you analyze primary sources.

*Graphic Organizer 1*

| ITEM | |
|---|---|
| What is it? | |
| Who created it? | |
| Where did it come from? | |
| When was it created? | |
| How does it relate to your research? | |
| Why is it important? | |

## IDENTIFYING POINT OF VIEW AND FRAME OF REFERENCE

*Point of view* is the way someone thinks about a subject. Often, point of view is influenced by a person's background or position in a situation. A consumer, for example, might have a different point of view about rising prices than a producer would.

*Frame of reference* is similar, but it refers to the methods by which someone develops a point of view. For example, an economist may have a different view of the effects of high unemployment than a sociologist would because each one is examining the topic from different frames of reference. An economist might look at the effects of high unemployment on other economic factors, such as consumer spending and overall economic growth. A sociologist might look at the effects of high unemployment on people's lifestyles, beliefs, and habits. Neither side is right or wrong, but they both will look at different data because of their different frames of reference. Using graphic organizers like those shown on page xxvii can help you identify points of view and frames of reference.

*Graphic Organizer 2*

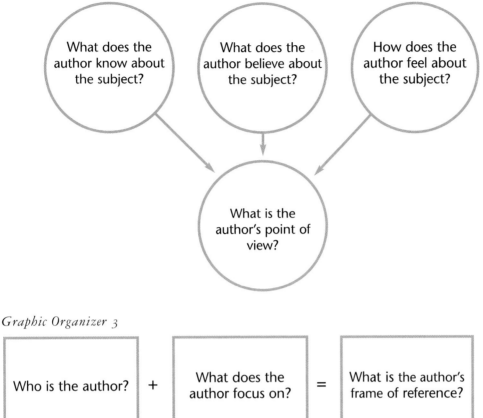

*Graphic Organizer 3*

| | | |
|---|---|---|
| Who is the author? | + What does the author focus on? | = What is the author's frame of reference? |

How does the author's frame of reference influence his or her point of view?

## DISTINGUISHING FACT AND OPINION

When reading information about a topic, it is very important to determine if what you are reading is fact or opinion. *Facts* are statements that can be checked for accuracy, such as the amount of money that something costs. *Opinions* are statements that reflect personal feelings and cannot be verified for accuracy, such as whether or not it is worth it to pay a certain price for an item.

Many times writers will combine facts and opinions. Writers who are trying to persuade a reader that their opinion on something is correct will use facts to support the opinion. However, readers should be very clear on which parts of the argument are opinion statements and which are facts. Misuse of facts also can be a sign of *bias*, or preconceived ideas not based on true facts. A reader who confuses facts and opinions easily can be led to a false conclusion about something.

In order to distinguish facts and opinions in writing, it is helpful to break the statements down and evaluate whether they can be tested for accuracy. For example, a writer might note that a certain state has suffered from increased inflation and high unemployment for more than a year. The writer might then state that these economic problems prove that the governor of the state is a bad leader. Increased inflation and high unemployment are facts that can be verified. That the governor is a bad leader is an opinion that may be supported or weakened by the introduction of more facts.

Clue words and phrases such as *bad, good, in my opinion, poor, strong,* and *weak* can help you identify opinions. Using a graphic organizer like the one below also can help you distinguish facts from opinions.

*Graphic Organizer 4*

| Statement | Fact | Opinion | Explain Why |
|-----------|------|---------|-------------|
|           |      |         |             |

## USING RELIABLE INFORMATION

When conducting research, it is important to use reliable information, or information that comes from a dependable source. In analyzing the reliability of information, you need to have all of the facts about where the information is coming from and recognize any biases from the source. You usually can find a great deal of reliable information in the library. Sources that provide footnotes or other indications of where the information came from usually are more reliable that undocumented sources. The Internet often provides fast, up-to-date information, but you have to be very careful about checking the reliability of Internet sources. Some that may initially look like they have come from a reliable source actually may have come from a biased source.

You also can check the reliability of a source by comparing its information with that of other sources. For example, if the reports of five major economic groups conclude that the economy is slowly entering a period of recession, but the report by a politically interested group concludes that there are no signs of recession, you may need to question the reliability of the last report.

Whenever possible, it is best to rely on the most original version of a source that is available. For example, if you were conducting research on a controversial speech by the U.S. Secretary of Commerce, you could read news accounts of the speech or commentaries on it by various people. However, if you really wanted to verify what the secretary said, the most reliable source would be a copy of the speech itself. Most speeches by government officials and other types of government information can be obtained on government web sites. Using a graphic organizer like the one below can help you check the reliability of sources.

*Graphic Organizer 5*

| Source | |
|--------|--|
| Who is the author? | |
| Who is the publisher? | |
| Does the author or publisher have any known biases? | |
| Where did the author get his or her information? | |
| Can the information be checked against other sources? | |

**SOCIAL STUDIES SKILLS**

## IDENTIFYING CAUSE AND EFFECT AND MAKING PREDICTIONS

A *cause* is something that makes an event happen. An *effect* is the result of that cause. A *prediction* is an educated guess about what the effect of a cause might be. Understanding the relationship between causes and effects can help you understand why an event occurred. It also can help you predict what might happen when certain actions are taken. For example, the cause of an increase in gasoline prices might be a decision by OPEC to cut oil supplies. One might predict, then, that gas prices would go down if OPEC reverses this policy.

There can be more than one cause for an effect. Likewise, one cause might have many effects. Clue words and phrases such as *accordingly, as a result of, because, for this reason, in order to, since, so,* and *then* can help you identify causes as you read. In examining causes and effects of actions and events, look for logical patterns. Once you understand the patterns, you can better predict what the next action or event will probably be. Using graphic organizers like the ones below can help you in this process.

*Graphic Organizer 6*

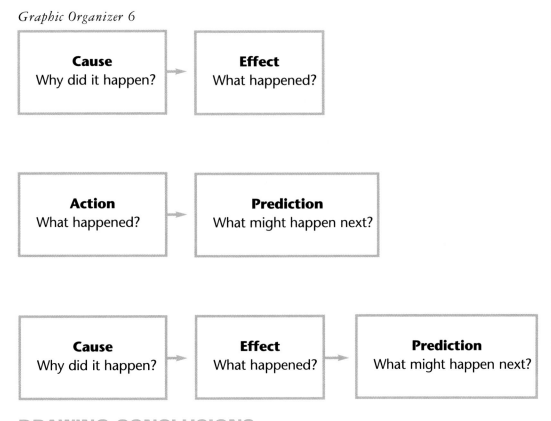

## DRAWING CONCLUSIONS

*Drawing conclusions* is the process by which people figure something out on their own, based on observations of facts or details. Writers do not always explain everything to readers. Like a good detective, readers must piece together clues within the text, combine this information with what they already know, and draw conclusions about the topic.

For example, you might read that consumer spending in the United States dropped during a certain year. You also might read that unemployment was very high during that year, and average household incomes dropped. From these facts you might conclude that people were spending less because they had less money to spend. Using graphic organizers like the ones on page xxx can help you draw conclusions as you read.

*Graphic Organizer 9*

*Graphic Organizer 10*

| Clues from Text | What I Already Know | My Conclusion |
|---|---|---|
| | | |

## DECISION MAKING AND PROBLEM SOLVING

Problem solving involves gathering information to develop a solution to a dilemma. During the course of solving a problem, you also must use good decision-making skills to choose the best possible solution to the problem. The first step in solving a problem is to identify what the problem is. For example, a company might have trouble selling a product it makes. In order to come up with a solution to this problem, you would have to gather as much information as you could about the subject. For example, if a product is not selling well, market research could be conducted to find as much information as possible about where it is being marketed, who is buying it, what competitors' products are selling better, and how the competitors' products differ.

Rarely will a problem have only one solution. Often there are multiple solutions that could be chosen. This is where the decision-making process comes into play. In the course of deciding between multiple solutions, you must consider all of the positive and negative aspects of each option, including their possible consequences. For example, a company might be considering revamping its current product to compete better in the marketplace. The positive aspects of this choice might be gaining a higher market share, but the negatives might be the need for huge amounts of money to be invested in changing the product and lost revenues on the original product. Another solution might call for keeping the original product, but targeting it only to demographic groups that tend to buy the product the most. A third solution might involve a compromise between the two—the company may decide to invest in revamping the old model, while at the same time remarketing the original product to gain a larger share of a target demographic group that likes the old product.

Using a graphic organizer like the one on page xxxi can help you to solve problems and make decisions.

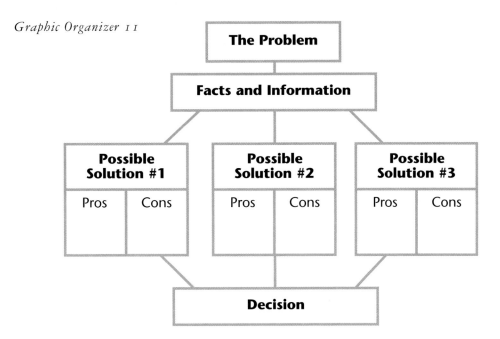

## SUPPORTING A POSITION

Part of identifying a point of view and distinguishing facts from opinions involves looking at the evidence the author presents to support his or her point of view. Whenever you take a position on a subject, you must be able to support that position with persuasive arguments and well-chosen facts. A weak argument will not convince others that your position is valid. For example, if an economist took the position that lowering taxes would help boost the economy but offered no evidence that this would happen, not many people would be convinced. If, however, the economist could show that lowering taxes would increase people's incomes and encourage them to spend money and include examples of when this has happened in the past, then others might be convinced that lowering taxes would be good for the economy.

When you put together an argument in support of a position, carefully think through why you have taken the position. Once you understand your own reasoning, present the most persuasive facts that help support your position. Using a graphic organizer like the one below can help you put together an argument to support your position.

*Graphic Organizer 12*

## COMPARING AND CONTRASTING

*Comparing* involves noting similarities between two or more things. *Contrasting* involves noting differences between these things. For example, if you were to compare and contrast the economies of two countries like the United States and China, you might note that they are similar in that they both are actively involved in trade and industrial growth. You might note that they are different in that the communist government of China still has much more direct control over its economy than the U.S. government has over the U.S. economy.

As you read, look for clue words that indicate if things are being compared or contrasted. Clue words or phrases that indicate comparison include *also, as well as, like, same as,* and *similar to.* Clue words or phrases that indicate contrast include *although, as opposed to, but, different from, however, instead of, on the other hand,* and *unlike.* Using graphic organizers like the ones below can help you compare and contrast information as you read.

*Graphic Organizer 13*

*Graphic Organizer 14*

|  | Item 1 | Item 2 | Different or Alike? |
|---|---|---|---|
| Characteristic A |  |  |  |
| Characteristic B |  |  |  |
| Characteristic C |  |  |  |

**SOCIAL STUDIES SKILLS**

## SEQUENCING

*Sequencing* is the process of placing events in chronological order to better understand why and how things happen as they do. Sometimes the text will make the chronology of an event clear and may even provide time lines for clarity. At other times, it is up to the reader to figure out what the order of events really was. Timelines provide a way to sequence information in *absolute chronology*, or the exact time when something happened.

Sometimes it is not clear, nor even important to know, exactly when something happened. However, it may be very important to know the *relative chronology* of events, or when things happened in relation to one another. Relative chronology tells us what happened first, second, and last. For example, if you were trying to understand how the Federal Reserve Board works, it would be helpful to note that during a given three-month period the rate of inflation was higher than average. At the end of those three months, the Federal Reserve raised interest rates to curb inflation. Over the next three months, inflation slowed, so at the end of that three-month period the Federal Reserve left interest rates unchanged.

Some clue words that may help you identify sequence include *after, before, finally, first, following, next, then,* and *when.* Using graphic organizers like the one below also can help you sequence information.

*Graphic Organizer 15*

What happened first?

What happened next?

What happened next?

What happened last?

Your textbook is a guide to help you learn new information, but you cannot retain that information without reading the text effectively. The following reading skills strategies can help you get the most out of your reading.

## BEFORE YOU READ

### Set a Purpose for Reading

✔ Think about what you will be reading and what you hope to learn from the reading. Consider how the topic might relate to your daily life and what you already know about the topic.

### Preview

✔ Look over the headings and visuals in the reading, including the chapter title, subheads, photos, graphs, charts, and maps. Look over any "preview" items the chapter provides, such as lists of bold-faced terms.

### Predict

✔ Using the information you examined in your preview, predict what you will learn from it.

✔ Use the following graphic organizer to help you prepare to read new materials.

| Purpose for Reading | Preview | Prediction(s) |
|---|---|---|
| I will be reading about _____ _____ _____ _____. I hope to learn _____ _____ _____ _____. The topic relates to my daily life in that _____ _____ _____ _____. I already know _____ _____ _____ _____. | The chapter title is _____ _____. The subheads are _____ _____ _____ _____. Chapter visuals include ____ _____ _____ _____ _____ _____. Chapter preview items include _____ _____ _____ _____. | Based on what I have previewed, I will probably learn _____ _____ _____ _____ _____ _____ _____ _____ _____ _____ _____ _____ _____ _____ |

### Find the Main Idea

The main idea is the most important idea in a reading passage. Sometimes the main idea of a passage is stated clearly, often in the first one or two sentences of a paragraph. But sometimes it is not stated so clearly, and you must read carefully to infer the main idea. You can test whether or not you have identified the correct main idea by offering details from the reading that support this idea. Using a graphic organizer like the one below can help you in this process.

### Draw Connections Between Items

As you read, pay particular attention to the relationships between people, places, events, and ideas. These relationships can include cause and effect, differences and similarities, sequencing, and problems or solutions. The Social Studies Skills section (pp. xxvi–xxxiii) contains several graphic organizers that can help you arrange this information as you read. It also contains some lists of clue words that can help you spot some relationships. Recognizing relationships between items can help you understand complicated information.

### Analyze Visual Information

Pay attention to the visual information in the text. Ask yourself why it is included and what it adds to the text. Think about how your understanding of the visuals as you read may have changed from when you looked at the visuals in your preview exercise.

## AFTER YOU READ

### Summarize

Once you have finished your reading, try to summarize, or state in the simplest way possible, what the reading passage is all about. The process of summarizing a reading passage is very similar to finding the main idea. As you prepare to summarize a passage, look at your notes on the most important details mentioned in the reading. Use these details to state what happened in the passage in the simplest way possible. Using a graphic organizer like the one below can help you in this process.

### Assess

After you have finished reading and summarizing, look back at your predictions about the chapter and analyze whether you learned what you thought you were going to learn. Consider how the information you learned may be put to use in your daily life.

### Analyze Visual Information—Tables

1. It shows unemployment rates from different countries over four decades.

2. You can learn how high unemployment was in different countries compared with other similar countries during the same time period.

3. For all of the countries, unemployment was higher in 2000 than in 1970, though some countries had greater highs and lows in between. Overall, Japan had the lowest average unemployment during the entire period, but its unemployment rate more than doubled between 1990 and 2000.

## ANALYZE VISUAL INFORMATION—TABLES

Often economic information is presented in the form of tables. *Tables* help to organize and display economic data in a clear form. Use the following steps to examine the table below.

1. Read the title of the table to understand what it is about.

2. Read all labels. They explain what information is being studied and describe the time period or range of items being compared.

3. Compare the data being presented in the columns to note changes over time or categories.

| UNEMPLOYMENT RATES IN VARIOUS COUNTRIES | | | | |
|---|---|---|---|---|
| Year | United States | France | Japan | United Kingdom |
| 1970 | 4.9 percent | 2.5 percent | 1.2 percent | 3.1 percent |
| 1980 | 7.1 percent | 6.5 percent | 2.0 percent | 7.0 percent |
| 1990 | 5.6 percent | 9.1 percent | 2.1 percent | 6.9 percent |
| 2000 | 4.0 percent | 9.1 percent | 4.8 percent | 5.5 percent |

Source: Bureau of Labor Statistics, U.S. Department of Labor.

### Use the Skill

1. What does the table show?

2. What types of information can you learn from the table?

3. What does the table tell you about trends in unemployment rates?

### Apply the Skill

Create your own chart on economic data by gathering information on earnings of students in your class. Have a group of students write down how much they earn in a week from outside jobs. The information should be anonymous to maintain privacy. Once you have collected the slips of paper, organize the information into a chart that shows the distribution of income among the students. You might also use this information to create a table that shows categories of income distribution to illustrate how many students fall within certain income ranges.

## ANALYZE VISUAL INFORMATION—BAR GRAPHS

A *bar graph* uses lengths of bars to show the relationship among different variables. Use the following steps to examine the bar graph below.

1. Read the title of the graph to understand what it is about.

2. Read all labels. They explain what information is being studied and how it is being measured. The labels on the vertical axis (left side) and horizontal axis (bottom) are the most important for understanding the information.

3. Compare the data being presented on the bars to note changes in measurements over time.

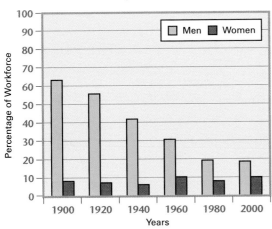

**Americans Over Age 65 in the Workforce**

Source: Bureau of the Census, U.S. Department of Commerce.

### Use the Skill

1. What does the graph show?
2. What are the advantages of showing this information in bar graph form?
3. What does the graph tell you about changes in the workforce over time?

### Apply the Skill

Take the information gathered for the "Apply the Skill" activity on the first page of this "Economic Measurement Skills" section, and use it to create a bar graph. To create the bar graph, label the vertical axis "Number of Students" and the horizontal axis "Income Categories."

**Analyze Visual Information—Bar Graphs**

1. It shows the percentage of Americans over age 65 in the workforce over a 100-year period.

2. It allows for the inclusion of a lot of information compared side by side, such as male and female figures. The visual approach allows for clearer observation of differences.

3. It shows that the percentage of men over age 65 in the workforce has dropped dramatically, but the percentage of women over age 65 in the workforce has remained fairly stable.

## ANALYZE VISUAL INFORMATION—LINE GRAPHS

A *line graph* shows the relationship among variables in the form of a line. A line graph looks simple, but it requires precise measurements along plot points to convey accurate information. A line graph is very effective for showing changes in information about the same item over time. Use the following steps to examine the line graph below.

1. Read the title of the graph to understand what it is about.

2. Read all labels. The vertical axis usually explains what is being compared. The horizontal axis usually marks periods of time.

3. Note what the lines on the graph stand for. Sometimes the lines will have labels on them. Sometimes, if there are multiple lines, there will be a legend to help you understand the lines, which will often be presented in different colors to distinguish them from one another.

4. To find information for an exact time, look for the location of that date along the horizontal axis and measure straight up to find the point of the line directly above that date. Then read to the left to find the corresponding measurement.

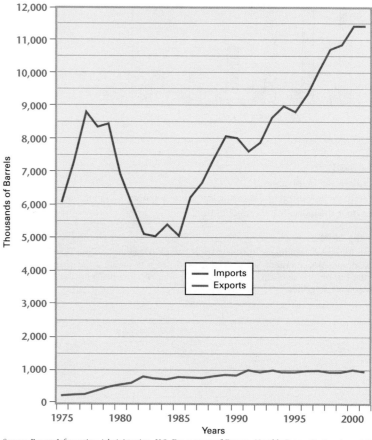

**Average Daily U.S. Petroleum Imports**

Source: Energy Information Administration. U.S. Department of Energy, *Monthly Energy Review*, August, 2002.

**ECONOMIC MEASUREMENT SKILLS**

## Use the Skill

1. What does the graph show?
2. What information does the graph reveal about the relationship between U.S. imports and exports of petroleum?
3. What general trends over time does the graph reveal?

## Apply the Skill

Take the bar graph that you create for the Apply the Skill activity on page xxxvii and change it into a line graph. Label the vertical axis "Number of Students" and the horizontal axis "Income Categories." Compare the different graphs and the table, and consider which is most effective at presenting the information.

## ANALYZE VISUAL INFORMATION—PIE GRAPHS

*Pie graphs* are used to show the breakdown of something by revealing the percentages of parts to the whole. Use the following steps to examine the pie graph below.

1. Read the title of the graph to understand what it is about.
2. Read all labels or legends to understand the breakdown of the various parts.
3. Compare the sizes of the different parts of the circle to understand how they relate to one another.

**Federal Budget Outlays, 2003**

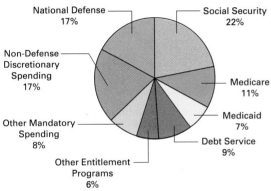

Source: Bureau of Industry and Security, Department of Commerce,
http://www.bxa.doc.gov/DefenseIndustrialBasePrograms/OSIES/DefMarketResearchRpts/a

## Use the Skill

1. What does the graph show?
2. How can a pie graph like this be useful?
3. What does the pie graph reveal about federal budget outlays?

## Apply the Skill

Take the information you have gathered for the previous "Apply the Skill" activities, and convert it into a pie graph to show the percentages of students among the entire survey who fall into certain earning categories. Think about how the presentation of the information in this pie graph is different from that of your previous tables and graphs.

**Analyze Visual Information— Line Graphs**

1. It shows U.S. imports and exports of petroleum over a 25-year period.
2. The United States imports much more petroleum than it exports.
3. The amounts of both imports and exports have gone up; imports have more than doubled while exports have more than quadrupled.

**Analyze Visual Information— Pie Graphs**

1. It shows federal budget outlays for 2003.
2. It can show what percentage of federal spending is going to what programs.
3. It shows that a higher percentage of spending is going toward Social Security than any other single service.

**Analyze Visual Information—Maps**

1. It shows the percentage of union membership in states and those states that are right-to-work states.

2. It visually shows the geographic distribution of union membership across the country.

3. New York

## ANALYZE VISUAL INFORMATION—MAPS

*Maps* illustrate information over a geographic area. Maps you use in the study of economics are special-purpose maps. They will usually display economic information in geographic locations. In this way, you can see differences in economic data between various regions, states, and countries. Use the following steps to examine the map below.

1. Read the title of the map to understand what it is about.

2. Note what kind of geographic breakdown of information is being shown.

3. Note what kind of economic information is being shown.

4. Read all labels or legends to understand the breakdown of the various parts.

**Right-to-Work States and Unionization Rates Per State**

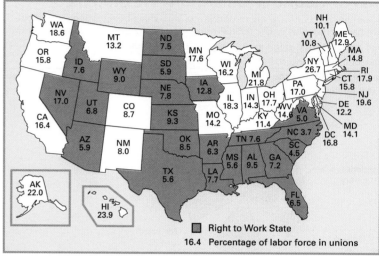

Source: National Right to Work Committee, http://www.nrtwc.org/. Unionization rates are for 2001 and right-to-work states are as of 2002.

### Use the Skill

1. What does the map show?

2. How does showing this information in map form help you understand it?

3. What state has the highest percentage of union members among its labor force?

### Apply the Skill

Choose an economic topic that would provide data for each state, such as unemployment rates or average income. Research the data for each state and create your own economic map, including a title, legend, and any important labels.

**xl**     **ECONOMIC MEASUREMENT SKILLS**

## USE MATH SKILLS—AVERAGES AND MEDIANS

Sometimes it is useful to summarize data in general rather than specific terms. The most common method of summarizing data is to average it. The average, or *mean*, can be found by adding together the values of all variables and dividing them by the number of variables. Sometimes it is also useful to calculate the *median*, or midpoint, in a distribution of data. Use the following steps to understand how the data below was calculated.

1. Add all the numbers together.
2. Divide that sum by the total amount of numbers listed to obtain the average, or mean.
3. To locate the median, arrange the numbers in order and find the number in the middle of the list.

### Costs of Food Items

| | |
|---|---|
| 1 lb bacon | $1.99 |
| 1 gal milk | $1.79 |
| 1 pt strawberries | $3.49 |
| 5 lb sugar | $1.41 |
| 1 pineapple | $2.99 |
| 1 lb tomatoes | $1.99 |
| 1 l bottled water | $ .89 |
| 1 lb ground beef | $2.99 |
| 1 bunch celery | $ .99 |
| **Total** | $18.53 |

Average price is $18.53 ÷ 9 = $2.59

| | |
|---|---|
| 1 pt strawberries | $3.49 |
| 1 lb ground beef | $2.99 |
| 1 pineapple | $2.99 |
| 1 lb bacon | $1.99 |
| 1 lb tomatoes | $1.99 ← median price is $1.99 |
| 1 gal milk | $1.79 |
| 5 lb sugar | $1.41 |
| 1 bunch celery | $ .99 |
| 1 l bottled water | $ .89 |

### Use the Skill

1. What do the lists show?
2. What are the average and median prices?
3. Are the average and median prices different? Why?
4. Which is more useful in this case, the mean or median price?

### Apply the Skill

Using the data on student income you generated in Apply the Skill for "Analyze Visual Information—Bar Graphs," calculate the average and median incomes for students in your group.

---

### Use Math Skills—Averages and Medians

1. Grocery prices
2. Average is $2.59; median is $1.99.
3. They are different. There are more items below the average than above it, but the highest prices are so high that they increase the average.
4. In this case, the average (mean) is probably more useful to help you know how much people would generally spend on food items.

## Use Math Skills—Ratios and Percentages

1. They show the number of independent, national, state, and total number of banks in the United States.

2. The ratio shows how many of the different types of banks there are, compared with one another. The percentages show how many different types of banks there are as a part of all banks.

3. You can calculate the ratio by subtracting all of the other numbers from the total of banks and, assuming the remaining number represents savings and loans, add that number to the ratio equation. You can calculate the percentage of all depository institutions that are savings and loans by subtracting all of the other percentage amounts from 100.

## USE MATH SKILLS—RATIOS AND PERCENTAGES

Sometimes it is useful to illustrate economic data in the form of ratios or percentages. *Ratios* show the relationship of one numerical value to another. *Percentages* show changes as parts of the whole, or part of 100 percent. Use the following steps to understand how the data below were calculated.

1. To find ratios, take two numbers and show them as a fraction, with the highest number on top. Reduce the fraction to its lowest terms.

2. Ratios also can be shown using more than two numbers by using colons and reducing all three numbers to their lowest terms.

3. To find the percentage relationship between two numbers, divide the smaller of the two numbers by the larger one. Then multiply the result by 100.

| Banks in the United States, 2001 | | | |
|---|---|---|---|
| **Independent** | **National** | **State** | **Total** |
| 4,971 | 2,137 | 972 | 9,631 |

Source: Federal Deposit Insurance Corp., December 2000.

**Ratios:**

Independent to National    $4{,}971/2{,}137 = 2.33/1$    For every one national bank, there are 2.33 independent banks.

Independent to State    $4{,}971/972 = 5.11/1$    For every one state bank, there are 5.11 independent banks.

National to State    $2{,}137/972 = 2.2/1$    For every one state bank, there are 2.2 national banks.

Independent to National to State    $5.11{:}2.2{:}1$    For every one state bank, there are 2.2 national banks and 5.11 independent banks.

**Percentages:**

Independent    $4{,}971 \div 9{,}631 = 0.52 \times 100 = 52\%$

National    $2{,}137 \div 9{,}631 = 0.22 \times 100 = 22\%$

State    $972 \div 9{,}631 = 0.10 \times 100 = 10\%$

Of the nation's banks, 52 percent are independent banks, 22 percent are national banks, and 10 percent are state banks.

### Use the Skill

1. What do the data show?

2. What are the advantages of showing the data as ratios or percentages?

3. The data do not include savings and loans, another type of depository institution. Based on the information above, can you calculate the ratio of savings and loans to the three types of banks? Can you calculate the percentage of savings and loans among all of these institutions?

### Apply the Skill

Think about how much money you earn in an average month. Then estimate how much you spend during a month and how much you save. Calculate (1) the ratio of your spending to savings and (2) the percentages of your earnings that you spend and that you save.

**ECONOMIC MEASUREMENT SKILLS**

## USING MATH SKILLS—RATES AND ABSOLUTE NUMBERS

In economics, information may sometimes be presented in *absolute numbers*, such as by showing that the cost of an item went from $500 to $700 in a six-month period. Economists also sometimes present information in the form of *rates*. These are percentages that are used to show how much something is rising or falling as a percentage of a whole or to reflect change. For example, economists often discuss the rate of inflation to show how quickly prices of goods are rising. You also might learn about *interest rates*, or the calculation of how much a loan will cost based on a percentage of the amount of money borrowed. Use the following steps to understand how the data below were calculated.

1. To calculate the rate of increase in the price of an item, plot the absolute price of the good over time.

2. Subtract the price you started with from the price you ended with.

3. Divide the result by the price you started with.

4. Multiply the result by 100 to get a percentage rate of change.

| AVERAGE COST OF A MOVIE TICKET | | |
|---|---|---|
| Year | Price | Annual Rate of Increase |
| 1992 | $4.15 | |
| 1993 | $4.14 | −0.24% |
| 1994 | $4.08 | −1.45% |
| 1995 | $4.35 | 6.62% |
| 1996 | $4.42 | 1.61% |
| 1997 | $4.59 | 3.84% |
| 1998 | $4.69 | 2.18% |
| 1999 | $5.06 | 7.89% |
| 2000 | $5.39 | 6.52% |
| 2001 | $5.65 | 4.82% |
| 2002 | $5.80 | 2.65% |

Source: National Association of Theater Owners, http://www.natoonline.org/statisticstickets.htm

Example: 1992 to 1993: $4.14 − 4.15/4.15 \times 100 = -0.24\%$

### Use the Skill

1. What do the data show?

2. What type of unusual change in prices does the rate of increase reveal?

3. How much was the 10-year rate of increase between 1992 and 2002?

### Apply the Skill

Research information about the average prices of other consumer goods for at least two years. Make a chart showing the annual rate of increase in prices for each product.

## USE MATH SKILLS—INDEX NUMBERS

Economists sometimes express changes in things like prices in terms of *index numbers*. Index numbers set a *base period* and measure changes from the base period to the present. The base period has a value of 100. All other numbers are expressed as a percentage of the prices of the base period. This would mean, for example, that if an item cost $1.00 during the base period and $1.08 during another period, the second period would be shown as a price index of 108, meaning 108% of the base period. The index system allows economists to summarize a great deal of information in a simple way. Use the following steps to understand the data below.

1. Find the base period.

2. Look at the indexes for the other periods. Remember that the index is a percentage of the price for the base period.

3. Calculate the average cost of an item that was $1.00 during the base period for other periods.

| CONSUMER PRICE INDEX, 1920–2002 | |
|---|---|
| (base year = 1967) | |
| 1920 | 60.0 |
| 1925 | 52.5 |
| 1930 | 50.0 |
| 1935 | 41.1 |
| 1940 | 42.0 |
| 1945 | 53.9 |
| 1950 | 72.1 |
| 1955 | 80.2 |
| 1960 | 88.7 |
| 1965 | 94.5 |
| 1970 | 116.3 |
| 1975 | 161.2 |
| 1980 | 248.8 |
| 1985 | 322.2 |
| 1990 | 391.4 |
| 1995 | 456.5 |
| 2002 | 535.8 |

Source: Bureau of Labor Statistics, U.S. Department of Labor.

**ECONOMIC MEASUREMENT SKILLS**

**Use the Skill**

1. What does the graph show?
2. What is the base year?
3. What did an item that cost $1.00 during the base year cost in 1935? In 2002?

**Apply the Skill**

Research the consumer price list for various consumer products. Note what year the prices were the lowest and the highest.

## USE MATH SKILLS—NOMINAL AND REAL VALUES

Economists sometimes express dollar amounts in nominal and real numbers. *Nominal numbers* reflect the actual amount of money on hand. *Real numbers* reflect the nominal numbers adjusted for inflation. For example, you might earn $30,000 at your job and get a 1 percent raise of $300, raising your salary to $30,300. However, if the rate of inflation during that year was 3 percent, you will not be able to buy as much with your salary as you could the year before. Economists use price indexes to adjust nominal numbers to real ones. Use the following steps to understand how the data below were calculated.

1. Obtain the nominal numbers for an amount of money.
2. Multiply the nominal amount of money by the price index (divided by 100) for the period of time you are examining.
3. The result is the real amount of the money.

| U.S. GROSS DOMESTIC PRODUCT (in billions of dollars) | | | |
|---|---|---|---|
| | **Nominal Dollars** | **Consumer Price Index (divided by 100)** | **Real Dollars** |
| 1990 | $5,546.1 ÷ | 3.914 = | $1,416.99 |
| 2000 | $9,824.6 ÷ | 5.358 = | $1,833.63 |

Source: Bureau of Economic Analysis, U.S. Department of Commerce.

**Use the Skill**

1. What do the data show?
2. What do the real dollar amounts reveal about the true value of GNP?
3. How do the data reveal the usefulness of converting nominal into real dollars?

**Apply the Skill**

Research to find out how much average personal income was in nominal dollars from 1990 to 2000. Then, using what you know about the Consumer Price Index, show what the real amount of average personal income was.

**Use Math Skills—Index Numbers**

1. It shows the Consumer Price Index over time.
2. 1967
3. $.41 in 1935; $5.36 in 2002

**Use Math Skills—Nominal and Real Values**

1. They show nominal and real gross domestic product figures for 1990 and 2000.
2. Looking at the nominal numbers, the GDP almost doubled, but the real numbers show that the value of the money had only a relatively small increase.
3. They show that the amount of nominal dollars does not reflect the real spending value of those dollars.

1

## National Content Standards in Economics

The following NCEE Standards are addressed in Unit 1:

| | |
|---|---|
| **Standard 1** | Scarcity |
| **Standard 2** | Marginal Cost/Benefit |
| **Standard 3** | Allocation of Goods and Services |
| **Standard 4** | Role of Incentives |
| **Standard 5** | Gain from Trade |
| **Standard 6** | Specialization and Trade |
| **Standard 7** | Markets—Price and Quantity Determination |
| **Standard 9** | Role of Competition |
| **Standard 10** | Role of Economic Institutions |
| **Standard 11** | Role of Money |
| **Standard 12** | Role of Interest Rates |
| **Standard 13** | Role of Resources in Determining Income |
| **Standard 14** | Profit and the Entrepreneur |
| **Standard 15** | Growth |
| **Standard 16** | Role of Government |
| **Standard 17** | Using Cost/Benefit Analysis to Evaluate Government Programs |
| **Standard 18** | Macroeconomy—Income, Employment, Prices |
| **Standard 20** | Monetary and Fiscal Policy |

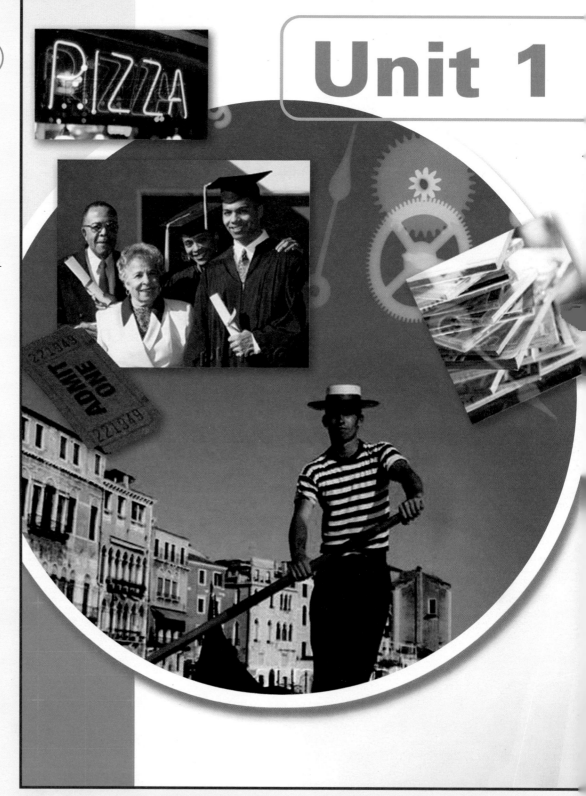

# Unit 1

| Pacing Guide | One-Semester Days of Study | Two-Semesters Days of Study | Block Schedule 90-Minute Blocks |
|---|---|---|---|
| **UNIT 1: INTRODUCTION TO ECONOMICS** | | | |
| Chapter 1: What Is Economics? | | | |
| **1.1** The Economic Problem | 2 | 3 | 2 |
| **1.2** Economic Theory | 1 | 3 | 1 |
| **1.3** Opportunity Cost and Choice | 2 | 4 | 2 |
| Chapter 2: Economic Systems and Economic Tools | | | |
| **2.1** Economic Questions and Economic Systems | 2 | 3 | 2 |
| **2.2** Production Possibilities Frontier | 1 | 3 | 1 |
| **2.3** Comparative Advantage | 2 | 4 | 2 |
| Chapter 3: U.S. Private and Public Sectors | | | |
| **3.1** The U.S. Private Sector | 1 | 2 | 1 |
| **3.2** Regulating the Private Sector | 1 | 2 | 1 |
| **3.3** Public Goods and Externalities | 1 | 3 | 1 |
| **3.4** Providing a Safety Net | 2 | 3 | 2 |

# Introduction to Economics

$\textcircled{1}$ **What Is Economics?**

.........................................................

$\textcircled{2}$ **Economic Systems and Economic Tools**

.........................................................

$\textcircled{3}$ **U.S. Private and Public Sectors**

Your aunt gives you $25 for your birthday. What will you do with that money? There are many possibilities. You could spend it on movies, pizza, CDs, gasoline, or a favorite brand of jeans. Or you could save the money toward a trip to Europe or a college education. You could even give the money to a worthy charity. Whatever you decide, you are making an economic choice. Economics focuses on how your choices and the choices of millions of others affect individual markets—such as the market for pizza—and shape the economy as a whole.

3

## Unit 1 Overview

Unit 1 introduces students to the study of economics. It is designed to help students develop a clearer understanding of familiar economic concepts and introduce them to the fundamental economics concepts and principles.

## Group Activity

Organize students into small groups and ask them to discuss the passage that appears on this page. Instruct students to discuss how their economic choices might shape the economy as a whole. Allow about 10 minutes for discussion. Ask a representative of each group to briefly summarize the discussion for the class.

## Think Critically Through Visuals

Direct students to study the images on the opposite page and think about how each image relates to economics. Ask them to work with a partner to create their own collage to illustrate the economy. Display the finished collages in the classroom while studying Unit 1.

## Look Beyond the Classroom

There is a wealth of economic experience and knowledge held by residents in every community. A good way to move beyond the classroom is to have students identify a person who owns or manages a local business. Ask students to investigate the following questions: How did the person become involved in the business? How does the person decide what products to produce, how to produce them, and to whom they should be marketed?

Instruct students to write a summary of their findings. Invite students who are particularly successful in this assignment to help you arrange for their subjects to visit your class as guest speakers.

An alternative would be to have students interview their subjects and present their findings to the class.

## Chapter Overview

**LESSON 1.1** *The Economic Problem:* This lesson explains the economic problem, identifies productive resources, and defines goods and services.

**LESSON 1.2** *Economic Theory:* This lesson focuses on the role of economic theory, explains the role of marginal analysis, and describes how market participants interact.

**LESSON 1.3** *Opportunity Cost and Choice:* In addition to defining opportunity cost, this lesson discusses how to choose among alternatives and explains the opportunity cost of attending college.

### Consider

Ask students to consider the questions posed on this page as they study Chapter 1. After studying all three lessons, students should be able to answer the questions. The content related to each question can be found on the pages indicated below.

- Why are characters in comic strips like Hagar the Horrible, Cathy, and Fox Trot missing a finger on each hand? See page 11—Simplify the Problem.

- Why are you reading this book right now rather than doing something else? See pages 11–12—Rational Self-Interest.

- Why is there no sense crying over spilt milk? See page 22—Ignore Sunk Cost.

- In what way are people who pound on vending machines relying on a theory? See page 12—Everybody Uses Theories.

### POINT YOUR BROWSER

Remind students that they can find additional resources for this chapter at **econxtra.swlearning.com**.

- Xtra! Study Tools
- Net Bookmarks
- Xtra! Quiz Prep
- econ@pps
- Ask the Xpert!
- Graphing Workshop

# What Is Economics?

The Economic Problem **1.1**

Economic Theory **1.2**

Opportunity Cost and Choice **1.3**

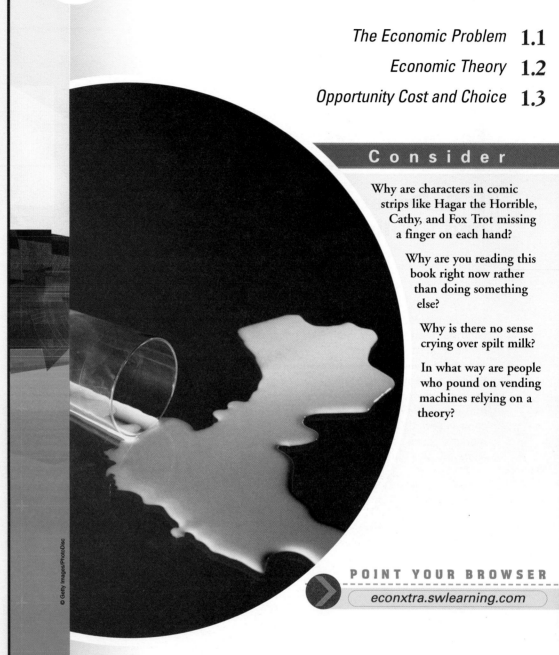

© Getty Images/PhotoDisc

### Consider

Why are characters in comic strips like Hagar the Horrible, Cathy, and Fox Trot missing a finger on each hand?

Why are you reading this book right now rather than doing something else?

Why is there no sense crying over spilt milk?

In what way are people who pound on vending machines relying on a theory?

### POINT YOUR BROWSER

econxtra.swlearning.com

**Teaching Resources for Chapter 1**

- Activities and Projects Masters
- Spanish Resources
- Econ Connection Interactive Tutorial CD
- **Exam***View*® CD
- Workbook Teacher's Edition
- Chapter Test Teacher's Edition
- NCEE Standards and Correlation
- Personal Finance Guide

- Social Studies Skills Review
- Instructor's Resource CD
  - PowerPoint Presentation
  - Lesson Plans
  - Video Discussion Guide
  - Answers to Graphing Exercises
- **econxtra.swlearning.com**

## 1.1 The Economic Problem

## Objectives

> Recognize the economic problem, and explain why it makes choice necessary.

> Identify productive resources, and list examples.

> Define goods and services, list examples, and explain why they are scarce.

## Overview

Economics is always in the news. If you read a newspaper, watch television, or go online, you are bombarded with current economic information. Economic issues are reported because they are important in people's lives. People want to know the latest about jobs, housing, prices, taxes, and other matters that affect their income and spending. Economics is concerned with identifying and clarifying your choices—the range of possibilities you face now and in the future. As you learn more about economics, you will begin to think more about the choices you face.

## Key Terms

**scarcity**

**productive resources**

**economics**

**human resources**

**labor**

**entrepreneur**

**natural resources**

**capital goods**

**good**

**service**

## [ In the News ]

### ● Rich or Poor, It's Good To Have Money

In a market economy such as the United States, the more money you have the more options you have. Alternatively, you could say that the more money you have, the fewer choices you have to make—because you can buy more of what you want. Either way, it's hard to argue against the goal of abundance over scarcity. A recent Gallup poll shows that although few Americans now label themselves as rich, many hope to reach that status some day. One third of those polled say becoming rich is "at least somewhat likely" for them. Ten percent say it is "very likely." Only a third reject the possibility. The dream of eventual wealth is particularly alive among the young. An amazing 51 percent of those 18 to 29 say becoming rich is "a likely possibility." That's important. For a market system to work well, young people must believe in the possibility of succeeding in that system.

### Think About It

Is it likely that you will become successful or even rich? Is this important to you? What choices for your future might you make differently if you thought you had little chance of success? How might you and the economy as a whole suffer as a result of your pessimism?

◄ | ►

**5**

Introduce this lesson by showing students pictures that depict expensive goods and services they are likely to want but are unlikely to be able to possess. These might include a sports car, a boat, a large-screen television, a mansion, or young people attending an important sporting event or rock concert. Ask them to explain why they are not able to own these items or attend the events. They will inevitably bring up the fact that they can't afford them. Lead this discussion to the concept of scarcity, our limited supply of productive resources, and differences between goods and services. Discuss how scarcity forces people to make decisions and therefore is the basis for the study of economics.

### Objectives

Remind students to read the lesson objectives to help focus their attention before reading the lesson.

### Key Terms

Direct students to use each of the key terms in a separate sentence or short paragraph that helps demonstrate the meaning of the term. For example: Hugo walked dogs to make extra money while he was in college. When he graduated, he developed his part-time job into a doggie daycare business. Hugo is an entrepreneur.

### [ In the News ]

Instruct students to read the passage and write down their answers. Point out that their answers might change after they finish studying Lesson 1.1.

### Answers to Think About It

Answers will vary. Possible answers: If you think you have little chance for success, you probably will lack ambition and drive. An economy without ambition and drive lacks innovation and productivity. A nation with this economy suffers as a whole.

### Visual Presentation

Use the PowerPoint presentation on the Instructor's Resource CD as an adjunct to your lecture. The presentation also can be used for review.

# Economic Choices

*Why are economists always talking about money and wealth?*

**scarcity**

A condition facing all societies because there are not enough productive resources to satisfy people's unlimited wants

**productive resources**

The inputs used to produce the goods and services that people want

**economics**

The study of how people use their scarce resources to satisfy their unlimited wants

Economics is about making choices. You make economic choices every day. You make choices about whether to get a part-time job or focus on your studies, buy a car or save for college, pack a lunch or buy a Subway sandwich. You already know more about economics than you realize. You bring to the subject a rich personal experience. This experience will be tapped throughout the book to reinforce your understanding of the basic ideas.

## The Economic Problem

Would you like a new car, a nicer home, better meals, more free time, more spending money, more sleep? Who wouldn't? But even if you can satisfy some of these desires, others keep popping up. Here's the economic problem: *Although your wants, or desires, are virtually unlimited, the productive resources available to help satisfy these wants are scarce.* Scarcity creates the economic problem. **Scarcity** is the condition facing all societies because there are not enough productive resources to satisfy people's unlimited wants.

**Productive resources**, or *factors of production*, are the inputs used to produce the goods and services that people want. *Because productive resources are scarce, goods and services are scarce too.*

A productive resource is *scarce* when it is not freely available. Because productive resources are scarce, you must choose from among your many wants. Whenever you choose, you must go without satisfying some other wants. The problem of scarce resources but unlimited wants exists for each of the six billion people on the planet.

Because you cannot have all the goods and services you would like, you must choose among them continually. Making choices means you must pass up some alternatives.

## Economics Defined

**Economics** examines how people use their scarce resources to satisfy their unlimited wants. A taxicab driver uses the cab and other scarce resources, such as knowledge of the city, driving skills, gasoline, and time, to earn income. That income, in turn, buys housing, groceries, clothing, trips to Disney World, and other goods and services that help satisfy some of the driver's unlimited wants.

### ✓ CHECKPOINT

What is the economic problem, and why does it make choice necessary?

**Main Idea**

Scarcity

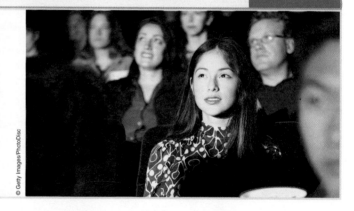

*Because productive resources are limited, you cannot have all the goods and services you want. You must choose some things and give up others. If you decide to attend a movie with your friends on a Saturday night, what alternatives might you have to pass up?*

© Getty Images/PhotoDisc

# Productive Resources

Productive resources, also called *factors of production*, or simply *resources*, sort into three broad categories: human resources, natural resources, and capital resources.

## Human Resources

The first category, **human resources**, is the broad category of human efforts, both physical and mental, used to produce goods and services. *Labor*, such as the labor of a cab driver or a brain surgeon, is the most important of the human resources. **Labor** is the physical and mental effort used to produce goods and services. Labor itself comes from a more fundamental human resource: time. Without time you can accomplish nothing. You allocate your time to alternative uses: You can sell your time as labor to earn a *wage*, or you can spend your time doing other things, such as sleeping, eating, studying, playing sports, surfing the Net, or watching TV.

Human resources also include the special skills supplied by an **entrepreneur**, who tries to earn a profit by developing a new product or finding a better way to produce an existing one. An entrepreneur seeks to discover profitable opportunities by purchasing resources and assuming the risk of business success or failure. *Profit* equals the *revenue* from sales minus the *cost* of production. If production costs exceed revenue, the entrepreneur suffers a loss. Profit provides the incentive that makes entrepreneurs willing to accept the risk of losing money. All companies in the world today began as an idea in the mind of an entrepreneur.

## Natural Resources

**Natural resources** are so-called "gifts of nature," including land, forests, minerals, oil reserves, bodies of water, and even animals. Natural resources can be divided into renewable resources and exhaustible resources. A *renewable resource* can be drawn on indefinitely if used wisely. Thus, timber is a renewable resource if

## NET Bookmark

What makes a good job good? Working for a good employer might be one factor. Each year, *Fortune* magazine lists the 100 best employers. The magazine includes this list on its web site, which you can access through econxtra.swlearning.com. What factors other than compensation are cited in the report as creating a favorable work environment?

**econxtra.swlearning.com**

felled trees are replaced to provide a steady supply. The air and rivers are renewable resources if they can recover from a certain level of pollutants. More generally, biological resources like fish, game, livestock, forests, rivers, groundwater, grasslands, and agricultural soil are renewable if managed properly.

An *exhaustible resource*—such as oil, coal, or copper ore—does not renew itself and so is available in a limited amount. Each gallon of oil burned is gone forever. Sooner or later, all oil wells will run dry. The world's oil reserves are exhaustible.

## Investigate Your Local Economy

With a partner, make a list of the natural resources found in your state. Research the impact these resources have on your local economy. Which industries use these natural resources in their production processes? How many people do these industries employ? How many dollars per year do these industries generate for the state? Report your results to the class.

**human resources**
The broad category of human efforts, both physical and mental, used to produce goods and services

**labor**
The physical and mental effort used to produce goods and services

**entrepreneur**
A profit-seeker who develops a new product or process and assumes the risk of profit or loss

**natural resources**
So-called "gifts of nature" used to produce goods and services; includes renewable and exhaustible resources

---

## TEACH

### Productive Resources

Introduce productive resources by asking students to consider the resources that were used to produce this textbook.

**Investigate Your Local Economy** Point out that almanacs and encyclopedias often contain information about a state's natural resources. The department of natural resources and the department of economic development for your state are also good sources.

### NET Bookmark

Direct students to **econxtra.swlearning.com**. Remind them to click on the link for Lesson 1.1 to find the appropriate link for the **NET Bookmark** on page 7.

**Answer**
Answers will vary. Possible answer: Other factors related to a favorable work environment include benefits, training, and programs to improve work/life balance.

### SPAN THE GLOBE

Direct students to read the short passage "A Yen for Vending Machines" on page 8. Use Think Critically as a starting point for class discussion on productive resources.

**Answers to Think Critically**
Vending machines are used more in Japan because labor is relatively scarce and expensive, and the Japanese prefer dealing with anonymous machines.

### ✓ CHECKPOINT
Invite a student to answer the checkpoint that appears on page 8.

---

## ENRICH

Construction projects are often taking place in or near schools. Identify such a project and ask students to make lists of human, natural, and capital resources that are being used. Is entrepreneurship demonstrated by the project? Choose several students to present their lists and classifications to the class. Do other students agree with the classifications? Why or why not? This activity may be completed by individual students or by asking students to work together in groups.

**Answer**
Three categories of productive resources are human resources, natural resources, and capital resources. Examples include labor (human resources), forest land (natural resources), and factories (capital resources).

### Goods and Services

Introduce goods and services by asking students to work as a class to make a list of all the things they would need in order to start a successful high school soccer team. When the list is complete, ask students to categorize the items as goods or services. The goods list will probably include soccer balls, a field, goals, shin pads, uniforms, and soccer shoes. The services list might include qualified coaches, scorekeepers, officials, fans, and players.

**CHECKPOINT**
Invite a student to answer the checkpoint that appears on page 9.

### Answer

A good is an item you can see, feel, and touch, requires scarce resources to produce, and satisfies human wants. Furniture, homes, and cars are examples of goods. A service is something not physical that requires scarce resources to produce and satisfies human wants. Concerts and sports games are examples of services. These goods are scarce because the amount that people desire of these is greater than the amount available at a zero price.

## APPLY

Assign Lesson 1.1 from the Contemporary Economics Workbook.

## ASSESS

Assign all or part of Lesson 1.1 Assessment on page 9 as homework or an in-class activity.

Direct students to the online study tools for Lesson 1.1 at **econxtra.swlearning.com**.

## CLOSE

**Revisit** the **In the News** feature on the first page of the lesson. Ask students to review their preliminary answers and discuss the questions, now that they have completed this lesson.

**Review** the objectives for Lesson 1.1.

---

## SPAN THE GLOBE

### A Yen for Vending Machines

Japan has more vending machines per capita than any other country on the planet—more than twice as many as the United States, and nearly ten times as many as Europe. The reasons are both economic and cultural. A low birthrate, virtually no immigration and an aging population have created a relative scarcity of labor and driven up the cost of that labor. Therefore, to sell products Japanese retailers rely on capital, particularly vending machines, which eliminates the need for sales clerks. Research shows that Japanese consumers prefer dealing with anonymous machines rather than having to exchange greetings and pleasantries with a real person.

### Think Critically

Compare the use of the vending machines in Japan with their use in the United States and Europe. Give specific reasons why you think vending machines are used relatively less in these countries as compared with Japan.

---

*capital goods*
All human creations used to produce goods and services; for example, factories, trucks, and machines

*good*
An item you can see, feel, and touch and that requires scarce resources to produce and satisfies human wants

*service*
Something not physical that requires scarce resources to produce and satisfies human wants

### Capital Resources

Capital resources, commonly called **capital goods**, include all human creations used to produce goods and services. Capital goods consist of factories, trucks, machines, tools, buildings, airports, highways, and other manufactured items employed to produce goods and services. Capital goods include the taxi driver's cab, the farmer's tractor, the interstate highway system, and your classroom.

**CHECKPOINT**
Name the three categories of productive resources, and provide examples of each.

---

**8**    **CHAPTER 1**   What Is Economics?

---

## Goods and Services

Resources are combined in a variety of ways to produce goods and services.

### Goods

A farmer, a tractor, 50 acres of land, seeds, and fertilizer come together to grow the good: corn. Corn is a **good** because it is tangible—something you can see, feel, and touch. It requires scarce resources to produce, and it satisfies human wants. This book, the chair you are sitting in, the clothes you are wearing, and your next meal are all goods.

### Services

One hundred musicians, musical instruments, chairs, a conductor, a musical score, and a music hall combine to produce the service: Beethoven's Fifth Symphony. The performance of the Fifth Symphony is a **service** because it is intangible—that is, not physical—yet it uses scarce resources to satisfy human wants. Movies, concerts, phone calls, Internet connections, guitar lessons, dry cleaning, and your next haircut are all services.

### No Free Lunch

You may have heard the expression "There is no such thing as a free lunch." This is so because all goods involve a cost to someone. The lunch may seem free to you, but it draws scarce resources away from the production of other goods. Also, whoever provides the free lunch often expects something in return. A Russian proverb makes a similar point but with a bit more bite: "The only place you find free cheese is in a mousetrap."

Because goods and services are produced using scarce resources, they are themselves scarce. A good or service is scarce if the amount people desire exceeds the amount available at a zero price. Rather than say "goods and services" every time, this book will sometimes use the term

---

## RETEACH

Ask students to make lists of general classifications of spending that they or their families undertake on a regular basis, such as food, clothing, entertainment, or housing. Once the lists are complete, have students identify each type of spending as being for a good or service. Do they believe their grandparents would have had similar spending patterns 50 years ago? Ask them to explain why people spend less on goods and more on services today.

---

"goods" to mean both goods and services.

A few goods seem free because the amount freely available (that is, available at a zero price) exceeds the amount people want. For example, air and seawater often seem free because you can breathe all the air you want and have all the seawater you can haul away. Yet, despite the old saying, "The best things in life are free," most goods are scarce, not free. Even those that appear to be free come with strings attached. For example, clean air and clean seawater have become scarce. *Goods that are truly free are not the subject matter of economics. Without scarcity, there would be no need for prices and no economic problem.*

Sometimes you may mistakenly think of certain goods as free because they involve no apparent cost to you. Subscription cards that fall out of magazines appear to be free. At least it seems you would have no problem rounding up a pile of them if necessary. Producing the cards, however, uses scarce resources. These resources were drawn away from other uses, such as producing higher-quality magazines.

✓ **CHECKPOINT**
Define goods and services, provide examples, and explain why they are scarce.

# 1.1 Assessment

## Key Concepts

1. What is the central problem that you face when you make economic choices?

2. What are examples of productive resources you use in your life?

3. How can you tell whether the food you eat from your refrigerator is scarce?

4. Identify each of the following as a human resource, natural resource, or capital resource:

   a. a hammer used to build a wooden box

   b. the tree that was cut down to make lumber to build a wooden box

   c. the effort used to nail lumber together to make a wooden box

## Graphing Exercise

5. Draw a pie chart that demonstrates how you spend the money you have (movies, CDs, clothing, food, transportation, etc). To draw a pie chart, draw a circle and divide it into slices. Label each slice with a type of spending, and identify it as either a good or a service. Each slice represents a percentage of the whole pie. The percents on the slices should add up to 100 percent.

## Think Critically

6. **Government** Identify a good or service provided by the government that has no apparent cost for you. Why is this good or service not really free?

**Xtra!**
Study Tools
econxtra.swlearning.com

Lesson 1.1 • *The Economic Problem* 9

---

# 1.1 Assessment

## Key Concepts

1. Scarcity—Although my desires are virtually unlimited, the productive resources available to help satisfy my wants are scarce.

2. Answers will vary. Students may identify rain that waters their lawn (a natural resource); their work at an after-school job cooking french fries (a human resource); or the shovel they use to clear their driveway when it snows (a capital good).

3. Any good or service that has a price that exceeds zero is scarce. Someone paid for the food in your refrigerator; therefore, it is scarce.

4. (a) A hammer is a capital good.
   (b) The tree is a natural resource.
   (c) The effort to construct the box is a human resource.

## Graphing Exercise

5. Answers will vary, depending on how much money students have to spend and how they spend it. Answers should demonstrate an understanding of the difference between goods and services. An example of a pie chart appears at the bottom of this page. It was created using the data shown below.

| Monthly Spending | | |
| --- | --- | --- |
| **Goods and Services** | **Amount** | **Good or Service** |
| CDs | $30 | Good |
| Clothing | $50 | Good |
| Food | $80 | Good |
| Gasoline | $40 | Good |
| Cell Phone | $20 | Service |
| Movies | $10 | Service |

## Think Critically

6. Answers will vary. Public schooling is a possible example. Although students receive their education with no direct cost, taxpayers support public schools, which allows scarce resources to be allocated to them.

---

**Monthly Spending**

Movies 4%
Cell Phone 9%
CDs 13%
Clothing 22%
Gasoline 17%
Food 35%

## Visualizing the Answer— Graphing Exercise

5. The answer to this exercise includes a graph. Students' graphs should look similar to the one shown here. The data used to create this example is shown above. An Excel spreadsheet containing the graph shown here, along with supporting data, is available on the Instructor's Resource CD.

**1.2 Economic Theory**

Tell students to imagine they are on a trip and are looking for a place to spend the night. Show them pictures of two motels or hotels. One picture should show a nice establishment with modern rooms, pleasant landscaping, and a swimming pool and fitness center. The other should be a more modest, perhaps older, facility without a pool or other amenities. Ask students to estimate the cost of a night's stay at each facility. Once they make their estimates, ask them to explain how they decided on a price. Point out that they used an economic theory that equates better quality with higher price.

#### Objectives

Remind students to read the lesson objectives to help focus their attention before reading the lesson.

#### Key Terms

Direct students to write each key term on a separate index card. Then write the matching definition and page reference on the back of the appropriate card. Encourage students to use the cards to study for quizzes and tests.

#### [ In the News ]

Instruct students to read the passage and write down their answers. Point out that their answers might change after they finish studying Lesson 1.2.

#### Answers to Think About It

Answers will vary. Possible answer: The Dow is not a useful means to measure economic trends from day to day because it fluctuates widely due to random events. However, the Dow does accurately capture year-to-year economic trends because in that greater span of time, the random fluctuations that happen on a daily basis cancel each other out.

#### Visual Presentation

Use the PowerPoint presentation on the Instructor's Resource CD as an adjunct to your lecture. The presentation also can be used for review.

## Objectives

> Explain the goal of economic theory.

> Understand the role of marginal analysis in making economic choices.

> Explain how market participants interact.

## Overview

An economy results from the choices that millions of individuals make in attempting to satisfy their unlimited wants. Because these choices lie at the very heart of the economic problem—coping with scarce resources but unlimited wants—they deserve a closer look. Learning about the forces that shape economic choice is the first step toward mastering economic analysis.

## Key Terms

**economic theory**

**marginal**

**market economics**

**national economics**

**market**

### [ In the News ]

#### ● How Now Dow?

The stock market's Dow Jones Industrial Average, or "the Dow," measures the average stock prices of 30 major U.S. companies. The Dow is reported widely on TV news shows and cable channels and often runs along the bottom of your TV screen. The simple ups and downs of the Dow are much easier for the general public to follow and understand than the more complicated measures of economic activity favored by economists. In fact, many Americans rely on the Dow for cues about where the economy is headed. Although the Dow is only one of many economic indicators, some people adjust their spending and saving behavior based on the Dow's movements. If the Dow is rising, people think the economy is improving, so they may spend more freely. Conversely, if the Dow is falling, they may hold back on spending. In reality, movements in the Dow may be linked to the economy's performance from year to year. Day-to-day fluctuations in the Dow, however, are likely caused more by random events that may or may not have any lasting effect on the economy.

#### Think About It

Would you consider the Dow a useful measure of economic trends from day to day? From year to year? Why or why not?

10

 **NCEE**

### National Content Standards in Economics

A complete list of the NCEE Standards appears on pages xxiv–xxv of this book. The following standards are addressed in Lesson 1.2.

Standard 2: Marginal Cost/Benefit

Standard 3: Allocation of Goods and Services

Standard 4: Role of Incentives

Standard 6: Specialization and Trade

Standard 7: Markets—Price and Quantity Determination

Standard 18: Macroeconomy—Income/ Employment, Prices

# The Role of Theory

Economists develop theories, or models, to help explain economic behavior. An **economic theory**, or *economic model*, is a simplification of economic reality that *is used to make predictions about the real world*. Thus the goal of economic theory is to make predictions about the real world, such as what happens to consumption of Pepsi when its price increases.

## Simplify the Problem

A theory captures the important elements of the problem under study. It need not spell out every detail and relationship. In fact, the more detailed a theory gets, the more difficult to understand it becomes, and the less useful it may be. The world is so complex that simplifying often is necessary to make sense of things. Think of comic strip characters, for example. Cartoonists often simplify their characters, leaving out fingers or even a mouth. You might think of economic theory as a stripped-down, or streamlined, version of economic reality. One way to strip down reality is by using simplifying assumptions.

## Simplifying Assumptions

To help develop a theory, economists make simplifying assumptions. One category of assumptions is the *other-things-constant assumption*. The idea is to identify the variables of interest and then focus exclusively on the relations among them, assuming that nothing else of importance changes—that other things remain constant.

Suppose you are interested in how a change in the price of Pepsi affects the number of bottles purchased. To isolate the relationship between these two variables—price and quantity purchased—you assume for purposes of the model that there are no changes in other relevant variables such as consumer income, the price of Coke, and the average outdoor temperature.

Economists also make assumptions about what motivates people—how people behave. These are called *behavioral assumptions*. Perhaps the most basic behavioral assumption is that people make choices based on their own self-interest.

## Rational Self-Interest

A key assumption about behavior is that in making choices, you rationally select alternatives you perceive to be in your best interests. By *rational*, economists mean that you try to make the best choices you can, given the information available.

**economic theory**

A simplification of economic reality used to make predictions about the real world

## The Role of Theory

Introduce the role of theory by asking students to identify products that are endorsed by famous people such as athletes or actors. Ask them to explain why manufacturers are willing to pay these people millions of dollars to wear shoes, drive cars, and appear in advertisements. Students will likely come up with the idea that the firms expect to increase their sales because of the endorsement. Then ask students to describe the theory that these firms assume consumers use when they make their buying decisions. They should come up with something like, "If this famous person, whom I admire and respect, chooses to use this product, it must be desirable, so I should use it, too." Ask students whether they ever use this type of theory when they shop. What simplifying assumption is the basis for this theory? (behavioral assumption)

# E-CONOMICS

Direct students to read the passage entitled "The Rational Choice Is to Stay Home from Work" on this page.

### Answers to Think Critically

Answers may vary. Possible answer: It might be in an individual's best interest to telecommute to avoid the traffic congestion encountered in commuting to an office or to avoid the rising costs of daycare.

Lesson 1.2 • *Economic Theory* **11**

## Outside Resources

**Fast-Food Menus** Menus can be obtained from most national chains such as Wendy's or McDonald's. Ask students to compare the selection and desirability of food offered at such restaurants with that provided by their school or another institutional cafeteria. Do students believe there are similarities between these two types of providers of food and those of market versus national economies? What incentives do school cafeterias have to offer desirable food selections?

## The Role of Theory

Use the following activity to help explain the role of theory. Direct students to write down the answers to the following questions related to preparing for an important test. When do you study? How long do you study? Where do you study? Do you study alone, with a partner, or in a group? Do you do anything else while you're studying, such as listen to music?

Ask several volunteers to read their answers to the class. They are likely to be quite different. Ask the students to explain why different people have different methods of studying. In what ways are these differences based on different theories they hold about the best way to earn good grades in their classes? Is it possible for different theories to be equally accurate for different students who have different learning styles?

### Think Critically Through Visuals

Direct students to focus their attention on the photograph on this page. Ask for a volunteer to answer the question posed in the caption.

### Answer

Volunteering at a soup kitchen is rational self-interest because it fits in with your personal interests. You are choosing to participate in an activity that will maximize your benefits and minimize your costs. The expected benefits include the satisfaction and enjoyment of helping others. The expected cost is the time you give up that could be used to do something else.

### CHECKPOINT

Invite a student to answer the checkpoint that appears on page 13.

### Answer

The goal of economic theory is to explain why and how the economy works.

---

In general, rational self-interest means that you try to maximize the expected benefit achieved with a given cost or to minimize the expected cost of achieving a given benefit.

Rational self-interest does not necessarily mean selfishness or greed. You probably know people who are tuned to radio station WIIFM (What's In It For Me). For most of you, however, self-interest often includes the welfare of your family, your friends, and perhaps the poor of the world. Even so, your concern for others is influenced by your personal cost of that concern. You may volunteer to drive a friend to the airport on Saturday afternoon but are less likely to offer a ride if the flight departs at 6:00 A.M. When you donate clothes to charitable organizations such as Goodwill Industries, these clothes are more likely to be old than new. People

© Getty Images/PhotoDisc

**How would choosing to volunteer at a soup kitchen that serves homeless people fit in with the concept of rational self-interest?**

tend to give more to a favorite charity if contributions are tax deductible.

The assumption of rational self-interest does not rule out concern for others. It simply means that concern for others is influenced to some extent by the same economic forces that affect other economic choices. The lower your personal cost of helping others, the more help you will offer.

Rationality implies that each consumer buys the products expected to maximize

his or her level of satisfaction. Rationality also implies that each firm supplies the products expected to maximize that firm's profit. These kinds of assumptions are called behavioral assumptions because they specify how economic decision makers are expected to behave—what makes them tick, so to speak.

### Everybody Uses Theories

Many people don't understand the role of theory. Perhaps you have heard, "Oh, that's fine in theory, but in practice it's another matter"—meaning that the theory provides little aid in practical matters. People who say this do not realize that they are merely substituting their own theory for a theory they either do not believe or do not understand. They really are saying, "I have my own theory that works better."

Everyone uses theories, however poorly defined or understood. Someone who pounds on a vending machine that just ate a quarter has a crude theory about how that machine works and what went wrong. One version of that theory might be, "The quarter drops through a series of whatchamacallits, but sometimes the quarter gets stuck. *If* I pound on the machine, *then* I can free up the quarter and send it on its way." This theory seems to be so widely used that many people continue to pound on vending machines that fail to perform. (This is a real problem for that industry and one reason why newer vending machines are fronted with glass.) Yet, if you asked any of these mad pounders to explain their "theory" of how the machine works, he or she would look at you as if you were crazy.

### Economists Tell Stories

Economists explain their theories by telling stories about how they think the economy works. To tell a good story, an economist relies on case studies, anecdotes, parables, listener's personal experience, and supporting data.

Throughout this book, you will hear stories that shed light on the ideas under consideration. Stories, such as the one about the vending machine, breathe life into economic theory.

---

Show students pictures of several different people. Ask them to write brief descriptions of what sort of person each individual is. They should include factors such as personality traits, careers, family situations, economic status, education, etc. After a few people have been described, ask students to compare their evaluations. Are they similar or different? Explain that they have based their descriptions on theories of what people with different appearances are like. People constantly evaluate other people based on incomplete information. Discuss why people do this. Why must economists use theories as well?

(Just as people cannot know or consider everything about others, economists cannot know or consider every factor that can affect future economic conditions. They must consider the most important relationships when they predict the future. Theories about economic relationships facilitate these predictions.)

## Normative Versus Positive Statements

Economists usually try to explain how the economy works. Sometimes they concern themselves not with how the economy *does* work but how it *should* work. Compare these two statements: "The U.S. unemployment rate is 5.8 percent" versus "The U.S. unemployment rate should be lower." The first is called a *positive economic statement* because it is a statement about economic reality that can be supported or rejected by reference to the facts. The second is called a *normative economic statement* because it reflects someone's opinion. An opinion is merely that—it cannot be shown to be true or false by reference to the facts.

Positive statements concern what *is*. Normative statements concern what, in someone's opinion, *should be*. Positive statements need not necessarily be true, but you should be able to find out whether they are true or false by referring to the facts. Economic theories are expressed as positive statements such as, "If the price increases, then the quantity purchased will decrease."

Most of the disagreement among economists involves normative debates—for example, what is the appropriate role of government—rather than statements of positive analysis. To be sure, many theoretical issues remain unresolved. However economists do agree on most basic theoretical principles—that is, about positive economic analysis.

Normative statements, or personal opinions, are relevant in debates about public policy (such as the proper role of government) provided that opinions are distinguished from facts. In such debates, you are entitled to your own opinions, but you are not entitled to your own facts.

**CHECKPOINT**
Explain the goal of economic theory.

## Marginal Analysis

Economic choice usually involves some adjustment to the existing situation, or the status quo. Your favorite jeans are on sale, and you must decide whether to buy another pair. You have just finished dinner at a restaurant and are deciding whether to eat dessert. Amazon.com must decide whether to add an additional line of products. The school superintendent must decide whether to hire another teacher.

### Compare Marginal Cost with Marginal Benefit

Economic choice is based on a comparison of the expected marginal benefit and the expected marginal cost of the action under consideration. **Marginal** means incremental, additional, extra, or one more. Marginal refers to a change in an economic variable, a change in the status quo.

*A rational decision maker will change the status quo as long as the expected marginal benefit from the change exceeds the expected marginal cost.* For example, you compare the marginal benefit you expect from eating dessert (the added satisfaction) with its marginal cost (the added dollar cost, time, and calories). Likewise, Amazon.com compares the marginal benefit expected from adding a new product line (the added sales revenue) with the marginal cost (the added cost of resources required).

Typically, the change under consideration is small, but a marginal choice can involve a major economic adjustment, as in your decision whether or not to go to college. For a firm, a marginal choice might mean building a factory in Mexico or even filing for bankruptcy protection.

Focusing on the effect of a marginal adjustment to the status quo cuts the analysis of economic choice down to a manageable size. Rather than confront a puzzling economic reality head-on, economic analysis can begin with a marginal choice and then show how that choice affects a particular market and shapes the economy as a whole.

**marginal**
Incremental, additional, extra, or one more; refers to a change in an economic variable, a change in the status quo

### Marginal Analysis

Introduce marginal analysis with the following demonstration. Select a student to help you who you believe will be cooperative. Ask this student whether he or she would be willing to help you clean your classroom for 20 minutes after school in exchange for a free pass to a local movie theater. The student is likely to agree. Explain that the time and work are the student's marginal cost and the value of the pass is the marginal benefit of the student's decision. Then ask the student whether he or she would stay an additional 20 minutes to receive another pass. Keep doing this until the student says he or she is unwilling to stay any longer to receive another pass. Explain that at this point, the marginal benefit of the additional pass is less than the marginal cost of staying 20 more minutes to clean the room. Make a table on the board to show the student's choices. Ask students how this demonstration relates to the way they make decisions in their own lives.

## Group Activity

Provide groups of students with identical copies of travel brochures for exotic vacations. Tell them they have $10,000 to spend and that any money they do not spend they can keep, as long as they choose to take one of the vacations. Ask them to keep a record of their discussion. After the groups have made their choices, discuss the marginal costs and benefits of their decisions. What additional information would have been useful to them? In real life, would they have made the effort to obtain this additional information? Why or why not?

## Marginal Analysis

To demonstrate marginal analysis, copy the table below on the board. Explain that the table illustrates the grade a student can expect to earn on an important assignment, relative to the time spent studying. Ask students how much time they would spend. What is the marginal cost and benefit of their decision? If they chose to study for 4 hours, their marginal cost was the extra 2 hours spent studying to achieve the extra benefit of earning a B instead of a C grade.

| Time Spent Studying | Grade Earned |
|---|---|
| 1 Hour | D |
| 2 Hours | C |
| 4 Hours | B |
| 10 Hours | A |

## Think Critically Through Visuals

Direct students to focus their attention on the photograph on this page. Ask for a volunteer to answer the questions posed in the caption.

### Answer

Answers will vary. Possible answers: The marginal benefit of purchasing another pair of your favorite jeans is that you would be getting the new pair at a reduced cost. The marginal cost of purchasing another pair of your favorite jeans is the additional monetary cost you must pay to attain those jeans.

### Main Idea

NCEE Standard 1:
**Marginal Cost/Benefit**

Effective decision making requires comparing the additional costs of alternatives with the additional benefits. Most choices involve doing a little more or a little less of something; few choices are "all or nothing" decisions.

**CHECKPOINT**
Invite a student to answer the checkpoint that appears on this page.

### Answer

If the marginal benefit of an activity or purchase exceeds the marginal cost, then people will choose to do that activity or make the purchase.

---

To the noneconomist, *marginal* usually means inferior, as in "a movie of marginal quality." Forget that meaning for this course and instead think of *marginal* as meaning incremental, additional, extra, or one more.

### Choice Requires Time and Information

Rational choice takes time and requires information, but time and information are scarce and valuable. If you have any doubts about the time and information required to make choices, talk to someone who recently purchased a home, a car, or a personal computer. Talk to a corporate official deciding whether to introduce a new product, sell over the Internet, build a new factory, or buy another firm. Or consider your own decision about going to college. You already may have talked to friends, relatives, teachers, and guidance counselors about it. You might review school catalogs, college guides, and web sites. You might even visit some campuses. The decision will take time and money, and probably will involve some hassle and worry.

Because information is costly to acquire, you are often willing to pay others to gather and digest it for you. College guides, travel agents, real estate brokers, career counselors, restaurant

**market economics**
Study of economic behavior in particular markets, such as the market for computers or for unskilled labor

**national economics**
Study of the economic behavior of the economy as a whole, especially the national economy

### Main Idea

**Marginal Cost/Benefit**

*To make effective consumer decisions, you need to compare the costs and benefits of alternative choices. If you find your favorite jeans on sale, what would be the marginal benefit of purchasing another pair of these jeans? What would be the marginal cost of this decision?*

---

critics, movie reviewers, specialized web sites, and *Consumer Reports* magazine all offer information to help improve your economic choices. *Rational decision makers will continue to acquire information as long as the marginal benefit expected from that information exceeds the marginal cost of gathering it.*

### Market Economics and National Economics

Although you have made thousands of economic choices, you probably have seldom thought about your own economic behavior. For example, why are you reading this book right now rather than doing something else? **Market economics**, or *microeconomics*, focuses on your economic behavior and the economic behavior of others who make choices involving what to buy and what to sell, how much to work and how much to play, how much to borrow and how much to save. Market economics examines the factors that influence individual economic choices and how markets coordinate the choices of various decision makers. For example, market economics explains how price and output are determined in the markets for breakfast cereal, sports equipment, or unskilled labor.

You probably have given little thought to what influences your own economic choices. You likely have given even less thought to how your choices link up with those made by hundreds of millions of others in the U.S. economy to determine economy-wide measures such as total production, employment, and economic growth. **National economics**, or *macroeconomics*, focuses on the performance of the economy as a whole, especially the national economy.

Thus market economics looks at the individual pieces of the economic puzzle. National economics fits all the pieces together to look at the big picture.

**CHECKPOINT**
Describe the role of marginal analysis in making economic choices.

14     **CHAPTER 1**  What Is Economics?

# Market Participants

There are four types of decision makers in the economy: households, firms, governments, and the rest of the world. Their interaction determines how an economy's resources get allocated.

## Four Types of Participants

*Households* play the leading role in the economy. As consumers, households demand the goods and services produced. As resource owners, households supply the resources used to produce goods and services.

*Firms, governments,* and *the rest of the world* demand the resources that households supply, and then use these resources to supply the goods and services that households demand. The rest of the world includes foreign households, firms, and governments that supply resources and products to U.S. markets and demand resources and products from U.S. markets.

## Markets

**Markets** are the means by which buyers and sellers carry out exchange. By bringing together the two sides of exchange, demand and supply, markets determine price and quantity. Markets may be physical places, such as super-markets, department stores, shopping malls, or flea markets. Markets also involve other ways for buyers and sellers to communicate, such as the stock market, telephones, bulletin boards, the Internet, and face-to-face bargaining.

Markets provide information about the quantity, quality, and price of products offered for sale. Goods and services are bought and sold in *product markets*. Resources are bought and sold in *resource markets*. The most important resource market is the labor, or job, market.

## A Circular-Flow Model

Now that you have learned a bit about economic decision makers, consider how they interact. Such a picture is conveyed by the *circular-flow model*, which describes the flow of resources, products, income, and revenue among economic decision makers. A simple circular-flow model focuses on the interaction between households and firms in a market economy. Figure 1.1 shows households on the left and firms on the right.

Households supply human resources, natural resources, and capital goods to firms through resource markets, shown in the lower portion of the figure. In return, households demand goods and services from firms through product markets, shown on the upper portion of the figure. Viewed from the business

*market*
The means by which buyers and sellers carry out exchange

A shopping mall is a familiar type of physical market. The Internet is a communications medium that enables markets to be conducted via computer. Compare physical markets with markets conducted via computer. How are they similar? How do they differ?

Lesson 1.2 • *Economic Theory*      **15**

## TEACH

### Market Participants

Introduce the concept of market participants by showing students a picture of a new pickup truck. Ask them to identify different groups of customers who might choose to purchase the truck. Encourage them to keep going until they have identified private consumers in the United States, a government agency, a business, and consumers in a foreign nation. Point out that a share of the trucks that are produced in the United States is purchased by each of these groups and that they are market participants in the U.S. economy. Ask students to describe how these participants are sellers as well as buyers in the U.S. market—people sell their labor, government sells the right to travel on toll roads, and businesses sell the goods and services they produce, as do foreign nations.

### *Think Critically Through Visuals*

Direct students to focus their attention on the photograph on this page. Ask for a volunteer to answer the questions posed in the caption.

### Answer

Answers will vary. Answers might compare the following aspects of a purchase: goods available, methods of payment, personal interaction, physical interaction, delivery, and convenience.

### *Think Critically Through Visuals*

Introduce the circular flow model by directing students to focus their attention on **Figure 1.1—Circular-Flow Model for Households and Firms** on page 16. Follow up with the **Team Work** activity on page 16.

## TEAM WORK

Remind students to use Figure 1.1 as a reference for their discussions. Instruct students to trace the flow on the model printed in the book using their finger or a closed pen. Suggest that students follow up by sketching the model as they explain it to each other.

## Curriculum Connection—Writing

For markets to work efficiently, buyers need accurate knowledge about products that are being offered for sale. Still, some advertising provides little useful information to consumers. Assign students to bring print advertisements to class that they believe are not particularly useful to consumers. Ask them to rewrite the ads in ways that would provide consumers with information that would help them make rational buying decisions. Ask students to explain why they think some businesses do not advertise in a way that informs consumers.

CHECKPOINT

Invite a student to answer the checkpoint that appears on this page.

## Answers

Households supply human resources, natural resources, and capital goods to firms through resource markets. In return, households demand goods and services from firms through product markets. Firms supply goods and services to households through product markets, and firms demand human resources, natural resources, and capital goods from households through resource markets.

### APPLY

Assign Lesson 1.2 from the Contemporary Economics Workbook.

### e-con @pps

Encourage students to apply their knowledge of concepts presented in this lesson as they explore economic news stories, policy debates, and data available at **econxtra.swlearning**.

### ASSESS

Assign all or part of Lesson 1.2 Assessment on page 17 as homework or an in-class activity.

### Xtra! Study Tools

Direct students to the online study tools for Lesson 1.2 at **econxtra.swlearning.com**.

### CLOSE

**Revisit** the **In the News** feature on the first page of the lesson. Ask students to review their preliminary answers and discuss the questions, now that they have completed this lesson.

**Review** the objectives for Lesson 1.2. Students should be able to:

- Explain the goal of economic theory.
- Understand the role of marginal analysis in making economic choices.
- Explain how market participants interact.

**Circular-Flow Model for Households and Firms**

Figure 1.1

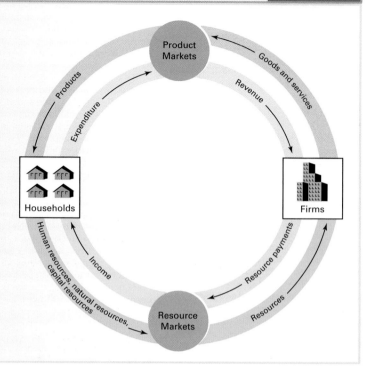

Households earn income by supplying resources to the resource markets, as shown in the lower portion of the model. Firms demand these resources to produce goods and services, which they supply to the product markets. This is shown in the upper portion of the model. Households spend their income to demand these goods and services. This spending flows through the product market to become revenue to firms.

end, firms supply goods and services to households through product markets, and firms demand human resources, natural resources, and capital resources from households through resource markets.

### TEAM WORK

Divide into groups of four students to study how market participants interact. One pair of students will work together to trace the flow in the circular model from households to firms. The other pair will trace the flow from firms through the product markets. Each pair of students will then explain the flow they have studied to the other pair.

The flows of resources and products are supported by the flows of income and expenditure—that is, *by the flow of money.* The supply and demand for resources come together in resource markets to determine resource prices, which flow as income to the households. The supply and demand for products come together in product markets to determine the prices for goods and services, which flow as revenue to firms.

Resources and products flow in one direction—in this case, counterclockwise—and the corresponding payments flow in the other direction—clockwise.

**CHECKPOINT**

How do market participants interact?

16     **CHAPTER 1**   What Is Economics?

### RETEACH

Some people believe consumer buying is the most important part of the circular flow of the economy because it provides businesses with money to buy resources and create products. Others argue that if businesses did not hire and pay workers, people could not buy products, and so this is the most important part of the circular flow. Assign students to sketch a circular flow model that shows their family's sources of income and types of spending. Do they believe their spending or their income is more important to the economy?

## Key Concepts

1. How are economic theories used in the real world?

2. Why do economists often use the other-things-constant assumption when they develop economic theories?

3. What does rational self-interest suggest that people want to achieve?

4. When Anthony went to watch another school's basketball team he saw that their center was nearly seven-feet tall. He immediately decided that this person would be that team's highest scorer. What theory did he use to draw this conclusion?

5. Identify each of the following as an example of either a positive or normative statement.

   a. Drew earns $7.50 per hour at his job.

   b. $250 is too much to pay for a prom dress.

   c. Schools should hire more math teachers.

   d. The unemployment rate in 2002 was 5.7%.

   e. The minimum wage ought to be increased.

6. Tomás bought two pairs of shoes for $60 each. He chose not to purchase a third pair at this price. What do you know about the marginal value of a third pair of shoes for Tomás?

## Graphing Exercise

7. Latischa works for a business that produces pocket calculators. She saves $50 from the $500 she earns each week. Yesterday she used part of her savings to make a $4,000 down payment on a new car. Draw and label a simple circular-flow model. Use the figure to the right as a guide. Place both of the transactions described on your model, and describe the flows between households and firms that result.

Xtra!
Study Tools
econxtra.swlearning.com

## Think Critically

8. **Research** Find the number of new claims for unemployment insurance compensation filed in a recent week in your state at www.dol.gov. If you do not have Internet access, use 60,403, the number of claims filed in the second week of October 2002 in California. Explain how unemployment relates to both market economics and national economics.

9. **Marketing** Examine some of the advertising that a college or university you might choose to attend uses to try to convince new students to apply for admission. Explain how this advertising is intended to help potential students make rational choices.

---

## Key Concepts

1. An economic theory or economic model is a simplification of economic reality. Economists use them to make predictions about what will happen in the real world. Consumers, entrepreneurs, and political leaders use these predictions when they make economic decisions.

2. They are trying to create a streamlined version of economic reality to make their theories easier to understand and use.

3. It means that people try to maximize the expected benefit achieved with a given cost, or to minimize the expected cost of achieving a given benefit.

4. He used a theory that relates tall basketball players with high scoring ability.

5. a. positive
   b. normative
   c. normative
   d. positive
   e. normative

6. Tomás believes that the marginal value of third pair of shoes is less than $60.00.

## Graphing Exercise

7. Latischa sells her labor for a wage in the resource market. Labor flows from households to firms through the resource market, while wages flow from firms to households. Latischa buys a new car in the product market. Goods flow from firms to households through the product market while revenue flows from households to firms.

   An example of an acceptable model appears at the bottom of this page.

*The Answer Key is continued on page 28.*

---

## Visualizing the Answer—Graphing Exercise

7. The exact labels that students use will vary; however, the labels should reflect the following categories and flows:

*Categories*

A      Latischa (household)

B1    Automobile market (product market)

B2    Calculator market (product market)

C1    Car dealership (firm)

C2    Calculator business (firm)

D      Resource market

*Flows*

1a    Car (good)

1b    Car (product)

2a    $4,000 down payment (expenditure)

2b    $4,000 down payment (revenue)

3a    Latischa's labor (human resources)

3b    Latischa's labor (resources)

4a    $500/week (resource payments)

4b    $500/week (income)

## FOCUS

Point out to students that a key assumption about behavior is that in making choices, you rationally select alternatives you perceive to be in your best interests. This feature demonstrates the concept of rational self-interest.

## TEACH

Instruct students to read the **Movers & Shakers** feature about Christopher Curtis. Point out that some students may find it helpful to read the article, read the questions at the bottom of the page, and then reread the article.

## ASSESS

Use the questions in Source Reading and Entrepreneurs in Action at the bottom of the profile to assess the students' understanding of this **Movers & Shakers** feature.

### Answers to Source Reading

The economic choice made by Curtis and his friend was to give themselves a half hour off every hour. The marginal cost of this decision was that they had to work harder during the other half hour. The marginal benefit of this decision was that they gained a half-hour break.

### Answers to Entrepreneurs in Action

Answers will vary. Encourage students to closely examine their interests and passions and to consider careers that would complement them.

# movers & shakers

## Christopher Curtis *Children's Book Author*

For 13 years after high school graduation, Christopher Curtis worked on an assembly line. His job was hanging doors on automobiles. It was boring, repetitive work, but he believes it helped him become a writer.

"My friend and I used to 'double up' on the assembly line. That means we would each hang 30 doors in a row instead of doing every other one, which allowed us each a half hour off every hour. I discovered that if I spent my half hour off the line writing, time would fly by for me." Writing every day helped Curtis develop the flexibility and confidence in his writing that he believes he might never have developed otherwise. Writing became his passion.

Curtis's wife, Kaysandra, knew he wanted to be a writer. Eventually, with her encouragement, he quit his job and began writing full-time. Curtis didn't own a computer, so armed with a stack of legal pads, he spent his days at the library writing his book with pen and paper. He also began attending college. He eventually earned a political science degree from the University of Michigan.

Curtis's first book, *The Watsons Go to Birmingham—1963,* is a fictional book for children. It received two honors: a Newbery Honor and a Coretta Scott King Honor. Such recognition encouraged him to begin work on his second children's book, *Bud, Not Buddy,* about a ten-year-old boy who leaves his foster home in search of his father. This book won the Newbery Medal, the most prestigious award in children's literature. It also won the Coretta Scott King Medal, given each year to a black writer for an inspirational and educational contribution to literature. His next book, to be published in 2004, is titled *Bucking the Sarge.*

Today, in addition to writing books, Curtis frequently visits schools. He meets with groups of children, explaining how he became a writer, and describing the steps he takes to write a book. He also reads to them from his books. "I tell kids that if I can do it, they can do it, too."

Aspiring writers often ask Curtis for advice. "I always tell them that the more they do it, the better they'll get. You have to be patient." He encourages everyone to look for opportunity in spite of barriers they may face. "Lack of money is a very real barrier, but it can be broken. If you are really passionate, do it for the sake of love. Plow right through."

### SOURCE READING

Curtis said that if he and his friend doubled up on their job of hanging doors in the automobile factory, it "allowed us each a half hour off every hour. I discovered that if I spent my half hour off the line writing, time would fly by for me." What was the economic choice that Curtis and his friend made in the situation he describes? What were the marginal cost and the marginal benefit of their decision?

### ENTREPRENEURS IN ACTION

Like everyone else, entrepreneurs make choices based on their own self-interests. Christopher Curtis chose to become a children's book author because of his passion for writing and his commitment to children. What are you passionate about? Into what type of career could you channel this passion? Write a paragraph to answer these questions.

18    **CHAPTER 1**    What Is Economics?

## ENRICH

Invite interested students to write a paragraph that describes how the concept of rational self-interest applies to Curtis and the choices he made.

### Answer

Answers will vary. A possible answer: Curtis applied the concept of rational self-interest to reach his work-related decision. He maximized the expected benefits achieved in his workday while minimizing the cost associated with achieving these benefits. To Curtis, the benefit was to get a break every half hour from his monotonous job to do something creative and stimulating—writing. The cost associated with this was that he had to work harder during his time on. For Curtis, this benefit outweighed the cost.

# 1.3 Opportunity Cost and Choice

## Objectives

> Define opportunity cost.

> Evaluate guidelines for making choices.

> Analyze the opportunity cost of attending college.

## Overview

Think about a decision you just made: the decision to read this chapter right now rather than study for another course, play sports, watch TV, go online, get some sleep, or do something else. Suppose your best alternative to reading this now is getting some sleep. The cost of reading this chapter is passing up the opportunity to sleep. Because of scarcity, whenever you make a choice you must pass up another opportunity—you experience an *opportunity cost*.

## Key Terms

**opportunity cost**

**sunk cost**

## [ In the News ]

### ● Women Continue to Move into Top Jobs

Women now hold 15.7 percent of the top-ranking executive positions at America's largest companies, compared with 12.5 percent in 2000 and 8.7 percent in 1995. According to a November 2002 Associated Press article, the number of female corporate officers at Fortune 500 companies increased 3.2 percentage points over the past two years. "It's clearly not as fast as anyone might like to see, but it's certainly measured progress, which is positive and sustainable in the right direction," said Diana Ferguson, vice president and treasurer of Sara Lee Corp. Women make up 17.9 percent of senior officers at Sara Lee. "One of the things I've been pleased to see and could be helpful in promoting more women is companies being willing to give high-potential individuals 'stretch assignments' to allow them to grow into their roles and get into the officer ranks," said Ferguson. This news is great for many women, but certainly not for all. As men have long learned, there is a heavy cost associated with the choice of aiming for the top rungs of the corporate ladder, and many opportunities lost.

#### Think About It

What are some of the opportunities a woman might miss out on if she aims for the top rungs of the corporate ladder?

◄ | ►

**19**

## National Content Standards in Economics

A complete list of the NCEE Standards appears on pages xxiv–xxv of this book. The following standards are addressed in Lesson 1.3.

Standard 1: Scarcity

Standard 2: Marginal Cost/Benefit

Standard 13: Role of Resources in Determining Income

Standard 15: Growth

---

## Opportunity Cost

Introduce opportunity cost by asking each student to imagine that she or he has decided to spend $10 to see a movie that has gotten very good reviews. Ask students to identify an alternative use of their money that they would have to give up in order to make this choice. Go around the room and ask students what their opportunity cost would be. There will probably be as many examples of opportunity costs as there are students. Use this to demonstrate that different people experience different opportunity costs, even when they make the same choice in how to use their money.

### Think Critically Through Visuals

Direct students to focus their attention on the photograph on this page. Ask for a volunteer to answer the questions posed in the caption.

#### Answer

Answers will vary. Possible answer: The opportunity costs you might face in being involved in school sports is that you do not have time for an after school job or you do not have time to be involved in other school organizations, such as student council.

### CHECKPOINT

Invite a student to answer the checkpoint that appears on page 21.

#### Answer

Opportunity cost is the value of the best alternative you must pass up. Sometimes this opportunity cost is "expensive" because the best alternative is very attractive. Other times, the opportunity cost is "inexpensive" because the best alternative does not appeal to you.

---

**opportunity cost**

The value of the best alternative passed up for the chosen item or activity

# Opportunity Cost

What do you mean when you talk about the cost of something? Isn't it what you must give up or go without to get that thing? The **opportunity cost** of the chosen item or activity is *the value of the best alternative you must pass up*. You can think of opportunity cost as the *opportunity lost*. Sometimes opportunity cost can be measured in dollar terms. However, as you shall see, money usually captures only part of opportunity cost.

## Nothing Better to Do?

How many times have you heard people say they did something because they "had nothing better to do"? They actually mean they had no alternative more attractive than the one they chose. Yet, according to the idea of opportunity cost, people *always* do what they do because they had nothing better to do. The choice selected seems, at the time, preferable to any other possible choice. You are reading this page right now because you have nothing better to do.

## Estimate Opportunity Cost

Only the individual decision maker can select the most attractive alternative. You, the chooser, seldom know the actual value of the best alternative you gave up, because that alternative is "the road not taken."

If you give up an evening of pizza and conversation with friends to work on a term paper, you will never know the exact value of what you gave up. You know only what you *expected*. You expected the value of working on that paper to exceed the value of the best alternative.

## Opportunity Cost Varies

Your opportunity cost depends on your alternatives. This is why you are less likely to study on a Saturday night than on a Tuesday night. On Saturday night, the opportunity cost of studying is higher because your alternatives are more attractive than they are on a Tuesday night, when there's less going on.

What if you go to a movie on Saturday night? Your opportunity cost is the value of the best alternative you gave up, which might be attending a basketball

© Getty Images/PhotoDisc

**Participating in a team sport such as soccer or basketball involves many opportunity costs. If you are involved in a team sport at your school, what opportunity costs do you face? If you are not involved in a team sport, were the opportunity costs of involvement a factor in your decision not to participate? Why or why not?**

20    **CHAPTER 1**   What Is Economics?

---

### Outside Resources

**School District Budgets** Provide students with copies of their local school district's budget. Ask them what trade-offs were made in how the district chose to spend its money. What opportunity costs resulted from these decisions?

**Catalog Delivery Charges** Mail-order and Internet marketers usually give customers a choice of delivery services. The faster they are, the more they cost. Provide students with an example of delivery charges and ask them to identify the opportunity cost customers face when they opt for the fastest delivery. Why do they make this choice?

# Ethics in Action

**A Question of Ethics** Kenneth Lay, Enron; Bernie Ebbers, WorldCom; and Dennis Kozlowski, Tyco. These are just three of the many disgraced CEOs and their corporations that have made business ethics a hot issue and personal ethics a major focus in schools across the nation. If you think about it, isn't the disgrace of these corporate leaders related to how they dealt with opportunity cost and choice?

## Think Critically

Where do we learn how to make the "right" choice, the ethical choice? Does the ability to make ethical or unethical choices begin with the core values taught by parents and reinforced by schooling? If you work in an unethical company, is it more difficult to make ethical decisions? Are the stories about Enron, WorldCom, and Tyco about evil individuals? Or are they stories of ordinary behavior within an unethical subculture?

---

game. Studying on Saturday night might rank well down the list of alternatives for you—perhaps ahead of cleaning your room but behind watching TV.

Opportunity cost is a personal thing, but in some cases, estimating a dollar cost for goods and services may work. For example, the opportunity cost of a new DVD player is the benefit of spending that $200 on the best alternative. In other cases, the dollar cost may omit some important elements, particularly the value of the time involved. For example, renting a movie costs not just the rental fee but the time and travel expense it takes to get it, watch it, and return it.

### ✓ CHECKPOINT
What is opportunity cost, and why does it vary with circumstances?

## Choose Among Alternatives

Now that you understand what opportunity cost is and how it can vary depending on the circumstances, consider what's involved in actually choosing among alternatives.

### Calculate Opportunity Cost

Economists assume that your rational self-interest will lead you to select the most valued alternative. This does not

mean you must calculate the value of all possible alternatives. Because acquiring information about alternatives is costly and time-consuming, you usually make choices based on limited or even faulty information. Indeed, some choices may turn out to be poor ones: You went for a picnic but it rained. Your new shoes pinch your toes.

Regret about lost opportunities is captured in the common expression "coulda, woulda, shoulda." At the time you made the choice, however, you believed you were making the best use of all your scarce resources, including the time required to gather information and assess your alternatives.

### Time—The Ultimate Limitation

The sultan of Brunei is among the world's richest people, with wealth estimated at $16 billion based on huge oil revenues that flow into his tiny country. He has two palaces, one for each wife. The larger palace has 1,788 rooms, with walls of fine Italian marble and a throne room the size of a football field.

Supported by such wealth, the sultan appears to have overcome the economic problem caused by scarcity. However, although he can buy just about whatever he wants, his time to enjoy these goods and services is scarce. If he pursues one activity, he cannot at the same time do something else. Each activity he undertakes has an opportunity cost. Consequently, the

---

### Choose Among Alternatives

Introduce the concept of choosing among alternatives by providing each student with a copy of a hypothetical assignment to write a major research report for a science, English, or history class. Tell them to imagine that the report will count half of their grade in this class. Ask them to decide how much time they would be willing to use over the next three weeks to complete the report. Ask them to identify and describe the opportunity cost(s) they could experience for the decision they make. Remind students that they might give up more than alternative uses of their time. They might forgo income they could have received from working, or better grades in other classes if they had spent more time studying for them instead. What opportunity cost might they pay for not allocating even more time to complete the report? Make sure they understand that by choosing to spend little time completing the report, they might give up the value of a passing grade in the class.

### Ethics in Action

Have students to work in pairs to discuss the ethical issue featured on this page, and develop answers to the questions presented.

#### Answers to Think Critically

Answers will vary. Possible answer: Most people learn to make the right choice from their family, friends, church, and work. The ability to make ethical choices begins with core values. If you work for an unethical company, it is harder to make ethical decisions because of your surroundings. Although some of the people involved in recent corporate scandals might be evil, many of the people involved made unethical decisions because they were influenced by their surroundings.

---

## ENRICH

Ask students to list several activities they enjoy, such as reading, watching TV, playing football, listening to their favorite music, etc. Then ask them to include the amount of time they spend doing each activity in an average week. Ask students to explain why they don't spend more time doing these favorite things. What opportunity costs would they pay to be able to do these things more often?

## Choose Among Alternatives

Describe the following situation to the class. Last year, Lamar bought a new bicycle for $500. It came with a six-month guarantee against all defects in parts or quality. For a little over one year, the bicycle worked perfectly. Last week, however, the gears began to slip from one to another while Lamar was peddling up a hill. He took the bicycle to the store where he bought it and was told that the rear-wheel sprocket was bent and it would cost $75 to replace it. To pay this amount, Lamar will have to give up going to a concert that he really wanted to see. But if he doesn't have his bicycle repaired, he won't have any transportation to get to his after-school job. Ask students to explain how Lamar should consider the $500 he spent to buy the bicycle last year when he makes his decision. Make sure they understand that Lamar should not consider the $500. It is a sunk cost. He should weigh only the value of a functional bicycle against the value of attending the concert.

### Think Critically Through Visuals

Direct students to focus their attention on the photograph on this page. Ask for a volunteer to answer the questions posed in the caption.

### Answer

You should move to the new line that opened. This illustrates the economic concept of sunk cost—the cost you have already incurred. In this case you ignore the time cost you have already incurred in the other line and switch to the line that just opened.

### ✓ CHECKPOINT

Invite a student to answer the checkpoint that appears on this page.

### Answer

1) Calculate Opportunity Cost: Calculate the cost of passing up each alternative.
2) Time: Consider which alternative requires the most time and how much time you have to offer.
3) Ignore Sunk Cost: Ignore any cost (time, money) that has been put into the alternatives prior to the decision. Consider only the costs that arise after the decision has been made.

---

**sunk cost**
A cost you have already incurred and cannot recover, regardless of what you do now

---

sultan must choose from among the competing uses of his scarcest resource, time. Although your alternatives are less exotic, you too face a time constraint, especially when term papers and exams demand your time.

### Ignore Sunk Cost

Suppose you have just finished shopping for groceries and are wheeling your grocery cart to the checkout. How do you decide which line to join? You pick the one you think will involve the least time. What if, after waiting ten minutes in a line that barely moves, you notice that a cashier has opened another line and invites you to check out. Do you switch to the open line, or do you think, "I've already spent ten minutes in this line. I'm staying here"?

The ten minutes you waited represents a **sunk cost**, which is a cost you have already incurred and cannot recover, regardless of what you do

now. You should ignore sunk cost in making economic choices, and you should switch to the newly opened line.

Economic decision makers should consider only those costs that are affected by their choice. Sunk costs already have been incurred and are not recoverable. Therefore, sunk costs are irrelevant and should be ignored. Likewise, you should walk out on a boring movie, even one that cost you $10. The irrelevance of sunk costs is underscored by the proverb, "There's no point crying over spilt milk." The milk has already spilled. What you do now cannot change that fact.

### ✓ CHECKPOINT

Evaluate guidelines for choosing among alternatives.

**You are standing in line at a movie theater's concession stand when suddenly, a cashier opens another line. The movie is about to begin. Should you stay in the line you have been waiting in, or move to the new line? What economic concept does this situation illustrate?**

---

*The Graphing Workshop* ——— See It

Use the Graphing Workshop feature to introduce students to the interpretation of graphs. Direct students to the Graphing Workshop for Chapter 1 at **econxtra.swlearning.com**. Instruct students to click on **See It** to view the tutorial "Interpreting Graphs."

# Sharpen Your Life Skills

## Understand Cause and Effect

Economic events don't just happen. They almost always result from other things that happened first. One of the best ways to understand an economic event is to investigate the factors that caused it to take place. An important benefit of learning about past economic events is the insight you will gain into what might happen if similar events take place in the future.

In 1974, for example, war broke out between Israel and some of her neighboring Arab states. As a result, the flow of crude oil from the Middle East to the United States and other nations was reduced by as much as [?] percent. Oil is a basic natural resource used to produce many goods and services. In 1974, as today, the economies of the United States and most other developed nations rely on imported oil. With a reduced supply of oil these nations were faced with different sets of opportunity costs when they chose how to use the oil that they had. With this in mind, answer the following questions.

## Apply Your Skill

Due to the shortage of oil in 1974, not enough gasoline could be produced for all the people who wanted to buy it. To try to address the problem, the government limited the amount of gasoline most people could purchase to ten gallons at one time. Later, people were allowed to buy gasoline only on every other day of the week and for a few months, no gasoline could be purchased on Sundays. Even so, some filling stations ran out of gasoline. There often were two- to three-hour waits in line to buy gasoline when it was available. Describe how events that took place nearly five thousand miles from the United States affected the economic decisions made by American consumers in 1974. How did this change the opportunity costs of their decisions?

2. Imagine that a large pipeline that carries 25 percent of the natural gas used in the Northeast is destroyed in an earthquake. It is the middle of winter and nearly half the homes in the Northeast are heated with natural gas. Further, 20 percent of the electrical power plants, and 15 percent of other businesses rely on natural gas to operate. What economic effects are likely to result from this event? How would it change the opportunity costs people face when they make decisions?

## Sharpen Your Life Skills

### Understand Cause and Effect

After studying Lesson 1.3, students should be able to answer the questions on this page.

### Apply Your Skill

Consider allowing students to work in pairs for this assignment.

### Answers

1. Answers will vary. The 1974 Arab-Israeli war reduced the amount of gasoline available to American consumers. They reacted by driving less and sharing rides when possible. This changed people's lifestyles and harmed the tourist industry in the United States and many other nations. In the years that followed 1974, many American drivers traded in their large "gas guzzlers" for smaller, more fuel-efficient vehicles. The opportunity cost of buying gasoline included the value of alternative uses of time that was spent waiting in line at filling stations.

2. Answers will vary. People who live in the Northeast will be forced to decide how to deal with the reduced supply of natural gas. They will not be able to heat their homes to the same degree, generate as much electricity, or keep all of their businesses in operation. Whatever choice is made, the opportunity cost paid for each use of natural gas will be greater than it was before. If more businesses are kept open, some of the value of warm homes and well-lit roads must be given up.

## Economic Headlines

Have students locate an article about the economic impact of another event in their lifetime. Instruct them to write a summary of the article. As an alternative or adjunct, invite students to interview a family member or adult acquaintance about the event. Possible topics appear in the list below.

- Corporate scandals
- September 11 terrorist attacks
- War in Iraq
- SARS epidemic
- Blaster worm
- August 2003 Northeast power failure

## The Opportunity Cost of College

Introduce the opportunity cost of college by asking students to estimate the amount they could earn if they took a job immediately after graduating from high school. Have them project the value of this flow of income over four years. Then ask them to estimate the costs of tuition, fees, books, and room and board at a college they might attend after graduating from high school. Direct them to use these amounts to make an estimate of their cost of earning a four-year college degree. Ask them to discuss the opportunity costs they might pay if they decide not to attend college after high school. Make sure they understand what they might be giving up—potentially higher salary in the future, knowledge and skills they would learn, and the enjoyment of a "college experience."
Continue the discussion by asking students to think about the opportunity cost of college for elite athletes and successful young entertainers.

### Think Critically Through Visuals

Direct students to focus their attention on the photograph on this page. Suggest that students take time to consider this section of the text in view of their own situation.

### THE WALL STREET JOURNAL

**Reading It Right**

Invite a student to explain the relevance of the statement from *The Wall Street Journal* that appears on page 25.

### Answer

Answers will vary. Possible answer: While the supply of qualified economics professors has risen, the demand has not. This has made becoming an economics professor a harder and more selective process.

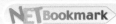

For the **NET Bookmark** on page 25, direct students to **econxtra.swlearning.com**. Remind them to click on the link for Lesson 1.3 to find the appropriate link for this **NET Bookmark**. This activity will take several hours. Consider allowing students to work in pairs.

# The Opportunity Cost of College

Now that you have some idea about opportunity cost and choice, you can apply these concepts in deciding whether or not to go to college.

What will be your opportunity cost of attending college full-time? What will be the most valued alternative you must give up to attend college? If you already know what kind of job you can get with a high school education, you have a fair idea of the income you must give up to attend college.

### Forgone Earnings

You may think that if you do not go to college, you could find a job paying $16,000 a year, after taxes. But wait a minute. Don't many college students also work part-time during the school year and full-time during the summer? If you do the same, suppose you could earn $7,000 a year, after taxes.

Thus, by attending college you give up the $16,000 you could earn from a full-time job, yet you could still earn $7,000 from part-time and summer work. Your annual earnings would be $9,000 lower ($16,000 minus $7,000) if you attend college. One part of your opportunity cost of college is the value of what you could have purchased with that additional $9,000 in income.

### Direct Costs of College

You also need to consider the direct costs of college itself. Suppose you must pay $5,000 a year for tuition, fees, and books at a public college (paying out-of-state rates would add about $5,000 to that, and attending a private college would add about $13,000). The opportunity cost of paying for tuition, fees, and books is the value of the goods and services that money could have purchased otherwise.

Have you made your decision about whether or not to attend college? If not, applying this section of the textbook to your own situation will help you carefully weigh the opportunity costs of this important decision.

24    **CHAPTER 1**   What Is Economics?

### Group Activity

Organize students into groups of four or five. Tell students to imagine that it is several years in the future and that for $8,000 they have purchased a used car with no guarantee. After they drive the car for about 3,000 miles, its transmission fails. In all other ways, the car seems to be in good condition. A mechanic says it will cost $2,000 to have it repaired, or it can be traded in for a similar used car that would cost an extra $5,000. Each group must decide whether to replace or repair the car. How does this situation demonstrate opportunity cost and sunk cost?

## Other College Costs

How about room and board? Expenses for room and board are not an opportunity cost of college because, even if you did not attend college, you would still need to live somewhere and eat something, though these costs could be higher at college. Likewise, whether or not you attended college, you would still incur outlays for items such as movies, CDs, clothing, toiletries, and laundry. Such expenses are not an opportunity cost of attending college. They are personal expenses that arise regardless of what you do. So, for simplicity, assume that room, board, and personal expenses will be the same whether or not you attend college.

The forgone earnings of $9,000 plus the $5,000 for tuition, fees, and books yield an opportunity cost of $14,000 per year for a student paying in-state rates at a public college. The opportunity cost jumps to about $19,000 for those paying out-of-state rates at a public college and to about $27,000 for those at a private college. Scholarships, but not loans, would reduce your opportunity cost.

## Other-Things-Constant Assumption

This analysis assumes that all other things are constant. If you expect college to be more painful than your best alternative, then the opportunity cost of attending college is even higher. In other words, if you expect to find college difficult, boring, and in most ways more unpleasant than a full-time job, then your money cost understates your opportunity cost. You not only pay the dollar cost of college, but you must also give up a more pleasant quality of life. If, however, you think college will be

To examine whether college would be a sensible investment for you, try Professor Jane Leuthold's COLLEGE CHOICE program. This program may be accessed through econxtra.swlearning.com.

**econxtra.swlearning.com**

more enjoyable than a full-time job, then the dollar cost overstates your opportunity cost—the next best alternative involves a less satisfying quality of life.

Evidently, most young people view college as a wise investment in their future, even though college is costly and perhaps even painful for some. College graduates on average earn about twice as much per year as high-school graduates.

Still, college is not for everyone. Some find the opportunity cost too high. For example, Tiger Woods, once an economics major at Stanford University, dropped out after two years to earn a fortune in professional golf, including a $100 million five-year endorsement contract with Nike. Some high school seniors who believe they are ready for professional basketball skip college altogether, as do most pro tennis players and many singers and actors. However, for most of you, the opportunity cost of attending college isn't nearly as high.

 **CHECKPOINT**
How do you measure the opportunity cost of attending college?

## THE WALL STREET JOURNAL

**Reading It Right** What's the relevance of the following statement from *The Wall Street Journal:* "With economics the most popular undergraduate major at many top colleges, demand for economics professors has led to a bidding war for the most highly regarded candidates."

---

**Lesson 1.3** • *Opportunity Cost and Choice* **25**

---

**CHECKPOINT**
Invite a student to answer the checkpoint that appears on this page.

### Answer

You decide whether the costs of forgone earnings outweigh the direct costs associated with college, or vice versa.

### APPLY

Assign Lesson 1.3 from the Contemporary Economics Workbook.

### e-con @pps

Encourage students to apply their knowledge of concepts presented in this lesson as they explore economic news stories, policy debates, and data available at **econxtra.swlearning.com**.

### ASSESS

Assign all or part of Lesson 1.3 Assessment on page 26 as homework or an in-class activity.

### Xtra! Study Tools

Direct students to the online study tools for Lesson 1.3 at **econxtra.swlearning.com**.

### CLOSE

**Revisit** the **In the News** feature on the first page of the lesson. Ask students to review their preliminary answers and discuss the questions, now that they have completed this lesson.

**Review** the objectives for Lesson 1.3. Students should be able to:

- Define opportunity cost.
- Evaluate guidelines for making choices.
- Analyze the opportunity cost of attending college.

## RETEACH

In economic analysis, the assumption of *other things constant* is almost always applied. In real life, things are rarely this simple. Tell students to assume that they have decided to purchase a new bicycle (or a similar product that they might want) for $500. They earn $75 each week from a part-time job and have no other major uses for this income. Ask students to list other things that might not be constant that could make this a bad choice. Have them explain why economists must make the *other-things-constant* assumption.

### Key Concepts

1. There is a best alternative for every choice. The value of the alternative you pass up is the opportunity cost of the choice that was made.

2. Answers will vary. The opportunity cost of a particular decision changes when the values of alternative choices change. The opportunity cost of staying home is often greater on a Saturday night than on a Monday night, when you have little else you could do.

3. The very wealthy are forced to pay opportunity costs by the limited time they have to enjoy the many products they are able to purchase.

4. Sunk costs that have been paid and cannot be recovered should not be considered when making new choices. Only the costs of benefits of each individual choice should be considered. If you pay $500 for a used motorcycle, that cost should have no bearing on whether you choose to have the motorcycle's clutch replaced for $250 six months later when it breaks.

5. The greatest cost of attending college for many students is the value of the lost earnings they could have received from working instead of completing their degree.

### Graphing Exercises

6. The answer to this exercise is at the bottom of this page.

7. Answers will vary. The value of buying a snow blower depends on the likelihood of a significant amount of snow. At the start of winter, people in North Dakota have an expectation of many snowstorms in their area. Therefore, the value of a snow blower increases when compared to alternative uses (opportunity costs) of people's scarce funds. As a result, people bought more of Harold's snow blowers in the fall than at any other time of the year.

*The Answer Key is continued on page 29.*

---

### Key Concepts

1. Why must there be an opportunity cost for every choice you make?

2. Why isn't the opportunity cost of using your time to do homework always the same?

3. What factor forces even people who are very wealthy to face opportunity costs?

4. Why should consumers ignore costs they have already paid when making decisions?

5. What is the greatest cost of attending college at publicly funded institutions?

### Graphing Exercises

6. Harold sells snowblowers at his hardware store in North Dakota. Although he never changes his price, his sales vary throughout the year. The following table shows his sales in each month of last year. Draw a line graph that demonstrates these data.

7. Explain how your graph shows that the value of buying a snowblower changes over time. What does this have to do with the opportunity cost of other uses for limited funds?

**Harold's Snowblower Sales**

| Month | Sales |
|-----------|-------|
| January | 13 |
| February | 11 |
| March | 3 |
| April | 0 |
| May | 0 |
| June | 0 |
| July | 0 |
| August | 0 |
| September | 8 |
| October | 32 |
| November | 38 |
| December | 21 |

### Think Critically

8. **Entrepreneurship** Wilma owns a 200-acre farm. She could plant either beans or tomatoes. If the weather is sunny and there is enough rain, she can earn $400 per acre of tomatoes. However, if it is dry or cloudy, tomatoes may earn her no profit at all. Beans are hardy and will grow well unless the weather is truly awful. Wilma can count on earning $200 per acre from beans. Explain why Wilma cannot be sure of the opportunity cost of any decision she might make. What do you think she will choose to do? Why?

9. **Office Technology** Ms. Morra teaches introductory classes in office technology. Her school board has approved $15,000 for her to buy new computers to replace her old outdated models. For this amount she can buy 20 low-end computers that just meet her student's current needs, or she can purchase 10 computers with greater speed and capabilities that she really would like her students to learn to use. What is her opportunity cost for either of these choices?

**Xtra!**
**Study Tools**
*econxtra.swlearning.com*

---

**Harold's Snow Blower Sales**

### Visualizing the Answer—Graphing Exercise

6. The answer includes a graph based on the data provided. Students' graphs should look similar to the one shown here.

An Excel spreadsheet containing this graph, along with supporting data, is available on the Instructor's Resource CD.

# to History

# Glassmaking in Jamestown

Despite failed attempts to establish a colony in the New World, in 1606 King James I of England granted a charter for this purpose to the Virginia Company of London. Because earlier enterprises had been expensive, the required funds were raised through a joint stock company. Colonists were instructed to settle land between the 34th and 41st parallels. The three ships arrived at the site of Jamestown Island on May 13, 1607.

Labor for the colony was provided by "colonists" hired by the company. Many of the colonists, lured by the promise of easy gold, were not prepared for the ordeal that followed. These gentlemen, often younger sons of wealthy families who were not used to hard work, struggled to survive. Still, these men perceived their opportunity cost as being small because they stood to inherit little at home. The colony seemed a way for them to gain the land and prominence they could not obtain in England. Well-to-do colonists who provided their own armor and weapons were paid in land, dividends, or additional shares of stock. Less-well-off colonists received clothes, food, and arms from the company, and then after seven years, they received land.

The Virginia Company was still recruiting colonists when Captain Christopher Newport returned to England, bringing word of a struggling colony. Although disappointed that gold and silver did not lie on the beach or grow on the trees, the entrepreneurs of the Virginia Company still saw profitable opportunities in various industries. They believed the colony could take advantage of the land's natural resources and manufacture products for sale in England. One such product was glass. Demand for glass products in England in the early seventeenth century was growing. However, scarce resources in England limited the growth of the industry. England's forests were being depleted,

and it took a lot of wood—about a week of burning two to three cords per day—to get the furnaces hot enough to produce glass. The New World, with its unlimited forests, appeared an ideal spot for a glassmaking industry.

Glassmaking in England also suffered from a shortage of labor, as few people were skilled in the craft. Although some glassmakers had come from foreign countries, England could not meet its glass wants domestically. Much of it had to be imported, leading the Company to believe that a Virginia-based enterprise could produce glass more cheaply than it could be imported. Because glassmakers in England were doing very well, the opportunity cost of their leaving for the uncertainty of a new and dangerous land was too great. Countries that exported large amounts of glass were better places to recruit workers. Among the early settlers in Virginia in the summer of 1608 were eight Germans and Poles for the glassmaking industry. Some glass was produced, but the enterprise was short lived. Workers had little time to devote to their industry because they were too busy trying to survive. When the newly appointed governor of Virginia arrived on May 24, 1610, with 150 new colonists, only 60 survivors remained. Ninety percent of the colonists had died, and with them, America's first industry.

## THINK CRITICALLY

Devise an economic theory that could have guided the Virginia Company's decision to begin a colony in the New World. What questions and variables might these entrepreneurs have considered? What might their assumptions have been? What might their hypotheses have been?

## FOCUS

Point out that entrepreneurs made a significant impact on the economy of colonial Jamestown. This feature about glassmaking in Jamestown helps demonstrate the connection between economics and history.

## TEACH

Instruct students to read the **Connect to History** feature and answer the questions.

## ASSESS

Use the questions at the bottom of the page to assess the students' understanding of this feature.

### Answers to Think Critically

The economic theory behind the Virginia Company's decision to begin a colony in the New World was that in England, they had a limit to resources needed for their production, but in the New World these resources were in abundance. The questions these entrepreneurs might have considered were (1) What are the transportation costs to bring the glass back to England? and (2) Where will the labor supply come from? Their assumptions might have been that survival in the New World was not difficult and that many would take the opportunity to go there. Their hypotheses might have been that glass would be produced over in the New World with little problem, it would be shipped to England for little cost, and they would make a large profit and relieve a scarcity problem.

Lesson 1.3 • *Opportunity Cost and Choice* **27**

## Bibliography

Cotton, Lee. "The Virginia Company of London: Success or Failure?" Colonial National Historical Park, National Park Service, Jamestown Historic Briefs. July 15, 2002. www.nps.gov/colo/Jthanout/VACompany.html

Fishwick, Marshall W. *Jamestown: First English Colony*. New York: American Heritage Publishing Company, 1974.

Harrington, J.C. *Glassmaking at Jamestown*. Richmond: Dietz Press, 1952.

Lieberman, Jethro K. *Companion to the Constitution: How the Supreme Court Has Ruled on Issues from Abortion to Zoning*. Los Angeles: University of California Press, 1999.

Short, John. "Glassmaking at Jamestown." Colonial National Historical Park, National Park Service, Jamestown Historic Briefs. February 1994. www.nps.gov/colo/Jthanout/Glassmak.html

Ask students to revisit the questions they were asked to consider at the beginning of the chapter. Remind students that they should be able to answer all of the questions after studying Chapter 1.

- Why are characters in comic strips like Hagar the Horrible, Cathy, and Fox Trot missing a finger on each hand? See page 11—Simplify the Problem.

- Why are you reading this book right now rather than doing something else? See pages 11–12—Rational Self-Interest.

- In what way are people who pound on vending machines relying on a theory? See page 12—Everybody Uses Theories.

- Why is there no sense crying over spilt milk? See page 22—Ignore Sunk Cost.

### Exam *View*

Use **Exam**View to assess student learning.

- Create a chapter test using questions from the existing test bank.
- Add your own questions to the existing test bank.
- Generate multiple forms of a chapter test.

### Study Skills

Offer the following study skills suggestions for students as they review this chapter.

- Outline the chapter.
- Review key terms.
- Review Checkpoints.
- Work in pairs to quiz each other.
- Use Xtra! Study Tools for each lesson.

Direct students to the online quiz preparation for Chapter 1 at **econxtra.swlearning.com**.

---

# ① Chapter Assessment

## Summary

### 1.1 The Economic Problem

**a** Economic choices are necessary because of our unlimited desires and the scarce supply of productive resources available to satisfy them. There are three basic types of productive resources. *Human resources* is the broad category of human efforts, both physical and mental, used to produce goods and services. *Natural resources* are so-called "gifts of nature." Natural resources can be divided into renewable resources and exhaustible resources. *Capital resources* commonly include all human creations used to produce goods and services.

**Xtra! Quiz Prep**
*econxtra.swlearning.com*

**b** Both goods and services are able to satisfy human desires but goods can be seen, felt, and touched while services cannot. Goods and services are scarce if their price exceeds zero. Because goods and services are produced using scarce resources, they are themselves scarce. Goods or services that are truly free are not a concern of economics.

### 1.2 Economic Theory

**a** Economic models are simplifications of economic reality that are used to make predictions about the real world. When economic theories are constructed, they are based on simplifying assumptions that include *other things being equal* and *rational self-interest*.

**b** Some economic statements involve facts that can be proven right or wrong. These are *positive statements*. Other statements that are based on individual opinion cannot be proven right or wrong and are *normative statements*.

**c** Economic choice usually involves a change in the status quo. The only relevant factors are the benefits and costs of the next choice that is made. This is called *marginal analysis*. A rational decision maker will change the status quo as long as the expected marginal benefit

from the change exceeds the expected marginal cost.

**d** *Markets* are the means by which buyers and sellers carry out exchange. By bringing together the two sides of exchange, demand and supply, markets determine price and quantity.

**e** Economics can be seen from two perspectives. *Market economics* concerns how individuals make decisions. *National economics* focuses on the condition of the economy as a whole. There are four participants in the economy: *households, firms, governments,* and the *rest of the world*.

**f** An economic system can be represented by a circular-flow diagram that includes households, firms, resource markets, and product markets. There are flows of goods, services, and resources that move in one direction through this model, and flows of money that move in the opposite direction.

### 1.3 Opportunity Cost and Choice

**a** Whenever an economic decision is made, an *opportunity cost* is paid. Opportunity cost is the value of the best alternative to a choice that is taken. It is often impossible to know the true value of a choice that is not taken. Decisions are based on the *expected* opportunity cost of a choice.

**b** Opportunity costs of a decision vary with circumstances. Calculating the value of an opportunity cost requires time and information. Although opportunity costs are often seen in how you spend your limited funds, time is the ultimate limiting factor that forces even the very wealthy to make choices.

**c** Sunk costs have already been paid and should not be considered when you make economic decisions.

**d** Many choices involve both direct and indirect opportunity costs. The decision to attend college, for example, requires spending funds that could be used for other purposes as well as forgoing income that could have been earned from other uses of scarce time.

---

### 1.2 Assessment

Continued from page 17.

#### Think Critically

8. Answers will vary. Each person who is laid off loses employment as the result of a decision made by an individual employer. Being laid off will affect how much a person is able to purchase. This is part of market economics. At the same time, a change in the number of new unemployment compensation claims is an indication of trends in national economics.

9. Answers will vary. Students should explain that rational choices for sources of higher education require information that is provided by the college or university's advertising. By providing this information, the institution is marketing its service and attempting to influence students' choices.

# Review Economic Terms

Choose the term that best fits the definition. On a separate sheet of paper, write the letter of the answer.

_____ 1. An item you can see, feel, and touch that requires scarce resources to produce and satisfies human wants

_____ 2. The means by which buyers and sellers carry out exchange

_____ 3. The broad category of human efforts, both physical and mental, used to produce goods and services

_____ 4. The value of the best alternative passed up for the chosen item or activity

_____ 5. The study of how people use their scarce resources to satisfy their unlimited wants

_____ 6. All human creations used to produce goods and services

_____ 7. Something not physical that requires scarce resources to produce and satisfies human wants

_____ 8. A profit-seeker who develops a new product or process and assumes the risk of profit or loss

_____ 9. So-called "gifts of nature" used to produce goods and services

_____ 10. Incremental, additional, extra, or one more; refers to a change in an economic variable, a change in the status quo.

a. **capital goods**

b. **economics**

c. **entrepreneur**

d. **good**

e. **human resources**

f. **marginal**

g. **market**

h. **natural resources**

i. **opportunity cost**

j. **service**

# Review Economic Concepts

11. **True or False** _Scarcity_ exists because our supplies of _productive resources_ are limited.

12. Which of the following is an example of a _natural resource_?
    a. lumber used to build a house
    b. a tree standing in a forest
    c. a carpenter who installs new cabinets
    d. gasoline you put in your car

13. A(n) __?__ is a person who tries to earn a profit by dreaming up a new product or finding a better way to produce an existing one.

14. When a firm's revenue from sales exceeds its costs of production, it will earn a(n) __?__.

15. **True or False** _Services_ are different from _goods_ because they are not able to satisfy human desires.

16. Which of the following is an exhaustible resource?
    a. crude oil in the ground
    b. corn growing in a field
    c. water in a river
    d. fish in the ocean

17. **True or False** When you play football in a public park you receive a _free good_ because you do not pay to use the park.

18. A(n) __?__ is a simplification of economic reality that is used to make predictions about the real world.

## Review Economic Terms

1. d. good
2. g. market
3. e. human resources
4. i. opportunity cost
5. b. economics
6. a. capital goods
7. j. service
8. c. entrepreneur
9. h. natural resources
10. f. marginal

## Review Economic Concepts

11. True
12. b. a tree standing in a forest
13. entrepreneur
14. profit
15. False. Services are different from goods because they are intangibles that require scarce resources to produce and satisfy human wants.
16. a. crude oil in the ground
17. False. It is not a free good because there is a cost for your playing football there. You are keeping the park from being used for an alternative reason, such as Frisbee or soccer.
18. economic theory or model

---

**1.3** **Assessment**

Continued from page 26.

## Think Critically

8. Answers will vary. Wilma does not know the value of the alternatives she has so she cannot be sure what the opportunity cost of any choice will be. She probably will choose to produce some of each crop to limit her risk and insure that she earns some profit.

9. If Ms. Morra chooses the less expensive computers, her students will not learn to use the more advanced computers. If she chooses the more expensive models, some of her students will have to use old, outdated models for at least part of their time in class.

## Review Economic Concepts

19. a. consider only variables that interest them
20. True
21. Positive
22. False. The assumption of rational self-interest does take into consideration concern for others.
23. d. Rose should be paid more than $8.00 an hour.
24. False. Most of the disagreement among economists involves debates over normative statements.
25. marginal, marginal
26. a. Tyrone received a 5 percent raise in his wage from his employer last year.
27. True
28. d. the value of the pizza she would have bought if she had not gone to the movie
29. False. The opportunity cost still exists: It is the decision to do nothing or to do the alternative.
30. False. The value of an opportunity cost of a particular choice varies for all people.
31. c. other uses of extra income earned because of the college education
32. True
33. b. the $30 monthly payment you already agreed to make to connect to the Internet

19. When economists use the *other-things-constant assumption* they are trying to
    a. consider only variables that interest them.
    b. duplicate reality in their ideas.
    c. establish economic laws that will last indefinitely.
    d. combine several ideas into one.

20. **True or False** In general, the assumption of *rational self-interest* means that individuals try to maximize the expected benefit achieved with a given cost.

21. __?__ statements concern what is.

22. **True or False** The assumption of *rational self-interest* rules out concerns for others.

23. Which of the following is a *normative statement*?
    a. On average, Rose works 30 hours a week.
    b. Rose is paid $8.00 per hour for her labor.
    c. Rose pays 7.65 percent of her earnings in Social Security tax.
    d. Rose works too many hours each week to do well in school.

24. **True or False** Most of the disagreement among economists involves debates over *positive statements*.

25. A rational decision maker will change the status quo as long as the expected __?__ benefit from the change exceeds the expected __?__ cost.

26. Which of the following is an example of *market economics*?
    a. Tyrone received a 5 percent raise in his wage from his employer last year.
    b. On average, prices increased by 2.3 percent last year.
    c. The federal government borrowed more than $100 billion last year.
    d. Businesses invested 3.1 percent more last year than in the year before.

27. **True or False** *Opportunity cost* is the value of the best alternative that you pass up whenever you make a choice.

28. Which of the following is Yo-chee's opportunity cost of spending $8 to go to a movie with her friends?
    a. the value of the $8 she spent
    b. the value of the time she worked to earn the $8
    c. the value of the enjoyment she received from seeing the movie
    d. the value of the pizza she would have bought if she had not gone to the movie

29. **True or False** If you have nothing better to do when you make a choice, you pay no opportunity cost for your decision.

30. **True or False** The value of the opportunity cost of a particular choice is the same for all people.

31. Which of the following would not be a possible opportunity cost of attending college?
    a. other uses of the money used to pay college tuition
    b. other uses of the time used to study and attend classes
    c. other uses of extra income earned because of the college education
    d. other uses of the money used to pay for room and board while attending college

32. **True or False** The opportunity cost you would incur for cleaning your room would probably be different on Saturday evening than on Tuesday afternoon.

33. Which of the following is a *sunk cost* that should be ignored when you choose whether or not to buy a new computer over the Internet?
    a. the $50 delivery charge
    b. the $30 monthly payment you already agreed to make to connect to the Internet
    c. the extra $200 you might pay to get a flat-screen monitor
    d. the $150 two-year service contract you could decide to buy

# Apply Economic Concepts

**34. Circular-Flow Model** Sketch a copy of the circular-flow model shown below on your own paper. Place each of the following in the correct location on your model.

   a. Brad watches Monday-night football on his new TV.

   b. The Sony Corporation produces a new TV.

   c. Brad works at a local drugstore.

   d. Brad buys a new TV from a Sears store.

**Circular-Flow Model**

**35. Opportunity Cost** Your uncle has offered to buy either a new computer or a good-quality bicycle for you as a graduation present. The prices of both items are the same. Write an essay that identifies which gift you would choose and describes the opportunity cost that would result from your choice. Why might other people make a different choice?

**36. Productive Resources** List the steps that need to be taken to produce a loaf of bread. Identify examples of each type of productive resource used in this process.

**37. Sharpen Your Life Skills: Cause and Effect** The owners of a bakery found they had more customers who wanted to buy their bread and cakes than they could serve. As a result they decided to expand the size of their business and employ twice as many workers. How does this example demonstrate cause and effect? What additional resources would the business require in order to increase its production?

*econxtra.swlearning.com*

**38.** Access **EconNews Online** at econxtra.swlearning.com. Click on e-con@pps and then click on the policy debate entitled "Are Americans Overworked?" Read the three quotations under "Issues and Background." If, as the textbook states, the fundamental human resource is "time," do you think it is a benefit or a problem for the U.S. economy that Americans are working more than ever before? Justify your answer with facts from the web site.

---

## Apply Economic Concepts

**34. a.** Brad watches Monday-night football on his new TV (households).

   **b.** The Sony Corporation produces a new TV (firms).

   **c.** Brad works at a local drugstore (resource market).

   **d.** Brad buys a new TV from a Sears store (product market).

**35.** Answers will vary. Students should demonstrate an understanding of opportunity cost and the fact that people have different opportunity costs because they have different values.

**36.** Answers will vary. Answers should include references to natural resources, human resources, and capital goods. Natural resources might include the land the wheat was grown on, the rain that fell on the field, or natural gas that was taken from the ground to heat the oven. Human resources might include the effort that was used to harvest the wheat, grind it into flour, or to knead the dough. Capital goods might include the tractor used to plow the field, the mill used to grind the wheat into flour, or the oven used to bake the bread.

**37.** Answers will vary. This situation demonstrates cause and effect by showing that if the amount of a product that customers want to consume increases (cause), more resources will be allocated to the production of that product (effect). Students may point out that the firm will need to purchase additional ingredients, ovens, and utensils for the new workers to use to produce additional bread and cakes.

**38.** From an individual's standpoint, it is a problem that he or she is working more and has less time to pursue personal interests and obligations outside work. From a firm's standpoint, it is a benefit that Americans are working more hours than ever before. Firms are gaining more of the scarce human resource of labor. However, there are costs associated with this increase in labor. The marginal product of labor that results from an additional hour worked is likely to decline as the length of the workweek increases beyond some point. Those who work more than 40 hours a week must get paid time and a half.

**LESSON 2.1** *Economic Questions and Economic Systems:* This lesson identifies the three questions that all economic systems must answer. The lesson also introduces the features and problems of economic systems.

**LESSON 2.2** *Production Possibilities Frontier:* The economy's production possibilities are described in this lesson through the use of a simple model.

**LESSON 2.3** *Comparative Advantage:* In addition to comparative advantage, this lesson focuses on specialization, division of labor, and exchange.

### Consider

Ask students to consider the questions posed on this page as they study Chapter 2. After studying all three lessons, students should be able to answer the questions. The content related to each question can be found on the pages indicated below.

- Why are economies around the world growing more market oriented? See page 38—Mixed, Transitional, and Traditional Economies.

- How much can an economy produce with the resources available? See page 42—Efficiency and the Production Possibilities Frontier.

- Can you actually save time by applying economic principles to your family chores? See page 51—Comparative Advantage.

- Why is experience a good teacher? See page 52—Gains from Specialization.

- Why is fast food so fast? See page 52—Gains from Specialization.

### POINT YOUR BROWSER

Remind students that they can find additional resources for this chapter at **econxtra.swlearning.com**.

- Xtra! Study Tools
- Net Bookmarks
- Xtra! Quiz Prep
- econ@pps
- Ask the Xpert!
- Graphing Workshop

# Economic Systems and Economic Tools

Economic Questions and Economic Systems **2.1**

Production Possibilities Frontier **2.2**

Comparative Advantage **2.3**

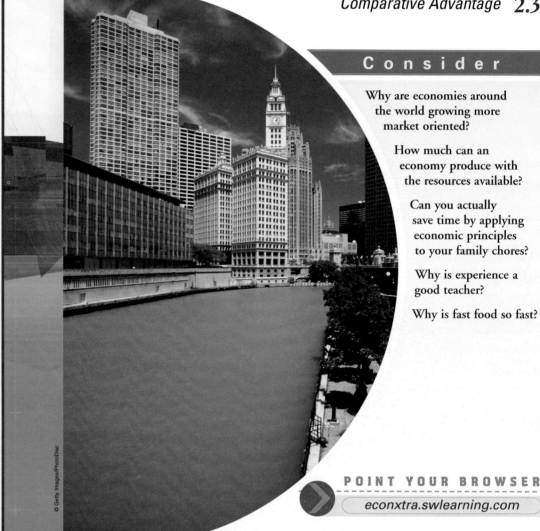

© Getty Images/PhotoDisc

### Consider

Why are economies around the world growing more market oriented?

How much can an economy produce with the resources available?

Can you actually save time by applying economic principles to your family chores?

Why is experience a good teacher?

Why is fast food so fast?

### POINT YOUR BROWSER

*econxtra.swlearning.com*

## Teaching Resources for Chapter 2

- Activities and Projects Masters
- Spanish Resources
- Econ Connection Interactive Tutorial CD
- **Exam***View*® CD
- Workbook Teacher's Edition
- Chapter Test Teacher's Edition
- NCEE Standards and Correlation
- Personal Finance Guide

- Social Studies Skills Review
- Instructor's Resource CD
  - PowerPoint Presentation
  - Lesson Plans
  - Video Discussion Guide
  - Answers to Graphing Exercises
- **econxtra.swlearning.com**

## Objectives

> Identify the three questions that all economic systems must answer.

> Describe a pure market economy, and identify its problems.

> Describe a pure centrally planned economy, and identify its problems.

> Compare mixed, transitional, and traditional economies.

## Overview

What should the economy produce? How should this output be produced? For whom should it be produced? More than 200 countries around the world attempt to answer these three economic questions, all using somewhat different economic systems. One way to distinguish among economic systems is to focus on the role of government. Imagine a range from the most free to the most government-controlled economic system. A *pure market economy* stands at one end of the range, and a *pure centrally planned economy* stands at the other. Although no economy in the world reflects either extreme in its purest form, knowing the features and problems of each extreme will help you understand differences around the world.

## Key Terms

**economic system**

**pure market economy**

**pure centrally planned economy**

**mixed economy**

**market economy**

**transitional economy**

**traditional economy**

Draw a two-foot horizontal line on the board. Label the left side of the line "Pure Market Economy." Label the right side "Pure Centrally Planned Economy." Explain that the line represents the range from the most free to the most government-controlled economic system.

### Objectives

Remind students to read the lesson objectives to help focus their attention before reading the lesson.

### Key Terms

Direct students to write each key term on a separate index card. Then write the matching definition and page reference on the back of the appropriate card. Suggest that students include a rough graph corresponding to the concept. Encourage students to use the cards to study for quizzes and tests.

## [ In the News ]

### ● Protectionism in a Free Market

Many industries in Japan have developed with the help of government protection. However, this protectionism has had a downside. A December, 2002 *Wall Street Journal* article reports that as most of the world benefited from an explosion of new drugs in the 1980s and 1990s, Japanese patients lacked access to some of the West's best-known medications. For years the Japanese government completely closed its markets to many Western drugs and intentionally delayed the introduction of other drugs. Though the government's actions obviously aided local drug producers, these actions were based mainly on the cultural prejudice that Japanese bodies differ significantly from those of Westerners. Due to this belief, pharmaceutical industry rules required that drug trials be conducted from scratch on Japanese subjects. Protectionist policies began to change in the late 1990s, when in an effort to re-energize its economy, Japan opened several of its industries to foreign competition. At the same time, patients began requesting more information from their doctors about drugs they had heard about. The new drug awareness led to increasing pressure on the government to remove the roadblocks to approval of pharmaceuticals from the West. Today the approval process for Western drug products is faster and easier. Western drug companies also have greater access to the Japanese market, and Western-style drug advertising is done through Japanese media outlets.

### Think About It

Were the Japanese government's protectionist policies helping or hurting consumers with regard to pharmaceuticals? What caused Japan to change its protectionist policies in the pharmaceutical industry?

**33**

◄ | ►

## [ In the News ]

Instruct students to read the passage and write down their answers. Point out that their answers might change after they finish studying Lesson 2.1.

### Answers to Think About It

Answers will vary. Possible answers: (1) Protectionist policies were hurting Japanese consumers. (2) Changes in Japan's protectionist policies are the result of an effort to re-energize the economy by opening the industry to foreign competition and pressure from consumers.

### Follow-Up Activity

Ask students how they think Japanese consumers learned about Western drugs. Explain that the Internet, global media, and foreign travel all played a role.

### Visual Presentation

Use the PowerPoint presentation on the Instructor's Resource CD as an adjunct to your lecture. The presentation also can be used for review.

### National Content Standards in Economics

A complete list of the NCEE Standards appears on pages xxiv–xxv of this book. The following standards are addressed in Lesson 2.1.

Standard 1: Scarcity

Standard 3: Allocation of Goods and Services

Standard 4: Role of Incentives

Standard 7: Markets—Price and Quantity Determination

Standard 10: Role of Economic Institutions

Standard 16: Role of Government

## The Three Economic Questions

Write the following short questions on the board: (1) What? (2) How? (3) For whom? Point out that every economic system must answer three questions: (1) What is to be produced? (2) How is it to be produced? and (3) For whom is it to be produced?

### *Think Critically Through Visuals*

Direct students to focus their attention on the photograph on this page. Ask for a volunteer to answer the question posed in the caption.

### Answer

Answers will vary. Possible answers: Suppose the clothes being produced were jeans for juniors. This choice affects how the clothing is produced and for whom it will be produced. Jeans are made out of denim in a factory, and junior-sized jeans are made for teenagers and young adults. Instead of jeans, suppose the clothes being produced were evening gowns designed by a top designer. This choice also affects how the clothing is produced and for whom it will be produced. These gowns would be hand-stitched, made out of the finest materials, and would be produced for wealthy women, including celebrities and socialites.

#### NCEE Standard 3: Allocation of Goods and Services

Students will understand that different economic systems answer the three economic questions differently. They also will recognize that the answers to the economic questions are closely related—the answer to one depends very much on the answers to the others.

### CHECKPOINT

Invite a student to answer the checkpoint that appears on page 35.

### Answer

All economic systems must answer these three questions: (1) What goods and services will be produced? (2) How will goods and services be produced? (3) For whom will goods and services be produced?

---

# The Three Economic Questions

All economies must answer three questions:

1. What goods and services will be produced?

2. How will they be produced?

3. For whom will they be produced?

An **economic system** is the set of mechanisms and institutions that resolves the *what, how,* and *for whom* questions. Some standards used to distinguish among economic systems are

1. Who owns the resources?

2. What decision-making process is used to allocate resources and products?

3. What types of incentives guide economic decision makers?

**economic system**
The set of mechanisms and institutions that resolves the *what, how,* and *for whom* questions for an economy

## What Goods and Services Will Be Produced?

Most people take for granted the many choices that go into deciding what gets produced—everything from which new kitchen appliances are introduced and which would-be novelists get published, to which roads are built. Although different economies resolve these and millions of other questions using different decision-making rules and mechanisms, all economies must somehow decide what gets produced.

## How Will Goods and Services Be Produced?

The economic system must determine how output is to be produced. Which resources should be used, and how should they be combined to produce each product? How much labor should be used and at what skill levels? What kinds of machines should be used? What type of fertilizer should be applied to grow the best strawberries? Should a factory be built in the city or closer to the interstate highway? Millions of individual decisions determine which resources are employed and how these resources are combined.

## For Whom Will Goods and Services Be Produced?

Who will actually consume the goods and services produced? The economic system must determine how to allocate the fruits of production among the population. Should equal amounts be provided to everyone? Should those willing to wait in line the longest get more? Should goods be allocated according to height? Weight? Religion? Age? Gender? Race? Looks? Strength? Political connections? The value of resources supplied?

**Main Idea**

**Allocation of Goods and Services**

An economic system determines how the three economic questions are answered *to allocate goods and services in an economy.* The *three economic questions* are closely interwoven. Why does the answer to one question depend so much on the answers to the other questions? Apply your answer to clothing products. How does what clothing is produced relate to *how it will be produced* and *for whom it will be produced*?

© Getty Images/PhotoDisc

**Outside Resources**

**Consumer Publications** *Consumer Reports* evaluates goods and services that consumers purchase in the United States. Ask students to read several product evaluations from this publication. Discuss why this type of magazine is more useful in a market economy than in a centrally planned economy.

The question "For whom will goods and services be produced?" often is referred to as the distribution question.

## Interdependent Questions

The three economic questions are closely interwoven. The answer to one depends very much on the answers to the others. For example, an economy that distributes goods and services in uniform amounts to all will, no doubt, answer the what-will-be-produced question differently from an economy that allows each person to choose goods and services.

**CHECKPOINT**
What three questions must all economic systems answer?

# Pure Market Economy

In a **pure market economy**, private firms account for all production. There is no government at all. Features of this economic system include the private ownership of all resources and the coordination of economic activity based on the prices generated in free, competitive markets. Any income derived from selling resources goes exclusively to the resource owners.

## The Invisible Hand of Markets

Resource owners have *property rights* to the use of their resources and are free to supply those resources to the highest bidder. Producers are free to make and sell whatever they believe will be profitable. Consumers are free to buy whatever they can afford. All this voluntary buying and selling is coordinated by competitive markets that are free from any government regulations.

Market prices guide resources to their most productive use and channel goods to those consumers who value them the most. Markets answer the *what, how,* and *for whom* questions. Markets transmit information about relative scarcity, provide incentives to producers and consumers, and distribute income among resource owners.

No single individual or small group coordinates these activities. Rather, the voluntary choices of many buyers and sellers responding only to their individual incentives direct resources and products to those who value them the most.

According to Adam Smith (1723–1790), market forces coordinate production as if by an "invisible hand." Smith argued that *although each individual pursues his or her self-interest, the "invisible hand" of market competition promotes the general welfare.* Voluntary choices in competitive markets answer the questions *what, how,* and *for whom.*

## Problems with Pure Market Economies

A pure market economy offers resource owners the freedom and the incentive to get the most from their resources. However a pure market economy has its flaws because markets do not always work on their own. The most notable *market failures* include:

1. **Difficulty Enforcing Property Rights** Market activity depends on people using their scarce resources to maximize their satisfaction. However, what if you were repeatedly robbed of your paycheck on your way home from work? What if, after you worked a week in a new job, your employer called you a fool and said you would not be paid? Why bother working? Private markets would break down if you could not safeguard your private property or if you could not enforce

**Adam Smith**

*pure market economy*
An economic system with no government involvement so that private firms account for all production

---

**THE WALL STREET JOURNAL**

**Reading It Right** What's the relevance of the following statement from *The Wall Street Journal:*

"Capitalism" is supposed to be the one economic system that puts consumers at the center." [Note: *Capitalism* is another term for *market economy.*]

---

**Pure Market Economy**

Ask students to think about Adam Smith's idea of the "invisible hand" as they study this section about pure market economy.

**THE WALL STREET JOURNAL**

**Reading It Right**

Invite a student to explain the relevance of the statement from *The Wall Street Journal* that appears on this page.

**Answer**

Answers will vary. Possible answer: Capitalism puts the consumers at the center of it all, because it allows the consumers to decide the what, how, and for whom of the economic system. The cumulative voluntary choices of many consumers determine what is wanted, how it is wanted, and for whom it is wanted.

Lesson 2.1 • *Economic Questions and Economic Systems* **35**

---

**ENRICH**

Ask students to identify situations in their community that they believe demonstrate problems that have resulted from our market economy. These situations might include examples of pollution, poverty, a lack of public goods, or abuse of monopoly power held by some businesses. Discuss how these situations came to exist and steps that could be taken to reduce or eliminate them. Is it possible or even wise to try to eliminate all of the problems that are associated with market economies? Could the effort cause other, even bigger, problems?

## Pure Market Economy

Direct students to focus their attention on the problems with pure market economies. Ask them to identify additional examples for each of the problems.

### Think Critically Through Visuals

Direct students to focus their attention on the photograph on this page. Ask for a volunteer to answer the questions posed in the caption.

### Answer

The market system fails to account for air pollution because it is an externality. An externality is a cost incurred by society during the production of a good and that is not taken into account in the true market price. Externalities can be solved for a society through government regulation, such as regulation of the amount of emissions allowed in the production of a good.

### CHECKPOINT

Invite a student to answer the checkpoint that appears on page 37.

### Answer

A pure market economy is an economy that runs strictly through capitalism. There is no government intervention. There is private ownership of all resources, and prices of all goods are determined in a free competitive market through consumer choice. The problems with a pure market economy are: (1) there is difficulty enforcing property rights, (2) some people have few resources to sell, (3) some firms try to monopolize markets, (4) there are no public goods, and (5) there are externalities.

---

contracts. In a pure market economy, there is no government, so there is no central authority to protect property rights, enforce contracts, and otherwise ensure that the rules of the game are followed.

2. **Some People Have Few Resources to Sell** Because of a poor education, disability, discrimination, the time demands of caring for small children, or bad luck, some people have few resources to sell in a market economy. Because markets do not guarantee even a minimum level of income, some people would have difficulty surviving.

3. **Some Firms Try to Monopolize Markets** Although the "invisible hand" of market competition usually promotes the general welfare, some producers may try to monopolize the market by either unfairly driving out competitors or by conspiring with competitors to fix prices. With less competition, firms can charge a higher

price to earn more profit. Thus, firms have a profit incentive to monopolize a market.

4. **No Public Goods** Private firms do not produce so-called *public goods*, such as national defense. Once produced, public goods are available to all, regardless of who pays and who does not pay for them. Suppliers cannot easily prevent those who fail to pay for a public good from benefiting from the good. For example, reducing terrorism benefits all in the economy. Because firms cannot sell public goods profitably, they are not produced in a pure market economy.

5. **Externalities** Market prices reflect the benefits to buyers and the costs to sellers. However, some production and consumption affect third parties—those not directly involved. For example, a paper mill fouls the air breathed by local residents, but the market price of paper fails to reflect such costs. Because the pollution

---

Air pollution from a paper mill affects the health of local residents. Why does the market system fail to account for such problems? How can such problems be solved for a society?

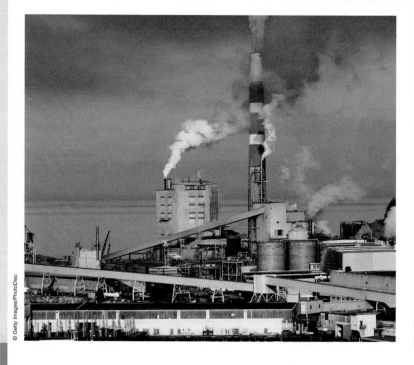
© Getty Images/PhotoDisc

**36**     **CHAPTER 2**   Economic Systems and Economic Tools

---

*Curriculum Connection—Visual Arts*

Have students create posters to explain how an advertisement printed in a newspaper or magazine relates to the three basic economic questions. The posters should indicate how the ads demonstrate that businesses influence the answers to *what, how,* and *for whom*. Display half of the posters on each side of the classroom. Have the creators of the posters on the left side of the room stand by their posters. Invite the other half of the class to visit the exhibit and discuss the posters with their creators. After 10 minutes, have the students switch roles.

costs are outside—or external to—the market transaction, they are called *externalities*. Private markets fail to account for externalities. Because of this type of market failure, even market economies allow a role for government.

**CHECKPOINT**
What is a pure market economy, and what are its problems?

# Pure Centrally Planned Economy

In a **pure centrally planned economy**, all resources are government-owned, and production is coordinated by the central plans of government. At least in theory, there is public, or *communal,* ownership of all resources. That is why central planning is sometimes called *communism.* Central planners answer the three economic questions by spelling out how many missiles, how many homes, and how much bread to produce. Central planners also decide how to produce these goods and who should get them.

## The Visible Hand of Planners

Rather than rely on competitive markets, central planners direct the allocation of resources and products. Central planners may believe that market economies produce too many consumer goods and too few capital goods, especially military hardware. They also may believe that central planning yields a more even distribution of goods across households than a market economy does.

In a pure centrally planned economy, the government, or state, owns all resources, including labor. Central planners direct production through state-owned enterprises, which usually face no competition. Some goods and serv-

ices are *rationed,* meaning that each household gets a certain amount. For example, each household gets so many square feet of living space. Other products are allocated based on prices set by central planners. Prices, once set, tend to be inflexible.

In short, market economies coordinate production through the invisible hand of market competition. Centrally planned economies use the visible hands of central planners.

## Problems with Centrally Planned Economies

A pure centrally planned economy ideally produces the combination of products that society desires. But this economic system has its flaws.

The most notable central planning failures include the following five failures. Because of these planning failures, countries have modified centrally planned economies to allow a greater role for private ownership and market competition.

1. **Consumers Get Low Priority**
   Central plans may reflect the preferences of central planners rather than those of consumers. Central planners decide what gets produced and who should consume the goods. When goods are rationed or offered for an inflexible price, severe shortages can result. Evidence of consumer goods shortage include empty store shelves, long waiting lines, and the "tips"—or bribes—shop operators expect for supplying scarce goods.

2. **Little Freedom of Choice** Because central planners are responsible for all production decisions, the variety of products tends to be narrower than in a market economy. Households in centrally planned economies not only have less choice about what to consume, but they also have less freedom in other economic decisions. Government planners may decide where people live and where they work.

3. **Central Planning Can Be Inefficient** Running an economy is so complicated that some resources

**pure centrally planned economy**
An economic system in which all resources are government-owned and production is coordinated by the central plans of government

**TEACH**

**Pure Centrally Planned Economy**
Direct students to focus their attention on the problems with centrally planned economies. Ask them to identify additional examples for each of the problems.

**NET Bookmark**

Direct students to **econxtra.swlearning.com**. Remind them to click on the link for Lesson 2.1 to find the appropriate link for the **NET Bookmark** on page 38.
Add interest to the assignment by asking each student to select a different country. Consider using a map or globe to aid in the selection process. Invite interested students to share what they learn by "briefing" their classmates. Encourage students to use visual aids such as maps and charts.

**CHECKPOINT**
Invite a student to answer the checkpoint that appears on page 38.

**Answer**
In a pure centrally planned economy, all resources are government-owned, and production is coordinated by the central plans of government. The problems with centrally planned economies are: (1) consumers get low priority, (2) there is little freedom of choice, (3) central planning can be inefficient, (4) resources owned by the state are sometimes wasted, and (5) environmental damage can occur.

## Group Activity: Economic Systems

Organize students into small groups. Instruct each group to produce a product that requires several steps to complete. These could be paper boxes, drawings, or other objects that are easy to make with available resources. The catch is that one student is assigned to be the group leader. This person must instruct each other member what to do and how to do it. Other students may not ask questions or make suggestions. The students are likely to discover that there are many misunderstandings and inefficiencies in their production. When they finish, ask them to discuss how their experience demonstrated the shortcomings of planned economic systems. How would their task have been easier to complete if they had worked in a market economy?

### Mixed, Transitional, and Traditional Economies

Point out that economic systems may be classified along a spectrum from pure market economy to a pure centrally planned economy. In reality, no economy achieves either polar extreme.

## TEAM WORK

Organize students into groups of four or five. Instruct teams to select a recorder and a spokesperson. Instruct students to complete the **Team Work** activity shown on page 39. Set a timer for 10 minutes. When the timer goes off, invite the spokesperson from each group to take a turn providing the evidence collected.

## *Ethics in Action*

Have students work in pairs to discuss the ethical issue featured on page 39, and develop an answer to the problem presented there.

### Answers to Think Critically

Answers will vary. Possible answer: The material being downloaded belongs to someone else. Taking property that belongs to someone else is wrong.

## CHECKPOINT

Invite a student to answer the checkpoint that appears on page 40.

### Answer

A market economy is a competitive market that is run strictly through private ownership of goods and the consumer demand for those goods. A mixed economy is comprised of both a market economy and a central planning economy. Transitional economies are markets that are in the process of shifting from publicly owned enterprises to private enterprises.

---

are used inefficiently. Consider all that's involved in growing and distributing farm products. Central planners must decide what to grow, what resources to employ (who, for example, should become farmers), and who gets to consume the harvest (should it be rationed or sold for a set price?). Mistakes along the way result in inefficiencies. For example, the former Soviet Union had a centrally planned economy. About one-third of the harvest there reportedly rotted on its way to consumers.

4. **Resources Owned by the State Are Sometimes Wasted** Because resources are owned by the state, nobody in particular has an incentive to see that they are employed in their highest-valued use. Some resources are wasted. For example, Soviet workers usually had little regard for equipment that belonged to the state. New trucks or tractors might be dismantled for parts, or working equipment might be sent to a scrap plant. Stealing state-owned property, though a serious crime, also was a common practice. In contrast to the lack of regard for state property, Soviet citizens took extremely good care of their personal property. For example, personal cars were so well maintained that they lasted more than 20 years on average—twice the official projected life of an automobile.

5. **Environmental Damage** In theory, a centrally planned economy, with its focus on "the common good," should

**mixed economy**
An economic system that mixes central planning with competitive markets

**market economy**
Describes the U.S. economic system, where markets play a relatively large role

The CIA World Factbook provides brief descriptions of all the world's economies. Access this web site through econxtra.swlearning.com. Choose one country and identify its economy. Write a paragraph explaining the characteristics of this country's economy.

*econxtra.swlearning.com*

take better care of the environment than a market economy. In practice, however, state enterprises often are more concerned with meeting the goals set by the central planners. For example, in its drive for military dominance, the former Soviet government set off 125 nuclear explosions *above* ground. The resulting bomb craters filled with water, forming contaminated lakes. Thousands of barrels of nuclear waste were dumped into Soviet rivers and seas.

## ✓ CHECKPOINT
What is a pure centrally planned economy, and what are its problems?

## Mixed, Transitional, and Traditional Economies

No country on earth represents either a market economy or centrally planned economy in its pure form. Economic systems have grown more alike over time. The role of government has increased in market economies, and the role of markets has increased in centrally planned economies. As a result, most economies now mix central planning with competitive markets and are called **mixed economies**.

### Mixed Economy

The United States is a mixed economy. Because markets play a relatively large role, it also is considered a **market economy**. Government accounts for about one-third of all U.S. economic activity.

Government also regulates the private sector in a variety of ways. For example, local zoning boards determine lot sizes, home sizes, and the types of industries allowed. Federal bodies regulate workplace safety, environmental

---

### *Economic Headlines*

Instruct students to locate an article in a current magazine or newspaper that relates to one of the topics in this lesson. For example, they might find articles about a developing country that is shifting to a market economy. Instruct students to read the article and write a brief summary that includes a reference citation. Identify the style you want them to use for the citation.
As an alternative, you might locate several articles of interest and provide citations for students to use in locating one of the articles. Direct students to read the article they have chosen and write a brief explanation of how it relates to this lesson.

quality, competition in markets, and many other activities.

Although both ends of the economic spectrum have moved toward the center, the market system has gained more converts in recent decades. Consider countries that have been cut in two by political and economic ideology. In such cases, the economies began with similar resources and income levels right after the split. Over time the market-oriented economies produced a much higher standard of living than the centrally planned economies. For example, income per capita in Taiwan, a market-oriented economy after it split from China, averages about four times that of China, a centrally planned economy. As another example, income per capita in market-oriented South Korea is about 12 times that of North Korea, perhaps the most centrally planned economy in the world.

Recognizing the power of markets to create incentives and provide information, even some of the most diehard central planners now reluctantly accept some market activity. For example, about 20 percent of the world's population lives in China, which grows more market oriented each day. The former Soviet Union dissolved into 15 independent republics. Most are now trying

to introduce more market incentives. Even North Korea has opened a special economic zone where market forces will be allowed to operate without government interference.

### Transitional Economy

More than two-dozen countries around the world are **transitional economies**, in the process of shifting orientation from central planning to competitive markets. This transition involves converting state-owned enterprises into private

*transitional economy*

An economic system in the process of shifting from central planning to competitive markets

## Ethics in Action

**Stealing Digital Property** The U.S. government works to protect property rights, enforce contracts, and otherwise ensure the rules of the game are followed. In protecting property rights, a major issue is how to handle piracy and "bootlegging" in the software, music, and movie industries. "Stealing someone else's work is no more legal on a computer than it is with your bare hands," said Peter Chernin, CEO of Fox Group, during the 2002 Fall Comdex consumer electronics trade show. His message was supported by George Lucas, producer-director of "Star Wars," who also spoke at the show. Lucas stressed that if piracy, unauthorized copying,

and counterfeiting of big, blockbuster films is not curtailed, it might no longer make economic sense to produce them. A student in the audience argued that if the companies would lower their prices, people's desire to bootleg would decrease. His opinion was that either the prices come down or people will not stop copying from their friend's music, film, and software collections, or downloading from the Internet.

### Think Critically

Explain the basic ethical problem with the college student's argument.

## Key Concepts

1. See the sample grid at the bottom of this page.

2. Answers will vary. Students may point out that Adam Smith argued that the "invisible hand" of market competition guides business owners to allocate resources to their most productive use and channels goods and services to those who value them the most.

3. Answers will vary. Students might point out that there would be little reason to produce goods and services to earn a profit without a guarantee that this profit could be used to buy resources to expand the firm's production or to purchase goods and services for the firm's owners to enjoy.

4. Answers will vary. Students might point out that in centrally planned economic systems, consumers are given a low priority in obtaining production and have little freedom of choice in the products they buy. Central planning is often inefficient and wasteful and, in some cases, leads to extensive environmental damage.

5. The market plays a large role in the U.S. economy, but the government controls about one-third of U.S. economic activity.

## Graphing Exercise

6. (1) From left to right: United States, Mexico, Sweden, Russia, Mainland China, North Korea. (2) Answers will vary. Possible answer: The United States is comprised mainly of competitive markets where the government accounts for about one-third of the market. North Korea is comprised of markets that are almost entirely owned and run by the government. Mexico, Sweden, Russia, and Mainland China fall in the middle, with Mexico having a higher percentage of private ownership and competitive markets (but not as high a percentage as the United States) and Mainland China having a higher percentage of government-owned, centrally planned markets (but not as high a percentage as North Korea).

## Think Critically

7. Answers will vary. Students might discuss the limited choice given to citizens or inefficiencies that took place in carrying out the project.

enterprises. This is a process called *privatization*. Altogether more than 150,000 large enterprises are trying to grow more competitive. Most of these enterprises have become more efficient and more productive. From Hungary to Mongolia, the transition now under way will shape economies for decades to come.

**traditional economy**
An economic system shaped largely by custom or religion

### Traditional Economy

Finally, some economic systems, known as **traditional economies**, are shaped largely by custom or religion. For example, caste systems in India restrict occupational choice. Family relations also play significant roles in organizing and coordinating economic activity.

Even in the United States some occupations still are dominated by women, and others by men, largely because of tradition. Your own pattern of consumption and choice of occupation may be influenced by some of these forces.

**CHECKPOINT**
Compare mixed, market, transitional, and traditional economies.

2.1 **Assessment**

## Key Concepts

1. Compare the answers to the three basic economic questions in a pure market economy with the answers to these questions in a pure centrally planned economy. Present your answers using a spreadsheet or grid.

2. What did Adam Smith mean when he talked about an "invisible hand" that guides production in market economies?

3. Why are property rights important to the efficient working of a market economy?

4. What problems are likely to occur in centrally planned economic systems?

5. Why is the U.S. economic system sometimes called a "mixed market economy"?

**Xtra!**
**Study Tools**
econxtra.swlearning.com

## Graphing Exercise

6. Draw a horizontal line. Label the left side of the line "Pure Market Economy" and the right side, "Pure Centrally Planned Economy." Place each of the following nations on your line at a place that you think accurately represents the current state of its economy: United States, Mainland China, North Korea, Sweden, Russia, Mexico. Research the economies of the countries not familiar to you. Be prepared to explain your placements.

## Think Critically

7. **Government** When governments decide how to spend money, they often behave in a way similar to centrally planned economies. Investigate an important spending decision that was made by your local government. Write a one-page paper that identifies problems that were encountered that have been common in centrally planned economies.

40  **CHAPTER 2**  Economic Systems and Economic Tools

### Visualizing the Answer

1. Answers will vary. The grid should be similar to the one shown below.

| Economic Questions | Pure Market Economy | Pure Centrally Planned Economy |
|---|---|---|
| What to produce | Goods that producers decide are profitable | Goods that planners decide are necessary |
| How to produce | Through resources available to producers | Through resources decided upon by central planners |
| For whom to produce | For consumers who can afford the good | For those whom central planners feel should receive the good |

## 2.2 Production Possibilities Frontier

## Objectives

> Describe the production possibilities frontier and explain its shape.

> Explain what causes the production possibilities frontier to shift.

## Overview

How much can the economy produce in a particular period if resources are used fully and efficiently? In reality, an economy, such as the U.S. economy, has millions of different resources that can be combined in all kinds of ways to produce millions of possible goods and services. A simple model is used to describe the economy's production possibilities.

## Key Terms

**production possibilities frontier (PPF)**

**efficiency**

**law of increasing opportunity cost**

**economic growth**

## FOCUS

### 2.2 Production Possibilities Frontier

Sketch a rough PPF on the board. Explain that the production possibilities frontier (PPF) is a simple model that shows society's menu of alternatives when goods are produced using all of society's resources fully and efficiently. The PPF curve is a boundary dividing points on the inside, which do not fully utilize society's resources, from points on the outside, which are unattainable with currently available resources and technology.

## Objectives

Remind students to read the lesson objectives to help focus their attention before reading the lesson.

## Key Terms

Direct students to write each of the key terms on a separate index card. Instruct students to write the complete definition of each key term on the back of the appropriate card along with the page number where the definition is located. Encourage students to use the cards to study for quizzes and tests.

## [ In the News ]

### ● Sometimes Frozen Possibilities Are a Good Thing

Starting with a small dairy herd, Lecherias Loncomilla Ltda. has expanded to become the leading producer of frozen desserts in Chile. However, in Chile, a country with 15 million consumers, the company's sales were beginning to top out at about $3 million a year. Owner Francisco Mac-Clure says, "Give us the U.S. and we'll grow and be twice as profitable." He is referring to the recently negotiated, first free-trade pact between the United States and Latin America since 1993. This United States–Chile trade pact can only help specialists like the frozen dessert maker Mac-Clure. Once the United States drops the imposed duties on ice cream and many other Chilean raw materials and products, Mr. Mac-Clure and his fellow producers will be free to sell the raw materials Chile has in greatly expandable supply. Chile's enormous crop of fresh fruit and huge dairy herds that produce rich cream and butterfat also will add to the price and quality competition in the market. Mac-Clure has another big reason to smile about the trade pact: Chile's summer is the opposite of that in the United States, and so the pact virtually doubles Chile's selling season for frozen desserts.

### Think About It

What effect, if any, do you think an increase in ice cream production in Chile will have on the country's production of capital goods?

◄ ❙ ▶

41

## [ In the News ]

Instruct students to read the passage and write down their answers. Point out that their answers might change after they finish studying Lesson 2.2.

### Answers to Think About It

Answers will vary. Possible answer: If Chile is using its available resources fully and efficiently, then an increase in ice cream production (a consumer good) in Chile will cause a decrease in the country's production of capital goods.

### Follow-Up Activity

Ask students whether they think Chile is using its available resources fully and efficiently. Based on the scenario described, it is likely that Chile is not using resources fully and efficiently. If Chile were using its resources fully and efficiently, it would not have the excess raw materials, such as produce and cattle, it now has.

### Visual Presentation

Use the PowerPoint presentation on the Instructor's Resource CD as an adjunct to your lecture. The presentation can also be used for review.

### National Content Standards in Economics

**NCEE**

A complete list of the NCEE Standards appears on pages xxiv–xxv of this book. The following standards are addressed in Lesson 2.2.

Standard 1: Scarcity

Standard 15: Growth

Standard 2: Marginal Cost/Benefit

**Efficiency and the Production Possibilities Frontier**

Make sure students understand that the PPF model is based on the four simplifying assumptions outlined in this section.

Use **Figure 2.1—Production Possibilities Frontier (PPF)** to illustrate the concept of the production possibilities frontier. Refer to the PPF curve to see that an increase in production of one (consumer good or capital good) will cause a decrease in the production of the other. The PPF curve shows the possible combinations of the two types of goods that can be produced when available resources are employed efficiently and fully. The point on the x-axis indicates that the economy is choosing to place all of its resources into capital goods production, while the point on the y-axis indicates that the country is choosing to place all of its resources into consumer goods production. Points in between on the PPF curve reflect varying combinations between these two extremes.

Direct students to the Graphing Workshop for Chapter 2 at **econxtra.swlearning.com** for an explanation of the production possibilities frontier using another example. Instruct students to click on **See It: The Production Possibility** to view the graph and listen to an explanation.

---

***production possibilities frontier (PPF)***

Shows the possible combinations of the two types of goods that can be produced when available resources are employed fully and efficiently

***efficiency***

Producing the maximum possible output from available resources

---

# Efficiency and the Production Possibilities Frontier

How much can an economy produce with the resources available? What are the economy's production capabilities? To help consider these questions, you need a simple model of the economy, beginning with some simplifying assumptions.

## Simplifying Assumptions

Here are the model's simplifying assumptions:

1. To reduce the analysis to manageable proportions, the model limits the output to two broad classes of products: consumer goods, such as pizzas and haircuts, and capital goods, such as pizza ovens and hair clippers.

2. The focus is on production during a given period—in this case, a year.

3. The resources available in the economy are fixed in both quantity and quality during the period.

4. Society's knowledge about how best to combine these resources to produce output—that is, the available *technology*—does not change during the year.

The point of these assumptions is to freeze the economy's resources and technology for a period of time to focus on what possibly can be produced during that time.

## PPF Model

Given the resources and the technology available in the economy, the **production possibilities frontier (PPF)** shows the possible combinations of the two types of goods that can be produced when available resources are employed fully and efficiently. **Efficiency** means producing the maximum possible output from available resources.

The economy's PPF for consumer goods and capital goods is shown by the curve *AF* in Figure 2.1. Point *A* identifies the amount of consumer goods produced per year if all the economy's resources are used efficiently to produce consumer goods. Point *F* identifies the amount of capital goods produced per year if all the economy's

---

**Production Possibilities Frontier (PPF)**
econxtra.swlearning.com

**Figure 2.1**

If the economy uses its available resources and technology fully and efficiently in producing consumer goods and capital goods, it will be on its production possibilities frontier curve *AF*. The PPF is bowed out to illustrate the law of increasing opportunity cost: Additional units of capital goods require the economy to sacrifice more and more units of consumer goods. More consumer goods must be given up in moving from *D* to *E* than in moving from *A* to *B*, although in each case the gain in capital goods is 10 million units. Points inside the PPF, such as *I*, represent inefficient use of resources. Points outside the PPF, such as *U*, represent unattainable combinations.

---

## Outside Resources

**Magazines** *Scientific American, Motor Trend, Popular Mechanics, Bike,* and *Popular Science* are only a few of many magazines that report on advancements in technology. Ask students to review a recent issue of one of these magazines and identify a technological advancement that may affect the cost of producing a specific product. Ask them to sketch and explain how this new technology could change a graph of the production possibilities frontier for firms that manufacture this product. Will it cause them to adjust the types of products they choose to produce? Ask students to explain why.

resources are used efficiently to produce capital goods.

Points along the curve between *A* and *F* identify possible combinations of the two goods that can be produced when the economy's resources are used efficiently. Resources are employed fully and efficiently when there is no change that could increase the production of one good without decreasing the production of the other good.

### Inefficient and Unattainable Production

Points inside the PPF, including *I* in Figure 2.1, represent combinations that do not employ resources fully, employ them inefficiently, or both. Note that point *C* yields more consumer goods and no fewer capital goods than point *I*. Point *E* yields more capital goods and no fewer consumer goods than point *I*. In fact, any point along the PPF between *C* and *E*, such as point *D*, yields both more consumer goods and more capital goods than *I*. So point *I* is *inefficient*. By using resources more efficiently or by using previously idle resources, the economy can produce more of at least one good without reducing the production of the other good.

Points outside the PPF, such as *U* in Figure 2.1, represent unattainable combinations, given the resources and the technology available. Thus the PPF not only shows efficient combinations of production but also serves as the border between inefficient combinations inside the frontier and unattainable combinations outside the frontier.

### The Shape of the PPF

Any movement along the PPF involves giving up some of one good to get more of the other. Movement down the curve indicates that the opportunity cost of more capital goods is fewer consumer goods. For example, moving from point *A* to point *B* increases the amount of capital goods produced from none to 10 million units and reduces production of consumer goods from 50 million to 48 million units, a decline of only 2 million units. Increasing production of capital goods to 10 million units causes the production of consumer goods to fall only a little. Capital production initially employs resources (such as road graders used to build highways) that add little or nothing to production of consumer goods but are quite productive in making capital goods.

**Study the two images and decide which one represents capital goods and which one represents consumer goods. If these goods were represented on a PPF, what would happen to the production of one type of good if the production of the other good increased?**

Lesson 2.2 • *Production Possibilities Frontier* **43**

## TEACH (continued)

### Efficiency and the Production Possibilities Frontier

Create a rough sketch of the PPF model shown in Figure 2.1 from page 42 on the board. As you draw the *AF* curve, ask students to explain what *A* and *F* represent. Use a pointer or pen to focus attention on a point along the curve and ask students to explain what the point represents. Focus attention on a point inside the curve and ask students for an explanation. Focus attention on a point outside the curve and ask for an explanation.

### Think Critically Through Visuals

Direct students to focus their attention on the photographs on this page. Ask for a volunteer to answer the question posed in the caption.

### Answer

(1) The photo on the left represents consumer goods and the photo on the right represents capital goods. (2) If the production of consumer goods were to increase, the production of capital goods would decrease and vice versa.

## E-CONOMICS

Direct students to read the passage entitled "A Growing Web" that appears on page 44.

### Answers to Think Critically

An increase in the availability of other resources such as Internet technology will allow an outward shift of the PPF curve. This outward shift of the PPF curve will allow greater production of both capital and consumer goods.

## ENRICH

Ask students to investigate the amount of shelf space that is devoted to DVD and VCR movies at a local video rental store such as Blockbuster or Hollywood Video. Point out that in the mid-1990s, no space was devoted to DVDs because this medium was not yet available to the public. By 2003, roughly one-half of the shelf space was devoted to DVDs in most rental stores. What do students find is now the case? What shift in these stores' production possibilities frontiers does this change show? What does new technology have to do with this change?

## Efficiency and the Production Possibilities Frontier

The production possibilities frontier is assumed to have a particular shape—bowed out from the origin. This shape reflects the fact that resources are not homogenous; some are specialized to the production of particular goods and services. When such resources are transferred from the production of Product A to the production of Product B, it follows that less productive, less specialized resources are applied to the production of Product B. This results in ever-increasing losses of output of Product A or ever-increasing opportunity costs.

Direct students to the Graphing Workshop for Chapter 2 at **econxtra.swlearning.com** for an activity related to a production possibilities frontier graph. Instruct students to click on **Try It: Understanding the Points on the PPF**.

### ✓ CHECKPOINT

Invite a student to answer the checkpoint that appears on page 45.

### Answer

The PPF model shows the possible combination of the two types of goods that can be used when available resources are employed fully and efficiently. The bow shape of the PPF curve reflects the law of increasing opportunity cost in that each additional increment of one good requires the economy to give up successively larger increments of the other good.

# E-CONOMICS

## A Growing Web

"The Internet is a total reversal of what Wall Street expected," says analyst Steven Vonder Haar of Interactive Media Strategies. "It delivers tailored and personalized services instead of entertainment and broadcast programming. In a word, it's practical." During the "dot-gone" era ending the 1990s, nearly 1,000 Internet companies that promised to greatly simplify our lives—such as Webvan, Furniture.com, and Pets.com—went belly-up and folded. However similar ideas live on in web sites that draw thousands, saving consumers time and money every day. These include health-related sites, grocery sites, map sites, stock-buying sites, government-services sites, clothes-shopping sites, and many others. Ken Cassar, an online retail analyst for Jupiter Research, says early results prove the Internet is "capable of allowing mass customization, better inventory management, and major cost savings in manufacturing." Internet sales have increased from $0.7 billion in 1996 to $62 billion in 2002.

### Think Critically

What effect do you think success of Internet commerce will have on the production possibilities frontier? Explain your answer.

---

**law of increasing opportunity cost**

Each additional increment of one good requires the economy to give up successively larger increments of the other good

As shown by the dashed lines in Figure 2.1, each additional 10 million units of capital goods reduces consumer goods by successively larger amounts. As more capital goods are produced, the resources drawn away from consumer goods are those that are increasingly better suited to making consumer goods and less suited to making capital goods. *The resources in the economy are not all perfectly adaptable to the production of both types of goods. Therefore, the opportunity cost of capital goods increases as the economy produces more capital goods and fewer consumer goods.*

The shape of the production possibilities frontier reflects the law of increasing opportunity cost. If the economy uses all resources efficiently, the **law of increasing opportunity cost** states that each additional increment of one good requires the economy to give up successively larger increments of the other good.

The PPF has a bowed-out shape due to the law of increasing opportunity cost. For example, whereas the first 10 million units of capital goods have an opportunity cost of only 2 million consumer goods, the final 10 million

capital goods—that is, the increase from point E to point F—have an opportunity cost of 20 million consumer goods. As the economy moves down the curve, the curve becomes steeper, reflecting the higher opportunity cost of capital goods in terms of forgone consumer goods.

The law of increasing opportunity cost also applies when moving from the production of capital goods to the production of consumer goods. When all resources in the economy are making capital goods, as at point F, certain resources, such as cows and farmland, are of little use in making capital goods. Thus, when resources shift from making capital goods to making consumer goods, few capital goods need be given up initially. As more consumer goods are produced, however, resources that are more productive in making capital goods must be used for making consumer goods, reflecting the law of increasing opportunity cost.

If resources were perfectly adaptable to the production of both types of

**44** **CHAPTER 2** Economic Systems and Economic Tools

---

## Curriculum Connection—Mathematics

Imagine that the ABC Glove Co. manufactures high-quality baseball gloves. Although it can produce both left- and right-handed gloves at the same cost, only 20 percent as many left-handed gloves are sold as right-handed models. What does the production possibilities frontier for ABC Gloves look like? How do the firm's managers choose what combination of left- and right-handed gloves to make? Why isn't a firm's ability to produce a product the only factor its managers consider when they decide what products to manufacture? (The production possibilities frontier is a straight diagonal line that slopes down from left to right because there is a one-for-one trade-off between the production of left-handed and right-handed gloves. ABC will make only 20 percent as many left-handed as right-handed gloves because the company must consider its ability to sell the gloves, as well as its costs of production.)

goods, the amount of consumer goods sacrificed to make more capital goods would remain constant. In this case, the PPF would be a straight line, reflecting a constant opportunity cost along the PPF.

**CHECKPOINT**
Describe the PPF model, and explain its shape.

# Shifts of the PPF

The production possibilities frontier assumes that resources available in the economy and the level of technology are fixed during the period. Over time, however, the PPF may shift as a result of changes in resource availability or in technology. An outward shift of the PPF reflects **economic growth**, which is an expansion in the economy's production possibilities or ability to produce. The economy's ability to make stuff grows.

## Changes in Resource Availability

If the labor force increases, such as through immigration, the PPF shifts outward, as shown in panel (a) of Figure 2.2. If people decide to work longer hours, retire later, or if the labor force becomes more skilled, this too would shift the PPF outward. An increase in the availability of other resources, such as new oil discoveries, also would shift the PPF outward.

In contrast, a decrease in the availability or quality of resources shifts the PPF inward, as shown in panel (b). For example, in 1990 Iraq invaded Kuwait, setting oil fields on fire and destroying much of Kuwait's physical capital. As a consequence, Kuwait's PPF shifted inward. In West Africa, the sands of the Sahara spread and destroy thousands of square miles of productive farmland each year, shifting the PPF of that economy inward.

## Increases in Stock of Capital Goods

An economy's PPF depends in part on its supply of the stock of capital goods. The more capital goods an economy produces during one period, the more output it can produce in the next period. Thus, producing more capital goods this period (for example, more factories) shifts the economy's PPF outward the next period.

The choice between consumer goods and capital goods is really between present consumption and future production. Again, the more capital goods produced this period, the greater the economy's production possibilities next period.

**economic growth**

An expansion in the economy's production possibilities or ability to produce

---

**Shifts of the Production Possibilities Frontier**  |  **Figure 2.2**

When the resources available to an economy change, the PPF shifts. If more resources become available, the PPF shifts outward, as in panel (a), indicating that more output can be produced. A decrease in available resources causes the PPF to shift inward, as in panel (b).

(a) Increase in available resources

(b) Decrease in available resources

---

**TEACH**

**Shifts of the PPF**

Explain that over time, with improvements in technology and the augmentation of resources, the production possibilities frontier can shift outward. This shifting is a graphical representation of economic growth. Shifts need not be proportional, because a technological advance seldom affects all sectors of the economy equally.

*Think Critically Through Visuals*

Direct students to focus their attention on **Figure 2.2—Shifts of the Production Possibilities Frontier**. Make sure students understand that a point inside the PPF curve represents inefficiency in that all the resources are not being efficiently used to produce all the consumer and capital goods possible. A point outside the PPF curve represents an unattainable point in that production is extending beyond the capability of the resources available.

*Think Critically Through Visuals*

Direct students to focus their attention on the photograph on page 46. Ask for a volunteer to answer the questions posed in the caption.

**Answers**

(1) Some decision makers might be citizens, businesses, and governments. (2) The citizens affect the amount of resources allocated for consumer goods. Businesses affect the amount of resources allocated for capital goods. Governments affect the amount of resources to both capital and consumer goods.

**NET Bookmark**

Direct students to **econxtra.swlearning.com**. Remind them to click on the link for Lesson 2.2 to find the appropriate link for the **NET Bookmark** on page 46.

---

## Extend the Content

Point out that the usefulness of the production possibilities frontier is its ability to simply depict the concepts of efficiency, scarcity, opportunity cost, the law of increasing opportunity cost, economic growth, choice, and the general need to specialize and trade in order to utilize resources efficiently.

## CHECKPOINT

Invite a student to answer the checkpoint that appears on this page.

### Answer

The PPF may shift as result of changes in resource availability or in technology.

### APPLY

Assign Lesson 2.2 from the Contemporary Economics Workbook.

## e-con @pps

Encourage students to apply their knowledge of concepts presented in this lesson as they explore economic news stories, policy debates, and data available at **econxtra.swlearning**. A sampling of the titles for this lesson appears below.

### Econ News

- The Federal Budget: What a Difference a Day Makes
- Trade Wars—in the U.S.

### ASSESS

Assign all or part of Lesson 2.2 Assessment on page 47 as homework or an in-class activity.

## Xtra! Study Tools

Direct students to the online study tools for Lesson 2.2 at **econxtra.swlearning.com**.

### CLOSE

**Revisit** the In the News feature on the first page of the lesson. Ask students to review their preliminary answers and discuss the questions.

**Review** the objectives for Lesson 2.2. Students should be able to:

- Describe the production possibilities frontier and explain its shape.
- Explain what causes the production possibilities frontier to shift.

## NETBookmark

USAID is an independent federal agency that administers the government's foreign-assistance programs. These programs generally promote economic growth in the receiving countries, thus expanding their production possibilities frontiers. Access the USAID web site through econxtra.swlearning.com. Surf the articles under "Press" to find specific examples of how USAID is promoting economic growth in specific countries. Then write a paragraph describing one example.

*econxtra.swlearning.com*

### Technological Change

Another change that could shift the economy's PPF outward is a technological discovery that employs available resources more efficiently. For example, the Internet has increased the efficiency of resource markets by boosting each firm's ability to identify resource suppliers. Such an increase expands the economy's PPF, as shown in panel (a) of Figure 2.2.

## Ask the Xpert!

*econxtra.swlearning.com*

Have computers affected worker productivity?

### Lessons from the PPF

The PPF demonstrates several concepts introduced so far. The first is *efficiency:* The PPF describes the efficient combinations of outputs that are possible, given the economy's resources and technology. The second is *scarcity.* Given the stock of resources and technology, the economy can produce only so much. The PPF slopes downward, indicating that, as the economy produces more of one good, it must produce less of the other good. This trade-off demonstrates *opportunity cost.*

The bowed-out shape of the PPF reflects the *law of increasing opportunity cost.* Not all resources are perfectly adaptable to the production of each type of good. A shift outward in the PPF reflects *economic growth.* Finally, because society must somehow choose a specific combination of output along the PPF, the PPF also emphasizes the need for *choice.* That choice will determine not only current consumption but also the capital stock available next period.

Each point along the economy's production possibilities frontier is an efficient combination of output. Whether the economy produces efficiently and how the economy selects the most preferred combination depends on the economic system.

## CHECKPOINT

What causes the production possibilities frontier to shift?

Economic decision makers play a key role in determining the PPF for an economy's consumer and capital goods. What types of decision makers are suggested in this image? (Hint: The buildings in the image house businesses, governments, and citizens.) How does each type of decision maker affect the PPF for consumer and capital goods?

© Getty Images/PhotoDisc

### RETEACH

Tell students that the Best Pasta Co. employs 20 workers. Ten of these employees are very skilled at producing spaghetti but can't make other pasta products well. The other 10 workers are really good at making lasagna noodles but are a disaster when they try to make other pasta products. Assign students to sketch a graph that shows the shape of Best Pasta's production possibilities frontier for these two products and explain why it is shaped the way it is. How do their graphs demonstrate the law of increasing opportunity cost? (The graphs of the production possibilities frontier should bend away from the origin. This demonstrates the law of increasing opportunity cost because when workers are required to make a type of pasta they are ill qualified to produce, they are inefficient. A large amount of one production must be given up to obtain a small amount of the other type of production.)

## Key Concepts

1. Explain why each of the following assumptions is made when a production possibilities frontier (PPF) is constructed.
   a. Only two goods or services are considered.
   b. The time considered is limited.
   c. The available resources are fixed in terms of quality and quantity.
   d. The available technology does not change in the time considered.

2. What does a production possibilities frontier for plastic tables and bowling balls identify?

3. What does it mean to say that a firm produces bowling balls efficiently?

4. If a firm that produces bowling balls and plastic tables is operating at a point inside its PPF, how efficiently is it using its resources?

5. Explain why the law of increasing opportunity cost causes PPFs to be bowed-out from the origin (corner) of their graphs.

6. Using consumer goods and capital goods in a production possibilities frontier, what combination would produce a straight-line PPF? What does this indicate about opportunity cost along the PPF, and why?

## Graphing Exercise

7. ABC Electronics Inc. can produce either digital cameras or DVD players in its factory. The more it makes of one product, the less it is able to make of the other. The table to the right shows different combinations of the two products it could manufacture next month. Use these data to construct a production possibilities frontier for this firm. Why isn't there a one-for-one trade-off between production of these two products?

**Combinations of Digital Cameras and DVD Players ABC Electronics Could Produce**

| Combination | Digital Cameras | DVD Players |
|---|---|---|
| A | 0 | 5,000 |
| B | 2,000 | 4,500 |
| C | 3,400 | 3,400 |
| D | 4,500 | 2,000 |
| E | 5,000 | 0 |

## Think Critically

8. **Math** Consider the table in graphing exercise 7 above. Suppose digital cameras generate $50 in profit per sale, while DVD players only earn $40 each. How much profit would ABC earn from each of the combinations of production indicated on the table? Which combination should it choose to produce?

9. **Government** Why has the federal government passed laws that are intended to encourage businesses to buy more capital goods? Given time, what should this do to the location of PPFs in the economy?

Xtra!
Study Tools
econxtra.swlearning.com

### PPF

*(graph: Digital Cameras vs. DVD Players)*

### Visualizing the Answer— Graphing Exercise

7. Answers to the question will vary. Students may point out that the law of increasing opportunity cost is based on the fact that not all resources are equally adaptable to all types of production. Some of ABC's resources are better suited to producing digital cameras, while others are more efficiently used to produce DVD players.

---

## Key Concepts

1. Answers will vary. Possible answers: (a) It is difficult to graph more than two products at once, (b) different amounts of production may take place given the same resources in different periods of time, (c) different amounts and qualities of resources will result in different amounts of production, and (d) different technologies can change the efficiency of producing the products.

2. A PPF identifies the possible combinations of plastic tables and bowling balls that can be produced when available resources are employed fully and efficiently.

3. The firm is producing the maximum number of bowling balls possible from its available resources.

4. Any point inside a PPF indicates inefficient production.

5. Answers will vary. Possible answer: PPFs are bowed out from the origin of their graphs because of the law of increasing opportunity cost—not all resources are perfectly adaptable to production of different goods or services. As more resources are devoted to one type of production, some of those resources will inevitably result in additional production that is less efficient. Therefore, the trade-off between production of the two products is not one-for-one, and the graph is not a straight line.

6. A straight-line PPF curve represents a one-for-one trade-off between the capital and consumer goods. This indicates that there is no opportunity cost along a straight line PPF. On a straight line PPF, the units you give up and attain are equal.

## Graphing Exercise

7. The answer and visual appear at the bottom of this page.

## Think Critically

8. Profit from each of the combinations: A, $20,000; B, $28,000; C, $30,600; D, $30,500; E, $25,000. If ABC Electronics is able to sell all products it manufactures, it should produce 3,400 of each product to maximize its profits.

9. Answers will vary. Students might point out that by encouraging businesses to buy more capital goods, the government hopes to cause increases in our production and to make PPFs move away from their origins.

## Sharpen Your Life Skills

### Interpret a Graph

After studying Lesson 2.2, students should be able to answer the questions on this page.

### Apply Your Skill

Consider allowing students to work in pairs for this assignment.

### Answers

1. If Apex produces 800 units of Product A, it can produce 300 units of Product B.

2. If Apex chooses to produce 400 units of Product A instead of 800, it can make roughly 160 more units of Product B—a total of 460.

3. According to the law of increasing opportunity cost, as more resources are allocated to one type of production, some of them will not be well suited to that type of production and will result in little additional production. To produce only Product B, the firm must use some of its resources in a way that produces few of these products.

4. At point *D* on the graph, production is inefficient. It could make additional products without adding additional resources.

5. Apex does not have enough resources to produce at point *E*. It can reach this level of production only by adding resources.

# Sharpen Your Life Skills

### Interpret a Graph

Apex Industries is able to produce either product A or product B from a fixed amount of resources it has each month. It also can produce different combinations of these products. However, for each additional amount of one of these products it produces, it must give up some of the other. Study the graph of Apex's production possibilities frontier, and then answer the following questions.

### Apply Your Skill

1. If Apex produces 800 units of product A, how many units of product B can it make?

2. If Apex chooses to produce 400 units of product A instead of 800, roughly how many more units of product B can it make?

3. If Apex chooses to produce 500 units of product B instead of 460 of them, why must it give up the production of 400 units of product A?

4. If Apex is producing at point *D* on the graph, what can you say about the efficiency of its production?

5. Why isn't Apex able to produce at point *E* given the current situation?

The Graphing Workshop

**Apex Industries' Production Possibilities Frontier**

C O N N E C T

*to History*

# Jamestown
## and the English Mercantile System

In 1612, John Rolfe began growing tobacco in Jamestown from seeds he obtained from the Spanish colonies. Rolfe acquired the seeds despite the Spaniards' threat of death to anyone selling tobacco seeds to a non-Spaniard. The local Indians may have aided Rolfe's acquisition of the seeds, as he was engaged to marry the chief's daughter, Pocahontas. By 1614, the first tobacco from Virginia was sold in London. Despite the disapproval of King James I, this "stinking weed" came into high demand in England and throughout Europe. With tobacco as a cash crop, the Virginia colony had the basis for its economic success in place.

With the success of tobacco, the demand for labor in the colony increased. Labor was first supplied by indentured servants, who sold their labor for passage to Virginia, food, clothing, and other necessities—but no wages. After filling the terms of the contract, usually three to seven years, the indentured servant would be given land, tools, and perhaps a small amount of money. A 20 percent death rate on the voyage over, and further exposure to hard work and disease, made it difficult to recruit indentured laborers. As time passed and the survival rate increased, more were willing to come. After indentured servants proved finally to be an unsatisfactory labor resource, slavery developed. Initially more expensive to purchase than indentured servants, slaves proved to be a cheaper form of labor, as their work was bought for life.

Although crops other than tobacco, such as wheat, could be grown in the South, the opportunity cost was high. By specializing in growing tobacco, a farmer could maximize his profits over what could be made from growing other crops. As planting tobacco became more profitable, laws had to be passed to require planters to devote some portion of their land to producing food. Tobacco was profitable on any size of farm. However, by specializing in tobacco, the

soil was worn out every four to seven years. Consequently, maintenance of soil fertility favored large-scale producers. From this the plantation system developed, and with it the *specialization* of labor. With this success, Virginia's *comparative advantage* lay in growing tobacco.

Virginia tobacco farmers were part of the English mercantile system. The object of the system was to increase a nation's wealth, as defined by the amount of gold it possessed. Gold could be acquired by a nation possessing a territory that produced gold. It also could be acquired by developing a positive balance of trade that brought in gold payments. For England, tobacco was an ideal mercantilist product. It was easy to ship and could replace the imports of tobacco from Spain. England did not allow Virginia tobacco to be shipped or sold anywhere but back to England, where it became a large source of import duties growing the English treasury. By 1639, at least 750 tons of Virginia tobacco had been shipped to England. After a profit was taken, it could be re-exported to Europe. Adam Smith criticized the mercantilist system. England's enforcing it became a contributing factor to the American Revolution.

## THINK CRITICALLY

The colonists in Jamestown were faced with the choice of producing food for consumption or producing tobacco for sale. Draw a *production possibilities frontier* for producing food and tobacco. Label the points where the PPF intersects the axes, as well as several other points along the frontier. What would it mean for the colonists to move upward and to the left along the PPF? Under what circumstances would the PPF shift outward?

### FOCUS

Point out that economics has been a driving force throughout history. This feature about Jamestown and the English mercantile system helps demonstrate the connection between economics and history.

### TEACH

Instruct students to read the **Connect to History** feature and answer the questions. Organize students into small groups and instruct them to prepare a short, in-class presentation, including visual aids, for their answers to the questions. Encourage students to be creative. For example, they might stage a scene where Adam Smith criticizes the mercantile system, or read a letter written by a colonist to a relative in England (explaining how the system works), or make a sales pitch for a newly invented piece of farm equipment.

### ASSESS

Use the questions at the bottom of the page to assess the students' understanding of this feature.

#### Answers to Think Critically

Student PPFs will vary, depending on the numbers they use.
Answers will vary. Possible answers: (1) To move upward and to the left along the PPF means the colonists would be utilizing Virginia's comparative advantage in tobacco. To move along the PPF curve in this way means giving up production of units of food to attain more production of units of tobacco. (2) The PPF would shift outward if a new technology were invented, such as a new technique for harvesting crops. (3) The shift would be parallel if the technology advancement were equally beneficial to tobacco and food production.

## Bibliography

Borio, Gene. "A Brief History of Jamestown, Virginia." *Tobacco News and Information*, 1998. Retrieved February 10, 2003 from the World Wide Web: http://tobacco.org/History/Jamestown.html.

Fishwick, Marshall W. *Jamestown: First English Colony*. New York: American Heritage Publishing Company, 1974.

Lieberman, Jethro K. *Companion to the Constitution: How the Supreme Court Has Ruled on Issues from Abortion to Zoning*. Los Angeles: University of California Press, 1999.

McEachern, William A. *Economics: A Contemporary Introduction*, sixth edition. Mason, Ohio: South-Western, 2003.

Middleton, Arthur Pierce. *Tobacco Coast*. Newport News, Va.: Mariners' Museum, 1953.

Scharf, J. Thomas. *History of Maryland: From the Earliest Periods to the Present Day*. Hatboro, Pa.: Tradition Press, 1967.

# FOCUS

### 2.3 Comparative Advantage

Explain that one of the oldest and most widely held propositions in economics is the concept of comparative advantage. Stated as a law, it asserts that the individual or country with the lowest opportunity cost of producing a particular good should specialize in the production of that good.

## Objectives

Remind students to read the lesson objectives to help focus their attention before reading the lesson.

## Key Terms

Direct students use each of the key terms in a separate sentence or short paragraph that helps demonstrate the meaning of the term. For example: Neighbors Margo and Hugo use the barter system—he walks her dog and she changes the oil in his car.

## [ In the News ]

Instruct students to read the passage and write down their answers. Point out that their answers might change after they finish studying Lesson 2.3.

### Answers to Think About It

Answers will vary. Possible answer: The two gains of specialization of cardiologists are (1) more focused attention to patients and (2) ability to provide patients with greater access to rehabilitation techniques.

## Visual Presentation

Use the PowerPoint presentation on the Instructor's Resource CD as an adjunct to your lecture. The presentation also can be used for review.

## Objectives

> Explain the law of comparative advantage.

> Understand the gains from specialization and exchange.

## Overview

The law of comparative advantage helps explain why even a person talented at many things can get more done by specializing. Division of labor allows firms to increase production by having each worker specialize. Specialization occurs not only among individual workers, but also among firms, regions, and entire countries.

## Key Terms

absolute advantage

law of comparative advantage

specialization

barter

money

division of labor

## [ In the News ]

### ● Live Longer with Specialized Care

Research has shown that people who have had a heart attack do better and recuperate faster if they are attended by a cardiac specialist rather than a general practitioner. As reported in the *New England Journal of Medicine,* a Boston research group studied Medicare data from 35,520 patients across the country. Studying a post-hospital time period of two years for the heart attack patients, the researchers found that 14.6 percent of patients with outpatient care from a cardiologist had died. In the same time period, 18.3 percent died while being treated solely by a family doctor, general practitioner, or internist. Reasons suggested for the greater success through specialization include: the patients treated by a cardiac specialist were likely to have received more focused attention, they underwent more medical procedures, and they were provided greater access to rehabilitation techniques.

### Think About It

Suggest two gains from specialization for cardiologists providing medical services to their patients.

50

### National Content Standards in Economics

A complete list of the NCEE Standards appears on pages xxiv–xxv of this book. The following standards are addressed in Lesson 2.3.

Standard 5: Gain from Trade

Standard 6: Specialization and Trade

Standard 11: Role of Money

Standard 15: Growth

# Comparative Advantage

You probably face some chores at home that your family expects you to do regularly. What if it is your responsibility to wash the two family cars and mow the lawn each week? It takes you 45 minutes to wash a car and an hour to mow the lawn. Altogether, you spend two and a half hours a week washing two cars and mowing the lawn.

Your high school friend David lives next door. He happens to face the same weekly chores—washing two family cars identical to yours and mowing a lawn identical to yours. David, however, is not nearly as quick as you. It takes him one hour to wash a car and three hours to mow the lawn. Altogether, David spends five hours a week on these chores.

## Absolute Advantage

Compared to David, you have an absolute advantage in both tasks, because you can do each using fewer resources. The resource here is your labor time. More generally, having an **absolute advantage** means being able to do something using fewer resources than other producers require.

If you and David each do your own weekly chores, you take two-and-a-half hours and he takes five hours. Because you can complete each task in less time than David can, you see no point in cooperating with him to save time. However, is this the best you can do?

## The Law of Comparative Advantage

It turns out that absolute advantage is not the best guide for deciding who should do what. A better guide is comparative advantage. According to the **law of comparative advantage**, the worker with the lower opportunity cost of producing a particular output should specialize in that output. **Specialization**, then, occurs when individual workers focus on single tasks, enabling each one to be more efficient and productive. Note that for the definitions of both the law of comparative advantage and specialization, the term *worker* may be replaced by the terms *firm, region,* or *country.*

What is your *opportunity cost* of washing each car? In the 45 minutes you take to wash a car, you could instead mow three-fourths of the lawn. So your opportunity cost of washing a car is mowing three-fourths of a lawn.

**law of comparative advantage**
The worker, firm, region, or country with the lowest opportunity cost of producing an output should specialize in that output

**specialization**
Occurs when individual workers focus on single tasks, enabling each one to be more efficient and productive

**absolute advantage**
To be able to make something using fewer resources than other producers require

**Study the two images and decide what the comparative advantages of the areas shown might be. (Hint: The locations in the images are New York City and Hawaii.)**

Lesson 2.3 • *Comparative Advantage* **51**

## Comparative Advantage

Point out that opportunity cost is based on relative rather than absolute resource requirements in the production of goods. Because comparative advantage implies the specialization of resource use, trade becomes important in allocating goods to consumers.

### SPAN THE GLOBE

Direct students to read the short passage entitled "Prison Labor" that appears on this page. Use the questions as a starting point for class discussion or have students write a short essay to answer the questions.

### Answers to Think Critically

Answers will vary. Some students will say that the economic advantages of importing prisoner-made products outweigh the social disadvantages. Other students will focus on the social issues and will support the U.S. ban.

 Allow students to use the business section of the local newspaper to jump-start their discussion. Remind students to choose a recorder and a spokesperson for their group before the brainstorming begins.

### NETBookmark

Direct students to **econxtra.swlearning.com**. Remind them to click on the link for Lesson 2.3 to find the appropriate link for the **NET Bookmark** on page 53.
Add interest to the assignment by inviting small groups of students with differing viewpoints to debate the issue in front of their classmates.

 **CHECKPOINT**

Invite a student to answer the checkpoint that appears on page 53.

### Answer

The law of comparative advantage says the worker with the lower opportunity cost of producing a particular output should specialize in that output.

---

# SPAN THE GLOBE

## Prison Labor

The United States has a number of laws designed to prevent importing products manufactured using prison labor. Despite the laws, prisoner-produced products from a number of nations continue to make their way into the U.S. market. Prison officials in northern Mexico have for years put their inmates to work manufacturing furniture. The furniture then finds its way into Texas. In general, Mexican inmates are paid the "minimum wage" of 45 pesos ($4.50) a day, which is about half the wage free workers across the border in Texas and Arizona are paid. The reason the use of prison labor is strongly criticized around the globe is because it undercuts union pay scales, steals jobs from law-abiding workers, and poses risks of human rights abuses.

### Think Critically

The law of comparative advantage states that whoever has the lower opportunity cost of producing a particular output should specialize in that output. In light of this, do you agree with the U.S. ban on imports of prisoner-made products? Why or why not?

---

**barter**
A system of exchange in which products are traded directly for other products

In the hour David takes to wash a car, he could instead mow one-third of the lawn. So his opportunity cost of washing a car is mowing one-third of a lawn. Because your opportunity cost of washing a car is mowing three-fourths of a lawn and David's is mowing one-third of a lawn, he faces the lower opportunity cost of washing cars.

Again, the law of comparative advantage says that the person with the lower opportunity cost should specialize in producing that output. In this example, David should specialize in washing cars.

Because David has a lower opportunity cost for washing cars, you must have a lower opportunity cost for

mowing lawns. So you should specialize in mowing lawns.

### Gains from Specialization

If you each specialize, David will wash your family cars, and you will mow his lawn. David washes the four cars in four hours, saving himself an hour. You cut both lawns in two hours, saving yourself a half hour. Through specialization and exchange, each of you saves time. Even though you can complete each task in less time than David can, your comparative advantage is mowing lawns. Put another way, David, although not as good as you at either task, is not as bad at washing cars as he is at mowing lawns. He has a comparative advantage in washing cars. You each specialize based on comparative advantage, and you each save time.

*Absolute advantage focuses on which of you uses the fewest resources, but comparative advantage focuses on what else those resources could have produced—that is, on the opportunity cost of those resources.* The law of comparative advantage indicates who should do what.

### Exchange

In this example, you and David specialize and exchange your output. No money is involved. In other words, you two engage in **barter**, a system of exchange in which products are traded directly for other products. Barter works

---

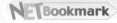 **Investigate Your Local Economy**

In small groups, brainstorm a list of possible resources that provide your local economy with a comparative advantage. After five minutes of brainstorming, each group will present its results to the class.

---

**ENRICH**

There was a time when many students in the United States attended rural one-room schools where one teacher taught all subjects to all grades of students. Ask students to write an essay or discuss the types of learning opportunities offered in large schools today that could not be offered to students in one-room schools of the past. How do these differences demonstrate advantages of a division of labor and specialization? Do students believe any single teacher could help them learn everything they need to know?

best in simple economies where there is little specialization and few types of goods to trade. For economies with greater specialization, *money* plays an important role in facilitating exchange.

**Money**—coins, bills, and checks—serves as a *medium of exchange* because it is the one thing that everyone is willing to accept in exchange for all goods and services.

### Wider Application

Due to such factors as climate, an abundance of labor, workforce skills, natural resources, and capital stock, certain parts of the country and certain parts of the world have a comparative advantage in producing particular goods. From Apple computers in California's Silicon Valley to oranges in Florida, from DVD players in Taiwan to bananas in Honduras—*resources are allocated most efficiently across the country and around the world when production and trade conform to the law of comparative advantage.*

**CHECKPOINT**
What is the law of comparative advantage?

## Specialization

Because of specialization based on comparative advantage, most people consume little of what they produce and produce little of what they consume. People specialize in particular activities, such as plumbing or carpentry, and then exchange their products for money, which in turn is exchanged for goods and services.

Did you make anything you are wearing? Probably not. Think about the degree of specialization that went into your cotton shirt. Some farmer in a warm climate grew the cotton and sold it to someone who spun it into thread, who sold it to someone who wove it into fabric, who sold it to someone who sewed the shirt, who sold it to a whole-

**NETBookmark**

To learn more about how barter works in the economy, see the web site of the International Reciprocal Trade Association (IRTA). IRTA's mission is to "advance the barter industry worldwide and raise the value of barter." Access this group's web site through econxtra.swlearning.com and press "Visitors Click Here." After reading the material on the web site, write a paragraph answering the following question: Do you think barter is an effective means of exchange in a market economy? Why or why not?

**econxtra.swlearning.com**

saler, who sold it to a retailer, who sold it to you. Many specialists produced your shirt.

### Division of Labor

Picture a visit to McDonald's: "Let's see, I'll have a Big Mac, an order of fries, and a chocolate shake." Less than a minute later, your order is ready. It would take you much longer to make a homemade version of this meal. Why is the McDonald's meal faster, cheaper, and—for some people—tastier than one you could make yourself? Why is fast food so fast?

McDonald's takes advantage of the gains resulting from the division of labor. The **division of labor** sorts the production process into separate tasks to be carried out by separate workers. Each worker specializes in a separate task. This division of labor allows the group to produce much more.

How is this increase in productivity possible? First, the manager can assign tasks according to individual preferences and abilities—that is, according to the law of comparative advantage. The worker with the nice smile and good personality can handle the customers up front. The muscle-bound worker with few social graces can do the heavy lifting in the back room.

**money**
Anything that everyone is willing to accept in exchange for goods and services

**division of labor**
An action that sorts the production process into separate tasks to be carried out by separate workers

*Lesson 2.3 • Comparative Advantage* **53**

## TEACH

### Specialization

Point out that specialization is a powerful way of organizing production, because it uses the most efficient means to produce output.

**CHECKPOINT**
Invite a student to answer the checkpoint that appears on page 54.

**Answer**

The gains from specialization and exchange are that everyone's time and resources are being allocated most efficiently.

## APPLY

Assign Lesson 2.3 from the Contemporary Economics Workbook.

## ASSESS

Assign all or part of Lesson 2.3 Assessment on page 54 as homework or an in-class activity.

**Xtra! Study Tools**

Direct students to the online study tools for Lesson 2.3 at **econxtra.swlearning.com**.

## CLOSE

**Revisit** the **In the News** feature on the first page of the lesson. Ask students to review their preliminary answers and discuss the questions, now that they have completed this lesson.

**Review** the objectives for Lesson 2.3. Students should be able to:
- Explain the law of comparative advantage.
- Understand the gains from specialization and exchange.

## RETEACH

Describe an athlete who participates in a team sport such as football, baseball, or hockey, who is good in only one aspect of the sport. A baseball player might be only a pinch hitter, a football player might only return punts, or a hockey player might play only when there is a penalty to kill off. Ask students why this type of specialization might cause problems for the individual player as well as for the team. How does this type of situation demonstrate a limit to the benefits of specialization? (The individual player might become bored and not work as hard as possible, or this person could fail to develop other skills that would allow him or her to become a well-rounded member of the team. The team might suffer because this player performs only one task and cannot contribute to other aspects of the game. Specialization can cause people to become bored and not make their best effort, and it can cause problems when there is little need for a particular specialty.)

## Key Concepts

1. Answers will vary. Students may point out that specializing in producing one good forces people to trade that product for other goods they do not produce.

2. Answers will vary. Students may point out that money is a medium of exchange that people are willing to accept in return for goods that they own or produce. Without money, people would have to rely on barter to complete exchanges, which would be time consuming and inefficient.

3. Answers will vary. Students may point out that a division of labor sorts the production process into separate steps, each of which is carried out by different workers. Through repetition and practice, each worker becomes better at his or her assigned task.

4. Answers will vary. Students may point out that a division of labor allows the introduction of labor-saving machinery to production.

## Graphing Exercise

5. Answers will vary. Students may point out that by specializing in the types of production that result in the lowest opportunity costs, Joel and Jamal are able to maximize their production of pies and iced cakes. See the table below and the graph at the bottom of this page.

|  | Situation A | | Situation B | |
| --- | --- | --- | --- | --- |
|  | Icing cakes | Making pies | Icing cakes | Making pies |
| Joel | 10 | 5 | 0 | 20 |
| Jamal | 8 | 1 | 32 | 0 |
| Total | 18 | 6 | 32 | 20 |

## Think Critically

6. Answers will vary. Students may point out that each team member is assigned to tasks according to his or her abilities. Once assigned, the division of labor allows them to become more efficient and to use specialized tools to further increase their efficiency.

---

Second, a worker who performs the same task again and again gets better at it: Experience is a good teacher. The worker filling orders at the drive-through, for example, learns how to deal with special problems that arise there. Third, there is no time lost in moving from one task to another.

Finally, and perhaps most important, the division of labor allows for the introduction of more sophisticated production techniques—techniques that would not make sense on a smaller scale. For example, McDonald's large milkshake machine would be impractical in your home. The division of labor allows for the introduction of specialized machines, and these machines make each worker more productive.

To review, the division of labor takes advantage of individual preferences and natural abilities. It allows workers to develop more experience at a particular task. It reduces the time required to shift between different tasks. Finally, it permits the introduction of labor-saving machinery. The specialization that results with the division of labor does not occur among individuals only. It also occurs among firms, regions, and entire countries.

### ✓ CHECKPOINT
What are the gains from specialization and exchange?

---

**2.3** *Assessment*

**Xtra!**
Study Tools
*econxtra.swlearning.com*

## Key Concepts

1. Why does specialization require people to complete exchanges?

2. How does money help people complete exchanges?

3. How is a division of labor accomplished?

4. What advantages may be offered by a division of labor in addition to allowing workers to become more accomplished at the tasks they complete?

## Graphing Exercise

5. Joel and Jamal work together at a bakery. In one hour Joel can ice ten cakes or prepare 5 pies. In the same time Jamal can ice eight cakes or prepare only one pie. Draw bar graphs to represent production of iced cakes and prepared pies for each of the following situations. Explain how your graphs demonstrate the law of comparative advantage.

   **Situation A**—Joel spends one hour icing cakes and three hours preparing pies. Jamal does the same. **Situation B**—Joel spends four hours preparing pies, while Jamal spends four hours icing cakes.

## Think Critically

6. **Research** Investigate the division of labor and specialization on a high-school sports team, such as basketball, football, or field hockey. Write a paragraph explaining the different positions, and how each one contributes to the team effort.

**54**    **CHAPTER 2** Economic Systems and Economic Tools

---

**Situation A**

Units

35
30
25
20
15
10
5
0

☐ Jamal
☐ Joel

Icing cakes    Making pies
Production

**Situation B**

Units

35
30
25
20
15
10
5
0

Icing cakes    Making pies
Production

## *Visualizing the Answer—Graphing Exercise*

5. In addition to the information shown here, a corresponding spreadsheet, including the graphs, is available on the Instructor's Resource CD.

# movers & shakers

## Susan Packard *President of Scripps Networks New Ventures*

Susan Packard began working in cable television at an exciting time. It was 1980, cable television was new, and cable operators were still developing their programs. Their salespeople were busy selling networks into viewer's homes while at the same time finding advertisers who wanted to reach each network's audience.

Packard worked for HBO at that time. She was part of a team that eventually made HBO available to every cable-ready home in the United States. To do her job well, Packard needed to be technically literate, so she climbed poles and learned to distinguish a receiver from a modulator and a head-end. Her willingness to learn kept her career on the fast track in the rapidly growing cable industry.

After eight years at HBO and then six years at CNBC, Packard took her knowledge of the cable industry to oversee the launch of HGTV—one of the most successful and fastest-growing new cable networks. She served as chief operating officer of HGTV, and then executive vice president of Scripps Networks, owner of HGTV. Today she is president of Scripps Networks New Ventures where her responsibilities include the development of new networks. Packard also is an officer of Scripps Networks, Inc., which includes Home & Garden Television, the Food Network, the Do It Yourself Network, and the Fine Living Network.

Each of these cable networks covers a different category of subjects, but they follow the same model. They package attractive visuals with how-to information aimed at the baby boomer and those with unique lifestyle interests and hobbies. These are audiences that advertisers often find difficult to reach. The networks are successful not only because of the programs they deliver, but because advertisers are eager to spend their money in order to reach these audiences.

Packard credits the meteoric success of these cable networks to the unique categories of programming they deliver to viewers. "We're nonviolent family fare. Everything on our air is TV-G. We appeal to specialized, passionate interests—gardeners, do-it-yourself types, hobbyists, cooks, and decorators, to name a few." Packard's knowledge and decision-making skills also deserve credit. Together they have earned her numerous awards including recognition as one of the "12 Most Powerful Women in Cable" by *Cablevision* magazine, as "One of 12 to Watch" by Electronic Media, and as one of the "Top 100" in the cable industry by *CableFax* magazine. Packard is the recipient of the 1998 Woman of the Year Award presented by Women in Cable & Telecommunications and in 1999 was profiled in *Modern Visionaries,* a book chronicling the contributions of pioneering women in the cable and telecommunications industry.

### SOURCE READING
Packard states, "We appeal to so many interests—gardeners, do-it-yourself types, hobbyists, and those with special interests." How are these networks incorporating the idea of specialization in ways that major television networks like ABC, NBC, and CBS are not?

### ENTREPRENEURS IN ACTION
Working in small groups, create a division of labor among five people producing a show about flower gardens. Could this same division of labor be used to produce a show about landscaping a home? Is it more efficient for a cable television network to produce shows about gardening and landscaping, or to produce shows about gardening and scuba diving?

Lesson 2.3 • *Comparative Advantage* **55**

---

## movers & shakers

## movers & shakers

### FOCUS

Point out to students that this feature is more than an interesting profile of Susan Packard. The feature is designed to integrate economic principles and ideas. In this case, the focus is specialization.

### TEACH

Instruct students to read the **Movers & Shakers** feature about Susan Packard. Point out that some students may find it helpful to read the article, read the questions at the bottom of the page, and then reread the article.

### ASSESS

Use the questions in Source Reading and Entrepreneurs in Action at the bottom of the profile to assess the students' understanding of this **Movers & Shakers** feature.

#### Answers to Source Reading

Cable networks are targeting a very specific market (do-it-yourselfers, gardeners, etc.). They target their programs to a narrower market than the markets of the major television networks. But advertisers are eager to reach these narrow markets, and so are willing to devote much of their money to advertising. This is why the cable networks are successful.

#### Answers to Entrepreneurs in Action

It is more efficient to produce similar programs. Gardening and landscaping involve similar products. The camerawork is similar. The locations are similar. The advertisers are similar and may even be the same. Gardening and scuba diving have very different requirements. Only a limited amount of knowledge and equipment can be shared. It is not likely that gardening and scuba diving advertisers would be the same.

---

## Extend the Content

Discuss the fact that in the real world, being very skilled and efficient in producing a product does not necessarily mean that a person should choose to produce this product. Consider Nora, for example. Nora is an American who went to France as a young woman to study French history. While living in Paris, she became interested in medieval French literature. After many years of study, she became one of the quickest and most accurate translators of medieval French literature in the world. If her goal was to earn a large salary, why might it not have been a good idea for her to specialize in this way?

(Specialization makes economic sense only when other people are willing to pay for products you make with a low opportunity cost. There is little advantage in being able to produce a product that no one wants to purchase.)

## Summary

### Consider

Ask students to revisit the questions they were asked to consider at the beginning of the chapter. Remind students that they should be able to answer all of the questions after studying Chapter 2.

- Why are economies around the world growing more market oriented? See page 38—Mixed, Transitional, and Traditional Economies.

- How much can an economy produce with the resources available? See page 42—Efficiency and the Production Possibilities Frontier.

- Can you actually save time by applying economic principles to your family chores? See page 51—Comparative Advantage.

- Why is experience a good teacher? See page 52—Gains from Specialization.

- Why is fast food so fast? See page 52—Gains from Specialization.

### Exam*View*

Use **Exam***View* to assess student learning.

- Create a chapter test using questions from the existing test bank.

- Add your own questions to the existing test bank.

- Generate multiple forms of a chapter test.

### Study Skills

Offer the following study skills suggestions for students as they review this chapter.

- Outline the chapter.

- Review key terms.

- Review Checkpoints.

- Work in pairs to quiz each other.

- Use Xtra! Study Tools for each lesson.

Direct students to the online quiz preparation for Chapter 2 at **econxtra.swlearning.com**.

---

 # Chapter Assessment

## Summary

### 2.1 *Economic Questions and Economic Systems*

**a** All economic systems must answer three basic questions: (1) What goods will be produced? (2) How will these goods be produced? (3) For whom will these goods be produced?

**b** In a pure market economy, all resources are privately owned and controlled. Competition forces businesses to serve the interest of consumers when they work to earn a profit. Property rights must be protected for a pure market economy to work. Owners would not operate firms if they were not sure they could use their profits to buy more resources or satisfy their personal desires.

**c** Pure market economies have some problems. These include the difficulty in enforcing property rights, the possibility that people who produce little of value will fall into poverty, the possibility of businesses monopolizing markets, and a lack of public goods. Externalities may cause costs or benefits of production to flow to individuals who are neither producers nor consumers.

**d** In a pure centrally planned economy, all resources are publicly owned and controlled. Government planners answer the three basic economic questions according to their own priorities or those of government leaders. Problems associated with these economies include consumer desires being given a low priority in production, little consumer freedom of choice, and inefficient use of resources.

**e** The problems of market and centrally planned economies have caused some nations to reorient their economies. Many nations have moved toward a market economy while other nations have increased the role of their governments. Nations moving from central planning to markets have *transitional economies*.

**f** Some nations have *traditional economies* in which resources are allocated and used to produce goods according to traditions that are passed from one generation to the next.

### 2.2 *Production Possibilities Frontier*

**a** Economists construct graphs called *production possibility frontiers* (PPFs) to demonstrate different combinations of two products that can be produced from a fixed amount of resources. Assumptions made to simplify PPFs include a time limitation, a fixed technology, and an inability to add more resources.

**b** The PPF for two products bows out from the corner of their graph because the trade-off in production between the two goods is not one-for-one. The *law of increasing opportunity cost* states that each additional unit of one good produced requires successively larger sacrifices of the other good. This happens because resources are not perfectly adaptable to the production of both goods.

**c** Any point below a PPF indicates inefficient production because more goods could be produced from the same resources. Any point above a PPF indicates a level of production that cannot be achieved without additional resources. A PPF will shift out if new resources are added, technology changes, or more time becomes available.

### 2.3 *Comparative Advantage*

**a** According to the law of comparative advantage, people should specialize in the type of production where their opportunity cost is the lowest.

**b** Specialization allows workers to become more efficient through practice. When people specialize, they must exchange what they produce for other goods they desire. These exchanges are easier when they are carried out through the use of money.

**c** There are many steps that must be completed to produce most goods. When individual workers specialize in specific steps in this process there is a division of labor. A division of labor results in greater efficiency because workers become more skilled in their tasks and are able to use more sophisticated production techniques.

---

# Review Economic Terms

Choose the term that best fits the definition. On a separate sheet of paper, write the letter of the answer. Some terms may not be used.

_____ 1. The set of mechanisms and institutions that resolve the what, how, and for whom questions for an economy

_____ 2. Organizing the production of goods into separate tasks to be carried out by separate workers

_____ 3. Ability to make something using fewer resources than other producers require

_____ 4. Anything that everyone is willing to accept in exchange for goods and services

_____ 5. The worker, firm, region, or country with the lowest opportunity cost of producing a particular output should specialize in that output

_____ 6. Producing the maximum possible output from available resources

_____ 7. An economic system with no government so that firms account for all production

_____ 8. Shows the possible combinations of two types of goods that can be produced when available resources are employed fully and efficiently

_____ 9. An economic system combining aspects of central planning and competitive markets

_____ 10. An expansion in the economy's ability to produce

a. **absolute advantage**

b. **barter**

c. **division of labor**

d. **economic growth**

e. **economic system**

f. **efficiency**

g. **law of comparative advantage**

h. **law of increasing opportunity cost**

i. **market economy**

j. **mixed economy**

k. **money**

l. **production possibilities frontier (PPF)**

m. **pure centrally planned economy**

n. **pure market economy**

o. **specialization**

p. **traditional economy**

q. **transitional economy**

# Review Economic Concepts

11. **True or False** According to the *law of comparative advantage,* only people who are the most efficient producers of a product can benefit from specialization.

12. _?_ is a system of exchange in which products are traded directly for other products.

13. Which of the following is the best example of a *division of labor?*

   a. Todd lives in a cabin in the woods where he does most things for himself.

   b. Julia works as a doctor, while her husband Ted is an automobile mechanic.

   c. Benito washes dishes after lunch, while his wife dries and puts them away.

   d. Brenda reads the front page of the newspaper while her husband studies the comics.

14. **True or False** The *law of comparative advantage* applies not only to individuals, but also to firms, regions of countries, and entire nations.

15. **True or False** All economic systems must decide what goods will be produced from the resources they have.

16. The economic question _?_ often is referred to as the *distribution question.*

17. Points _?_ the PPF represent unattainable combinations given the resources and technology available.

*Chapter Assessment*    **57**

## Review Economic Terms

1. e. economic system
2. c. division of labor
3. a. absolute advantage
4. k. money
5. g. law of comparative advantage
6. f. efficiency
7. n. pure market economy
8. l. production possibilities frontier (PPF)
9. j. mixed economy
10. d. economic growth

## Review Economic Concepts

11. True
12. Barter
13. c. Benito washes dishes after lunch, while his wife dries and puts them away.
14. True
15. True
16. for whom
17. outside

## Review Economic Concepts

18. b. The prices of the goods produced do not change.

19. opportunity cost

20. a. successively larger increments of the other good

21. False. Resources are publicly owned and controlled in a pure centrally planned economy.

22. market competition

23. False. In a centrally planned economy little focus is given to consumer needs and wants.

24. True

25. Privatization

26. d. traditional economy

## Apply Economic Concepts

27. Answers will vary. By assigning people to jobs that are well suited to their skills, personality, and abilities, each person should maximize his or her production. This will take advantage of the law of comparative advantage and should improve the firm's opportunity for success.

28. The new PPF reflects an increase in the resources allocated toward the production of wheat and a decrease in the resources allocated toward the production of cloth.

29. a. The PPF curve would shift inward with an increase in vacation length (decrease in labor).

b. The PPF curve would shift outward with an increase in immigration (increase in labor).

c. The PPF curve would shift outward with a decrease in the average retirement age (increase in labor).

d. The PPF curve would shift inward with the migration of workers to another country (decrease in labor).

---

18. Which of the following is *not* a simplifying assumption made when a *production possibilities frontier* (PPF) is created?

    a. Only two goods are considered.

    b. The prices of the goods produced do not change.

    c. Production is limited to a fixed period of time.

    d. There is a set amount of resources that may be used.

19. Movement down the PPF curve indicates that the _?_ of more capital goods is fewer consumer goods.

20. According to the *law of increasing opportunity cost,* each additional increment of one good requires the sacrifice of

    a. successively larger increments of the other good.

    b. equal increments of the other good.

    c. successively smaller increments of the other good.

    d. the level of productive efficiency.

21. **True or False** In a *pure market economy,* resources are publicly owned and controlled.

22. Adam Smith argued that although each individual pursues his or her self-interest in a market economy, the "invisible hand" of _?_ promotes the general welfare.

23. **True or False** One problem with *centrally planned economies* is too much focus on consumer needs and wants.

24. **True or False** In *centrally planned economies,* state enterprises often are more concerned with meeting the goals set by the central planners than they are about the environment.

25. _?_ is a process that involves converting state-owned enterprises into private enterprises.

26. An economic system in which the means and methods of production are passed from one generation to the next is a definition of a

    a. pure market economy.

    b. pure centrally planned economy.

    c. transitional economy.

    d. traditional economy.

# Apply Economic Concepts

27. **Create a Division of Labor** Make a list of five friends who you know well. Assume that the six of you have decided to open a small restaurant. Assign each of your friends, and yourself, to one of the following job descriptions in the way that you believe would result in the most efficient operation of your restaurant. Briefly explain the reasons for each of your assignments. How does this demonstrate the advantages of specialization and a division of labor?

    a. Greet customers and take them to their tables

    b. Take customer's orders and bring food to their tables

    c. Be the chief cook in the kitchen

    d. Clear tables and wash dishes

    e. Keep the books, accept payments, order supplies, and pay the bills

    f. Be the chief cook's assistant

28. **Apply Production Possibilities** Imagine an economy that uses two resources, labor and capital, to produce two goods, wheat and cloth. Capital is relatively more useful in producing cloth, and labor is relatively more useful in producing wheat. If the supply of capital falls by 10 percent and the supply of labor increases by 10 percent, how will the PPF for wheat and cloth change?

29. **Apply Shifts of Production Possibilities** Determine whether each of the following would cause the economy's PPF to shift inward, outward, or not at all.

    a. Increase in average vacation length

    b. Increase in immigration

    c. Decrease in the average retirement age

    d. Migration of workers to other countries

### 30. Marcy and Gloria's Production Last Monday

| Marcy's Production | | | Gloria's Production | | |
|---|---|---|---|---|---|
| Time used | # books catalogued | # books shelved | Time used | # books catalogued | # books shelved |
| 2 hours | 0 | 200 | 2 hours | 20 | 0 |
| 6 hours | 150 | 0 | 6 hours | 0 | 540 |
| Total books: 170 catalogued and 740 shelved | | | | | |

**30. Measure the Benefit of Specialization** Both Marcy and Gloria work eight-hour days at a public library. At present, neither worker has assigned tasks, they just do what needs to be done. They never seem to finish all their work. Last Monday, Marcy spent two hours reshelving 200 returned books. Then she catalogued 150 new books during the remaining six hours of her shift. Gloria used her first six hours shelving 540 returned books and then cataloged 20 new books before she went home.

Copy and complete the following table to show Marcy and Gloria's production last Monday. Create another table that demonstrates how they could increase their total production through specialization. How much more could they produce if they each specialized in the type of production that has their lowest possible opportunity cost?

**Marcy and Gloria's Production Last Monday**

| Marcy's Production | | | Gloria's Production | | |
|---|---|---|---|---|---|
| Time used | # books catalogued | # books shelved | Time used | # books catalogued | # books shelved |
| 2 hours | | | 2 hours | | |
| 6 hours | | | 6 hours | | |
| Total books catalogued: | | | | | |
| Total books shelved: | | | | | |

**Marcy and Gloria's Possible Production with Specialization**

| Marcy's Production | | Gloria's Production | |
|---|---|---|---|
| Time used | # books catalogued or shelved | Time Used | # books catalogued or shelved |
| hours | | hours | |
| hours | | hours | |
| Total books catalogued: | | | |
| Total books shelved: | | | |
| Additional books catalogued: | | | |
| Additional books shelved: | | | |

econxtra.swlearning.com

**31. Access EconNews Online** at econxtra.swlearning.com. Read the article entitled "Trade Wars in the U.S." According to the article, what percent of the population believes that foreign trade is bad for the U.S. economy? What, according to the article, is the basis for this belief? Do you agree or disagree? Justify your answer with facts from the article.

## Apply Economic Concepts

30. Production Last Monday

Marcy: 200 books shelved (2 hours); 150 books catalogued (6 hours)

Gloria: 540 books shelved (6 hours); 20 books catalogued (2 hours)

Totals: 740 books shelved; 170 books catalogued

Production with Specialization

Marcy: 0 books shelved (0 hours); 200 books catalogued (8 hours)

Gloria: 720 books shelved (8 hours); 0 books catalogued (0 hours)

Totals: 720 books shelved; 200 books catalogued

31. According to the article, 58 percent of the population believes that foreign trade is bad for the U. S. economy. This belief is based on the idea that cheap imports hurt wages and jobs.

Students who disagree that foreign trade is bad for the U.S. economy are likely to state that that even though trade might result in some job losses, it is possible that net employment will increase, as it did in North Carolina between 1988 and 1994.

Students who agree that foreign trade is bad for the U.S. economy might point out that the jobs lost because of foreign trade often pay higher wages than the new jobs that are created. Even though more people are employed, individual income might not be as high.

**Marcy and Gloria's Possible Production with Specialization**

| Marcy's Production | | Gloria's Production | |
|---|---|---|---|
| Time used | # books catalogued or shelved | Time Used | # books catalogued or shelved |
| 8 hours | 200 catalogued | 8 hours | 720 shelved |
| 0 hours | | 0 hours | |
| Additional books catalogued: +30 | | | |
| Additional books shelved: -20 | | | |

## Chapter Overview

**LESSON 3.1** *The U.S. Private Sector:* This lesson addresses the evolution of the household and the firm. It also introduces international trade.

**LESSON 3.2** *Regulating the Private Sector:* This lesson illustrates the role of government in the private sector. Government regulations, fiscal policy, and monetary policy are addressed.

**LESSON 3.3** *Public Goods and Externalities:* This lesson describes and provides examples of four types of goods. Externalities, both positive and negative, are examined.

**LESSON 3.4** *Providing a Safety Net:* Income and poverty are the focus of this lesson. How income differs across households is addressed. Poverty is defined and government programs for the poor are explained.

### Consider

Ask students to consider the questions posed on this page as they study Chapter 3. After studying all four lessons, students should be able to answer the questions. The content related to each question can be found on the pages indicated below.

- Why did households go from self-sufficiency to relying on markets? See page 62—Evolution of the Household.

- How did firms evolve to take advantage of large-scale production? See page 63—Evolution of the Firm.

- Why do countries trade? See page 65—International Trade.

- If the "invisible hand" of competitive markets is so great, why do governments get into the act? See page 71—Market Competition and Natural Monopolies.

- Why are some people poor even in the world's most productive economy? See page 83—Why Household Incomes Differ.

### POINT YOUR BROWSER

Remind students that they can find additional resources for this chapter at **econxtra.swlearning.com**.

- Xtra! Study Tools
- Net Bookmarks
- Xtra! Quiz Prep
- econ@pps
- Ask the Xpert!

# 3 U.S. Private and Public Sectors

### Consider

Why did households go from self-sufficiency to relying on markets?

How did firms evolve to take advantage of large-scale production?

Why do countries trade?

If the "invisible hand" of competitive markets is so great, why do governments get into the act?

Why are some people poor even in the world's most productive economy?

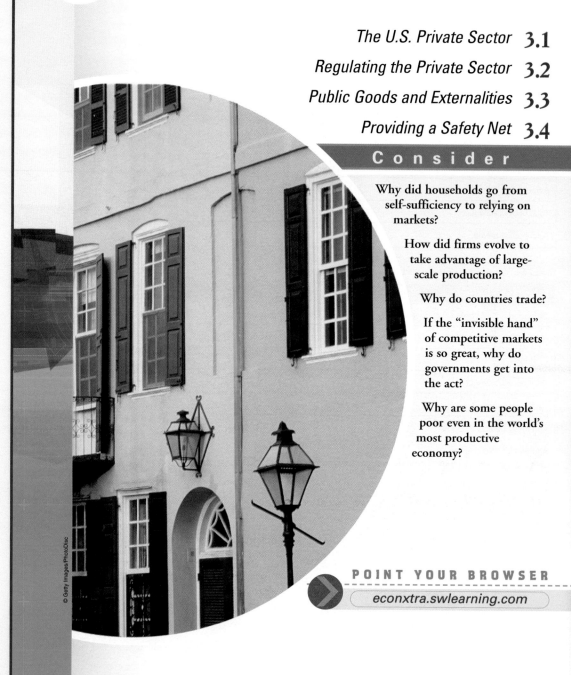

© Getty Images/PhotoDisc

### POINT YOUR BROWSER

*econxtra.swlearning.com*

---

### *Teaching Resources for Chapter 3*

- Activities and Projects Masters
- Spanish Resources
- Econ Connection Interactive Tutorial CD
- **Exam***View*® CD
- Workbook Teacher's Edition
- Chapter and Unit Test Teacher's Edition
- NCEE Standards and Correlation
- Personal Finance Guide

- Social Studies Skills Review
- Instructor's Resource CD
  – PowerPoint Presentation
  – Lesson Plans
  – Video Discussion Guide
  – Answers to Graphing Exercises
- **econxtra.swlearning.com**

## Objectives

> Describe the evolution of households.

> Explain the evolution of the firm with respect to the changes in production processes.

> Demonstrate your understanding of why international trade occurs.

## Overview

The U.S. private sector includes three groups of economic decision makers: households, firms, and the rest of the world. To develop a better feel for how the economy works, you must become more acquainted with these key players. You already know more about them than you may realize. You grew up as a member of a household. You have interacted with firms all your life, from Wal-Mart to Subway. You have a growing awareness of the rest of the world, from imported cars to international web sites.

## Key Terms

household

utility

firm

Industrial Revolution

## FOCUS

**3.1** **The U.S. Private Sector**

Show students a boxed cake mix, frozen pizza box, or a similar convenience food container. Ask them whether such products are used in their households. Make a list on the board of advantages offered to consumers by such products. Lead a discussion of why consumers are much less self-sufficient than they were 100 or 150 years ago. How has the trend toward interdependency increased our nation's use of economic markets? How do U.S. consumers benefit from this trend? Are there costs that they pay because of it?

### Objectives

Remind students to read the lesson objectives to help focus their attention before reading the lesson.

### Key Terms

Direct students to create a database using the key terms for this lesson. The database fields should include terms, definitions, and page numbers. Point out that the process of keying the data is an effective way to study key terms.

### [ In the News ]

Instruct students to read the passage and write down their answers. Point out that their answers might change after they finish studying Lesson 3.1.

### Answers to Think About It

Answers will vary. Possible answer: Nebraska might have a high percentage of dual working parents because the family is not making enough from farming alone and requires a second income. Connecticut might have a high percentage of dual working parents because the cost of living in Connecticut is high, compared with that of other states.

### Visual Presentation

Use the PowerPoint presentation on the Instructor's Resource CD as an adjunct to your lecture. The presentation also can be used for review.

## [ In the News ]

### ● Mom and Pop Missing in Action

In 1950 only about 15 percent of married women with children under 18 years old were employed outside the home. Now, according to data from the 2000 U.S. Census, more young children are growing up with both parents working. A wide range of socioeconomic forces during the 1990s expanded child-rearing options for many working parents. Some won more flexible schedules from their employers or arranged for job sharing with another parent. Others decided to open Internet-based businesses at home. The 1996 welfare law, which pushed more people from public-assistance rolls into the work force, also played a part in the 1990s trend.

### Think About It

In Connecticut, nearly 62 percent of children under age 6 had both parents working, up from 56 percent in 1990. In Nebraska, nearly 70 percent of young children had both parents in the labor force. Connecticut has a relatively affluent population. Nebraska has a large farm economy. What might be explanations for each of those states having such a high percentage of dual working parents?

◀ | ▶

61

### National Content Standards in Economics

A complete list of the NCEE Standards appears on pages xxiv–xxv of this book. The following standards are addressed in Lesson 3.1.

Standard 1: Scarcity

Standard 2: Marginal Cost/Benefit

Standard 3: Allocation of Goods and Services

Standard 4: Role of Incentives

Standard 5: Gain from Trade

Standard 6: Specialization and Trade

Standard 14: Profit and the Entrepreneur

Standard 15: Growth

## Households

Introduce the topic of households by reminding students that 50 years ago, most mothers did not work outside the home. This is no longer the case. Ask students to identify ways in which this trend has changed the types of goods and services households purchase. What products do consumers purchase, how have businesses changed the way they operate, and which markets have grown? Are there markets that have diminished?

### *Think Critically Through Visuals*

Direct students to focus their attention on the photographs on this page. Ask for a volunteer to answer the question posed in the caption.

#### Answer

Answers will vary. Possible answer: All households must decide what to buy, how much to save, where to live, and where to work.

 **Investigate Your Local Economy** Point out that the required information can be obtained by using a variety of resources including libraries, government offices, and the Internet. Local and regional planning commissions and the local chamber of commerce are good places to start this research.

 **CHECKPOINT** Invite a student to answer the checkpoint that appears on page 63.

#### Answer

Over time, there are more two-earner households due to the higher education levels among women and the increased demand for labor. Therefore, there is less production at home and more purchasing in the market. Additionally, members of many households have moved from working on a farm to working in an office or a factory.

# Households

Households play the starring role in a market economy. All those who live under one roof are considered part of the same **household**. Households' demand for goods and services determines what gets produced. The human resources, natural resources, and capital goods they sell help to produce that output. As buyers of goods and services and sellers of resources, households make all kinds of economic choices. These choices include what to buy, how much to save, where to live, and where to work.

**household**
 The most important economic decision maker, consisting of all those who live under one roof

## Evolution of the Household

In 1850 about two-thirds of America's labor force worked on farms. The economy was primarily agricultural, and each farm household was largely self-sufficient. Individual family members specialized in specific farm tasks—preparing meals, sewing clothes, tending livestock, growing crops, and so on. These households produced most of what they consumed and consumed most of what they produced.

With the introduction of labor-saving machinery, disease-resistant seeds, and better fertilizers, farm productivity increased sharply. Because each farmer produced much more, fewer farmers were needed to grow enough food to feed the nation. At the same time, the growth of urban factories increased the need to hire factory labor. As a result, many workers and their families moved from farms to cities, where they became less self-sufficient. Now, only about 2 percent of the U.S. labor force works on farms.

**Investigate Your Local Economy**

Research to find how many households there are in your community. How many of those are two-earner families? How many are headed by a single parent? What is the average annual income of households in the community? What conclusions can you draw from your research?

**Although the makeup of households differs, each one makes a variety of economic choices. What types of choices must all households make?**

*Outside Resources*

**National Academy of Engineering** Invite students to visit the National Academy of Engineering web site at www.greatachievements.org to learn more about technology or engineering advancements of the twentieth century. Instruct students to choose an achievement that influences their lives today. Direct students to create a poster that explains the economic impact of the advancement they choose. Display posters in the classroom.

U.S. households have evolved in other important ways. For example, in 1950 only about 15 percent of married women with children under 18 years old were in the labor force. Since then, higher education levels among married women and a growing need for workers increased women's earnings, raising their opportunity cost of not working. Today, more than half of married women with young children are in the labor force.

The rise of two-earner households has affected the family as an economic unit. Less production occurs in the home. More goods and services are purchased in markets. Reduced household production has led to increased availability of child-care services and greater varieties of restaurants to meet these needs. The rise of two-earner families has reduced the significance of specialization within the household.

## Households Maximize Utility

There are more than 110 million U.S. households. Economists consider each household as acting like a single decision maker. Households, like other economic decision makers, are assumed to pursue their rational self-interest. This means they try to act in their best interests by selecting products and services that are intended to make them better off.

But what exactly do households attempt to accomplish in making decisions? Economists assume that households attempt to maximize their **utility**—their level of satisfaction or sense of well-being. Utility maximization depends on each household's personal goals, not on some objective standard. For example, some households maintain neat homes with well-groomed lawns. Other households pay little attention to their homes and yards.

**CHECKPOINT**
In what ways has the household evolved over time?

# Firms

Household members once built their own homes, made their own clothes and furniture, grew their own food, and entertained themselves. Over time, however, the efficiency arising from comparative advantage resulted in a greater specialization among resource providers. Resource providers often organize as firms. A **firm** is an economic unit formed by a profit-seeking entrepreneur who combines resources to produce goods and services and accepts the risk of profit and loss. What led to the development of the firm as we know it today?

## Evolution of the Firm

Specialization and comparative advantage help explain why households are no longer self-sufficient. But why is a firm the natural outgrowth? For example, rather than make a woolen sweater from scratch, couldn't a consumer take advantage of specialization by hiring someone to produce the wool, another person to spin the wool into yarn, and a third to knit the yarn into a sweater? Why is a firm even necessary?

Here's the problem with that model: If the consumer had to visit and make agreements with each of these specialists, the resulting *transaction costs*—the cost of time and information required for exchange—could easily cancel out the efficiency gained from specialization. Instead of visiting and dealing with each specialist, the consumer can pay someone else to do this. The consumer can pay an entrepreneur to purchase all the resources necessary to make the sweater. *An entrepreneur, by hiring specialists to make many sweaters rather than just one, is able to reduce the transaction costs per sweater.*

During the seventeenth and eighteenth centuries, entrepreneurs provided raw material, such as wool and cotton, to rural households. The entrepreneur hired households to turn this raw

**firm**
A business unit or enterprise formed by a profit-seeking entrepreneur who combines resources to produce goods and services

**utility**
The level of satisfaction from consumption or sense of well-being

**Firms**
Direct students to identify a local business they believe is particularly successful. Does this firm offer goods or services that consumers could not produce as efficiently for themselves? Direct students to write several sentences identifying and explaining advantages the firm has in productive efficiency that individual consumers would not share. Ask several students to read their sentences to the class.

Lesson 3.1 • *The U.S. Private Sector* **63**

**ENRICH**

Remind students that many people in the United States are physically able to care for their lawns but choose to hire others to do this task for them. A truck pulls up to a house and workers unload lawnmowers, trimmers, and blowers. There is a whirlwind of activity for 15 minutes, the job is done, and then the workers leave for their next job. Ask students to explain why lawn-care firms can be more efficient than individuals in producing this service. What does this example have to do with entrepreneurship?

## Firms

Ask students to identify new technology-based products that they use regularly but that their parents or grandparents do not use. Ask students to explain how new businesses and markets have developed to satisfy their desires for these technology-based products. In what ways has the technology revolution of the past 20 or 30 years been similar to the Industrial Revolution of the nineteenth century? Do students expect further changes in the goods and services firms offer for sale? Can businesses be successful if they fail to keep up with new technologies that will be developed in the future? How will consumers benefit from these changes?

### *Think Critically Through Visuals*

Use **Figure 3.1—Evolution of Production** to illustrate the evolution from self-sufficient rural households to the cottage industry system to the Industrial Revolution.

✔ **CHECKPOINT**

Invite a student to answer the checkpoint that appears on page 65.

### Answer

In the seventeenth century, entrepreneurs provided raw materials to rural households that produced the goods. This system was called the cottage industry system. The Industrial Revolution began in the eighteenth century. During the Industrial Revolution, all the stages of production began to be organized under one roof and in an urban factory instead of on rural homesteads. Technological developments increased the productivity of each worker. Today, entrepreneurs conduct business by combining resources in firms.

material into finished products, such as woolen goods made from yarn. The system developed in the British Isles, where workers' rural cottages served as tiny factories. Production usually occurred during the months when farming tasks were few—when the opportunity cost for farm workers was lower.

This approach, which came to be known as the *cottage industry system,* still exists in some parts of the world. You can view this system as the bridge between the self-sufficient farm household and the modern firm that depends on trade.

**Industrial Revolution**
Development of large-scale production during the eighteenth century

### The Industrial Revolution

As the economy expanded in the eighteenth century, entrepreneurs began organizing the stages of production under one roof. Technological developments, such as water power and later steam power, increased the productivity of each worker and contributed to the shift of employment from rural farm to urban factory.

Work, therefore, became organized in large, centrally powered factories that

1. promoted more efficient division of labor

2. allowed for the direct supervision of production

3. reduced transportation costs

4. facilitated the use of specialized machines far larger than anything that had been used in the home

The development of large-scale factory production, known as the **Industrial Revolution**, began in Great Britain around 1750. The Industrial Revolution quickly spread to the rest of Europe, North America, and Australia. Production evolved from self-sufficient rural households to the cottage industry system, where specialized production occurred in the household, to the Industrial Revolution of handling most production under one roof. Figure 3.1 shows this evolution.

Today, entrepreneurs combine resources in firms such as factories, mills, offices, stores, and restaurants. The entrepreneurs accept the risk of profit and loss from the enterprise. Just as households attempt

**Evolution of Production** **Figure 3.1**

The production process evolved from self-sufficient rural households to the cottage industry system, where specialized production occurred in the household. From there, the Industrial Revolution saw the organization of the various stages of production under one roof with the development of large-scale factory production.

64    CHAPTER 3   U.S. Private and Public Sectors

*Curriculum Connection—Performing Arts*

Invite students to work in small groups to act out the concepts illustrated in Figure 3.1. Direct students to create three short acts that parallel the three components of the illustration. Suggest that they develop their presentations based on the history of a particular community or on the development of a particular industry.

Instruct students to write a script, including stage directions, and to practice their performance. Encourage the use of costumes, scenery, and props to enrich the production value of the performances. Arrange a time for each group to perform for the other members of the class.

to maximize utility, firms attempt to maximize profit. Profit is the entrepreneur's reward for accepting the risks involved. Profit equals revenue—the money made from the sales of the firm's goods and services—minus the cost of production.

Profit = Revenue − Cost of Production

There are more than 25 million profit-seeking firms in the United States. Two-thirds of these are small retail businesses, small service operations, part-time home-based businesses, and small farms. Each year more than a million new businesses start up and nearly as many fail. Despite the challenges, the lure of profit provides entrepreneurs with the incentive to keep trying.

**CHECKPOINT**
How have production processes changed over time?

# The Rest of the World

So far, the focus has been on private-sector institutions within the United States—that is, U.S. households and firms. This initial focus has been appropriate because the primary objective is to understand the workings of the U.S. economy, by far the largest in the world.

The rest of the world affects what U.S. households consume and what U.S. firms produce. For example, firms in Japan and South Korea supply U.S. markets with autos, electronic equipment, and other goods, thereby affecting U.S. prices, employment, wages, and profit. Political unrest in the Persian Gulf can drive up the price of oil, increasing U.S. production costs.

Foreign decision makers have a significant effect on the U.S. economy—on what Americans consume and on what they produce. The *rest of the world* consists of the households, firms, and governments in the more than 200 sovereign nations throughout the world.

## International Trade

The gains from comparative advantage and specialization explain why households stopped trying to do everything for themselves and began to sell their resources to specialized firms. International trade arises for the same reasons. *Gains from international trade occur because the opportunity cost of producing specific goods differs across countries.*

Trade allows the countries involved to specialize and thereby increase production. Americans buy raw materials such as crude oil, diamonds, and coffee beans and finished goods such as cameras, DVD players, and automobiles

# SPAN THE GLOBE

## Chinese Food for Thought

December 2004 marks the third anniversary of China's membership in the World Trade Organization (WTO), the rules-making body of modern global commerce. China became a member of this group because it is moving from a planned economy to a more market-driven system. Thus far, exports and imports are rising. Economic growth remains around 8 percent per year, though growth in 2003 was slowed by the SARS virus. Economists credit WTO membership with convincing foreign investors that the Chinese marketplace will treat them according to international practices. At the same time, the government is wary of creating instability by opening markets too quickly. As China overhauls its state firms, millions of people have been put out of work in heavy industry, migrants are streaming into cities, and farmers are jittery about an invasion of cheap foreign food. The Communist Party is concerned with keeping progress moving, yet retaining its monopoly on power.

## Think Critically

Compare current-day China's economic situation to that of the United States during the Industrial Revolution. What are the similarities and differences?

## The Rest of the World

Point out that at the end of the nineteenth century, the United States was one of the world's most important exporters of petroleum products. Crude oil was pumped from the ground in Western Pennsylvania, refined into lubricants or kerosene, and sold to consumers in Europe, South America, and the Far East. Today, more than 100 years later, the United States imports over half the petroleum used in this nation.

Ask students to identify and explain changes in the U.S. and global economies in the twentieth century that resulted in this change in the market for U.S. petroleum products. How might the U.S. economy be affected if low-cost petroleum could not be purchased from other nations? How might the lives of students and their families be changed?

**SPAN THE GLOBE**

Direct students to read the short passage entitled "Chinese Food for Thought" that appears on this page. Use the questions as a starting point for class discussion or have students write a short essay to answer the question.

### Answers to Think Critically

Answers will vary. Possible answer: The similarity is that both were faced with dealing with increases in production and competition. The difference is that China's increases are coming from expanding itself to the world market, while the Industrial Revolution's increases came from technological advances.

### *Think Critically Through Visuals*

Direct students to focus their attention on **Figure 3.2—U.S. Production as a Percentage of U.S. Consumption** on page 66. Ask students how much of the oil consumed in the United States must be imported. Students should be able to look at the graph and determine that U.S. oil production accounts for only about 45 percent of U.S. oil consumption. Therefore, we must import approximately 55 percent of the oil we consume.

## Group Activity

This activity requires a deck of playing cards or colored index cards. Divide students into four groups that represent four countries. Tell group #1 that it can produce 12 heart cards, 9 spades, 6 clubs, or 3 diamonds from its resources. Do the same for the other groups but rotate the types of cards they can produce most efficiently. Ask the groups to decide what cards they would choose to produce and give them the appropriate number of cards. Then tell them to trade to get an equal number of all cards. When they have finished, discuss how this activity demonstrates the advantages offered by specialization and international trade.

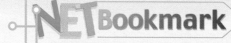

**NET Bookmark**

What goods and services does the United States trade? With whom? Who are our largest trading partners? Answers to these and many other trade-related questions can be found at the U.S. Census Bureau's Trade Data Web site. Access this site through

**econxtra.swlearning.com**

from other countries. U.S. producers sell to other countries sophisticated products such as computer hardware and software, aircraft, movies, and agricultural products.

International trade between the United States and the rest of the world has increased in recent decades. In 1970, only about 6 percent of U.S. production was sold to other countries. That figure has now increased to 14 percent.

## Trade in Raw Materials

To give you some idea of how international trade works, consider the trade in raw materials. Figure 3.2 shows U.S.

production as a percentage of U.S. consumption for 12 key commodities. If production exceeds consumption, the United States sells the difference to other countries. If production falls short of consumption, the United States purchases the difference from other countries. For example, because the United States grows little coffee, nearly all coffee is purchased from other countries. U.S. production of coffee is only 1 percent of U.S. consumption.

The figure also shows that U.S. production falls short of consumption for oil and for metals such as lead, zinc, copper, and aluminum. At the other extreme, U.S.-grown wheat is nearly double U.S. wheat consumption. Nearly half of the U.S. wheat crop is exported. When it comes to raw materials, the United States is a net importer of oil and metals and a net exporter of crops.

**CHECKPOINT**

Why does international trade occur?

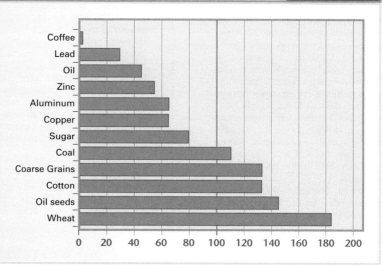

**U.S. Production as a Percentage of U.S. Consumption**     **Figure 3.2**

If production exceeds consumption, the United States sells the difference to other countries. If production falls short of consumption, the United States buys the difference from other countries. For example, because the United States produces only 1 percent of its coffee consumption, 99 percent is purchased from other countries. Because U.S.-grown wheat amounts to 184 percent of U.S. wheat consumption, the 84 percent in excess of 100 percent is sold to other countries.

Source: Based on annual figures from *The Economist World in Figures: 2001 Edition* (London: Profile Books, 2001).

## RETEACH

This text makes reference to changes in production that resulted from the Industrial Revolution. It has been said that there were also revolutions in technology and communications in the twentieth century. Ask students to identify a specific advancement that took place in the last century that they believe was important to the way products are manufactured. Ask them to discuss how this advancement increased the benefits offered by specialization and international trade. How did it affect their lives?

# Key Concepts

1. Describe three tasks that would probably have been done within most households 100 years ago that your family now pays others to do.

2. Identify a product that you often buy and use. Describe the steps that are taken to produce this good. Explain why you do not produce this product for yourself.

3. What are several advantages that a large automobile repair shop would have over a small one?

4. In what ways is working at home on a computer today similar to, and different from, the cottage industry system that existed in the eighteenth century?

5. Think of a recent event that took place in a different part of the world that had an impact on the U.S. economy. Explain how the event affected the U.S. economy.

## Graphing Exercise

6. Draw a bar graph that demonstrates the declining size of the average U.S. household, based on the data in the table below. Explain why smaller households might encourage people to purchase more of the goods and services they use.

| Year | Average Size of U. S. Household |
|------|--------------------------------|
| 1975 | 3.14 members |
| 1980 | 2.94 |
| 1985 | 2.76 |
| 1990 | 2.63 |
| 1995 | 2.65 |
| 2000 | 2.62 |

Source: *Statistical Abstract of the United States 1999*, p. 60, and *2001*, p. 49.

## Think Critically

7. **Research** Choose a foreign country that one of your ancestors came from or a country that interests you. Investigate this nation's economy and identify products it trades. Explain how this nation benefits from trade by using its comparative advantage.

8. **History** In 1825, Robert Owen bought a community called New Harmony in Indiana. He told people who lived in New Harmony to contribute whatever they produced to a community storehouse. They could also take whatever they needed from this storehouse for free. Look up New Harmony and find out how Owen's experiment worked out. Why weren't residents of New Harmony able to benefit from their comparative advantages?

Xtra!
**Study Tools**
*econxtra.swlearning.com*

**Lesson 3.1** • *The U.S. Private Sector* **67**

## Key Concepts

1. Answers will vary. Possible answers: Growing or preparing foods, cleaning, yard work, or making clothing.

2. Answers will vary. Possible answers: People today may lack the skills, tools, and other resources that would allow them to produce the product efficiently. They benefit from a division of labor and specialization when they buy from others.

3. Answers will vary. Possible answer: The larger shop can afford to purchase more specialized resources (workers and tools) than can a smaller one. It will therefore be more efficient.

4. Answers will vary. Possible answer: People working on computers at home is similar to the cottage industry system in that the workers do not travel to a central location. The type of work they perform, however, is quite different, since the "products" they produce quite often are documents.

5. Answers will vary. Possible answers: Students should provide an event that interrupted the flow of trade either into or out of the United States. The interruption would have harmed U.S. producers of exports or consumers of imports.

## Graphing Exercise

6. Graphs will vary slightly. An example of an acceptable graph appears at the bottom of this page. Answers to the questions will vary. Possible answer: With fewer household members, people have less need and less ability to produce for themselves the variety of goods and services they desire.

## Think Critically

7. Answers will vary. Possible answer: The nation benefits from specializing in types of production that result in its lowest opportunity costs while purchasing from other nations goods that have greater opportunity costs.

8. Answers will vary. Possible answer: When people don't have to pay for goods, they have little incentive to produce or to use their skills in the most productive way.

**Average Size of U.S. Household**

## Visualizing the Answer— Graphing Exercise

6. The answer includes a graph. Students' graphs should look similar to the one shown here. An Excel spreadsheet containing this graph, along with supporting data, is available on the Instructor's Resource CD.

## FOCUS

**3.2  Regulating the Private Sector**

Introduce this lesson by asking students to identify some of their favorite possessions. Make a list of these items on the board. Then ask students to describe how they would react if someone tried to take these items from them. What would they expect the government to do to help them defend their property rights?

Then ask students to describe what would happen if the government provided no legal recourse for people to defend their property rights. Continue the discussion by asking the following questions: How would this affect our economy? Would people be willing to work, produce, or operate a business if they could not be reasonably sure that they would receive the fruits of their labor? Why would the profit motive have little importance without an associated right to hold private property?

### Objectives

Remind students to read the lesson objectives to help focus their attention before reading the lesson.

### Key Terms

Direct students to use each of the key terms in a separate sentence or short paragraph that helps demonstrate the meaning of the term.

### [ In the News ]

Instruct students to read the passage and write down their answers. Point out that their answers might change after they finish studying Lesson 3.2.

### Answers to Think About It

Answers will vary. Possible answer: The United States should not step in to prevent dumping within the United States. If foreign countries can sell a good at a lower cost, it is because they have a comparative advantage in the production of this good. Consumer consumption of a good should go to those with the comparative advantage.

### Visual Presentation

Use the PowerPoint presentation on the Instructor's Resource CD as an adjunct to your lecture. The presentation also can be used for review.

# Regulating the Private Sector  3.2

## Objectives

> Explain how government, by establishing laws and regulations, can improve operation of the private sector.

> Distinguish between regulations that promote competition and those that control natural monopolies.

> Describe how fiscal policy and monetary policy reduce the ups and downs of the business cycle.

## Overview

The private sector would not run smoothly on its own in a pure market economy. With no government, there would be no laws protecting your life and property. People could rob you of your earnings and possessions. They also could steal your inventions and ideas. Business contracts would have no binding force without laws and the authority to enforce those laws. Some firms could drive competitors out of the market. Firms also could sell unsafe or defective products or otherwise cheat consumers. These actions could bring about reduced economic activity and result in high unemployment. Government regulations address these market shortcomings.

## Key Terms

**private property rights**

**antitrust laws**

**natural monopoly**

**fiscal policy**

**monetary policy**

### [ In the News ]

#### ● Ball-Bearing Bonanza

Some government regulations are created to protect U.S. interests in international trade. One new law, the Continued Dumping and Subsidy Offset Act of 2000, affects the prices that foreign trading partners can charge for products they export to the United States. The law allows U.S. manufacturers to inform the government if they believe imports in their market are being "dumped"—or sold at less than fair-market value—by foreign competitors. If the government agrees, it will impose tariffs (taxes) on those imports. The manufacturers then receive the proceeds of those tariffs. The law's chief beneficiaries for 2001 were two ball-bearing companies whose lawyers helped to write the legislation. One New Jersey company, Torrington Co., took in $63 million, and Timken Co. in Ohio took in $31 million. The $94 million was collected from ball-bearing makers in Japan, the United Kingdom, Romania, Sweden, and six other countries. U.S. trading partners have criticized the law as violating international trade rules by unfairly favoring U.S. companies. The World Trade Organization (WTO) agrees. More than a few U.S. companies also agree. They say the law "promotes litigation, violates our WTO commitments, and undercuts U.S. competitiveness."

#### Think About It

Do you think the U.S. government should step in to prevent "dumping" of foreign goods in such a way? Why or why not?

68

### *National Content Standards in Economics*

A complete list of the NCEE Standards appears on pages xxiv–xxv of this book. The following standards are addressed in Lesson 3.2.

Standard 2: Marginal Cost/Benefit

Standard 9: Role of Competition

Standard 10: Role of Economic Institutions

Standard 11: Role of Money

Standard 12: Role of Interest Rates

Standard 14: Profit and the Entrepreneur

Standard 15: Growth

Standard 16: Role of Government

# Rules for a Market Economy

The effects of government regulations are all around you. Government-required labels that provide washing instructions are stitched into the clothes you wear. The condition of the vehicle you drive to school is regulated by the government. The government also regulates how fast you can drive and prohibits you from driving under the influence of alcohol. Government has a pervasive influence on many aspects of your life as well as on the economy.

## Establishing Property Rights

In a market system, specific individuals usually own the rights to resources. **Private property rights** guarantee individuals the right to use their resources as they choose or to charge others for the use. Owners therefore have a strong incentive to get the most value from their resources. This ensures that resources will find their most productive use.

However if people could not safeguard their property, they would have less incentive to work, to save, to invest, to buy things, or to pursue other market activity. Markets could break down. For example, less investment would occur if potential investors believed their capital goods might be stolen by thieves, damaged by civil unrest, destroyed by war, or blown up by terrorists. You would have less incentive to work if your employer refused to pay you or if you were repeatedly robbed of your earnings.

Governments play a role in safeguarding private property by establishing legal rights of ownership. They then enforce these rights through national defense, police protection, legal contracts, and the judicial system.

## Intellectual Property Rights

Laws also grant property rights to the creators of new ideas and new inventions. Inventors reap the rewards of

**private property rights**
Legal claim that guarantees an owner the right to use a resource or to charge others for its use

---

# E-CONOMICS

## Digital Crackers

Due to the lightning speed of advancements in Internet and e-commerce technology, the government is working fast to enact laws to regulate this new area. One law enacted was the 1998 Digital Millennium Copyright Act. This law covered a variety of issues including the lawful uses of copyrighted works in the electronic environment. The law had strong support from Silicon Valley companies who were trying to protect their lucrative software programs. The first criminal prosecution under this law was the case against Elcomsoft Co. Ltd. Elcomsoft was charged with selling software that allows users to disable security features in the "eBook." The eBook is reader software made by Adobe Systems. It is used to access digital publications like novels and nonfiction works. Adobe's software allows publishers to sell books online in formats that prevent the content from being copied, printed, or transferred. The Elcomsoft product, called the Advanced eBook Processor Program, *cracks* the security protections in eBook software and allows the removal of publisher-imposed usage restrictions. Elcomsoft says its program simply lets users make backup copies or transfer content to other devices, something permitted under the "fair use" concept of copyright law. When Elcomsoft began selling its product on the Internet, Adobe Systems complained to the FBI.

### Think Critically

A federal jury found Elcomsoft not guilty on all counts in the case, which ended December 17, 2002. What effect, if any, do you think this decision will have on the software market?

---

## TEACH

### Rules for a Market Economy

Display some common household or classroom items on your desk or a table in the classroom, and ask students to group them by the type of intellectual property right protection that applies. Ask students to give examples of how someone might infringe on the patent, trademark, or copyright of these items.

## E-CONOMICS

Direct students to read the passage entitled "Digital Crackers" that appears on this page.

### Answers to Think Critically

This decision will increase the growth of the software market. It provides an incentive for more start-up software companies to develop in the future.

---

## Outside Resources

**Music Web Sites** In 2003, the music industry took on web sites that helped people share music over the Internet. In September of that year, several hundred individuals were sued for downloading music from Kazaa, "a completely distributed peer-to-peer file sharing service." Ask students to investigate what has happened to this and other similar web services since 2003. How does this demonstrate intellectual property rights?

**The Federal Reserve System** Invite interested students to search the Federal Reserve System web site at www.federalreserve.gov for *monetary policy* (discussed on page 72), and write a short report on their findings.

(continued) **TEACH**

## Rules for a Market Economy

Hold up a helmet, kneepads, or some other piece of equipment that is designed to protect athletes. Ask students to explain whether they believe the government has a responsibility to set and enforce safety standards for such products. What would happen if a helmet shattered upon impact or a catcher's mask bent when struck by a foul ball? Are consumers qualified to judge the quality of this type of equipment without government regulation? What other types of safety regulations do students believe the government should set and enforce? Do they believe it is possible for the government to go too far in setting safety standards for products consumers buy? What responsibilities do people have to protect their own interests in consumer markets?

### Think Critically Through Visuals

Direct students to focus their attention on the photograph on this page. Ask for a volunteer to answer the question posed in the caption.

### Answer

Answers will vary. Possible answer: Labels on food products imply that the products are safe. Labels also help consumers make informed decisions about their purchases.

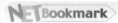

Direct students to **econxtra.swlearning.com**. Remind them to click on the link for Lesson 3.2 to find the appropriate link for the **NET Bookmark** on this page.

### Answer

Only the inventor of a product may apply for a patent.

## CHECKPOINT

Invite a student to answer the checkpoint that appears on this page.

### Answer

Laws and regulations improve the operation of the private sector by providing a standard that everyone must meet and abide by. They allow the private sector to operate with order and fairness.

---

## NET Bookmark

To learn more about patents, go to the U.S. Patent and Trademark Office's web page on General Information Concerning Patents. Access this web site through econxtra.swlearning.com. In your own words, describe who may apply for a patent.

**econxtra.swlearning.com**

their creations so they have more incentives to create.

Patent laws encourage inventors to invest the time and money required to discover and develop new products and processes. If others could simply copy successful products, inventors would be less willing to incur the up-front costs of invention. Patents also provide the stimulus to turn inventions into marketable products, a process called *innovation*.

Thus, the patent system establishes property rights to inventions and other technical advances. Likewise, a *copyright* assigns property rights to original expressions of an author, artist, composer, or computer programmer. A *trademark* establishes property rights to unique commercial marks and symbols, such as McDonald's golden arches and Nike's swoosh.

### Measurement and Safety

Much market exchange involves products sold by weight, such as a pound of hamburger, or by volume, such as a gallon of gasoline. To ensure buyers don't get cheated, governments test and certify the accuracy of various measuring devices. For example, the U.S. Bureau of Weights and Measures is responsible for the annual inspection and testing of all commercial devices used to buy, sell, and ship products.

Consumers also want to be confident that the products they buy are safe. The U.S. Food and Drug Administration (FDA) regulates the safety of foods, prescription and over-the-counter drugs, and medical devices. The U.S. Department of Agriculture helps the FDA by inspecting and grading meat and poultry for freshness and quality. The Consumer Product Safety Commission, a federal agency, monitors the safety of all consumer products, from baby cribs to dishwashers.

## CHECKPOINT

How can laws and regulations improve the operation of the private sector?

The FDA requires that labels appear on packages of most prepared foods, such as breads, cereals, canned and frozen foods, snacks, desserts, and drinks. How do consumers benefit from nutrition information on labels of food products?

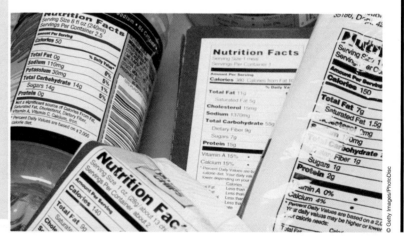

© Getty Images/PhotoDisc

---

## ENRICH

The Consumer Products Safety Commission lists product recalls on its web site at www.cpsc.gov/. Ask students to research this web site and identify a recall they believe involved a particularly dangerous product. Ask them to explain why this dangerous product was brought to market and what might have happened if its recall had not been required by the CPSC. Do they believe the CPSC should do more to protect consumers? If the CPSC did do more, what could happen to the choices of products consumers enjoy?

# Market Competition and Natural Monopolies

It's been said that businesspeople praise competition, but they love monopoly. Their praise of competition echoes Adam Smith's argument that the invisible hand of market competition harnesses self-interest to promote the general good. However, competition imposes a discipline that most businesses would rather avoid. A business owner would prefer to be a monopolist—that is, to be the only seller of a product. As an only seller, a monopolist can usually charge a higher price and earn a greater profit than would be possible with greater competitive pressure.

## Promoting Market Competition

Although competition typically ensures the most efficient use of resources, an individual firm would prefer the higher price and higher profit of monopoly. Here's the problem. When a few firms account for most of the sales in a market, such as the market for steel, those firms may join together to fix a price that is higher than one that would result from greater market competition. These firms try to act like a monopolist to boost the price and profits. An individual firm also may try to become a monopolist by driving competitors out of business or by merging with competitors.

Thus, a monopoly or a group of firms acting like a monopoly tries to charge a higher price than would result through competition. This higher price hurts consumers more than it benefits producers, making society worse off. Monopoly may harm social welfare in other ways as well. If a monopoly is insulated from market competition, it may be less innovative than aggressive competitors would be. Worse still, monopolies may try to influence the political system to protect and enhance their monopoly power.

Antitrust laws attempt to promote competition and reduce anticompetitive behavior. These laws prohibit efforts to create a monopoly in a market in which competition is desirable. Antitrust laws are enforced in the courts by government attorneys. They also are enforced by individual firms bringing lawsuits against other firms for violating these laws.

## Regulating Natural Monopolies

Competition usually forces the product price lower than it would be if the product were sold by a monopoly. In rare instances, however, a monopoly can produce and sell the product for less than could several competing firms. For example, electricity is delivered more efficiently by a single firm that wires the community than by competing firms each stringing their own sets of wires. A city's subway service is delivered more efficiently by a single firm digging one tunnel system than by competing firms each digging their own. The cost per customer of delivering electricity or subway service is lower if each of these markets is served by a single firm.

When it is cheaper for one firm to serve the market than for two or more firms to do so, that firm is called a **natural monopoly**. But a natural monopoly, if unregulated by government, maximizes profit by charging a higher price than is optimal from society's point of view.

Government can increase social welfare by forcing the monopolist to lower its price. To do this, the government can either operate the monopoly itself, as it does with most urban transit systems, or regulate a privately owned monopoly, as it does with local phone services and electricity transmission. Government-owned and government-regulated monopolies are called *public utilities*.

> **CHECKPOINT**
> Why does government promote competition in some markets and control natural monopolies in others?

**antitrust laws**
Laws that prohibit anticompetitive behavior and promote competition in markets where competition is desirable

**natural monopoly**
One firm that can serve the entire market at a lower per-unit cost than two or more firms

---

### Market Competition and Natural Monopolies

Emphasize that the government regulates market competition and natural monopolies in the private sector. With these regulations, the government typically promotes competition and reduces anticompetitive behaviors. Ask students to think of examples of anticompetitive behaviors that companies might engage in. (A recent example is the government's accusing Microsoft of monopolizing the market for operating systems, as discussed in the **E-conomics** feature in Lesson 7.3.) Tell students they will learn more about market structures, including the forms of competition and monopoly, in Chapter 7.

> **CHECKPOINT**
> Invite a student to answer the checkpoint that appears on this page.

**Answer**

Government promotes competition in some industries, such as retail, because the industry operates more efficiently under competition. In other cases, such as utilities, government promotes natural monopolies because the industry operates more efficiently in monopolies. For industries that require regulation, it is easier for the government to provide that regulation in a monopoly setting.

## TEACH

### Growth and Stability of the U.S. Economy

Provide students with the most recent rate of unemployment available at the Bureau of Labor Statistics web site. Ask them to discuss their attitudes toward people who are unemployed. Do they believe that anyone who really wants employment can find it, or do they believe that it is possible for economic conditions to make it impossible for some people to find work? Do they believe the government should help those who are unemployed find work? What are some of the possible benefits and costs to the economy of trying to create more jobs through additional government spending?

---

## Extend the Content

To help students understand fiscal policy, use the following examples. In recent years, the Japanese government has cut taxes and increased spending to stimulate its troubled economy. In his first state-of-the-union message, President George W. Bush proposed a tax cut to "get the country moving again."

To help students better understand how too much money circulating in an economy results in higher inflation, refer to the example about wild inflation in Brazil in 1994 that appears on page 72. Explain that with similar inflation in the United States, a pair of jeans that sold for $25 in 1988 would have cost $90 million in 1994!

Extend the example from the book to help students better understand the impact of high inflation. Explain that with such high inflation, everyone, including merchants, had difficulty keeping track of prices. People lost faith in the Brazilian currency and often used barter to complete economic transactions. This situation led to declines in production and employment. Brazil's economy suffered.

**Answer**

Fiscal policy works by allowing the government to offset a slowdown in economic activity in the private sector by cutting taxes to stimulate consumption and investment. The monetary policy works by putting more money into circulation during slow economic times to lower interest rates and encourage borrowing and spending.

## APPLY

Assign Lesson 3.2 from the Contemporary Economics Workbook.

## ASSESS

Assign all or part of Lesson 3.2 Assessment on page 73 as homework or an in-class activity.

## Xtra! Study Tools

Direct students to the online study tools for Lesson 3.2 at **econxtra.swlearning.com**.

## CLOSE

**Revisit** the **In the News** feature on the first page of the lesson. Ask students to review their preliminary answers and discuss the questions, now that they have completed this lesson.

**Review** the objectives for Lesson 3.2. Students should be able to:

- Explain how government, by establishing laws and regulations, can improve operation of the private sector.

- Distinguish between regulations that promote competition and those that control natural monopolies.

- Describe how fiscal policy and monetary policy reduce the ups and downs of the business cycle.

---

**monetary policy**
The central bank's attempts to control the money supply to influence the national economy

**fiscal policy**
The federal government's use of taxing and public spending to influence the national economy

---

# Growth and Stability of the U.S. Economy

The U.S. economy and other market economies experience alternating periods of growth and decline in their level of economic activity, especially employment and production. *Business cycles* reflect the rise and fall of economic activity relative to the long-term growth trend of the economy. Governments try to reduce these fluctuations, making the bad times not so bad and the good times not quite so good. Pursuing these objectives through taxing and spending is called *fiscal policy*. Pursuing them by regulating the money supply is called *monetary policy.*

## Fiscal Policy

**Fiscal policy** uses taxing and public spending to influence national economic variables such as how much is produced, how many people have jobs, and how fast the economy grows. The idea behind fiscal policy is that when economic activity in the private sector slows down, the government should offset this by cutting taxes to stimulate consumption and investment. The government also may increase its own spending to offset a weak private sector.

If, on the other hand, the economy is growing so fast as to cause higher *inflation,* which is an increase in the economy's average price level, the government should increase taxes and reduce its own spending to cool down the economy. This will keep inflation from getting too high.

When economists study fiscal policy, they usually focus on the federal government, although governments at all levels affect the economy. The federal, state, and local governments in the United States spend about $3.5 trillion per year, making the public sector a significant part of the country's $11 trillion economy.

## Monetary Policy

Just as oil makes the gears in a car move more smoothly, money reduces the friction—the transaction costs—of market exchange. Too little money can leave parts creaking. Too much money can gum up the works.

**Monetary policy** tries to supply the appropriate amount of money to help stabilize the business cycle and promote healthy economic growth. In the United States, monetary policy is the responsibility of the Board of Governors of the Federal Reserve System, the U.S. central bank established by Congress in 1913. The Federal Reserve System, or Fed, used monetary policy in 2001 and 2002 to try to revive the nation's stalled economy. By putting more money into circulation, the Fed pushed interest rates to their lowest levels in more than 40 years. This action was intended to encourage more borrowing and spending that would lead to economic recovery.

Too much money in circulation results in higher inflation. For example, in 1994 huge increases in Brazil's money supply resulted in wild inflation. Prices in Brazil were on average about 3.6 million times higher in 1994 than in 1988.

At the other extreme, too little money in an economy can make market exchange more difficult. For example, people tried to cope with a severe money shortage in the early American colonies by maintaining very careful records, showing who owed what to whom. However, the transaction costs of all this record keeping used up scarce resources and reduced output in the economy.

---

## RETEACH

During the summer of 2003, President George W. Bush led Congress to pass a variety of tax cuts designed to stimulate the economy. Assign students to investigate changes in employment, production, prices, and the national debt that took place thereafter. To what extent do they believe the tax cuts were successful? How does this demonstrate the government's use of fiscal policy?

## Key Concepts

1. Describe one way your life might be different if the government did not protect individual property rights.

2. Study the contents label of a cereal box. Explain how the government attempts to protect consumers when it requires manufacturers to place these labels on food products.

3. In 2001 the government passed laws that reduced many federal taxes. Explain why this could be seen as an example of *fiscal policy* that was intended to cause the economy to produce more goods and services.

4. During the economic expansion of the late 1990s, the Federal Reserve System took steps to reduce the rate of growth of money in the U.S. economy. Was this an example of monetary policy that was intended to slow the growth of production? Why or why not?

## Graphing Exercise

5. Draw a double line graph of changes in the money supply and interest rates charged to large businesses in the U.S. economy, based on the data at the right. Describe how these two sets of data appear to be related to each other.

## Think Critically

6. **Math** Calculate the amount of the federal government's surplus or deficit in different years, using data in the table at the right. Are you concerned about the government spending more than it receives in taxes? Explain your point of view.

7. **Research** In the 1970s, American Telephone and Telegraph (AT&T) was a good example of a natural monopoly. At that time, AT&T provided almost all of the local and long-distance telephone service in the country. To prevent AT&T from setting high prices, the government told the company how much it could charge its customers. Research the history of AT&T. Describe what has taken place in the past 30 years to reduce this firm's monopoly power and the government's need to set its prices.

Xtra!
**Study Tools**
econxtra.swlearning.com

**Changes in the Money Supply and Interest Rates, 1993–2001**

| Year | % change in money [M1] | % interest charged to businesses [prime] |
|------|------------------------|------------------------------------------|
| 1993 | + 10.3% | 6.0% |
| 1994 | + 1.8 | 7.2 |
| 1995 | − 2.0 | 8.8 |
| 1996 | − 4.2 | 8.3 |
| 1997 | − 0.6 | 8.4 |
| 1998 | + 2.3 | 8.4 |
| 1999 | + 2.5 | 8.0 |
| 2000 | − 3.2 | 9.2 |
| 2001 | + 8.3 | 6.9 |

Source: *Economic Indicators,* October, 2002, pp. 26 & 30.

**Federal Spending and Tax Revenue, 1996–2002**
**Amounts in billions of dollars, 2002 values estimated**

| Year | Spending | Tax Revenue | Difference |
|------|----------|-------------|------------|
| 1996 | 1,560 | 1,453 | _____ |
| 1997 | 1,601 | 1,579 | _____ |
| 1998 | 1,652 | 1,722 | _____ |
| 1999 | 1,702 | 1,828 | _____ |
| 2000 | 1,789 | 2,025 | _____ |
| 2001 | 1,863 | 1,991 | _____ |
| 2002 | 2,012 | 1,853 | _____ |

Source: *Economic Indicators,* October, 2002, p. 32.

**Lesson 3.2** • *Regulating the Private Sector* **73**

## Key Concepts

1. Answers will vary. Possible answer: It could be difficult to either buy or sell a house or car if the government did not provide titles to prove ownership of property.

2. Answers will vary. Possible answer: By reading these labels, consumers are able to choose foods that will give them a more balanced diet. Before the government required these labels, few manufacturers made this type of information available to consumers.

3. Answers will vary. Possible answer: Lower taxes gave people and businesses more money to spend, which could stimulate activity in the economy.

4. Answers will vary. Possible answer: Yes. A slower rate of growth in the money supply would result in higher interest rates, which would discourage additional borrowing and spending.

## Graphing Exercise

5. Graphs will vary slightly. An example of an acceptable graph appears at the bottom of this page.

   Answers will vary. Possible answer: Faster growth in money seems to cause lower interest rates, while slower growth or decline in money cause higher interest rates.

   *The Answer Key is continued on page 92.*

**Changes in the Money Supply and Interest Rates 1993–2001**

% interest charged to businesses [prime]

% change in Money [M1]

## Visualizing the Answer— Graphing Exercise

5. The answer includes a graph. Students' graphs should look similar to the one shown here. An Excel spreadsheet containing this graph, along with supporting data, is available on the Instructor's Resource CD.

movers & shakers

## FOCUS

Ask students to name all the businesses they can think of that are owned by or specialize in serving people of different nationalities, races, or genders. Write their suggestions on the board. Ask students why these people might have started their specialty or niche businesses. Direct students to write one page about obstacles these people might have had to overcome on their road to success. What advantages might they have had?

## TEACH

Instruct students to read the **Movers & Shakers** feature about George Herrera. Point out that some students may find it helpful to read the article, read the questions at the bottom of the page, and then reread the article.

## ASSESS

Use the questions in Source Reading and Entrepreneurs in Action at the bottom of the profile to assess the students' understanding of this **Movers & Shakers** feature.

## Answers to Source Reading

It is good news that one million small business are owned by Hispanics because small businesses are a pathway to success for many Americans, especially minorities such as Hispanics.

## Answers to Entrepreneurs in Action

This assignment has three distinct parts: research, interview, and presentation. Consider asking students to submit a written report about their research findings along with a list of interview questions, prior to setting up a meeting with a business owner.

**George Herrera** *President and CEO, United States Hispanic Chamber of Commerce*

George Herrera has always been interested in helping Hispanic businesses grow. For 17 years he worked at Burgos and Associates, Inc., a company that provides management and technical help to minority businesses throughout the United States. This work was the ideal training ground for his next job as president and chief executive officer of the United States Hispanic Chamber of Commerce (USHCC). Herrera has held this job since 1998.

The USHCC, headquartered in Washington, D.C., promotes the interests of more than 1.2 million Hispanic-owned businesses in the United States and Puerto Rico. Herrera's goal is to help these businesses and their owners succeed. As the number of U.S. Hispanic residents grows, so too does the number of Hispanic businesses grow. According to the 2000 U.S. Census, 12.5 percent of the U.S. population, more than 35 million, are Hispanic or Latino. Herrera believes it is important to help this growing segment of the U.S. population succeed.

Herrera has been instrumental in encouraging President George W. Bush to recognize the Hispanic community. He has called President Bush "a tremendous asset, not only to Hispanic businesses, but also to the Hispanic people." President Bush placed Hispanics in key positions in his administration. He appointed Mel Martinez as Secretary of Housing and Urban Development and Hector V. Barreto, Jr., as Administrator of the Small Business Administration. In a recent address to the USHCC, President Bush stated, "Small businesses are the pathway to advancement and success for many Americans, especially women and new arrivals to our country, and to minorities. I believe in small business because I know that two-thirds of all new jobs created in America every year come from small businesses. More than one million small businesses are owned by Hispanic Americans. And this is good news for America."

Herrera has been recognized by *Hispanic Business Magazine* as one of the 100 Most Influential Hispanics in the United States. *Black Enterprise Magazine* has named him one of the 30 future leaders for economic empowerment of minority communities. One of Herrera's most significant accomplishments was the creation of the first-ever national Hispanic television show, *Hispanics Today*, which is syndicated across the United States.

### SOURCE READING

Analyze the quotation from President Bush's address to the USHCC. Explain why you think he said, "More than one million small businesses are owned by Hispanic Americans. And this is good news for America."

### ENTREPRENEURS IN ACTION

Working with a partner, choose a minority group, such as African Americans, Asian Americans, Native Americans, Hispanic Americans, etc. Research the number of small businesses in the United States owned by members of this minority. Interview a successful small business owner who is a member of this minority group. Ask about his or her education and work background. Also ask what advice he or she has for students thinking about becoming small business owners. Present your findings in class.

## Extend the Content

The United States Hispanic Chamber of Commerce "advocates, promotes, and facilitates the success of Hispanic business" through its web site at http://ushcc.com. Have students visit this site and select a topic that interests them, such as one of the studies or reports posted on the site. They should write a one-page report on the topic they chose.

## Objectives

> Describe and provide examples of four types of goods.

> Define negative externalities and positive externalities, and discuss why government intervenes in such markets.

## Overview

Government focuses on improving the performance of the private sector—enforcing property rights, promoting competition, regulating natural monopolies, and smoothing out the economy's ups and downs. However the private sector can't profitably supply some goods that people want. The government is in a better position to supply goods such as national defense or a highway system. What's more, the private sector sometimes affects people not involved in the market transaction, such as the factory that pollutes the air breathed by nearby residents. In such cases, the government often intervenes to improve the market's performance.

## Key Terms

private goods

public goods

quasi-public goods

open-access goods

negative externalities

positive externalities

## FOCUS

### 3.3 Public Goods and Externalities

Introduce the concept of public goods by showing students a road map of their community. Ask them to describe locations where they frequently travel and the route they take. Locations might include their school, a store, a restaurant, and so on. Then ask them to describe how their lives would change if there were no public roads and all land was privately owned by individuals. Could they afford to build roads of their own? Would they be willing to pay tolls to cross property that belonged to their neighbors? Could businesses or schools operate successfully without public roads? What other examples can they cite of goods or services that must be provided by the government for the economy and society to function efficiently?

### Objectives

Remind students to read the lesson objectives to help focus their attention before reading the lesson.

### Key Terms

Direct students to look up key terms in a business or economics dictionary. Some students will find it helpful to read another definition. In addition to a definition, many entries will include a brief explanation and an example.

## [ In the News ]

### ● The Healthcare Dilemma

Should a country's healthcare system be a private good or a public good? With the exception of Medicare and Medicaid, the United States currently has a private healthcare system. If the United States had a national health system, like its national defense system, health services would be available to all in an equal amount. The following issue in the news highlights one problem with the private U.S. healthcare system. Lobbying interests in Washington are pressing for limitations on when, where, and how consumers can file healthcare-related lawsuits. They argue that lawsuit limitations will help save struggling medical-related businesses, preserve jobs in the health field, and protect the public's access to healthcare. The American Medical Association (AMA), a group representing the nation's doctors, contends that limits on consumers' right to sue would benefit consumers. The group points to statistics showing that physicians have left some parts of the country because of costly malpractice lawsuits and the expensive insurance they must carry to protect themselves. The AMA also is lobbying for a federal law limiting damage awards in medical lawsuits, such as those for pain and suffering, to $250,000. Opponents of further limits, particularly the American Trial Lawyers Association (ATLA) are gearing up for battle.

### Think About It

Do you think limitations on lawsuits would protect the public's access to healthcare and reduce costs, or would these limitations likely only protect bad doctors and insurance companies? Explain your answer. Do you think healthcare should be available to everyone in an equal amount, regardless of an individual's ability to pay? Why or why not?

◄ I ►

## [ In the News ]

Instruct students to read the passage and write down their answers. Point out that their answers might change after they finish studying Lesson 3.3.

### Answers to Think About It

Answers will vary. Possible answer: Limitations on lawsuits would protect American's healthcare system because they would keep small, struggling doctor's offices and medical companies from going out of business. They would also keep down the cost of malpractice insurance, which has been rising at an alarming rate.

### Visual Presentation

Use the PowerPoint presentation on the Instructor's Resource CD as an adjunct to your lecture. The presentation also can be used for review.

75

### National Content Standards in Economics

**NCEE**

A complete list of the NCEE Standards appears on pages xxiv–xxv of this book. The following standards are addressed in Lesson 3.3.

Standard 16: Role of Government      Standard 17: Using Cost/Benefit Analysis to Evaluate Government Programs

## Private Goods, Public Goods, and In Between

Point out that short of the point of congestion, additional people can benefit from a golf course, swimming pool, or rock concert without diminishing the benefit to others. These goods, when not congested, are nonrival. Yet producers can, with relative ease, exclude those who don't pay the greens fee, pool admission, or ticket price. These goods, when not crowded, are both nonrival and exclusive and are therefore quasi-public goods. If congestion sets in, however, these goods become rival. Space grows scarce on a backed-up golf course, in a crowded swimming pool, or at a packed rock concert. Once congestion sets in, these become private goods—both rival and exclusive.

### TEAM WORK

Organize students into groups of four or five. Instruct teams to select a recorder and a spokesperson. Instruct students to complete the **Team Work** activity shown on this page. Set a timer for 10 minutes. When the timer goes off, invite the spokesperson from each group to take a turn naming an example of a public good. Ask the class to confirm that the example is, indeed, a public good by explaining how it is both nonrival and nonexclusive. As each public good is confirmed, have a student write it on the board. Continue until all groups have exhausted their lists.

### Answer

Parks, lakes, forests, and the air around us are examples of public goods typically consumed by individuals and families. All are nonrival, because one person's consumption does not reduce the amount available to others. All are nonexclusive, because everyone has equal access to the goods.

---

# Private Goods, Public Goods, and In Between

So far this book has been talking mostly about private goods, such as tacos, toasters, and telephone service. Other categories of goods exist as well. At the other extreme are public goods, with various categories in between, including quasi-public goods and open-access goods.

## Private Goods

**Private goods** have two important features. First, they are *rival in consumption*. This means that the amount consumed by one person is unavailable for others to consume. For example, when you and some friends share a pizza, each slice they eat is one less available for you. A second key feature of a private good is that suppliers can easily exclude those who don't pay, so a private good is said to be *exclusive*. Thus a private good is both *rival* and *exclusive*.

## Public Goods

In contrast to private goods, **public goods**, such as national defense, the Centers for Disease Control, or a neighborhood mosquito-control program, is nonrival in consumption. One person's benefit does not reduce the amount available to others. Such goods are available to all in equal amount. The marginal cost of providing the good to an additional consumer is zero.

Public goods cannot be provided through the market system because of the problem of who would pay for

them. Public goods are both nonrival and nonexclusive. Once produced, public goods are available for all to consume, regardless of who pays and who doesn't. As a consequence, for-profit firms cannot profitably sell public goods. For example, if a private firm were to spray a neighborhood for mosquitoes, all of the households in the neighborhood would benefit. However, some households might not pay, figuring that they would still benefit from the spraying. These households would be called *free riders*. If this service is provided by a local government, all the households would pay for it with their tax money.

The government provides public goods and funds them through enforced taxation. Sometimes nonprofit agencies also provide public goods, funding them through charitable contributions and other revenue sources.

## Quasi-Public Goods

The economy consists of more than just private goods and public goods. Some goods are nonrival but exclusive. For example, additional households can tune to a TV show without harming the TV reception of other viewers. Television signals are nonrival in consumption. Yet the program's producer can make viewers "pay" for the show, either by adding commercials or by charging each household for the show, as with cable TV. So the TV signal is nonrival but exclusive. Goods that are nonrival but exclusive are called **quasi-public goods**.

## Open-Access Goods

Finally, some other goods are *rival* but *nonexclusive*. The fish in the ocean are rival because every fish caught is not available for others to catch. The same goes for migratory game, like wild geese. Ocean fish and migratory game are nonexclusive in that it would be costly or impossible for a private firm to prevent access to these goods. Goods that are rival but nonexclusive are

---

**private goods**
Goods with two features: (1) the amount consumed by one person is unavailable to others and (2) nonpayers can easily be excluded

**public goods**
Goods that, once produced, are available to all, but nonpayers are not easily excluded

**quasi-public goods**
Goods that, once produced, are available to all, but nonpayers are easily excluded

### TEAM WORK

In small groups, brainstorm a list of public goods that you and your families consume. Make sure that each good you list is both nonrival and nonexclusive.

---

### Outside Resources

**Online Budgets** Most states provide information about their budgets online. New York, for example, maintains a web site at www.budget.state.ny.us. Invite students to locate online budget information for one of the 50 states and investigate planned capital spending. Ask students to report on a specific type of capital spending that will create or expand a public good such as roads, public parks, or police protection. Direct students to prepare a short report, slide presentation, or poster based on their findings.

© Getty Images/PhotoDisc

**Some households receive television signals through satellite-dish technology. What type of good is the television signal that is received this way? Explain your answer.**

called **open-access goods** because it would be difficult and costly to block access to these goods.

In the absence of any regulations, open-access goods are overfished, over-hunted, and overused. For example, the United Nations reports that 11 of the world's 15 primary fishing grounds are seriously depleted.

By imposing restrictions on open-access resource use, governments try to keep renewable resources from becoming depleted. Output restrictions are aimed at reducing resource use to a sustainable rate. For example, in the face of the tendency to overfish, governments now impose a variety of restrictions on the fishing industry.

### Summary Table

Figure 3.3 summarizes the four types of goods in the economy. Across the top, goods are either *rival* or *nonrival*, and along the left margin, goods are either *exclusive* or *nonexclusive*. Private goods usually are provided by the private sector. Quasi-public goods are sometimes provided by government, as with a municipal golf course, and sometimes provided by the private sector, as with a private golf course. Government usually regulates open-access goods, such as with fishing licenses. Government usually provides public goods, funding them with enforced taxation.

 **CHECKPOINT**
Name the four categories of goods, and provide an example of each.

## Externalities

The rivers in Jakarta, Indonesia, are dead—killed by acid, alcohol, and oil. Some coral reefs in the South Pacific have been ripped apart by dynamite fishing. The air in some U.S. cities does not meet health standards. These are all examples of *negative externalities*, which are by-products of production and consumption. Some externalities are

**open-access goods**
Goods that are rival in consumption but exclusion is costly

---

### Private Goods, Public Goods, and In Between

Show students a photograph of high-rise apartments along the shoreline of a city. Point out that when many of the older and shorter buildings were constructed, they had excellent views of the water. Later, as newer and taller buildings were built, these views were reduced or eliminated. Ask students to explain how the view of the water in these cities might be considered an open-access good. Students should understand that these views might be considered open-access goods because they are rival but nonexclusive. There are only so many locations from which the water can be seen, but anyone who builds a taller or closer building can take advantage of the view.

### *Think Critically Through Visuals*

Direct students to focus their attention on the photograph on this page. Ask for a volunteer to answer the question posed in the caption.

**Answer**

Answers will vary. Possible answer: Television that is received through a satellite is a quasi-public good because it is nonrival but exclusive.

 **CHECKPOINT**
Invite a student to answer the checkpoint that appears on this page.

**Answer**

Private goods are those that are rival in consumption, such as clothes. Public goods are nonrival in consumption, such as public parks. Quasi-public goods are nonrival but exclusive, such as TV or radio. Open-access goods are rival but nonexclusive, such as fish.

### *Think Critically Through Visuals*

Direct students to focus their attention on **Figure 3.3—Categories of Private and Public Goods** on page 78. Ask for a volunteer to answer the question posed in the caption.

**Answer**

Private: cars and homes
Quasi-public: TV and garbage collection
Open-access: hunting and fishing
Public: air and lakes

---

## ENRICH

Assign students to list as many exclusive and nonexclusive goods as they can that exist in, or are associated with, their school. Examples of exclusive goods include textbooks and lockers that are distributed and assigned to individual students. Nonexclusive goods might be lectures given by teachers, morning announcements made on the PA system, or watching team sports. Discuss which of these items are public or quasi-public goods.

## Externalities

Present the following scenario about Ted, a professional musician. Ted practices the piano in his apartment four hours each day. He often leaves his windows open while he practices. Ask students how Ted's music could be considered a positive externality by some of his neighbors while others might regard it as a negative externality. Students should understand that the neighbors who enjoy listening to the music benefit from Ted's practice, but those who do not like the music or would prefer quiet are harmed by his practice.

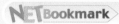

Direct students to **econxtra.swlearning.com**. Remind them to click on the link for Lesson 3.3 to find the appropriate link for the **NET Bookmark** on this page.

## Answer

Answers should include four of the following.

- National Environmental Policy Act of 1969 (NEPA)
- Chemical Safety Information, Site Security and Fuels Regulatory Relief Act (1999)
- The Clean Air Act (CAA) (1970)
- The Clean Water Act (CWA) (1977)
- Comprehensive Environmental Response, Compensation, and Liability Act (CERCLA or Superfund)
- The Emergency Planning & Community Right-To-Know Act
- The Endangered Species Act (ESA)
- Federal Insecticide, Fungicide and Rodenticide Act (FIFRA) (1972)
- Federal Food, Drug, and Cosmetic Act (FFDCA)
- Food Quality Protection Act (FQPA)
- The Freedom of Information Act (FOIA) (1966)
- The Occupational Safety and Health Act (OSHA) (1970)
- The Oil Pollution Act of 1990 (OPA)
- The Pollution Prevention Act (PPA)
- The Resource Conservation and Recovery Act (RCRA) (1976)
- The Safe Drinking Water Act
- The Superfund Amendments and Reauthorization Act (SARA) (1986)
- The Toxic Substances Control Act

---

**Categories of Private and Public Goods**                    Figure 3.3

The four types of goods—private, quasi-public, open-access, and public—are characterized as being either rival or nonrival in consumption and either exclusive or nonexclusive. Can you think of two more examples for each type of good?

Private

Quasi-public

Open-access

Public

---

**negative externalities**

By-products of production or consumption that impose costs on third parties, neither buyers nor sellers

*positive.* For example, if you get vaccinated, you reduce your chances of contracting that disease. However you also reduce the chances that others will catch it from you, so they benefit too. The private sector, operating on its own, produces too many negative externalities and too few positive externalities. Government intervenes in the market to improve the outcome.

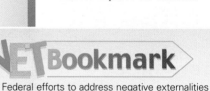

Federal efforts to address negative externalities that harm the air, water, and soil are coordinated by the Environmental Protection Agency (EPA). Access the EPA web site through econxtra.swlearning.com. Identify four of the major U.S. environmental laws.

*econxtra.swlearning.com*

## Negative Externalities

A renewable resource can be used indefinitely if used conservatively. Some renewable resources also are open-access resources, and this creates a special problem for the environment. The atmosphere and waterways are renewable resources to the extent they can absorb and neutralize a certain level of pollutants yet still remain relatively clean.

**Negative externalities** generally are by-products of production or consumption that impose costs on third parties (those who are neither buyer nor seller in the transaction). For example, some spray cans once released chlorofluorocarbons into the atmosphere, affecting those not directly involved in the purchase or sale of the spray cans. These gases were suspected of causing a thinning of the ozone layer that protects people from the sun's ultraviolet rays. The use of chlorofluorocarbons as a propellant in aerosol cans now is outlawed in the United States.

---

### Extend the Content

Point out that pollution and other negative externalities arise because there are no practical, enforceable, private property rights to open-access resources, such as the air. Market prices usually fail to include the cost that negative externalities impose on society. For example, in the past, the cost of a can of hair spray powered by chlorofluorocarbons did not reflect the effect of gas emissions on the atmosphere's ozone layer. Note that externalities may be unintended side effects of actions that are themselves useful and productive. Hair spray producers, for example, did not mean to pollute the air.

## Correcting for Negative Externalities

Polluters of the atmosphere, waterways, and other open-access resources tend to ignore the impact of their pollution on other people and on the resource's ability to renew itself. Therefore, the quality and quantity of an open-access resource tends to deteriorate over time.

Government restrictions can improve the allocation of open-access resources. For example, antipollution laws limit the kind and amount of gases that can be released into the atmosphere from factories, automobiles, and other pollution sources. Restrictions aimed at maintaining water quality limit what can be dumped into the rivers, lakes, and oceans. Noise restrictions aim at maintaining the peace and quiet. Local zoning laws limit where firms can locate and in what condition homes must be maintained. In short, government restrictions try to reduce negative externalities.

Market prices can direct the allocation of resources as long as property rights are well defined and can be enforced at a reasonable cost. Pollution of air, land, water, peace and quiet, scenery, and so on arises not so much from the misdeeds of producers or consumers as from the fact that open-access resources are overused.

## Positive Externalities

Some externalities are positive, or beneficial. **Positive externalities** occur when the by-products of consumption or production benefit third parties—those who are neither buyers nor sellers in the transaction. For example, people who get inoculated against a disease reduce their own likelihood of contracting the disease. In the process they also reduce the risk of transmitting the disease to others. Inoculations thus provide external benefits on others.

Education also generates positive externalities. Society as a whole receives external benefits from education because those who acquire more education become better citizens, can read road signs, and become more productive workers who are better able to support themselves and their families. Educated people also are less likely to require public assistance or to resort to

*positive externalities*

By-products of consumption or production that benefit third parties, who are not buyers or sellers

# Ethics in Action

**Wildlife Refuge at Stake** Soaring energy prices and uncertainty about the availability of Persian Gulf oil are increasing the chances Congress will approve oil drilling in the Arctic National Wildlife Refuge. Millions of barrels of oil are thought to be under the coastal plain of the refuge in the far northeastern corner of Alaska. Extraction of this oil for domestic use has been at the heart of President Bush's energy agenda. Many Democrats are determined to protect the 100-mile sliver of tundra. Such protection has been an obsession among some environmentalists who insist that drilling will destroy its value as a sanctuary for polar bears, musk oxen, caribou, and migratory birds. While

Bush has argued that the refuge's oil should be tapped to reduce U.S. dependence on foreign crude, the refuge oil won't be available for at least three to four years, even if Congress gives the go-ahead. Though drilling in the refuge may increase oil production and thus reduce the price of fuel, the unintended side effects may cause irreversible problems for animals and the environment.

## Think Critically

Draw conclusions regarding the specific positive and negative externalities that you think could result from drilling oil in the Arctic National Wildlife Refuge. What do you think the government should do in this situation?

## Externalities

Before the class period begins, recruit a student to help you with this activity. Instruct the student to agree to buy your product for 10 cents. Provide this student with a dime.
Begin your demonstration by standing in front of a different student's desk and cutting out a string of paper dolls, letting the scraps fall on the desk. Make no effort to pick up the scraps. Offer to sell the dolls to anyone in the class for 10 cents. Complete the transaction with the cooperating student. Ask students to explain how the production of the paper dolls and their eventual sale demonstrates the problem of negative externalities.

## Ethics in Action

Have students work in pairs to discuss the ethical issue featured on this page, and develop an answer to the question presented there.

### Answers to Think Critically

Answers will vary. Possible answer: Positive externalities of drilling would be a rich oil supply for U.S. consumption. The negative externalities associated with drilling for oil include harming Alaskan wildlife.

### *Think Critically Through Visuals*

Direct students to focus their attention on the photographs on page 80. Ask for a volunteer to answer the question posed in the caption.

### Answer

Answers will vary. Possible answer: The benefits of the government policies outweigh the costs because the policies protect the country's citizens from negative externalities.

## Group Activity

Describe the following scenario. Coal-burning power plants are emitting compounds into the atmosphere that cause acid rain. Plants, animals, and bodies of water are being harmed. Organize students into groups of three or four, and instruct each group to formulate a policy to reduce this negative externality. Point out that they might tax emissions, curtail production, or develop their own policy. Each group should report on their choice and the impact it would have on the economy.

**Main Idea**

### NCEE Standard 16: Role of Government

Students will understand that there is an economic role for government in a market economy whenever the benefits of a government policy outweigh its costs. Governments often provide for national defense, address environmental concerns, define and protect property rights, and attempt to make markets more competitive. Most government policies also redistribute income.

**CHECKPOINT**
Invite a student to answer the checkpoint that appears on this page.

**Answer**

Negative externalities are by-products of consumption that impose a cost on third parties. Positive externalities occur when the by-products of consumption benefit third parties. Governments intervene to protect these third parties who are indirectly involved.

**APPLY**

Assign Lesson 3.3 from the Contemporary Economics Workbook.

**ASSESS**

Assign all or part of Lesson 3.3 Assessment on page 81 as homework or an in-class activity.

**Xtra! Study Tools**

Direct students to the online study tools for Lesson 3.3 at **econxtra.swlearning.com**.

**CLOSE**

**Revisit** the **In the News** feature on the first page of the lesson. Ask students to review their preliminary answers and discuss the questions, now that they have completed this lesson.

**Review** the objectives for Lesson 3.3. Students should be able to:

● Describe and provide examples of four types of goods.

● Define negative externalities and positive externalities, and discuss why government intervenes in such markets.

---

 Main Idea

**Role of Government**

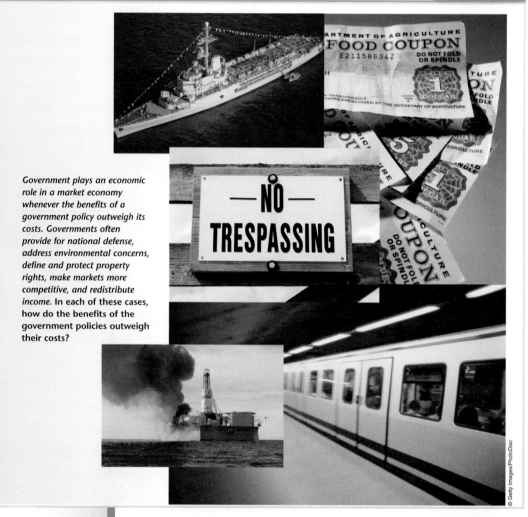

*Government plays an economic role in a market economy whenever the benefits of a government policy outweigh its costs. Governments often provide for national defense, address environmental concerns, define and protect property rights, make markets more competitive, and redistribute income.* **In each of these cases, how do the benefits of the government policies outweigh their costs?**

crime for income. Thus, education benefits those getting the education, but it also confers benefits on others.

When there are positive externalities, governments aim to increase the level of production beyond what would be chosen privately. For example, governments try to increase the level of education by providing free primary and secondary education, by requiring students to stay in school until they reach 16

years of age, by subsidizing public higher education, and by offering tax breaks for some education expenditures.

**CHECKPOINT**
What are negative externalities and positive externalities, and why does government intervene to regulate them?

---

**RETEACH**

When some people visit public parks, they bring their music with them. They play rock, rap, or classical music, sometimes at volumes that force other visitors to the park to listen to that music, too. Ask students to explain how this situation can demonstrate both negative and positive externalities. If the government passed and enforced a law that required people to keep the volume of their music low, how could it both harm and benefit park goers?

## Key Concepts

1. In 2002, there was a debate over whether smallpox vaccinations should be given to the general public. Would vaccinations be an example of a *public good*. Why or why not?

2. Identify and describe an example of each of the following types of goods that you encounter in your life.

   a. Private good

   b. Quasi-public good

   c. Open-access good

   d. Public goods

3. Describe an example of a negative externality that has been a problem in your community.

4. Describe steps that have been taken in your community to try to eliminate or reduce the negative externality you identified in exercise 3 above.

## Graphing Exercise

5. Construct a pie chart for 1990 and another for 2000 that show federal spending on natural resources and the environment. Base your charts on the data in the table. What parts of this spending may have been dedicated to trying to reduce negative externalities?

## Think Critically

6. **Government** Determine the open-access goods that exist in your county or state. Investigate whether the county or state government regulates these goods. If they do, what are the regulations? If not, why do you think these goods are not regulated?

7. **Business Management** Although trucks powered by natural gas are expensive to purchase, they create little pollution when they are operated. Why do you think some states have passed laws that give tax reductions to businesses that use natural gas-powered trucks? Explain how this is an effort by these states to reduce a negative externality. Do you think this is a good idea?

**Xtra!**
Study Tools
econxtra.swlearning.com

**Federal Spending for Natural Resources and the Environment 1990–2000**
**Amounts in Billions of Dollars**

| Type of Spending | 1990 | % of total | 2000 | % of total |
|---|---|---|---|---|
| Water Resources | $ 4.4 | 25.7% | $5.1 | 21.3% |
| Conservation | 3.6 | 21.1 | 5.9 | 24.6 |
| Recreation | 1.9 | 11.1 | 3.4 | 14.2 |
| Pollution control | 5.2 | 30.1 | 7.4 | 30.8 |
| Other | 2.0 | 11.7 | 3.0 | 12.1 |
| Total | $17.1 | 100.0 | $24.8 | 100.0 |

Source: *Statistical Abstract of the United States,* 2001, p. 307.

## Key Concepts

1. Vaccinations are not public goods. They are both rival and exclusive.

2. Answers will vary. Examples of acceptable answers include: bicycles or CD players (private), radio signals or school libraries (quasi-public), fish in a river or deer in a forest (open-access), and police protection or road construction (public).

3. Answers will vary. Students may point out pollution as an example of a negative externality in their community.

4. Answers will vary. Students should describe steps that were taken to redistribute costs of the negative externality to the buyers or sellers of the product that caused the problem.

## Graphing Exercise

5. An example of an acceptable graph appears at the bottom of this page.

   Answers will vary. Possible answer: Much of this spending is intended to reduce or eliminate negative externalities. Spending that polices pollution can reduce these costs.

## Think Critically

6. Answers will vary. Possible answer: Any fees people must pay to enjoy the parks would be an attempt to reduce the chances of having a free-rider problem. Excluding non-residents from the parks would do the same.

7. Answers will vary. Possible answer: Taxes are a cost of doing business. By reducing one cost (taxes), the government may encourage businesses to accept other costs that are higher (buying the trucks). If this happens, third parties will not have to breathe as much air pollution, and a negative externality of the business will be reduced.

## Visualizing the Answer—Graphing Exercise

5. Students' graphs should look similar to the ones shown here. An Excel spreadsheet containing these graphs, along with supporting data, is available on the Instructor's Resource CD.

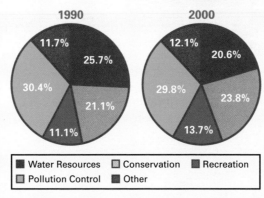

1990    2000

■ Water Resources   □ Conservation   ■ Recreation
□ Pollution Control   ■ Other

## FOCUS

Introduce this lesson by showing students photographs of people who appear to be living in poverty. Ask students to identify reasons why some people live in poverty. Do they believe poverty happens because of forces that are beyond these people's control, or do they think many of these people could escape poverty if they made other decisions? What do students believe the government's role should be in helping those who live in poverty in the United States? How would they decide how much help is appropriate and how much help is too much?

### Objectives

Remind students to read the lesson objectives to help focus their attention before reading the lesson.

### Key Terms

Direct students to write each of the key terms on a separate index card. Instruct students to write the complete definition of each key term on the back of the appropriate card, along with the page number where the definition is located.

## [ In the News ]

Instruct students to read the passage and write down their answers. Point out that their answers might change after they finish studying Lesson 3.4.

### Answers to Think About It

Answers will vary. Possible answer: These findings indicate that the social safety net within the United States is stronger than ever. There is more protection and safety now than in the past.

### *Visual Presentation*

Use the PowerPoint presentation on the Instructor's Resource CD as an adjunct to your lecture. The presentation also can be used for review.

### Ask the Xpert!

Direct students to **econxtra.swlearning.com** to hear an expert answer the question, "Will there always be poverty?"

## Objectives

> Determine why incomes differ across households, and identify the main source of poverty in the United States.

> Describe government programs that provide a safety net for poor people.

## Overview

Operating on its own, the private sector offers no guarantee that people will earn enough to survive. Some people may have few resources that are valued in the market. Because markets do not assure even a minimum level of income, society has made the political choice that poor families should receive short-term public assistance, or welfare. This assistance reflects society's attempt to provide a social safety net. However public assistance could reduce incentives to work, because welfare benefits decrease as earnings from work increase.

## Key Terms

**median income**

**social insurance**

**income-assistance programs**

## [ In the News ]

### ● Good News/Bad News for U.S. Kids

In July 2002, the Federal Interagency Forum on Child and Family Statistics reported encouraging news on the health, economics, and education of some 70 million children in the United States. The best news was a drop in the infant mortality rate—from 7.2 deaths per 1,000 babies under age one in 1998, down to 6.9 deaths per 1,000 babies in 2000. Other positive trends: More children were covered by health insurance; fewer eighth and tenth graders smoked; more children were read to every day by a family member; and more youngsters ages two to five had a good diet. However, numerous measures did not change: In 2000, 16 percent of children lived in poverty; only 76 percent of toddlers got the recommended immunizations; and only 87 percent of young adults finished high school. Drug and alcohol use among junior high and high school students held steady. The report also found that in 2001, 19 percent of children had at least one parent born outside the United States, up from 14 percent in 1994.

### Think About It

What do the above statistics say about the social safety net in the United States?

◀ ▮ ▶

82

### *National Content Standards in Economics*

**NCEE**

A complete list of the NCEE Standards appears on pages xxiv–xxv of this book. The following standards are addressed in Lesson 3.4.

Standard 3: Allocation of Goods and Services

Standard 13: Role of Resources in Determining Income

Standard 16: Role of Government

Standard 20: Monetary and Fiscal Policy

# Income and Poverty

In a market economy, income depends primarily on earnings, which depend on the value of each person's contribution to production. The problem with allocating income according to productivity is that some people are not able to contribute much value to production. Individuals born with mental or physical disabilities tend to be less productive and may be unable to earn a living. Others may face limited job choices and reduced wages because of advanced age, poor health, little education, discrimination, bad luck, or the demands of caring for small children. Consider first why incomes differ across households.

## Why Household Incomes Differ

The **median income** of households is the middle income when incomes are ranked from lowest to highest. In any given year, half the households are above the median income and half are below it.

The main reason household incomes differ is that the number of household members who are working differs. For example, the median income for house-

holds with two earners is nearly double that for households with only one earner and about four times that for households with no earners. Household incomes also differ for all the reasons that labor earnings differ, such as differences in education, ability, job experience, and so on.

At every age, people with more education earn more on average. For example, those with a professional degree earn about four times as much as those with only a high school education. Age itself has an important effect on income. As workers mature, they typically

**median income**
The middle income when a group of incomes is ranked from lowest to highest

## Ask the Xpert!
econxtra.swlearning.com

*Will there always be poverty?*

**Main Idea**

### Role of Resources in Determining Income

*Income for most people is determined by the market value of the productive resources they sell. What they earn depends on the market value of what they produce and how productive they are. What are the products of the two people shown in the photos? Which one do you think should earn more than the other, and why?*

© Getty Images/PhotoDisc
© Getty Images/PhotoDisc

Lesson 3.4 • *Providing a Safety Net*    **83**

---

## Outside Resources

**Statistical Abstract of the United States** The most recent version of the *Statistical Abstract* can be found online at www.census.gov/prod/www/statistical-abstract-us.html. Invite students to visit this site and search the Income, Earnings, and Wealth section for data about people living below the poverty level. Have students write a report that answers the following questions.

- How do the current data compare with data presented in the textbook?
- What changes have taken place in recent years?
- How can these changes be explained?

---

## Income and Poverty

Organize the class into groups of four. Each group represents a family with an annual income of $20,000. The major difference between these families is where they live. Choose varied locations such as a large city in the northeast, a small town in the southeast, a rural area in the northwest, a rural area in the west, and a large city in the southwest. Be sure to pick one location that is similar to the area where your school is located.

Ask each "family" to research how it could live on the $20,000, and create a budget for the family. Have each family present its budget to the class.

After the presentations, ask students to explain why equal amounts of income do not always equate to the same levels of poverty in different geographic regions. Students may point out that rents will be higher in urban areas. Utilities will be more expensive in the north. People who live in rural areas may be able to grow some of their own food.

### *Think Critically Through Visuals*

Direct students to focus their attention on **Figure 3.4—Number and Percentage of U.S. Population in Poverty: 1959–2001.** Ask for a volunteer to answer the question posed in the caption.

## Answer

During a recession, the number in poverty and the poverty rate increase.

acquire valuable job experience, get promoted, and earn more.

Differences in earnings based on age and education reflect a normal life-cycle pattern of income. In fact, most income differences across households reflect the normal workings of resource markets, whereby workers are rewarded according to their productivity. Because of these lifetime patterns, it is not necessarily the same households that remain rich or poor over time. There is much income mobility among households.

Despite this mobility over time, generalizations can be made about rich and poor households at a point in time. High-income households typically consist of well-educated couples with both spouses employed. Low-income households typically are headed by a single mother who is young, poorly educated, and unemployed.

Young, single motherhood is a recipe for poverty. Often the young mother drops out of school, which reduces her future earning possibilities when and if she seeks work outside the home. Even a strong economy is little aid to households with nobody in the labor force.

### Official Poverty Rate

Because poverty is such a relative concept, how can it be measured objectively over time? The federal government determines the official poverty level and adjusts this benchmark over time to account for inflation. For example, the official poverty level for a family of four was $18,104 in 2001.

U.S. poverty since 1959 is presented in Figure 3.4. Poverty is measured both in millions of people living below the official poverty level and the percentage of the U.S. population below that level. Periods of U.S. recession are shaded. A *recession* is defined as a decline in the nation's total production that lasts at least six months. Note that poverty increases during recessions.

The biggest decline in U.S. poverty occurred before 1970. The poverty rate dropped from 22 percent in 1959 to 12 percent in 1969. During that period, the number of poor people decreased from about 40 million to 24 million. More recently, the rate declined from 15 percent in 1993 to 12 percent in 2001, one of the lowest rates since 1973. The 33 million people in poverty in 2001 was 6 million below the 1993 level.

**Number and Percentage of U.S. Population in Poverty: 1959–2001** | **Figure 3.4**

On the line graph, the "number in poverty" line shows how many millions of people were living below the official poverty level. The "poverty rate" line shows the percentage of the U.S. population below that level. Periods of U.S. recession are shaded. What happens to the number in poverty and the poverty rate during a recession?

Source: U.S. Census Bureau, *Poverty in the United States: 2001,* Current Population Reports, September 2002, Figure 3, www.census.gov/hhes/www/poverty01.html.

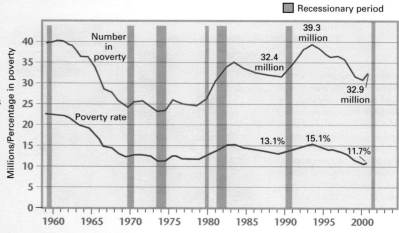

## ENRICH

The official federal measure of poverty was created during the early 1960s. It was based on the cost of providing a "minimal standard of living" in urban areas. Roughly one-third of this cost was for food. In following years, the government used this relationship to measure poverty. It calculated the cost of providing a minimally adequate diet in urban areas and multiplied this amount by a factor of roughly 3. Explain these facts to your students, and discuss whether they believe this was a good way to determine poverty.

Poverty is a relative term. If you examined income differences across countries, you would find huge gaps between rich and poor nations. The U.S. official poverty level of income is many times greater than the average income for most of the world's population. Many other countries set a much lower income level as their poverty level. For example, the poverty level for a family of four in the United States in 2001 worked out to be about $12 per person per day. China uses a poverty level of only $0.30 per person per day. In China, $0.30 can purchase more goods and services than it can in the United States.

## Poverty and Marital Status

One way of measuring poverty is based on the marital status of the household head. Figure 3.5 compares poverty rates during the last three decades for

1. families headed by females with no husband present

2. families headed by males with no wife present

3. married couples

Three trends are clear. First, poverty rates among female-headed families are five to six times greater than rates among married couples. Second, poverty rates among female-headed families are two to three times greater than those for male-headed families. And third, since the mid-1990s poverty rates have trended down for all types of families, before rising slightly in the recession year of 2001.

The percentage of births to unmarried mothers is five times greater today than in 1960. Many of these births are to teenage mothers. The United States has the highest teenage pregnancy rate in the developed world—twice the rate of Great Britain and more that 12 times that of Japan. Because the father in such cases typically assumes little responsibility for child support, children born outside marriage are much more likely to be poor than other children. Births to single mothers make up the primary source of poverty in the United States.

### CHECKPOINT
Why do incomes differ across households, and what is the main source of poverty in the U.S. economy?

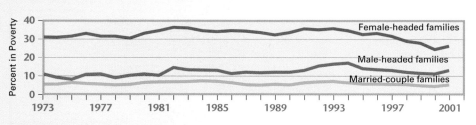

**U.S. Poverty Rates and Types of Households**

**Figure 3.5**

*Percent in Poverty* (y-axis: 0, 10, 20, 30, 40)

Female-headed families
Male-headed families
Married-couple families

(x-axis: 1973, 1977, 1981, 1985, 1989, 1993, 1997, 2001)

**Female-headed families have the highest poverty rate in the United States, followed by male-headed families and married couples.**

Source: Developed from U.S. Census Bureau, *Poverty in the United States: 2001,* Current Population Reports, September 2002, Table A-3.

Lesson 3.4 • *Providing a Safety Net* 85

# TEACH (continued)

## Income and Poverty

Point out that a person who earned $1,000 a year in the United States would be regarded as living in deep poverty, while a person earning the same income in India would be reasonably well off. Ask students to explain why the same amount of income can support very different standards of living in different countries. What does this difference have to do with the prices charged for the basic necessities of life in these countries? How much of the meaning of poverty is a matter of social values and expectations?

### *Think Critically Through Visuals*

Direct students to focus their attention on **Figure 3.5—U.S. Poverty Rates and Types of Households.** Point out that even though there are fluctuations across time, poverty rates among female-headed families are greater than rates for male-headed families and married-couple families.

### CHECKPOINT
Invite a student to answer the checkpoint that appears on this page.

### Answer

Incomes differ across households because of the number of individuals in the household who work and the age and education of these individuals. Families headed by females with no husband present are the number-one source of poverty in the United States.

## *Economic Headlines*

Direct students to find an article in a newspaper or newsmagazine about a government-sponsored social service. Ask students to picture a United States in which no social services are provided to the poor. There would be no welfare payments, food stamps, subsidized housing, Medicaid, etc. Ask them to either describe or write an essay about differences that would result in our society, political, and economic situations. Do they think their own lives would be better or worse? Ask them to explain their points of view.

## Programs to Help the Poor

Point out that one of the undesirable consequences of income assistance is that it creates a high marginal tax on earned income. Individuals who are currently on welfare but who can find work may discover that, after figuring cuts in welfare benefits as a result of working, their net income earned is not worth the effort. This creates an incentive to remain on public assistance.

### *Think Critically Through Visuals*

Direct students to focus their attention on the photograph on this page. Ask for a volunteer to answer the question posed in the caption.

### Answer

Answers will vary. To help students answer this question, explain that the cost of health insurance and the benefits paid out generally are not based on income. For example, when a company offers group health insurance to its employees, the employee usually pays a portion of the cost of the coverage. All employees who opt for similar coverage pay the same amount, regardless of their income. Similarly, when a benefit is paid, the patient's income is not considered.

**social insurance**
Cash transfers for retirees, the unemployed, and others with a work history and a record of contributions to the program

**income-assistance programs**
Government programs that provide money and in-kind assistance to poor people

# Programs to Help the Poor

What should be society's response to poverty? Families with a full-time worker are nine times more likely to escape poverty than are families with no workers. Thus, the government's first line of defense in fighting poverty is to promote job opportunities. Yet even when the unemployment rate is low, some people still remain poor.

Since the 1960s, spending for income redistribution at all levels of government has increased significantly. These programs divide into two broad categories: social insurance and income assistance.

## Social Insurance

**Social insurance** programs are designed to help make up for the lost income of people who worked but are now retired, temporarily unemployed, or unable to work because of disability or work-related injury. The federal government funds all these programs. The major social insurance program is Social Security, established during the Great Depression of the 1930s. *Social Security*

provides retirement income for those with a work history and a record of making payments to the program.

*Medicare,* another social insurance program, provides health insurance for short-term medical care, mostly to those age 65 and older, regardless of income. There were about 40 million Social Security and Medicare beneficiaries in 2001.

The social insurance system tends to redistribute income from rich to poor and from young to old. Most current Social Security beneficiaries receive far more in benefits than they paid into the program, especially those with a brief work history or a record of low wages.

Other social insurance programs include unemployment insurance and workers' compensation, which supports workers injured on the job. Both programs require that beneficiaries have a prior record of employment.

## Income-Assistance Programs

**Income-assistance programs**—typically called *welfare programs*—provide money and in-kind assistance to poor people. In-kind assistance is help in the form of goods and services. Programs

Medicare is a social insurance program that provides health insurance for short-term medical care, mostly to people age 65 and older. Why do you think this insurance is provided regardless of income level?

© Getty Images/PhotoDisc

**86** CHAPTER 3 U.S. Private and Public Sectors

## *Group Activity*

Provide each group with a weekly grocery-store shopping supplement. Tell them they are required to select food for a family of four that will last them one week. Provide each group with progressively smaller amounts to spend; one might have $200, another $150, and so on. Ask the groups to report their purchase decisions to the class. Compare their choices. What does this show about the impact of poverty on the way people eat? Can a nutritious diet be purchased for relatively little? How can this be accomplished?

that pay money directly to recipients are called cash transfer programs. Other forms of assistance, such as housing and healthcare, are provided through in-kind transfer programs.

Unlike social insurance programs, income-assistance programs do not require a work history or a record of contributions. Instead, income-assistance programs are means tested. In a *means-tested program,* a household's income and assets must fall below a certain level to qualify for benefits. The federal government funds two-thirds of welfare spending, and state and local governments fund one-third.

### Cash Transfer Programs

The two main cash transfer programs are *Temporary Assistance for Needy Families (TANF),* which provides cash to poor families with dependent children, and *Supplemental Security Income (SSI),* which provides cash to the elderly poor and the disabled. Cash transfers vary inversely with family income from other sources. The federal government gives each state a fixed grant to help fund TANF programs. Each state determines eligibility standards.

The SSI program provides support for the elderly and disabled poor, including people addicted to drugs and alcohol, children with learning disabilities, and, in some cases, the homeless. SSI is the fastest-growing cash- transfer program, with outlays of $33 billion in 2001, double the TANF outlays that year.

### In-Kind Transfer Programs

A variety of *in-kind transfer programs* provide goods and services such as food stamps, healthcare, housing assistance, and school lunches to the poor. *Medicaid* funds medical care for those with incomes below a certain level who are elderly, blind, disabled, or are living in families with dependent children. Medicaid is the largest welfare program, costing nearly twice as much as all cash transfer programs combined. It has grown more than any other poverty program, quadrupling in the last decade and accounting for nearly a quarter of the typical state's

budget. States get federal grants covering half or more of their Medicaid budget.

The qualifying level of income is set by each state. Some states are quite strict. Therefore, the proportion of poor covered by Medicaid varies greatly across states. In 2001, more than 36 million people received free medical care under Medicaid at a total cost of more than $200 billion. Outlays averaged about $5,600 per recipient. In all, there are about 75 means-tested federal welfare programs.

To get some idea of how much the federal government spends on programs to help the poor, also called *income redistribution programs,* look at Figure 3.6. This figure shows the composition of federal outlays since 1960. As you can see, income redistribution, including Social Security, Medicare, and various welfare programs, increased from about one-fifth of federal outlays in 1960 to about half by 2000. Conversely, defense spending fell from more than half of federal outlays in 1960 to less than one-fifth by 2000. Thus, income redistribution claims a growing share of the federal budget.

### Earned-Income Tax Credit

The *earned-income tax credit* supplements wages of the working poor. For example, a family with two children and earning $13,000 in 2001 would not pay federal income tax and would receive a cash transfer of about $4,000. The idea is to increase income and to provide incentives for people to work. More than 18 million working families received such transfers in 2001, requiring federal outlays exceeding $30 billion.

### Welfare Reform

The biggest reform of the welfare system in the last 60 years came with 1996 legislation that created the current system, Temporary Assistance for Needy Families (TANF). The earlier program established eligibility rules that guaranteed the federal government would pay most of the cost. Families could stay

### Programs to Help the Poor

Explain that welfare reform had an impact. Welfare caseloads declined. In January 1994, the number of welfare recipients in the United States peaked at 14.2 million, mostly single women with children. By December 2001, the rolls fell by two-thirds to 5.3 million. It helped that the national economy was healthy and growing during most of that period.

Because the welfare rolls have declined but federal grants to states remained constant, welfare spending per recipient has increased significantly. Most states are combining tough new work requirements with an expanded menu of welfare services. States have made large investments in work-related services, such as job placement, transportation to work, and especially childcare.

Other positive developments from welfare reform may include falling rates of crime and drug abuse, the greatest decline in child poverty since the 1960s, and a substantial increase in employment among mothers who head families, especially those who never married.

### *Think Critically Through Visuals*

Direct students to focus their attention on **Figure 3.6—Income Redistribution—Composition of Federal Outlays** on page 88. Point out the significant changes in the percent of federal outlays for defense and redistributions between 1960 and 2000.

## THE WALL STREET JOURNAL

### Reading It Right

Invite a student to explain the relevance of the statement from *The Wall Street Journal* that appears on page 88.

### Answer

Answers will vary. Possible answer: These figures indicate the government's priority is to provide safety nets, such as earned-income tax credit and welfare, to single-parent families headed by mothers.

**Answer**

The main government programs that try to offer a safety net are social insurance programs and income-assistance programs. The main social insurance programs are Social Security and Medicare. The main income-assistance programs are TANK, SSI, and Medicaid.

## APPLY

Assign Lesson 3.4 from the Contemporary Economics Workbook.

## ASSESS

Assign all or part of Lesson 3.4 Assessment on page 90 as homework or an in-class activity.

## Xtra! Study Tools

Direct students to the online study tools for Lesson 3.4 at **econxtra.swlearning.com**.

## CLOSE

**Revisit** the **In the News** feature on the first page of the lesson. Ask students to review their preliminary answers and discuss the questions, now that they have completed this lesson.

**Review** the objectives for Lesson 3.4. Students should be able to:

• Determine why incomes differ across households, and identify the main source of poverty in the United States.

• Describe government programs that provide a safety net for poor people.

---

## THE WALL STREET JOURNAL

**Reading It Right** What's the relevance of the following statement from *The Wall Street Journal?* "Family households maintained by women without a husband present saw incomes rise 4.0 percent to $28,116 from 1999 to 2000, the Census Department said. Other types of households had no significant change in their median household income."

on welfare for a decade or more. Under the new system, states get a fixed amount of aid from the federal government and can run their own welfare programs. The system requires welfare recipients to look for jobs and limits cash transfers to five years.

About half the states impose time limits shorter than five years. Some observers fear that states now have an incentive to keep welfare costs down by cutting benefits. To avoid becoming destinations for poor people—that is, to avoid becoming "welfare magnets"—

states may be tempted to offer relatively low levels of benefits.

Welfare reform has reduced welfare rolls and increased employment. However, because most people on welfare are poorly educated and have few job skills, wages for those who find jobs remain low. Part-time work also is common, as is job loss among those who initially find jobs.

On the plus side, however, the earned-income tax credit provided up to $4,000 in 2001 in additional income to low-income workers. Most of those going to work also can receive food stamps, child care, and Medicaid. All this has helped reduce the overall poverty rate.

**CHECKPOINT**

What are the main government programs that try to offer a safety net?

---

### Income Redistribution—Composition of Federal Outlays    Figure 3.6

Since 1960, spending on income redistribution has increased and spending on defense has decreased as a share of federal outlays.

Source: Computed based on figures from the *Economic Report of the President*, January 2001, Table B-80. Access the most current report through econxtra.swlearning .com.

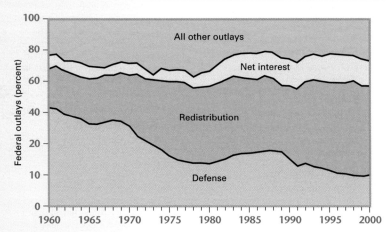

88    **CHAPTER 3**   U.S. Private and Public Sectors

---

## RETEACH

Some people believe that persons who live in poverty are likely to spend transfer payments they receive in ways that waste their money. They argue that transfers in kind are more likely to truly help the poor. Benefits of food stamps, subsidized housing, and Medicaid care are harder to misuse. Ask your students whether they believe this is a reasonable position to take. Does it deny freedom of choice or constitutional rights to the poor that are enjoyed by people who do not receive support from the government?

# Sharpen Your Life Skills

## Use Mathematics to Draw Conclusions

Federal, state, and local governments receive a large part of the income that is generated from production in the U.S. economy through taxes, fees, and borrowing. Some of the government's revenue is used to purchase goods or services while other parts become transfer payments. Welfare, Social Security, and unemployment compensation payments are examples of government transfers of income to individuals. Use data in the table below to calculate the percent of total income earned from production that has flowed through the government in recent years. What conclusions could you draw from these data about the importance of government in deciding how income in our nation will be used?

## Apply Your Skill

1. Assume that all people currently alive will live to an age of at least 67. Use the *Statistical Abstract of the United States* to find the approximate number of people who will become eligible for Social Security benefits (67 years of age) in the 2010s, 2020s, and 2030s. Do this by finding the number of people who are currently in age groups that will reach 67 in each of these decades. Explain why these data indicate that government spending for Social Security and Medicare insurance is likely to grow as a share of total income in the future.

2. In 2000, the federal government's spending for national defense totaled $294.5 billion, or about 3 percent of the value of all production in the U.S. economy during that year. If spending for defense had grown by 5 percent in each of the following five years, how much would it total by 2005? If the value of total U.S. production increased by 3 percent in each of these years, what would happen to the share of that production that would have been devoted to our national defense?

**Government Spending and Transfers as a Percent of Total Production, 1980–2000 Values in Billions of Dollars**

| Year | Government Spending and Transfers | Value of Total Production | Government Spending & Transfers as a Percent of Total Production |
|------|-----------------------------------|---------------------------|------------------------------------------------------------------|
| 1980 | $   812.0 | $2,795.8 | |
| 1990 | $1,778.0 | $5,803.2 | |
| 2000 | $2,772.5 | $9,963.1 | |

## Sharpen Your Life Skills

### Use Mathematics to Draw Conclusions

After studying Lesson 3.4, students should be able to answer the questions on this page.

### Answer

The percent of total income earned from production for each year is shown in the table below. A spreadsheet showing the correct formulas appears at the bottom of this page.

| Year | Percent of Total Income Earned from Production |
|------|------------------------------------------------|
| 1980 | 29.0% |
| 1990 | 30.6% |
| 2000 | 27.8% |

Answers will vary. Possible answer: The share of total income flowing through the government declined during the 1990s. This may be a temporary situation as our need for government-funded programs changes over time.

### Apply Your Skill

Consider allowing students to work in pairs for this assignment.

### Answers

1. Answers will vary. Students should find that there will be approximately 38 million people reaching 67 in the 2010s, 45 million in the 2020s, and 31 million in the 2030s. This large number of people will require the government to allocate more of its funds to Social Security and Medicare, unless the level of these benefits is reduced.

2. At a 5 percent rate of growth, spending for national defense would total $375.9 billion by 2005. If the value of total U.S. production grew at 3 percent in these years, the share devoted to national defense would have increased to roughly 3.3 percent. Whether or not an increase in spending is likely to take place depends on recent national and international events.

## Visualizing the Answer

Suggest students practice using spreadsheet skills, using the data on this page. Students should recreate the table on this page and enter the appropriate formula for calculating the percentages. The formulas are shown in column E of the spreadsheet below.

| A | B | C | D | E |
|---|---|---|---|---|
| 1 | Year | Government Spending and Transfers | Value of Total Production | Government Spending & Transfers as a Percent of Total Production |
| 2 | 1980 | $   812.0 | $2,795.8 | +C3/D3 |
| 3 | 1990 | $1,778.0 | $5,803.2 | +C4/D4 |
| 4 | 2000 | $2,772.5 | $9,963.1 | +C5/D5 |

## Key Concepts

1. Answers will vary. Possible answer: Few people would work to produce goods and services if they received the same income no matter what they chose to do.

2. Answers will vary. Possible answer: People are considered to live in poverty when they have significantly fewer goods and services to enjoy than the majority of people in their society. Their poverty is relative to what most people have.

3. Answers will vary. Possible answer: Poverty often is caused by more factors than simply not having enough money. Using more resources to help the poor does not mean that poverty will be reduced if the resources are poorly used.

4. Answers will vary. Students may point out the growing number of older people and the increasing costs of treatments that are able to help them live longer.

5. Answers will vary. Possible answer: Some people left the welfare program because they used up their benefits or they took jobs that did not pay well because they were afraid they would lose their benefits and have no income to live on. These people are off the welfare rolls but often still live in poverty.

## Graphing Exercise

6. An example of an acceptable graph appears at the bottom of this page.

   Answers will vary. Students may point out that households headed by a single woman are more likely to be in poverty, and a large part of these households is made up of children. The economic downturn after 2000 probably increased the share of people living in poverty. You may ask students to find out what actually happened.

## Think Critically

7. Answers will vary. Students may point out that with so many people living in poverty, government leaders found it necessary to create programs to help the poor.

8. Answers will vary. Students may point out that householders who have less education, are younger, or are from a minority group have higher poverty rates than those who are well educated, older, or white.

**Xtra!**
**Study Tools**
*econxtra.swlearning.com*

## Key Concepts

1. Explain why a pure market economy would not work well if all people were guaranteed the same income by the government.

2. Why is *poverty* a relative term?

3. Think of a person you know who you think lives in poverty. What steps could the government take to help this person escape poverty? Do you think the government should do these things? Would you be willing to pay more taxes to support this type of help?

4. Why do you think that spending for Medicare is the most rapidly growing part of the social insurance program?

5. Between 1996 and 2002 the number of welfare cases in the United States fell by more than half. Explain why this does not mean that the number of people living in poverty was also cut in half during these years.

## Graphing Exercise

6. Draw a double line graph of the percent of U.S. residents and children who were officially designated as living in poverty from 1991 through 1999, based on the data in the table to the right. As a percent, why do more children live in poverty than adults? What do you think happened to these percentages during the downturn in the U.S. economy after 2000?

**Percent of U.S. Residents and Children Living in Poverty, 1991–1999**

| Year | % of total population living in poverty | % of children living in poverty |
|------|------|------|
| 1991 | 14.2% | 21.1% |
| 1993 | 15.1% | 22.0% |
| 1995 | 13.8% | 20.2% |
| 1997 | 13.3% | 19.2% |
| 1999 | 11.6% | 16.3% |

Source: *Statistical Abstract of the United States*, 2001, p. 442.

## Think Critically

7. **English** Read *The Grapes of Wrath* by John Steinbeck or a summary of this novel. This book describes what it was like for poor people to live through the Great Depression of the 1930s. Describe why these conditions led the government to create many of the programs that help people living in poverty today.

8. **Research** Find current data concerning poverty as it relates to education, race, and age by searching the Internet for the *Statistical Abstract of the United States*. Look for useful data in a table titled "Families Below Poverty Level by Selected Characteristics" in the *Income, Expenditures, and Wealth* section of the *Abstract*. What relationships can you draw see in these data?

**90** CHAPTER 3 U.S. Private and Public Sectors

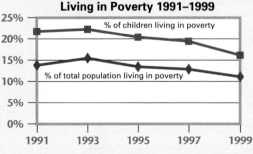

**Percent of U.S. Residents and Children Living in Poverty 1991–1999**

% of children living in poverty

% of total population living in poverty

## Visualizing the Answer—Graphing Exercise

6. The answer includes a graph. Students' graphs should look similar to the one shown here. An Excel spreadsheet containing this graph, along with supporting data, is available on the Instructor's Resource CD.

# CONNECT to *History*

## The Commerce Clause

In September, 1786, at a meeting held in Annapolis, Maryland, delegates from five states met to discuss the problems of interstate commerce. Realizing that the problems were beyond their power to resolve, the Virginia delegation and Alexander Hamilton called for a general convention to be held in Philadelphia the next year. When the convention met on May 25, it was with the purpose of revising the Articles of Confederation. The delegates decided to abandon the Articles and write a new plan of government. By September 17, the 55 delegates representing 12 of the 13 states had drafted the U.S. Constitution. Although inspired by economic circumstances, the U.S. Constitution is not just an economic document. Even so, the Constitution contains the basis of the country's economic success.

Much of the federal government's regulatory power comes from Article 1, Section 8, the Commerce Clause, of the U.S. Constitution. This section states that Congress shall have the power to "regulate commerce with foreign nations, and among the several states, and with Indian tribes." The first major case involving the Commerce Clause was *Gibbons v. Ogden.* In its decision the U.S. Supreme Court, led by Chief Justice John Marshall, established the government's right to regulate interstate commerce. However, Marshall didn't stop there. He used the case as an opportunity to expand the power of the federal government by broadening the definition of commerce. Reading the phrase "to regulate commerce ... among the several states," Marshall rejected the notion that "commerce" meant only the transportation of goods across state lines for sale. In his opinion, the term "commerce" came to include nearly every commercial activity that sooner or later will include the transportation of persons, things, services or power across state lines. This opinion was confirmed by subsequent Court rulings.

The 1887 Interstate Commerce Act, which created the Interstate Commerce Commission (ICC), and the Sherman Antitrust Act (1890) were the federal government's first major use of the Commerce Clause as the authority for its regulation of the economy. This introduced the Progressive Era of the early twentieth century, which saw the government increase its regulatory power with the Hepburn Act (1906), the Mann-Elkins Act (1910), and the creation of the Federal Trade Commission (1914). The Commerce Clause has been used as justification to expand government into many aspects of the national life and economy. For example, it has been used to justify laws prohibiting child labor, to regulate business-labor relations, to create a federal minimum wage, and to prosecute gangsters.

The Commerce Clause has been the subject of more Supreme Court cases between 1789 and 1950 than any other Constitutional clause. The Court's actions have made it an important, if not *the most* important, source of government power over the economy. President Ronald Reagan tried to roll back some of that power in the 1980s, when he attempted to abolish the Interstate Commerce Commission (ICC). He argued that deregulation had made the agency unnecessary. Congress refused to go along. Today the power of the federal government to regulate any business activity that even remotely affects interstate commerce seems well established.

### THINK CRITICALLY

Read and analyze the Fifth Amendment and the rest of the Commerce Clause of the U.S. Constitution. What parts of these affect the U.S. economic system and how?

---

## CONNECT to *History*

### FOCUS

Explain to the students that the thousands of laws and regulations that shape our economy get their authority from a few words in our Constitution, as shaped by the U.S. Supreme Court. While the founding fathers could not have imagined the size and complexity of today's economy, their efforts provided a foundation for laws and regulations needed for modern commerce.

### TEACH

Instruct students to read the **Connect to History** feature and answer the question.

### ASSESS

Use the question at the bottom of the page to assess the students' understanding of this feature. Provide students with a copy of the text of the Fifth Amendment and the Commerce Clause.

### Answers to Think Critically

The Fifth Amendment affects the economic system in its affirmation of private property rights ("nor shall private property be taken for public use, without just compensation"). The Commerce Clause of the U.S. Constitution (Article 1, Section 8) affects the economic system through the passages that start with the following phrases: (1) The Congress shall have Power To lay and collect Taxes... (2) To borrow Money on the credit of the United States; (3) To regulate Commerce with foreign Nations... (4) To coin Money... (5) To promote the Progress of Science and useful Arts...

---

### Bibliography

Hall, Kermit L., ed. *The Oxford Companion to the Supreme Court of the United States.* New York: Oxford University Press, 1992.

Lieberman, Jethro K. *Companion to the Constitution: How the Supreme Court Has Ruled on Issues from Abortion to Zoning.* Los Angles: University of California Press, 1999.

McEachern, William A. *Economics: A Contemporary Introduction,* 6th ed. Mason, Ohio: South-Western, 2003.

Puth, Robert C. *American Economic History.* New York: The Dryden Press, Harcourt Brace Jovanovich College Publishers, 1988.

## Consider

Ask students to revisit the questions they were asked to consider at the beginning of the chapter. Remind students that they should be able to answer all of the questions after studying Chapter 3.

- Why did households go from self-sufficiency to relying on markets? See page 62—Evolution of the Household.

- How did firms evolve to take advantage of large-scale production? See page 63—Evolution of the Firm.

- Why do countries trade? See page 65—International Trade.

- If the "invisible hand" of competitive markets is so great, why do governments get into the act? See page 71—Market Competition and Natural Monopolies.

- Why are some people poor even in the world's most productive economy? See page 83—Why Household Incomes Differ.

## Exam *View*

Use **Exam***View* to assess student learning.

- Create a chapter test using questions from the existing test bank.

- Add your own questions to the existing test bank.

- Generate multiple forms of a chapter test.

## Study Skills

Offer the following study skills suggestions for students as they review this chapter.

- Outline the chapter.
- Review key terms.
- Review Checkpoints.
- Work in pairs to quiz each other.
- Use Xtra! Study Tools for each lesson.

Xtra! **Quiz Prep**

Direct students to the online quiz preparation for Chapter 3 at **econxtra.swlearning.com**.

---

# ③ Chapter Assessment

## Summary

 **3.1** *The U.S. Private Sector*

**a** There are four groups of decision makers in the U.S. economy: *households, firms, government,* and *the rest of the world.*

**b** Firms expanded their importance in the economy during the Industrial Revolution. By gathering factors of production into one location, businesses are able to create a more efficient *division of labor.*

*Xtra! Quiz Prep*
*econxtra.swlearning.com*

**c** Decisions made by the rest of the world affect the consumption and production of U.S. households. The United States buys goods from other nations that have lower opportunity costs of production and sells goods that have lower opportunity costs to U.S. producers.

**3.2** *Regulating the Private Sector*

**a** The private sector of the U.S. economy would not run smoothly without government regulation. Economic rules created and enforced by the government set standards for quality and weights and measures, and protect property rights and consumer safety.

**b** The federal government promotes competition in the market and limits monopoly power through enforcing *antitrust laws* and regulating *natural monopolies.*

**c** The government promotes economic growth and stability through *fiscal* and *monetary policies.* Fiscal policy uses taxes and public spending to influence economic conditions. Monetary policy adjusts the amount of money in the economy to influence interest rates, borrowing, spending, and production.

**3.3** *Public Goods and Externalities*

**a** All goods can be classified as *private goods, public goods, quasi-public goods,* or *open-access goods.*

**b** Public goods are nonrival and nonexclusive. If a public good is used by one person that does not prevent another from benefiting from using it.

**c** Quasi-public goods are nonrival but exclusive. The use of a public park by one person does not prevent others from enjoying it, too, unless it is very crowded. The government, however, may impose a fee to enter the park, which makes it exclusive for those who choose to pay.

**d** Open-access goods are rival but nonexclusive. If you collect seashells at the beach, the shells you gather cannot be collected by others, but you are free to collect as many as you can find.

**e** *Negative externalities* are costs of production that are imposed on people who are neither the producer nor the consumer of the product.

**3.4** *Providing a Safety Net*

**a** In a pure market economy, people would receive income in proportion to the value of their contribution to production. Individuals unable to work could fall into poverty and starve. The U.S. government provides social services for those who otherwise might live in poverty.

**b** The official poverty rate in the United States declined in most years since the government began to measure poverty. Poverty is most common among households headed by single mothers.

**c** The government has established many programs to help specific groups of people. Among these are *social insurance programs, income-assistance programs, the earned-income credit for federal income tax,* and *in-kind transfers.*

**d** The nation's *welfare programs* were reformed in 1996, when the Temporary Assistance for Needy Families Program was created.

**92** **CHAPTER 3** U.S. Private and Public Sectors

---

 **3.2** *Assessment*

### Think Critically

| Year | Spending | Revenue | Difference |
|------|----------|---------|------------|
| 1996 | 1,560 | 1,453 | **–107** |
| 1997 | 1,601 | 1,579 | **–22** |
| 1998 | 1,652 | 1,722 | **70** |
| 1999 | 1,702 | 1,828 | **126** |
| 2000 | 1,789 | 2,025 | **236** |
| 2001 | 1,863 | 1,991 | **128** |
| 2002 | 2,012 | 1,853 | **–159** |

Continued from page 73.

6. The completed table should look similar to this. A greater federal debt will increase the amount of government funds that must be allocated to pay interest on the debt. This could reduce the amount of funds allocated to other government programs in the future.

7. Because of the break-up of AT&T and the growth in the number of cellular telephone companies, there is more competition in the communications industry. Consumers now have many choices in telephone services, so there is less need to regulate the firm's prices.

# Review Economic Terms

Choose the term that best fits the definition. On a separate sheet of paper, write the letter of the answer. Some terms will not be used.

_____ 1. The satisfaction received from consumption

_____ 2. Laws that prohibit anticompetitive behavior and promote competition

_____ 3. Legal claims that guarantee an owner the right to use a good or resource exclusively or to charge others for its use

_____ 4. The federal government's use of taxing and public spending to influence the national economy

_____ 5. The Federal Reserve System's attempts to control the money supply to influence the national economy

_____ 6. One firm that can serve an entire market at a lower per-unit cost than can two or more firms

_____ 7. A good with two features: (1) the amount consumed by one person is unavailable to others and (2) nonpayers can easily be excluded

_____ 8. A good that, once produced, is available for all to consume, but the producer cannot easily exclude nonpayers

_____ 9. A good that is rival in consumption but exclusion is costly

_____ 10. The most important economic decision maker, consisting of all those who live under one roof.

a. **antitrust laws**

b. **firm**

c. **fiscal policy**

d. **household**

e. **income-assistance programs**

f. **Industrial Revolution**

g. **median income**

h. **monetary policy**

i. **natural monopoly**

j. **negative externalities**

k. **open-access good**

l. **positive externalities**

m. **private good**

n. **private property rights**

o. **public good**

p. **quasi-public good**

q. **social insurance**

r. **utility**

# Review Economic Concepts

11. All those who live under one roof are considered to be part of the same _?_.

12. Firms organizing production in large, centrally powered factories did all of the following except

   a. promote a more efficient division of labor.

   b. reduce transportation costs.

   c. reduce consumer reliance on trade.

   d. enable the use of specialized machines.

13. In the evolution of the firm, the _?_ was the bridge between the self-sufficient farm household and the modern firm.

14. Which of the following is correct?

   a. Revenue = Profit − Cost of Production

   b. Profit = Cost of Production − Revenue

   c. Profit = Revenue − Cost of Production

   d. Cost of Production = Revenue + Profit

15. **True or False** International trade occurs because the opportunity cost of producing specific goods differs among countries.

16. A(n) _?_ awards an inventor the exclusive right to produce a good for a specific period of time.

## Review Economic Terms

1. r. utility
2. a. antitrust laws
3. n. private property rights
4. c. fiscal policy
5. h. monetary policy
6. i. natural monopoly
7. m. private good
8. o. public good
9. k. open-access good
10. d. household

## Review Economic Concepts

11. household
12. c. reduce consumer reliance on trade
13. cottage industry system
14. c. Profit = Revenue − Cost of Production
15. True
16. patent

## Review Economic Concepts

17. b. By maximizing profits, monopolies ultimately benefit social welfare.

18. d. set prices for distributing natural gas to homes

19. False. Public goods can be used by all consumers, but they do impose an economic cost.

20. Quasi-public goods

21. True

22. c. an increase in the amount of money in the economy

23. b. income-assistance program

## Apply Economic Concepts

24. Exclusive and Rival: E. Your television set; H. Your uncle's fishing boat

Exclusive and Nonrival: D. Picnic tables in a national park; F. An unused public tennis court

Nonexclusive and Rival: B. Shrimp in the ocean; G. Seashells on a beach

Nonexclusive and Nonrival: A. Police protection

---

17. Which of the following is *not* a true statement about monopolies?

    a. Monopolies try to charge higher prices than would result through competition.

    b. By maximizing profits, monopolies ultimately benefit social welfare.

    c. Antitrust laws attempt to reduce monopoly power.

    d. Monopolies may try to influence the political system in order to protect and enhance their power.

18. Which of the following is the *best* example of the government regulating a *natural monopoly*?

    a. emission standards for automobiles

    b. required testing and approval to market new drugs

    c. rules for selling new shares of corporate stock

    d. set prices for distributing natural gas to homes

19. **True or False** *Public goods* can be used by all consumers and have no economic cost.

20. _?_ are nonrival but exclusive, such as cable TV signals.

21. **True or False** *Poverty* is a relative term that has different meanings at different times and in different locations.

22. Which of the following would be an example of an attempt by the Federal Reserve System to stimulate the economy through *monetary policy*?

    a. a 5 percent reduction in federal income tax rates

    b. an increase in government spending for road construction

    c. an increase in the amount of money in the economy

    d. an increase in the tax on goods purchased from other countries

23. Another term for *welfare* is

    a. job-placement program.

    b. income-assistance program.

    c. social insurance program.

    d. tax rebate program.

# Apply Economic Concepts

24. **Identifying Goods** Copy the figure below. Place the letter of each of the following in the correct box of the figure.

    A. Police protection

    B. Shrimp in the ocean

    C. Public vaccinations

    D. Picnic tables in a national park

    E. Your television set

    F. An unused public tennis court

    G. Seashells on a beach

    H. Your uncle's fishing boat

|  | Rival | Nonrival |
|---|---|---|
| **Exclusive** |  |  |
| **Nonexclusive** |  |  |

|  | Rival | Nonrival |
|---|---|---|
| **Exclusive** | EH | DF |
| **Nonexclusive** | BG | AC |

25. **Examples in Your Community** Make a second copy of the figure in Exercise 24. Place two examples of each type of good that exist in your community in the appropriate boxes. Use examples that are different from those in exercise 24.

26. **Your Share of the Cost** In 2001, the cost of national defense for the United States was just over $300 billion. At that time, there were approximately 280 million people living in this country. Calculate the cost of national defense per person in 2001. Explain why it is difficult to charge individuals their "fair share" of the cost of national defense.

27. **Sharpen Your Life Skills—Use Mathematics to Draw Conclusions** In 2001, the value of total production in the United States was $10.442 trillion. In that year, the federal government spent or transferred $1.864 trillion. What percent of the nation's total income flowed through federal government in 2001? The table below shows the experience over a longer period. On a separate sheet, fill in the right-hand column. What has been the trend over the period? What do these data show about the importance of federal government spending and transfers in the economy in these years? Considering recent history, would you expect this trend to continue in the future?

**Government Spending and Transfers as a Percent of Total Production, 1980–2000**
**Values in Billions of Dollars**

| Year | Federal Government Spending and Transfers | Value of Total Production | Federal Spending & Transfers as a Percent of Total Production |
|------|---------------------------------|------------------|-----------------------------------------|
| 1980 | $   812.0 | $2,795.8 | _____ |
| 1990 | $1,778.0 | $5,803.2 | _____ |
| 2000 | $3,012.4 | $9,963.1 | _____ |

Source: *Statistical Abstract of the United States,* 2002, p. 305.

*e*-con @pps    econxtra.swlearning.com

28. Access **EconData Online** at econxtra. swlearning.com. Click on "Microeconomics," "Income Distribution and Poverty," and then "Civilian Unemployment Rate." After analyz-ing the information available, write a paragraph to explain why the unemployment rate is inversely related to the growth rate of real GDP over the business cycle.

## Apply Economic Concepts

25. Answers will vary. Students should demonstrate an understanding of each type of good through their choices.

26. Answers will vary. Possible answer: The cost of national defense per person in 2001 was roughly $1,071. Possible answer: Charging a "fair share" for any public good is virtually impossible because of unequal income (ability to pay) and the complex tax system that would be necessary to impose such charges.

27. Answers will vary. Possible answer: Students may point out that the trend in federal government spending between 1980 and 2000 was a slow growth in the 1980s, followed by a significant decline in the 1990s. It is doubtful that this trend will continue, considering the increase in federal spending for homeland security and the war on terror, both here and abroad. The expansion of Medicare to include some prescription drug costs also will add to federal spending.

*e*-con @pps

28. Answers will vary. Possible answer: When there is an increase in the growth rate of the real GDP in the business cycle, there is a corresponding increase in the number in the labor force. The growth rate of real GDP and the number in the labor force are therefore directly related. Because the number in the labor force is, by definition, indirectly related to the unemployment rate, the growth rate of the real GDP also is indirectly related.

*Chapter Assessment*    **95**

# Investing In Your Future

## The Situation

Aleesha Johnson had a big decision to make. For years, animals had fascinated her. She devoured every television program, book, and movie she could find about the animal kingdom. Now, the metropolitan area's new zoo was opening, and there were jobs available for interns. However, the new zoo was some 12 miles away, located even outside the ring of suburbs that surrounded the city. Aleesha's guidance counselor said that with her excellent grades and level of interest, she was a shoe-in for one of the positions. Unfortunately, however, Aleesha had no way to get there. Of course, she just turned 16 and, if her parents would co-sign a loan for her as they promised, she could buy a car and drive to work. Her parents made it clear that she would need to make the car payments and pay for the maintenance and insurance herself.

## The Decision

Thanks to a long-term grant received by the zoo, an intern's pay was $1 an hour above the minimum wage. That would probably pay for her car expenses, but Aleesha wasn't sure. She was convinced, however, that with working 20 hours a week as an intern after school and on some weekends, she would lose her positions on the school's track and basketball teams. Her honor-roll GPA also might suffer. Then there was her social life, which was just starting to get interesting.... Still, the intern position appealed to her. It wasn't just animals that Aleesha had observed and learned about in her life. She recognized that some of the really successful people in the world took special steps early in their lives to follow their dreams. The internship would be a chance to learn the nuts and bolts of how a state-of-the-art zoo operates. Who knew what doors would open as a result?

## PREPARE

This project can be completed in the classroom or as an outside assignment. The activities call for students to work in teams, but students working alone can complete the activities successfully. If you organize the class into teams, consider identifying specific roles for team members such as recorder, discussion leader, researcher, etc.

Although the project has five components, you might consider using only the first four if time is limited. Teaching suggestions are offered for all six steps.

## TEACH

### The Situation

This initial problem statement has been created as an example of the types of decisions the students will be making in their lives at this time. The implications of these decisions are far reaching and should be made through a process that involves long-range planning to identify and commit to long-range goals. Point out that economic analysis can and should be used to help Aleesha make a decision about this opportunity.

### The Decision

Remind students that commitment to goals involves choosing between competing opportunities and then applying their scarce resources (generally time and money) toward achieving a desired goal. Explain that Aleesha serves as a good example because she has identified a rewarding individual goal at an early age. Economics-related techniques of budgeting, detailed research, and comparative analysis all are valuable tools she can use to help achieve her goals.

## RESEARCH

Encourage students to use Internet and library resources to learn more about the costs of operating a vehicle, the level of the minimum wage, and the earning potential for careers related to zoos. Consider inviting the school librarian or media specialist to offer suggestions on how to research these areas.

## Activities

**Divide into teams or work individually, as directed by your teacher, to perform the following tasks.**

Apply the steps in the following decision-making process to Aleesha's situation:

**1.** *Define the problem.* Define Aleesha's problem in a way that will allow a clear solution.

**2.** *Identify the choices.* List the various alternatives among which she must choose.

**3.** *Evaluate the pluses and minuses of each choice.* Carefully weigh the value Aleesha puts on each alternative and the opportunity cost(s) for each.

**4.** *Make a choice.* Which course of action should she choose? Be prepared to present and defend your choice in class.

**5.** *Provide "action" steps that are appropriate to the decision.* Make sure these are realistic and timely to ensure the necessary actions are taken to resolve the problem.

**6.** *Critique the decision.* The class will assist in the review and evaluation of your plan of action. In real life, you should review not only the decision and its result, but also the process by which you make it. Set a time to initiate reviewing the decision or identify an event that would trigger its review.

## Research

Research for the information you need to effectively make the decision, such as how much it would cost to operate her car, the level of the minimum wage, the career opportunities for zookeepers, etc.

## Present

Arrive at a decision. Then prepare a presentation for the class on the six steps you took to achieve this decision. Be ready for questions and criticisms.

*Project 1*    **97**

### Activities

The six steps in the decision-making process provide a road map for students as they complete this project. Point out that students also can use these steps in making decisions in their own lives.

**Step 1:** Answers should reflect how to allocate scarce resources.

**Step 2:** The choices should be spelled out in sufficient detail so as to be clearly understood. Encourage students to think "outside the box." Do not discourage any choice.

**Step 3:** The evaluations should involve "pushing the numbers" by budgeting both time and money. This type of detailed planning helps develop the insight into the situation that promotes the student's emotional attachment with the ultimate decision and then learning from it.

**Step 4:** Students should recognize that the basic choice for Aleesha is whether to take her life in her own hands or to wait to see what happens.

**Step 5:** Make sure students produce detailed plans that follow through on Aleesha's choice. These should involve not only the resources to be committed but also a timetable for execution of the steps of the plan and means of evaluating ongoing success or failure.

**Step 6:** Students should recognize that it is important to set up periodic reviews at appropriate points such as applying to college, graduating from high school, choosing a college major, etc. Remind students that not every decision they make will be the correct one. All decisions can be valuable if they help refine their decision-making ability and enhance the chances of making a better decision next time.

---

**ASSESS**

**Presentation** Consider using a rubric or evaluation form for student presentations. Make sure you share the rubric or form with students before they start working on the project. A sample evaluation form appears on the Instructor's Resource CD. The categories to be evaluated include: **Content** (organization, specific content, and accurate information); **Presentation Skills** (eye contact, grammar and pronunciation, volume, and pitch); **Audiovisual Aids** (appropriate content, style, and spelling); and **Handouts** (appropriate content; grammar, punctuation, and spelling).

### *National Content Standards in Economics*

The following NCEE Standards are addressed in Unit 2:

| | |
|---|---|
| **Standard 1** | Scarcity |
| **Standard 2** | Marginal Cost/Benefit |
| **Standard 4** | Role of Incentives |
| **Standard 5** | Gain from Trade |
| **Standard 6** | Specialization and Trade |
| **Standard 7** | Markets—Price and Quantity Determination |
| **Standard 8** | Role of Price in the Market System |
| **Standard 9** | Role of Competition |
| **Standard 10** | Role of Economic Institutions |
| **Standard 13** | Role of Resources in Determining Income |
| **Standard 14** | Profit and the Entrepreneur |
| **Standard 16** | Role of Government |
| **Standard 17** | Using Cost/Benefit Analysis to Evaluate Government Programs |

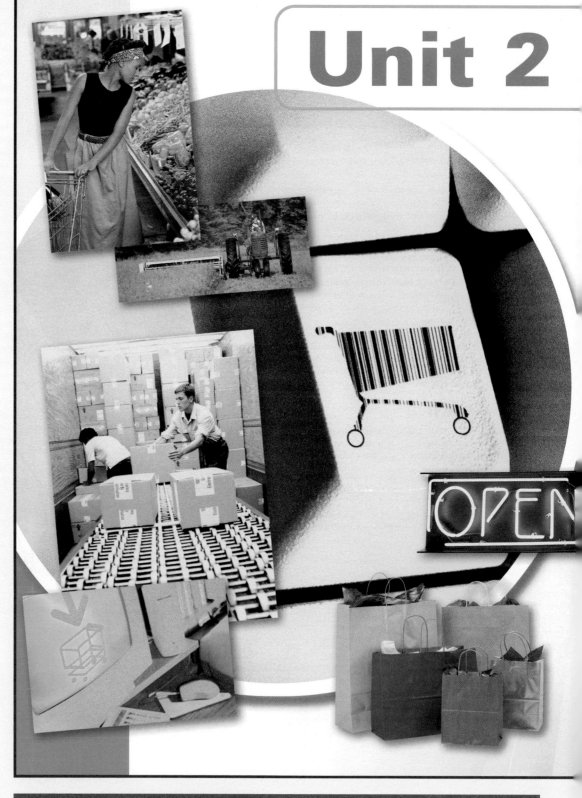

# Unit 2

| **Pacing Guide** | One-Semester Days of Study | Two-Semesters Days of Study | Block Schedule 90-Minute Blocks |
|---|---|---|---|
| **UNIT 2: THE MARKET ECONOMY** | | | |
| Chapter 4: Demand | | | |
| **4.1** The Demand Curve | 2 | 3 | 2 |
| **4.2** Elasticity of Demand | 1 | 3 | 1 |
| **4.3** Changes in Demand | 2 | 4 | 2 |
| Chapter 5: Supply | | | |
| **5.1** The Supply Curve | 2 | 3 | 2 |
| **5.2** Shifts of the Supply Curve | 1 | 3 | 1 |
| **5.3** Production and Cost | 2 | 4 | 2 |
| Chapter 6: Market Forces | | | |
| **6.1** Price, Quantity, and Market Equilibrium | 2 | 3 | 2 |
| **6.2** Shifts of Demand and Supply Curves | 1 | 3 | 1 |
| **6.3** Market Efficiency and Gains from Exchange | 2 | 4 | 2 |

# The Market Economy

In 1962, Sam Walton opened his first store in Rogers, Arkansas, with a sign that read: "Wal-Mart Discount City. We sell for less." Wal-Mart now sells more than any other retailer in the world because prices there are the lowest around. As a consumer, you understand why people buy more at a lower price. Wal-Mart, for example, sells on average more than 20,000 pairs of shoes *an hour*. Buyers love a bargain, but sellers must make sure their prices cover the costs of supplying the goods. Differences between the desires of buyers and sellers are sorted out by competitive pressures in a market economy.

99

## Unit 2 Overview

In Unit 2, students are introduced to the concepts of demand and supply. They then apply these concepts to study the effects of market forces on demand and supply curves. Next, they explore the various market structures. Finally, they explore government regulation of the private sector through antitrust regulation.

## Group Activity

Organize students into small groups and ask them to discuss the passage that appears on this page. Instruct students to discuss some of the differences betweens the desires of buyers and sellers. Ask a representative of each group to briefly summarize the discussion.

## Think Critically Through Visuals

Direct students to study the images on the opposite page and think about how each image relates to the market economy. Ask them to work with a partner to create their own collage. Display the finished collages in the classroom.

## Contemporary Economics Video

From the *Contemporary Economics* video, the segment entitled "Record Technology" can be used to introduce or recap the concepts presented in Unit 2. A Video Discussion Guide is available on the Instructor's Resource CD.

## Look Beyond the Classroom

The forces of demand and supply interact to determine the equilibrium price that is paid for goods and services in every community. Have students identify a product they often purchase and visit several local retail outlets to compare the prices charged for this good or service. Direct students to record the prices and calculate differences as a percent of the lowest price. Instruct students to write a summary of their findings and to explain why price differences exist for the product they investigated. If the product is the same at each store, how can some stores charge more than others? Are the retail outlets selling anything beyond the actual product? How valuable is convenience?

| Pacing Guide *continued* | One-Semester Days of Study | Two-Semesters Days of Study | Block Schedule 90-Minute Blocks |
|---|---|---|---|
| **UNIT 2: THE MARKET ECONOMY** | | | |
| Chapter 7: Market Structures | | | |
| **7.1** Perfect Competition and Monopoly | 2 | 3 | 2 |
| **7.2** Monopolistic Competition and Oligopoly | 1 | 3 | 1 |
| **7.3** Antitrust, Economic Regulation, and Competition | 2 | 4 | 2 |

## Chapter Overview

**LESSON 4.1** *The Demand Curve:* This lesson explains the law of demand and introduces the concepts of demand schedule and demand curve.

**LESSON 4.2** *Elasticity of Demand:* In addition to introducing the concept, this lesson explains the relevance of elasticity of demand. Factors that influence elasticity of demand are also discussed.

**LESSON 4.3** *Changes in Demand:* This lesson identifies the determinants of demand and explains how a change in each will affect the demand curve. The distinction between money price and time price is addressed.

### Consider

Ask students to consider the questions posed on this page as they study Chapter 4. After studying all three lessons, students should be able to answer the questions. The content related to each question can be found on the pages indicated below.

- Why are newspapers sold in vending machines that allow you to take more than one copy? See page 103—Diminishing Marginal Utility.

- How much do you eat when you can eat all you want? See page 103—Diminishing Marginal Utility.

- What cures spring fever? See page 103—Diminishing Marginal Utility.

- What economic principle is behind the saying, "Been there, done that"? See page 103—Diminishing Marginal Utility

- Why do higher cigarette taxes cut smoking by teenagers more than by other age groups? See page 115— An Application: Teenage Smoking.

### POINT YOUR BROWSER

Remind students that they can find additional resources for this chapter at **econxtra.swlearning.com**.

- Xtra! Study Tools
- Net Bookmarks
- Xtra! Quiz Prep
- econ@pps
- Ask the Xpert!
- Graphing Workshop

# 4 Demand

### Consider

Why are newspapers sold in vending machines that allow you to take more than one copy?

How much do you eat when you can eat all you want?

What cures spring fever?

What economic principle is behind the saying, "Been there, done that"?

Why do higher cigarette taxes cut smoking by teenagers more than by other age groups?

© Getty Images/PhotoDisc

### POINT YOUR BROWSER

*econxtra.swlearning.com*

---

### Teaching Resources for Chapter 4

- Activities and Projects Masters
- Spanish Resources
- Econ Connection Interactive Tutorial CD
- **Exam***View*® CD
- Workbook Teacher's Edition
- Chapter Test Teacher's Edition
- NCEE Standards and Correlation
- Personal Finance Guide

- Social Studies Skills Review
- Instructor's Resource CD
  - PowerPoint Presentation
  - Lesson Plans
  - Video Discussion Guide
- **econxtra.swlearning.com**

# 4.1 The Demand Curve

## Objectives

> Explain the law of demand.

> Interpret a demand schedule and a demand curve.

## Overview

The primary building blocks of a market economy are demand and supply. Consumers demand goods and services that maximize their utility, and producers supply goods and services that maximize their profit. As a consumer in the United States' market economy, you demand all kinds of goods and services. You buy less of a good when its price increases and more of it when the price decreases. This section draws on your experience as a consumer to help you understand demand, particularly the demand curve.

## Key Terms

demand

law of demand

marginal utility

law of diminishing marginal utility

demand curve

quantity demanded

individual demand

market demand

To introduce this lesson, bring an item of food to class that students are likely to desire, such as a giant chocolate chip cookie or bag of chips. By show-of-hands, ask students whether they would be willing to buy the item for $5. Make a chart of their responses on the board. Then make the same offer at progressively lower prices keeping track in a table of the number of items that would be sold at each price. Students will realize that at lower prices, the number of items purchased will be greater. The table that demonstrates their buying decisions is a demand schedule that can be converted into a demand curve. A presentation of the law of demand can be based on this demand schedule. It can also be used to demonstrate diminishing marginal utility.

### Objectives

Remind students to read the lesson objectives to help focus their attention before reading the lesson.

### Key Terms

Direct students to write each key term on a separate index card. Then write the matching definition and page reference on the back of the appropriate card. Encourage students to use the cards to study for quizzes and tests.

## [ In the News ]

### ● Demand Rising Slowly For Digital HDTV

Officials at the most recent National Association of Broadcasters Exposition (NAB) say that sales of digital, high-definition television (HDTV) sets are slowly gaining momentum. Little by little, consumers are learning about the new technology's clearer picture and better sound quality versus standard analog TV. However, there are a few obstacles to demand for this product. One obstacle is the limited availability of digital programming for HDTVs. Another is the relatively high cost. Although a small number of consumers will buy the newest technologies regardless of price, most people have learned that if you wait a bit for new electronics products, the prices will come down. For example, big-screen TVs started out selling at $4,000 to $5,000, and then a year later sold for less than half that price. A 27-inch set that cost $700 to $800 five years ago sells for $180 today. Because they know the law of demand, consumer electronics marketers plan their strategies to sell to the early adopters at a higher price, and then begin lowering the price to increase the quantity demanded.

### Think About It

Why do most consumers wait to purchase new consumer electronics products such as HDTVs?

◀ ▮ ▶

**101**

## [ In the News ]

Instruct students to read the passage and write down their answers. Point out that their answers might change after they finish studying Lesson 4.1.

### Answers to Think About It

Answers will vary. Possible answer: Consumers wait to purchase because the price will go down.

### Visual Presentation

Use the PowerPoint presentation on the Instructor's Resource CD as an adjunct to your lecture. The presentation also can be used for review.

---

### National Content Standards in Economics

A complete list of the NCEE Standards appears on pages xxiv–xxv of this book. The following standards are addressed in Lesson 4.1.

Standard 1: Scarcity

Standard 2: Marginal Cost/Benefit

Standard 4: Role of Incentives

Standard 7: Markets—Price and Quantity Determination

Standard 8: Role of Price in Market System

## Law of Demand

Hold up a cell phone and ask your students why most young people want to own and use a cell phone of their own. Then tell them to imagine that they own a cell phone but they are required to pay a set per-minute price for the time they spend talking. Ask them to make a table that shows how many minutes they believe they would talk on their phone each month if they were required to pay 20 cents per minute. Progressively lower the per-minute charge until it is only half-a-cent per minute. Point out that they have created a demand schedule for their demand for cell phone use, and that as the price declined they were willing to purchase (demand) more minutes. This example demonstrates the law of demand.

### *Think Critically Through Visuals*

Direct students to focus their attention on the photograph on this page. Ask for a volunteer to answer the question posed in the caption.

### Answer

Answers will vary. Possible answer: The quantity of dogs demanded would decrease since the price/cost of owning a dog has increased.

---

**demand**
A relation showing the quantities of a good that consumers are willing and able to buy at various prices per period, other things constant

**law of demand**
The quantity of a good demanded per period relates inversely to its price, other things constant

---

# Law of Demand

How many 12-inch pizzas will people buy each week if the price is $12? What if the price is $9? What if it's $6? The answers reveal the relationship between the price of pizza and the quantity purchased. Such a relationship is called the *demand* for pizza.

**Demand** indicates how much of a product consumers are both *willing* and *able* to buy at each possible price during a given period, other things remaining constant. Because demand pertains to a specific period—a day, a week, a month—you should think of demand as the desired *rate of purchase per time period* at each possible price. Also, notice the emphasis on *willing* and *able*. You may be *able* to buy a rock concert ticket for $30 because you can afford one. However you may not be *willing* to buy one if the performers do not interest you.

This relation between the price and the quantity demanded is an economic law. The **law of demand** says that quantity demanded varies inversely with price, other things constant. Thus, the higher the price, the smaller the quantity demanded. The lower the price, the greater the quantity demanded.

## Demand, Wants, and Needs

Consumer demand and consumer wants are not the same thing. You know that wants are unlimited. You may want a new Mercedes-Benz SL500 roadster convertible, but the $95,000 price tag is likely beyond your budget. (The quantity you demand at that price is zero.) Nor is demand the same as need. You may have outgrown your winter coat and so need a new one. But if the price is $200, you may decide your old coat will do for now. If the price drops enough—say, to $100—then you become both willing and able to buy a new coat.

## Substitution Effect

What explains the law of demand? Why, for example, is more of a product demanded when the price falls? The explanation begins with unlimited wants meeting scarce resources. Many goods and services are capable of satisfying your particular wants. For example, you can satisfy your hunger by eating pizza, tacos, burgers, chicken, sandwiches, salads, or hundreds of other items. Similarly, you can satisfy your desire for warmth in the winter with warm clothing, a home-heating system, a trip to Hawaii, or in other ways.

Some ways of satisfying your wants will be more appealing than others. A trip to Hawaii is more fun than wearing warm clothing. In a world without scarcity, everything would be free, so you would always choose the most attractive alternative. Scarcity, however, is a reality, and the degree of scarcity of one good relative to another helps determine each good's relative price.

Notice that the definition of *demand* includes the other-things-constant assumption. (A Latin phrase you may

© Getty Images/PhotoDisc

**The law of demand applies even to personal choices, such as whether or not to own a pet. For example, after New York City passed an anti-dog-litter law, owners had to follow their dogs around the city with scoopers and plastic bags. The law raised the cost, or price, of owning a dog. What do you think happened to the quantity of dogs demanded as a result of this law, and why?**

**102**   **CHAPTER 4**  Demand

---

*Outside Resources*

**Direct mail** Direct mail advertising sales fliers can be used to demonstrate the law of demand. Retailers often reduce prices to try to increase the quantities of products they are able to sell, possibly eliminating inventories of outdated products. Fliers also can be used as a jumping-off place to discuss diminishing marginal utility. Ask students why prices for products are most often high when they are first introduced to the market and lower as more people come to own them over time.

hear for "other things constant" is *ceteris paribus*.) Among the "other things" assumed to remain constant are the prices of other goods. For example, if the price of pizza declines while other prices remain constant, pizza becomes relatively cheaper. Consumers are more *willing* to purchase pizza when its relative price falls. People tend to substitute pizza for other goods. This is called the *substitution effect of a price change*. On the other hand, an increase in the price of pizza, other things constant, causes consumers to substitute other goods for the now higher-priced pizza, thus reducing their quantity demanded.

Remember that *the change in the relative price—the price of one good relative to the prices of other goods—causes the substitution effect*. If all prices changed by the same percentage, there would be no change in relative prices and no substitution effect.

### Income Effect

A fall in the price of a product increases the quantity demanded for a second reason. What if you take home $36 a week from a Saturday job, and your money income is $36 per week. Your *money income* is simply the number of dollars you receive per period, in this case $36 per week. Suppose you spend all your income on pizza, buying four a week at $9 each. What if the price drops to $6? At that price you can now afford six pizzas a week.

Your money income remains at $36 per week, but the decrease in the price has increased your *real income*—that is, your income measured in terms of how many goods and services it can buy. The price reduction, other things constant, increases the purchasing power of your income, thereby increasing your *ability* to buy pizza and, indirectly, other goods. The quantity of pizza you demand likely will increase because of this *income effect of a price change*. You may not increase your quantity demanded to six pizzas, but you can now afford six. If you purchase five pizzas a week when the price drops to $6, you would have $6 left to buy other goods.

Thus, the income effect of a lower price increases your real income and

thereby increases your *ability* to purchase pizza and other goods. Because of the income effect of a price decrease, other things constant, consumers typically increase their quantity demanded as the price decreases. Conversely, an increase in the price of pizza, other things constant, reduces real income, thereby reducing the ability to purchase pizza. Because of the income effect of a price increase, consumers typically reduce their quantity demanded as the price increases.

### Diminishing Marginal Utility

After a long day of school, studies, and sports, you are starved, and so you visit a local pizzeria. That first slice tastes great and puts a serious dent in your hunger. The second is not quite as good as the first. A third is just fair. You don't even consider a fourth slice. The satisfaction you derive from an additional unit of a product is called your **marginal utility**. For example, the additional satisfaction you get from a second slice of pizza is your marginal utility of that slice.

The marginal utility you derive from each additional slice of pizza declines as your consumption increases. Your experience with pizza reflects the **law of diminishing marginal utility**. This law states that the more of a good an individual consumes per period, other things constant, the smaller the marginal utility of each additional unit consumed.

Diminishing marginal utility is a feature of all consumption. A second foot-long submarine sandwich at one meal would probably yield little or no marginal utility. You might still enjoy a second movie on Friday night, but a third one is probably too much to take.

Consumers make purchases to increase their satisfaction, or utility. In deciding what to buy, people make rough estimates about the marginal utility, or marginal benefit, they expect from the good or service. Based on this marginal benefit, people then decide how much they are willing and able to pay. Because of diminishing marginal

**Ask the Xpert!**
*econxtra.swlearning.com*

*Why do consumers buy less of an item when its price rises?*

**marginal utility**
The change in total utility resulting in a one-unit change in consumption of a good

**law of diminishing marginal utility**
The more of a good a person consumes per period, the smaller the increase in total utility from consuming one more unit, other things constant

### Law of Demand

The income and substitution effects can be presented as the direct consequence of the *ceteris paribus* assumption. Holding other prices constant while changing the price of the good whose demand curve is being constructed results in a change in its opportunity cost because its relative price has changed. Holding money income constant while changing the price of the good results in a change in the purchasing power or real income of the person whose demand curve is being constructed.

You should use examples to discuss how the demand for a particular good changes when the price of a substitute changes. Students may have trouble with this concept, but if concrete examples are used, it becomes clear. For example if Pepsi is on sale, those who normally purchase Coca-Cola may switch to Pepsi, causing the demand for Coca-Cola to decline (substitutes).

**Ask the Xpert!**

Direct students to **econxtra.swlearning.com** to hear an expert answer the question, "Why do consumers buy less of an item when its price rises?"

---

### ENRICH

Tell students that they have been put in charge of setting the price for tickets to a concert given by a musical group that is currently popular among young people. Although they want to collect as much money from sales as possible, they also want to fill an 8,000-seat auditorium because the performance is going to be filmed. It is important that there are no empty seats for publicity reasons. Ask them to explain how they would set the price for tickets and how this demonstrates the law of demand.

## Law of Demand

Consider using an example from the school cafeteria menu to illustrate the law of demand.

### Think Critically Through Visuals

Direct students to focus their attention on the photograph this page. Ask for a volunteer to answer the question posed in the caption.

### Answer

The law of diminishing marginal utility applied to pizza states that each additional piece of pizza you consume offers less and less satisfaction.

Direct students to **econxtra.swlearning.com**. Remind them to click on the link for Lesson 4.1 to find the appropriate link for the **NET Bookmark** on this page. Students' answers should demonstrate an understanding of the law of diminishing marginal utility. For example, they might point out that the pricing of the ticket package ("five days for the price of two") or hotel rooms ("fourth night free") show that Universal understands this law.

### TEAM WORK

Organize students into groups of four or five. Set a time limit for each of the three components of this activity. Remind students that their group is to come up with the list of products such as lattes, slices of pizza, etc. After the list is established, individuals are to work independently as they apply the law of diminishing marginal utility to each item. The activity should end with group members sharing their answers with each other.

### ✓ CHECKPOINT

Invite a student to answer the checkpoint that appears on page 105.

### Answer

The law of demand says that quantity demanded varies inversely with price, other things constant.

---

### NETBookmark

For an example of pricing that uses the law of diminishing marginal utility, visit the Universal Studios Orlando web site. Access this web site through econxtra.swlearning.com. Click on "Tickets and Vacations." Which offer or offers demonstrate the theme park's understanding of the law of diminishing marginal utility? Explain your answer.

**econxtra.swlearning.com**

---

utility, you would not be willing to pay as much for a second slice of pizza as for the first. This is why it takes a decrease in price for you to increase your quantity demanded.

Suppose pizza sells for $2 a slice. How many slices will you buy? You will increase consumption as long as the marginal benefit you expect from another slice exceeds the price. You stop buying more when your expected marginal benefit is less than the price. Simply put, you aren't willing to pay $2 for something that's worth less to you.

What if the price of pizza drops from $2 to $1 a slice? You buy more if the marginal benefit of another slice exceeds $1. *The law of diminishing marginal utility helps explain why people buy more when the price decreases.*

Diminishing marginal utility has wide applications. Restaurants depend on the law of diminishing marginal utility when they offer all-you-can-eat specials—and no doggie bags. The deal is all you can eat now, not all you can eat now and for as long as the doggie bag holds out.

After a long winter, that first warm day of spring is something special and is the cause of "spring fever." The fever is cured by many warm days like the first. By the time August rolls around, most people get much less marginal utility from yet another warm day.

© Getty Images/PhotoDisc

**How does the law of diminishing marginal utility apply to pizza consumption?**

---

### Group Activity

Tell the members of each group that they are assigned to set the price for candy bars sold by a local drugstore and that the price must maximize the store's total revenue from candy sales. To do this, they must determine how many candy bars members of their group would purchase each week at different prices you provide, such as $1, $.80, $.60, and so on. By multiplying these quantities by the prices, they can calculate the store's potential revenue. What would happen to the store's sales and revenue if a neighboring bakery had a sale on cupcakes and cookies? How does this activity demonstrate the substitution effect?

For some goods, the drop in marginal utility after the first unit is dramatic. For example, a second copy of the same daily newspaper would likely provide you with no marginal utility. In fact, the design of newspaper vending machines relies on the fact that you will not want to take more than one.

More generally, the expressions "Been there, done that" and "Same old, same old" convey the idea that, for many activities, things start to get old after the first time. Your marginal utility, or marginal benefit, declines.

**CHECKPOINT**
Explain the law of demand in your own words.

# Demand Schedule and Demand Curve

Demand can be expressed as a *demand schedule* and as a *demand curve*. Panel (a) of Figure 4.1 shows a hypothetical demand schedule for pizza. When you

describe demand, you must specify the units being measured and the period considered. In this example, the price is for a 12-inch regular pizza and the period is a week. The schedule lists possible prices, along with the quantity demanded at each price.

At a price of $15, for example, consumers demand 8 million pizzas per week. As you can see, the lower the price the greater the quantity demanded, other things constant. If the

## TEAM WORK

In small groups, brainstorm a list of products that most members of the group consume in a typical week. Then, working on your own, apply the law of diminishing marginal utility to each item. How many units of each item would you consume before the marginal benefit is less than the price of each unit? Compare your answers with those of other group members.

**The Graphing Workshop**
econxtra.swlearning.com

**Demand Schedule and Demand Curve for Pizza**                    **Figure 4.1**

**(a) Demand schedule**

Market demand curve *D* shows the quantity of pizza demanded, at various prices, by all consumers.

| | Price per Pizza | Quantity Demanded per Week (millions) |
|---|---|---|
| a | $15 | 8 |
| b | 12 | 14 |
| c | 9 | 20 |
| d | 6 | 26 |
| e | 3 | 32 |

**(b) Demand curve**

## Extend the Content

The distinction between *demand* and *quantity demanded* is difficult for some students to grasp. Such confusion can be reduced by continually reminding students that *demand is a curve* that depicts the relationship between price and quantity demanded assuming that all other factors (which may affect demand) are held constant. *Quantity demanded is a point on the curve* that shows the quantity demanded at a given price.

## TEACH

### Demand Schedule and Demand Curve

Share the following demand schedule with students.

| Demand for Servings of French Fries at Mel's Diner | |
|---|---|
| Price | Quantity Demanded per Day |
| $1.25 | 50 |
| 1.00 | 75 |
| .75 | 150 |
| .50 | 350 |

Discuss how it demonstrates the law of demand and can be used to construct a demand curve for sales of french fries at Mel's Diner. Ask students to discuss what might happen to sales of other food items at Mel's Diner if he charged only $.50 for french fries. (Answer: People might demand fewer of them as they substituted french fries for the alternative food items.)

**See It**

Use **Figure 4.1—Demand Schedule and Demand Curve for Pizza** to illustrate the law of demand. Direct students to the Graphing Workshop for Chapter 4 at **econxtra.swlearning.com**. Instruct students to click on **See It: Demand and Shifts in Demand** to view the graph and listen to an explanation. Tell students they should view the first part of this workshop, which explains the demand schedule and demand curve.

---

### THE WALL STREET JOURNAL

**Reading It Right**

Invite a student to explain the relevance of the statement from *The Wall Street Journal* that apears on page 106.

**Answer**

Answers will vary. Possible answer: As price falls quantity demanded increases because consumers have more real income to work with.

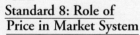
● **Reading It Right** What's the relevance of the following statement from *The Wall Street Journal:* "Few things are as gratifying to American consumers as finding a good bargain. . . . The psychology of this is simple: It feels good to pay less."

**demand curve**

A curve or line showing the quantities of a particular good demanded at various prices during a given time period, other things constant

**quantity demanded**

The amount demanded at a particular price

price drops as low as $3, consumers demand 32 million per week. As the price falls, consumers substitute pizza for other goods. As the price falls, the real income of consumers increases, causing them to increase the quantity of pizza they demand. As pizza consumption increases, the marginal utility of pizza declines, so quantity demanded will increase only if the price falls.

The *demand schedule* in panel (a) of Figure 4.1 appears as a **demand curve** in panel (b), with price on the vertical axis and the quantity demanded per week on the horizontal axis. Each combination of price and quantity listed in the demand schedule in the left panel becomes a point in the right panel. Point *a*, for example, indicates that if the price is $15, consumers demand 8 million pizzas per week. These points connect to form the demand curve for

pizza, labeled *D.* Note that some demand curves are straight lines and some are curved lines, but all of them are called demand *curves.*

The demand curve slopes downward, reflecting the *law of demand*—that is, price and quantity demanded are inversely, or negatively, related, other things constant. Several things are assumed to remain constant along the demand curve, including the prices of other goods. Thus, along the demand curve for pizza, the price of pizza changes *relative to the prices of other goods.* The demand curve shows the effect of a change in the *relative price* of pizza—that is, relative to other prices, which do not change.

### Demand Versus Quantity Demanded

Be sure to distinguish between *demand* and *quantity demanded.* An individual point on the demand curve shows the **quantity demanded** at a particular price. For example, point *b* on the demand curve in Figure 4.1 indicates that 14 million pizzas are demanded when the price is $12. The *demand* for pizza is not a specific quantity, but the *entire relation* between price and quantity

## Ethics in Action

**Demand Can Be Deadly** Misjudging demand can have an enormous effect on a company's sales or profits, but it can have more devastating, even tragic, effects as well. On a quiet Sunday morning in Bangladesh, at least 30 women and children were killed and hundreds more injured in a stampede, as thousands of poor people scrambled for clothes being handed out as charity. The clothes were being distributed by a businessman in conjunction with the Islamic Eid Al-Fitr festival. The Associated Press reported that the stampede happened outside an abandoned jute mill in a village in northern Bangladesh. Those in charge woefully under-

estimated the response to the news of the giveaway—they failed to predict what the demand for the clothing would be at a price of $0. Consequently, they were totally unprepared for the more than 10,000 people who showed up to get the free clothes. Two men in charge of distributing the clothes were arrested for possible negligence.

### Think Critically

Analyze this situation. Do you think the two men, attempting to be charitable, should be punished for underestimating the demand and not preparing for the crowds? Why or why not?

**106**     **CHAPTER 4**   Demand

demanded. This relation is represented by the demand schedule or the demand curve. To recap, quantity demanded is represented by one point on the demand curve or schedule, whereas demand is represented by the entire demand curve or schedule.

### Individual Demand and Market Demand

It is useful to distinguish between **individual demand**, which is the demand of an individual consumer, and **market demand**, which sums the individual demands of all consumers in the market. *The market demand curve shows the total quantity demanded per period by all consumers at various prices.*

In most markets, there are many consumers, sometimes millions. To give you some feel for how individual demand curves sum to the market demand curve, assume that there are only three consumers in the market for pizza: Hector, Brianna, and Chris.

Figure 4.2 shows how three individual demand curves are added together to get the market demand curve. When the price of pizzas is $8, for example, Hector demands two pizzas a week, Brianna demands one, and Chris demands none. The market demand at a price of $8 is therefore three pizzas. At a price of $4, Hector demands three per week, Brianna two, and Chris one, for a market demand of six. Panel (d) sums across each individual's demand curve to arrive at the market demand curve.

*The market demand curve is simply the sum of the individual demand curves for all consumers in the market.* Unless otherwise noted, this book will focus on market demand.

**individual demand**
The demand of an individual consumer

**market demand**
The sum of the individual demands of all consumers in the market

 **CHECKPOINT**
What do a demand schedule and demand curve show?

**Role of Price in Market System: Market Demand for Pizzas**

**Figure 4.2**

Prices send signals and provide incentives to buyers. When demand changes, market prices adjust, affecting buyers' incentives. For example, at a price of $8 per pizza, Hector demands 2 per week, Brianna demands 1, and Chris demands none. Market demand at a price of $8 is 2 + 1 + 0 = 3 pizzas per week. At a lower price of $4, Hector demands 3, Brianna demands 2, and Chris demands 1. Market demand at a price of $4 is 6 pizzas. The market demand curve D is the horizontal sum of individual demand curves $d_H$, $d_B$, and $d_C$.

Assign Lesson 4.1 from the Contemporary Economics Workbook.

### e-con @pps

Encourage students to apply their knowledge of concepts presented in this lesson as they explore economic news stories, policy debates, and data available at **econxtra.swlearning.com**. A sampling of the titles for this lesson appears below.

**Econ News**
- Broadband Market Growth Narrows
- Cold Comfort: Heating Oil Aid
- European Airlines: Too Many for Their Own Good?
- GB: Great Bargains
- Government and Cigarette Manufacturers Butt Heads
- Happy Holidays for Retailers
- Hard Drive to Increase Computer Sales; Prices Lowest in Memory
- Health Maintenance Organizations Fail to Maintain Health Benefits
- Higher Health Costs: Who Pays?
- House Prices Go Through the Roof
- State Try to Trump Video Poker Machine owners
- Upscale Hotels' Concern: Sleeping with the Enemy

### ASSESS

Assign all or part of Lesson 4.1 Assessment on page 108 as homework or an in-class activity.

### Xtra! Study Tools

Direct students to the online study tools for Lesson 4.1 at **econxtra.swlearning.com**.

### CLOSE

**Revisit** the In the News feature on the first page of the lesson.

**Review** the objectives for Lesson 4.1. Students should be able to:
- Explain the law of demand.
- Interpret a demand schedule and demand curve.

### RETEACH

Ask students to construct a demand schedule for the number of times they would visit a beach, amusement park, or other popular location during an entire summer. Instruct them to include different logical prices. Amusement park tickets might be priced at $18, $15, $12, and so on. Ask them to discuss how their schedules demonstrate diminishing marginal utility. What would happen to their demand schedules if they accepted a summer job that paid $100 per week? They would have more money to spend but less time to spend it.

## Key Concepts

1. Answers will vary. Students may point out that most of the students who want to own a sports car are not able to afford one. When nothing is purchased there is no demand.

2. Answers will vary. Students may point out that many consumers would substitute the relatively less-expensive burgers for the relatively more-expensive burgers.

3. Answers will vary. Students may point out that at the lower price more people could afford to purchase tickets than at the higher price. In effect, their real income increased.

4. Answers will vary. Students may point out that the second taco is worth less to Joe than the first because he will not pay $1.50 to buy it. This shows that the utility he receives from tacos diminishes as he receives more of them within a particular period of time.

5. Answers will vary. Students may point out that demand is the entire relationship between the price of tickets and the quantity demanded, while the quantity demanded is the specific relationship between a price of $8 and the average number of tickets purchased (285) at that price.

6. Answers will vary. Students may point out that per day market demand for school lunches is made up of all meals that would be purchased by students and teachers at every possible price.

## Graphing Exercise

7. Answers will vary. Students may point out that the demand curve shows that people are only willing to purchase more pairs of shoes at lower prices which means that they must receive less utility from extra pairs as they buy more. See the visual at the bottom of this page.

## Think Critically

8. Answers will vary. Students may point out that many customers will substitute shoes from the competing store because of their lower price.

9. Answers will vary. Students may point out that the first television sets were quite expensive. Although many people wanted to own one, they often were not able to afford a television set.

---

Xtra!
**Study Tools**
*econxtra.swlearning.com*

## Key Concepts

1. Many students would like to own an expensive sports car. Is this considered demand? Why or why not?

2. Why would demand for one fast food restaurant's hamburgers grow if the price of the hamburgers at the fast food restaurant across the street increased by $0.50?

3. How would the *income effect of a price change* be demonstrated by a $10 reduction in the price of tickets to a concert that resulted in a sell-out crowd?

4. Joe is willing to pay $1.50 for one taco after basketball practice but chooses not to purchase a second taco for the same price. How does this illustrate the *law of diminishing marginal utility*?

5. On Saturday nights, lots of people attend movies at the State Theater. The number who attend depends at least in part on the price of tickets. At the current price of $8 per ticket, an average of 285 tickets are sold each Saturday night. What is the *demand* and what is the *quantity demanded* in this example?

6. What is the market demand per day for lunches in the cafeteria at your school?

## Graphing Exercise

7. The owners of a local shoe store surveyed their customers to determine how many pairs of running shoes they would buy each month at different prices. The results of the survey appear in the demand schedule below. Use these data to construct a demand curve for running shoes. Explain how your graph demonstrates the law of diminishing marginal utility.

**Demand for Running Shoes**

| Price | Quantity Demanded |
|-------|-------------------|
| $70   | 40                |
| $60   | 50                |
| $50   | 60                |
| $40   | 70                |
| $30   | 80                |

## Think Critically

8. **Marketing**  Nancy is the sales manager of the shoe store. The owner has told her that she must set a price that allows the store to sell at least 50 pairs of running shoes next month. What price should she set? If another local store has a big sale and lowers its price for running shoes by 25 percent, will Nancy's employer reach the sales goal? Why or why not?

9. **History**  When television sets first became available to consumers in the late 1940s, many people wanted one. Still, very few sets were sold at first. Explain why people's desire to own televisions did not result in a great demand for this product.

---

**Demand for Running Shoes**

A scatter/line graph titled "Demand for Running Shoes" with Price (y-axis, $0.00 to $100.00) and Quantity (x-axis, 0 to 100), labeled "Quantity Demanded," showing a downward-sloping demand curve.

## Visualizing the Answer— Graphing Exercise

7. The answer includes a graph. Students' graphs should look similar to the one shown here. An Excel spreadsheet containing this graph along with supporting data is available on the Instructor's Resource CD.

## Objectives

> Compute the elasticity of demand, and explain its relevance.

> Discuss the factors that influence elasticity of demand.

## Overview

Knowing the law of demand is useful, but a demand curve can provide even more information. It can tell how sensitive quantity demanded is to a change in price. For example, a fast-food restaurant would like to know what will happen to its total revenue if it introduces a dollar menu. The law of demand indicates that a lower price increases quantity demanded, but by how much? A firm's success or failure depends on how much it knows about the demand for its product. This section measures how sensitive quantity demanded is to a change in price.

## Key Terms

**elasticity of demand**

**total revenue**

### FOCUS

**4.2    Elasticity of Demand**

To introduce elasticity, hold up a piece of elastic and a piece of rope of equal lengths. Explain that the rope represents the amount of a cancer-curing drug that will be sold and the elastic represents the amount of a brand of laundry soap that will be sold.
Have two students pull on the ends of the rope and point out that the length does not change. Have two other students pull on the ends of the elastic and point out that the length changes. The rope is inelastic and so is the amount of the drug sold. The quantity demanded does not change if the price is lower—people who need the drug will buy the amount they need regardless of price.
The fact that the length changes shows that the other band is elastic. The same is true of the demand for the laundry soap. People will demand more at lower prices as they substitute this brand for more expensive ones.

#### Objectives

Remind students to read the lesson objectives to help focus their attention before reading the lesson.

#### Key Terms

Direct students use each of the key terms in a separate sentence or short paragraph that helps demonstrate the meaning of the term.

#### [ In the News ]

Instruct students to read the passage and write down their answers. Point out that their answers might change after they finish studying Lesson 4.2.

#### Answers to Think About It

Answers will vary. Possible answer: It depends on the elasticity of demand for avocados. If the demand for avocados is elastic, meaning demand changes with price, there will be an increase in revenue. If the demand for avocados is inelastic, there will be a decrease in revenue.

#### Visual Presentation

Use the PowerPoint presentation on the Instructor's Resource CD as an adjunct to your lecture. The presentation also can be used for review.

## [ In the News ]

### ● Super Bowl of Avocados

Super Bowl Sunday is the biggest single day of avocado consumption in the United States, thanks to the serving up of bowls and bowls of the zesty green dip known as guacamole. More than 40 million pounds of avocados are smashed, mashed, whipped, and eaten with blue and white corn chips, flour tortillas, tacos, and chunks of bread during Super Bowl festivities, according to the California Avocado Commission. California growers sold a record 400 million pounds of avocados for a very profitable $398 million (nearly a dollar a pound) in the 2001–2002 season. California is home to 86 percent of the nation's crop, and 46 percent of the state's avocados come from San Diego County. The more than 6,000 avocado growers see a huge potential for growth in the market. Until fairly recently, the avocado, originally from southern Mexico, was either unknown or considered odd and exotic in most of the United States. But the expanding popularity of California cuisine and the spread of Hispanic populations over the years have opened a host of new markets for avocado growers. Today only 18 percent of the population, mainly in the Southwest, eat nearly half of all avocados sold in the United States. Avocados are consumed in nearly 45 percent of U.S. homes, but in the West the portion is 80 percent.

### Think About It

What if in the following season the growers reduce the price of avocados from approximately $1 a pound to 90 cents a pound? Based on the expanding market predictions, would the total revenue probably be less than $398 million, remain the same, or be more than $398 million? Explain your answer.

◀ ▮ ▶

**109**

### National Content Standards in Economics

**NCEE**

A complete list of the NCEE Standards appears on pages xxiv–xxv of this book. The following standards are addressed in Lesson 4.2.

Standard 4: Role of Incentives

Standard 7: Markets—Price and Quantity Determination

Standard 8: Role of Price in Market System

## Computing the Elasticity of Demand

Continue with the example about Mel's Diner. Tell students that Mel decided to lower the price of his fries from $1.00 per serving to $.75 (a 25 percent change in price). As a result, the quantity of fries demanded increased from 75 to 150 servings per day (a 100 percent change in the quantity demanded). In this example, a 25 percent change in price resulted in a 100 percent change in the quantity demanded. The elasticity of demand for Mel's fries in this example is 4 (100 ÷ 25 = 4). A value of 4 indicates demand that is quite elastic. Products that are easily substituted, such as fries, almost always have demand that is elastic. An alternative example is demand for insulin that is used to control diabetes. If the price of a month's supply of this medication decreased from $20 to $15 (a 25 percent decrease) the amount purchased might increase by only 1.0 percent because people who need this drug are already buying it at a price of $20. The new lower price would not cause them to buy more or cause other people who do not need the drug to purchase it. In this case the elasticity of demand would be 0.04 (0.01 ÷ 0. 25 = 0.04). A value of 0.04 indicates demand that is very inelastic. Products that are necessary and cannot be substituted, such as insulin, almost always have demand that is inelastic.

See It

Use **Figure 4.3—The Demand for Pizza** to illustrate elasticity of demand. Direct students to the Graphing Workshop for Chapter 4 at **econxtra.swlearning.com**. Instruct students to click on **See It: Demand, Price Elasticity, and Total Revenue** to view the graph and listen to an explanation.

# Computing the Elasticity of Demand

Figure 4.3 shows the downward sloping demand curve for pizza developed earlier. As you can see, if the price of pizzas falls from $12 to $9, the quantity demanded increases from 14 million to 20 million. Is such a response in quantity demanded a little or a lot? The demand elasticity measures consumer responsiveness to the price change. *Elasticity* is another word for *responsiveness*. Specifically, the **elasticity of demand** measures the percentage change in quantity demanded divided by the percentage change in price, or

Elasticity of demand =

$$\frac{\text{Percentage change in quantity demanded}}{\text{Percentage change in price}}$$

What's the demand elasticity when the price of pizza falls from $12 to $9? The percentage increase in quantity demanded is the change in quantity demanded, 6 million, divided by 14 million. So, quantity demanded

**elasticity of demand**
Measures how responsive quantity demanded is to a price change; the percentage change in quantity demanded divided by the percentage change in price

increases by 43 percent. The percentage change in price is the price change of $3 divided by $12, which is 25 percent.

The elasticity of demand is the percentage increase in quantity demanded, 43 percent, divided by the percentage decrease in price, 25 percent, which equals 1.7.

## Elasticity Values

Does an elasticity of 1.7 indicate that consumers are sensitive to the price change? To offer some perspective, economists sort elasticity into three general categories. If the percentage change in quantity demanded exceeds the percentage change in price, the resulting elasticity exceeds 1.0. Such a demand is said to be *elastic*, meaning that a percentage change in price will result in a larger percentage change in the quantity demanded. Thus quantity demanded is considered relatively *responsive* to a change in price. The demand for pizza is elastic when the price falls from $12 to $9.

If the percentage change in quantity demanded just equals the percentage change in price, the resulting elasticity is 1.0, and this demand is called *unit-elastic*. Finally, if the percentage change in quantity demanded is less than the percentage change in price, the resulting

**The Demand for Pizza**
*econxtra.swlearning.com*

**Figure 4.3**

If the price falls from $12 to $9, the quantity of pizza demanded increases from 14 million to 20 million per week.

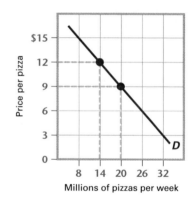

---

### Outside Resources

**Mackinac Center** The Mackinac Center for Public Policy is an organization that supports economics education. It provides current estimates of the elasticity of demand for various products at its web site located at www.educationreport.org/1247. Ask students to investigate this site and find products that have either elastic or inelastic demand. Ask them to explain reasons for the types of demand for the products they choose.

elasticity lies between 0 and 1.0, and this demand is said to be *inelastic*.

In summary, *demand is elastic if greater than 1.0, unit elastic if equal to 1.0, and inelastic if between 0 and 1.0.* Also, the measure of the price elasticity of demand usually is different at different points on a demand curve. Demand is almost always more elastic at higher prices and less elastic at lower prices. This is particularly true when the demand curve is a straight line that slopes down from left to right.

Elasticity expresses a relationship between two amounts: the percentage change in price and the resulting percentage change in quantity demanded. Because the focus is on the percentage change, you need not be concerned with how output or price is measured. For example, suppose the good in question is apples. It makes no difference in the elasticity formula whether you measure apples in pounds, bushels, or even tons. All that matters is the percentage change in quantity demanded. Nor does it matter whether you measure price in U.S. dollars, Mexican pesos, French francs, or Zambian kwacha. All that matters is the percentage change in price.

## Elasticity and Total Revenue

Knowledge of elasticity is especially valuable to producers, because it indicates the effect a price change will have on how much consumers spend on this product. **Total revenue** is price multiplied by the quantity demanded at that price. What happens to total revenue when price decreases? A lower price means producers are paid less for each unit sold, which tends to decrease total revenue. However, according to the law of demand, a lower price increases quantity demanded, which tends to increase total revenue.

The impact of a lower price on total revenue can be estimated using the product's price elasticity of demand. When the elasticity is greater than 1.0, or *elastic*, reducing the price by 5 percent will cause sales to grow by more than 5 percent. Thus the total

revenue will increase. When the elasticity is equal to 1.0, or *unit elastic*, reducing the price by 5 percent will cause sales to grow by 5 percent. In this

# SPAN THE GLOBE

## We Ate All the Big Fish

"Fisherman used to go out and catch these phenomenally big fish," said a fisheries biologist in Nova Scotia. "But they cannot find them anymore. They're not there. We ate them." He adds that about 90 percent of big fish—such as giant tuna, swordfish, and Chilean sea bass—are gone from the world's oceans. In fact, at a UN summit meeting in 2002, 192 nations signed a declaration to try to restore fish to healthy levels by 2015. Chilean sea bass is a good example of what happened to the big fish. Eight to ten years ago, very few people had heard of this fish. There wasn't much demand, and it was selling at $3 or $4 a pound. After several years of word-of-mouth and magazine advertising, and strong recommendations from food critics and TV chefs, Chilean sea bass became "the hot new fish." All the publicity increased the demand, and the low price increased the quantity demanded. Suddenly, Chilean sea bass was featured on thousands of restaurant menus and sold in every supermarket. Fishermen couldn't catch enough sea bass to keep up with the rising demand, though they tried. They were overfishing and not giving the fish enough time to replenish their populations. Today, Chilean sea bass sells for $18 to $20 a pound, and is on the menu of only upscale, "trendy" restaurants. The once inexpensive, great-tasting fish is now gone from most supermarkets. At $20 per pound, the quantity demanded has decreased considerably. Unfortunately, the species also is nearly gone from our oceans.

### Think Critically

Suppose that at a price of $3 a pound, the quantity of Chilean sea bass demanded is 500,000 pounds, and at a price of $18 a pound, the quantity demanded is 100,000 pounds. At these prices and quantities, is the demand elastic, unit elastic, or inelastic?

*total revenue*
Price multiplied by the quantity demanded at that price

## Computing the Elasticity of Demand

Return to the example of Mel's decision to lower the price of his french fries. Remind students that at a price of $1.00, Mel sold 75 servings per day. His total revenue from these sales was $75 ($1.00 x 75 = $75). After he lowered the price of the fries to $.75, his sales grew to 150 servings per day. At the lower price his total revenue increased to $112.50 ($.75 x 150 = $112.50). When the price of a product with elastic demand is lowered, its total revenue will grow.

In the case of the lowered price for insulin, tell students to imagine that a drug store sold 1,000 vials per month at $20 each. The store's total revenue at that price was $20,000 ($20 x 1,000 = $20,000). When the price was lowered to $15, the quantity sold increased by 1 percent to 1,010. The store's total revenue fell to $15,150 ($15 x 1010 = $15,150). When the price of a product with inelastic demand is lowered its total revenue will fall.

### SPAN THE GLOBE

Direct students to read the short passage titled "We Ate All the Big Fish" on this page. Ask students to answer the question and provide the calculation(s) used to determine the answer.

### Answers to Think Critically

The good is inelastic because the elasticity of demand is less than 1.0. The percentage change in quantity is 80 percent (400,000 ÷ 500,000) and the percentage change in price is 500 percent ($15 ÷ $3). Elasticity of demand is 0.16; it is calculated by dividing the percentage change in quantity by the percentage change in price. (0.80 ÷ 5.00 = 0.16).

### ✓ CHECKPOINT
Invite a student to answer the checkpoint that appears on page 112.

### Answer

The elasticity of demand measures the percentage change in quantity demanded divided by the percentage change in price.

### Determinants of Demand Elasticity

To help students understand the determinants of demand elasticity, ask them to identify a popular musical group that they would be willing to pay to see. Tell them to assume that this group is going to give only one local concert before it disbands and never performs again. There are only 300 unsold tickets available for this concert. Ask them to discuss the elasticity of demand for these tickets. They should agree that the demand would be inelastic. Then ask them to change their assumptions. This time the group has contracted to perform at eight different locations within 50 miles of your school (this makes over 25,000 tickets available), and they have made public statements that they intend to perform at least this often every year for the foreseeable future. What would this do to the elasticity of demand for tickets to their concerts? Students should agree that the demand for the tickets will be much more elastic. Use these examples to lead into a discussion of factors that make demand either elastic or inelastic. When many items of a particular type are available, the demand for these items is much more likely to be elastic.

### *Think Critically Through Visuals*

Direct students to focus their attention on the photograph on this page. Ask for a volunteer to answer the question posed in the caption.

### Answer

Answers will vary. Some students may suggest that the demand for particular brands of sunglasses is elastic. When the price of one brand increases, consumers will substitute a different brand. The demand might be inelastic only if all brands of sunglasses increased in price.

---

case the total revenue will remain unchanged. When the elasticity is less than 1.0, or *inelastic*, reducing the price by 5 percent will cause the sales to grow, but by less than 5 percent. So, total revenue will fall.

Knowing a product's elasticity can help businesses when they set their prices. If demand is inelastic, producers will never willingly cut the price since doing so would reduce total revenue. The percentage increase in quantity demanded would be less than the percentage decrease in price. Why cut the price if selling more reduces total revenue?

**CHECKPOINT**
What does the elasticity of demand measure?

# Determinants of Demand Elasticity

So far you have explored the link between elasticity of demand and what happens to total revenue when the price changes. However, you have not yet considered why elasticity differs for different goods. Several characteristics influence the elasticity of demand.

## Availability of Substitutes

As noted earlier, your individual wants can be satisfied in a variety of ways. A rise in the price of pizza makes other foods relatively cheaper. If close substitutes are available, an increase in the price of pizza will prompt some consumers to switch to substitutes. But if nothing else satisfies like pizza, the quantity of pizza demanded will not decline as much. *The greater the availability of substitutes for a good and the more similar the substitutes are to the good in question, the greater that good's elasticity of demand.*

The number and similarity of substitutes depend on the definition of the good. *The more broadly a good is defined, the fewer substitutes there are and the less elastic the demand.* For example, everyone needs some sort of shoes, so the demand for shoes as a general category of product is quite inelastic. If the price of all shoes goes up 20 percent, most people will still buy shoes. If you consider one particular brand of shoes, however, the demand is sure to be elastic because there are many other brands of shoes you could buy instead. For example, if only one shoe manufacturer raises the price of its shoes by 20 percent, most consumers will substitute a different brand of shoes that have not increased in price.

Certain goods—many prescription drugs, for instance—have no close substitutes. The demand for such goods tends to be less elastic than for goods with close substitutes, such as Bayer aspirin. Much advertising is aimed at establishing in the consumer's mind the uniqueness of a particular product—an effort to convince consumers "to accept no substitutes."

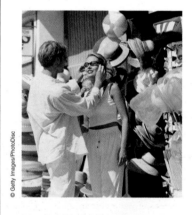

**Do you think demand for sunglasses is elastic or inelastic? Identify the determinant of demand that supports your answer.**

---

Tell students that they operate a movie theater. On average, 500 people used to purchase $8 tickets at their theater every Saturday evening. Last month, they raised their price to $9 only to see the average number of tickets sold fall to 450. Ask students to calculate the elasticity of demand for these tickets and to state whether the demand is elastic or inelastic. What happened to the total revenue as a result of the price increase? *(0.10 divided by 0.125 = 0.8, the demand is inelastic, total revenue increased from $4,000 to $4,050)*

## Share of Consumer's Budget Spent on the Good

Recall that a higher price reduces quantity demanded in part because a higher price reduces the real spending power of consumer income. A demand curve reflects both the *willingness* and *ability* to purchase a good at alternative prices. Because spending on some goods represents a large share of the consumer's budget, a change in the price of such a good has a substantial impact on the amount consumers are *able* to purchase.

An increase in the price of housing, for example, reduces consumers' ability to purchase housing. The income effect of a higher price reduces the quantity demanded. In contrast, the income effect of an increase in the price of, say, paper towels is less significant because paper towels represent such a tiny share of any budget. *The more important the item is as a share of the consumer's budget, other things constant, the greater is the income effect of a change in price, so the more price elastic is the demand for the item.* This explains why the quantity of housing demanded is more responsive to a given percentage change in price than is the quantity of paper towels demanded.

## A Matter of Time

Consumers can substitute lower-priced goods for higher-priced goods, but finding substitutes usually takes time. For example, between 1973 and 1974, the OPEC oil cartel raised the price of oil sharply. The result was a 45-percent increase in the price of gasoline, but the quantity demanded decreased only 8 percent. As more time passed, however, people purchased smaller cars and made greater use of public transportation. Because the price of oil used to generate electricity and to heat homes increased as well, people bought more energy-efficient appliances and insulated their homes better. As a result, the change in the amount of oil demanded was greater over time as consumers adjusted to the price hike.

The longer the adjustment period, the greater the consumers' ability to substitute relatively higher-priced products with lower-priced substitutes. Thus, the longer the period of adjustment, the more responsive the change in quantity demanded is to a given change in price.

Figure 4.4 demonstrates how demand for gasoline becomes more elastic over time. Given an initial price of $1.00 a gallon, let $D_w$ be the demand curve one week after a price change; $D_m$, one

© Getty Images/PhotoDisc

© Getty Images/PhotoDisc

Compare the income effect of an increase in the price of a car to the income effect of an increase in the price of a grocery store item. For which product is demand more price elastic?

Lesson 4.2 • *Elasticity of Demand* **113**

## Determinants of Demand Elasticity

Ask students to imagine that they are about to start a major test such as the SAT or ACT and they realize that they do not have a No. 2 pencil. Only one person has an extra pencil, but he refuses to sell it for less than $5. Ask students if they would pay $5. What does this show about time and the elasticity of demand for products?

### Think Critically Through Visuals

Direct students to focus their attention on **Figure 4.4—Demand Becomes More Elastic Over Time**. Point out the labels on the three demand curves.

### Reading It Right

Invite a student to explain the relevance of the statement from *The Wall Street Journal* that appears on this page.

### Answer

Answers will vary. Possible answer: By maintaining close contact with their customers, Dell can change their responsiveness to price increases and price decreases. This helps them effectively run a successful business by being aware of consumer reactions to price.

### Think Critically Through Visuals

Direct students to focus their attention on **Figure 4.5—Selected Elasticities of Demand** on page 115. Point out that in the long run, elasticity for demand is greater for all the products shown.

### ✓ CHECKPOINT

Invite a student to answer the checkpoint that appears on page 115.

### Answer

The determinants of demand elasticity are: the availability of substitutes, the share of the consumer's budget spent of the good, and the time frame in which the consumer has to work.

---

**Demand Becomes More Elastic Over Time**   Figure 4.4

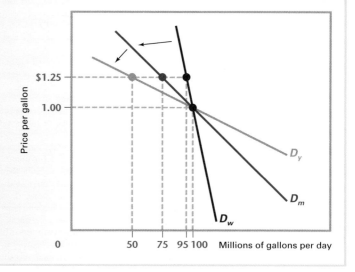

$D_w$ is the demand curve one week after a price increase from $1.00 to $1.25. Along this curve, quantity demanded per day falls from 100 to 95 million gallons. One month after the price increase, quantity demanded has fallen to 75 million gallons along $D_m$. One year after the price increase, quantity demanded has fallen to 50 million gallons along $D_y$. At any given price, $D_y$ is more elastic than $D_m$, which is more elastic than $D_w$.

---

month after; and $D_y$, one year after. Suppose the price increases to $1.25. The more time consumers have to respond to the price increase, the greater the reduction in quantity demanded. The demand curve $D_w$ shows that one week after the price increase, the quantity demanded has not declined much—in this case, from 100 to 95 million gallons per day. The demand curve $D_m$ indicates a reduction to 75 million gallons per day after one month, and demand curve $D_y$ shows a reduction to 50 million gallons per day after one year.

### Some Elasticity Estimates

Let's look at some estimates of the elasticity of demand for particular goods and services. As noted earlier, the substitution

### THE WALL STREET JOURNAL

● **Reading It Right**  What's the relevance of the following statement from *The Wall Street Journal*: "By selling directly via the Internet, catalogs, and the telephone, Dell maintains direct contact with customers and can regularly gauge their sensitivity to price changes."

of lower-priced goods for a good whose price has just increased often takes time. Thus, when estimating elasticity, economists often distinguish between a period during which consumers have little time to adjust—call it the short run—and a period during which consumers can more fully adjust to a price change—call it the long run. Figure 4.5 provides some short-run and long-run elasticity estimates for selected products.

*The elasticity of demand is greater in the long run because consumers have more time to adjust.* For example, if the price of electricity rose today, consumers in the short run might cut back a bit on their use of electrical appliances, and those in homes with electric heat might lower the thermostat in winter. Over time, however, consumers would switch to more energy-efficient appliances and might convert from electric heat to oil or natural gas. So the demand for electricity is more elastic in the long run than in the short run, as noted in Figure 4.5. In fact, in every instance where estimates for both the short run and the long run are available, the long run is more elastic than the short run.

---

### Curriculum Connection—Literature

Author J. K. Rowling has written a series of books about the imaginary wizard Harry Potter that has sold many millions of copies in almost every nation of the world. Ask students to discuss the elasticity of demand for these books. What would happen to the number of these books sold if their price were 10 or 20 percent higher? Is demand for Harry Potter books elastic or inelastic? How do they know? Why might the publisher choose to sell the books for less as time goes by?

## Selected Elasticities of Demand

Figure 4.5

When estimating elasticity, economists distinguish between the short run (a period during which consumers have little time to adjust) and the long run (a period during which consumers can more fully adjust to a price change). The elasticity of demand is greater in the long run because consumers have more time to adjust.

| Product | Short Run | Long Run |
|---|---|---|
| Electricity (residential) | 0.1 | 1.9 |
| Air travel | 0.1 | 2.4 |
| Medical care and hospitalization | 0.3 | 0.9 |
| Gasoline | 0.4 | 1.5 |
| Movies | 0.9 | 3.7 |
| Natural gas (residential) | 1.4 | 2.1 |

**CHECKPOINT**
What are the determinants of demand elasticity?

### An Application: Teenage Smoking

As the U.S. Surgeon General warns on each pack of cigarettes, smoking cigarettes can be hazardous to your health. Researchers estimate that smoking causes more than 400,000 deaths a year in the United States—nearly 10 times the fatalities from all traffic accidents.

One way to reduce smoking is to raise the price of cigarettes through higher cigarette taxes. Economists estimate the demand elasticity for cigarettes among teenage smokers to be about 1.3, so a 10 percent increase in the price of cigarettes would reduce smoking by 13 percent. Among adult smokers, the estimated elasticity is only 0.4, or only about one-third that of teenagers.

Why are teenagers more sensitive to price changes than adults? First, recall that one of the factors affecting the elasticity of demand is the importance of the item in the consumer's budget. The share of income that a teenage smoker spends on cigarettes usually exceeds the share for adult smokers. Second, peer pressure is more influential in a young

person's decision to smoke than in an adult's decision to continue smoking. (If anything, adults face peer pressure not to smoke.) The effects of a higher price get multiplied among young smokers because a higher price reduces smoking by peers. With fewer peers smoking, there is less pressure to smoke. And third, because smoking is addictive, young people who are not yet hooked are more sensitive to price increases than are adult smokers, who are already hooked.

### NETBookmark

For more information about the dangers of smoking, The Campaign for Tobacco Free Kids maintains a web site with a page devoted to articles on the economics of tobacco policy. Access this site through econxtra.swlearning.com. Click on Tobacco Facts. According to this article, is the total number of smokers in the world increasing or decreasing? The article states that between 80,000 and 100,000 young people around the world become addicted to tobacco every day. If this trend continues, how many children alive today will die from tobacco-related disease?

*econxtra.swlearning.com*

Lesson 4.2 • *Elasticity of Demand* **115**

## Key Concepts

1. Answers will vary. Students may point out that it would have to determine the percentage decline in sales that would result from this increase in price and then divide the percentage change in sales by the 10 percent change in price.

2. There is elastic demand for running shoes at the current price.

3. The store's total revenue from running shoes would decline because the demand is elastic.

4. Answers will vary. Students may point out that there are many brands of cake mix consumers could buy. If the price of one goes up, people are likely to substitute other brands. A small percentage change in price should cause a much larger percentage change in the quantity demanded.

## Graphing Exercise

5. The price elasticity of demand is 1.20 (0.20 ÷ 0.167 = 1.20). This is elastic demand. The total revenue would decrease.

## Think Critically

6. Answers will vary. Students may point out that people who are lactose intolerant are not responsive to changes in the price of dairy products. On Easter many Christians buy eggs to color and hide for their children, regardless of the price.

7. Answers will vary. Students may point out that when there are many bakeries, it is easy for consumers to substitute one firm's products for another when prices change. Opening a bakery in such a location would not allow a new firm to raise prices without losing many customers. To do so would cause the firm's total revenue to fall.

Xtra!
Study Tools
econxtra.swlearning.com

## Key Concepts

1. What would a shoe store need to do to calculate the price elasticity of demand for the running shoes it sells if it decides to raise its prices by 10 percent?

2. If the shoe store found that the measure of elasticity for its running shoes is 1.3, is there elastic, unit elastic, or inelastic demand for this product at the current price?

3. If the shoe store increases its price for running shoes by 10 percent, what would happen to the store's total revenue from these products?

4. Why should you expect the demand for a particular brand of cake mix to be elastic?

## Graphing Exercise

5. Consider this graph for running shoes. Note that if the store's manager increases the price for running shoes from $60 to $70 (16.7%), the store's sales would fall from 50 to 40 pairs per month (20.0%). What is the elasticity of demand? Is this price elasticity of demand elastic, unit elastic, or inelastic? Will the store's total revenue increase, decrease, or remain unchanged?

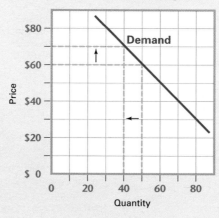

Demand Curve for Running Shoes

## Think Critically

6. **Sociology** The elasticity of demand for some products is affected by the personal values of possible customers. Consider people who practice the Hindu faith. They believe it is wrong to eat meat. In Hindu communities, the price elasticity of demand for meat products is 0.0, or completely inelastic—consumers won't buy meat no matter what happens to its price. Describe several other situations where other factors are more important to the buying decision than price.

7. **Entrepreneurship** If there are 10 bakeries in a small city, why might the price elasticity of demand for the products they supply be high? Why might this not be a good location for you to open another bakery?

**Demand for Running Shoes**

Demand

Quantity Demanded

## Visualizing the Answer— Graphing Exercise

5. Students' graphs should look similar to the one shown here. An Excel spreadsheet containing this graph along with supporting data is available on the Instructor's Resource CD.

# movers & shakers

**Julie Azuma** *President, Different Roads to Learning*

Finding appropriate toys for her autistic daughter was always a challenge for Julie Azuma. In 1995 she met that challenge by starting a business selling educational toys for learning disabled children via the Internet. Her first obstacle—she was not computer literate. With determination and courage, Azuma met the obstacle head-on, and within months her web site was established. Her company, Different Roads to Learning, received its first orders by December of that year.

Selling product via the Internet meant Azuma didn't need a storefront. This was something she originally wanted but quickly learned she couldn't afford. Selling via the Internet had its advantages, however. Azuma was able to reach potential customers throughout the world, and today 10 percent of her customers are from Canada, the United Kingdom, and Australia.

From the start, Different Roads to Learning's web site included a complete line of products. "But as soon as the site went up, we received requests for a printed catalog, too." Azuma responded by printing 3,000 catalogs for customers who requested them. It was a good decision. Although catalog requests typically came from parents, "we found that parents were bringing the catalog to their child's school, asking their school districts to purchase many of the items." That resulted in larger orders for more products. Today Azuma prints 50,000 to 100,000 catalogs a year.

Azuma prides herself on serving her customers the best she can. She's quick to advise parents on what materials may be appropriate for their child, as well as what toys may not be a good fit. "We try to ship all of our orders on the day we receive them if at all possible," she explains. "Parents of autistic children need to have their materials as soon as possible."

In response to the increased demand for advice on helping an autistic child to learn, in 1999 Azuma started a publishing company, DRL Books, Inc. Her first book, a comprehensive handbook for parents of autistic children, sold more than she projected. She began to look for more books that met her high standards of assisting parents and teachers. By 2002, the company had published eight books with sales of $175,000. While the first books she published were extremely popular, not every book has met Azuma's expectations. "I thought that all of our books would have the same appeal, but there are a lot of autism books available now."

In 1996, Different Roads to Learning's first year in business, gross sales were $8,000. By 2000, sales exceeded expenses and the company became profitable. Gross sales in 2002 exceeded $1,000,000, and in 2003 sales were expected to increase even more. In addition to increasing sales, Azuma also has learned how to make her business more profitable. Azuma's efforts to help parents of autistic children have earned her New York State's prestigious Martin Luther King Award for community service.

## SOURCE READING
Although the first books published by DRL Books, Inc. exceeded sales goals, the books she published later were not as popular. Azuma said, "I thought that all of our books would have the same appeal, but there are a lot of autism books available now." What influenced the elasticity of demand for the company's later books?

## ENTREPRENEURS IN ACTION
If Azuma's first book sold for $22 and 875 copies were sold, what was her total revenue? What would likely happen to Azuma's total revenue if she decreased the price of the book to $18? If demand is inelastic, would Azuma's decision to lower the price be a good one? Why or why not?

---

# movers & shakers

## FOCUS

Remind students that Julie Azuma's business has been in existence since 1995. By now her success has been recognized by other people, some of whom have started their own businesses to compete with hers. This has created a wider selection of products from which consumers may choose. Ask students to discuss what this has probably done to the elasticity of demand for her products. What steps could Azuma take to maintain a relatively inelastic demand for the products she sells? Why is any business that is successful likely to face more elastic demand for its products as time passes? Success invites competition. Competition gives consumers a wider variety of products from which to choose. Therefore, the elasticity of demand for these products will increase over time.

## TEACH

Instruct students to read the **Movers and Shakers** about Julie Azuma. Point out that some students may find it helpful to read the article, read the questions at the bottom of the page, and then reread the article.

## ASSESS

Use the questions in Source Reading and Entrepreneurs in Action at the bottom of the profile to assess the students' understanding of this **Movers and Shakers** feature.

### Answers to Source Reading
The availability of substitutes influenced the elasticity of demand for the company's later books.

### Answers to Entrepreneurs in Action
Azuma's revenue was $19,250 (875 x $22 = $19,250). If Azuma decided to lower the price of the first book, her total revenue would probably have been less. This is because the demand for the first book was inelastic because there were no substitutes for the book at that time.

# FOCUS

## 4.3 Changes in Demand

Ask students to identify a clothing style they once thought was attractive, but that is now out of style. How much would they have been willing to pay for these garments when they were popular? How much would they be willing to pay for them now? Ask students to discuss how this change in demand came about. Did people just get bored with the style or was it replaced with a new style that was clearly better? Why does the fashion industry come out with new styles every year? In 2003, the jeans industry was having a particularly difficult time because the sales of designer jeans had fallen by more than 50 percent since the late 1990s. The demand for designer jeans had become much more elastic.

## Objectives

Remind students to read the lesson objectives to help focus their attention before reading the lesson.

## Key Terms

Direct students to create a database using the key terms for this section. The database fields should include terms, definitions, and page numbers. Point out that the process of keying the data is an effective way to study the key terms.

## [ In the News ]

Instruct students to read the passage and write down their answers. Point out that their answers might change after they finish studying Lesson 4.3.

## Answers to Think About It

Answers will vary. Possible answer: Airlines' tests will cause a shift in the demand curve because it will result in an increase in the number of consumers participating in the airline industry market.

## Visual Presentation

Use the PowerPoint presentation on the Instructor's Resource CD as an adjunct to your lecture. The presentation also be can used for review.

## Objectives

> Identify the determinants of demand, and explain how a change in each will affect the demand curve.

> Distinguish between the money price of a good and the time price of a good.

## Overview

So far the discussion of demand has been limited to the relationship between price and quantity demanded. That is, the focus has been on movement along a particular demand curve. A demand curve isolates the relation between the price of a good and the quantity demanded when other factors that could affect demand remain unchanged. What are these other determinants of demand, and how would changes in them affect demand?

## Key Terms

tastes

movement along a given demand curve

shift of a demand curve

## [ In the News ]

### ● Will Business-Fare Cuts Bring Business Flyers Back?

Major airlines have experienced a huge drop in demand that will result in roughly $4 billion in losses in a year. This loss has airlines searching for ways to generate more revenue. One way being tested is to offer business travelers lower fares. This contradicts the airlines' long-held belief that business travelers would pay whatever they had to for their necessary business trips. That belief may have been true when the economy was soaring and planes were full on the popular routes. However, it's a much harder argument in light of tighter travel budgets and lots of empty seats offering travelers more choices. Business travelers have been staying at home or in the office, buying well in advance of their trip to get the discounts, or going to "no-frills" discount airlines. The airlines have been cutting back their sky-high business-travel fares in selected markets to see if lower fares will bring these flyers back. The early test results are encouraging some carriers to believe that they can in fact cut business fares and maintain or even increase their revenues. Delta Air Lines has cut business fares by about 21 percent in more than 400 small markets with no announcement. The company was rewarded with a double-digit increase in revenue. Continental Airlines also has been quietly conducting tests of lower business fares in a number of select markets with "mixed but not discouraging" results, according to Continental officials.

### Think About It

Will the airlines' tests cause a movement along the demand curve or a shift in the demand curve? Explain.

◁ ▷

118

### National Content Standards in Economics

A complete list of the NCEE Standards appears on pages xxiv–xxv of this book. The following standards are addressed in Lesson 4.2.

Standard 4: Role of Incentives

Standard 7: Markets—Price and Quantity Determination

Standard 8: Role of Price in Market System

# Changes That Can Shift the Demand Curve

A demand curve isolates the relation between price and quantity when other factors that could affect demand are assumed constant. These other factors, often referred to as *determinants of demand*, include

1. Consumer income
2. The prices of related goods
3. The number and composition of consumers
4. Consumer expectations
5. Consumer tastes

How does a change in each affect demand?

## Changes in Consumer Income

Figure 4.6 shows the market demand curve *D* for pizza. Consumers' money income is assumed to remain constant along a demand curve. Suppose money income increases. Some consumers will then be willing and able to buy more pizza at each price, so market demand increases. The demand curve shifts to the right from *D* to *D'*. For example, at a price of $12, the amount of pizza demanded increases from 14 million to 20 million per week, as indicated by the movement from point *b* on demand curve *D* to point *f* on demand curve *D'*. In short, *an increase in demand–that is, a rightward shift of the demand curve–means that consumers are more willing and able to buy pizza at each price.*

### Normal Goods

Goods are classified into two broad categories, depending on how the demand for the good responds to changes in money income. The demand for a *normal good* increases as money income increases. Because pizza is a normal good, the demand curve for pizza shifts rightward when consumer income increases. Most goods are normal.

### Inferior Goods

In contrast, the demand for an *inferior good* actually decreases as money income increases. Examples of inferior

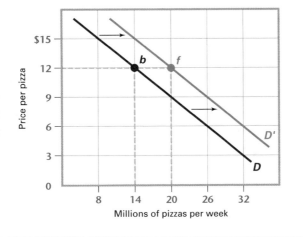

**An Increase in the Market Demand for Pizza**

An increase in the demand for pizza is reflected by a rightward shift of the demand curve. After the increase in demand, the quantity of pizza demanded at a price of $12 increases from 14 million (point *b*) to 20 million (point *f*).

econxtra.swlearning.com

**Figure 4.6**

---

### Changes That Can Shift the Demand Curve

Point out that in 2003 the federal government lowered tax rates for all people who paid income taxes. Effectively, most workers received more take-home pay. Ask students to discuss what this would have done to the demand for most normal and most inferior goods. You might ask them to describe how increased income would have affected demand for movie tickets and restaurant meals. Why might it have had less of an impact on sales of board games and other at-home forms of entertainment? (Answer: With greater take-home income, consumers may have increased their demand for more expensive forms of entertainment and felt less need to stay at home to save money.)

**See It**

Use **Figure 4.6**—An Increase in the Market Demand for Pizza to illustrate a shift in the demand curve. Direct students to the Graphing Workshop for Chapter 4 at **econxtra.swlearning.com**. Instruct students to click on **See It: Demand and Shifts in Demand** to view the graph and listen to an explanation. The first part of this workshop will be a review of the demand schedule and demand curve. The last part covers shifts in demand, the topic of Figure 4.6.

---

## Outside Resources

**Local Television News Reports** Events that can shift demand are constant features on local television news reports. Assign students to identify a story about an event that will cause consumers to purchase more or less of a product. Each student should explain, either to the class or in a written assignment, how the news feature will affect demand.

**Celebrity Endorsements** Ask students to identify a celebrity who has endorsed a product. An example might be Tiger Woods and Buick automobiles. What does Buick hope will happen to the elasticity of demand for its cars because of the endorsement?

## Changes That Can Shift the Demand Curve

Ask students to imagine that the price of energy they use to heat their homes has increased by 100 percent over the past year. Ask them to identify different ways such a price increase would affect their lives. What products would they buy more of (home insulation, sweaters, better windows), and which they would demand fewer of (water for long showers, new home additions, heated swimming pools). How do these changes demonstrate changes in demand that result from changes in the price of substitute and complementary products?

Use **Figure 4.7—A Decrease in the Market Demand for Pizza** to illustrate a shift in the demand curve. Direct students to the Graphing Workshop for Chapter 4 at **econxtra.swlearning.com**. Instruct students to click on **See It: Demand and Shifts in Demand** to view the graph and listen to an explanation. The first part of this workshop will be a review of the demand schedule and demand curve. The last part covers shifts in demand, the topic of Figure 4.7.

 Answers will vary. Students might point out the need for day care centers, grocery stores, and gasoline stations in an area that is experiencing growth due to construction of affordable housing, an influx of young families, and a high birthrate. In an older community where the population is aging, there might be an increase in the demand for travel agencies, home repair services, and medical services.

goods include bologna sandwiches, used furniture, used clothing, trips to the Laundromat, and bus rides. As money income increases, consumers switch from consuming these inferior goods to consuming normal goods— like roast beef sandwiches, new furniture, new clothing, a washer and dryer, and automobile or plane rides.

### Changes in the Prices of Related Goods

As you've seen, the prices of other goods are assumed to remain constant along a given demand curve. Now you are ready to consider the impact of changes in the prices of other goods.

#### Substitutes

Products that can be used in place of each other are called substitutes. Consumers choose among substitutes partly on the basis of their relative prices. For example, pizza and tacos are substitutes, though not perfect ones. Yet an increase in the price of tacos, other things constant, reduces the quantity of tacos demanded along a given taco demand curve and shifts the demand curve for pizza right, as shown in Figure 4.6. Two goods are *substitutes* if an increase in the price of one shifts the demand for the other rightward and, conversely, if a decrease in the price of one shifts demand for the other leftward.

A decrease in the price of tacos would reduce the demand for pizza, as shown in Figure 4.7, where the demand curve for pizza shifts to the left from $D$ to $D''$. As a result, consumers are less willing and able to buy pizza at every price. For example, at a price of $12, the amount demanded decreases from 14 million to 10 million per week, as indicated by the movement from point $b$ on demand curve $D$ to point $j$ on demand curve $D''$.

#### Complements

Certain goods are often used in combination. Pizza and soft drinks, milk and cookies, computer hardware and software, and airline tickets and rental cars are complements. When two goods are complements, a decrease in the price of one shifts the demand for the other rightward. For example, a decrease in the price of soft drinks shifts the demand curve for pizza rightward.

**A Decrease in the Market Demand for Pizza**

*econxtra.swlearning.com*

**Figure 4.7**

A decrease in the demand for pizza is reflected by a leftward shift of the demand curve. After the decrease in demand, the quantity of pizza demanded at a price of $12 decreases from 14 million (point *b*) to 10 million (point *j*).

The price of imported crude oil has fluctuated widely in recent years from as low as $10 to as high as nearly $40 per barrel. As a result, the price of gasoline has also fluctuated. Ask students to identify goods or services that are complementary products to gasoline and explain how the demand for these products would have increased or declined because of the changes in the price of gasoline. Examples would include automobile tires, hotel stays, admission to national parks, and crossings purchased at toll bridges.

## Changes in the Size or Composition of the Population

As mentioned earlier, the market demand curve is the sum of the individual demand curves of all consumers in the market. If the population grows, the number of consumers in the market increases. For example, if the population grows, the demand curve for pizza will shift rightward. Even if the total population remains unchanged, demand could shift as a result of a change in the composition of the population. For example, a bulge in the teenage population could shift pizza demand rightward. A baby boom would shift rightward the demand for car seats and baby food.

## Changes in Consumer Expectations

Another factor assumed to be constant along a given demand curve is consumer expectations about factors that influence demand, such as the future income and the future price of the good. A change in

**Investigate Your Local Economy**

Examine changes or trends in the composition of the population of your city or town. What products or categories of products might these changes affect?

consumer expectations can shift the demand curve. For example, you may spend a little more after lining up a summer job, even before summer arrives.

Changes in price expectations also can shift demand. For example, if you expect pizza prices to jump next week, you may buy an extra one now for the freezer, thereby shifting the demand for pizza rightward. Or if consumers come to believe that home prices will climb

# E-CONOMICS

## Technology Is a Girl's Best Friend

Banners flying the headline "Technology Is a Girl's Best Friend" greeted attendees to the 2003 International Consumer Electronics Show (CES) in Las Vegas. The show included a product showcase devoted specifically to female-friendly products. Also featured at the annual show was a series of conferences and events concerned with understanding and promoting women's increased role in the consumer electronics world. A few years earlier, about 70 percent to 80 percent of the show's attendees were men. These days, however, the attendance ratio is down to about 60–40 in favor of men. In 2003, women's spending accounted for about $55 billion of the projected $100 billion U.S. consumer electronics market, according to a CES vice president. She also said that women initiate nearly 75 percent of such purchases on their own or with a spouse. Consumer electronics companies are realizing that female buyers are a demographic worthy of their attention. They also realize that young girls are more receptive to technology than older women, according to Ann Shoket of *Cosmo Girl* magazine. "This generation of girls is going to change everything," Shoket said. "They don't see technology as some sort of alien, strange thing they're afraid of."

### Think Critically

Identify the determinant of demand this situation illustrates. Explain your answer.

---

### Changes That Can Shift the Demand Curve

Point out that the demand for many products is seasonal. Ask students how much their family would be willing to pay for a cut evergreen tree in July. Why are many families willing to pay as much as $100 for this item at the beginning of December? Why would a business be unlikely to sell many colored eggs in November or pumpkins in February? How do these situations demonstrate changes in demand that take place as tastes change during each year?

## E-CONOMICS

Direct students to read the passage entitled "Technology Is a Girl's Best Friend" on this page.

### Answers to Think Critically

This situation illustrates the "composition of consumers" determinant of demand. Demand is changing because the percentage of women that represent the consumer body as a whole is increasing in the technology industry.

### ✓ CHECKPOINT

Invite a student to answer the checkpoint that appears on page 122.

### Answer

The five determinants of demand are: (1) Consumer income—a rise in income causes an outward shift of the demand curve. (2) The price of related goods—a rise in this causes an outward shift of the demand curve. (3) Number of consumer's in the market—a rise in this causes an outward shift of the demand curve. (4) Consumer expectations—a rise in this causes an inward shift of the demand curve. (5) Consumer tastes—a change in this could shift the demand curve either inward or outward.

---

## Extend the Content

Firms that produce products that have inelastic demand enjoy a degree of monopoly power in their markets. They know that if they increase their prices they will lose relatively few sales and their total revenue will grow, at least in the short run. In the long run, however, this can cause problems. In the 1960s demand for U.S. automobiles was quite inelastic. As prices were raised by manufacturers sales remained strong. In the 1970s, foreign competition caused great difficulties for U.S. automakers. Discuss what happened to the elasticity of demand for U.S. automobiles as a result of foreign competition.

### Extensions of Demand Analysis

Point out that some families make a point of eating together and sharing their daily experiences around the dinner table. These families do not care what the price of fast food might be because they almost never choose to buy any. Then ask students how such a family's demand for fast food might change if the person who normally does the cooking became ill and could no longer prepare the family's meals. In such a case, is it food alone that is being demanded? What does fast food offer consumers in addition to sustenance?

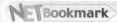

Direct students to the **econxtra.swlearning.com** web site. Remind them to click on the link for Lesson 4.3 to find the appropriate link for the NET Bookmark on this page.

**Answer**

According to the article, the rise in the value of time has resulted in increased spending on timesaving services such as store-bought clothing, processed foods, and restaurant meals.

## CHECKPOINT

Invite a student to answer the checkpoint that appears on page 123.

**Answer**

Money price is how much a good costs. Time price is the monetary value you place on having a good that works faster or is more convenient.

Assign Lesson 4.3 from the Contemporary Economics Workbook.

Assign all or part of Lesson 4.3 Assessment on page 124 as homework or an in-class activity.

## Xtra! Study Tools

Direct students to the online study tools for Lesson 4.3 at **econxtra.swlearning.com**.

---

next year, some will increase their demand for housing this year, shifting the demand for housing rightward.

### Changes in Consumer Tastes

Do you like anchovies on a pizza? How about sauerkraut on a hot dog? Is music to your ears more likely to be rock, country, heavy metal, hip-hop, reggae, jazz, new age, or classical? Choices in food, music, clothing, reading, movies, TV shows—indeed, all consumer choices—are influenced by consumer tastes.

**Tastes** are your likes and dislikes as a consumer. What determines your tastes? Your desires for food when hungry and liquid when thirsty are largely biological. So is your preference for shelter, comfort, rest, personal safety, and a pleasant environment. Your family background shapes many of your tastes. Other influences include the surrounding culture and peer influence. Generally, economists claim no special expertise in understanding how tastes develop.

Economists recognize, however, that tastes are important in shaping demand. For example, although pizza is a popular food, some people just don't like it and others might be allergic to the cheese or tomatoes. Thus, some people like to eat pizza and others don't. A change in the tastes for a particular good shifts the demand curve. For example, a discovery that the combination of cheese and tomato sauce on pizza promotes overall health could affect consumer tastes, shifting the

**tastes**
Consumer preferences; likes and dislikes in consumption; assumed to be constant along a given demand curve

**movement along a given demand curve**
Change in quantity demanded resulting from a change in the price of the good, other things constant

**shift of a demand curve**
Increase or decrease in demand resulting from a change in one of the determinants of demand other than the price of the good

## NETBookmark

To learn more about the economics of consumption, read Jane Katz's "The Joy of Consumption: We Are What We Buy," in the Federal Reserve Bank of Boston's *Regional Review*. Access this article through econxtra.swlearning.com. What evidence does Katz cite about how the rising value of time has affected consumer spending patterns?

**econxtra.swlearning.com**

---

demand curve for pizza to the right.

But a change in tastes is difficult to isolate from other economic changes. That's why economists attribute a change in demand to a change in tastes only after ruling out other possible explanations.

### Movement Along a Demand Curve Versus a Shift of the Curve

You should remember the distinction between a movement along a demand curve and a shift of a demand curve. A change in price, other things constant, causes a **movement along a demand curve**, changing the quantity demanded. A change in one of the determinants of demand other than price causes a **shift of a demand curve**, changing demand.

## CHECKPOINT

What are the five determinants of demand, and how do changes in each shift the demand curve?

## Extensions of Demand Analysis

Because consumption does not occur instantaneously, time plays an important role in demand analysis.

### Role of Time in Demand

The cost of consumption has two components: the *money price* of the good and the *time price* of the good. Goods are demanded because of the benefits they provide. Thus, you are willing to pay more for medicine that works faster. Similarly, it is not the microwave oven, personal computer, or airline trip that you value but the services they provide. Other things constant, the good that provides the same benefit in less time is preferred. That's also why you are willing to pay more for ready-to-eat foods that you don't need to prepare yourself.

---

Propose the following scenario. A major computer manufacturer, G-Tech, is having a giant 35% off sale for its laptop computers while other producers of laptops have left their prices unchanged. Ask students to explain what will happen to the demand curves for both G-Tech computers and other manufacturers' products. Remind them that when the price of a product changes there will be movement along its demand curve so there will be no shift in the demand curve for G-Tech computers. The other manufactures, however, produce substitutes for G-Tech computers. The demand curves for their products will shift to the left as more people buy G-Tech computers instead of other brands.

Your willingness to pay more for time-saving goods and services depends on the opportunity cost of your time. Differences in the value of time among consumers help explain differences in the consumption patterns observed in the economy. For example, a retired couple has more leisure time than a working couple. The retired couple may clip coupons and search the newspapers for bargains, sometimes going from store to store for particular grocery items on sale that week. The working couple usually will ignore the coupons and sales and will eat out more often and purchase more at convenience stores, where they are willing to pay extra for the convenience. The retired couple will be more inclined to drive across country on vacation, whereas the working couple will fly to a vacation destination.

## The Cost of Waiting In Line

Just inside the gates at Disneyland, Disney World, and Universal Studios, visitors see signs posting the waiting times of each attraction and ride. At that point, the visitor already has paid the dollar cost of admission, so the marginal dollar cost of each ride and attraction is zero. The waiting times offer a menu of the marginal *time cost* of each ride or attraction. The opportunity cost of waiting in line is not enjoying other rides or attractions. Incidentally, people who are willing to pay up to $55 an hour at Disney World and $60 an hour at Disneyland (plus the price of admission) could until recently take VIP tours that bypass the lines.

Differences in the opportunity cost of time among consumers shape consumption patterns and add another dimension to demand analysis.

**CHECKPOINT**
What's the difference between the money price of a good and its time price?

# Sharpen Your Life Skills

## Draw Conclusions

Demand for many products can be affected by a single important event. In September 2002, for example, Hurricane Isadore plowed into the southern coast of Louisiana, leaving widespread destruction in its wake. Thousands of homes were destroyed along with many businesses, roads, and public buildings.

Consider how this disaster must have changed people's demand for goods and services in Louisiana. Divide the following businesses into two lists: one made up of firms that would have had increased demand for their products because of Isadore, the other of businesses that would have experienced reduced demand. Explain your placement of each business.

- building contractors
- swimming pool installers
- luxury hotels
- apartment buildings
- lumber yards
- amusement parks

## Apply Your Skill

Imagine that the United States mobilizes its military forces to fight a war in a foreign country. It calls up 250,000 reserve soldiers and increases its purchases of military equipment. Many factories operate 24 hours a day to keep up with government orders. Describe several ways in which this would shift demand for products in the U.S. economy.

**Revisit** the In the News feature on the first page of the lesson. Ask students to review their preliminary answers and discuss the questions now that they have completed this lesson.

**Review** the objectives for Lesson 4.3. Students should be able to:

- Identify the determinants of demand, and explain how a change in each will affect the demand curve.
- Distinguish between the money price of a good and the time price of a good.

### Sharpen Your Life Skills

#### Draw Conclusions

See the answers at the bottom of this page.

#### Apply Your Skill

Answers will vary. Students may point out that many workers will have more income to spend which will shift many demand curves to the right. Certainly the demand curve for military equipment will shift to the right. It is possible, however, that taxes could be raised to help pay for the war which would shift consumer demand for products to the left. Further, some consumers might buy more products because they are worried that they might not be available in the future. This would shift demand to the right.

## Draw Conclusions

| | |
|---|---|
| Building contractors | **Increased demand** to replace destroyed structures |
| Apartment buildings | **Increased demand** as people need to find a place to live while homes are rebuilt |
| Lumber yards | **Increased demand** as people buy lumber and other building products to repair or replace their homes |
| Swimming pool installers | **Reduced demand** because people choose to spend limited income for other products needed to rebuild |
| Luxury hotels | **Reduced demand** as fewer people choose to vacation in damaged area |
| Amusement parks | **Reduced demand** because people choose to spend limited income for other products needed to rebuild |

## Key Concepts

1. Answers will vary. Students may point out that an increase will cause people to substitute bus transportation for driving a car. The demand curve for bus tickets would shift to the right because of this change in the price of a related good.

2. Answers will vary. Students may point out that this would cause people to demand more of the product. It would change their tastes and cause the demand curve for the shampoo to shift to the right.

3. Answers will vary. Students may point out that the ad would cause people to put off buying until next week. The change in their expectations of future prices would cause their demand curve for towels to shift to the left.

4. The demand curve for hot dogs will stay in the same location. This is an example of a change in the quantity demanded. There will be movement from one point on the demand curve to a different point indicated by the higher price.

5. Answers will vary. Students may point out that consumers demand more "Quick Oats" because they value the time they spend preparing their breakfast.

## Graphing Exercise

6. a. The demand curve shifts right because of a change in tastes.

   b. The demand curve shifts left because of a change in tastes.

   c. The demand curve shifts left because workers have less income to spend.

   d. The demand curve shifts right because there are more potential customers near the store.

## Think Critically

7. Answers will vary. Students may point out that the stock market crash caused many people to feel poor so they spent less of their income on new goods or services. This reduced sales, caused workers to be laid off, and contributed to the failure of many businesses.

8. Answers will vary. Students may point out that these warnings are intended to change smokers' tastes for cigarettes by convincing them that smoking is bad for their health. If successful, the warnings shift the demand curve to the left.

---

**Xtra!**
**Study Tools**
econxtra.swlearning.com

## Key Concepts

1. What would happen to the demand curve for bus tickets if the price of gasoline increased to $5 per gallon? Which of the determinants of demand does this demonstrate?

2. What would happen to the demand curve for a particular brand of shampoo if a famous movie actress with beautiful hair announces that it is the best shampoo she has ever used? Which of the determinants of demand does this demonstrate?

3. What would happen to the demand curve for towels today if a large store advertises that it will have a 50 percent off sale on towels next week? Which of the determinants of demand does this demonstrate?

4. If the price of hot dogs increases by $.20 per pound when the price of substitute products remains the same, will the demand curve for hot dogs shift to the right, shift to the left, or stay in the same location? Explain your answer.

5. Why is the demand for "Quick Oats" that cook in 2.5 minutes greater than the demand for regular oats that take 5 minutes to prepare?

## Graphing Exercise

6. To the right is the demand curve for running shoes at a local retailer. Make a copy of the demand curve. Draw the shift in demand on your copy that would result from each of the following events. Label each shift in the demand curve.

   a. Many people decide to buy new running shoes to run in a local marathon.

   b. Three months of almost uninterrupted rain keeps most people inside.

   c. Income tax rates for most workers are increased by 10 percent.

   d. A new housing development is built near a store.

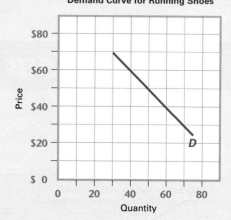

Demand Curve for Running Shoes

## Think Critically

7. **History** When the stock market crashed in 1929, demand for most consumer products fell. Explain why this happened and how it contributed to the causes of the Great Depression that took place during the 1930s.

8. **Health** For many years, cigarette manufacturers have been required to place health warnings on their products. What are these warnings intended to do to smokers' demand curves for cigarettes?

**Demand for Running Shoes**

Quantity Demanded

*a* and *d*

*b* and *c*

## Visualizing the Answer—Graphing Exercise

6. The answer includes a graph. Students' graphs should look similar to the one shown here. An Excel spreadsheet containing this graph along with supporting data is available on the Instructor's Resource CD.

# The
## Industrial Revolution in England:
## The Demand for Cotton

The Industrial Revolution began with England's textile industry in the late 1700s. Cotton had been around since the 1630s, when it was introduced to Europe from India. Although popular, cotton was considered a threat to the British wool, linen, and silk industries. In response, Parliament restricted cotton imports. The restrictions lasted until 1736, when Great Britain changed the laws allowing the manufacture and sale of cotton. This marked the beginning of cotton manufacturing in the West.

The two basic stages of manufacturing cotton textiles were spinning and weaving. Typically these tasks were done in the home in what was called a cottage industry. Entrepreneurs supplied raw materials, such as raw cotton or thread, to a household. Then members of the household would produce thread or cloth for the entrepreneur. Of the two tasks, spinning was simpler and the spinners produced more thread than the weavers could weave. John Kay's 1733 invention, the flying shuttle, changed much of that. It allowed one weaver rather than two to operate a loom and produce more cloth. The demand for thread began to rise.

To satisfy this demand, James Hargreaves invented the spinning jenny in the 1760s. With his invention, a single worker could spin multiple threads, but it produced a relatively weak product. Richard Arkwright invented the water frame in 1769. This innovation produced a stronger, coarser thread. Finally, Samuel Crompton's 1779 spinning mule produced a strong yet fine thread. Once again spinners were producing more than what weavers could use.

Edmund Cartwright's power loom, patented in 1785, enabled the British cotton textile industry to explode. In 1796, the country manufactured 21 million yards of cotton cloth. That number increased to 347 million by 1830. The demand for cotton cloth proved to be highly elastic. The technological advances, coupled with a source supply in the United States, caused the price of cotton cloth to drop. By the early part of the century, Britain was even able to sell cotton cloth in India. With this increased technology, the demand for raw cotton increased. Great Britain found in the United States a willing and able supplier.

## THINK CRITICALLY

Indicate how the demand curve for cotton would shift with each of the Industrial Revolution's technological inventions. Use $D_1$ for the cottage industry demand, $D_2$ for John Kay's flying shuttle, $D_3$ for Samuel Crompton's spinning mule, and $D_4$ for Edmund Cartwright's power loom.

C O N N E C T
*to History*

### FOCUS

Set the stage for the **Connect to History** feature by reminding students that the Industrial Revolution marked a fundamental change in human history. The use of machinery and the techniques developed in the textile industry would spread to other industries. The technology of the Industrial Revolution was stimulated because each new advance created and increased demand for the processes that went before it. The result would be a production bottleneck until technology could catch up.

### TEACH

Instruct students to read the **Connect to History** feature and respond to the problem.

### ASSESS

Use the Think Critically question at the bottom of the page to assess the students' understanding of this feature.

**Answers to Think Critically**

The demand curve for cotton would shift with each of the Industrial Revolution's technological inventions.

## Bibliography

Cannon, John, ed. *Oxford Companion to British History.* New York: Oxford University Press, 1997

Carson, Thomas and Mary Bonk, eds. *Gale Encyclopedia of U.S. History.* Detroit: Gale Group, 1999.

Michl, H.E. *The Textile Industries.* Washington, D.C.: The Textile Foundation, 1938.

Puth, Robert C. *American Economic History.* New York: The Dryden Press, 1988.

Watkins, James. *King Cotton: A Historical and Statistical Review.* New York: Negro University Press, 1969.

## Summary

### Consider

Ask students to revisit the questions they were asked to consider at the beginning of the chapter. Remind students that they should be able to answer all of the questions after studying Chapter 4.

- Why are newspapers sold in vending machines that allow you to take more than one copy? See page 103—Diminishing Marginal Utility.

- How much do you eat when you can eat all you want? See page 103—Diminishing Marginal Utility.

- What cures spring fever? See page 103—Diminishing Marginal Utility.

- What economic principle is behind the saying, "Been there, done that"? See page 103—Diminishing Marginal Utility.

- Why do higher cigarette taxes cut smoking by teenagers more than by other age groups? See page 115—An Application: Teen Smoking.

### Exam*View*

Use **Exam***View* to assess student learning.

- Create a chapter test using questions from the existing test bank

- Add your own questions to the existing test bank.

- Generate multiple forms of a chapter test.

### Study Skills

Offer the following study skills suggestions for students as they review this chapter.

- Outline the chapter.
- Review Key Terms.
- Review Checkpoints.
- Work in pairs to quiz each other.
- Use Xtra! Study Tools for each lesson.

 **Xtra!** Quiz Prep

Direct students to the online quiz preparation for Chapter 4 at **econxtra.swlearning.com**.

---

## Summary

 **Xtra!Quiz Pr**
*econxtra.swlearning.co*

### 4.1 The Demand Curve

a *Demand* indicates how much of a product consumers are willing and able to buy at each possible price during a given period, other things remaining equal. The *law of demand* states that the higher the price, the smaller the quantity demanded, and vice versa.

b The *quantity demanded* of a product grows as prices fall because of the *substitution effect*, *income effect*, and *diminishing marginal utility*. The law of diminishing marginal utility states that additional units of a product normally provide smaller additional amounts of utility to a consumer within a period of time.

c Demand for a product can be expressed in a *demand schedule* or a graph called a *demand curve*. Most demand curves slope down from left to right, indicating an inverse relationship between changes in price and quantity. This means that as prices decline, the quantity demanded of the product will grow.

### 4.2 Elasticity of Demand

a The *price elasticity of demand* measures the responsiveness of the quantity demanded to a change in price. Elasticity is calculated by dividing the percentage change in the quantity demanded by the percentage change in price.

b The price elasticity of demand may be *elastic*, *unit elastic*, or *inelastic*. Elastic demand is indicated by a value greater than 1.0. When there is elastic demand, a percentage change in price will result in a larger percentage change in the quantity demanded. Unit elastic demand is indicated by a value of 1.0. When there is unit elastic demand, a percentage change in price will result in the same percentage change in the quantity demanded. Inelastic demand is indicated by a value less than 1.0. When there is inelastic demand, a percentage

change in price will result in a smaller percentage change in the quantity sold.

c The price elasticity of demand can be used to predict what will happen to a firm's *total revenue* when it changes the price of its product. When there is elastic demand, an increase in price will result in reduced total revenue. When there is unit elastic demand, an increase in price will result in unchanged total revenue. When there is inelastic demand, an increase in price will result in increased total revenue.

d Products that have many substitutes tend to have elastic demand. Those that are very important and have few substitutes, or that represent a small proportion of the consumer's budget, tend to have inelastic demand. As a general rule, the more time that passes, the more elastic demand will be.

### 4.3 Changes in Demand and the Time Price of Goods

a There are five general classifications of events that can cause the location of a demand curve to move. These are: (1) a change in consumer income, (2) a change in the price of related goods, (3) a change in the number and composition of consumers, (4) a change in consumer expectations, and (5) a change in consumer tastes.

b *Substitute* products may be used interchangeably. An increase in the price of one will cause demand for the other to increase. *Complementary* products are normally used together. An increase in the price of one will cause the demand for the other to fall.

c The demand for products can be influenced by time. Customers who must wait in line to buy a product may choose not to wait. They are being required to pay in time as well as money to purchase the product.

# Review Economic Terms

Choose the term that best fits the definition. On a separate sheet of paper, write the letter of the answer.

1. The sum of the individual demand of all consumers in the market

2. A graph that shows the quantities of a particular good that will be demanded at various prices during a given time period, other things constant

3. The demand of a single consumer in the market

_____ 4. The amount of a product that is demanded at a particular price

_____ 5. An increase or decrease in demand that results from a change in a determinant of demand

_____ 6. A change in the quantity of a product demanded that results from a change in the product's price

_____ 7. The change in total utility resulting from a one-unit increase in consumption of a particular product

_____ 8. The more of a good a person consumes per period, the smaller the increase in total utility from consuming one more unit, other things constant

_____ 9. The quantity of a good demanded per period relates inversely to its price, other things constant

10. Price multiplied by the quantity demanded at that price

11. A relation showing the quantities of a good that consumers are willing and able to buy at various prices per period, other things constant

_____ 12. Measures how responsive quantity demanded is to a price change

_____ 13. Consumer preferences; assumed to be constant along a given demand curve

a. demand
b. demand curve
c. elasticity of demand
d. individual demand
e. law of demand
f. law of diminishing marginal utility
g. marginal utility
h. market demand
i. movement along a given demand curve
j. quantity demanded
k. shift of a demand curve
l. tastes
m. total revenue

# Review Economic Concepts

14. **True or False** A change in the price of a product will not cause that product's *demand curve* to shift.

15. The __?__ is demonstrated by the fact that people will buy more hot dogs and hamburgers when the price of pizza increases.

16. *Elasticity* expresses a relationship between the percentage change in __?__ and the resulting percentage change in __?__.

17. Which of the following is false about demand curves?

a. They normally slope down from left to right.

b. They show the relationship between price and the quantity demanded.

c. They can be used to calculate a product's price elasticity of demand.

d. They show how much profit is earned by businesses that sell the product.

18. **True or False** *Quantity demanded* at a particular price is represented by an individual point on the demand curve.

*Chapter Assessment* **127**

## Review Economic Concepts

19. d. % change in the quantity demanded ÷ % change in the price of the product
20. True
21. elastic
22. True
23. b. availability of substitute products
24. False. Market demand is the demand of all the consumers together.
25. b. a particular brand of hand soap
26. True
27. d. all of the above would affect demand when other factors are assumed constant
28. False. Demand for a normal good increases as money increases.
29. c. make a product's demand more elastic
30. disposable
31. a. blank sheets of paper and copy machines
    e. peanut butter and jelly
    i. golf clubs and golf balls
32. determinant of demand
33. True

---

19. Which of the following is the correct formula for the *price elasticity of demand*?

    a. $\dfrac{\text{change in the price of the product}}{\text{change in the quantity demanded}}$

    b. $\dfrac{\text{change in the quantity demanded}}{\text{change in the price of the product}}$

    c. $\dfrac{\text{\% change in the price of the product}}{\text{\% change in the quantity demanded}}$

    d. $\dfrac{\text{\% change in the quantity demanded}}{\text{\% change in the price of the product}}$

20. **True or False** A firm's *total revenue* will increase if it raises the price of a product that has a price elasticity of demand equal to 0.73.

21. If the *total revenue* from selling a product declines when the product's price is increased, the demand for that product is __?__.

22. **True or False** A business is more likely to increase the price of its products if the demand for these products is elastic than if the demand is inelastic.

23. Which of the following does *not* influence the *elasticity of demand*?

    a. availability of substitute products

    b. availability of complementary products

    c. the share of the consumer's budget spent on the good

    d. the timeframe of the purchase

24. **True or False** *Market demand* is the demand of an individual consumer.

25. Which of these products is most likely to have very elastic demand?

    a. a cable television service

    b. a particular brand of hand soap

    c. ground black pepper

    d. taxi service in a large city

26. **True or False** When consumers earn more income, their demand for all products will increase.

27. Which of the following is *not* a determinant of demand?

    a. consumer income

    b. prices of related goods

    c. consumer expectations and tastes

    d. all of the above would affect demand when other factors are assumed constant

28. **True or False** Demand for a *normal good* decreases as money income increases.

29. The purpose of advertising is to

    a. shift a product's demand curve to the right.

    b. shift a product's demand curve to the left.

    c. make a product's demand more elastic.

    d. point out a product's substitutes to its consumers.

30. Your __?__ income is your income measured in terms of how many goods and services it can buy.

31. Which of the following pairs of products are examples of *complementary goods*?

    a. blank sheets of paper and copy machines

    b. dining room tables and floor lamps

    c. heating oil and natural gas

    d. warm gloves and trips to Florida

    e. peanut butter and jelly

    f. private and public transportation

    g. Coke and Pepsi

    h. alarm clocks and automobiles

    i. golf clubs and golf balls

32. A change in a __?__ will change demand for a product when there is no change in price.

33. **True or False** If a person's income falls to zero, he or she will still demand some products.

# Apply Economic Concepts

**34. Graphing Shifts in Demand** The owner of Rita's Tacos bought ads in a local newspaper. As a result, the demand for her tacos increased as demonstrated in the demand schedule below.

Draw a graph of her demand as it was before the ads were printed. On the same graph, draw the new demand curve for tacos. Explain why many businesses advertise their products.

**Old and New Demand Schedule for Rita's Tacos**

| Price Per Taco | Old Quantity Demanded | New Quantity Demanded |
|---|---|---|
| $2.00 | 25 | 75 |
| $1.75 | 50 | 100 |
| $1.50 | 75 | 125 |
| $1.25 | 100 | 150 |
| $1.00 | 125 | 175 |
| $0.75 | 150 | 200 |

**35. Price Elasticity of Demand** If Rita changed the price of her tacos from $1.75 to $1.50 each, her sales would grow from 100 to 125 per day. Calculate the percentage change in price and quantity demanded and then the price elasticity of demand. Is this demand elastic, unit elastic, or inelastic?

**36. Total Revenue** Calculate the total revenue Rita received from the tacos when she sold them at a price of $1.75 and now that she sells them at a price of $1.50. Can you be sure that her business is more profitable at the lower price? Explain why.

**37. Market Demand** Working in small groups, determine your group's market demand for gasoline. Make up a chart listing a variety of

prices per gallon of gasoline, such as $1.00, $1.25, $1.50, $1.75, $2.00, $2.25. Each group member should determine how many gallons *per week* they would purchase at each possible price. Then do the following:

a. Plot each group member's demand curve. Check to see whether each person's responses are consistent with the law of demand.

b. Derive the "market" demand curve by adding up the quantities demanded by all students at each possible price.

c. What do you think will happen to that market demand curve after your class graduates and your incomes rise?

econxtra.swlearning.com

**38.** Read the Real Per Capita Disposable Income article in the **EconDataOnline** section at econxtra.swlearning.com. What happens to

quantity of goods demanded when real per capita disposable income increases?

---

## Apply Economic Concepts

**34.** Answers will vary. Students may point out that businesses pay for advertising because they hope to increase the demand for their products. They believe that this will increase their profitability. See visual at the bottom of this page.

**35.** The percentage change in price is 14.3 (25 ÷ 175 = 0.143).

The percentage change in quantity demanded is 25.0 (25 ÷ 100 = 0.25).

The price elasticity of demand is 1.75 (25.0 ÷ 14.3 = 1.75).

The price elasticity of demand is elastic.

**36.** She received $175.00 in total revenue at the old price ($1.75 × 100 = $175.00).

She receives $187.50 in total revenue at the new price ($1.50 × 125 = $187.50).

We can't be sure her business is more profitable at the lower price because we don't know how much she spends to produce tacos.

**37.** Answers to items a and b will vary, depending on group members' demand for gasoline.
c. The market demand will increase as incomes increase.

**38.** The quantity of goods demanded will increase when real per capita disposable income increases.

---

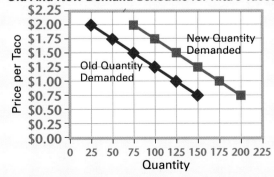

**Old And New Demand Schedule for Rita's Tacos**

## Chapter 4 Assessment

### Apply Economic Concepts

**34.** Students' graphs should look similar to the one shown here. An Excel spreadsheet containing this graph along with supporting data is available on the Instructor's Resource CD.

## Chapter Overview

**LESSON 5.1** *The Supply Curve:* This lesson introduces and defines the supply curve. A description of elasticity of supply is provided along with an explanation of how it is measured.

**LESSON 5.2** *Shifts of the Supply Curve:* The focus of this lesson is the identification of the determinants of supply and how changes affect the supply curve. This lesson also contrasts movement along the supply curve with a shift of the supply curve.

**LESSON 5.3** *Production and Cost:* This lesson includes explanations of how marginal product varies as a firm employs more labor in the short run and the shape of the firm's marginal cost curve. Economies of scale are distinguished from diseconomies of scale in the long run.

### Consider

Ask students to consider the questions posed on this page as they study Chapter 5. After studying all three lessons, students should be able to answer the questions. The content related to each question can be found on the pages indicated below.

- Why might a firm decide to store its products in a warehouse rather than offer them for sale? See page 143—Changes in Producer Expectations.
- What's the meaning of the old expression "Too many cooks spoil the broth"? See page 148—Law of Diminishing Returns.
- Can a firm shut down without going out of business? See page 152—Short-Run Losses and Shutting Down.
- Why do movie theaters have so many screens? See page 154—Economies of Scale.

### POINT YOUR BROWSER

Remind students that they can find additional resources for this chapter at **econxtra.swlearning.com**.

- Xtra! Study Tools
- Net Bookmarks
- Xtra! Quiz Prep
- econ@pps
- Ask the Xpert!
- Graphing Workshop

# 5 Supply

The Supply Curve **5.1**

Shifts of the Supply Curve **5.2**

Production and Cost **5.3**

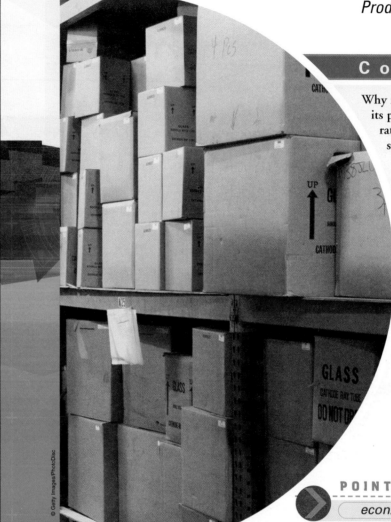

© Getty Images/PhotoDisc

### Consider

Why might a firm decide to store its products in a warehouse rather than offer them for sale?

What's the meaning of the old expression "Too many cooks spoil the broth"?

Can a firm shut down without going out of business?

Why do movie theaters have so many screens?

### POINT YOUR BROWSER

econxtra.swlearning.com

---

### Teaching Resources for Chapter 5

- Activities and Projects Masters
- Spanish Resources
- Econ Connection Interactive Tutorial CD
- **Exam**View® CD
- Workbook Teacher's Edition
- Chapter Test Teacher's Edition
- NCEE Standards and Correlation
- Personal Finance Guide

- Social Studies Skills Review
- Instructor's Resource CD
  - PowerPoint Presentation
  - Lesson Plans
  - Video Discussion Guide
  - Answers to Graphing Exercises
- **econxtra.swlearning.com**

## Objectives

> Understand the law of supply.

> Describe the elasticity of supply, and explain how it is measured.

## Overview

Just as consumer behavior shapes the demand curve, producer behavior shapes the supply curve. When studying demand, you should think like a consumer, or a demander. When studying supply, however, you must think like a producer, or a supplier. You may feel more natural as a consumer—after all, you are a consumer. But you know more about producers than you may realize. You have been around them all your life—Wal-Mart, Sony, Blockbuster, Exxon, McDonald's, Microsoft, Kinko's, Ford, Home Depot, Sears, Gap, and hundreds more. You will draw on this knowledge to develop an understanding of supply and the supply curve.

## Key Terms

**supply**

**law of supply**

**supply curve**

**elasticity of supply**

## [ In the News ]

### ● Pay Phones Don't Pay Anymore

Where will Clark Kent change into his Superman outfit now that it's getting harder and harder to find a phone booth? Pay phones are being eliminated from all the familiar spots—shopping centers, gasoline stations, restaurants, and street corners. It seems they're just not profitable anymore. In the mid-1990s, there were as many as 2.7 million pay phones across the country. That number is down to about 1.9 million now, and dropping. For the most part, they have been replaced by wireless cell phones. The few small companies that collect the monies and service pay phones are leaving the business. These companies have found that even with an increased price of 50 cents a call, the majority of pay phones operate at a loss when factoring in the costs of cleaning, maintaining, and repairing them. For the time being, pay phones continue to be supplied and maintained in the low-income areas of cities. Many people who live in these areas can't afford to own any type of phone, and so pay phones are still profitable there.

### Think About It

What, if anything, can suppliers of pay phones do to save their industry?

131

### National Content Standards in Economics

A complete list of the NCEE Standards appears on pages xxiv–xxv of this book. The following standards are addressed in Lesson 5.1.

Standard 1: Scarcity

Standard 2: Marginal Cost/Benefit

Standard 4: Role of Incentives

Standard 7: Markets—Price and Quantity Determination

Standard 8: Role of Price in Market System

Standard 14: Profit and the Entrepreneur

Explain that this lesson investigates the relationship between prices and the quantity of goods or services businesses are willing to offer for sale. One of the relationships considered is how businesses react to changes in the price they are able to charge. Tell students to imagine that they are earning money for a class trip by selling candy bars at football games. Ask them how they would react if they discovered that they could sell their candy for $1.50 per bar instead of the $1.00 price they had been charging. Would they work to sell even more candy than they had in the past? How would they decide the amount of candy to offer for sale?

### Objectives

Remind students to read the lesson objectives to help focus their attention before reading the lesson.

### Key Terms

Direct students to look up key terms in a business or economics dictionary. Some students will find it helpful to read another definition. In addition to a definition, many entries will include a brief explanation and an example.

### [ In the News ]

Instruct students to read the passage and write down their answers. Point out that their answers might change after they finish studying Lesson 5.1.

### Answers to Think About It

Answers will vary. Possible answer: Suppliers of pay phones can take away all pay phones except for those in the low-income areas, where the phones are used often. In this way, they lower the overhead cost of maintaining and repairing phones, and do it only for the phones that have a high volume of calls.

### Visual Presentation

Use the PowerPoint presentation on the Instructor's Resource CD as an adjunct to your lecture. The presentation also can be used for review.

## Law of Supply

Hold up an empty soft drink can. Tell students to imagine that there is a five-cent deposit on these containers and that they are trying to earn money by collecting them and returning (supplying) them to a grocery store. Lead the class in a discussion of how many students would work to collect containers and how many containers they think they could collect. Then ask them the same questions, assuming that the deposit value was 10 cents, 25 cents, and 50 cents. Construct a table on the board that relates the deposit value (price) to the number of containers that would be collected (supplied). Students should notice that as the deposit value increases, the number of students who choose to participate and the quantity of containers collected also grow.

### Think Critically Through Visuals

Direct students to focus their attention on the photograph and caption on this page.

 **Main Idea**

### NCEE
### Standard 14: Profit and the Entrepreneur

Entrepreneurs are people who take the risks of organizing productive resources to make goods and services. Profit is an important incentive that leads entrepreneurs to accept the risks of business failure.

# Law of Supply

With demand, the assumption is that consumers try to maximize utility, a goal that motivates their behavior. With supply, the assumption is that producers try to maximize profit. Profit is the goal that motivates the behavior of suppliers.

## Role of Profit

In trying to earn a profit, firms transform productive resources into products. Profit equals total revenue minus total cost. Total revenue is the total sales, or total dollars, received from consumers for the day, week, or year. Total cost includes the cost of all resources used by a firm in producing goods or services, including the entrepreneur's opportunity cost.

**Main Idea**

### Profit and Entrepreneur

**supply**
A relation showing the quantities of a good producers are willing and able to sell at various prices during a given period, other things constant

**law of supply**
The quantity of a good supplied during a given time period is usually directly related to its price, other things constant

**supply curve**
A curve or line showing the quantities of a particular good supplied at various prices during a given time period, other things constant

© Getty Images/PhotoDisc

*Entrepreneurs take the risks of organizing productive resources to make goods and services. A restaurant venture is an especially risky business that uses the productive resources of people and food to prepare and serve meals to customers. The profit incentive leads restaurant entrepreneurs to accept the risks of business failure.*

Profit = Total revenue − Total Cost

When a firm *breaks even,* total revenue just covers total cost. Over time, total revenue must cover total cost for the firm to survive. If total revenue falls short of total cost year after year, entrepreneurs will find more attractive uses for resources, and the firm will fail.

Each year, millions of new firms enter the U.S. marketplace and nearly as many leave. The firms must decide what goods and services to produce and what resources to employ. Firms must make plans while facing uncertainty about consumer demand, resource availability, and the intentions of other firms in the market. The lure of profit is so strong that entrepreneurs are always eager to pursue their dreams.

## Supply

Just as demand is a relation between price and quantity demanded, supply is a relation between price and quantity supplied. **Supply** indicates how much of a good producers are *willing* and *able* to offer for sale per period at each possible price, other things constant. The **law of supply** says that the quantity supplied is usually directly related to its price, other things constant. Thus, the lower the price, the smaller the quantity supplied. The higher the price, the greater the quantity supplied.

Figure 5.1 presents the market *supply schedule* and market **supply curve** S for pizza. Both show the quantities of 12-inch pizzas supplied per week at various possible prices by the many pizza makers in the market. As you can see, price and quantity supplied are directly (or positively) related, other things constant. The supply curve shows, for example, that at a price of $6 per pizza, the quantity supplied is 16 million per week. At a price of $9 per pizza, the quantity supplied increases to 20 million.

Like the demand curve, the supply curve represents a particular period of time. It shows quantity supplied per period. For any supply curve, it is assumed that the prices of other goods

### Outside Resources

**Telephone Directory** The business pages of the telephone book can be used to start discussions about supply. Assign students to count the number of pizza or Asian restaurants that are listed in their local Yellow Pages. Compare this total with the number of restaurants that offer fine French cuisine. Which type of restaurant is likely to serve more meals per day? Why are there fewer French restaurants? Do students believe that the supply of meals served by French restaurants is elastic or inelastic? What about pizza restaurants? Do they believe a new French restaurant would be more successful than a new pizza restaurant? Why?

**The Supply Schedule and Supply Curve for Pizza**

Figure 5.1

(a) Supply schedule

| Price per Pizza | Quantity Supplied per Week (millions) |
|---|---|
| $15 | 28 |
| 12 | 24 |
| 9 | 20 |
| 6 | 16 |
| 3 | 12 |

Market supply curve *S* shows the quantity of pizza supplied, at various prices, by all pizza makers.

(b) Supply curve

### Law of Supply

Revisit the candy bar example introduced on page 131 of this Teacher's Edition. Tell students that while they were able to increase the price of the candy they sold to $1.50, the amount they had to pay for the bars also increased, from $.75 to $1.25. At the same time, they could have sold slices of pizza for $1.00 that cost them $.50 each. How might these facts alter the number of candy bars they supply? Why might they decide to offer slices of pizza for sale instead of candy? Lead this discussion into an explanation of the relationship between profit and supply. The fact that the profit earned per slice of pizza is greater than that which is earned from candy bars will encourage students to supply pizza instead of candy. Point out that producers allocate scarce resources to the type of production that promises the greatest total profit.

The Graphing Workshop — See It

Use **Figure 5.1**—The Supply Schedule and Supply Curve for Pizza to illustrate the law of supply. Direct students to the Graphing Workshop for Chapter 5 at **econxtra.swlearning.com** for another example of a supply curve. Instruct students to click on **See It: Supply, and Shifts in Supply** to view the graph and listen to an explanation. Tell students they should view the first part of this workshop, which explains the supply schedule and supply curve.

the business could produce remain unchanged. Thus, along the supply curve for pizza, the price of pizza changes *relative to other prices*, which do not change. The supply curve shows the effect of a change in the *relative price* of pizza—that is, relative to the prices of other goods the resources could supply. Producers supply more pizza at a higher price than at a lower price, so the supply curve slopes upward.

### More Willing to Supply

Producers offer more for sale when the price rises for two reasons. First, as the price increases, other things constant, a producer becomes more *willing* to supply the good. Prices act as signals to existing and potential suppliers about the rewards for producing various goods. An increase in the price of pizza, with other prices remaining constant, creates an incentive to shift some resources out of producing other goods, whose prices are now relatively lower, and into pizza, whose price is now relatively higher. *A higher pizza price makes pizza production more profitable and attracts resources from lower-valued uses.*

### More Able to Supply

Higher prices also increase the producer's *ability* to supply the good. The cost of producing an additional unit of a good usually rises as output increases—that is, the *marginal cost* of production increases as output increases. (You will learn more about marginal cost in Lesson 5.3.) Because suppliers face a higher marginal cost for producing the good, they must receive a higher price to be *able* to increase the quantity supplied. *A higher price makes producers more able to increase quantity supplied.*

For example, a higher price for gasoline in recent decades increased producers' ability to explore for oil in less-accessible areas, such as the remote jungles of the Amazon, the stormy waters of the North Sea, and the frozen tundra above the Arctic Circle. Thus, the quantity of oil supplied increased as the price increased. On the other hand, a two-decade long slide in the price of gold means producers are no longer able to mine gold in less-accessible regions or where each ton of ore holds less gold. As the price declined, the quantity supplied decreased.

Lesson 5.1 • *The Supply Curve* **133**

Tell students that a popular author is coming to town to autograph her most recent novel. She will do this for only one hour, but she will do it for free. Discuss why this author might autograph books for a longer time if she felt she could charge $5 per autograph. How does this situation demonstrate the law of supply?

## Law of Supply

Extend the pizza sales example by explaining that the reason the class was not able to sell even more pizza was the fact that they had rented a very small booth for $50 per game. In this limited space, there was not enough room to serve more than two customers at a time. Ask students how they would react if a larger booth became available at twice the cost but would allow them to serve four customers at a time. Would they agree to pay this higher cost? If they did rent the larger booth, what would happen to their ability to supply pizza? What other steps would the students need to take to increase the quantity of pizza they supply? Required steps might include recruiting more students to serve customers and buying more pizza to resell.

### Think Critically Through Visuals

Direct students to focus their attention on **Figure 5.2—Summing Individual Supply Curves to Find the Market Supply Curve**. Point out that the market supply curve shown on the graphs at the far right is the horizontal sum of each individual supply curve.

**CHECKPOINT**

Invite a student to answer the checkpoint that appears on page 135.

### Answer

Answers will vary. Possible answer: Quantity supplied is directly related to price. The lower the price, the less supplied. The higher the price, the more supplied.

---

In short, a higher price makes producers more *willing* and better *able* to increase quantity supplied. Suppliers are more *willing* because production of the higher-priced good now is more profitable than the alternative uses of the resources involved. Suppliers are better *able* because the higher price allows them to cover the higher marginal cost that typically results from increasing production.

## Supply Versus Quantity Supplied

As with demand, economists distinguish between *supply* and *quantity supplied*. *Supply* is the entire relation between the price and quantity supplied, as reflected by the supply schedule or supply curve. *Quantity supplied* refers to a particular amount offered for sale at a particular price, as reflected by a point on a given supply curve. Thus, it is the *quantity supplied* that increases with a higher price, not *supply*. The term *supply* by itself refers to the entire supply schedule or supply curve.

## Individual Supply and Market Supply

Economists also distinguish between *individual supply* (the supply of an individual producer) and *market supply* (the supply of all producers in the market). *The market supply curve shows the total quantity supplied by all producers at various prices.*

In most markets, there are many suppliers, sometimes thousands. Assume for simplicity, however, that there are just two suppliers in the market for pizza: Pizza Palace and Pizza Castle. Figure 5.2 shows how the supply curves for two producers in the market are added together to yield the market supply curve. Individual supply curves are summed across to get a market supply curve.

For example, at a price of $9, Pizza Palace supplies 400 pizzas per week and Pizza Castle supplies 300. Thus, the quantity supplied in the market for pizza at a price of $9 is 700. At a price of $12, Pizza Palace supplies 500 and Pizza Castle supplies 400, for a market supply of 900 pizzas per week. The market supply curve in panel (c) of Figure 5.2 shows the horizontal sums of the individual supply curves in panels (a) and (b).

*The market supply curve is simply the horizontal sum of the individual supply curves for all producers in the market.* Unless otherwise noted, when this book talks about supply, you can take that to mean market supply.

---

**Summing Individual Supply Curves to Find the Market Supply Curve**  **Figure 5.2**

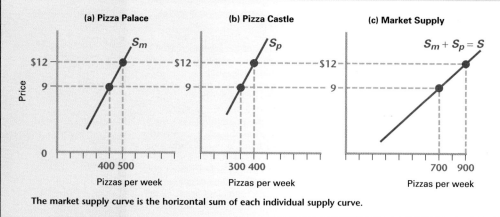

The market supply curve is the horizontal sum of each individual supply curve.

---

### Economic Headlines

Instruct students to locate an article in a newspaper or newsmagazine about some aspect of supply. For example, they might find an article about a hot fashion trend, a wildly popular video game, or a once-in-a-lifetime concert event. Instruct them to write a paragraph summarizing the article and drawing a connection to this lesson. Encourage the use of graphs to help illustrate the ideas presented.

Consider asking students to attach a copy of the original article along with a properly formatted reference citation.

# Elasticity of Supply

Prices are signals to both sides of the market about the relative scarcity of products. High prices discourage consumption but encourage production. The elasticity of demand measures how responsive consumers are to a price change. Likewise, the elasticity of supply measures how responsive producers are to a price change.

## Measurement

The elasticity of supply is calculated in the same way as the elasticity of demand. The **elasticity of supply** equals the percentage change in quantity supplied divided by the percentage change in price.

Elasticity of supply =

$$\frac{\text{Percentage change in quantity supplied}}{\text{Percentage change in price}}$$

Suppose the price increases. Because a higher price usually results in an increased quantity supplied, the percentage change in price and the percentage change in quantity supplied move in the same direction. So, the price elasticity of supply usually is a positive number.

Figure 5.3 depicts the typical upward-sloping supply curve presented earlier. As you can see, if the price of pizza increases from $9 to $12, the quantity supplied increases from 20 million to 24 million. What's the elasticity of supply? The percentage change in quantity supplied is the change in quantity supplied—4 million—divided by 20 million. So quantity supplied increases by 20 percent. The percentage change in price is the change in price—$3—divided by $9, which is 33 percent.

The elasticity of supply is, therefore, the percentage increase in quantity

**elasticity of supply**
A measure of the responsiveness of quantity supplied to a price change; the percentage change in quantity supplied divided by the percentage change in price

## Elasticity of Supply

Return to the soft-drink container example given on page 132. Remind students that when the deposit value was increased from 5 cents to 10 cents per container, the number of containers that would be collected increased, demonstrating the law of supply. Point out that this increase in the price of the returned containers was 100 percent ($.10 – $.05 = $.05, $.05 / $.05 = 1.0 = 100%). Calculate the percentage increase in the number of containers supplied as a result of this price increase by dividing the increase in the number collected at a price of 10 cents by the number collected at 5 cents. If the percentage change in the number of containers collected was greater than 100 percent, the supply is elastic. If the percentage change in the number of containers collected was less than 100 percent, the supply is inelastic. Remind students that elasticity measures the responsiveness of either the quantity demanded or supplied to changes in price. The elasticity of supply can be found by dividing the percentage change in price into the percentage change in the quantity supplied.

See It

Use **Figure 5.3—The Supply of Pizza** to illustrate elasticity of supply. Direct students to the Graphing Workshop for Chapter 5 at **econxtra.swlearning.com**. Instruct students to click on **See It: Supply, and Shifts in Supply** to view the graph and listen to an explanation. Students may have already viewed the first part of this workshop, as directed for Figure 5.1. The first part of the workshop also pertains to Figure 5.3.

**The Graphing Workshop**    **The Supply of Pizza**

econxtra.swlearning.com

If the price increases from $9 to $12, the quantity of pizza supplied increases from 20 million to 24 million per week.

**Figure 5.3**

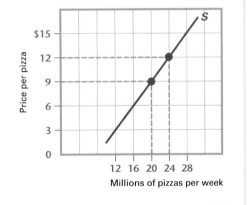

Lesson 5.1 • *The Supply Curve*    **135**

## Group Activity

Organize students into small groups. Assign groups to calculate the market supply for hours they would be willing to work at an after-school job in a fast-food restaurant at different wage rates. These rates might be $6, $7, $8, $9, or $10 per hour. Ask them to explain how their supply schedule demonstrates the law of supply. Is their supply of hours worked elastic or inelastic when the wage rate changes from $8 to $9 per hour? [Percent change in hours worked divided by percentage change in price of their labor (12.5%) = elasticity of supply]

Direct students to read the short passage entitled "Mongolian Goats and the Price of Cashmere Sweaters" that appears on this page. Use the questions as a starting point for class discussion or have students write a paragraph to answer the questions.

## Answers to Think Critically

Answers will vary. In the short run, the supply of cashmere is elastic because the Mongolians responded to the price decrease by lowering the supply of cashmere. Over the long run, however, the supply of cashmere is inelastic. At some point, the Mongolians are going to sell regardless of the price because they will need money to feed their goat herds and themselves.

## *Think Critically Through Visuals*

Use **Figure 5.4—Market Supply Becomes More Elastic Over Time** on page 137 to illustrate how the supply of gasoline becomes more elastic over time, with a different supply curve for each of three periods—a week, a month, and a year.

## TEAM WORK

Organize students into groups of four or five. Instruct teams to select a recorder and a spokesperson. Instruct students to complete the **Team Work** activity shown on page 137. Set a timer for 10 minutes. When the timer goes off, invite the spokesperson from each group to take a turn providing their group's findings.

## Answer

Answers will vary. Possible answer: In the short run, this is how five different industries would be able to respond from shortest to longest: farming (1), oil industry (2), clothing retailers (3), electronic industry (4), and automobile industry (5).

supplied—20 percent—divided by the percentage increase in price—33 percent—which equals 0.6.

### Categories of Supply Elasticity

The terminology for supply elasticity is the same as for demand elasticity. If supply *elasticity* exceeds 1.0, supply is *elastic*. If it equals 1.0, supply is *unit elastic*. If supply is less than 1.0, it is *inelastic*. Because 0.6 is less than 1.0, the supply of pizza is inelastic when the price increases from $9 to $12. Note that elasticity usually varies along a supply curve.

### Determinants of Supply Elasticity

The elasticity of supply indicates how responsive producers are to a change in price. Their responsiveness depends on how costly it is to alter output when the price changes. If the marginal cost of supplying additional units rises sharply as output expands, then a higher price will generate little increase in quantity supplied, so supply will tend to be inelastic. However, if the marginal cost rises slowly as output expands, the profit lure of a higher price will prompt a relatively large boost in output. In this case, supply will be more elastic.

One important determinant of supply elasticity is the length of the adjustment period under consideration. Just as demand becomes more elastic over time as consumers adjust to price changes, supply also becomes more elastic over time as producers adjust to price changes. The longer the time period under consideration, the more easily producers can adjust. For example, a higher oil price will prompt suppliers to pump more from existing wells in the short run. However, in the long run, suppliers can explore for more oil.

Figure 5.4 demonstrates how the supply of gasoline becomes more elastic over time, with a different supply curve for each of three periods. $S_w$ is the supply curve when the period of adjustment is a week. As you can see, a higher gasoline price will not prompt much of a response in quantity supplied because firms have little time to adjust. This supply curve is inelastic if the price increases from $1.00 to $1.25 per gallon.

$S_m$ is the supply curve when the adjustment period under consideration is a month. Firms have a greater ability to

## SPAN THE GLOBE

### Mongolian Goats and the Price of Cashmere Sweaters

Think there's a connection? Cashmere comes from the hair of cashmere goats, the majority of which (some 10 million) are raised primarily in Mongolia and northern China. Although that's a lot of goats, each one yields only about 2½ pounds of fleece per shearing. That 2½ pounds, in turn, produces only about 5 ounces of usable cashmere fiber after the labor-intensive job of cleaning and de-hairing. Consequently, the price of the warmer, softer cashmere usually is far higher than its competitor, wool. In past years, Mongolia's exports of this unique product have grown dramatically and, up until 2003, totaled around 2,000 tons with its internal usage of the product between 1,600 and 2,000 tons annually. Unfortunately for the Mongolian producers, the price of cashmere currently is down from a high of almost $20 per pound in 2002 to $9 a pound. This price decline has caused the Mongolian herdsmen to stockpile more than 3,000 tons of the material.

### Think Critically

In the short run (over the next few months), is Mongolia's supply of cashmere elastic or inelastic along the supply curve at the price of $9 per pound? Mongolia barely raises enough food for its people, much less its animals, and more than a million of the goats recently have starved to death. In view of this, would you consider the longer-term response to the $9 price to be elastic or inelastic? Explain your answer.

*Curriculum Connection—Foreign Language*

In the past 20 years, the number of high schools that teach Spanish has almost doubled. In many schools, it has been relatively easy to find teachers who are certified to teach Spanish. What has happened to increase the supply of qualified Spanish teachers in the United States? If the salary for Spanish teachers fell by 30 percent, what would happen to the number of qualified Spanish teachers who would be willing to teach in our high schools? (There has been an influx of people from Spanish-speaking countries to the United States. Many of them have become certified teachers.)

vary output in a month than they do in a week. Thus, supply is more elastic when the adjustment period is a month than when it's a week. Supply is even more elastic when the adjustment period is a year, as is shown by $S_y$. A given price increase in gasoline prompts a greater quantity supplied as the adjustment period lengthens. Research confirms the positive link between the elasticity of supply and the length of the adjustment period. *The elasticity of supply is typically greater the longer the period of adjustment.*

The ease of increasing quantity supplied in response to a higher price differs across industries. The long run will be longer for producers of electricity and timber (where expansion may take years) than for window washing and hot-dog vending (where expansion may take only days).

# TEAM WORK

Working in small groups, think of five industries other than those given as examples in this textbook. For each industry, describe the product or services sold, as well as the means of distribution, such as retail stores, online, or wholesale. Rank these industries in order of the time the industry needs to adjust to a price change. Give a ranking of 1 to industries that would require the least amount of time to adjust fully to a price change and a 5 to those that would require the most time. Provide an explanation for each of your rankings. Discuss your group's rankings in class.

 **CHECKPOINT**
What does the elasticity of supply measure, and what factors influence its numerical value?

**Market Supply Becomes More Elastic Over Time**                    Figure **5.4**

The supply curve one week after a price increase, $S_w$, is less elastic, at a given price, than the curve one month later, $S_m$, which is less elastic than the curve one year later, $S_y$. Given a price increase from $1.00 to $1.25, quantity supplied per day increases to 110 million gallons after one week, to 140 gallons after one month, and to 200 million gallons after one year.

Lesson 5.1 • *The Supply Curve* **137**

 **CHECKPOINT**
Invite a student to answer the checkpoint that appears on this page.

### Answer
The elasticity of supply measures the responsiveness of quantity supplied to price change. The percentage change in quantity supplied affects the elasticity of supply directly, and the percentage change in price affects the elasticity of supply indirectly.

### APPLY

Assign Lesson 5.1 from the Contemporary Economics Workbook.

 *e*-con @pps

Encourage students to apply their knowledge of concepts presented in this lesson as they explore economic news stories, policy debates, and data available at **econxtra.swlearning.com**. A sampling of the titles for this lesson appears below.

### EconNews
- The Blackout of 2003 May Increase Gasoline Prices

### ASSESS

Assign all or part of Lesson 5.1 Assessment on page 138 as homework or an in-class activity.

## Xtra! Study Tools

Direct students to the online study tools for Lesson 5.1 at **econxtra.swlearning.com**.

### CLOSE

**Revisit** the **In the News** feature on the first page of the lesson. Ask students to review their preliminary answers and discuss the questions, now that they have completed this lesson.

**Review** the objectives for Lesson 5.1. Students should be able to:
- Understand the law of supply.
- Describe the elasticity of supply, and explain how it is measured.

## RETEACH

The supply of many agricultural products is inelastic in the short run. This is particularly true for products that are grown on trees that take many years to mature. Ask students to explain why a 25 percent increase in the price of apples would have no immediate impact on the quantity of apples supplied by local growers. As a matter of fact, the supply of apples might increase five years later when the price of apples had fallen. Why is farming a risky business?

### Key Concepts

1. Answers will vary. Possible answer: The owner is motivated to maximize profit while the customers are interested in maximizing their personal satisfaction.

2. Answers will vary. Possible answer: The higher price will cause firms to shift resources from the production of other goods to the production of additional jackets. They may also attract new producers to the market.

3. The individual supply is the number of breakfasts sold by each individual restaurant. The market supply is the total number of breakfasts sold by all three restaurants.

4. The price elasticity of supply is elastic because a percentage change in price resulted in a greater percentage change in the quantity supplied. The elasticity in this case is 2.0 (20.0 / 10.0 = 2.0).

5. Answers will vary. Possible answer: It is easy to allocate more wood and labor to the production of wooden bowls; but only so many natural pearls are found each year, so a higher price is not likely to change this number very much.

### Graphing Exercise

6. The law of supply is demonstrated by the upward sloping supply curve. It shows that the owner is willing to supply greater quantities of shoes at higher prices. The graph for this answer appears at the bottom of this page.

### Think Critically

7. The percentage change in price is 33.3% ($1.00 / $3.00 = 0.333). The percentage change in the quantity supplied is 40.0% (2,000 / 5,000 = 0.40). The price elasticity of supply is 1.20 (0.40 / .333 = 1.20). It is elastic.

### Key Concepts

1. In what ways are the motives of a pizza restaurant owner different from the motives of customers who buy the restaurant's pizza?

2. Why should the quantity of winter jackets supplied increase when there is an increase in the price of these jackets?

3. There are three restaurants that open at 7:00 A.M. to serve breakfast in a small community. Each one charges $4.00 for two eggs, bacon, toast and a cup of coffee. Together they sell 220 breakfasts on an average weekday morning. What is the individual and market supply in this situation?

4. When the market price of kitchen chairs increases by 10 percent, producers of these chairs increase the quantity supplied by 20 percent. Is supply elastic, unit elastic, or inelastic? Explain how you know your answer is correct. What is the measure of elasticity in this situation?

5. Why is the price elasticity of supply likely to be greater for wooden bowls than for natural pearls?

### Graphing Exercise

6. The owner of a shoe store reviewed her costs to determine how many pairs of running shoes she would be willing to supply each month at different prices. The results of her research appear in the supply schedule at the right. Use this data to construct her supply curve for running shoes. Explain how the graph demonstrates the law of supply.

**Supply of Running Shoes**

| Price | Quantity Supplied |
|-------|-------------------|
| $70 | 100 |
| $60 | 80 |
| $50 | 60 |
| $40 | 40 |
| $30 | 20 |

### Think Critically

7. **Mathematics** The table below shows how much cheese three dairies in a small community supply each month at the current price of $3.00 per pound. It also shows how much each one would supply if the price increased to $4.00. Calculate the percentage change in price and quantity supplied that would result from this price increase. What is the price elasticity of supply for cheese in this market? Is the supply elastic, unit elastic, or inelastic?

**Supply of Cheese at $3.00 and $4.00 per pound**

| Dairy | Quantity Supplied at $3.00 | Quantity Supplied at $4.00 |
|-------|----------------------------|----------------------------|
| A | 1,000 pounds | 1,300 pounds |
| B | 1,700 pounds | 2,600 pounds |
| C | 2,300 pounds | 3,100 pounds |
| Total Production | 5,000 pounds | 7,000 pounds |

**Supply of Running Shoes**

### Visualizing the Answer— Graphing Exercise

6. The answer includes a graph. Students' graphs should look similar to the one shown here. An Excel spreadsheet containing this graph, along with supporting data, is available on the Instructor's Resource CD.

# Sharpen Your Life Skills

## Understand Cause and Effect

In economics, as in most other fields of study, things don't "just happen." There is a logical reason, or a cause, for almost every economic event. The goal of studying economic events that have taken place in the past is to learn about their causes so we can predict what will happen when similar events take place in the future. Consider each of the following events from American history and their results. What can you learn that could help you better understand future economic events?

In 1892, workers at the Carnegie Steel Plant in Homestead, Pennsylvania, went on strike, closing down this factory. This reduced the supply of steel and may have contributed to workers at other factories that used steel being laid off.

In 1903, the Wright brothers were credited with having made the first powered flight. This led to a new mode of transportation that millions of Americans now use each year. With a few exceptions, the supply curve of air transportation has steadily moved to the right over time.

In 1929, the stock market crash contributed to the failure of thousands of U.S. businesses and the onset of the Great Depression of the 1930s. The supply of many products fell during the early years of the Great Depression.

In 1938, the Fair Labor Standards Act was passed that established the 40-hour workweek. This caused some businesses to hire additional workers to avoid paying workers overtime wages and may have increased their cost of production. If this was true, the supply curve for these firms' products would have shifted to the left.

## Apply Your Skill

1. At the beginning of 2003, President George W. Bush suggested reducing taxes for businesses that purchased new machinery or hired additional workers. Describe the effect that this suggested policy was intended to cause. How would it affect the supply of many products in the U.S. economy?

2. In 2003, farmers in central California were told that they were taking more than their share of water from the Colorado River. They were ordered to plan to reduce the amount of water they took for irrigation. Nearly a third of the lettuce and many other vegetables grown in the United States are produced in central California. If this ruling were enforced, what might happen to the supply of vegetables American consumers could buy?

**Understand Cause and Effect**

After studying Lesson 5.1, students should be able to answer the questions on this page.

**Apply Your Skill**

Consider allowing students to work in pairs for this assignment.

**Answers**

1. Answers will vary. Students may point out that this policy was intended to encourage growth in U.S. production. Lower taxes and new technology could reduce the cost of production and shift supply curves to the right.

2. Answers will vary. Students may point out that these farmers may not be able to produce as many vegetables in the future. This would shift their supply curve to the left.

**Follow-Up Activity**

Invite interested students to research one of the topics to learn the actual effect of the tax cut or the water ruling in California.

## Extend the Content

Invite interested students to choose a major economic event that occurred in your community or a nearby community. Instruct students to write a short paragraph describing cause and effect. Suggest that students use the four events described on this page as models for their work. Encourage students to include a visual, such as a drawing or photograph, to illustrate their work. This activity is suitable for students working in pairs.

Explain that this lesson identifies events that may cause a business to supply more or fewer products when there is no change in the price of the product. Remind students that entrepreneurs operate businesses to earn a profit. Events that increase a firm's profits usually cause that firm to supply more products, even if the price remains unchanged. Events that decrease a firm's profits usually cause that firm to supply fewer products, even if the price remains unchanged. Return to the example of candy bars being sold at football games. How would the students have reacted if the cost of the candy bars they sold had fallen from $1.25 to $.75 while they continued to charge their customers $1.50? Why would they have been willing to supply more candy bars, even though the price they charged did not change?

## Objectives

Remind students to read the lesson objectives to help focus their attention before reading the lesson.

## Key Terms

Direct students to write each key term on a separate index card. Then write the matching definition and page reference on the back of the appropriate card. Suggest that students include a rough graph corresponding to the concept. Encourage students to use the cards to study for quizzes and tests.

### [ In the News ]

Instruct students to read the passage and write down their answers. Point out that their answers might change after they finish studying Lesson 5.2.

### Answers to Think About It

Answers will vary. Possible answer: The Clean Diamond Trade Act will shift the supply curve of diamonds in the United States downward.

## Visual Presentation

Use the PowerPoint presentation on the Instructor's Resource CD as an adjunct to your lecture. The presentation also can be used for review.

## Objectives

> Identify the determinants of supply, and explain how a change in each will affect the supply curve.

> Contrast a movement along the supply curve with a shift of the supply curve.

## Overview

The supply curve illustrates the relation between the price of a good and the quantity supplied, other things constant. Assumed constant along a supply curve are the determinants of supply other than the good's price. There are five such determinants of supply. A change in one of these determinants of supply causes a shift of the supply curve. This contrasts with a change in price, other things constant, that causes a movement along a supply curve.

## Key Terms

**movement along a supply curve**

**shift of a supply curve**

### [ In the News ]

#### ● Conflict vs. Clean Diamonds

In 2003, President George W. Bush signed the Clean Diamond Trade Act. The Act should decrease markedly the importation and sale of diamonds from several nations where brutal regimes control their production. The Act institutionalizes the Kimberley Process Certification Scheme. This scheme or plan is intended to insure that diamonds entering the United States are certified as not being "conflict diamonds." These are diamonds that have been mined and sold to finance decades-long wars and atrocities in Africa and have reportedly financed al-Qaeda as well. More than 50 countries, both producing and importing nations, have agreed to participate in the plan. In addition, the diamond industry has agreed to establish a system of warranties under which dealers purchase stones only from sellers who can prove the merchandise's legitimacy.

#### Think About It

What effect(s) do you think this Act will have on the supply curve of diamonds in the United States?

140

### National Content Standards in Economics

A complete list of the NCEE Standards appears on pages xxiv–xxv of this book. The following standards are addressed in Lesson 5.2.

Standard 4: Role of Incentives

Standard 7: Markets—Price and Quantity Determination

Standard 8: Role of Price in Market System

# Determinants of Supply

Because each firm's supply curve is based on the cost of production and profit opportunities in the market, anything that affects production costs and profit opportunities helps shape the supply curve. Following are the five determinants of market supply other than the price of the good:

1. The cost of resources used to make the good

2. The price of other goods these resources could make

3. The technology used to make the good

4. Producer expectations

5. The number of sellers in the market

## Changes in the Price of Resources

Any change in the costs of resources used to make a good will affect the supply of the good. For example, suppose the price of mozzarella cheese falls. This reduces the cost of making pizza. Producers are therefore more willing and able to supply pizza at each price, as reflected by a rightward shift of the supply curve from *S* to *S'* in Figure 5.5. After the shift, the quantity supplied increases at each price level. For example, at a price of $12, the quantity supplied is higher from 24 million to 28 million pizzas a week, as shown by the movement from point *g* to point *h*. In short, *an increase in supply—that is, a rightward shift of the supply curve—means that producers are more willing and able to supply more pizzas at each price.*

What if there is an increase in the price of a resource used to make pizza? This means that at every level of output, the cost of supplying pizza increases. An increase in the price of a resource will reduce supply, meaning a leftward shift of the supply curve. For example, if the wage of pizza workers increases, the higher labor cost would increase the cost of making pizza.

Higher production costs decrease supply, so pizza supply shifts leftward, as from *S* to *S''* in Figure 5.6. After the decrease in supply, producers offer less for sale at each price. For example, at a price of $12 per pizza, the quantity supplied falls from 24 million to 20 million

**An Increase in the Supply of Pizza**

econxtra.swlearning.com

**Figure 5.5**

An increase in the supply of pizza is reflected by a rightward shift of the supply curve, from *S* to *S'*. After the increase in supply, the quantity of pizza supplied at a price of $12 increases from 24 million pizzas (point *g*) to 28 million pizzas (point *h*).

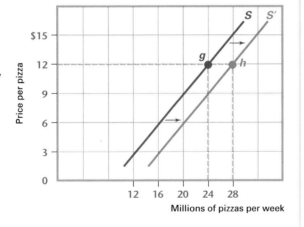

Lesson 5.2 • *Shifts of the Supply Curve*    **141**

## Outside Resources

***The Statistical Abstract of the United States*** This valuable resource can be found at www.census.gov/prod/www/statistical-abstract-us.html. A table titled "Selected Timber Products— Producer Price Indexes" appears in the Natural Resources section. This table indicates changes in the price of basic lumber products. Ask students to find this table, or download it and provide it to them. Discuss how changes in the costs of materials used in construction would affect the supply of new houses.

## TEACH

### Determinants of Supply

Point out that 30 years ago, the only telephones offered to the public were hard wired into the AT&T telephone system. At that time, making long distance calls was quite expensive. Ask students to discuss changes that have taken place during their lives that have increased the supply of long distance telephone communication, even though the price has not increased and is in fact lower. How has new communications technology caused the supply curve for telephone communications to shift? Lead this into a discussion of the impact that technology has on the costs of production and therefore on the location of many firms' supply curves.

See It

Use **Figure 5.5—An Increase in the Supply of Pizza** to illustrate a shift of the supply curve. Direct students to the Graphing Workshop for Chapter 5 at **econxtra.swlearning.com** for another example of a supply curve. Instruct students to click on **See It: Supply, and Shifts in Supply** to view the graph and listen to an explanation. The first part of this workshop will be a review of the supply schedule and supply curve. The last part covers shifts in supply, the topic of Figure 5.5.

**Investigate Your Local Economy** Assign the activity on page 143. In addition to contacting the local government's bureau of taxation, suggest that students search local newspaper archives (often available online) to find stories related to the impact of taxation on local business. Consider allowing students to work in pairs.

## Determinants of Supply

Tell students to imagine that a way to convert water into gasoline has been discovered. Although it will take several years to supply all the gasoline needed, it is only a matter of time before the price of gasoline falls to 5 cents per gallon. They should also imagine that they own a refinery that has stored 5 billion gallons of gasoline. What will happen to the amount of gasoline they are willing to supply at the current price? The supply curve for gasoline will shift to the right because of this change in expectations.

### *Think Critically Through Visuals*

Use **Figure 5.6—A Decrease in the Supply of Pizza** to illustrate a shift of the supply curve.

Instruct students to click on **See It: Supply, and Shift in Supply** to view the graph and listen to an explanation. The first part of this workshop will be a review of the supply schedule and supply curve. The last part covers shifts in supply, the topic of Figure 5.6.

### CHECKPOINT

Invite a student to answer the checkpoint that appears on page 143.

### Answer

The five determinants of supply are:

1. *Cost of resources:* An increase in the cost of resources will shift the supply curve inward.

2. *The price of other goods the resources could make:* An increase of this will shift the supply curve inward.

3. *Technology used to make the good:* An increase in this will shift the supply curve outward.

4. *Producer expectations:* An increase in this will cause the supply curve to shift outward.

5. *The number of sellers in the markets:* An increase in this will cause the supply curve to shift outward.

---

per week. This is shown in Figure 5.6 by the movement from point *g* to point *i*.

## Changes in the Prices of Other Goods

Nearly all resources have alternative uses. The labor, building, machinery, ingredients, and knowledge needed to make pizza could produce other products, such as bread sticks, rolls, and other baked goods.

A change in the price of another good these resources could make affects the opportunity cost of making pizza. For example, if the price of rolls falls, the opportunity cost of making pizza declines. These resources are not as profitable in their best alternative use, which is making rolls. So pizza production becomes relatively more attractive. As resources shift from baking rolls to making pizza, the supply of pizza increases, or shifts to the right, as shown in Figure 5.5.

On the other hand, if the price of rolls increases, so does the opportunity cost of making pizza. Some pizza makers may bake more rolls and less pizza, so the supply of pizza decreases, or shifts to the left, as in Figure 5.6. A change in the price of another good these resources

could produce affects the profit opportunities available to producers.

## Changes in Technology

The state of technology represents the economy's stock of knowledge about how to combine resources efficiently. Discoveries in chemistry, biology, electronics, and many other fields have created new products, improved existing products, and lowered the cost of production. For example, the first microprocessor, the Intel 4004, could execute about 400 computations per second when it hit the market in 1971. Today a standard PC often can handle more than 2 billion computations per second, *or 5 million* times what the 1971 Intel 4004 could handle. Technological change—in this case, faster computers—lowers the cost of producing goods whose production involves computers, from automobile manufacturing to document processing.

Along a given market supply curve, technological know-how about how this good can be manufactured is assumed to remain unchanged. If a more efficient technology is discovered, the cost of production will fall, making this market more profitable. Improvements in technology make firms more willing and

---

**A Decrease in the Supply of Pizza**

**Figure 5.6**

A decrease in the supply of pizza is reflected by a leftward shift of the supply curve, from *S* to *S″*. After the decrease in supply, the quantity of pizza supplied at a price of $12 decreases from 24 million pizzas (point *g*) to 20 million pizzas (point *i*).

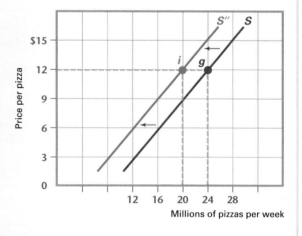

---

At the beginning of the twenty-first century, many automobile manufacturers made little profit producing standard family sedans. Their profits were being generated almost entirely by huge SUVs and luxury models. As a result, manufacturers introduced a wide variety of new, expensive cars. Ask students to sketch supply curves and explain how this situation would have caused a shift in supply both for luxury models and standard family sedans. What problem are manufacturers likely to encounter as more luxury models are brought to market? (The supply for sedans shifted to the left while supply for luxury models shifted to the right, as resources were reallocated from low-profit to high-profit production.)

able to supply the good at each price. Consequently, supply will increase, as reflected by a rightward shift of the supply curve. For example, suppose a new high-tech oven bakes pizza in half the time. Such a breakthrough would shift the supply curve rightward, as from *S* to *S'* in Figure 5.5, so that more is supplied at each possible price.

## Changes in Producer Expectations

Producers transform resources into goods they hope can be sold for a profit. Any change that affects producer expectations about profitability can affect market supply. For example, if pizza prices are expected to increase in the future, some pizza makers may expand production capacity now. This would shift the supply of pizza rightward, as shown in Figure 5.5.

Some goods can be stored easily. For example, crude oil can be left in the ground and grain can be stored in a silo. Expecting higher prices in the future might prompt some producers of these goods to *reduce* their current supply while awaiting the higher price. This would shift the supply curve to the left, as shown in Figure 5.6. Thus, an expectation of higher prices in the future could either increase or decrease current supply, depending on the good.

## Changes in the Number of Sellers in the Market

General changes in the market environment also can affect the number of sellers in the market. For example, government regulations may influence market supply. As a case in point, for decades government strictly regulated the prices and entry of new firms in a variety of industries including airlines, trucking, and telecommunications. During that period, the number of firms in the market was artificially limited by these government restrictions. When these restrictions were eliminated, more firms entered these markets, increasing supply.

Any government action that affects a market's profitability, such as a change in business taxes, could shift the supply curve. Lower business taxes will increase supply and higher business taxes will reduce supply.

The increase in the number of firms is not simply a response to a price change. Along a given market supply curve, there usually are fewer suppliers at lower prices than higher prices. Higher prices attract producers and increase the quantity supplied along the supply curve.

### Investigate Your Local Economy

Businesses generally pay income taxes to local, state, and the federal government. Contact your local government's bureau of taxation. Find out the current tax rate for businesses. Also find the rate for the past five years. Has an increase or decrease in the tax rate affected supply in your area? Write a paragraph to explain your findings.

✓ **CHECKPOINT**
What are the five determinants of supply, and how do changes in each affect the supply of a good?

# Movements Along a Supply Curve Versus Shifts of a Supply Curve

Note again the distinction between a *movement along a supply curve* and a *shift of a supply curve*. A change in *price*, other things constant, causes a **movement along a supply curve** from one price-

**movement along a supply curve**

Change in quantity supplied resulting from a change in the price of the good, other things constant

Lesson 5.2 • *Shifts of the Supply Curve* **143**

---

### *Curriculum Connection—Journalism*

Invite a journalist who covers business or government for a local newspaper to speak to your class about the local economy. Ask the speaker to share some of the resources and sources that are routinely used by journalists who write about the economy. Encourage the speaker to provide a handout, such as a copy of a recently published story.

---

**CHECKPOINT**

Invite a student to answer the checkpoint that appears on this page.

**Answer**

A change in price causes a movement along the supply curve from one price-quantity combination to another. A change in one of the determinants of supply other than price causes a shift of a supply curve. This results in a change in the quantity supplied at each price.

### APPLY

Assign Lesson 5.2 from the Contemporary Economics Workbook.

Encourage students to apply their knowledge of concepts presented in this lesson as they explore economic news stories, policy debates, and data available at **econxtra.swlearning.com**.

### ASSESS

Assign all or part of Lesson 5.2 Assessment on page 145 as homework or an in-class activity.

## Xtra! Study Tools

Direct students to the online study tools for Lesson 5.2 at **econxtra.swlearning.com**.

### CLOSE

**Revisit** the In the News feature on the first page of the lesson. Ask students to review their preliminary answers and discuss the questions, now that they have completed this lesson.

**Review** the objectives for Lesson 5.2.

- Identify the determinants of supply, and explain how a change in each will affect the supply curve.
- Contrast a movement along the supply curve with a shift of the supply curve.

---

**shift of a supply curve**

Increase or decrease in supply resulting from a change in one of the determinants of supply other than the price of the good

quantity combination to another. A change in one of the determinants of supply other than the price causes a **shift of a supply curve**, changing supply. A shift of the supply curve means a change in the quantity supplied at each price.

A change in price, other things constant, changes quantity supplied along a given supply curve. A change in a determinant of supply other than the price of the good—such as the prices of resources used to make the good, technology used to make the good, the price of other goods these resources could produce, producer expectations, and the number of firms in the market—shifts the entire supply curve to the right or left.

**CHECKPOINT**

Explain the difference between a movement along a supply curve and a shift of a supply curve.

## NETBookmark

Read the E-conomics feature, below, about the use of credit-card technology at fast-food restaurants. McDonald's Corporation is working with eMac Digital in developing its new point-of-sale (POS) software system. To learn more about the relationship between McDonald's and eMac, access two press releases through econxtra.swlearning.com. Why did McDonald's sell its ownership interest in eMac? How is this consistent with McDonald's focus on specialization and division of labor? What determinant of supply does the POS system represent?

*econxtra.swlearning.com*

## E-CONOMICS

**Faster Fast Food** Pay for your Big Mac with a credit card? McDonald's has been testing the system and says customers soon will be able to pay for their burgers and fries with credit cards. In a world of charging everything on plastic cards, fast-food chains have been slow to get with the program. But customers want to be able to put just about everything they buy on a credit card. According to a market research firm, if credit-card use really takes hold, service at fast-food outlets will become even faster. The lines will move more quickly because the latest high-speed technologies and fiber-optic networks are making credit-card transactions even faster than paying

with cash. Current technologies enable a customer to call out an order at the drive-through, or at the counter, and then swipe a credit card and have it approved in less than 5 seconds. On the other hand, cash transactions take an average of 8 to 10 seconds. With widespread use of credit cards, fast-food outlets will be able to supply more hungry customers in the same amount of time.

**Think Critically**

Will the use of credit-card technology at fast-food restaurants be likely to cause a movement along the supply curve or a shift of the supply for fast food? Explain your answer.

144   **CHAPTER 5**  Supply

---

### RETEACH

Tell students to imagine Gus, a 10-year-old who earns money by walking dogs after school. He charges $4 for a 30-minute walk. Lots of people would like to hire him but he is unwilling to work for anyone who lives more than a few blocks from his home because he walks to their houses to pick up their dogs. It would take too much time to work for anyone who lives further away. Then Gus buys a bicycle and is willing to work for people who live up to a mile from his home. Ask students to discuss why this change in technology would cause the supply curve for dog walks to shift to the right.

## Key Concepts

1. One year a farmer grows corn on his 200 acres of land. He sells his corn in September for $3.00 per bushel. Early the next spring he notices that the price of soybeans has gone up 50 percent while the price of corn has remained the same. What will probably happen to his supply curve for corn? Explain your answer.

2. The Apex Plastics Corp. finds a new way to produce plastic outdoor furniture from recycled milk bottles at very low cost. What will happen to the supply curve for plastic furniture? Explain your answer.

3. A big storm destroys most of the sugarcane crop in Louisiana. Most people expect this to cause a large increase in the price of sugar in the next few months. What will happen to the supply curve for sugar?

4. The cost of crude oil increases by 25 percent. Crude oil is the basic raw material used to produce plastic. What will this do to the supply curve for plastic toys?

5. How might an increase in the minimum wage shift both the demand curve and supply curve for pizza?

## Graphing Exercise

6. Make a copy of the supply curve. Draw and explain the shifts of the market supply on your copy that would result from each of the following events. Label each shift of the supply curve.

a. There is an increase in the cost of rubber used to produce the soles of running shoes.

b. There is a decrease in the market price of rubber tires.

c. A new machine is invented that produces running shoes with only one-third as many workers.

d. A new mall is built in town with three stores that offer running shoes for sale.

**Supply Curve for Running Shoes**

## Think Critically

7. **Research** Use newspapers, magazines, or the Internet to research a world event that could have an impact of the supply of a product consumed in the United States. Describe this event and explain how it might shift the U.S. supply curve.

8. **Technology** Choose a single product many consumers buy, and write a paragraph that discusses whether the creation of the Internet has shifted the supply curve for this product.

**Xtra!**
Study Tools
econxtra.swlearning.com

**Supply Curve for Running Shoes**

*Visualizing the Answer—*
*Graphing Exercise*

6. The answer includes a graph. Students' graphs should look similar to the one shown here.

*Key Concepts*

1. Answers will vary. Possible answer: The increase in the price of soybeans might cause the farmer to grow them instead of corn. This would cause his supply curve for corn to shift to the left.

2. Answers will vary. Possible answer: This new technology that reduces the cost of producing plastic furniture will shift the supply curve for this product to the right.

3. Answers will vary. Possible answer: The businesses that have sugar to sell may hold it back so they can sell it later at a higher price. This will shift the supply curve for sugar to the left.

4. Answers will vary. Possible answer: The increased cost of oil will increase the cost of plastic used to make toys. This will shift the supply curve for plastic toys to the left.

5. Answers will vary. Possible answer: An increased minimum wage could provide consumers with more income so they could buy more pizza. This would shift demand to the right. However, the higher wage would cause pizza suppliers to have higher costs, so the supply curve for pizza might shift to the left.

*Graphing Exercise*

6. The graph for this answer appears at the bottom of this page.

a. The supply curve will shift left because of an increase in the cost of rubber.

b. The supply curve will shift right because of a decrease in the price of a product that rubber could be used to produce.

c. The supply curve will shift right because of more efficient technology.

d. The supply curve will shift to the right because there are more firms offering running shoes for sale.

*Think Critically*

7. Answers will vary. Possible answer: A war, storm, or political unrest in a nation that exports important products to the United States could shift the supply curve for these products in this country.

8. Answers will vary. Possible answer: The Internet has increased the number of businesses from which consumers may buy goods and services. This has caused the supply curve for most consumer products to shift to the right.

# movers & shakers

Point out that businesses supplying similar products are not always equally successful. Ask students to explain the factors they consider when they choose to purchase a pizza. Are they looking for low price, quality, convenience, or some other quality? By supplying superior products or greater convenience, some firms are able to succeed even when they charge a premium price. Furthermore, higher prices encourage them to open more stores and supply even more products in the future. This will shift their supply curves to the right over time. Ask students to consider this **Movers & Shakers** feature and explain how John Schnatter was able to become successful by supplying superior-quality pizza.

## TEACH

Instruct students to read the **Movers & Shakers** feature about John Schnatter. Point out that some students may find it helpful to read the article, read the questions at the bottom of the page, and then reread the article.

## ASSESS

Use the questions in Source Reading and Entrepreneurs in Action at the bottom of the profile to assess the students' understanding of this **Movers & Shakers** feature.

### Answers to Source Reading

John Schnatter's determination and attention to detail and quality make him a successful entrepreneur.

### Answers to Entrepreneurs in Action

The company needs to make its price comparable to that of frozen pizzas. Additionally, it needs to make sure that it is always more convenient to order a pizza from Papa John's than to go to the grocery store for one.

# movers & shakers

**John Schnatter** *Founder, Papa John's Pizza*

During high school and college, John Schnatter earned spending money by working part-time in national-chain pizzerias. He noticed something missing from every one of them: No one was making a superior-quality pizza that could be delivered directly to the customer. He dreamed of one day opening his own pizza restaurant, doing everything right.

In 1984, Schnatter graduated from Ball State University with a degree in business administration and then returned home to Jeffersonville, Indiana. There he took the first step to introduce the world to his own superior pizza. First he knocked out a broom closet in the rear of his father's business. Then he sold his beloved 1972 Camaro in order to purchase $1,600 worth of used restaurant equipment, including his first pizza oven. The first Papa John's restaurant opened in 1985. Less than twenty years later 3,000 Papa John's restaurants operate in 49 states and 12 international markets.

Schnatter's successful business philosophy is to focus on one thing and do it better than anyone else. He keeps the menu simple and uses only superior-quality ingredients. He insists on using fresh (never frozen) water-purified traditional dough, vine-ripened fresh-packed tomato sauce, and 100 percent mozzarella cheese.

For four consecutive years, Papa John's was rated number one in customer satisfaction among all national fast-food restaurants in the American Customer Satisfaction Index. Papa John's also was rated number one in product quality in the Restaurants & Institutions' Choice in Chains consumer survey for seven consecutive years. In 2000, Papa John's become the third-largest pizza company in the world.

Schnatter established his company headquarters in Louisville, Kentucky, and is one of Louisville's most successful business leaders. Now in his early forties, this young entrepreneur is generous with his annual earnings, which exceed $1 million a year.

The pizza market has presented Papa John's with some obstacles. In 2001, the industry became stagnant, partly because of increasingly strong competition from frozen grocery pizzas. When things didn't change in 2002, Papa John's largest rivals, Pizza Hut and Dominos, focused on offering deep discounts to customers to increase sales. Instead of following suit, Schnatter decided his company would focus on product quality and manager retention. He spent between $6 million and $7 million on these two efforts alone. Schnatter said he believes that "consistently getting a better product out the door" will result in improved sales, adding that one way to enhance quality is to reduce staff turnover. The company also has begun online ordering.

As Papa John's founder, Chairman of the Board, President, and Chief Executive Officer, Schnatter continues to be enthusiastic about making superior-quality pizzas that can be delivered directly to the customer. "I love the product, I like the people, I love the business. You've got to understand I've been doing this since I was 15...It's all I know."

## SOURCE READING

Analyze the quotations attributed to John Schnatter. From these statements, what qualities do you think he possesses that make him a successful entrepreneur?

## ENTREPRENEURS IN ACTION

In small groups, role-play Papa John's Board of Directors, with one student portraying Schnatter. The company is faced with stiff competition from frozen grocery pizzas and deep discounting from its direct competitors. Discuss the steps management needs to take in order to keep the company growing.

### Extend the Content

Have students visit the Papa John's web site at www.papajohns.com. Instruct them to read the Core Values and Mission Statements, and then write a short report about how these ideas contribute to the success of the company. Extend this activity by asking students to prepare an oral presentation of their findings.

## Objectives

> Understand how marginal product varies as a firm employs more labor in the short run.

> Explain the shape of the firm's marginal cost curve and identify what part of that is the firm's supply curve.

> Distinguish between economies of scale and diseconomies of scale in the long run.

## Overview

How much will a firm supply in order to maximize profit? The answer to this question requires a brief introduction to how a firm converts productive resources into outputs. In general, a profit-maximizing firm will supply more output to the market as long as the marginal revenue from each unit sold exceeds its marginal cost.

## Key Terms

short run
long run
total product
marginal product
law of diminishing returns
fixed cost
variable cost
total cost
marginal cost
marginal revenue
competitive firm's supply curve
economies of scale
long-run average curve cost

Point out that this lesson demonstrates the types of costs businesses pay when they supply goods or services to the market. Remind students that businesses exist to earn a profit and that profit is equal to the revenue they receive from their sales less the costs they paid to supply products. Any factor that either increases or decreases their costs will affect their profits, and therefore the amount of product they are willing to supply. By studying costs of production, businesses can determine how many products they should supply at each possible price.

### Objectives

Remind students to read the lesson objectives to help focus their attention before reading the lesson.

### Key Terms

Direct students to create a database using the key terms for this lesson. The database fields should include terms, definitions, and page numbers. Point out that the process of keying the data is an effective way to study key terms.

### [ In the News ]

Instruct students to read the passage and write down their answers. Point out that their answers might change after they finish studying Lesson 5.3.

### Answers to Think About It

Answers will vary. Possible answer: This reading illustrates the economic principle of economies of scale.

### Visual Presentation

Use the PowerPoint presentation on the Instructor's Resource CD as an adjunct to your lecture. The presentation also can be used for review.

## [ In the News ]

### ● At the Local Megaplex

Have you ever wondered why movie theaters seem to be offering moviegoers more and more screens? Think about it in this way: A theater with one screen needs someone to sell tickets, someone to sell popcorn, and someone to operate the projector. If another screen is added, the same staff can perform these tasks for both screens. Thus, the ticket seller becomes more productive by selling tickets to both movies. Also, construction costs per screen are reduced because only one lobby and one set of rest rooms are required. The theater can run bigger, more noticeable newspaper ads and can spread the cost over more films. From 1990 to 2000, the number of screens in the United States grew faster than the number of theaters, so the average number of screens per theater increased.

### Think About It

As you read this section, look for the economic principle this situation illustrates. What do economists call this principle?

**147**

### National Content Standards in Economics

**NCEE**

A complete list of the NCEE Standards appears on pages xxiv–xxv of this book. The following standards are addressed in Lesson 5.3.

Standard 2: Marginal Cost/Benefit

Standard 6: Specialization and Trade

Standard 7: Markets—Price and Quantity Determination

Standard 8: Role of Price in Market System

Standard 9: Role of Competition

Standard 13: Role of Resources in Determining Income

Standard 14: Profit and the Entrepreneur

**short run**
A period during which at least one of a firm's resources is fixed

**long run**
A period during which all resources can be varied

**total product**
The total output of the firm

**marginal product**
The change in total product resulting from a one-unit change in a particular resource, all other resources constant

**law of diminishing returns**
As more of a variable resource is added to a given amount of fixed resources, marginal product eventually declines and could become negative

# Production in the Short Run

A firm tries to earn a profit by converting productive resources, or *inputs,* into goods and services, or *outputs.* Consider production at a hypothetical moving company called Hercules at Your Service.

## Fixed and Variable Resources

All producers, like Hercules, use two categories of resources: fixed and variable. Resources that cannot be altered easily—the size of the building, for example—are called *fixed resources.* Hercules' fixed resources consist of a warehouse, a moving van, and some moving equipment. Resources that can be varied quickly to change output are called *variable resources.* In this example, assume that labor is the only variable resource.

When considering the time required to change the quantity of resources employed, economists distinguish between the short run and the long run. In the **short run**, at least one resource is fixed. In the **long run**, no resources are fixed. Hercules is operating in the short run because some resources are fixed. In this example, labor is the only resource that varies in the short run. A firm can enter or leave a market in the long run but not in the short run.

Figure 5.7 relates the amount of labor employed to the amount of furnishings moved. Labor is measured in worker-days, which is one worker for one day, and output is measured in tons of furnishings moved per day. The first column shows the total product per day, measured in tons of furniture moved. **Total product** is the total output of the firm. The second column shows the number of workers required for that total product. The third column shows the **marginal product** of each worker—that is, the amount by which the total product changes with each additional worker, assuming other resources remain unchanged.

## Increasing Returns

Without labor, nothing gets moved, so total product is zero when no workers are hired. If one worker is hired, that person must do all the driving, packing, and moving. A single worker cannot easily move some of the larger items. Still, one worker manages to move 2 tons per day. When a second worker is hired, some division of labor occurs, and two can move the big stuff more easily, so production more than doubles to 5 tons per day. The marginal product of the second worker is 3 tons per day.

Adding a third worker allows for an even better division of labor, which contributes to increased production. For example, one worker can specialize in packing fragile items while the other two do the heavy lifting. The total product of three workers is 9 tons per day, 4 tons more than with two workers. The firm experiences *increasing returns* from labor as each of the first three workers is hired, meaning that marginal product increases as more labor is hired.

## Law of Diminishing Returns

Hiring a fourth worker adds to the total product but not as much as was added by a third. Hiring still more workers increases total product by successively smaller amounts, so the marginal product in Figure 5.7 declines after three workers. Beginning with the fourth worker, the **law of diminishing returns** takes hold. This law states that as more units of one resource are added to all other resources, marginal product eventually declines. *The law of diminishing returns is the most important feature of production in the short run.*

As long as marginal product is positive, total product continues to increase. However, as additional workers are hired, total product may eventually decline. For example, an eighth worker would crowd the work area so much that people get in each other's way. As a result, total output would drop, meaning a negative

---

### Outside Resources

**Utility Bills** Use a utility bill to start a discussion about the different types of costs producers pay. Electric bills typically feature a relatively high rate for the first units of power used. As more electricity is consumed, however, the rate per KWH generally falls. Students can be shown copies of such bills and asked to explain the price structure. They should come up with the idea that the first units are expensive, to cover the fixed cost of producing electricity. Then, additional units are less expensive because the marginal cost of producing additional electricity is lower.

**Short-Run Relationship Between Units of Labor and Tons of Furniture Moved**   **Figure 5.7**

As each of the first three workers is hired, the firm experiences increasing returns from labor. Marginal product increases as more labor is hired. Beginning with the fourth worker, the law of diminishing returns takes hold. This law states that as more units of one resource are added to all other resources, marginal product eventually declines.

| Total Product (tons moved per day) | Units of the Variable Resource (worker-days) | Marginal Product (tons moved per day) |
|---|---|---|
| 0 | 0 | — |
| 2 | 1 | 2 |
| 5 | 2 | 3 |
| 9 | 3 | 4 |
| 12 | 4 | 3 |
| 14 | 5 | 2 |
| 15 | 6 | 1 |
| 15 | 7 | 0 |
| 14 | 8 | −1 |

marginal product. Likewise, a restaurant can hire only so many workers before congestion and confusion cut total product. "Too many cooks spoil the broth."

## Marginal Product Curve

Figure 5.8 shows the marginal product of labor, using data from Figure 5.7. Note that because of increasing returns, marginal product increases with each of the first three workers. Beginning with the fourth worker, diminishing returns cut marginal product. Marginal product turns negative if an eighth worker is hired. Figure 5.8 identifies three ranges of marginal product:

1. Increasing marginal returns

2. Diminishing but positive marginal returns

3. Negative marginal returns.

As you will soon learn, firms normally produce in the range of diminishing but positive marginal returns.

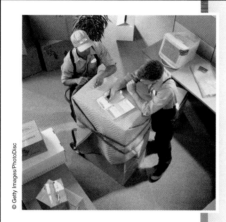
© Getty Images/PhotoDisc

**When Hercules at Your Service hires a second worker, division of labor occurs, and production more than doubles. What is total product and marginal product with two workers? With three workers? What happens when a fourth worker is hired?**

*Lesson 5.3 • Production and Cost*   **149**

## TEACH (continued)

### Production in the Short Run

Give one student a blanket and ask this person to fold it neatly. Time and record the student's progress. Then have two students complete the same task. They will be able to fold the blanket much more quickly because they can hold it better. Add a third and then a fourth student. Require each student to participate in the folding process. The time it takes to fold the blanket will begin to grow as they get in each other's way. Use this example to begin a discussion of decreasing and increasing returns of employing additional factors of production—in this case, additional workers.

### *Think Critically Through Visuals*

Direct students to look at the photograph on this page along with the table in Figure 5.7. Ask for a volunteer to answer the questions posed in the photo caption.

### Answer

With two workers, the total product is five tons moved per day and the marginal product is three tons moved per day. With three workers, the total product is nine tons and the marginal product is four. With four workers, the total product is twelve and the marginal product is three.

### *Think Critically Through Visuals*

Point out that **Figure 5.8—The Marginal Product of Labor** on page 150 is a graphic representation of the data shown in Figure 5.7.

The Graphing Workshop ——— See It

Direct students to the Graphing Workshop for Chapter 5 at **econxtra.swlearning.com**. Instruct students to click on **See It: Production in the Short Run**, which explains Figures 5.7 and 5.8.

## ENRICH

Tell students that a farmers' market is held in Wellsville every Saturday. The farmers rent stalls for $50 per day, where they market their produce. Ask students to explain why the farmers try to sell as many products as they possibly can each day. How does this example demonstrate fixed, variable, and marginal costs of production? What happens to the proportionate amount of fixed cost per item as more produce is sold?

CHAPTER 5   Supply

### Answer

As more workers are hired, the marginal product increases. Then, after a while, there is diminishing but positive marginal product as the firm hires more labor. Finally, there is negative marginal product as the firm hires even more labor.

## TEACH

### Costs in the Short Run

Remind students that in the short run, some costs businesses pay are fixed while others are variable. Show the class a copy of a newspaper that is offered free of charge to residents of their community. In many locations, it is called the Penny Saver. Ask the students to identify fixed costs that the publishers of this newspaper would have to pay in the short run (rent, insurance, leasing a computer, or monthly payments for delivery truck loans) and others that would be variable (production workers' wages, newsprint, or electricity to operate the firm's printing press). This discussion can be directed to the topic of differences between the short run and long run in which all costs are variable.

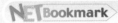

Direct students to **econxtra.swlearning.com**. Remind them to click on the link for Lesson 5.3 to find the appropriate link for the **NET Bookmark** on page 151.

### Answer

The current trend is a decrease in labor costs. The number of individuals wanting to enter the workforce may be the cause of this decrease in labor costs. This decrease in labor costs increases the profitability of firms.

---

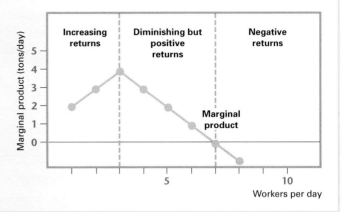

The marginal product of the first three workers shows increasing returns. The next four workers show diminishing but positive returns, and the eighth worker shows negative returns.

# Costs in the Short Run

Now that you have some idea about production in the short run, consider how the firm's costs vary with output. A firm faces two kinds of costs in the short run: fixed cost and variable cost.

## Fixed and Variable Costs

**fixed cost**
Any production cost that is independent of the firm's output

**variable cost**
Any production cost that changes as output changes

**total cost**
The sum of fixed cost and variable cost

A **fixed cost** is one that does not change in the short run, no matter how much output is produced. A firm must pay a fixed cost even when nothing gets produced. Even if Hercules hires no labor and moves no furniture, the firm must pay for the warehouse, property taxes, insurance, vehicle registration, and equipment. By definition, fixed cost is just that—fixed. It does not vary with output in the short run. Fixed cost is sometimes called *overhead.* Hercules's fixed cost is $200 per day.

**Variable cost** varies with the amount produced. With Hercules, only labor

varies in the short run, so labor is the only variable cost. For example, if Hercules hires no labor, output is zero, so variable cost is zero. As more labor is employed, output increases, as does variable cost. Variable cost depends on the amount of labor employed and on the wage. If the firm can hire each worker for $100 a day, variable cost equals $100 times the number of workers hired.

## Total Cost

Figure 5.9 offers cost information for Hercules. The table lists the daily cost of different output totals. Column 1 shows the number of tons of furniture moved per day. Column 2 indicates the fixed cost for each output total. By definition, fixed cost remains at $200 per day regardless of output. Column 3 shows the quantity of labor needed to produce each level of output. For example, moving 2 tons a day requires one worker, 5 tons requires two workers, and so on. Only the first six workers are listed, because more workers add nothing to total product.

Column 4 lists variable cost, which equals $100 times the number of workers employed. For example, the variable cost of moving 9 tons of furniture per day is $300 because this output requires three workers. Column 5 lists the **total cost**, which sums fixed cost

---

*Curriculum Connection—Science*

In the United States, many aspects of different crops have been changed through genetic engineering. Strains of wheat and corn have been developed that are resistant to disease; tomatoes are grown that are firmer in order to ship better; and other fruits have been altered to last longer on store shelves. Ask students to investigate developments in genetically engineered foods and to discuss how these technological advancements have changed the supply of food products available for purchase.

and variable cost. As you can see, when output is zero, variable cost is zero, so total cost consists entirely of the fixed cost of $200.

## Marginal Cost

Of special interest to the firm is how much total cost changes with output. In particular, what is the marginal cost of moving another ton? As shown in columns 6 and 7, the **marginal cost** of production is simply the change in total cost divided by the change in quantity, or

$$\frac{\text{Change in total cost}}{\text{Change in quantity}} = \text{Marginal cost}$$

For example, increasing output from 0 to 2 tons increases total cost by $100. The marginal cost of each of the first 2 tons is the change in total cost, $100, divided by the change in output, 2 tons, or $100/2, which equals $50. The marginal cost of each of the next 3 tons is the change in total cost, $100, divided by the change in output, 3 tons, or $100/3, which equals $33.33.

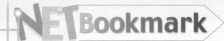

**NET Bookmark**

*Unit labor cost* is the term used to describe the cost of labor per unit of output. Because labor costs generally represent the largest share of costs, this value is closely watched by businesspeople and analysts at the Federal Reserve. Look at the most recent data on unit labor costs at the Bureau of Labor Statistics web site. Access this web site through econxtra.swlearning.com. What is the current trend? What forces may be pushing unit labor costs downward? What does this mean for the profitability of firms?

**econxtra.swlearning.com**

Notice in column 7 that marginal cost first decreases and then increases. Changes in marginal cost reflect changes in the productivity of the variable resource, labor. The first three workers show increasing returns. This rising marginal product of labor reduces

**marginal cost**
The change in total cost resulting from a one-unit change in output; the change in total cost divided by the change in output

### Costs in the Short Run

Return to the example of the free shopping newspaper. Tell students that the publishers of this paper generate income by selling advertising. The amount they charge depends on the number of households that receive the newspaper. The owners of this business are considering adding a neighboring community with 2,500 homes to their area of circulation. This would increase their variable costs by 25 percent in the short run. The owners believe that this increased circulation would allow them to increase their advertising income by 30 percent. Ask students to explain how the owners should make their decision. What additional information might they need? This example can be used to illustrate the concepts of marginal cost and marginal revenue.

### Think Critically Through Visuals

Use **Figure 5.9—Short-Run Cost Data for Hercules at Your Service** to illustrate the cost information for Hercules.

**Short-Run Cost Data for Hercules at Your Service**

**Figure 5.9**

| 1 Tons Moved per Day | 2 Fixed Cost | 3 Workers per Day | 4 Variable Cost | 5 Total Cost | 6 Change in total cost ÷ Change in tons moved = | 7 Marginal Cost |
|---|---|---|---|---|---|---|
| 0 | $200 | 0 | $ 0 | $200 | — | |
| 2 | 200 | 1 | 100 | 300 | $100 ÷ 2 | $ 50.00 |
| 5 | 200 | 2 | 200 | 400 | $100 ÷ 3 | 33.33 |
| 9 | 200 | 3 | 300 | 500 | $100 ÷ 4 | 25.00 |
| 12 | 200 | 4 | 400 | 600 | $100 ÷ 3 | 33.33 |
| 14 | 200 | 5 | 500 | 700 | $100 ÷ 2 | 50.00 |
| 15 | 200 | 6 | 600 | 800 | $100 ÷ 1 | 100.00 |

Column 7 shows the marginal cost of moving another ton of furnishings.
It is the change in total cost divided by the change in tons moved.

Lesson 5.3 • *Production and Cost*    **151**

## Group Activity

Organize students into small groups. Tell each group that they manufacture filing cabinets. Their fixed costs total $5,000 per week, and they must pay a marginal cost of $40 for each additional cabinet they produce. They are currently selling 250 cabinets each week at a price of $60. A foreign customer has offered to buy 50 additional cabinets per week but is willing to pay only $50 per extra cabinet. Ask each group to decide whether they would agree to sell the cabinets at this discounted price. Ask them to explain their decisions. (They should agree to the offer. The $50 price is greater than their marginal cost of $40. They will earn a $500 profit per week instead of breaking even, which they are doing now.)

## Costs in the Short Run

Use the free newspaper example again. Tell students that the owners have found that they must pay 6 cents per copy to have the paper delivered, instead of the 2 cents they paid in the past. This increased cost has resulted in a loss for the firm. The firm is obligated to pay $2,000 for fixed costs each month, and it paid $9,000 in variable costs last month. Its total revenue for that month was $10,000. Ask students to calculate the firm's total costs ($11,000) and the amount it lost ($1,000). How much would the firm lose if it closed? ($2,000, the fixed costs) Discuss why firms continue to operate at a loss in the short run if their revenue pays for their fixed costs. In the long run, the firm will fail if it continues to lose money.

Use **Figure 5.10—Marginal Cost Curve for Hercules at Your Service** to illustrate a marginal cost curve. Direct students to the Graphing Workshop for Chapter 5 at **econxtra.swlearning.com**. Instruct students to click on **See It: Costs in the Short Run** to view the graph and listen to an explanation. As an enrichment exercise, students may also complete **Try It: Understanding the Relationship between ATC (Average Total Cost) and MC (Marginal Cost)**. This enrichment exercise presents concepts more advanced than those discussed in the textbook.

### Think Critically Through Visuals

Use **Figure 5.11—Supply Curve for Hercules at Your Service** to illustrate the quantity supplied at each price. Point out the relationship between the supply curve in Figure 5.11 and the marginal cost curve in Figure 5.10. The supply curve is the upward-sloping portion of the firm's marginal cost curve.

---

marginal cost for the first 9 tons moved. Beginning with the fourth worker, the firm experiences diminishing returns from labor, so the marginal cost of output increases. Thus, marginal cost in Figure 5.9 first falls and then rises, because returns from labor first increase and then decrease.

### Marginal Cost Curve

Figure 5.10 shows the marginal cost curve for moving furniture based on the data in Figure 5.9. Because of increasing returns from labor, the marginal cost curve at first slopes down. Because of diminishing marginal returns from labor, the marginal cost curve slopes up after 9 tons. Keep in mind that economic analysis is marginal analysis. Marginal cost is one key to the firm's production decision.

### Marginal Revenue

To understand how firms work, it may help to draw on your knowledge of demand. Remember that demand is based on the marginal benefit that consumers get from buying each additional unit of the good. Likewise, supply is based on the marginal benefit that producers get from selling each additional unit of a good. The marginal benefit that producers get from supplying another unit is the **marginal revenue** they receive. This is the change in total revenue from selling that unit. In competitive markets, the firm's marginal revenue is the market price. A competitive firm receives the market price for selling one more unit.

**marginal revenue**

The change in total revenue from selling another unit of the good

### Short-Run Losses and Shutting Down

In general, producers sell additional units as long as the marginal revenue they receive exceeds the marginal cost. In competitive markets, the firm supplies additional units as long as the price exceeds marginal cost. The firm settles on the level of output where *marginal revenue equals marginal cost.*

There is one qualification to this output rule. Sometimes the market price may be so low that production makes no economic sense. At the level of output where marginal revenue equals marginal cost, the firm's total revenue must at least cover its variable cost. A firm that can't cover variable cost will lose less in the short run by shutting down.

Here's the logic behind the shutdown decision. Even if the firm produces nothing in the short run, it must still pay fixed cost. If nothing is produced, the firm's loss equals fixed cost. For example, Hercules would lose $200 a day if no furniture gets moved.

What if the market price is really low, but the firm decides to produce anyway and hires two workers for $200? Because the price is so low, the total revenue received from selling that output is only $150. That amount pays none of the fixed cost and only a portion of the variable cost. The firm would not only lose its fixed cost of $200, but it also would lose $50 of variable cost. The firm would lose less—only $200—by shutting down. Why produce when doing so only increases any loss?

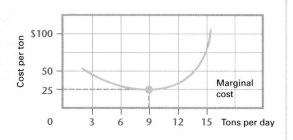

**Marginal Cost Curve for Hercules At Your Service**

**Figure 5.10**

*econxtra.swlearning.com*

Marginal cost first declines, reflecting increasing marginal returns, and then increases, reflecting diminishing marginal returns.

---

### Extend the Content

At the time of this writing, there were only three important manufacturers of large passenger airplanes in the world: Boeing, Lockheed-Martin, and Airbus of Europe. The cost of designing a new passenger jet, constructing prototypes, and testing them before any sales are made is typically several billion dollars or more. Ask students to explain why there aren't more of these firms. What does this situation have to do with fixed costs, long-run average costs, and economies of scale?

A firm's *minimum acceptable price* is a price high enough to ensure that total revenue at least covers variable cost. If the market price is below that minimum, the firm will shut down. Note that shutting down is not the same as going out of business. A firm that shuts down keeps its productive capacity intact—paying the rent, fire insurance, and property taxes, keeping water pipes from freezing in the winter, and so on. For example, auto factories sometimes shut down for a while when sales are soft. Businesses in summer resorts often close for the winter. These firms do not escape fixed cost by shutting down, because fixed cost by definition is not affected by changes in output.

If in the future the price increases enough, the firm will resume production. If market conditions look grim and are not expected to improve, the firm may decide to leave the market. But that's a long-run decision. The short run is defined as a period during which some resources and some costs are fixed. A firm cannot escape those costs in the short run, no matter what it does. The firm cannot enter or leave the market in the short run.

### The Firm's Supply Curve

To produce in the short run, the price must be high enough to ensure that total revenue covers variable cost. The **competitive firm's supply curve** is the upward sloping portion of its marginal cost curve at and above the minimum acceptable price. This supply curve shows how much the firm will supply at each price.

In the Hercules example, a price of $33.33 allows the firm to at least cover variable cost. Hercules's short-run supply curve is presented in Figure 5.11 as the upward-sloping portion of the marginal cost curve starting at $33.33. At that price, Hercules will supply 12 tons of moving a day. At a price of $50 per ton, the company will move 14 tons, and at a price of $100 per ton, the company will move 15 tons. The market supply curve sums individual supply curves for firms in the market.

**competitive firm's supply curve**
The rising portion of a firm's marginal cost curve at or above the price that will allow the firm to cover variable cost

✓ **CHECKPOINT**
Why does the firm's marginal cost curve slope upward in the short run?

## Production and Costs in the Long Run

So far, the analysis has focused on how short-run costs vary with output for a firm of a given size. In the long run, all

---

**Supply Curve for Hercules at Your Service**

**Figure 5.11**

A competitive firm's supply curve shows the quantity supplied at each price. The supply curve is the upward-sloping portion of its marginal cost curve, beginning at the firm's minimum acceptable price. The minimum acceptable price, in this case $33.33, is the price that allows the firm's total revenue to cover its variable cost.

---

### Costs in the Short Run

Explain that the newspaper owners have returned to profitability by extending their circulation to the neighboring community. This increased their income to $13,000 per month, while their variable costs grew to $10,000. Ask students to calculate the marginal cost of producing and delivering an additional 2,500 papers ($1,000 / 2,500 = $.40). The firm was willing to supply additional newspapers because its marginal revenue exceeded its marginal costs. This expansion was so successful that the owners are thinking of adding yet another community to their circulation. To do this, they would have to rent a larger building. Ask students what this might do to the firm's costs and its ability to earn a profit. They should understand that if the firm rents a new building, it is no longer in the short run. The increased cost might eliminate the firm's profits in the long run.

The Graphing Workshop ————  Apply It

Direct students to the Graphing Workshop for Chapter 5 at **econxtra.swlearning.com**. As an enrichment exercise, instruct students to complete **Apply It: Short Run and Long Run Average Total Costs**. This enrichment exercise presents concepts more advanced than those discussed in the textbook.

✓ **CHECKPOINT**
Invite a student to answer the checkpoint that appears on this page.

### Answer

The firm's marginal cost curve slopes upward in the short run because of the initial fixed costs associated with starting a business.

---

Explain the following situation to your students. Harold owns a small business that manufactures shoelaces. He can sell as many pairs of laces as he can make at the price of $1 per pair. If he charges a higher price, no one will buy any of his laces. To produce more laces, he must ask his employees to work longer hours and pay them overtime. As a result, his variable costs per pair of laces grow as he produces more. Ask students to explain how Harold should decide when to stop making more shoelaces. (Harold's marginal revenue for each additional pair of laces is $1. He should stop making more when the marginal cost exceeds $1.)

## Production and Costs in the Long Run

Point out that, as a general rule, economies and diseconomies of scale occur for different size firms in the long run, while increasing and diminishing returns can occur for firms of any given size in the short run.

### THE WALL STREET JOURNAL

**Reading It Right**

Invite a student to explain the relevance of the statement from *The Wall Street Journal* that appears on this page.

### Answer

Answers will vary. Possible answer: OLED backers expect that as the production of OLED increases, the long-run average cost declines as the firm's size increases. This decrease in the average cost will cause a decrease in the price of OLED display screens.

### *Think Critically Through Visuals*

Use **Figure 5.12—A Firm's Long-Run Average Cost Curve** on page 155 to illustrate the lowest average cost for producing each level of output.

---

### Ethics in Action

Have students work in pairs to discuss the ethical issue featured on page 155, and develop answers to the question presented there.

### Answers to Think Critically

Answers will vary. Possible answers: An ethical issue involved with worker's compensation insurance is the laying off of honest and moral employees because of the hike in insurance cost. Another ethical issue involves dishonest employees cheating the system by faking injuries. An increase in worker's compensation insurance increases the firm's long-run average cost curve.

---

**long-run average cost curve**

A curve that indicates the lowest average cost of production at each rate of output when the firm's size is allowed to vary

**economies of scale**

Forces that reduce a firm's average cost as the firm's size, or scale, increases in the long run

---

inputs can be varied, so there are no fixed costs. What should be the size of the firm?

### Economies of Scale

Because all resources can vary in the long run, the focus is on the average cost of production, not the marginal cost. *Average cost* equals total cost divided by output. The firm's owner would like to know how the average cost of production varies as the size, or scale, of the firm increases. A firm's *long-run average cost* indicates the lowest average cost of producing each output when the firm's size is allowed to vary.

If the firm's long-run average cost declines as the firm size increases, this reflects **economies of scale**. Consider some reasons for economies of scale. *A larger-size firm often allows for larger, more specialized machines and greater specialization of labor.* Typically, as the scale of the firm increases, capital substitutes for labor. Production techniques such as the assembly line can be introduced only if the firm is sufficiently large.

### Diseconomies of Scale

As the scale of the firm continues to increase, however, another force may eventually take hold. If the firm's long-run average cost increases as production increases, this reflects *diseconomies of scale*. As the amount and variety of resources employed increase, so does the *task of coordinating all these inputs.* As the workforce grows, additional layers of management are needed to monitor production. Information may not be correctly passed up or down the chain of command.

### THE WALL STREET JOURNAL

**Reading It Right** What's the relevance of the following statement from *The Wall Street Journal*: "As with any new technology, the early OLED (organic light-emitting diode) display screens are expensive, perhaps six times more than liquid-crystal-display screens. But OLED backers say that problem will in part be addressed once mass production gears up and economies of scale are reached."

---

It is possible for long-run average cost to neither increase nor decrease with changes in firm size. If neither economies of scale nor diseconomies of scale occur as the scale of the firm expands, a firm experiences *constant returns to scale* over some range of production.

### Long-Run Average Cost Curve

Figure 5.12 presents a firm's **long-run average cost curve**, showing the lowest average cost of producing each level of output. The curve is marked into segments reflecting economies of scale, constant returns to scale, and diseconomies of scale. Production must reach quantity *A* for the firm to achieve the *minimum efficient scale*, which is the smallest scale, or size, that allows the firm to take full advantage of economies of scale. At the minimum efficient scale, long-run average cost is at a minimum. From output *A* to output *B*, the firm experiences constant returns to scale. Beyond output rate *B*, diseconomies of scale increase long-run average cost.

Firms try to avoid diseconomies of scale. Competition weeds out firms that grow too large. To avoid diseconomies of scale, IBM divided into six smaller decision-making groups. Other large corporations have spun off parts of their operations to create new companies. HP started Agilent Technologies, and AT&T started Lucent Technologies.

The long-run average cost curve guides the firm toward the most efficient plant size for a given level of output. However, once a plant of that scale is built, the firm has fixed costs and is operating in the short run. A firm in the short run chooses the output rate where marginal revenue equals marginal cost. Firms plan for the long run, but they produce in the short run.

**CHECKPOINT**
How are economies of scale and diseconomies of scale reflected in a firm's long-run average cost curve?

Average cost declines until production reaches output level *A*. The firm is experiencing economies of scale. Output level *A* is the minimum efficient scale—the lowest rate of output at which the firm takes full advantage of economies of scale. Between *A* and *B*, the economy has constant returns to scale. Beyond output level *B*, the long-run average cost curve reflects diseconomies of scale.

 CHECKPOINT
Invite a student to answer the checkpoint that appears on page 154.

**Answer**

Economies of scale occur when the firm's long-run average cost declines as the firm size increases. This is reflected by a downward sloping long-run average cost curve. Diseconomies of scale occur when the firm's long-run average cost increases as the firm size increases. This is reflected by an upward-sloping long-run average cost curve.

### APPLY

Assign Lesson 5.3 from the Contemporary Economics Workbook.

 e-con @pps

Encourage students to apply their knowledge of concepts presented in this lesson as they explore economic news stories, policy debates, and data available at **econxtra.swlearning.com**. A sampling of the titles for this lesson appears below.

**EconDebate**

- Should there be a market for human organs?

**EconNews**

- AT&T Wireless Cuts Costs to Gain Long-Run Profits
- Cell Phones Sell Well
- Fliers Fly Less Frequently
- No More Annoying Sales People
- Optimizing Operations
- Precision Plowing

### ASSESS

Assign all or part of Lesson 5.3 Assessment on page 156 as homework or an in-class activity.

# Ethics in Action

**Worker's Compensation** All across the nation, the cost of worker's compensation insurance has been spiking upward at a frightening rate. A seafood wholesaler in Los Angeles saw its rates climb 68 percent in one year to almost $7,000 per employee. Most insurance costs have risen for companies in the past few years, but "worker's comp," as it is often called, is a major problem because firms have no control over cost increases. By law, companies must provide worker's comp insurance, which pays for medical treatment for job-related injuries and for wages lost as a result of those injuries. Because every employee must have worker's comp insurance, the only way a company can reduce this cost is to eliminate employees. Increased insurance costs have caused both large and small companies to lay off workers, and—in many cases—it has forced them out of business. The main reasons for the sharp increases in worker's comp costs are soaring medical and legal costs, and fraud. Workers fake injuries and stay out of work longer than necessary. Doctors, chiropractors, and lawyers work together to cheat the system. Companies also manipulate their employee reports and downplay the dangers involved in the work that's being done in order to pay less than they should.

**Think Critically**

What are the ethical issues involved with worker's compensation insurance? How does the increase in worker's compensation insurance affect a firm's long-run average cost curve?

## CLOSE

**Revisit** the In the News feature on the first page of the lesson. Ask students to review their preliminary answers and discuss the questions, now that they have completed this lesson.

**Review** the objectives for Lesson 5.3. Students should be able to:

- Understand how marginal product varies as a firm employs more labor in the short run.
- Explain the shape of the firm's marginal cost curve and identify what part of that is the firm's supply curve.
- Distinguish between economies of scale and diseconomies of scale in the long run.

Xtra! Study Tools

Direct students to the online study tools for Lesson 5.3 at **econxtra.swlearning.com**.

## Key Concepts

1. Answers will vary. Possible answer: In the small room, the three workers got in each other's way and couldn't work efficiently. This demonstrates the law of diminishing returns because Tanya found that additional workers eventually added little or nothing to her output.

2. This payment is a fixed cost because she must make it no matter how many computers she repairs.

3. The marginal cost is equal to two hours of labor, or $30.00. She would have to know how much her fixed or overhead costs are per hour to set her price. She wants to be sure that her marginal revenue exceeds her marginal cost.

4. Answers will vary. Possible answer: Her total revenue of $6,000 paid for her assistant ($2,500), the value of her own labor ($3,000), and was able to contribute $500 toward her fixed cost. If she shut down, she would have to pay the entire fixed cost ($1,000) out of other income. Therefore, she should continue to operate her business at present.

## Graphing Exercise

5. The graph for this answer appears at the bottom of this page.

   Tony needs to know what his marginal revenue for selling additional pizzas will be at different levels of production. This will tell him when the marginal cost exceeds marginal revenue and when he should stop producing additional pizzas.

## Think Critically

6. Answers will vary. Possible answer: The firm's marginal revenue from staying open late at night is only $150 per hour. Its marginal cost includes the $35 and $125 for the gasoline that is sold. The additional revenue does not cover these costs; therefore, the business should be closed at night.

## Key Concepts

1. Tanya runs a computer repair business in a small room in her basement. Many people wanted her to fix their computers so she hired another worker, who doubled the number of computers she could fix each day. But when she hired a third worker, she found that the number of computers she could service hardly changed at all. Explain how this demonstrates the law of diminishing returns.

2. Tanya has borrowed more than $10,000 to buy special equipment she needs in order to repair computers. Is the $750 she pays each month to repay her loan a fixed or a variable cost? Explain your answer.

3. Tanya pays her worker $15.00 per hour. If, on average, he can repair one computer in two hours, what is the marginal cost of fixing one more computer? What other information does she need to have before she can decide how much to charge her customers for computer repairs?

4. Tanya's monthly fixed costs total $1,000. She pays her assistant $2,500 each month. She could take a job with a different business that would pay her $3,000 each month. Her total revenue from sales last month amounted to $6,000. Should she continue to operate the business or shut it down?

## Graphing Exercise

5. Construct a graph of fixed cost, variable cost, and total cost, and then a second graph of marginal cost for Tony's Pizza, using the data in the cost table below. What other information does Tony need in order to determine how many pizzas he should produce per week? Explain your answer.

**Weekly Cost Data for Tony's Pizza**

| Output | Fixed Cost | Variable Cost | Total Cost | Marginal Cost |
|--------|-----------|---------------|-----------|---------------|
| 0 | $500 | 0 | $ 500 | - - - |
| 10 | $500 | $1,000 | $1,500 | $100 |
| 20 | $500 | $1,500 | $2,000 | $ 50 |
| 30 | $500 | $1,800 | $2,300 | $ 30 |
| 40 | $500 | $2,100 | $2,600 | $ 30 |
| 50 | $500 | $2,600 | $3,100 | $ 50 |
| 60 | $500 | $3,600 | $4,100 | $100 |

## Think Critically

6. **Entrepreneurship** You own a gasoline station. You have found that the cost of keeping your store open is $35 per hour for labor and power. Between midnight and 5:00 A.M., sales are not that great. On average, during this time you sell only 100 gallons of gasoline per hour. At the current price of $1.50 per gallon, your markup on gasoline is $.25 per gallon. Should you keep your business open all night?

**Fixed, Variable and Total Costs for Tony's Pizza**

**Marginal Cost for Tony's Pizza**

## Visualizing the Answer— Graphing Exercise

5. The answer includes two graphs. Students' graphs should look similar to the two shown here. An Excel spreadsheet containing these graphs, along with supporting data, is available on the Instructor's Resource CD.

# The Industrial Revolution in the United States: The Supply of Cotton

The increases in the production of cotton textiles in the late 1700s brought about the Industrial Revolution. As production became more industrialized, suppliers of raw cotton were faced with heavy demand. In the United States, growing cotton was profitable only along a narrow strip along the coast of Georgia and the Carolinas. It was the only place Sea Island cotton could be grown. Another strain, which could be grown in the interior, was unprofitable because it produced a lot of seeds, which could be removed only by hand. It took a day's work to separate the seeds from the lint, making it too slow and too expensive to satisfy the demands of the industry.

Eli Whitney changed all this in 1793 with his invention of the cotton gin. Whitney's invention allowed one man to produce what it had previously taken 50 men, mostly slaves, to produce. Cotton now could be grown where it formerly had been cost prohibitive, enabling the American South to supply Great Britain's growing demand for raw cotton. Within two years, cotton exports from the United States to Great Britain rose from 487,000 pounds to 6,276,300. Because Great Britain's textile mills were demanding ever-increasing amounts of cotton, Southern planters were willing to move inland and devote more land and resources to producing cotton. The quantity of cotton supplied increased rapidly, keeping pace with the growing British cotton textile industry.

The British government, protective of its textile industry, passed laws preventing anyone with knowledge of the workings of a textile mill from leaving the country. Despite that prohibition, an English textile mechanic, Samuel Slater, was attracted by a prize being offered for information about the English textile industry. He disguised himself as a farm laborer and came to the United States. Slater established a mill at Pawtucket, Rhode Island. Building its machinery entirely from memory, he started the American textile industry on December 20, 1790. Still, American mills had a difficult time competing with British imports and could afford only cheaper cotton imported from the West Indies. Southern states sold all of their cotton at a better price to English mills.

## THINK CRITICALLY

What variable cost did the invention of the cotton gin allow Southern cotton producers to lower? How were the growers able to create "economies of scale"? Why do you think the American cotton mills, using essentially the same equipment, had difficulty competing with the British cotton imports?

### FOCUS

Review with students how innovation and technology can impact the supply of a good. The cotton gin dramatically increased the supply of cotton available to the textile mills of Great Britain and transformed the economy of the South.

### TEACH

Instruct students to read the **Connect to History** feature and answer the questions.

### ASSESS

Use the questions at the bottom of the page to assess the students' understanding of this feature.

#### Answers to Think Critically

The invention of the cotton gin allowed southern producers to lower the variable cost of labor. The growers were able to create economies of scale by lowering the long-run average cost curve through the invention of the cotton gin. The American cotton mills had trouble competing because they were using cheaper cotton in their production of textiles.

## Bibliography

Cannon, John, ed. *Oxford Companion to British History*. New York: Oxford University Press, 1997.

Carson, Thomas, and Mary Bonk, eds. *Gale Encyclopedia of U.S. History*. Detroit: Gale Group, 1999.

Michl, H.E. *The Textile Industries*. Washington, D.C.: The Textile Foundation, 1938.

Puth, Robert C. *American Economic History*. New York: The Dryden Press, 1988.

Watkins, James L. *King Cotton: A Historical and Statistical Review*. New York: Negro University Press, 1969.

### Consider

Ask students to revisit the questions they were asked to consider at the beginning of the chapter. Remind students that they should be able to answer all of the questions after studying Chapter 5.

- Why might a firm decide to store its products in a warehouse rather than offer them for sale? See page 143—Changes in Producer Expectations.

- What's the meaning of the old expression "Too many cooks spoil the broth"? See page 148—Law of Diminishing Returns.

- Can a firm shut down without going out of business? See page 152—Short-Run Losses and Shutting Down.

- Why do movie theaters have so many screens? See page 154—Economies of Scale.

### Exam*View*

Use **Exam***View* to assess student learning.

- Create a chapter test using questions from the existing test bank.
- Add your own questions to the existing test bank.
- Generate multiple forms of a chapter test.

### Study Skills

Offer the following study skills suggestions for students as they review this chapter.

- Outline the chapter.
- Review Key Terms.
- Review Checkpoints.
- Work in pairs to quiz each other.
- Use Xtra! Study Tools for each lesson.

Direct students to the online quiz preparation for Chapter 5 at **econxtra.swlearning.com**.

---

 **Chapter Assessment**

## Summary

 **5.1** *The Supply Curve*

**a** Firms are motivated to produce products out of their desire to earn profit. *Supply* indicates how much of a good producers are willing and able to offer for sale per period at each possible price, other things constant. The *law of supply* states that the quantity of a product supplied will be greater at a higher price than at a lower price, other things constant.

 **Xtra! Quiz Prep**
*econxtra.swlearning.com*

**b** Businesses supply more products at higher prices because they can shift resources from the production of other products that have lower prices. Further, higher prices encourage producers to find new sources of resources, or more efficient means of production. *Individual supply* is the quantity of product supplied by one firm in a market. *Market supply* is the total quantity of product supplied by all firms in a market.

**c** The *price elasticity of supply* is the relationship between a percentage change in the price of a product and the resulting percentage change in the quantity supplied. Supply may be elastic, unit elastic, or inelastic. As a general rule, the more difficult or costly it is to change the quantity of a product produced, the less elastic supply will be.

**5.2** *Shifts of the Supply Curve*

**a** There are five determinants of supply that shift the location of a supply curve when they change. They are (1) changes in the cost of resources used to make the good, (2) changes in the price of other goods these resources could make, (3) changes in the technology used to make the good, (4) changes in the producers' expectations, and (5) changes in the number of sellers in the market.

**b** A change in the price of a product will cause movement along a supply curve that is called a change in the quantity supplied. A change in a determinant of supply will cause a supply curve to move or shift to the left or right.

**5.3** *Production and Cost*

**a** Production in the *short run* takes place in a period during which at least one productive resource cannot be changed or is fixed. Variable resources may be changed in the short run. In the *long run*, all resources are variable.

**b** The *marginal product* of an additional worker is the change in total production that results from employing one more worker. When production of a product is increased, there are typically first increasing returns and then diminishing returns.

**c** *Fixed cost* must be paid in the short run and does not change with the quantity produced. *Variable cost* is zero when output is zero and increases when output increases.

**d** *Marginal cost* equals the change in total cost divided by the change in total quantity. *Marginal revenue* is the additional revenue resulting from selling one more unit of output. Businesses will sell more output as long as the marginal revenue exceeds the marginal cost. In the short run, a firm's supply curve is that portion of its marginal cost curve rising above the minimum acceptable price.

**e** In the short run, firms that are losing money will continue to produce as long as their total revenue is greater than their variable cost. If they shut down, they would lose more than they would if they continued to make products.

**f** In the long run, firms face *economies* and *diseconomies of scale*. The *long-run average cost curve* first slopes downward as the scale of the firm expands, reflecting economies of scale. At some point it may flatten out, reflecting constant returns to scale. As the scale of the firm increases, the long-run average cost curve may begin to slope upward, reflecting diseconomies of scale.

# Review Economic Terms

Choose the term that best fits the definition. On a separate sheet of paper, write the letter of the answer. Some terms may not be used.

1. A period of time during which at least one of a firm's resources is fixed

2. The change in total revenue from selling another unit of a product

3. Any cost that does not change with the amount of production in the short run

____ 4. A period of time during which all of a firm's resources can be varied

____ 5. The change in total cost resulting from producing one more unit of output.

____ 6. Any production cost that changes as output changes

____ 7. A measure of the responsiveness of the quantity of a product supplied to a change in price

____ 8. The change in total product that results from an increase of one unit of resource input

____ 9. As more of a variable resource is added to a given amount of fixed resources, marginal product eventually declines and could become negative

10. Forces that reduce a firm's average cost as the firm's size grows

11. The total output of the firm

a. **competitive firm's supply curve**

b. **economies of scale**

c. **elasticity of supply**

d. **fixed cost**

e. **law of diminishing returns**

f. **law of supply**

g. **long run**

h. **long-run average cost curve**

i. **marginal cost**

j. **marginal product**

k. **marginal revenue**

l. **short run**

m. **supply**

n. **supply curve**

o. **total cost**

p. **total product**

q. **variable cost**

# Review Economic Concepts

12. A shift of a product's *supply curve* will be caused by each of the following *except*

  a. an increase in the cost of the resources used to produce the product.

  b. an improvement in the technology used to produce the product.

  c. an increase in consumer demand for the product.

  d. a decrease in the price of other products that resources could be used to produce.

13. **True or False** If a product's *elasticity of supply* is 0.8, a 2 percent increase in price will cause a greater than 2 percent increase in the quantity supplied.

14. Typically, the longer the period of time, the __?__ a product's *elasticity of supply* will be.

15. Which of the following events would cause the supply curve to shift to the left?

  a. A firm's employees negotiate a 5 percent increase in their wages.

  b. A firm's managers buy new, more efficient machinery for workers to use.

  c. A firm provides its workers with training to better use their tools.

  d. A firm finds a new, less expensive source of raw materials.

## Review Economic Terms

1. l. short run
2. k. marginal revenue
3. d. fixed cost
4. g. long run
5. i. marginal cost
6. q. variable cost
7. c. elasticity of supply
8. j. marginal product
9. e. law of diminishing returns
10. b. economies of scale
11. p. total product

## Review Economic Concepts

12. c. an increase in consumer demand for the product

13. False. If a product's elasticity of supply is 0.8, a 2 percent increase in price will cause a less than 2 percent increase in the quantity supplied.

14. greater or more elastic

15. a. A firm's employees negotiate a 5 percent increase in their wages.

## Review Economic Concepts

16. movement along

17. True

18. movement along

19. b. the next worker hired will add less to production than the last worker hired

20. c. the cost of raw materials used to produce goods

21. fixed

22. False. A firm's marginal cost of production increases as output increases.

23. Economies of scale

24. a. elastic

25. marginal revenue

26. True

27. c. face diseconomies of scale as its long-run average cost curve slopes up

28. True

## Apply Economic Concepts

29. The firm will produce 500 units. The additional cost of making unit 501 would be greater than the price that is the firm's marginal revenue. It would lose money on product 501.

---

16. An increase in the price of a firm's product will cause __?__ the firm's supply curve.

17. **True or False** In the long run, all costs of production are variable.

18. An increase in the price of a product will cause __?__ the supply curve for that product.

19. If a firm experiences diminishing returns, it finds that

    a. there will be no increase in production when it hires another worker.

    b. the next worker hired will add less to production than the last worker hired.

    c. it will earn no profit if it hires additional workers.

    d. it must lay off workers to earn a profit.

20. Which of the following is an example of a variable cost?

    a. the cost or wages for night security guards

    b. the cost of fire insurance for a firm's factory

    c. the cost of raw materials used to produce goods

    d. the cost of renting a computer for a firm's accounting office

21. In the short run, __?__ cost does not change as a firm produces additional output.

22. **True or False** A firm's *marginal cost* of production decreases as output increases.

23. __?__ are forces that reduce a firm's average cost of production as the firm grows in size.

24. If a 1 percent change in price results in a 2 percent change in the quantity of the product that is supplied, the supply of that product is

    a. elastic.

    b. unit elastic.

    c. inelastic.

    d. perfectly elastic.

25. A producer's __?__ is the change in its total revenue that results from selling one more unit of a product.

26. **True or False** The *law of supply* states that the quantity of a product that is supplied will grow as the price of that product increases.

27. In the long run, a firm will

    a. face economies of scale as its long-run average cost curve slopes up.

    b. face diseconomies of scale as its long-run average cost curve slopes down.

    c. face diseconomies of scale as its long-run average cost curve slopes up.

    d. face economies of scale after its long-run average cost curve reaches its lowest point.

28. **True or False** On the left side of a firm's long run average cost curve, its average costs decline as production increases.

# Apply Economic Concepts

29. A firm has the following marginal costs at different levels of production. If it is able to sell all the products it can produce at $5 each, how many will it produce? Explain your answer.

| Units | Marginal Cost Per Unit |
|-------|------------------------|
| 100 | $6 |
| 200 | $4 |
| 300 | $3 |
| 400 | $4 |
| 500 | $5 |
| 600 | $6 |

30. The lowest long-run average cost for whatsits is $50 per unit. To take advantage of economies of scale and produce whatsits at this low cost, a firm would need to build a factory that could produce 5,000,000 whatsits per year. There are only 20,000 people who are willing to pay anything to buy a whatsit per year. Why won't a large whatsits factory be built?

**Price Elasticity of Supply for Dozens of Bagels**

| Price | Percentage Change | Quantity Supplied | Percentage Change | Elasticity | Elastic/Inelastic |
|---|---|---|---|---|---|
| $8 | - - - | 100 | - - - | - - - | - - - |
| $7 | 12.5% | 90 | 10.0% | _____ | _____ |
| $6 | 14.3% | 80 | 11.1% | _____ | _____ |
| $5 | 16.6% | 70 | 12.5% | _____ | _____ |
| $4 | 20.0% | 60 | 14.3% | _____ | _____ |
| $3 | 25.0% | 50 | 16.6% | _____ | _____ |

31. **Calculating the Price Elasticity of Supply** Complete the table below by calculating each missing elasticity of supply value. Is the supply elastic or inelastic?

32. **Sharpen Your Life Skills: Cause and Effect** During the summer of 2003, Americans were warned that shortages of natural gas could cause its price to increase by as much as 50 percent or more during the following winter. Natural gas is a primary ingredient used in the production of artificial fertilizer. Much of the fertilizer used by U.S. farmers during the spring of 2004 was produced during the preceding winter. If the cost of producing this fertilizer increased as predicted, what would have happened to the location of the supply curve for agricultural products in 2004? Explain your answer.

33. **Accounting** Classify each of the following costs as variable or fixed. Explain your decision for each cost.

- The cost of a leased delivery truck
- The cost of a night security service
- The cost of delivering finished products
- The cost of fire insurance
- The cost of electricity used to run production machinery

*e*-con *@*pps   *econxtra.swlearning.com*  ▶▮▮▮

34. Access **EconData Online** at econxtra .swlearning.com. Read the article entitled "Labor Cost Per Unit of Output." Find the answers to the following questions from the article: (1) What is the relationship between labor productivity and worker's compensation insurance? (2) Why is labor cost an important indicator of trends in production costs? Write your answers in complete sentences on a sheet of paper.

## Apply Economic Concepts

30. Answers will vary. Students may point out that there is no reason to produce a product at a low cost if it cannot be sold at any price. Businesses that produce whatsits need to be relatively small, even if they are less efficient than they could be, because they cannot sell enough of these products to justify building a large factory.

31. The completed table appears at the bottom of this page.

32. The supply curve for agricultural products would shift inward because there is an increase in the cost of a resource used to grow agricultural goods.

33. Delivery truck—fixed (this must be paid regardless of production)

    Security service—fixed (this must be paid regardless of production)

    Delivering finished products—variable (this cost will increase with production)

    Fire insurance—fixed (this must be paid regardless of production)

    Electricity—variable (this cost will increase with production)

*e*-con *@*pps

34. (1) Together, labor productivity and worker's compensation insurance determine unit labor costs. If labor productivity increases and worker's compensation insurance remains constant, then unit labor costs decrease. (2) Labor cost is an important indicator of trends in production costs because labor is the single largest component of production costs.

## Visualizing the Answer

31. The completed table is shown below.

**Price Elasticity of Supply for Dozens of Bagels**

| Price | Percentage Change | Quantity Supplied | Percentage Change | Elasticity | Elastic/Inelastic |
|---|---|---|---|---|---|
| $8 | - - - | 100 | - - - | - - - | - - - |
| $7 | 12.5% | 90 | 10.0% | 0.80 | inelastic |
| $6 | 14.3% | 80 | 11.1% | 0.78 | inelastic |
| $5 | 16.6% | 70 | 12.5% | 0.75 | inelastic |
| $4 | 20.0% | 60 | 14.3% | 0.72 | inelastic |
| $3 | 25.0% | 50 | 16.6% | 0.66 | inelastic |

### Consider

Ask students to consider the questions posed on this page as they study Chapter 6. After studying all three lessons, students should be able to answer the questions. The content related to each question can be found on the pages indicated below.

- How is market competition different from competition in sports and in games? See page 166—Market Exchange Is Voluntary.
- Why do car dealers usually locate together on the outskirts of town? See page 167—Markets Reduce Transaction Costs.
- What's the difference between making stuff right and making the right stuff? See page 179—Productive Efficiency and Allocative Efficiency.
- Why do government efforts to keep rents low usually lead to a housing shortage? See page 180—Price Ceiling.
- Why do consumers benefit nearly as much from a low price as from a zero price? See page 181—Consumer Surplus.

### ▶ POINT YOUR BROWSER

Remind students that they can find additional resources for this chapter at **econxtra.swlearning.com**.

- Xtra! Study Tools
- Net Bookmarks
- Xtra! Quiz Prep
- econ@pps
- Ask the Xpert!
- Graphing Workshop

# 6 Market Forces

Price, Quantity, and Market Equilibrium **6.1**

Shifts of Demand and Supply Curves **6.2**

Market Efficiency and Gains from Exchange **6.3**

### Consider

How is market competition different from competition in sports and in games?

Why do car dealers usually locate together on the outskirts of town?

What's the difference between making stuff right and making the right stuff?

Why do government efforts to keep rents low usually lead to a housing shortage?

Why do consumers benefit nearly as much from a low price as from a zero price?

CLEARANCE

© Getty Images/PhotoDisc

### ▶ POINT YOUR BROWSER

*econxtra.swlearning.com*

---

### Teaching Resources for Chapter 6

- Activities and Projects Masters
- Spanish Resources
- Econ Connection Interactive Tutorial CD
- **Exam***View*® CD
- Workbook Teacher's Edition
- Chapter Test Teacher's Edition
- NCEE Standards and Correlation
- Personal Finance Guide
- Social Studies Skills Review

- Instructor's Resource CD
  - PowerPoint Presentation
  - Lesson Plans
  - Video Discussion Guide
  - Answers to Graphing Exercises
- **econxtra.swlearning.com**

## Objectives

> Understand how markets reach equilibrium.

> Explain how markets reduce transaction costs.

## Overview

Markets allow you to buy and sell for a price. Price is the amount you pay when you buy a good and the amount you receive when you sell it. As a buyer, or demander, you have a different view of the price than a seller, or supplier, does. That's because demanders pay the price and suppliers receive it. As the price rises, consumers reduce their quantity demanded along their demand curve, and producers increase their quantity supplied along their supply curve. How is this conflict between producers and consumers resolved? Market forces resolve the differences.

## Key Terms

**equilibrium**

**surplus**

**shortage**

**transaction cost**

## FOCUS

Point out that this lesson is devoted to learning how the forces of demand and supply determine the market price for goods and services. Ask students how they would react if a music store advertised new CDs for either $1 or $100 each. How would these prices affect the quantity of CDs they would demand? Remind students that businesses also react to changes in price. How would the owner of a different music store react to these prices? Would the owner offer the same price? Would a greater or lesser quantity of CDs be supplied? (There is a good chance that the other store would ignore the very high or low price because their competition is not likely to be able to maintain the price for long. If it continued, they would be more likely to try to meet it and change the quantity of CDs they would supply to the market.)

### Objectives

Remind students to read the lesson objectives to help focus their attention before reading the lesson.

### Key Terms

Direct students to create a database using the key terms for this section. The database fields should include terms, definitions, and page numbers. Point out that the process of keying the data is an effective way to study key terms.

## [ In the News ]

### The Toy Business Is Not Child's Play

U.S. toy sales exceeded $25 billion a year in 2001, but the business is not much fun for toy makers. Most toys don't make it from one season to the next, turning out to be costly duds. A few have staying power—like G.I. Joe, who could retire after more than 30 years of military service; Barbie, who is pushing 40; and the Wiffle Ball, still a hit after 40 years. Most store buyers must order in February for Christmas delivery. Can you imagine the uncertainty of this market? Who, for example, could have anticipated the phenomenal success of Tickle Me Elmo, Beanie Babies, Teletubbies, Furbies, Pokemon, or PlayStation 2? A few years ago, the Mighty Morphin Power Rangers were hot. Within a year, the manufacturer increased production tenfold, with 11 new factories churning out nearly $1 billion worth of Rangers. Still, at a selling price of $13, quantity demanded exceeded quantity supplied. Why don't toy manufacturers simply let the price find equilibrium? Suppose, for example, that the market-clearing price for Power Rangers was $26, twice the actual selling price. Consumers might have resented paying so much for such a small toy. Toy manufacturers usually make a variety of toys and may not want to be viewed as price gougers. After all, a firm's reputation is important, and surveys indicate that consumers consider some price hikes to be unfair. Suppliers who hope to retain customers over the long haul may want to avoid appearing greedy.

### Think About It

What other factors can you think of that would lead a company to set the price for its product rather than letting supply and demand determine the price?

**163**

## [ In the News ]

Instruct students to read the passage and write down their answers. Point out that their answers might change after they finish studying Lesson 6.1.

### Answers to Think About It

Answers will vary. Possible answer: By keeping the price lower, companies can appeal to a wider range of income groups in the market because there are more people who can afford the toy at a lower price. Appealing to a wider range of the market gives a company a greater share of the market.

### Visual Presentation

Use the PowerPoint presentation on the Instructor's Resource CD as an adjunct to your lecture. The presentation also can be used for review.

### National Content Standards in Economics

A complete list of the NCEE Standards appears on pages xxiv–xxv of this book. The following standards are addressed in Lesson 6.1.

Standard 4: Role of Incentives

Standard 5: Gain from Trade

Standard 7: Markets—Price and Quantity Determination

Standard 8: Role of Price in Market System

Standard 9: Role of Competition

## Market Equilibrium

Assemble a selection of products students are likely to buy and create a display similar to one seen on a television game show. Ask students to guess the price of each product on display and to record their guesses on a sheet of paper. Compare the price estimates for each item to the actual price you paid. Ask students how they guessed the correct price or how they knew what the price was.

Discuss how the market arrived at the price for each item. Discuss events that might increase or decrease the price. Why might an increase in price be caused by a shortage of a product? Why might a decrease in price be caused by a surplus of the product? What would price changes do to the quantities demanded and supplied?

### Think Critically Through Visuals

Direct students to focus their attention on the photograph on this page. Ask for a volunteer to answer the questions posed in the caption.

### Answer

Answers will vary. Possible answers: If there were excess bananas, the manager would lower the price in order to sell the bananas before they went bad. The consumers would then purchase and consume more bananas due to the lower price.

**NCEE Standard 4: Role of Incentives**

People respond predictably to positive and negative incentives.

Use **Figure 6.1—Equilibrium in the Pizza Market** on page 165 to illustrate the concept of market equilibrium. Direct students to the Graphing Workshop for Chapter 6 at **econxtra.swlearning.com**. Instruct students to click on **See It: Market Equilibrium** to view the graph and listen to an explanation.

---

## Investigate Your Local Economy

Go to a local shopping center. Look for evidence of specific goods that seem to be experiencing a surplus and those that seem to be experiencing a shortage. Make a list of at least four examples of each. Share your list of goods in class, and discuss the evidence that led you to choose each one.

**equilibrium**
The quantity consumers are willing and able to buy equals the quantity producers are willing and able to sell

**surplus**
At a given price, the amount by which quantity supplied exceeds quantity demanded; a surplus usually forces the price down

### Main Idea

**Role of Incentives**

*Suppliers and consumers respond predictably to positive and negative incentives.* Suppliers view a surplus as a negative incentive, and they act to eliminate it by lowering the price of the good. Consumers, on the other hand, view a surplus as a positive incentive, and increase the quantity they buy due to the lower price. If a fruit market had an excess supply of bananas, what would the manager probably do with the price? How would consumers likely respond?

© Getty Images/PhotoDisc

---

## Market Equilibrium

When the quantity that consumers are willing and able to buy equals the quantity that producers are willing and able to sell, that market reaches **equilibrium**. In equilibrium, the independent plans of buyers and sellers exactly match, and there is no incentive for change. Therefore, market forces exert no further pressure to change price or quantity.

### Surplus Forces the Price Down

To understand how a particular market reaches equilibrium, you need to consider demand *and* supply. Figure 6.1 shows the market for pizza, using schedules in panel (a) and curves in panel (b). What if the price initially is $12 per pizza? At that price, producers supply 24 million pizzas per week, but consumers demand only 14 million, resulting in an *excess quantity supplied*, or a **surplus**, of 10 million pizzas per week. This surplus means that suppliers are stuck with 10 million pizzas they can't sell at $12.

Suppliers' desire to eliminate the surplus puts downward pressure on the price. The arrow pointing down in the graph represents this pressure. As the price falls, producers reduce their quantity supplied and consumers increase their quantity demanded. As long as quantity supplied exceeds quantity demanded, the surplus forces the price lower.

### Shortage Forces the Price Up

What if the initial price is $6 per pizza? Figure 6.1 shows that at that price, consumers demand 26 million pizzas a week, but producers supply only 16 million. This results in an *excess quantity demanded,* or a **shortage**, of 10 million pizzas per week. Producers soon notice that the quantity supplied has sold out and the consumers unable to buy pizza for $6 are frustrated. Profit-maximizing producers and frustrated consumers create market pressure for a higher price. The arrow pointing up in the graph represents this pressure. As the price rises, producers increase their quantity supplied and consumers reduce their quantity demanded. The price continues to rise as long as quantity demanded exceeds quantity supplied.

Thus, *a surplus puts downward pressure on the price, and a shortage puts upward pressure.* As long as quantity demanded and quantity supplied differ, this difference forces a price change. Note that a shortage or a surplus is always measured at a particular

**164   CHAPTER 6   Market Forces**

---

An important but sometimes ignored transaction cost consumers pay is the value of the time they use when they go shopping. Ask students to identify an important purchase they, or a member of their family, recently made. Have them describe the process that was completed to make this purchase. How much time was spent identifying alternatives, evaluating them, and finally making the choice? Do they believe this time was well spent? If the purchase had been made quickly with little time spent for finding the best deal or the best product, would they have been as satisfied?

price. There is no such thing as a general shortage or a general surplus.

## Market Forces Lead to Equilibrium Price and Quantity

In Figure 6.1, the demand and supply curves intersect at the *equilibrium point*, identified as point *c*. The *equilibrium price*, which equates quantity demanded with quantity supplied, is $9 per pizza. The *equilibrium quantity* is 20 million per week. At that price and quantity, the market is said to *clear*. That's why the equilibrium price also is called the *market-clearing price*. Because there is no shortage and no surplus, there is no longer any pressure for the price to change. The equilibrium price will remain at $9 unless there is some shift in demand or supply.

A market finds equilibrium through the independent and voluntary actions of thousands, or even millions, of buyers and sellers. In one sense, the market is personal because each consumer and each producer makes a personal decision regarding how much to buy or sell at a given price. In another sense, the market is impersonal because it requires no conscious coordination among consumers or producers. *The independent decisions of many individual buyers and many individual sellers cause the price to move to reach equilibrium in competitive markets.*

✓ **CHECKPOINT**
How do markets reach equilibrium?

# Market Exchange

Buyers and sellers have different attitudes about the price of a particular good. Markets help sort out those differences. Markets answer the questions of *what to produce, how to produce it*, and *for whom to produce it*.

## Adam Smith's Invisible Hand

Market prices guide resources to their most productive uses and channel goods to those consumers who value

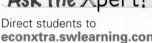

*Why do some prices adjust more slowly?*

**shortage**
At a given price, the amount by which quantity demanded exceeds quantity supplied; a shortage usually forces the price up

### The Graphing Workshop

**Equilibrium in the Pizza Market** — Figure 6.1

econxtra.swlearning.com

**(b) Market curves**

**(a) Market schedules**

**Millions of Pizzas per Week**

| Price per Pizza | Quantity Demanded | Quantity Supplied | Surplus or Shortage | Effect on Price |
|---|---|---|---|---|
| $15 | 8 | 28 | Surplus of 20 | Falls |
| 12 | 14 | 24 | Surplus of 10 | Falls |
| 9 | 20 | 20 | Equilibrium | Remains the same |
| 6 | 26 | 16 | Shortage of 10 | Rises |
| 3 | 32 | 12 | Shortage of 20 | Rises |

Market equilibrium occurs at a price at which the quantity demanded by consumers is equal to the quantity supplied by producers. This is shown at point *c*. At prices above the equilibrium price, the quantity supplied exceeds the quantity demanded. At these prices there is a surplus, and a downward pressure on the price. At prices below equilibrium, quantity demanded exceeds quantity supplied. The resulting shortage puts upward pressure on the price.

Lesson 6.1 • *Price, Quantity, and Market Equilibrium* **165**

---

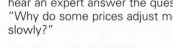

**Investigate Your Local Economy** Before assigning the **Investigate Your Local Economy** activity, make sure that students understand that a surplus puts downward pressure on the price. For example, locally grown fruits and vegetables are often abundant during the summer. This can result in a reduced price during the summer months.

### Ask the Xpert!

Direct students to **econxtra.swlearning.com** to hear an expert answer the question "Why do some prices adjust more slowly?"

✓ **CHECKPOINT**
Invite a student to answer the checkpoint that appears on this page.

**Answer**
Market equilibrium is reached when the quantity consumers are willing and able to buy equals the quantity that producers are willing and able to sell.

### TEACH

**Market Exchange**
As another example of how markets reduce transaction costs, think about the auto dealers in your area. They tend to locate together. The dealers gather not because someone told them to or because they like one another's company. They do so because each wants to be where customers shop for cars—that is, near other auto dealers.

✓ **CHECKPOINT**
Invite a student to answer the checkpoint that appears on page 167.

**Answer**
Markets reduce transaction costs by decreasing the amount of time and information needed to carry out an exchange.

---

### RETEACH

Ask students to consider reasons Wal-Mart Super Stores have been so successful. Remind them that these stores offer a wide variety of hardware, clothing, automotive goods, household goods, and food items that include almost everything any shopper might want to buy. How do Wal-Mart Super Stores reduce the transaction costs of shopping? What competitive advantages do they have over stores that sell only one type of product?

## E-CONOMICS

Direct students to read the passage entitled "Shortage of Internet Access Creates Hot Spots" on this page.

### Answers to Think Critically

Demand for wireless Internet connections is increasing at a fast rate, and demand for hard-wired ISPs is decreasing. This increasing demand for wireless Internet connection is reflected in a higher market price than for hard-wired ISPs. By having a higher price, wireless Internet providers can reach and maintain market equilibrium.

### Shortage of Internet Access Creates Hot Spots

You're grabbing a quick bite at McDonald's and use your laptop's Internet connection to check the price of a stock you bought earlier today. You're flying to Santa Fe and are on a layover in Dallas. You check your e-mail using your hand-held game device's Internet connection. A few years ago none of these functions would have been possible due to the shortage or non-availability of hard-wired access points to an Internet service provider (ISP). Today, the widespread demand for Internet access has a new type of supplier creating "hot spots" or zones where wireless connectors can stream information at an incredible speed. Access to wireless hot spots is available for about $20 per month for nationwide service. Compare this to phone dial-up ISPs' flat rates of around $10 per month. As wireless Internet coverage expands, you may find such hot spots just about anywhere.

### Think Critically

How is the demand for such wireless service reflected in the relative pricing of wireless versus hard-wired ISPs?

### APPLY

Assign Lesson 6.1 from the Contemporary Economics Workbook.

Encourage students to apply their knowledge of concepts presented in this lesson as they explore economic news stories, policy debates, and data available at **econxtra.swlearning.com**.

### ASSESS

Assign all or part of Lesson 6.1 Assessment on page 167 as homework or an in-class activity.

## Xtra! Study Tools

Direct students to the online study tools for Lesson 6.1 at **econxtra.swlearning.com**.

### CLOSE

**Revisit** the In the News feature on the first page of the lesson. Ask students to review their preliminary answers and discuss the questions, now that they have completed this lesson.

**Review** the objectives for Lesson 6.1. Students should be able to:

• Understand how markets reach equilibrium.

• Explain how markets reduce transaction costs.

them the most. Market prices transmit information about relative scarcity and provide incentives to producers and consumers. Markets also distribute earnings among resource owners.

The coordination that occurs through markets takes place not because of some central plan but because of Adam Smith's "invisible hand." No individual or small group coordinates market activities. Rather, it is the voluntary choices of many buyers and sellers responding only to their individual incentives. Buyers and sellers direct resources and products to those who value them the most. Although each individual pursues his or her own self-interest, the "invisible hand" of market competition promotes the general welfare.

### Market Exchange Is Voluntary

Your experience with competition likely comes from sports, games, and the like, where one side wins and the other side loses. Market exchange is not like that. Market exchange is a voluntary activity in which both sides of the market expect to benefit and usually do. Neither buyers nor sellers would participate in the market unless they expected to be better off. A buyer values the product purchased at least as much as the money paid for it. A seller values the money received at least as much as the product sold.

For example, a consumer will pay $9 for a pizza only if he or she thinks the marginal benefit of that pizza is worth at least $9. The pizza maker will supply a pizza for $9 only if he or she thinks its marginal cost will be no more than $9. Again, voluntary exchange usually makes both sides better off.

Market prices serve as signals to both buyers and sellers about the relative scarcity of the good. A higher price encourages consumers to economize by finding substitutes for the good or even going without it. A higher price also encourages producers to allocate more resources to the production of this good and fewer resources to the production of other goods.

In short, prices help people recognize market opportunities to make better choices as consumers and as producers. The beneficial effects of market exchange include trade between people or organizations in different parts of the country, and among people and organizations in different countries.

## Markets Reduce Transaction Costs

A market sorts out the conflicting views of price between demanders and suppliers. Markets reduce **transaction costs**, or the cost of time and information needed to carry out market exchange. The higher the transaction cost, the less likely the exchange will actually take place. For example, imagine you are looking for a summer job. One approach might be to go from employer to employer looking for openings. This would be time consuming and could have you running around for days. A more efficient strategy would be to read the help-wanted ads in the local paper or go online to look for job openings. Classified ads and web sites, which are elements of the job market, reduce the transaction costs required to bring workers and employers together. Thus, *markets reduce transaction costs*.

**transaction cost**

The cost of time and information needed to carry out market exchange

✓ **CHECKPOINT**
How do markets reduce transaction costs?

# 6.1 *Assessment*

## Key Concepts

1. How would the owner of a dress shop react if she found she had 30 extra prom dresses that she could not sell at the current price?

2. How would the owners of a nursery react if hundreds of customers wanted to buy yucca plants at the current price of $15 when they have only 25 plants to sell?

3. How is it possible for both you and the owner of a fast-food restaurant to benefit when you choose to buy a hamburger for $2.00?

4. What are the transaction costs involved in shopping for shoes at your local mall?

## Graphing Exercise

5. Construct a graph of the demand and supply for running shoes from the data in the demand and supply schedule. What is the equilibrium price? What would happen to the price and quantity demanded and supplied if the current price was $60?

## Think Critically

6. **Science** Scientists have created tomatoes through genetic engineering that are resistant to many diseases. Over time this has caused the equilibrium price of tomatoes to fall. Explain why this has happened.

**Demand and Supply for Running Shoes**

| Price | Quantity Demanded | Quantity Supplied |
|-------|-------------------|-------------------|
| $70 | 40 | 100 |
| $60 | 50 | 80 |
| $50 | 60 | 60 |
| $40 | 70 | 40 |
| $30 | 80 | 20 |

**Xtra!**
**Study Tools**
econxtra.swlearning.com

### Demand and Supply for Running Shoes

## Visualizing the Answer— Graphing Exercise

5. The answer includes a graph. Students' graphs should look similar to the one shown here. An Excel spreadsheet containing this graph, along with supporting data, is available on the Instructor's Resource CD.

## 6.1 Assessment

### Key Concepts

1. Answers will vary. Possible answer: The surplus of dresses indicates the current price is above the equilibrium price. This will force the owner to lower her price to eliminate the surplus.

2. Answers will vary. Possible answer: The shortage of yucca plants indicates that the $15 price is below the equilibrium price. This may cause the owners to raise its price, which will decrease the quantity demanded and encourage the business to acquire additional yucca plants to sell.

3. Answers will vary. Possible answer: Both parties in a voluntary exchange benefit because they have different values. The student values the hamburger more than the $2.00, while the owner of the restaurant places a higher value on the money than the hamburger.

4. Answers will vary. Possible answer: The cost of getting to the mall and the value of alternative uses of your time are transaction costs in this situation.

### Graphing Exercise

5. The equilibrium price is $50, at which the quantity demanded and supplied are both 60 pairs of running shoes. If the current price were $60, the quantity demanded would be 50, while 80 pairs would be supplied. There would be a surplus of 30 pairs, which would cause the firm to lower its price to $50. This would increase the quantity demanded to 60 and reduce the quantity supplied to 60.

A sample of an acceptable graph appears at the bottom of this page.

### Think Critically

6. Answers will vary. Possible answer: Developing disease-resistant tomatoes has increased the quantity farmers are willing and able to supply at each possible price. This may have created a surplus of tomatoes that caused their equilibrium price to fall.

Show students a selection of current magazines that might appeal to young people. These could include *Sports Illustrated*, *Vogue*, or *People*. Ask students to identify the type of readers who would demand each of the magazines. How do publishers encourage more people to demand their publications? Why are some magazines successful when others have been discontinued? Would an increase in demand for these magazines lead to a higher equilibrium price? The laws of demand and supply suggest it will, but does this always happen in real life? After discussing these magazines, invite students to look at a copy of *Mary Engelbreit's Home Companion*. What does this magazine offer that the others do not? How can serving a special niche in a market help a business to succeed?

## TEACH

Instruct students to read the **Movers & Shakers** feature about Mary Engelbreit. Point out that some students may find it helpful to read the article, read the questions at the bottom of the page, and then reread the article.

## ASSESS

Use the questions in Source Reading and Entrepreneurs in Action at the bottom of the profile to assess the students' understanding of this **Movers & Shakers** feature.

### Answers to Source Reading

The market forces used by Mary to determine the price and quantity of greeting cards were the supply of greeting cards already in the market and the demand by consumers in that market.

### Answers to Entrepreneurs in Action

Answers will vary. Possible answer: All these companies sell and promote Mary Engelbreit's artwork in some way. Another company that would also promote and sell her artwork might be a gallery that displays and sells Mary Engelbreit original art and limited edition prints.

# movers & shakers

## Mary Engelbreit *Artist and Entrepreneur*

When Mary Engelbreit was 11 years old, she moved into her first art studio—a closet in her home in St. Louis, Missouri. After high school graduation, Engelbreit went to work in an art supply store and then in a small advertising agency. She accepted freelance art projects, held independent showings of her work, and for a short time worked as an editorial cartoonist for the St. Louis Post-Dispatch. Although she learned a lot, Engelbreit felt she did her best work when it came from her imagination.

In 1977, newly married and with encouragement from her husband, Engelbreit took her portfolio to New York City and called on some well-known publishing houses. One New York art director suggested she try greeting cards. "I was kind of crushed," she recalls, but then she saw how suitable the suggestion might be. Engelbreit's open-mindedness toward new possibilities became one of the keys to her success.

Engelbreit sold her first three greeting-card designs for $150. But she didn't like depending on the whims of the card companies. So in 1983 Engelbreit began her own greeting-card company. While some may have thought the timing was not right to start her own company—she was due to have a baby in just one month—Engelbreit said, "There's always a reason not to do things; it's too expensive, or it's not the best time, or this, or that; but I believe there are always wonderful opportunities sailing by, and you have to be ready to grab them."

Engelbreit has been grabbing opportunities ever since. In just a few years, her greeting cards blossomed into a million dollar business. Today she is the leader of three companies:

- Mary Engelbreit Studios develops licensed products—including greeting cards, books, calendars, gifts, frames, dinnerware, and fabrics—sold by thousands of retailers throughout the United States and in many foreign countries.

- The Mary Engelbreit Store in St. Louis, Missouri, carries more than 1,000 products, including the exclusive ME products that are available only in her store.

- *Mary Engelbreit's Home Companion* magazine has a readership of more than two million and covers topics including family life, food, home décor, crafts, gardening, and collectibles. Today, most of Engelbreit's products are sold through specialty stores and major retailers, as well as through online stores, including her own, which opened in July 2003.

Each of Engelbreit's products reaches a similar audience, and she clearly is a success. In 2000, she was named by *Giftware Business* magazine as the second best-selling licensed property (a close second to Winnie the Pooh). In 2001 and 2003, the International Licensing Industry Merchandisers' Association honored Mary Engelbreit with the prestigious Best Art License of the Year award.

### SOURCE READING

Mary Engelbreit was not thrilled with the idea of illustrating greeting cards. After some thought, however, she reconsidered. What were some of the market forces that would have helped Mary determine the price of her greeting cards and the quantity she should produce?

### ENTREPRENEURS IN ACTION

In small groups, discuss the similarities in the markets for Mary Engelbreit's three companies. Think of one or more companies that Engelbreit might consider starting, based on these similarities.

## *Curriculum Connection—Visual Arts*

Using Mary Engelbreit as a model, instruct students to develop some ideas for how to market the work of a well-known artist. For example, in addition to selling paintings of ballet dancers, Edgar Degas might create a line of dance apparel. Mary Cassatt might be interested in opening a boutique featuring stationery, teas, and needlework. Georg Dionysius Ehret might develop a line of botanical beauty products. Encourage students to look through art books and visit art museum web sites to get ideas.

Have students work in groups of three or four to create a sample catalog page including at least three products. The catalog listing for each product should include some kind of illustration, a name, a brief description, and a price.

## Objectives

> Explain how a shift of the demand curve affects equilibrium price and quantity.

> Explain how a shift of the supply curve affects equilibrium price and quantity.

> Explain what happens to equilibrium price and quantity if both curves shift.

## Overview

When a market reaches equilibrium, the quantity of products demanded and supplied are the same. The equilibrium price and quantity will continue until one of the determinants of demand or supply changes. This section examines how a change in any one of these determinants will shift the demand curve or the supply curve, and in the process change equilibrium price and quantity. The adjustment to a new equilibrium is usually swift. At times, however, often because of government intervention, markets fail to achieve equilibrium.

## Key Terms

**increase in demand**

**decrease in demand**

**increase in supply**

**decrease in supply**

## FOCUS

### Shifts of Demand and Supply Curves

Ask students whether they have ever wanted something so much they did not care how much they had to pay to own it. Request specific examples and write the names of the product on the board as students identify them. Question students about why they wanted these products. How did the producers of these products capitalize on people's desire for these products? Ask what happened to the location of their demand curves for the products as time passed. (The curves shifted to the left.)

### Objectives

Remind students to read the lesson objectives to help focus their attention before reading the lesson.

### Key Terms

Direct students to write each key term on a separate index card. Then write the matching definition and page reference on the back of the appropriate card. Suggest that students include a rough graph corresponding to the concept. Encourage students to use the cards to study for quizzes and tests.

### [ In the News ]

Instruct students to read the passage and write down their answers. Point out that their answers might change after they finish studying Lesson 6.2.

### Answers to Think About It

Answers will vary. Possible answers: The demand curve for natural gas shifted out during the cold snap. The effect was to drive up the price and reduce the quantity of natural gas.

### Visual Presentation

Use the PowerPoint presentation on the Instructor's Resource CD as an adjunct to your lecture. The presentation also can be used for review.

## [ In the News ]

### ● A Cold Slap in the Face

In February 2003, a cold snap and a quick rise in natural gas prices drove up monthly heating costs for some U.S. homeowners to nearly twice what they had been in February 2002. A retired Long Island, N.Y., executive reported a gas bill of $425, which was 107 percent more than he paid the year earlier. The unexpected cold snap drove up demand for the limited supply of gas. Adding to the problem was that the price of oil also was high at that time. (Because oil and natural gas are interchangeable for many industrial uses, their prices often rise together.) The 2003 supply of gas in the United States was less than half of what it had been the year before. Experts foresee continued increases in the demand for gas, while available resources will remain in decline. "All the big, easy-to-get gas got pulled out to provide for us in the [19]90s," said a spokesperson for the American Gas Association. "For the next three to five years, this is what we're going to be seeing." Oddly enough, homebuilders say the high heating costs don't seem to bother many of today's home buyers, who keep demanding bigger and bigger homes. A home-building industry spokesperson estimates that improved construction and insulation in the last decade has cut the amount of gas required to heat a new house by more than 30 percent.

### Think About It

Which curve for natural gas—supply or demand—was affected by the cold snap, and which way did it shift? What was the effect on price and quantity?

◀ | ▶

**169**

### National Content Standards in Economics

A complete list of the NCEE Standards appears on pages xxiv–xxv of this book. The following standards are addressed in Lesson 6.2.

Standard 4: Role of Incentives

Standard 6: Specialization and Trade

Standard 7: Markets—Price and Quantity Determination

Standard 8: Role of Price in Market System

## Shifts of the Demand Curve

On separate slips of paper, write the situations listed below, excluding the text in parentheses. Sketch a demand curve on the board and tell students it represents their demand for meals at a steakhouse on Saturday night. One at a time, have students pick a slip, read the situation aloud, and explain how their demand curve for restaurant meals would change because of what they read.

- You just found out you will be laid off from your after-school job at the end of next week. (The demand will shift left because there is a change in your expectations of income in the future.)

- Your best friend wants you to go to the steakhouse on Saturday. (The demand will shift right because of a change in tastes.)

- Your parents won't let you go out on Saturday unless you clean your room and wash the minivan. (The demand will shift left because of a change in tastes.)

- Your cousin is visiting you next weekend and wants to go to the steakhouse. (The demand will shift right because there are more customers.)

- You didn't earn your allowance this week because you did not do your chores. (The demand will shift left because of a change in income.)

- A friend tells you that the service at the steakhouse is extremely slow. (The demand will shift left because of a change in tastes.)

- The movie theater next to the restaurant is offering half-price tickets to anyone who buys a meal at the steakhouse. (The demand will shift right because of a change in the price of complementary goods.)

Suggest students go to the Graphing Workshop for Chapter 6 at **econxtra.swlearning.com**. At this point, students may complete **Apply It: The Impact of Changing Tastes on the Market for Veggies**.

---

The Graphing Workshop

**increase in demand**
Consumers are more willing and able to buy the product at every price

# Shifts of the Demand Curve

In Figure 6.2, demand curve $D$ and supply curve $S$ intersect at the equilibrium price of $9 and the initial equilibrium quantity of 20 million 12-inch pizzas per week. What happens to equilibrium price and quantity when the demand curve shifts? A shift of the demand curve means that quantity demanded changes at each price.

## What Could Shift the Demand Curve?

If one of the factors that determine the demand for pizza changes in a way that increases demand, this would shift the demand curve to the right from $D$ to $D'$. Any of the following could shift the demand for pizza rightward:

1. An increase in the money income of consumers (because pizza is a normal good)

2. An increase in the price of a substitute, such as tacos, or a decrease in the price of a complement, such as beverages

3. A change in expectations that encourages consumers to buy more pizza now

4. A growth in the population of pizza consumers

5. A change in consumer tastes in favor of pizza

### An Increase in Demand

Any one of those five changes could increase the demand for pizza. An **increase in demand** means that consumers are now more willing and able to buy the product at every price. Note that none of these changes will shift the supply curve.

After the demand curve shifts rightward to $D'$ in Figure 6.2, the amount demanded at the initial price of $9 increases to 30 million pizzas. Because producers supply only 20 million pizzas at that price, there is a shortage of 10 million pizzas. Many consumers are frustrated because they can't find pizza at that price. Producers realize that they could charge more for pizza. This shortage puts upward pressure on the price.

As the price increases, the quantity demanded decreases along the new demand curve, $D'$, and the quantity supplied increases along the existing supply curve, $S$, until the two quantities are once again equal. The new equilibrium price is $12, and the new equilib-

The Graphing Workshop
**Effects of an Increase in Demand**
econxtra.swlearning.com

**Figure 6.2**

After an increase in demand shifts the demand curve from $D$ to $D'$, quantity demanded exceeds quantity supplied at the old price of $9 per pizza. As the price rises, quantity supplied increases along supply curve $S$, and quantity demanded falls along demand curve $D'$. When the new equilibrium price of $12 is reached, the quantity demanded once again equals the quantity supplied. Both price and quantity are higher following the increase in demand.

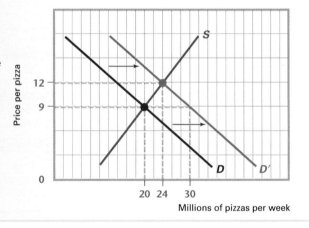

---

## Outside Resources

**Newspapers** Local and national newspapers often report on events that can change our demand for various goods and services. Assign students to find an article about an event that will cause the demand for a specific product to shift. One possible example would be the 2003 finding that hormone replacement therapy (HRT) may increase older women's chances of suffering strokes, heart attacks, and some types of cancer. Ask students how this announcement might affect the location of the demand curve for HRT.

rium quantity is 24 million pizzas per week. *As long as the supply curve slopes upward, a rightward shift of the demand curve increases both price and quantity.*

## A Decrease in Demand

What if one of the determinants of demand changed in a way that reduced demand—such as a decrease in consumer income, a decrease in the price of a substitute, or a reduction in the number of consumers? This results in a **decrease in demand** and consumers are now less willing and able to buy the product, pizza, at every price.

The effect of a decrease in demand is shown in Figure 6.3. The demand for pizza shifts leftward from *D* to *D''*. The amount demanded at the initial price of $9 is now 10 million pizzas. Because producers supply 20 million at that price, there is a surplus of 10 million pizzas. To eliminate the surplus, the price must fall. Thus, this surplus puts downward pressure on the price.

As the price falls, the quantity demanded increases along the new demand curve *D''* and the quantity supplied decreases along the existing supply curve *S* until the two quantities are equal once again. The new equilibrium price is $6, and the new equilibrium quantity is 16 million pizzas per week.

week. *As long as the supply curve slopes upward, a leftward shift of the demand curve reduces both price and quantity.*

### Summary of Demand Shifts

*Given an upward-sloping supply curve, a rightward shift of the demand curve increases both price and quantity and a leftward shift of the demand curve decreases both price and quantity.* One way to remember this is to picture the demand curve shifting along a given upward-sloping supply curve. If the demand curve shifts rightward, price and quantity increase. If the demand curve shifts leftward, price and quantity decrease.

**CHECKPOINT**
How does a shift of the demand curve affect equilibrium price and quantity?

**decrease in demand**
Consumers are less willing and able to buy the product at every price

# Shifts of the Supply Curve

What happens to equilibrium price and quantity when there is a shift of the supply curve? A shift of the supply curve

**Effects of a Decrease in Demand**                **Figure 6.3**

econxtra.swlearning.com

After a decrease in demand shifts the demand curve from *D* to *D''*, quantity supplied exceeds quantity demanded at the old price of $9 per pizza. As the price falls, quantity supplied decreases along supply curve *S*, and quantity demanded increases along demand curve *D''*. When the new equilibrium price of $6 is reached, the quantity demanded once again equals the quantity supplied. Both price and quantity are lower following the decrease in demand.

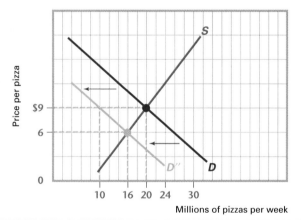

Price per pizza

$9

6

0

10  16  20  24   30

Millions of pizzas per week

*S*

*D''*

*D*

**TEACH**                    (continued)

## Shifts of the Demand Curve

Show your class a video of several typical television advertisements. At least one should appeal to their emotions. Another should provide specific information about the product's price, qualities, or usefulness. Ask students to discuss how these advertisements are attempting to shift consumer demand curves. Why do so few television advertisements include much specific information about the product being promoted? Which of the advertisements do your students believe would be the most successful in shifting consumer demand to the right? What is it about this ad that makes it better (from the business's point of view) than the others?

### *Think Critically Through Visuals*

Use **Figure 6.2—Effects of an Increase in Demand** to illustrate the concept of shifts in the demand curve. Use **Figure 6.3—Effects of a Decrease in Demand** to illustrate the decrease in demand for pizza. Point out that the demand for pizza shifts leftward from *D* to *D''*.

See It — Try It
Apply It

Direct students to the Graphing Workshop for Chapter 6 at **econxtra.swlearning.com**. Instruct students to review **See It: Market Equilibrium** and complete **Try It: Changes in Wealth and the Demand Model**. Students also may try **Apply It: Analyzing the Impact of Multiple Shifts in Supply and Demand in the Market for Gasoline**.

**CHECKPOINT**
Invite a student to answer the checkpoint that appears on this page.

**Answer**
A rightward shift of the demand curve increases both price and quantity, while a downward shift of the demand curve decreases both price and quantity.

## Shifts of the Supply Curve

Remind students that businesses supply products because they intend to earn a profit. Events that cause their ability to earn a profit to change will cause their willingness to supply products to change as well. If a product's price remains unchanged, the only way a producer can earn more profit from each product sold is to find a way to reduce the product's cost of production.

### *Think Critically Through Visuals*

Direct students to focus their attention on the photograph on this page. Ask for a volunteer to answer the question posed in the caption.

### Answer

Answers will vary. Possible answer: A new technology breakthrough, such as a pizza oven, would shift the supply curve outward, or increase the supply of pizzas.

### *Think Critically Through Visuals*

Use **Figure 6.4—Effects of an Increase in Supply** to illustrate the increase in supply for pizza. Point out that the supply for pizza shifts rightward from *S* to *S˜*.

 **Try It**

Suggest that students go to the Graphing Workshop for Chapter 6 at **econxtra.swlearning.com** to complete **Try It: Technology and the Supply and Demand Model.**

---

means that quantity supplied changes at each price. In Figure 6.4, demand curve *D* and supply curve *S* intersect to yield the initial equilibrium price of $9 and the initial equilibrium quantity of 20 million 12-inch pizzas per week.

© Getty Images/PhotoDisc

**increase in supply**
Producers are more willing and able to supply the product at every price

> What would happen to the supply curve for pizza in your area if many of the pizza restaurants invested in a new type of pizza oven?

### What Could Shift the Supply Curve?

If one of the factors that determine supply changes in a way that increases supply, this would shift the supply curve to the right from *S* to *S'*. Any of the following could shift the pizza supply curve rightward:

1. A reduction in the price of a resource used to make pizza, such as mozzarella cheese

2. A decline in the price of another good these resources could make, such as Italian bread

3. A technological breakthrough in pizza ovens

4. A change in expectations that encourages pizza makers to expand production

5. An increase in the number of pizzerias

### An Increase In Supply

Any of the above changes will shift the supply curve, but none will shift the demand curve. An **increase in supply** means that producers are more willing and able to supply pizza at every price. After the supply curve shifts rightward to *S'* in Figure 6.4, the amount supplied

---

### *The Graphing Workshop* — Effects of an Increase in Supply

econxtra.swlearning.com

**Figure 6.4**

An increase in supply is depicted as a shift to the right of the supply curve, from *S* to *S'*. At the new equilibrium, quantity is greater and price is lower than before the increase in supply.

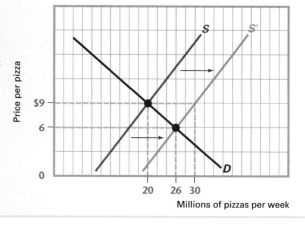

---

Tell students that they are going to bid on several desirable items such as a candy bars, tickets to a school play, or certificates good for free homework assignments. They will use faux money provided by you. Give each student a different amount of fake money and auction off the products. Find the average selling price. Do this a second time, but give each student twice as much money. Ask students to explain what happened to the demand curve for these items when their incomes increased. What would have happened if they had had only half as much money in the second round?

at the initial price of $9 increases from 20 million to 30 million. Producers supply 10 million more pizzas than consumers demand. The build up of unsold pizzas frustrates producers stuck with pizzas they can't sell for $9 each. This surplus forces the price down.

As the price falls, the quantity supplied declines along the new supply curve and the quantity demanded increases along the existing demand curve until a new equilibrium point is reached. The new equilibrium price is $6, and the new equilibrium quantity is 26 million pizzas per week. *As long as the demand curve slopes downward, a rightward shift of the supply curve reduces the price but increases the quantity.*

## A Decrease In Supply

What if one of the determinants of supply changed in a way that reduced supply—such as an increase in the price of a resource used to make pizza, an increase in the price of another good these resources could make, or a decrease in the number of pizzerias?

A **decrease in supply** means that producers are less willing and able to supply pizza at every price. After the supply curve shifts leftward to *S''* in Figure 6.5, the amount supplied at the initial price of $9 decreases from 20 million to 10 million. Producers supply 10 million

fewer pizzas than consumers demand. This shortage forces the price up.

As the price rises the quantity supplied increases along the new supply curve and the quantity demanded decreases along the existing demand curve until a new equilibrium point is reached. The new equilibrium price is $12, and the new equilibrium quantity is 14 million pizzas per week. *As long as the demand curve slopes downward, a leftward shift of the supply curve increases the price but reduces the quantity.*

## Summary of Supply Shifts

Thus, *given a downward-sloping demand curve, a rightward shift of the supply curve decreases price but increases quantity, and a leftward shift of the supply curve increases price but decreases quantity.* Picture the supply curve shifting along a given downward-sloping demand curve. If the supply curve shifts rightward, price decreases but quantity increases. If supply shifts to the left, price increases but quantity decreases.

 **CHECKPOINT**
How does a shift of the supply curve affect equilibrium price and quantity?

**decrease in supply**
Producers are less willing and able to supply the product at every price

---

**Effects of a Decrease in Supply**

**Figure 6.5**

A decrease in supply is depicted as a shift to the left of the supply curve, from *S* to *S''*. At the new equilibrium, quantity is lower and price is higher than before the increase in supply.

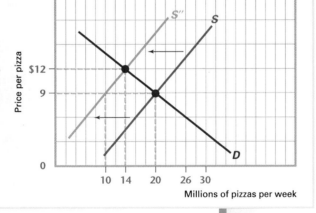

---

## Shifts of the Supply Curve

Ask students to imagine that they own a firm that produces and markets snowboards. Ask them to explain how their willingness to supply the product would be affected by each event listed below. What would each of these shifts do to the equilibrium price, assuming no corresponding change in demand?

- The cost of raw materials increased by 30 percent. (Supply curve shifts left, and equilibrium price grows.)
- The cost of advertising falls by 10 percent. (Supply curve shifts right, and equilibrium price falls.)
- A competing firm increases the wage by $3 per hour and tries to hire some of your workers. You give workers a raise to retain them. (Supply curve shifts left, and equilibrium price grows.)
- A new process allows you to produce boards with fewer workers. (Supply curve shifts right, and equilibrium price falls.)

*Think Critically Through Visuals*

Use **Figure 6.5—Effects of a Decrease in Supply** to illustrate the decrease in supply of pizza. Point out that the supply for pizza shifts leftward from *S* to *S''*.

---

**Ethics in Action**

Have students work in pairs to discuss the ethical issue featured on page 174, and develop an answer to the question presented there.

**Answers to Think Critically**

Answers will vary. Possible answer: The oil industry has its OPEC cartel, which fixes prices. Gas stations have been accused of colluding to fix prices. The pharmaceutical industry has often been accused of price-fixing, etc.

---

## Group Activity

Give each group of students several sheets of blank paper. Give them two minutes to divide each sheet of paper into four equal parts and then make "works of art" from the pieces of paper. They are not allowed to use anything except their own hands and the paper. They are likely to manufacture paper airplanes, hats, or wads of paper. Then give each group a pair of scissors, crayons, adhesive tape, a ruler, and additional sheets of paper. Make the same assignment. Their production this time is likely to be much greater. Discuss how this shows that a change in technology can lead to a shift in supply.

 **CHECKPOINT**
Invite a student to answer the checkpoint.

**Answer**

A rightward shift of the supply curve decreases price but increases quantity, and a leftward shift of the supply curve increases price but decreases quantity.

## Both Curves Shift

Point out that as long as only one curve shifts, you can determine what will happen to both equilibrium price and equilibrium quantity. If both curves shift, the outcome is less certain.

## Think Critically Through Visuals

Ask for a volunteer to answer the question posed in the caption for the photograph on this page.

### Answer

If the demand for housing increases more than the supply, the price of homes will increase, and the quantity of homes will decrease.

## Think Critically Through Visuals

Direct students to focus on **Figure 6.6—Effects of Changes in Both Supply and Demand** on page 175. Use this figure to summarize the effects of various combinations of shifts.

### ✓ CHECKPOINT

Invite a student to answer the checkpoint that appears on page 175.

### Answer

If both the demand and supply increase, all you can say is that equilibrium quantity will increase. Whether the equilibrium price increases or decreases depends on which curve shifts more.
If the demand curves move in opposite directions, you can say what will happen to the price. Equilibrium price will increase if demand increases and supply decreases. Equilibrium price will decrease if demand decreases and supply increases. You can't say for sure what will happen to quantity when the curves move in opposite directions.

# *Ethics in Action*

**Face the Music** The music business always has been fiercely competitive, with frequent unethical attempts to manipulate supply and demand and to control prices. Back in the 1960s, music companies fiddled with demand using an unethical practice that came to be known as "payola." Distributors would give under-the-table pay-offs, or bribes, to radio disc jockeys to play certain recordings and not play others. More recently, two major companies were ordered to stop fixing prices of certain popular CDs. In June 2002, as reported by the Associated Press, an administrative law judge ruled that two music companies joined forces to sell recordings of the opera stars known as the Three Tenors and illegally fixed prices. The illegal "piracy" of music recordings and films has for years created chaos on the supply side of the business. Also, the Internet continues to create ethical and legal issues surrounding the duplicating and distribution of music and other copyrighted art forms.

### Think Critically

The music industry is not alone in its attempts to manipulate supply, demand, and prices. Can you think of how other industries might apply similar unethical or illegal practices?

# Both Curves Shift

As long as only one curve shifts, you can determine what will happen to equilibrium price and quantity. If both curves shift, the outcome is less certain.

## If Curves Shift in the Same Direction

If both demand and supply increase, buyers are more willing and able to demand the good at every price and sellers are more willing and able to sell it at every price. All you can say for sure is that equilibrium quantity will

**Main Idea**

**Market—Price and Quantity Determination**

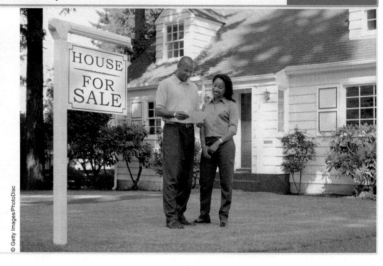

The housing market exists when people who want to purchase a home interact with people who have a house for sale. How are prices in the housing market determined? If the demand for housing increases more than the supply, what happens to the price and quantity of homes on the market?

© Getty Images/PhotoDisc

**174**     **CHAPTER 6**   Market Forces

## *Extend the Content*

In 2003, Congress approved temporary tax cuts. Without further action, the cuts will expire and tax rates will increase to their previous level by 2011. Ask students to assume that Congress will not take action to extend these cuts and tax rates will go up. Have them explain what this will do to the demand and supply curves for most consumer goods. Also discuss the impact this will have on the market price for goods and services. (This will reduce consumers' take-home income and increase the cost of producing many products. There will be a shift to the left for both demand and supply for most consumer products, everything else being equal.)

increase. What happens to price depends on which curve shifts more.

If the demand curve increases more than the supply curve, equilibrium price will increase. For example, in the last decade, the demand for housing has increased more than the supply, so both price and quantity have increased.

If the supply curve increases more than the demand curve, equilibrium price will decrease. For example, in the last decade, the supply of personal computers has increased more than the demand, so price has decreased and quantity has increased.

Conversely, if both the demand and supply curves decrease, or shift to the left, this means that buyers are less willing and able to demand the good and sellers are less willing and able to supply it. So equilibrium quantity decreases. But again, you cannot determine what will happen to equilibrium price unless you examine the relative shifts. If the demand curve shifts more than the supply curve, the price will fall. If the supply curve shifts more, the price will rise.

## If Curves Shift in Opposite Directions

If demand and supply shift in opposite directions, you can determine what will happen to equilibrium price.

**THE WALL STREET JOURNAL**

● **Reading It Right** What's the relevance of the following statement from *The Wall Street Journal*?

"California officials attribute generally lower electricity prices to relatively mild weather in recent days, conservation efforts in the state, and the return of some power plants to full operation."

Equilibrium price will increase if demand increases and supply decreases. Equilibrium price will decrease if demand decreases and supply increases. Without knowledge of particular shifts, however, you cannot say what will happen to equilibrium quantity.

Figure 6.6 summarizes the four possible combinations of changes. Keep in mind that demand curves shift due to factors that determine demand, and supply curves shift due to factors that determine supply.

✓ **CHECKPOINT**
What happens to equilibrium price and quantity if both curves shift in the same direction?

---

**Effects of Changes in Both Supply and Demand**  **Figure 6.6**

When the supply and demand curves shift in the same direction, equilibrium quantity also shifts in that direction. The effect on equilibrium price depends on which curve shifts more. If the curves shift in opposite directions, equilibrium price will move in the same direction as demand. The effect on equilibrium quantity depends on which curve shifts more.

|  | **Change in Demand** | |
|  | Demand increases | Demand decreases |
| **Change in Supply** | | |
| Supply increases | Equilibrium price change is indeterminate.<br><br>Equilibrium quantity increases. | Equilibrium price falls.<br><br>Equilibrium price change is indeterminate. |
| Supply decreases | Equilibrium price rises.<br><br>Equilibrium quantity change is indeterminate. | Equilibrium price change is indeterminate.<br><br>Equilibrium quantity decreases. |

---

## RETEACH

Ask students to sketch a graph of demand and supply for tickets sold to a high school homecoming football game. They should assume the team has won half its games this year. Tell them there are exactly 600 seats in the stadium; therefore, the supply curve will be a vertical line touching the horizontal axis at a quantity of 600. The current price of tickets is $2, and 300 seats remain empty. Ask students what the school could do to fill the stadium. What would happen if the opposing team was an old school rival? What would happen if the team had lost every game so far this year?

---

**THE WALL STREET JOURNAL**

● **Reading It Right**

Invite a student to explain the relevance of the statement from *The Wall Street Journal* that appears on page 175.

**Answer**

Answers will vary. Possible answer: The demand for electricity is decreasing due to milder weather, and the supply is increasing due to conservation efforts; therefore, the market equilibrium price of electricity is decreasing.

**APPLY**

Assign Lesson 6.2 from the *Contemporary Economics Workbook.*

*e*-con @pps

Encourage students to apply their knowledge of concepts presented in this lesson as they explore economic news stories, policy debates, and data available at **econxtra.swlearning.com**.

**ASSESS**

Assign all or part of Lesson 6.2 Assessment on page 177 as homework or an in-class activity.

 **Study Tools**

Direct students to the online study tools for Lesson 6.2 at **econxtra.swlearning.com**.

**CLOSE**

**Revisit** the **In the News** feature on the first page of the lesson. Ask students to review their preliminary answers and discuss the questions, now that they have completed this lesson.

**Review** the objectives for Lesson 6.2. Students should be able to:

● Explain how a shift of the demand curve affects equilibrium price and quantity.

● Explain how a shift of the supply curve affects equilibrium price and quantity.

● Explain what happens to equilibrium price and quantity if both curves shift.

## Analyze Visuals

After studying Lesson 6.2, students should be able to answer the questions on this page.

## Apply Your Skill

Consider allowing students to work in pairs for this assignment.

## Answers

1. The increased travel would cause the demand for disposable cameras to increase, shifting the demand curve for these cameras to the right. This would cause a shortage of the product at the old equilibrium price of $15. This shortage would cause the price of the cameras to increase to $20, the new equilibrium price.

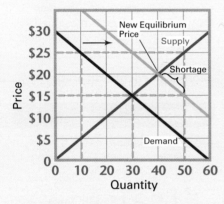

2. The supply curve for disposable cameras will shift left because firms will have to pay more to manufacture the cameras. The equilibrium price will increase.

3. The demand curve for disposable cameras shifts left, as many people substitute the new digital cameras. The equilibrium price will fall.

4. The supply curve for disposable cameras will shift right because the firms will no longer need to pay as many workers. The equilibrium price will fall.

# Sharpen Your Life Skills

## Analyze Visuals

The demand, supply, and equilibrium price for a product are unlikely to stay the same over long periods of time. Economists often demonstrate changes on graphs of demand and supply with arrows. Horizontal arrows that point to the right (→) indicate an increase in either demand or supply that shifts a curve to the right. Horizontal arrows that point to the left (←) indicate a decrease in either demand or supply that shifts a curve to the left. When the demand or supply curve for a product shifts, there will be a shortage or surplus of the product. When there is a surplus of a product, the producer will have an incentive to lower the price to a new equilibrium price. This change often is demonstrated on a graph of demand and supply with a vertical arrow that points down (↓). When there is a shortage of a product, the producer will have an incentive to increase the price to a new equilibrium price. This change often is demonstrated on a graph of demand and supply with a vertical arrow that points up (↑).

## Apply Your Skill

Consider the graph of demand and supply for disposable cameras below. Redraw the graph to show what would happen as a result of each of the following events. Use arrows to show the shift in demand or supply, the resulting shortage or surplus, and the change in the price that would eliminate these amounts. Explain what you have done in each case.

**Demand and Supply for Disposable Cameras**

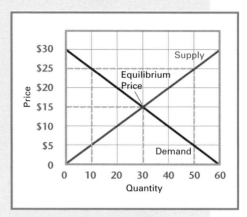

1. Travel increases during the summer months. This leads many more people to take vacation photographs.

2. There is an increase in the cost of film that causes the cost of producing a disposable camera to grow by 10 percent.

3. A new type of digital camera is marketed that is inexpensive and takes excellent photographs. Many people who used to buy disposable cameras choose to purchase these new digital cameras instead.

4. A new process is invented that allows the producer to assemble disposable cameras with half as many workers. This causes the firm to be willing to offer more cameras for sale at each possible price.

## Key Concepts

1. What would happen to a student's demand curve for movie tickets if she lost her after-school job?

2. What would happen to a student's demand curve for movie tickets if the price of DVD movies rentals increased by $4.00 each?

3. What would happen to the equilibrium price and demand curve for New York Yankee baseball caps if the Yankees had just won the World Series?

4. What would happen to the equilibrium price and location of a bakery's supply curve for loaves of bread if it agreed to give its workers a 10 percent raise in pay?

5. What would happen to the locations of a bowling alley's demand and supply curves if the Social Security rate of taxation was increased from 7.65 percent to 9.0 percent for both workers and employers? What would happen to the equilibrium price per game of bowling?

## Graphing Exercise

6. Suppose that running becomes much more popular. As a result, consumers are willing to purchase 30 more pairs of running shoes at each possible price. The demand and supply schedule below shows this increase in demand. Construct a graph showing this shift of demand and the unchanged supply for running shoes. What is the new equilibrium price? Explain why the equilibrium price changed from $50.

**Demand and Supply for Running Shoes**

| Price | Quantity Demanded | | Quantity Supplied |
|---|---|---|---|
| | Old | New | |
| $70 | 40 | 70 | 100 |
| $60 | 50 | 80 | 80 |
| $50 | 60 | 90 | 60 |
| $40 | 70 | 100 | 40 |
| $30 | 80 | 110 | 20 |

## Think Critically

7. **Advertising** Find an advertisement for a well-known brand of candy. Explain what the firm is trying to do to the location of its product's demand curve. If the firm is successful, what will probably happen to its profits?

8. **History** During 1974, there was a war in the Middle East that caused many petroleum-exporting nations to stop shipping oil to the United States. Explain what this did to the location of the supply curve and price for gasoline in the United States.

Xtra!
**Study Tools**
econxtra.swlearning.com

## Key Concepts

1. Her demand curve for movie tickets would shift to the left because she had less money income to spend on all goods and services.

2. His demand curve for movie tickets would shift to the right because he would substitute the purchase of movie tickets for the more expensive DVD rentals.

3. The equilibrium price would increase, and the demand curve for New York Yankees baseball caps would shift to the right because many more consumers would want to wear a Yankees cap. Their tastes would have changed.

4. The equilibrium price would increase, and the bakery's supply curve would shift to the left because the higher wages would increase its costs of production.

5. The demand curve would shift to the left because all workers would have less take-home pay to spend on bowling. The firm's supply curve would also shift to the left because it would have to pay more to employ its workers. The equilibrium price could go up or down, depending on whether the demand or supply curve shifted more.

## Graphing Exercise

6. The new equilibrium price is $60. It changed from $50 because at $50 there was a shortage of 30 pairs. This encouraged the firm to raise the price to $60, where the quantity demanded and supplied was the same—80 pairs.

   A sample of an acceptable graph appears at the bottom of this page.

## Think Critically

7. Answers will vary. Possible answer: Successful advertising will change consumer tastes and cause their demand curve for the candy to shift to the right. This will result in a higher equilibrium price and probably cause greater profits for the firm.

8. The supply curve for gasoline in the United States shifted to the left because oil is the basic raw material for producing gasoline. This shift caused the equilibrium price of gasoline to increase.

**Demand and Supply for Running Shoes**

### Visualizing the Answer—
### Graphing Exercise

6. The answer includes a graph. Students' graphs should look similar to the one shown here. An Excel spreadsheet containing this graph, along with supporting data, is available on the Instructor's Resource CD.

# Market Efficiency and Gains from Exchange — 6.3

## FOCUS

### 6.3 Market Efficiency and Gains from Exchange

Ask students whether being able to do something better than anyone else will ensure them an ability to earn a good income. Many are likely to answer in the affirmative. Then show the class a picture of an old-fashioned dress with lots of petticoats or a bustle. Tell students to imagine they are able to produce this type of garment at a lower cost than anyone else in the world. Ask them how much good this will do them. Will it ensure them a good income? Point out that productive efficiency does not necessarily ensure that there will also be allocative efficiency.

### Objectives

Remind students to read the lesson objectives to help focus their attention before reading the lesson.

### Key Terms

Direct students to look up key terms in a business or economics dictionary. Some students will find it helpful to read another definition. In addition to a definition, many entries will include a brief explanation and an example.

### [ In the News ]

Instruct students to read the passage and write down their answers. Point out that their answers might change after they finish studying Lesson 6.3.

### Answers to Think About It

Answers will vary. Possible answers: Some practices that can be used to maintain blood supply are: (1) promoting blood donation to the general public at all times, not just during an emergency and (2) making it easier to donate blood, by having more traveling donor vans.

### Visual Presentation

Use the PowerPoint presentation on the Instructor's Resource CD as an adjunct to your lecture. The presentation also can be used for review.

## Objectives

> Distinguish between productive efficiency and allocative efficiency.

> Explain what happens when government imposes price floors and ceilings.

> Identify the benefits that consumers and producers get from market exchange.

## Overview

Demand and supply are the foundation of a competitive market economy. Although a market usually involves the interaction of many buyers and sellers, few markets are consciously designed. Just as the law of gravity works whether or not you understand Newton's principles, market forces operate whether or not buyers and sellers understand the laws of demand and supply. Market forces arise naturally, much the way car dealers gather together in the city's outskirts.

## Key Terms

**productive efficiency**

**allocative efficiency**

**disequilibrium**

**price floor**

**price ceiling**

**consumer surplus**

## [ In the News ]

### ● Blood Pressure

In June 2002, the United States blood supply reached its lowest level in decades. America's Blood Centers (the federation that provides half the U.S. public blood supply) and the blood-collection centers of the American Red Cross both reported huge shortfalls. The shortages had a direct and measurable impact on healthcare across the nation. Hospitals were forced to cancel scheduled surgeries, and surcharges were imposed on blood usage. The problem was a surprise. Just one year earlier, after the tragic 9-11 terrorist attacks, there was a surge in the number of Americans who rolled up their sleeves to bolster the blood supply. In fact, the Red Cross tripled its supply in the weeks following the attacks. One explanation for the drop in the number of donors was that, after the public's burst of generosity in 2001, people were just plain drained of giving, regardless of the need. The phenomenon was termed "compassion fatigue." But, most doctors said that even compassion fatigue doesn't fully explain the apathy toward donating blood.

#### Think About It

What are some ideas that might ensure that the nation's supply of blood keeps up with demand?

◀ | ▶

178

### National Content Standards in Economics

A complete list of the NCEE Standards appears on pages xxiv–xxv of this book. The following standards are addressed in Lesson 6.3.

Standard 2: Marginal Cost/Benefit

Standard 6: Specialization and Trade

Standard 7: Markets—Price and Quantity Determination

Standard 8: Role of Price in Market System

Standard 9: Role of Competition

Standard 16: Role of Government

# Competition and Efficiency

How do competitive markets stack up in terms of efficiency? To judge market performance, economists employ two measures of efficiency. The first, called *productive efficiency,* refers to producing output at the lowest possible cost. The second, called *allocative efficiency,* refers to producing the output that consumers value the most. Market competition promotes both productive efficiency and allocative efficiency.

## Productive Efficiency: Making Stuff Right

**Productive efficiency** occurs when a firm produces at the lowest possible cost per unit. The firms that survive and thrive in a competitive market are those that supply the product at their lowest price. *Competition ensures that firms produce at the lowest possible cost per unit.* Firms that are not efficient must either shape up or leave the industry.

## Allocative Efficiency: Making the Right Stuff

Producing at the lowest possible cost per unit is no guarantee that firms are producing what consumers most prefer. This situation is like the airline pilot who announces to passengers that there's some good news and some bad news: "The good news is that we're making record time. The bad news is that we're lost!" Likewise, firms may be producing efficiently but producing the wrong goods—that is, making stuff right but making the wrong stuff.

**Allocative efficiency** occurs when firms produce the output that is most valued by consumers. How do economists know that market competition guarantees allocative efficiency? The answer lies with the market demand and supply curves. The demand curve reflects the marginal benefit that consumers attach to each unit of the good, so the market price is the amount of money people are willing and able to pay for the final unit they purchase.

You also know that the equilibrium price equals the marginal cost of supplying the final unit sold. Marginal cost measures the opportunity cost of resources employed by the firm to produce that final unit sold. Thus the supply curve reflects the opportunity cost of producing the good.

The supply and demand curves intersect at the combination of price and quantity at which *the marginal benefit that consumers attach to the final unit purchased just equals the marginal cost of the resources employed to produce that unit.*

As long as marginal benefit equals marginal cost, that last unit purchased is worth as much as, or more than, any other good that could have been produced using those same resources. There is no way to reallocate resources to increase the total value of output to society. Thus, there is no way to reallocate resources to increase the total benefit consumers reap from production.

*When the marginal benefit that consumers derive from a good equals the marginal cost of producing that good, that market is said to be allocatively efficient.* Competition among sellers encourages producers to supply more of what consumers value the

**productive efficiency**
Occurs when a firm produces at the lowest possible cost per unit

**allocative efficiency**
Occurs when a firm produces the output most valued by consumers

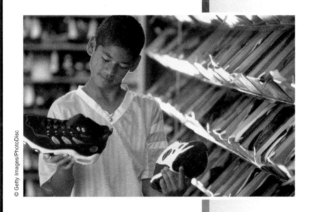

Competition among running shoe brands encourages shoe producers to supply the types of shoes that consumers want to buy. What type of efficiency does this statement suggest?

Remind students that businesses may find they have surpluses or shortages of products and are able to eliminate this disequilibrium by adjusting prices. Place a stack of textbooks or old magazines on a desk in the front of the room. Tell a student that he or she is responsible for selling these materials for you. You would like to receive $10 per item, but if you can't receive that amount, you'll take what you can get. Anything is better than nothing. The student's job is to hold a pretend auction in which members of the class pretend to bid for the books. What the student is likely to find is that the quantity of the books that is demanded won't equal the quantity supplied until the price falls to five cents or less per text. Use this activity to introduce the idea of disequilibrium and how the forces of supply and demand work to eliminate this condition.

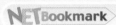

Direct students to **econxtra.swlearning.com**. Remind them to click on the link for Lesson 6.2 to find the appropriate link for the **NET Bookmark** on this page.

### Answer

When a price floor is imposed, the quantity of labor demanded is lower than the quantity of labor supplied. This results in an excess of labor.

---

*disequilibrium*

A mismatch between quantity demanded and quantity supplied as the market seeks equilibrium; usually temporary, except where government intervenes and sets the price

*price floor*

A minimum legal price below which a product cannot be sold

*price ceiling*

A maximum legal selling price above which a product cannot be sold

---

most. Firms not only are making stuff right, they are making the right stuff.

## Disequilibrium

One way to appreciate markets is to examine instances when they are slow to adjust or where they are not free to work. A surplus of goods exerts downward pressure on the price, and a shortage of goods exerts upward pressure. But markets do not always reach equilibrium quickly. During the time required for adjustment, the market is said to be in disequilibrium. **Disequilibrium** is usually a temporary condition when the plans of buyers do not match the plans of sellers. Sometimes, usually as a result of government intervention in markets, disequilibrium can last a while.

### Price Floor

At times public officials set the price above its equilibrium level. For example, the federal government often regulates the prices of agricultural products in an attempt to ensure farmers a higher and more stable income than they would earn otherwise. To achieve higher prices, the federal government establishes a price floor for a product, making it illegal to sell below the floor price. A **price floor** is a minimum selling price that is above the equilibrium price.

Panel (a) of Figure 6.7 shows the effect of a $2.50 per gallon price floor for milk. At that price, farmers supply 24 million gallons per week, but consumers demand only 14 million gallons. Thus, the price floor results in a surplus of 10 million gallons. This surplus milk will accumulate on store shelves and eventually sour. So, as part of the price-support program, the government usually agrees to buy up the surplus milk to take it off the market. The federal government, in

---

**NETBookmark**

The *minimum wage* is a price floor in the market for labor. The government sets a minimum price per hour of labor in certain markets, and no employer is permitted to pay a wage lower than that. Access the Department of Labor web site through econxtra.swlearning.com to learn more about the mechanics of the program. Then use a supply and demand graph to illustrate the effect of a minimum wage above equilibrium on a particular labor market. What happens to quantity demanded and quantity supplied as a result?

**econxtra.swlearning.com**

fact, has spent billions buying and storing surplus agricultural products.

### Price Ceiling

Sometimes public officials try to keep prices below their equilibrium levels by establishing a **price ceiling**, or a *maximum* selling price. For example, concern about the rising cost of rental housing in some cities prompted public officials to impose rent ceilings, making it illegal to charge more than the ceiling price. Panel (b) of Figure 6.7 represents the demand and supply for rental housing in a hypothetical city. The vertical axis shows the monthly rent, and the horizontal axis shows the quantity of units rented. The equilibrium, or market-clearing, rent is $1,000 per month. The equilibrium quantity is 50,000 housing units.

Suppose government officials are concerned that rents of $1,000 per month are not affordable to enough households. They pass a law that sets a maximum rent of $600 per month. At that ceiling price, 60,000 rental units are demanded, but only 40,000 are supplied, resulting in a housing shortage of 20,000 units.

Because of the price ceiling, the rental price no longer allocates housing to those who value it the most. Other devices emerge to ration housing, such as waiting lists, personal connections, and

---

In 2003, a power outage affected nearly 100 million people in the northeastern United States. Although there were many causes, limited investment in the power grid over the preceding 20 years was probably the greatest. To prevent another blackout, experts estimated that $100 billion would have to be invested in new equipment. This would require an increase in the price of electricity by as much as 15 percent. Others suggested that rationing would be a better choice. Ask your students to evaluate these alternatives. What would probably happen if the government forced utilities to keep prices at the same level?

**Figure 6.7**

**(a) Price floor for milk**

Surplus

Price per gallon

$2.50
1.90

0

14 19 24

Millions of gallons per month

**(b) Price ceiling for rent**

$1,000

600

Shortage

Monthly rental price

S

D

0

40 50 60

Thousands of rental units per month

**If a price floor is established above the equilibrium price, a permanent surplus results. A price floor established at or below the equilibrium price has no effect. If a price ceiling is established below the equilibrium price, a permanent shortage results. A price ceiling established at or above the equilibrium price has no effect.**

the willingness to make under-the-table payments, such as "key fees," "finder's fees," high security deposits, and the like.

*To have an impact, a price floor must be set above the equilibrium price, and a price ceiling must be set below the equilibrium price.* A floor price above the equilibrium price creates a surplus, and a ceiling price below the equilibrium price creates a shortage. Various nonprice devices emerge to cope with the disequilibrium resulting from the market interference.

Price controls distort market prices and interfere with the market's ability to allocate resources efficiently. Prices no longer provide consumers and producers accurate information about the relative scarcity of goods. The good intentions of government officials create shortages and surpluses that often are economically wasteful.

### Other Sources of Disequilibrium

Government intervention in the market is not the only source of disequilibrium. Sometimes, when new products are intro-

duced or when demand or supply changes suddenly, the market takes a while to adjust. For example, popular toys, best-selling books, and chart-busting CDs often sell out and are unavailable while suppliers produce more. In these cases, there is a temporary shortage.

On the other hand, some new products attract few customers and pile up unsold on store shelves, awaiting a "clearance sale." In this case, there is a temporary surplus.

> ✓ **CHECKPOINT**
> What happens when governments impose price floors and price ceilings?

## Consumer Surplus

In equilibrium, the marginal benefit of pizza just equals its marginal cost. The cost to the economy of bringing that

Lesson 6.3 • *Market Efficiency and Gains from Exchange* **181**

### Disequilibrium

Ask students to imagine that they are farmers and each own 100 dairy cows, which produce milk used to make cheese or yogurt. If they produce cheese, the government will guarantee a price of at least $4.00 per pound. This price should earn them a profit of $50,000 for their cheese. If they produce yogurt, there is no guaranteed price. They might earn $100,000 if the price of yogurt is high. They might earn nothing if it is low. What would the students choose to produce? What will their decision do the relative supplies of cheese and yogurt? Why does a price floor such as the $4.00 per pound of cheese tend to cause a lasting surplus? (Producers supply more of a product that has a guaranteed profit [cheese] and use fewer resources for production that involves greater risk [yogurt]. This results in a lasting disequilibrium in the market.)

### *Think Critically Through Visuals*

Direct students to focus on **Figure 6.7—Effects of a Price Floor and a Price Ceiling**. Point out that the panel on the left illustrates the price floor for milk, and the panel on the right illustrates the price ceiling for rent.

### SPAN THE GLOBE

Direct students to read the short passage "Oil for One and One for Oil" on page 182. Use the question as a starting point for class discussion.

### Answers to Think Critically

Answers will vary. Possible answer: The United States could develop reserves of oil it could tap if OPEC reduced production in the future. It could also develop alternative sources of energy using geothermal power, wind, or energy from the sun.

> ✓ **CHECKPOINT**
> Invite a student to answer the checkpoint that appears on this page.

### Answer

When governments impose price floors or ceilings, market prices are distorted and interfere with the market's ability to allocate resources efficiently. This results in disequilibrium of the market.

### *Economic Headlines*

Instruct students to locate an article in a current magazine or newspaper that relates to one of the topics in this lesson. For example, they might find articles about competition, rent control, or consumer surplus. Instruct students to read the article and write a brief summary, making sure to include a reference citation. Identify the style you want them to use for the citation.

As an alternative, you might locate several articles of interest and provide citations for students to use to locate one of the articles. Direct students to read the article they have chosen and write a brief explanation of how it relates to this lesson.

### Consumer Surplus

Choose several products that many students would like to own. Display the products, or pictures of the products, and ask students to write down an amount that they would be willing and able to pay for each product. After everyone has written down the amounts, tell them to imagine that a store is having a sale on these items. Announce an absurdly small amount for the price of each product. Instruct students to subtract the amount that they would need to pay to buy the product from the amount that they would have been willing to pay. This amount is called a consumer surplus.

### Answers

Answers will vary. Possible answers: The consumers win because they are getting something at a reduced cost; suppliers lose because they are selling items at a lower profit, or, in some cases, at a loss. These clearance sales raise the price of other goods in the store so that these suppliers can recover some of their lost profit.

### Think Critically Through Visuals

Direct students' attention to **Figure 6.8—Market Demand and Consumer Surplus** on page 183. Point out that the darkest area represents the consumer surplus when the price is $2. The shaded area between $1 and $2 shows the additional surplus when the price is $1.

**The Graphing Workshop** — (See It)

Direct students to the Graphing Workshop for Chapter 6 at **econxtra.swlearning.com**. Instruct students to click on **See It: Consumer Surplus** to view the graph and listen to an explanation. 👁 ((∘))

---

final pizza onto the market just equals the marginal benefit that consumers get from that pizza. Does this mean that consumers get no net benefit from the good? No. Market exchange usually benefits both consumers and producers.

### Market Demand and Consumer Surplus

A demand curve shows the marginal benefit consumers attach to each unit of the good. For example, based on the demand curve for pizza presented earlier, consumers demanded 8 million pizzas at a

**consumer surplus**
The difference between the total amount consumers are willing and able to pay for a given quantity of a good and what they actually pay

### TEAM WORK

In small groups, discuss the pros and cons of "clearance sales" with regard to consumers and suppliers. Who wins? Who loses? What impact do you think these sales have on the prices of other goods the store sells?

---

## SPAN THE GLOBE

### Oil for One and One for Oil

The Organization of Petroleum Exporting Countries (OPEC) is an 11-member, international group that works together to control the output and price of oil. OPEC pumps about a third of the world's crude oil. Its production policies can have a profound effect on the price consumers pay to drive their cars and heat their homes. Representatives of the 11 countries meet periodically and agree to increase or decrease the number of barrels of crude oil they supply in order to maintain the price levels they want. If the price drops, OPEC will cut back production (lower the ceiling). If the price rises, OPEC increases its oil output. OPEC has no control over the demand for oil. However, by using its control over supply, OPEC's goal is to artificially create an equilibrium and maintain the price of oil at the level it wants.

### Think Critically

What are some safeguards the United States could employ to keep OPEC from raising petroleum prices unreasonably in the future?

---

price of $15. Apparently, those consumers believed the marginal benefit of pizza was worth at least $15. Consumers demanded 14 million pizzas at a price of $12. At a price of $9, consumers demanded 20 million pizzas, even though some were willing to pay $15 each for 8 million pizzas and $12 each for 14 million pizzas.

Consumers enjoy a consumer surplus because they get to buy all 20 million pizzas for $9 each even though they would have been willing to pay more for lesser amounts. At a given price, **consumer surplus** is the difference between the total amount consumers would have been willing and able to pay for that quantity and the total amount they actually do pay.

To get a clearer idea of consumer surplus, refer to the demand curve in Figure 6.8. If the price is $2 per unit, each person adjusts his or her quantity demanded until the marginal benefit of the final unit he or she purchases equals at least $2. Each consumer gets to buy all other units for $2 each as well. The dark-shaded area bounded above by the demand curve and below by the price of $2 depicts the consumer surplus when the price is $2.

The light-shaded area shows the increase in consumer surplus if the price drops to $1. If this good were free, the consumer surplus would be the entire area under the demand curve. Notice that at a price of zero, the consumer surplus is not that much greater than when the price is $1. Competitive markets maximize the amount of consumer surplus in the economy.

---

### Curriculum Connection—Geography

In 1900, the United States was the world's largest exporter of petroleum. Oil had not yet been discovered in the Middle East or in South America. Today, the United States imports roughly 60 percent of the oil it consumes. Ask students to sketch graphs of demand and supply curves for petroleum, *within* the United States, as they would have existed in 1900 and 2000. (The 1900 graph should show a surplus of oil that would have been shipped to other nations, while the 2000 graph would show a shortage that was filled by importing oil into the U.S.)

## An Application of Consumer Surplus: Free Medical Care

Certain Americans, such as the elderly and those receiving public assistance, are provided government-subsidized medical care. Taxpayers spent more than $420 billion in 2000 to provide medical care to 75 million Medicare and Medicaid recipients, for an average annual cost of about $5,600 per beneficiary. The dollar cost to most beneficiaries was usually little or nothing. The problem with giving something away is that beneficiaries consume it to the point where their marginal benefit from the final unit is zero. However, the marginal cost to taxpayers can be substantial.

This is not to say that beneficiaries derive no benefit from free medical care. Although they may not value the final unit consumed very much, most derive a large consumer surplus from the other units they consume. For example, suppose that Figure 6.8 represents the demand for medical care by Medicaid beneficiaries. Because the dollar price to them is zero, they consume medical care up to the point where the demand curve intersects the horizontal axis. Their consumer surplus is the entire area under the demand curve.

The cost to taxpayers of providing that final unit of medical care may be $100 or more. One way to reduce the total cost to taxpayers of such programs without really harming beneficiaries is to charge a small price—say, $1 per physician visit. Beneficiaries would eliminate visits they value less than $1. This would yield significant savings to taxpayers but would still leave beneficiaries with good health care and a substantial consumer surplus. This is measured in Figure 6.8 as the area under the demand curve but above the $1 price.

As a case in point, one Medicaid experiment in California required some beneficiaries to pay $1 per visit for their first two office visits per month (after two visits, the price of additional visits went back to zero). A cost of at most $2 per month would not impose much of a

burden on recipients. As a means of comparison, another group continued to receive completely free medical care. The $1 charge reduced office visits by 8 percent compared to the group not charged.

Medical care, like other goods and services, is also sensitive to a time price. For example, a 10 percent increase in the average travel time required to visit a free outpatient clinic reduced visits by 10 percent. Similarly, when the relocation of a free clinic at one college campus increased students' walking time by 10 minutes, student visits dropped by 40 percent.

These findings do not mean that certain groups shouldn't receive low-cost medical care. The point is that when something is provided for free, people consume it until their marginal benefit is zero. Even a modest money cost or time cost would reduce program costs yet still leave beneficiaries with a substantial consumer surplus.

## The Graphing Workshop

### Market Demand and Consumer Surplus

**Figure 6.8**

econxtra.swlearning.com

Consumer surplus at a price of $2 is shown by the darker area. If the price falls to $1, consumer surplus increases to include the lighter area.

✓ **CHECKPOINT**
How do consumers benefit from market exchange?

✓ **CHECKPOINT**
Invite a student to answer the checkpoint that appears on this page.

### Answer

Consumers benefit from market exchange by receiving the goods they demand and want at a price they are willing to pay. Consumers benefit even further from market exchange when there is a consumer surplus. When this occurs, consumers receive goods at a lower price than what they would have originally been willing to pay.

### APPLY

Assign Lesson 6.3 from the Contemporary Economics Workbook.

### e-con @pps

Encourage students to apply their knowledge of concepts presented in this lesson as they explore economic news stories, policy debates, and data available at **econxtra.swlearning.com**.

### ASSESS

Assign all or part of Lesson 6.3 Assessment on page 184 as homework or an in-class activity.

### Xtra! Study Tools

Direct students to the online study tools for Lesson 6.3 at **econxtra.swlearning.com**.

### CLOSE

**Revisit** the **In the News** feature on the first page of the lesson. Ask students to review their preliminary answers and discuss the questions, now that they have completed this lesson.

**Review** the objectives for Lesson 6.3. Students should be able to:

- Distinguish between productive efficiency and allocative efficiency.
- Explain what happens when government imposes price floors and ceilings.
- Identify the benefits that consumers and producers get from market exchange.

### RETEACH

Ask students to make lists of products that are marketed to U.S. consumers that they believe waste scarce resources (SUVs, gold-plated bath tubs, palatial houses for sports superstars, etc.). Do your students believe anything should be done to limit "consumer excesses" that often exist in competitive market economies? If they do, how would they impose such limits without harming individual rights and personal freedoms? Remember, for the producers of these products to continue to exist there must be demand for the products they make.

### Key Concepts

1. Answers will vary. Possible answer: Competition leads to productive efficiency because inefficient firms cannot afford to offer food products at competitive prices; they cannot earn a profit and so will fail. Only efficient firms are able to offer the food products consumers demand, at prices that are no higher than those charged by other firms, and still earn a profit.

2. Answers will vary. Possible answer: The business that produces these cameras will be encouraged to produce more of them by consumers who are willing to pay relatively high prices for them. Firms will purchase resources to make these products as long as managers believe they can sell them for a profit.

3. Answers will vary. Possible answers: Almost all students would look for work if they expected to be paid $20 per hour. However, few employers would be willing to hire unskilled workers at this rate. There would be a surplus of workers who could not find employment. The government would have created a price (wage) floor that would result in a surplus of labor.

4. Answers will vary. Possible answer: It would be difficult for ISPs to earn a profit if they could charge only $5 per month. Many would stop offering their service, while the low price would encourage more consumers to seek to subscribe. This price ceiling would cause a shortage of the service.

5. You will receive $3.75 worth of consumer surplus (5 × $.75 = $3.75).

6. Answers will vary. Possible answer: The money costs of providing an education are not the only costs of learning. They have to consider the opportunity cost of time used to study as well. Extra homework may help them learn more but they will give up alternative uses for the time they spend studying.

### Graphing Exercise

7. At a price ceiling of $40, the quantity demanded would be 70 and the quantity supplied would be 40. There would be a shortage of 30 pairs of shoes. This would cause many consumers to be upset because they would not be able to find running shoes to buy. See the visual at the bottom of this page.

*The Answer Key is continued on page 186.*

### Key Concepts

1. How does market competition ensure that consumers will be offered a selection of low-priced foods?

2. How does market competition ensure that a new type of camera you want to own will eventually be available for you to purchase?

3. If the minimum wage were increased to $20 per hour, how many of your classmates do you believe would look for a job? How many jobs do you expect they would find? How is this an example of a price floor?

4. If the government set a price ceiling of $5 per month to subscribe to an Internet Service Provider (ISP), what would happen to the number of ISPs that offer Internet access and the number of people who wished to purchase their service?

5. Suppose you buy a salad for lunch every day for $2.75. This is the most you would be willing to pay for your salad. One week there is a special on salads and the price is reduced to $2.00. What is the value of the consumer surplus you will receive if you buy five salads during that week?

6. Most students pay no direct cost in terms of money for public education. To them the value of their education is a consumer surplus. Why doesn't this result in lots of students demanding extra homework and remedial classes after school?

### Graphing Exercise

7. Suppose the government became concerned about the high price of running shoes and imposed a price ceiling of $40 per pair. Given the data in the demand and supply schedule at the right, what would the results of such a regulation be? Why would many consumers and producers be upset with this result? Construct a graph that demonstrates the result of such a regulation.

**Demand and Supply for Running Shoes**

| Price | Quantity Demanded | Quantity Supplied |
|-------|-------------------|-------------------|
| $70 | 40 | 100 |
| $60 | 50 | 80 |
| $50 | 60 | 60 |
| $40* | 70 | 40 |
| $30 | 80 | 20 |

*(government price ceiling)*

### Think Critically

8. **History** In the early 1900s, many businesses produced horse-drawn wagons at very low cost. Still, many of these firms were forced out of business due to a lack of consumer demand. Many people chose to purchase automobiles instead of wagons. Explain how this fact demonstrates the importance of allocative efficiency.

**Demand and Supply for Running Shoes**

### Visualizing the Answer— Graphing Exercise

7. The answer includes a graph. Students' graphs should look similar to the one shown here. An Excel spreadsheet containing this graph, along with supporting data, is available on the Instructor's Resource CD.

# *to History*

## The Rocky Mountain Fur Company

On March 20, 1823, an ad appeared in the *Missouri Republican:*

> "... to enterprising young men. The subscriber wishes to engage one hundred young men to ascend the Missouri River to its source, there to be employed for one, two, or three years. For particulars enquire of Major Henry, near the lead mines in the country of Washington, who will ascend with, and command, the party of the subscriber near St. Louis."
>
> *William H. Ashley*

This call for young men began the era of the Mountain Men and the fur trade in the American Far West. To the north, the French and the British had long established a profitable fur trade in North America, but Americans did not reach the Far West until after the Lewis and Clark expedition. The trade was driven by the demand of the markets in the eastern United States and Europe for furs, but the Napoleonic Wars and the War of 1812 closed many of these markets. Following the peace, the demand once again rose in the United States and Europe.

With the establishment of trading posts, most furs were obtained by trading with the Native Americans. Some were obtained by company-employed hunters and trappers. The average take was 120 beaver skins a season. A third method was by purchasing them from independent hunters and trappers. Ashley and Henry's company, the Rocky Mountain Fur Company, cut costs by taking an innovative approach that would send groups of trappers into the wilderness. Each would trade or trap furs and then would meet at the end of the season at a predetermined location, where a rendezvous was held. At the rendezvous, the Mountain Men would sell their furs and obtain more supplies for the next season. This method allowed the company to cut costs by avoiding the building and maintaining of expensive trading posts.

### THINK CRITICALLY

Using supply and demand curves, demonstrate the following situations:
1. The effects of the end of the War of 1812 on the market for fur
2. The effects of the depletion of the supplies of fur
3. The effect of the substitute of silk for fur in men's hats

### FOCUS

The fur trade of the early nineteenth century had a significant effect on American history. A small number of Mountain Men paved the way for the groups of men and women who settled the American West. Markets in the eastern United States and Europe, as well as the number of animals available, directed their fortunes. The era of the Mountain Men lasted only about 25 years before the demand for furs and the supply of animals both ended.

### TEACH

Point out that many events in history can be illustrated using the tools of economics. Instruct students to read the **Connect to History** feature and answer the questions.

### ASSESS

Use the problems at the bottom of the page to assess the students' understanding of this feature. Instruct students to use the following labels for their graphs: S1—War of 1812; S2—depletion of fur; and S3—silk substitute.

#### Answers to Think Critically

1. The end of the War of 1812 would shift the demand and supply curves for furs to the right.
2. The effects of the depletion of the supplies of fur would shift the supply curve to the left.
3. The effects of substituting silk for fur in men's hats would shift the demand curve to the left.

### *Bibliography*

Carlos, Ann M. *The North American Fur Trade, 1804-1821: A Study in the Life Cycle of a Duopoly.* New York: Garland Publishing, Inc., 1986.

Chittenden, Hiram Martin. *American Fur Trade of the Far West.* Vols. 1 & 2. Lincoln: University of Nebraska Press, 1987.

Fuchs, Victor R. *The Economics of the Fur Industry.* New York: Columbia University Press, 1957.

Lewis, Jon E. *The Mammoth Book of the West.* New York: Carrol & Graf Publishers, Inc., 1996.

Milner, Clyde A., Carol A. O'Connor, and Martha A. Sandweiss, eds. *Oxford History of the American West.* New York: Oxford University Press, 1994.

### Consider

Ask students to revisit the questions they were asked to consider at the beginning of the chapter. Remind students that they should be able to answer all of the questions after studying Chapter 6.

- How is market competition different from competition in sports and in games? See page 166—Market Exchange Is Voluntary.

- Why do car dealers usually locate together on the outskirts of town? See page 167—Markets Reduce Transaction Costs.

- What's the difference between making stuff right and making the right stuff? See page 179—Productive Efficiency and Allocative Efficiency.

- Why do government efforts to keep rents low usually lead to a housing shortage? See page 180—Price Ceiling.

- Why do consumers benefit nearly as much from a low price as from a zero price? See page 181—Consumer Surplus.

### Exam *View*

Use **Exam***View* to assess student learning.

- Create a chapter test using questions from the existing test bank.
- Add your own questions to the existing test bank.
- Generate multiple forms of a chapter test.

### Study Skills

Offer the following study skills suggestions for students as they review this chapter.

- Outline the chapter.
- Review Key Terms.
- Review Checkpoints.
- Work in pairs to quiz each other.
- Use Xtra! Study Tools for each lesson.

 Xtra! Quiz Prep

Direct students to the online quiz preparation for Chapter 6 at **econxtra.swlearning.com**.

---

 **6** # Chapter Assessment

## 6.1 *Price, Quantity, and Market Equilibrium*

**a** In a competitive market, the forces of demand and supply push prices to their *equilibrium* level where the quantity demanded and supplied are the same.

**b** Any price above the equilibrium price will cause a *surplus* that will force producers to lower their price to the equilibrium price. Any price below the equilibrium price will cause a *shortage* that will encourage producers to increase their price to the equilibrium price.

**c** In competitive markets, buyers and sellers are free to exchange goods or services for money voluntarily. When there is a voluntary exchange, both parties gain because of the different values they place on goods, services, or money.

**d** *Transaction costs* are costs that are necessary to carry out market exchanges. Markets encourage exchanges by reducing transaction costs. Similar businesses often choose to be located in the same area to reduce the transaction costs of shopping.

## 6.2 *Shifts of Demand and Supply Curves*

**a** There are five types of factors that can shift the demand curve for a product. These are (1) changes in consumer money income, (2) changes in the price of substitute or complementary products, (3) changes in consumer expectations, (4) changes in consumer population, and (5) changes in consumer tastes.

**b** There also are five types of factors that can shift the supply curve for a product. These are (1) changes in the cost of a resource used to make the product, (2) changes in the price of other goods that these resources could be used to produce, (3) changes in technology that reduce the cost of making the product, (4) changes in producer expectations, and (5) a change in the number of producers.

**c** When either the demand or supply curve for a product shifts, there will be a corresponding change in the equilibrium price and the quantity of the product.

## 6.3 *Market Efficency and Gains from Exchange*

**a** Competitive markets exhibit productive and allocative efficiency. *Productive efficiency* occurs when products are manufactured at the lowest possible cost. *Allocative efficiency* occurs when firms produce the products that are most valued by consumers.

**b** *Disequilibrium* occurs when the quantity of a product consumers demand is not equal to the quantity producers supply. It is usually a temporary condition, but can continue over time, particularly when government intervenes in the market. Government-imposed *price floors* are likely to result in surpluses of a product, while government *price ceilings* usually cause shortages.

**c** A *consumer surplus* is the difference between the amount of money consumers would have been willing to pay for a product and what they actually pay for it. Government price regulations or subsidized services often result in consumer surpluses. Free or low-cost medical care provided by the government to the poor and elderly are examples of this type of situation.

---

 **6.3** *Assessment*

Continued from page 184.

### Think Critically

8. Answers will vary. Possible answer: Firms that had productive efficiency (made horse-drawn wagons well) still failed because they lacked allocative efficiency (consumers demanded more automobiles and fewer horse-drawn wagons).

# Review Economic Terms

Choose the term that best fits the definition. On a separate sheet of paper, write the letter of the answer. Some terms may not be used.

1. The quantity of a product demanded is not equal to the quantity supplied

2. Quantity demanded equals quantity supplied and the market clears

3. A situation achieved when a firm produces output most desired by consumers

_____ 4. A minimum legal price below which a product cannot be sold

_____ 5. The amount of a product that cannot be sold at a given price

_____ 6. Consumers are more willing and able to buy a product at every price

_____ 7. A maximum legal price above which a product cannot be sold

_____ 8. A situation achieved when a firm produces output at the lowest possible cost

_____ 9. The amount by which the amount of a product demanded exceeds the amount supplied at a particular price

10. The cost of time and information needed to carry out market exchange

11. Producers are less willing and able to supply a product at every price

a.  **allocative efficiency**

b.  **consumer surplus**

c.  **equilibrium**

d.  **decrease in demand**

e.  **decrease in supply**

f.  **disequilibrium**

g.  **increase in demand**

h.  **increase in supply**

i.  **price ceiling**

j.  **price floor**

k.  **productive efficiency**

l.  **shortage**

m.  **surplus**

n.  **transaction cost**

# Review Economic Concepts

12. **True or False**  A price below a product's *equilibrium* price will result in a surplus of the product.

13. When there is a voluntary exchange, it is reasonable to believe
    a. both the buyer and seller gained.
    b. neither buyer nor seller gained.
    c. the buyer gained more than the seller.
    d. the seller gained more than the buyer.

14. **True or False**  A market is always in a state of equilibrium.

15. **True or False**  Government regulations affect equilibrium in the markets for some goods and services.

16. Given an upward sloping supply curve, a rightward shift of the demand curve
    a. decreases both equilibrium price and quantity.

    b. increases both equilibrium price and quantity.
    c. decreases equilibrium price only.
    d. increases equilibrium price only.

17. **True or False**  A shift of the supply curve results from a change in quantity demanded at all prices.

18. A market will stay in equilibrium until
    a. one of the factors that determines demand changes.
    b. one of the factors that determines supply changes.
    c. all the suppliers go out of business.
    d. both a and b

19. __?__ are costs that must be paid to complete a market exchange.

1. f. disequilibrium
2. c. equilibrium
3. a. allocative efficiency
4. j. price floor
5. m. surplus
6. g. increase in demand
7. i. price ceiling
8. k. productive efficiency
9. l. shortage
10. n. transaction cost
11. e. decrease in supply

**Review Economic Concepts**

12. False. A price above a product's equilibrium will result in a surplus of the product.
13. a. both the buyer and seller gained
14. False. A market is not always in a state of equilibrium.
15. False. Government regulations affect equilibrium for all goods and services.
16. b. increases both equilibrium price and quantity
17. True
18. d. both a and b
19. Transaction costs

## Review Economic Concepts

20. c. an increase in the number of people who are unemployed

21. True

22. d. a number of experienced workers retire and are replaced by new workers

23. False. Both the supply curve and demand curve are shifting outward (to the right) in this example. This results in a definitive increase in the equilibrium quantity. What happens to the equilibrium price is indecisive.

24. productive efficiency

25. c. the quantity demanded to grow and the quantity supplied to fall

26. Consumer surplus

## Apply Economic Concepts

27. Columns 1, 4, and 5 of the schedule appear below.

| Price Per Taco | Surplus/ Shortage | Will the price rise or fall? |
|---|---|---|
| $2.00 | +150 | fall |
| $1.75 | +100 | fall |
| $1.50 | +50 | fall |
| $1.25 | ____ | ____ |
| $1.00 | −50 | rise |
| $0.75 | −100 | rise |

28. A sample of an acceptable graph appears at the bottom of this page.

---

20. Each of the following will cause the demand for butter to increase *except*

   a. an increase in the price of margarine.

   b. a scientific study that shows butter is good for people's health.

   c. an increase in the number of people who are unemployed.

   d. an increase in the number of people who might purchase butter.

21. **True or False** An increase in a firm's cost of production will cause its supply curve to move to the left.

22. Each of the following will cause a firm's supply to increase *except*

   a. the firm's workers are trained to be more efficient.

   b. the firm finds a new, lower-cost source of electric power.

   c. the firm invests in new technology that reduces its costs of production.

   d. a number of experienced workers retire and are replaced by new workers.

---

23. **True or False** If a firm's costs of production fall while the demand for its product grows, you can be sure the equilibrium price for its product will fall.

24. There is __?__ when a firm produces products at the lowest possible cost.

25. Suppose the current equilibrium price for natural gas is $1.05 per thousand cubic feet. The government decides to impose a price ceiling of $.90. This will cause

   a. the quantity demanded to fall and the quantity supplied to fall.

   b. the quantity demanded to fall and the quantity supplied to grow.

   c. the quantity demanded to grow and the quantity supplied to fall.

   d. the quantity demanded to grow and the quantity supplied to grow.

26. __?__ is the difference between the total amount consumers would be willing and able to pay for a product and what they actually had to pay.

---

# Apply Economic Concepts

27. **Equilibrium** On a separate sheet of paper, complete the table below:

**Demand and Supply Schedule for Tacos**

| Price Per Taco | Quantity Demanded | Quantity Supplied | Surplus/ Shortage | Will the price rise or fall? |
|---|---|---|---|---|
| $2.00 | 25 | 175 | _____ | _____ |
| $1.75 | 50 | 150 | _____ | _____ |
| $1.50 | 75 | 125 | _____ | _____ |
| $1.25 | 100 | 100 | _____ | _____ |
| $1.00 | 125 | 75 | _____ | _____ |
| $0.75 | 150 | 50 | _____ | _____ |

---

**Demand and Supply Schedule for Tacos**

*Apply Economic Concepts*

28. The answer includes a graph. Students' graphs should look similar to the one shown here. An Excel spreadsheet containing this graph, along with supporting data, is available on the Instructor's Resource CD.

**28. Graphing Demand and Supply** Construct a graph of the demand and supply for tacos from the data provided in the table in exercise 27.

**29. Graphing Shifts in Demand and Supply** On your graph, draw and label the shifts in demand and supply curves for tacos that would result from each of the following events.

   a. The cost of corn meal increases 50 percent.

   b. The price of pizza goes down 25 percent.

   c. The number of people who like tacos increases by 30 percent.

   d. A new machine is invented that makes tacos automatically.

**30. Sharpen Your Life Skills: Analyze Supply and Demand Graphs** Between 2000 and June of 2003, the unemployment rate in the United States grew from 4.0 percent to 6.4 percent. This 2.4 percent increase added more than 3.6 million workers to the ranks of the unemployed in this country. People who are out of work may receive unemployment compensation payments from the government. These payments, however, replace only a portion of the income they had been earning. After unemployed people pay for food, clothing, and shelter for their families, they often have little left over to purchase other goods or services. Increased unemployment in the United States between 2000 and June of 2003 contributed to a decline in demand for many household appliances. Sketch a graph similar to the one to the right that shows what happened to the demand and supply for refrigerators in these years. Place arrows on your

graph to show shifts in demand, the surplus of products, and change in the equilibrium price. Label the changes that took place and explain what happened.

**Demand and Supply for Home Refrigerators, 2000**

**31. Make Predictions** Predict how the equilibrium price of coffee would be affected by the following changes:

   a. Poor growing conditions for coffee beans (demand remains constant)

   b. Major advertising campaign in the United States by a group of the world's coffee growers (supply remains constant)

   c. The publication of a new medical study warning against coffee consumption in excess of one cup per week (supply remains constant)

   d. Trade prohibition against a country in South America that produces a significant share of the U.S. coffee supply (demand remains constant)

*e*-con *@*pps    econxtra.swlearning.com

**32.** Access **EconNews Online** at econxtra. swlearning.com. Read the article entitled "PC Price Cuts."

   a. Draw a graph showing the price and quantity of personal computers. Then show the effects of the recession on the demand curve and the quantity at a given price.

   b. Draw a second graph of the demand for computers. Assume computer suppliers responded by offering price discounts on new computers. Illustrate what happened on your graph.

*Chapter Assessment*    **189**

## Apply Economic Concepts

**29.** The exact location of the supply and demand lines cannot be determined from the information provided, but students' graphs should indicate shifts in the appropriate direction.

   a. Supply shifts to the left.

   b. Demand shifts to the left.

   c. Demand shifts to the right.

   d. Supply shifts to the right.

**30.** Answers will vary. Possible answer: The increase in unemployment in these years decreased workers' income and caused their demand for refrigerators to shift to the left. This created a surplus of refrigerators that caused producers to lower the price of refrigerators from the old equilibrium price of $500 to a new equilibrium price of $400 per product. Even at this lower price, 10 million fewer refrigerators were sold.

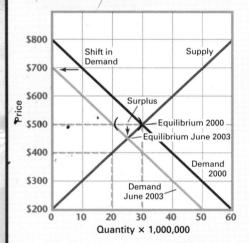

**31.** a. Supply curve shifts to the left. Results in an increase in the equilibrium price.

   b. Demand curve shifts to the right. Results in an increase in the equilibrium price.

   c. Demand curve shifts to the left. Results in a decrease in equilibrium price.

   d. Supply curve shifts to the left. Results in an increase in equilibrium price.

**32.** a. Demand curves should show the curve moving leftward to indicate a decrease in demand.

   b. Graphs should indicate that quantity demanded will increase as price decreases.

**LESSON 7.1** *Perfect Competition and Monopoly:* This lesson describes the features of perfect competition and the barriers to entry that can create a monopoly. Market structures of monopoly and perfect competition are compared in terms of efficiency.

**LESSON 7.2** *Monopolistic Competition and Oligopoly:* This lesson identifies the features of monopolistic competition and oligopoly.

**LESSON 7.3** *Antitrust, Economic Regulation, and Competition:* This lesson focuses on U.S. antitrust laws and distinguishes between the two views of government regulation. Why U.S. markets have grown more competitive in recent decades is explained.

### Consider

Ask students to consider the questions posed on this page as they study Chapter 7. After studying all three lessons, students should be able to answer the questions. The content related to each question can be found on the pages indicated below.

- What does a bushel of wheat have in common with a share of Microsoft stock? See page 192— Perfect Competition.
- What's so perfect about perfect competition? See page 192—Perfect Competition.
- Why don't most monopolies last? See page 196—True Monopolies Are Rare.
- Why are some panty hose sold in egg-shaped cartons? See page 202—Product Differentiation.
- Why was OPEC created? See page 204—When Oligopolists Collude.
- Is the U.S. economy more competitive now than it used to be? See page 211—Competitive Trends in the U.S. Economy.

### ▶ POINT YOUR BROWSER

Remind students that they can find additional resources for this chapter at **econxtra.swlearning.com**.

- Xtra! Study Tools
- Net Bookmarks
- Xtra! Quiz Prep
- econ@pps
- Ask the Xpert!
- Graphing Workshop

# 7 Market Structure

Perfect Competition and Monopoly **7.1**

Monopolistic Competition and Oligopoly **7.2**

Antitrust, Economic Regulation, and Competition **7.3**

### Consider

What does a bushel of wheat have in common with a share of Microsoft stock?

What's so perfect about perfect competition?

Why don't most monopolies last?

Why are some panty hose sold in egg-shaped cartons?

Why was OPEC created?

Is the U.S. economy more competitive now than it used to be?

© Getty Images/PhotoDisc

### ▶ POINT YOUR BROWSER

*econxtra.swlearning.com*

## Teaching Resources for Chapter 7

- Activities and Projects Masters
- Spanish Resources
- Econ Connection Interactive Tutorial CD
- **Exam***View*® CD
- Workbook Teacher's Edition
- Chapter and Unit Tests Teacher's Edition
- NCEE Standards and Correlation
- Personal Finance Guide

- Social Studies Skills Review
- Instructor's Resource CD
  – PowerPoint Presentation
  – Lesson Plans
  – Video Discussion Guide
  – Answers to Graphing Exercises
- **econxtra.swlearning.com**

## 7.1 Perfect Competition and Monopoly

### Objectives

> Distinguish the features of perfect competition.

> Describe the barriers to entry that can create a monopoly.

> Compare the market structures of monopoly and perfect competition in terms of efficiency.

### Overview

A firm's decision about how much to supply depends on the structure of the market. Market structure describes the important features of a market, including the number of buyers and sellers, the product's uniformity across suppliers, the ease of entry into the market, and the forms of competition among firms. All firms that supply output to a particular market—such as the market for cars, shoes, or wheat—are referred to as an *industry*. Therefore, the terms *industry* and *market* are used interchangeably. The first two market structures you will examine are perfect competition and monopoly.

### Key Terms

**market structure**

**perfect competition**

**commodity**

**monopoly**

**barriers to entry**

**market power**

Point out that firms in perfect competition market a single product that is identical from firm to firm. In this situation, consumers base their buying decisions solely on price. Monopolies, however, are single producers of a product that has no close substitute. Consumers are forced to buy this product from its single producer or go without. This gives the producer power to charge higher prices without losing many sales. Ask students to identify businesses they know of that are examples of firms in perfect competition or monopolies.

#### Objectives

Remind students to read the lesson objectives to help focus their attention before reading the lesson.

#### Key Terms

Direct students to create a database using the key terms for this lesson. The database fields should include terms, definitions, and page numbers. Point out that the process of keying the data is an effective way to study key terms.

### [ In the News ]

#### All that Glitters

At the start of 2003, economists who specialize in precious metals and jewels were predicting that the price of gold was going to rise dramatically. The predictions were based on three factors: a rocky U.S. economy, the unsettling war on terrorism, and a worldwide decrease in the production of gold. International events and the uncertainties they create often cause the price of an ounce of gold to rise. When people don't trust their national currencies, they often invest in precious metals and jewels as an alternative. Since the start of the millennium, worldwide demand for gold has been growing at a steady 2 percent to 3 percent a year. Yet, while demand increased, production remained the same or was cut back. Some observers suggest that the rising price might be just the spark that motivates mining companies to invest heavily and quickly in gold exploration. Others remind us that world economic conditions that could decrease the demand for gold also might arise, such as a great improvement in the U.S. economy or an easing of tensions in the Middle East and Asia. The decrease in demand would then drive down the price of gold.

#### Think About It

Read the first section of this lesson on perfect competition. Assuming that the market for gold is perfectly competitive, what effect would each of the following have on the supply and demand graph: (1) growing mistrust of national currencies, (2) an easing of international tensions, and (3) the opening of new gold mines?

◀ ▐ ▶

191

### [ In the News ]

Instruct students to read the passage and write down their answers. Point out that their answers might change after they finish studying Lesson 7.1.

#### Answers to Think About It

Answers will vary. Possible answers:

1. A growing mistrust of national currencies would increase the demand for gold (shift the demand curve to the right).

2. An easing of international tensions would decrease the demand for gold (shift the demand curve to the left).

3. The opening of new gold mines would increase the supply of gold (shift the supply curve to the right).

#### Visual Presentation

Use the PowerPoint presentation on the Instructor's Resource CD as an adjunct to your lecture. The presentation also can be used for review.

**NCEE** | ### National Content Standards in Economics

A complete list of the NCEE Standards appears on pages xxiv–xxv of this book. The following standards are addressed in Lesson 7.1.

Standard 4: Role of Incentives

Standard 7: Markets—Price and Quantity Determination

Standard 9: Role of Competition

Standard 10: Role of Economic Institutions

Standard 16: Role of Government

## Perfect Competition

Describe the following scenario. A homeowner looking for someone to do yard work placed a classified ad in a community newspaper. Ten potential workers answered the ad. All were equally qualified and motivated. Point out that each of the potential workers was acting like a business that is in perfect competition. They all offered the same service, so the only difference to the consumer was the price they charged. The homeowner likely hired the worker who was willing to work for the lowest pay.

### Think Critically Through Visuals

Direct students to focus on **Figure 7.1—Market Structure**. Suggest that students familiarize themselves with this table as they begin their study of different market structures.

### Think Critically Through Visuals

Direct students to focus on **Figure 7.2—Market Equilibrium and a Firm's Demand Curve in Perfect Competition**. Point out that the panel on the left illustrates market equilibrium and the panel on the right illustrates the demand curve facing the perfectly competitive firm.

**See It**

Direct students to the Graphing Workshop for Chapter 7 at **econxtra.swlearning.com**. Students may want to click on the **See It** enrichment exercise entitled **Short-Run Profit Maximization and Market Equilibrium**. They may also want to do the **Try It** enrichment exercise entitled **Identifying Short-Run Profit for a Perfectly Competitive Firm** at that time.

---

**market structure**

Important features of a market, including the number of buyers and sellers, product uniformity across sellers, ease of entering the market, and forms of competition

**perfect competition**

A market structure with many fully informed buyers and sellers of an identical product and ease of entry

**commodity**

A product that is identical across sellers, such as a bushel of wheat

---

# Perfect Competition

To begin your study of different **market structures**, familiarize yourself with the descriptions of market features shown in Figure 7.1. The first market structure to consider is **perfect competition**. Perfectly competitive markets are assumed to have the following features:

1. There are many buyers and sellers—so many that each buys or sells only a tiny fraction of the total market output. This assumption ensures that no individual buyer or seller can influence the price.

2. Firms produce a standardized product, or a **commodity**. A commodity is a product that is identical across producers, such as a bushel of wheat or a share of Microsoft stock. A buyer is not willing to pay more for one particular supplier's product. Buyers are concerned only with the price.

3. Buyers are fully informed about the price, quality, and availability of products, and sellers are fully informed about all resources and technology.

4. Firms can easily enter or leave the industry. There are no obstacles preventing new firms from entering profitable markets.

If these conditions exist in a market, individual buyers and sellers have no control over the price. Price is determined by market demand and supply. Once the market establishes the price, each firm is free to produce whatever quantity maximizes its profit or minimizes its loss. *A perfectly competitive firm is so small relative to the size of the market that the firm's choice about how much to produce has no effect on the market price.*

### Example Markets

Examples of perfect competition include markets for the shares of large corporations such as Microsoft or General Electric; foreign exchange, such as yen, euros, and pounds; and those for most agricultural products, such as livestock, corn, and wheat. In these markets, there are so many buyers and sellers that the actions of any one cannot influence the market price.

In the perfectly competitive market for wheat, for example, a single firm in this market is a wheat farm. In the world market for wheat, there are tens of thousands of farms, so any one supplies just a tiny fraction of market output. For example, the thousands of wheat farmers in Kansas together produce less than 3 percent of the world's supply of wheat. No single wheat farmer can influence the market price for a bushel of wheat.

### Market Price

In Figure 7.2, the market price of wheat of $5 per bushel is determined in panel (a) by the intersection of the market demand curve *D* and the market supply curve *S*. Once the market price is established, farmers can sell all they want at that market price.

---

| Market Structure | Figure 7.1 |
|---|---|

Market structure describes the important features of a market.

| Market Feature | Questions to Ask |
|---|---|
| 1. Number of buyers and sellers | Are there many, only a few, or just one? |
| 2. Product's uniformity across suppliers | Do firms in the market supply identical products, or are products differentiated across firms? |
| 3. Ease of entry into the market | Can new firms enter easily, or do natural or artificial barriers block them? |
| 4. Forms of competition among firms | Do firms compete based only on prices, or are advertising and product differences also important? |

**Market Equilibrium and a Firm's Demand Curve in Perfect Competition**　**Figure 7.2**

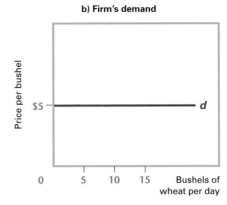

a) Market equilibrium

b) Firm's demand

In panel (a), the market price of $5 is determined by the intersection of the market demand and supply curves. The individual perfectly competitive firm can sell any amount at that price. The demand curve facing the perfectly competitive firm is horizontal at the market price, as shown by demand curve *d* in panel (b).

Each farm is so small relative to the market that each has no impact on the market price. Because all farmers produce an identical product—bushels of wheat—anyone who charges more than the market price will sell no wheat. For example, if a farmer charged $5.25 per bushel, wheat buyers would simply turn to other sellers.

Of course, any farmer is free to charge less than the market price. But why do that when all wheat can be sold at the market price? *The demand curve facing an individual farmer is, therefore, a horizontal line drawn at the market price.* In this example, the demand curve in panel (b) is drawn at the market price of $5 per bushel.

It has been said, "In perfect competition there is no competition." Two neighboring wheat farmers in perfect competition are not really rivals. They both can sell all they want at the market price. The amount one sells has no effect on the market price or on the amount the other can sell. Likewise, no two buyers compete for the product because they both can buy all they want at the market price. Each farm, or firm, tries to maximize profit. Firms that ignore this strategy don't survive.

 **CHECKPOINT**
What are the features of perfect competition?

# Monopoly

The monopoly market structure is the extreme opposite of the perfect competition structure. **Monopoly** is the sole supplier of a product with no close substitutes. *Monopoly* is from a Greek word meaning "one seller." A monopolist has more market power than does a business in any other market structure. **Market power** is the ability of a firm to raise its price without losing all sales to rivals. A perfect competitor has no market power.

*monopoly*

A sole supplier of a product with no close substitutes

*market power*

The ability of a firm to raise its price without losing all sales to rivals

 **TEACH** (continued)

**Perfect Competition**

Bring three apples to class. The apples need to be indistinguishable—similar shape, color, and size. Display the apples and tell students to imagine that they are hungry and want to buy one of the apples. Ask them if they care about where the apple was grown. Tell them that each apple came from a different farmer, and that there are at least 100 other similar apples they could buy from other farmers at a local market. Ask them how they would choose among the apples. (They would choose the apple with the lowest price if there were any difference in price.)

Explain that this situation demonstrates firms in perfect competition. Because consumers see no difference among the products, they care only about price when they choose which apple to buy. What would happen to an individual farmer who attempted to charge more for apples than other farmers? (No one would buy from this farmer because apples can be purchased for less from other farmers.)

**CHECKPOINT**

Invite a student to answer the checkpoint that appears on this page.

**Answer**

The features of perfect competition are: (1) There are many buyers and sellers. (2) Firms produce a standardized product or commodity. (3) Buyers are fully informed about the price, quality, and availability of products, and sellers are fully informed about all resources and technology. (4) Firms can easily enter or leave the industry.

---

*Outside Resources*

**Internet** The Internet provides many examples of competition. Ask students to complete a search for marketers of mountain bikes, laptop computers, digital cameras, or other products they might wish to purchase. How many web addresses do they find? Ask them to compare this way of shopping with the methods consumers used when the students' parents and grandparents were young adults.

## Monopoly

Point out that monopolies have a good deal of market power but not total market power. Return to the previous example using the apples. This time, display only one apple and announce there are no other apples or fruits available. In this situation, how much could the owner of the apple charge? Ask each student to write on a slip of paper the most he or she would be willing to pay for the apple, and use these to create a demand schedule for the apple on the board. Point out that above some price, no one will be willing to buy the apple, and the apple's owner will receive no revenue because the apple will not be sold. Other firms with monopoly power face the same limitation on their pricing power.

### SPAN THE GLOBE

Direct students to read the passage entitled "Flower Auction Holland" on this page. Use the questions as a starting point for class discussion or have students write a short essay to answer the questions.

## Answers to Think Critically

This is not an example of perfect competition because the buyers are not fully informed about the price and quantity of the commodity in a Dutch auction.

---

**barriers to entry**
Restrictions on the entry of new firms into an industry

## Barriers to Entry

A monopolized market has high **barriers to entry**, which are restrictions on the entry of new firms into an industry. Barriers to entry allow a monopolist to charge a price above the competitive price. There are three types of entry barriers: legal restrictions, economies of scale, and control of an essential resource.

# SPAN THE GLOBE

## Flower Auction Holland

Five days a week in a huge building 10 miles outside Amsterdam, some 2,500 buyers gather to participate in Flower Auction Holland. At this auction, more than 14 million flowers from 5,600 growers around the globe are auctioned off each day. The auction is held in the world's largest commercial building, and it is spread across the equivalent of 100 football fields. Flowers are grouped and auctioned off by type—long-stemmed roses, tulips, and so on. Hundreds of buyers are seated in theater settings with their fingers on buttons. Once the flowers are presented, a clock-like instrument starts ticking off descending prices until a buyer stops it by pushing a button. The winning bidder gets to choose how many and which items to take. The clock starts again until another buyer stops it, and so on, until all flowers are sold. Buyers also can bid from remote locations. Flower auctions occur swiftly—on average one transaction occurs every four seconds. This is an example of a *Dutch auction*, which starts at a high price and works down. Dutch auctions are common where multiple lots of similar, though not identical, items are sold, such as flowers in Amsterdam, tobacco in Canada, and fish in seaports around the world.

### Think Critically

Is Flower Auction Holland a perfect example of a perfectly competitive market? Why or why not?

---

## Legal Restrictions

One way to prevent new firms from entering a market is to make entry illegal. Patents, licenses, and other legal restrictions imposed by the government provide some producers with legal protection against competition.

Governments confer monopoly rights to sell hot dogs at civic auditoriums, collect garbage, offer bus and taxi service, and supply other services ranging from electricity to cable TV. The government itself may become a monopolist by outlawing competition. For example, many states are monopoly sellers of liquor and lottery tickets. The U.S. Postal Service (USPS) has the exclusive right to deliver first-class mail.

## Economies of Scale

A monopoly sometimes emerges naturally when a firm experiences substantial economies of scale, as reflected by the downward-sloping, long-run average cost curve shown in Figure 7.3. A single firm can sometimes satisfy market demand at a lower average cost per unit than could two or more smaller firms. Put another way, market demand is not great enough to allow more than one firm to achieve sufficient economies of scale.

Thus, a single firm will emerge from the competitive process as the sole supplier in the market. The transmission of electricity involves economies of scale. Once wires are run throughout a community, the marginal cost of linking additional households to the power grid is relatively small. Consequently, the average cost per household declines as more and more households are wired into the system.

A monopoly that emerges from the nature of costs is called a *natural monopoly.* A new entrant cannot sell enough output to experience the economies of scale enjoyed by an established natural monopolist. Therefore, entry into the market is naturally blocked.

In less-populated areas, natural monopolies include the only grocery store, movie theater, or restaurant for miles around. These are *geographic*

---

For many years, silk could be purchased only from China because Chinese law outlawed the exportation silk worms. Some people were executed when they were caught trying to smuggle silk worms. In the long run, however, some smugglers were successful, and silk production was established in other countries.
Invite students to research this topic and prepare a short paper that answers the following questions. Why did China outlaw the exportation silk worms in the first place? How was the Chinese economy changed when silk could be produced in other countries? What did this situation have to do with monopoly power and competition? Encourage students to provide additional information, including information about the current impact of silk production on the economies of China and other countries.

$

Cost per unit

Long-run average cost

Quantity per period

A monopoly sometimes emerges naturally when a firm experiences economies of scale as reflected by a downward-sloping, long-run average cost curve. An individual firm can satisfy market demand at a lower average cost per unit than could two or more firms operating at smaller rates of output.

*monopolies* for products sold in local markets.

**Control of Essential Resources**

Sometimes the source of monopoly power is a firm's control over some resource critical to production. Following are some examples of the control of essential resources barrier to entry.

• For decades Alcoa controlled the world's supply of bauxite, the key raw material in aluminum.

• China is a monopoly supplier of pandas to the world's zoos. The zoo in Washington, D.C., for example, rents a pair of pandas from China for $1 million a year. As a way of controlling the panda supply, China stipulates that any offspring from the Washington pair become China's property.

• Since the 1930s, the world's diamond trade has been controlled primarily by De Beers Consolidated Mines. De Beers mines diamonds and also buys most of the world's supply of rough diamonds.

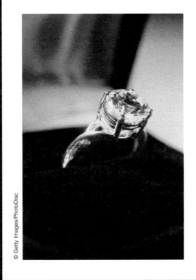

© Getty Images/PhotoDisc

**The Graphing Workshop**

De Beers's advertising slogan is "A diamond is forever." What results do you think the company hopes to achieve with this slogan?

Lesson 7.1 • *Perfect Competition and Monopoly*     **195**

**Monopoly**

Describe the following scenario: Clay is desperate to attend the Super Bowl. His favorite team is playing, and he is willing to pay almost any price to attend the sold-out game. Two days before the game, Clay meets Vivian. She has a ticket and is willing to sell it for $500.

Ask the following questions: Will Clay pay $500 for the ticket, and, if he will, why? If Clay decides not to buy the ticket, will Vivian be able to sell the ticket to someone else? What does this situation have to do with monopoly power? (Vivian is the only supplier that Clay knows about. There are no close substitutes. Even if Clay does not buy the ticket, Vivian can probably find someone who is willing to pay $500, or more, because of monopoly power.)

***Think Critically Through Visuals***

Direct students to focus on **Figure 7.3—Economies of Scale as a Barrier to Entry**. Point out that a single firm sometimes can satisfy market demand at a lower average cost per unit than can two or three smaller firms.

**The Graphing Workshop**  ( See It )

Direct students to the Graphing Workshop for Chapter 7 at **econxtra.swlearning.com**. As an enrichment exercise, students may click on the **See It: Regulating Natural Monopoly**, which covers concepts that go beyond what is taught in this lesson. For an additional enrichment activity, suggest they click on **See It: Monopoly Behavior in the Short-Run**, which explains this topic using the DeBeers example.

***Think Critically Through Visuals***

Direct students to focus their attention on the photograph on this page. Ask for a volunteer to answer the question posed in the caption.

**Answer**

Answers will vary. Possible answer: The company hopes to see an increase in the amount that consumers are willing to spend on a diamond because it will last forever.

**Group Activity**

For this activity you need play money and eight sets of cards lettered A through E. Randomly select five students to be suppliers, and divide the remaining students into four consumer groups. The goal for each consumer group is to purchase a complete set of cards—one card of each letter, A through E. Each supplier should try to earn as much income as possible. Give *all* the C cards to one of the suppliers. Mix the remaining cards together and then give eight cards to each of the remaining suppliers. Give each consumer group the same amount of play money, and instruct the groups to negotiate the purchase of cards from the various suppliers. Have suppliers keep track of the price they get for each card they sell. When all transactions are completed, have the suppliers share their sales figures with the class. Ask students to explain the results as they relate to competition and monopoly.

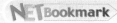

Direct students to **econxtra.swlearning.com**. Remind them to click on the link for Lesson 7.1 to find the appropriate link for the **NET Bookmark** on this page.

**Answers**

Competition plays no role. The Postal Service Governors and the Postal Rate Commission set rates. If the USPS determines that its revenue needs require raising rates, public hearings on the request are held before the Postal Rate Commission. The PRC makes a recommendation to the Governors, who make the final decision.

# CHECKPOINT

Invite a student to answer the checkpoint that appears on this page.

**Answer**

The barriers to entry into a market are: legal restrictions, economies of scale, and control of essential resources.

## TEACH

**Monopoly and Efficiency**

Remind students that monopolies have no effective competition for their products. In this situation, firms have little reason to be efficient because customers have only one alternative to paying the price the firm charges—doing without the product. For this reason, monopolies are not motivated to keep wage rates low, to avoid waste, to use resources effectively, or to invest in new technology. They are often able to pass higher costs that result from inefficiency on to customers through higher prices.

*Think Critically Through Visuals*

Direct students to focus on **Figure 7.4—Monopoly, Perfect Competition, and Consumer Surplus** on page 197. Use the figure to compare monopoly and perfect competition.

## Monopolists May Not Earn a Profit

Because a monopoly, by definition, supplies the entire market, the demand curve for a monopolist's output also is the market demand curve. That demand curve, therefore, slopes downward, reflecting the law of demand. Price and quantity demanded are inversely related.

Even a monopolist with iron-clad barriers to entry may go broke. Although a monopolist is the sole producer of a good with no close substitutes, the demand for that good may not be great enough to keep the firm in business. After all, many inventions are protected from direct competition by patents, yet most patented products never get produced and many that are produced fail to attract enough customers to survive.

## True Monopolies Are Rare

Long-lasting monopolies are rare because a profitable monopoly attracts competitors and substitutes. Even where barriers to entry are initially strong, technological change tends to create substitutes. For example, railroads at one time enjoyed a natural monopoly in shipping goods across country. The monopoly ended when the trucking industry was born.

The development of wireless transmission of long-distance telephone calls created competitors for the monopolist AT&T and may soon erase the monopoly held by some local cable TV

Access the rate page of the USPS web site through econxtra.swlearning.com. Describe the process by which the USPS sets its postage rates. What role, if any, do the forces of competition play in rate setting?

*econxtra.swlearning.com*

providers and some local phone services. Likewise, fax machines, e-mail, the Internet, and firms such as FedEx have all cut into the U.S. Postal Service's monopoly on first-class mail.

# CHECKPOINT

Name and describe the three barriers to entry into a market.

# Monopoly and Efficiency

Monopolists are not guaranteed a profit. Monopolies can lose money. Monopolies are relatively rare. So, then, what's the problem?

## Monopoly Versus Perfect Competition

One way to understand the problem is to compare monopoly to perfect competition. Competition forces firms to be *efficient*—that is, to produce the maximum possible output from available resources—and to supply the product at the lowest possible price. Consumers get a substantial consumer surplus from this low price. However, a successful monopolist typically will charge a higher price than would competitive firms. Thus, fewer consumers will be able to afford to buy the product.

To compare monopoly and perfect competition, suppose $D$ in Figure 7.4 is the *market demand* for a product sold in perfect competition. The market price is $P_c$ and the market quantity is $Q_c$. Consumer surplus for the perfectly competitive price is the triangular area below the demand curve and above the price, measured by $acp_c$. (Recall that *consumer surplus* is the difference between the total amount consumers are willing to pay for a given quantity of a good and what they actually pay.)

What if one firm buys up all the individual firms in the perfectly competitive market, creating a giant

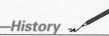

*Curriculum Connection—History*

Assign students to research the effect the transcontinental railroad had on the United States upon its introduction. Have them write a short report that answers this question: How did the building of a transcontinental railroad affect both the economy and people's lives? (Answers will vary. Possible answer: The railroads affected the U.S. economy as they brought together the economies of the East and West. They affected people's lives by helping Western settlers with transporting supplies such as lumber, farming tools, and food. The railroads also changed the way people told time, as the railroad companies set up a system of standard time in order to develop regular schedules.)

**Figure 7.4**

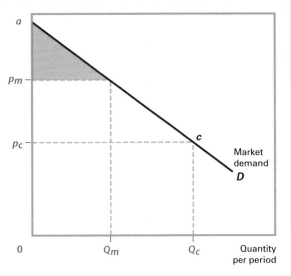

A perfectly competitive industry would produce output $Q_c$ and sell at a price $p_c$. A monopoly that could produce at that same minimum average cost would produce output $Q_m$ and sell at price $p_m$. Thus, output is lower and price is higher under monopoly than under perfect competition. With perfect competition, the consumer surplus is the entire triangle $acp_c$, reflected by the shaded area. With monopoly, consumer surplus shrinks to the blue-shaded triangle.

monopoly? In this case, the market demand curve becomes the monopolist's demand curve. What if average cost per unit is the same with monopoly as with perfect competition? The monopolist will restrict quantity to $Q_m$ and will increase the price to $p_m$. With monopoly, consumer surplus shrinks to the blue triangle, which is much smaller than consumer surplus with perfect competition.

### Other Problems with Monopoly

Monopolies may reduce social welfare for other reasons besides higher prices to consumers. These include a possible waste of resources and inefficiencies that may develop in their operation.

### Resources Wasted Securing Monopoly Privilege

Because of their size and economic importance, monopolies may have too much influence on the political system, which they use to protect and strengthen their monopoly power. Lawyers' fees,

lobbying expenses, and other costs associated with gaining a special privilege from government are largely a social waste because they use up scarce resources but add not one unit to output.

### Monopolies May Grow Inefficient

The monopolist, insulated from the rigors of market competition, could grow fat and lazy, and thus become inefficient. Corporate executives might waste resources by creating a more comfortable life for themselves. Lavish salaries and corporate perks boost the average cost of production above the competitive level. Monopolists also have been criticized for being slow to adopt the latest production techniques, reluctant to develop new products, and generally lacking in innovation.

### Monopoly Might Not Be So Bad

For several reasons, some monopolies may not be as socially wasteful as was just described.

## Ask the Xpert!

*econxtra.swlearning.com*

*Why are cable rates so high?*

## Monopoly and Efficiency

Describe this scenario: The world's only golf cart producer has trouble keeping up with demand from golf courses that are willing to pay $5,000 per cart. The firm's workers are already well paid, but they are demanding a 10 percent raise, more vacation time, and a longer lunch period in their labor negotiations. If the firm refuses to grant these demands, there may be a strike that could interrupt production for weeks or even months.
Ask students how they would respond to the workers' demands. How would they respond if there were 50 other golf cart manufacturers? (Students might agree to the workers' demands to avoid a strike and then pass the increased costs on to customers through higher prices. A monopoly can do this. But, if the firm were in competition, it would be more likely to refuse because it would be difficult to pass on the added costs to customers.)

## Ask the Xpert!

Direct students to **econxtra.swlearning.com** to hear an expert answer the question "Why are cable rates so high?"

### Ethics in Action

Have students work in pairs to discuss the ethical issue featured on page 198, and develop an answer to the question presented there.

### Answers to Think Critically

Answers will vary. Possible answer: Yes, it is ethical for the state to try to force drug companies to lower their prices, because it is forcing them into competition. Forcing the drug companies into competition also forces them to be more efficient.

## Extend the Content

Microsoft has been accused of being a monopoly and was forced to alter its business practices to avoid being broken up by the government. Although many people believe Microsoft used its market power to abuse customers, this business is one of the most important exporters in the U.S. economy. Over the past 20 years, Microsoft has sold billions of dollars worth of software to other nations. This increased employment in the United States and helped pay for imports we receive from other nations. Ask students to discuss whether they believe Microsoft's market power has done more good or bad for the U.S. economy.

### ✓ CHECKPOINT

Invite a student to answer the checkpoint that appears on page 198.

### Answer

Monopolies, insulated from the rigors of market competition, could grow inefficient—unlike perfect competition, which is always efficient.

Assign Lesson 7.1 from the Contemporary Economics Workbook.

Encourage students to apply their knowledge of concepts presented in this lesson as they explore economic news stories, policy debates, and data available at **econxtra.swlearning.com**. A sampling of the titles for this lesson appears below.

### EconDebate

- Can open-source software survive?
- Does public investment in municipal sports stadiums pay off?

### EconNews

Among the news articles appropriate for this chapter are the following:

- Cranberry Giant Made to Look Like a Turkey
- FCC Is Making Waves in The Radio Business

Assign all or part of Lesson 7.1 Assessment on page 199 as homework or an in-class activity.

## Xtra! Study Tools

Direct students to the online study tools for Lesson 7.1 at **econxtra.swlearning.com**.

**Revisit** the In the News feature on the first page of the lesson. Ask students to review their preliminary answers and discuss the questions, now that they have completed this lesson.

**Review** the objectives for Lesson 7.1. Students should be able to:

- Distinguish the features of perfect competition.
- Describe the barriers to entry that can create a monopoly.
- Compare the market structures of monopoly and perfect competition in terms of efficiency.

### Economies of Scale

If economies of scale are substantial, a monopolist might be able to produce output at a lower average cost than could competitive firms. Therefore, the price, or at least the cost of production, could be lower with monopoly than with perfect competition.

### Government Regulation

Government intervention can increase social welfare by forcing the monopolist to lower price and increase output. The government can either operate the monopoly itself, as it does with most urban transit systems, or it can regulate a privately owned monopoly, as it does with local phone services and electricity transmission. You will read more about government regulation later in the chapter.

### Keeping Prices Low to Avoid Regulation

A monopolist might keep prices below the profit-maximizing level to avoid government regulation. For example, the prices and profits of drug companies, which individually are monopoly producers of patented medicines, come under scrutiny from time to time by public officials who threaten to regulate drug prices. Drug firms might try to avoid such treatment by keeping prices below the level that would maximize profit.

### Keeping Prices Low to Avoid Competition

Finally, a monopolist might keep the price below the profit-maximizing level to avoid attracting competitors. For example, at one time Alcoa was the only U.S. producer of aluminum. Industry observers claimed that the company kept prices and profits below their maximum to discourage competition.

**CHECKPOINT**
How does monopoly compare to perfect competition in terms of efficiency?

## Ethics in Action

### Price-Control Program Challenged

The state of Maine recently enacted legislation designed to make prescription medicine less expensive for the neediest of its citizens. This legislation currently is being challenged in the U.S. Supreme Court. In recent years, the cost of prescription drugs has jumped by more than 15 percent annually. In addition to Maine, a dozen other states have indicated they would like to enact similar laws. Maine's approach is to use the combined buying power of citizens in an entire state to bargain for savings of 25 percent or more on prescription drugs. Sponsors of Maine's legislation have stated that their program does for its citizens what a number of other nations have done for theirs: put pressure on the drug companies to bargain. The pharmaceutical companies take the point of view that Maine is illegally strong-arming them into reducing prices. These firms argue that they have spent hundreds of millions of dollars developing and testing each drug, and they should be allowed to recover those costs. They claim that if they are forced to lower prices in one state, the rest of the country would get stuck with the bill to make up the difference.

### Think Critically

The pharmaceutical industry has market power—that is, the ability to raise price without losing all sales. Is it ethical for a state to try to force these firms to lower their prices?

Describe the following scenario: Many teenaged baby-sitters live in a large subdivision or apartment complex. All these baby sitters charge $5 per hour for watching a toddler. Two new teenagers move into the area and offer to baby-sit for $10 per hour. Ask students how successful the new arrivals will be. Why is it unlikely that they will succeed in earning this higher wage? What does this show about competition?

Extend the example by describing another situation where there is only one teenager living in an area with many toddlers. How might this teenager take advantage of monopoly power?

## Key Concepts

1. What characteristics of farms demonstrate that these firms operate in perfectly competitive markets?

2. Three years ago, the town of Mt. Utopia had three fast-food restaurants. The town's population has grown rapidly in the past two years. As the town grew, the sales and profits of these restaurants increased. There now are seven fast-food restaurants in Mt. Utopia. None of them earns a large profit. What feature of competitive markets does this demonstrate? Explain your answer.

3. Identify a firm that operates in your community that you think has a significant amount of monopoly power. Explain why you chose this firm.

4. At one time, the American Telephone and Telegraph Corp. (AT&T) had a great deal of monopoly power and earned large profits. In recent years AT&T has lost money, and it could be purchased by another firm. What happened to AT&T's monopoly power?

## Graphing Exercise

5. Use data in the table to construct two graphs: the market demand and supply curve, and the individual demand curve for the Apex Coal Mine. Apex is able to produce a maximum of 1,000 tons of coal per month. What is the market equilibrium price? Explain how you were able to construct the individual demand curve for Apex Coal.

**Market Coal Demand and Supply Schedule Per Month**

| Price per Ton | Market Demand (tons) | Market Supply (tons) |
|---|---|---|
| $200 | 4,000,000 | 8,000,000 |
| $175 | 5,000,000 | 7,000,000 |
| $150 | 6,000,000 | 6,000,000 |
| $125 | 7,000,000 | 5,000,000 |
| $100 | 8,000,000 | 4,000,000 |

## Think Critically

6. **Advertising** Although individual farmers do not purchase advertising for their products, it is common for groups of farmers to join together to do this. In New York, for example, the Upstate Milk Cooperative collects funds from thousands of dairy farmers and uses the money to buy advertisements for milk products. Explain why this makes sense. What are the farmers trying to accomplish?

7. **History** Between 1880 and 1900, the Standard Oil Company came to control almost 90 percent of the production of oil products in the United States. It did this by buying up or driving other firms out of business. With this monopoly power, the firm's owners were able to earn as much as a 20 percent profit on the value of the firm's assets, such as its refineries, pipelines, etc. Much of the firm's profit was used to develop new technologies that, according to the owners, contributed to lower prices. In your opinion, is it possible for monopolies to be good for consumers? Explain your answer.

**Market Coal Demand and Supply Schedule per Month**

**Individual Demand for Apex Mines**

## Visualizing the Answer— Graphing Exercise

5. The answer includes a graph. Students' graphs should look similar to the one shown here. An Excel spreadsheet containing this graph, along with supporting data, is available on the Instructor's Resource CD.

---

## Key Concepts

1. Answers will vary. Possible answer: Many farms and consumers of farm products exist in the market, many farms produce essentially the same products, both buyers and sellers are aware of the market price, and it is relatively easy for firms to enter or leave markets for farm products.

2. This example demonstrates the many-buyers-and-many-sellers aspect of competitive markets. When there are many buyers and sellers, each one owns only a tiny part of the market, as was the case in this example.

3. Answers will vary. Students should describe features of the firm they choose that demonstrate that the firm possesses a degree of monopoly power in its market.

4. Answers will vary. Possible answer: AT&T was harmed by advances in technology that allowed other firms to offer local, long distance, and cellular telephone services at lower prices. By not keeping up with the competition, AT&T lost many of its customers.

## Graphing Exercise

5. Answers will vary. The equilibrium price is $150. Students may point out that they are able to draw the individual firm's demand curve because it is a horizontal line at the market price of $150. It is able to sell all of its coal at that price and none of it at any higher price.

   Samples of acceptable graphs appear at the bottom of this page.

## Think Critically

6. Answers will vary. Possible answer: The farmers are trying to increase demand for their products and thus raise prices. If the advertisements convince many consumers to buy more milk, a higher market price will result, which will benefit each individual dairy farmer.

7. Answers will vary. Possible answer: Firms that drive other firms out of business inevitably do harm to the other firms' owners. Larger profits do not have to be a bad thing if they are used to reduce costs of production and, eventually, prices.

# Sharpen Your Life Skills

## Read Pie Graphs

Study the pie graphs to the right that show the approximate percentage of motor vehicle sales in this country made by each of the three largest U.S. producers, foreign-owned producers, and other U.S.-owned producers in 1980 and 2002. Summarize the changes in the U.S. automobile market that these graphs show.

## Apply Your Skill

1. If U.S. producers wanted to regain a larger share of the U.S. motor vehicle market, how might they achieve their goal?

2. How might the U.S. government help U.S. producers regain their share of the U.S. motor vehicle market? Do you think the U.S. government should do these things? Explain your answer.

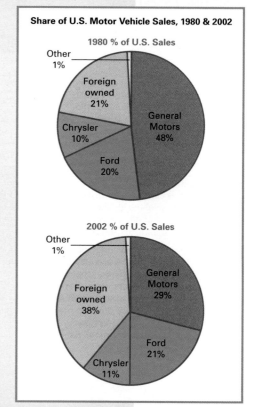

**Share of U.S. Motor Vehicle Sales, 1980 & 2002**

1980 % of U.S. Sales

Other 1%
Foreign owned 21%
Chrysler 10%
Ford 20%
General Motors 48%

2002 % of U.S. Sales

Other 1%
Foreign owned 38%
General Motors 29%
Ford 21%
Chrysler 11%

## Objectives

> Identify the features of monopolistic competition.

> Identify the features of oligopoly, and analyze firm behavior when these firms cooperate and when they compete.

## Overview

You are now aware of the two extreme market structures of perfect competition and monopoly. Now you will learn about monopolistic competition and oligopoly, the two structures that exist in between. These are the market structures in which most firms operate. Firms in each of these market structures face downward-sloping demand curves for their products, so each has some control over the price. Monopolistic competition is like a golf tournament in which each player strives for a personal best. Firms in oligopoly are more like players in a tennis match, where each player's actions depend on how and where the opponent hits the ball.

## Key Terms

**monopolistic competition**

**oligopoly**

**cartel**

Point out that many businesses operate in markets that are neither perfect competition nor monopolies. These firms have some control over their prices, but not total control. Economists divide these firms into two classifications: those in monopolistic competition and those in oligopoly. Although both of these groups of businesses have some monopoly power, they behave very differently. Their impacts on the economy and consumers are also different.

### Objectives

Remind students to read the lesson objectives to help focus their attention before reading the lesson.

### Key Terms

Direct students to look up key terms in a business or economics dictionary. Some students will find it helpful to read another definition. In addition to a definition, many entries will include a brief explanation and an example.

## [ In the News ]

### The Unfriendly Skies

At one time, airline routes were straight lines from one city to another. Now they radiate like the spokes of a wagon wheel from a "hub" city. From 29 hub airports across the country, the airlines send out planes along the spokes to about 400 commercial airports and then quickly bring them back to the hubs. Major airlines dominate hub airports. For example, United Airlines accounts for half the passengers at the Dallas-Fort Worth airport. A new airline trying to enter the industry must secure a hub airport as well as landing slots at crowded airports around the country. This is not an easy task because all the viable hubs are taken, and landing slots are scarce. Another trend in the airline industry is the offering of frequent-flyer mileage programs. The biggest airlines fly more national and international routes, and so they offer greater opportunities for fliers to both accumulate frequent-flyer miles and to use the mileage for free flights. Thus, the biggest airlines have the most attractive programs.

### Think About It

What are the barriers to entry in the airline industry discussed in this feature?

◄ | ►

**201**

## [ In the News ]

Instruct students to read the passage and write down their answers. Point out that their answers might change after they finish studying Lesson 7.2.

### Answers to Think About It

Answers will vary. Possible answer: One barrier to entry in the airline industry involves economies of scale. Specifically, it would be difficult for a new airline to compete with an established airline's frequent-flyer program. Another barrier involves scarcity of landing spots and hubs around the country's airports.

### Visual Presentation

Use the PowerPoint presentation on the Instructor's Resource CD as an adjunct to your lecture. The presentation also can be used for review.

**NCEE**

### National Content Standards in Economics

A complete list of the NCEE Standards appears on pages xxiv–xxv of this book. The following standards are addressed in Lesson 7.2.

Standard 7: Markets—Price and Quantity Determination

Standard 9: Role of Competition

Standard 16: Role of Government

## Monopolistic Competition

Show students photographs of several brands of jeans. At least one should be a designer brand and another should be a generic brand. Tell students the price for each pair. Ask them to describe differences between the brands. How important are these differences? What do these manufactures have a monopoly on? (They have a monopoly on their public image and trademark.)

### Think Critically Through Visuals

Direct students to focus their attention on the photograph on this page. Ask for a volunteer to answer the question posed in the caption.

### Answer

Answers will vary. Possible answer: Yes, I would be willing to pay more for food because more choices mean a greater chance of customer satisfaction.

 Assign the activity on page 203. Suggest that students look for stores that seem to have an abundance of stock on hand. For example, in the winter, a gas station might have a display of hundreds of gallons of windshield wiper fluid.

The Graphing Workshop ——— (See It)

Direct students to the Graphing Workshop for Chapter 7 at **econxtra.swlearning.com**. As an enrichment exercise, students may complete **See It: The Monopolistically Competitive Firm in the Short Run**.

### CHECKPOINT

Invite a student to answer the checkpoint that appears on page 203.

### Answer

The important features of monopolistic competition are product differentiation, costs of product differentiation, and excess capacity.

---

**monopolistic competition**

A market structure with low entry barriers and many firms selling products differentiated enough that each firm's demand curve slopes downward

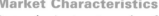 The Graphing Workshop

## Monopolistic Competition

In monopolistic competition, many firms offer products that differ slightly. As the expression **monopolistic competition** suggests, this structure contains elements of both monopoly and competition. The "monopolistic" element is that each firm has some control over its price. Because the products of different suppliers differ slightly, each firm's demand curve slopes downward. The "competition" element of monopolistic competition is that barriers to entry are so low that any short-run profit will attract new competitors, erasing profit in the long run.

### Market Characteristics

Because barriers to entry are low, firms in monopolistic competition can, in the long run, enter or leave the market with ease. Consequently, there are enough

Monopolistic competition may result in higher costs for firms, but it also provides more choices for consumers, such as a choice among many restaurants. Would you be willing to pay more for food if it means you would have more restaurants to choose from?

© Getty Images/PhotoDisc

---

sellers that they behave competitively. There also are enough sellers that each tends to get lost in the crowd. A particular firm, in deciding on a price, does not worry about how other firms in the market will react. For example, in a large city, an individual restaurant, gas station, drugstore, dry cleaner, or convenience store tends to act *independently* from its competitors.

### Product Differentiation

In perfect competition, the product is identical across suppliers, such as a bushel of wheat. In monopolistic competition, the product differs slightly among sellers, as with the difference between one rock radio station and another. Sellers differentiate their products in four basic ways.

#### Physical Differences

The most obvious way products differ is in their physical appearance and their qualities. The differences among products are seemingly endless. Shampoos, for example, differ in color, scent, thickness, lathering ability, and bottle design. Packaging also is designed to make a product stand out in a crowded field, such as panty hose in a plastic eggshell and yogurt in a tube.

#### Location

The number and variety of locations where a product is available also are means of differentiation. Some products seem to be available everywhere, including the Internet. Finding other products requires some search and travel.

#### Services

Products also differ in their accompanying services. For example, some takeout restaurants deliver. Others don't. Some retailers offer product demonstrations by a well-trained staff. Others are mostly self-service.

#### Product Image

A final way products differ is in the image the producer tries to foster in the consumer's mind. For example, some products use celebrity endorsements to boost sales.

---

### Outside Resources

**Consumer Products** A visit to any drugstore, grocery store, or big-box merchandiser can demonstrate a wide selection of products that are sold in monopolistic competition. Hair care and beauty products may be the best examples. Ask students to examine product packaging to discover how manufacturers work to distinguish their products from each other. How much factual information is provided?

This activity can be completed in the classroom by bringing an assortment of hair care products to class or by asking each student to bring a product to class.

## Costs of Product Differentiation

Firms in monopolistic competition spend more on advertising and other promotional expenses to differentiate their products. This increases average cost. Some economists argue that monopolistic competition results in too many firms and in product differentiation that is artificial. Others argue that consumers are willing to pay a higher price for a wider choice.

## Excess Capacity

Firms in monopolistic competition are said to operate with excess capacity. *Excess capacity* means that a firm could lower its average cost by selling more. Such excess capacity exists, for example, with gas stations, drugstores, banks, convenience stores, restaurants, motels, bookstores, and flower shops.

As a specific example, industry analysts argue that the nation's 22,000 funeral homes could efficiently handle 4 million funerals a year, but only about 2.4 million people die. So the industry operates at 60 percent capacity. This results in a higher average cost per funeral because resources remain idle much of the time.

**CHECKPOINT**
What are the important features of monopolistic competition?

In small groups, brainstorm a list of markets in your area in which firms seem to be operating with excess capacity. Then for each market listed, cite evidence of the excess capacity.

# Oligopoly

Oligopoly is a Greek word meaning "few sellers." When you think of "big business," you are thinking of **oligopoly**, a market dominated by just a few firms. Perhaps three or four firms account for three-quarters of market output. Because an oligopoly has only a few firms, each must consider the effect of its own actions on competitors' behavior. Oligopolistic industries include the markets for steel, oil, automobiles, breakfast cereals, and tobacco.

In some oligopolies, such as steel or oil, the product is identical, or undifferentiated, across producers. Thus, an *undifferentiated oligopoly* sells a commodity, such as an ingot of steel or a barrel of oil. In other oligopolies, such as automobiles or breakfast cereals, the product is differentiated across producers. A *differentiated oligopoly* sells products that differ across producers, such as Ford versus Toyota or General Food's Wheaties versus Kellogg's Corn Flakes.

Firms in an oligopoly are interdependent. Therefore, each firm knows that any changes in its price, output, or advertising may prompt a reaction from its rivals. Each firm may react if another firm alters any of these features.

## Barriers to Entry

Why have some industries evolved into an oligopolistic market structure, dominated by only a few firms, whereas other industries have not? Although the reasons are not always clear, *an oligopoly often can be traced to some barrier to entry, such as economies of scale or brand names built up by years of advertising.* Most of the barriers that applied to monopoly also apply to oligopoly.

### Economies of Scale

Perhaps the most significant barrier to entry is economies of scale. The *minimum efficient scale* is the lowest rate of output at which the firm takes full advantage of economies of scale. If a firm's minimum efficient scale is relatively large compared to industry output, then only a few firms are needed to produce the total amount

*oligopoly*
A market structure with a small number of firms whose behavior is interdependent

### Oligopoly

Remind students that some types of production are so expensive that only large businesses can do them efficiently. If only a few firms manufacture a product and they are interdependent, the market is an oligopoly. Ask students to imagine that they want to buy a repair manual for small gasoline engines. They find that only three firms publish this type of book. Each firm charges $20 for its products, which all seem to be about the same. They are roughly 120 pages long, have lots of pictures and diagrams, and contain step-by-step directions for rebuilding engines. Ask students why these publishers may be an oligopoly. (They produce similar products. What one does would have an immediate impact on the others because there are so few of them. If one raised or lowered the price, the others would be influenced by the substitution effect. They are interdependent.)

### THE WALL STREET JOURNAL

**Reading It Right**

Invite a student to explain the relevance of the statement from *The Wall Street Journal* that appears on page 204.

**Answer**

Answers will vary. Possible answer: This article indicates that without spare production, the members of OPEC have not been tempted to cheat the cartel by selling above quota. Selling above quota would increase the supply that was put into the market place and drive down prices, which would affect all members of the cartel.

## Answers

Answers will vary. Possible answers:

- Perfect Competition—cattle, coal, timber, grain, and milk
- Monopolistic Competition—clothing, bottled drinking water, lightbulbs, hand lotion, and pasta sauce
- Oligopoly—overnight delivery service, carbonated soft drinks, gasoline, film, and oil.
- Monopoly—cable TV, trash collection; newly introduced products (such as a new hybrid flower); a new type of technology (for example, the first developers to come out with the DVD had a monopoly on that market at first).

## Think Critically Through Visuals

Direct students to focus on **Figure 7.5—Comparison of Market Structures** on page 205. Point out that this table compares the features of the four market structures presented in this lesson.

## Ask the Xpert!

Direct students to **econxtra.swlearning.com** to hear an expert answer the question "What are the major differences among the four market structures?"

## ✓ CHECKPOINT

Invite a student to answer the checkpoint that appears on page 205.

## Answer

An oligopoly is a market determined by three or four firms that account for three-quarters of the market output. These firms are interdependent. Cooperating oligopolists agree on a fixed price; competing oligopolists compete to have the lowest price.

---

demanded in the market. For example, an automobile factory of minimum-efficient scale could make enough vehicles to supply nearly 10 percent of the U.S. market. To compete with existing producers, a new entrant must sell enough automobiles to reach a competitive scale of operation.

**cartel**
A group of firms that agree to act as a single monopolist to increase the market price and maximize the group's profits

### The High Cost of Entry

The total investment needed to reach the minimum-efficient size often is huge. A new auto factory or new computer chip plant can cost more than $1 billion. The average cost of developing and testing a new drug exceeds $300 million. Advertising a new product enough to compete with established brands also could require enormous outlays. A failed attempt at securing a place in the market could cripple a new firm. That's why most new products usually come from existing firms, which can better withstand the possible loss. For example, McDonald's spent $100 million in its unsuccessful attempt to introduce the Arch Deluxe. Unilever lost $160 million when its new detergent, Power, failed to catch on.

### Product Differentiation Costs

Oligopolists often spend millions and sometimes billions trying to differentiate their products. Some of these expenditures provide valuable information to consumers and offer them a wider array of products. However, some forms of product differentiation appear to be of little value. Slogans such as "Generation Next" or "Always Cola-Cola" convey little information, yet Pepsi and Coke spend huge sums on such messages. In 2000, Coke spent nearly $2 billion on advertising. Product differentiation expenditures create barriers to entry.

## THE WALL STREET JOURNAL

**Reading It Right** What's the relevance of the following statement from *The Wall Street Journal:* "Few OPEC members other than Saudi Arabia have had significant spare production. That means quota-busting, the usual foil to OPEC unity, has been minimal."

---

## When Oligopolists Collude

To decrease competition and increase profit, oligopolistic firms, particularly those that offer identical products, may try to *collude,* or agree on a price. *Collusion* is an agreement among firms in the industry to divide the market and fix the price. A **cartel** is a group of firms that agree to act as a single monopolist to increase the market price and maximize the group's profits.

Compared with competing firms, colluding firms usually produce less, charge higher prices, earn more profit, and try to block the entry of new firms. Consumers lose consumer surplus because of the higher prices, and potential entrants suffer from being denied the chance to compete.

Collusion and cartels are illegal in the United States. However, monopoly profit can be so tempting that some U.S. firms break the law. Some other countries are more tolerant of cartels. Some even promote them, as with the 11 nations of OPEC, the world oil cartel. If OPEC members were ever to meet in the United States, those officials could be arrested for price fixing. Even though they are outlawed in some countries, cartels can operate worldwide because there are no international laws banning them.

The biggest obstacle to maintaining a profitable cartel is the powerful temptation to cheat on the agreement. By offering a price slightly below the established price, individual firms in the cartel usually can increase their own sales and profit. A cartel collapses when cheating becomes widespread.

A second obstacle to cartel success is the entry of rival firms. The profit of the cartel attracts entry, entry increases market supply, and increased supply forces down the market price. A cartel's continued success therefore depends on the ability to block the entry of new firms or to get new firms to join the cartel.

Finally, cartels, like monopolists, must be concerned that technological change can erode their market power. For example, hydrogen-powered

---

Concentration ratios are often used to measure the degree of monopoly power held by firms in oligopoly. Ask students to search the Internet for information about four- or eight-firm concentration ratios. Have them report their findings to the class.

fuel cells may replace gasoline in automobiles.

OPEC's initial success attracted so many other oil suppliers that OPEC now accounts for less than half the world's oil output. As a result, OPEC has lost much of its market power. Efforts to form cartels in the world markets for bauxite, copper, coffee, and some other products have failed so far.

## When Oligopolists Compete

Because oligopolists are interdependent, analyzing their behavior is complicated. At one extreme, the firms in the industry may try to coordinate their behavior so they act collectively as a single monopolist, forming a cartel, as was just discussed. At the other extreme, oligopolists may compete so fiercely that price wars erupt, such as those that flare up in markets for cigarettes, computers, airline fares, and long-distance phone service.

You have now worked through the four market structures, including perfect competition, monopolistic competition, monopoly, and oligopoly. Features of the four are compared in Figure 7.5.

✔ **CHECKPOINT**
What are the important features of oligopoly, and how do oligopolists that cooperate compare to those that compete?

## TEAM WORK

In small groups, brainstorm five additional examples to those given in Figure 7.5 of industries that compete in each of the four market structures (perfect competition, monopolistic competition, oligopoly, and monopoly).

**Ask the Xpert!**
econxtra.swlearning.com

*What are the major differences among the four market structures?*

### Comparison of Market Structures | Figure 7.5

|  | Perfect Competition | Monopolistic Competition | Oligopoly | Monopoly |
|---|---|---|---|---|
| **Number of firms** | most | many | few | one |
| **Control over price** | none | limited | some | complete |
| **Product differences** | none | some | none or some | none |
| **Barriers to entry** | none | low | substantial | insurmountable |
| **Examples** | wheat, shares of stock | convenience stores, books | automobiles, cigarettes | local electricity and phone service |

## APPLY
Assign Lesson 7.2 from the Contemporary Economics Workbook.

## e-con @pps
Encourage students to apply their knowledge of concepts presented in this lesson as they explore economic news stories, policy debates, and data available at **econxtra.swlearning.com**. A sampling of the titles for this lesson appears below.

### EconDebate
● Should the antitrust exemption for baseball be eliminated?

### EconNews
● Anonymous Consumers Increasingly Faceless, Too
● Irregular Remedy for Iridium
● Just-in-Time State of the Art Fashion

## ASSESS
Assign all or part of Lesson 7.2 Assessment on page 206 as homework or an in-class activity.

## Xtra! Study Tools
Direct students to the online study tools for Lesson 7.2 at **econxtra.swlearning.com**.

## CLOSE
**Revisit** the In the News feature on the first page of the lesson. Ask students to review their preliminary answers and discuss the questions, now that they have completed this lesson.

**Review** the objectives for Lesson 7.2. Students should be able to:
● Identify the features of monopolistic competition.
● Identify the features of oligopoly, and analyze firm behavior when these firms cooperate and when they compete.

## RETEACH

Ask students to identify a product that is used in their households on a regular basis. Assign them to write an essay that describes how this product's manufacturer works to differentiate its product from other similar products. Do students believe the firm has been successful? Why? What could this firm's competitors do that would cause their families to switch brands? Why is it often easier for consumers to always purchase one particular brand of a product? Do they believe there is such a thing as brand loyalty? What does this have to do with monopolistic competition?

## Key Concepts

1. Answers will vary. Possible answer: They are differentiated by advertising, scent, packaging, or appearance. Brands that are successfully differentiated have a "monopoly" on their reputation or image and can be priced higher than other detergents without losing sales.

2. Answers will vary. Possible answer: The cost of setting up a large oil refinery is so great that most oil producers could not afford to compete with these firms.

3. Answers will vary. Possible answer: Cheating by individual producers is likely to prevent almost any cartel from succeeding.

## Graphing Exercise

4. Answers will vary. Possible answer: The firm is trying to shift customers' demand to the right by changing their tastes for Sleepwell Mattresses. If the firm is successful, the marginal revenue curve will also move right. This would cause the intersection between the firm's new demand curve and its long-run average cost curve to occur at a lower average cost ($100 as it has been drawn here). With lower costs and greater sales (275 per day instead of 100), the firm should be able to sell more mattresses at a higher price to earn a greater profit.

A sample of an acceptable graph appears at the bottom of this page.

## Think Critically

5. Answers will vary. Possible answer: To differentiate their products in the market, firms try to convince consumers that their products are better than competing products. In 2003, an estimated 43 million households, or nearly 100 million viewers, tuned in to the Super Bowl.

---

Xtra!
Study Tools
econxtra.swlearning.com

## Key Concepts

1. There are probably 20 or more brands of laundry detergent in the grocery store where your family shops. Make a list of different ways in which producers try to differentiate one detergent brand from another. Why can some brands have prices that are much higher than the price of others and still sell well?

2. Why can't most oil producers compete successfully with large oil refiners such as Texaco, Shell Oil, or Mobil Oil?

3. In the 1990s, many nations that grew coffee beans tried to set up a cartel that would have limited coffee production and stabilized prices at a higher level. This effort failed. Explain why it is so hard to create a successful cartel when there are many members.

## Graphing Exercise

4. The graph below shows the current demand and long-run average cost curves (discussed in Chapter 5) for Sleepwell Mattresses, one of more than 50 firms that manufacture mattresses. At the present, the firm is just breaking even—its total costs equal its total revenue. The firm's owners want to differentiate their product by convincing consumers that their mattresses are better than those offered by other firms. This would increase demand for their products and decrease their average cost by taking advantage of economies of scale. To do this, they undertake a major advertising campaign. If it is successful, what will happen to the location of the firm's demand curve and the location of the intersection between the demand curve and the firm's long-run average cost curve? Make a copy of the graph and sketch in the new demand curve. Assuming the firm continues to sell mattresses for $150 each, what happens to the firm's average cost and profit?

**Demand and Long-Run Average Cost for Sleepwell Mattresses**

## Think Critically

5. **Research** In 2003, the American Broadcasting Company (ABC) charged $2.2 million for a 30-second advertisement on television during the Super Bowl. Investigate the cost of this type of advertising during the latest Super Bowl. Why are businesses willing to spend this amount for a 30-second advertisement? What are they trying to accomplish?

206    **CHAPTER 7** Market Structure

---

**Demand and Long-Run Average Cost for Sleepwell Mattresses**

## *Visualizing the Answer— Graphing Exercise*

4. The answer includes a graph. Students' graphs should look similar to the one shown here.

# movers & shakers

**Dwight Cooper** *Co-Owner, Professional Placement Resources*

Dwight Cooper met his friend and business partner, Keith Frein, when the two attended Florida State University. After graduating, they became co-workers at a medical staffing company. Each man dreamed of one day running his own business. In 1996, their dreams became reality when they invested their combined savings of $10,000 to found Professional Placement Resources (PPR). The company placed physical therapists, occupational therapists, and speech language pathologists into jobs. Because a shortage of workers in these fields had left organizations desperate for such qualified workers, PPR grew quickly.

Within a year, the company settled into offices in Jacksonville Beach, Florida, and employed five people. They added a travel service, allowing the therapists to work for 13 weeks in one city and then either move to a new assignment in a new city, remain in the same assignment for another 13 weeks, or take some time off before accepting a new assignment. The lure of travel, combined with attractive salaries and benefits (including free housing), helped PPR triple in size in just two years. When the therapist shortage ended in 1998, PPR began placing nurses instead. The nursing field continues to face a severe shortage throughout the United States. For the next two years, PPR recorded average annual growth of 244 percent.

Although PPR was founded when the market was expanding, "start-up was not easy," Cooper says. He credits the company's initial success to a lot of hard work and a little bit of luck. Although the company's growth was welcome, it also presented challenges. "We grew really fast from early on," Cooper explains. "And as we grew, our business became more complex. We had so many more relationships to manage, and we no longer had the luxury or the time to discuss every issue among ourselves."

Cooper found the challenge of quickly building systems and processes suitable for the company to be "a bit overwhelming." He compares it to "living in a society with no laws and rules...imagine having to establish laws and rules for that first time."

Today PPR competes with more than 200 companies that also provide traveling nurses to hospitals across the United States. For PPR, "this healthy marketplace lets the customer decide what is a fair price for a nurse, and lets the nurse ultimately decide what is a fair wage," Cooper explains. "The market keeps all companies in this industry honest."

PPR's revenues will exceed $30 million in 2003. Its oceanfront headquarters have grown to 6,000 square feet. The company employs a staff of 65 dedicated employees who place more than 300 nurses in positions throughout the United States. Recognizing the need to expand its search for qualified nurses, PPR now recruits from as far away as Australia, India, and the Philippines to fill jobs in the United States.

In recognition of their accomplishments, Cooper and Frein were selected as finalists for Ernst and Young's Entrepreneur of the Year Award in 2000 and 2001. PPR twice was named one of the fastest-growing companies in north Florida by the *Jacksonville Business Journal*. Further, *Inc. Magazine* included PPR on its list of fastest-growing privately held companies in 2001 and 2002.

---

**SOURCE READING**
Dwight Cooper said, "The market keeps all companies in this industry honest." What do you think he means by this?

**ENTREPRENEURS IN ACTION**
As the company grew, Cooper said it was a challenge to establish rules quickly, without the time to discuss every issue with his partner. In small groups, discuss how you might handle this situation.

Lesson 7.2 • *Monopolistic Competition and Oligopoly* **207**

## FOCUS

Introduce the concept of antitrust policies by asking students to imagine that only one business supplies all the gasoline sold in their community. They either buy gasoline from this firm or they cannot drive their car. This firm sets a price that is $.50 more per gallon than is charged in other parts of the country. It also keeps its stations open only from 8:00 A.M. to 6:00 P.M., six days a week. Do students believe this is fair? What do they believe the government should do to stop the firm from setting such high prices and providing such limited service?

### Objectives

Remind students to read the lesson objectives to help focus their attention before reading the lesson.

### Key Terms

Direct students use each of the key terms in a separate sentence or short paragraph that helps demonstrate the meaning of the term.

### [ In the News ]

Instruct students to read the passage and write down their answers. Point out that their answers might change after they finish studying Lesson 7.3.

### Answers to Think About It

Answers will vary. Possible answers: For some markets it is more efficient to have monopolies because of the economies of scale that monopolies are able to achieve. To correct the situation above, the government should begin slowly re-regulating the industry. In doing so, they will "weed" out the poor suppliers, leaving an oligopoly of knowledgeable and capable suppliers.

### Visual Presentation

Use the PowerPoint presentation on the Instructor's Resource CD as an adjunct to your lecture. The presentation also can be used for review.

# Antitrust, Economic Regulation, and Competition  **7.3**

## Objectives

> Explain the goal of U.S. antitrust laws.

> Distinguish between the two views of government regulation.

> Discuss why U.S. markets have grown more competitive in recent decades.

## Overview

More than 225 years ago, Adam Smith remarked, "People of the same trade seldom meet together, even for merriment or diversion, but the conversation ends in a conspiracy against the public, or in some contrivance to raise prices." The tendency of firms to seek monopolistic advantage is understandable in light of their drive to maximize profit. But monopoly often harms the economy. Public policy can promote competition in markets where competition seems desirable. It can reduce the harmful effects of monopoly in markets where the output can be most efficiently produced by one or a few firms.

## Key Terms

**antitrust activity**

**merger**

**deregulation**

## [ In the News ]

### Foot-Tingling Deregulation

When the power industry's natural monopoly was deregulated at the federal level, experts hoped the action would create competition in power generation throughout the country. The same experts warned, however, that deregulation also could lead to neglect of the transmission grids that delivered the generated power to the customers. The accuracy of this warning was made obvious when testimony before a federal panel pinpointed the triggering incident for the great northeastern blackout of mid-August, 2003: an overheated, melting electrical transmission line outside Cleveland that eventually sagged enough to touch a tree and short-circuit. The utility responsible for that part of the transmission grid already had a bad enough summer. Its New Jersey operation had been under fire for rolling blackouts that injured shore businesses and for inadequate maintenance that allowed stray electricity to run through the ground. This neglect left residents of Brick, N.J., tingling when they stepped into pools and Jacuzzis. In addition, one of its nuclear power plants had been shut down to prevent an accident when an acid leak had eaten through the steel lid of a reactor. A federal judge ruled it had violated the Clean Air Act by not installing pollution-control equipment at a coal-fired plant.

### Think About It

What do you think this says about deregulation of some natural monopolies? What would you recommend to a government panel trying to correct the situation in the power industry?

### National Content Standards in Economics

A complete list of the NCEE Standards appears on pages xxiv–xxv of this book. The following standards are addressed in Lesson 7.3.

Standard 6: Specialization and Trade

Standard 7: Markets—Price and Quantity Determination

Standard 9: Role of Competition

Standard 16: Role of Government

Standard 17: Using Cost/Benefit Analysis to Evaluate Government Programs

# Antitrust

Although competition typically promotes the most efficient use of the nation's resources, an individual firm would prefer to operate as a monopoly. If left alone, a firm might try to create a monopoly by driving competitors out of business, by merging with competitors, or by colluding with competitors to rig prices and increase profits. **Antitrust activity** attempts to prohibit efforts to monopolize markets in which competition is desirable.

## U.S. Antitrust Activity

Antitrust activity tries to

1. Promote the market structure that will lead to greater competition, and

2. Reduce anticompetitive behavior.

## Antitrust Laws

*Antitrust laws attempt to promote socially desirable market performance.* Three early laws dealt with the growing problem of antitrust activity. These included the Sherman Antitrust Act, the Clayton Act, and the Federal Trade Commision Act.

The Sherman Antitrust Act of 1890 outlawed the creation of trusts, restraint of trade, and monopolization. A *trust* is any firm or group of firms that tries to monopolize a market. The Clayton Act of 1914 was passed to outlaw certain practices not prohibited by the Sherman Act and to help government stop a monopoly before it developed. The Federal Trade Commission (FTC) Act of 1914 established a federal body to help enforce antitrust laws. The FTC has five full-time commissioners assisted by a staff of mostly economists and lawyers.

These three laws provide the U.S. antitrust framework. This framework has been clarified and enhanced by amendments and court decisions over the years.

## Mergers and Antitrust

One way that firms may try to reduce competition is by merging with competing firms. A **merger** is the combination of two or more firms to form a single firm. Much of what federal antitrust officials do today is to approve or deny proposed mergers. These officials consider the merger's impact on the share of sales by the largest firms in the industry. If a few firms account for a relatively large share of sales in the market (say, more than half), any merger that increases that share may be challenged.

Federal guidelines sort all mergers into two categories. *Horizontal mergers* involve firms in the same market, such as a merger between competing oil companies. *Nonhorizontal mergers* include all other types of mergers. Horizontal mergers currently hold greater interest for antitrust officials. When determining whether to challenge a particular merger, officials consider factors such as the ease of entry into the market and possible efficiency gains from the merger. They would ask, for example, can the merger increase the resulting firm's economies of scale?

## Flexible Merger Policy

In recent years, the government has shifted from rules that restrict big mergers to a more flexible approach. This new approach allows big companies to merge if the combination is more efficient or more competitive with other big firms in the market. For example, the government approved Boeing's $15 billion acquisition of McDonnell Douglas, another aircraft manufacturer, because Boeing still competes fiercely with Airbus, a European rival, in the world market for aircraft. As one antitrust official put it, "I do not believe that size alone is a basis to challenge a merger." However, just the threat of a legal challenge has stopped many potentially anticompetitive mergers.

**CHECKPOINT**
What is the goal of antitrust laws?

*antitrust activity*
Government efforts aimed at preventing monopoly and promoting competition in markets where competition is desirable

*merger*
The combination of two or more firms to form a single firm

### Antitrust

Point out that there are two main reasons for business mergers. Businesses merge to increase their productive efficiency by taking advantage of economies of scale. Larger firms often are more efficient than smaller firms. Another reason is to reduce competition. Ask students what might happen if all the pizza restaurants in their community joined together to form one big chain of restaurants. They all had the same menu and charged the same prices. What type of merger would this be? (horizontal) Why might this be a bad thing for consumers? Do students believe the government should prevent this type of merger from taking place?

**CHECKPOINT**
Invite a student to answer the checkpoint that appears on this page.

### Answer

The goal of antitrust laws is to promote socially desirable market performance.

---

### Outside Resources

**The Department of Justice** The DOJ maintains a listing of current antitrust cases at its web site at www.usdoj.gov/atr/cases.html. Ask students to visit this site and review a current antitrust case that interests them. Have them write a brief description of the issues involved in the case and explain how they believe the case should be resolved. Ask several of your students to report their findings to the class.

## Regulation of Natural Monopolies

Remind students that some businesses need to be monopolies to be efficient. Absent government regulation, these natural monopolies could take advantage of consumers by charging high prices or providing inferior products or services. Ask students to imagine that they are members of a regulatory agency and that a natural gas delivery service has requested a rate increase of 10 percent. What factors would they consider when they decide whether or not to grant the increase? What might happen if the firm was not able to charge enough to cover its costs? (When a utility is unable to charge enough to cover its costs, it is likely to cut back on investment and maintenance. In the long run, this may prevent the utility from providing quality service to its customers.)

### *Think Critically Through Visuals*

Direct students to focus their attention on the photograph on this page. Ask for a volunteer to answer the question posed in the caption.

### Answer

Answers will vary. Possible answers: Phone companies are regulated because of social interest (lower prices and increased output) and special interest of the producers (limited entry).

 **CHECKPOINT**

Invite a student to answer the checkpoint that appears on this page.

### Answer

Both views are concerned with protecting and promoting a certain group. Social interest promotes consumers by offering increased output and lower prices. Special interest promotes producers by offering limited entry.

# Regulation of Natural Monopolies

Antitrust laws try to prevent monopoly in those markets where competition seems desirable. On the other hand, the *regulation of natural monopolies* tries to control price, output, the entry of new firms, and the quality of service in industries in which monopoly appears inevitable or even desirable. *Natural monopolies,* such as local electricity transmission, local phone service, or a city subway system, are regulated. Several other industries, such as land and air transportation, were regulated in the past based on the same idea.

## Two Views of Government Regulation

Why do governments regulate the price and output of certain markets? There are two views of regulation. The first view has been the one discussed so far—namely, such regulation is in the *public interest.* Regulation promotes social welfare by reducing the price and increasing the output when a market is served most efficiently by one or just a few firms.

A second view is that such regulation is not in the public interest but is in the *special interest* of producers. According to this view, well-organized producer groups expect to profit from government regulation by persuading public officials to impose restrictions that these groups find attractive. Such restrictions include limiting entry into the industry and preventing competition among existing firms.

Producer groups may argue that competition in their industry would hurt consumers. For example, the alleged problem of "cutthroat" competition among taxi drivers has led to regulations that eliminated price competition and restricted the number of taxis in most large metropolitan areas. The problem is that regulation has made taxis more expensive and harder to find.

The special-interest theory may be valid even when the initial intent of the legislation was in the consumer interest. Over time, the regulators may start acting more in the special interests of producers.

© Getty Images/PhotoDisc

**Why do you think it is desirable for local phone service to be regulated by government?**

 **CHECKPOINT**

Compare the two views of government regulation of monopoly.

**210**    **CHAPTER 7**   Market Structure

Another federal law that was passed to limit the power of big business was the Interstate Commerce Act of 1887. This law made it illegal for businesses to conspire to set "unreasonable" railroad rates. At that time, many railroad companies, particularly in the western United States, charged rates that were very high. Invite interested students to investigate the impact of the Interstate Commerce Act of 1887.

# Competitive Trends in the U.S. Economy

The U.S. economy has grown more competitive in the last half century. The number of industries judged to be competitive increased from about half of all industries in 1960 to more than three-fourths of all industries today. Causes of increased competition include antitrust activity, deregulation, international trade, and technological change. Consider the impact of each.

## Antitrust Activity

Antitrust officials now spend most of their time evaluating the impact of proposed mergers on market competition. Although not many mergers ultimately are challenged by government, just the threat of a legal challenge has deterred many potentially anticompetitive mergers.

Perhaps the most significant antitrust case in recent years not involving a merger was the agreement antitrust officials reached with Microsoft. Microsoft was charged with having a monopoly in operating-system software and with attempting to extend this monopoly to the Web browser market. Among other

# E-CONOMICS

## Microsoft on Trial

The most significant antitrust case in the last decade was the U.S. Justice Department's (DOJ's) case against Microsoft Corporation. The DOJ accused Microsoft of engaging in a pattern of "predatory conduct" to protect its operating-system monopoly and to extend that monopoly into Internet software. Microsoft disputed the charges and said the government was interfering with its right to create new products that benefit consumers. After 78 days of testimony and months of deliberation, Judge Thomas Penfield Jackson ruled that Microsoft maintained a monopoly in operating-system software by anticompetitive means. He also found that Microsoft attempted to monopolize the Web browser market by unlawfully "tying" Internet Explorer with Windows. As a remedy, Judge Jackson proposed restricting Microsoft's business practices and dividing the firm into a Windows-based operating-system company and an applications-software company. Microsoft appealed the decision to the U.S. Court of Appeals. This court upheld the finding that Microsoft violated antitrust laws and acted illegally in maintaining a monopoly in

its operating system. However, they also found that Judge Jackson had engaged in "serious judicial misconduct" in making negative comments about Microsoft to the media. The court ordered a new judge to decide on the punishment. In September 2001, however, the DOJ announced it would not seek a breakup of Microsoft, but would ask the court for a series of tough restrictions. In November 2001, Microsoft reached a settlement with the DOJ and with most of the state attorneys general. The settlement gave personal-computer makers greater freedom to install non-Microsoft software on new machines and to remove access to competing Microsoft features, such as Internet browsers. It also banned exclusive contracts and prohibited Microsoft from acting against companies that take advantage of these freedoms. Further, it required Microsoft to disclose design information to hardware and software makers, so they can build competing products that will run smoothly with Windows.

### Think Critically

Who benefits from the settlement Microsoft reached with the Justice Department?

things, the settlement with Microsoft gives personal-computer makers greater freedom to install non-Microsoft software on new machines. Read more about this important antitrust case in the E-conomics feature on page 211.

### Deregulation

For most of the twentieth century, industries such as trucking, airlines, securities trading, banking, and telecommunications were regulated by the government to limit price competition and restrict entry. The trend in recent decades has been toward **deregulation**, which reduces or eliminates government regulations. For the most part, deregulation has increased competition and benefited consumers.

Take, for example, the regulation and deregulation of airlines. The Civil Aeronautics Board (CAB), established in 1938, once strictly regulated the U.S. interstate airline business. Any potential entrant interested in serving an interstate route had to persuade the CAB that the route needed another airline, a task that proved impossible. During the 40 years of regulation, potential entrants submitted more than 150 applications for long-distance routes, *but not a single new interstate airline was allowed.* The CAB also forced strict compliance with regulated prices. A request to lower prices on any route would result in a rate hearing, during which both the CAB and competitors scrutinized the request. In effect, the CAB created a cartel that fixed prices

**deregulation**
A reduction in government control over prices and firm entry in previously regulated markets, such as airlines and trucking

A review of the history of airline deregulation from a conservative viewpoint is available online from the Heritage Foundation's magazine. Access this web site through econxtra.swlearning.com. What actions was the Department of Transportation considering at the time this review was written? What nonregulatory alternatives does the author suggest?

*econxtra.swlearning.com*

among the 10 existing major airlines and blocked new entry.

In 1978, despite opposition from the existing airlines and their labor unions, Congress passed the Airline Deregulation Act, which allowed price competition and new entry. By 2000, airfares averaged 27 percent below previously regulated prices. Passenger miles nearly tripled. Airlines became more productive by filling a greater percentage of seats. The net benefits of deregulation to consumers now exceed $20 billion a year, or about $75 per U.S. resident.

Regulations that limited competition also have been repealed in trucking, securities trading, banking, and telecommunications. For the most part, these industries have become more competitive as a result of deregulation. Consumers benefit from lower prices and better products.

### International Trade

Foreign imports increased competition in many industries, including autos, tires, and steel. Many imported goods were attractive to U.S. consumers because of their superior quality and lower prices. Finding themselves at a cost and technological disadvantage, U.S. producers initially asked for government protection from foreign competitors through trade barriers, such as quotas and tariffs. Despite their efforts to block foreign goods, U.S. producers still lost market share to imports.

For example, General Motors dominates U.S. auto manufacturing. GM's sales account for half of U.S. automobile sales by U.S. firms. However, when sales by Japanese and European producers are included, GM's share of the U.S. auto market falls to less than one third. To survive in the market, U.S. producers improved quality and offered products at more competitive prices.

### Technological Change

Some industries are growing more competitive as a result of technological change. Here are some examples: In the last two decades, the prime-time audience share of the three major television networks (NBC, CBS, and ABC)

*Group Activity*

Organize students into small groups. Tell each group that it must decide how much a natural gas company may charge its customers for delivering gas. At the current rate, the firm has not been able to pay for new gas lines or even to maintain the ones it has. The firm would like to increase its rates by 25 percent so it can invest in improving its system. Many consumers say they can't afford to heat their homes at the current prices. Ask the groups to agree on a pricing policy and explain their choice to the class. How does this demonstrate problems in regulating natural monopolies?

dropped from 91 percent to 46 percent as satellite and cable technology delivered many more channels.

Despite Microsoft's dominance in operating systems, the packaged software market for personal computers barely existed in 1980. It now thrives in a technology-rich environment populated by thousands of software makers. Also, the Internet has opened possibilities for greater competition in a number of industries, from online stock trading to all manner of electronic commerce.

Some web sites offer consumers ready information about the price and availability of products. This makes comparison shopping easier and lowers the transaction costs of buying and selling.

 **CHECKPOINT**
Why have U.S. markets grown more competitive in recent decades?

 **Main Idea**
**Role of Competition**

The trend toward e-commerce has led to greater competition in the U.S. economy. For example, *competition among online sellers lowers costs and prices and encourages producers to make more of the products buyers want. Competition among online buyers increases price and allocates goods and services to people who are willing and able to pay for them.*

© Getty Images/PhotoDisc

Lesson 7.3 • *Antitrust, Economic Regulation, and Competition* **213**

 **APPLY**

Assign Lesson 7.3 from the Contemporary Economics Workbook.

**e-con @pps**

Encourage students to apply their knowledge of concepts presented in this lesson as they explore economic news stories, policy debates, and data available at **econxtra.swlearning.com**. A sampling of the titles for this lesson appears below.

**EconDebate**
- Has deregulation caused the energy shortage in California?
- Should Napster and similar MP3 distribution mechanisms be banned?
- Is Microsoft a monopoly?

**EconNews**
- Duty-Free Sales No Longer Free
- Maximizing and Minimizing the Minimum Wage
- Paying the Price of Pollution

**ASSESS**

Assign all or part of Lesson 7.3 Assessment on page 214 as homework or an in-class activity

**Xtra! Study Tools**

Direct students to the online study tools for Lesson 7.3 at **econxtra.swlearning.com**.

**CLOSE**

**Revisit** the **In the News** feature on the first page of the lesson. Ask students to review their preliminary answers and discuss the questions, now that they have completed this lesson.

**Review** the objectives for Lesson 7.3. Students should be able to:
- Explain the goal of U.S. antitrust laws.
- Distinguish between the two views of government regulation.
- Discuss why U.S. markets have grown more competitive in recent decades.

**RETEACH**

Ask students to identify a business that produces a good or service in their community and that they believe has a substantial amount of monopoly power. What benefits, if any, do they derive from this firm? In what ways, if any, does this firm harm them? Ask them to find out what types of regulation are imposed on this firm by the government. What reasons can they give that could explain the government's current policy toward the firm? If they were in charge, what rules would they enforce on the firm? How would their rules change the situation?

Have students present their findings in a short paper or as an oral presentation. Consider allowing students to work in pairs to complete this assignment.

## Key Concepts

1. Answers will vary. Possible answer: A single discount store might take the reduced competition as an opportunity raise prices, or it might have better sales that would allow it to stock a wider range of products and hire more employees to provide better service.

2. Answers will vary. Possible answer: It is the responsibility of the executive branch of the government to bring antitrust cases to court. Different administrations have had different ideas about how aggressively these laws should be enforced.

3. Answers will vary. Possible answer: Foreign producers were able to offer shoes at lower prices because their resource costs were lower than those paid by U.S. producers. This reduced the monopoly power of U.S. producers.

4. Answers will vary. Possible answer: Millions of people would want to take this drug to prevent themselves from being infected with HIV and would be willing to pay a high price to purchase the drug. The firm, however, might not choose to charge an exceptionally high price in order to avoid a public outcry and possible government regulation.

## Graphing Exercise

5. Answers will vary. Possible answer: Consumers of Product A will demand almost the same quantity regardless of the price, while consumers of Product B will change the quantity they demand when the price changes. The demand for product A is inelastic while the demand for B is elastic. Product A must be the drug while product B is the shampoo. Firms that have inelastic demand for their products have more monopoly power because they are able to raise their prices without losing many customers.

## Think Critically

6. Answers will vary. Students might point out that the Postal Service has gained or lost monopoly power. Their assessment of any change should be based on reason and logic.

---

## Key Concepts

1. Imagine there are two large discount stores in a small town. Describe one way in which consumers might be harmed if these stores merged and one way they might benefit.

2. The basic antitrust laws in the United States have not changed very much in many years. Still, over time, there has been a significant difference in the way these laws have been enforced. What could explain this situation?

3. Fifty years ago, the vast majority of shoes sold in the United States were manufactured in this country. In recent years, U.S.-made shoes have accounted for less than 10 percent of this market. How has foreign competition reduced the monopoly power of U.S. shoe producers?

4. What would happen to the market power of a firm that found, patented, and received FDA approval to market a drug that prevents HIV infections? Why might such a firm not charge an extremely high price for this drug?

## Graphing Exercise

5. Study the two demand curves below. One is for a drug manufactured by Acme Pharmaceuticals that thousands of people need in order to stay healthy. The other is for a particular brand of shampoo. In which case is demand elastic and in which case is it inelastic? Which of these products is Product A and which is Product B? How did you make this determination? Which of these firms has greater monopoly power? In general, do firms with elastic or inelastic demand have more monopoly power?

## Think Critically

6. **Government** The U.S. Postal Service (USPS) lost billions of dollars in the decade between 1992 and 2002. In 2003, some people argued that the USPS should be privatized or sold to private businesses to be run. What has happened to the USPS since then? Has its monopoly power been increased or decreased? Does it remain as a government monopoly or has it been sold? Do you think the situation has improved or worsened for consumers?

214

**CHAPTER 7** Market Structure

# The North American Fur Trade

From 1804 to 1816, two companies—the Hudson Bay Company (HBC) headquartered in London, and the Northwestern Company (NWC) of Montreal—dominated the North American fur trade. Both companies operated over large areas of the Canadian wilderness. For the most part, each company respected the other's territory and business operation without a formal market-sharing agreement.

With the start of the Napoleonic War in Europe, the demand for furs in Britain declined 50 percent as the European markets were closed off from British trade. The HBC suffered greater losses than its rival, because the HBC's charter prohibited it from trading anywhere but England. The NWC, on the other hand, was able to find markets in China, the United States, and even Europe. Despite the drop in demand, the HBC refused to slow down its operations in the hope that the war would be short. It also did not want to jeopardize its business relations with the Native Americans, from whom it purchased the pelts. Instead, in an attempt to control supply and maintain prices, it chose to store the furs it collected.

However, where the two companies previously had respected each other's territory, the HBC's financial problems led it to end their informal agreement. It began to move into the area in which the NWC had been trapping exclusively. The cost of obtaining furs rose as competition between the companies drove up the price each had to pay the Native Americans. Both companies also engaged in attempts to disrupt the other's operation by employing "bully boys." This harmful competition ended in 1821, when the companies agreed to merge and form a monopoly. The new company brought an end to the destructive practices and lowered costs by taking advantage of the economies of scale. The combined company also provided a unified front in purchasing from the Native Americans.

## THINK CRITICALLY

Referring to the characteristics of monopolistic competition and oligopoly, analyze the behavior of the Hudson Bay Company and the Northwest Company during the period from 1804 to 1821. What effect do you think the merger of the two companies had on the price of fur?

CONNECT

*to History*

## FOCUS

Point out that agreements between firms to work together (collude) may be imposed by government rules rather than by the firms' owners. Such situations are likely to be short-lived because governments have a history of not setting consistent policies or rules over extended periods of time. This was the case with the Hudson Bay Company (HBC) and Northwestern Company (NWC). The rule that forced HBC to trade with England prevented it from adjusting to changes in the market and world politics. This destroyed its agreement with the NWC and prevented the firm from benefiting from the ologpolistic market it had done business in.

## TEACH

Instruct students to read the **Connect to History** feature and answer the question.

## ASSESS

Use the question at the bottom of the page to assess the students' understanding of this feature.

### Answers to Think Critically

The merger of the two companies lowered costs because of the economies of scale achieved and joint control of essential resources.

Lesson 7.3 • *Antitrust, Economic Regulation, and Competition* **215**

## Bibliography

Carlos, Ann M. *The North American Fur Trade, 1804-1821: A Study in the Life Cycle of a Duopoly.* New York: Garland Publishing, Inc., 1986.

Chittenden, Hiram Martin. *American Fur Trade of the Far West.* Vols. 1 and 2. Lincoln: University of Nebraska Press, 1987.

Fuchs, Victor R. *The Economics of the Fur Industry.* New York: Columbia University Press, 1957.

Lewis, Jon E. *The Mammoth Book of the West.* New York: Carroll & Graf Publishers, Inc., 1996.

Milner, Clyde A., Carol A. O'Connor, and Martha A. Sandweiss, eds. *Oxford History of the American West.* New York: Oxford University Press, 1994.

## Summary

## Summary

### Consider

Ask students to revisit the questions they were asked to consider at the beginning of the chapter. Remind students that they should be able to answer all of the questions after studying Chapter 7.

- What does a bushel of wheat have in common with a share of Microsoft stock? See page 192—Perfect Competition.

- What's so perfect about perfect competition? See page 192—Perfect Competition.

- Why don't most monopolies last? See page 196—True Monopolies Are Rare.

- Why are some panty hose sold in egg-shaped cartons? See page 202—Product Differentiation.

- Why was OPEC created? See page 204—When Oligopolists Collude.

- Is the U.S. economy more competitive now than it used to be? See page 211—Competitive Trends in the U.S. Economy.

### Exam*View*

Use Exam*View* to assess student learning.

- Create a chapter test using questions from the existing test bank.

- Add your own questions to the existing test bank.

- Generate multiple forms of a chapter test.

### Study Skills

Offer the following study skills suggestions for students as they review this chapter.

- Outline the chapter.
- Review Key Terms.
- Review Checkpoints.
- Work in pairs to quiz each other.
- Use Xtra! Study Tools for each lesson.

Direct students to the online quiz preparation for Chapter 7 at **econxtra.swlearning.com**.

### 7.1 Perfect Competition and Monopoly

**Xtra! Quiz Prep**
*econxtra.swlearning.com*

**a** *Perfectly competitive* markets share four features: (1) they have many buyers and sellers; (2) producers sell the same standard product; (3) buyers are fully informed about the price, quality, and availability of products and sellers are fully informed about all resources and technology used to make them; and (4) firms and resources are free to enter or leave the market.

**b** The price that individual producers in perfect competition charge is determined by market supply and market demand. A firm that charged more than the prevailing market price would have no customers.

**c** A *monopoly* is the only supplier of a product that has no close substitutes. For monopolies to exist in the long run, there must be *barriers to entry*. These may include legal restrictions such as patents, economies of scale that make established firms more efficient than new firms, and control of essential resources not available to other firms.

**d** The demand curve for a monopoly slopes down from left to right. This means that the firm must lower its price on all products to sell additional products.

**e** Many people believe that monopolies harm the general welfare because they may waste resources, exert undue influence on the government, or grow lazy and inefficient. Others believe that monopolies may have lower costs and prices because of economies of scale and that government regulation can prevent them from exploiting consumers.

### 7.2 Monopolistic Competition and Oligopoly

**a** *Monopolistic competition* is a market structure with many firms offering similar but not identical products. Each monopolisticcom-petitor tries to attract customers by differentiating its product. Forms of product differentiation include physical differences, sales locations, services offered with the product, and the product's image.

**b** *Oligopoly* is a market structure in which a few businesses dominate production in the market and are interdependent. Oligopolies typically exist in markets where there are economies of scale and high costs of entry.

**c** Oligopolists sometimes cooperate with each other in pricing their products. When they actually agree to set prices, they collude. Internationally, some nations have worked together to establish *cartels* that are intended to increase or stabilize prices by controlling supply.

### 7.3 Antitrust, Economic Regulation, and Competition

**a** The federal government has passed three basic *antitrust* laws intended to limit the monopoly power of large businesses: (1) the Sherman Antitrust Act, (2) the Clayton Act, and (3) the Federal Trade Commission Act.

**b** Many of the firms that became monopolies gained their power through merger. Mergers are either horizontal—when firms supplying the same market join—or nonhorizontal—when firms not supplying the same product join. Much of the federal antitrust activity today is directed toward limiting the ability of firms to merge if doing so would result in businesses with significant monopoly power.

**c** An alternative to limiting the ability of firms to merge is to regulate those that have a significant amount of monopoly power. The federal government and all states have regulatory agencies that are designed to protect the public's interests.

**d** In recent years there has been a trend toward *deregulation* of many parts of the economy. The monopoly power of many U.S. businesses has been reduced as a result of new technologies and foreign competition.

# Review Economic Terms

Choose the term that best fits the definition. On a separate sheet of paper, write the letter of the answer.

1. A market structure with many fully informed buyers and sellers of an identical product with no barriers to entry

2. A sole supplier of a product with no close substitutes

3. Restrictions on the entry of new firms into an industry

_____ 4. The ability of a firm to raise its price without losing all its sales

_____ 5. A market structure with no entry barriers and many firms selling products differentiated enough that each firm's demand curve slopes downward

_____ 6. A market structure with a small number of firms whose behavior is interdependent

_____ 7. A group of firms that agree to act as a monopolist to increase the market price and maximize the group's profits

_____ 8. Government efforts aimed at preventing monopoly and promoting competition in markets where competition is desirable

_____ 9. The combination of two or more firms into a single firm

10. A product that is identical across sellers

11. A reduction in government control over prices and firm entry in previously regulated markets

_____12. Important features of a market, including the number of buyers and sellers and the product's uniformity across sellers.

a. **antitrust activity**

b. **barriers to entry**

c. **cartel**

d. **commodity**

e. **deregulation**

f. **market power**

g. **market structure**

h. **merger**

i. **monopolistic competition**

j. **monopoly**

k. **oligopoly**

l. **perfect competition**

# Review Economic Concepts

13. Which of the following statements is *not* true of firms in *perfect competition*?

   a. All producers charge the same price.

   b. All producers make the same product.

   c. Each firm tries to sell more by reducing its price.

   d. There are no barriers to entry.

14. **True or False** The demand curve for a single firm in competition is a horizontal line.

15. A firm operating in the __?__ market structure has no market power.

16. **True or False** *Monopolies* may emerge naturally when a firm has substantial economies of scale.

17. *Monopolies* must lower the price of the products they sell to

   a. sell more output.

   b. earn a profit.

   c. shift the demand curve.

   d. meet their competition.

18. **True or False** By definition, all *monopolies* earn substantial profits.

19. **True or False** Most *monopolies* tend to last for a long time.

20. Suppose a giant *monoply* is created when one firm buys up all the individual firms in a perfectly competitive market. In this case, the __?__ curve becomes the monopolist's demand curve.

## Review Economic Terms

1. l. perfect competition
2. j. monopoly
3. b. barriers to entry
4. f. market power
5. i. monopolistic competition
6. k. oligopoly
7. c. cartel
8. a. antitrust activity
9. h. merger
10. d. commodity
11. e. deregulation
12. g. market structure

## Review Economic Concepts

13. c. Each firm tries to sell more by reducing its price.
14. True
15. perfect competition
16. True
17. a. sell more output
18. False. Not all monopolies earn substantial profits.
19. False. Long-lasting monopolies are rare.
20. market demand

## Review Economic Concepts

21. d. all work to differentiate their products
22. True
23. c. collusion
24. excess capacity
25. b. is a horizontal line drawn at the market price
26. undifferentiated
27. b. are interdependent
28. True
29. b. electrical service
30. True
31. a. the Fair Labor Standards Act of 1938
32. True

## Apply Economic Concepts

33. Answers will vary. Possible answer: Boeing could raise its prices, too. If Boeing's prices remain unchanged, Airbus likely will be forced to lower its prices back to the original level. This would not help either firm earn a greater profit. Each firm depends on the other's decisions.

34. Answers will vary. Students may point out that some people regard downloading anything from the Internet as being protected by the First Amendment. Others believe that copyright laws should apply to the Internet no less than to other media. A problem that must be resolved is how to limit this type of activity when programs to accomplish it are so readily available.

35. Answers will vary. Possible answer: Store brands now are offered at lower prices than the major brands. Many people choose to buy these less expensive products. Several of the large, nationally advertised producers have merged. Those that remain are still interdependent, but they do not enjoy the same degree of market power as in the past.

21. Firms in *monopolistic competition*
    a. all produce exactly the same product.
    b. all charge the same price.
    c. all earn the same profit.
    d. all work to differentiate their products.

22. **True or False** One problem for society resulting from *monopoly* is that the monopoly may have too much influence on the political system.

23. Which of the following is not a way in which sellers in *monopolistic competition* differentiate their products?
    a. physical differences
    b. location and services
    c. collusion
    d. product image

24. A firm that has __?__ can lower its average cost by selling more of the good.

25. The demand curve facing an individual firm operating in perfect competition
    a. is a vertical line drawn at the number of units.
    b. is a horizontal line drawn at the market price.
    c. slopes down from left to right.
    d. slopes up from left to right.

26. In a(n) __?__ *oligopoly,* the product is identical across producers.

27. Firms in an *oligopoly*
    a. are totally independent from each other.
    b. are interdependent.
    c. always have excess capacity.
    d. none of the above is true.

28. **True or False** The minimum efficient scale is the highest rate of output at which a firm takes full advantage of economies of scale.

29. Which of the following industries is most likely to be regulated by government?
    a. consumer products
    b. electrical service
    c. dry-cleaning service
    d. precious jewels

30. **True or False** Government regulatory agencies are designed to protect the public's interests.

31. Each of the following is a basic federal antitrust law in the United States *except*
    a. the Fair Labor Standards Act of 1938.
    b. the Clayton Act of 1914.
    c. the Sherman Act of 1890.
    d. the Federal Trade Commission Act of 1914.

32. **True or False** Consumers usually benefit from *deregulation* because of the resulting lower prices.

# Apply Economic Concepts

33. **Analyze Pricing in Oligopoly** The two largest producers of commercial aircraft in the world are Airbus of Europe and the Boeing Corporation of the United States. Most economists regard the market for large commercial aircraft as a good example of an oligopoly. Describe what you think Boeing would do if Airbus increased the price of its airplanes by 20 percent. How does this show the interdependency of these firms?

**34. Business Law** An important question today is whether limits should be placed on what consumers may download from the Internet. According to copyright law, those who produce literature, music, films or works of art should be able to profit from what they create. They should, in effect, have a monopoly on their work. Indeed, if their work is placed on the Internet for others to copy for free, they may choose not to produce anything at all. Investigate the current status of this issue, and state your opinion of what should be done.

**35. History** There was a time when Nabisco, Post Cereals, Kellogg's, and General Mills sold nearly 75 percent of the breakfast cereal purchased in the United States. These firms were part of an oligopoly, but those days are now gone. Describe what has happened to reduce the monopoly power of these firms in the market. Think about the breakfast cereal shelves in your grocery store.

**36. Sharpen Your Life Skills: Auto Industry** Review changes in the distribution of sales in the U.S. automobile market that were presented in the Sharpen Your Life Skills activity on page 200 of this chapter. Assume that the trend in sales between 1980 and 2002 demonstrated by the pie graphs continues for another 22 years to 2024. How would the U.S. economy be affected? Would U.S. consumers benefit or be harmed? What would happen to businesses and people employed in the U.S. auto industry?

econxtra.swlearning.com

**39.** Access **EconDebate Online** at econxtra.swlearning.com. Read the policy debate entitled "Should the antititrust exemption for baseball be eliminated?" Analyze this issue from both points of view, and write a paragraph summarizing each side.

**37. Problems with Monopoly** During the 1960s the three largest U.S. producers of automobiles (Ford, General Motors, and Chrysler) sold nearly 90 percent of the cars purchased by U.S. consumers. During the 30 years between 1970 and 2000 these firms lost about one-third of their market to foreign competition that was more technologically advanced. What problem common to monopolies does this situation demonstrate?

**38. Distinguish Between Competition and Monopoly** The graph below provides demand curves for two different firms. One of them is for a competitive firm and the other is for a firm with monopoly power. Identify the firm that is competitive and the one that is a monopoly. Explain how you know which is which. What would happen to the sales of the competitive firm if it tried to raise its price? What would happen to the firm that is a monopoly? Why do businesses prefer to have monopoly power?

**Apply Economic Concepts**

36. The U.S. economy would lose even more automobile sales with the majority of the sales going overseas. The U.S. consumers would increase competition among sellers and from the entry of more sellers into the market. People in the automobile industry would see a decrease in wages and a smaller workforce, due to the loss in market share.

37. Answers will vary. Students may point out that firms with monopoly power sometimes feel little need to buy new technology to improve the efficiency of their production or quality of their products. These firms can suffer when they are forced to compete with firms that are more technologically advanced

38. Firm 1 is competitive because it sells no products until its price falls to $6. At that price, Firm 1 can sell all the products it can produce. Lowering the price further results in no additional sales because it is unable to produce additional products. If Firm 1 tried to charge more than $6, it would have no sales. Firm 2 has monopoly power because it must lower the price of all its products to sell additional products. If Firm 2 increases its price, it will lose some, but not all, of its customers. Firms prefer to have monopoly power because it gives them the ability to increase their price without losing all their customers.

e-con @pps

39. Yes. Major League Baseball should not be exempted from the antitrust laws. By exempting MLB, we are exposing the American public to higher prices at baseball games. In addition, we are forcing American cities to spend millions in public funds to go into new and better stadiums.

No. Major League Baseball should be exempted from the antitrust laws. In exempting MLB, we are allowing baseball to maintain its level of professionalism by limiting the number of teams and players. In addition, we are not making MLB a monopoly by exempting it. It still faces competition from other entertainment industries (other sports, movies, etc.).

*Chapter Assessment*      **219**

# Investing In Your Future

This project can be completed in the classroom or as an outside assignment. The activities call for students to work in teams, but students also can complete the assignment working alone.

## The Situation

As with Project 1, this description of Aleesha's life is meant to provide situations students can identify with. It also incorporates the decisions she had to make in the first installment and the consequences of them. Because Aleesha has remained in control of her life, she again is faced with decisions that are a two-edged sword. She gets to choose the direction(s) her life will follow instead of having them forced on her, and she remains responsible for her choices. Will she "settle" at this stage in life or go on to seek other levels of alternatives in the pursuit of her lifetime goals/dreams?

## The Decision

Emphasize that, because Aleesha identified and pursued her potential career field at an earlier age than most, she has been empowered with the choices presented in this problem. Instead of being forced into a job to which she is not committed in order to achieve a short-term goal (such as flipping burgers to make a car payment), she has positioned herself so that her actions are aligned with her long-term goals. In addition, because she is "working" where her true interest lies, her natural instincts to learn more about animals, their care, and development, have made her a great employee and brought opportunities her way (a job offer and the potential scholarship). Now she must use her natural abilities and some economic insights to help her make more decisions.

## The Situation

Graduation from high school was just around the corner for Aleesha. She had worked for the zoo as an intern for almost two years now, and had become a trusted and valued employee. The zoo manager had offered her a full-time position as his administrative assistant upon her graduation. The used car her father helped her pick out had held up well, but it was just about worn out. Aleesha had managed to keep her grades high, but she had let her participation in sports drop away. Of course, even though she had lots of opportunities, her social life had suffered, at least up until the last few months. Then she had met Charles, an associate manager at the local convenience store. He had been persistent in his invitations, and they had been dating on weekends for about two months. He was even talking about their getting married after she graduated, and starting a family.

## The Decision

However, Aleesha's basic love for the zoo and its animals remained strong. She cared for them, kept a personal set of records on the ones she tended, read articles about them in professional zoo journals, and did her own research in the field. She was filled with ideas about better ways to provide for their well-being and improve the relationship between the animals and the public. Aleesha knew that to develop her ideas and someday have a position where they could be applied, she would have to go to college. However, the nearest college with an appropriate degree program was a long distance away. She would have to live near campus rather than at home. On the positive side, the zoo manager was confident that she could get a scholarship from the zoological society. The award would cover tuition and books for a year, and it could be renewed as long as Aleesha maintained a B average.

Encourage students to use Internet and library resources to obtain information to use in developing budgets. They also can find information relative to applying for loans and grants on the Internet or in the school's guidance office. To discount future earnings streams back to the present day at a suitable compounding rate, students can access tables available on the Internet, along with explanatory remarks that simplify this tool of analysis. See http://www.creatework.com/articles/sample-bus-forms/Business%20Finance/npvtab_1.rtf or http://www.toolkit.cch.com/tools/npvtab_m.asp

Chapters 1 and 2 of *Investing in Your Future* (South-Western Publishing, 2001) also will aid in this analysis. Specifically, see charts and narrative on Mean Monthly Income per Educational Level, p. 12, and the Growth Rate Table, p. 37.

## Activities

**Divide into teams or work individually, as directed by your teacher, to perform the following tasks.**

Apply the steps in the following decision-making process to Aleesha's situation:

**1.** *Define the problem.* Define Aleesha's problem in a way that will allow a clear solution.

**2.** *Identify her choices.* List the various alternatives among which she must choose. Develop budgets and project the quality of life for each of the following choices. See econxtra.swlearning.com for links to tools of analysis that will help you to perform this step.

**a.** Aleesha takes the assistant's position and marries Charles.

**b.** Aleesha takes the assistant's position at the zoo but does not marry. Due to the needs of her brothers and sisters, she has to move out of the home within a year of graduation.

**c.** Aleesha applies for and receives the scholarship to college. Her parents are unable to help her financially but she is eligible for loans and grants.

**3.** *Evaluate the pluses and minuses of each choice.* Carefully weigh the value Aleesha puts on each alternative and the opportunity costs for each.

**a.** Project Aleesha's lifetime income level for each choice. See econxtra.swlearning.com for links to tools of analysis that will help you to perform these steps.

**b.** What personal, emotional, and psychological factors do you think will affect Aleesha's choice?

**4.** *Make a choice.* Which course of action should she choose? Be prepared to present and defend your choice in class.

**5.** *Provide "action" steps that are appropriate to the decision.* Make sure these are realistic and timely to ensure the necessary actions are taken to resolve the problem.

**6.** *Critique the decision.* The class will assist in the review and evaluation of your plan of action. In real life, you should review not only the decision and its result, but also the process by which you make it. Set a time to initiate reviewing the decision or identify an event that would trigger its review.

## Research

Research for the information you need to effectively make the decision, such as the lifetime income levels Aleesha could expect for each choice.

## Present

Arrive at a decision. Then prepare a presentation for the class on the six steps you took to achieve this decision. Be ready for questions and criticisms.

*Project 2*  **221**

**APPLY**

### Activities

**Step 1:** The important aspect to this activity is to listen to the students and how they define the "problem." Do they consider it an opportunity or a burden to make such a decision? How strong are their characters?

**Step 2:** The budgets must display insight into the various choices. Remind the students of the hidden costs of living on their own or in partnership with someone. Emphasize the necessity of budgeting for disposable income and saving for unforeseen situations.

**Step 3:** The key here is twofold. First, the project is about Aleesha. So, when considering the possibility of marriage, the focus should still remain on her and the level of separate income she would need to allow her to reach her life goals. How she would get this income and find the time (either concurrent with child-rearing or later in life) is a subject worthy of research and discussion. Second, this is a perfect time to develop and apply the concept of comparison of the present value of a future stream of income as an enabler of choice. Have students discount Aleesha's future earnings streams back to the present day at a suitable compounding rate—for example, 6%.

**Step 4:** The teacher should focus on the individual traits that Aleesha has shown in reaching this stage of her life. She is disciplined, far-sighted, goal-oriented, wise, and has the inner strength of character to take responsibility for the decisions she is empowered to make.

**Step 5:** Listening to students advocate the various choices will reveal a great deal about their own personal traits as well as the challenges they face. After all have presented their choices, appoint one student to state the consensus of the class.

**Step 6:** Students should recognize that it is important to set up periodic reviews at appropriate points such as applying to college, graduating from high school, choosing a college major, etc.

**ASSESS**

**Presentation** Consider using a rubric or evaluation form for student presentations. Make sure you share the rubric or form with students before they start working on the project. A sample evaluation form appears on the Instructor's Resource CD. The categories to be evaluated include: **Content** (organization, specific content, and accurate information); **Presentation Skills** (eye contact, grammar and pronunciation, volume, and pitch); **Audiovisual Aids** (appropriate content, style, and spelling); and **Handouts** (appropriate content; grammar, punctuation, and spelling).

## National Content Standards in Economics

The following NCEE Standards are addressed in Unit 3:

| | |
|---|---|
| Standard 1 | Scarcity |
| Standard 2 | Marginal Cost/Benefit |
| Standard 4 | Role of Incentives |
| Standard 5 | Gain from Trade |
| Standard 6 | Specialization and Trade |
| Standard 8 | Role of Price in the Market System |
| Standard 9 | Role of Competition |
| Standard 10 | Role of Economic Institutions |
| Standard 11 | Role of Money |
| Standard 12 | Role of Interest Rates |
| Standard 13 | Role of Resources in Determining Income |
| Standard 14 | Profit and the Entrepreneur |
| Standard 15 | Growth |
| Standard 16 | Role of Government |

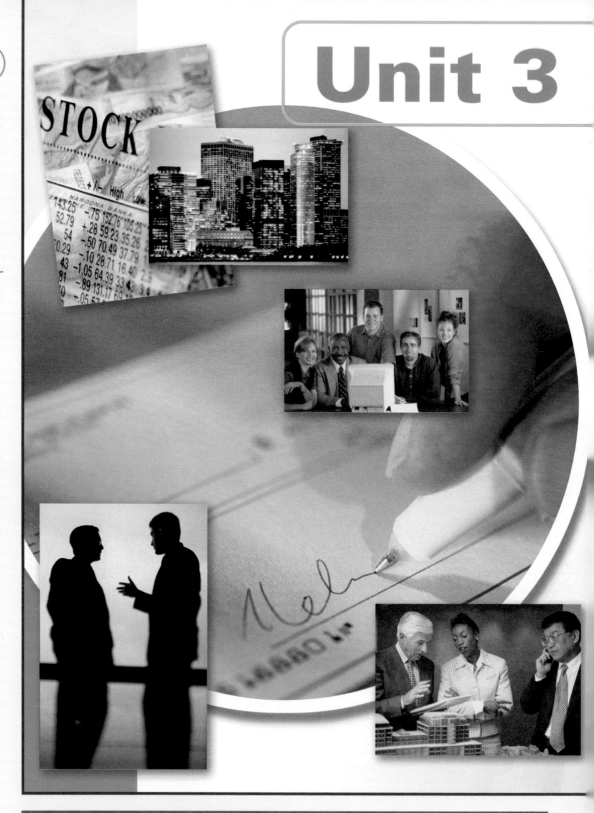

# Unit 3

| Pacing Guide | One-Semester Days of Study | Two-Semesters Days of Study | Block Schedule 90-Minute Blocks |
|---|---|---|---|
| **UNIT 3: MARKET INSTITUTIONS** | | | |
| Chapter 8: Businesses | | | |
| **8.1** Entrepreneurs | 2 | 3 | 2 |
| **8.2** Sole Proprietorships and Partnerships | 1 | 3 | 1 |
| **8.3** Corporations and Other Organizations | 2 | 4 | 2 |
| Chapter 9: Labor Markets | | | |
| **9.1** Demand and Supply of Resources | 2 | 3 | 2 |
| **9.2** Wage Determination | 1 | 3 | 1 |
| **9.3** Labor Unions | 2 | 4 | 2 |
| Chapter 10: Financial Markets and Business Growth | | | |
| **10.1** Production, Consumption, and Time | 2 | 3 | 2 |
| **10.2** Banks, Interest, and Corporate Finance | 1 | 3 | 1 |
| **10.3** Business Growth | 2 | 4 | 2 |

# Market Institutions

 **Businesses**

 **Labor Markets**

 **Financial Markets and Business Growth**

One important decision maker in a market economy is you. Your consumption choices and those of other consumers determine what gets produced. To help supply the products that you and others demand, several institutions have developed to nurture a market economy. Among the most important are businesses, labor markets, and financial markets. You already have some acquaintance with all three. You have interacted with businesses all your life. Most of you have observed labor markets first hand. You are even familiar with financial markets—from credit cards to bank accounts.

223

## Unit 3 Overview

Unit 3 introduces students to the institutions that interact in a market economy. They learn the importance of the entrepreneur to the economy and are introduced to the types of business organizations an entrepreneur can operate. In addition, students explore labor markets, financial markets, and the ways in which business organizations grow.

## Group Activity

Organize students into small groups and ask them to discuss the passage that appears on this page. Instruct students to discuss how they interact with market institutions. Allow about 10 minutes for discussion. Ask a representative of each group to briefly summarize the discussion for the class.

## Think Critically Through Visuals

Direct students study the images on the opposite page and think about how each image relates to market institutions. Ask them to work with a partner to create their own collage to illustrate market institutions. Display the finished collages in the classroom while studying Unit 3.

## Contemporary Economics Video

From the *Contemporary Economics* video, the segment entitled "Wahoo's Fish Tacos" can be used to introduce or recap the concepts presented in Unit 3.

A Video Discussion Guide for this video is available on the Instructor's Resource CD.

## Look Beyond the Classroom

Production requires the organization of human, natural, and capital resources to create goods and services. A good way to move beyond the classroom is to ask students who hold jobs to describe how they contribute to production. Ask several employed students to answer these questions:
- What type of business organization does your employer use?
- What is the nature of your contribution to production (job)?
- How is your level of compensation determined?
- How is your employer's business financed?

Ask the class to answer the following questions regarding the jobs described by classmates:
- How important is this job to production in the economy?
- Could a different resource be substituted for the classmate's labor?
- How is pay related to the value of the classmates' contribution to production?

**LESSON 8.1** *Entrepreneurs:* This lesson focuses on the role of the entrepreneur in a market economy.

**LESSON 8.2** *Sole Proprietorships and Partnerships:* This lesson explains the advantages and disadvantages of sole proprietorship and partnership business forms.

**LESSON 8.3** *Corporations and Other Organizations:* This lesson describes how a corporation is established and explains the advantages and disadvantages of this business form. Other types of organizations that business people use to accomplish their goals are also addressed.

### Consider

Ask students to consider the questions posed on this page as they study Chapter 8. After studying all three lessons, students should be able to answer the questions. The content related to each question can be found on the pages indicated below.

- Why do some people want to call themselves "boss"? See page 234—Sole Proprietorship.
- Why start a business if most new businesses don't last five years? See page 226—Role of Entrepreneurs.
- What does your summer lawn-mowing operation have in common with General Motors? See page 229—Who Isn't an Entrepreneur?
- What do *Corp.* or *Inc.* in a company's name tell you about how the owners treat debt? See page 242—Incorporating.
- How could it be possible that most U.S. businesses have no paid employees? See page 234—Who Is a Sole Proprietor?

### ▶ POINT YOUR BROWSER

Remind students that they can find additional resources for this chapter at **econxtra.swlearning.com**.

- Xtra! Study Tools
- Net Bookmarks
- Xtra! Quiz Prep
- econ@pps
- Ask the Xpert!

# ⑧ Businesses

Entrepreneurs **8.1**

Sole Proprietorships and Partnerships **8.2**

Corporations and Other Organizations **8.3**

### Consider

Why do some people want to call themselves "boss"?

Why start a business if most new businesses don't last five years?

What does your summer lawn-mowing operation have in common with General Motors?

What do *Corp.* or *Inc.* in a company's name tell you about how the owners treat debt?

How could it be possible that most U.S. businesses have no paid employees?

© Getty Images/PhotoDisc

### ▶ POINT YOUR BROWSER

econxtra.swlearning.com

---

### *Teaching Resources for Chapter 8*

- Activities and Projects Masters
- Spanish Resources
- Econ Connection Interactive Tutorial CD
- **Exam***View*® CD
- Workbook Teacher's Edition
- Chapter Test Teacher's Edition
- NCEE Standards and Correlation
- Personal Finance Guide

- Social Studies Skills Review
- Instructor's Resource CD
    - PowerPoint Presentation
    - Lesson Plans
    - Video Discussion Guide
    - Answers to Graphing Exercises
- **econxtra.swlearning.com**

---

# 8.1 Entrepreneurs

## Objectives

> Understand the role of the entrepreneur in a market economy.

> Differentiate entrepreneurs from people who perform a limited entrepreneurial role.

## Overview

In a market economy, people are free to risk their time and their savings to start a business. If the business succeeds, they are rewarded with profit. If the business fails, they could lose a bundle. Chances of success are not great. Most new businesses fail in the first five years. On the other hand, some businesses survive, a few thrive, and a tiny few make their founders wealthy. Despite the high rate of business failure, the promise of profit attracts many prospective entrepreneurs. By putting their ideas into action, entrepreneurs drive the economy forward.

## Key Terms

financial capital

innovation

## [ In the News ]

### Hip-Hop's Surprise Entrepreneur

From its first downbeat, hip-hop music has been dominated by urban and inner-city African-American artists—with a few exceptions like the white artists Eminem and the Beastie Boys. Now there's another white face gaining prominence in the rap and hip-hop music scene. His name is Devin Lazerine, and he's from a suburban town outside Los Angeles. Just 19 years old, Lazerine began his career with a web site. Then, with financial backing and other assistance from media giant Time Warner, he started a "fan 'zine" called *Rap-Up*. The glossy publication is targeted to a new market referred to as "Generation Y" —hip-hop's rapidly growing base of fans. *Rap-Up*'s first issue sold an amazing 200,000 copies. In March 2003, Lazerine made *Fast Company* magazine's list of top 50 "Champions of Innovation," entrepreneurs whose achievements are having a major impact on both the business world and our culture. Lazerine's first celebrity interview for *Rap-Up* was with the group Destiny's Child. He hooked their agent's interest with a phone call talking up the new magazine, and she called back the next day. When Lazerine's mom answered the phone and told the agent he was in school, the agent thought it was a joke. Lazerine persisted and ultimately did get the interview. In his own interview with *USA Weekend* magazine, Lazerine talked about how difficult it was getting respect at such a young age. However, he also said, ". . . if you have a love for something, I don't think age or color or anything should make a difference."

### Think About It

How do you think Devin Lazerine overcame the obstacle of age to become a successful entrepreneur? How big a part did creativity play in his success?

225

## National Content Standards in Economics

A complete list of the NCEE Standards appears on pages xxiv–xxv of this book. The following standards are addressed in Lesson 8.1.

Standard 1: Scarcity

Standard 2: Marginal Cost/Benefit

Standard 4: Role of Incentives

Standard 9: Role of Competition

Standard 10: Role of Economic Institutions

Standard 11: Role of Money

Standard 14: Profit and the Entrepreneur

Standard 15: Growth

## FOCUS

### 8.1 Entrepreneurs

Remind students that production requires human, natural, and capital resources. Entrepreneurship is a human resource. Without this resource, the other resources will not bring about production. Although entrepreneurship can occur in many ways, without it, production will not take place. Ask students to give examples of entrepreneurship that they are aware of in their community.

### Objectives

Remind students to read the lesson objectives to help focus their attention before reading the lesson.

### Key Terms

Direct students use each of the key terms in a separate sentence or short paragraph that helps demonstrate the meaning of the term.

### [ In the News ]

Instruct students to read the passage and write down their answers. Point out that their answers might change after they finish studying Lesson 8.1.

### Answers to Think About It

Answers will vary. Possible answers: Devin Lazerine overcame the obstacle of age through persistence, professionalism, and determination. Creativity played a large role in his success. He thought outside the box when devising a hip-hop web site and magazine.

### Visual Presentation

Use the PowerPoint presentation on the Instructor's Resource CD as an adjunct to your lecture. The presentation also can be used for review.

### Role of Entrepreneurs

Display photographs of lumber, hand tools, and a production worker. Ask students whether anything will be produced if there is no one to direct or pay for these resources. Then add an entrepreneur to your display. Explain that the entrepreneur will tell the worker how to use the other resources to produce a wooden table. This person will have the financial resources needed to buy the resources and pay the worker to produce the table. Point out that production will not take place without someone to organize it, fund it, and take the risks inherent in operating a business.

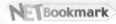

Direct students to **econxtra.swlearning.com**. Remind them to click on the link for Lesson 8.1 to find the appropriate link for the **NET Bookmark** on this page.

#### Think Critically Through Visuals

Direct students to focus their attention on the photograph on this page. Ask for a volunteer to answer the questions posed in the caption.

#### Answer

Answers will vary. Possible answers: Yes, I do feel that the Segway™ Human Transporter will succeed in the marketplace because I believe there is a demand for it. For example, it could be used in warehouses, airports, convention centers, and other locations where employees need to move around large areas.

# Role of Entrepreneurs

An *entrepreneur* is a profit-seeker who develops a new product or process and assumes the risk of profit or loss. The entrepreneur is the prime mover in the market economy—a visionary, someone who can see what others can't. The entrepreneur's role is to discover and introduce new and better products and more efficient ways of doing things. Because new products often involve long and costly development, they are risky. Entrepreneurs must have the confidence to accept that risk and must inspire confidence in others, such as resource suppliers and lenders. In short, *an entrepreneur comes up with an idea, turns that idea into a marketable product, accepts the risk of success or failure, and claims any resulting profit or loss.*

To learn more about the Segway™ Human Transporter, access the company's web site through

**econxtra.swlearning.com**

An entrepreneur goes into business to earn a profit by satisfying consumer wants. A business can consist simply of one self-employed person earning a few thousand dollars by mowing lawns during the summer. Or, a business can be as complex as General Motors, with 365,000 employees, factories around the world, and annual revenue of $200 billion. The lawn-mowing operation and General Motors are both businesses. There are about 25 million businesses in the United States. Most of these businesses consist of just one self-employed person. Most of these self-employed enterprises will remain tiny. A handful will become the largest businesses in the world.

### Entrepreneurs and Creative Change

The introduction of new or better products and new production methods are sources of technological progress and economic growth in the economy. Entrepreneurs initiate four types of creative changes in a market economy.

1. **Introduce New Products** Some entrepreneurs try to come up with new products, opening up markets that had not existed. For example, the Segway™ Human Transporter, a personal transport device, was developed by Dean Kamen and introduced in 2003. The product is marketed as an alternative to walking or riding a bicycle.

With some new products, entrepreneurs invent a whole new market, like the market for the Segway™ Human Transporter. Do you think this new product will succeed in the marketplace? Why or why not?

© Rick Friedman/CORBIS

**226      CHAPTER 8**   Businesses

---

*Outside Resources*

**Small Business Administration** The mission of the U.S. Small Business Administration is to "maintain and strengthen the nation's economy by aiding counseling, assisting, and protecting the interests of small businesses." In carrying out their mission, the SBA provides programs and resources for people who are considering starting a business. The SBA web site at www.sba.gov covers topics such as startup basics, business planning, finance, legal issues, taxes, and employees. Instruct students to visit this web site and investigate its offerings. Ask students whether the information on the web site might encourage them to or dissuade them from starting a business of their own some time in the future.

**2. Improve Quality of Existing Products** Some entrepreneurs begin with an existing product and make it better. For example, Howard Schultz took the simple cup of coffee and turned it into liquid gold by offering higher quality and greater variety in a more inviting atmosphere. Founded by Schultz in 1985, Starbucks Coffee now is a multibillion-dollar operation with more than 70,000 employees in thousands of locations around the world.

**3. Introduce New Production Methods** Some entrepreneurs combine resources more efficiently to reduce production costs. They use less costly materials, employ better technology, or combine resources in more economical ways. Henry Ford, for example, introduced the assembly line, where automobiles move along a conveyer and the workers stay put. Ford didn't invent the automobile, but his assembly line made owning one affordable to millions of households.

**4. Introduce New Ways of Doing Business** Some entrepreneurs step outside existing business models to create a new way of doing business. For example, Michael Dell began in 1984 with $1,000 and the idea to sell computers directly to customers rather than through retailers. His made-to-order computers are sold by phone and over the Internet. Dell is now the largest computer seller in the world, with sales exceeding $50 million *a day*. Mary Kay Ash did the same for skin care products and cosmetics, selling $2 billion a year directly to consumers around the world through independent Mary Kay consultants.

### Financing the Business

A good idea in itself does not guarantee profit. To succeed, entrepreneurs must figure out how best to transform their ideas into reality. They must acquire the necessary resources, including hiring employees and buying supplies. They also must obtain **financial capital**, that is, the money needed to start or expand the business.

## THE WALL STREET JOURNAL

● **Reading It Right** What's the relevance of the following statement from *The Wall Street Journal:* "The new activity in certain technologies reminds some industry observers of past investment bubbles, where eager venture capitalists piled too much money into supposedly hot technologies, only to see most investments fizzle."

Financial capital may be obtained through bank loans or from *venture capitalists*—individuals or companies that specialize in financing start-up firms. Entrepreneurs also often draw from their own savings to invest in the new enterprise. Some even sell all they own to get the business off the ground. For example, the filmmaker Michael Moore sold all his possessions to finance his first documentary film, *Roger and Me.* To accept such risks, entrepreneurs must have confidence in their ideas.

**Ask the Xpert!**
econxtra.swlearning.com

*How do businesses raise cash to finance startups and expansions?*

**financial capital**
Money needed to start or expand a business

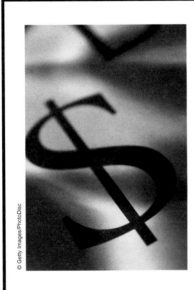

© Getty Images/PhotoDisc

**Describe the ways in which entrepreneurs may obtain financial capital for their business.**

Lesson 8.1 • *Entrepreneurs*    **227**

**TEACH**    (continued)

### Role of Entrepreneurs
Explain to students that in the 1960s, fast-food restaurants spread rapidly across the nation, often replacing small lunch-counter restaurants that cooked to order. Ask students to discuss changes in production methods that took place during this time and what such changes had to do with entrepreneurship. What changes in the American lifestyle brought about this transformation in how restaurant food is produced? (Over the last few decades, many Americans have chosen to use less time to eat. Restaurants that took more than a few minutes to supply food often could not compete for these customers. Entrepreneurs who were able to direct production to supply meals quickly were in a much better position to compete in the marketplace because they satisfied consumers' desires.)

**Ask the Xpert!**

Direct students to **econxtra.swlearning.com** to hear an expert answer the question "How do businesses raise cash to finance start-ups and expansions?"

## THE WALL STREET JOURNAL

● **Reading It Right**

Invite a student to explain the relevance of the statement from *The Wall Street Journal* that appears on this page.

**Answer**
Answers will vary. Possible answer: The statement is relevant because it indicates that there are risks involved in financing businesses.

**ENRICH**

In an attempt to better meet the mobility needs of people with disabilities, Independence Technology, a Johnson & Johnson company, introduced the iBOT™ Mobility System. This mobility device uses sensors, gyroscopes, and electric motors to climb stairs and even stand upright on two wheels. The price tag for the iBOT was $29,000 in 2003. Ask students to research the technology and entrepreneurial effort involved in bringing it to market. Suggest that they search the Internet to find more information about this innovative product. To learn more about iBOT before you assign this activity, visit www.independencenow.com.

## Role of Entrepreneurs

Display a pair of inline skates or a picture of the skates. Explain that prior to 1980, this product was not available to consumers in most parts of the market. Inline skates were produced and used by a few individuals, but there was no large production. Then a few entrepreneurs took the risk to produce and mass market this product. At first there were few producers, so consumers had relatively few products to choose from. As these firms enjoyed growing sales and good profits, many new entrepreneurs entered the market. As a result, consumers had more products to choose from, and prices for the products fell. Ask students to explain how this example demonstrates that entrepreneurship benefits consumers.

### Think Critically Through Visuals

Direct students to focus their attention on the photographs on this page. Ask for a volunteer to explain how the photographs depict growth.

### Answer

Answers will vary. Possible answer: Investment in a factory and the training of people can raise future standards of living. The first panel depicts a worker on a construction project, the second illustrates training, and the third shows a couple moving to a new home.

### NCEE
### Standard 15: Growth

Investment in factories, machinery, new technology, and in the health, education, and training of people can raise future standards of living.

### CHECKPOINT

Invite a student to answer the checkpoint that appears on this page.

### Answer

The role of entrepreneurs is to be the prime movers in the market economy—that is, to be visionaries. They discover new and better products and more efficient ways of doing things.

## Profit Attracts Competitors

If an innovation succeeds in the market, many people benefit. The entrepreneur is rewarded with profit and the satisfaction of creating something of value. Workers are rewarded with more and better jobs. Consumers are rewarded with new and better products. The government benefits from higher tax revenue, which can be used to fund public goods and services or to lower other taxes. Overall the economy reaches a higher level of business activity. This translates into a higher standard of living for the people who live in the economy.

Entrepreneurs may earn profit in the short run. However, it is profit in the long run that attracts competitors and substitutes. Other businesses will enter the market and try to duplicate the success of the original entrepreneur. Competitors try to offer a better product or a lower price. Because these copycats must be creative and take risks, they, too, are entrepreneurs.

The original entrepreneur must fight to remain profitable in the long run.

Ultimately, the pursuit of profit can lead to a chain of events that creates new and better products, more competition, more production, higher quality, and lower prices. Entrepreneurs are the key players in a market economy. They supply the creative sparks that drive the economy forward.

If the new business loses money and has no prospects for a turnaround, this tells the entrepreneur to find a better use for the resources. Profits tell entrepreneurs they are on the right track. Losses tell them to change tracks. You could think of profits as a way of keeping score, a way of telling entrepreneurs whether they are winning or losing. When an entrepreneur wins, many others in the economy win as well. When an entrepreneur loses, it's mostly the entrepreneur who suffers.

### CHECKPOINT

Explain the role of entrepreneurs in a market economy.

**Main Idea** 💡 **Growth**

An entrepreneur's investment in a new business venture benefits the economy as a whole. The *investment leads to* a higher level of business activity, and ultimately to a *higher standard of living* for the people who live in the economy.

© Getty Images/PhotoDisc

**228**  **CHAPTER 8**  Businesses

### *Economic Headlines* ✒

Instruct students to locate an article in a newspaper or newsmagazine about some aspect of entrepreneurship. For example, they might find an article about a local entrepreneur or a resource for entrepreneurs. Ask students to write a paragraph summarizing the article and drawing a connection to this lesson. Consider asking students to attach a copy of the original article along with a properly formatted reference citation.

# Who Isn't an Entrepreneur?

Some people may carry out just one of the functions of an entrepreneur. For example, they may dream up a new product or process, they may manage resources, or they may assume the risk of success or failure. Carrying out just one of the roles alone does not make you an entrepreneur, however. A way of determining more about who is an entrepreneur is to learn more about people in business who are not entrepreneurs.

## Invention, Innovation, and Entrepreneurs

**Innovation** is the process of turning an invention into a marketable product. Inventors are entrepreneurs if they bear the risk of success or failure. Most inventors work for firms as paid employees. For example, corporations such as Pfizer, Dow Chemical, or Intel employ thousands of scientists to improve existing products and develop new ones. These corporate inventors, sometimes referred to as *intrapreneurs*, are paid even in years when their creative juices slow down. Because these hired inventors take no more risks than most other employees, they are not considered to be entrepreneurs.

Figure 8.1 shows the source of inventions since 1980 as measured by U.S. patents awarded. The number of patents more than doubled from 1980 to 2000. The number of patents awarded to individuals fell from 22 percent to only 14 percent, however. Some of these individual inventors are in the business of inventing new products and selling the idea to others. These inventors accept risks in a way that the inventors working for corporations do not. Therefore, individual inventors usually are entrepreneurs.

## Managers and Entrepreneurs

Most entrepreneurs do more than simply sell their good ideas to others. They try to bring their ideas to the market by paying resource owners for the right to control these resources in the businesses. Then they claim any profit or loss that results. This right to control resources does not necessarily mean the entrepreneur must manage the firm. The entrepreneur does have the power to hire and fire the manager.

For example, Dean Kamen, inventor

*innovation*
The process of turning an invention into a marketable product

---

### Source of U.S. Patents Awarded for Inventions by Year

Figure 8.1

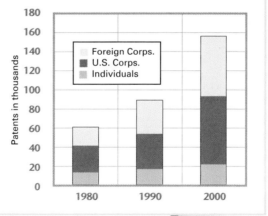

The number of patents grew from 61,800 in 1980 to 157,500 in 2000. In 1980, 22 percent of all patents were awarded to individuals. By 2000, only 14 percent went to individuals.

Source: U.S. Bureau of the Census, *Statistical Abstract of the United States*, 2001.

Legend:
- Foreign Corps.
- U.S. Corps.
- Individuals

Patents in thousands: 0, 20, 40, 60, 80, 100, 120, 140, 160, 180
Years: 1980, 1990, 2000

---

## TEACH

### Who Isn't an Entrepreneur?
Explain that most people who hold jobs and produce goods or services are employees rather than entrepreneurs. Entrepreneurs direct production. They finance it and take the risks of success or failure. Ask several students to describe their after-school jobs. Have the class determine whether they are employees or entrepreneurs. It is possible that some may be entrepreneurs. For example, a student who has a paper route is likely to be an entrepreneur because this person is free to determine exactly how to deliver the papers. He or she may ride a bicycle, walk, or use a skateboard.

### *Think Critically Through Visuals*
Direct students to focus on **Figure 8.1—Source of U.S. Patents Awarded for Inventions by Year.** Ask students to explain why the percentage of patents awarded to individuals has gone down since 1980. (Students should recognize that many inventors are employees of corporations.)

### SPAN THE GLOBE
Direct students to read the short passage "Are We Deporting Our Future?" that appears on page 230. Use the questions at the bottom of the feature as a starting point for class discussion or have students write a short essay to answer the questions.

### Answers to Think Critically
Answers will vary. Students should explain their point of view and give examples.

---

## *Group Activity*

Organize students into small groups and ask each group to construct a sentence outline for the steps involved in starting a new business. Outlines should identify the product they want to produce, the amount and types of resources they need, the number of workers they need to employ, the amount of money they must invest, their method of marketing the product, etc.

In addition to turning in an outline, ask each group to convert their outline to a slide presentation using computer software such as PowerPoint or Freelance Graphics.

**CHECKPOINT**
Invite a student to answer the checkpoint that appears on this page.

**Answer**

Managers and stockholders perform part of the entrepreneur's role. Managers run the business for entrepreneurs, while stockholders, through the purchasing of stock, share with the entrepreneur some of the risk of the company's success or failure.

## APPLY

Assign Lesson 8.1 from the Contemporary Economics Workbook.

## ASSESS

Assign all or part of Lesson 8.1 Assessment on page 231 as homework or an in-class activity.

## Xtra! Study Tools

Direct students to the online study tools for Lesson 8.1 at **econxtra.swlearning.com**.

## CLOSE

**Revisit** the In the News feature on the first page of the lesson. Ask students to review their preliminary answers and discuss the questions, now that they have completed this lesson.

**Review** the objectives for Lesson 8.1. Students should be able to:

• Understand the role of the entrepreneur in a market economy.

• Differentiate entrepreneurs from people who perform a limited entrepreneurial role.

---

of the Segway personal transporter, created a company to make and sell his invention. Kamen also hired a chief executive officer to run the business. Even though he doesn't run the business himself, Kamen still is an entrepreneur

## SPAN THE GLOBE

### Are We Deporting Our Future?

Have events since the September 11, 2001, terrorist attacks made the United States hostile to newcomers? By withdrawing the welcome mat, will we suffer the loss of much-needed skills and energetic entrepreneurial spirit? Both the public and the government have overreacted in some cases: A Sikh gas-station owner from India was murdered by a crazed revenge seeker. A high-tech company executive was yanked from a routine commercial flight and questioned because, though he was actually a peaceful Hindu from India wearing $500 shoes and a $4,000 suit, he looked suspicious. More than a third of Silicon Valley's software engineers have emigrated from India. If the United States discourages the influx of professionals from this area, will the Valley and the nation as a whole suffer as a result? For many years, the United States was a haven for talented people seeking a safe and inviting home to pursue their professional passions. However, the professional climate for immigrants has changed dramatically. Entrepreneurs around the world are getting the message that foreigners who even remotely fit the terrorist profile no longer are welcome in the United States, no matter how talented they are. Paul Saffo, Director of the Institute for the Future, says, "We can't afford to deport our future. Our country cannot sustain the technology sector without brilliant minds from all over the planet. If we stay on our current path, we will enjoy an illusory sense of security, but it will come at the cost of strangling the nation's technological and economic future."

### Think Critically

Do you think Mr. Saffo's concern is justified? Why or why not?

**230**     **CHAPTER 8**   Businesses

---

because he has the power to hire and fire the manager. Kamen's chief executive officer is a well-paid employee, but he is not an entrepreneur.

### Stockholders and Entrepreneurs

More than half of all households in the United States—over 50,000,000 of them—now own corporate stock. If a corporation fails, stockholders could lose the amount they paid for that particular stock. If the corporation thrives, the stock value will increase and stockholders will benefit.

People buy a corporation's stock because they believe in the managers' ability to increase the value of the business. They think the managers can make more profitable use of their funds than they themselves can. At the same time, the stockholders assume the risk of the company's success or failure. Does this make the stockholders entrepreneurs? No, it does not. True entrepreneurs do more than take the risk of success or failure. They decide what to produce and usually figure out how to produce it profitably. Stockholders, on the other hand, usually have little say in the firm's operation.

**CHECKPOINT**
What groups perform part of the entrepreneur's role but are not considered entrepreneurs?

---

## RETEACH

*Entrepreneur* magazine is a monthly publication available at many libraries and on the Internet at www.entrepreneur.com. Instruct students to read an article from this magazine that describes an entrepreneur who runs a successful business. Ask students to identify actions that the person took to become successful. These might include finding a better way to produce something, inventing a new good or service, or improving the quality of an existing product. Ask students to review the risks this person took and the rewards he or she is likely to receive.
Instruct students to use the information they gather to create a poster or fact sheet. They should use the content of this lesson as a guide.

## Key Concepts

1. Which of the following describes an entrepreneur? (a) a person employed to mow lawns by a landscaping firm or (b) a person who buys a lawn mower to cut her neighbor's lawn for $20. Explain your answer.

2. What creative changes have fast-food restaurant owners used to distinguish their products from similar products offered by other firms?

3. Why aren't entrepreneurs likely to earn large profits from their businesses for many years?

4. Why wasn't the Bell Labs employee who invented the first transistor an entrepreneur?

5. What role do entrepreneurs play in the U.S. economy?

## Graphing Exercise

6. Many entrepreneurs begin their businesses by inventing a product and then patenting it. Construct a bar graph from the data in the table that concerns patents granted by the federal government. What does your graph show about the number of inventions that are being made by individuals and corporations? Why are only some of these inventions examples of entrepreneurship?

**Patents Granted by the Federal Government, 1980–2000**

| Year | Patents Granted to Individuals | Patents Granted to U.S. Corporations |
|------|-------------------------------|--------------------------------------|
| 1980 | 13,800 | 27,700 |
| 1985 | 12,900 | 31,200 |
| 1990 | 17,300 | 36,100 |
| 1995 | 17,400 | 44,000 |
| 2000 | 22,400 | 70,900 |

Source: U.S. Bureau of the Census, *Statistical Abstract of the United States*, 2001, p. 494.

## Think Critically

7. **History** Review an American history textbook to identify a historical figure who was an important entrepreneur. Explain what this person did and the influence he or she had on the development of the United States.

8. **Marketing** Entrepreneurship may involve finding a new way to market an existing product. For example, Wal-Mart sells the same products as many other discount stores, but it is much more successful than most. What did Sam Walton do differently that made him a successful entrepreneur?

**Xtra!**
**Study Tools**
econxtra.swlearning.com

Lesson 8.1 • *Entrepreneurs* **231**

**8.1** *Assessment*

*Key Concepts*

1. The person who buys a lawnmower to cut her neighbor's lawn for $20 is an entrepreneur. The person who works for the landscaping firm has taken no risks, while the person who buys a lawnmower has.

2. Answers will vary. Possible answer: The owners of fast-food restaurants introduce new production methods that allow them to offer products more quickly and at lower prices than other similar firms.

3. Answers will vary. Possible answer: A firm that is profitable will encourage other firms to compete with it. Over time, this will increase the supply of the product, lower the market price, and reduce the profits earned by the firm

4. Answers will vary. Possible answer: The inventor of the first transistor took no risk and did not attempt to produce or market his invention commercially.

5. Answers will vary. Possible answer: Entrepreneurs are responsible for developing many new products, creating additional jobs, and paying many of the taxes that allow our economy to grow and provide a better standard of living for all Americans.

*Graphing Exercise*

6. Answers will vary. Possible answers: The number of patents granted to corporations has grown more rapidly than the number granted to individuals. Those granted to individuals are more likely to be examples of entrepreneurship. Many inventions patented by corporations are made by employees rather than by entrepreneurs.

   A sample of an acceptable graph appears at the bottom of this page.

*Think Critically*

7. Answers will vary. Possible answer: Thomas Edison invented the electric light, which was successfully marketed and changed the way Americans live.

8. Answers will vary. Possible answer: Sam Walton created a store that consistently offers a wide selection of products at lower prices than its competitors. Consumers learned they could rely on his stores for quality products and low prices.

**Patents Granted by the Federal Government, 1980 to 2000**

*Visualizing the Answer—*
*Graphing Exercise*

6. The answer includes a graph. Students' graphs should look similar to the one shown here. An Excel spreadsheet containing this graph, along with supporting data, is available on the Instructor's Resource CD.

Ask students to explain what makes one entrepreneur succeed while many others fail. Is it a matter of having a better idea, a well-thought-out business plan, luck, or simply that she or he was willing to work harder and give up more? As students read about Roxanne Quirnby and Burt's Bees, have them identify the qualities that made this business a success.

## TEACH

Instruct students to read the **Movers & Shakers** feature about Roxanne Quimby. Point out that some students may find it helpful to read the article, read the questions at the bottom of the page, and then reread the article.

## ASSESS

Use the questions in Source Reading and Entrepreneurs in Action at the bottom of the profile to assess the students' understanding of this **Movers & Shakers** feature.

### Answers to Source Reading

Answers will vary. Possible answers: The focus on goal setting is vital. If she had focused solely on the big picture, developing a $50 million business, it would have been overwhelming. However, Roxanne's looking at it as smaller goals made achieving success more manageable and realistic.

### Answers to Entrepreneurs in Action

Answers will vary. Examples of plans for product development and ideas for handling growth include:
*Travel to flea markets*—Visit many flea markets all over the country so that a large portion of the market can be hit.
*Listen to your customers*—This will help develop a product that people want and that is in demand.
*Develop a web site*—This will enable you to target an even larger portion of the market (those who do not go to flea markets).

# movers & shakers

### Roxanne Quimby, *Burt's Bees*

Roxanne Quimby learned at a young age that hard work pays off. As a child, she worked with her grandmother selling sandwiches at a Boston beach. An immigrant from Siberia, her grandmother "demonstrated to me what it was like to start from nothing and make a living," Roxanne remembers. Roxanne tried her own hand at business early on. She began by selling homemade cookies, and later made and sold yarn dolls in her Massachusetts neighborhood.

By the early 1980s, Roxanne was the divorced mother of twins living in a cabin she built herself in Maine. She raised chickens and rabbits, and waited tables to support her family. That's when she met Burt Shavitz, her town's local beekeeper. Burt agreed to teach Roxanne about beekeeping if she would help him sell his honey. Before long, in addition to selling honey, Roxanne put her degree from the San Francisco Art Institute to use by making candles and furniture polish from the discarded beeswax. She traveled to flea markets and crafts fairs selling the products she and Burt created. In addition to selling, however, Roxanne spent a lot of time listening to her customers. She heard over and over that what they wanted was personal-care products made from natural ingredients.

Soon Roxanne stopped selling furniture polish and began to make and sell new personal-care items. To accommodate the changes, she and Burt moved their operation from Roxanne's kitchen to an old bowling alley. Within a year their small company needed more room, and they relocated again. By 1992, Burt's Bees was manufacturing about half a million beeswax candles a year along with personal-care items. By 1994, Burt's Bees' sales totaled $3 million.

As their business once again outgrew its walls, Burt and Roxanne decided to move the company to North Carolina, home to numerous cosmetics manufacturers. Although in favor of moving the company, Burt opted to remain in Maine, taking a lesser role in the company. A few years later he sold his share of Burt's Bees to Roxanne, leaving Roxanne solely in charge of the ever-growing company.

Today 120 employees work at Burt's Bees headquarters in Raleigh, North Carolina. They make more than 150 products, including lip color, facial creams, hair products, natural remedies, and specialty items for men and for babies. Most of Burt's Bees' products are 100 percent natural, harvested from nature. All of the products contain only natural colors and natural preservatives. They are sold in retail stores, online, and through the mail.

Roxanne keeps her business growing by setting daily, weekly, and monthly goals. "Sometimes I don't know how I'm going to reach them, but it's important to set them. People tend to get bogged down in the process [of setting goals], but that's backwards," she states. Her first goal was sales of $10,000 a year. In 2002, her goal was sales of $50 million. Keeping a focus on the customer is her means of reaching her goals. "I call myself a media junkie. Keeping abreast of what's happening gives you a clear understanding of what your customer is all about," she says.

### SOURCE READING
Re-read Roxanne Quimby's comments about setting goals. How important do you think her focus on goal setting was to the success of Burt's Bees? Explain your answer.

### ENTREPRENEURS IN ACTION
Imagine you are Roxanne Quimby and selling beeswax candles at flea markets. Write a business plan that would incorporate each of the steps she took from that point forward to become a successful entrepreneur. Include plans for product development and ideas for handling growth.

232      **CHAPTER 8** Businesses

## Extend the Content

Many businesses in your community are privately owned franchises. As franchisees, the owners of these firms have limited control over their businesses. They must follow a basic business plan set forth by the franchiser and sell only products approved by the franchiser. Invite the owner of a local franchise business to speak to your class. Ask the speaker to explain the process of purchasing and operating a franchise. Encourage the speaker to share the ups and downs of being a franchisee. Prepare for the guest speaker by sharing the speaker's name and identifying the business. Ask students to prepare some questions they would like to ask after the presentation.

## 8.2 Sole Proprietorships and Partnerships

### Objectives

> Describe the advantages and disadvantages of sole proprietorships.

> Describe the advantages and disadvantages of partnerships.

### Overview

Entrepreneurs make all kinds of decisions when they start a business. One of the first is to decide how to organize the firm. What form of business would work best? Entrepreneurs may organize their firm in one of three ways: as a sole proprietorship, a partnership, or a corporation. Each type has its advantages and disadvantages. Sole proprietorships and partnerships are the easiest business forms to start, but they each also present a great deal of risk for the business owner.

### Key Terms

sole proprietorship

liability

partnership

general partnership

limited partnership

---

## [ In the News ]

### Tougher Bankruptcy Laws

A major disadvantage of the sole proprietorship form of business is unlimited personal liability for any loss. If a business goes bankrupt, the owner may have to draw on personal savings or sell personal assets in order to pay the business's debts. Under a measure recently approved by the U.S. House of Representatives, debtors who file for bankruptcy would not be protected from as many bills as they are under current law. The new legislation would make it much more difficult for bankruptcy filers to completely eliminate unpaid balances, even after liquidating their assets. The new law also would require bankruptcy filers to take a means test. They might also be subjected to an in-depth investigation to determine if they have additional resources that could be used to pay off more of their debt. Credit card companies, banks, and retailers have applied their top lobbyists to push for this new legislation. The legislation's supporters argue that there are widespread abuses under the former bankruptcy laws. They also argue that these abuses are the main reason for rising interest rates on both business and consumer credit. Opponents argue that the bill will only serve to make people and businesses in trouble even more desperate, especially in a weak economy. They say it will provide greater profits to the credit industry without reducing the interest rates charged.

### Think About It

How would the new legislation and its harsher treatment of bankruptcy filers affect owners of small businesses, and the economy itself?

◄ I ►

233

---

### National Content Standards in Economics

A complete list of the NCEE Standards appears on pages xxiv–xxv of this book. The following standards are addressed in Lesson 8.2.

Standard 4: Role of Incentives

Standard 10: Role of Economic Institutions

Standard 14: Profit and the Entrepreneur

Standard 15: Growth

Standard 16: Role of Government

---

## FOCUS

### 8.2 Sole Proprietorships and Partnerships

Point out that the great majority of businesses in the United States are sole proprietorships. Ask students to identify types of businesses that they could reasonably hope to own one day. What characteristics do these businesses share? It is likely that they all will require relatively small amounts of money and expertise to operate. Most of them will be centered on providing a service rather than producing a good. Businesses that require more financial capital are most often organized as corporations.

### Objectives

Remind students to read the lesson objectives to help focus their attention before reading the lesson.

### Key Terms

Direct students to look up key terms in a business or economics dictionary. Some students will find it helpful to read another definition. In addition to a definition, many entries will include a brief explanation and an example.

### [ In the News ]

Instruct students to read the passage and write down their answers. Point out that their answers might change after they finish studying Lesson 8.2.

### Answers to Think About It

Answers will vary. Possible answer: The proposed new legislation would make it even riskier for people to start small businesses. Because of the increased risk, entrepreneurs will be more resistant to starting businesses. Fewer small businesses will result in a slowdown of the economy.

### Visual Presentation

Use the PowerPoint presentation on the Instructor's Resource CD as an adjunct to your lecture. The presentation also can be used for review.

---

## Sole Proprietorship

Remind students that almost all entrepreneurs start their first business as a sole proprietorship. This is no accident. Students will learn that there are both advantages and disadvantages of this, and other, forms of business organization. But the advantages of starting a sole proprietorship for new entrepreneurs almost always outweigh any disadvantages.

### *Think Critically Through Visuals*

Direct students to focus on Figure 8.2—Distribution of Sole Proprietorships Based on Annual Sales and by Industry. Instruct students to look at the largest (blue) and smallest (yellow) slices of the pie chart on the left. Point out that most sole proprietors, 68 percent, earn $25,000 or less per year. Only 0.4 percent have yearly earnings of $1,000,000 or more. Ask students to direct their attention to the largest (orange) and smallest (purple) slices of the pie chart on the right. Point out that almost half the sole proprietorships are service businesses and that less than 0.2 percent are manufacturing concerns.

**sole proprietorship**

The simplest form of business organization; a firm that is owned and managed by one person, but sometimes hires other workers

# Sole Proprietorship

The simplest form of business organization is the **sole proprietorship**, where a firm is owned and managed by a single individual. That person, the sole proprietor, earns all the firm's profits and is responsible for all the firm's losses. Although some sole proprietorships have many employees, most do not. Most have just one self-employed individual. *A self-employed person is not considered to be a paid employee.*

## Who Is a Sole Proprietor?

The majority of businesses in your community are owned by sole proprietors. These include self-employed plumbers, farmers, hair stylists, truckers, lawyers, doctors, and dentists. Most sole proprietorships consist of just one self-employed person. A self-employed person may work at the business all the time throughout the year, or only part of the year, or part-time. For example, most self-employed farmers hold other jobs that are their primary occupations.

About three quarters of all businesses in the United States are owned by sole proprietors. There were about 19 million sole proprietorships in 2000. Because this type of business is typically small, however, sole proprietorships generate only 5 percent of all U.S. business sales.

Figure 8.2 shows the distribution of sole proprietorships based on firm revenue and based on the industry in which the business operates. You can see in the pie chart on the left that nearly all sole proprietorships are small. About two thirds reported annual sales, or revenue, of less than $25,000. Only 0.4 percent had sales of $1 million or more.

The pie chart on the right in Figure 8.2 shows the industry breakdown of sole proprietors. Nearly half provide services, such as health services and business services. About one in ten works in agriculture.

## Advantages of Sole Proprietorships

The sole proprietorship is the most common type of business for a reason. It offers several advantages.

**1. Easy to Start** A sole proprietorship is easy to start. This form involves minimum red tape and legal expense.

 **Figure 8.2**

### Distribution of Sole Proprietorships Based on Annual Sales and by Industry

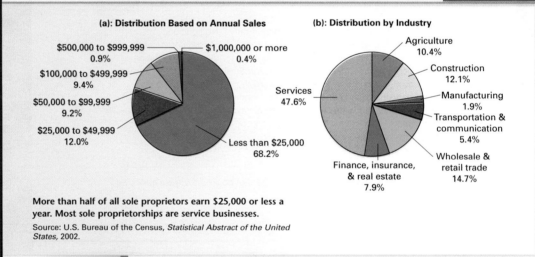

**(a): Distribution Based on Annual Sales**

- $500,000 to $999,999 — 0.9%
- $100,000 to $499,999 — 9.4%
- $50,000 to $99,999 — 9.2%
- $25,000 to $49,999 — 12.0%
- $1,000,000 or more — 0.4%
- Less than $25,000 — 68.2%

**(b): Distribution by Industry**

- Agriculture 10.4%
- Construction 12.1%
- Manufacturing 1.9%
- Transportation & communication 5.4%
- Wholesale & retail trade 14.7%
- Finance, insurance, & real estate 7.9%
- Services 47.6%

More than half of all sole proprietors earn $25,000 or less a year. Most sole proprietorships are service businesses.

Source: U.S. Bureau of the Census, *Statistical Abstract of the United States,* 2002.

**234    CHAPTER 8   Businesses**

### *Outside Resources*

**CCH Business Owner's Toolkit™** This resource bills itself as "total know-how for small business." Ask students to visit www.toolkit.cch.com and click on link "Starting Your Business." Suggest that students spend about 15 minutes exploring this site. Instruct them to write down five interesting facts, ideas, or tips they found on the web site.
Organize students into small groups for a brief discussion of what they learned. Invite a spokesperson from each group to share the group's findings with the class.

A sole proprietor might need to secure a local business license and a permit to collect state or local sales taxes.

**2. Few Government Regulations** Once established, a sole proprietorship faces relatively few government regulations beyond maintaining accurate tax records and complying with employment laws. As noted, most sole proprietors have no employees.

**3. Complete Control** The sole proprietor is the boss, with complete authority over all business decisions, such as what to produce, what resources to hire, and how to combine these resources.

**4. Owner Keeps All Profit** The sole proprietor does not have to share profits with anyone.

**5. Lower Taxes** Income from a sole proprietorship is taxed only once as the owner's personal income. As you will learn later, corporate income is taxed twice.

**6. Pride of Ownership** Creating a successful business and watching it grow can provide a sole proprietor tremendous satisfaction.

## Disadvantages of Sole Proprietorships

There are also some significant disadvantages of sole proprietorships, when compared to other forms of business.

**1. Unlimited Personal Liability** A sole proprietor faces unlimited personal liability for any loss. **Liability** is the legal obligation to pay any debts of the business. Sole proprietors are personally responsible for paying all their business debts. If the business goes bankrupt or is sued, the owner is personally responsible. He or she may have to draw from personal savings or sell personal assets, such as a home or automobile.

**2. Difficulty Raising Financial Capital** Because the sole proprietor has no partners or other financial backers, raising enough money to get the business going can be a problem. Banks

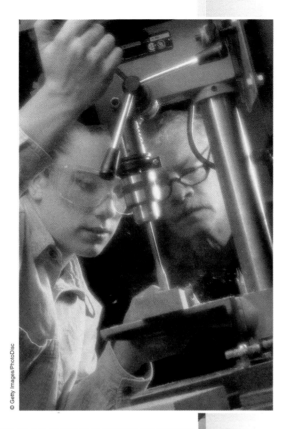
© Getty Images/PhotoDisc

Only about 2 percent of sole proprietorships are manufacturing companies. Why do you think this number is so small?

are reluctant to lend money to a new business with no track record and few assets. Even a sole proprietorship that's been around for a while may seem risky to lenders.

**3. Limited Life** With a sole proprietorship, the business and the owner are one and the same. The business ends when the owner dies or leaves the business. The firm's assets can be sold or turned over to someone else, who may restart the business. The result is a new firm with new ownership.

*liability*
The legal obligation to pay any debts of the business

### Sole Proprietorship

Ask students to identify some local businesses that are likely organized as sole proprietorships. Write the business names on the board and then ask students to categorize the businesses, using the industries shown in Figure 8.2.

*Think Critically Through Visuals*

Direct students to focus their attention on the photograph on this page. Ask for a volunteer to answer the question posed in the caption.

### Answer

Answers will vary. Possible answer: This number is so small because starting a manufacturing company usually requires significant capital investment and labor. It is difficult for one individual to supply both of these things without partners or investors.

Lesson 8.2 • *Sole Proprietorships and Partnerships* **235**

## ENRICH

Tell students that each one of them has inherited $50,000 to use to start a business. Ask them to identify a type of business they believe could be started with this amount of liquid capital. Have them write an essay explaining why it would be easier and quicker to start this business as a sole proprietorship than as a partnership. What advantages would this type of business organization offer them in their chosen business? What limitations might they face?

## Sole Proprietorship

Show students a photograph of a person operating a business as a street vendor. The person might be selling wristwatches, scarves, or pushing a cart of hot pretzels. Ask students to list the reasons that such an entrepreneur is almost certainly operating as a sole proprietor. What advantages does this type of organization offer the entrepreneur? (Relatively little money and expertise is required to start this type of business. It is easy to organize, and there is no need to share responsibilities or profits with others. Sole proprietors can also leave this type of business quickly if it is not successful.)

### ✓ CHECKPOINT

Invite a student to answer the checkpoint that appears on this page.

### Answer

*Advantages*
1. Easy to start
2. Few government regulations
3. Complete control
4. Owner keeps all profits
5. Lower taxes
6. Pride of ownership

*Disadvantages*
1. Unlimited personal liability
2. Difficulty raising financial capital
3. Limited life
4. Difficulty finding and keeping good workers
5. Unlimited responsibility

---

*partnership*
Two or more people agree to contribute resources to the business in return for a share of the profit

4. **Difficulty Finding and Keeping Good Workers** Because of its lack of permanence and difficulty raising financial capital, sole proprietors have trouble offering workers the job security and opportunity for advancement available in larger businesses. Therefore, a sole proprietorship may have difficulty attracting and retaining talented employees.

5. **Unlimited Responsiblity** Sole proprietors shoulder a great deal of responsibility. They must manage the firm, maintain financial records, oversee production, market the product, keep up with competition, and perform dozens of other tasks. It is not likely that one person can do all of these things well. However, small firms typically cannot afford to hire experts to carry out these functions. This may lead to long work days—and a lot of stress—for the sole proprietor.

### ✓ CHECKPOINT

What are the advantages and disadvantages of sole proprietorships?

---

# Partnerships

Another relatively simple form of business organization is the **partnership**, which involves two or more individuals who agree to contribute resources to the business in return for a share of the profit. A partnership sometimes consists of one person who is talented at running the business and one or more who supply the money needed to get the business going. In 2000, there were about 2 million partnerships in the United States. They accounted for about 8 percent of all businesses and about 8 percent of all business sales.

Law, accounting, real estate, and medical partnerships typify this business form. Figure 8.3 shows the distribution of partnerships by annual revenue on the left, and by industry on the right. More than half of all partnerships had annual sales of less than $25,000. Only 5.6 percent had sales of $1 million or more. About half of all partnerships are in finance, insurance, or real estate. Though not shown in the pie chart, real-estate firms alone

---

**Distribution of Partnerships Based on Annual Sales and Industry** | **Figure 8.3**

**(a): Distribution Based on Annual Sales**

- $500,000 to $999,999 — 4.0%
- $100,000 to $499,999 — 16.7%
- $50,000 to $99,999 — 11.3%
- $25,000 to $49,999 — 8.2%
- $1,000,000 or more — 5.6%
- Less than $25,000 — 54.2%

**(b): Distribution by Industry**

- Services — 17.6%
- Agriculture — 15.1%
- Construction — 6.3%
- Manufacturing — 1.7%
- Transportation & communication — 6.5%
- Wholesale & retail trade — 2.0%
- Finance, insurance, & real estate — 50.8%

Most partnerships had annual sales of less than $25,000. About half of all partnerships are in finance, insurance, or real estate.

Source: U.S. Bureau of the Census, *Statistical Abstract of the United States*, 2002.

---

**236** **CHAPTER 8** Businesses

---

### *Economic Headlines*

Instruct students to locate an article in a newspaper or newsmagazine about the business operations of a sole proprietorship or partnership. Ask students to write a paragraph summarizing the article and drawing a connection to this lesson. Consider asking students to attach a copy of the original article along with a properly formatted reference citation.

As an alternative, you can have students summarize pre-selected articles. You can either give students copies of the articles or you can have them find the articles based on reference citations you provide.

account for about 40 percent of all partnerships.

## Types of Partnerships

There are two broad categories of partnerships: general partnerships and limited partnerships. Each divides responsibilities and liabilities differently.

### General Partnerships

The most common type of partnership is the **general partnership**, where partners share both in the responsibility for running the business and in any liability from its operation. Professional groups such as doctors, lawyers, and accountants often form general partnerships.

### Limited Partnerships

With a **limited partnership**, at least one partner is required to be a general partner. General partners manage the business and have unlimited personal liability for the partnership. The other partners don't manage the business. Their contribution is strictly financial. The most they can lose is the amount they have invested in the firm. Because their liability is limited, they are called *limited* partners. A limited partnership can have any number of limited partners.

## Advantages of Partnerships

Partnerships offer several advantages.

1. **Easy to Start** As with the sole proprietorship, partnerships are easy to start. The partners need only agree on how they will share business responsibilities, rewards, and losses. Some partnerships are formed with articles of partnership, a legal agree-

*general partnership*

Partners share both in the responsibility of running the business and in any liability from its operation

*limited partnership*

At least one general partner runs the business and bears unlimited personal liability; other partners provide financial capital but have limited liability

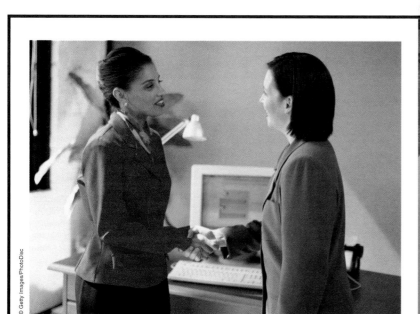

In a general partnership with two partners, both are responsible for running the business and for any liability that results from its operation. If you were to start a business, would you rather be a partner or a sole proprietor? Give reasons for your answer.

Lesson 8.2 • *Sole Proprietorships and Partnerships* **237**

## TEACH

### Partnerships

Partnerships are formed by two or more people who agree to share the responsibilities and risks of operating a business. The fact that this is the least common of the three major types of business organization in the United States is telling. This must mean that for many entrepreneurs, the disadvantages of this form of business organization outweigh its advantages, at least in comparison to those offered by other forms of business organization entrepreneurs may choose.

#### *Think Critically Through Visuals*

Direct students to focus on **Figure 8.3—Distribution of Partnerships Based on Annual Sales and Industry.** Instruct students to look at the largest (blue) and smallest (green) slices of the pie chart on the left. Point out that most partnerships, 54 percent, earn $25,000 or less per year. Only 0.4 percent have yearly earnings of $1,000,000 or more. Ask students to direct their attention to the largest (blue) and smallest (purple) slices of the pie chart on the right. Point out that almost half the partnerships are involved in finance, insurance, and real estate. Less than 0.2 percent are manufacturing concerns.

#### *Think Critically Through Visuals*

Direct students to focus their attention on the photograph on this page. Ask for a volunteer to answer the question posed in the caption.

#### Answer

Answers will vary. Possible answer: I would rather be a partner so I could share the start-up costs, liability, and responsibility with another individual.

### TEAM WORK

Organize students into groups of four or five. Instruct teams to select a recorder and a spokesperson. Instruct students to complete the **Team Work** activity that appears on page 238. Set a timer for 10 minutes. When the timer goes off, invite the spokesperson from each group to take a turn providing the evidence collected.

### *Group Activity*

Organize students into groups of five. Tell the members of each group that they have formed a partnership that sells computers. Each person has a different responsibility in the business. One keeps the books. Another makes sure parts and computers are in stock. A third oversees repairs, while a fourth is in charge of sales. The last person does advertising. Each person feels overworked. The firm has enough money to hire one employee. Everyone wants to hire someone to help with his or her job. Ask the students to explain why it is hard for partnerships to make quick decisions.

## Partnerships

Ask students to identify some local businesses that are likely organized as partnerships. Write the business names on the board, and then ask students to categorize the businesses, using the industries shown in Figure 8.3.

## E-CONOMICS

Direct students to read the passage entitled "Partnering for Start-Ups" on page 239.

### Answers to Think Critically

The major disadvantages to the entrepreneur and her associates are that they will have to share decision making on business issues and share profits.

### *Think Critically Through Visuals*

Direct students to focus their attention on the photograph on page 239. Ask for a volunteer to answer the question posed in the caption.

### Answer

Answers will vary. Possible answer: To avoid arguments, potential partners should map out how they would like to see the business run. By doing this before the business starts, they can make sure they share a common vision and can decide how disputes will be handled.

---

ment spelling out each partner's rights and responsibilities. In most states, partnerships that do not have their own agreement are governed by the Uniform Partnership Act (UPA), which established partnership rules.

2. **Few Government Regulations** Once the partnership has begun operating, it faces relatively few government regulations. Like the sole proprietorship, the partnership must maintain accurate tax records and comply with employment laws.

3. **Shared Decision Making and Increased Specialization** A sole proprietor makes all key business decisions. But general partners usually share decision-making responsibilities. On average there were about 8 partners per partnership in 2000. By discussing important decisions, partners may make better decisions than a sole proprietor can make alone. By relying on the different skills of each partner, general partnerships also may be more efficient than sole proprietors. For example, one partner may be good at dealing with the public while another excels at record keeping and paperwork.

4. **Greater Ability to Raise Financial Capital** Partnerships often find it easier than sole proprietors to raise the financial capital needed to get a business going. First, the partners themselves can come up with money

from their own sources, such as a savings account. Second, banks may be more willing to lend money to a partnership than to a sole proprietor. With a partnership, the loans are backed by the promise and property of each partner.

5. **More Able to Attract and Retain Workers** Compared to sole proprietors, partnerships offer employees more opportunities for advancement. For example, a partnership can make a key employee, such as a promising lawyer or accountant, a partner. A partnership typically is more able to attract and retain talented workers than is a sole proprietorship.

6. **Lower Taxes** Partners pay personal income taxes on their share of partnership income. The partnership itself does not have to pay a separate tax, as does the corporation.

### Disadvantages of Partnerships

There also are disadvantages to partnerships. Some of these drawbacks are the same as for sole proprietorships.

1. **Unlimited Personal Liability** In a general partnership, each partner is personally responsible for paying all business debts. If the business fails or is sued, the partners may have to draw from personal savings or sell personal assets, such as a home, to pay debts. This means one partner could lose it all because of another's blunder. In a limited partnership, the limited partners have less liability than the general partners. Their liability for the firm's debts and losses is limited to the amount of capital they have invested.

2. **Limited Life of the Business** A partnership has no life of its own, independent of the partners. The partnership ends when one partner dies or leaves the business. A new partnership can be formed to continue the business, but the transition could be tricky. A partnership might end even if remaining partners would like it to continue.

## TEAM WORK

Divide into small groups. Your group is starting a general partnership. Decide the type of business your partnership will run. Then decide the area of responsibility each team member will handle. Match each member's strengths and interests with the tasks to be done.

---

### *Curriculum Connection—English*

Ask students to write a report or create a multimedia presentation about a successful American business leader, inventor, or entrepreneur. Encourage students to choose an unfamiliar subject. Instruct students to highlight the subject's successes and failures as they relate to the content of this chapter.

Consider offering students suggestions, including any of the following people:

| | | |
|---|---|---|
| Wally Amos | Ruth Handler | Harriet Williams Russell Strong |
| Clarence Birdseye | Conrad Hilton | Nikola Tesla |
| Frank Braniff | Stephanie Kwolek | Earl C. Tupper |
| Bessie Coleman | Jean Nidetch | Madam C.J. Walker |
| Philo Farnsworth | Ida Rosenthal | An Wang |
| Henry Morrison Flagler | John G. Sperling | Orla Watson |

**3. Partners May Disagree** Partners may not always agree on important decisions. Unlike a sole proprietorship, where the one owner makes all the decisions, partners must reach a consensus. Disagreements and disputes may hamper operations and could end the partnership.

**4. Profits Must Be Shared** Partners must share any profits according to the original partnership agreement. This may seem unfair to a partner who accounts for most of the profit. Unless the sharing agreement is revised, the most productive partner may look for a better deal elsewhere. This could end the partnership. Some major law partnerships have dissolved recently because of this.

✓ **CHECKPOINT**
What are the advantages and disadvantages of the partnership form of business?

**Partners may not always agree on all business matters. What advice do you have for potential partners to help them avoid arguments?**

# E-CONOMICS

## Partnering for Start-Ups

Although Silicon Valley in California continues to lose thousands of jobs, some potential entrepreneurs think the time has never been better for creating a start-up company. One software designer wants to introduce a new service she says will permanently end spam for e-mail users. "Computers are incredibly inexpensive now, network bandwidth is essentially free, and there is surplus equipment," she said. Her business premise is that consumers will pay a small annual fee for a solution to spam. Coming from a creative background, this entrepreneur has decided to form a limited partnership to finance her venture. She knows that many feature film and Broadway show producers get financing without giving up creative control under this form of organization. She also is aware of many e-commerce start-ups that began as limited partnerships. In the new venture, this entrepreneur and her close associates will be the general partners, manage the business, and make all the creative decisions. The investors will be limited partners, and their contribution will be strictly financial.

### Think Critically

What is the major disadvantage to the entrepreneur and her close associates of their role as general partners?

Lesson 8.2 • *Sole Proprietorships and Partnerships* **239**

---

**CHECKPOINT**
Invite a student to answer the checkpoint that appears on this page.

**Answer**

*Advantages*
1. Easy to start
2. Few government regulations
3. Shared decision making and increased specialization
4. Greater ability to raise financial capital
5. More able to attract and retain workers
6. Lower taxes

*Disadvantages*
1. Unlimited personal liability
2. Limited life of the business
3. Partners may disagree
4. Profits must be shared

## APPLY

Assign Lesson 8.2 from the Contemporary Economics Workbook.

## ASSESS

Assign all or part of Lesson 8.2 Assessment on page 240 as homework or an in-class activity.

## Xtra! Study Tools

Direct students to the online study tools for Lesson 8.2 at **econxtra.swlearning.com**.

## CLOSE

**Revisit** the In the News feature on the first page of the lesson. Ask students to review their preliminary answers and discuss the questions, now that they have completed this lesson.
**Review** the objectives for Lesson 8.2. Students should be able to:
• Describe the advantages and disadvantages of sole proprietorships.
• Describe the advantages and disadvantages of partnerships.

---

## RETEACH

Ask students to identify a local sole proprietorship that competes with a corporation. Hardware stores, hair salons, and drugstores are examples. Ask students to list and explain advantages and disadvantages the sole proprietorship experiences as compared with the larger corporation. Do they believe the advantages outweigh the disadvantages? If they intended to start this type of business, would they organize as a sole proprietorship or a corporation?

## Key Concepts

1. Answers will vary. Possible answer: The cost of starting a restaurant can be relatively low, but the cost of the equipment necessary to complete industrial construction can be many millions of dollars, exceeding the financial capacity of most individuals.

2. Answers will vary. Possible answer: Sole proprietors are often unable to complete all necessary tasks as their businesses grow but may be unwilling to delegate responsibility for completing these tasks to others.

3. Answers will vary. Possible answer: Many sole proprietorships are so small that they do not generate enough profit for the owner to live on. The owner must find some other way to provide his or her support.

4. Answers will vary. Possible answer: Many opportunities arise for partners to disagree with each other and dissolve their partnership agreements as a result.

5. Answers will vary. Possible answer: The time and cost of establishing an independent law practice can prevent a new lawyer from earning an adequate income for many years. By joining and becoming a partner in a firm, however, the new lawyer can share the cost of establishing a practice and can take advantage of the legal reputation the firm has earned over its years of existence.

## Graphing Exercise

6. Answers will vary. Possible answer: Businesses that require large investments are better suited to be partnerships than sole proprietorships. They are also less likely to market nationally than in a specific part of the nation.

   A sample of an acceptable graph appears at the bottom of this page.

*The Answer Key is continued on page 250.*

---

**Xtra! Study Tools**
econxtra.swlearning.com

## 8.2 Assessment

### Key Concepts

1. Why are more restaurants organized as sole proprietorships than are industrial construction firms?

2. Why do many sole proprietorships become less efficient as they grow?

3. Why are many sole proprietorships run by part-time entrepreneurs who earn most of their income by being employed by another firm?

4. Why do most partnerships last for only a few years or less?

5. Why do many new lawyers seek to become partners in established law firms?

### Graphing Exercise

6. In 1998, all U.S. partnerships had a total of $1.5 trillion in sales. The federal government classified partnerships into 20 categories. However, the bulk of the sales were made by partnerships in seven of the federal classifications, as listed in the table to the right. Use the data in this table to construct a pie graph showing partnerships' sales. Why do you think some types of businesses lend themselves to being organized as partnerships?

**Gross Sales by Partnerships in 1998**
**Values in Millions of Dollars**

| Business Classification | Sales | Percent of Total |
|---|---|---|
| Manufacturing | $247,489 | 16.1% |
| Finance and insurance | 184,489 | 12.0 |
| Retail trade | 170,809 | 11.1 |
| Professional, scientific, and technical services | 147,765 | 9.6 |
| Wholesale trade | 133,261 | 8.7 |
| Real estate and rental and leasing | 110,831 | 7.2 |
| Construction | 106,321 | 6.9 |
| All other | 432,788 | 28.4 |

Source: U.S. Bureau of the Census, *Statistical Abstract of the United States,* 2001, p. 476

### Think Critically

7. **Management** Make a list of all the management functions a sole proprietor must perform to be successful. What types of courses should a person who wants to own a business take? What types of experience should such a person look for in a job he or she might work in while going to school?

8. **Research** Review listings for physicians in your local Yellow Pages. How many of them are partners in a group and how many of them practice independently? Why do you think so many physicians prefer to participate in partnerships with other physicians?

---

**Sales by Business Classification**

Retail trade 11.1%
Finance and insurance 12.0%
Manufacturing 16.1%
All other 28.2%
Construction 6.9%
Real estate and rental and leasing 7.2%
Wholesale trade 8.7%
Professional, scientific, and technical services 9.6%

### Visualizing the Answer— Graphing Exercise

6. The answer includes a graph. Students' graphs should look similar to the one shown here. An Excel spreadsheet containing this graph, along with supporting data, is available on the Instructor's Resource CD.

## Objectives

> Describe how a corporation is established.

> Understand why the corporate form is favored by large businesses.

> Recognize other types of organizations businesspeople use to accomplish their goals.

## Overview

Sole proprietorships and partnerships may suit small businesses, but they are not appropriate for larger, more complex businesses. They need a more flexible business organization that allows the firm to raise a sufficient amount of financial capital and cope with a changing business environment. The corporation is the favored type of business organization for large businesses. Additionally, business owners may choose to organize as a limited liability company, limited liability partnership, cooperative, or not-for-profit organization.

## Key Terms

corporation

articles of incorporation

private corporation

publicly traded corporation

S corporation

limited liability company (LLC)

limited liability partnership (LLP)

cooperative

not-for-profit organizations

## [ In the News ]

### • Open Season on CEOs

The widespread corporate scandals shaking the United States have corporate CEOs (Chief Executive Officers) feeling less than proud of their titles. "Clearly it's open season on CEOs," said the CEO of Ford Motor Company. "But the broad brush with which everyone is tainted isn't really justified." Most CEOs resent having to spend time defending their reputations and distancing themselves from the ugly shadow cast by executives at Enron, WorldCom, and other companies. Most assert that their companies' accounting records are accurate and that their employees are honest and ethical. They're angry that the negative attitudes towards corporate America are destroying their companies' reputations, stock prices, and overall value. Congress is calling for more independent directors on corporate boards. It also is asking for closer scrutiny of the hiring and firing of CEOs—including their salaries, bonuses, expense accounts, and termination packages.

### Think About It

Do you think the public outrage against CEOs is justified? Do CEOs who receive multi-million dollar salaries deserve to earn that much money? Why or why not?

◄ | ►

241

### National Content Standards in Economics

A complete list of the NCEE Standards appears on pages xxiv–xxv of this book. The following standards are addressed in Lesson 8.3.

Standard 10: Role of Economic Institutions     Standard 15: Growth

Standard 14: Profit and the Entrepreneur     Standard 16: Role of Government

---

Point out that almost all large businesses in the United States are corporations. This shows that for entrepreneurs who operate a large business, the advantages of the corporate form of business organization must outweigh any disadvantages. Ask students to try to think of any large firms that are not corporations or small firms that are. They not are likely to be able to come up with many examples.

### Objectives

Remind students to read the lesson objectives to help focus their attention before reading the lesson.

### Key Terms

Direct students to create a database using the key terms for this lesson. The database fields should include terms, definitions, and page numbers. Point out that the process of keying the data is an effective way to study key terms.

### [ In the News ]

Instruct students to read the passage and write down their answers. Point out that their answers might change after they finish studying Lesson 8.3.

### Answers to Think About It

Answers will vary. Possible answers: Although generalized public outrage is probably not warranted, there have been enough examples of bad behavior to make the public wary. Considering the high salaries that elite celebrities and athletes receive, it is not unreasonable for top executives to be well-compensated.

### Follow-Up Activity

Point out that major companies often pay top executives more than a million dollars a year plus lots of stock options. Invite interested students to research the compensation package of a CEO of a publicly held corporation with ties to your community.

### Visual Presentation

Use the PowerPoint presentation on the Instructor's Resource CD as an adjunct to your lecture. The presentation also can be used for review.

## Incorporating

Ask students to form a corporation that will manufacture mountain bicycles. They will need $10 million to start the business and cover their costs until their sales become large enough to generate much income. Ask them to make a list of things they will need to do to achieve this as they read this lesson. They should make two additional lists of advantages and disadvantages of forming their business as a corporation.

### *Think Critically Through Visuals*

Direct students to focus on **Figure 8.4—Comparing Corporations with Sole Proprietorships and Partnerships**. For the top pie chart, point out the relative size of the slice representing sole proprietorships compared with the other two smaller slices. Ask students to look at the bottom pie chart and notice that the largest slice represents corporations. Even though sole proprietorships represent the largest share of businesses by type, corporations are much more important, based on sales.

---

# Incorporating

*corporation*

A legal entity with an existence that is distinct from the people who organize, own, and run it

*articles of incorporation*

A written application to the state seeking permission to form a corporation

By far the most influential and most complex form of business organization is the corporation. A **corporation** is a legal entity with an existence that is distinct from the people who organize it, own it, and run it. The corporation can earn a profit, lose money, be sued, and even be found guilty of a crime.

There were about five million corporations in the United States in 2000, accounting for about one fifth of all businesses. Because they tend to be much larger than the other two business types, however, corporations account for 86.5 percent of all business sales. Figure 8.4 summarizes the three types of businesses in terms of business type and business sales. Even though sole proprietors represent the largest share of businesses by type, corporations are much more important, based on business sales.

Figure 8.5 shows the distribution of corporations based on sales and on the industry. Whereas the median-sized sole proprietorship or partnership had annual sales of less than $25,000, the median-sized corporation had sales of $100,000 to $499,999. Virtually all the nation's large businesses are corporations. Compared with the other types of businesses, a smaller share of corporations is in agriculture and a larger share is in manufacturing.

## Articles of Incorporation

A corporation is established through **articles of incorporation**, a written application to a state seeking permission

**Comparing Corporations with Sole Proprietorships and Partnerships** — **Figure 8.4**

**(a): As a Share of All Businesses**

Corporations 19.0%
Partnerships 7.8%
Sole proprietorships 73.2%

**(b): As a Share of Business Sales**

Corporations 86.5%
Partnerships 8.2%
Sole proprietorships 5.3%

Sole proprietorships account for nearly three quarters of all U.S. businesses, but corporations account for most business sales.

Source: U.S. Bureau of the Census, *Statistical Abstract of the United States,* 2002.

**Distribution of Corporations by Annual Sales and by Industry** — **Figure 8.5**

**(a): By Annual Sales**

$1,000,000 or more 18.7%
$500,000 to $999,999 12.1%
Less than $25,000 24.0%
$25,000 to $49,999 5.8%
$100,000 to $499,999 30.1%
$50,000 to $99,999 9.3%

**(b): By Industry**

Finance, insurance, & real estate 15.2%
Wholesale & retail trade 19.7%
Transportation & communication 5.4%
Services 37.8%
Agriculture 4.3%
Construction 11.3%
Manufacturing 6.4%

Nearly one in five corporations had annual sales of $1 million or more. About four in ten corporations are in services, such as health care.

Source: U.S. Bureau of the Census, *Statistical Abstract of the United States,* 2002.

---

*Outside Resources*

**United Way** In many communities, the United Way sponsors a speaker's bureau featuring volunteers who can speak about the organization's programs and nonprofit agencies. Contact the local United Way to arrange for a speaker who can talk to students about the structure of a nonprofit organization. To locate the United Way affiliate for your community, go to the national web site at national.unitedway.org and key in your zip code.

to form a corporation. If these articles comply with state and federal laws, a charter is issued and the corporation becomes a legal entity. A *charter* offers the legal authorization to organize a business as a corporation.

A board of directors is elected by stockholders to oversee the firm's operation. The board sets major goals and decides major policy issues, and it appoints and sets salaries of top officers. Day-to-day duties of running the business are delegated to the corporate executives the board hires.

The owners of a corporation are issued *shares of stock,* entitling them to corporate profits and to vote for members of the board of directors and on various other issues in proportion to their stock ownership. For example, a stockholder who owns 1 percent of the stock has a right to 1 percent of the firm's profit paid in dividends and can vote 1 percent of the shares. *Dividends* are a share of a corporation's profits paid to its stockholders.

## Types of Corporations

A **private corporation** issues stock to just a few people, sometimes only family members. Such stockholders rarely sell their stock. Instead they pass it on within the family. Private corporations account for the overwhelming share of corporations in the United States.

In contrast, a **publicly traded corporation** has many shareholders—sometimes numbering in the millions—who can buy or sell shares. Stocks are bought and sold in financial markets called stock exchanges. You will read more about these in a later chapter.

By any measure of size, whether it be sales or employment, publicly traded corporations are larger than private corporations. Publicly traded corporations account for less than 1 percent of all corporations.

✔ **CHECKPOINT**
How is a corporation established?

# Advantages and Disadvantages

Here are the advantages and disadvantages of establishing of corporation.

## Advantages of Incorporation

The corporate form offers advantages to the stockholders and to the business itself.

1. **Easier to Raise Financial Capital** The corporate form is the most effective structure for raising financial capital. This is especially true if large sums are needed to start or expand a business. Many investors—hundreds, thousands, even millions—can exchange their money for company shares, giving the firm a huge pool of funds. Corporations have more ways to raise money than either sole proprietors or partnerships.

2. **Limited Liability** In most cases, stockholders, the owners of the corporation, are responsible for the firm's debts only up to the amount they paid for their shares. Stockholders are said to have limited liability. Their personal assets cannot be seized to pay the debts of the business. Use of the abbreviations "Inc." or "Corp." in the company name serves as a warning that stockholders will not accept personal liability for corporate debts.

3. **Unlimited Life** Unlike sole proprietorships and partnerships, a corporation does not cease to exist if a major stockholder dies or leaves the business. In fact, even if all stockholders die, the shares would pass on to others and the corporation would continue. Because stock is transferable—that is, it can be bought and sold or given to someone else—corporations can exist indefinitely, independently of its owners.

4. **Specialized Management** In sole proprietorships and general partnerships, the firms' owners and

*private corporation*

Ownership limited to just a few people, sometimes only family members; shares are not publicly traded

*publicly traded corporation*

Owned by many shareholders; shares can be bought or sold

### Incorporating

Return to the example of the new corporation that will produce mountain bicycles. Ask half the students to use aspects of this firm to demonstrate each of the advantages of corporations identified in the text. The other students should do the same for disadvantages of corporations. When they have completed this task, ask students to read and evaluate each other's answers.

*Think Critically Through Visuals*

Direct students to focus on **Figure 8.5—Distribution of Corporations by Annual Sales and by Industry** on page 242. Ask students to identify examples of corporations with ties to their lives that fit into the industry categories shown in this figure. (Students should recognize that many corporations have ties to their lives even if the corporation does not have a farm, factory, or other facility in your community. For example, students probably eat Chiquita bananas even though most bananas are not grown in the United States and Chiquita is headquartered in Ohio.)

✔ **CHECKPOINT**
Invite a student to answer the checkpoint that appears on this page.

### Answer

A corporation is established through articles of incorporation.

**ENRICH**

Fifty years ago, almost all farms in the United States were operated as sole proprietorships. Although many farms still operate in this way, most of them are relatively small. Corporations currently operate many large farms. Ask your students to write an essay that explains why this change has taken place. What does this have to do with the inefficiency of small farms, technological advancements in farming, and the need farmers have to raise large amounts of capital?

## Advantages and Disadvantages

Write down the four advantages and four disadvantages of incorporation on separate pieces of paper and put the pieces in a box. Organize students into eight groups and have a representative of each group draw a topic from the box. Allow the groups to meet for 10 minutes to prepare an explanation, including examples, for their topic. Reconvene and have the groups make their presentations in the order that the topics appear in the textbook.

### Ethics in Action

Have students work in pairs to discuss the ethical issue featured on this page, and develop answers to the questions presented.

### Answers to Think Critically

Answers will vary. Students who think "bad-guy" executives should get lighter sentences might believe that a bank robber is more dangerous and more likely to offend again. An executive might return to be a productive member of society after serving a light sentence. Students who do not think "bad-guy" executives should get lighter sentences might point out that executives have the advantage of an education and the means to make an honest living. The executive "should have known better" and should be held accountable.

### ✓ CHECKPOINT

Invite a student to answer the checkpoint that appears on page 245.

### Answer

Answers will vary. Students may list one or more of the following in their answer: easier to raise financial capital, limited liability, unlimited life, and/or specialized management.

---

managers often are one and the same. Therefore, owners usually must possess management skills. However, the owners of a corporation—the stockholders—need no special management skills. Because ownership is separated from management, a corporation can hire experts to run the firm.

### Disadvantages of Incorporation

The U.S. economy depends heavily on the corporate form. However, this business type also has some disadvantages when compared to sole proprietors and partnerships.

1. **Difficult and Costly to Start** Compared to the two other business forms, a corporation is more complicated to start. Articles of incorporation can be difficult and costly to draw up and get approved by government.

2. **More Regulated** Corporations, especially those publicly traded, face more regulations and red tape than other forms of business. For example, publicly traded corporations must issue financial reports every three months and issue annual reports prepared by an outside accounting firm. These reports must be filed with the Securities and Exchange Commission (SEC), a federal agency that regulates trading of corporate stocks.

3. **Owners Have Less Control** Owners of large, publicly traded corporations usually are far removed from the day-to-day operations of the business. The firm's owners have little direct control over the firm they own. Professional managers run the business, but they may not always act in the owners' best interests, as evidenced by some management failures in large corporations such as Enron and WorldCom.

4. **Double Taxation** In the eyes of the law, a corporation is a legal entity separate from its owners. The corporation therefore pays taxes on any earnings. Stockholders must then pay personal income taxes on any earnings they receive from the corporation. Thus, each dollar of corporate

## Ethics in Action

### Execs Corrupted by Corporate Culture?
According to a 2002 Gallup Poll taken in the aftermath of the Enron and WorldCom scandals, the only people less trusted than corporate CEOs were health maintenance organization managers and car dealers. Curiously, while only 23 percent of Americans said they trusted heads of big businesses, 75 percent believed that most people who run small businesses can be trusted. Responding to the scandals and subsequent outrage against corporations, 120 top executives met to brainstorm the subject of how to restore public confidence in corporate America. Warren Buffett, one of the richest men in America, was the keynote speaker at the meeting titled "The Forum for Corporate Conscience." Buffett said that the need to restore corporate integrity was "vital to this country." He argued that, for the most part, the scandals were not created by absolute crooks. Rather, he said the problem was that basically good people got caught up in a corporate culture that blurred the lines and led them to do bad things.

### Think Critically
In view of Buffett's remarks, do you think a "bad-guy" executive corrupted by the corporate culture should get a lighter sentence than a bank robber who claims he was corrupted by a poor upbringing? Why or why not?

**244**      CHAPTER 8   Businesses

---

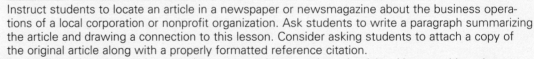

### Economic Headlines

Instruct students to locate an article in a newspaper or newsmagazine about the business operations of a local corporation or nonprofit organization. Ask students to write a paragraph summarizing the article and drawing a connection to this lesson. Consider asking students to attach a copy of the original article along with a properly formatted reference citation.

As an alternative, you can have students summarize pre-selected articles. You can either give students copies of the articles or you can have them find the articles based on reference citations you provide.

earnings gets taxed twice—first by the corporate income tax and then by the personal income tax.

**CHECKPOINT**
Why is the corporation the preferred business form for large businesses?

# Other Organizations

So far you have considered the three basic business forms: sole proprietorships, partnerships, and corporations. Other ways of doing business have developed that combine attractive features of the basic forms.

## Hybrid Businesses

A big advantage of sole proprietorships and partnerships is that business earnings are taxed only once—as income to the business owners. A big advantage of the corporation is that all owners are protected by limited liability. Some new business hybrids have developed that offer the protection of limited liability while avoiding the double taxation of business income. Here are the most important new business types.

### S Corporation

The **S corporation** was introduced about two decades ago to combine the limited liability protection of the corporate form with the single taxation feature of a partnership. To qualify as an S corporation, a business must be incorporated in the United States, must have no more than 75 stockholders, and must not have foreign stockholders. Because of these restrictions, S corporations tend to be smaller than other corporations. About half of all U.S. corporations are S corporations.

### Limited Liability Company (LLC)

Like an S corporation, a **limited liability company (LLC)** combines the limited liability feature of the corporation with the single-tax provisions of a

partnership. An LLC does not have the ownership restrictions of the S corporation, making it ideal for a business with foreign investors. An LLC must have at least two members, and a member can personally guarantee certain obligations of the LLC. This gives a new business more financial flexibility. For example, a prospective landlord about to lease office space to a new business most likely will require a personal guarantee from a business owner. The LLC structure would allow one or more company members to make such a guarantee. Because of its more flexible management structure, the LLC has become a common way to own and operate a business.

### Limited Liability Partnership (LLP)

An existing partnership may find it difficult to convert to an LLC. This is the reason the **limited liability partnership (LLP)**, a newer type of organization, was created. An LLP has the advantages of an LLC and is easier to establish, especially if a business needs to convert from a partnership. An existing partnership usually can be converted to an LLP simply by changing the partnership agreement and registering as an LLP. Both LLPs and LLCs are taxed as partnerships.

### Cooperatives

A **cooperative** is a group of people who pool their resources to buy and sell more efficiently than they could independently. The government grants most cooperatives tax-exempt status.

*limited liability company (LLC)*
Business with limited liability for some owners, single taxation of business income, and no ownership restrictions

*limited liability partnership (LLP)*
Like a limited liability company but more easily converted from an existing partnership

*S corporation*
Organization that offers limited liability combined with the single taxation of business income; must have no more than 75 stockholders with no foreign stockholders

*cooperative*
An organization consisting of people who pool their resources to buy and sell more efficiently than they could independently

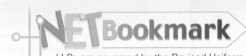
**NETBookmark**
LLPs are governed by the Revised Uniform Partnership Act (RUPA). Access the text of this Act through econxtra.swlearning.com. The LLP amendments to RUPA deal with four major issues. List these issues, and write a sentence summarizing each one.

*econxtra.swlearning.com*

## Other Organizations

Explain that there are situations in which none of the three basic forms of business organization meets the needs of entrepreneurs who want to operate a business. In these situations, several hybrid organizations combine aspects of other forms of business organization to better serve the entrepreneurs' needs. Many businesses that are smaller than large corporations but larger than most sole proprietorships are organized in one of these ways.

**NETBookmark**

Direct students to **econxtra.swlearning.com**. Remind them to click on the link for Lesson 8.3 to find the appropriate link for the **NET** Bookmark on this page.

### Answer

The four major issues are: the scope of a partner's liability shield, the voting requirements to become an LLP, the effect of becoming an LLP on the partnership agreement, and the annual filing requirement.

**Investigate Your Local Economy** For the feature appearing on page 246, suggest students choose a not-for-profit organization that has touched their lives. For example, students who have participated in a charity walk might choose that charity. If students are having trouble finding an organization, suggest they visit the United Way web site at www.national.unitedway.org.

**CHECKPOINT**
Invite a student to answer the checkpoint that appears on page 246.

### Answer

Answers should include the following types of organizations along with a brief explanation: S corporation, limited liability company, limited liability partnership, cooperatives, and not-for-profit organizations.

## Group Activity

Organize students into small groups. Provide each group with a copy of a recent issue of a general-interest magazine such as *Newsweek, Time,* or *U.S. News & World Report.* Ask each group to look for and count the full- and multi-page advertisements to determine how many of the ads were placed by a large corporation. Ask them to explain why they think many of the advertised products are produced by large rather than small corporations. How does the size of a firm benefit or hurt consumers?

APPLY

Assign Lesson 8.3 from the Contemporary Economics Workbook.

ASSESS

Assign all or part of Lesson 8.3 Assessment on page 247 as homework or an in-class activity.

Xtra! Study Tools

Direct students to the online study tools for Lesson 8.3 at **econxtra.swlearning.com**.

CLOSE

**Revisit** the In the News feature on the first page of the lesson. Ask students to review their preliminary answers and discuss the questions, now that they have completed this lesson.
**Review** the objectives for Lesson 8.3. Students should be able to:

• Describe how a corporation is established.

• Understand why the corporate form is favored by large businesses.

• Recognize other types of organizations businesspeople use to accomplish their goals.

**not-for-profit organizations**
Groups that do not pursue profit as a goal; they engage in charitable, educational, humanitarian, cultural, professional, or other activities, often with a social purpose

There are two types: consumer cooperatives and producer cooperatives.

### Consumer Cooperative

A *consumer cooperative* is a retail business owned and operated by some or all of its customers in order to reduce costs. Some cooperatives require members to pay an annual fee and others require them to work a certain number of hours each year. Members sometimes pay lower prices than other customers or may share in any revenues that exceed costs. In the United States, consumer cooperatives operate credit unions, electric-power facilities, health plans, and grocery stores, among others. If you go to college, your college bookstore may be a cooperative.

### Producer Cooperative

In a *producer cooperative,* producers join forces to buy supplies and equipment and to market their output. Each producer's objective is to reduce costs and increase profits. For example, farmers pool their funds to purchase machinery and supplies. Farm cooperatives also provide storage facilities, processing, and transportation to market, thereby eliminating wholesalers. Federal legislation allows farmers to cooperate in this way without violating antitrust laws.

**Investigate Your Local Economy**

Identify a not-for-profit organization in your area. Research to discover how this organization affects your local economy. For example, find out what services the organization provides and how many paid employees and volunteers work for the organization. Share your findings in class.

Firms in other industries could not do this legally.

### Not-for-Profit Organizations

So far, you have learned about organizations that try to maximize profits or, in the case of cooperatives, minimize costs. Some organizations have neither as a goal. **Not-for-profit organizations** engage in charitable, educational, humanitarian, cultural, professional, and other activities, often with a social purpose.

Like businesses, not-for-profit organizations evolved to help people accomplish their goals. Examples include nonprofit hospitals, private schools and colleges, religious organizations, the Red Cross, charitable foundations, orchestras, museums, labor unions, and professional organizations such as the National Education Association. There are about 300,000 not-for-profit organizations in the United States. They employ about nine million workers, with hospitals accounting for about half of these jobs.

Even not-for-profit organizations must somehow pay the bills. Revenues typically include some combination of voluntary contributions and service charges, such as college tuition and hospital charges. In the United States, not-for-profit organizations usually are exempt from taxes.

 **CHECKPOINT**
Name and describe other types of organizations businesspeople may choose.

246    **CHAPTER 8** Businesses

RETEACH

Tell students they have discovered a chemical that, when applied to fabric, will repel any type of stain. Blood, oil, dye, dirt—it doesn't matter; nothing sticks to it. What's more, the chemical does not change the appearance or texture of the fabric. They are sure that the carpet industry alone will buy 100 million gallons of the chemical each year. There is a problem, however. It will cost $500 million to build a factory to produce the chemical commercially. Ask students to explain how they would organize a business to make this type of investment. How could they convince others to invest in their business?

## Key Concepts

1. Why would most people not invest in corporations if there were no limited liability for stock owners?

2. Why might a family business organize as a private corporation rather than as a sole proprietorship?

3. Although stockholders do not need to be professional managers, they should stay aware of decisions made by the people who run the firm. Why is this true?

4. If publicly traded corporations account for only 1 percent of all corporations, why should society care what they do?

5. Identify a local not-for-profit organization that operates in your community. In what ways is this firm different from other businesses?

**Xtra!**
Study Tools
*econxtra.swlearning.com*

## Graphing Exercise

6. In the years between 1995 and 2000, many publicly held corporations in the United States reported large and growing profits. Although some of their profits were paid to stockholders in dividends, a large part was kept as retained earnings. Use the data in the table to construct a double line graph that shows the change in corporate profits and dividends in these years. Why do you think these firms chose not to pay a larger share of their profits in dividends?

**Corporate After-Tax Profits and Dividends, 1995–2000**
**Values in Billions of Dollars**

| Year | After-Tax Profits | Dividends | Dividends as a Percent Of After-Tax Profits |
|------|-------------------|-----------|---------------------------------------------|
| 1995 | $458 | $254 | 55.5% |
| 1996 | 503 | 298 | 59.1 |
| 1997 | 555 | 335 | 60.4 |
| 1998 | 514 | 352 | 68.5 |
| 1999 | 567 | 371 | 65.4 |
| 2000 | 641 | 397 | 61.9 |

Source: U.S. Bureau of the Census, *Statistical Abstract of the United States,* 2001, p. 501.

## Think Critically

7. **History** Investigate the history of a major U.S. corporation. How did it begin? What factors led to its growth? What impact has it had on the lives of American consumers?

Lesson 8.3 • *Corporations and Other Organizations*     **247**

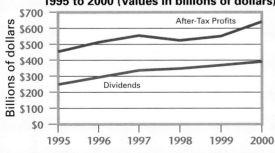

**Corporate After-Tax Profits and Dividends, 1995 to 2000 (Values in billions of dollars)**

*Visualizing the Answer—Graphing Exercise*

6. The answer includes a graph. Students' graphs should look similar to the one shown here. An Excel spreadsheet containing this graph, along with supporting data, is available on the Instructor's Resource CD.

*Key Concepts*

1. Answers will vary. Possible answer: Few people would be willing to invest in stock in a firm over which they had little control if they could be held responsible for all of that firm's debts.

2. Answers will vary. Possible answer: Sole proprietorships must be reorganized when the owner dies. Corporations, however, continue to operate when an owner dies. Decisions are made by surviving owners.

3. Answers will vary. Possible answer: The decisions of the firm's managers will affect the firm's profits and the value of its stock. Stockholders should keep up with the firm's day-to-day operation to protect the value of their investments and to know when they might wish to sell their stock.

4. Answers will vary. Possible answer: Although there are relatively few publicly held corporations, they tend to be very large and have an important impact on the economy as a whole.

5. Answers will vary. Possible answer: Not-for-profit organizations do not generate income solely from sales; they usually provide a good or service to members of the community at or below cost, and they judge their success in ways that are not related to profits.

*Graphing Exercise*

6. Answers will vary. Possible answer: Many corporations finance their growth through retained earnings. If they pay more dividends, they will either grow less or need to find other sources for investment capital.

A sample of an acceptable graph appears at the bottom of this page.

*Think Critically*

7. Answers will vary. Possible answers: Firms such as General Motors or IBM grew because they produced products people wanted and were able to sell them for prices that were lower than competitors' prices.

## Draw Conclusions

After studying Lesson 8.3, students should be able to answer the questions on this page.

## Apply Your Skill

Consider allowing students to work in pairs for this assignment.

## Answers

1. Answers will vary. Students may point out that she needs $50,000 altogether to start her business. She could borrow the remaining $25,000 from a bank, find another person to be a partner in her business, or form a private corporation by selling stock to several of her friends.

2. Answers will vary. Students may point out that Rita would have to charge $12 per ornament to be able to receive $9 for each item if she pays a marketing person a 25 percent commission. She would need to charge $18 per item to receive $9 per item from the mail-order firm.

3. Answers will vary. Students may point out that because of the small size of Rita's firm, she should form a sole proprietorship, or she could form a partnership with another person who has money to invest and/or knowledge of marketing and financial practices.

## *Follow-Up Activity*

Use the following questions to extend this activity:

4. Rita could employ her teenage niece and nephew after school and on weekends. Another option is to hire a woman she knows who needs a job. She expects to pay her workers $9 per hour. Which choice would you recommend she make, and why? (Answers will vary. Students may point out that her teenage niece and nephew may not be as reliable as an adult worker. If she pays $9 per hour and it takes 20 minutes to produce each ornament, there will be $3 of labor cost in each item.)

5. Construct a business plan that explains how Rita should organize her business in its first year. Include an estimate of her costs and business revenues. Make up the additional information you think should be included in the plan. (Answers will vary. Students should create plans that are logical and realistically project the firm's expenses and revenues in the future.)

# Sharpen Your Life Skills

## Draw Conclusions

In drawing a conclusion, you first must gather information about the issue at hand. Then you must consider all aspects of the information before reaching your conclusion. Consider Rita, who for many years has made brightly colored glass Christmas ornaments for her friends and relatives. Everyone who has received one of Rita's ornaments has been thrilled. She has decided to go into business manufacturing and selling ornaments.

Rita has asked you to help her translate her ideas into a successful business. Here's the information she has gathered so far. The materials in each ornament cost $1.00, and it takes 20 minutes to produce one by hand. In addition, Rita has determined that she will need to do the following:

• Invest $10,000 in equipment and supplies and have $40,000 to cover her costs until her products begin to sell

• Hire and train one full-time or two part-time employees

• Manufacture and sell 12,000 ornaments each year

• Receive $9 for each ornament

• Keep track of the business's income and expenditures

## Apply Your Skill

1. Rita has $25,000 to invest in the business. How much more does she need to start her business? What method would you advise her to use to raise the rest of the money? Explain the reasons for your advice.

2. Rita doesn't know very much about marketing. She could hire someone to market her ornaments and pay that person a 25 percent commission. Or, she might try to convince a mail-order firm to sell her ornaments. If she makes this choice, the firm will keep half the revenue from her sales. So, she would have to charge a higher price.

3. What sort of organization should Rita use to start her business—a sole proprietorship, a partnership, or a corporation? Explain the reasons for your choice.

# Andrew Carnegie—
## Entrepreneur and Philanthropist

When he was 12, Andrew Carnegie moved with his family from Scotland to the United States. Soon after arriving in this country, he got a job working in a cotton mill for $1.20 a week. At age 18, he took a job as a telegrapher for the Pennsylvania Railroad. While working there, he won the favor of Thomas A. Scott, a top official in the company. With Scott's help, Carnegie rose quickly through the company ranks. By age 24, he had become the superintendent of the

© Hulton-Deutsch Collection/CORBIS

© Richard Cummins/CORBIS

western division of the railroad. He invested much of his earnings in stocks.

By age 30, Carnegie was earning $50,000 a year—a fortune at the time—and turned all his efforts and investments to the steel industry. This industry would make him the richest man in America. He believed that the new Bessemer process would cause the industry to grow. He hired good managers and reinvested the profits back into his companies. He used what he learned from his railroad experience to lower costs and keep prices low. By controlling costs and reinvesting profits, he was able to take advantage of economies of scale. Smaller companies unable to undertake all the phases of production were at a disadvantage. He was able to increase his market share and expand his holdings. Carnegie purchased iron ore deposits and coke fields. Adding these to his steel mills, ships, and railroads, Carnegie was able to control the entire steel-making process, from ore to finished products.

When he sold his company to J.P. Morgan in 1901, Carnegie received $250 million—worth $4.5 billion today. He then set out to give away much of his fortune. In 1889, Carnegie wrote in an essay for the *American Review* that the man who dies rich, dies disgraced. Although at his death in 1919 he was worth more than $22 million, Carnegie did not die disgraced. He had given away 90 percent of his fortune—$350 million—to libraries, concert halls, and other public institutions across the nation and the world.

### THINK CRITICALLY
Research the life of another successful American entrepreneur. What were the keys to his or her success, and what lessons can be learned from that success?

### FOCUS

Explain to students that America of the late 1800s was a period of unprecedented industrial growth. Industrialists who built vast empires in railroads and oil dominated the country's economy. Today, questions as to whether they should be classified as "Captains of Industry" or "Robber Barons" are debated. Andrew Carnegie was one of the foremost industrialists of the era. His "rags to riches" story and subsequent charity remains one of the major examples of the "American Dream."

### TEACH

After introducing the **Connect to History** feature, have students read it and answer the questions. Lead a discussion about Carnegie and the nature of his accomplishments. How typical was Carnegie's life? Could something similar be accomplished today?

### ASSESS

Use the activity at the bottom of the page to assess the students' understanding of this feature. Suggest students pattern their reports on the **Connect to History** feature on this page, including illustrations.

**Answers to Think Critically**
Answers will vary. In addition to biographical information, reports should include the keys to the person's success and the lessons that can be learned.

## Bibliography

Engerman, Stanley L. and Robert E. Gallman. *The Cambridge Economic History of the United States: The Long Nineteenth Century.* Vol. II. Cambridge, England: Cambridge University Press, 2000.

Foner, Eric and John A. Garraty, eds. *The Reader's Companion to American History.* New York: Houghton Mifflin, 1991.

Heilbroner, Robert L. "Carnegie & Rockefeller" in *A Sense of History: The Best Writing from the Pages of American Heritage.* New York: American Heritage, 1985.

Puth, Robert C. *American Economic History.* Ft. Worth: Dryden Press, 1988.

Wall, J.F. *Andrew Carnegie.* New York: Oxford University Press, 1970.

Warren, Kenneth. *Big Steel: The First Century of the United States Steel Corporation, 1901-2001.* Pittsburgh: University of Pittsburgh Press, 2001.

### Consider

Ask students to revisit the questions they were asked to consider at the beginning of the chapter. Remind students that they should be able to answer all of the questions after studying Chapter 8.

- Why do some people want to call themselves "boss"? See page 234—Sole Proprietorship.
- Why start a business if most new businesses don't last five years? See page 226—Role of Entrepreneurs.
- What does your summer lawn-mowing operation have in common with General Motors? See page 229—Who Isn't an Entrepreneur?
- What do *Corp.* or *Inc.* in a company's name tell you about how the owners treat debt? See page 242—Incorporating.
- How could it be possible that most U.S. businesses have no paid employees? See page 234—Who Is a Sole Proprietor?

### Exam *View*

Use **Exam***View* to assess student learning.

- Create a chapter test using questions from the existing test bank.
- Add your own questions to the existing test bank.
- Generate multiple forms of a chapter test.

### Study Skills

Offer the following study skills suggestions for students as they review this chapter.

- Outline the chapter.
- Review Key Terms.
- Review Checkpoints.
- Work in pairs to quiz each other.
- Use the Xtra! Study Tools for each lesson.

Direct students to the online quiz preparation for Chapter 8 at **econxtra.swlearning.com**.

---

# 8 Chapter Assessment

## Summary

### 8.1 *Entrepreneurs*

a *Entrepreneurs* are the prime movers in our market economy. They bring about creative change through their effort to earn profits.

b Entrepreneurs take risks when they operate businesses. They must obtain and risk *financial capital* to get their businesses off the ground. When entrepreneurs are successful, their success attracts other entrepreneurs to the same type of production. This creates competition that improves the quality of products and lowers prices for consumers.

**Xtra! Quiz Prep**
econxtra.swlearning.com

c Not all businesspeople are entrepreneurs. Many employees are paid to be innovative or to manage businesses. If they are not risking their own funds, they are not entrepreneurs. Stockholders are not entrepreneurs because they do not generally participate in day-to-day management.

### 8.2 *Sole Proprietorships and Partnerships*

a The three basic types of business organization in the United States are sole proprietorships, partnerships, and corporations.

b *Sole proprietorships* are the most common type of business organization. A sole proprietorship is owned by a single person who is totally responsible for its operation, receives all of its profits, or incurs all its losses. It exists only as long as the owner lives. Sole proprietorships are relatively easy to start, enjoy a lower level of government regulation, and are taxed only once on the profits they earn.

c *General partnerships* are created when two or more owners form a business by agreeing to share responsibilities for the firm and any resulting profits or losses. *Limited partnerships* are formed when at least one owner is a general partner and other owners contribute funds to become limited partners.

**250**     **CHAPTER 8** Businesses

d Partnerships also are relatively easy to start, and general partners have unlimited *liability* for the debts of the firm. Partnerships are better able to raise financial capital than sole proprietorships, and their profits are taxed only once. The lives of partnerships are limited to the lives of the partners.

### 8.3 *Corporations and Other Organizations*

a *Corporations* are able to raise large amounts of financial capital by selling stock. Almost all large firms in the United States are corporations. They may either be private or publicly traded. *Private corporations* issue stock to a limited number of people, who often are members of a family. *Publicly traded corporations* raise funds by selling stock to anyone who is willing to buy it. Stockholders receive a vote for each share owned for important business decisions that are made. They also have a claim to a share of the firm's profits.

b Corporations are established through *articles of incorporation*. Corporations are legal entities separate from the individual owners of their stock. The owners of corporate stock enjoy limited liability. They risk no more than the funds they use to purchase stock. Corporations have unlimited life. If an owner dies, the remaining owners may make decisions for the firm without the participation of the deceased owner.

c Corporations are more difficult and costly to start than other forms of business organizations. They are more closely regulated by the government, and their profits are taxed twice—once when they are earned by the firm and again when they are paid to the stockholders in dividends or when shareholders gain by selling shares.

d Some special forms of business organizations are called hybrid businesses. These include *S corporations, limited liability companies,* and *limited liability partnerships.* Other ways of organizing production that help people accomplish their goals include *cooperatives* and *not-for-profit organizations.* Each of these forms of organization was created to fill the specific needs of a particular group of people.

---

### 8.2 Assessment

#### Think Critically

Continued from page 240.

7. Successful sole proprietors must have a basic understanding of accounting, human resource management, inventory control, marketing, advertising, and taxes. Such a person should register for small-business management courses and seek employment that would provide firsthand experience in these areas before starting a business.

8. Answers will vary. Possible answer: Many physicians choose to work in partnerships to share the cost and responsibilities of their practice. The cost of setting up a medical office can be too great for most new physicians to afford.

---

# Review Economic Terms

Choose the term that best fits the definition. On a separate sheet of paper, write the letter of the answer. Some terms may not be used.

1. The process of turning an invention into a marketable product

2. Two or more people agree to contribute resources to a business in return for a share of the profit

3. Ownership is limited to just a few people, sometimes only family members; shares are not publicly traded

____ 4. An organization consisting of people who pool their resources to buy and sell more efficiently than they could independently

____ 5. The legal obligation to pay any debts of a business

____ 6. The simplest form of business organization; a firm that is owned and run by one person

____ 7. A legal entity with an existence that is distinct from the people who organize, own, and run it

____ 8. Owned by many shareholders; shares can be bought and sold

____ 9. Limited liability combined with the single taxation of business income; must have no more than 75 stockholders and no foreign stockholders

10. Money needed to start or expand a business

11. Partners share both in the responsibility of running the business and in any liability from its operation

____ 12. At least one general partner runs the business and bears unlimited personal liability; other partners provide financial capital but have limited liability

____ 13. A written application to the state seeking permission to form a corporation

____ 14. Business with limited liability for some owners, single taxation of business income, and no ownership restriction

____ 15. Groups that do not pursue profit as a goal and often engage in activities with a social purpose

a. articles of incorporation

b. cooperative

c. corporation

d. financial capital

e. general partnership

f. innovation

g. liability

h. limited liability company (LLC)

i. limited liablility partnership (LLP)

j. limited partnership

k. not-for-profit organization

l. partnership

m. private corporation

n. publicly traded corporation

o. S corporation

p. sole proprietorship

# Review Economic Concepts

16. *Entrepreneurs* bring about creative change in each of the following ways *except*

   a. they improve the quality of existing products.

   b. they introduce new products.

   c. they find ways to eliminate competition.

   d. they introduce new production methods.

17. **True or False** Once established, most *entrepreneurs* are able to maintain a substantial profit margin on the products they produce and sell.

18. Competitors are attracted to a market that yields

   a. profit in the short run.

   b. unlimited liability.

   c. lower prices for consumers.

   d. higher tax revenues.

## Review Economic Terms

1. f. innovation
2. l. partnership
3. m. private corporation
4. b. cooperative
5. g. liability
6. p. sole proprietorship
7. c. corporation
8. n. publicly traded corporation
9. o. S corporation
10. d. financial capital
11. e. general partnership
12. j. limited partnership
13. a. articles of incorporation
14. h. limited liability company (LLC)
15. k. not-for-profit organization

## Review Economic Concepts

16. c. they find ways to eliminate competition

17. False. Only a handful of entrepreneurs are able to maintain a substantial profit margin on the products they produce and sell.

18. a. profit in the short run

## Review Economic Concepts

19. a. A scientist invents a long-lasting paint and sells it to a large manufacturer.
20. True
21. b. It is easy for them to gather large amounts of financial capital.
22. unlimited liability
23. c. the type of business organization that is best able to raise funds
24. True
25. False. If a firm files for bankruptcy, the firm's stockholders are responsible for the firm's debts only up to the amount they paid for that particular stock.
26. b. reduce costs of buying goods or services for its members
27. False. Private corporations account for the overwhelming share of corporations in the United States.
28. a. S corporation
29. Securities and Exchange Commission
30. True
31. b. less regulated
32. b. They must reorganize when an owner dies.
33. False. These abbreviations indicate that the owners are not personally liable for the company's debts.
34. Answers will vary. Students may point out that Gretchen has invented a new product, but to be an entrepreneur she must produce and market the lubricant commercially. To do this, she must acquire financing, hire employees, and create and implement a marketing plan. If she is successful, she could earn great profits; but if she fails, she could lose her entire investment.

19. Which of the following examples demonstrates *entrepreneurship*?
    a. A scientist invents a long-lasting paint and sells it to a large manufacturer.
    b. A government official creates a new tax form that is easier to complete.
    c. A technician discovers a new type of wax that is used by the firm that employs her.
    d. A student cuts his elderly neighbor's lawn for free.

20. **True or False** *Sole proprietorships* are the most common form of business organization in the United States.

21. *Sole proprietors* enjoy each of the following advantages *except*
    a. they receive all the profit their businesses earn.
    b. it is easy for them to gather large amounts of financial capital.
    c. they can make business decisions quickly.
    d. it is easy for them to form their business.

22. Owners of *sole proprietorships* and *partners* both have __?__ for the firm's debts if the firm fails to pay its bills.

23. *Corporations* are
    a. the most common type of business organization.
    b. the easiest form of business to start.
    c. the type of business organization that is best able to raise funds.
    b. the least-regulated form of business organization.

24. **True or False** Most large businesses in the United States are *corporations*.

25. **True or False** A *corporation's* stockholders are held responsible to pay off all the firm's debts if the firm files for bankruptcy.

26. A *consumer cooperative* generally is formed to
    a. earn a profit for its owners.
    b. reduce costs of buying goods or services for its members.

    c. avoid paying income tax on its profits.
    d. limit the type of people who can shop at specific stores.

27. **True or False** Almost all corporations in the United States are *publicly traded corporations*.

28. Which of the following types of business organizations cannot have a foreign owner?
    a. S corporation
    b. limited liability company
    c. limited liability partnership
    d. not-for-profit organization

29. *Publicly traded corporations* must issue financial reports and file them with the __?__, a federal agency that regulates trading of corporate stocks.

30. **True or False** An important disadvantage of *corporations* is the fact that their profits are taxed twice.

31. Which of the following does not describe a disadvantage of a *corporation*?
    a. difficult to start
    b. less regulated
    c. owners have little control
    d. earnings are taxed twice

32. Which of the following is not true of *private corporations*?
    a. They exist to earn a profit.
    b. They must reorganize when an owner dies.
    c. Their income is taxed more than employee earnings.
    d. They are treated as an individual separate from their owners by the law.

33. **True or False** Use of the abbreviations "Inc." or "Corp." in a company name indicates that the owners are personally liable for the company's debts.

# Apply Economic Concepts

34. **Entrepreneurship** Gretchen has invented a new lubricant that reduces friction between moving parts in an engine to almost nothing. This product should increase automobile gas mileage by at least 50 percent and make automobile engines last almost forever. Explain how Gretchen could become an entrepreneur through her invention.

35. **Assess Limitations of Sole Proprietorships** Paul opened a florist business that marketed tropical flowers as a sole proprietorship. His idea was that by offering flowers that no other local store sold, he could charge high prices and earn a good profit. This may have been a good idea, but his business failed. First, he had only $30,000 to get started, so he was never able to keep many flowers in stock. Although he knew flowers, he didn't know much about advertising, accounting, or how to direct employees. Even when he put in 80-hour weeks, things didn't get done on time. When the business failed, he owed $40,000. The bankruptcy court took his house and car to pay his debts. Explain why Paul's business might have been more successful if it had been organized as a corporation.

36. **Limited Liability** Gretchen has successfully tested her lubricant on small engines. She has not tried to use it in large engines or for extended periods of time. To complete these tests, she needs many thousands of dollars to buy equipment and run the tests. If the tests are successful, Gretchen thinks her product could earn many millions of dollars in profit every year. If they fail, all the funds invested in the tests could be lost. Why would Gretchen want to limit her liability when she starts her business?

37. **Forms of Business Organization** Identify the type of business organization Gretchen should form to be able to produce and market 10,000,000 gallons of her lubricant each year.

38. **Sharpen Your Life Skills: Draw Conclusions** After five years, Rita's business has become very successful. Her annual sales have reached $450,000 and she employs three full-time workers. She is convinced she could double her sales if she employed three more workers and spent $500,000 to purchase additional equipment. Rita has saved only $100,000 that she could invest. She spends almost all of her time working. She never takes a day off, and still, some orders can't be filled on time. Rita once again has come to you for advice. Her business is still organized as it was when she started out. (See your answer to Question 3 for *Sharpen Your Life Skills* on page 248.) What are the issues and the possible solutions?

What would you advise Rita to do?

39. **Access EconLinks Online** through econxtra.swlearning.com. In the Government listing, click on Federal Independent Agencies and Organizations. Then click on the link to the Securities and Exchange Commission web site. Under "About the SEC," click on "Laws and Regulations." Read the information about the Sarbanes-Oxley Act of 2002. Write a paragraph explaining the purpose of this Act.

*Chapter Assessment* **253**

## Apply Economic Concepts

35. If the business had been organized as corporation, Paul would not have been personally responsible for the debts of the business. His losses would have been limited to what he invested in the business. He would not have lost his car and home in the bankruptcy proceedings. He could have shared the responsibilities for running the business with other owners who had business management skills he lacked.

36. Answers will vary. Students may point out that Gretchen would like to avoid the possibility that all of her property could be taken to satisfy the debts of her firm if the product fails to work as expected. She would prefer to have the limited liability offered by corporate business organizations.

37. Answers will vary. Students may point out that the cost of building a factory that can produce 10,000,000 gallons of lubricant is probably greater than any single person or small group of individuals can afford. Gretchen will probably need to create a private or publicly traded corporation.

38. The issues are that Rita does not have enough money or time to spend on her business. Students might recommend that she look for a manager to run the business and stockholders to finance the business. Adding these two individuals will divide the responsibilities and allow each person to focus on his or her own area and strength. Adding specialized staff and investors will bring stability and opportunity for growth.

39. Students' paragraphs should include the following information about the Sarbanes-Oxley Act of 2002: (1) President George W. Bush signed the Act into law on July 30, 2002. (2) The Act deals with reforms that promote corporate responsibility, enhance financial disclosure, and combat fraud. (3) Sarbanes-Oxley created the Public Company Accounting Oversight Board to oversee activities of auditors.

**LESSON 9.1** *Demand and Supply of Resources:* This lesson focuses on the shape of a resource demand curve and a resource supply curve. It also deals with the causes of a shift of a labor demand curve and the causes of a shift of a labor supply curve.

**LESSON 9.2** *Wage Determination:* This lesson provides an explanation of why wages differ across labor markets. The rationale and the impact of the minimum wage are addressed.

**LESSON 9.3** *Labor Unions:* This lesson describes the history and tools of U.S. labor unions. Analysis of how labor unions try to increase wages is presented along with a discussion of recent trends in union membership.

### Consider

Ask students to consider the questions posed on this page as they study Chapter 9. After studying all three lessons, students should be able to answer the questions. The content related to each question can be found on the pages indicated below.

- Why do truck drivers in the United States earn at least 20 times more than rickshaw drivers in Asia? See page 259—Prices of Other Resources.
- Why do some professional basketball players earn 50 times more than others? See page 267—Why Wages Differ.
- Among physicians, why do surgeons earn twice as much as general practitioners? See page 267—Differences in Training, Education, Age, and Experience.
- What's the payoff for a college education? See page 267—Differences in Training, Education, Age, and Experience.

### ▶ POINT YOUR BROWSER

Remind students that they can find additional resources for this chapter at **econxtra.swlearning.com**.

- Xtra! Study Tools
- Net Bookmarks
- Xtra! Quiz Prep
- econ@pps
- Ask the Xpert!
- Graphing Workshop

# Labor Markets

*Demand and Supply of Resources* **9.1**

*Wage Determination* **9.2**

*Labor Unions* **9.3**

© Getty Images/PhotoDisc

### Consider

Why do truck drivers in the United States earn at least 20 times more than rickshaw drivers in Asia?

Why do some professional basketball players earn 50 times more than others?

Among physicians, why do surgeons earn twice as much as general practitioners?

What's the payoff for a college education?

### ▶ POINT YOUR BROWSER

*econxtra.swlearning.com*

## Teaching Resources for Chapter 9

- Activities and Projects Masters
- Spanish Resources
- Econ Connection Interactive Tutorial CD
- **Exam***View*® CD
- Workbook Teacher's Edition
- Chapter Test Teacher's Edition
- NCEE Standards and Correlation

- Personal Finance Guide
- Social Studies Skills Review
- Instructor's Resource CD
  - PowerPoint Presentation
  - Lesson Plans
  - Video Discussion Guide
  - Answers to Graphing Exercises
- **econxtra.swlearning.com**

## Objectives

> Determine the shape of a resource demand curve and a resource supply curve.

> Identify what can shift a labor demand curve.

> Identify what can shift a labor supply curve.

## Overview

As with all prices, prices of productive resources—the inputs used to produce goods and services—are determined by the interaction of demand and supply. Demand and supply in resource markets determine the price and quantity of resources employed. The distribution of resource ownership determines the distribution of income throughout the economy. Your earnings will depend on the market value of the resources you supply. In deciding upon your career—the labor market in which you will work—you should consider the income you could expect from alternative occupations.

## Key Terms

**derived demand**

**productivity**

**equilibrium wage**

**resource substitutes**

**resource complements**

## FOCUS

### 9.1 Demand and Supply of Resources

Explain that part of running a business is deciding the number of workers to hire, whom to hire, and how much to pay workers for their labor. Businesses routinely make trade-offs when they choose which resources to use. Remind students that the best way for competitive businesses to earn profits is to control costs. In some cases, this means replacing a worker with a machine.

### Objectives

Remind students to read the lesson objectives to help focus their attention before reading the lesson.

### Key Terms

Direct students to look up key terms in a business or economics dictionary. Some students will find it helpful to read another definition. In addition to a definition, many entries will include a brief explanation and an example.

### [ In the News ]

Instruct students to read the passage and write down their answers. Point out that their answers might change after they finish studying Lesson 9.1.

### Answers to Think About It

Answers will vary. Possible answer: Prices would increase if worker productivity fell because the unit cost of labor would increase.

### Visual Presentation

Use the PowerPoint presentation on the Instructor's Resource CD as an adjunct to your lecture. The presentation also can be used for review.

## [ In the News ]

### • Higher Productivity, Fewer Workers

In 2003, figures from the U.S. Department of Labor reflected trends that suggested both the good news and the bad news about the current state of the American economy. The good news was that productivity—one of the most important indicators of a dynamic and growing economy—increased by a seasonally adjusted 7.2%. This information was provided in the Labor Department's report on the economy's performance in the second quarter of 2003. However, this strong showing on the part of American workers was offset by the fact that the gains were accomplished using fewer employees. By restructuring and tightening management controls, businesses are able to get maximum production out of their workers. At the same time, the rise in productivity helps to lower unit labor costs and hold off inflationary price increases. Though it hurts the job market in the short run, many economists argue that in the long run, gains in productivity are not only good for the economy, but help workers as well. Gains in productivity allow businesses to increase workers' pay without increasing prices.

### Think About It

What do you think would happen to prices if worker productivity fell?

255

### National Content Standards in Economics

A complete list of the NCEE Standards appears on pages xxiv–xxv of this book. The following standards are addressed in Lesson 9.1.

Standard 8: Role of Price in Market System

Standard 10: Role of Economic Institutions

Standard 13: Role of Resources in Determining Income

Standard 15: Growth

## Demand and Supply of Resources

Point out that the wage rate employers pay is similar to the price consumers pay for goods and services. There is an equilibrium wage rate for workers with a special skill, just as there is an equilibrium price for pizza. The wage rate for a worker depends on the demand and the supply for the tasks this person is able to accomplish. Ask students what is likely to happen to the demand for, supply of, and wage rate paid to people with tax preparation skills as April 15 approaches each year. (Each year, as the deadline approaches for filing federal income tax returns, the demand for workers with these skills will grow while the supply remains unchanged. This will increase the wage rate they receive.)

### *Think Critically Through Visuals*

Direct students to focus their attention on the photographs on this page. Ask for a volunteer to answer the questions posed in the caption.

### Answer

Answers will vary. Possible answers: The doctor should earn more than the construction worker because the physician's labor, assisting the sick, is in higher demand than the construction worker's labor. Fewer individuals can supply the doctor's labor because it is so specialized; more individuals can supply the construction worker's labor.

**NCEE
Standard 13: Role of Resources in Determining Income**

Income for most people is determined by the market value of the productive resources they sell. What workers earn depends, primarily, on the market value of what they produce and how productive they are.

---

*derived demand*

The demand for a resource that arises from the demand for the product that resource produces

# Demand and Supply of Resources

In the market for goods and services—the *product market*—households are demanders and firms are suppliers. Households demand the goods and services that maximize utility. Firms supply the goods and services that maximize profit. In the *resource market*, roles are reversed. Households are suppliers and firms are demanders. Households supply resources to maximize utility. Firms demand resources to maximize profit. Any differences between the utility-maximizing goals of households and the profit-maximizing goals of firms are sorted out through voluntary exchange in markets.

## Market Demand for Resources

Why do firms employ productive resources? Firms use resources to produce goods and services. They try to sell the goods and services to earn a profit. A firm values not the resource itself but the resource's ability to produce goods and services. Because the value of any resource depends on the value of what it produces, the demand for a resource is said to be a *derived demand*. Another term for "derive" is "arise from." Thus, **derived demand** arises from the demand for the good or service produced by the resource. For example, demand for a carpenter arises, or derives, from the demand for the carpenter's output, such as a cabinet or a new deck. Demand for professional baseball players derives from the demand for ballgames. Demand for truck drivers derives from the demand for transporting goods.

The derived nature of resource demand helps explain why professional baseball players usually earn more than professional hockey players, why brain surgeons earn more than tree surgeons, and why tractor-trailer drivers earn more than delivery-van drivers. *The more a worker produces and the higher the price of that product, the more valuable that worker is to a firm.* Thus the demand for a

 **Role of Resources in Determining Income**

*Income for most people is determined by the market value of the productive resources they sell. What they earn depends on the market value of what they produce and how productive they are.* **What outputs do the two people shown in the photos produce? Which one do you think should earn more than the other, and why?**

256    **CHAPTER 9**   Labor Markets

---

*Outside Resources*

**Bureau of Labor Statistics** This federal agency provides extensive data about average wage rates earned by workers in different occupations. Its web site is located at www.bls.gov/bls/blswage.htm. Ask students to think of an occupation that might interest them and to visit this site to find out what they could expect to earn in this type of job. Ask them to discuss the demand and supply for workers who possess the skills needed to hold this job. What might happen in the next few years to change the equilibrium wage rate for these workers?

resource is tied to the value of the output produced by that resource, or its **productivity**. The more productive a resource, the more a firm is willing to pay for it.

The market demand for a particular resource is the sum of demands for that resource in all its different uses. For example, the market demand for carpenters adds together the demand for carpenters in residential and commercial construction, remodeling, cabinetmaking, and so on. Similarly, the market demand for the resource, timber, sums the demand for timber as lumber, railway ties, furniture, pencils, toothpicks, paper products, firewood, and so on. The demand curve for a resource, like the demand curves for the goods produced by that resource, slopes downward. This is depicted by the demand curve for carpenters, *D,* in Figure 9.1.

As the price of a resource falls, firms are more willing and more able to employ that resource. Consider first the firm's greater *willingness* to hire resources as the resource price falls. In developing the demand curve for a particular resource, the prices of other resources are assumed to remain constant. If the wage of carpenters falls, this type of labor becomes relatively cheaper com-

The demand for architects is derived from the demand for new construction, particularly commercial buildings. The American Institute of Architects maintains a career center with a job board. Access this web site through econxtra.swlearning.com. You can find analysis and forecasts for many jobs in the Bureau of Labor Statistics' *Occupational Outlook Handbook (OOH).* Access the prospectus for architects in the OOH through econxtra.swlearning.com. What is the future employment outlook for professional architects?

*econxtra.swlearning.com*

pared with other resources the firm could employ to produce the same output. Firms, therefore, are more willing to hire carpenters rather than hire other, now relatively more costly, resources.

Firms may make *substitutions in production.* For example, a homebuilder can employ more carpenters and fewer prefabricated sections made at a factory. Likewise firms can substitute coal for oil

*The Graphing Workshop*

**productivity**
The value of output produced by a resource

**Labor Market for Carpenters**

**Figure 9.1**

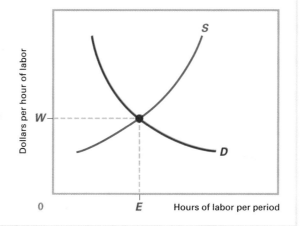

The intersection of the upward-sloping supply curve of carpenters with the downward-sloping demand curve determines the equilibrium wage rate, *W,* and the level of employment, *E.*

**Demand and Supply of Resources**

Ask several students who are employed to describe the work they accomplish on their jobs. Use the following questions to stimulate the discussion: What do you do that has value to your employer? What gives your labor value? Would your labor have value if your employer could not sell the good or service you help produce? Why is the demand for your labor a derived demand?

**NETBookmark**

Direct students to the **econxtra.swlearning.com**. Remind them to click on the link for Lesson 9.1 to find the appropriate link for the **NET Bookmark** on this page.

**Answer**

Answers will vary. Possible answer: Employment for architects is projected to grow about as fast as the average for all occupations through 2010. Additional job openings will come from replacing architects who leave the labor force. Architects face competition for entry-level positions, and even in times of overall good job opportunities, there are areas of the country with few opportunities. Architects face particularly strong competition for jobs or clients during recessions.

***Think Critically Through Visuals***

Direct students to focus their attention on **Figure 9.1—Labor Market for Carpenters**. Point out that at the equilibrium wage, the quantity of labor firms want to hire exactly matches the quantity carpenters want to supply.

*The Graphing Workshop* ——— **Try It**

Direct students to the Graphing Workshop for Chapter 9 at **econxtra.swlearning.com**. Instruct students to click on **Try It: Demand and Supply of Labor in the NBA**. As an enrichment exercise, students may complete **Try It: The Effect of a Change in Demand for Labor on the Aggregate Production Function**. This enrichment exercise presents concepts more advanced than those discussed in the textbook.

**ENRICH**

Identify a local business that employs many workers. Describe a situation in which the firm's sales grow by 50 percent over a single year. Ask students to explain what would happen to the firm's demand for labor and other resources it uses to produce its products. What would happen if the firm's sales fell by 50 percent instead? Ask students to write a one-page paper using this example to demonstrate why the demand for labor is a derived demand.

## Demand and Supply of Resources

Point out that employers do not hire workers if there is no demand for the good or service they supply to the market.

---

**SPAN THE GLOBE**

Direct students to read the short passage "The Immigration Issue" on this page. Use the questions as a starting point for class discussion or have students write a short essay to answer the questions.

### Answers to Think Critically

Answers will vary. In the short run, there would be an increase in the wage rate because the United States would experience a labor shortage. In the long run, producers would not be able to hire as many workers due to the wage increase, and unemployment might result.

 — **Try It**

Direct students to the Graphing Workshop for Chapter 9 at **econxtra.swlearning.com**. As enrichment, students may complete one or both of the following exercises—**Try It: The Bank Teller and the Automated Teller** or **Try It: The Effect of a Change in the Supply of Labor on the Aggregate Production Function**. These enrichment exercises present concepts more advanced than those discussed in the textbook.

 **CHECKPOINT**

Invite a student to answer the checkpoint that appears on page 259.

### Answer

As the price of a resource falls, firms are more willing and able to employ that resource. Therefore, the resource demand curve slopes downward. The more productive a resource, the more a firm is willing to pay for it. On the other side, resource suppliers are more willing and able to supply the resource as the price increases. Therefore, the resource supply curve is upward sloping.

---

**The Graphing Workshop**

**equilibrium wage**
The wage at which the quantity of labor firms want to hire exactly matches the quantity workers want to supply

or security alarms for security guards, as the relative price of coal or security alarms declines.

A lower price for a resource also increases a firm's *ability* to hire that resource. For example, if the wage for carpenters falls, homebuilders can hire more carpenters for the same total cost. The lower resource price means the firm is *more able* to buy the resource. Because producers are more willing and

## SPAN THE GLOBE

### The Immigration Issue

According to recent polls, the U.S. public is more opposed to any kind of immigration than their elected officials realize. Whether legal or illegal, the public seems to be canceling America's invitation engraved on the Statue of Liberty: "Give me your tired, your poor, your huddled masses yearning to breathe free...." However, it seems legislators and other national leaders charged with shaping legal policy on the issue haven't heard the news. According to a poll by the Chicago Council on Foreign Relations, 70 percent of 2,862 people interviewed said that "controlling and reducing illegal immigration" should be a "very important" policy goal. Only 22 percent of 400 of leaders from Congress, business, the media, labor, and religious and academic groups agreed. Moreover, 55 percent of the general public also wants to reduce quotas and legal immigration, compared to only 18 percent of the country's leaders. Many suggest the reason for the opinion gap between the public and its leaders is that a great many Americans are afraid of immigrants taking their jobs. The nation's leaders, on the other hand, have little fear of job competition from immigrants.

### Think Critically

What if Congress eliminated immigration into the United States? In the short run, what would happen to the wage rate and level of employment in the United States? What might happen in the long run?

more able to employ a resource when the price of the resource declines, the demand curve for a resource slopes downward, as shown in Figure 9.1.

## Market Supply of Resources

On the other side of the market, resource suppliers tend to be both more *willing* and more *able* to supply the resource as its price increases. This explains the upward-sloping market supply curve, as shown in Figure 9.1 by the supply curve of carpenters, *S*. Resource suppliers are more *willing* because a higher resource price, other things constant, means more goods and services can be purchased with the earnings from each unit of the resource supplied.

Resource prices are signals about the rewards for supplying resources to alternative activities. A high resource price tells the resource owner, "The market really values your resource and is willing to pay you well for what you supply." Higher prices will draw resources from lower-valued uses. For example, as the wage for carpenters increases, the quantity of labor supplied will increase. Some carpenters will give up leisure time to work more hours. Also, people in other lines of work will be attracted to carpentry.

The second reason a resource supply curve slopes upward is that resource owners are more *able* to supply the resource at a higher price. For example, a higher carpenter's wage means more apprentices will choose to undergo training to become carpenters. The higher wage *enables* resource suppliers to increase their quantity supplied. Similarly, a higher timber price enables loggers to harvest trees in more remote regions. A higher oil price enables drillers to explore more remote parts of the world.

The interaction in Figure 9.1 of the labor demand curve, *D*, and the labor supply curve, *S*, determines the equilibrium wage for carpenters, *W*, and the equilibrium employment of carpenters, *E*. At the **equilibrium wage**, the quantity of labor firms want to hire exactly

---

*Economic Headlines*

Instruct students to locate an article in a current magazine or newspaper describing a new product that is being brought to market. Tell them to imagine that this product is very successful and that millions of units are demanded. Ask them to describe the impact this would have on the labor market, wage rates, and the ability of other businesses to attract and keep workers. (The demand for workers to produce the product would grow, increasing the equilibrium wage rate for workers with the needed skills. This would force other employers to raise their wage rates to hire or keep these workers.)

matches the quantity carpenters want to supply. At the equilibrium wage, there is neither an excess quantity of carpenters demanded nor an excess quantity supplied. The interaction of labor demand and labor supply determines the market wages and thereby allocates the scarce resource, labor.

 **CHECKPOINT**
Describe the shape of a resource demand curve and a resource supply curve.

# Nonwage Determinants of Labor Demand

The quantity of labor demanded increases as the wage decreases, other things constant, because a lower wage makes employers more willing and more able to hire workers. Thus the labor demand curve slopes downward, other things constant, as you saw in Figure 9.1. What are the other things that are assumed to remain constant along a

given demand curve? In other words, what are the nonwage factors that help shape the labor demand curve?

## Demand for the Final Product

Labor demand is derived from the demand for the output produced by that labor. For example, the demand for carpenters derives from the demand for what they produce. Because the demand for labor is *derived* from the demand for that labor's output, any change in the demand for that output affects resource demand. For example, an increase in the demand for housing will increase the demand for carpenters. As shown in Figure 9.2, this causes the demand curve for that labor to shift to the right, from *D* to *D'*. A rightward shift of the demand for carpenters will increase the market wage and employment.

## Prices of Other Resources

The prices of other resources are assumed to remain constant along the downward sloping demand curve for labor. A change in the price of other resources could shift the demand for labor. Some resources substitute for each other in production. For example, as mentioned already, prefabricated

## Nonwage Determinants of Labor Demand

Remind students that labor is only one of many resources used to produce goods and services. A change in the cost of other resources, or a change in how resources are used, will change the demand for workers. Ask students why it would be difficult for most ski instructors to find employment during the summer months, or why the number people who work on farms has fallen so much in the past 50 years.

### *Think Critically Through Visuals*

Direct students to focus their attention on **Figure 9.2—An Increase in the Demand for Carpenters**. Point out that the rightward shift of the demand for carpenters will increase the market wage and employment.

The Graphing Workshop ——— Apply It

Direct students to the Graphing Workshop for Chapter 9 at **econxtra.swlearning.com**. As an enrichment exercise, students may complete **Apply It: Disequilibrium in the Labor Market: IT Workers**. This enrichment exercise presents concepts more advanced than those discussed in the textbook.

 **An Increase in the Demand for Carpenters**

Figure 9.2

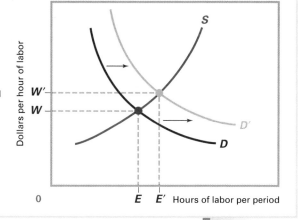

An increase in the demand for carpenters is shown by a rightward shift of that labor demand curve. This will increase the market wage and increase employment of carpenters.

## Group Activity

Divide students into four groups with four students left over. Tell each group that it is a business that wants to hire a new manager at the lowest possible cost. They may offer up to $50,000 per year and two of the following fringe benefits: (1) health insurance, (2) retirement plan, (3) life insurance, (4) company car, or (5) four weeks of vacation. The four extra students are qualified workers who are seeking work. Give each group time to interview and make an offer to each worker. Which offers are accepted and which are not? How does this demonstrate the importance of nonwage determinants of labor supply?

# TEACH (continued)

## Nonwage Determinants of Labor Demand

Ask why it is unrealistic for a worker to say something like, "I've graduated with a degree in accounting. I know what I need to know. I won't ever need to go back to school again." Either show your class a manual typewriter or a photograph of one. Point out that prior to 1980, virtually all written businesses correspondence required the use of such a device. Ask students to compare the skills needed to operate a manual typewriter with those needed to use a word processing program on a computer. What happened to the demand for workers who could operate only a typewriter after 1980? Why do technological advancements almost always require workers to learn new skills?

## Think Critically Through Visuals

Direct students to focus their attention on the photograph on this page. Ask for a volunteer to answer the question posed in the caption.

### Answer

Answers will vary. Possible answer: The truck driver earns more than the rickshaw driver because the truck driver is more productive than the rickshaw driver—that is, the truck driver is able to carry a larger load for a much greater distance, and faster, than the rickshaw driver.

 **CHECKPOINT**

Invite a student to answer the checkpoint question that appears on page 261.

### Answer

The nonwage determinants of labor supply are (1) demand for the final product, (2) prices of other resources, and (3) technology.

---

**resource substitutes**

One resource can replace another in production; an increase in the price of one resource increases the demand for the other

**resource complements**

One resource works with the other in production; a decrease in the price of one increases the demand for the other

---

home sections built mostly by machine at the factory substitute for on-site home construction by carpenters. Substitutes can replace each other in production. With **resource substitutes**, an increase in the price of one increases the demand for the other. For example, an increase in the price of prefabricated home sections will increase the demand for carpenters. This will shift the demand for carpenters to the right, as in Figure 9.2.

Some resources are complements in production—carpenters and lumber, for example. Complements go together in production. With **resource complements**, a decrease in the price of one leads to an increase in the demand for the other. If the price of lumber decreases, the quantity of lumber demanded increases, which increases the demand for carpenters, shifting the demand for carpenters to the right.

As another example, trucks and truck drivers are complements. Any increase in the quantity or quality of a complementary resource, such as trucks, boosts the productivity of the resource in question, such as truck drivers. This, in turn, increases the demand for truck drivers. Bigger and better trucks make truck drivers more productive.

## Technology

A labor demand curve assumes a given level of technology in that market. Thus, technology is assumed to be constant along a labor demand curve. A change in technology can shift the labor demand curve. More technologically sophisticated capital can increase the productivity of labor, thus increasing the demand for labor. For example, better power tools, such as a pneumatic nail driver, enable carpenters to be more productive, thus shifting the demand for carpenters to the right. Alternatively, improved technology could make some workers unnecessary, thus shifting the demand for carpenters to the left. An example of this would be a factory

© Getty Images/PhotoDisc

One reason truck drivers in the United States earns at least 20 times more than rickshaw drivers in Asia is the nature of the vehicles themselves. Compare the photograph of a rickshaw on the first page of this chapter to the tractor-trailer shown here. What specific characteristics of the tractor-trailer would make it a more productive resource than the rickshaw?

**260**   **CHAPTER 9**   Labor Markets

---

## Curriculum Connection—Business

Many businesses provide training for their workers. This may be formal training in an accredited program or on-the-job training provided by co-workers. In either case, training costs time and money. Ask students to discuss why businesses provide training, and how it might change their labor supply curve. Do students believe there are potential disadvantages to businesses that provide training? (Businesses that provide training may attract more or better workers because this is a nonwage benefit of employment. It might cause employees to look for other work after they are trained.)

using a robot to perform a delicate task once performed by a human worker.

Sometimes a technological improvement can boost the productivity of some resources but reduce the demand for others. For example, the development of computer-generated animated movies increased the demand for computer programmers with that skill. At the same time, it decreased the demand for animators who drew each frame by hand.

## CHECKPOINT
What are the nonwage factors that help shape the labor demand curve?

# Nonwage Determinants of Labor Supply

The quantity of labor supplied increases with the wage, other things constant, so the labor supply curve slopes upward, as shown in Figure 9.1. What are the other things that are assumed to remain constant along a given supply curve? In

other words, what are the nonwage factors that help shape the labor supply curve?

## Worker Wealth

Although some jobs are rewarding in a variety of nonmonetary ways, the main reason people work is to earn money to buy goods and services. The wealthier people are, the less they need to work for a living. Thus, a person's supply of labor depends, among other things, on his or her wealth, including homes, cars, savings, stock holdings, and other assets. A person's wealth is assumed to remain constant along the labor supply curve.

A decrease in wealth would prompt people to work more, thus increasing their supply of labor. For example, the stock market decline between 2000 and 2003 reduced significantly the wealth that many people planned to draw on during retirement. As a result, they had to put retirement plans on hold and instead work more and longer to rebuild their retirement nest egg. This increased the supply of labor, as shown by the rightward shift of the labor supply curve from $S$ to $S'$ in Figure 9.3. This will reduce the wage and increase employment.

## An Increase in the Supply of Carpenters

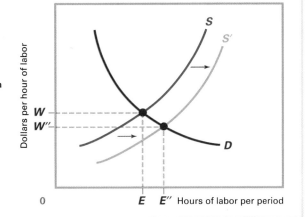

**Figure 9.3**

An increase in the supply of carpenters is shown by a rightward shift of the labor supply curve. This will reduce the market wage and increase employment of carpenters.

Lesson 9.1 • *Demand and Supply of Resources* **261**

## RETEACH
Ask students to identify several jobs they regard as being unpleasant or dangerous. These might include collecting garbage, cleaning floors, working in high places, or disposing of toxic waste. Ask them to describe the labor demand and supply curves for these jobs. Why do these employees often receive higher wages than other workers with similar skills and training who work in more desirable occupations? Is there such a thing as a nonwage cost of labor supply?

## TEACH

### Nonwage Determinants of Labor Supply

Remind students that jobs are more than a way to earn income. People's willingness to work often depends on their values as well as their financial situation. Why does the number of people willing to work often grow when employment begins to fall as the economy enters a recession? (When one family member is laid off, others are more likely to seek employment.)

### *Think Critically Through Visuals*

Direct students to focus their attention on **Figure 9.3–An Increase in the Supply of Carpenters**. Point out that the rightward shift of the labor supply curve shows an increase in the supply of labor.

**Investigate Your Local Economy** Assign the activity on page 262. Consider having students create a short survey that can be administered to a large group of students. For example, you might help the students arrange to have homeroom teachers administer the survey to all juniors and seniors.

### *Think Critically Through Visuals*

Direct students to focus their attention on the photograph on page 262. Ask for a volunteer to answer the questions posed in the caption.

### Answer

Answers will vary. Possible answer: The job of a steel worker might have a smaller supply of labor because the job is labor intensive, exhausting, and dirty.

## CHECKPOINT
Invite a student to answer the checkpoint that appears on page 262.

### Answer

The nonwage factors that help shape the labor supply curve are (1) worker wealth, (2) working conditions, and (3) tastes for work.

As an example of the opposite effect, winners of multimillion-dollar lotteries often announce they plan to quit their jobs. This would reduce their supply of labor in response to the increase in their wealth. In your own life, if you were to inherit some money from a relative, you might decide not to work next summer. This would decrease your labor supply.

### Working Conditions

Labor supply to a particular market depends on the working conditions, such as the difficulty of the job and the attractiveness of the work environment. Working conditions are assumed to remain constant along a given labor supply curve. Any improvement in working conditions would shift the labor supply curve rightward. For example, if employers offer carpenters more flexible hours, many will find this more attractive than a rigid work schedule. These carpenters will increase their supply of labor, shifting the labor supply curve to the right.

More generally, people supply less labor to jobs that are dirty, dangerous, dull, exhausting, illegal, low status,

dead-end, and involve inconvenient hours. They choose to supply more labor to jobs that are clean, safe, interesting, energizing, legal, high status, have advancement potential, and involve convenient hours.

### Tastes for Work

Just as consumer tastes for goods and services are assumed to remain constant along a demand curve, worker tastes for jobs are assumed to remain constant along a given labor supply curve. Job tastes are relatively stable. They don't change overnight. Still, over time the supply of labor could change because of a change in the tastes for a particular job. For example, suppose carpentry becomes more appealing because people become more attracted to jobs that provide exercise, fresh air, and the satisfaction of building something. In this case, the supply of labor to carpentry would shift rightward, as in Figure 9.3.

As another example of how worker tastes can change over time, most teenagers a decade ago found jobs at fast-food restaurants relatively attractive. Teenagers today seem to prefer upscale employers such as Starbucks and the Gap.

**Based on working conditions, do you think that the job of steel worker would have a large supply of labor? Why or why not?**

### CHECKPOINT

What are the nonwage factors that help shape the labor supply curve?

## Key Concepts

1. What is the demand for workers in your school cafeteria derived from?

2. Why would the demand for roofers increase if the price of shingles falls by 50 percent?

3. Why would an increase in the price of heating oil increase the quantity of heating oil supplied to the market?

4. What would happen to the demand for technicians who produce computer chips if a new chip-manufacturing process using only half as much raw material was introduced?

5. Why might the supply of high-school students who are willing to work in fast-food restaurants decrease if there was an economic boom and a large increase in stock values?

## Graphing Exercise

6. Draw a labor supply curve for students who are willing to work, based on the data in the table. Explain what would happen to the location of this labor supply curve as a result of each of the listed events.

| Hourly Wage Rate | Number of Students Willing to Work |
| --- | --- |
| $6 | 5 |
| $7 | 10 |
| $8 | 15 |
| $9 | 20 |
| $10 | 25 |

a. A large employer in town closes and thousands of workers are laid off.

b. Wearing old clothes becomes popular among students. This style causes many young people to stop buying new clothing.

c. The state board of education raises the grade requirement to graduate.

## Think Critically

7. **Management** Make a list of nonwage determinants of labor supply that managers could use to increase the number of workers who are willing to be employed.

8. **Science** Identify scientific developments that have taken place in the last 50 years that have changed the demand for labor in the marketplace.

**Xtra!**
**Study Tools**
econxtra.swlearning.com

Lesson 9.1 • *Demand and Supply of Resources*    **263**

**Labor Supply**

(Graph: Wage rate on y-axis from $6 to $10, Students willing to work on x-axis from 5 to 25)

### Visualizing the Answer— Graphing Exercise

6. The answer includes a graph. Students' graphs should look similar to the one shown here. An Excel spreadsheet containing this graph, along with supporting data, is available on the Instructor's Resource CD.

## Key Concepts

1. The demand for food served by the cafeteria creates the demand for cafeteria workers.

2. The lower price for shingles would reduce the cost of new roofs, so more people would hire roofers to install new roofs.

3. Answers will vary. Possible answer: Higher heating oil prices would cause businesses to change from the production of gasoline and other products to the production of more heating oil. The higher price also would encourage exploration for new sources of crude oil.

4. Answers will vary. Possible answer: The lower cost process would reduce the price of computer chips and should increase the quantity demanded. This would result in a greater demand for the technicians who produce the chips.

5. Answers will vary. Possible answer: When students' parents are earning large salaries and feel wealthy because the value of their stocks has increased, they may be more willing to give their children money. This could reduce the willingness of high-school students to accept low-paying employment at fast-food restaurants.

## Graphing Exercise

6. Graphs will vary. An example of an acceptable graph appears at the bottom of this page.

   a. With reduced family incomes, more students will be willing to work, causing the supply curve for labor to shift to the right.

   b. Fewer students will choose to work because they don't need money to buy new clothing, causing the supply curve for labor to move to the left.

   c. Fewer students will choose to work because they don't have time, causing the supply curve for labor to move to the left.

The Answer Key is continued on page 282.

## Sharpen Your Life Skills

### Working with Percentages

After studying Lesson 9.1, students should be able to answer the questions on this page.

### Apply Your Skill

Consider allowing students to work in pairs for this assignment.

### Answers

1. The increase in the CPI from 1990 through 2002: 180.9 − 130.7 = 50.2

   The increase in prices between 1990 and 2002 as measured by the CPI: 50.2 / 130.7 = 0.384 = 38.4%

   Increase in value of $1.59 from 1990 to 2002: $1.59 × .384 = $.61

   Value of $1.59 in 1990 adjusted to 2002 prices: $1.59 + $.61 = $2.20

   The $2.29 price of 2-by-4 lumber went up more rapidly than other prices on average. This indicates that the demand for lumber grew and/or the supply was reduced to bring about a higher real equilibrium price.

2. The increase in the CPI from the end of 2002 to the end of 2005: 196.7 − 180.9 = 15.8

   The increase in prices between 2002 and 2005 as measured by the CPI: 15.8 / 180.9 = 0.087 = 8.7%

   Amount to adjust 2005 income by to convert it to 2002 values: $14.00 × 0.087 = $1.22

   The 2002 value of $14.00 earned in 2005: $14.00 − $1.22 = $12.78

   Your real hourly income will be $2.78 greater than it is now.

# Sharpen Your Life Skills

## Working with Percentages

Raw economic data can be difficult to interpret. It often is more meaningful if expressed in terms of percentages. For example, your father might have said something like this in December 2002: "In 1980, when I was 16 years old, I earned only $3.10 an hour." You might believe that what he said was true. However, would this information give you an accurate idea of how well he was paid? Probably not. In order to compare values over time, many economists adjust them for inflation and then express the values as percentages. The most common tool they use for comparing values is the Consumer Price Index (CPI). In 1980, the CPI was 82.4. At the end of 2002, it was 180.9. But again, what do these values mean? You can answer this question by finding the percentage change in the CPI and using it to adjust the value of your father's 1980 income.

To calculate the percentage change in the CPI, you need to find the change in the index (180.9 − 82.4 = 98.5) and divide this change by the original index (98.5 ÷ 82.4 = 1.20 or 120%). According to the CPI, prices increased by 120% between 1980 and 2002.

To find the purchasing power of the 1980 wage in 2002, you need to mul-

tiply $3.10 times the percentage increase in the CPI and then add the result to the 1980 wage of $3.10:

$$\$3.10 \times 1.2 = \$3.72$$

$$\$3.72 + \$3.10 = \$6.82$$

Knowing that the purchasing power of your father's 1980 wage was $6.82 is more meaningful to you than simply knowing he earned $3.10 at that time.

## Apply Your Skill

1. In 1990, the CPI was 130.7 and the average price for an eight-foot 2-by-4 used to construct houses was $1.59. In December 2002, the same 2-by-4 cost $2.29. Use the method demonstrated above to calculate whether the price of 2-by-4s increased more or less rapidly than the CPI.

2. Suppose you earned $10.00 per hour in December 2002. Further, suppose that by December 2005, the CPI is 196.7. If you earn $14.00 per hour at that time, what will the real value of your wage be in terms of December 2002 dollars? Will you be better off or worse off than you are now?

264        **CHAPTER 9**   Labor Markets

### Extend the Content

Every summer, millions of young people look for work. Some are recent graduates. Others want to find summer employment before they return to school in the fall. Ask students to discuss how this influx of new workers is likely to affect the supply of labor and wage rates offered to lower-skill workers. Why are most well-paid workers unaffected by this situation? (Lower-skill workers may receive lower wage rates because of the increased supply of labor. Well-paid workers are not likely to be affected because the young workers lack skills that experienced workers possess.)

# movers & shakers

## Dr. Tim Kremchek *Orthopedic Surgeon*

Tim Kremchek started college with two goals in mind—to play baseball and to have fun. Academics were not high on his priority list, and after two years of college his grade-point average was 2.2.

During a holiday break, Tim's father, an orthopedic surgeon, invited Tim to join him at work. "He knew I was clueless about my future, but he didn't pressure me to make a decision about life after college." While watching his father work, Tim observed how much his father loved what he was doing. It seemed more like fun than work. After the break Tim returned to college knowing he wanted to become an orthopedic surgeon. From that point on, he earned a 4.0 grade-point average.

After four years of college, Tim attended four more years of medical school, followed by a two-year residency in general surgery. Wanting to specialize in orthopedics meant an additional four years of training. Then, because he wanted to specialize in treating athletes, Tim opted to participate in an orthopedic sports-medicine fellowship for a year. Finally, at the age of 34—after 15 years of schooling beyond high school—this highly trained surgeon began his life's work.

Today Tim Kremchek, M.D., is not only the director of sports medicine and chief orthopedic surgeon for the TriHealth hospital system in Cincinnati, Ohio. He also is the medical director and chief orthopedic surgeon for the Cincinnati Reds major league baseball team. He provides the team with medical advice and has performed multiple surgeries on such major league players as Ken Griffey, Jr., and

Barry Larkin. Because of his expertise, out-of-town athletes now regularly travel to Dr. Kremchek for surgery and physical therapy. Asked why he thinks athletes opt to travel to Cincinnati instead of larger cities for their medical care, he said, "I think they trust me and appreciate my straightforward approach to diagnosing their problem. I offer a team approach to care and have surrounded myself with expert personnel to assist in that care." High school and college athletes also routinely seek his expertise in their desire to overcome injuries and return to the playing field.

In addition to his busy practice, Dr. Kremchek's role with the Cincinnati Reds has meant his attendance at every Reds home game. Of 81 home games played each year, Kremchek has missed only one in the last seven years. Although it's not a requirement for the job, Dr. Kremchek attends each game because "by being there and getting to know each athlete, I'm able to develop relationships with them and understand them. It builds my credibility not only with the Reds players but with visiting players as well, some who come to me for treatment from other parts of the world."

Married with five children, Dr. Kremchek bases his success on his love for his work. He proudly states that in addition to his family, "I love baseball. I like the challenge of taking care of baseball players. I'm very good at it, and I'm so lucky to be able to say that."

### SOURCE READING

Dr. Kremchek admits that after two years of college, he "was clueless" about his future. However, he made some decisions that drastically altered his career course. What were those decisions? How did his decisions affect his life as it is now?

### ENTREPRENEURS IN ACTION

Dr. Kremchek found a career that combined his love of baseball with his desire to be successful in business. What special interests do you have? What career will enable you to use those interests? What training do you need for this goal?

---

## movers & shakers

### FOCUS

This feature addresses the nonwage factors that help shape the labor supply by focusing on the career of Dr. Tim Kremchek, orthopedic surgeon. Have students apply the nonwage determinants of labor—worker wealth, working conditions, and tastes for work—to Dr. Kremchek's career, as described in this feature.

### TEACH

Instruct students to read the **Movers & Shakers** feature about Dr. Tim Kremchek. Point out that some students may find it helpful to read the article, read the questions at the bottom of the page, and then reread the article.

### ASSESS

Use the questions in Source Reading and Entrepreneurs in Action at the bottom of the profile to assess the students' understanding of this **Movers & Shakers** feature.

#### Answers to Source Reading

Dr. Kremchek decided he wanted to be an orthopedic surgeon and that he was going to work really hard in school to achieve this goal. His decision enabled him to get where he is today.

#### Answers to Entrepreneurs in Action

Answers will vary. Possible answer: Encourage students to check the training requirements for their field of interest using a resource such as the *Occupational Outlook Handbook* at the U.S. Department of Labor Bureau of Labor Statistics at www.bls.gov.

#### Extend the Content

Developing aptitudes into skills through education, practice, and training is thought to be one of the best ways to achieve a good income. Ask students what else besides education, practice, and training contributed to Dr. Tim Kremchek's satisfying career. (Answer: patience, persistence, and drive.) Ask students whether they feel similarly goal-driven by their current interests. What must people be willing to do to become part of the demand for workers with special talents and abilities?

## Objectives

> Explain why wages differ across labor markets.

> Describe minimum wage legislation, and discuss its impact on employment and nonwage compensation.

## Overview

Because of the division of labor and comparative advantage, the U.S. work force is becoming more specialized. For example, the U.S. Census of 1850 identified 322 job titles. In the 2000 Census, there were 31,000 job titles—about 100 times the number in 1850. The pay for each of these specialties is determined by the intersection of a labor demand curve and a labor supply curve. The resulting differences in pay across job specialties can be huge.

## Key Terms

minimum wage law

### [ In the News ]

#### ● Winner-Take-All Labor Markets

Each year *Forbes* magazine reports on the multimillion-dollar earnings of top entertainers and professional athletes. Entertainment and sports have come to be called "winner-take-all" labor markets because a few key people critical to the overall success of an enterprise are richly rewarded. For example, the credits at the end of a movie list the dozens of people involved in its production. Hundreds, sometimes thousands, more are employed behind the scenes. Despite a huge cast and crew, the difference between a movie's financial success and its failure depends on the performance of just a few people—the lead actors, the director, and the screenwriter. These are the people who are compensated the most. The same happens in sports. Although thousands of players compete each year in professional tennis, for example, the value of television time, ticket sales, and endorsements is based on the drawing power of just the top players. In professional golf, attendance and TV ratings are significantly higher for tournaments in which Tiger Woods is in the running. Compensation for top performers is determined through open competition for their talents. The competition bids up their pay to extremely high levels, such as the $20 million per movie earned by some top stars. This is more than 1,000 times the average annual earnings of Screen Actors Guild members.

#### Think About It

Do you think it is fair that top entertainers and sports figures earn as much money as they do? Why or why not?

266

### National Content Standards in Economics

A complete list of the NCEE Standards appears on pages xxiv–xxv of this book. The following standards are addressed in Lesson 9.2.

Standard 1: Scarcity

Standard 2: Marginal Cost/Benefit

Standard 4: Role of Incentives

Standard 10: Role of Economic Institutions

Standard 13: Role of Resources in Determining Income

Standard 15: Growth

# Why Wages Differ

Wages differ substantially across labor markets. Figure 9.4 shows the average hourly wages for the 128 million U.S. workers in 2001. Workers are sorted into 22 occupations from the highest to the lowest average wage. Management earns the highest wage, at $34 an hour, and food workers earn the lowest, at $8 an hour. Wage differences across labor markets can be attributed to differences in labor demand, labor supply, or both.

## Differences in Training, Education, Age, and Experience

Some jobs pay more because they require a long and expensive training period. Costly training reduces market supply because fewer individuals are willing to undergo the time and expense required. However, extensive training increases the productivity of labor. This in turn increases the demand for workers with those skills. For example, certified public accountants (CPAs) earn more than file clerks because the extensive training for CPAs limits the supply to this field and because this training increases the productivity of CPAs compared to file clerks. Reduced supply and increased demand both increase the market wage. Even among physicians, some specialties earn more than others because of a longer training period. This is why, for example, surgeons on average earn twice as much as general practitioners.

Figure 9.5 shows how education and experience affect earnings. Age groups are shown on the horizontal axis and

**Ask the Xpert!**
*econxtra.swlearning.com*

*What would happen if everyone were paid the same?*

---

**Average Hourly Wage by Occupation**

Figure 9.4

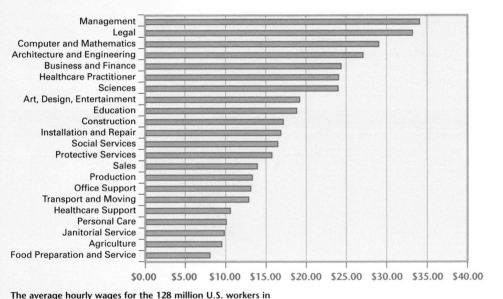

The average hourly wages for the 128 million U.S. workers in 2001 are sorted from the highest to the lowest in this graph. Wage differences across labor markets can be attributed to differences in labor demand, labor supply, or both.

Source: U.S. Bureau of Labor Statistics. Figures are for 2001.

---

## Outside Resources

**College Brochures** Universities and colleges publish brochures and catalogs describing the academic programs offered at the institution. In many high schools, these publications are available for review in the guidance office. Many institutions also provide these resources online. Ask students to review a brochure and identify a field of study that they believe they would enjoy. Instruct them to write an essay that explains how completing a degree in this field would improve their employment opportunities. Why would employers be more willing to demand their labor?

---

## TEACH

### Why Wages Differ

Point out that workers should not expect to receive the same wage rate for any job they might accept. In theory, workers in a market economy are paid in relation to the value of their contribution to production. Being skilled, hard working, or experienced is not enough to guarantee a high wage rate. A worker who is the best, most efficient, and hardest working soap carver in the world is not likely to earn much income. The value of anything, including labor, is best measured by finding out what others are willing to pay for it.

### Ask the Xpert!

Direct students to **econxtra.swlearning.com** to hear an expert answer the question "What would happen if everyone were paid the same?"

### Think Critically Through Visuals

Direct students to focus their attention on **Figure 9.4–Average Hourly Wage by Occupation**. Ask students to use the graph to explain how education influences the average hourly wage of various occupations. Students should recognize that the occupations at the top of the graph generally require a college degree.

### The Graphing Workshop — See It

Direct students to the Graphing Workshop for Chapter 9 at **econxtra.swlearning.com**. As an enrichment exercise, students may complete **See It: Wage Differentials**. This enrichment exercise presents concepts more advanced than those discussed in the textbook.

### Why Wages Differ

Write the subheadings from this section on the board and invite students to offer examples of wage differences for each category.

## TEAM WORK

Organize students into groups of four. Instruct teams to select a recorder and a spokesperson. Instruct students to complete the **Team Work** activity shown on this page. Set a timer for 10 minutes. When the timer goes off, invite the spokesperson from each group to take a turn providing their group's findings.

Make sure each group understands that wage differences are based upon the difference in labor specialization, training, education, and skill that each one of these jobs requires. Wage differences also arise from the different working conditions for each of these occupations.

### Think Critically Through Visuals

Direct students to focus their attention on **Figure 9.5—Education Pays More for Every Age Group**. Ask students to explain the shape of the lines in this graph. For example, the bottom line shows that workers without a high school education do not see a significant increase in earnings with age, while college graduates gradually earn more with additional experience until their earnings flatten out in middle age.

## TEAM WORK

Divide into groups of four. Each group member should choose one of the occupation categories shown in Figure 9.4. Make sure that each member chooses a different occupation. As a group, discuss the reasons for the wage differences among the four occupations.

average annual earnings, on the vertical axis. Earnings are for all full-time, year-round workers in 2001. The lines are labeled to reflect the highest level of education achieved and range from "Less Than Ninth Grade" (bottom line) up to "Professional Degree" (top line). Professional degrees include graduate degrees in law, medicine, business administration, and the like.

The relationship between income and education is clear. At every age, those with more education earned more. For example, in the 35-to-44 age group, those with a professional degree earned five times more on average than those with less than a ninth-grade education.

Age itself also has an important effect on income. Earnings increased as workers gained more job experience and became more productive.

Notice that the pay increase with age is greater for more-educated workers. For example, among those with less than a ninth-grade education, workers in the 45-to-54 age group earned on average only 8 percent more than those in the 25-to-34 age group. But among those with a professional degree, workers in the 45-to-54 age group earned on average 86 percent more than those in the 25-to-34 age group.

These earnings differences reflect the normal operation of labor markets. More education and more job experience increase labor productivity, and more productive workers earn more.

### Differences in Ability

Because they are more able and more productive, some workers earn more than others with the same training and education. For example, two college graduates majoring in economics may have identical educations, but one earns more because of greater ability and higher productivity. Most business executives have extensive training and business experience, but few become chief executives of large corporations.

---

**Education Pays More for Every Age Group**　　　　　　　　　　**Figure 9.5**

**At every age, those with more education earned more. Earnings increased as workers gained more job experience and became more productive.**

Source: U.S. Bureau of Labor Statistics. Figures are average earnings for all full-time, year-round workers in 2001.

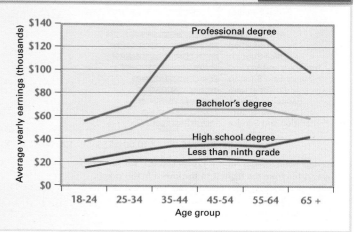

---

## ENRICH

Many careers traditionally have been dominated by either male or female workers. In the past, most nurses, secretaries, elementary teachers, and beauticians were women, while most truck drivers, mechanics, business managers, and lawyers were men. This situation is changing. Ask students to discuss whether they would consider pursuing a career that traditionally has been followed by members of the opposite gender. What has the blurring of gender links in occupations done to wage rates? Has there been any equalization? Do they believe this is a good trend? Ask them to explain their points of view.

The same goes for professional athletes. In the National Basketball Association, for example, Kevin Garnet of Minnesota was paid $25.2 million in 2002, which was about 50 times that of the lowest-paid player. Being tall helps boost productivity and pay. Nine of the ten highest-paid players were at least 6 feet 9 inches tall.

## Differences in Risk

Jobs with a higher probability of injury or death, such as coal mining and fishing, pay more than safer jobs, other things constant. Workers also earn more, other things constant, in seasonal jobs such as construction and fishing. This is due to the higher risk of unemployment at certain times of the year.

Some jobs are both dangerous and seasonal. For example, deckhands on fishing boats in the winter waters of the Bering Sea off Alaska earn more than $4,000 for five days of work. The temperature on the boats is seldom above zero and daily shifts allow only three hours for sleep.

## Geographic Differences

People have a strong incentive to supply their resources in the market where they earn the most, other things constant. For example, place kickers in the National Football League come from around the world for the attractive salaries available. Likewise, because physicians earn more in the United States than elsewhere, thousands of foreign-trained physicians migrate here each year. The flow of labor is not all one way. Some Americans seek their fortune abroad, with basketball players going to Europe and baseball players headed to Japan.

## Job Discrimination

Some people earn lower wages because of discrimination in the job market based on race, ethnicity, or gender. Although such discrimination is illegal, history shows that certain groups—including African Americans, Hispanics, and women—have systematically earned less than others of apparently equal ability.

Job-market discrimination can take many forms. An employer may fail to

© Getty Images/PhotoDisc

The workplace today is increasingly diverse. However, many forms of discrimination result in fewer opportunities for some workers. Propose a solution to the problem of job discrimination.

hire a minority job applicant because the applicant lacks training. But this lack of training can arise from discrimination in the schools, in union apprenticeship programs, or in employer-run training programs. For example, evidence suggests that black workers receive less on-the-job training than otherwise similar white workers.

The Equal Employment Opportunity Commission, established by the Civil Rights Act of 1964, monitors cases involving unequal pay for equal work and unequal access to promotion. Research suggests that civil rights legislation has helped narrow the black-white earnings gap.

The gap between male and female pay also has narrowed. For example, among all full-time, year-round U.S. workers, females in 1980 earned only 60 percent of what males earned. By 2002, females earned 77.5 percent of male pay. In addition to discrimination as a source of the pay gap, women do more housework and childcare than men do. This tends to reduce female job experience. It also causes some to seek more flexible positions, which often pay less.

## Union Membership

Finally, workers represented by labor unions earn more on average than other workers. The final section of this chapter discusses the effects of labor unions on the market for labor.

### CHECKPOINT
Why do wages differ across labor markets?

Lesson 9.2 • *Wage Determination*  **269**

## The Minimum Wage

Remind students that the minimum wage in the United States was created as a result of the Great Depression, when many adults could not earn enough from their jobs to support themselves or a family. Today, the minimum wage (when adjusted for inflation) is much lower than it was in the late 1930s.

### Ethics in Action

Have students work in pairs to discuss the ethical issue featured on this page, and develop answers to the questions presented.

#### Answers to Think Critically

Answers will vary. Students should recognize social factors, including cultural and religious influences. They should also recognize the social influence of the traditional role of women as it related to reproduction and child-rearing.

### NETBookmark

Direct students to **econxtra.swlearning.com**. Remind them to click on the link for Lesson 9.2 to find the appropriate link for the **NET Bookmark** on this page.

#### Answer

In January 2004, the federal minimum wage was $5.15 per hour. Various minimum wage exceptions apply under specific circumstances to workers with disabilities, full-time students, youth under age 20 in their first 90 consecutive calendar days of employment, tipped employees, and student learners.

### THE WALL STREET JOURNAL

#### Reading It Right

Invite a student to explain the relevance of the statement from *The Wall Street Journal* that appears on page 271.

#### Answer

Answers will vary. Possible answer: If the minimum wage increases, companies can afford less labor and fewer workers. There will be more layoffs and unemployment if the labor price rises.

---

# Ethics in Action

**Women Trail Men** Statistically, women make up about 51 percent of the country's approximately 285 million people, but men outnumber women in the workforce 53 to 47 percent. In the age-old battle about "equal pay for equal work," women have come a long way. They now hold almost half the executive and managerial jobs in the United States. However, at the top-most rungs of the ladder, the statistics aren't quite as good. Among men working full time, almost 16 percent earned at least $75,000 a year. Only 6 percent of full-time women workers earned that much. "In my lifetime, there will still be a wage gap," said the president of the National Association of Female Executives. "It's up to women in senior positions to bring other women up, or else it's not going to happen." Women's leaders say that discrimination is at least partly to blame for differences between men's and women's compensation.

### Think Critically

What are the social factors behind gender discrimination? Do you think it should be up to the government to correct this wage gap? Why or why not?

---

**minimum wage law**
Establishes a minimum amount that an employer can pay a worker for an hour of labor

# The Minimum Wage

In March 2000, Congress sent the president a measure to increase the U.S. minimum wage by $1.00 to $6.15. The legislation was vetoed. The **minimum wage law** establishes a minimum amount that an employer can pay a worker for an hour of labor.

## Coverage of the Law

When the legislation was vetoed, about 7 percent of the U.S. workforce earned between $5.15 and $6.15 an hour and thus could have been affected by an increased minimum wage. This group included workers with few job skills. Most were young, the majority worked only part time, and they were employed primarily in service and sales occupations. For example, while 8 of 10 working teenagers earned less than a dollar above the minimum wage, fewer than 1 in 10 workers in their mid-40s earned that little.

## Effects of the Minimum Wage

Advocates of minimum-wage legislation argue that it increases the income of the poorest workers at little or no cost to overall employment. Critics argue that a minimum wage established above the equilibrium wage causes employers either to reduce the quantity of labor employed or change something else about the job.

Most research on the effects of the minimum wage finds either no effect on employment or a negative effect, particularly among teenage workers. Employers often react to a minimum wage increase by

- substituting part-time jobs for full-time jobs

### NETBookmark

The U.S. Department of Labor maintains a Minimum Wage web page. Access this page through econxtra.swlearning.com. What is the current federal minimum wage? Which groups of workers are exempt from minimum wage laws?

**econxtra.swlearning.com**

---

## Group Activity

Organize students into groups of four or five. Tell each group that they operate a small business that produces baseball caps. The business employs 50 workers, most of whom are paid the minimum wage. Ask them how they would react to a $1 increase in the minimum wage. Which of the following steps would they take? (1) Increase the price of caps by $.50 each, (2) never pay workers more than the minimum wage, (3) spend $100,000 to buy a machine that would replace 10 workers, or (4) demand that workers make two more caps per hour to keep their jobs. What effect would each step have on the number of people they employ?

- substituting more-qualified minimum-wage workers (such as high school graduates) for less-qualified workers (such as high school dropouts)
- adjusting some nonwage features of the job to reduce employer costs or increase worker productivity.

## Nonwage Job Features

Congress may be able to legislate a minimum wage, but employers can still adjust many other conditions of the employment. Here are some of the nonwage job components that an employer could alter to offset the added cost of a higher minimum wage: the convenience of work hours, expected work effort, on-the-job training, time allowed for meals and breaks, wage premiums for night shifts and weekends, paid vacation days, paid holidays, sick leave policy, health-care benefits, and so on. For example, one study found that restaurants responded to a higher minimum wage by reducing fringe benefits, particularly vacation time, and reducing the higher wages offered for less-desirable shifts.

## Higher Opportunity Cost of School

A higher minimum wage also raises the opportunity cost of staying in

## THE WALL STREET JOURNAL

▶ **Reading It Right** What's the relevance of the following statement from *The Wall Street Journal*: "'I'm afraid you are going to unemploy more people,' Sen. Don Nickles, R-Oklahoma, said of what would happen if a minimum wage increase is included."

school. According to one study, an increase in the minimum wage encouraged some 16- to 19-year-olds to quit school and look for work, though many failed to find jobs. Those who had already dropped out of school were more likely to become unemployed because of a higher minimum wage. Thus, an increase in the minimum wage may have the unintended consequence of encouraging some students to drop out of school. The unemployment rate is highest for high-school dropouts. In 2003, 11 states had a minimum wage higher than the federal level.

### ✓ CHECKPOINT

How might an increase in the minimum wage affect nonwage compensation for low-wage workers?

Jobs high school students find, such as waitressing, often pay minimum wage. One study found that if the minimum wage were increased, some students would drop out of high school to pursue full-time work. What is your opinion on this issue? Should government keep the minimum wage lower so the dropout rate won't increase?

**Lesson 9.2** • *Wage Determination* **271**

***Think Critically Through Visuals***

Direct students to focus their attention on the photograph on this page. Ask for a volunteer to answer the question posed in the caption.

**Answer**

Possible answer: The government should keep the minimum wage low enough to dissuade students from dropping out of school. The longer students stay in school, the more earning power they have.

### ✓ CHECKPOINT

Invite a student to answer the checkpoint that appears on this page.

**Answer**

If the minimum wage increases, low-wage workers might experience less on-the-job training, shorter breaks, less convenience, and fewer paid holidays.

### APPLY

Assign Lesson 9.2 from the *Contemporary Economics Workbook*.

Encourage students to apply their knowledge of concepts presented in this lesson as they explore economic news stories, policy debates, and data available at **econxtra.swlearning.com**.

### ASSESS

Assign all or part of Lesson 9.2 Assessment on page 272 as homework or an in-class activity.

## Xtra! Study Tools

Direct students to the online study tools for Lesson 9.2 at **econxtra.swlearning.com**.

### CLOSE

**Revisit** the In the News feature on the first page of the lesson. Ask students to review their preliminary answers and discuss the questions, now that they have completed this lesson.

**Review** the objectives for Lesson 9.2.

### RETEACH

In the past, political leaders have suggested setting a lower minimum wage rate for workers under the age of 18. Their goal was to help young people find jobs that would provide them with experience to help them get better jobs later in life. Ask your students to evaluate this idea. How would this policy affect adults earning the minimum wage or slightly more? What would this do to the number of young people willing to work at the minimum wage? Why do your students believe this idea failed to be passed into law?

### Key Concepts

1. Answers will vary. Possible answer: Consumers are willing to pay more to have their computers repaired than they are to have their clothing mended. They may prefer to replace clothing when it is old and in need of repair.

2. Answers will vary. Possible answer: Liberal arts majors are often less able to provide high-valued labor than are electrical engineers. This difference is reflected in the amounts they typically are able to earn.

3. Answers will vary. Possible answer: When people are not able to reach their full potential because of discrimination, they also are less able to produce goods or services that would benefit society.

4. Answers will vary. Possible answer: An increased minimum wage could cause some low-skill workers to be laid off, rather than to be paid the higher wage. It also could attract new workers to look for employment they may not find.

### Graphing Exercise

5. Answers will vary. Possible answer: Although there was a steady growth in the number of people in the labor force, the increase in employment was even greater, resulting in a smaller pool of unemployed workers who were available for new jobs.

   An example of an acceptable graph appears at the bottom of this page.

### Think Critically

6. Answers will vary. Possible answer: Government leaders were more interested in lower-paid workers being employed than in the amount they earned. These lower minimum wages probably increased the number of jobs offered to workers who were willing to accept lower wages.

---

econxtra.swlearning.com

### Key Concepts

1. Why are people who are trained to repair computers paid more than people who are trained to mend clothing?

2. Why is the earning power of a college liberal arts major less than that of an electrical engineering major?

3. Why does job discrimination harm not only the people who are discriminated against but also society in general?

4. Why might an increase in the minimum wage cause greater unemployment among low-skill workers?

### Graphing Exercise

5. When data are gathered about the labor supply in the United States, people are divided into several categories. Some people are not considered because they are too young or unable to work for other reasons. The remaining people comprise the *civilian noninstitutional population (CNP)*. Of this group, some people do not choose to seek employment and so are not considered to be in the labor force. The remaining people are in the labor force and are either employed or unemployed. Use the data in the table to construct a multiple line graph that illustrates the data given below. What does your graph tell you about the growth in the labor supply available to U.S. employers during the 1990s?

**Labor Force Data, 1990–2000**
**Values in Millions of People**

| Year | CNP | Not in Labor Force | In Labor Force | Employed | Unemployed |
|------|-------|-----|-------|-------|------|
| 1990 | 189.2 | 63.5 | 125.8 | 118.8 | 7.0 |
| 1992 | 192.8 | 64.7 | 128.1 | 118.4 | 9.7 |
| 1994 | 196.8 | 65.8 | 131.0 | 123.1 | 7.9 |
| 1996 | 200.6 | 66.6 | 134.0 | 126.7 | 7.3 |
| 1998 | 205.2 | 67.5 | 137.7 | 131.5 | 6.2 |
| 2000 | 209.7 | 68.8 | 140.9 | 135.2 | 5.7 |

### Think Critically

6. **Government** In 1968, the federal minimum wage was $1.60 per hour. This might seem to be a small amount. However, when adjusted for inflation it had the same purchasing power as $7.92 per hour in 2000 dollars. In 2000, the federal minimum wage was $5.15 per hour. Therefore, the real (adjusted for inflation) value of the minimum wage fell by about 35 percent between 1968 and 2000. Why do you think the federal government did not increase the minimum wage at the same rate as inflation? How might this have affected the number of minimum-wage jobs offered to workers?

---

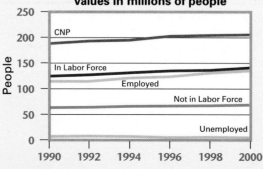

**Labor Force Data, 1990 to 2000**
**Values in millions of people**

### Visualizing the Answer— Graphing Exercise

5. The answer includes a graph. Students' graphs should look similar to the one shown here. An Excel spreadsheet containing this graph, along with supporting data, is available on the Instructor's Resource CD.

# Objectives

> Describe the history and tools of U.S. labor unions.

> Analyze how labor unions try to increase wages.

> Discuss recent trends in union membership.

# Overview

The aspect of labor markets that makes the most news headlines is the activity of labor unions. Labor negotiations, strikes, picket lines, and heated confrontations between workers and employers all fit neatly into TV's "action news" format. But despite all the media attention, only about one in seven U.S. workers belongs to a labor union. What's more, the overwhelming share of union contracts are reached without a strike. The typical union member is more likely to be a government employee than a steelworker or autoworker. Labor unions focus on negotiating higher pay and more benefits for members.

# Key Terms

**labor union**

**right-to-work law**

**collective bargaining**

**mediator**

**binding arbitration**

**strike**

**featherbedding**

---

## [ In the News ]

### ● Union Activity at Amazon.com

Labor unions made minor efforts toward organizing at Amazon.com as early as 1998. A serious organizing campaign began nearly four years later when about 50 employees from the company's 400-person customer service center in Seattle gathered to strategize. The employees had many concerns, including job security, mandatory overtime shifts, and erratic schedules. About the same time, the United Food and Commercial Workers (UFCW) began a drive to unionize workers in eight of the company's distribution centers. The UFCW drive has focused on educating workers about what unions can do for them. They're taking it slow and waiting for the right time to ask workers to sign union cards and prompt a formal election for union representation. To counter the union's moves, Amazon has started its own campaign. The company has staged mandatory employee meetings to respond to union arguments. They've coached managers on the best ways to deal with organizing efforts. They also continually post responses to employees' frequently asked questions. It's a gentle battle of education and persuasion but a very serious battle nonetheless. Amazon has devoted its best people to the issue as well as significant resources to combat the union. For now, it remains a war of words and ideas.

### Think About It

Do you think it would be easier to unionize high-tech workers today than it was at the beginning of the "Dot-Com" revolution? Why or why not?

◀ | ▶

**273**

---

## National Content Standards in Economics

A complete list of the NCEE Standards appears on pages xxiv–xxv of this book. The following standards are addressed in Lesson 9.3.

Standard 4: Role of Incentives

Standard 10: Role of Economic Institutions

Standard 13: Role of Resources in Determining Income

---

## FOCUS

9.3 **Labor Unions**

Remind students that large groups are usually in a stronger bargaining position when they negotiate than are small groups. Tell them to imagine one worker who decided to tell her boss, "I can't take it any more. I work too hard and earn too little. I can't pay my bills. If you don't raise my wage, I'm going to walk out the door and never come back." And she does, but there are 500 other workers at the plant who stay and just as many unemployed people who want a job. Ask students how things will work out for this worker. What does this have to do with why workers often have chosen to join together in unions?

### Objectives

Remind students to read the lesson objectives to help focus their attention before reading the lesson.

### Key Terms

Direct students to write each of the key terms on a separate index card. Instruct students to write the complete definition of each key term on the back of the appropriate card along with the page number where the definition is located. Encourage students to use the cards to study for quizzes and tests.

## [ In the News ]

Instruct students to read the passage and write down their answers. Point out that their answers might change after they finish studying Lesson 9.3.

### Answers to Think About It

Answers will vary. Possible answers: I think that it would be harder to unionize high-tech workers now than at the beginning because firms are doing everything in their power to train and hold on to IT workers. Firms are already offering many fringe benefits and high wages, so there is little that unions can further offer IT workers.

### Visual Presentation

Use the PowerPoint presentation on the Instructor's Resource CD as an adjunct to your lecture. The presentation also can be used for review.

## TEACH

### Organized Labor

Remind students that organized labor originated, at least in part, because of exploitation of workers that took place during the nineteenth century. Some of these unions were quite successful while others accomplished little for their members. Point out that workers who form successful unions usually share a number of personal and job characteristics. Ask students to explain why each of the following worker characteristics is important to a union's success:

- They usually have a special skill or expertise.
- They usually expect to stay in the same job for a number of years.
- They usually share common objectives.
- They usually earn enough to have saved in the past.
- They usually work for an employer that is reasonably profitable.

### CHECKPOINT

Invite a student to answer the checkpoint that appears on page 275.

### Answer

Collective bargaining and strikes are the tools used by labor unions.

---

**right-to-work law**

State law that says a worker at a union company does not have to join the union or pay union dues to hold a job there

**labor union**

A group of workers who join together to seek higher pay and better working conditions by negotiating a labor contract with their employers

**collective bargaining**

The process by which representatives of the union and the employer negotiate wages, employee benefits, and working conditions

**mediator**

An impartial observer brought in when labor negotiations break down, to suggest how to resolve differences

**binding arbitration**

When labor negotiations break down and the public interest is involved, a neutral third party is brought in to impose a settlement that both sides must accept

**strike**

A labor union's attempt to withhold labor from the firm

274

---

# Organized Labor

In the late nineteenth century, factory workers averaged 11-hour days, 6 days a week. Those in steel mills, paper mills, and breweries averaged 12-hour days, 7 days a week. Child labor was common, and working conditions often were dangerous. For example, according to one estimate, fatal accidents in the steel mills of Pittsburgh accounted for one-fifth of all male deaths in that city during the 1880s. Despite the long hours and dreadful working conditions, millions of immigrants entered the work force, increasing the supply of labor and keeping wages low.

## History of Labor Unions

Through a **labor union**, workers join together to improve their pay and working conditions by negotiating a labor contract with their employers. The first labor unions in the United States were *craft unions*, where membership was limited to workers with a particular skill, or craft—such as carpenters, shoemakers, or printers. Craft unions eventually formed their own national organization, the *American Federation of Labor (AFL)*, in 1886. The AFL was not a union itself but rather an organization of national unions, each retaining its own independence.

The Clayton Act of 1914 exempted labor unions from antitrust laws, meaning that *union members at competing companies could join forces legally in an effort to raise wages and improve working conditions*. Unions also were exempt from taxation. This favorable legislation encouraged the union movement.

The *Congress of Industrial Organizations (CIO)* was formed in 1935 to serve as a national organization of unions in mass-production industries. Whereas the AFL organized workers in particular crafts, the CIO organized all workers in a particular industry. These *industrial unions* organized all workers in an industry, such as all autoworkers or all steelworkers. They still had to organize workers company by company, however. Workers at a company became unionized if a majority of them voted for union representation.

After World War II, economic conditions and public sentiment seemed to turn against unions. In 1947, Congress passed the *Taft-Hartley Act*, which authorized states to approve right-to-work laws. A **right-to-work law** says that a worker at a union company does not have to join the union or pay union dues to hold a job there. Twenty-two states have passed right-to-work laws. These states are mostly in the South, the Plains, and the Mountain states. Union membership rates in the right-to-work states average only half the rates in other states. For more information on the history of labor unions, see the Connect to History feature on page 281.

## Collective Bargaining

**Collective bargaining** is the process by which representatives of a union and an employer negotiate wages, employee benefits, and working conditions. Once a preliminary agreement is reached, union representatives present it to the membership for a vote. If the agreement is accepted, union representatives and the employer sign a labor contract. If the agreement is rejected, the union can strike or can continue negotiations.

If the negotiators cannot reach a decision, and if the public interest is involved, government officials may ask a mediator to step in. A **mediator** is an impartial observer who listens to both sides separately and then suggests a solution. The mediator has no power to impose a settlement on the parties.

In the provision of certain vital services such as police and fire protection, a strike could harm the public. The government may impose **binding arbitration** in these cases. This means that a neutral third party evaluates both sides of the dispute and issues a ruling that both sides must accept. Some disputes skip the mediation and arbitration steps and go directly to a strike.

## The Strike

A major source of union power in the bargaining relationship is the threat of a **strike**. This is a union's attempt to withhold labor from the firm. The purpose of a strike is to stop production

**CHAPTER 9** Labor Markets

---

### Outside Resources

**The American Federation of Labor–Congress of Industrial Organizations (AFL-CIO)** is the largest labor organization in the United States. Its web site at www.aflcio.org describes the organization's goals and objectives as well as reports on current labor negotiations. Instruct your students to visit this site and report on what they find. What issues seem to be most important to labor organizations? What benefits does the AFL-CIO offer workers? Why might a worker choose to join or not join a union if he or she is given the choice?

so as to force the firm to accept the union's position. Strikes also can hurt union members, who suffer a drop in income and who may lose their jobs permanently. The threat of a strike hangs over labor negotiations and can encourage an agreement. *Although neither party usually wants a strike, rather than give in on key points, both sides act as if they could and would go through one.*

If a strike is called, unions usually picket the targeted employer to prevent or discourage so-called strikebreakers from "crossing the picket lines." With non-striking employees and temporary workers, a firm sometimes can maintain production during a strike. That's bad news for the union.

**CHECKPOINT**
What are the tools used by U.S. labor unions?

# Union Wages and Employment

The union's focus usually is on higher wages. Here are two approaches unions employ to increase the wages of their members: (1) reduce the supply of labor and (2) increase the demand for union labor.

## Reduce the Supply of Labor

One way to increase wages is for the union to somehow reduce the supply of labor. This occurs with craft unions, such as unions of carpenters or plumbers. The effect of a supply restriction is shown as a leftward shift of the labor supply curve from $S$ to $S''$ in panel (a) of Figure 9.6. The result is a higher wage and reduced employment.

Successful supply restrictions of this type require the union first to limit its membership and second to force all employers in the market to hire only union members. The union can restrict membership with high initiation fees,

long apprenticeship periods, difficult qualification exams, restrictive licensing requirements, and other devices aimed at slowing down or discouraging new membership. But, even if unions can restrict membership, they have difficulty requiring all firms in the market to hire only union workers. In right-to-work states, for example, workers do not have to belong to a union even if the company is unionized.

Professional groups—doctors, lawyers, and accountants, for example—also impose entry restrictions through education and examination requirements. These restrictions usually are defended by the professions on the grounds that they protect the public. Some observers, however, see the restrictions as attempts to increase pay among existing professionals by limiting the labor supply.

## Increase the Demand for Union Labor

Another way to increase the wage is to increase the demand for union labor. This strategy is reflected by a rightward shift of the labor demand curve from $D$ to $D'$ in panel (b) of Figure 9.6. This is an attractive alternative because *it increases both the wage and employment.* Here are some ways unions try to increase the demand for union labor.

Does it make a difference to the quality of a job if the workplace is unionized? The AFL-CIO, an umbrella organization for most of the nations' unions, certainly believes it makes a difference. Access the AFL-CIO web site through econxtra.swlearning.com to read about how and why people join unions. In your opinion, what would be the biggest benefit of union membership? Are there any benefits cited that you do not think would be helpful? If so, what are they?

*econxtra.swlearning.com*

## TEACH

### Union Wages and Employment

Remind students that employers who are required to negotiate a labor agreement with large groups of unionized workers are more likely to offer higher wage rates than they would offer to individual workers. The power of a union lies in its ability to threaten, and carry out, a strike that forces a business to close. A closed business earns nothing while the owners continue to pay fixed costs, at least in the short run. To avoid such losses, many owners are willing to pay union workers more than they would otherwise. This is particularly likely to happen when the firm has a degree of monopoly power in the market where it sells its final product. Then it can pass the added costs on in higher prices.

### NETBookmark

Direct students to **econxtra.swlearning.com**. Remind them to click on the link for Lesson 9.3 to find the appropriate link for the **NET Bookmark** on this page.

### Answer

Answers will vary. The benefits cited by students should be consistent with the information presented at the web site. According to the web site, benefits of union memberships include:

- A voice in improving the quality of products and services
- Better wages and benefits
- Better working conditions
- More flexibility for work and family needs
- Protection against discrimination
- Quality health care
- Respect on the job
- Retirement protection
- Safer and more secure workplaces

## ENRICH

The ultimate weapon of labor organizations is their ability to withdraw labor from an enterprise, thus forcing the business to close. To accomplish this, unions traditionally have relied on strikes and picket lines intended to prevent other workers from replacing them. Discuss the ethical issues involved in a strike. What groups will be harmed? What benefits may be won eventually? (Groups harmed include workers who lose pay, owners who lose profit, customers who lose products to buy, governments that lose tax revenue, and suppliers who are unable to sell to the business. In the long run, union members may benefit from higher wages.)

# (continued) TEACH

## Union Wages and Employment

Point out that people who want to achieve something often work together to change rules or get support for their cause. This is true in the labor market as well as in other situations. Ask students to share their own experiences with working together.

### Think Critically Through Visuals

Direct students to focus their attention on **Figure 9.6—Effect of Reducing Supply or Increasing Labor Demand**. Point out that reducing labor supply increases wages but reduces employment. Increasing labor demand increases wages and the level of employment.

  **Apply It**

Direct students to the Graphing Workshop for Chapter 9 at **econxtra.swlearning.com**. As an enrichment exercise, students may complete **Apply It: Analyzing the Impacts of Multiple Shifts in Labor Demand and Supply**. This enrichment exercise presents concepts more advanced than those discussed in the textbook.

### Think Critically Through Visuals

Direct students to focus their attention on **Figure 9.7—Median Weekly Earnings: Unions vs. Nonunion** on page 277. Point out that unions are more competitive in raising wages in less competitive industries.

## CHECKPOINT

Invite a student to answer the checkpoint that appears on page 277.

### Answer

Unions try to increase labor wages by reducing the supply of labor or by increasing the demand for union labor.

## Increase Demand for Union-Made Products

The demand for union labor may be increased through a direct appeal to consumers to buy only union-made products. Increasing the demand for union-made products increases the demand for union labor.

## Restrict Supply of Nonunion-Made Products

Another way to increase the demand for union labor is to restrict the supply of products that compete with union-made products. The United Auto Workers, for example, supports restrictions on imported cars. Fewer imported cars means greater demand for cars produced by U.S. workers, who are mostly union members.

## Increase Productivity of Union Labor

In the absence of a union, a dissatisfied worker may simply look for another job. Losing workers in this way is costly to the firm because the departing worker often leaves with abundant on-the-job experience that makes the worker more productive. Unions sometimes try to keep workers from quitting or goofing off. This increases worker productivity, thereby increasing the demand for union labor.

## Featherbedding

Another way unions try to increase the demand for union labor is by **featherbedding**. This is an attempt to ensure that more union labor is hired than employers would prefer. For example, union rules require that each Broadway theater hire a permanent "house" carpenter, electrician, and property manager. Once the play begins, these workers appear only on payday. In addition, the theater's box office must be staffed by at least three people. With featherbedding, the union tries to set not only the wage but also the number of workers that must be hired at that wage.

*featherbedding*
Union efforts to force employers to hire more workers than demanded for the task

### The Graphing Workshop | Effect of Reducing Supply or Increasing Labor Demand | Figure 9.6

 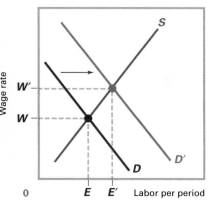

If a union can restrict labor supply to an industry, the supply curve shifts to the left from *S* to *S''*, as in panel (a). The wage rate rises from *W* to *W''*, but at the cost of a reduction in employment from *E* to *E''*. In panel (b), an increase in labor demand from *D* to *D'* raises both the wage and the level of employment.

**276**    **CHAPTER 9**  Labor Markets

## Economic Headlines

Instruct students to locate an article in a current magazine or newspaper that describes a strike that is either taking place or is threatened. Ask them to report on the issues involved and whether they believe the union is in a position to win its demands. Ask them to assume the union wins its demands. How would the contract affect them or other U.S. consumers? What would it do to our nation's ability to compete in the global marketplace?

## Union Pay Is Higher

Studies have shown that unions increased members' wages by an average of about 15 percent above the wages of similarly qualified nonunion workers. Figure 9.7 compares the median weekly earnings of union and nonunion workers. Unions are more successful at raising wages in less-competitive industries. For example, unions have less impact on service industries, where product markets tend to be competitive. Unions have greater impact on wages in government, transportation, and construction, which tend to be less competitive.

When there is more competition in the product market, employers cannot easily pass along higher union wages as higher product prices. New firms can enter the industry, pay lower wages, and sell the product for less.

✔ **CHECKPOINT**
How do unions try to increase the wages of union workers?

# Trends in Union Membership

In 1955, about one-third of workers in the United States belonged to unions. Union membership as a fraction of the workforce has since declined. Now only about one-seventh of all workers belong to a union. Government workers now make up nearly half of all union members, even though they account for just one-sixth of U.S. workers. Compared with other advanced economies, the United States ranks relatively low in the number of workers who belong to a union. However, rates abroad have declined as well.

**Median Weekly Earnings: Union vs. Nonunion**

**Figure 9.7**

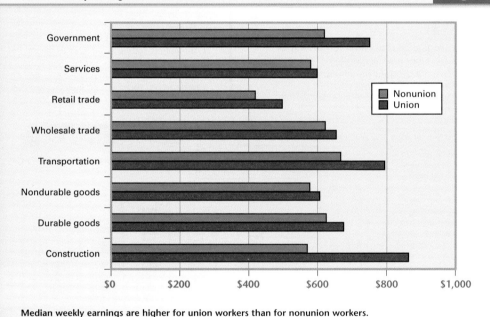

Median weekly earnings are higher for union workers than for nonunion workers.

Source: U.S. Bureau of Labor Statistics. Figures are for full-time workers in 2001.

Lesson 9.3 • *Labor Unions*   **277**

## TEACH

### Trends in Union Membership

Remind students that union membership has fallen rapidly in recent years. This decline has had an impact that extends well beyond negotiations between labor and management. One of the primary sources of union power in the past was the unions' ability to swing elections one way or another. Imagine an election in which 49 percent of the voters want one candidate and 51 percent want the other. Only 10 percent of the voters are union members. If the union leaders could guarantee their members would vote for one candidate or the other, they could decide the election. This would give them a great deal of power to influence what legislation the candidates would support. This is how a number of laws that protected workers' rights were passed. As union memberships have declined, unions are less able to deliver votes or influence legislation.

### *Think Critically Through Visuals*

Direct students to focus their attention on the photograph on page 278. Ask for a volunteer to answer the question posed in the caption.

### Answer

Answers will vary. Reasons given for wanting to join a union will likely include higher wages, better benefits, and safer working conditions. possible reasons for not wanting to join will likely include declining membership, union dues, and concern about possibly having to participate in a strike.

---

*Group Activity* ✎

Organize students into groups of four or five. Tell each group that it is in charge of a union that is negotiating a new contract. The members have been asked by their employer to accept a wage freeze for two years and then receive 2-percent raises for the next two years. In return, all current workers will be guaranteed employment for the next four years. If they refuse this offer, they are told that 2 percent of their members will be laid off for each percent increase in the wage rate. The assignment is to develop a bargaining position and write a letter to union members explaining the situation. Ask groups to explain their decisions to the class.

## Trends in Union Membership

There are many possible reasons for the decline in union membership in recent years. Ask students to evaluate each of the following possible reasons. Which do they believe are the most important reasons? Are there any other reasons they could add to the list?

- Workers already earn good wages.
- Unions have not benefited workers lately.
- There are fewer industrial workers today.
- More workers are professionals who rarely join unions.
- More workers are in the service industries.
- People change jobs much more often today.
- The government has been anti-union in its policies.
- More women are in the workforce, and they don't join unions as often as men do.

### *Think Critically Through Visuals*

Direct students to focus their attention on **Figure 9.8—U.S. Union Membership for Men and Women by Age**. Point out the lower rate of union membership for women. This is because women are employed more in the service sector, where union membership historically has been lower. The rise in union membership as workers age is likely due to increasing work experience and increasing family responsibilities. The decline during later working years is likely the result of retirement. For example, many government employees, including police officers and firefighters, retire during their 50s, after 20 or 30 years of service.

### *Think Critically Through Visuals*

Direct students to focus their attention on **Figure 9.9–Right-to-Work States and Unionization Rates per State** on page 279. Point out that most states in the Northeast, once known for heavy industry and manufacturing, are right-to-work states. Most Southern states and many Midwestern states, once known for agriculture, do not have right-to-work laws.

## Membership by Gender, Age, and Geography

The bar graph in Figure 9.8 indicates U.S. union membership rates by age and gender. The rates for men, shown by the green bars, are higher than the rates for women. This, in part, is due to the fact that men are employed more in manufacturing. Women are employed more in the service sector, where union membership historically has been lower. The highest membership rates are for middle-aged males.

## Membership Across States

Union membership rates also vary across states. Figure 9.9 shows union membership as a percent of those employed by state. The figure also shades right-to-work states, where workers in unionized companies do not have to join the union or pay union dues. As noted earlier, unionization rates in right-to-work states average only half the rates in other states. New York has the highest unionization rate at 26.7 percent. North Carolina has the lowest, at 3.7 percent.

## Reasons for Declining Membership

Improvements in the conditions of the average worker since the late nineteenth century have been remarkable. The average workweek in some industries has been cut in half. The workplace now is monitored more closely for health and safety hazards. Child labor was outlawed decades ago. Wages have increased substantially.

These improvements cannot be entirely credited to labor unions. Competition among employers to attract qualified workers helps explain some of the improvements. The increase in wages can be traced mostly to an increase in labor productivity. This is because

**Assembly-line workers in factories often belong to unions. If you worked on an assembly line and had to decide whether or not to join the union, do you think you would join? Why or why not?**

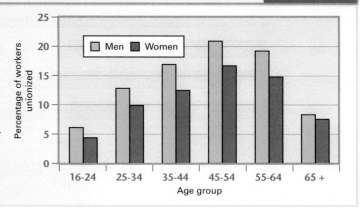

**U.S. Union Membership for Men and Women by Age**

**Figure 9.8**

Men in the United States have higher rates of union membership than women, due to the nature of the work each group typically performs.

Source: U.S. Bureau of Labor Statistics. Percentages are for 2001.

**278**  **CHAPTER 9**  Labor Markets

---

### *Curriculum Connection—Science*

Advancements in technology are making many occupations obsolete. For example, no one is likely to be successful operating a typewriter repair shop anymore. The same was true of technological advancements in the past. Ask students to identify a specific technological advancement that took place near 1900 and to discuss how it affected workers. What types of jobs were eliminated, and what types increased in number?

## Right-to-Work States and Unionization Rates per State

Figure 9.9

Shaded areas show right-to-work states, where workers in unionized companies do not have to join the union or pay union dues. Percentages indicate union membership as a fraction of those employed by state. States that have right-to-work laws have only about half the unionization rates (percent of workers who belong to unions) of other states.

Source: National Right to Work Committee, http://www.nrtwc.org/. Unionization rates are for 2001 and right-to-work states are as of 2002.

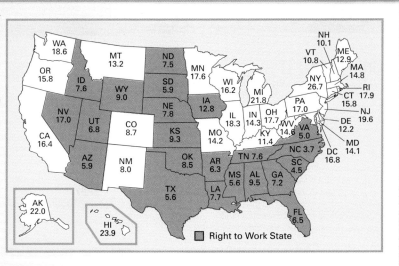

| State | Rate |
|-------|------|
| WA | 18.6 |
| OR | 15.8 |
| ID | 7.6 |
| MT | 13.2 |
| ND | 7.5 |
| MN | 17.6 |
| WI | 16.2 |
| NH | 10.1 |
| VT | 10.8 |
| ME | 12.9 |
| NY | 26.7 |
| MA | 14.8 |
| RI | 17.9 |
| CT | 15.8 |
| NV | 17.0 |
| UT | 6.8 |
| WY | 9.0 |
| SD | 5.9 |
| IA | 12.8 |
| NE | 7.8 |
| IL | 18.3 |
| MI | 21.8 |
| IN | 14.3 |
| OH | 17.7 |
| PA | 17.0 |
| NJ | 19.6 |
| DE | 12.2 |
| CA | 16.4 |
| CO | 8.7 |
| KS | 9.3 |
| MO | 14.2 |
| KY | 11.4 |
| WV | 14.6 |
| VA | 5.0 |
| MD | 14.1 |
| DC | 16.8 |
| AZ | 5.9 |
| NM | 8.0 |
| OK | 8.5 |
| AR | 6.3 |
| TN | 7.6 |
| NC | 3.7 |
| SC | 4.5 |
| TX | 5.6 |
| LA | 7.7 |
| MS | 5.6 |
| AL | 9.5 |
| GA | 7.2 |
| FL | 6.5 |
| AK | 22.0 |
| HI | 23.9 |

▢ Right to Work State

---

workers now have more education and training and benefit more from physical capital. However, unions played a crucial role in improving wages and working conditions and in calling public attention to labor problems.

Because working conditions and wages are now much better, workers today feel less inclined to join a union, especially in those states where they don't need to join to enjoy union benefits. Fewer union members mean fewer voters who belong to unions, so unions also have lost some political clout. Unions have, in a sense, become the victims of their own success. Here are some other reasons why union membership has declined.

### Changes in the Economy
The decline in union membership is due partly to changes in the industrial structure of the U.S. economy. Unions have long been more important in the goods-producing sector than in the service-producing sector. But employment in the goods-producing sector, which includes manufacturing and construction, has fallen in recent decades as a share of all jobs.

### Competition from Nonunion Firms
Another factor in the decline of union membership is the growth in market competition, particularly from imports. Increased competition from nonunion employers, both foreign and domestic, has reduced the ability of unionized firms to pass higher labor costs on as higher prices.

### Strikes Are Fewer and Less Effective
Finally, the near disappearance of the strike has reduced union power. The 1970s averaged nearly 300 strikes a year involving 1,000 or more workers in the United States. Since 1995, there have been only about 30 such strikes a year. Many recent strikes ended badly for union workers because companies hired permanent replacements. Union members now are more reluctant to strike because of the increased willingness of employers to hire replacements and the increased willingness of workers—both union and nonunion—to cross picket lines.

✓ **CHECKPOINT**
In what sense is the union movement a victim of its own success?

---

**Answer**
Unions in the 1970s improved working conditions and wages. Now that conditions and wages are better, even where workers are not unionized, workers feel less inclined to join a union.

### APPLY
Assign Lesson 9.3 from the Contemporary Economics Workbook.

### e-con @pps

Encourage students to apply their knowledge of concepts presented in this lesson as they explore economic news stories, policy debates, and data available at **econxtra.swlearning.com**.

### ASSESS
Assign all or part of Lesson 9.3 Assessment on page 280 as homework or an in-class activity.

### Xtra! Study Tools
Direct students to the online study tools for Lesson 9.3 at **econxtra.swlearning.com**.

### CLOSE
**Revisit** the In the News feature on the first page of the lesson. Ask students to review their preliminary answers and discuss the questions, now that they have completed this lesson.

**Review** the objectives for Lesson 9.3. Students should be able to:

- Describe the history and tools of U.S. labor unions.
- Analyze how labor unions try to increase wages.
- Discuss recent trends in union membership.

---

### RETEACH

Ask students to make a list of reasons why workers would choose to form or join a union. Considering these reasons, how would they explain the declining membership in labor organizations? Have workers achieved many of their goals or are they discouraged because they feel that that union membership is unlikely to benefit them? Why are many unions now willing to work without a contract rather than go on strike as they might have in the past? What do students believe unions could do to regain some of their lost power in the economy?

Direct students to read the passage entitled "Unionizing IT".

## Answers to Think Critically

The focus on higher wages might not appeal to IT workers because they are more concerned with benefits such as hiring bonuses, health insurance, and stock options, which they might already be receiving.

## 9.3 Assessment

### Key Concepts

1. Answers will vary. Possible answer: Union members who strike may be able to achieve better compensation and working conditions. They risk losing their jobs and will lose pay while they are out on strike.

2. Answers will vary. Possible answer: It is easier for firms with monopoly power to pass on increased wage costs to consumers than for firms that are in strong competition.

3. Answers will vary. Possible answer: Some workers prefer not to pay dues or fees to unions and therefore withdraw or refuse to join when membership is not a required condition of employment. With fewer members, unions tended to be less successful in states with right-to-work laws.

### Graphing Exercise

4. Answers will vary. Possible answer: With fewer members, labor organizations have had less power in the economy.

   An example of an acceptable graph appears at the bottom of this page.

### Think Critically

5. Answers will vary. Possible answer: Wages, working conditions, and medical insurance were issues that led to the strike. Results might include increased pay for workers and increased costs for the employer. In a few cases, workers may have been eliminated or the firm might actually have chosen to move or close.

---

▸ E-CONOMICS

## Unionizing IT
Information technology (IT) workers make up the fastest-growing sector of the labor force. IT workers are the people in an organization responsible for keeping all the computer operations and networks running smoothly. Why aren't labor unions focusing on unionizing these workers? Well, they have tried, but this group poses some special challenges. To succeed, a union must be able to convince workers that it can make a difference for them. Most employers, on the other hand, make every effort to hire and retain IT workers. Incentives and fringe benefits include hiring bonuses, health insurance, retirement plans, stock options, free cell phones, laptops, flex-time, and a relaxed work environment. Another problem for union organizers is that IT workers are a collection of full-time workers, telecommuters, part-timers, temporary workers, free-lancers, and a growing number of foreign workers on short-term work visas. Unions have a hard time even communicating with such a diverse, independent bunch.

### Think Critically
Why might union membership not appeal to IT workers?

## 9.3 Assessment

Xtra!
Study Tools
econxtra.swlearning.com

### Key Concepts
1. What are the potential costs and benefits for striking union members?
2. Why are unions more often successful in negotiating for higher wages with firms that have monopoly power than with firms that are in strong competition?
3. Why is union membership often lower in states that passed right-to-work laws? How did this affect the effectiveness of unions in these states?

### Graphing Exercise
4. In the late 1950s, nearly one-third of workers in the United States belonged to a labor union. Since then the share of organized workers has declined steadily. Use data in the table to construct a line graph to show this decline since 1985.

### Think Critically
5. **Research** Investigate a recent strike in your state. What issues were involved? What was the result of the strike?

**Union Membership as a Percent of the Labor Force, 1985–2000**

| Year | % of Labor Force Organized |
|------|----------------------------|
| 1985 | 18.0% |
| 1990 | 16.1 |
| 1995 | 14.9 |
| 2000 | 13.5 |

**280**    CHAPTER 9   Labor Markets

---

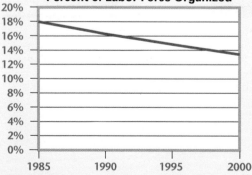

**Percent of Labor Force Organized**

### Visualizing the Answer— Graphing Exercise

4. The answer includes a graph. Students' graphs should look similar to the one shown here. An Excel spreadsheet containing this graph, along with supporting data, is available on the Instructor's Resource CD.

# to History

## Labor Unions

The United States labor movement had its roots in craft industries and skilled workers. The National Trades Union, the country's first national labor union, did not survive the panic of 1837. Only after the Civil War and the great boom in industrial growth in the United States did the union movement grow, as labor organizers realized the bargaining power of national organizations. The first major union to attempt a national reach was the National Labor Union. Started in 1866 in Baltimore, it grew to 60,000 members by 1872. Unwieldy with a diverse membership drawn from many industries, it failed to survive an economic downturn—the panic of 1873.

A third attempt at a national union was the Knights of Labor. Founded in 1869 in Philadelphia, the Knights had a goal of organizing all workers, skilled and unskilled, men and women. The union took a long-term view of labor reform with issues such as pay equity, the eight-hour workday and the abolition of child labor. The Knights of Labor shied away from using the strike as a tool and played down higher wages as a goal. The broad reforms it sought, and its attempts to unite all segments of the work force, proved difficult, as its members wanted more immediate results. Still, by 1886 it had grown to 750,000 members. In that year, the union was unjustly accused of the bombing of Haymarket Square in Chicago. This led to a public backlash against it and, ultimately, its demise.

Studies show that, unlike those of today, strikes of the 1880s rarely ended in compromise. Only about 10 percent led to something other than total victory for management or labor. The successful strikes for labor—about 50 percent of the total—occurred if the union was supported and the strikes were short. If strikebreakers were employed, the strike likely would fail.

National unions of skilled trades created the American Federation of Labor (AFL), the nation's oldest large-scale labor organization. Unlike the Knights, the AFL wanted to organize skilled workers by craft. Skilled workers were more difficult to replace, giving the unions more bargaining power. It concentrated on small companies that were less likely to be able to bust the unions. Led by Samuel Gompers, the AFL emphasized basic issues such as higher wages, shorter hours, and better working conditions. It pressed for the "closed shop," a workplace where only union members could be hired. Although it questioned the effectiveness of strikes and boycotts, it did use those methods to force employers to engage in collective bargaining. Mediation also came into more common use to settle labor disputes.

### THINK CRITICALLY

Using the concepts of supply and demand, explain how a closed shop could be used to control the labor market within an industry.

---

C O N N E C T
to History

### FOCUS

Explain to the students that the movement to unionize workers in the late 1800s was a long and difficult one. Often, union activities were characterized by violence and even death. For the most part, the government sided with the industrialists. Even Andrew Carnegie, who would later give away millions of dollars, was involved in large, violent clashes with his workers.

### TEACH

After introducing the selection, have the students read it and answer the questions. Discuss the conditions that led workers to form unions and brought about the often-violent clashes with management. Ask students how the past compares with workers and working conditions today. Do they believe the issues that led to the formation of unions in the late 1800s are still issues today? Are there examples of union activity in their own community? Ask the students what would cause them to join or reject union membership.

### ASSESS

Use the problem at the bottom of the page to assess the students' understanding of this feature.

### Answers to Think Critically

A "closed shop"—a shop that employs only union members—helps limit increases in labor supply in that market. This is because workers outside the union cannot be hired.

### Bibliography

Engerman, Stanley L., and Robert E. Gallman. *The Cambridge Economic History of the United States: The Long Nineteenth Century.* Vol. II. Cambridge, England: Cambridge University Press, 2000.

Foner, Eric, and John A. Garraty, eds. *The Reader's Companion to American History.* New York: Houghton Mifflin, 1991.

Puth, Robert C. *American Economic History.* Ft. Worth, Texas: Dryden Press, 1988.

## Summary

### Consider

Ask students to revisit the questions they were asked to consider at the beginning of the chapter. Remind students that they should be able to answer all of the questions after studying Chapter 9.

- Why do truck drivers in the United States earn at least 20 times more than rickshaw drivers in Asia? See page 259—Prices of Other Resources.

- Why do some professional basketball players earn 50 times more than others? See page 267—Why Wages Differ.

- Among physicians, why do surgeons earn twice as much as general practitioners? See page 267—Differences in Training, Education, Age, and Experience.

- What's the payoff for a college education? See page 267—Differences in Training, Education, Age, and Experience.

### Exam*View*

Use Exam*View* to assess student learning.

- Create a chapter test using questions from the existing test bank.
- Add your own questions to the existing test bank.
- Generate multiple forms of a chapter test.

### Study Skills

Offer the following study skills suggestions for students as they review this chapter.

- Outline the chapter.
- Review Key Terms.
- Review Checkpoints.
- Work in pairs to quiz each other.
- Use the Xtra! Study Tools for each lesson.

 Xtra! Quiz Prep

Direct students to the online quiz preparation for Chapter 9 at **econxtra.swlearning.com**.

## Summary

### 9.1 Demand and Supply of Resources

a The demand for resources is a *derived demand* that arises from the demand for final goods and services.

b A firm's willingness to hire workers depends on the wage rate and the cost of other resources it needs to produce the products it sells. If the cost of one type of resource increases, the firm will try to substitute a less costly resource. If wage rates fall, the firm will hire more workers because they are relatively less expensive than other resources.

 Xtra! Quiz Prep
*econxtra.swlearning.com*

c The quantity of resources available for a firm to purchase depends on the price businesses are willing and able to pay and the alternative uses of those resources. When a wage rate results in the same number of workers seeking employment as there are job openings, the labor market is at the *equilibrium wage.*

d There are many nonwage determinants of labor demand and supply. Nonwage determinants of labor demand include demand for the final product, prices of other resources, and the technology used in production. Nonwage determinants of supply include workers' wealth and working conditions as well as current tastes for work.

### 9.2 Wage Determination

a Wages differ across labor markets for a variety of reasons, including differences in education, training, and experience. People who contribute labor that has greater value to production tend to be better paid.

b There are many factors related to jobs that result in different levels of compensation for workers. Those who have jobs that involve significant levels of risk, unpleasant locations, or disagreeable tasks often are paid more for their labor. Discrimination also can cause some workers to be paid more or less for their labor.

c The purpose of *minimum wage* legislation is to increase levels of compensation for the nation's lowest-paid workers. Supporters of higher minimum wages say the laws can help low-paid workers improve their standards of living. Opponents suggest that higher minimum wages will reduce the number of jobs offered to low-skill workers.

### 9.3 Labor Unions

a *Labor unions* are formed when workers join together to improve their pay and working conditions by negotiating labor contracts with their employers. Labor unions fall into two general classifications—craft unions and industrial unions. Craft unions limit membership to workers with a particular skill. Industrial unions are formed by workers in a particular industry who join together.

b Union and management negotiations are carried out through a process called *collective bargaining*. Once a preliminary agreement is reached between the union bargaining team and management, union members vote to either ratify or reject the proposal. Negotiations can be assisted through *mediation* or *binding arbitration*, which involve a neutral third party.

c Unions work to improve wages and working conditions for their members by reducing the supply of labor available to employers or by increasing the demand for labor. This may be accomplished by limiting union membership, increasing demand for union-made products, restricting the supply of non-union-made products, or increasing the productivity of union workers. *Featherbedding* takes place when contracts are negotiated that require employers to hire more workers than they think are needed.

d In recent years union membership has declined. There are many possible reasons for this, including improved wages and working conditions, a reduction in the number of industrial jobs in the U.S. economy, competition from nonunion businesses either within or outside the United States, and the apparent ineffectiveness of *strikes* in recent history.

**282    CHAPTER 9** Labor Markets

### 9.1 Assessment

Continued from page 263.

#### Think Critically

7. Answers will vary. Possible answer: By allowing workers to have more flexible hours, a greater voice in how they do their jobs, or more variety in the tasks that they perform, employers can increase the number of workers willing to be employed without increasing wage rates.

8. Answers will vary. Possible answers: Electronic calculators changed the demand for accountants and bookkeepers. New varieties of seeds have changed the demand for farm workers. New communications equipment has changed the demand for telephone operators.

# Review Economic Terms

Choose the term that best fits the definition. On a separate sheet of paper, write the letter of the answer. Some terms may not be used.

_____ 1. A labor union's attempt to withhold labor from a firm

_____ 2. An impartial observer brought in when labor negotiations break down, to suggest how to resolve differences

_____ 3. The process by which representatives of the union and the employer negotiate wages, employee benefits, and working conditions

_____ 4. A state law that says workers do not have to join a union or pay union dues to hold a job

_____ 5. When labor negotiations break down and the public interest is involved, a neutral third party is brought in to impose a settlement both sides must accept

_____ 6. The demand for a resource that arises from the demand for the product that resource produces

_____ 7. One resource works with the other in production; a decrease in the price of one resource increases the demand for the other

_____ 8. One resource can replace another in production; an increase in the price of one resource increases the demand for the other

_____ 9. The wage at which the quantity of labor firms want to hire exactly matches the quantity workers want to supply

_____ 10. The value of output produced by a resource

_____ 11. Establishes a minimum amount that an employer can pay a worker for an hour of labor

_____ 12. A group of workers who join together to seek higher pay and better working conditions by negotiating a labor contract with their employers

_____ 13. Union efforts to force employers to hire more workers than demanded for a task

a. **binding arbitration**

b. **collective bargaining**

c. **derived demand**

d. **equilibrium wage**

e. **featherbedding**

f. **labor union**

g. **mediator**

h. **minimum wage law**

i. **productivity**

j. **resource complements**

k. **resource substitutes**

l. **right-to-work law**

m. **strike**

# Review Economic Concepts

14. The demand for resources is derived from

   a. the demand for products the resources are used to produce.

   b. the demand for higher wages for workers.

   c. the demand for profits by business owners.

   d. the demand for taxes to pay for government services.

15. **True or False** Resource prices provide information to producers that allow them to use resources in a way that maximizes their value.

16. If two resources are __?__, an increase in the price of one will cause businesses to demand less of the other.

17. The market supply of labor will change as a result of each of the following *except*

   a. a change in the amount of wealth workers hold.

   b. a change in the conditions in which employees are expected to work.

   c. a change in the demand for products workers produce.

   d. a change in workers' tastes for being employed in a particular career.

*Chapter Assessment*     **283**

---

## Review Economic Terms

1. m. strike
2. g. mediator
3. b. collective bargaining
4. l. right-to-work law
5. a. binding arbitration
6. c. derived demand
7. j. resource complements
8. k. resource substitutes
9. d. equilibrium wage
10. i. productivity
11. h. minimum wage law
12. f. labor union
13. e. featherbedding

## Review Economic Concepts

14. a. the demand for products the resources are used to produce
15. True
16. complements
17. c. a change in the demand for products workers produce

## Review Economic Concepts

18. True

19. d. a worker who helped design Microsoft's Windows 2000 software

20. Job discrimination

21. False. Membership in craft unions is limited to workers with a particular skill.

22. b. binding arbitration has taken place

23. Featherbedding

24. d. have the same skill

25. Collective bargaining

26. True

## Apply Economic Concepts

27. Answers will vary. Possible answer: Apex might decide to replace some or all of the workers with machines rather than pay higher wages. The workers might justify the requested raise by finding a way to increase the number of products they can produce per minute.

28. Answers will vary. Possible answer: The owner of the restaurant could reduce the number of people employed and require each remaining worker to do more work. Fringe benefits could be cut. All raises above the minimum wage could be eliminated. Higher-skilled workers might be employed to replace the current low-skilled workers. Machines could be purchased to perform tasks currently done by workers.

29. Answers will vary but should include evidence of an actual interview.

30. Answers will vary. Possible answer: The arbitrator is not likely to award the union any less than the amount the city has offered. Still, this could happen. Further, if a larger raise is awarded, the city may lay off some fire fighters to get the money to pay the raises. This could endanger the lives of citizens and firefighters if there are not enough people to do the job.

---

18. **True or False** Some workers are better paid because they have acquired special training that makes their labor more valuable to employers.

19. Which of the following workers would be best paid?

    a. a worker who has not graduated from high school

    b. a worker who just completed a master's degree in English literature

    c. a worker who is willing to stay up all night to guard a bank's deposit box

    d. a worker who helped design Microsoft's Windows 2000 software

20. __?__ takes place when a person is not employed because of his or her race, ethnicity, or gender.

21. **True or False** Membership in industrial unions is limited to workers with a particular skill.

22. When a labor settlement is imposed on management and a union by a neutral third party,

    a. there is a right-to-work law.

    b. binding arbitration has taken place.

    c. there has been mediation.

    d. there is likely to be a strike.

23. __?__ takes place when a contract requires management to hire more workers than it feels are necessary.

24. A craft union is formed when workers who all __?__ join together to form a union.

    a. have the same employer

    b. work in the same area

    c. work in a particular industry

    d. have the same skill

25. __?__ takes place when unions and management negotiate to reach a labor contract.

26. **True or False** In recent years, union membership has declined.

# Apply Economic Concepts

27. **Resource Substitutes** The Apex Pot company manufactures high-quality kitchen pans. Currently it employs 500 workers, who produce stainless steel pans one at a time on individual machines. It takes a worker six minutes to produce each item. The workers are paid $12 per hour for their labor. Apex managers have found that they can purchase machines that will produce products with equal quality automatically. One machine costs $200,000 but can produce one pan per minute. So far, management has chosen not to purchase any of the machines. The workers' contract is due to expire next month. Their union has asked to have the wage rate increased to $14 per hour. Apex management has stated that the firm cannot afford to pay them any more than they currently receive. What factors should each side consider during collective bargaining?

28. **Minimum Wage Laws** Imagine that you own a fast-food restaurant. The restaurant employs 20 workers, who are paid the minimum wage of $5.15 per hour. Next month, Congress passes a law that will increase the minimum wage you must pay your workers to $6.15 per hour. What steps could you take to control your production costs and protect your profits?

29. **Labor Unions** Interview a friend or relative who is a member of a labor union. Ask why this person joined a union. Ask what the biggest benefit is of union membership. Write a paragraph summarizing your interview.

30. **Binding Arbitration** You are the president of a fire fighter's union in a large city. There is a law that provides for binding arbitration for vital public employees in your state. The current contract between your union and the

city is about to expire. Your members want at least a 4 percent increase in their wages in each of the next three years. The city has offered a 2 percent raise per year. Negotiators have not been able to reach a decision. The city has said it will call for binding arbitration unless the union accepts its "final offer." If an arbitrator is called in, he or she might award the union more than the city's 2 percent offer. But, you know the city is in a financial bind. The arbitrator could award less than the 2 percent. What recommendation would you make to your members? Explain your reasons for this recommendation.

31. **History** Investigate the Knights of Labor organization after the Civil War. Why was this industrial union largely unsuccessful? What led to its end after 1886? How were the problems it faced different from those labor organizations face today?

32. **Dealing with a Labor Shortage** Consider Marcy, who owns a wedding photography business. She currently employs four photographers, whom she pays $25 per hour. She has more customers than she can serve and would hire another employee if she could find a qualified worker. Unfortunately, few photographers meet her standards. She could hire a photographer away from one of her competitors if she were willing to pay this person $30 per hour. Her current employees then would expect to be paid more, too. Assume that each of her photographers works a 40-hour week. How much more would Marcy have to pay each week to employ this fifth worker? Why might an employer choose not to hire a worker away from a competitor when there is a labor shortage?

33. **Assess a Strike** Garbage collectors in several cities in a state went on strike for better wages and a continuation of their employer-paid medical insurance coverage. At that time, the state and many of its local governments had large budget deficits. They argued that they could not afford to pay the garbage collectors more and demanded that these workers contribute to the cost of their medical coverage. Write an essay that addresses two issues: (1) Should garbage collectors be allowed to strike? Why or why not? (2) Should the garbage collectors be forced to pay all or part of the cost for their medical insurance when it has been totally paid by their employers in the past?

34. **Sharpen Your Life Skills: Working with Percentages** Every month the Bureau of Labor Statistics calculates the *labor force participation rate (LFPR)* This is the percentage of the *civilian noninstitutional population (CNP)* that is either employed or looking for work. Economists believe that this value provides insight into workers' attitudes about the economy by showing how interested they are in working. It is found by dividing the labor force (the total of employed workers and those looking for work) by the CNP. In 2000, the CNP was 209.7 million people. In that same year, there were 135.2 million employed workers and 5.7 million unemployed workers who were actively seeking employment. Calculate the LFPR for 2000. If the LFPR was 67.0% in 2001, what might it show about the economy?

econxtra.swlearning.com

35. Access **EconDebate Online** at econxtra.swlearning.com. Click on the following policy debate: "Does an increase in the minimum wage result in a higher unemployment rate?" Choose one article that argues in support of increasing the minimum wage and one that argues against it. Summarize each article in a paragraph. Then write a paragraph explaining your opinion on this issue.

## Apply Economic Concepts

31. Answers will vary. Possible answer: The Knights of Labor was poorly organized and lacked strong leadership. Although its leaders never approved a single strike, its members went out on strike anyway. It faced government opposition and several of its members were convicted of inciting violence and were executed for their crimes. Unions today have the legal right to organize and negotiate with management.

32. Marcy will have to pay $2,000 more each week if she hires a new worker—$1,200 for the new employee and $800 for current employees (4 employees ? $5 ? 40 hours). The table at the bottom of the page illustrates the difference between the two situations.

    Answers will vary. Possible answer: Employers might not hire additional workers when there is a labor shortage because the added cost of higher wages might be more than they are worth.

33. Answers will vary but should reflect logic and reason as well as student values.

34. 67.2% (140.9 / 209.7)

    Answers will vary. Possible answer: The smaller LFPR in 2001 might indicate a less optimistic attitude about seeking employment.

35. Answers will vary but should include evidence that the articles were read. Consider asking students to include a reference citation for the articles they use.

### Marcy's Photography Business

| | Current Situation | | | Situation with Additional Worker | | |
|---|---|---|---|---|---|---|
| | Rate | Hours | Weekly Pay | Rate | Hours | Weekly Pay |
| Worker 1 | $25 | 40 | $1,000 | $30 | 40 | $1,200 |
| Worker 2 | $25 | 40 | $1,000 | $30 | 40 | $1,200 |
| Worker 3 | $25 | 40 | $1,000 | $30 | 40 | $1,200 |
| Worker 4 | $25 | 40 | $1,000 | $30 | 40 | $1,200 |
| Worker 5 | | | | $30 | 40 | $1,200 |
| Total payroll | | | $4,000 | | | $6,000 |

# Financial Markets and Business Growth

## Chapter Overview

**LESSON 10.1** *Production, Consumption, and Time:* This lesson explains why production requires savings and why people often pay more to consume now.

**LESSON 10.2** *Banks, Interest, and Corporate Finance:* This lesson focuses on the role of banks in bringing borrowers and savers together. It also addresses the reasons for differing interest rates among types of loans and the sources of financial capital.

**LESSON 10.3** *Business Growth:* This lesson addresses the main sources of corporate growth: profit, franchising, mergers, and multinational corporations. An historical perspective on the four merger waves of the past century is included.

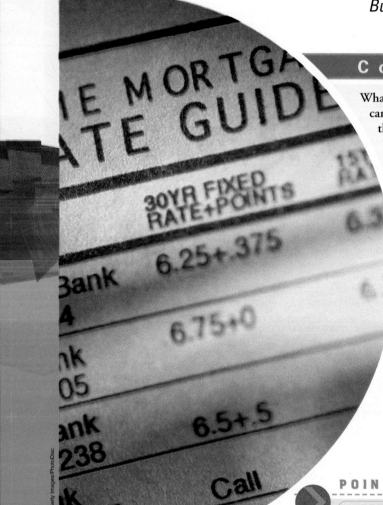

© Getty Images/PhotoDisc

### Consider

Ask students to consider the questions posed on this page as they study Chapter 10. After studying all three lessons, students should be able to answer the questions. The content related to each question can be found on the pages indicated below.

- What's seed money, and why can't Farmer Jones grow anything without it? See page 288—Production Takes Time.

- Why are you willing to pay more at a first-run movie theater than at other theaters? See page 290—Paying More to Consume Now.

- Why do you repeatedly burn your mouth eating pizza, despite knowing the risk? See page 290—Paying More to Consume Now.

- Why is a bank more likely to be called Security Trust than Benny's Bank? See page 295—Banks as Intermediaries.

- Why do banks charge more interest on car loans than on home loans? See page 297—Why Interest Rates Differ.

### Consider

What's seed money, and why can't Farmer Jones grow anything without it?

Why are you willing to pay more at a first-run movie theater than at other theaters?

Why do you repeatedly burn your mouth eating pizza, despite knowing the risk?

Why is a bank more likely to be called Security Trust than Benny's Bank?

Why do banks charge more interest on car loans than on home loans?

### POINT YOUR BROWSER

*econxtra.swlearning.com*

### POINT YOUR BROWSER

Remind students that they can find additional resources for this chapter at **econxtra.swlearning.com**.

- Xtra! Study Tools
- Net Bookmarks
- Xtra! Quiz Prep
- econ@pps
- Ask the Xpert!
- Graphing Workshop

### Teaching Resources for Chapter 10

- Activities and Projects Masters
- Spanish Resources
- Econ Connection Interactive Tutorial CD
- **Exam***View*® CD
- Workbook Teacher's Edition
- Chapter and Unit Tests Teacher's Edition
- NCEE Standards and Correlation
- Personal Finance Guide

- Social Studies Skills Review
- Instructor's Resource CD
  - PowerPoint Presentation
  - Lesson Plans
  - Video Discussion Guide
  - Answers to Graphing Exercises
- **econxtra.swlearning.com**

# 10.1 Production, Consumption, and Time

## Objectives

> Explain why production requires savings.

> Explain why people often pay more to consume now.

> Apply demand and supply analysis to the market for loans.

## Overview

Time plays an important role in both production and consumption. From an entrepreneur's bright idea for a new product to its delivery to market, production takes time. For example, consider the textbook you are now reading. This book was years in the making and required dozens of specialists, including an author, a project manager, editors, supplement writers, designers, photographers, reviewers, typesetters, paper makers, printers, binders, and marketers. All this effort was made before a single copy was sold, so no revenue was coming in. During the long production process, how did these resource suppliers survive?

## Key Terms

interest rate

demand for loans curve

supply of loans curve

market for loans

equilibrium interest rate

## [ In the News ]

### ● Current Trends in the Mortgage Market

You are sitting quietly in front of your computer monitor, surfing the Internet. Suddenly a pop-up ad appears: "Obtain a 4.25% mortgage. Credit problems are not problems. Approvals on same day of application. Cash Outs. Lender Does Battle for Your Business." Roadside billboards, some with flashing electronic signs, also greet you with current mortgage rates and invitations to visit nearby lenders. Well-known entertainment and sports figures assure you on television that now is the time to refinance your home. Whether you are a 55-year-old suburban dweller or a 15-year-old high-school student, you suddenly are aware that the once-conservative mortgage industry is changing. The industry has evolved overnight into an aggressive, customer-pursuing, market-creating force. Why is this happening now? After all, interest rates were quite low in the late 1990s, but this marketing approach was not in use then. The answer is that vast numbers of homeowners today see refinancing as a way not only to lower the payments on their home mortgage, but also to consolidate all forms of high-interest debt into one low-interest loan. According to mortgage companies, refinancing once made up about 10 to 15 percent of their business. It now makes up about 40 percent. The refinancing homeowners increase the size of their loans by an average of more than $40,000.

### Think About It

What do you think has caused the change in approach among mortgage companies? Why are so many homeowners choosing to refinance their homes? What long-term effects do you think this will have on home ownership?

◀ | ▶

287

---

## National Content Standards in Economics

A complete list of the NCEE Standards appears on pages xxiv–xxv of this book. The following standards are addressed in Lesson 10.1.

Standard 2: Marginal Cost/Benefit

Standard 10: Role of Economic Institutions

Standard 11: Role of Money

Standard 12: Role of Interest Rates

Standard 15: Growth

---

## Production and Time

Remind students that production doesn't just happen. Gathering resources takes time. This can be seen in entrepreneurship as well. Finding a better way to produce a good or service implies that the entrepreneur took the time to consider how the previous method could be improved. Ask students how much time they spend thinking about their assignments before they start to work. Do they do as well if they just start to work without taking the time to think first? Remind them that completing assignments is a type of production, too.

### Think Critically Through Visuals

Direct students to focus their attention on the photograph on this page. Ask for a volunteer to answer the question posed in the caption.

### Answer

The plow will allow him to plant more land and so grow more corn. Adding 50 more bushels a year does outweigh the one-time cost of 200 bushels if Farmer Jones continues to harvest for more than four years after making the plow.

# Production and Time

Jones is a primitive farmer in a simple economy. Isolated from any neighbors or markets, he literally scratches out a living on a plot of land, using only crude sticks. While a crop is growing, none of it is available for current consumption.

© Getty Images/PhotoDisc

Farmer Jones must decide whether to invest his time in making a plow. Does adding 50 more bushels a year outweigh the one-time cost of 200 bushels? If you were Farmer Jones, how would you decide?

## Production Takes Time

None of the crop is ready for consumption until it grows, so to survive, Jones must rely on food saved from prior harvests while the new crop comes in. The longer the growing season, the more Jones must have saved during prior periods. In this simple example, it is clear that *production cannot occur without savings from prior periods.*

## Investment Takes Time

With his current resources of land, labor, seed corn, fertilizer, and some crude sticks, Jones grows about 200 bushels of corn a year. He soon realizes that if he had a plow—*a capital good*—his productivity would increase. Making a plow in such a primitive setting, however, would take time and keep him away from his fields for a year. Thus, the plow has an opportunity cost of 200 bushels of corn. Jones would be unable to survive this drop in production unless he has saved enough from prior harvests. The question is: Should he invest his time in the plow? The answer depends on the costs and benefits of the plow. You already know that the plow's opportunity cost is 200 bushels—the forgone output. The benefit depends on how much the plow will increase production and how long the plow will last. Jones figures that the plow will boost his yield by 50 bushels a year and will last his lifetime. In making the investment decision, he compares current costs to the future stream of benefits.

## Capital Increases Labor Productivity

Rather than work the soil with his crude sticks, Jones produces capital to increase his future productivity. Making the plow is an investment of his time. For the economy as a whole, more investment means more capital goods, increasing the economy's ability to produce in the future. This growth can be shown by an expansion of the economy's production possibilities frontier. Advanced industrial economies invest more than other economies.

**288**   CHAPTER 10   Financial Markets and Business Growth

### Outside Resources

**GE Credit** One of many organizations that offers credit to large and small businesses, GE Credit has a web site at www.ge.com/en/financial/index.htm. Ask students to search this, or a similar web site, to find out how easy it is for a business to borrow funds. How is GE able to acquire the funds it lends to businesses?

**The FDIC's Learning Bank Web Site** This site provides a wide range of information for young people at www.fdic.gov/about/learn/learning/who/index.html. Topics include banking, saving, borrowing, and the FDIC itself. Ask students to evaluate this site.

These additions to capital accumulate over time. Figure 10.1 shows the value of capital goods in the United States in recent years. The combined value of business equipment and business structures, such as factories and buildings, increased from $7.5 trillion in 1991 to $10.2 trillion in 2001. This increase in capital makes U.S. workers more productive.

You can see from the Farmer Jones example why most production cannot occur without prior saving. *Production depends on savings because production of both consumer goods and capital goods takes time. This is time during which consumer goods are not available for current consumption.*

## Financial Intermediaries

To modernize the example, suppose Farmer Jones can borrow money. Many farmers visit the bank each spring to borrow enough "seed money" to survive until the crops come in. Likewise, other businesses often borrow at least a portion of the financial capital needed until output gets sold.

The **interest rate** is the price of borrowing—the annual interest expressed as a percentage of the amount borrowed. For example, if the interest rate is 5 percent, the interest

Bloomberg.com's financial news network provides quick links to the latest key interest rates at its markets web site. Access this site through econxtra. swlearning.com. Click on "Rates and Bonds" under "Market Data." Analyze the trends in the key rates and mortgage rates over the one-year period.

*econxtra.swlearning.com*

charged is $5 per year for each $100 borrowed. The lower the interest rate, the lower the price of borrowing. The lower the price of borrowing, the more Farmer Jones and other producers are willing and able to borrow.

In a modern economy, producers need not rely exclusively on their own savings. They can borrow the funds needed to help finance a business.

## Ask the Xpert!

*econxtra.swlearning.com*

*Why are some rates of interest so much higher than others?*

✔ **CHECKPOINT**
Why does production require savings?

**interest rate**
Annual interest expressed as a percentage of the amount borrowed or saved

---

### Value of Business Structures and Equipment in the United States

**Figure 10.1**

The combined value of business equipment and business structures increased nearly $3 trillion from 1991 to 2001.

Source: Developed from estimates in the U.S. Department of Commerce, *Survey of Current Business,* September 2002, Table 15. Structures include factories, buildings, and other permanent business fixtures. Figures are adjusted to eliminate the effects of inflation.

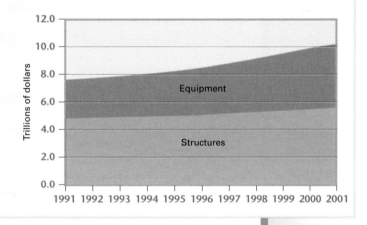

---

## ENRICH

Fifty years ago, homes were constructed by workers who performed most tasks by hand. Today, new machines have reduced the average number of hours of labor needed to construct a typical three-bedroom home by almost 50 percent. Ask students to identify some of these machines and to estimate their costs. Why has investment been a necessary part of the effort to construct new homes more efficiently? What might have happened to construction in the United States if firms had not been able to borrow funds to make investments?

---

## TEACH          (continued)

### Production and Time

Give each student a sheet of paper. Without any warning, tell them that they must fold it into a perfect square in the next 10 seconds. Many won't complete the assignment and those who do are likely to produce messy or misshapen squares. Give them a second sheet of paper and ask them to accomplish the same task, but this time give them a full minute to produce the square. (They will also have had time to think about what they are doing by now.) The quality and quantity of their production is likely to improve. Discuss the need for time to achieve efficient production. Ask students to explain why technological advancements such as Henry Ford's production line for Model Ts involved an investment of time as well as other resources.

### NETBookmark

Direct students to **econxtra.swlearning.com**. Remind them to click on the link for Lesson 10.1 to find the appropriate link for the **NET Bookmark** on this page.

### Ask the Xpert!

Direct students to **econxtra.swlearning.com** to hear an expert answer the question "Why are some rates of interest so much higher than others?"

### *Think Critically Through Visuals*

Direct students to focus their attention on **Figure 10.1—Value of Business Structures and Equipment in the United States.** Point out that the value of capital increased during the 10-year period shown in the graph.

✔ **CHECKPOINT**
Invite a student to answer the checkpoint that appears on this page.

**Answer**
Production requires savings because production takes time.

## Consumption and Time

Review the concept of time value. Remind students that the value of a pizza is greater when they are hungry than when they are not. Time value can affect the amount they are willing to pay for a good or service. Ask them how much they would be willing to pay to hire a lawyer at the present. Then ask them how much they would be willing to pay if they were unjustly accused of committing a crime. They would probably be willing to pay quite a bit to avoid going to jail. They probably would be willing to borrow money to hire the lawyer. Emphasize the idea that people borrow to spend now when they value current consumption more than future consumption.

**CHECKPOINT**

Invite a student to answer the checkpoint that appears on this page.

### Answers

People are willing to pay more to consume now because they value present consumption more than future consumption.

# Consumption and Time

Did you ever burn the roof of your mouth biting into a slice of pizza that hadn't sufficiently cooled? Have you done this more than once? Why do you continue to do this when you know what is likely to happen? You continue because that bite of pizza is worth more to you now than the same bite two minutes from now. You are so anxious to eat that pizza that you are willing to risk burning your mouth rather than wait until it can no longer harm you. In a small way, this reflects the fact that you and other consumers often value *present* consumption more than *future* consumption.

### Paying More to Consume Now

*When you value present consumption more than future consumption you are willing to pay more to consume now rather than wait.* Prices often reflect your greater willingness to pay to consume sooner. Consider the movies. You pay more to see a movie at the theater rather than wait until it comes out on video or DVD. The same is true for books. By waiting for the paperback, you usually save more than half the price of the hardback. Photo developers, dry cleaners, fast-food restaurants, convenience stores, and other suppliers advertise the speed of their services. They know that consumers are willing to pay more for earlier availability.

Thus, *impatience* is one reason you may value present consumption more than future consumption. Another is *uncertainty.* If you wait, something might prevent you from consuming the good. A T-shirt slogan captures this point best: "Life is uncertain. Eat dessert first."

One way to ensure that goods and services can be consumed now is to borrow money to buy these products. Home mortgages, car loans, personal loans, and credit cards are examples of household borrowing. People borrow more when the interest rate declines,

**demand for loans curve**

A downward-sloping curve showing the negative relationship between the interest rate and the quantity of loans demanded, other things constant

other things constant. For example, home purchases increase when mortgage rates decline.

**CHECKPOINT**

Why are people often willing to pay more to consume now?

# The Market for Loans

You already know that producers are willing to pay interest to borrow money: This borrowing finances the production of consumer goods and capital goods. The simple principles developed for Farmer Jones can be generalized to other producers.

### The Demand for Loans

Firms borrow to help fund production and investment. Firms need money to pay for resources until output is produced and sold. Firms also need money to invest in capital, such as machines, trucks, and buildings. The interest rate is the cost of borrowing. The lower the interest rate, other things constant, the more firms are willing and able to borrow. So the demand for loans is a downward-sloping curve. It shows that firms borrow more when the interest rate declines.

Firms are not the only demanders of loans. Households borrow to pay for homes, cars, college tuition, and more. The lower the interest rate, the more willing and able households are to borrow. Therefore, households, like firms, borrow more when the interest rate declines, other things constant.

The downward-sloping **demand for loans curve**, labeled $D$ in Figure 10.2, reflects the negative relationship between the interest rate and the quantity of loans demanded. The lower the interest rate, the greater the quantity of loans demanded, other things constant.

**290**

**CHAPTER 10** Financial Markets and Business Growth

---

### *Economic Headlines*

Instruct students to locate an article or advertisement in a current magazine or newspaper that describes a change in interest rates. Ask students to decide whether this change is the result of a change in the demand for loans or in the supply of loans. Or, is there some other reason for the interest rate to have changed? Could a business be trying to encourage people to buy its product by providing low-cost loans, effectively lowering its price? Do students believe that low-cost interest is an effective marketing tool?

## Main Idea

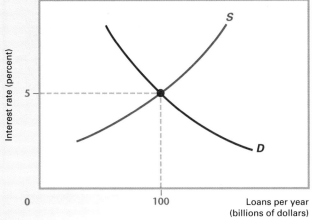

**Role of Interest Rates: Market for Loans**

 **Figure 10.2**

The quantity of loans demanded is inversely related to the rate of interest. The quantity of loans supplied is directly related to the interest rate. The equilibrium rate of interest, 5 percent, is determined at the intersection of the demand curve and supply curve for loans.

*The interest rate rises or falls to balance the amount saved with the amount borrowed.* **What if the initial interest rate was 8 percent?** *The equilibrium interest rate determines the allocation of scarce resources in the economy between present uses and future uses.* **In the market for loans, who trades present spending for future spending, and who trades future spending for the ability to spend now?"**

## The Supply of Loans

What about the supply of loans? Because you and other consumers often value present consumption more than future consumption, you must be rewarded to postpone consumption. The amount saved during the year equals income minus consumption. When they save a portion of their incomes in financial institutions such as banks, households give up present consumption in return for interest. *Interest is the reward for not consuming now.*

People delay present consumption for a greater ability to consume in the future. The higher the interest rate, other things constant, the greater the reward for saving, so the more people save. Savers are the suppliers of loans.

The more saved, the greater the quantity of loans supplied.

The **supply of loans curve**, labeled S in Figure 10.2, shows the positive relationship between the interest rate and the quantity of loans supplied, other things constant. As you can see, this supply of loans curve slopes upward.

## Market Interest Rate

The demand for loans and the supply of loans come together in the market for loans to determine the market interest rate, as in Figure 10.2. The **market for loans** brings together borrowers, or demanders of loans, and savers, or suppliers of loans, to determine the market rate of interest. The interest rate is the price of borrowing and the reward for

**supply of loans curve**
An upward-sloping curve showing the positive relationship between the interest rate and the quantity of loans supplied, other things constant

**market for loans**
The market that brings together borrowers (the demanders of loans) and savers (the suppliers of loans) to determine the market interest rate

Lesson 10.1 • *Production, Consumption, and Time* **291**

## TEACH

### The Market for Loans
Remind students that the benefits of saving include interest income earned from savings while the costs of borrowing include interest paid for a loan.

*Think Critically Through Visuals*

Direct students to focus their attention on **Figure 10.2—Role of Interest Rates: Market for Loans**. Point out that in the market for loans, the borrower trades future spending for the ability to spend now, while the saver trades present spending for future spending.

### Main Idea
**NCEE Standard 12: Role of Interest Rates**

Interest rates, adjusted for inflation, rise and fall to balance the amount saved with the amount borrowed, which affects the allocation of scarce resources between present and future uses.

*Think Critically Through Visuals*

Direct students to focus their attention on the photograph on page 292. Ask for a volunteer to answer the question posed in the caption.

**Answer**
Answers will vary. Possible answer: The couple completing the application is demanding loans, while the bank is supplying loans.

Have students work in pairs to discuss the ethical issue and develop an answer to the question presented in the **Ethics in Action** feature on page 292.

**Answers to Think Critically**
Answers will vary. Possible answer: Subprime lending is not unethical; it helps people who don't qualify for traditional mortgages realize their dreams of homeownership. Consumers need to educate themselves before borrowing money. There is no need to regulate this practice.

## Group Activity
Divide students into an equal number of small groups. Half of the groups have $1,000 to lend, and the others want to borrow $500. Each lending group is free to set its own interest rate, but its objective is to earn the most interest possible. Each borrowing group is trying to borrow the $500 it needs at the lowest rate possible. Let the groups negotiate loans for a set time of 5 to 10 minutes. The resulting interest rates should be quite low. Then reverse the amounts. The lenders have $500 to lend while the borrowers want to borrow $1,000. How can students explain the higher interest rates?

## CHECKPOINT

Invite a student to answer the checkpoint that appears on page 292.

**Answer**

The demand for loans and the supply for loans come together in the market for loans to determine the market interest rate.

## APPLY

Assign Lesson 10.1 from the Contemporary Economics Workbook.

### e-con @pps

Encourage students to apply their knowledge of concepts presented in this lesson as they explore economic news stories, policy debates, and data available at **econxtra.swlearning.com**.

## ASSESS

Assign all or part of Lesson 10.1 Assessment on page 293 as homework or an in-class activity.

### Xtra! Study Tools

Direct students to the online study tools for Lesson 10.1 at **econxtra.swlearning.com**.

## CLOSE

**Revisit** the In the News feature on the first page of the lesson. Ask students to review their preliminary answers and discuss the questions, now that they have completed this lesson.

**Review** the objectives for Lesson 10.1. Students should be able to:

• Explain why production requires savings.

• Explain why people often pay more to consume now.

• Apply demand and supply analysis to the market for loans.

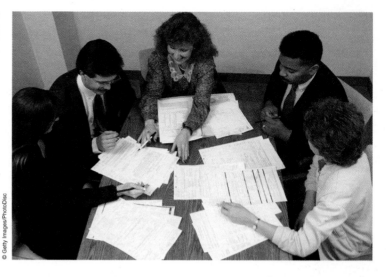

The demand for loans and the supply of loans come together in the market for loans to determine the market interest rate. In this photograph, representatives of the bank are working with the couple on the left to fill out loan applications. Who is demanding the loans, and who is supplying the loans?

**equilibrium interest rate**

The only interest rate at which the quantity of loans demanded equals the quantity of loans supplied

saving. In this case, the **equilibrium interest rate** of 5 percent is the only one that exactly matches the intentions of savers and borrowers. Here, the equilibrium quantity of loans is $100 billion per year.

## CHECKPOINT

How does demand and supply analysis apply to the market for loans?

# Ethics in Action

**Predatory Lending** Consumer organizations and subprime mortgage lenders are in a legislative battle in Washington over so-called predatory lending. "Subprime" refers to less-desirable mortgage terms or rates. This term applies to loans geared primarily to people or businesses who have credit problems and who can't qualify for the best terms or rates. These loans also are targeted to customers who generally are ignorant about what loans are available to them. The mortgage industry is lobbying for federal legislation that would reverse state and local laws that protect consumers against unfair lending practices. Consumer groups argue that enacting a strict national standard would prevent millions of Americans from

losing these protections. In the most abusive instances, predatory lending activities have destroyed the equity borrowers had built up in their homes over many years. In far too many cases, borrowers have lost their homes. Many of these people, particularly older Americans, have been persuaded or fooled by unethical salespeople into borrowing against their home equity, often to pay for unnecessary, high-priced home renovations. Still others have been charged sky-high fees and interest rates.

**Think Critically**

Do you think that laws against predatory lending should be at the state or local level or at the national level? Explain your answer.

292   CHAPTER 10   Financial Markets and Business Growth

## RETEACH

Instruct students to decide whether they will buy a new $500 bicycle now by borrowing at 10 percent interest, or later by saving for a year and paying cash for the product. To make their decision, they should first list the benefits and costs of each alternative. These lists should include the value of having the product now, the cost of the interest, the interest they might earn on their savings, and the possibility that the price of the product could increase. If the interest rate were only 3 percent, would their decision be different? How do interest rates influence people's willingness to borrow?

## Key Concepts

1. Why couldn't you open up a pizza restaurant tomorrow if you wanted to?

2. Before the 1970s there were no hand-held electronic calculators. When these products first became available, they cost about $100 each. Why were people willing to invest so much in a calculator that could only add, subtract, multiply, and divide? How did the calculator change workers' productivity?

3. Why were many more consumers willing to buy automobiles when manufacturers offered special 0 percent interest rates in 2002?

4. Why do most people borrow funds to purchase a home or an automobile rather than wait until they can afford to pay cash?

5. What happens to the demand for loans that causes the equilibrium interest rate to fall during a downturn in the economy?

## Graphing Exercise

6. Home mortgage interest rates change over time with the demand and supply for loans. Use data given in the table to construct a line graph that shows the annual average for new-home mortgage interest rates from 1993 through 2002. How much did this interest rate fall from 2000 through 2002? How important is a change of 1 percent in the mortgage interest rate to a person who wants to borrow $100,000 to buy a home?

### New Home Mortgage Interest Rates, 1993–2002

| Year | Interest Rate | Year | Interest Rate |
|------|---------------|------|---------------|
| 1993 | 7.20% | 1998 | 7.07% |
| 1994 | 7.49 | 1999 | 7.04 |
| 1995 | 7.87 | 2000 | 7.52 |
| 1996 | 7.80 | 2001 | 7.00 |
| 1997 | 7.71 | 2002 | 6.43 |

## Think Critically

7. **Financial Management** Most businesses rely on borrowed money. In the early 1980s, interest rates were very high in the United States, reaching levels of 20 percent of more. How would such high interest rates affect businesses and, therefore, the overall economy?

8. **Advertising** Businesses that market expensive consumer products such as refrigerators, computers, and home furnishings typically include statements about "easy payment plans" in their ads. Why do they include this information? If many consumers choose to borrow to finance their purchases, what will this do to the demand for loans and interest rates?

**Xtra!**
Study Tools
*econxtra.swlearning.com*

---

## Key Concepts

1. Answers will vary. Possible answer: Opening any type of business requires time, money, and planning. To open a pizza restaurant, a student would need to identify a location, purchase supplies and equipment, hire employees, and prepare to market the product. None of this can happen over night.

2. Answers will vary. Possible answer: Being able to perform basic mathematical calculations saved accountants and scientists a great deal of time and increased their productivity so much that $100 seemed a small price to pay.

3. Answers will vary. Possible answer: Zero percent interest rates reduced their cost of borrowing and the effective price they had to pay to purchase a new automobile.

4. Answers will vary. Possible answer: It would take most people many years to accumulate enough money to purchase these expensive products. They prefer to borrow the funds so they are able to consume now.

5. Answers will vary. Possible answer: When the economy is not doing well, many consumers are worried about becoming unemployed and are not willing to take on the responsibility of additional debt. This causes the demand for loans to decline and the equilibrium interest rate to fall.

## Graphing Exercise

6. Answers will vary. The decline in interest rates from 2000 through 2002 was 1.09%. Possible answer: This decline would have reduced the annual interest cost of a $100,000 loan by more than $1,000.

A sample of an acceptable graph appears at the bottom of this page.

*The Answer Key is continued on page 312.*

---

### New Home Mortgage Interest Rates

### Visualizing the Answer— Graphing Exercise

6. The answer includes a graph. Students' graphs should look similar to the one shown here. An Excel spreadsheet containing this graph, along with supporting data, is available on the Instructor's Resource CD.

## FOCUS

### 10.2 Banks, Interest, and Corporate Finance

Point out that people who save and people who borrow are not the same individuals. Further, those who save most often are not well qualified to judge whether a potential borrower is worthy of credit. In general, savers must rely on financial intermediaries to help them earn a return on their savings. Without these intermediaries, funds might not flow from savers to borrowers and the economy would not work as well.

### Objectives

Remind students to read the lesson objectives to help focus their attention before reading the lesson.

### Key Terms

Direct students to look up key terms in a business or economics dictionary. Some students will find it helpful to read another definition. In addition to a definition, many entries will include a brief explanation and an example.

### [ In the News ]

Instruct students to read the passage and write down their answers. Point out that their answers might change after they finish studying Lesson 10.2.

### Answers to Think About It

Answers will vary. Possible answers: With the additional competition from online banks, interest rates on savings accounts will rise. Online banking offers consumers another option that makes them more money, and if local banks are unable to meet this interest rate increase for savings accounts, then consumers will switch to online banking.

### Visual Presentation

Use the PowerPoint presentation on the Instructor's Resource CD as an adjunct to your lecture. The presentation also can be used for review.

## Objectives

> Explain the role of banks in bringing borrowers and savers together.

> Understand why interest rates differ among types of loans.

> Identify and discuss a corporation's sources of financial capital.

## Overview

You now understand why borrowers are willing to pay interest and why savers expect to be paid interest. Banks serve both groups. Banks are willing to pay interest on consumer savings because the banks can, in turn, charge higher rates of interest to those who need credit, such as farmers, home buyers, college students, and entrepreneurs looking to start or expand a business. Banks bring borrowers and savers together and try to earn a profit by serving both groups.

## Key Terms

**financial intermediaries**

**credit**

**line of credit**

**prime rate**

**collateral**

**initial public offering (IPO)**

**dividends**

**retained earnings**

**bond**

**securities**

### [ In the News ]

#### ● The Bank that Never Closes

Juniper Bank never closes. It's open 24 hours a day, 365 days a year. With Internet access, bank customers can pay bills, check account balances, and borrow money from anywhere in the world. Juniper was one of the nation's first virtual banks—one of the first authorized to offer banking services on the Internet. The bank can accept deposits from customers in all 50 states. All accounts are FDIC insured. Because Internet banks don't have to spend money on buildings and bank tellers, they can offer their customers higher interest rates on savings accounts. When it comes to getting cash and making deposits, however, virtual bank customers do need a physical connection. Juniper Bank customers can get cash at thousands of ATM locations. Deposits are accepted at ATMs, through the mail, direct deposit, electronic transfers, and at any of the 4,200 Mail Boxes Etc. locations. With the easy access offered by Internet banks such as Juniper Bank, customers increasingly are shopping nationwide for the best rates for deposits, credit cards, and loans.

#### Think About It

What, if any, impact do you think additional competition from online banks will have on interest rates on savings accounts?

◄ | ►

294

## National Content Standards in Economics

A complete list of the NCEE Standards appears on pages xxiv–xxv of this book. The following standards are addressed in Lesson 10.2.

Standard 4: Role of Incentives

Standard 10: Role of Economic Institutions

Standard 11: Role of Money

Standard 12: Role of Interest Rates

Standard 15: Growth

# Banks as Intermediaries

Banks accumulate funds from savers and lend these funds to borrowers, thereby serving as **financial intermediaries** between the two groups. Savers need a safe place for their money. Borrowers need **credit**, which is the ability to borrow now, based on the promise of repayment in the future.

## Serving Savers and Borrowers

Savers are looking for a safe place for their money. Banks try to inspire confidence among savers. Banks usually present an image of trust and assurance. For example, banks are more likely to be called First Trust or Security National than Benny's Bank or Easy Money Bank and Trust.

Banks gather various amounts from savers and repackage these funds into the amounts demanded by borrowers. Some savers need their money back next week, some next year, and others, only after retirement. Likewise, different borrowers need credit for different lengths of time. Some need credit only for a short time, such as the farmer who borrows until the crop comes in. Homebuyers need credit for up to 30 years. Banks, as intermediaries, offer desirable durations to both savers and borrowers.

## Banks Specialize in Loans

As lenders, banks try to identify borrowers who are willing to pay interest and are able to repay the loans. Because of their experience and expertise, banks can judge the creditworthiness of loan applicants better than an individual saver could. Because banks have experience in drawing up and enforcing contracts with borrowers, they can do so more efficiently than an individual saver lending money directly to a borrower.

Thus, savers are better off dealing with banks than making loans directly to borrowers. The economy is more efficient because banks develop expertise in evaluating borrowers, structuring loans, and enforcing loan contracts. In short, *banks reduce the transaction costs of channeling savings to creditworthy borrowers.*

## Reducing Risk Through Diversification

By lending funds to many borrowers rather than lending just to a single borrower, banks reduce the risk to each individual saver. A bank, in effect, lends a tiny fraction of each saver's deposit to each of the many borrowers. If one borrower fails to repay a loan, this failure will hardly affect a large, diversified bank. However, if someone lends his or her life's savings directly to a borrower who defaults on the loan, that would be a financial disaster for the lender.

**financial intermediaries**

Banks and other institutions that serve as go-betweens, accepting funds from savers and lending them to borrowers

**credit**

The ability to borrow now, based on the promise of repayment in the future

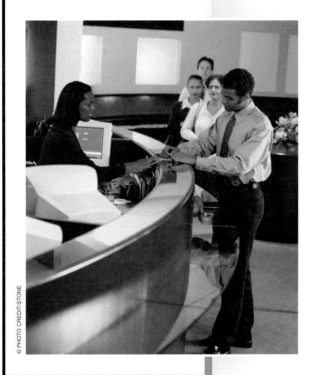

© PHOTO CREDIT/STONE

**What are the benefits of saving your money in a bank?**

TEACH

## Banks as Intermediaries

Use the following role-play activity to demonstrate how banks and other financial intermediaries help funds flow from savers to borrowers in the economy and therefore help the economy be more productive. Ask two students to sit on chairs at the front of the class. Give one a small piece of paper labeled $1,000. Tell the class this represents $1,000 that the student has saved over time. Tell the other student that he or she wants to borrow the $1,000 to help pay for a used car. This student should explain why the money is needed and why the first student should extend the loan. Ask the first student whether he or she would be willing to make the loan and under what conditions. Ask students to explain why this person would demand a higher interest rate to lend the money than a bank. (The student is not well qualified to judge the credit worthiness of the other student and so demands a high interest rate.) Why would the owner of the $1,000 be willing to accept a lower interest rate if the money were deposited in a bank? (The deposit in a bank is insured by the government, and there is very little risk involved.)

### *Think Critically Through Visuals*

Direct students to focus their attention on the photograph on this page. Ask for a volunteer to answer the question posed in the caption.

### Answer

Saving your money in a bank is beneficial because a bank offers a safeguard against loss or theft of your money and you earn money through interest rates.

## *Outside Resources*

**Federal Reserve Banks** Each of the 12 Federal Reserve District Banks has a variety of educational programs that concern banking in general and the Federal Reserve in particular. These banks can be accessed through the Fed's web site at www.federalreserve.gov. Ask students to find the home page of the district bank that is responsible for banking in their community. Ask them to review the site and evaluate the information it provides. Are there any programs in which they or their classmates could participate?

### Banks as Intermediaries

Explain that banks are only one, but the most important, financial intermediary in the U.S. economy. Millions of savers rely on banks to protect their savings and to help them earn a return from their savings when they deposit them. Banks in turn make loans to borrowers that fund spending for consumer goods and services and capital investment. This spending creates greater aggregate demand in the economy, stimulates production, and provides additional employment. Banks help the economy to be more productive.

## ➤ E-CONOMICS

Direct students to read the passage entitled "Identity Theft" on this page.

### Answers to Think Critically

Identity theft increases the interest rate on credit cards because it increases the cost associated with credit cards.

Direct students to **econxtra.swlearning.com**. Remind them to click on the link for Lesson 10.2 to find the appropriate link for the **NET Bookmark** on this page.

### Answer

Answers will vary. Answers should include the following points.

- Confirm that an online bank is legitimate and that your deposits are insured.
- Keep your personal information private and secure.
- Understand your rights as a consumer.
- Learn where to go for more assistance from banking regulators.

 **CHECKPOINT**

Invite a student to answer the checkpoint that appears on this page.

### Answer

Banks serve as financial intermediaries by accumulating funds from savers and lending these funds to borrowers.

## ➤ E-CONOMICS

### Identity Theft

The Federal Trade Commission (FTC) reports that more than 40 percent of all consumer complaints it receives involve identity theft. Identity theft basically is someone assuming your identity for the purpose of stealing your money or obtaining and using credit in your name. Many experts expect this problem to grow, due to easy access to personal information via the Internet and the minimal penalties given to identity thieves who are caught. One identity-theft ring stole the personal data and complete credit histories of more than 30,000 people, generating $2.7 million in fraud. The theft was traced to a credit bureau employee who used the Internet and stolen passwords in the scheme. To obtain a new credit card in your name, all an identity thief needs is your Social Security number and a birth date. With a few additional bits of your personal data, the thief is able to get loans, start up utility accounts—even wipe out your bank accounts.

Not only do you end up in debt with no money in the bank, but your credit is destroyed as well. Businesses are doing what they can to stop the thieves. Some banks now include photos and special holograms on credit cards. Many restaurants are installing a new wireless device that allows customers to swipe their own credit cards at the table. Individuals also must take personal responsibility to avoid becoming victims. The experts' best advice is to avoid revealing any part of your Social Security number to anyone. Shredding papers with personal information and destroying your credit card receipts also is strongly advised. Once targeted, experts estimate that the victim of identity theft can expect to spend more than 175 hours and more than $1,100 on setting things right.

#### Think Critically

How does identity theft affect interest rates on the credit cards you have?

### Line of Credit

**line of credit**
An arrangement with a bank through which a business can quickly borrow needed cash

Businesses often need to borrow during the year to fund those stretches when sales are low. For example, many retail businesses sell most of their output during the Christmas shopping season. These firms may need to borrow to get through those months when little is sold. Because of these fluctuations in cash needs, many businesses negotiate a **line of credit** with a bank. This allows the business to access cash as needed during the year. For example, the business applies for a line of credit of, say, $200,000. If the application is approved, the business can draw on that line of credit as needed without having to fill out a loan application each time. This line of credit is equivalent to a consumer's credit-card limit.

Access tips for safe Internet banking from the Federal Deposit Insurance Corporation (FDIC) web site through econxtra.swlearning.com. What can you do to protect your privacy if you choose to do your banking online? Write a paragraph explaining your answer.

*econxtra.swlearning.com*

✓ **CHECKPOINT**
How do banks serve as financial intermediaries between borrowers and savers?

**ENRICH**

In 2003, a bank offered mortgage loans at different rates, depending on the term of the loan. A 6.75% rate was offered for a 30-year mortgage, while people who agreed to a 15-year mortgage paid only 6.50 percent. Ask students to explain why the bank was willing to accept a lower interest rate for the shorter-term loan. What types of risks does a lender take besides the risk of nonpayment? (If there is unexpected inflation, the value of money that is repaid can be less than the value of the money loaned. The longer the term of the loan, the greater is this risk.)

# Why Interest Rates Differ

So far, the discussion has focused on the market rate of interest, as if there were only one interest rate in the economy. At any particular time, however, a range of interest rates coexists. For example, there are different interest rates applied to home mortgages, car loans, personal loans, business loans, and credit card balances. Figure 10.3 shows interest rates for loans in various markets. The lowest is the so-called **prime rate**, the interest rate lenders charge the most trustworthy business borrowers. The highest is the rate charged on credit card balances. Why do interest rates differ?

## Risk

Some borrowers are more likely than others to *default* on their loans—that is, to not pay them back. Before a bank lends money, it usually requires that a borrower put up **collateral**. This is an asset owned by the borrower that can be sold to repay the loan in the event of a default. With business loans, any valuable assets owned by the firm serve as collateral. With a home mortgage, the home itself becomes collateral. With car loans, the car becomes collateral.

Identify three banks in your area. Contact the banks or access their web sites to find the interest rates they currently apply to home mortgages, car loans, personal loans, business loans, and credit card balances. Compare the results in spreadsheet format. Share your results in class. Are the interest rates consistent among banks for each of the categories?

The more valuable the collateral backing up the loan, the lower the interest rate charged on that loan. The interest rate charged on car loans is higher than on home loans. A car loses its value more quickly than a home, and it can be driven away by a defaulting borrower. Thus, a car is not as good collateral as a home. Interest rates are

**prime rate**
The interest rate lenders charge for loans to their most trustworthy business borrowers

**collateral**
An asset owned by the borrower that can be sold to pay off the loan in the event the loan is not repaid

## Interest Rates Charged for Different Types of Loans

**Figure 10.3**

**Generally, the less collateral associated with a loan, the higher the interest rate will be.**

Source: Federal Reserve Board. Interest rates are annual averages during 2002, except for prime rate, which is for December 2002.

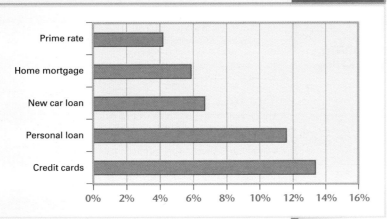

## Why Interest Rates Differ

Remind students that there is always some risk involved in making a loan. Those who have money to lend demand compensation for perceived greater risk in the form of higher interest rates. At some point, the risk becomes too great and no money will be loaned. To facilitate this process, banks and other financial intermediaries have developed credit scoring and other systems to evaluate the risk associated with loans they might make.

 Consider making a list of local banks and asking each student to choose a different bank.

### Think Critically Through Visuals

Direct students to focus their attention on **Figure 10.3—Interest Rates Charged for Different Types of Loans**. Point out that personal loans and credit card balances are unsecured loans.

## Economic Headlines

Instruct students to locate an article in a current magazine or newspaper that concerns an expansion worth millions of dollars being made by a large corporation. Ask students to identify and explain factors that determine the interest rate the firm will pay to borrow the needed funds. Would a smaller firm be able to borrow funds at a similar rate? What does the firm's size have to do with its ability to borrow money? Why is its risk perceived to be different from a smaller firm's risk? Is it good for the economy that larger firms are often able to borrow at relatively low interest rates?

## Why Interest Rates Differ

Tell students to imagine they are loan officers at a bank. The following people visit their bank and complete a loan application. Ask students to decide which applications would be approved and which would not. For those approved, what interest rate would be charged? When this is completed, call on students to state and explain their decisions.

- Mike and Sharon want to borrow $90,000 to purchase a house. They have a $20,000 down payment and a good credit history. They are both employed, and their combined gross income is $75,000 per year. Sharon tells you she is planning to quit her job next year to stay home and raise a family.

- Nadine is a single mother who wants to borrow $5,000 to buy a used car so she can drive to her new job, where she will earn $9.50 per hour. She has been unemployed for the past two years. In the past she missed a few loan payments but made them up later. She has no outstanding debt. She owns almost nothing of value.

### THE WALL STREET JOURNAL

**Reading It Right**

Invite a student to explain the relevance of the statement from *The Wall Street Journal* that appears on this page.

**Answer**

Answers will vary. Possible answer: The delinquency rates for FHA loans are much higher than those not insured by FHA.

 **CHECKPOINT**

Invite a student to answer the checkpoint that appears on this page.

**Answer**

Interest rates for loans differ, based upon the risk associated with the loan, the duration of the loan, the cost of administering the loan, and the tax treatment of the loan.

### THE WALL STREET JOURNAL

**Reading It Right** What's the relevance of the following statement from *The Wall Street Journal:* "The Mortgage Bankers Association of America said the percentage of borrowers who fell behind on their mortgage loans rose to a seasonally adjusted 4.62% in the second quarter, from 4.52% the previous quarter. The delinquency rate for loans insured by the Federal Housing Administration, a government program that helps first-time home buyers, rose more sharply to a record 12.59%, from 11.65% in the first quarter."

*The Graphing Workshop*

higher still for personal loans and credit cards, because there usually is no collateral at all with these loans.

### Duration of the Loan

The future is uncertain, and the further into the future a loan is to be repaid, the more uncertain that repayment becomes. Thus, under normal circumstances, as the duration of a loan increases, the interest rate charged increases to compensate for the greater risk. For example, the annual interest rate on a 10-year loan typically is higher than on a 1-year loan.

### Cost of Administration

The costs of executing the loan agreement, monitoring the loan, and collecting payments are called the *administration costs* of the loan. These costs, as a proportion of the loan, decrease as the size of the loan increases. For example, the cost of administering a $100,000 loan is not much greater than the cost of administering a $10,000 loan. The relative cost of administering the loan declines as the size of the loan increases. This reduces the interest rate for larger loans, other things constant.

### Tax Treatment

Differences in the tax treatment of different types of loans also will affect the interest rate. For example, the interest earned on loans to state and local governments is not subject to federal income taxes. Because people do not have to pay federal income taxes on this interest, they are more willing to lend money to state and local governments.

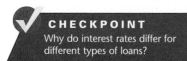 **CHECKPOINT**
Why do interest rates differ for different types of loans?

## Corporate Finance

During the Industrial Revolution, labor-saving machinery made large-scale production more profitable. However, building huge factories filled with heavy machinery required substantial sums—more money than any single bank would lend. The corporate structure became the easiest way to finance such investments, and by 1920, corporations accounted for most employment and output in the U.S. economy.

You know that a corporation is a legal entity, distinct from its shareholders. The corporation may own property, earn a profit, borrow, and sue or be sued. Stockholders, the owners of the corporation, are liable for company debts up to the amount of their investment in the firm.

### Corporate Stock

Suppose you have developed a recipe for a spicy chili that your friends have convinced you will be a best seller. You start a sole proprietorship called Six-Alarm Chili. As the founder, you are that firm's entrepreneur. Recall that entrepreneurs are profit-seeking decision makers. They begin with a good idea, organize a business to make that idea happen, and assume the risk of its operation.

Your chili company meets with early success. You believe, however, that you need to achieve economies of scale to remain competitive. To do that, you need to grow faster than your own savings or company profits would allow. To obtain the funds you need for expansion, you decide to incorporate the business. The newly incorporated company issues 1,000,000 shares of stock. You award yourself 100,000 shares. You, in effect, pay for your

### Group Activity

Organize students into groups of four or five. Each group represents a board of directors for a corporation that wants to make a $10 million investment in new equipment. The corporation can acquire the money in one of three ways. It can (1) borrow the money from a bank at a flexible interest rate that would be set at 6 percent in the first year; (2) sell 20-year bonds at a rate of 7.5 percent; or (3) sell 1 million shares of new stock at $10 per share. In recent years, the corporation has paid a $.40 dividend on its stock each year. Ask each group to identify the costs and benefits of each alternative. They are then to decide how they will raise the money and explain to the class why they made their choice.

shares with "sweat equity," or all the hard work you did to get the company rolling. The remaining shares are sold to the public for $10 per share. This raises $9 million for the company.

Corporations issue and sell stock to fund operations and to pay for new plants and equipment. The initial sale of stock to the public is called an **initial public offering (IPO)**. A share of corporate stock represents a claim on the net income and assets of a corporation. Each share gives the shareholder one vote on corporate issues.

Corporations must pay corporate income taxes on any profit. After-tax profit is either paid as **dividends** to shareholders or reinvested in the corporation. Reinvested profit, or **retained earnings**, allows the firm to grow more. The corporation is not required to pay dividends. Young firms usually pay no dividends. They prefer instead to put any profit back into the firm so it can grow faster. For example, Six-Alarm Chili might use its retained earnings to enter additional geographic markets.

Once shares of stock are issued, their price tends to fluctuate directly with the firm's potential for earning a profit. People buy stock because of the dividends they hope to receive. They also hope the value of the stock will increase over time.

### Corporate Borrowing

Your corporation can acquire financial capital by issuing stock, retaining earnings, or borrowing. To borrow money, the corporation can go to a bank for a loan. Such loans usually are for short durations—from a matter of months to two or three years. For longer-term borrowing, corporations will usually issue bonds. A **bond** is the corporation's promise to pay back the holder a fixed sum of money on the designated *maturity date* plus make annual interest payments until that date. For example, a corporation might sell bonds of $1,000 each, which promise the bond buyer annual interest of, say, $50 plus the $1,000 back at the end of 20 years. Corporate bonds have maturity dates as short as two years and as long as 30 years.

The payment stream to those who own bonds is more predictable than that for those who own stocks. Unless the corporation goes bankrupt, it must pay bondholders the promised amounts. On the other hand, stockholders are last in line when resource holders get paid. Because bondholders get paid before stockholders, bonds are considered less risky than stocks. Less risk means lower returns. Stocks have outperformed bonds in all decades.

### Securities Exchanges

Both stocks and bonds are called **securities**. Securities are represented on pieces of paper. In the case of a share of stock, the security shows how much of the corporation the stockholder owns. In the case of a bond, it shows how much the corporation owes the bondholder.

Once corporations have issued stocks and bonds, owners of these securities are usually free to resell them on *security exchanges*. In the United States, there are seven security exchanges registered with the Securities and Exchange

*initial public offering (IPO)*
The initial sale of corporate stock to the public

*dividend*
That portion of after-tax corporate profit paid out to shareholders

*retained earnings*
That portion of after-tax corporate profit reinvested in the firm

*bond*
A contract promising to repay borrowed money on a designated date and pay interest along the way

*securities*
Corporate stock and corporate bonds

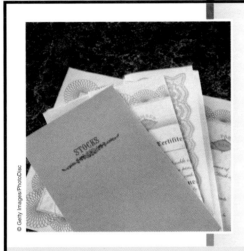
© Getty Images/PhotoDisc

**Stock certificates show how much of the corporation a shareholder owns. How does the information on a stock certificate differ from the information on a bond certificate?**

### Corporate Finance

Remind students that corporations are able to raise money in ways that are not available to other types of business, or to individuals. The best known of these is the sale of corporate stock. It might be difficult to find a bank or single investor who would be willing to risk $10,000,000 to implement a new type of production. But, it is possible that there could be 10,000 people who would each be willing to risk $1,000 to buy stock in a new corporation.

*Think Critically Through Visuals*

Direct students to focus their attention on the photograph on this page. Ask for a volunteer to answer the question.

**Answer**

A bond certificate shows how much money a corporation has borrowed from an individual, when the money will be repaid, and the associated interest. A bondholder does not own part of the company. A stockholder, on the other hand, does own part of the company. Stockholders are not lending the corporation money but, rather, are purchasing part of the corporation.

**The Graphing Workshop**  Try It • Apply It

Direct students to the Graphing Workshop for Chapter 10 at **econxtra.swlearning.com**. Instruct students to click on **Try It: The Effect of Changes in a Firm's Product Market on Its Stock Price**. As an enrichment exercise, students may complete **Apply It: The Impact of a Change in the Product Market on a Firm's Stock Price**. This exercise presents concepts more advanced than those discussed in the textbook.

*Think Critically Through Visuals*

Direct students to focus their attention on the photograph on page 300. Ask for a volunteer to answer the question.

**Answer**

Securities transactions take place in a secondary market because the corporation has already sold them. The money goes from a securities buyer to a securities seller.

### Curriculum Connection—Government

The Securities Exchange Commission (SEC) is charged with overseeing this nation's stock transactions from the issuance of new stock to the sale of "second-hand" stock on stock exchanges. In recent years, problems associated with stock trading have resulted in individuals and businesses being fined billions of dollars for inappropriate activities. Ask your students to identify and research one such event. For example, they might research market timing, insider trading, or money laundering. Do they feel the SEC has been successful in protecting the public's interests in stock trading? Ask them to explain their findings.

**CHECKPOINT**

Invite a student to answer the checkpoint that appears on this page.

**Answer**

The sources of financial capital for a corporation are stocks and bonds.

---

**APPLY**

Assign Lesson 10.2 from the Contemporary Economics Workbook.

*e*-con @pps

Encourage students to apply their knowledge of concepts presented in this lesson as they explore economic news stories, policy debates, and data available at **econxtra.swlearning.com**. A sampling of the titles for this lesson appears below.

**EconData**

- Interest Rate Spread
- Stock Prices; S&P 500

---

**ASSESS**

Assign all or part of Lesson 10.2 Assessment on page 301 as homework or an in-class activity.

Xtra! Study Tools

Direct students to the online study tools for Lesson 10.2 at **econxtra.swlearning.com**.

---

**CLOSE**

**Revisit** the In the News feature on the first page of the lesson. Ask students to review their preliminary answers and discuss the questions, now that they have completed this lesson.

**Review** the objectives for Lesson 10.2. Students should be able to:

- Explain the role of banks in bringing borrowers and savers together.
- Understand why interest rates differ among types of loans.
- Identify and discuss a corporation's sources of financial capital.

---

Commission (SEC), the federal body that regulates securities markets. The two largest are the New York Stock Exchange, which trades the stock of more than 3,300 major corporations, and the NASDAQ, which trades more than 4,000 corporate stocks, many of them technology companies.

Nearly all the securities traded each day are *secondhand securities* in the sense that they have already been sold by the corporation. Therefore, the bulk of daily transactions do not finance firms in need of investment funds. The money goes from a securities buyer to a securities seller. By providing a *secondary market* for securities, exchanges enhance the *liquidity* of these securities—that is, the exchanges make the securities more easily sold for cash. This ready conversion into cash makes securities more attractive.

More than half the trading volume on major exchanges is done by *institutional investors*, such as banks, insurance com-panies, and mutual funds. A *mutual fund* issues stock to individual investors and with the proceeds buys a portfolio of securities.

The secondary market for stocks also determines the current market value of a corporation. The market value of a firm at any given time can be found by multiplying the share price by the number of shares outstanding. The share price reflects the current value of the expected profit. For example, General Electric, one of the most valuable U.S. corporations, had a market value of $315.9 billion at the close of business on September 16, 2003. At that time, the market value of all publicly traded U.S corporations was more than $15 trillion.

**CHECKPOINT**

What are the sources of financial capital for a corporation?

**Buyers and sellers of securities come together through their representatives in the trading room of stock exchanges. Why are most securities transactions said to take place in the secondary market for securities?**

**300**   CHAPTER 10   Financial Markets and Business Growth

---

**RETEACH**

Large corporations often borrow funds by selling bonds to the public. Explain that bonds represent debt to the issuing firm. The firm must pay interest for a specific period of time, after which it must repay the original principal of the bond. Bonds are rated by several services according to their risk. Standard & Poor's, for example, rates bonds from *D* for those in default to *AAA* for those with maximum safety. Ask students to identify a local utility and investigate the firm's bond rating. They may do this online or by visiting their local library. Would they consider buying this firm's bonds if they had money to invest?

## Key Concepts

1. Why are banks often unwilling to provide mortgage loans to people who want to purchase homes in urban neighborhoods with high crime rates and decreasing home values?

2. Would you rather lend a friend $50 until she gets paid tomorrow or until the end of the school year when she hopes to find a summer job? What does this tell you about the interest rates that are charged for short- and long-term loans?

3. Why might a corporation prefer to raise funds by selling stock than by borrowing money from a bank?

4. Why are stock exchanges necessary for corporations to successfully market stocks to the public?

## Graphing Exercise

5. Corporations sell new issues of stock to the public to finance expansion and to obtain operating funds. The amount of new stock sold is one indicator of how much business activity is taking place in the economy. Construct a bar graph from the data in the table that shows the value of new stock sold by U.S. corporations between 1992 and 2000. What does your graph tell you about the U.S. economy during these years?

**New Public Stock Issues, 1992–2002 Values in Billions of Dollars**

| Year | New Stock Issues |
|------|------------------|
| 1992 | $ 88.3 |
| 1993 | 122.5 |
| 1994 | 84.6 |
| 1995 | 99.7 |
| 1996 | 149.6 |
| 1997 | 154.4 |
| 1998 | 176.6 |
| 1999 | 217.4 |
| 2000 | 291.2 |

## Think Critically

6. **History** Investigate the development of the NASDAQ market. Why have many high-tech corporations chosen to be listed on the NASDAQ rather than on a centralized exchange, such as the New York Stock Exchange?

7. **Communication** Identify a publicly traded corporation that does business in your community. Imagine that this firm wants to raise funds by issuing new stock. Write a letter that could be sent to potential investors that explains why they should consider buying shares of this firm's newly issued stock.

**Xtra!**
Study Tools
*econxtra.swlearning.com*

### Key Concepts

1. Answers will vary. Possible answer: Homes in deteriorating urban neighborhoods may lose value and be poor collateral for a loan. If the borrower fails to repay the loan, the bank may not be able to sell the home for enough to cover the amount that is owed.

2. Answers will vary. Possible answer: Waiting one day to have a loan repaid involves less risk than waiting until the end of the year. There is no way to know whether the friend will find a summer job so she can afford to repay the loan. Interest rates usually are higher for long-term loans.

3. Answers will vary. Possible answer: A corporation does not have to repay the amount it receives when it sells stock, and it will pay dividends only if it chooses to do so. Loans must be repaid with interest, regardless of whether the firm earns a profit.

4. Answers will vary. Without stock exchanges, corporations would not be able to have successful initial public offerings to raise money for the firm.

### Graphing Exercise

5. Answers will vary. Possible answer: During later years in the 1990s, there were increasing amounts of new stock being issued. This seems to indicate that U.S. corporations were expanding during these years.

   A sample of an acceptable graph appears at the bottom of this page.

### Think Critically

6. Answers will vary. Possible answer: It was easier for firms to be listed on the NASDAQ as it was growing during the 1990s than on the NYSE. It may have seemed more appropriate for high-tech firms to be listed there because the NASDAQ relied more on technology to carry out stock transactions than did other centralized exchanges.

7. Answers will vary. Possible answer: Students might suggest that the firm is well established and has a record of financial success. They may explain how the firm intends to use the money raised through the sale of new stock.

**New Public Stock Issues, 1992 to 2002**

*Visualizing the Answer—*
*Graphing Exercise*

5. The answer includes a graph. Students' graphs should look similar to the one shown here. An Excel spreadsheet containing this graph, along with supporting data, is available on the Instructor's Resource CD.

## Sharpen Your Life Skills

### Make Inferences

After studying Lesson 10.2, students should be able to answer the questions on this page.

### Answer

Answers will vary. Possible answer: The Fed increased interest rates in the mid- and late 1990s, when the economy was booming. It lowered interest rates when the economy slowed after 2000.

### Apply Your Skill

Consider allowing students to work in pairs for this assignment.

### Answers

1. Answers will vary. Possible answer: A stronger economy would cause people and businesses to demand more loans. At the same time, those who have saved funds will have more alternative uses for their money and may choose to lend fewer dollars. The increased demand for loans and decreased supply of money to lend will cause interest rates to increase. This is probably why the Fed would want to reduce inflationary pressure on the economy.

2. Answers will vary. Possible answer: More people will be willing to save and lend funds because they can keep all the interest income they receive. As a result, the supply of loans will increase and the prevailing interest rates will fall.

# Sharpen Your Life Skills

### Make Inferences

One of the most important factors businesses consider when they decide whether to make an investment is the interest rate they must pay to borrow funds. Large businesses pay the *prime rate*. Smaller firms usually pay prime plus one or two percent. The prime interest rate often is influenced by the Federal Reserve System (the Fed). If the Fed wants to encourage businesses to borrow and invest more money, it can push the prime interest rate down. If it wants businesses to invest fewer dollars, the Fed can pull the prime rate up. The table indicates the average prime interest rates charged by banks from 1993 through 2002. What do these data show about the Fed's interest-rate policies in these years?

### Apply Your Skill

1. Suppose that economic conditions improve by 2005 and the economy is booming. What would this do to the demand for loans, the supply of loans, and the level of interest rates that the Fed would like to have banks change? Considering all of these factors, what would you expect to happen to interest rates under these conditions? Explain your reasons.

2. Suppose Congress passes a law that eliminates the federal income tax on interest income. As a result, individuals and banks are able to keep all the interest income they receive. What would this do to the supply of loans available and the prevailing interest rates charged to those who borrow?

**Prime Interest Rates Charged by U.S. Banks, 1993–2002**

| Year | Prime Interest Rate | Year | Prime Interest Rate |
|------|--------------------|------|--------------------|
| 1993 | 6.00% | 1998 | 8.35 |
| 1994 | 7.15 | 1999 | 8.00 |
| 1995 | 8.83 | 2000 | 9.23 |
| 1996 | 8.27 | 2001 | 6.91 |
| 1997 | 8.44 | 2002 | 4.67 |

**302    CHAPTER 10**   Financial Markets and Business Growth

# 10.3 Business Growth

## Objectives

> Recognize the role of profit and franchising in business growth.

> Identify the types of corporate mergers and the four merger waves that occurred during the last century.

> Examine the multinational corporation as a source of corporate growth.

## Overview

Some owners of small businesses, such as grocers, plumbers, or pizza makers, are quite content running a small operation. They have no plans for expanding their businesses. However, many entrepreneurs who develop a profitable business want to see the business grow. Perhaps the business needs to grow to achieve economies of scale or to become more competitive in its market. Maybe the owner believes the product could be profitably sold across the country or around the world. Whatever the reason, owners often believe that growth is desirable to maximize profits. Several growth strategies are available for business owners. These include franchising the business, merging with other firms, and operating globally with a multinational corporation.

## Key Terms

vertical merger

conglomerate merger

multinational corporation (MNC)

## [ In the News ]

### ● Banks Are Changing the Combination

In the 1990s, banks began a merger spree, making new and bigger combinations to provide consumers with one-stop shopping for insurance, stocks, bonds, credit cards, checking accounts, and every other kind of financial service. Why the change? In the past, banks would lend you money, charge some interest, and wait for you to repay it. Today, that simple approach has changed. Banks continue to make loans and charge interest on car loans, mortgages, credit cards, and the like. However, instead of handling the loans themselves, they now package loans together and sell them to pension funds or insurance companies that have huge sums of money to invest. Banks no longer hold your mortgage for the money it would make on the interest charged. Rather, the bank now makes money from you by charging upfront fees for selling you the loan. It then charges the group that bought the loan package fees for collecting the payments from you. Banks are merging into bigger and more diverse institutions to maximize their assets and expand their fee-based services.

### Think About It

What do you think are the advantages and disadvantages to consumers of the growth of banks through mergers and acquisitions?

◀ | ▶

**303**

### National Content Standards in Economics

A complete list of the NCEE Standards appears on pages xxiv–xxv of this book. The following standards are addressed in Lesson 10.3.

Standard 5: Gain from Trade
Standard 10: Role of Economic Institutions
Standard 12: Role of Interest Rates
Standard 14: Profit and the Entrepreneur
Standard 15: Growth

---

## FOCUS

### 10.3 Business Growth

Point out that when a business is exceptionally successful, it is able to expand by reinvesting its own profits or by encouraging others to invest their money and resources in greater production.

### Objectives

Remind students to read the lesson objectives to help focus their attention before reading the lesson.

### Key Terms

Direct students to write each of the key terms on a separate index card. Instruct students to write the complete definition of each key term on the back of the appropriate card along with the page number where the definition is located. Encourage students to use the cards to study for quizzes and tests.

### [ In the News ]

Instruct students to read the passage and write down their answers. Point out that their answers might change after they finish studying Lesson 10.3.

### Answers to Think About It

Answers will vary. Possible answers: Consumers benefit from one-stop shopping for insurance, stock, bonds, credit cards, and many other financial services. A disadvantage is that large banks are more impersonal than small banks, and customer service may not be as good.

### Visual Presentation

Use the PowerPoint presentation on the Instructor's Resource CD as an adjunct to your lecture. The presentation also can be used for review.

## Profit and Growth

Remind students that three things can be said of any business that earns a profit: (1) it produces a product that customers are willing to purchase, (2) the product is priced at a level customers are willing to pay, and (3) the firm's total revenue exceeds its total costs. When a firm meets these three criteria, it is able to earn a profit that can be reinvested to expand its production. Few firms can earn enough profit to grow quickly. For this reason, most firms that grow quickly find ways to attract investments from alternative sources.

Direct students to **econxtra.swlearning.com**. Remind them to click on the link for Lesson 10.3 to find the appropriate link for the **NET Bookmark** on this page.

### Answer

A franchisee needs $100,000 to $175,000 in cash (liquid assets), depending on the type of purchase (conventional or Business Facilities Lease). Partners are not allowed. McDonald's selects the site and constructs the building.

### CHECKPOINT

Invite a student to answer the checkpoint that appears on page 305.

### Answer

More profitable firms grow faster because they find it easier to borrow from banks or to sell bonds. The more profitable the corporation, the lower the interest charged on bank loans and on corporate bonds.

# Profit and Growth

Profitability is the surest path to firm growth, regardless of the type of business. A profitable firm can reinvest earnings, and the more profit, the faster that firm can grow. This is true whether the firm is a sole proprietorship, partnership, or corporation. Firm owners are more willing to invest their own savings in a business if it is profitable. Profitable firms also find it easier to borrow the financial capital needed for expansion. Banks are more willing to lend to businesses that are profitable, because such firms are more able to pay back their loans.

To summarize, more profitable firms can grow faster because

1. more profits can be reinvested into the firm

2. owners are willing to invest more of their own money in such firms

3. banks are more willing to lend to such firms.

## Corporate Profits and Growth

Corporate profitability opens up paths of growth that are not available to sole proprietorships or partnerships. The greater a corporation's profit, other things constant, the higher the value of shares on the stock market. The higher the value of the shares, the more money a corporation can raise by issuing new shares. Unprofitable corporations cannot sell new shares easily. More profitable corporations also find it easier to borrow from banks or to sell bonds. The more profitable the corporation, the lower the interest charged on bank loans and on corporate bonds.

Thus, financial markets allocate funds more readily to profitable corporations than to corporations in financial difficulty. Some corporations may be in such poor shape that they cannot issue stocks or bonds. *Securities markets promote the survival of the fittest by lending financial capital to those firms that seem able to make the most profitable use of those funds.*

## Franchises

One way a business with a successful product can grow quickly is by franchising that product. A *franchise* is a contract between a parent company (franchiser) and another business or individual (franchisee). For a fee, the parent company grants the franchisee the exclusive right to sell a certain product in a given region.

The franchiser supplies the retailer with a brand name, production and marketing experience, and other expertise. The parent firm can achieve economies of scale in research and development, building design, business practices, and promoting the brand name.

Franchises allow people with limited experience to enter a business. They are guided by the franchise plan, which can reduce their risk of failure. Most important is the brand name and reputation that comes with a franchise. Popular franchise programs also increase customer awareness of the business because many businesses operate in different locations using the same franchise name and promotions.

The franchise has been common for decades with gas stations and auto dealers. Of growing importance are franchise structures for hotels, fast-food outlets, and restaurants. There are now more than 4,000 franchisers in the United States.

### NETBookmark

McDonald's maintains a web page devoted to information about obtaining a franchise. Access this web page through econxtra.swlearning.com. Look over the FAQ file. How much cash does a potential franchisee currently need to qualify? How many partners can be involved in a McDonald's franchise? Who selects the sites? Who constructs the building?

***econxtra.swlearning.com***

**304**  **CHAPTER 10**  Financial Markets and Business Growth

---

### Outside Resources

**Financial Publications** *Barron's, Money, Fortune,* and other magazines print advertisements for franchises that may be purchased for as little as several thousand dollars or as much as several million dollars. Ask students to find, copy, and bring to class such an advertisement. What does the ad indicate they should do to take advantage of the offer? What promises does it make? What other information would they need before they could make a rational decision about investing in the business? Why do many first-time entrepreneurs buy franchises?

# Corporate Mergers

One way a firm can double its size overnight is by merging with another firm of equal size. Mergers represent the quickest path to growth.

## Types of Mergers

Horizontal mergers occur when one firm combines with another firm making the same product, such as Exxon merging with Mobil. With a **vertical merger**, one firm combines with another from which it buys inputs or to which it sells output. An example of a vertical merger would be one between a steel producer and an automaker. Finally, a **conglomerate merger** is a combination of firms in different industries, such as a merger between a plastics maker and an electronics firm. There have been four merger waves in this country over the last century. They are summarized in Figure 10.4.

## First Merger Wave: 1887–1904

In the last half of the nineteenth century, two important developments caused firms to get big quickly. First, technological breakthroughs led to more extensive use of capital, increasing the minimum efficient size of manufacturing firms. Second, transportation costs declined as railroads increased from 9,000 miles of track in 1850 to 167,000 miles of track by 1890. *Economies of scale and cheaper transportation costs extended the geographical size of markets.* Firms grew larger to reach markets over a broader geographical area. Mergers offered an opportunity to get bigger quicker.

Mergers during this first wave tended to be horizontal. For example, the firm that is U.S. Steel today was created in 1901 through a billion-dollar merger that involved dozens of individual steel producers and two-thirds of the industry's production capacity. During this first wave, similar merger trends occurred in Canada, Great Britain, and elsewhere. This first merger wave created dominant firms, some of which still survive today, more than a century later.

**vertical merger**
One firm combines with another from which it buys inputs or to which it sells output, such as a merger between a steel producer and an automaker

**conglomerate merger**
One firm combines with another firm in a different industry, such as a merger between a plastics maker and an electronics firm

### Corporate Mergers

Remind students that many firms become more efficient as they move down their long-run average cost curves by taking advantage of economies of scale. This movement often can take place only with vast investments that require time and large amounts of financial capital. However, it may be possible to achieve growth and economies of scale through merger. When two or more related firms join to work as one, they may be able to cut costs by eliminating duplicated costs. A merged firm might require fewer managers or enjoy a more efficient marketing system than could the separate firms from which it was formed.

### *Think Critically Through Visuals*

Direct students to focus their attention on **Figure 10.4—Merger Waves in the Past Century**. Point out that this table provides a snapshot of the merger waves.

---

**Merger Waves in the Past Century**                          **Figure 10.4**

Four distinct merger waves took place in the United States between 1887 and 2000.

| Wave | Years | Dominant Type of Merger | Examples | Stimulus |
|------|-------|--------------------------|----------|----------|
| First | 1887–1904 | Horizontal | U.S. Steel, Standard Oil | Span national markets |
| Second | 1916–1929 | Vertical | Copper refiners with fabricators | Stock market boom |
| Third | 1948–1969 | Conglomerate | Litton Industries | Diversification |
| Fourth | 1982–2000 | Horizontal and vertical | Banking, tele-communications, health services, insurance | Span national and global markets, stock market boom |

Lesson 10.3 • *Business Growth*     **305**

---

Mergers are not always successful. One example of this was the 1991 merger of AT&T and NCR. Differences in these firms' managements, organizations, and corporate environments were never overcome. As a result, their merger was dissolved in 1997. Ask students to investigate how other mergers have worked out. Which ones appear to have worked and which have failed? Can they explain what makes the difference? How have consumers and the economy in general been affected by these mergers? The AOL-Time Warner merger might be a good place to begin.

## Corporate Mergers

Select five students to help you with a demonstration. Each student represents a firm that completes a separate step in the production and distribution of baseball bats.

- Student #1 owns many acres of mature ash trees.
- Student #2 pays student #1 for the right to cut down select ash trees and make them into lumber.
- Student #3 buys lumber from student #2 and makes it into baseball bats.
- Student #4 buys bats from student #3 and sells them to retail sporting goods stores.
- Student #5 buys bats from student #4 and sells them to consumers.

The owners of each of these firms are interested in making a profit. This suggests that each will charge as much as possible for the products they sell. What will this do to the final price charged to the consumer? (It will tend to make it high.) If these firms joined in a vertical merger, could the merged firms sell bats for a lower price to consumers? Ask students to explain their answers. Why have vertical mergers often been able to dominate their markets? (Because the firms were joined, they were better able to control costs and sell their product at a lower price. This enabled them to drive other firms in their industry out of business because the other firms were less able to control their costs.)

✔ **CHECKPOINT**

Invite a student to answer the checkpoint that appears on page 307.

### Answer

The break up of the Soviet Union in 1991 expanded market economies around the world and motivated the most recent wave of corporate mergers. Companies tried to achieve stronger, more competitive positions in global markets by merging. This wave of mergers ended with the stock market plunge that began in 2000.

### Second Merger Wave: 1916–1929

The first merger wave cooled with the introduction of antitrust laws. Because these laws restrained horizontal mergers, vertical mergers became more common during the second merger wave. This wave of mergers took place between 1916 and 1929. A vertical merger combines firms at different stages of the production process. For example, a copper refiner merges with a copper fabricator. The stock market boom of the 1920s fueled this second wave, but the stock market crash in 1929 stopped it cold.

### Third Merger Wave: 1948–1969

The Great Depression and World War II slowed merger activity for two decades. The third merger wave began after the war. More than 200 of the 1,000 largest firms in 1950 had disappeared by the early 1960s as a result of this merger wave. Between 1948 and 1969, many large firms were absorbed by other, usually larger, firms. The third merger wave peaked in a frenzy of activity between 1964 and 1969. During this time, conglomerate mergers accounted for four-fifths of all mergers.

Merging firms were looking to diversify their product mix and perhaps reduce costs by producing a variety of goods. For example, Litton Industries combined firms that made calculators, appliances, electrical equipment, and machine tools. As it turned out, this strategy didn't seem to work very well. Conglomerate mergers stretched management expertise and lost the efficiency gains that spring from specialization and comparative advantage. The firm resulting from a conglomerate merger no longer focused on producing a particular product efficiently. It tried to produce all kinds of different products efficiently, which proved too challenging for some corporate executives.

### Fourth Merger Wave: 1982–2000

The fourth merger wave began in 1982 and involved both horizontal and vertical mergers. Some large conglomerate mergers of the 1960s were undone during this latest wave as firms tried to focus on what they did best and sell off unrelated operations. About one-third of mergers during the 1980s resulted from *hostile takeovers,* where one firm would buy control of another against the wishes of the target firm's management. Hostile takeovers dwindled to less than one-tenth of mergers during the 1990s.

The break up of the Soviet Union in 1991 expanded market economies around the world. Companies tried to achieve a stronger competitive position in global markets by merging with other firms here and abroad. Merger activity gained momentum during the latter half of the 1990s, with the dollar value of each new merger topping the previous record. Most mergers during this period were financed by the exchange of corporate stock and were fueled by a booming stock market.

The largest mergers in history occurred during the late 1990s and in 2000. During this time, the most merger activity took place in banking, radio and television, telecommunications, health services, and insurance. The latest merger wave ended with the stock market plunge that began in 2000.

Not all the mergers during this latest wave turned out well. Corporate scandals engulfed some companies that had used mergers aggressively to grow, such as Enron and WorldCom. A recent deal that experienced difficulties was the $103 billion merger of AOL and Time Warner. In 2002, the merged company lost $99 billion, a world record.

With a fading stock market and slumping economy, merger activity fell sharply after 2000, thus ending the fourth wave. For example, among Internet and software companies, the value of merger deals in 2002 was less than one-tenth their value in 2000.

## *Economic Headlines*

Instruct students to locate an article in a current magazine or newspaper that discusses a proposed corporate merger. Ask them to identify costs and benefits stakeholders in the merger—including employees, customers, and owners—are likely to encounter. Ask students whether they believe the merger will be a good thing for the economy in general. Should the government allow or oppose the merger? What reasons can they give for their points of view?

## CHECKPOINT
What motivated the most recent wave of corporate mergers and what ended it?

# Multinational Corporations

The developer of a successful product has a profit incentive to sell the product around the world. Because of high shipping costs and differences in labor costs, a firm often finds it more profitable to make products around the world as well. Many large corporations operate factories overseas and sell their products globally.

A corporation that operates globally is called a **multinational corporation (MNC)**. These companies also may be called transnational corporations, international corporations, or global corporations.

### Running Multinationals

An MNC is usually headquartered in its native country and has affiliates in other countries. Most of the world's largest multinationals are headquartered in the United States, such as General Electric, General Motors, and Coca-Cola. Some are headquartered in Japan, such as Toyota, Honda, and Sony. Others are in Western Europe, such as Shell, BP, and Nestlé.

An MNC usually develops new products in its native country. It manufactures some or all of the goods abroad, where production costs are usually lower. For example, Whirlpool, the world's leading manufacturer of major home appliances, is headquartered in the United States but operates in more than 170 countries. The company motto is "Every home...Everywhere."

The multinational can take advantage of a successful brand by selling it around the world. Multinationals benefit consumers and workers worldwide by supplying products and creating jobs. Multinationals also spread the latest technology and the best production techniques around the globe. This allows the firms located in less-developed countries to adopt cutting-edge technologies.

### Problems of Multinationals

Running a multinational is more complicated than running a domestic firm. It requires coordinating far-flung operations, adapting operations and products to suit local cultures, and coping with different business regulations, different tax laws, and different currencies.

> **multinational corporation (MNC)**
> A large corporation that makes and sells its products around the world

# SPAN THE GLOBE

## Betting Dollars to Doughnuts

Dick Clark, TV personality and producer, is betting dollars to doughnuts on a new venture in England. In the 1960s, Clark helped introduce several hot British rock bands to the United States through his *American Bandstand* program. With his new venture, he'll help introduce a hot American product to the United Kingdom—the Krispy Kreme doughnut. Mr. Clark's partnership wants to open as many as 25 Krispy Kreme stores throughout the United Kingdom. Clark and his franchise partners are betting that Krispy Kreme's assortment of sugar-powdered, glazed, and custard- or berry-filled delicacies will become a number-one hit with the British people. Their bet is a pretty good one. Each year about 25 percent of all Europe's sugar products and nearly 34 percent of its chocolate are consumed in the United Kingdom. Krispy Kreme's future franchise plans include a major international expansion. After the U.K. openings, more stores are scheduled to open in Australia, New Zealand, Japan, South Korea, Spain, and Mexico.

### Think Critically

Krispy Kreme thinks its franchise stores will be a big hit in Britain. What, if any, holes do you see in that thinking?

Lesson 10.3 • *Business Growth* **307**

## TEACH

### Multinational Corporations
Remind students that most large corporations are multinationals because they produce their products in many countries. This allows them to produce their products in the place where they are best able to control their costs. Or, they may complete part of a production process in one nation and finish it in another. Ask students whether they have ever seen a garment label that says, "Assembled in Malaysia from fabric produced in the USA"?

### SPAN THE GLOBE
Direct students to read the short passage "Betting Dollars to Doughnuts." Use Think Critically as a starting point for class discussion or have students write a short essay to answer the questions.

**Answers to Think Critically**
Answers will vary. Possible answer: Krispy Kreme cannot assume people in the United Kingdom will like Krispy Kreme doughnuts just because, as a country, they consume large amounts of sugar.

### TEAM WORK
Organize students into groups of four or five. Instruct teams to select a recorder and a spokesperson. Instruct students to complete the **Team Work** activity shown on page 308. Set a timer for 10 minutes. When the timer goes off, invite the spokesperson from each group to take a turn providing the group's findings.

### Think Critically Through Visuals
Direct students to focus their attention on the photograph on page 308. Ask for a volunteer to answer the question posed in the caption.

**Answer**
Answers will vary. Possible answer: The advantage to these advanced economies would be that U.S. multinationals supply many job opportunities and increase the earning potential of the citizens of that country.

## Group Activity
Organize students into small groups. Tell each group that they are the managers of a large multinational corporation that manufactures auto parts. They have factories in the United States, Canada, Greece, India, and Mexico. They have just received an order for 5 million fuel injection systems from an American car producer. The fuel injection units could be produced in any of the five countries where they own factories. Ask each group to list factors they would consider in making the most profitable choice. Would they consider the political consequences of where they chose to produce the products? Why or why not?

**CHECKPOINT**
Invite a student to answer the checkpoint that appears on page 308.

**Answer**
The developer of a successful product has a profit incentive to sell the product around the world. Because of high shipping costs and differences in labor costs, a firm often finds it more profitable to make products around the world as well.

**APPLY**

Assign Lesson 10.3 from the Contemporary Economics Workbook.

**e-con @pps**

Encourage students to apply their knowledge of concepts presented in this lesson as they explore economic news stories, policy debates, and data available at **econxtra.swlearning.com**.

**ASSESS**

Assign all or part of Lesson 10.3 Assessment on page 309 as homework or an in-class activity.

Direct students to the online study tools for Lesson 10.3 at **econxtra.swlearning.com**.

**CLOSE**

**Revisit** the In the News feature on the first page of the lesson. Ask students to review their preliminary answers and discuss the questions, now that they have completed this lesson.

**Review** the objectives for Lesson 10.3. Students should be able to:

• Recognize the role of profit and franchising in business growth.

• Identify the types of corporate mergers and the four merger waves that occurred during the last century.

• Examine the multinational corporation as a source of corporate growth.

**TEAM WORK**

In small groups, identify and debate the controversies involving multinational corporations. Do the benefits of multinationals to consumers and workers worldwide outweigh the problems associated with their operation?

Union leaders in the United States have claimed that multinationals are hiring workers overseas because wages there are lower. It's true that wages are lower in poorer countries. However, the wages paid there by multinationals are usually higher than wages offered by local employers for the jobs otherwise available. Some experts say workers in those poorer countries are better off because multinationals provide jobs that offer relatively good wages. U.S. multinationals export more to their foreign affiliates than they import from their foreign affiliates. As a result, foreign operations may tend to *create* U.S. jobs on balance.

Some critics also charge that multinationals have too much influence on the culture and the politics in the countries where they operate. However, foreign production by U.S. multinationals account on average for less than 4 percent of the value of all production in the countries in which they operate. Of the countries where U.S. multinationals account for the largest share of output, most are not poor countries but advanced economies such as Canada, the United Kingdom, and the Netherlands. Advanced economies would seem to be less affected by cultural or political influences by U.S. multinationals.

**CHECKPOINT**
Why do firms become multinational corporations?

© Getty Images/PhotoDisc

Of the countries where U.S. multinationals account for the largest share of output, most are advanced economies such as the Netherlands. What do you think would be the benefits to advanced economies of the presence of U.S. multinationals?

308    **CHAPTER 10**   Financial Markets and Business Growth

**RETEACH**

Some experts believe the growth of electronic communications and the Internet have made it easier for mergers and multinational corporations to be successful. Ask students to evaluate this perspective. What are large businesses and multinationals able to do today because of new communications technology that they could not have done 20 years ago? How have U.S. consumers benefited from the growth of these firms? Does the value of these benefits exceed their costs? Ask students to explain their points of view.

## Key Concepts

1. Why are some people willing to invest in new firms that have not yet made any profit and do not expect to earn a profit for several years?

2. Suppose you have inherited $50,000 and want to use the money to start a business. Would you rather organize the business by yourself or purchase a franchise? Explain your reasons.

3. Do you think mergers are more often helpful or harmful for consumers? Explain your reasons.

4. When firms merge, they often lay off some workers to reduce their costs. Is it possible that this could be good for the economy?

5. Why have multinationals tended to "level the playing field" among workers and businesses in different nations?

## Graphing Exercise

6. Mergers have an important impact on the U.S. economy, and they can be a sign of economic activity as well. More mergers tend to take place when the economy is booming and stock prices are high. They are less likely to occur when businesses are not earning good profits or when it is difficult to obtain funding to finance mergers. Use the data in the table to construct two bar graphs of merger activity in the U.S. economy from 1985 through 1999. One graph should show the number of mergers that took place. The other should show their value. What do your graphs show about economic conditions in the United States during these years?

**Mergers With a Value in Excess of $5 Million, 1985–1999**

| Year | Number of Mergers | Value of Mergers in Billions of Dollars |
|------|-------------------|------------------------------------------|
| 1985 | 1,719 | $ 149.6 |
| 1990 | 4,239 | 205.6 |
| 1995 | 4,981 | 895.8 |
| 1999 | 9,599 | 3,401.6 |

## Think Critically

7. **Business Management** Many firms that offer franchise opportunities promote their organizations on the Internet. Identify a particular franchise business that exists in your community. Search the Internet for information about this franchise. What does the organization offer its members? What is the cost of becoming a franchisee? Would you consider ever starting this type of business yourself?

8. **History** In the years surrounding the turn of the nineteenth to the twentieth century, John D. Rockefeller created the Standard Oil Company primarily by merging many smaller firms. Investigate how he accomplished this and what the impact was for the owners and customers of the merged firms. What costs and benefits may have resulted from these mergers for the economy as a whole?

Xtra!
Study Tools
econxtra.swlearning.com

Lesson 10.3 • *Business Growth*    **309**

**10.3** *Assessment*

*Key Concepts*

1. Answers will vary. Possible answer: People invest in a corporation's stock in anticipation of future performance. While developing a new product, a firm may not earn any profit, but future success could result in large profits.

2. Answers will vary. Possible answer: With limited experience, it is unlikely that a person will be able to start a successful business. A franchise provides the franchisee training and an established business plan that can help be successful.

3. Answers will vary. Possible answer: Larger merged firms may be more efficient and provide consumers with better quality products and services than smaller firms. However, they also may obtain monopoly power that could result in higher prices and a reduced selection of products.

4. Answers will vary. Possible answer: Employing fewer workers will lower the merged firm's costs of production, which may allow it to lower the price it charges consumers. This could make the firm more competitive in the global marketplace. If the firm is more profitable, it may reinvest in new technologies to increase efficiency, develop new products, or hire additional workers in the long run.

5. Answers will vary. Possible answer: Multinationals quickly transfer new ideas and technologies among nations, and they often move production to those nations that have the lowest costs. This tends to make the competitive position of different nations more equal in international trade.

*Graphing Exercise*

6. Answers will vary. Possible answer: The value of mergers grew much more rapidly than the number of mergers. This indicates that larger firms were merging, possibly creating businesses with some monopoly power in our economy. The rapid growth in mergers probably indicates a booming economy.

A sample of an acceptable graph appears at the bottom of this page.

*The Answer Key is continued on page 313.*

**Number of Mergers With a Value in Excess of $5 Million from 1985 through 1999**

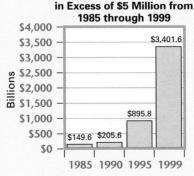

**Value of Mergers With a Value in Excess of $5 Million from 1985 through 1999**

*Visualizing the Answer— Graphing Exercise*

6. The answer includes a graph. Students' graphs should look similar to the one shown here. An Excel spreadsheet containing these graphs, along with supporting data, is available on the Instructor's Resource CD.

Point out that by choosing to purchase a franchise, people gain access to a proven business plan and often are provided extensive training that can help them create a successful business. Ask students whether they believe they possess the skills, experience, and knowledge necessary to be a successful entrepreneur. Would they ever consider purchasing a franchise such as the one purchased by Paul Gbodi?

### TEACH

Instruct students to read the **Movers & Shakers** feature about Paul Gbodi. Point out that some students may find it helpful to read the article, read the questions at the bottom of the page, and then reread the article.

### ASSESS

Use the questions in Source Reading and Entrepreneurs in Action at the bottom of the profile to assess the students' understanding of this **Movers & Shakers** feature.

### Answers to Source Reading

Answers will vary. Possible answer: Paul's college education, research capabilities, and perseverance make him a successful entrepreneur.

### Answers to Entrepreneurs in Action

Answers will vary. Possible answer: *Pros*—The franchise provides ongoing marketing support and invoicing of clients. You are buying into an already established business. *Cons*—You pay the franchise a percentage of your gross revenues. The start-up fees of buying into the franchise can be costly.

# movers & shakers

## Paul Gbodi *Jani-King Franchise Owner*

Paul Gbodi was 24 years old when he came to the United States from Nigeria. Although he had attended a junior college in Nigeria, he said, "I wanted to come to the United States because of the educational opportunities it provides." After earning his bachelor's degree from Langston University in Langston, Oklahoma, Paul went on to earn his master's degree from the University of Central Oklahoma in Edmond, Oklahoma.

Paul originally intended to return to Nigeria after earning his college degrees. "But after spending some time in the United States, I realized the tremendous opportunities in business that it held for me," he said. So he, his wife, and daughter decided to remain in Oklahoma. After finishing college, Paul began working in the restaurant and food service industries. In 1990, he decided his best career option was to start his own business.

After months of research, Paul and a friend selected the $17.8 billion commercial cleaning market. They decided to purchase a franchise cleaning business instead of starting a company on their own. "Because we were foreigners, we knew it would be difficult to convince the owner of a company to give us the keys to their building so that we could clean it in the evening while they were away," Paul said. In 1990, they purchased a Jani-King commercial cleaning franchise. Within months of starting the business, Paul was making more money than he did in his previous full-time job.

Jani-King is the world's largest commercial cleaning franchiser with more than 9,500 franchise owners in 15 countries. Jani-King franchises typically cost between $8,000 and $50,000 in start-up fees. The fees depend on the number of established customers the purchaser receives and the services the purchaser wishes to provide. Like Paul, each franchise owner operates independently and has a full stake in the success of his or her company.

Today, Paul is the sole owner of the Jani-King franchise in Oklahoma City. His company has more than 200 clients. Paul's staff provides daily, weekly, monthly, or semi-annual cleaning, trash removal, window washing, floor care, and other specialty cleaning services. His office staff includes an accountant, a payroll clerk, and an office manager. The Jani-King regional office provides franchisers with ongoing marketing support and invoicing of clients. Paul pays Jani-King 10 percent of gross revenues each month for these services. He spends most of his time training his employees and doing paperwork at home.

Paul doesn't find much time for vacations, but he is thrilled with his work. "I love what I'm doing," he says enthusiastically. In 2003, selected from among all the Jani-King franchisees, Paul was named Jani-King Franchisee of the Year by the International Franchise Association. He credits his success to a positive attitude and the support and training provided to him by Jani-King. "The people at Jani-King really believed in me from the start. The support they provide me has definitely helped me live a better life, own a home, and make my family proud," he said. He is quick to point out that anyone can be successful "if you put your mind to it, stay positive, and work hard."

---

**SOURCE READING**
Re-read the quotations from Paul Gbodi. What characteristics does he possess that make him a successful entrepreneur?

**ENTREPRENEURS IN ACTION**
Divide into pairs. You and your partner are considering starting a residential maid service. Decide whether to start your business from scratch or purchase a franchise from a franchiser. List the pros and cons of both starting from scratch and purchasing a franchise.

**310**   CHAPTER 10   Financial Markets and Business Growth

# CONNECT to History

## United States Steel

On December 12, 1900, Charles M. Schwab, president of the Carnegie Steel Company, spoke before a group of 80 industrial executives at the University Club of New York. He discussed the advantages of consolidation in such industries as steel. Whether Carnegie Steel owner Andrew Carnegie encouraged Schwab to make the speech—or if Carnegie even was in attendance—is not known. Within five months, however, the largest corporation in the world, United States Steel, was created.

The U.S. steel industry was growing quickly during the last two decades of the nineteenth century. In 1880, the United States produced only half the amount of crude pig iron as Britain. By 1900, it was making 50 percent more than Britain, as production rose from 4 to 14 million metric tons. Up to 1880, the steel industry was driven by the railroad industry, and 85 percent of production went to making rails. By 1900, rail production had increased almost 300 percent, but rails represented only 31 percent of the rolled steel output.

As demand grew, advantages in economies of scale became apparent. However, integrating the various stages of production and modernizing plants to achieve the economies were costly. Some in the industry viewed acquisition as a safer method of growth. Still, as long as prices remained high, success was insured for most steel producers. When competition turned more predatory, however, prices dropped, causing the smaller, weaker companies to struggle.

Consolidation of the industry already had begun by the late 1900s. Many of the companies that specialized in finished steel were combining horizontally as the market diversified. Sheet making, wire making, and tube making were just a few of the activities that were subject to mergers. For these companies, most of the semi-finished steel was supplied along regional lines by one of two steel-producing giants—Federal or Carnegie Steel.

Two developments threatened to upset this arrangement. First, some of the companies that made finished steel began trying to reduce costs by producing their own steel. Some new companies were formed just to supply steel to these finishing companies. The reaction of Federal Steel and Carnegie Steel was to go into the finished steel business as well. At the threat of cutthroat competition, smaller companies feared that lower profits would destroy them.

J.P. Morgan was in attendance during Schwab's University Club speech. Morgan had been involved in the formation of both Federal Steel and National Steel, and railroads were an important part of his business empire. Morgan recognized that he could secure the financial success of his companies by following Schwab's proposal. After the speech, Morgan pulled Schwab aside and spoke with him for half an hour. He followed up the conversation with a meeting a few weeks later. Morgan secured a list of the companies Schwab had proposed for consolidation in his speech. The list also included values for what each company was worth. Morgan then asked Schwab to find out the amount for which Carnegie would sell his steel company. Carnegie came up with a figure of $480 million. Morgan accepted Carnegie's price, and U.S. Steel was created on April 1, 1901.

### THINK CRITICALLY

Economies of scale were critical to the success of U.S. Steel. Still, some believe that the firm eventually became too large and difficult to manage. Its plants were spread over a large area. Also, because it was profitable, it was hard to justify modernizing old plants. What kind of diagram would you use to illustrate economies of scale? Draw a suitable diagram and show the effect of economies of scale in the long run.

---

# CONNECT to History

### FOCUS

Point out that in the late 1800s, acquisition and merger created ever-larger companies. Many companies such as Standard Oil used destructive business practices to acquire other companies.

### TEACH

After introducing the selection, have the students read it and answer the questions. Discuss with them the reasons for corporate acquisition. Explore with them why a company like U.S. Steel may want to own not only raw steel production facilities but also mines and finished steel production facilities.

### ASSESS

Use the questions at the bottom of the page to assess the students' understanding of this feature.

**Answers to Think Critically**

Students' diagrams will vary. An example of an acceptable diagram appears below.

---

## Bibliography

Engerman, Stanley L., and Robert E. Gallman, eds. *The Cambridge Economic History of the United States: The Long Nineteenth Century.* Vol. II. Cambridge, England: Cambridge University Press, 2000.

Foner, Eric, and John A. Garraty, eds. *The Reader's Companion to American History.* New York: Houghton Mifflin, 1991.

Heilbroner, Robert L. "Carnegie and Rockefeller." *A Sense of History: The Best Writing from the Pages of American Heritage.* New York: American Heritage, 1985.

Puth, Robert C. *American Economic History.* Ft. Worth: Dryden Press, 1988.

Wall, J.F. *Andrew Carnegie.* New York: Oxford University Press, 1970.

Warren, Kenneth. *Big Steel: The First Century of the United States Steel Corporation, 1901–2001.* Pittsburgh: University of Pittsburgh Press, 2001.

## Summary

## Summary

### Consider

Ask students to revisit the questions they were asked to consider at the beginning of the chapter. Remind students that they should be able to answer all of the questions after studying Chapter 10.

- What's seed money, and why can't Farmer Jones grow anything without it? See page 288—Production Takes Time.

- Why are you willing to pay more at a first-run movie theater than at other theaters? See page 290—Paying More to Consume Now.

- Why do you repeatedly burn your mouth eating pizza, despite knowing the risk? See page 290—Paying More to Consume Now.

- Why is a bank more likely to be called Security Trust than Benny's Bank? See page 295—Banks as Intermediaries.

- Why do banks charge more interest on car loans than on home loans? See page 297—Why Interest Rates Differ.

### Exam*View*

Use **Exam***View* to assess student learning.

- Create a chapter test using questions from the existing test bank.

- Add your own questions to the existing test bank.

- Generate multiple forms of a chapter test.

### Study Skills

Offer the following study skills suggestions for students as they review this chapter.

- Outline the chapter.
- Review Key Terms.
- Review Checkpoints.
- Work in pairs to quiz each other.
- Use the Xtra! Study Tools for each lesson.

Direct students to the online quiz preparation for Chapter 12 at **econxtra.swlearning.com**.

 **Production, Consumption, and Time**

Xtra! Quiz Prep
econxtra.swlearning.com

a It takes time to produce goods and services. Investments in capital can increase labor productivity but also require time and an accumulation of savings to use while investments are being made. Financial intermediaries help financial capital flow from savers to borrowers.

b Consumers generally value current consumption more than future consumption. This can be seen in their willingness to pay interest to borrow funds that allow them to consume now. A *demand for loans curve* slopes down. As interest rates decline, the amount of loans demanded increases.

c Loans are supplied by people willing to give up current consumption to consume more later. Interest is their reward for giving up current consumption. The higher the interest rate, the more money will be made available for loans. This is why the *supply of loans curve* slopes up. As interest rates increase, the amount of loans supplied also increases.

 **Banks, Interest, and Corporate Finance**

a Banks act as *financial intermediaries* when they accumulate funds from savers and lend these funds to borrowers. By depositing funds in banks, savers earn interest. The banks then lend these funds at higher interest rates to borrowers that have been evaluated for their creditworthiness. If one borrower defaults, other borrowers are still likely to keep up their repayments.

b Interest rates differ for many reasons. The most important reason is the risk associated with a loan. Higher risks require borrowers to pay higher rates of interest. Other factors that influence interest rates include the duration of the loan, its cost of administration, and the way in which interest is taxed.

c Corporations raise money in a variety of ways. They may sell stock to the public or corporate bonds. Funds received from the sale of stock do not have to be repaid. *Dividends* will be paid on stock only when the corporation's board of directors chooses to do so. *Bonds* are debts of the business that must be repaid with interest, regardless of whether the firm earns a profit. Transactions of corporate stocks and bonds are carried out on stock exchanges.

**10.3** **Business Growth**

a Businesses that are profitable are better able to grow than those that are not profitable. Profits may be reinvested in a firm. Banks are more likely to make loans to firms that are profitable. Individual investors are more likely to purchase stocks or bonds issued by profitable firms.

b Many entrepreneurs go into business by purchasing a franchise. These businesses benefit from having an established and successful business plan. The franchisees typically receive training from the franchiser. Although franchises have a better chance of being successful, there are significant fees that must be paid to the franchiser.

c There have been four waves of mergers in U.S. history. Although most mergers have created stronger, more successful businesses, some have not. A number of giant mergers in the 1990s lost billions of dollars, and some of these mergers were dissolved.

d In recent years many corporations have expanded beyond the borders of any individual nation. These *multinationals* often are better able to control their costs and market their products in many countries. It has been suggested that multinationals may exploit workers by producing goods and services in nations that have the lowest wage rates. But the wages offered by multinationals are typically higher than prevailing wages in those low-wage countries. Critics also claim that multinationals also may inappropriately influence governments because of their great economic power.

**312** **CHAPTER 10** Financial Markets and Business Growth

---

**10.1** **Assessment**

### Think Critically

Continued from page 293.

7. Answers will vary. Possible answer: With such high interest rates, businesses would avoid borrowing if they could. This would reduce business investment in new capital and decrease the number of jobs available to U.S. workers. High interest rates were a contributing cause for the recession of 1980 through 1982.

8. Answers will vary. Possible answer: Manufacturers know that many consumers cannot afford their products unless they borrow funds, so they try to encourage borrowing. If many consumers choose to borrow, the demand for loans will grow and interest rates will increase.

# Review Economic Terms

Choose the term that best fits the definition. On a separate sheet of paper, write the letter of the answer. Some terms may not be used.

1. An asset owned by the borrower that can be sold to pay a loan in the event the loan is not repaid

2. The interest rate banks charge their most trustworthy business borrowers

3. Banks and other institutions that serve as go-betweens, accepting funds from savers and lending them to borrowers

____ 4. A large corporation that makes and sells products in many different nations

____ 5. An arrangement with a bank through which a business can quickly borrow needed cash

____ 6. Corporate stock and corporate bonds

____ 7. The portion of after-tax corporate profit that is reinvested in the firm

____ 8. The initial sale of corporate stock to the public

____ 9. The ability to borrow now, based on a promise of repayment in the future

10. Annual interest as a percentage of the amount borrowed or saved

a.  bond
b.  collateral
c.  conglomerate merger
d.  credit
e.  demand for loans curve
f.  dividend
g.  equilibrium interest rate
h.  financial intermediaries
i.  initial public offering (IPO)
j.  interest rate
k.  line of credit
l.  market for loans
m.  multinational corporation (MNC)
n.  prime rate
o.  retained earnings
p.  securities
q.  supply of loans curve
r.  vertical merger

# Review Economic Concepts

11. **True or False** Production depends on savings because it requires time during which consumer goods cannot be produced.

12. The fact that people generally prefer to consume now rather than in the future is shown by their willingness to

    a.  pay tuition to attend college.

    b.  pay interest for an automobile loan.

    c.  pay for life insurance.

    d.  deposit their savings in a bank account.

13. The __?__ brings together borrowers and savers to determine the market rate of interest.

14. **True or False** The more valuable the collateral backing a loan, the higher the interest rate charged on the loan.

15. When the quantity supply of money supplied for loans exceeds the quantity of money for loans, there will be a

    a.  shortage of loans, and interest rates will soon fall.

    b.  surplus of loans, and interest rates will soon grow.

    c.  shortage of loans, and interest rates will soon grow.

    d.  surplus of loans, and interest rates will soon fall.

16. A(n) __?__ is extended to businesses by banks to provide them with funds when their sales are low.

17. __?__ are profits that a corporation earns but does not pay to its stockholders in dividends.

## Review Economic Terms

1. b. collateral
2. n. prime rate
3. h. financial intermediaries
4. m. multinational corporation (MNC)
5. k. line of credit
6. p. securities
7. o. retained earnings
8. i. initial public offering (IPO)
9. d. credit
10. j. interest rate

## Review Economic Concepts

11. True
12. b. pay interest for an automobile loan
13. market for loans
14. False. The more valuable the collateral, the lower the interest rate.
15. d. surplus of loans, and interest rates will soon fall
16. line of credit
17. Retained earnings

 **Assessment**

Continued from page 309.

## Think Critically

7. Franchise opportunities offer potential entrepreneurs a proven business plan and training. However, franchisees must generally make a large initial investment, pay a significant annual franchise fee, and share a portion of the sales.

8. Many of the former owners of the merged firms lost control of their businesses and often were not fairly compensated for their property. Customers often benefited, at least at first, from lower prices. These prices, however, did tend to increase over time. The growth of Standard Oil made the United States one of the foremost producers of oil products in the world but also gave Rockefeller a great deal of economic and political power.

## Review Economic Concepts

18. a. A loan is to be paid off in 60 days instead of 3 years.

19. d. diagonal mergers

20. False. The more profitable a firm is, the more it is able to grow through issuing new stock shares and borrowing from banks.

21. multinational corporation

22. b. MNCs usually manufacture products in their native countries because costs usually are lower there.

## Apply Economic Concepts

23. Answers will vary. Possible answer: A horizontal merger would be formed by joining XYZ Soap, Mom's Detergent, and the Clean Soap companies. A vertical merger would be formed by joining XYZ Soap, Ajax Trucking, Joe's Wholesale, and Apex Super Markets. A conglomerate merger would be formed by joining Dad's Ice Cream, Mom's Detergent, Sue's Sandwich Co., and Harold's Fruit companies.

24. Answers will vary. Possible answer: Although Justin and Carla's firm earned almost $112,000 in profit, there were many months when they needed borrowed funds to pay their bills. This situation is true for most businesses that have seasonal sales.

25. Students may say they expect the Fed to decrease the amount of money entering into the economy. A decrease in the supply of money entering the economy would stave off inflation and would increase the interest rates in the near future, because there would be a decreased supply of money for consumers to borrow.

---

18. Which of the following situations will cause a bank to charge a lower *interest rate*?

   a. A loan is to be paid off in 60 days instead of 3 years.

   b. A loan is used to purchase an automobile instead of a house.

   c. A loan is made to a person who just changed jobs rather than a person who has been employed at the same job for 10 years.

   d. A loan is made to a small business instead of one that is very large.

19. Which is not a form of merger used by U.S. firms in the past?

   a. vertical mergers

   b. conglomerate mergers

   c. horizontal mergers

   d. diagonal mergers

20. **True or False** A firm's profits have little to do with that firm's ability to grow.

21. A corporation that operates globally is called a(n) __?__.

22. Which of the following statements about *multinational corporations* is not true?

   a. MNCs usually develop new products in their native countries.

   b. MNCs usually manufacture products in their native countries because costs usually are lower there.

   c. MNCs introduce less-developed countries to new technologies.

   d. MNCs benefit consumers and workers around the world by supplying products and creating jobs.

# Apply Economic Concepts

23. **Different Types of Mergers** Organize these businesses into three groups as they would form horizontal, vertical, and conglomerate mergers. You may not need to use all of the firms to complete this activity.

   Ajax Trucking Co.

   Apex Super Markets

   Clean Soap Co.

   Dad's Ice Cream Co.

   Harold's Fruit Co

   Joe's Wholesale Co.

   Mom's Detergent Co.

   Sue's Sandwich Co.

   XYZ Soap Co.

24. **Lines of Credit** Justin and Carla own a ski resort. All of their income is earned in the months between November and April, but they have expenses throughout the year. During the summer, they must repair their equipment and clear their ski trails. The table to the right shows their income and expenses from the end of last year's ski season through April of this year. Explain why Justin and Carla need a line of credit from their bank.

**Justin and Carla's Income and Expenses**

| Month | Income | Expenses |
|-------|--------|----------|
| May | $0 | $ 42,810 |
| June | $0 | $ 38,291 |
| July | $0 | $ 36,743 |
| Aug. | $0 | $ 34,805 |
| Sept. | $0 | $ 40,283 |
| Oct. | $0 | $ 52,939 |
| Nov. | $ 10,832 | $ 66,380 |
| Dec. | $134,640 | $103,592 |
| Jan. | $288,902 | $154,021 |
| Feb. | $275,010 | $152,831 |
| March | $152,345 | $100,438 |
| April | $ 56,832 | $ 83,921 |
| Total | $918,561 | $806,576 |

**25. Sharpen Your Life Skills: Make Inferences** Imagine that in the past few months, interest rates have been growing steadily. They now stand about two percentage points higher for most types of loans than they did just one year ago. However, the demand for loans seems to be strong. Leaders of the Fed have announced that they are worried about increasing rates of inflation. Given this situation, what is the Fed likely to do, and what do you expect will happen to interest rates in the near future? Explain your answers.

**26. Demand and Supply for Loans** On a separate sheet of paper complete the table, indicating what would happen in each situation by placing a (+) for increase, (−) for decrease, or (0) for stay the same, in each box to the right of the event. Also, explain the reasons for each of the signs you place in the table.

| Event | Demand for Loans | Supply of Loans | Interest Rates |
|---|---|---|---|
| A new electric motor is invented that is expensive but uses only half as much electricity as older motors. | | | |
| There is a new baby boom, and millions of children are born. | | | |
| There is a downturn in the economy and many workers are laid off. | | | |
| Many foreigners decide they want to buy more U.S.-made products. | | | |

 econxtra.swlearning.com

**27.** Access **EconData Online** through econxtra.swlearning.com. Read the article entitled "Stock Prices: S&P 500." Write a paragraph that describes the S&P 500, and why this index is useful to investors.

## Apply Economic Concepts

**26.** Answers and explanations for each event appear below.

Event: Invention of a new electric motor

Demand for loans: (+) Many businesses want to borrow to be able to buy the new motors.

Supply of loans: (0) There is no reason for this invention to change the supply of loans.

Interest rates: (+) The increased demand for loans will cause the interest rates to increase.

Event: Baby boom

Demand for loans: (+) Many families want to borrow to buy baby furniture and add new rooms to their homes.

Supply of loans: (−) Many families cut back on their saving so they can buy things for their babies.

Interest rates: (+) The increased demand for loans and decreased supply causes interest rates to grow.

Event: Downturn in the economy and layoffs.

Demand for loans: (−) Fewer people and businesses want to borrow because they are worried about repaying loans.

Supply of loans: (−) The people who are laid off are not able to save and must draw on funds they have saved in the past.

Interest rates: (−) Interest rates will probably fall, but it is not certain. The Fed will probably encourage lower rates.

Event: Foreigners want to buy more U.S.–made products.

Demand for loans: (+) Businesses will want to borrow more to expand their factories.

Supply of loans: (0) There is no reason that the greater foreign demand for U.S. products should change the supply of loans.

Interest rates: (+) The increased demand for loans will cause the interest rates to increase.

**27.** Students' paragraphs should demonstrate that they have read the two paragraphs about the S&P 500 in EconData Online at **econxtra.swlearning.com**.

# Investing In Your Future

### The Situation

The major emphasis here should be on the idea of the student investing in her or himself. The loss of personal relationships, the postponement of immediate gratification possibilities, and similar benefits of settling for more comfortable and easier choices should be contrasted with the likelihood of future well-being and enjoyment of life brought about through advanced education. Have students identify people they know who have had to make similar choices and evaluate the observed results in terms of opportunity "payoffs." This should be rewarding to students in terms of clarity and motivation for their personal choices.

### The Decision

This problem has been constructed to present several real-life themes. The first is the idea of assessment and planning to gain proximity—the advantage of being close to and familiar with the area of one's career choice. Such commitment of time and focus allows both knowledge and opportunity to flow to the person so placed. The second of these is the idea of cross-fertilization of ideas from general study (such as the Egyptian level's application to animal management). The third theme, from Chapter 8 especially, is the agony and the ecstasy of being an innovator and potential entrepreneur. Chances like the one afforded Aleesha never occur when someone has plenty of resources, time, and money to devote to the project at hand. The opportunity costs and the risks of seizing this chance are huge. The question really is—does Aleesha, who has excelled to this point at assessing life and planning her progress, have the capability to RISK the failure of all those plans and go for it? That risk-taking ability marks the entrepreneur. Others stay on the safe road. Class discussion on this issue should be very revealing as to each student's predisposition.

| Project 3 | INVESTING IN YOURSELF |

## The Situation

Aleesha sat quietly in her room at home, lost in thought about her junior year at college. Since moving away to go to school, a great deal had changed in Aleesha's life, yet some things had remained constant. She broke up with her boyfriend—their relationship a victim of the priority Aleesha placed on her studies. She still felt the passion for animals and their care that had carried her to this point. This had been reinforced by working at the zoo during the summers.

She declared a major in zoology, one of the educational cornerstones for a career in zoo keeping. This year, she would begin to take the courses specific to her career plan, including animal management and animal behavior. Her first two years at school had been pretty rough. She forced herself to concentrate, but some of the required courses seemed to have little to do with her area of interest. Even so, she maintained an A- average and easily retained her scholarship. Now, just before the beginning of junior year, she faced another major choice.

## The Decision

The decision facing Aleesha at the moment came out of her sophomore history class. Aleesha had written a research report on the tools used by ancient engineers, such as those used to build the pyramids. One of these tools, an Egyptian level, had sparked in her an idea for a new type of animal-restraint muzzle. During the summer, Aleesha had created a prototype of the device and had adjusted it for various species. The result was an innovative product that was far more animal friendly and cost-effective than current alternatives on the market. The head zookeeper allowed her to test the device throughout the zoo. Several of the animal keepers suggested that she patent the product, and then make and sell it commercially.

Unfortunately, patenting the idea would take money—at least half her budget for the upcoming school year. She then would have

Encourage students to use Internet and library resources to obtain information to research the issues in this project. Students can access the U.S. Patent Office for information on the patent process via www.uspto.gov/. For information regarding college business curricula, students may refer to college catalogs, either online or in the school's guidance office. To learn about forms of business organization, they may consult the chapters in this unit or refer to pertinent information in business textbooks.

to make and sell the devices to earn money in order to stay in school spring semester. She knew little about business. However, that could be remedied by switching her minor to business and changing some fall-semester courses. Aleesha knew that if she did not act soon, someone else would claim the idea for the device.

## Activities

**Divide into teams or work individually, as directed by your teacher, to perform the following tasks.**

Apply the steps in the following decision-making process to Aleesha's situation:

1. *Define the problem.* Define Aleesha's problem in a way that will allow a clear solution. Should Aleesha become an entrepreneur?

2. *Identify the choices.* List the various alternatives among which she must choose.

a. Research the patent-application process. Also research firms that offer help in securing patents.

b. Which business courses would be most advantageous for Aleesha to take to enhance her chances in marketing her idea?

c. What form of business organization would be best for Aleesha?

3. *Evaluate the pluses and minuses of each choice.* Carefully weigh the value Aleesha puts on each alternative and the opportunity cost(s) for each.

4. *Make a choice.* Which course of action should she choose? Be prepared to present and defend your choice in class.

5. *Provide "action" steps that are appropriate to the decision.* Make sure these are realistic and timely to ensure the necessary action(s) are taken to resolve the problem.

6. *Critique the decision.* The class will assist in the review and evaluation of your plan of action. In real life, you should review not only the decision and its result, but also the process by which you make it.

## Research

Research for the information you need to effectively make the decision, such as the patent-application process, business courses Aleesha might take, and the forms of business organization she might choose.

## Present

Arrive at a decision. Then prepare a presentation for the class on the six steps you took to achieve this decision.

*Project 3*          **317**

### APPLY

**Activities**

**Step 1:** In defining the problem, students should focus on the decision of whether Aleesha should pursue the opportunity to become an entrepreneur before graduating from college.

**Step 2 (a):** Several firms offering to help people patent their ideas are shams, and students should distinguish these from legitimate programs. Often patent lawyers unaffiliated with these programs can offer help to the inventors with whom they work. Aside from the idea itself, a patent application requires properly drafted plans and appropriate claims (how the current invention is significantly different from any previous patented idea) to be successful. The date of application is crucial, and time is generally of the essence—in this case especially, because Aleesha has used her device throughout the zoo. Once the patent is acquired, Aleesha could consider licensing the product to current producers of like products instead of producing and selling it herself. **(b)** Many collegiate business schools offer courses in entrepreneurship as a starting point. If such a course is not available, an introduction to business course along with basic accounting and law, would be advisable at this initial stage of Aleesha's business. **(c)** Given the burden of finding time and money to develop this product, Aleesha might consider taking on a limited or full partner in the enterprise. The corporate form ultimately would be ideal for the venture (especially given the potential liability should a muzzle fail). But, due to the expense of incorporating relative to Aleesha's resources, assuming such a form may have to be postponed for a time.

**Step 4:** The recommended course of action and its justification for Aleesha will reveal a lot about the students' aspirations, personal confidence, and risk-taking ability. It should be very interesting to the teacher to observe the students in these regards, not only currently but in the future.

### ASSESS

**Presentation** Consider using a rubric or evaluation form for student presentations. Make sure you share the rubric or form with students before they start working on the project. A sample evaluation form appears on the Instructor's Resource CD. The categories to be evaluated include: **Content** (organization, specific content, and accurate information); **Presentation Skills** (eye contact, grammar and pronunciation, volume, and pitch); **Audiovisual Aids** (appropriate content, style, and spelling); and **Handouts** (appropriate content; grammar, punctuation, and spelling).

## *National Content Standards in Economics*

The following NCEE Standards are addressed in Unit 4:

| | |
|---|---|
| **Standard 1** | Scarcity |
| **Standard 2** | Marginal Cost/Benefit |
| **Standard 4** | Role of Incentives |
| **Standard 5** | Gain from Trade |
| **Standard 7** | Markets—Price and Quantity Determination |
| **Standard 9** | Role of Competition |
| **Standard 10** | Role of Economic Institutions |
| **Standard 12** | Role of Interest Rates |
| **Standard 13** | Role of Resources in Determining Income |
| **Standard 14** | Profit and the Entrepreneur |
| **Standard 15** | Growth |
| **Standard 16** | Role of Government |
| **Standard 17** | Using Cost/Benefit Analysis to Evaluate Government Programs |
| **Standard 18** | Macroeconomy—Income, Employment, Prices |

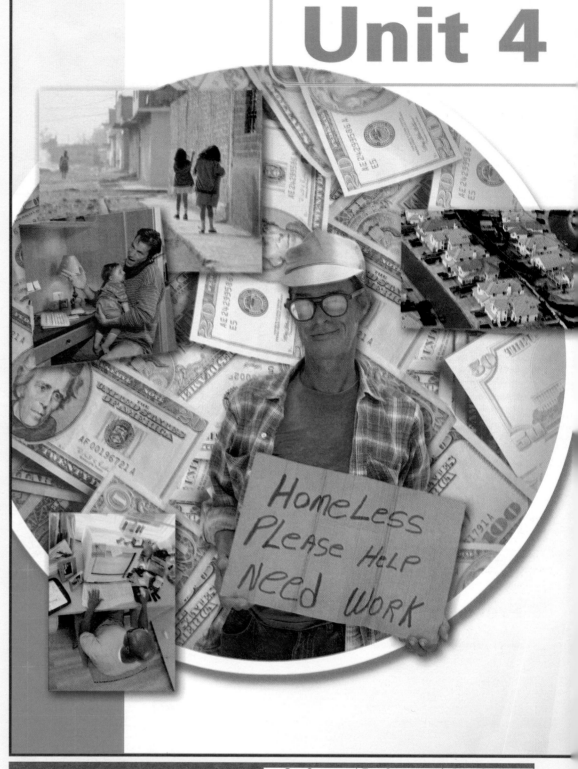

# Unit 4

| Pacing Guide | One-Semester Days of Study | Two-Semesters Days of Study | Block Schedule 90-Minute Blocks |
|---|:---:|:---:|:---:|
| **UNIT 4: THE NATIONAL ECONOMY** | | | |
| Chapter 11: Economic Performance | | | |
| **11.1** Gross Domestic Product | 1 | 2 | 1 |
| **11.2** Limitations of GDP Estimation | 1 | 2 | 1 |
| **11.3** Business Cycles | 1 | 3 | 1 |
| **11.4** Aggregate Demand and Aggregate Supply | 2 | 3 | 2 |
| Chapter 12: Economic Growth | | | |
| **12.1** The PPF, Economic Growth, and Productivity | 2 | 3 | 2 |
| **12.2** Living Standards and Labor Productivity Growth | 1 | 3 | 1 |
| **12.3** Issues of Technological Change | 2 | 4 | 2 |
| Chapter 13: Economic Challenges | | | |
| **13.1** Unemployment | 1 | 2 | 1 |
| **13.2** Inflation | 1 | 2 | 1 |
| **13.3** Economic Instability | 1 | 3 | 1 |
| **13.4** Poverty | 2 | 3 | 2 |

# The National Economy

 **Economic Performance**

 **Economic Growth**

 **Economic Challenges**

Since 1776, when Adam Smith inquired into the *Wealth of Nations,* economists have been trying to figure out why some economies prosper while others don't. Because a market economy is not the product of conscious design, it does not reveal its secrets readily. There is no clear blueprint of the economy, so policy makers can't simply push here and pull there to create prosperity for everyone. Still, economists are learning more every day about how the U.S. economy works. You, too, can discover the challenges and opportunities facing the largest and most complex economy in world history.

**319**

## Unit 4 Overview

The focus of Unit 4 shifts to the macro-economic topics of the national economy. Students explore how the performance of the economy is measured, how the economy grows, and economic challenges such as unemployment, inflation, economic instability, and poverty.

## Group Activity

Organize students into small groups and ask them to discuss the passage that appears on this page. Instruct students to discuss current challenges and opportunities facing the U.S. economy. Allow about 10 minutes for discussion. Ask a representative of each group to briefly summarize the discussion for the class.

## Think Critically Through Visuals

Direct students study the images on the opposite page and think about how each image relates to the national economy. Ask them to work with a partner to create their own collage to illustrate the national economy. Display the finished collages in the classroom while studying Unit 4.

## Look Beyond the Classroom

A good way to move beyond the classroom is to ask students to identify and investigate situations in their community that give them an idea of how the local economy is doing. These may include things as simple as seeing many people shopping during the holiday season, the number of new buildings being constructed, or the ease or difficulty students have in finding after-school jobs. Help students make a comprehensive list of these situations on the board.

Instruct students to describe in writing what the list tells them about the state of their local economy. Do they expect that production in their local economy will grow, remain unchanged, or decline in the next year? What reasons can they give for their points of view?

An alternative would be to ask students to review recent newspapers to find articles about the state of the national economy. Ask them to use the information they find to write an essay that evaluates likely changes in production in the national economy over the next year.

## Chapter Overview

**LESSON 11.1** *Gross Domestic Product:* This lesson describes what the gross domestic product measures and explains how to calculate the GDP.

**LESSON 11.2** *Limitations of GDP Estimation:* This lesson identifies the types of production neglected by the GDP. It also addresses why and how to adjust the GDP for changes over time in the general price level.

**LESSON 11.3** *Business Cycles:* This lesson distinguishes between the two phases of the business cycle and compares the average length of each. It also differentiates among leading, coincident, and lagging economic indicators.

**LESSON 11.4** *Aggregate Demand and Aggregate Supply:* This lesson explains the aggregate output and the economy's price level. Aggregate demand curve and aggregate supply curve are addressed.

### Consider

Ask students to consider the questions posed on this page as they study Chapter 11. After studying all four lessons, students should be able to answer the questions. The content related to each question can be found on the pages indicated below.

- How is the economy's performance measured? See page 322—Gross Domestic Product.
- What's gross about the gross domestic product? See page 322—Gross Domestic Product.
- What's the impact on gross domestic product if you make yourself a sandwich for lunch? See page 323—Calculating GDP.
- How can you compare the value of production in one year with that in other years if prices change over time? See page 344—Real Gross Domestic Product.
- What's the business cycle? See page 336—Recessions and Expansions.
- What's the big idea with the national economy? See page 339—Economic Indicators.

▶ **POINT YOUR BROWSER**

Remind students that they can find additional resources for this chapter at **econxtra.swlearning.com**.

# Economic Performance

### Consider

How is the economy's performance measured?

What's gross about the gross domestic product?

What's the impact on gross domestic product if you make yourself a sandwich for lunch?

How can you compare the value of production in one year with that in other years if prices change over time?

What's the business cycle?

What's the big idea with the national economy?

© Getty Images/PhotoDisc

**POINT YOUR BROWSER**

*econxtra.swlearning.com*

---

### Teaching Resources for Chapter 11

- Activities and Projects Masters
- Spanish Resources
- Econ Connection Interactive Tutorial CD
- **Exam***View*® CD
- Workbook Teacher's Edition
- Chapter Test Teacher's Edition
- NCEE Standards and Correlation
- Personal Finance Guide

- Social Studies Skills Review
- Instructor's Resource CD
  – PowerPoint Presentation
  – Lesson Plans
  – Video Discussion Guide
  – Answers to Graphing Exercises
- **econxtra.swlearning.com**

# Gross Domestic Product

## Objectives

> Describe what the gross domestic product measures.

> Learn two ways to calculate the gross domestic product, and explain why they are equivalent.

## Overview

The Great Depression of the 1930s convinced economists and the government to get a better handle on what was happening with the economy. Economists began assembling huge quantities of data collected from a variety of sources across America. These data were organized and reported periodically by the federal government. The resulting system for measuring the nation's economy has been hailed as one of the great achievements of the twentieth century. Its primary developers won a Nobel Prize for their work.

## Key Terms

economy

gross domestic product (GDP)

consumption

investment

aggregate expenditure

aggregate income

Ask a student what chores he or she is expected to do at home. Then ask how the student's work is evaluated in terms of quality, timeliness, or amount of resources used to complete the task. How would a parent react to a room being "cleaned" but still having dirt and dust everywhere, or if it were cleaned late at night, or if an entire bottle of furniture polish were spilled on a upholstered chair? Is there a relationship between the quality and quantity of work that is accomplished and what students receive from their parents or guardians? If a student wanted an extra $10, what work (production) could he or she do to justify this extra payment?

### Objectives

Remind students to read the lesson objectives to help focus their attention before reading the lesson.

### Key Terms

Direct students to look up key terms in a business or economics dictionary. Some students will find it helpful to read another definition. In addition to a definition, many entries will include a brief explanation and an example.

### [ In the News ]

Instruct students to read the passage and write down their answers. Point out that their answers might change after they finish studying Lesson 11.1.

### Answers to Think About It

Answers will vary. Possible answers: The United States government keeps track of the size of the economy in order to ensure the welfare of citizens and businesses.

### *Visual Presentation*

Use the PowerPoint presentation on the Instructor's Resource CD as an adjunct to your lecture. The presentation also can be used for review.

## [ In the News ]

### ● Tracking a $12 Trillion Economy

How does the government keep track of the most complex economy in history? Ever since Article I of the U.S. Constitution required that a census be taken every 10 years, the federal government has been gathering data. The three main data-gathering agencies are the Census Bureau, the Bureau of Economic Analysis, and the Bureau of Labor Statistics. Since 1980, the market value of all final goods and services produced in the United States has doubled. Employment has increased by nearly 40 million workers. Foreign trade has tripled. Yet the federal budget for these agencies has declined. Only 0.2 percent of the federal budget goes toward keeping track of the economy. Federal budget cuts have eliminated some data-collection efforts and have slowed down others. For example, the monthly household sample that tracks unemployment was cut from 60,000 to 50,000. Some agencies must do more with the same staff. In 1980, the Bureau of Labor Statistics had 18 analysts to keep track of productivity in 95 different industries. The number of industries they now track has increased four times. However, the number of analysts has changed little.

### Think About It

Why do you think it is important for the U.S. government to keep track of the size of the economy?

◄ ❘ ►

**321**

### *National Content Standards in Economics*

**NCEE**

A complete list of the NCEE Standards appears on pages xxiv–xxv of this book. The following standards are addressed in Lesson 11.1.

Standard 5: Gain from Trade

Standard 10: Role of Economic Institutions

Standard 12: Role of Interest Rates

Standard 15: Growth

Standard 18: Macroeconomy—Income/ Employment, Prices

## The National Economy

Point out that measuring the value of production for the national economy is a challenge. Tens of millions of products are produced in the United States by millions of producers. The values of these products are determined by the prices at which they are sold. But, the same product often sells at different prices in different locations. Sometimes the price charged at a single location varies when the product is put on sale. How can the government keep track of all this production and all of these prices? In this lesson, students will learn about the two primary methods used to measure GDP: the income and expenditures approaches.

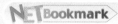

Direct students to **econxtra.swlearning.com.** Remind them to click on the link for Lesson 11.1 to find the appropriate link for the **NET Bookmark** on this page.

### CHECKPOINT
Invite a student to answer the checkpoint that appears on page 323.

### Answers

The gross domestic product (GDP) measures the market value of all final goods and services produced in the United States during a given period, usually a year.

---

# The National Economy

*economy*
The structure of economic activity in a locality, a region, a country, a group of countries, or the world

National economics, or macroeconomics, focuses on the overall performance of the *economy*. The term **economy** describes the structure of economic activity in a locality, a region, a country, a group of countries, or the world. You could talk about the Chicago economy, the Illinois economy, the Midwest economy, the U.S. economy, the North American economy, or the world economy.

### Gross Domestic Product

An economy's size can be measured in different ways. The value of production, the number of people employed, or their total income can be measured. The most commonly used measure is the *gross product*. This is the market value of production in a geographical region during a given period, usually one year.

*gross domestic product (GDP)*
The market value of all final goods and services produced in the United States during a given period, usually a year

The **gross domestic product**, or **GDP**, measures the market value of all final goods and services produced in the United States during a given period, usually a year. GDP measures production during the year by individuals and businesses located in the United States. GDP includes production in the United States by foreign firms, such as a Japanese auto plant in Kentucky. It excludes foreign production by U.S.

firms, such as a General Motors plant in Mexico.

GDP measures the economy's total production of goods and services, from trail bikes to pedicures. GDP can be used to track the same economy over time. It also may be used to compare different economies at the same time.

### National Income Accounts

*National income accounts* organize huge quantities of data collected from a variety of sources across the United States. These data are summarized and reported periodically by the federal government. National income accounts keep track of the value of *final goods and services*. These are goods and services sold to the final, or end, users. A toothbrush, a pair of contact lenses, and a bus ride are examples of final goods and services.

Gross domestic product includes the value of only final goods and services. Your purchase of chicken from a grocer is reflected in GDP. When KFC purchases chicken, however, this transaction is not recorded in GDP because KFC is not the final consumer. Only after KFC deep fries that chicken and sells it to customers is the sale recorded as part of GDP.

### No Double Counting

*Intermediate goods and services* are those purchased for additional processing and resale, such as the chicken purchased by KFC. This additional processing may be minor, as when a grocer buys canned goods to stock the shelves. The intermediate goods may be altered dramatically. For instance, oil paint costing $20 and a canvas costing $25 may be transformed into a work of fine art that sells for $5,000.

Sales of intermediate goods and services are excluded from GDP to avoid the problem of *double counting*. This is counting an item's value more than once. For example, suppose the grocer buys a can of tuna for $0.60 and sells it for $1.00. If GDP counted both the intermediate transaction of $0.60 and the final transaction of $1.00, that can of

---

**NET**Bookmark

The Bureau of Economic Analysis is charged with estimating GDP and its components. You can access selected National Income and Product Account tables through econxtra.swlearning.com. Summary Table S1 tells you by how much each component has grown. Summary Table S2 shows the contribution of each component to GDP growth. Can you explain the difference between these two types of statistics?

*econxtra.swlearning.com*

---

---

### *Outside Resources*

**Council of Economic Advisers** *Economic Indicators* is one of the best sources of current data concerning national income accounting. This monthly publication can be found online at www.access.gpo.gov/congress. Nominal and real values for GDP are provided for the preceding 10 years, as well as the composition of GDP.

tuna would be counted twice in GDP. Its recorded value of $1.60 would exceed its final value of $1.00 by $0.60. Therefore, GDP counts only the final value of the product.

GDP also ignores most of the secondhand value of used goods, such as existing homes and used cars. These goods were counted in GDP when they were produced. However, the value of services provided by realtors and used-car dealers is counted in GDP. For example, suppose a new-car dealer gives you a $1,500 trade-in allowance for your used car. The dealer cleans and repairs the car, and then resells it for $2,500. The $1,000 increase in the car's value is included in GDP.

### CHECKPOINT
What does the gross domestic product measure?

# Calculating GDP

The national income accounts are based on the idea that *one person's spending is another person's income.* This is expressed in a double-entry bookkeeping system of accounting. Spending on final goods and services is recorded on one side of the ledger and income created by that spending is recorded on the other side. GDP can be measured either by total spending on U.S. production or by total income earned from that production.

## GDP Based on the Expenditure Approach

The *expenditure approach to GDP* adds up the spending on all final goods and services produced in the economy during the year. The easiest way to understand the spending approach is to divide spending into its four components: consumption, investment, government purchases, and net exports.

**Consumption** consists of purchases of final goods and services by households during the year. Examples of *services* include dry cleaning, haircuts, and air travel. Consumption of goods includes *nondurable goods,* such as soap and soup, and *durable goods,* such as televisions and furniture. Durable goods are those expected to last at least three years. On average, consumption makes up about two-thirds of all spending in the economy. Figure 11.1 shows the composition of U.S. spending since 1960.

**consumption**
Household purchases of final goods and services

---

**U.S. Spending Components as Percentages of GDP Since 1960**

**Figure 11.1**

Consumption's share of total U.S. spending increased slightly from 1960 to 2002. Most recently, it accounted for about 67 percent of the total.

Source: Computed from annual estimates from the U.S. Department of Commerce.

---

---

## Calculating GDP

Return to the example of the cake that was sold for $10. Provide students with the following cost data:

| | |
|---|---|
| Cake mix | $1.89 |
| Other ingredients | $0.83 |
| Electricity | $0.21 |
| Share of rent | $0.33 |
| Share of marketing | $0.25 |
| Share of management | $0.20 |
| Other costs | $0.48 |
| Total | $5.19 |

Ask students to measure the value of Marvin's contribution to GDP. How much of the $10 price of the cake should be allocated to profit for the owner's entrepreneurship? Why is it much easier to measure the value of labor by finding out how much a worker is paid? Assume that Marvin earns $7.00 per hour and used 30 minutes to bake the cake. What was Marvin's labor worth? ($7.00 ÷ 2 = $3.50) How much gross profit did the owner receive? ($10.00 − 3.50 − 5.19 = $1.31)

### *Think Critically Through Visuals*

Direct students to focus their attention on the photographs on this page. Ask for a volunteer to answer the question posed in the caption.

### Answer

Answers will vary. Possible answers: The woman shopping for gifts is shopping for a nondurable good, while the man shopping for chairs is shopping for a durable good.

**Which of the shoppers in these photos is shopping for durable goods, and which one is shopping for nondurable goods?**

**investment**

The purchase of new plants, new equipment, new buildings, new residences, and net additions to inventories

**Investment** consists of spending on new capital goods and additions to inventories. More generally, investment consists of spending on current production that is not used for current consumption. The most important category of investment is new *physical capital,* such as new buildings and new machinery purchased by firms and used to produce goods and services. Spending by households on new residential construction also is considered to be investment.

Changes in firms' inventories are another category of investment. Inventories include stocks of goods in process, such as computer parts. They also include stocks of finished goods, such as new computers awaiting sale. Investment changes more from year to year than any other spending component. On average it accounts for about 15 percent of U.S. GDP.

In the national income accounts, investment does not include purchases of *existing* buildings and machines. Nor does it include purchases of financial assets, such as stocks and bonds. Existing buildings and machines were counted in GDP in the year they were produced. Purchases of stocks and bonds sometimes provide firms with the funds to invest. However, stocks and bonds are not investments. They are simply indications of ownership.

*Government purchases* include spending by all levels of government for goods

324         **CHAPTER 11**   Economic Performance

### *Economic Headlines*

Data that concern nominal and real GDP are regularly reported in the media and used by politicians. Most politicians point to GDP data to try to prove a point. Incumbents use the data to show how well the economy is doing. Those who are seeking office for the first time are more likely to use the data to show that things could be better. Ask students to complete an online search for articles that report GDP data. What information do they provide? What is equally important is how these data are used. How is it possible for different people to draw different conclusions from the same data?

and services—from clearing snowy roads to clearing court dockets, from library books to the librarian's pay. Government purchases at all levels account for about 20 percent of U.S. GDP. Government purchases, and therefore GDP, exclude transfer payments such as those for Social Security, welfare, and unemployment. These transfer payments are outright grants from the government to the recipients and are not true purchases by the government or true earnings by the recipients. Transfer payments typically are used by recipients to purchase consumer goods. This portion of transfer payments is, therefore, counted in consumption totals.

The final component of the expenditure approach to GDP is net exports. This results from the interaction between U.S. residents and the rest of the world. Some spending for consumption, investment, and government purchases goes for imports. However, spending on imports does not count as part of U.S. GDP. To figure out the net effect of the rest of the world on GDP, the value of imports must be subtracted from the value of exports. *Net exports* equal the value of U.S. exports of goods and services minus the value of U.S. imports of goods and services.

The expenditure approach considers the nation's *aggregate expenditure*. Any time an economist uses the term *aggregate*, you can substitute the word *total* for it to determine the meaning. **Aggregate expenditure** equals the sum of consumption, *C*, investment, *I*, government purchases, *G*, and net exports, which is the value of exports, *X*, minus the value of imports, *M*, or $(X - M)$. Summing these spending components yields aggregate expenditure, or GDP:

$$C + I + G + (X - M) = GDP$$

The value of U.S. imports has exceeded the value of U.S. exports nearly every year since the 1960s. This means U.S. net exports $(X - M)$ have been negative. Negative net exports means that the sum of consumption, investment, and government purchases exceeds GDP. You can see negative net exports in Figure 11.1. It is that portion of consumption, investment, and government purchases that exceeds 100 percent of GDP.

## GDP Based on the Income Approach

The expenditure approach sums, or aggregates, spending on production. The income approach sums, or aggregates, income arising from that production. The *income approach to GDP* adds up the aggregate income earned during the year by those who produce that output. Again, double-entry bookkeeping ensures that the value of aggregate output equals the aggregate

**aggregate expenditure**

Total spending on all final goods and services produced in the economy during the year

# SPAN THE GLOBE

## Japanese Economic Revival Plan

Japan once was a powerful economic force in the world. But as of 2003, the country had not yet recovered from more than a decade-long downturn in its GDP. Falling prices, lack of growth, and increasing unemployment continued. Japan's successful economy began to contract in the early part of the 1990s, when sky-high real-estate prices suddenly dropped. The drop in prices wiped out the value of much of the collateral that Japanese banks were holding against business loans. To make matters worse, Japan's export-driven companies were under increasing pressure to reduce prices—and therefore profits. They faced intense competition from other Asian nations with much lower labor costs. In October 2002, the Japanese government launched an economic revival plan. The plan involved a special loan program that rewarded companies that hired people who had been laid off. Its goal was to erase more than $336 billion of the banks' bad debts and create more jobs for Japanese workers. Though it seems like a big step and a lot of money, most observers think the Japanese government will need to spend much more money to effectively stimulate the economy.

### Think Critically

How would creating more jobs for Japanese workers help to raise the GDP in Japan?

# APPLY

Assign Lesson 11.1 from the Contemporary Economics Workbook.

## e-con @pps

Encourage students to apply their knowledge of concepts presented in this lesson as they explore economic news stories, policy debates, and data available at **econxtra.swlearning. com**. A sampling of the titles for this lesson appears below.

### EconData
- Current Account
- Housing Starts
- Real GDP

### EconNews
- A Growing Surprise
- It Ain't Over 'til It's Over

# ASSESS

Assign all or part of Lesson 11.1 Assessment on page 327 as homework or an in-class activity.

## Xtra! Study Tools

Direct students to the online study tools for Lesson 11.1 at **econxtra.swlearning.com**.

# CLOSE

**Revisit** the In the News feature on the first page of the lesson. Ask students to review their preliminary answers and discuss the questions, now that they have completed this lesson.

**Review** the objectives for Lesson 11.1. Students should be able to:
- Describe what the gross domestic product measures.
- Learn two ways to calculate the gross domestic product, and explain why they are equivalent.

**aggregate income**
The sum of all the income earned by resource suppliers in the economy during a given year

income paid for resources used to produce that output. **Aggregate income** equals the sum of all the income earned by resource suppliers in the economy. Thus

Aggregate expenditure
= GDP
= Aggregate income

A finished product usually is processed by several firms on its way to the consumer. A wooden desk, for example, starts as raw timber, which usually is cut by one firm. It is milled by another, made into a desk by a third, and retailed by a fourth. You avoid double counting either by focusing only on the market value of the desk when it is sold to the final user or by *calculating the value added at each stage of production.*

The *value added* by each firm equals that firm's selling price minus the amount paid for intermediate goods, This is the amount spent on inputs purchased from other firms. The value added at each stage represents income to individual resource suppliers at that stage. *The sum of the value added at all stages equals the market value of the final good. The sum of the value added for all final goods and services equals GDP based on the income approach.*

For example, suppose you buy a wooden desk for $200, which is the final market value counted in GDP. Consider the production of that desk. Suppose the tree that gave its life for your studies was cut into a log that was sold to a mill for $20. That log was milled into lumber and sold for $50 to a manufacturer, who built your desk and sold it for $120 to a retailer. The retailer then sold it to you for $200. If all these transactions were added up, the total of $390 would exceed the $200 market value of the desk.

To avoid double counting, you include only the value added at each stage of production. In this example, the logging company adds $20, the miller $30, the manufacturer $70, and the retailer $80. The total value added is $200, which also is the selling price of the desk. All this is illustrated in Figure 11.2.

**CHECKPOINT**
What are two ways of calculating gross domestic product, and how are they equivalent?

---

## Computation of Value Added for a New Desk | Figure 11.2

The value added at each stage of production is the sale value minus the cost of intermediate goods, or column (1) minus column (2). The sum of the values added at all stages equals the market value of the final good, shown at the bottom of column (3).

| Stage of Production | (1) Sale Value | (2) Cost of Intermediate Goods | (3) Value Added |
|---|---|---|---|
| Logger | $ 20 | — | $ 20 |
| Miller | 50 | $ 20 | 30 |
| Manufacturer | 120 | 50 | 70 |
| Retailer | 200 | 120 | 80 |
| | | Market value of final good | **$200** |

**326**    **CHAPTER 11**   Economic Performance

---

# RETEACH

Review the circular-flow model introduced in Chapter 1. Ask students to identify flows of money in the model that would be counted with the income approach and others that would be counted with the expenditures approach in measuring GDP. When a consumer buys a television set in the product market, the value of that payment is spending in the expenditures approach. When a worker is paid a wage in the resource market, that payment is income to the worker. The fact that the values of money and goods and services that flow though the model in these transactions are equal and counted in both methods helps show that these two methods of measurement will arrive at the same value for GDP.

## Key Concepts

1. Why should people care about the amount of production that takes place within the economy?

2. Why wouldn't you add $100 to GDP if you produced a table that you sold for $100?

3. Why are the values of spending and income always assumed to be the same?

4. In what way are investment by businesses and some spending by the government similar?

5. What would your teacher mean if she said, "The aggregate income of all students in this class was $52,315.28 last year?"

Xtra!
**Study Tools**
econxtra.swlearning.com

## Graphing Exercise

6. Use the data in the table to construct two grouped bar graphs showing the percentage of spending for $C + I + G + (X - M)$ for the U.S. GDP in 1970 and 2000. The vertical axis should show the percent of GDP purchased. Each of the spending types should be represented by bars placed along the horizontal axis. Make separate bars for each of the different types of spending. Show the negative net exports in 2000 by extending that bar below the horizontal axis of the graph. What conclusions about changes in the economy can you draw from your graphs?

**Different Types of Spending in 1970 and 2000**
**Values in Billions of Dollars**

| Spending | 1970 | % of GDP | 2000 | % of GDP |
|---|---|---|---|---|
| Consumption | $648.1 | 62.6% | $6,728.4 | 68.2% |
| Investment | 150.2 | 14.5 | 767.5 | 18.0 |
| Government | 236.1 | 22.8 | 741.0 | 17.7 |
| Net Exports | 1.2 | 0.1 | −364.0 | −3.9 |
| Total GDP | $1,035.6 | 100.0 | $9,872.9 | 100.0 |

## Think Critically

7. **Mathematics** Calculate the final price consumers would pay for a gallon of gasoline given the following costs. How does this example demonstrate the need for calculating added value when measuring GDP?

   • Crude oil is extracted from the ground at a cost of $20 per 40-gallon barrel.

   • Crude oil is transported to a refinery at a cost of 18 cents per gallon.

   • It takes 1.25 gallons of crude oil to produce 1 gallon of gasoline.

   • Crude oil is refined into gasoline at a cost of 7 cents per gallon of finished product.

   • Gasoline is transported to gas stations at a cost of 8 cents per gallon.

8. **Consumer Economics** A 5-pound bag of potatoes can be purchased for $2.49. At the same time, a 24-ounce bag of frozen french fries is priced at $2.99. Explain why the frozen potatoes are more expensive. What impact does this difference have on the measurement of GDP?

**Lesson 11.1** • *Gross Domestic Product*

**327**

---

# 11.1 Assessment

## Key Concepts

1. Answers will vary. Possible answer: People should care about the amount of production because it will give them an insight into the health of the economy, which could help them make better personal decisions.

2. Answers will vary. Possible answer: You had to pay for wood, screws, and varnish to construct the table. Therefore, including the entire price of the table in the GDP would have resulted in double counting.

3. Answers will vary. Possible answer: Money spent by one person is income received by someone else. Further, this is the only way to receive income. (Wages are a form of spending because employers are buying labor. Interest is a form of spending because borrowers are buying the use of someone else's money, etc.) Therefore, the value of spending must equal the value of income.

4. Answers will vary. Possible answer: When a business builds a new factory and the government builds a new road, they are both using current production in ways that do not add to current consumption.

5. Students should explain that "aggregate" means "total." So, this statement means that the total income received by all students in the class was $52,315.28 last year.

## Graphing Exercise

6. Answers will vary. Possible answer: Government spending and investment were larger parts of GDP in 1970. This corresponded to a relatively smaller share of GDP being allocated to personal consumption. A large part of 2000 spending was used to buy imported goods that caused a negative net trade.

   A sample of an acceptable graph appears at the bottom of this page.

*The Answer Key is continued on page 352*

---

## Visualizing the Answer— Graphing Exercise

6. The answer includes a graph. Students' graphs should look similar to the one shown here. An Excel spreadsheet containing this graph, along with supporting data, is available on the Instructor's Resource CD.

**Different Types of Spending**

Legend: Consumption, Investment, Government, Net trade

Y-axis: Billions of dollars

1970: 648.1, 150.2, 236.1, 1.2
2000: 6,728.4, 767.5, 741.0, −364.0

**11.2 Limitations of GDP Estimation**

Explain that measuring the value of GDP is complicated by deciding which types of production to include and which to exclude. Ask students to imagine a person who is marooned on a deserted island. To fill his time, this person takes up carving wood and over many years becomes very skilled. He fills the island with beautiful carvings that remind him of his home. Eventually he dies, and his carvings are never found. Clearly the carvings had value to this person, but were they part of anyone else's GDP? How can the government measure the value of production that it does not know takes place? Is this type of production less valuable than production that is sold, reported to the government, and therefore included in GDP?

## Objectives

Remind students to read the lesson objectives to help focus their attention before reading the lesson.

## Key Terms

Direct students to write each of the key terms on a separate index card. Instruct students to write the complete definition of each key term on the back of the appropriate card, along with the page number where the definition is located.

## [ In the News ]

Instruct students to read the passage and write down their answers. Point out that their answers might change after they finish studying Lesson 11.2.

## Answers to Think About It

Answers will vary. Possible answers: People participate in underground markets by purchasing items at farmer's markets and craft shows and by earning money by baby-sitting and mowing lawns. Goods purchased in this activity are not included in the national GDP because the government is unaware of the amount or extent of these underground purchases or earnings.

## Visual Presentation

Use the PowerPoint presentation on the Instructor's Resource CD as an adjunct to your lecture. The presentation also can be used for review.

## Objectives

> Identify what types of production GDP calculations neglect.

> Determine why and how to adjust GDP for changes over time in the general price level.

## Overview

Imagine the difficulty of developing an accounting system that must describe such a complex and dynamic economy. In the interest of clarity and simplicity, certain features are neglected. Features that are easier to measure and to explain may get too much attention. The problem is that the more comprehensive the national income accounts become, the more complicated they get. Trackers of the U.S. economy are always making tradeoffs between simplicity and comprehensiveness. Some production is not accounted for in GDP, however. GDP also must be adjusted for changes in the general price level over time.

## Key Terms

**depreciation**

**nominal GDP**

**real GDP**

**consumer price index (CPI)**

## [ In the News ]

### ● The Yard Sale Police Are Coming

Given the current state of the economy, the underground economy—also called the informal economy, the shadow economy, or the black market—is flourishing. You may associate the underground economy with the drug trade, money laundering, and other such activities. However, this uncharted sector of the U.S. GDP is booming and spreading into all walks of life. It's found in the market for recycled aluminum cans, day labor, pawnshops, and unreported tips at restaurants. It's at farmer's markets, under-the-table work sites, used book and clothing stores, and—yes—even yard sales. U.S. governmental agencies largely have ignored the underground economy—until now, that is. The IRS and state tax departments currently are developing programs to keep track, and get their share, of tax money from the underground activities. The focus of these new big-brother programs is the dollar, the exchange medium of choice in the black market. The new identification markers in almost all new currency will allow tracking of the currency. It also will allow the government to pinpoint large amounts of unexplained cash placed in people's bank accounts or used for purchases. So be careful: The Yard Sale Police are recruiting and getting ready for a yard sale near you.

### Think About It

Do you participate in the underground economy? If so, do you buy or sell in it? If not, do you think you will in the future? What it is about this activity that keeps it from being included in the GDP measurement?

328

### National Content Standards in Economics

A complete list of the NCEE Standards appears on pages xxiv-xxv of this book. The following standards are addressed in Lesson 11.2.

Standard 12: Role of Interest Rates
Standard 15: Growth
Standard 18: Macroeconomy—Income, Employment, Prices

Standard 19: Unemployment and Inflation

# What GDP Misses

With some minor exceptions, GDP includes only those products that are sold in legal markets. It thereby neglects all household production and all illegal production. GDP accounting also has difficulty capturing changes in the quality and variety of products, and in the amount of leisure time available.

## Household Production

Do-it-yourself household production, such as childcare, meal preparation, house cleaning, and home repair, is not captured in GDP. Consequently, an economy in which householders are largely self-sufficient will have a lower GDP than will an otherwise similar economy in which households specialize and sell products to one another.

During the 1950s, more than 80 percent of American mothers with small children stayed at home, caring for the family. All this care did not add one cent to GDP, however. Today more than half of all mothers with small children are in the workforce. Their market labor is counted in U.S. GDP. What's more, GDP also has increased because meals, childcare, and the like are now more apt to be purchased in markets than provided by households. In less-developed economies, more economic activity is do-it-yourself or provided by the extended family.

*Because official GDP figures ignore most home production, these figures understate actual production in economies where families do more for themselves and buy less in the market.*

## Underground Economy

GDP also ignores production in the *underground economy,* which includes activity that goes unreported either because it's illegal or because those involved want to evade taxes on otherwise legal activity. The underground economy also is called the black market or "working off the books." A federal study suggests production in the underground economy is the equivalent of

7.5 percent of GDP. This amounted to about $750 billion in 2003.

## Leisure, Quality, and Variety

GDP indicates the value of goods and services produced in the economy. This gives economists some idea of the economy's *standard of living,* or its level of economic prosperity. However, GDP fails to capture some features of the economy that also play a part in living standards. For example, more leisure time contributes to a higher standard of living, but GDP offers no information

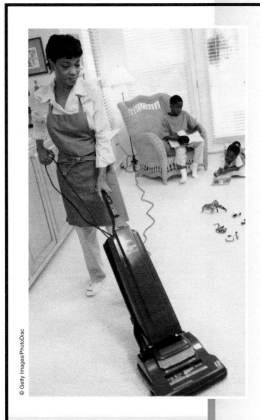

© Getty Images/PhotoDisc

**Is the value of the activity of the woman in this photograph captured in GDP? Explain your answer.**

## What GDP Misses

Describe the following situation to students: Reggie and Sharon own the first house on the first street of a pleasant subdivision next to a busy street. The lot at the corner of their street and the busy street was undeveloped until six months ago, when construction began on a 24-hour diner. After months of construction, the diner opened for business. The parking lot is well lit, and the building has neon signs. The owners of the diner are getting rich, the patrons are enjoying their meals, and Reggie and Sharon haven't had a good night's sleep in weeks. Ask students to explain the aspect of value produced at this diner that is missed in the measure of its contribution to GDP. (It does not consider the cost Reggie and Sharon pay in terms of lost sleep.)

### THE WALL STREET JOURNAL

**Reading It Right**

Invite a student to explain the relevance of the statement from *The Wall Street Journal* that appears on this page.

**Answer**

Answers will vary. Possible answer: The statement indicates a significant amount of activity in Italy's underground economy and that the Italian government is interested in measuring it.

**CHECKPOINT**

Invite a student to answer the checkpoint that appears on page 331.

**Answer**

Calculation of GDP neglects household production, underground economy, leisure, quality, variety, depreciation, and environmental damage.

---

**depreciation**
The value of the capital stock that is used up or becomes obsolete in producing GDP during the year

---

about the amount of leisure time available in an economy. If the amount of leisure remained relatively constant over time, then ignoring leisure would not change the picture.

However, the average U.S. workweek is much shorter now than it was a century ago. This means people work less to produce today's output. People also retire at an earlier age, and they live longer after retirement. Thus, over the years, there has been an increase in the amount of leisure time available. However, leisure is not reflected in GDP because leisure is not explicitly bought and sold in a market.

The quality and variety of products available also have improved over the years because of technological advances and market competition. Recording systems, computers, tires, running shoes, and thousands of other products have been improved. Also, new products are introduced all the time, such as high-definition television, the Internet, and wireless Internet connectors. Yet most of these improvements and innovations are not captured in GDP.

*The gross domestic product fails to capture changes in the availability of leisure time. It also often fails to reflect changes in the quality of existing products and the availability of new ones. These factors make GDP a less-reliable measure of an economy's standard of living.*

### Depreciation

In the course of producing GDP, some capital wears out, such as the delivery truck that finally dies. Other capital becomes obsolete, such as an aging computer that can't run the latest software. A new truck that logs 100,000 miles its first year has been subject to wear and tear. It is now less valuable as a productive resource.

### THE WALL STREET JOURNAL

**Reading It Right** What's the relevance of the following statement from *The Wall Street Journal:* "The economic package approved by the Italian Parliament includes measures to encourage firms operating in the underground economy to come out in the open."

**Depreciation** measures the value of the capital stock that is used up or becomes obsolete in the production process. Gross domestic product is called "gross" because it does not take into account this depreciation. A picture of the *net* production that actually occurs during a year is found by subtracting this depreciation from GDP. *Net domestic product* equals gross domestic product minus depreciation, the value of the capital stock used up in the production process. By failing to account for depreciation, GDP gives a misleading total of what's actually produced.

Economists distinguish between two definitions of investment. *Gross investment* measures the value of all investment during a year. Gross investment is used in computing GDP. *Net investment* equals gross investment minus depreciation. The economy's production possibilities depend on what happens to net investment. If net investment is negative—that is, if depreciation exceeds gross investment—the capital stock declines, so its contribution to output will decline as well. If net investment is zero, the capital stock remains constant, as does its contribution to output. If net investment is positive, the capital stock grows, as does its contribution to output. As the names indicate, *gross* domestic product reflects gross investment and *net* domestic product reflects net investment.

### GDP Does Not Reflect All Costs

Some production and consumption degrades the quality of the environment. Trucks and cars pump carbon monoxide into the atmosphere. Housing developments gobble up forests. Paper mills foul lungs and burn eyes. These negative externalities—costs that fall on those not directly involved in the market transactions—largely are ignored in GDP accounting, even though they diminish the quality of life and may limit future production. To the extent that growth in GDP also involves growth in such negative externalities, a rising GDP may not be as attractive as it would first appear.

Net national product captures the depreciation of buildings, machinery,

---

**ENRICH**

Bring an appliance or device to class that is many years out of date. A mechanical adding machine, typewriter, slide rule, or a corrugated washboard would be appropriate. Ask students to compare the item with a modern device that could accomplish the same task today. Discuss why it is hard to account for changes in the quality and price of these items when GDP values are compared over time. Fifty years ago, a mechanical adding machine, for example, was an expensive item, costing much more than an electronic calculator does today. Can this difference be captured adequately? What does this tell students about limitations on GDP when it is used to compare the value of production over time?

vehicles, and other manufactured capital. Both GDP and net national product ignore the depletion of natural resources, such as standing timber, fish stocks, and soil fertility. The federal government is now in the process of developing so-called *green accounting*, or green GDP, to reflect the impact of production on air pollution, water pollution, lost trees, soil depletion, and the loss of other natural resources.

Despite the limitations and potential distortions associated with official GDP estimates, the trend of GDP over time provides a fairly accurate picture of the overall performance of the U.S. economy. Inflation, however, distorts comparisons of dollar amounts from one year to the next. That problem is discussed next.

 **CHECKPOINT**
What types of production does the calculation of GDP neglect?

# Adjusting GDP for Price Changes

The national income accounts are based on the market values of final goods and services produced in a particular year. Gross domestic product measures the value of output in *current dollars*—that is, in the dollar values at the time the output is produced. The system of national income accounting based on current dollars allows for comparisons among income or expenditure components in a particular year. For example, you could say that consumption last year was about five times greater than investment. Because the economy's general price level changes over time, however, current-dollar comparisons across years can be misleading.

## Nominal GDP versus Real GDP

When GDP is based on current dollars, the national income accounts measure the *nominal value* of national output. Thus, the current-dollar GDP, or

The Bureau of Labor Statistics (BLS) web site features an "Inflation Calculator." You can access this tool through econxtra.swlearning.com. The inflation calculator lets you adjust for inflation the price of a good in one year to its price in another year. Use this tool to find the current year's prices for the following goods: (1) Bicycle purchased in 1992 for $250. (2) Candy bar purchased in 1980 for $.50. (3) College tuition of $3,000 per year in 1974.

**econxtra.swlearning.com**

### TEAM WORK

Choose a partner. Each partner should list five goods and the cost of each good today. Next to each item, write a year as early as 1913. Your partner, using the BLS inflation calculator, will determine the price of each good on your list in the year you have indicated.

**nominal GDP**, is based on the prices when the output is produced. Because of inflation, however, focusing on the nominal value of GDP over time distorts the true picture. For example, between 1979 and 1980, nominal GDP increased by about 9 percent. That sounds impressive, but the economy's general price level rose more than 9 percent. So the growth in nominal GDP resulted entirely from inflation. **Real GDP**, or GDP adjusted for inflation, in fact declined. Recall that *inflation* is an increase in the economy's average price level.

If nominal GDP increases in a given year, part of this increase may simply result from inflation—pure hot air. To make meaningful comparisons of GDP across years, you must take out the hot air, or *deflate* nominal GDP. To focus on *real* changes in production,

**nominal GDP**
GDP based on prices at the time of the transaction; current-dollar GDP

**real GDP**
The economy's aggregate output measured in dollars of constant purchasing power; GDP measured in terms of the goods and services produced

---

## Adjusting GDP for Price Changes

Ask students whether they would accept a job that paid $.90 per hour. How long would it take them to earn enough to buy a meal at a fast-food restaurant at that wage rate? Then tell students to imagine it is 1959, and McDonald's menu includes hamburgers for $.15, fries for $.10 and soft drinks for $.12. How much would you pay for a meal of two hamburgers, an order of fries, and a soft drink? ($.52) Ask how this affects their perception of the value of a job that pays $.90 per hour. Would they have been willing to accept the job in 1959? Why must production and income values in GDP be adjusted for changes in price to make them meaningful over time?

 **E-CONOMICS**

Direct students to read the passage "Computer Prices and GDP Estimation" on this page.

### Answers to Think Critically

There has been a sharp decline in the price of computers because of technological advancements. As a result, the supply of computers has increased and their cost has decreased.

*Think Critically Through Visuals*

Direct students to focus their attention on **Figure 11.3—Example of a Price Index**. Review how the price index is calculated. Extend the example by adding subsequent years to the table and having students calculate the price index.

*Think Critically Through Visuals*

Direct students to focus their attention on **Figure 11.4—Example Market Basket Used to Develop the Consumer Price Index** on page 333. Point out that this figure is for illustration only; the actual market basket used to develop the CPI has hundreds of items.

---

## E-CONOMICS

### Computer Prices and GDP Estimation

Computer prices have fallen by an average of about 13 percent per year since 1982. Based on this rate of decline, a computer that cost, say $10,000 in 1982 cost about $5,000 in 1987 but only about $650 in 2001. According to these prices, that computer cost about the same in 1982 as a minivan. In 2001, you could buy about 35 computers for the cost of a minivan. So computers became much less expensive between 1982 and 2001. The sharp decline in computer prices spurred purchases of computers for offices and homes. Suppose the number of computers jumped from 1 million in 1982 to 5 million in 2001. If computers are valued at their 1987 price of $5,000, computer spending would have increased five times, from $5 billion in 1982 to $25 billion in 2001. If priced in current, or nominal, dollars of $10,000 in 1982 and $650 in 2001, spending on computers would have declined two-thirds from $10 billion in 1982 to only $3.3 billion in 2001.

### Think Critically

How would you explain the sharp decline in computer prices from 1982 to 2001?

---

you must eliminate changes due solely to inflation.

### Price Indexes

To compare the price level over time, you need a point of reference, a base year to which prices in other years can be compared. An *index number* compares the value of a variable in a particular year to its value in a base year, or reference year. Suppose bread is the only good produced in the economy. As a reference point, consider the price in some specific year. The year selected is called the base year. Prices in other years are expressed relative to the base-year price.

Suppose the base year is 2002, when a loaf of bread sold for $1.25. The price of bread increased to $1.30 in 2003 and to $1.40 in 2004. To construct a *price index*, each year's price is divided by the price in the base year and then multiplied by 100, as shown in Figure 11.3. For 2002, the base year, the base price of bread is divided by itself, $1.25/$1.25, which equals 1. So the price index equals $1 \times 100 = 100$. *The price index in the base year, or base period, is always 100.*

**Example of a Price Index (base year = 2002)**                    **Figure 11.3**

The price index equals the price in the current year divided by the price in the base year, all multiplied by 100.

| Year | (1) Price of Bread in Current Year | (2) Price of Bread in Base Year | (3) Price Index (3) = (1)/(2) × 100 |
|------|------|------|------|
| 2002 | $1.25 | $1.25 | 100 |
| 2003 | 1.30 | 1.25 | 104 |
| 2004 | 1.40 | 1.25 | 112 |

---

## Curriculum Connection—Literature

Many students have seen *Gone with the Wind* or have read Margaret Mitchell's classic novel on which the movie is based. In this story, Rhett and Scarlett are affected very differently by inflation as the South begins to lose the war against the North. Ask students to discuss why Rhett is able to prosper while Scarlett's life is torn apart. Why would it have been difficult to measure the GDP of the South in those years? (Rhett was active in the black market. He had goods to sell in a time of shortage and so received the benefit of higher prices. Scarlett was a consumer. She had limited funds to buy scarce products and was forced to pay high prices or do without. She was harmed by the high prices.)

The price index in 2003 is $1.30/$1.25, which equals 1.04, which multiplied by 100 equals 104. In 2004, the index is $1.40/$1.25, or 1.12, which multiplied by 100 equals 112. Thus, when compared to the base year, the price index is 4 percent higher in 2003 and is 12 percent higher in 2004.

The price index permits comparisons between any two years. For example, what if you were presented with the indexes for 2003 and 2004 and were asked what happened to the price level between the two years? By dividing the 2004 price index by the 2003 price index, 112/104, you find that the price level rose by 7.7 percent.

## Consumer Price Index

The **consumer price index (CPI)**, measures changes over time in the cost of buying a "market basket" of goods and services purchased by a typical family. For simplicity, suppose that market basket for the year includes 365 pounds of bananas, 500 gallons of fuel oil, and 12 months of cable TV. Prices in the base year are listed in column (2) of Figure 11.4. Multiplying price by quantity yields the total cost of each product in the base year, as shown in column (3). The cost of the market basket in the base year is $1,184.85, shown as the total of column (3).

Prices in the current year are listed in column (4). Note that not all prices changed by the same percentage since the base year. The price of fuel oil increased by 50 percent, but the price of bananas fell. The cost of purchasing that same basket in the current year is $1,398.35, shown as the total of column (5).

To compute the consumer price index for the current year, you simply divide the total cost in the current year by the total cost of that same basket in the base year, $1,398.35/$1,184.85, and then multiply by 100. This yields a price index of 118. You could say that between the base year and the current year, the "cost of living" increased by 18 percent, although not all prices changed by the same percentage.

The federal government uses the years 1982 to 1984 as the base period for calculating the CPI for a market basket of 400 goods and services. The CPI is reported monthly, based on prices from thousands of sellers across the country.

## GDP Price Index

Price indexes are weighted sums of various prices. Whereas the CPI focuses on just a sample of consumer purchases, a more comprehensive price index, the *GDP price index*, includes all goods and services produced. The GDP price index is found by dividing the

*consumer price index (CPI)*

Measure of inflation based on the cost of a fixed "market basket" of goods and services purchased by a typical family

### Example Market Basket Used to Develop the Consumer Price Index

Figure **11.4**

| Good or Service | (1) Quantity in Market Basket | (2) Prices in Base Year | (3) Cost of Basket in Base Year (3) = (1) × (2) | (4) Prices in Current Year | (5) Cost of Basket in Current Year (5) = (1) × (4) |
|---|---|---|---|---|---|
| Bananas | 365 pounds | $0.89/pound | $ 324.85 | $ 0.79 | $ 288.35 |
| Fuel Oil | 500 gallons | 1.00/gallon | 500.00 | 1.50 | 750.00 |
| Cable TV | 12 months | 30.00/month | 360.00 | 30.00 | 360.00 |
| | | | $1,184.85 | | $1,398.35 |

**The cost of a market basket in the current year, shown at the bottom of column (5), sums the quantities of each item in the basket, shown in column (1), times the price of each item in the current year, shown in column (4).**

**Answer**
GDP is adjusted for changes in the general price level so that comparisons of prices can be made across years. This adjustment is made by discounting for inflation across the given years.

**APPLY**

Assign Lesson 11.2 from the Contemporary Economics Workbook.

Encourage students to apply their knowledge of concepts presented in this lesson as they explore economic news stories, policy debates, and data available at **econxtra.swlearning. com**. A sampling of the titles for this lesson appears below.

**EconNews**
● Moving Along
● Rocky(?) Road to a Record

**ASSESS**

Assign all or part of Lesson 11.2 Assessment on page 334 as homework or an in-class activity.

## Xtra! Study Tools

Direct students to the online study tools for Lesson 11.2 at **econxtra.swlearning.com**.

**CLOSE**

**Revisit** the In the News Feature on the first page of the lesson. Ask students to review their preliminary answers and discuss the questions, now that they have completed this lesson.

**Review** the objective for Lesson 11.2. Students should be able to:
● Identify what types of production GDP calculations neglect.
● Determine why and how to adjust GDP for changes over time in the general price level.

## RETEACH

Remind students that measures of GDP do not include the value of all types of production, including that which takes place in the home. Read aloud a brief description of an American pioneer's typical day. Many books provide this type of description, including Barbara Greenwood's *A Pioneer Sampler: The Daily Life of a Pioneer Family in 1840*. Ask students to explain why most of the production that took place in this story would not have been included in the measure of GDP. What production takes place in students' homes that is not included in the measure of GDP today?

## Key Concepts

1. Answers will vary. Possible answer: GDP includes only the value of production that is purchased or generates income.

2. Answers will vary. Possible answer: Earnings from many jobs held by young people, such as baby-sitting and lawn-care jobs, are not reported to the government.

3. Answers will vary. Possible answer: If the new truck replaces an old truck that has worn out, its value is not entirely a new investment in the economy.

## Graphing Exercise

4. Answers will vary. Possible answer: There is no way to place a value on time spent watching television. Including the value of television in GDP would be impossible.

   A sample of an acceptable graph appears at the bottom of this page.

## Think Critically

5. Answers will vary. Possible answer: Federal spending increased by 42.7 percent in the 1990s ($1,788.8 / $1,253.2 = 1.427; 1.427 − 1 = 0.427 = 42.7%). In these years, the CPI increased by 31.8 percent (172.2 / 130.7 = 1.318; 1.318 − 1 = 0.318 = 31.8%). Therefore, the real value of federal spending declined by 10.9 percent (42.7% − 31.8% = 10.9%). If you had been a nonincumbent running for election, you might have emphasized the nominal increase in federal spending. If you had been an incumbent, you might have pointed out the real decline in federal spending.

---

nominal GDP by the real GDP and then multiplying by 100:

GDP price index

$$= \frac{\text{Nominal GDP}}{\text{Real GDP}} \times 100$$

Nominal GDP is the dollar value of this year's GDP measured in current-year prices. Real GDP is the dollar value of this year's GDP measured in base-year prices. If you know both nominal GDP and real GDP, then finding the GDP price index is easy. The federal government most recently has used 1996 as the base year for computing real GDP. The base year moves forward every few years and could be a later year by the time you read this.

**✓ CHECKPOINT**
Why and how is GDP adjusted for changes in the general price level?

---

**11.2** *Assessment*

**Xtra!**
Study Tools
econxtra.swlearning.com

## Key Concepts

1. Why wouldn't our nation's GDP grow if you mow your own lawn, but would grow if you were paid to mow your neighbor's lawn?

2. How do many young people participate in the underground economy?

3. Why wouldn't the purchase of a $20,000 truck by a business necessarily represent a $20,000 net investment in the economy?

## Graphing Exercise

4. U.S. citizens watch television for more hours than people in any other nation. Although they value their time in front of the "tube," this value is not included in GDP. Construct a bar graph showing the hours the average U.S. citizen spends watching TV from the data in the table. Is there a way the value of this time should or could be included in national income accounting? Explain your point of view.

**Average Hours Spent Watching Television Programming Per Year, 1996–2004**

| Year | Average Viewing Hours |
|------|----------------------|
| 1996 | 1,559 |
| 1998 | 1,551 |
| 2000 | 1,633 |
| 2002 | 1,655 |
| 2004 | 1,673 |

(Values for 2002 and 2004 are projected.)

## Think Critically

5. **Government** In 1990, the federal government spent $1,253.2 billion when the CPI was 130.7. Ten years later, in 2000, the federal government spent $1,788.8 billion when the CPI was 172.2. Did the federal government's real spending increase in these years? If you had been a politician running for election in 2002, how would you have used this information? Explain your answer.

---

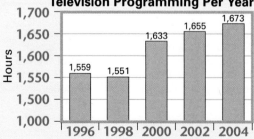

**Average Hours Spent Watching Television Programming Per Year**

## Visualizing the Answer—Graphing Exercise

4. The answer includes a graph. Students' graphs should look similar to the one shown here. An Excel spreadsheet containing this graph, along with supporting data, is available on the Instructor's Resource CD.

## 11.3 Business Cycles

### Objectives

> Distinguish between the two phases of the business cycle, and compare the average length of each.

> Differentiate among leading, coincident, and lagging economic indicators.

### Overview

Economic activity, like cycles in nature, fluctuates in a fairly regular way. The U.S. economy and other industrial market economies historically have experienced alternating periods of expansion and contraction in the level of economic activity. These fluctuations vary in length and intensity, yet some features appear common to all. The ups and downs usually involve the entire nation and often the world. They affect nearly all dimensions of economic activity, not simply employment and production. Despite these ups and downs, the U.S. economy has grown dramatically over the long run.

### Key Terms

**business cycle**

**recession**

**expansion**

**leading economic indicators**

### [ In the News ]

#### • Taking the Pulse of the Economy

In mid-April 2003, after the war in Iraq, the U.S. economy was in a state of flux. Financial market observers and Washington policymakers were paying attention to economic indicators that provided a general picture of what the economy looked like right then. Some of the best of these indicators—termed coincident indicators—are the financial markets. Fluctuations in the prices of stocks and bonds offer investors a reasonable basis for predictions about inflation, earnings, and economic growth. Additionally, investors also can keep close tabs on other indicators—from weekly sales reports of major retailers to home mortgage applications. By the time most official government data are released, they're more than a month old. The coincident indicators can provide an up-to-the-moment snapshot of how the economy is performing. However, caution must be used in looking at these indicators. Coincident indicators can change quickly and register sharp spikes, false starts, or temporary dips. On April 15, 2003, the coincident data showed the economy was reacting positively to the quick end of the war in Iraq. Jobless claims were down by 38,000 and Wal-Mart sales were up 5 to 7 percent. However, complete economic recovery was a long time coming.

#### Think About It

What would be the problems associated with using only coincident indicators in making economic decisions?

335

### National Content Standards in Economics

A complete list of the NCEE Standards appears on pages xxiv–xxv of this book. The following standards are addressed in Lesson 11.3.

Standard 18: Macroeconomy—Income/ Employment, Prices

Standard 19: Unemployment and Inflation

## U.S. Economic Fluctuations

Remind students that the U.S. econo-my increased its real production at an average real rate of more than 2.5 per-cent per year during the twentieth cen-tury. Ask whether students think gov-ernment, businesses, or consumers should be satisfied or pleased if the current real growth rate in GDP is 1 percent. This would indicate that the economy is growing, but is it growing fast enough? What growth rate do they believe the economy should achieve? Remind them that rapid growth is likely to lead to inflation.

### *Think Critically Through Visuals*

Direct students to focus their attention on **Figure 11.5—Business Cycles**. Point out the two areas of recession and remind students that expansions last longer than recessions, but the length of the full cycle varies.

**business cycle**

Fluctuations reflecting the rise and fall of economic activity relative to the long-term growth trend of the economy

**recession**

A decline in total production lasting at least two consecutive quarters, or at least six months

# U.S. Economic Fluctuations

The **business cycle** reflects the rise and fall of economic activity relative to the long-term growth trend of the economy. Perhaps the easiest way to understand the business cycle is to examine its components. During the 1920s and 1930s, Wesley C. Mitchell, director of the National Bureau of Economic Research (NBER), noted that the economy experiences two phases: periods of expansion and periods of contraction.

## Recessions and Expansions

A contraction might be so severe as to be called a *depression*. This is a sharp reduction in the nation's total production lasting more than a year and accompanied by high unemploy-ment. A milder contraction is called a **recession**, which is a decline in total production lasting at least two consecutive quarters, or at least six months. The U.S. economy experi-enced both recessions and depressions before World War II. Since then, there have been recessions but no depressions.

## Long-Term Growth

Despite these ups and downs, the U.S. economy has grown dramatically over the long run. The economy in 2003 was more than 11 times larger than it was in 1929, as measured by real gross domes-tic product, or real GDP. With real GDP, the effects of changes in the economy's price level have been stripped away. Therefore, the remaining changes reflect real changes in the value of goods and services produced.

Production tends to increase over the long run because of

1. increases in the amount and quality of resources, especially labor and capital

2. better technology

3. improvements in the *rules of the game* that facilitate production and exchange, such as property rights, patent laws, legal systems, and customs of the market.

Figure 11.5 shows a long-term growth trend in real GDP as an upward-sloping straight line. Economic fluctuations reflect movements around this growth trend. A recession begins after the previ-ous expansion has reached its *peak*, or high point, and continues until the economy reaches a *trough*, or low point. The period between a peak and trough is a recession. The period between a

---

**Business Cycles**

**Figure 11.5**

Business cycles reflect movements of economic activity around a trend line that shows long-term growth. A recession (shown in pink) begins after a previous expansion (shown in blue) has reached its peak and continues until the economy reaches a trough. An expansion begins when economic activity starts to increase and continues until the economy reaches a peak. A complete business cycle includes both the recession phase and the expansion phase.

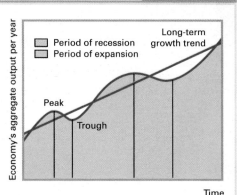

---

## *Outside Resources*

***The Grapes of Wrath*** John Steinbeck's *The Grapes of Wrath* provides a well-known description of the impact of the Great Depression. Read aloud several pages from this book, and ask students to imagine what it must have been like to be destitute and on the move in the 1930s. Discuss why knowing what will happen in the economy over the next few years is so important to people, busi-nesses, and the government. Ask students to describe how their families have been affected by changes in the business cycle.

trough and subsequent peak is an **expansion**, or the phase of economic activity during which the economy's total output increases. Note that expansions last longer than recessions, but the length of the full cycle varies.

## History of U.S. Business Cycles

Economists at the NBER have been able to track the U.S. economy back to 1854. Since then, the nation has experienced 31 business cycles. No two have been exactly alike. The longest expansion began in the spring of 1991 and broke the record during the first quarter of 2001. The longest contraction lasted five and a half years from 1873 to 1879.

Output changes since 1929 appear in Figure 11.6. The figure shows the annual percentage change in real GDP, with declines in red and increases in green. The big decline during the Great Depression of the early 1930s and the sharp jump during World War II stand in stark contrast. Growth since 1929 has averaged 3.4 percent a year.

## Different Impact on States

The intensity of the business cycle varies from region to region across the United States. A recession hits hardest those regions that produce durable goods, such as appliances, furniture, and automobiles. This is because the demand for these goods falls more during hard times than does the demand for other goods and services.

Because of seasonal fluctuations and random events, the economy does not move smoothly through phases of business cycle. At the time of their occurrence, economists cannot always distinguish between temporary setbacks in economic activity and the beginning of a downturn. The drop in production in a particular quarter may result from a snowstorm or a poor harvest rather than

### NETBookmark

The National Bureau of Economic Research maintains a Web page devoted to business cycle expansions and contractions. Take a look at this page and see if you can determine how the business cycle has been changing in recent decades. Has the overall length of cycles been changing? Have recessions been getting longer or shorter?

*econxtra.swlearning.com*

### Ask the Xpert!

*econxtra.swlearning.com*

*Gross Domestic Product increased between 1973 and 1974, but they say we had a recession. How could this be?*

**expansion**
The phase of economic activity during which the economy's total output increases

**Annual Percentage Change in U.S. Real GDP Since 1929**

Figure **11.6**

Since the end of World War II in 1945, the economy has gone through 10 business cycles. Expansions averaged just under five years. Recessions averaged just under one year. Note: In this chart, declines are shown in red and increases, in blue.

Source: Based on annual estimates from the U.S. Department of Commerce.

Lesson 11.3 • *Business Cycles*    **337**

## TEACH    (continued)

### U.S. Economic Fluctuations

Describe the following scenario: Alan has decided to purchase a new car at some time in the next year. He has noticed in news reports that the economy is growing rapidly and that price levels are rising at an increasing rate. The car he wants to purchase is priced at $20,000 today. He is worried that if he waits a year, the same car might cost as much as $21,500. To buy the car now, he will need to borrow $10,000 for one year at 8 percent per year. Should Alan buy the car now or wait? If he buys it now, how much will the loan cost? ($400) Why do expectations of rapid growth and higher rates of inflation often contribute to higher growth and rates of inflation? (When people expect prices to go up, they may choose to buy more now to avoid the higher prices later. This contributes to greater current demand and production, as well as to accelerating rates of inflation.)

### NETBookmark

Direct students to the **econxtra.swlearning.com**. Remind them to click on the link for Lesson 11.3 to find the appropriate link for the **NET Bookmark** on this page.

**Answer**

Answers will vary, depending on when students complete the activity.

### Ask the Xpert!

Direct students to the **econxtra.swlearning.com** to hear an expert answer the question "Gross domestic product increased between 1973 and 1974, but they say we had a recession. How could this be?"

### *Think Critically Through Visuals*

Direct students to focus their attention on **Figure 11.6—Annual Percentage Change in U.S. Real GDP Since 1929.** Point out that even though there have been periods of recession, growth since 1929 has averaged 3.4 percent a year.

## ENRICH

Remind students of the fable "The Ant and the Grasshopper." In this story, an ant worked day after day to gather and store food during the summer because he knew winter was on its way. The grasshopper just played, never thinking of the future. But when winter arrived, he had nothing to eat. Many people behave like the grasshopper. They spend when the economy is doing well and have little to spend when the economy turns bad. Ask students why this sort of behavior tends to make the business cycle larger. (It causes more spending when the economy is growing and less spending when the economy is in a recession.)

Invite students to write a modern-day fable related to a topic in this lesson.

## U.S. Economic Fluctuations

XYZ Contractor Supply sells lumber, concrete blocks, flooring, windows, and similar products to construction contractors. XYZ is able to purchase the products it sells at reduced costs when it buys them in large quantities. For example 5,000 sheets of quarter-inch plywood costs $8.50 per sheet. But, if XYZ orders 20,000 sheets, the price per sheet falls to $7.50. Similar discounts are available for most of the other products XYZ stocks. Ask students to explain why the owners of this firm would be interested in the future of the business cycle in the United States. Why would they be particularly interested in the number of new housing starts, mortgage interest rates, and the backlog of unfinished construction projects?

### *Think Critically Through Visuals*

Direct students to focus their attention on the photograph on this page. Ask for a volunteer to answer the question posed in the caption.

### Answer

The job security of a construction worker who builds homes is likely to be affected because the demand for expensive goods, including new homes, declines during hard times.

### *Think Critically Through Visuals*

Direct students to focus their attention on **Figure 11.7—U.S. and U.K. Growth Rates**. Point out the similarities of the growth rate of the United Kingdom and the United States.

 **CHECKPOINT**

Invite a student to answer the checkpoint that appears on page 339.

### Answer

The two phases of the business cycle are recession and expansion. Recessions are declines in total production lasting at least two consecutive quarters. Expansions are the phase of economic activity during which the economy's total output increases. Expansions last longer than recessions, but the length of the full cycle varies.

**Is the job security of a construction worker who helps to build new homes likely to be affected by a recession? Why or why not?**

mark the onset of a recession. Turning points—peaks and troughs—are thus identified by the NBER only after the fact. Because recession means that output declines for at least two consecutive quarters, a recession is not so designated until at least six months after it begins.

### Business Cycles Around the Globe

Business cycles usually involve the entire nation. Indeed, market economies around the world often move together. Though economic fluctuations do not also happen at the same time across countries, a link often is apparent. Consider the recent experience of two leading economies—the United States and the United Kingdom. Figure 11.7 shows for both economies the year-to-year percentage change since 1985 in their real GDP. Again, *real* means that the effects of inflation have been erased. Remaining changes reflect *real* changes in the total amount of goods and services produced.

If you follow the annual changes in each economy, you will notice the similarities. For example, in 1991, U.S. real GDP declined, or had a negative growth

**U.S. and U.K. Growth Rates**  **Figure 11.7**

Growth rates of output in the United States and the United Kingdom are similar.

Source: *OECD Economic Outlook* and *Economic Report of the President*, February 2003, Table B-112.

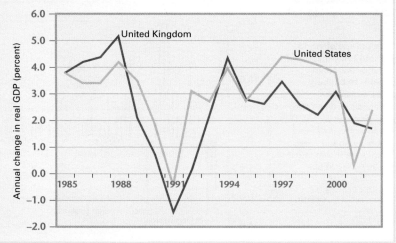

**338**  **CHAPTER 11**  Economic Performance

### *Economic Headlines*

Ask students to find a magazine or newspaper article that concerns the status of the economy. Does the article suggest the economy is expanding or falling into recession? To what does the article attribute the status of the economy? How is the economy affecting consumers, businesses, and/or the government? Is there any way people could have predicted this economic condition, or did it happen because of external events such as wars, droughts, or political conditions?

rate, reflecting a recession. The United Kingdom also experienced a recession that year. Likewise, in both economies, growth in 1994 jumped to at least 4 percent, and then slowed the following year.

One problem with the linkage across economies is that a slump in other major economies could worsen a recession in the United States, and vice versa. For example, the terrorist attacks on the United States in September 2001 affected economies and stock markets around the world.

Although year-to-year fluctuations in output are of interest, even more important to an economy's standard of living is its long-term growth trend. U.S. real GDP growth averaged 3.1 percent per year between 1985 and 2002, compared with 2.6 percent in the United Kingdom. This seemingly small difference compounded over the years to raise the level of real GDP much more in the United States. For example, if U.S. GDP had averaged only 2.6 percent growth since 1985, output by 2002 would have been $600 billion below that achieved with its 3.1 percent growth. The lower growth rate would have reduced U.S. production and income in 2002 by about $2,100 per person.

**CHECKPOINT**

What are the two phases of the business cycle, and what has been the average length of each?

# Economic Indicators

During the Great Depression, economists identified measures that would keep better track of the economy. These economic indicators are classified according to their timing relative to the ups and downs of the business cycle. Those that predict future changes are called *leading indicators*. Those that measure the ups and downs as they

occur are called *coincident indicators*. Those that measure the ups and downs after they have already occurred are called *lagging indicators*.

To understand economic indicators better, consider weather indicators as an example. A leading indicator tells you what the weather will be like tomorrow. A coincident indicator tells you what's it's like outside right now. The lagging indicator tells you what the weather was yesterday. Leading economic indicators get the most attention because people want to know where the economy is headed.

## Leading Indicators

Certain events foretell a turning point in economy. Months before a recession begins, changes in leading economic indicators point to the coming storm. In the early stages of a recession, business slows, orders for machinery and computers slip, and the stock market, anticipating lower profits, turns down. Consumer confidence in the economy's future also begins to sag. Households cut back on their spending, especially for big-ticket items like new cars and new homes.

All these activities are called **leading economic indicators** because they usually predict, or *lead to*, a downturn. There are 10 leading indicators combined into the *index of leading indicators* and reported monthly. Upturns in leading indicators point to an economic recovery. The index of leading indicators is a closely followed measure of economic activity.

Leading indicators cannot predict precisely *when* a turning point will occur, or even *whether* one will occur. Sometimes the leading indicators sound a false alarm. Leading indicators also do not work when there is an external shock to the economy, such as a terrorist attack, drought, earthquake, or hurricane. For example, when Iraq invaded Kuwait, the price of crude oil increased from $25 to $40 per barrel. This caused an economic downturn throughout the world that could not have been predicted by the leading indicators.

*leading economic indicators*

Measures that usually predict, or *lead to,* recessions or expansions

Lesson 11.3 • *Business Cycles*     **339**

## TEACH

### Economic Indicators

Point out that economic measures change during the business cycle. The three measures are called leading indicators, coincident indicators, and lagging indicators. Recall the example of the building supply wholesaler on page 338. What kinds of indicators would this firm be most interested in? Why would this firm probably be more interested in the course of the business cycle than a firm that sold groceries? (Consumers buy groceries even when the economy is in a recession. They will cut back on buying homes and other expensive products when the economy is in a recession.)

**Investigate Your Local Economy** Direct students to answer the question in the **Investigate Your Local Economy** on page 340. Students' findings will vary, depending on when and where this assignment is completed.

### *Think Critically Through Visuals*

Direct students to focus their attention on the photograph on page 340. Ask for a volunteer to answer the question posed in the caption.

**Answer**

Answers will vary. Possible answer: The stock market is a leading indicator. The stock market is a measure that usually predicts, or leads to, recessions or expansions.

**CHECKPOINT**

Invite a student to answer the checkpoint that appears on page 340.

**Answer**

Leading indicators predict future changes. Coincident indicators measure ups and downs as they occur. Lagging indicators measure ups and downs after they have already occurred.

## *Group Activity*

Organize students into small groups. Provide recent copies of newspapers to the groups. Ask each group to locate and summarize articles that report on economic conditions. Ask students to use information in these articles to predict the condition in which the economy will be, one year in the future. What are the leading indicators they used? What other types of information could be gathered to help them make more reliable predictions?

Encourage students to apply their
knowledge of concepts presented in
this lesson as they explore economic
news stories, policy debates, and data
available at **econxtra.swlearning.
com**. A sampling of the titles for this
lesson appears below.

### EconData
- Interest Rate Spread

### EconNews
- Is the Recession Really Over?
- Some News Is Good
- Brazil Sí, Argentina No
- Going, Going, Hopefully Gone
- A Shrinking Product
- Gloom in the Forecast
- Border Crossing
- A Stitch in Time Could Be Harmful
- Signs of Some Slowing
- GDP Will Recover, but Will We?
- Hard Landing Ahead
- A Never-Ending Story?

## ASSESS

Assign all or part of Lesson 11.3
Assessment on page 341 as homework or an in-class activity.

## Xtra! Study Tools

Direct students to the online study
tools for Lesson 11.3 at
**econxtra.swlearning.com**.

## CLOSE

**Revisit** the **In the News** feature on the
first page of the lesson. Ask students
to review their preliminary answers
and discuss the questions, now that
they have completed this lesson.

**Review** the objectives for Lesson 11.3.
Students should be able to:
- Distinguish between the two phases
of the business cycle, and compare
the average length of each.
- Differentiate among leading,
coincident, and lagging economic
indicators.

## Coincident Indicators

Some economic indicators measure
what's going on in the economy right
now. *Coincident economic indicators* are
those measures that reflect peaks and
troughs as they happen. There are four
coincident indicators combined into the
*index of coincident indicators,* including
total employment, personal income, and
industrial production.

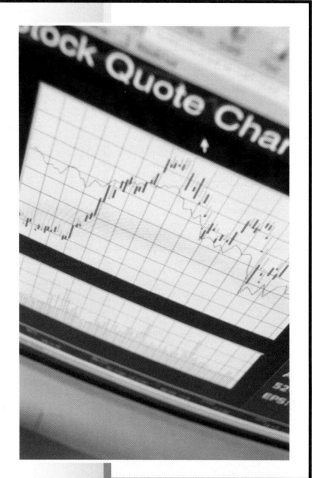

**What type of economic indicator is
provided in a chart that tracks the
daily activity of a particular stock?**

### Investigate Your Local Economy

Before new houses may
be constructed, contrac-
tors must obtain building
permits from local gov-
ernment. Find out the
number of building
permits issued in your
community in the last two
months. In light of this
information, what will
probably happen to the
local economy in the next
few months?

## Lagging Indicators

Some economic indicators measure
what has already happened. *Lagging
economic indicators* follow, or trail,
changes in overall economic activity.
There are seven economic measures
combined into *the index of lagging
indicators,* including the interest rate,
measures of loans outstanding,
and the average duration of
unemployment.

This introduction to the business
cycle has been largely mechanical,
focusing on the history and measurement of these fluctuations. Why
economies fluctuate has not been
addressed, in part because such a discussion requires a fuller understanding
of the economy and in part because
the causes are not always clear. The
next section begins to build a framework by introducing a key model of
the national economy.

### CHECKPOINT
What are the differences among
leading, coincident, and lagging
economic indicators?

## RETEACH

Remind students that the business cycle does not hit all regions of the country equally. The recession of 2001-2002, for example, hit very hard in the states of the Pacific Northwest. This was the
home of the Boeing Corporation and of many high-tech electronics firms. Ask students why the
downturn in the economy would have harmed these businesses more than other types of businesses located in other parts of the country. (Boeing was hurt by a decline in orders for new airplanes following the September 11, 2001, terrorist attacks. The recession caused many businesses
and individual consumers to put off buying new computers and software. This hurt many firms that
were located in the Pacific Northwest.)

340          **CHAPTER 11**   Economic Performance

## 11.3 Assessment

### Key Concepts

1. Decide whether the U.S. economy is currently in an expansion or a recession. Identify and explain the types of information that allow you to make this decision.

2. Do you think a recession would harm your community more or less than the average of all communities in the United States? Explain your answer.

3. How would a major expansion of the economies in Europe affect the U.S. economy?

4. If the GDP increased from $1.1 trillion last year to $1.6 trillion this year, would you think the economy is in a recession or an expansion? Explain your answer.

### Graphing Exercise

5. Use data in the table to construct a line graph that shows the rate of growth in the real GDP from 1990 through 2001. If the long-range growth rate averaged 3.4 percent per year, which years exceeded this growth rate and which had lower rates of growth? How does your graph demonstrate the business cycle?

**Real GDP Growth Rates, 1990–2001**

| Year | Real GDP Growth | Year | Real GDP Growth |
|------|-----------------|------|-----------------|
| 1990 | 1.8% | 1996 | 3.6% |
| 1991 | −0.5% | 1997 | 4.4% |
| 1992 | 3.1% | 1998 | 4.3% |
| 1993 | 2.7% | 1999 | 4.1% |
| 1994 | 4.4% | 2000 | 3.8% |
| 1995 | 2.7% | 2001 | 0.3% |

### Think Critically

6. **History** During the early years of the Great Depression of the 1930s, average prices fell in the United States. Explain what this would have done to the real value of the products that were produced in these years.

7. **Management** Explain why the managers of a home construction business would be more concerned with the business cycle than would the owners of a dairy.

Xtra!
**Study Tools**
econxtra.swlearning.com

---

### Visualizing the Answer— Graphing Exercise

5. The answer includes a graph. Students' graphs should look similar to the one shown here. An Excel spreadsheet containing this graph, along with supporting data, is available on the Instructor's Resource CD.

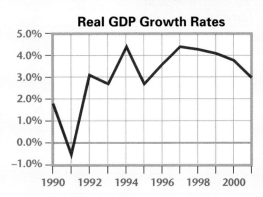

**Real GDP Growth Rates**

---

### 11.3 Assessment

### Key Concepts

1. Answers will vary. Possible answer: Factors including change in GDP, unemployment, business profits, and the number of people who are receiving social assistance can be used to judge whether the economy is in expansion or recession.

2. Answers will vary. Possible answer: Communities that rely on businesses that produce durable goods are more likely to be harmed by recessions than those that are home to businesses that produce non-durable goods or services that are demanded regardless of the status of the economy. When the economy is in recession, many businesses and consumers are not willing to take on the cost of major purchases of durable goods.

3. Answers will vary. Possible answer: An expansion of European economies would cause them to buy more U.S. goods and services, which would cause the U.S. economy to expand as well.

4. Answers will vary. Possible answer: There was an increase of 5.5 percent in the real GDP in the past year (1.6 / 1.1 = 1.455, 1.455 − 1 = 0.455 = 4.5%). This exceeds the 3.4 percent long-term growth rate for the U.S. economy. Therefore the economy is in an expansion.

### Graphing Exercise

5. Answers will vary. Possible answer: The real rate of growth in GDP exceeded the long-range growth rate in 1996 through 2000. There appears to have been a recession in the early 1990s and 2001.

   A sample of an acceptable graph appears at the bottom of this page.

### Think Critically

6. Answers will vary. Possible answer: With prices falling, the real value of the individual products produced would have increased. This does not change the fact that reduced amounts of production caused total GDP to fall both in nominal and real terms.

7. Answers will vary. Possible answer: Home construction varies directly with the condition of the economy. When times are good, more homes are built; when times are bad, few people are willing to purchase new home. Dairy products, however, are likely to be purchased regardless of the condition of the economy.

Remind students that businesses are able to earn a profit by achieving total revenues that exceed their total costs. Firms best able to control their costs are likely to be most successful, regardless of the current stage of the business cycle that is found in the economy. A firm such as Dorothy Lane Markets has reduced its marketing costs by eliminating advertising. This has allowed the firm to concentrate on quality, services, and prices. If the economy is in a recession or a boom, this firm is able to offer good quality at low prices to enhance its profitability.

## TEACH

Instruct students to read the **Movers & Shakers** feature about Norman Mayne. Point out that some students may find it helpful to read the article, read the questions at the bottom of the page, and then reread the article.

## ASSESS

Use the questions in Source Reading and Entrepreneurs in Action at the bottom of the profile to assess the students' understanding of this **Movers & Shakers** feature.

### Answers to Source Reading

Answers will vary. Possible answer: Other major retailers reward anyone who stops into their store with coupons and lower prices. Because of the large number of people they reward, they can cut cost only so much. However, Norman Mayne rewards only members. With a limited number of people to reward, he can lower the prices more. In a recession, Mayne's business will gain because he will be able to offer the lowest price to his members.

### Answers to Entrepreneurs in Action

Answers will vary. Possible answers: Call customers to remind them it is time for routine service. Offer a loaner car for service that takes more than a day. Drive customers to work after they drop off their cars. Offer regular customers routine services (i.e., oil changes) at a reduced price. Offer free informational classes to your customers on car maintenance. Sponsor a youth sports team.

# movers & shakers

**Norman Mayne** *CEO, Dorothy Lane Markets*

Headquarters for one of the nation's largest grocery store chains is less than an hour away. Even so, Norman Mayne is proud to say that his three Dorothy Lane Markets are nothing like the chains. In fact, "we ignore what they do," he says.

Mayne is CEO of Dorothy Lane Markets in Dayton and Springboro, Ohio. His father started the business as a fruit stand in 1948. The fruit stand, located on Dorothy Lane, brought in $35 on its first day of business. This was the start of what would become one of the world's leading independent grocery stores. The stores attract visiting grocers from as far away as Europe, Japan, and Australia. The grocers are eager to learn as much as they can about how Dorothy Lane Markets operate.

"Most companies advertise three things," according to Mayne. These are "cheapest prices, best quality, and best service." But, as Mayne has learned, "it's impossible to do all three." In order to offer the cheapest prices, you have to compromise one of the other two, he explains. So after years of spending thousands of dollars each week advertising special prices, Mayne decided to focus his stores on quality and service. He ran his last ad in 1995. He now spends his promotional dollars rewarding his best, most loyal customers, all members of Club DLM.

Mayne gives members of Club DLM special prices. "It's not ethical *not* to give our best customers the best deal," he says. In addition, members receive a monthly newsletter. During Christmas, each store's 100 best customers typically receive a gift and a thank-you note. One year the company's 5,000 best customers received invitations to a popular oldies show that played for one night only in the Dayton area.

Overall, Club DLM allows Mayne and his staff to focus attention on their customers instead of on the competition. Here's how he responded to a recent price war on milk: "Grocers were paying $1.70 for a gallon of milk, yet during the price war they were selling it for 99 cents. We knew that one way to go broke was to lose 71 cents on an item that people buy 200 times a year. So, for Dorothy Lane's best customers we printed coupons that let them buy milk for 49 cents a gallon, limit five. People who just stopped into the store paid full price."

Half of Dorothy Lane's profits come in the fourth quarter of each calendar year. "The three biggest holidays—Thanksgiving, Christmas, and New Year's—all occur during this quarter and are built around great meals," says Mayne. Grocery stores are somewhat recession-proof because people continue to eat during a recession. However, Mayne does notice a difference in spending when customers' pocketbooks are tighter. "We might see our customers purchase lesser-priced cuts of meat, or a less-expensive brand," he says. But one thing seems certain. With Mayne at the helm, Dorothy Lane customers will continue to be rewarded for their business, and Dorothy Lane Markets will continue to be rewarded with loyal customers.

## SOURCE READING

Norman Mayne states, "It's not ethical *not* to give our best customers the best deal." How does this thinking differ from that of many major retail chains? When the economy is in a recession, how might Mayne's business gain from this type of thinking?

## ENTREPRENEURS IN ACTION

Pretend you are the owner of a car repair shop. A major car repair chain moves in across the street, offering better prices. Think of three things that you and your staff can do to retain customers and continue to grow your business.

### Extend the Content

Another American story of business success is Sam Walton's Wal-Mart stores. This firm has been successful in good times and bad. Ask students to identify and discuss reasons for this firm's success despite what is going on in the rest of the economy. Why have its sales grown in some years when the economy has been poor? (If you cannot afford to shop at expensive stores, you may shop at ones that are relatively inexpensive.)

# Objectives

> Explain what is meant by aggregate output and the economy's price level.

> Describe the aggregate demand curve and the aggregate supply curve, and show how they determine the equilibrium level of price and aggregate output.

# Overview

In the study of market economics, the focus is on a particular market, such as the market for pizza. However, the national economy is so complex that you need to simplify in order to focus on the big picture. The perspective broadens from the market for pizza, computers, or cell phones to the market for everything produced in the economy. Aggregate demand and supply curves help you understand how the price and output for the economy as a whole are determined. Like other theoretical models, these can be used to predict what will happen as a result of economic policies and events.

# Key Terms

aggregate output

aggregate demand

price level

aggregate demand curve

aggregate supply curve

## [ In the News ]

### • Defense Spending and the Economy

In 2003, the war on terrorism and a war in Iraq caused government spending on defense and homeland security to increase dramatically. The spending helped a number of areas of the economy and several industries. Spending on new military equipment increased quite a bit in 2003, and the Pentagon planned to continue increasing its budgets. However, in a growing economy, billions in increased spending should have prompted industry to expand facilities and increase hiring. That didn't happen after the war in Iraq. A major reason sharp economic growth didn't take place was that most companies had excess capacity. Defense spending was preventing some layoffs and allowing some firms to maintain profitability. However, many industries still had a shortage in their private-sector orders. Firms had no need to add workers or open new factories to address increased demands. The increased spending by government to support the war in Iraq did not benefit the economy as much as it did following earlier wars. For example, increased defense spending to support the Korean War between late 1950 and the end of 1951 amounted to about 8 percent of the economy. In today's dollars, that amount would be about $800 billion. Total government spending for defense and homeland security was projected to be almost $600 billion in 2003. That's equal to about 6 percent of projected 2003 GDP.

### Think About It

Why do you think the increased spending for defense in 2003 had a smaller impact on the economy than did the increased spending on defense for the Korean War?

343

## National Content Standards in Economics

A complete list of the NCEE Standards appears on pages xxiv–xxv of this book. The following standards are addressed in Lesson 11.4.

Standard 13: Role of Resources in Determining Income

Standard 15: Growth

Standard 18: Macroeconomy—Income, Employment, Prices

Standard 19: Unemployment and Inflation

---

# FOCUS

 **11.4** *Aggregate Demand and Aggregate Supply*

Many students are confused by the use of the word aggregate. There is value in explaining that they can substitute the word "total" for "aggregate" in almost every case to better understand the meaning of a statement. For example the statement "When aggregate demand is equal to aggregate supply, the economy is in equilibrium" becomes "When total demand is equal to total supply, the economy is in equilibrium." Most students will find the second statement easier to understand.

## Objectives

Remind students to read the lesson objectives to help focus their attention before reading the lesson.

## Key Terms

Direct students to create a database using the key terms for this lesson. The database fields should include terms, definitions, and page numbers. Point out that the process of keying the data is an effective way to study key terms.

## [ In the News ]

Instruct students to read the passage and write down their answers. Point out that their answers might change after they finish studying Lesson 11.4.

### Answers to Think About It

Answers will vary. Possible answers: The increased spending for defense in 2003 had a smaller impact because companies had excess capacity. They did not have to hire additional people to meet the increased demand stemming from defense spending.

## Visual Presentation

Use the PowerPoint presentation on the Instructor's Resource CD as an adjunct to your lecture. The presentation also can be used for review.

## Aggregate Output and the Price Level

Remind students that there is an inverse relationship between the quantity of products supplied and the prices charged in competitive market economies. When businesses choose to supply more products (a shift to the right in aggregate supply), they will end up with a surplus of products unless there is a corresponding rightward shift in demand. This surplus will cause them to lower their prices until the quantity of aggregate demand is equal to the quantity of aggregate supply. Supply and demand interact to determine market prices whether the market considered is a single product or encompasses all of aggregate demand and aggregate supply.

**CHECKPOINT**

Invite a student to answer the checkpoint that appears on this page.

### Answer

Aggregate output is the total amount of goods and services produced in the economy during a given period. The average price of aggregate output is the price level.

---

**aggregate output**

A composite measure of all final goods and services produced in an economy during a given period; real GDP

**aggregate demand**

The relationship between the economy's price level and the quantity of aggregate output demanded, with other things constant

**price level**

A composite measure reflecting the prices of all goods and services in the economy relative to prices in a base year

**aggregate demand curve**

A curve representing the relationship between the economy's price level and real GDP demanded per period, with other things constant

---

# Aggregate Output and the Price Level

Picture a pizza. Now picture food more generally. Food includes not just pizza but thousands of edibles, from eggplant to omelets. Although food is more general than pizza, you probably have no difficulty picturing food. Now make the leap from food to all goods and services produced in the economy— food, housing, clothing, entertainment, education, transportation, medical care, and so on.

## Aggregate Output

**Aggregate output** is the total amount of goods and services produced in the economy during a given period. The best measure of aggregate output is *real GDP*. Just as you can talk about the demand for pizza or the demand for food, you can talk about the demand for aggregate output. **Aggregate demand** is the relationship between the average price of aggregate output and the quantity of aggregate output demanded.

## The Price Level

The average price of aggregate output is called the **price level**. You are more familiar than you may think with these aggregate measures. Headlines refer to changes in the growth of aggregate output—as in "Growth Slows in Second Quarter." News accounts also report on changes in the economy's price level— as in "Prices Up Slightly in June." You already have some idea how the economy's price level is computed. What you need to know now is that the price level in any year is an *index number,* or reference number. This compares average prices that year to average prices in some base, or reference, year. If you say that the price level is higher, you mean it's higher compared to where it was. The focus here is on the *price level* of all goods and services produced in the economy *relative to the price level in some base year.*

As discussed in the section about price indexes, the price level in the *base year* has a benchmark value of 100. Price levels in other years are expressed relative to the base-year price level. The price level, or price index, is used not only to compare price levels across time but also to make accurate comparisons of real aggregate output over time.

## Real Gross Domestic Product

Economists use the GDP price index to eliminate any year-to-year changes in GDP due solely to changes in the general price level. After this adjustment is made, remaining changes are simply changes in real output, or changes in the amount of goods and services produced. After adjusting GDP for price changes, you end up with real GDP.

**CHECKPOINT**
What is aggregate output, and what is the economy's price level?

# Aggregate Demand and Aggregate Supply Curves

In Chapters 4 and 5, you learned about the demand and supply of a particular product. Now the focus turns to the demand and supply of the total measure of output—aggregate output, or real GDP.

## The Aggregate Demand Curve

Just as you can talk about the demand for pizza or the demand for movie tickets, you can talk about the demand for aggregate output in the economy. The **aggregate demand curve** shows the relationship between the price level in the economy and the real GDP

---

**Outside Resources**

**Trade Journals** There are trade journals for all kinds of industries—automobiles to zoos. These publications typically report on events of particular interest to businesses that produce or sell products in the relevant industry. Ask students to choose an industry that interests them. Instruct them to go online or to visit a large public library to find a trade journal for that industry. Direct them to report on articles that describe how the industry is doing financially and in terms of its production. What part of the business cycle does the industry appear to be in? Is it doing better than, worse than, or the same as the rest of the economy?

demanded, other things constant. Figure 11.8 shows a hypothetical aggregate demand curve, *AD*. The vertical axis measures an index of the economy's price level relative to a 1996 base-year price level of 100. The horizontal axis shows real GDP, which measures aggregate output in dollars of constant purchasing power (here, based on 1996 prices).

The aggregate demand curve in Figure 11.8 reflects an inverse relationship between the price level in the economy and real GDP demanded. Aggregate demand sums the demands of the four economic decision makers: households, firms, governments, and the rest of the world. As the price level increases, other things constant, households demand less housing and furniture, firms demand fewer trucks and tools, governments demand less computer software and military hardware, and the rest of the world demands less U.S. grain and U.S. aircraft.

Here's a quick explanation of the inverse relationship between price level and real GDP demanded. Real GDP demanded depends in part on household wealth. Some wealth is typ-ically held in bank accounts and in currency. An increase in the price level, other things constant, decreases the purchasing power of bank accounts and currency. Households, therefore, are poorer in real terms when the price level increases, so the quantity of real GDP demanded decreases. Conversely, a reduction in the price level increases the purchasing power of bank accounts and currency. Because households are richer as the price level decreases, the quantity of real GDP demanded increases.

Among the factors held constant along a given aggregate demand curve are the price levels in other countries as well as the exchange rates between the U.S. dollar and foreign currencies. When the U.S. price level increases, U.S. products become more expensive relative to foreign products. Consequently, households, firms, and governments both here and abroad decrease the quantity of U.S. real GDP demanded. On the other hand, a lower U.S. price level makes U.S. goods relatively cheap compared with foreign goods, so the quantity of U.S. real GDP demanded increases.

**The Graphing Workshop**

**Aggregate Demand Curve**                    Figure **11.8**

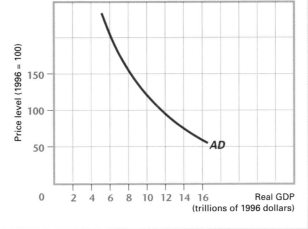

The quantity of output demanded is inversely related to the price level, other things constant. This inverse relationship is reflected by the aggregate demand curve AD.

**Aggregate Demand and Aggregate Supply Curves**

Remind students that many factors can change the total (aggregate) quantity of goods and services demanded and supplied in the economy. Among these is the average price level. When goods and services become more expensive, people who have income that remains the same are not able to buy as many products. Higher prices are often associated with a falling quantity of aggregate demand. Higher prices, however, contribute to greater quantities of goods and services being offered for sale, everything else equal. Changes in the equilibrium price level inevitably result from shifts in aggregate demand, aggregate supply, or both.

***Think Critically Through Visuals***

Direct students to focus their attention on **Figure 11.8—Aggregate Demand Curve**. Point out that the aggregate demand curve in this figure reflects an inverse relationship between the price level in the economy and real GDP demanded.

*The Graphing Workshop* ——— ( See It )

Direct students to the Graphing Workshop for Chapter 11 at **econxtra.swlearning.com**. Students may want to view the **See It** enrichment exercises related to aggregate demand and aggregate supply entitled: **Deriving the Aggregate Demand Curve, Determining Aggregate Output Demanded,** and **Shifting the Aggregate Demand Curve.**

**ENRICH**

Have students locate and copy several advertisements containing price information that were published at least 10 years ago. Based on the information in the ads, ask students to explain what has happened to aggregate demand and supply since the ads were published to change the equilibrium price. What has happened to the nominal and real prices of these products over time?

## Think Critically Through Visuals

Direct students to focus their attention on illustration on this page. Point out that the arrows both go in the same direction.

### NCEE Standard 18: Macroeconomy— Income/Employment, Prices

A nation's overall levels of income, employment, and prices are determined by the interaction of spending and production decisions made by all households, firms, government agencies, and others in the economy.

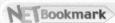

The Graphing Workshop ———— **See It**

Direct students to the Graphing Workshop for Chapter 11 at **econxtra. swlearning.com**. Students may want to click on the **See It** enrichment exercise entitled **Aggregate Supply**.

## Think Critically Through Visuals

Direct students to focus their attention on **Figure 11.9—Aggregate Demand and Supply** on page 347. Point out the positive relationship between the price level and the quantity of aggregate output.

**NET Bookmark**

Direct students to **econxtra. swlearning.com**. Remind them to click on the link for Lesson 11.4 to find the appropriate link for the **NET Bookmark** on page 347.

## Answer

Economic changes were the driving force behind other changes during the twentieth century.

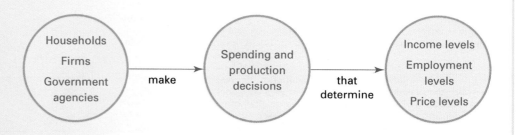

*Households, firms, and government agencies make spending and production decisions that determine income levels, employment levels, and price levels.*

---

**aggregate supply curve**

A curve representing the relationship between the economy's price level and real GDP supplied per period, other things constant

The Graphing Workshop

## The Aggregate Supply Curve

The **aggregate supply curve** shows how much output U.S. producers are willing and able to supply at each price level, other things constant. How does the quantity supplied respond to changes in the price level? The upward-sloping aggregate supply curve *AS* in Figure 11.9 shows a positive relationship between the price level and the quantity of aggregate output that producers supply, other factors remaining constant.

Assumed constant along an aggregate supply curve are (1) resource prices, (2) the state of technology, and (3) the rules of the game that provide production incentives, such as patent and copyright laws. Wage rates are typically assumed to remain constant along the aggregate supply curve. With wages constant, firms find a higher price level more profitable, so they increase real GDP supplied. *Whenever the prices firms receive rise faster than the cost of production,*

*firms find it profitable to expand output. Therefore, real GDP supplied varies directly with the economy's price level, other things constant*

## Equilibrium

The intersection of the aggregate demand curve and aggregate supply curve determines the equilibrium levels of price and real GDP in the economy. Figure 11.9 is a rough depiction of aggregate demand and supply in 2002. Equilibrium real GDP in 2002 was about $9.4 trillion, measured in dollars of 1996 purchasing power. The equilibrium price level in 2002 was 110.6, compared with a price level of 100 in the base year of 1996. At any other price level, quantity demanded would not match quantity supplied.

Although employment is not measured directly along the horizontal axis, firms usually must hire more workers to produce more output. Greater levels of real GDP are beneficial because (1) more goods and services are available

The total output of the economy and its price level are determined at the intersection of the aggregate demand and aggregate supply curves. The equilibrium reflects real GDP and the price level for 2002, using 1996 as the base year.

in the economy and (2) more people are employed.

## Seven Decades of Real GDP and Price Levels

Figure 11.10 traces the U.S. real GDP and price level since 1929. Aggregate demand and aggregate supply curves for 2002 are shown as an example, but all points in the series reflect such intersections. Years of growing GDP are indicated as blue points and years of declining GDP as red ones. Despite the Great Depression of the 1930s and 10 recessions since World War II, the long-term trend of economic growth is unmistakable.

Real GDP, measured along the horizontal axis in 1996 constant dollars, grew from $0.8 trillion in 1929 to $9.4 trillion in 2002—an eleven-fold increase and an average annual growth rate of 3.4 percent. The price level also rose, but not as much, rising from only 12.6 in 1929 to 110.6 in 2002—an eight-fold increase and an average inflation rate of 3.0 percent per year.

Because the U.S. population is growing all the time, the economy must create new jobs just to employ the addi-

tional people looking for work. For example, the U.S. population grew from 122 million in 1929 to 289 million in 2002, a rise of 137 percent. Fortunately, employment grew even faster, from 48 million in 1929 to 134 million in 2002, for a growth of 179 percent. During the last seven decades, employment grew more than enough to keep up with a growing population. The United States has created more jobs than any other economy in the world.

Not only did the number of workers more than double, but workers' average level of education increased as well.

### NETBookmark

Would you like to learn more about the economic history of the past century? J. Bradford De Long's brief article, "Slouching Toward Utopia," provides one economist's evaluation of key developments. Access this article through econxtra.swlearning.com. According to the article, what changes were history's driving force during the twentieth century?

*econxtra.swlearning.com*

## Group Activity

Ask groups of students to compare their favorite stories from their parents or grandparents about how much harder things were when they were young. ("When I was your age, I had to walk three miles to school through the snow and I didn't even own a pair of ear muffs.") Each group should choose the story that best illustrates why it is difficult to compare standards of living over long periods of time. Ask the groups to act out the story they chose and explain what information they would need in order to be able to make an accurate comparison of their own lives to the lives of their older relatives.

---

### Think Critically Through Visuals

Direct students to focus their attention on **Figure 11.10—U.S. Real GDP and Price Level Since 1929** on page 348. Point out that despite the Great Depression and the 10 recessions since World War II, the long-term trend of economic growth is unmistakable.

### The Graphing Workshop

See It

Direct students to the Graphing Workshop for Chapter 11 at **econxtra.swlearning.com**. Students may want to click on the **See It** enrichment exercise entitled **Temporary Supply Shocks in the Aggregate Supply and Demand Model**.

### Think Critically Through Visuals

Direct students to focus their attention on the photograph on page 348. Ask for a volunteer to answer the question posed in the caption.

**Answer**

Answers will vary. Possible answers: Technology, education, and higher qualities of human capital and physical capital lead to increases in the productivity of individual workers.

### CHECKPOINT

Invite a student to answer the checkpoint that appears on page 348.

**Answer**

The aggregate demand curve shows the relationship between the price level in the economy and the real GDP demanded, other things constant. The aggregate supply curve shows how much output U.S. producers are willing and be able to supply at each price level, other things constant. The intersection of the aggregate demand curve and aggregate supply curve determine equilibrium levels of price and real GDP in the economy.

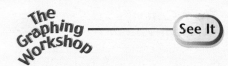

The Graphing Workshop

**See It**

Direct students to the Graphing
Workshop for Chapter 11 at
**econxtra.swlearning.com**.
Students may want to click on the **See
It** enrichment exercise entitled **The
Circular Flow Model**.

## Ethics in Action

Have students work in pairs to
discuss this ethical issue and
develop an answer to the question presented on page 349.

### Answers to Think Critically

The government would benefit
from more accurate measures of
the CPI because 30 percent of federal outlays are tied to the CPI.
Those receiving the federal outlays
would be hurt by the CPI adjustment. The government should use
the most accurate measure possible because it would save the government $180 billion annually.

## APPLY

Assign Lesson 11.4 from the
Contemporary Economics Workbook.

Encourage students to apply their
knowledge of concepts presented in
this lesson as they explore
**econxtra.swlearning.com**.

## ASSESS

Assign all or part of Lesson 11.4
Assessment on page 350 as homework or an in-class activity.

## Xtra! Study Tools

Direct students to the online study
tools for Lesson 11.4 at
**econxtra.swlearning.com**.

## CLOSE

**Revisit** the In the News feature on the
first page of the lesson.
**Review** the objectives for Lesson 11.4.

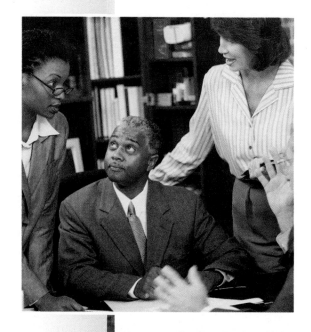

The Graphing Workshop

**What factors led to the increase in
the productivity of the individual
worker?**

Employment of other resources, especially capital goods, also rose sharply.
What's more, the level of technology
improved steadily, thanks to breakthroughs such as the computer chip.
The availability of more and higher-
quality human capital and physical
capital increased the productivity of
each worker. This contributed to the
eleven-fold jump in real GDP since
1929.

Real GDP is important, but the best
measure of the standard of living in an
economy is *real GDP per capita*, which
indicates how much an economy produces on average per resident. Because
real GDP grew much faster than the
population since 1929, real GDP *per
capita* jumped five-fold from $6,740 in
1929 to about $32,800 in 2002. The
United States is the largest economy in
the world and has been a leader in real
GDP per capita.

**CHECKPOINT**

What are the aggregate demand
and aggregate supply curves, and
how do they determine the
economy's equilibrium price level
and aggregate output?

**U.S. Real GDP and Price Level Since 1929**

**Figure 11.10**

Both real GDP and the
price level increased
since 1929. Blue points
indicate years of
growing real GDP, and
red points are years of
declining real GDP. Real
GDP in 2002 was more
than 11 times greater
than it was in 1929. The
price level was more
than 8 times greater.

Source: Based on annual
estimates from the U.S.
Department of Commerce.

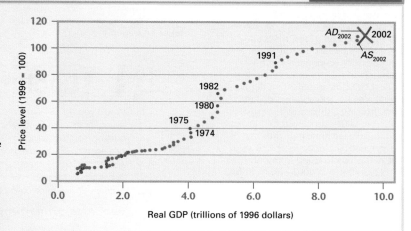

**348**        **CHAPTER 11**   Economic Performance

*Curriculum Connection—Mathematics*

In September 2003, the seasonally adjusted consumer price index stood at 185.0. Ask students to
visit the government web site at www.access.gpo.gov/congress to find the current index in
*Economic Indicators*. Instruct them to determine how much inflation has taken place since
September 2003 by dividing 185.0 into the current index and subtracting 1 from the answer. What
does this show about changes in nominal prices in recent years?

# Ethics in Action

**A New, Improved CPI** There is no perfect way to measure changes in the price level. The Consumer Price Index (CPI) tends to overstate the true impact of inflation on the price level. The problem occurs in part because the CPI does not take into consideration that higher prices could result from improved quality rather than inflation. Another reason CPI tends to overstate inflation is that it does not recognize that the prices of items in the market basket may change at different rates. Researchers have concluded that the CPI overestimates inflation by about 1 percentage point per year. About 30 percent of all federal outlays are tied to changes in the CPI. The Internal Revenue Service uses the CPI to determine changes in tax brackets. Firms and unions determine changes in cost-of-living allowances based on the CPI. The government also bases Social Security benefits and welfare payments on changes in the CPI. A 1 percent downward correction in the CPI would save the federal budget $180 billion annually by the year 2008. The Bureau of Labor Statistics is now working on this problem. It has introduced an experimental version of the CPI that would reduce measured inflation.

## Think Critically

Who would benefit from a more accurate measurement of CPI? Who would be hurt financially? Should government use the more accurate measurement? Why or why not?

# Sharpen Your Life Skills

## Evaluate Data

he data in the table below can be sed to draw conclusions about the verage standard of living enjoyed y people in Mexico between 1997 d 2000. In evaluating data, you st identify the subject. Next, iden-y the types of data given. Then termine the quantities in which e data are recorded. Lastly, mpare the values of the data.

## Apply Your Skill

1. What happened to the real GDP in Mexico during these years?

2. What impact would the growth in population have had on the standard of living in Mexico?

3. Why would lower rates of inflation tend to cause most people in Mexico to have better standards of living?

4. Why do nations that have lower birth rates tend to have higher standards of living?

**ta About Mexico, 1997–2000**

| ear | 1997 | 1998 | 1999 | 2000 |
|---|---|---|---|---|
| Jominal GDP (billions of U.S. dollars) | $401 | $421 | $480 | $574 |
| opulation (millions of people) | 97.6 | 98.6 | 99.5 | 100.4 |
| hange in Prices | —— | 15.9% | 16.6% | 9.5% |

## Evaluate Data

After studying Lesson 11.4, students should be able to answer the questions on this page.

## Answer

Answers will vary. Possible answer: By adjusting the nominal GDP for inflation and population growth, the real GDP per capita can be determined. Students might also want to know how evenly income is distributed in Mexico.

## Apply Your Skill

Consider allowing students to work in pairs for this assignment.

## Answers

1. Answers will vary. Possible answer: Although the nominal GDP increased in these years, the real GDP declined in most of them. For example, in 1998, nominal GDP increased by almost 5 percent. However, when the 15.9 percent increase in prices is considered, the real GDP fell by more than 10 percent.

2. When the 1 percent increase in population is included the real GDP, per capita declined by more than 11 percent in 1998. This indicates that the average standard of living in Mexico fell in 1998. Similar conclusions can be drawn from the data about other years until 2000, when the real GDP per capita increased.

3. Answers will vary. Possible answer: Inflation does not harm all people equally. Those who are unemployed or work on a part-time basis will be less able to deal with higher prices than those who have full-time jobs. These people are most likely to receive higher incomes to make up for the higher prices.

4. Lower birth rates mean that production needs to be divided among fewer people.

## RETEACH

Remind students that prices of some goods change throughout the year due to seasonal fluctuations. For example, it is reasonable to expect fresh strawberries to cost more in December than they do in May. For this reason, the government provides two indexes for the Consumer Price Index. One is adjusted for these annual changes and the other is not. Which index do students believe would be a better indicator of how the economy is doing? What other prices would they expect to fluctuate at specific times of each year? (heating oil in the winter, gasoline in the summer)

### Key Concepts

1. Answers will vary. Possible answer: Higher prices will reduce consumers' ability to purchase goods and services. This will reduce the aggregate demand for products throughout the economy.

2. Answers will vary. Possible answer: Aggregate output will fall when nominal GDP grows if the rate of inflation exceeds the rate of growth in aggregate output.

3. Answers will vary. Possible answer: Increased resource prices will reduce firms' profit margins and cause them to produce fewer goods and services. This will shift the location of the aggregate supply curve to the left, causing a higher equilibrium price.

4. Answers will vary. Possible answer: Students would need to know the nominal value of last year's GDP and this year's GDP, the rate of inflation, and the U.S. population in each of these years.

### Graphing Exercise

5. Answers will vary. Possible answer: The average rate of growth in real GDP per capita from 1990 through 2001 was 1.81% ($32,646 / 26,834 = 1.217; 1.217 − 1 = 0.217 = 21.7%; 21.7% / 12 = 1.81%).

   A sample of an acceptable graph appears at the bottom of this page.

### Think Critically

6. Answers will vary. Possible answer: The reduced real GDP per capita must have significantly reduced the average standard of living enjoyed by U.S. citizens. Between 1929 and 1933, the real per capita GDP fell by more than 31 percent.

---

Xtra!
Study Tools
econxtra.swlearning.com

### Key Concepts

1. Explain how your spending would be affected by a 10 percent average increase in prices. How would this change affect aggregate demand for goods and services throughout the economy?

2. How is it possible for aggregate output to fall at the same time that nominal GDP increases by 2 percent?

3. What effect would an increase in the cost of productive resources have on the aggregate supply curve and on the equilibrium prices of products?

4. What would you need to know to be able to determine whether the real GDP per capita increased from last year?

### Graphing Exercise

5. Use the data in the table to construct a bar graph that shows the change in real GDP per capita in the years from 1990 through 2001. What was the average rate of growth in the value over these years?

**Real GDP Per Capita, 1990–2001**

| Year | Real GDP Per Capita | Year | Real GDP Per Capita |
|------|---------------------|------|---------------------|
| 1990 | $26,834 | 1996 | $28,993 |
| 1991 | $26,354 | 1997 | $29,915 |
| 1992 | $26,804 | 1998 | $30,834 |
| 1993 | $27,160 | 1999 | $31,727 |
| 1994 | $27,914 | 2000 | $32,663 |
| 1995 | $28,321 | 2001 | $32,646 |

### Think Critically

6. **History** Study the data in the table. How do you think the lives of many U.S. citizens changed during the Great Depression of the 1930s?

**Real GDP Per Capita, 1929–1938**
**Values in 1929 Prices**

| Year | Real GDP Per Capita | Year | Real GDP Per Capita |
|------|---------------------|------|---------------------|
| 1929 | $857 | 1934 | $639 |
| 1930 | $772 | 1935 | $718 |
| 1931 | $721 | 1936 | $787 |
| 1932 | $611 | 1937 | $845 |
| 1933 | $590 | 1938 | $794 |

---

**Real GDP Per Capita
1990 to 2001**

### Visualizing the Answer—Graphing Exercise

5. The answer includes a graph. Students' graphs should look similar to the one shown here. An Excel spreadsheet containing this graph, along with supporting data, is available on the Instructor's Resource CD.

# The Panic of 1907

During the 1800s, economic panics were a familiar feature of the American economy. Before 1907, the economy had suffered through four such events in the course of 34 years. In the summer of 1907, the American economy began another downturn. Each fall, the financial system suffered stress because money was needed to move crops from the Midwest to the markets in the East and Europe. Thousands of banks across the country, needing to maintain their reserves, withdrew cash from the country's 47 regional banks. These banks, in turn, withdrew cash from other banks in one of three cities that acted as central reserves—most notably, New York City. While not unexpected, the situation did cause short-term interest rates to rise. What was different in 1907 was that the money supply did not increase to meet the demand for money. Gold that usually would have flowed into the United States from Europe due to the higher interest rate did not do so. In 1907, the banking system that had been able to contain the earlier panics failed.

The panic accentuated an already declining stock market, which had lost 8.9 percent of its value since March 12. It would bottom out on November 15 with a decline of 39 percent as people turned their investments into cash.

Although the New York banking community publicly pledged to support the New York banks, depositors of the Knickerbocker Trust Company began a run. Another bank, not wanting to be stuck with worthless checks, refused to process checks from the Knickerbocker bank. On October 22, $8 million was paid out to depositors and the company closed it doors. New Yorkers lined up outside their banks, fearing for their deposits.

Financier J.P. Morgan decided to take action to restore confidence and end the panic. He called a committee of bankers, which first decided that the Knickerbocker's finances were in such bad shape that it could not be helped. It would be allowed to fail while other more sound banks were helped. The panic extended to banks around the country as they worried that New York banks would refuse them loans, and they began to pull out their reserves.

Morgan and his bankers could not contain the crisis and turned to the federal government. After making a direct plea to President Theodore Roosevelt, Morgan secured the aid of the U.S. government, which agreed to deposit $25 million in New York banks. Industrialist John D. Rockefeller also contributed $10 million in an effort to boost depositor confidence. Morgan also was able to get New York bankers to put another $25 million into ailing banks.

Over the next several weeks, the situation slowly got better. By mid-October, the panic had subsided, but the downturn in the business cycle lasted until June 1908. Banks around the country, afraid of being cut off by larger banks, continued to draw down their reserves and hoarded what cash they had. They stopped extending credit to their customers and suspended making cash payments. Thousands of firms that depended on short-term loans went bankrupt, and thousands of individuals lost their jobs. Much of the trade in the country ground to a halt.

## THINK CRITICALLY

Draw a diagram illustrating the effect that a panic and the drawing down of reserves had on local, regional, and national (or central reserve) banks. Your diagram should show the cause and effect of a situation that could cause a banking panic such as that described above for (1) central reserve banks, (2) regional banks, and (3) local banks.

---

## CONNECT to History

### FOCUS

By the early 1900s, recessions and depressions were accepted as a part of the business cycle. But many persons came to believe that the government had a responsibility to control the ups and downs of the economy. The story of the Panic of 1907 was, in many ways, the last straw. J.P. Morgan's efforts to control the scope of the panic pushed the country to the tipping point. Many people wondered what would happen if the country did not have a J.P. Morgan. They did not want the nation's economic fortunes left unregulated to private individuals. This situation would lead to the formation of the Federal Reserve Bank and to more government control over the economy.

### TEACH

Instruct students to read the **Connect to History** feature and complete the assignment at the bottom of the page. A role-play activity can be used to reinforce the concepts presented in this feature. Consider dividing the class into two groups and having the groups take turns playing play out the scenes described here.

### ASSESS

Use the questions at the bottom of the page to assess the students' understanding of this feature.

**Answers to Think Critically**

Answers will vary. Diagrams should clearly show the relationship of the three banks and include causes and effects. An example of an acceptable diagram appears below.

Central banks honor withdrawal requests from regional banks
↓
Regional banks withdraw money from central banks
↓
Regional banks honor withdrawal requests from local banks
↓
Local banks withdraw money from regional banks to maintain reserve
↓
Local banks honor withdrawal requests from depositors
↓
Depositors withdraw money

---

## Bibliography

Chernow, Ron. *The House of Morgan.* New York: Atlantic Monthly Press, 1990.

Foner, Eric, and John A. Garraty, eds. *The Reader's Companion to American History.* Boston: Houghton Mifflin Company, 1991.

Greider, William. *Secrets of the Temple: How the Federal Reserve Runs the Country.* New York: Simon and Schuster, 1987.

Morris, Richard B., and Jeffrey B. Morris. *Encyclopedia of American History.* New York: HarperCollins, 1996.

Parish, Peter J., ed. *Reader's Guide to American History.* Chicago: Fitzroy Dearborn Publishers, 1997.

Puth, Robert C. *American Economic History.* New York: Dryden Press, 1982.

## Summary

### Consider

Ask students to revisit the questions they were asked to consider at the beginning of the chapter. Remind students that they should be able to answer all of the questions after studying Chapter 11.

- How is the economy's performance measured? See page 322—Gross Domestic Product.

- What's gross about the gross domestic product? See page 322—Gross Domestic Product.

- What's the impact on gross domestic product if you make yourself a sandwich for lunch? See page 323—Calculating GDP.

- How can you compare the value of production in one year with that in other years if prices change over time? See page 344—Real Gross Domestic Product.

- What's the business cycle? See page 336—Recessions and Expansions.

- What's the big idea with the national economy? See page 339—Economic Indicators.

### Exam*View*

Use **Exam***View* to assess student learning.

- Create a chapter test using questions from the existing test bank.

- Add your own questions to the existing test bank.

- Generate multiple forms of a chapter test.

### Study Skills

Offer the following study skills suggestions for students as they review this chapter.

- Outline the chapter.
- Review key terms.
- Review Checkpoints.
- Work in pairs to quiz each other.
- Use Xtra! Study Tools for each lesson.

Direct students to the online quiz preparation for Chapter 11 at **econxtra.swlearning.com**.

 **11** # Chapter Assessment

## Summary

### 11.1 Gross Domestic Product

a  *Gross domestic product (GDP)* measures the market value of all final goods and services produced in a country in a year. GDP can be used to track an economy's performance over time or compare different economies with each other at a point in time.

**Xtra! Quiz Prep**
econxtra.swlearning.com

b  To measure GDP accurately, it is necessary to avoid double counting. This can be done only by totaling the value of final goods and services produced or by finding the sum of the value added at each step in producing a product.

c  The expenditure approach to calculating GDP counts all spending carried out to purchase goods and services produced. The income approach totals the value of all income earned producing goods and services.

d  These two methods reach the same total because one person's spending is automatically another person's income.

### 11.2 Limitations of GDP Estimation

a  There are several difficulties that must be overcome to measure GDP. Chief among these is complex nature of production. A number of simplifications are made. GDP includes only products that are sold in legal markets. GDP is sometimes adjusted for *depreciation* to calculate *net domestic product.* Finally, GDP usually ignores the cost of pollution arising from production.

b  GDP often is adjusted for price changes. When prices increase, it is possible for the *nominal GDP* to grow with no actual increase in the amounts of goods and services produced.

c  The *Consumer Price Index (CPI)* measures the change in prices charged for a market basket of 400 goods and services sold by retailers across the nation. The GDP price index is found by dividing nominal GDP by *real GDP* and multiplying by 100.

### 11.3 Business Cycles

a  Over time, the level of economic activity fluctuates in a fairly regular way. These fluctuations are commonly called the *business cycle.*

b  Business cycles involve periods of *expansion* and periods of *recession.* Expansions are periods of time in which production grows. Recessions occur when real GDP declines for at least two successive quarters, or at least six months.

c  Production tends to increase over time because of (1) increases in the amount and quality of resources, especially labor and capital, (2) improvement in technology, and (3) improvement in the *rules of the game.*

d  There are factors within the economy that change with the business cycle. Factors that change before the overall economy are *leading indicators.* Those that change at the same time as the overall economy are *coincident indicators.* Those that change after the overall economy are *lagging indicators.*

### 11.4 Aggregate Demand and Aggregate Supply

a  The total production of all goods and services within an economy is called the *aggregate output.* The total demand for all goods and services within an economy is called the *aggregate demand.* Price levels in an economic system are determined by the interaction of aggregate output and aggregate demand.

b  The *aggregate demand curve* slopes downward, indicating that the quantity of aggregate output demanded increases as the price level falls. The *aggregate supply curve* slopes upward, indicating that the quantity of aggregate output supplied increases as the price level increases.

c  Over the past seven decades, real GDP in the United States has increased by 1,100 percent. The best measure of a nation's standard of living is its real GDP per capita.

**352**  **CHAPTER 11**  Economic Performance

### 11.1 Assessment

Continued from page 327

#### Think Critically

7. The price of a gallon of gasoline would be $1.00.

$20 / 40 = \$.50$

$\$.50 + \$.18 = \$.68$

$\$.68 \times 1.25 = \$.85$

$\$.85 + \$.07 = \$.92$

$\$.92 + \$.08 = \$1.00$

If the value of the gasoline at each step in its production process were added, the total value would far exceed the price charged to consumers. This is why only the final price is included when calculating GDP.

8. French fries were produced using more resources, particularly labor. This justifies their greater value and contribution.

# Review Economic Terms

Choose the term that best fits the definition. On a separate sheet of paper, write the letter of the answer. Some terms may not be used.

_____ 1. The market value of all final goods and services produced in the United States during a given period, usually a year

_____ 2. The structure of economic activity in a locality, a region, a country, a group of countries, or the world

_____ 3. Fluctuations reflecting the rise and fall of economic activity relative to the long-term growth trend of the economy

_____ 4. Measures that usually predict recessions or expansions in the economy

_____ 5. Household purchases of final goods and services except for new residences, which count as investment

_____ 6. Total spending on all final goods and services produced in the economy during the year

_____ 7. The purchase of new plants, new equipment, new buildings, new residences, and net additions to inventories

_____ 8. The value of capital stock that is used up or becomes obsolete in producing GDP

_____ 9. GDP based on prices at the time of the transaction; current-dollar GDP

_____ 10. The economy's aggregate output measured in dollars of constant purchasing power, GDP measured in terms of the goods and services produced

_____ 11. A composite measure reflecting the prices of all goods and services in the economy relative to prices in a base year

_____ 12. A measure of inflation based on the cost of a fixed market basket of goods and services purchased by a typical family

_____ 13. A decline in total production lasting at least two consecutive quarters, or at least six months

_____ 14. The phase of economic activity during which the economy's total output increases

a.  **aggregate demand**

b.  **aggregate demand curve**

c.  **aggregate expenditure**

d.  **aggregate income**

e.  **aggregate output**

f.  **aggregate supply curve**

g.  **business cycle**

h.  **consumer price index (CPI)**

i.  **consumption**

j.  **depreciation**

k.  **economy**

l.  **expansion**

m.  **gross domestic product (GDP)**

n.  **investment**

o.  **leading economic indicators**

p.  **nominal GDP**

q.  **price level**

r.  **real GDP**

s.  **recession**

# Review Economic Concepts

15. Which of the following would be included in GDP?

 a. the value of a used car your family purchased

 b. the amount you received in your pay check

 c. the weekly allowance your parents give you

 d. the $30 you received from your aunt for your birthday

16. The __?__ is a method of measuring GDP that adds up all spending on final goods and services produced in the economy.

## Review Economic Terms

1.  m. gross domestic product (GDP)
2.  k. economy
3.  g. business cycle
4.  o. leading economic indicators
5.  i. consumption
6.  c. aggregate expenditure
7.  n. investment
8.  j. depreciation
9.  p. nominal GDP
10. r. real GDP
11. q. price level
12. h. consumer price index (CPI)
13. s. recession
14. l. expansion

## Review Economic Concepts

15. b. the amount you received in your pay check
16. expenditure approach

*Chapter Assessment*     **353**

## Review Economic Concepts

17. False. This does not count toward the real GDP because it is underground activity.

18. Nominal

19. d. 4.0%

20. True

21. Leading economic indicators

22. False. The intensity of the business cycle varies from region to region across the United States.

23. a. expansions and recessions

24. d. real GDP and the price level

## Apply Economic Concepts

25.
- Buying a used bicycle (no)
- Paying for a movie ticket (yes, expenditure approach)
- Being paid to sell magazines (yes, income approach)
- Buying a new coat (yes, expenditure approach)
- Mending your own shirt (no)
- Earning interest on your savings (yes, income approach)
- Earning profit from a business (yes, income approach)
- Paying a toll to use a bridge (yes, expenditure approach)

26. Germany's nominal GDP increased by 4.1 percent (3,560 / 3,420 = 1.041; 1.041 − 1 = 0.041 = 4.1%). The rate of inflation was 2% (122.4 / 120.0 = 1.02; 1.02 − 1 = 0.02 = 2%). Therefore, the real increase in Germany's GDP was 2.1% (4.1% − 2.0% = 2.1%).

27.
- The value of the stock market increased by 12 percent. (When the value of stocks increase, people feel richer and are more likely to spend. This should cause economic activity to increase in the future.)
- The number of orders businesses have received but not filled falls by 8 percent. (When businesses have fewer orders booked, they are less likely to hire workers or produce as many products. This should cause economic activity to decrease in the future.)
- The number of hours employees work each week grows from 42.1 to 44.6. (When employees work more hours, they have more income to spend. This should cause economic activity to increase in the future.)

17. **True or False** If you bake a cake from a cake mix and sell it for $8, you have added $8 to GDP.

18. __?__ GDP has not been adjusted for changes in price.

19. If last year's *consumer price index* was 185.0, and this year's is 192.4 how much inflation has there been in the past year?

    a. 7.4%

    b. 3.8%

    c. 5.0%

    d. 4.0%

20. **True or False** The value of capital *depreciation* is not considered when GDP is calculated.

21. __?__ usually predict what is likely to happen to the economy in the near future.

22. **True or False** A *business cycle* will affect all states, people, and businesses equally.

23. The *business cycle* consists of two phases that are called

    a. expansions and recessions.

    b. recessions and contractions.

    c. inflation and recessions.

    d. expansions and inflation.

24. *Aggregate demand* and *aggregate supply* interact to determine

    a. business profits.

    b. government tax receipts.

    c. investment.

    d. real GDP and the price level.

# Apply Economic Concepts

25. **Measuring GDP** Identify which of the following activities would be included in the measurement of GDP. For those that would be included, tell whether they would be used in the income approach or expenditure approach.

| Activity | Included in GDP? | Expenditure Approach | Income Approach |
|---|---|---|---|
| Buying a used bicycle | _____ | _____ | _____ |
| Paying for a movie ticket | _____ | _____ | _____ |
| Being paid to sell magazines | _____ | _____ | _____ |
| Buying a new coat | _____ | _____ | _____ |
| Mending your own shirt | _____ | _____ | _____ |
| Earning interest on your savings | _____ | _____ | _____ |
| Earning profit from a business | _____ | _____ | _____ |
| Paying a toll to use a bridge | _____ | _____ | _____ |

26. **Calculating Real GDP** Suppose the gross domestic product of Germany was 3,420 billion euros in 2004 and 3,560 billion euros in 2005. Between the same years, the German CPI increased from 120.0 to 122.4. What was the real growth in Germany's real GDP in this time period?

27. **Evaluating Leading Indicators** Suppose the following events took place in the U.S. economy. Explain why each would be a leading indicator and what each would predict about future economic activity in the U.S. economy.

- The value of the stock market increases by 12 percent.

- The number of orders businesses have received but not filled falls by 8 percent.

- The number of hours employees work each week grows from 42.1 to 44.6.

- Business inventories of finished goods decline by 20 percent.

**Real Spending in the U.S. Economy, 1996–2000**
**Values in Billions of 1996 Dollars**

| Year | Consumption | Investment | Government | Net Exports |
|------|-------------|------------|------------|-------------|
| 1996 | $5,237.5 | $1,242.7 | $1,422.9 | − $ 89.0 |
| 1997 | $5,423.9 | $1,392.8 | $1,455.4 | −$113.3 |
| 1998 | $5,683.7 | $1,557.7 | $1,483.3 | −$221.1 |
| 1999 | $5,968.4 | $1,659.0 | $1,531.8 | −$316.9 |
| 2000 | $6,257.8 | $1,772.7 | $1,572.6 | −$399.1 |

29. **Mathematics** In 2001, real GDP was $10,208 billion. Suppose that the real GDP for the United States increased at the following rates in the five years following 2001.

| Year | Rate of Increase in Real GDP | Real GDP in Billions |
|------|------------------------------|----------------------|
| 2002 | 2.4% | _____ |
| 2003 | 2.6% | _____ |
| 2004 | 3.3% | _____ |
| 2005 | 4.1% | _____ |
| 2006 | 2.5% | _____ |

econxtra.swlearning.com

30. Access **EconData Online** through econxtra.swlearning.com. Read the article on Real Gross Domestic Product (GDP). Is it possible for nominal GDP to rise at the same time real GDP declines? Why or why not? For help

28. **Skills Check: Evaluate Data** The data in the table indicate real spending in the economy in the years from 1996 through 2000. Use these data to calculate the real GDP for each of these years. How much growth was there in the real GDP from 1996 through 2000? What does the real GDP per capita in 2000 show about the state of the economy in that year?

Calculate the real value of GDP in 2001 dollars for each of these years. What would this mean for aggregate demand and supply in our economy?

with answering this question, access the data series for nominal GDP and real GDP. These links are provided on the second page of the article.

- Business inventories of finished goods decline by 20 percent. (When inventories decline, businesses normally increase production to replace these inventories. This should cause economic activity to increase in the future.)

## Apply Economic Concepts

28.
| Year | Real GDP in Billions |
|------|----------------------|
| 1996 | $7,814.1 |
| 1997 | $8,158.8 |
| 1998 | $8,503.6 |
| 1999 | $9,842.3 |
| 2000 | $9,204.0 |

There was 17.8 percent growth in the real GDP in these years ($9,204.0 / $7,814.1 = 1.178; 1.178 − 1 = 0.178 = 17.8%). The smaller real GDP per capita in 2000 probably shows that the economy was entering a recession.

29.
| Year | Real GDP in Billions |
|------|----------------------|
| 2002 | $10,382 |
| 2003 | $10,651 |
| 2004 | $11,003 |
| 2005 | $11,454 |
| 2006 | $11,740 |

Answers will vary. Students may point out that the increased rate of growth in the real GDP from 2002 through 2004 would show an expansion of aggregate supply (production) and demand in our economy. The lower rate of growth in 2006 might indicate that the economy was entering a recession.

*e*-con @pps

30. Yes, it is possible for nominal GDP to increase while the real GDP decreases. This will occur when inflation is large enough to overcompensate for a decline in the nation's real GDP.

# Economic Growth

## Chapter Overview

**LESSON 12.1** *The PPF, Economic Growth, and Productivity:* This lesson uses the production possibilities frontier to analyze economic growth. Labor productivity is defined and discussed.

**LESSON 12.2** *Living Standards and Labor Productivity Growth:* This lesson provides an explanation of standard of living. It also addresses the record of U.S. labor productivity growth and explains why even small differences in average growth are important.

**LESSON 12.3** *Issues of Technological Change:* This lesson includes a discussion of the impact of research and development on the standard of living. It explains the relationship between technological change and employment levels. Industrial policy is described.

### Consider

Ask students to consider the questions posed on this page as they study Chapter 12. After studying all three lessons, students should be able to answer the questions. The content related to each question can be found on the pages indicated below.

- Why do surgeons earn more than barbers, and accountants earn more than file clerks? See page 360—Human and Physical Capital.
- Why is the standard of living so much higher in some countries than in others? See page 367—Standard of Living.
- How can a nation boost its standard of living? See page 367—Standard of Living.
- Why is the economy's long-term growth rate more important than short-term fluctuations in economic activity? See page 358—The PPF and Economic Growth.
- What is labor productivity, and why has it grown faster in recent years? See page 368—U.S. Labor Productivity and Output Per Capita.

### POINT YOUR BROWSER

Remind students that they can find additional resources for this chapter at **econxtra.swlearning.com**.

- Xtra! Study Tools
- Net Bookmarks
- Xtra! Quiz Prep
- econ@pps
- Ask the Xpert!

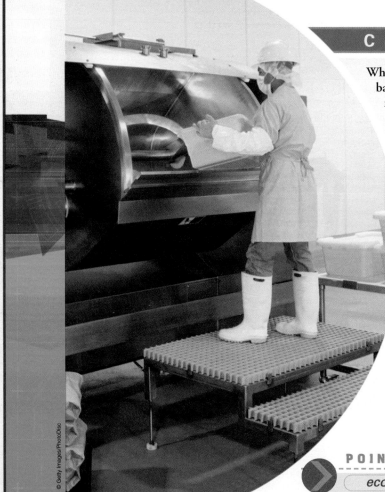

© Getty Images/PhotoDisc

### Consider

Why do surgeons earn more than barbers, and accountants earn more than file clerks?

Why is the standard of living so much higher in some countries than in others?

How can a nation boost its standard of living?

Why is the economy's long-term growth rate more important than short-term fluctuations in economic activity?

What is labor productivity, and why has it grown faster in recent years?

### POINT YOUR BROWSER
*econxtra.swlearning.com*

## Teaching Resources for Chapter 12

- Activities and Projects Masters
- Spanish Resources
- Econ Connection Interactive Tutorial CD
- **Exam**View® CD
- Workbook Teacher's Edition
- Chapter Test Teacher's Edition
- NCEE Standards and Correlation

- Personal Finance Guide
- Social Studies Skills Review
- Instructor's Resource CD
    - PowerPoint Presentations
    - Lesson Plans
    - Video Discussion Guide
    - Answers to Graphing Exercises
- **econxtra.swlearning.com**

# 12.1 The PPF, Economic Growth, and Productivity

## Objectives

> Use the production possibilities frontier to analyze economic growth.

> Define labor productivity, and discuss what can increase it.

## Overview

Throughout history, economic growth has been the primary way of easing poverty and raising living standards. Over the last century, there has been an incredible increase in the U.S. standard of living as measured by the goods and services available per capita. An economy's standard of living grows because of (1) increases in the amount and quality of resources, (2) better technology, and (3) improvements in the rules of the game—such as tax laws, property rights, patent laws, the legal system, and customs of the market—that enable production and exchange.

## Key Terms

**standard of living**

**productivity**

**labor productivity**

**human capital**

**physical capital**

**capital deepening**

**rules of the game**

Review production possibilities frontiers (PPF) that were introduced in Chapter 2. Point out that PPFs may represent the ability to produce all goods and services in an entire economic system, just as they may represent two products. Point out that in this lesson, students will learn why the ability to allocate larger proportions of current production to capital goods will accelerate an economy's rate of growth. This type of allocation of resources is often shown on a PPF.

### Objectives

Remind students to read the lesson objectives to help focus their attention before reading the lesson.

### Key Terms

Direct students to create a database using the key terms for this lesson. The database fields should include terms, definitions, and page numbers. Point out that the process of keying the data is an effective way to study key terms.

## [ In the News ]

Instruct students to read the passage and write down their answers. Point out that their answers might change after they finish studying Lesson 12.1.

### Answers to Think About It

Answers will vary. Possible answers: This one-child policy might have a downward effect on China's future economic growth because there will be fewer people to contribute to the nation's GDP.

### Visual Presentation

Use the PowerPoint presentation on the Instructor's Resource CD as an adjunct to your lecture. The presentation also can be used for review.

## [ In the News ]

### • The Chinese Are Coming on Strong

China's GDP grew approximately 8.3 percent in 2002. Its projected rate for GDP growth in 2004 was 8.5 percent. If China keeps up this rate of growth, it should have the third largest GDP in the world—behind only the United States and Japan and ahead of France, Great Britain and Germany—in three to four years. For 2002 in particular, Chinese GDP totaled $1.2 trillion. In comparison, France's GDP for that year totaled $1.4 trillion, Great Britain's $1.6, and Germany's $2.0. Significantly, however, the growth rates of these three competitors were much lower than China's 8.3 percent rate. France's economy grew at a 1.2 percent rate in 2002. Great Britain's grew at 1.9 percent, and Germany's, at less than 0.75 percent. Of course, it should be many years before the Chinese come close to Japan's $4.0 trillion economy or the United States' 2002 GDP of $10.4 trillion, which exceeded the total GDPs of all other nations in the top six. Nonetheless, the Chinese are in the race and accelerating.

### Think About It

China's current population is about 1.3 billion people. To control its population growth rate, the government enforces a "one-child" policy that penalizes people for having more than one child and rewards them for having only one. What effects, if any, do you think this policy might have on China's future economic growth?

◀ ▮ ▶

**357**

### National Content Standards in Economics

A complete list of the NCEE Standards appears on pages xxiv–xxv of this book. The following standards are addressed in Lesson 12.1.

Standard 1: Scarcity

Standard 2: Marginal Cost/Benefit

Standard 4: Role of Incentives

Standard 10: Role of Economic Institutions

Standard 13: Role of Resources in Determining Income

Standard 14: Profit and the Entrepreneur

Standard 15: Growth

**The PPF and Economic Growth**

Consider having students work in pairs to reinforce the concepts presented in this section. Ask one student to read the section aloud as the other student studies Figure 12.1. Then, have the student who has been studying the figure explain it to the reader.

***Think Critically Through Visuals***

Direct students to focus their attention on **Figure 12.1—Economic Growth Shown by Outward Shifts of the Production Possibilities Frontier.** Point out that understanding this figure is key to understanding the PPF and economic growth.

# The PPF and Economic Growth

The easiest way to introduce the idea of economic growth is to begin with the production possibilities frontier, or PPF. The *production possibilities frontier,* first introduced in Chapter 2, shows alternative combinations of goods that the economy can produce if available resources are used efficiently. Here are the assumptions used to develop the frontiers shown in Figure 12.1. During the period under consideration, usually a year, the quantity of resources in the economy and the level of technology are assumed to remain unchanged. Also assumed fixed during the period are the rules of the game that enable production and exchange. These "rules" will be discussed at the end of this section.

In Figure 12.1, production is sorted into two broad categories—consumer goods and capital goods. Capital goods are used to produce other goods. For example, the economy can make both pizzas and pizza ovens. Pizzas are consumer goods, and pizza ovens are capital goods.

When resources are employed efficiently, the production possibilities frontier *CI* in each panel of Figure 12.1 shows the possible combinations of consumer goods and capital goods that can be produced in a given year. Point *C* depicts the quantity of consumer goods produced if all the economy's resources are employed efficiently to produce them. Point *I* depicts the same for capital goods. Points inside the frontier are inefficient. Points outside the frontier are unattainable, given the resources, technology, and rules of the game. The production possibilities frontier is bowed out because resources are not perfectly adaptable to the production of both goods. Some resources are specialized and better suited for a particular good.

## Economic Growth and the PPF

*An outward shift of the production possibilities frontier reflects economic growth.* This is shown in each panel of Figure 12.1. What can generate this growth? Any increase in the availability of resources, such as a growth in the labor supply or in the capital stock, shifts the frontier outward. Labor can increase because of an increase in either the quantity or the quality of labor. For example, growth in

---

**Economic Growth Shown by Outward Shifts of the Production Possibilities Frontier**  | **Figure 12.1**

An economy that produces more capital goods will grow more, as shown by a shifting outward of the production possibilities frontier. More capital goods and fewer consumer goods are produced in panel (b) than in panel (a), so the PPF shifts outward more in panel (b).

**(a) Lower growth**

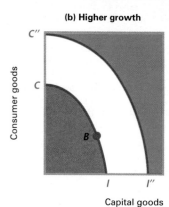

**(b) Higher growth**

---

***Outside Resources***

**Government Statistics** The *Statistical Abstract of the United States* provides recent data about labor productivity and business investments in new tools and machinery. The *Statistical Abstract* can be accessed at www.census.gov/statab/www.

the population can increase the number of workers. An increase in education levels can increase the quality of workers. The greater the quantity or quality of workers, the more the economy can grow, as shown by an outward shift of the PPF.

The capital stock expands if the economy produces more capital goods this year. Any improvement in technology also expands the frontier by making more efficient use of existing resources. Technological change often improves the quality of capital goods. It also can increase the productivity of any resource.

Finally, any improvements in the rules of the game—such as tax laws, property rights, patent laws, the legal system, and customs of the market—that encourage production and exchange will promote growth and expand the frontier. For example, the economy can grow as a result of a patent law revision that encourages more inventions or legal reforms that reduce transaction costs. In summary, *the economy grows because of a greater availability of resources, an improvement in the quality of resources, technological breakthroughs that make better use of resources, or improvements in the rules of the game that enhance production incentives.*

### Capital and Growth

The amount of capital produced this year will affect the location of the PPF next year. For example, in panel (a) of Figure 12.1, the economy has chosen point *A* from possible points along *CI*. The capital produced this year shifts the PPF next year out to *C'I'*. However, if more capital is produced this year, as reflected by point *B* in panel (b), the economy will grow more next year. The PPF will shift farther outward next year, to *C"I"*.

An economy that produces more capital this year is said to *invest* more in capital. As you can see, to invest more in capital goods, people must give up some consumer goods. Thus, the opportunity cost of more capital goods this year is having fewer consumer goods available this year. More generally, to invest in capital, people in the economy must save more now—that is,

they must give up some current consumption. Investment cannot occur without saving. Economies that save more can invest and grow more.

**CHECKPOINT**
How does the PPF show economic growth?

# Productivity

Productivity measures how efficiently resources are employed. In simplest terms, the greater the productivity, the more goods and services can be produced from a given amount of resources. Economies that use resources more efficiently create a higher **standard of living**, meaning that more goods and services are produced per person.

## Labor Productivity

**Productivity** compares total output to a specific measure of input. It usually reflects an average, expressing total output divided by the amount of a particular kind of resource employed, such as bushels of grain per acre of farm land. **Labor productivity** is the output per unit of labor. It measures total output divided by the hours of labor employed to produce that output.

Economists can focus on the productivity of any resource, such as labor, capital, or land. When agriculture made up the bulk of output in the economy, land productivity, such as bushels of grain per acre, shaped the standard of living. Where soil was rocky and barren, people were less well off than where soil was fertile and fruitful. Even today, in many countries around the world, land productivity determines the standard of living.

Industrialization and trade have freed many economies from dependence on land fertility. Today some of the world's most productive economies have relatively little land or have land of poor fertility. For example, Japan has a relatively

**standard of living**
An economy's level of economic prosperity; best measured by the value of goods and services produced per person

**productivity**
Compares output to a specific measure of input; usually reflects an average, such as bushels of grain per acre of farm land

**labor productivity**
Output per unit of labor; measured as total output divided by the hours of labor employed to produce that output

## Productivity

Remind students that productivity is a measure of the amount or value of production that can be achieved from a fixed set of resources. The more efficiently resources are used, the greater productivity will be, and the better the standard of living is likely to become.

## Answer

Answers will vary. Possible answer: In the third quarter of 2003, productivity in the manufacturing sector increased 9 percent; productivity in durable goods manufacturing increased 14.8 percent, and nondurable goods increased 3.1 percent.

## Think Critically Through Visuals

Direct students to focus their attention on the photographs on page 361. Ask for a volunteer to answer the question posed in the caption.

## Answer

In the photo on the left, an office worker depicts human capital, and a computer depicts physical capital. In the photo on the right, a farmer depicts human capital, and a tractor depicts physical capital. As an economy accumulates more human and physical capital per worker, labor productivity increases and the standard of living increases.

---

*human capital*

The accumulated knowledge, skill, and experience of the labor force

*physical capital*

The machines, buildings, roads, airports, communications networks, and other manufactured creations used to produce goods and services; also called capital goods

*capital deepening*

An increase in the quantity and quality of capital per worker; one source of rising labor productivity

*rules of the game*

The formal and informal institutions that provide production incentives and promote economic activity, such as laws, customs, and conventions

---

high living standard even though its population, which is about 40 percent that of the United States, lives on a land area that is only 4 percent of the U.S. land area. Put another way, compared to the United States, Japan has only one tenth the land area per capita.

### Human and Physical Capital

Labor is the resource most commonly used to measure productivity. Why labor? First, labor accounts for a large share of the cost of production—about 70 percent on average. Second, labor is more easily measured than other inputs, whether it's in hours of work per week or number of full-time workers per year. Measures of employment and hours worked are more readily available and more reliable than measures of other resources.

The resource most responsible for increasing labor productivity is capital. The two broad categories of capital are human capital and physical capital. **Human capital** is the accumulated knowledge, skill, and experience of the labor force. As individual workers acquire more human capital, their productivity and incomes grow. That's why surgeons earn more than barbers, and accountants earn more than file clerks. You are reading this book right now to increase your human capital.

**Physical capital**, or *capital goods*, includes the machines, buildings, roads, airports, communications networks, and other manufactured cre-

**NET**Bookmark

Access the Bureau of Labor Statistics (BLS) web page on Quarterly Labor Productivity through econxtra. swlearning.com. Find the latest news release on productivity. Read the information about productivity growth in the manufacturing sectors of the U.S. economy. Then summarize the trends in productivity growth in one or two sentences.

*econxtra.swlearning.com*

---

ations used to produce goods and services. Think about the difference between digging a ditch with your bare hands and digging it with a shovel. Now compare that shovel to an excavating machine, such as a backhoe. More physical capital obviously makes a digger more productive.

As an economy accumulates more human and physical capital per worker, labor productivity increases and the standard of living grows. The most productive combination of all is human capital combined with physical capital. For example, one certified public accountant with a computer and specialized software can sort out a company's finances more quickly and more accurately than could a hundred high-school-educated file clerks with pencils and paper.

### Capital Deepening

Two kinds of changes in capital can improve worker productivity:

**1.** An increase in the *quantity* of capital per worker, and

**2.** An improvement in the *quality* of capital per worker, as reflected by technological change.

More capital per worker and better capital per worker generally result in more output per worker.

An increase in the quantity and quality of capital per worker is called **capital deepening**. This is one source of rising labor productivity. *Capital deepening contributes to labor productivity and to economic growth.* Over time, more output per worker translates into more output per person, meaning a higher standard of living.

Changes in the *quantities* of labor and capital account for less than half of economic growth. Most growth comes from improvements in the *quality* of resources. As technological breakthroughs lead to new and better capital, total output increases. Thus, capital serves as the primary engine for economic growth.

### Rules of the Game

Perhaps the most complex ingredients of productivity and growth are the **rules of the game**. These include the

---

*Economic Headlines*

Ask students to find newspaper or magazine articles describing a technological breakthrough that will enhance productivity in the economy. Instruct students to read the article and write a brief summary, making sure to include a reference citation. Identify the style you want them to use for the citation.

As an alternative, you might locate several articles of interest and provide citations for students to use in locating one of the articles. Direct students to read the article they have chosen, and write a brief explanation of how it relates to this lesson.

Identify the human capital and physical capital in each of these images. Why do you think human capital is more productive in combination with physical capital?

# Ethics in Action

## Training Foreign Workers to Take Your Job

To reduce costs, a growing number of technology companies in the United States are replacing U.S. workers with less-expensive foreigners. In many cases, the U.S. workers are paid to train their own replacements before being laid off. The situation is spurred by the government's nonimmigrant visa program and the L-1 classification. The L-1 visa permits companies to transfer workers from overseas offices to the United States for up to three years. Moreover, the L-1 allows those companies to pay the foreign workers the lower wage they would be earning in their own country. An American computer programmer earns about $60 per hour in wages and benefits. Indian, Pakistani, or Chinese programmers working in their native countries receive about $10 an hour.

### Think Critically

Do you think importing less-expensive foreign workers via the L-1 visa classification is an ethical business practice? Why or why not?

## Curriculum Connection—History

Ask students to identify an invention that changed production and the way Americans lived in the nineteenth century. Obvious choices would include electric lights, railroads, the telegraph, and the use of interchangeable parts. They should write an essay describing the conditions that contributed to the creation of the invention and how it changed productivity in the United States. How were these changes similar to new production methods introduced in the twentieth century?

Direct students to focus their attention on the photograph at the top of page 362. Point out that investment in new technology can raise future standards of living.

### Main Idea

### NCEE Standard 15: Growth

Investment in factories, machinery, new technology, and in the health, education, and training of people can raise future standards of living.

## THE WALL STREET JOURNAL

**Reading It Right**

Invite a student to explain the relevance of the statement from *The Wall Street Journal* that appears on page 362.

**Answer**

Answers will vary. Possible answer: The terrorist attacks were a destabilizing event in our country's history and have discouraged many investments in the economy. This decrease in investments will have a long-lasting effect on the country's production growth.

*Think Critically Through Visuals*

Direct students to focus their attention on the photograph at the bottom of page 362. Ask for a volunteer to answer the questions posed in the caption.

**Answer**

The sign represents the "rules of the game." In this case, it is laws that protect economic productivity. If something were to happen to the electrical transformer, there would be a decrease in productivity.

## CHECKPOINT

Invite a student to answer the checkpoint that appears on page 362.

**Answer**

Labor productivity is the output produced by a laborer. An increase in the quality of capital can increase it.

**Main Idea** Growth

*Investments that increase the quality and quantity of capital per worker contribute to rising labor productivity. This, in turn, leads to more output per worker, and higher standards of living.*

© Getty Images/PhotoDisc

## THE WALL STREET JOURNAL

**Reading It Right** What's the relevance of the following statement from *The Wall Street Journal:* "Some economists say productivity growth will take an additional and longer-lasting hit in the terrorist attack's aftermath."

What "rule" do you think this sign represents? How would it affect productivity in the economy?

© Getty Images/PhotoDisc

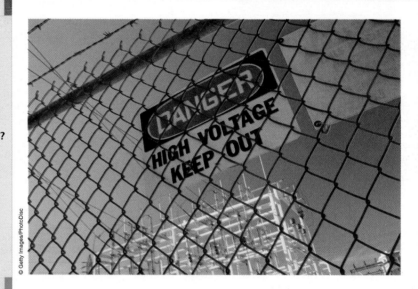

**362** CHAPTER 12 Economic Growth

formal and informal institutions that provide production incentives and promote economic activity. Rules of the game include the laws, customs, and conventions that encourage people to undertake productive activity. A stable political environment and a system of well-defined property rights are important. Little investment will occur if potential investors think their capital might be taken over by government, stolen by thieves, destroyed by civil unrest, or blown up by terrorists.

Improvements in the rules of the game can affect the incentives that reward successful innovation and investment. Better incentives can boost economic growth and improve the standard of living. For example, a more stable political climate could promote investment in the economy. Conversely, destabilizing events such as wars and terrorist attacks can discourage investment and harm productivity and economic growth.

✔ **CHECKPOINT**
What is labor productivity, and what can increase it?

## RETEACH

Starting in the late 1950s, the U.S. government undertook a major construction program designed to link the nation's economic centers with a limited-access highway system. Although such roads existed in some states prior to that time, the majority of states relied on two-lane roads with many stop signs and traffic crossings for transportation. Ask students to explain how productivity in the United States has been affected by the construction of the interstate highway system.

## Key Concepts

1. Why does the U.S. production possibilities frontier shift outward in May and June of each year? What does this have to do with the graduation of many students from high school or college?

2. Why is it more difficult for poorer nations to invest in capital goods than it is for wealthier nations?

3. Why wouldn't the act of giving new computers to the rural residents of a less-developed country add much to that nation's labor productivity?

4. How is capital deepening demonstrated by an increased number of students who purchase computers to help them in their studies?

5. How could a cut in payroll taxes make businesses more productive?

## Graphing Exercise

6. Use the data in the table to construct a bar graph of investment in physical capital during the 1990s. Explain how changes in the level of investment in physical capital are likely to affect productivity in our economy.

| Year | Investment in Physical Capital (in billions of real 1996 dollars) |
|------|---------------------------|
| 1992 | $ 630.6 |
| 1994 | $ 744.6 |
| 1996 | $ 899.4 |
| 1998 | $1,135.9 |
| 2000 | $1,350.7 |

## Think Critically

7. **Management** You are the president of a small corporation. Your firm made good profits last year and could afford to pay increased dividends. You, however, think those funds should be used to purchase a new computer system to improve the efficiency of your firm's production. Write a letter to your firm's stockholders, explaining the benefits of your proposed use of the firm's profits.

8. **Research** Use newspapers or Internet sources to find information about college programs you might enroll in to improve your human capital. Explain how completing a college degree could increase your productivity.

Xtra!
Study Tools
econxtra.swlearning.com

Lesson 12.1 • *The PPF, Economic Growth, and Productivity* **363**

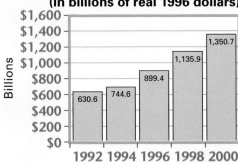

**Investment in Physical Capital (in billions of real 1996 dollars)**

630.6  744.6  899.4  1,135.9  1,350.7
1992 1994 1996 1998 2000

*Visualizing the Answer— Graphing Exercise*

6. The answer includes a graph. Students' graphs should look similar to the one shown here. An Excel spreadsheet containing this graph, along with supporting data, is available on the Instructor's Resource CD.

*Key Concepts*

1. Answers will vary. Possible answer: Millions of students graduate from high school or college each May or June and join the labor force. This causes the production possibilities frontier to shift outward.

2. Answers will vary. Possible answer: Poorer nations need to devote a larger share of their limited production to consumption so that their residents can have even a minimal standard of living. This leaves them little to invest.

3. Answers will vary. Possible answer: Physical capital can add to productivity only when there is sufficient human capital to allow people to use it effectively.

4. Answers will vary. Possible answer: Students who are familiar with computer technology often learn more quickly and have a higher productivity rate.

5. Answers will vary. Possible answer: Lower payroll taxes (i.e., Social Security taxes) would reduce the costs of production for businesses and cause them to employ more workers and produce more products.

*Graphing Exercise*

6. Answers will vary. Possible answer: The steady increase in investment in physical capital allowed our economy's productivity to increase and contributed to an improved standard of living in our nation during these years.

   A sample of an acceptable graph appears at the bottom of this page.

*Think Critically*

7. Answers will vary. Possible answer: The firm will become more productive with the new computer system, and it will earn greater profits in the future from lower costs, and increased production and sales.

8. Answers will vary. Possible answer: Many college programs are designed to provide students with knowledge that will increase the value of what they are able to contribute to production. Learning how to use spreadsheet programs on computers, for example, can make them more productive accountants.

## Sharpen Your Life Skills

### Categorize Information

After studying Lesson 12.1, students should be able to answer the questions on this page.

### Answers

A. *Physical and human capital*: Some of these funds were used for training researchers, and some were used to purchase supplies and equipment. Greater R&D contributes to increased productivity.

B. *Human capital*: High school graduates are better able to contribute to production than are people who do not graduate.

C. *Human capital*: Students who become educated are better able to contribute to production.

D. *Physical and human capital*: Providing Internet access and training students to use it allows them to make greater contributions to productivity.

E. *Physical and human capital*: Some of these funds were used for training researchers, and some were used to purchase supplies and equipment. Greater R&D contributes to increased productivity.

F. *Physical capital*: Funds provided through the SBA are used to purchase new equipment that increases production.

G. *Physical capital*: New machines are used by businesses to increase production.

H. *Human capital*: Many adults take continuing education courses in order to become more productive—thereby often qualifying for better paying jobs.

### Apply Your Skill

Consider allowing students to work in pairs for this assignment.

### Answers

1. Answers will vary. Possible answer: The intent of the elimination of federal tax on interest earned on savings bonds was to encourage more people to save for their college education, enabling them to increase their human capital.

2. Answers will vary. Possible answer: This tax credit was intended to encourage taxpayers in New York state to purchase more efficient automobiles that would reduce our nation's reliance on foreign oil and increase our nation's physical capital.

## Sharpen Your Life Skills

### Categorize Information

Each of the following events contributed to the stock of either human capital or physical capital in the United States. Make two lists. The term *human capital* should head the first one and *physical capital* should head the second. Then place each event in the appropriate list. Some of these events may have contributed to stocks of both human and physical capital. Describe how each event contributed to increased productivity in the U.S. economy.

A. In 2000, more than $264 billion was spent on research and development in the United States.

B. In 2000, more than 2.5 million students graduated from high school.

C. In 2000, the U.S. government provided more than $85 billion in aid for education.

D. In 1999, 81 percent of all public-school students attended schools that had some access to the Internet. Fifty-three percent of all schools provided access to the Internet for instruction in at least one classroom.

E. In 2000, U.S. government agencies provided grants of more than $17 billion to colleges and universities for research and development.

F. In 2000, the federal Small Business Administration (SBA) provided more than $48 billion in loans to businesses.

G. In 2000, U.S. businesses spent more than $758 billion to purchase new machinery

H. In 1999, more than 88 million seats were taken by adults in continuing education courses.

### Apply Your Skill

1. In 1998, a law was passed that eliminated federal taxes on interest earned on U.S. savings bonds that was used to pay for the education of taxpayers or their children. Was this law intended to encourage investment in human or physical capital? Explain your answer.

2. Soon after 2000, the state of New York passed a law that allowed residents to deduct as much as $2,000 from their state income tax liability if they purchased a new hybrid gasoline/electric-powered automobile. Was this law intended to encourage investment in human or physical capital? Explain your answer.

# movers & shakers

## Jerry Yang and David Filo *Founders, Yahoo!*

When Jerry Yang was 10 years old, his mother moved him and his brother from Taipei, Taiwan, to San Jose, California. Although his mother was an English teacher, Yang knew just one word of English when he moved to the United States. He quickly caught on to the language, however, and within three years he was a straight-A student. Yang's good grades earned him a spot in Stanford University's electrical engineering program. After earning bachelor's and master's degrees, Yang intended to look for a job. Because the labor market was in a slump at the time, however, he stayed at Stanford instead to work toward a Ph.D.

David Filo grew up in Moss Bluff, Louisiana, and attended nearby Tulane University. There he earned a bachelor's degree in computer engineering. Afterwards he attended Stanford University and earned a master's degree in electrical engineering. Filo, too, remained at Stanford to work towards a Ph.D.

Then the two got sidetracked.

"I was terribly bored," Filo recalls, as he discussed the outline of his unfinished graduate thesis. Yang was not anxious to complete his coursework, either. To fight the boredom, the two began surfing the still-developing World Wide Web. "Really, we'd do anything to keep from working on our theses," Yang remembers. In February 1994, as a hobby, Yang and Filo started a guide to keep track of their favorite online destinations on the Internet. Eventually their lists became too long, so they broke the lists into categories. When the categories became too full, the partners created subcategories.

Yang and Filo first called their web site "Jerry's Guide to the World Wide Web." Later, with the help of a dictionary, they settled on "Yahoo!" Although the guide was initially created for their own use, they later shared it with fellow students. "And then, a funny thing happened," Yang smiles. Within months, Yahoo! celebrated its first million-hit day.

"The first ingredient in our success was that we created Yahoo! as a hobby while students at Stanford—we never thought it would become a business," Yang explains. They created the site "because we loved it . . . not to make money." In March 1995, Yang and Filo incorporated the business and met with dozens of venture capitalists. Just one month later, Sequoia Capital agreed to an initial investment of almost $2 million.

Today, Yahoo! Inc. is a leading Internet communications, commerce, and media company that provides services to more than 237 million people each month worldwide. Total sales for 2002 reached just over $953 million with net income close to $43 million. In October 2003, the stock market valued the company at $25 billion. Not bad for a couple of college guys who started their business as a way to avoid completing their college coursework!

### SOURCE READING
Using direct quotations from this feature, describe the human capital that Yang and Filo brought to the venture at its start. What type of physical capital do you think is used in running Yahoo today?

### ENTREPRENEURS IN ACTION
In small groups, brainstorm a list of hobbies that might provide the potential for wealth. Are there specific areas of the country, or the world, that would provide a performance advantage for each business? Who might be interested in investing in the business? Why?

---

## movers & shakers

### FOCUS

Remind students of the meaning of transaction costs. Much of the cost of many purchases is the value of the time and effort used to find and choose the product to buy. A service that reduces transaction costs can enhance productivity and add to the standard of living people enjoy. You may have $100 to buy a new product, but if you can't find the product you want for that price, your $100 won't satisfy your desire. Jerry Yang and David Filo provided a service that has value because of its ability to reduce the cost of searching the Internet. Ask students how Yahoo.com and other similar services increase productivity in the U.S. economy.

### TEACH

Instruct students to read the **Movers & Shakers** feature about Jerry Yang and David Filo. Point out that some students may find it helpful to read the article, read the questions at the bottom of the page, and then reread the article.

### ASSESS

Use the questions in Source Reading and Entrepreneurs in Action at the bottom of the profile to assess the students' understanding of this **Movers & Shakers** feature.

#### Answers to Source Reading

Answers will vary. Possible answer: "Really, we'd do anything to keep from working on our theses," describes the human capital that went into starting up Yahoo. Physical capital in the form of computers is running Yahoo today.

#### Answers to Entrepreneurs in Action

Answers should be logical and show an understanding of the feature.

---

### Extend the Content

Tell students that the government passed a law in 1981 allowing businesses to subtract 10 percent of the cost of any new tools or machines they bought from the amount of tax they owed. Effectively, the government was offering to pay one-tenth of the cost of new physical capital businesses purchased. Ask students to discuss what this law was intended to accomplish. How was it intended to increase productivity in the U.S. economy?

**12.2** *Living Standards and Labor Productivity Growth*

Tell students that much of what they learn in this lesson is, like many ideas in economics, a matter of common sense. Logic tells us that in most situations, the more that workers are able to produce, the better they will be able to live. Much of this lesson will be devoted to learning about factors that allow workers to be more productive and therefore enjoy a better standard of living.

## Objectives

Remind students to read the lesson objectives to help focus their attention before reading the lesson.

## Key Terms

Direct students use each of the key terms in a separate sentence or short paragraph that helps demonstrate the meaning of the term

## [ In the News ]

Instruct students to read the passage and write down their answers. Point out that their answers might change after they finish studying Lesson 12.2.

## Answers to Think About It

Answers will vary. Possible answer: The United States has a duty to feed the poor. Those who are fortunate to have enough also have a responsibility to care for those who don't have enough.

## Visual Presentation

Use the PowerPoint presentation on the Instructor's Resource CD as an adjunct to your lecture. The presentation also can be used for review.

## Objectives

> Explain why there is such a difference among countries in the standard of living.

> Evaluate the record of U.S. labor productivity growth, and explain why even small differences in growth rates are important.

## Overview

The single most important determinant of a nation's standard of living over the long run is the productivity of its resources. A nation prospers by getting more from its resources. Even a relatively small growth in productivity, if continued for years, can have a huge effect on the average living standard—that is, on the average availability of goods and services per capita. Growing productivity is critical to a rising standard of living. It has kept the United States ahead of every other major economy in the world.

## Key Terms

**industrial market countries**

**developing countries**

**Group of Seven (G-7)**

## [ In the News ]

### • Standard of Living and the Poverty Threshold

Living standards vary both within a country and among countries. However, no matter what the standard of living, poverty exists in all countries to some degree. In 1963, Mollie Orshansky of the U.S. Social Security Administration developed the idea of identifying a certain income level that she termed the "poverty threshold." If an individual or family received less than that amount in income each year, they would be considered as living in poverty. Orshansky started with the fact that food expenditures usually were 30 percent of total expenditures for food, clothing, and shelter. She then based her figures on how much it would cost to buy the necessary amount of food called for in the Department of Agriculture's "economy food plan." The percentage living in poverty in the United States has been at or near its all-time low for more than a decade—between 11 and 12 percent, or about 33 million people. Compare this figure to the approximately 23 percent living in poverty in Scotland, more than 55 percent in Zambia, and 60 percent of Palestinians living in the West Bank and Gaza. Over the years, the dollar amounts of the U.S. poverty-threshold income level have been increasing, due to inflation and other factors. For individuals it is now at $8,980, up from $1,539 in 1963. Similarly, the level for a family of four has risen from $3,169 in 1963 to $18,400 in 2003. The poverty threshold will continue to rise with the general level of prices in the economy.

### Think About It

According to the latest estimates, more than half the world's population lives on less than the equivalent of $2 per day. Do you think the United States has a duty to help feed the poor of the world? Why or why not?

366

## National Content Standards in Economics

A complete list of the NCEE Standards appears on pages xxiv–xxv of this book. The following standards are addressed in Lesson 12.2.

Standard 13: Role of Resources in Determining Income

Standard 15: Growth

# Standard of Living

There are vast differences in the standards of living among countries. For example, per capita output in the United States is more than 50 times that of the world's poorest countries. With only 5 percent of the world's population, the United States produces more than the nations making up the bottom 50 percent of the world's population put together. You might say that poor countries are poor because they experience low labor productivity.

## Industrial and Developing Economies

The world's economies can be sorted into two broad groups. **Industrial market countries**, or *developed countries*, make up about 20 percent of the world's population. They include the advanced market economies of Western Europe, North America, Australia, New Zealand, and Japan. Industrial market countries were the first to experience long-term economic growth during the nineteenth century. Today they have the world's highest standard of living, based on their abundant human and physical capital.

The rest of the world—the remaining 80 percent of the population—consists of **developing countries**, which have a lower standard of living because they have relatively little human and physical capital. On average, more than half the workers in developing countries are in agriculture. Farming methods in developing countries are primitive. Labor productivity there is low, and most people barely subsist. In the United States, only about 2 percent of all workers are in agriculture. However, U.S. farmers are so productive that they grow enough to feed the nation and export to other countries.

## Education and Economic Development

An important source of productivity is the quality of labor—the skill, experience, and education of workers. If

knowledge is lacking, other resources may not be used efficiently. For example, a country may have fertile land, but farmers lack knowledge of irrigation and fertilization techniques.

What exactly is the contribution of education to the process of economic development? Education makes workers aware of the latest production techniques and more receptive to new ideas and methods. Countries with the most advanced educational systems also were the first to develop.

One distinguishing feature between industrial economies and developing economies is the literacy of the population. Literacy is the ability to read and write. Among countries that make up the poorest third of the world's population, most adults are illiterate. In contrast, fewer than 5 percent of adults in industrial market economies are illiterate.

*industrial market countries*

The advanced market economies of Western Europe, North America, Australia, New Zealand, and Japan; also called developed countries

*developing countries*

Countries with a lower standard of living because they have relatively little human and physical capital

© Getty Images/PhotoDisc

**The farm workers in this photo are planting onions. Do you think this photo was taken in a developed country or in a developing country? Why?**

Lesson 12.2 • *Living Standards and Labor Productivity Growth*     **367**

---

# TEACH

## Standard of Living

Ask students to identify factors that determine the standard of living they enjoy. Point out that the amount of money they receive is less important than what they are able to buy with it. Also point out that in this lesson, students will learn about factors that affect their standards of living and about changes in the average standard of living that people in the United States have experienced in recent years.

## *Think Critically Through Visuals*

Direct students to focus their attention on the photograph on this page. Ask for a volunteer to answer the question posed in the caption.

### Answer

Answers will vary. Possible answer: It is more likely a picture of workers in a developing country because agriculture accounts for more than half of the workers in developing countries.

## Standard of Living

Place a collection of small objects on your desk. Invite a student to carry the objects as quickly as possible to the opposite side of the room. There should be so many things that several trips are necessary. Then ask for a second volunteer to do the same, but give this student a box to use so the objects can easily be moved in one trip. Be sure to time both students. Point out that the second student's productivity was much greater because of the capital (the box) available. This allowed the objects to be moved in less time. If the students had been paid $1 to move the objects, how much could each have earned per hour? What does productivity have to do with income and with the standard of living workers are able to enjoy?

 Divide students into small groups to complete this assignment. For example, two students in each group could be responsible for finding the average years of schooling. One source of this information is the state or local boards of education. Other students in the group could be responsible for finding the gross product for the state for one or more years. The groups should work together to analyze the information and determine whether a correlation exists between the average years of schooling and gross products.

### *Think Critically Through Visuals*

Direct students to focus their attention on **Figure 12.2—Average Years of Education of Working-Age Populations in 1970 and 1998**. In 1970, the average years of education of the U.S. working population was higher than in any other country. By 1998, the United States had slipped to third place.

 **CHECKPOINT**
Invite a student to answer the checkpoint that appears on this page

### Answer

There is a difference among countries in standard of living because of the difference in the skill, experience, and education of their workers.

---

**Group of Seven (G-7)**
The seven leading industrial market economies, including the United States, United Kingdom, France, Germany, Italy, Japan, and Canada

Figure 12.2 shows the average years of schooling of the working-age population in the United States and six other leading industrial market economies. Together these seven economies are called the **Group of Seven (G-7)**. In 1970, the average education of the U.S. working population was 11.6 years. This was higher than any other nation in the world. Among other advanced economies, average education ranged from a low of 6.6 years in Italy to 11.3 years in Canada. By 1998, the U.S. edu-

Research the average years of schooling in your school district for more than one year. Then determine the gross state product per capita for your state for the same years. Is there a correlation?

cation average had grown to 12.7 years, but other countries had become even more educated. Americans ranked third behind Germany, at 13.6 years, and Canada, at 12.9 years.

**CHECKPOINT**
Why is there such a difference among countries in standard of living?

## U.S. Labor Productivity and Output Per Capita

Labor productivity is measured by real output per work hour. The higher the level of labor productivity, the more output per labor hour and the higher the standard of living in the economy. Thus, differences across economies in labor productivity determine differences in living standards. The key to a rising standard of living is the growth in labor productivity.

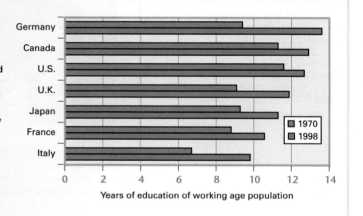

**Average Years of Education of Working-Age Populations in 1970 and 1998**    **Figure 12.2**

The United States has been surpassed by Germany and Canada in average years of education of its working-age population.

Source: Based on estimates developed by the Organization for Economic Cooperation and Development. The 1998 figure for Japan is based on 1990 data.

*(bar chart: Years of education of working age population, 0 to 14, for Germany, Canada, U.S., U.K., Japan, France, Italy; series for 1970 and 1998)*

**368    CHAPTER 12**  Economic Growth

---

**ENRICH**

At the end of World War II, the economies of Germany and Japan were largely destroyed. Although their physical capital was damaged, their skilled workers helped them to rebuild quickly much of their productive capacity. Ask students to discuss why countries that were once in productive shambles were able to become world leaders in productivity and standards of living. (These countries were forced to invest in new productive facilities because their old ones were destroyed. They still had many skilled workers who were able to use new facilities to become more productive and increase their standards of living.)

## Record Over the Long Run

Figure 12.3 offers a long-run perspective, showing U.S. productivity growth stretching back more than a century. Annual productivity growth is averaged by decade. Note the slowdown during the 1930s because of the Great Depression and the rebound during the 1940s because of World War II. Productivity growth slowed again during the 1970s and 1980s but recovered somewhat after 1990.

For the entire period since 1870, productivity growth averaged 2.1 percent per year. This may not seem like much, but growth has a powerful cumulative effect. Real output per work hour has grown a total of 1,400 percent since 1870. To put this in perspective, if a carpenter in 1870 could build one house in a year, today's carpenter could build 15 houses in a year.

*Small differences in productivity growth can amount to huge differences in the economy's ability to produce and, therefore, in the standard of living.* For example, if productivity growth had averaged only 1.1 percent per year instead of 2.1 percent, output per work hour since 1870 would have increased by only 325 percent, not 1,400 percent. On the other hand, if productivity growth had averaged 3.1 percent per year, output per work hour since 1870 would have jumped 5,500 percent! The wheels of progress seem to grind slowly, but the cumulative effect can be powerful.

### Slowdown and Rebound in Productivity Growth

You can see in Figure 12.3 that productivity growth declined during the 1970s and 1980s and recovered somewhat since 1990. To focus on productivity

### U.S. Labor Productivity and Output Per Capita

Remind students that real production in the United States grew at a rate of more than 2.5 percent per year during the twentieth century. This growth allowed a significant improvement in the standard of living enjoyed by U.S. residents from one generation to the next. Tell students that they will learn in this lesson that this growth did not occur at a constant rate. Some periods of growth were rapid while others were slow. In some years, production actually fell. They will also study the relationship between changes in production and the average standard of living.

### *Think Critically Through Visuals*

Direct students to focus their attention on **Figure 12.3—Long-Term Trend in U.S. Labor Productivity Growth: Annual Average by Decade.** This figure offers a long-run perspective, showing U.S. productivity growth stretching back more than a century.

---

**Long-Term Trend in U.S. Labor Productivity Growth: Annual Average by Decade** | Figure **12.3**

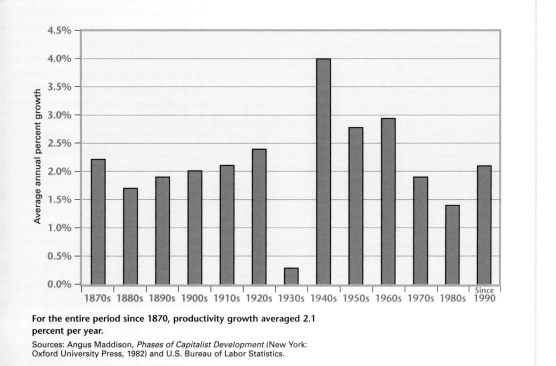

**For the entire period since 1870, productivity growth averaged 2.1 percent per year.**

Sources: Angus Maddison, *Phases of Capitalist Development* (New York: Oxford University Press, 1982) and U.S. Bureau of Labor Statistics.

Lesson 12.2 • *Living Standards and Labor Productivity Growth* **369**

---

## Group Activity

|  | List 1 | List 2 | List 3 | List 4 | List 5 |
|---|---|---|---|---|---|
| Mortgage | 4,000 | 3,000 | 2,000 | 1,000 | 500 |
| Rent | 1,000 | 1,000 | 1,000 | 500 | 500 |
| Car payment | 1,500 | 1,200 | 900 | 600 | 300 |
| Transit pass | 100 | 100 | 50 | 50 | 30 |
| Groceries | 2,000 | 1,600 | 1,200 | 100 | 800 |
| Cell phone | 50 | 50 | 50 | 30 | 30 |
| Cable TV | 200 | 150 | 100 | 100 | 50 |

Before class, prepare five monthly price lists, using the information shown at left. Organize students into five groups and explain that each group will pretend to be a family with a monthly income of 5,000 curns (the currency of an imaginary country). Provide one of the monthly price lists to each family and instruct them to figure out how to spend the money to purchase the best standard of living possible. Have students share their spending plans. Point out that the amount of income is less important than what the money will buy. Why do nations with greater productivity often have price structures that make goods and services more affordable for consumers?

## U.S. Labor Productivity and Output Per Capita

You will need notebook paper, a pen, and a computer to complete this demonstration. Ask two students to volunteer. Both should be proficient in using word processing software. Flip a coin to determine which student will use the paper and pencil and which will use the computer.

Give one student a sheet of paper, a pen, and two or three paragraphs of text. Instruct the student to use the paper and pen to copy the paragraphs neatly. After one minute, give the same two or three paragraphs to the student sitting at the computer and instruct this volunteer to make a copy of the text using the computer. Have a third student time the progress of the students making the copies.

The person using the computer is likely to finish long before the other student. Explain that the minute when the second student was not working could represent a recession in the economy. This shows that with skilled labor and better technology, an economy is often able to recover quickly from a recession. This is true of industrial market economies such as the U.S. economy. Less developed economies are likely to suffer longer from downturns in their production.

### *Think Critically Through Visuals*

Direct students to focus their attention on **Figure 12.4—U.S. Labor Productivity Growth.** This figure illustrates the average annual growth for four distinct periods.

## E-CONOMICS

Direct students to read the passage entitled "Computers and Productivity Growth" on page 372.

### **Think Critically**

Computers have had a positive effect on the quality of human capital in the United States through the increase in the skill and efficiency of the workers who use them. This has resulted in an increase in productivity.

### Ask the Xpert!

Direct students to **econxtra. swlearning.com**. to hear an expert answer the question "Have computers affected worker productivity?"

---

trends since World War II, Figure 12.4 offers the average annual growth for four distinct periods. Labor productivity growth declined from an average of 2.9 percent per year between 1948 and 1973 to only 0.8 percent between 1974 and 1982. The rate of growth in labor productivity from 1974 to 1982 was less than a third the rate during the quarter century following World War II. Except for the Great Depression, the rate of growth in labor productivity during this period was less than the average for any decade during the previous century.

Why the slowdown? First, the price of oil quadrupled from 1973 to 1974 as a result of OPEC actions. Spikes in energy prices fueled inflation during the period. This contributed to three recessions, which slowed productivity growth. Second, in the early 1970s, several laws were passed to protect the environment and improve the quality and safety of the workplace. These measures ultimately led to cleaner air, purer water, and safer working conditions. However, they also required more costly production methods. Productivity growth slowed down as these costlier methods were introduced.

Fortunately, productivity rebounded off the lows that occurred from 1974 to 1982, growing 1.7 percent from 1983 to 1995 and 2.7 percent from 1996 to 2002.

Why the rebound? The most dramatic technological development in recent years has been the information revolution powered by computers and the Internet. New technology helps workers produce more. Computers also increase the flexibility of machines, which can be reprogrammed for different tasks. See the E-conomics feature on page 372 for a discussion about the effects of computers on productivity growth.

Higher labor productivity growth easily can make up for output lost during recessions. For example, if over the next 10 years the U.S. labor productivity grows an average of 2.7 percent per year (the average from 1996 to 2002) instead of 1.7 percent (the average from 1983 to 1995), that higher growth would add more than $1 trillion to real GDP in the tenth year. This would more than make up for the output lost during two typical recessions. *This cumulative power of productivity growth is why economists now worry less about short-term fluctuations in output related to the business cycle and more about long-term growth.*

### Output Per Capita

So far, the focus has been on rising labor productivity as an engine of economic growth—that is, growth achieved by getting more output from each hour worked.

---

**U.S. Labor Productivity Growth**                    **Figure 12.4**

Growth in labor productivity in the United States slowed during 1974 to 1982 and then rebounded.

Source: Averages based on annual estimates from the U.S. Bureau of Labor Statistics.

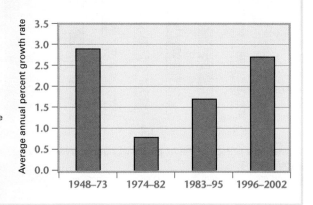

---

## *Curriculum Connection—Government*

In the 1850s, the federal government decided to give government land to businesses that agreed to build railroads in the western United States. The companies would be given one square mile to the left of a new rail line and then the next square mile on the right. This provided an incentive to the company and assured the government that it would own half the land along any new rail line. Ask students how this policy was intended to increase productivity in the U.S. economy. Can they think of similar uses of government power that have taken place more recently? (By encouraging construction of railroads, transportation costs were reduced. which made production less costly.)

Even if labor productivity remained unchanged, real GDP would grow if the quantity of labor increased. Total output can grow as a result of greater labor productivity, more labor, or both.

The best measure of an economy's standard of living is output per person, or per capita. *Output per capita*, or real GDP divided by the population, indicates how much an economy produces on average per resident. Labor productivity in the U.S. economy in 2002 was about $65,600 per worker per year. In the United States, one of every two people in the economy is a worker. Therefore, *output per capita* equals output per worker divided by two. In this example, output per capita would be $65,600/2, or $32,800.

Figure 12.5 presents real GDP per capita for the United States since 1959. Notice the general upward trend, interrupted by seven recessions, indicated by the pink shading. Real GDP per capita more than doubled (measured in 1996 dollars) from about $13,100 in 1959 to

about $32,800 in 2002 for an average annual growth rate of 2.2 percent. Since 1959, labor productivity grew an average of 2.1 percent. Output per capita grew faster than did labor productivity because the number of workers grew faster than did the population.

### International Comparisons

How does U.S. output per capita compare with that of other major industrial economies? Figure 12.6 compares GDP per capita for the United States and the six other leading industrial nations. The United States produced more output per capita than any other major economy.

## Ask the Xpert!
econxtra.swlearning.com

*Have computers affected worker productivity?*

**CHECKPOINT**
What has been the record of U.S. labor productivity growth, and why are even small differences in average growth important?

---

**U.S. Real GDP Per Capita Since 1959**

**Figure 12.5**

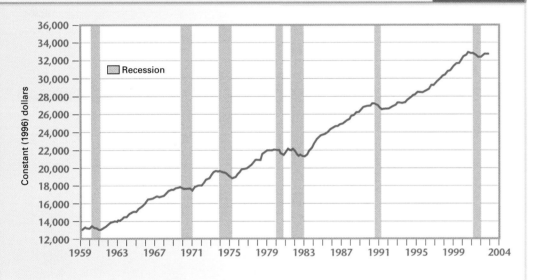

Despite the recessions since 1959, U.S. real GDP per capita has more than doubled. Periods of recession are indicated by the pink-shaded columns.

Source: U.S. Department of Commerce.

Lesson 12.2  •  *Living Standards and Labor Productivity Growth*  **371**

---

## TEACH  (continued)

### U.S. Labor Productivity and Output Per Capita

Write the following sentence on the board: "Next year, the U.S. economy will produce 500,000 more automobiles than it did this year." Ask each student to write a sentence or two that states what this sentence tells them about the standard of living U.S. residents will enjoy next year. Have several students read their sentences and list their ideas on the board. Did any of them mention the impact of population growth on their predictions? What would a 2-million-person increase in the number of licensed drivers do to their predictions? At the present, there are roughly the same number of licensed drivers as there are registered automobiles. Adding 2 million more drivers but only 500,000 new cars will reduce the car-to-driver ratio. This discussion can be directed to the general concept that changes in GDP need to be related to changes in population to provide them with greater meaning.

### *Think Critically Through Visuals*

Direct students to focus their attention on **Figure 12.5—U.S. Real GDP Per Capita Since 1959.** Point out the general upward trend, interrupted by seven recessions, indicated by the pink shading.

### *Think Critically Through Visuals*

Direct students to focus their attention on **Figure 12.6—U.S. GDP Per Capita as Compared to Other Major Economies** on page 372. Point out that the United States produces more output per capita than any other major economy.

**CHECKPOINT**
Invite a student to answer the checkpoint that appears on this page.

### Answer

Overall, the trend of U.S. labor productivity growth has been an upward one. Small differences in average growth are important because these average changes are multiplied by the U.S. workforce (millions) to get the overall change.

## APPLY

Assign Lesson 12.2 from the Contemporary Economics Workbook.

### e-con @pps

Encourage students to apply their knowledge of concepts presented in this lesson as they explore economic news stories, policy debates, and data available at **econxtra.swlearning.com**. A sampling of the titles for this lesson appears below.

### EconDebate

- Do technological advances result in higher unemployment?

### EconData

- Average Weekly Hours, Manufacturing
- Consumer Price Index
- Labor Cost Per Unit of Output

### EconNews

- Amazing Gains
- Australia Goes for the Gold
- Pleasing Progress of Productivity

## ASSESS

Assign all or part of Lesson 12.2 Assessment on page 373 as homework or an in-class activity.

### Xtra! Study Tools

Direct students to the online study tools for Lesson 12.2 at **econxtra.swlearning.com**.

## CLOSE

**Revisit** the **In the News** feature on the first page of the lesson. Ask students to review their preliminary answers and discuss the questions.

**Review** the objectives for Lesson 12.2. Students should be able to:

- Explain why there is such a difference among countries in the standard of living.
- Evaluate the record of U.S. labor productivity growth, and explain why even small differences in average growth are important.

# E-CONOMICS

## Computers and Productivity Growth

The first microprocessor, the Intel 4004, could carry out about 400 computations per second when it hit the market in 1971. Today desktop computers can crunch 2 billion computations per second. This is 5 million times what the Intel 4004 could handle. Such advances in computing power have fueled a sharp increase in computer use. Since 1982, the growth rate of the computer sector has averaged 26 percent annually. PCs are moving beyond word processing and spreadsheet analysis to help people work together. For example, design engineers in California use the Internet to test new ideas with marketers in New York. This cuts development time for new products in half. Sales representatives on the road can use laptops or wireless devices to log orders and provide customer service. New-generation computer systems even monitor themselves and send messages to service centers detailing problems when they arise. For example, General Electric uses these systems and the Internet to keep tabs on factory equipment thousands of miles away. A recent study concludes that information technology (IT) was a leading force behind the improved productivity growth during the second half of the 1990s. Computers affect productivity through two channels: (1) efficiency gains in the production of computers and (2) greater computer use by industry.

### Think Critically

Since their introduction to the workplace, what effects have computers had on the quality of human capital in the United States? How has this influenced productivity?

**U.S. GDP Per Capita as Compared to Other Major Economies**  **Figure 12.6**

The U.S. per capita income in 2000 stood 25 percent above that of second-ranked Canada and 48 percent above that of France, ranked last among these major economies.

Source: Based on OECD figures, which are adjusted across countries using the purchasing power of the local currency as of 2000.

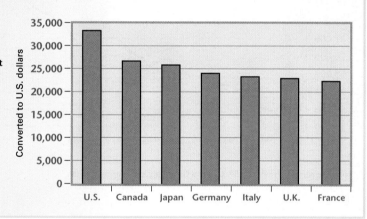

## RETEACH

Show students a picture related to unemployment, such as workers waiting in line for unemployment compensation payments. Ask them to discuss why unemployment is a drag on production and the standard of living in an economy. Some people suggest that unemployment compensation causes people to reject job offers they might otherwise accept. Do students believe this is a reasonable point of view? Why can some economic systems recover more quickly from lost production caused by unemployment than others?

## Key Concepts

1. Do you think your standard of living is better than that of your parents when they were your age? Explain your answer.

2. Why is providing education to all residents a difficult task for many developing countries?

3. What if by earning a high-school diploma you are able to produce 25 percent more each year than you could have produced without graduating from high school? How important would this extra production be to you, your family, and the economy in general if you work until you are 67 years old?

4. Identify a specific event or new technology that you think has increased labor productivity in the past five years. Explain how this increase has been accomplished.

5. Measures of output per capita do not consider production that takes place within households. In the past 50 years, a much larger share of U.S. citizens work outside the home. How may this have affected output per capita?

**Xtra!**
Study Tools
econxtra.swlearning.com

## Graphing Exercise

6. As labor productivity grows, the value of output per hour worked increases. The data in the table show the increase in the real output per hour worked in the years from 1992 through 2001. The year 1992 represents 100 percent. Values for years after 1992 show the percentage growth from 1992. For example, the value 101.9 for 1994 shows that 1.9 percent more was produced per hour worked in 1994 than in 1992. Use these data to construct a line graph that shows the change in output per hour worked for these years. Explain what this information shows about the economy.

**Real Output Per Hour Worked, 1992–2001**

| Year | Output | Year | Output | Year | Output |
|------|--------|------|--------|------|--------|
| 1992 | 100.0 | 1996 | 105.4 | 1999 | 113.4 |
| 1993 | 100.5 | 1997 | 107.8 | 2000 | 117.3 |
| 1994 | 101.9 | 1998 | 110.7 | 2001 | 119.5 |
| 1995 | 102.6 | | | | |

## Think Critically

7. **Science** Identify and describe a scientific advancement you have studied that has contributed to increases in labor productivity in this country or other countries in the world.

8. **Literature** Identify and describe advances in communications technology that have changed the way books are written and published in recent years. If Shakespeare had lived today, how might his work have been different?

Lesson 12.2 • *Living Standards and Labor Productivity Growth* **373**

**Real Output Per Hour Worked**

### Visualizing the Answer— Graphing Exercise

6. The answer includes a graph. Students' graphs should look similar to the one shown here. An Excel spreadsheet containing this graph, along with supporting data, is available on the Instructor's Resource CD.

### Key Concepts

1. Answers will vary. Possible answer: Students' standard of living is better because our economy is more productive than it was in the past. They might also discuss new types of products that they enjoy that their parents could not own because the products did not exist at that time.

2. Answers will vary. Possible answer: Many developing countries need to use the labor of most adults to produce goods and services that provide a minimal standard of living. The return on investments in education is long term and does little to help people live better at the present.

3. Answers will vary. Possible answer: This extra production will increase students' life-span income. This will improve the standard of living they and their family enjoy, and their extra production will benefit the economy by increasing the quantity of aggregate output available for all consumers to buy.

4. Answers will vary. Possible answer: New telephones allow people to communicate from any location and at any time. This allows people to use more of their time to be productive.

5. Answers will vary. Possible answer: People who work within a household produce goods and services that are not included in output per capita data. Therefore, as more people choose to work outside the home, the value of this production grows more rapidly.

### Graphing Exercise

6. Answers will vary. Possible answer: Although the increase in real output per hour worked was not constant, it averaged more than 2 percent per year. This increase in labor productivity should have contributed to an improved standard of living for U.S. citizens in these years.

A sample of an acceptable graph appears at the bottom of this page.

*The Answer Key is continued on page 382.*

Remind students that an individual's ability to produce is closely related to the tools and technology available. Tell them they will learn about relationships between productivity and technology in this lesson. Ask a student how he or she would go about communicating with a relative who lives hundreds of miles away if there were no telephone or Internet. How long would it take? How do electronic communications add to production and therefore improve productivity? (Electronic communications speed the acquisition of resources and facilitate the distribution of finished products.)

## Objectives

Remind students to read the lesson objectives to help focus their attention before reading the lesson.

## Key Terms

Direct students to write each of the key terms on a separate index card. Instruct students to write the complete definition of each key term on the back of the appropriate card along with the page number where the definition is located. Encourage students to use the cards to study for quizzes and tests.

## [ In the News ]

Instruct students to read the passage and write down their answers. Point out that their answers might change after they finish studying Lesson 12.3.

## Answers to Think About It

Answers will vary. Possible answers: The United States is spending enough on defense because the country and its citizens are relatively safe and secure. For the most part, our freedom and way of life are not being threatened.

## Visual Presentation

Use the PowerPoint presentation on the Instructor's Resource CD as an adjunct to your lecture. The presentation also can be used for review.

## Objectives

> Discuss the impact of research and development on the standard of living.

> Explain the relationship between technological change and employment levels.

> Describe industrial policy, and argue for and against its use.

## Overview

A major contributor to productivity growth and a rising standard of living is an improvement in the quality of human and physical capital. Improvement of human capital results from better education and more job training. Improvement of physical capital springs from better technology. Some other issues of technological change include the role of research and development and the relationship between technological change and the employment level.

## Key Terms

**basic research**

**applied research**

**industrial policy**

**cluster**

## [ In the News ]

### • Defense Spending: How Much Is Enough?

The U.S. defense budget for the fiscal year 2004 stood at almost $400 billion—up from $283 billion in 1999—with more funding requested by President George W. Bush for the war on terror and operations in Afghanistan and Iraq. The $400 billion represented approximately 4.1 percent of projected GDP for the period. Critics said that such an amount was unnecessary, as it took away needed funding from other programs. In addition, they argued that the United States was preparing to fight twenty-first century wars with needless spending on outmoded twentieth-century defense programs. Others maintained that we were not spending enough: that we could and should spend almost double the projected $400 billion without hardship. Such a level, they maintained, would allow us to "go it alone" in many future conflicts and not be subject to potential "vetoes" from allies. Compare U.S. 2004 defense spending to that of other countries for the same year:

- Russia, $65 billion, about 6 percent of its GDP
- Japan, $42.6 billion, about 1 percent of its GDP
- China, $47 billion, about 6 percent of its GDP
- United Kingdom, $38.4 billion, about 2.7 percent of its GDP

Also, contrast the 4 percent of 2004 GDP spent on defense with the percentages the United States spent during earlier wars and conflicts. In the Vietnam War, the country spent approximately 10 percent of GDP on defense; during Korea, 15 percent; during World War II, 43 percent; and during World War I, 14 percent.

### Think About It

Is the United States spending enough on defense? Why or why not?

374

## National Content Standards in Economics

A complete list of the NCEE Standards appears on pages xxiv–xxv of this book. The following standards are addressed in Lesson 12.3.

Standard 9: Role of Competition

Standard 13: Role of Resources in Determining Income

Standard 15: Growth

Standard 16: Role of Government

# Research and Development

Improvements in technology arise from scientific discovery, which is the product of research. Economists distinguish between basic research and applied research.

## Basic and Applied Research

The search for knowledge without regard to how that knowledge will be used is called **basic research**. Basic research is a first step toward technological advancement. In terms of economic growth, however, scientific discoveries are meaningless until they are implemented, which requires applied research.

**Applied research** seeks to answer particular questions or to apply scientific discoveries to the development of specific products. Technological breakthroughs may or may not have commercial possibilities. Thus the payoff is less immediate with basic research than with applied research.

## R&D Comparisons Across Countries

Technological change is the fruit of research and development (R&D). Investment in R&D reflects the economy's efforts to improve productivity through technological discoveries. One way to track R&D spending is to measure it relative to gross domestic product, or GDP. Figure 12.7 shows R&D spending as a share of GDP for the United States and the six other major economies for the 1980s and 1990s. Overall R&D spending in the United States averaged 2.7 percent of GDP in both the 1980s and the 1990s. During the 1990s, R&D as a share of GDP ranked the United States second among the major economies. It ranked slightly behind Japan, at 2.9 percent, but well ahead of last-place Italy, at only 1.1 percent.

Bar segments in the chart distinguish between R&D by businesses and R&D by governments and nonprofit institutions. Business R&D is more likely for applied research and innovations. R&D spending by governments

**basic research**
The search for knowledge without regard to how that knowledge will be used; a first step toward technological advancement

**applied research**
Research that seeks answers to particular questions or applies scientific discoveries to develop specific products

Which of these photos best illustrates basic research, and which best illustrates applied research? Justify your answers with evidence from the photos.

© Getty Images/PhotoDisc

© Getty Images/PhotoDisc

## TEACH

### Research and Development

Ask students to consider a country where all resources are allocated to the production of either consumer goods or capital goods that are used to replace machines and tools that are worn out in production. Nothing is allocated to finding better ways to produce goods or services. Ask why this country's economy would not grow rapidly.

### *Think Critically Through Visuals*

Direct students to focus their attention on the photographs on this page. Ask for a volunteer to answer the question posed in the caption.

### Answer

Answers will vary. Possible answers: The photo of the technician working on a computer circuit board illustrates applied research, and the photo of the people working in the sterile lab illustrates basic research.

## *Outside Resources*

**National Science Foundation** The National Science Foundation (NSF) gathers and publishes data about research and development in the United States. Many publications are available online at the NSF web site: www.nsf.gov/. One of these publications is *U.S. Corporate R&D: Volume 1: Top 500 Firms in R&D by Industry Category*. Ask students to visit this site and investigate the information it provides. Which U.S. industries are investing the most in R&D and which are investing less? How may these levels of R&D investment affect the future of these industries?

## Research and Development

Ask students to complete the following calculation without the use of an electronic calculator: 83,728,640 / 1,280. Allow only 30 seconds. Most students will not be able to calculate the correct answer (65,413) in the allotted time. Ask for a volunteer to complete the same problem using a calculator. It should take less than 15 seconds to complete. Tell students that the R&D to develop the first electronic calculator was about $100 million. Do they believe it was money and resources spent well? How have electronic calculators increased productivity and therefore the standard of living of U.S. residents?

### *Think Critically Through Visuals*

Direct students to focus their attention on **Figure 12.7—Growth: R&D Spending as a Percentage of GDP for Major Economies During the 1980s and 1990s.** Point out that the chart distinguishes between R&D by businesses and R&D by governments and nonprofit institutions.

 **NCEE**
### Standard 15: Growth

Investment in factories, machinery, new technology, and in the health, education, and training of people can raise future standards of living.

## Ask the Xpert!

Direct students to **econxtra.swlearning.com** to hear an expert answer the question "Does technological change destroy jobs and lead to unemployment?"

✔ **CHECKPOINT**
Invite a student to answer the checkpoint that appears on this page.

### Answer

Research and development have a positive impact on the standard of living.

---

 **Main Idea**

**Growth: R&D Spending as a Percentage of GDP for Major Economies During the 1980s and 1990s**     **Figure 12.7**

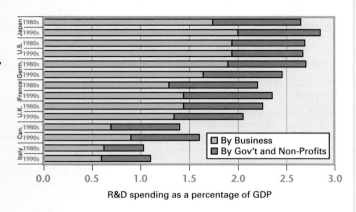

The United States devotes relatively more resources to R&D than most other advanced economies. *Investment in R&D results in a higher standard of living for Americans.*

Source: Based on figures from the Organization for Economic Cooperation and Development.

---

## Ask the Xpert!
**econxtra.swlearning.com**

*Does technological change destroy jobs and lead to unemployment?*

and nonprofits, such as universities, is more likely for basic research. This basic research may generate valuable ideas that ultimately have specific applications. For example, the Internet developed out of U.S. government research for a national defense communications system.

R&D by U.S. businesses averaged 1.9 percent of GDP in the 1990s, the same as in the 1980s. Three of the six other major countries experienced an increase in business R&D between the 1980s and 1990s, and three saw a decrease. Again, only Japan had higher business R&D than the United States in the 1990s, at 2.0 percent of GDP. Italy had the lowest at 0.6 percent.

In short, the United States devotes relatively more resources to R&D than most other advanced economies. This results in a higher standard of living for Americans.

✔ **CHECKPOINT**
What is the impact of research and development on the standard of living?

**376    CHAPTER 12   Economic Growth**

---

# Technological Change and Employment Levels

Technological change affects the economy in a variety of ways. Most of these effects are beneficial. However, technological change usually reduces the number of workers needed to produce a given amount of output. Consequently, some critics charge that new technology will throw people out of work and lead to lower employment levels.

## Technological Change and Labor Productivity

Technological change may increase production and employment by making products more affordable. For example, the introduction of the assembly line made automobiles more affordable to the average household. This stimulated production and employment in the auto industry. The same happened with personal computers.

Technological change also may lead to workers losing their jobs—or being displaced—in some industries. Even in

---

**ENRICH**

The National Science Foundation receives millions of dollars from the federal government each year to fund basic research at U.S. academic institutions. Descriptions of recent awards of NSF grants can be found at the NSF web site at www.nsf.gov/. Ask students to visit this web site, click on a link for a recent award, and read the grant abstract. Instruct students to print the abstract and write a brief explanation of how the research might add to the productivity of the U.S. economy in the long run.

industries where some workers are displaced by machines, those who keep their jobs are more productive, so they earn more. As long as human wants are unlimited, displaced workers usually will find jobs producing other goods and services demanded in a growing economy. Sometimes finding another job requires a worker to be retrained for a new occupation.

## Technological Change and Employment Levels Across Countries

There is no evidence that employment levels today are any lower than they were in 1870. Since then, however, worker productivity has increased more than 1,400 percent. The length of the average workweek has been cut nearly in half. Although technological change may displace some workers in the short run, long-run benefits include higher real incomes on average and more leisure—in short, a higher standard of living.

If technological change leads to lower levels of employment, then employment levels should be higher in economies where the latest technology has not yet been introduced, such as in developing countries. In fact, employment levels there usually are much lower. Those who do find work earn relatively little because they are not very productive.

Again, there is no question that technological change sometimes creates hardships in the short run, as workers scramble to adjust to a changing world. Some workers who lose their jobs due to advances in technology may not find jobs that pay as well as the ones they lost. These lost jobs are one price of progress. Over time, however, most of these workers find other jobs, often in new industries created by technological change. In a typical year, the U.S. economy creates many more jobs than it eliminates.

### ✓ CHECKPOINT
How does technological change affect employment levels?

© Getty Images/PhotoDisc

**Human workers on some assembly lines have been replaced by automated systems. In a growing economy, what happens to workers who become displaced by technological change?**

## Industrial Policy

Because technological change is so important to a rising standard of living, some argue that government should become more involved in shaping an economy's technological future. One concern is that technologies of the future will require huge sums to develop and implement. An individual firm cannot easily raise these sums and so will be put at risk. Another concern is that individual firms have less incentive to carry out basic research even though that research eventually has a high payoff for the economy as a whole. The fruits of basic research are not immediately embodied in something the firm can sell. Therefore, an individual firm may go bankrupt before applications are marketable.

### Technological Change and Employment Levels

Remind students that one of the primary determinants of labor productivity is a worker's ability to use other resources efficiently. A worker who really wants to work hard and produce computer microchips is unlikely to add much to production if he or she has completed only the sixth grade. New technologies require workers to learn new skills. Those who do not possess these skills are not likely to remain employed. People who do posses these skills are likely to benefit from a high demand for their labor.

### *Think Critically Through Visuals*

Direct students to focus their attention on the photograph on this page. Ask for a volunteer to answer the question posed in the caption.

**Answer**

Answers will vary. Possible answers: Workers displaced by technological change in a growing economy will find jobs producing other goods and services.

### ✓ CHECKPOINT
Invite a student to answer the checkpoint that appears on this page.

**Answer**

Technological change can increase or decrease employment levels. In a constant economy, technological change stimulates production and can lead to an increase in employment levels. However, in the same economy, technological change can replace human jobs.

### *Economic Headlines*

Assign students to find a newspaper or magazine article on a business that plans to lay off workers because of a change in technology. Instruct students to read the article and write a brief summary, making sure to include a reference citation. Identify the style you want them to use for the citation.

As an alternative, you might locate several articles of interest and provide citations for students to use in locating one of the articles. Direct students to read the article they have chosen, and write a brief explanation of how it relates to this lesson.

## Industrial Policy

Remind students that government intervention in a market economy normally is minimal. In recent times, however, some governments have chosen to encourage specific types of production through what has been called industrial policy.

### SPAN THE GLOBE

Direct students to read the short passage "European Industrial Policy" on this page. Use the Think Critically as a starting point for class discussion or have students write a short paragraph to answer the question.

### Answers to Think About It

Airbus enjoys government backing to promise special advantages to its customers, including landing rights at key European airports and easing of regulatory constraints.

### Think Critically Through Visuals

Direct students to focus their attention on the photograph on page 379. Ask for a volunteer to answer the questions posed in the caption.

### Answer

Answers will vary. Possible answers: Some of the careers associated with the movie business include actor, cinematographer, director, editor, producer, and writer. It would be beneficial to live near Hollywood because it is the industry cluster for filmmaking.

### TEAM WORK

Organize students into groups of four or five. Instruct teams to select a recorder and a spokesperson. Instruct students to complete the **Team Work** activity shown on page 379. Set a timer for 15 minutes. When the timer goes off, invite the spokesperson from each group to take a turn providing the results of the brainstorming session.

---

**industrial policy**
The view that government—using taxes, subsidies, and regulations—should nurture the industries and technologies of the future, thereby giving domestic industries an advantage over foreign competition

## Government Involvement

One possible solution to the problem of underinvestment is greater government involvement to promote investment in particular industries. **Industrial policy** is the idea that government—using taxes, subsidies, regulations, and coordination in the private sector—could help nurture the industries and technologies of the future. This would give U.S. industries an advantage over foreign competition. The objective of U.S. industrial policy is to ensure adequate investment in research and to secure a

## SPAN THE GLOBE

### European Industrial Policy

Airbus, a four-nation aircraft maker, exemplifies European industrial policy in which companies from two or more countries combine efforts to compete more effectively in world markets. Airbus was established as a consortium of French, German, Spanish, and British companies in order to compete effectively with U.S. aircraft manufacturers. In its infancy, Airbus had to integrate the four different business cultures involved. It also had to agree on a common set of measurements and a common language. The company was first created in 1970 between Aerospatiale of France and Deutsche Aerospace of Germany. CASA of Spain and two British companies joined in 1971. The company has received an estimated $20 billion in government aid from the countries involved. It has now become Boeing's main rival. When Airbus seeks aircraft orders around the world, it can draw on government backing to promise special advantages. These include landing rights at key European airports and an easing of regulatory constraints. U.S. aircraft producers do not receive such government backing.

### Think Critically

What advantages does Airbus enjoy that U.S. aircraft producers do not?

378    **CHAPTER 12**   Economic Growth

---

leading global role for U.S. industry. See the Span the Globe feature for an example of European industrial policy.

U.S. industrial policy over the years was aimed at creating the world's most advanced military production capacity. With the demise of the Soviet Union, however, defense technologies became less important.

### Identifying Industry Clusters

Economists have long recognized that firms in some industries gain a performance advantage by forming a **cluster**. That is, they locate in a region already thick with firms in that same industry or in related industries. Examples of industry clusters include the movie business in Hollywood, Broadway theaters, Wall Street finances, Silicon Valley software, and Orlando theme parks.

Clusters aid communication and promote healthy competition among cluster members. The flow of information and cooperation between firms, as well as the competition among firms located together, stimulates regional innovation and promotes growth. By locating in a region that has similar businesses, a firm also can tap into an established customer base and into local markets for specialized labor and for other inputs.

Many state and local governments are trying to identify the industries that should be promoted in their area. Governments try to attract firms in favored technologies by adopting favorable tax policies. They also may help to pay for the construction of support facilities.

### Pitfalls of Picking Technological Winners

Skeptics of industrial policy wonder whether the government should be trusted to identify emerging technologies and to pick the industry clusters that will lead the way. Critics of industrial policy say that markets allocate scarce resources better than governments do. For example, in the early 1980s, the U.S. government spent $1 billion to help military contractors

---

### Group Activity

For this activity you will need five linear measuring tools, including a 1-foot ruler, a yardstick, a 6-foot tape measure, and a 25-foot tape measure. If possible, also include a laser tape measure. Organize student into six groups. Give a measuring tool to five of the groups and give nothing to the sixth group. Tell each group to measure the same room and draw a floor plan. You can have them measure your classroom, the gymnasium, or another room in the school. After they complete their floor plans, ask students what technological advancements have taken place in recent years that could have made the task easier and quicker. How have these advancements added to productivity and the standard of living in the United States?

develop a high-speed computer circuit. However, Intel, a company that received no federal support, actually was the first to develop the circuit.

Japan has had the most aggressive policy for regulating and supporting favored industries. Its approach includes discouraging competition in the industry and encouraging joint research. Those Japanese industries

# TEAM WORK

In small groups, brainstorm to identify any business clusters in your region. Then discuss the effects you think the clusters have on economic growth in the region.

subject to the most regulation and support, such as chemicals and aircraft manufacturing, simply became uncompetitive in the world market. Meanwhile, the Japanese industries that had received little government backing, such as automobiles, cameras, and video games, turned out to be dynamic, innovative world competitors.

There also is concern that the government aid and the competitive advantages would be awarded based on political connections rather than on the promise of the technologies. Most economists would prefer to let private firms bet their own money on the important technologies of the future.

**cluster**

Firms in the same industry or in related industries that group together in a region, such as Wall Street, Hollywood, or Silicon Valley

 **CHECKPOINT**
What is industrial policy, and what are the arguments for and against its use?

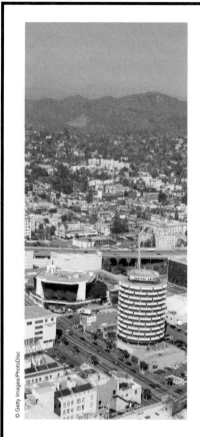

The business of making movies is carried out primarily in Hollywood, California. What are the careers associated with the movie business? Why would people working in these fields benefit from living in or near Hollywood?

 **NETBookmark**

The Bureau of Labor Statistics compiles international data on manufacturing productivity. Access this information through econxtra.swlearning.com. For the most recent period, which nations have enjoyed the most rapid growth in manufacturing productivity? Which nations have experienced the slowest growth?

*econxtra.swlearning.com*

**NETBookmark**

Direct students to **econxtra.swlearning.com**. Remind them to click on the link for Lesson 12.3 to find the appropriate link for the **NET Bookmark**. Instruct students to click on the International Page, then on Foreign Labor Statistics, then on Productivity and Unit Labor Cost, and then on International Comparisons.

**Answer**

Answers will vary, depending on when the students access the web site.

 **CHECKPOINT**

Invite a student to answer the checkpoint that appears on this page.

**Answer**

Industrial policy is the idea that government, using taxes, subsidies, and regulations, could help nurture the industries and technologies of the future.

**APPLY**

Assign Lesson 12.3 from the Contemporary Economics Workbook.

**e-con @pps**

Encourage students to apply their knowledge of concepts presented in this lesson as they explore economic news stories, policy debates, and data available at **econxtra.swlearning.com**

**ASSESS**

Assign all or part of Lesson 12.3 Assessment on page 380 as homework or an in-class activity.

**Xtra! Study Tools**

Direct students to the online study tools for Lesson 12.3 at **econxtra.swlearning.com**.

**CLOSE**

**Revisit** the In the News feature on the first page of the lesson. Ask students to review their preliminary answers and discuss the questions, now that they have completed this lesson.
**Review** the objectives for Lesson 12.3.

**RETEACH**

When Benjamin Franklin wrote *Poor Richard's Almanack* in the mid-1700s, his original manuscripts were prepared with a quill pen and printed with type that was set by hand. Ask students to identify and explain technological advancements that have taken place since then that make publishing much more efficient than it was in the past. How have these advancements made other types of production more efficient? (Anything that facilitates printing and learning will make human capital easier to attain and add to labor productivity.)

## Key Concepts

1. Answers will vary. Possible answer: The development of new genetically engineered plants may increase the productivity of our land and farmers quickly while research into how genes control the development of fish embryos is not likely to have any immediate impact on productivity.

2. Answers will vary. Possible answer: These products are part of our nation's GDP. If they have greater value, the R&D used to create them would contribute to our nation's productivity.

3. Answers will vary. Possible answer: People who have skills that become technologically obsolete need training to become qualified for a new job. This training is likely to be expensive and take a good deal of time to complete. While this training is taking place, the government might offer special support to these workers. The alternative might be to have many workers unemployed and unproductive for many years.

4. Answers will vary. Possible answer: By helping students pay for higher education, the government is increasing our nation's stock of human capital. Although this does not directly help specific industries, it does increase the number of skilled and therefore more productive workers in our economy.

## Graphing Exercise

5. Answers will vary. Possible answer: The steady rate of growth in spending for new computer hardware must have increased the efficiency of U.S. workers and their productivity. This spending is even more significant when the falling price of most computer hardware and its improved capabilities are considered.

   A sample of an acceptable graph appears at the bottom of this page.

The Answer Key is continued on page 383.

---

Xtra!
Study Tools
econxtra.swlearning.com

## Key Concepts

1. Which of the following research topics would have a more immediate impact on our nation's productivity: research into new types of genetically engineered plants or research about how genes control the development of fish embryos? Explain your choice.

2. A good deal of R&D in the United States and other countries is devoted to creating new types of consumer products such as shampoo, dish soap, or frozen pizza. Do you think this type of R&D adds significantly to our nation's productivity? Explain your answer.

3. There are many fewer manufacturing jobs in the U.S. economy today than there were in the past. Many people who once held manufacturing jobs have not been able to find new jobs that allow them to earn as much as they did in the past. Do you think government should provide such workers with special benefits? Why or why not?

4. Do you think that government-supported student aid for college students is similar to industrial policy in any way? Explain your answer.

## Graphing Exercise

5. The use of computer technology in production in the United States has dramatically increased productivity. Use the data in the table to create a line graph that shows the growth of spending on new computer hardware in the United States during the 1990s. To what extent do you think this investment was responsible for the rapid growth in productivity in these years? Explain your answer.

**Spending for New Computer Hardware in the United States, 1990 Through 1999**
**Values in Billions of Dollars**

| Year | Spending | Year | Spending |
|------|----------|------|----------|
| 1990 | $102.7 | 1997 | $197.4 |
| 1995 | $155.4 | 1998 | $210.9 |
| 1996 | $171.9 | 1999 | $225.4 |

## Think Critically

6. **Government** In 1981, Congress passed a law that allowed businesses to deduct 10 percent of the cost of investments they made from their federal income taxes. A firm that purchased a $1 million machine could subtract $100,000 from its federal taxes. This law expired in 1986. Some people think a similar law should be passed today. Would you support such a law? Why or why not?

7. **Science** The federal government has provided many billions of dollars to the National Science Foundation (NSF) to support scientific research and development. Although some of the discoveries made by researchers supported by NSF grants have been of great value to our economy, others have not. Do you think that using several billion dollars each year for the NSF research is a good use of your tax payments? Explain your answer.

---

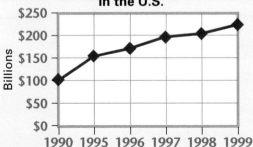

**Spending for New Computer Hardware in the U.S.**

## Visualizing the Answer—Graphing Exercise

5. The answer includes a graph. Students' graphs should look similar to the one shown here. An Excel spreadsheet containing this graph, along with supporting data, is available on the Instructor's Resource CD.

# CONNECT to History

## Interchangeable Parts and the Assembly Line

First proposed for the gun industry, the idea of interchangeable parts depended on machinery and precise measurements to build parts that were exactly the same. This allowed lesser-skilled workers to use machines to construct identical parts that could be assembled quickly and easily. The result was that productivity increased and cost was reduced. The amount of work that skilled craftspeople did in half a day now could be completed in three-and-a-half minutes.

By the 1850s, meat packers in Cincinnati began to combine slaughtering and processing under one roof. Set up as "disassembly" lines, they were noted as models of efficiency. The hogs were killed with a sledgehammer. Their bodies were then hung from a hook and moved along a pulley through the slaughterhouse. Along the line they were bled, scalded, gutted, and cleaned. Finally the carcasses were dismembered in about 35 seconds by a team of butchers.

Ransom Olds was the first person to mass-produce automobiles. Before mass production, the cars remained stationary in the factory. The workers moved from chassis to chassis assembling parts. Other workers would bring the parts to the workers wherever they were needed. Olds manufactured the cars by bringing all the material, including both the chassis and the parts, to the workers, who remained in one place. Henry Ford used the same process. Frames were arranged in a line in the plant, and teams of assemblers moved down the line performing one assembly operation. Parts already delivered to each station were ready for installation when the assemblers arrived. Following a suggestion by scientific management expert Clarence Avery, Ford installed conveyer belts to deliver the parts.

In 1913, Ford adopted the moving assembly line to automobile manufacturing in his Highland Park plant. Assembly time dropped from 17 hours to six. Workers were more productive, and the cost of the automobile fell—making it affordable to most Americans. Ford was able to give his unskilled workers wages that previously had been available only to skilled workers. In 1914, Ford was selling cars at $440. By 1916 the price had dropped to $345. Following World War I, the Model T roadster was priced at $260.

© Hulton Archive

### THINK CRITICALLY

Look at your own life and home and determine the things that make your life more productive, such as computers, telephones, dishwashers, etc. Ask your parents, grandparents, or both to estimate the time they spent on household tasks when they were young, and compare it to the time spent doing them today. What is the effect on everyday life? Write your findings down, and be prepared to compare them with what your classmates have found.

### FOCUS

Industrial technology such as interchangeable parts and the assembly line changed the nature of work. The need for muscle and skill in creating unique products no longer was the main requirement in manufacturing. Now, machines performed many jobs much faster than people could, and the human workers performed repetitive motions in doing their jobs. Industrial technology has given us modern conveniences and a standard of living that is impossible otherwise, but it also made us into a cookie-cutter society.

### TEACH

Instruct students to read the **Connect to History** feature and answer the questions.

### ASSESS

Use the questions at the bottom of the page to assess the students' understanding of this feature.

**Answers to Think Critically**
Answers will vary. Answers should include evidence of conversations with family members who have seen a change in the productivity in everyday life. Students should provide specific examples of household tasks. For example, they might compare a grandparent's description of laundry day, including backyard clotheslines and clothespins, with their own experience of tossing clothes in the washer and then in the dryer.

## Bibliography

Bryant, Keith L., and Henry C. Dethloff. *A History of American Business*. Edgewood Cliffs, N.J.: Prentice Hall, 1990.

Chandler, Alfred D. *Giant Enterprise: Ford General Motors and the Automobile Industry*. New York: Harcourt, Brace, and World, 1964.

Foner, Eric, and John A. Garraty, eds. *The Reader's Companion to American History*. Boston: Houghton Mifflin Company, 1991.

Hurley, Daniel. *Cincinnati, the Queen City*. Cincinnati: The Cincinnati Historical Society, 1982.

Kross, Herman E., and Charles Gilbert. *American Business History*. Edgewood Cliffs, N.J.: Prentice Hall, 1972.

Morris, Richard B., and Jeffrey B. Morris. *Encyclopedia of American History*. New York: Harper Collins, 1996.

Murdock, Eugene. *The Buckeye Empire: An Illustrated History of Ohio Enterprise*. Northridge, Calif.: Windsor Publications, 1988.

Parish, Peter J., ed. *Reader's Guide to American History*. Chicago: Fitzroy Dearborn Publishers, 1997.

Puth, Robert C. *American Economic History*. New York: Dryden Press, 1982.

## Summary

### Summary

### Consider

Ask students to revisit the questions they were asked to consider at the beginning of the chapter. Remind students that they should be able to answer all of the questions after studying Chapter 12.

- Why do surgeons earn more than barbers, and accountants earn more than file clerks? See page 360—Human and Physical Capital.

- Why is the standard of living so much higher in some countries than in others? See page 367—Standard of Living.

- How can a nation boost its standard of living? See page 367—Standard of Living.

- Why is the economy's long-term growth rate more important than short-term fluctuations in economic activity? See page 358—The PPF and Economic Growth.

- What is labor productivity, and why has it grown faster in recent years? See page 368—U.S. Labor Productivity and Output Per Capita.

### Exam *View*

Use **Exam** *View* to assess students' learning

- Create a chapter test using questions from the existing test bank.

- Add your own questions to the existing test bank.

- Generate multiple forms of a chapter test.

### Study Skills

Offer the following study skills suggestions for students as they review this chapter.

- Outline the chapter.
- Review Key Terms.
- Review Checkpoints.
- Work in pairs to quiz each other.
- Use Xtra! Study Tools for each lesson.

Direct students to the online quiz preparation for Chapter 12 at **econxtra.swlearning.com**.

### 12.1 The PPF, Economic Growth, and Productivity

econxtra.swlearning.com

a Economic growth is the primary way to reduce poverty and raise living standards. When a greater share of a nation's resources is allocated to the production of capital goods, there will be increased rates of economic growth. When this is graphed on a production possibilities frontier, the frontier will shift out over time.

b *Productivity* measures how efficiently resources are employed to create goods and services. The more efficiently resources are used, the higher a nation's *standard of living* is likely to be. Measures of productivity include *labor productivity,* capital productivity, and land productivity. Labor productivity can be enhanced through investments in *human capital.*

c Investments in *physical capital* can take the form of *capital deepening,* which involves adding more or better physical capital to production. Investment in physical capital also may involve the creation and use of new types of capital. Capital embodies the fruits of technological breakthroughs and serves as the primary engine for economic growth.

### 12.2 Living Standards and Labor Productivity Growth

a The single most important determinant of a nation's standard of living is the productivity of its resources. There are great differences in the standards of living among nations. *Developing countries* have a lower standard of living than *industrial market countries* because they have less human and physical capital.

b The quality of a nation's labor is an important source of productivity. Countries with the most advanced educational systems also are those that were first to develop. Over the past 130 years, the productivity has grown at an average rate of just over 2 percent per year in

the United States. Small differences in productivity growth can cause huge differences in an economy's ability to produce over time.

c The best measure of an economy's standard of living is its output per capita. There has been an upward trend in this measure of productivity in the United States that has been interrupted by recessions in our economy. The output per capita in the United States is much greater than that in most other nations, whether they are industrial market economies or developing economies.

### 12.3 Issues of Technological Change

a Improvements in technology arise from scientific discovery, which is the product of research that may either be basic or applied. *Basic research* investigates general fields of knowledge but has no direct application to production. *Applied research* seeks to answer particular questions that will assist in the production of specific products. As a greater share of a nation's resources are devoted to research and development, that nation should enjoy a greater increase in its productivity.

b Technological improvements that are brought about through research lead to increases in *labor productivity.* Workers who are trained to use new technologies are able to produce goods and services that have greater value. New technologies, however, can cause some workers who lack needed skills to become unemployed. This unemployment may occur within a nation or across national boundaries.

c Some nations have created and implemented *industrial policies* that are intended to shape their economies' futures. These nations use taxes, subsidies, and regulations to coordinate business activity in their private sectors to nurture industries and technologies of the future. This type of government policy has been used in a limited way in the United States. It has been much more common in Europe and Japan. Although industrial policies have assisted some types of production, they also have resulted in allocating resources to industries that could not use them efficiently.

**382    CHAPTER 12** Economic Growth

### 12.2 Assessment

#### Think Critically

7. Answers will vary. Possible answer: The invention of the electric motor has contributed to the construction of many labor-saving devices that have increased labor productivity. These include electric drills, saws, and lathes that allow carpenters to be more productive.

Continued from page 373.

8. Answers will vary. Possible answer: Spell checks, computerized thesauruses, word processing, and desktop publishing have made the job of writing much easier today than it was in the past. Shakespeare might have been able to write hundreds of plays today instead of only 36 or 37.

# Review Economic Terms

Choose the term that best fits the definition. On a separate sheet of paper, write the letter of the answer. Some terms may not be used.

1. The machines, buildings, roads, airports, communications networks, and other manufactured creations used to produce goods and services

2. An economy's level of economic prosperity

3. Firms in the same industry or in related industries that group together in a region

_____ 4. The advanced market economies that include Western Europe, North America, Australia, New Zealand, and Japan

_____ 5. Output per unit of labor

_____ 6. The accumulated knowledge, skill, and experience of the labor force

_____ 7. Countries with a lower standard of living because they have relatively little human and physical capital

_____ 8. The search for knowledge without regard to how that knowledge will be used

_____ 9. The ratio of output to a specific measure of input

10. Research that seeks answers to particular questions or applies scientific discoveries to develop specific products

11. The view that government—using taxes, subsidies and regulations—should nurture the industries and technologies of the future, thereby giving domestic industries an advantage over foreign competition

_____12. The formal and informal institutions—such as laws, customs, and conventions—that provide production incentives and promote economic activity

a. **applied research**
b. **basic research**
c. **capital deepening**
d. **cluster**
e. **developing countries**
f. **Group of Seven (G-7)**
g. **human capital**
h. **industrial market countries**
i. **industrial policy**
j. **labor productivity**
k. **physical capital**
l. **productivity**
m. **rules of the game**
n. **standard of living**

# Review Economic Concepts

13. **True or False** *Capital deepening* involves adding more or better physical capital to production.

14. __?__ measures how efficiently resources are employed to create goods and services.

15. **True or False** The more of a nation's resources that are allocated to the production of capital goods, the greater that nation's rate of economic growth will be.

16. __?__ takes place when there is an increase in the quantity or quality of capital per worker.

17. Which of the following will shift a nation's production possibilities frontier outward over time?

a. switching production away from capital goods

b. an increase in resources that are devoted to Social Security benefits

c. switching production away from consumer goods towards capital goods

d. an increase in resources that are devoted to employee salaries

## Review Economic Terms

1. k. physical capital
2. n. standard of living
3. d. cluster
4. h. industrial market countries
5. j. labor productivity
6. g. human capital
7. e. developing countries
8. b. basic research
9. l. productivity
10. a. applied research
11. i. industrial policy
12. m. rules of the game

## Review Economic Concepts

13. True
14. Productivity
15. True
16. Capital deepening
17. c. switching production away from consumer goods towards capital goods

---

 **Assessment**

### Think Critically

6. Answers will vary. Possible answer: This type of tax reduction could cause businesses to purchase more machines that would replace workers. This could contribute to higher rates of unemployment.

Continued from page 380.

7. Answers will vary. Possible answer: Few private businesses would be willing or able to support the basic research carried out under NSF grants. Many important discoveries that improve the quality of our lives have been made because of NSF support. Several drugs that have extended the lives of those who suffer from AIDS were discovered with NSF support. This is a legitimate use of tax payments.

## Review Economic Concepts

18. a. Farmers are given a tax deduction when they buy new farm equipment.
19. developing
20. c. quality of its natural resources
21. industrial policies
22. Basic research
23. b. output per capita
24. Applied research
25. False. Technological advancements can reduce the number of workers needed to produce a given output.
26. d. Industrial policy may prevent businesses from investing in new technologies.
27. False. Productivity in the United States has increased at a varying rate over the past century.
28. b. can cause some workers who lack needed skills to become unemployed

## Apply Economic Concepts

29. Answers will vary. Possible answer: Each employee worked 2,000 hours (40 × 50 = 2,000) and produced 24,000 pins (480,000 ÷ 20 = 24,000) that were sold for $60,000 (24,000 × $2.50 = $60,000). The average value of each worker's hourly production was $30 ($60,000 ÷ 2,000 = $30). Labor was not the only cost ABC would have paid. The firm also needed to pay for raw materials and its physical capital.

---

18. Which of the following is an example of a change in the *rules of the game* that should increase a nation's productivity?

    a. Farmers are given a tax deduction when they buy new farm equipment.

    b. Lunches are provided free to students at an elementary school.

    c. Taxes on imported automobiles are increased.

    d. Welfare payments are increased for the nation's poor.

19. *Labor productivity* in most __?__ countries is very low, so most of their residents barely subsist.

20. The single most important determinant of a nation's *standard of living* is the

    a. productivity of its resources.

    b. size of its population.

    c. quality of its natural resources.

    d. nature of its government.

21. Some nations have created and implemented __?__ that are intended to nurture the industries and technologies of the future.

22. __?__ investigates general fields of knowledge but has no direct application to production.

23. Which of the following is regarded as the best measure of a nation's *standard of living*?

    a. total output

    b. output per capita

    c. spending on research and development

    d. spending on capital goods

24. __?__ seeks to answer particular questions or to use scientific discoveries to develop specific products.

25. **True or False** Technological advances will benefit all people equally.

26. Which of the following is not a common argument applied against the use of *industrial policy*?

    a. Industrial policy may result in investments that do not add to productivity.

    b. Industrial policy may give politicians too much control over the economy.

    c. Industrial policy may cause businesses to become uncompetitive in international trade.

    d. Industrial policy may prevent businesses from investing in new technologies.

27. **True or False** Productivity in the United States has increased at a constant rate of 2.1 percent per year over the past century.

28. Although technological improvements can lead to increased *labor productivity*, they also

    a. often reduce the quality of production.

    b. can cause some workers who lack needed skills to become unemployed.

    c. can weaken a nation's ability to compete in the global economy.

    d. may lower a nation's average standard of living.

# Apply Economic Concepts

29. **Calculating Labor Productivity** The ABC Bowling Pin Company employs 20 workers who all work 40 hours per week, 50 weeks per year. Last year ABC produced 480,000 bowling pins that were sold for $2.50 each. What was the average hourly value of each ABC's worker's production?

**30. Graphing Land Productivity** The amount of corn that Sara is able to grow on her farm depends on many things, including the amount of fertilizer she adds to the soil. She has studied her production over many years and has found the data in the table. Use these data to construct a bar graph that relates the land productivity per acre of Sara's farm to the amount of fertilizer she applies. Why does production per acre decrease when she applies more than 5 tons of fertilizer per 100 acres?

**Fertilizer Use and Corn Production Per Acre**

| Tons of Fertilizer Applied Per 100 Acres | Bushels of Corn Produced Per Acre |
|---|---|
| 0 | 100 |
| 1 | 130 |
| 2 | 160 |
| 3 | 185 |
| 4 | 200 |
| 5 | 210 |
| 6 | 200 |

**31. Comparing Growth Rates in Different Nations** Suppose that two nations currently have exactly the same GDP this year. Country A allocates 10 percent of its resources to producing capital goods, while country B devotes only 6 percent of its resources to this type of production. As a result, country A's production grows at a rate of 2.5 percent per year while country B's rate of growth is only 1.8 percent per year. After five more years, how much larger will country A's GDP be than country B's? Make the amount of production in the first year equal to 100 in both countries.

**32. Sharpen Your Life Skills: Categorizing Information** Identify which of the following activities would add to human capital, which would add to physical capital, and which would add to neither type of capital.

- Ted buys a new bicycle so he can deliver more newspapers in his neighborhood.
- Shakir buys a new pizza oven for her restaurant.
- Tyekeesha buys a take-out pizza on her way home from work.
- Carmen buys a calculator to help her keep records for her pet shop.
- Martin reads a book that teaches him how to repair his lawn mower.
- Tanya completes a class in automotive repair at a community college.

  econxtra.swlearning.com

**33.** Access **EconData Online** through econxtra.swlearning.com. Read the article entitled "What Is Labor Productivity?". Then click on "Diagrams/Data" and examine the line graph entitled "Labor Productivity and the Consumer Price Index." Judging from the graph, describe the relationship between production and inflation. Explain why you think this type of relationship exists.

---

## Apply Economic Concepts

**30.** Answers will vary. Possible answer: At some point, the plants will produce less corn because they have too much fertilizer.

A sample of an acceptable graph appears at the bottom of this page.

**31.** Answers will vary. Possible answer: Country A's GDP will have increased by 3.81 percent more than country B's (113.14 − 109.33 = 3.81).

| Year | Country A | Country B |
|---|---|---|
| 1 | 100.00 | 100.00 |
| 2 | 102.50 | 101.80 |
| 3 | 105.06 | 103.63 |
| 4 | 107.69 | 105.50 |
| 5 | 110.38 | 107.40 |
| 6 | 113.14 | 109.33 |

**32.** Ted—adds to physical capital

Shakir—adds to physical capital

Tyekeesha—adds to neither human nor physical capital

Carmen—adds to physical capital

Martin—adds to human capital

Tanya—adds to human capital

**33.** Production and inflation appear to be inversely related; an increase in inflation results in a decrease in production and vice versa. This relationship may exist because, during a period of inflation, there is less money to spend on technological advancements, which have a positive effect on production.

---

*Visualizing the Answer—*
*Apply Economic Concepts*

**30.** The answer includes a graph. Students' graphs should look similar to the one shown here. An Excel spreadsheet containing this graph, along with supporting data, is available on the Instructor's Resource CD.

**Fertilizer Used and Corn Production per 100 Acres**

## Chapter Overview

**LESSON 13.1** *Unemployment:* This lesson identifies types of unemployment and how unemployment is measured.

**LESSON 13.2** *Inflation:* The types and sources of inflation are presented in this lesson. Problems created by unexpected inflation are identified.

**LESSON 13.3** *Economic Instability:* This lesson demonstrates the use of aggregate demand and aggregate supply to analyze the Great Depression, demand-side economics, stagflation, and supply-side economics.

**LESSON 13.4** *Poverty:* The links between poverty and jobs and poverty and unmarried motherhood are explored. Some unplanned results of income-assistance programs are also discussed.

### Consider

Ask students to consider the questions posed on this page as they study Chapter 13. After studying all three lessons, students should be able to answer the questions. The content related to each question can be found on the pages indicated below.

- Would a high school senior who is not working be considered unemployed? See page 390—Unemployment Rate.
- What type of unemployment might be healthy for the economy? See page 388—Frictional Unemployment.
- What's bad about inflation? See page 400—Impact of Inflation.
- What's stagflation? See page 406—The Great Stagflation: 1973–1980.
- Why don't some families benefit from a strong economy? See page 400—Impact of Inflation.
- How might government transfers change work incentives? See page 414—Unplanned Results of Income Assistance.

### POINT YOUR BROWSER

Remind students that they can find additional resources for this chapter at econxtra.swlearning.com.

- Xtra! Study Tools
- Net Bookmarks
- Xtra! Quiz Prep
- econ@pps
- Ask the Xpert!
- Graphing Workshop

# 13 Economic Challenges

© Getty Images/PhotoDisc

### Consider

Would a high school senior who is not working be considered unemployed?

What type of unemployment might be healthy for the economy?

What's bad about inflation?

What's stagflation?

Why don't some families benefit from a strong economy?

How might government transfers change work incentives?

### POINT YOUR BROWSER

*econxtra.swlearning.com*

---

### Teaching Resources for Chapter 13

- Activities and Projects Masters
- Spanish Resources
- Econ Connection Interactive Tutorial CD
- **Exam***View*® CD
- Workbook Teacher's Edition
- Chapter and Unit Test Teacher's Edition
- NCEE Standards and Correlation
- Personal Finance Guide

- Social Studies Skills Review
- Instructor's Resource CD
  – PowerPoint Presentations
  – Lesson Plans
  – Video Discussion Guide
- Answers to Graphing Exercises
- **econxtra.swlearning.com**

## Objectives

> Distinguish among four types of unemployment.

> Discuss the unemployment rate, and describe how it differs over time and across groups.

> Explain who is eligible for unemployment benefits in the United States.

## Overview

"They scampered about looking for work.... They swarmed on the highways. The movement changed them. The highways, the camps along the road, the fear of hunger and the hunger itself, changed them. The children without dinner changed them, the endless moving changed them." There is no question, as John Steinbeck wrote in *The Grapes of Wrath*, that a long stretch of unemployment deeply affects the individual and the family. Unemployment also imposes costs on the economy. When there is high unemployment, the economy will not achieve its potential level of output. Not all unemployment harms the economy, however. Even in a healthy economy, some of the unemployment reflects the voluntary choices of workers and employers seeking their own self-interests.

## Key Terms

**full employment**

**underemployment**

**labor force**

**unemployment rate**

**labor force participation rate**

**unemployment benefits**

## FOCUS

13.1

### *Unemployment*

Remind students that unemployment can be seen from at least two perspectives. From a macro point of view, unemployment represents lost production and income that can reduce productivity and growth in an economy. From the individual worker's point of view, being unemployed interrupts one's flow of income, affects one's ability to purchase goods and services, and diminishes the standard of living.

### Objectives

Remind students to read the lesson objectives to help focus their attention before reading the lesson.

### Key Terms

Direct students to look up key terms in a business or economics dictionary. Some students will find it helpful to read another definition. In addition to a definition, many entries will include a brief explanation and an example.

### [ In the News ]

Instruct students to read the passage and write down their answers. Point out that their answers might change after they finish studying Lesson 13.1.

### Answers to Think About It

Answers will vary. Depression, sadness, anger, and anxiety are common emotional responses to job loss.

### Follow-Up Activity

Consider inviting a social worker, psychologist, or outplacement counselor to speak about the impact of job loss.

### *Visual Presentation*

Use the PowerPoint presentation on the Instructor's Resource CD as an adjunct to your lecture. The presentation also can be used for review.

## [ In the News ]

### ● Will Work for Anything

Vicky K. was laid off from her job as a computer engineer. At the time, she earned $21.50 per hour with full benefits. To make ends meet after the layoff, she took a seasonal job at an amusement park for $7.00 per hour with no benefits. Joseph B. lost his job as a computer programmer and worked part-time as a gas meter reader while he looked for full-time work for more than two years. One morning, Joseph joined 700 other people who lined up to answer a want ad for 18 technical jobs in city government. According to some economists, the U.S. economy slowly began to recover from a recession in the fall of 2001. However, despite some small improvements in the stock market and other parts of the economy, jobs continued to disappear. Some 9 million people were out of work on Labor Day, 2003. Many were finding it difficult to find any jobs in their field, especially if they had worked in high-tech industries. Almost a quarter of all people without jobs in 2003 spent more than six months looking for employment before they were hired again. Those who had used up all of their unemployment benefits were forced to look for any work they could find. Many people were forced to change careers just a few years before they had once expected to retire.

### Think About It

Has anyone close to you ever lost a job? What emotional impact did this job loss have on him or her?

◀ ▮ ▶

**387**

### *National Content Standards in Economics*

**NCEE**

A complete list of the NCEE Standards appears on pages xxiv–xxv of this book. The following standards are addressed in Lesson 13.1.

Standard 18: Macroeconomy—Income, Employment, Prices

Standard 19: Unemployment and Inflation

Standard 20: Monetary and Fiscal Policy

### Types of Unemployment

Tell students that although being unemployed may seem the same to those who experience this condition, there are different types of unemployment that have dissimilar impacts on the economy and those who suffer unemployment. Describe each of the four types of unemployment that economists have identified. Ask students to provide examples of each type from their own experiences. Tell students not to identify individuals in their examples by name or relationship to avoid any possible personal embarrassment. List these examples on the board. Discuss which examples were most harmful to the economy or to the people who were unemployed. Point out that some frictional unemployment is good for the economy and the unemployed individuals. People move from less productive jobs to alternative types of employment that allow them to increase their production, income, and standard of living.

## Ask the Xpert!

Direct students to **econxtra.swlearning.com** to hear an expert answer the question "What are the principal types of unemployment?"

## Ask the Xpert!

**econxtra.swlearning.com**

*What are the principal types of unemployment?*

**full employment**
Occurs when there is no cyclical unemployment; relatively low unemployment

# Types of Unemployment

Think about all the ways people can become unemployed. They may quit or be fired from their job. They may be looking for a first job, or they may be re-entering the labor force after an absence. A look at the reasons behind unemployment in 2000 indicates that 42 percent of the unemployed lost their previous jobs, 13 percent quit their previous jobs, 9 percent were entering the labor market for the first time, and 36 percent were re-entering the market.

The help-wanted section of a big-city newspaper may list thousands of job openings, from accountants to yoga instructors. Why are people unemployed when so many jobs are available? To understand the answer to this question, take a look at the four types of unemployment: frictional, structural, seasonal, and cyclical.

## Frictional Unemployment

Just as employers do not always hire the first applicant who comes through the door, job seekers do not always accept their first offer. Both employers and job seekers need time to explore the job market. Employers need time to learn about the talent available, and job seekers need time to learn about employment opportunities. The time required to bring together labor suppliers and labor demanders creates *frictional unemployment*. Frictional unemployment does not usually last long and results in a better match-up between workers and jobs. The entire economy becomes more efficient. A marketing major who graduated in June and is taking the summer to look for the perfect sales job is frictionally unemployed. A high school teacher who quits his job at the end of the school year to look for a job in another field is frictionally unemployed.

## Structural Unemployment

In a dynamic economy, the demand for some labor skills declines while the demand for other labor skills increases.

For example, automatic teller machines have put many bank tellers out of work. At the same time, those with certain computer skills are in greater demand. *Structural unemployment* results when job seekers do not have the skills demanded. Structural unemployment poses more of a problem than frictional unemployment because the unemployed may need to retrain to develop the required skills.

## Seasonal Unemployment

Unemployment caused by seasonal changes in labor demand during the year is called *seasonal unemployment*. During cold winter months, for example, demand for farm hands, lifeguards, and construction workers shrinks. Workers in these seasonal jobs know they will probably be unemployed in the off-season. Some may have even chosen a seasonal occupation to complement their lifestyles or academic schedules.

## Cyclical Unemployment

As output declines during recessions, firms reduce their demand for inputs, including labor. *Cyclical unemployment* is the increase in unemployment caused by the recession phase of the business cycle. Cyclical unemployment increases during recessions and decreases during expansions.

## Full Employment

In a dynamic, growing economy, changes in consumer demand and in technology continually affect the market for particular types of labor. Thus, even in a healthy, growing economy, there will be some frictional, structural, and seasonal unemployment. The economy is said to be at **full employment** if there is no cyclical unemployment.

When economists talk about "full employment," they do not mean zero unemployment but relatively low unemployment, say between 4 and 5 percent. Even when the economy is at full employment, there will be some frictional, structural, and seasonal unemployment.

## *Outside Resources*

**Unemployment Information** The U.S. Department of Labor provides extensive information about unemployment, including its causes and results, at its web site, which is located at www.dol.gov/. Ask students to visit this web site, use the Index to find unemployment information, pick a topic, and report on what they find. Some specific topics from the web site are listed below.

- Job & Training Information
- Layoff Resources
- Wages & Work Hours
- Workplace Safety & Health

- Retirement & Health Benefits
- Disability Resources
- Statistical Information

## Problems with Official Unemployment Estimates

Official unemployment statistics have limitations. For example, some people may have become so discouraged by a long, unsuccessful job search that they have given up looking for work. These *discouraged workers* have, in effect, dropped out of the labor force, so they are not counted as unemployed. Because the official unemployment rate ignores discouraged workers, it may underestimate unemployment in the economy.

Official employment figures also ignore the problem of **underemployment**. This arises because people are counted as employed even if they can find only part-time jobs or are overqualified for their job. For example, if someone with a Ph.D. in English can find work only as a bookstore clerk, that individual would be considered underemployed.

## NET Bookmark

The Bureau of Labor Statistics provides abundant data on labor market conditions, including unemployment rates, labor force estimates, and earnings data. Access the web site through econxtra.swlearning.com. What is the unemployment rate for the most recent month listed in the table?

*econxtra.swlearning.com*

Counting the underemployed as employed tends to understate the true amount of unemployment.

On the other hand, there are reasons why unemployment figures may overstate the true extent of employment. For example, to qualify for some government transfer programs, beneficiaries must look for work. If some of these

**under-employment**

Workers are overqualified for their jobs or work fewer hours than they would prefer

**What type of unemployment results for members of the ski patrol when changing weather patterns no longer permit skiing in an area?**

© Getty Images/PhotoDisc

---

The U.S. dot-com industry suffered a "meltdown" at the beginning of the twenty-first century. Workers who had been earning well into six figures found themselves out of work. Even though they possessed many specialized skills that had once been in great demand, many were either looking for jobs or working for considerably less pay, often in lesser positions. Discuss how this situation demonstrates cyclical and structural unemployment, and in many cases underemployment as well. (People became unemployed because of the downturn in the economy; because they lacked skills that were in demand; and, in many cases, accepted jobs that did not take advantage of their skills.)

---

## The Cost and Measure of Unemployment

Explain that it can be difficult for the government to measure unemployment accurately. In 2003, the civilian noninstitutional population was roughly 220 million people. The labor force in that year exceeded 140 million individuals. It would be impossible for the government to ask all of these people about their employment status every month. The Bureau of Labor Statistics, therefore, uses a scientific survey in which various groups are surveyed in proportion to the share they represent of the nation's population. If 13 percent of the total population is African American, then 13 percent of those surveyed are African American, and so on. The results of this scientific survey are projected to the entire population to calculate the official national employment data. This methodology assumes that the survey method used is reliable. Although most economists believe that it is, some are less sure. Remind students that only workers who are actively seeking employment are counted as unemployed. Wanting a job is not enough. To be counted, a person must actually go out and look for work.

### *Think Critically Through Visuals*

Direct students to focus their attention on the photograph on this page. Ask for a volunteer to answer the questions posed in the caption.

### Answer

Answers will vary. Possible answers: One cost of unemployment for individual is the loss of a steady paycheck. A loss of self-esteem may accompany this. Unemployment also produces a cost on the economy because fewer goods and services are produced.

### NCEE Standard 19: Unemployment and Inflation

Main Idea

Unemployment imposes costs on individuals and nations. Unexpected inflation imposes costs on many people and benefits some others because it arbitrarily redistributes purchasing power. Inflation can reduce the rate of growth of national living standards because individuals and organizations use resources to protect themselves against the uncertainty of future prices.

---

people do not in fact want to find a job, then counting them as unemployed overstates the true unemployment rate. Also, people working in the underground economy may not readily admit they have a job if their intent is to evade taxes or skirt the law. Many of those in the underground economy end up being counted as unemployed even though they are working.

**CHECKPOINT**
What are the four types of unemployment?

# The Cost and Measure of Unemployment

The most obvious cost of unemployment is the loss of a steady paycheck for the unemployed individual. However, many who lose their jobs also suffer a loss of self-esteem. No matter how much people complain about their jobs, they rely on them not only for income but also for part of their personal identity. A long stretch of unemployment can have a lasting effect on both self-esteem and economic welfare.

Main Idea

**labor force**
Those in the adult population who are either working or looking for work

**unemployment rate**
The number looking for work divided by the number in the labor force

**Unemployment**

What are *the costs of unemployment for unemployed individuals?* What are some other costs associated with unemployment?

© Getty Images/PhotoDisc

---

In addition to these personal costs, unemployment imposes a cost on the economy as a whole because fewer goods and services are produced. When the economy does not generate enough jobs to employ all who seek work, that unemployed labor is lost forever. *This lost output together with the economic and psychological damage to unemployed workers and their families represents the true cost of unemployment.*

## Unemployment Rate

The most widely reported measure of the nation's economic health is the unemployment rate. To see what the unemployment rate measures, you need to understand its components. A measurement of unemployment begins with the U.S. *noninstitutional adult population,* which consists of all those 16 years of age and older, except people in the military, in prisons, or in mental hospitals. When the expression "adult population" is referred to in this section, it means the noninstitutional adult population.

The **labor force** consists of those in the adult population who are either working or looking for work. *Those with no job who are looking for work are counted as unemployed.* Thus, a high school student at least 16 years of age, Nicole Kidman, and Barry Bonds would all be counted as unemployed if they want a job but can't find one. The **unemployment rate** equals the number unemployed—that is, people without jobs who are looking for work—divided by the number in the labor force.

Unemployment rate

$$= \frac{\text{Number unemployed}}{\text{Number in the labor force}}$$

Only a fraction of those not working are considered unemployed. People may not be working for all kinds of reasons. They may be full-time students, retirees, homemakers, or disabled. Or they may simply not want to work.

## Labor Force Participation Rate

Employment measures are illustrated in Figure 13.1. In this figure, circles represent the various groups, and the millions of people in each category and subcategory are shown in parentheses. The circle on the left depicts the entire U.S. labor force, including both those employed and those looking for work. The circle on the right represents members of the adult population who are not working. Together, these two circles include the adult population.

The overlapping area identifies *unemployed* workers—that is, people in the labor force who are not working but looking for work. Using the fomula given above, in this example 8.4 million people were unemployed in a labor force of 145.9 million. This resulted in a U.S. unemployment rate of 5.8 percent.

The productive capability of any economy depends in part on the proportion of adults in the labor force, measured as the *labor force participation rate*. In Figure 13.1, the U.S. adult population equals those in the labor force (145.9 million) plus those not in the labor force (74.2 million), for a total

**Investigate Your Local Economy**

Research to find the unemployment rates in your city and state. Compare these rates with the most current unemployment rate for the United States. If these rates differ, propose an explanation for why they differ.

of 220.1 million. The **labor force participation rate** therefore equals the number in the labor force divided by the adult population. For February 2003, that was 145.9 million divided by 220.1 million, which equals 66.3 percent. So, on average, two out of three adults were in the labor force then. The labor force participation rate increased from about 60 percent in 1970 to about 67 percent in 1990. Since then, it has remained relatively constant.

**labor force participation rate**

The number in the labor force divided by the adult population

---

**Composition of Adult Population, February 2003 (in millions)**

**Figure 13.1**

The labor force consists of employed and unemployed people. Those not working consist of individuals not in the labor force and those unemployed. The adult population sums the employed, the unemployed, and people not in the labor force.

Source: U.S. Bureau of Labor Statistics.

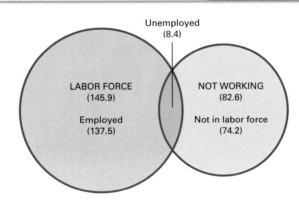

Unemployed (8.4)

LABOR FORCE (145.9)

Employed (137.5)

NOT WORKING (82.6)

Not in labor force (74.2)

Lesson 13.1 • *Unemployment* 391

---

---

*Group Activity*

Give groups copies of recent financial newspapers such as *The Wall Street Journal* or *Barron's*. Ask them to find articles that report on a change in production, or economic conditions that are likely to affect the labor force participation rate for a particular group of workers. Many of these will involve the opening or closing of a business in a particular community. The creation or elimination of many jobs in a community is likely to affect the number of people who join the labor force, and thereby also affect the labor force participation rate. What does an awareness of job opportunities have to do with people's willingness to seek employment?

(continued) **TEACH**

## The Cost and Measure of Unemployment

Provide five students with the following job descriptions. Ask them to read them to the class. Then tell the class that the economy has gone into a recession. Ask the class to predict which workers would be most likely to become unemployed. Call on students to explain their predictions to the class. If these workers became unemployed, how might the economy be affected?

- You are employed as a stock clerk in a grocery store where you have worked for the past 17 years. You are a member of a labor union.

- You are employed as an airline representative. Your job is to take telephone orders for tickets. You have held your job for two years.

- You are employed as a production worker by an office-furniture manufacturer. You have held your job for five years. There is no union at this business.

- You are a research chemist employed by a large pharmaceutical manufacturer. You have made an important discovery in the past year that should help the firm earn a good profit.

- You design web pages for online retail sales firms. You are self-employed.

### *Think Critically Through Visuals*

Direct students to focus their attention on **Figure 13.2—The U.S. Unemployment Rate Since 1900.** Point out the dramatic increase in unemployment starting in 1929.

### *Think Critically Through Visuals*

Direct students to focus their attention on **Figure 13.3—Unemployment Among Various Groups Since 1972** on page 393. Point out the difference in the scale used for the y-axis in the two graphs.

**CHECKPOINT**

Invite a student to answer the checkpoint that appears on page 393.

### Answer

The unemployment rate is the number unemployed divided by the number in the labor force. Unemployment rates tend to be higher for African Americans and for individuals under the age of 20.

## Changes in Unemployment Rate

Figure 13.2 shows the U.S. unemployment rate since 1900, with shading to indicate periods of recession and depression. As you can see, the rate increased during recessions and fell during expansions. Perhaps the most striking feature of the graph is the dramatic jump that occurred during the Great Depression of the 1930s, when the unemployment rate reached 25.2 percent.

## Unemployment for Various Groups

The unemployment rate says nothing about who is unemployed or for how long. Even a low overall rate often hides wide differences in unemployment rates across age, race, gender, and geographic area. For example, when the U.S. unemployment rate was 5.8 percent, the rate was 17.1 percent among teenagers, 10.5 percent among blacks, and 7.7 percent among Hispanics. These reflect differences in job opportu-nities, work experience, education, skills, as well as discrimination.

Unemployment rates for different groups appear in Figure 13.3. As you can see, rates are higher among blacks than among whites. They also are higher among teenagers than among those aged 20 and older. During recessions, the rates climbed for all groups. Rates peaked during the recession of 1982 and then trended down. After the recession of the early 1990s, unemployment rates continued downward, with the rate among blacks falling in 2000 to the lowest on record. Rates then turned up again with the recession of 2001.

Why are unemployment rates among teenagers so much higher than among workers age 20 and older? Because young workers enter the job market with little training, they take unskilled jobs and are the first to be fired if the economy slows down. Young workers also move in and out of the job market more frequently during the year as they juggle school demands. Even those who have left school often shop around for jobs more than older workers do.

**The U.S. Unemployment Rate Since 1900**  **Figure 13.2**

Since 1900, the unemployment rate has fluctuated widely, rising during recessions and falling during expansions. During the Great Depression of the 1930s, the rate rose as high as 25.2 percent.

Sources: U.S. Census Bureau, *Historical Statistics of the United States: Colonial Times to 1970* (Washington, D.C.: U.S. Government Printing Office, 1975); *Economic Report of the President,* February 2003; and U.S. Bureau of Labor Statistics.

**392**   **CHAPTER 13**  Economic Challenges

---

### *Curriculum Connection—History*

During the nineteenth century, there were no meaningful child labor laws in the United States. Young people could be hired to do virtually any job and work under any conditions. As a matter of fact, children were often sought out as workers because of their size. It was not uncommon for children to be employed when adults could not find work. One example of this can be seen in the textile industry, where children's small hands allowed them to manipulate thread more easily in automated looms than could adults' hands. Many children were injured operating these powerful, high-speed machines. Ask students to discuss the economic results of child-labor laws that prohibited the use of children in most industrial situations after the turn of the twentieth century.

**Figure 13.3**

### (a) 20 years of age or older

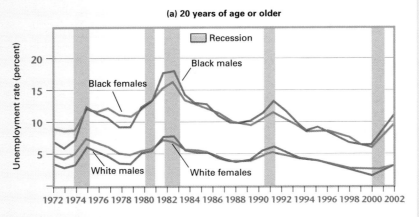

**Unemployment affects different groups in different ways. The unemployment rate is higher for blacks than for whites and higher for teenagers than for older persons.**

Sources: *Economic Report of the President,* February 2003; U.S. Bureau of Labor Statistics.

### (b) 16 to 19 years of age

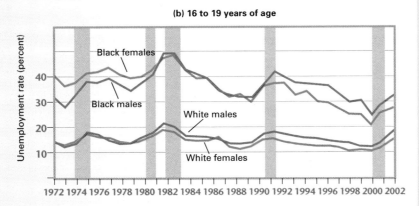

The U.S. unemployment rate also covers up much variation in rates across the country. For example, recent unemployment rates in Alaska, Oregon, and Washington were more than double those in Nebraska, North Dakota, and South Dakota.

 **CHECKPOINT**
What is the unemployment rate and how has it differed over time and across groups?

# Unemployment Benefits

As noted earlier, unemployment often imposes both an economic and psychological hardship on the unemployed worker and the family. Today, a large proportion of households have two workers in the labor force, so if one becomes unemployed, another is likely to still have a job that may provide health insurance and other benefits. Having more than one family member

**Lesson 13.1** • *Unemployment*    **393**

**TEACH**

**Unemployment Benefits**
Point out that every state provides some level of unemployment compensation to workers who have been laid off. These benefits allow unemployed workers to continue to spend and support their families for limited periods of time (most often 26 weeks). Although the unemployed workers clearly benefit from these payments, employed workers do, too. The spending that is supported by unemployment compensation payments helps to maintain aggregate demand in the economy and the derived demand for labor and other resources.

***Think Critically Through Visuals***
Direct students to focus their attention on the photograph on page 394. Ask for a volunteer to answer the question posed in the caption.

**Answer**
Answers will vary. Possible answer: One advantage of having more than one family member in the work force is that it can cushion the shock of unemployment.

 **CHECKPOINT**
Invite a student to answer the checkpoint that appears on page 394.

**Answer**
Workers who have lost their jobs are eligible for unemployment benefits.

## Extend the Content

Before 1935, there was no national program to provide unemployment compensation benefits. During this time, it was much easier for employers to exploit workers than it is today. Ask students to discuss how unemployment compensation helped to "level the playing field" in negotiations between workers and employers after 1935. (After 1935, workers knew that they would receive unemployment compensation payments if they were laid off from their jobs. Although such payments generally are not made when there is a strike, this still gave workers greater flexibility in seeking new employment when they did get laid off.)

**unemployment benefits**

Cash transfers to unemployed workers who actively seek work and who meet other qualifications

in the labor force cushions the economic shock of unemployment.

## Unemployment Compensation

Workers who lose their jobs today often receive unemployment benefits. In response to the massive unemployment of the Great Depression, Congress passed the Social Security Act of 1935. This act provided unemployment insurance financed by a tax on employers. Unemployed workers who meet certain qualifications can receive **unemployment benefits** for up to six months, provided they actively seek work.

During recessions, unemployment benefits often extend beyond six months in states with especially high unemployment. Insurance benefits go mainly to people who have lost jobs. Individuals just entering or re-entering the labor force are not covered, nor are those who quit their last job or those fired for just cause, such as excessive absenteeism or theft. Because of these restrictions, fewer than half of all unemployed workers receive unemployment benefits.

Unemployment benefits averaged about $240 per week in 2002. This replaced on average about 40 percent of a person's take-home pay, with a higher share for those whose jobs paid less.

## Unemployment Benefits and Work Incentives

Because unemployment benefits reduce the opportunity cost of remaining unemployed, they also may reduce the incentive to find work. For example, what if you faced the choice of taking a job washing dishes that pays $200 per week or collecting $150 per week in unemployment benefits?

Evidence suggests that those who receive unemployment benefits tend to search less actively than those who don't. Those who receive benefits step up their job search as the end of benefits approaches.

Although unemployment benefits provide a safety net for the unemployed, they also may reduce the need to find work. They may increase the average length of unemployment and the unemployment rate as well.

On the plus side, unemployment benefits allow for a more careful job search, because the job seeker has some money and need not take the first job that comes along. As a result of a better search, there is a better match between job skills and job requirements, and this promotes economic efficiency. In addition, unemployment compensation payments allow the unemployed to continue to spend. This spending reduces the likelihood that other workers will be laid off.

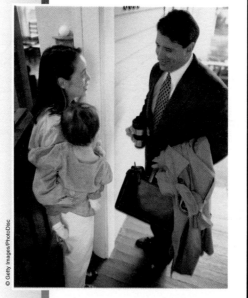

© Getty Images/PhotoDisc

**What are the advantages of having more than one family member in the labor force?**

 **CHECKPOINT**
Who is eligible for unemployment benefits in the United States?

394   **CHAPTER 13**   Economic Challenges

## Key Concepts

1. How may people who keep their jobs be harmed by high levels of unemployment?

2. Are you currently a member of the labor force? Explain your answer.

3. Why do you think the government considers as unemployed only those adults who are without employment but are looking for work?

4. Do you know anyone who has chosen to change jobs? Why did this person make this choice? How long was he or she unemployed? Was this person satisfied with the job he or she eventually accepted? Do you think this person made a rational choice?

5. Unemployment compensation payments can make up for some of the income workers lose when they are laid off. However, such payments do not provide medical insurance coverage. Why might this be an important incentive for a person who is out of work to seek new employment as quickly as possible?

6. How can unemployment compensation payments help workers who are not unemployed?

## Graphing Exercise

7. In general, young people suffer from higher rates of unemployment than older people. Use data from this table to construct a double line graph that compares the rates of unemployment for people who are 16–19 years of age with the average for all members of the labor force. Identify and explain three possible reasons for young people having higher unemployment rates.

**Unemployment Rates, 1985–2002**

| Year | Unemployment Rate For People 16–19 | Unemployment Rate For Entire Labor Force |
|------|-----------------------------------|------------------------------------------|
| 1985 | 18.6% | 7.2% |
| 1990 | 15.5% | 5.6% |
| 1995 | 17.3% | 5.6% |
| 2000 | 13.1% | 4.0% |
| 2002 | 16.5% | 5.8% |

## Think Critically

8. **History** The Great Depression of the 1930s was the deepest and most well-known economic downturn in recent U.S. history. There have been many other recessions since 1776. Years in which these recessions occurred include 1837, 1873, 1893, and 1907. Investigate one of these events. What happened to employment in the recession you chose to study?

9. **Sociology** Look through a sociology textbook or on the Internet to find information about how society is affected by high rates of unemployment. You should particularly investigate its impact on families. Are there more divorces when unemployment is high? Why might this be true?

**Xtra!** Study Tools
econxtra.swlearning.com

---

## Key Concepts

1. Answers will vary. Possible answer: When many people are unemployed, production falls and the average standard of living in a nation will decline. This can affect people who are employed because they have fewer products to choose from and may not be able to work as many hours or earn as much income. They may also have to contribute more to government assistance programs.

2. Answers will vary. Students may point out that they would be included in the labor force if they are 16 or over and either employed or looking for work.

3. Answers will vary. Possible answer: Counting people who are not looking for employment as unemployed might give an unrealistically high picture of unemployment and an inaccurate impression of the state of the economy.

4. Answers will vary. Possible answer: A person who chooses to quit a job is probably dissatisfied with that job and is therefore likely not to be as productive as he or she could be. By leaving the job and finding other employment, the person may be more satisfied and more productive.

5. Answers will vary. Students may point out that medical insurance is very expensive and important for people to have. An unemployed person who receives a job offer from an employer who will provide medical insurance is likely to accept that offer to avoid being uninsured.

6. The spending that is supported by unemployment compensation payments helps to maintain aggregate demand in the economy and the derived demand for labor and other resources.

## Graphing Exercise

7. Answers will vary. Students may point out that young people often lack experience, training, and seniority that could prevent them from becoming unemployed.

A sample of an acceptable graph appears at the bottom of this page.

*The Answer Key is continued on pages 421–422.*

---

**Unemployment Rates, 1985 through 2001**

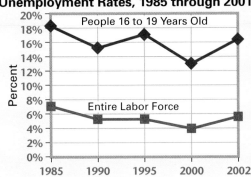

### Visualizing the Answer— Graphing Exercise

7. The answer includes a graph. Students' graphs should look similar to the one shown here. An Excel spreadsheet containing this graph, along with supporting data, is available on the Instructor's Resource CD.

# movers & shakers

## FOCUS

A visit to Monster.com is a good way to introduce this feature. Consider showing the Monster.com home page and then clicking on the link for new visitors. Point out that the site looks fun and inviting. Suggest that students visit the site after reading about Jeff Taylor.

## TEACH

Instruct students to read the **Movers & Shakers** feature about Jeff Taylor. Point out that some students may find it helpful to read the article, read the questions at the bottom of the page, and then reread the article.

## ASSESS

Use the questions in Source Reading and Entrepreneurs in Action at the bottom of the profile to assess the students' understanding of this **Movers & Shakers** feature.

### Answers to Source Reading

Answers will vary. Possible answers: Monster.com affects frictional unemployment—that is, the unemployment that results from the time it takes employers to find job seekers. Monster.com makes the economy more efficient by reducing the amount of time it takes these two population groups to find each other.

### Answers to Entrepreneurs in Action

Answers will vary. Possible answer: Jeff's ingenuity in developing a good or service in a market where there is an existing demand for that good or service led to his success.

# movers & shakers

### Jeff Taylor *CEO, Monster.com*

Being a leader is part of Jeff Taylor's make-up. While attending the University of Massachusetts, he set his sights on becoming pledge master of the Pi Kappa Alpha fraternity. Not only did he achieve that goal, Taylor eventually became fraternity vice-president and then president. At the same time, he also managed the university's tour guide service. As advertising manager and later business manager for the University of Massachusetts paper, *The Collegian,* Taylor helped make the paper profitable after a 30-year history of operating in the red. To earn living expenses during college, Taylor came up with the idea to assemble and sell "freshmen survival kits," a box of snacks intended to help freshmen survive exam week.

After graduating, Taylor earned an executive MBA from Harvard Business School. In 1989, he started his own advertising agency, Adion. The name, he explains, "stood for what we did, which was create ads, and for the particle of energy—ion—that represented the energy we put into creating ads." While running his ad agency, Taylor became intrigued by the then-new concept of computer bulletin boards. "So I started learning everything I could about them. At the same time, the World Wide Web was being invented." Taylor combined his interests in advertising and the new communications technologies, and what resulted was Monster.com.

Now the company's CEO, Taylor created Monster.com for companies looking for employees and individuals looking for jobs. At its inception, the site posted 200 job openings at 20 different companies.

Today, the Monster web site typically posts more than 400,000 job openings and is visited by more than 15 million job seekers each month. It is the largest careers web site in the world. In 2003, Monster.com had 8,500 employees and annual sales of more than $1 billion. The stock market valued the company at $3.2 billion as of October 2003.

Monster.com has special services that enable visitors to develop one or more online resumes that can be stored for free. Visitors also can apply online for jobs, all at no charge. For a membership fee, users can utilize software components that will continuously search for their self-described "ideal" job.

At 39 years of age, Taylor is not your typical CEO. He equipped the company's headquarters, located in Maynard, Massachusetts, with pool, ping-pong, and foosball tables. "We encourage our employees to be excellent foosball players as long as they have some other core competency, like doing their job well." He practices what he preaches. "I can hold my own during employee foosball tournaments."

Taylor's leadership abilities have made him an attractive employer. "I think a big part of being a leader is learning how to identify talent. The people you surround yourself with are going to directly influence your ability to build a successful organization, so you must be very careful and selective of the people you hire." He adds, "Being able to recognize good ideas from okay ideas is also a key aspect of leadership." Taylor is a fan of the saying that the shortest distance between two points is a good idea. A popular speaker, Taylor likes to tell his audience, "If you have good ideas, pursue them!" His other favorite expression—one that promotes his belief in hard work—is, "you can only coast one way, and that is downhill."

---

### SOURCE READING

What type of unemployment do you think Monster.com affects? Explain your answer. How does Monster.com help to make the economy more efficient?

### ENTREPRENEURS IN ACTION

Jeff Taylor's success is self-made. In small groups, discuss the qualities Jeff Taylor possesses that helped lead to his success.

**396**      **CHAPTER 13**   Economic Challenges

## 13.2 Inflation

## Objectives

> Describe the types of inflation, and identify two sources of inflation.

> Identify the problems that unexpected inflation creates.

## Overview

As a result of incredibly high inflation, Brazilian prices in 1994 were 3.6 million times higher than in 1988. To put this in perspective, with such inflation in the United States, the price of gasoline would have climbed from $1.25 a gallon in 1988 to $4.5 million a gallon in 1994. A pair of jeans that sold for $25 in 1988 would have cost $90 million in 1994. With such wild inflation, Brazilians had difficulty keeping track of prices. People couldn't lug around enough money to make even small purchases. Inflation, particularly high inflation, makes market exchange much more difficult.

## Key Terms

**inflation**

**demand-pull inflation**

**cost-push inflation**

**nominal interest rate**

**real interest rate**

## [ In the News ]

### ● Who's the Box Office Champion?

Almost every year, the total amount of movie box office receipts increases. The 1997 movie *Titanic* grossed more than $600 million in the United States—more than any movie ever. However, in 1997 the average ticket price for a movie was around $5.00. When adjusted for inflation, *Titanic* was only the seventh highest-grossing film of all time. The film that made the most money, when adjusted for inflation, was the 1939 epic *Gone with the Wind*. At the time it came out, the average price of a movie ticket was only 25 cents. When its revenues are adjusted for inflation, it earned the equivalent of $1.3 billion in 1997 dollars, more than twice as much as *Titanic*. This means that many more people actually saw *Gone with the Wind* when it came out than saw *Titanic*. This trend is reflected in movie attendance records as well. Even though films today gross much more than films of the 1930s, more people went to the movies back then. Today about 25 million Americans see a movie each week. In the 1930s, about 90 million people went to the movies every week. Because of this difference, it is very unlikely that even the most popular modern film will ever surpass *Gone with the Wind*, or even the second-runner up, *Snow White and the Seven Dwarves* (1937), which, in inflation-adjusted dollars, grossed more than $1 billion in the United States.

### Think About It

Why is it necessary to adjust for inflation when comparing economic situations from different eras, such as movie box office receipts?

◀ | ▶

**397**

### National Content Standards in Economics

A complete list of the NCEE Standards appears on pages xxiv–xxv of this book. The following standards are addressed in Lesson 13.2.

Standard 18: Macroeconomy—Income, Employment, Prices

Standard 19: Unemployment and Inflation

Standard 20: Monetary and Fiscal Policy

## FOCUS

### 13.2 Inflation

Remind students that inflation is a sustained increase in the average price level. There are different types of inflation that affect the economy in different ways. Not only are the effects of inflation different but the causes can be different as well.

### Objectives

Remind students to read the lesson objectives to help focus their attention before reading the lesson.

### Key Terms

Direct students to create a database using the key terms for this lesson. The database fields should include terms, definitions, and page numbers. Point out that the process of keying the data is an effective way to study key terms.

### [ In the News ]

Instruct students to read the passage and write down their answers. Point out that their answers might change after they finish studying Lesson 13.2.

### Answers to Think About It

Answers will vary. Possible answer: It is necessary to adjust for inflation when comparing economic situations from different time periods because there are changes in prices from time period to time period. In order to make comparisons across time periods, one needs to compensate for those differences in cost.

### Follow-Up Activity

Invite interested students to create a poster or model to illustrate one of the key concepts presented in this feature. Consider allowing students to work in pairs or small groups.

### Visual Presentation

Use the PowerPoint presentation on the Instructor's Resource CD as an adjunct to your lecture. The presentation also can be used for review.

## Inflation Basics

Remind students that inflation is the result of an imbalance between the quantity of products demanded and the quantity supplied at an existing price level. A shortage of products that will cause prices to rise may be caused either by an increase in demand (demand-pull inflation) or a decrease in supply (cost-push inflation). In either situation, pressure will be exerted on prices to increase.

### *Think Critically Through Visuals*

Direct students to focus their attention on Figure 13.4—Inflation Caused by Shifts in the Aggregate Demand and Aggregate Supply Curves. Point out that although the two graphs are similar, the graph on the left illustrates demand-pull inflation and the one on the right illustrates cost-push inflation.

Direct students to **econxtra.swlearning.com.** Remind them to click on the link for Lesson 13.2 to find the appropriate link for the NET Bookmark on this page.

### Answer

Answers will vary, depending on when students visit the web site. The answer should be expressed as a percentage.

### Follow-Up Activity

Invite interested students research the inflation rate of another country. Suggest that they choose a country currently in the news.

### Ask the Xpert!

Direct students to **econxtra.swlearning.com** to hear an expert answer the question "Which is worse: demand-pull inflation or cost-push inflation?"

# Inflation Basics

**inflation**
An increase in the economy's general price level

**demand-pull inflation**
Inflation resulting from a rightward shift of the aggregate demand curve

You were introduced to the concept of inflation earlier in this book. **Inflation** is an increase in the economy's general price level. Inflation reduces the value of money and is usually measured on an annual basis. The *annual inflation rate* is the percentage increase in the general price level from one year to the next.

## Types of Inflation

Extremely high inflation, such as the experience in Brazil, is called *hyperinflation*. A reduction in the rate of inflation is called *disinflation*, as occurred in the United States during the 1980s. A decrease in the general price level is called *deflation*, as occurred in the United States during the Great Depression and most recently in Japan, Hong Kong, and Taiwan.

## Two Sources of Inflation

Inflation is an increase in the economy's price level resulting from an increase in aggregate demand or a decrease in aggregate supply. Panel (a) of Figure 13.4 shows an increase in aggregate demand that raises the price level from $P$ to $P'$. Inflation resulting from increases in aggregate demand is often called **demand-pull inflation**. In such cases, a rightward shift of the aggregate demand curve *pulls up* the price level.

### NETBookmark

The Brazilian embassy in Washington, D.C., maintains a web site that you can access through econxtra.swlearning.com. Put your cursor on "The Economy" and then click on "Brazil Economic Briefing" to access the latest news and reports on the Brazil's economy. What's the current status of Brazil's inflation rate?

*econxtra.swlearning.com*

---

**Inflation Caused by Shifts of the Aggregate Demand and Aggregate Supply Curves** | Figure 13.4

**(a) Demand-pull inflation: inflation caused by an increase of aggregate demand**

**(b) Cost-push inflation: inflation caused by a decrease of aggregate supply**

Panel (a) illustrates demand-pull inflation. An outward shift of the aggregate demand curve to *AD'* "pulls" the price level up from *P* to *P'*. Panel (b) shows cost-push inflation, in which a decrease of aggregate supply to *AS'* "pushes" the price level up from *P* to *P'*.

398    **CHAPTER 13**   Economic Challenges

---

## *Outside Resources*

**Financial Periodicals** Many financial periodicals provide extensive information about inflation and its impact on the economy. Among these is *Kiplinger's Personal Finance Magazine*. This monthly publication contains many articles about changes in price. These articles can be used to help illustrate concepts presented in this textbook. Recent articles can be accessed online at www.kiplinger.com. Registration is required, but there is no fee.
A table showing the monthly Consumer Price Index since 1970 is available without registration at www.special.kiplinger.com/kbftables/usecon/inflation/CPIbymonth.htm.

To generate continuous demand-pull inflation, the aggregate demand curve would have to keep shifting out along a given aggregate supply curve. Rising U.S. inflation rates during the late 1960s resulted from demand-pull inflation. At this time, federal spending for the Vietnam War and for expanded social programs boosted aggregate demand.

Alternatively, inflation can arise from reductions in aggregate supply. This is shown in panel (b) of Figure 13.4, where a leftward shift of the aggregate supply curve raises the price level. For example, crop failures and cuts in OPEC oil supplies reduced aggregate supply during 1974 and 1975, thereby raising the price level.

Inflation stemming from decreases in aggregate supply is called **cost-push inflation**, suggesting that increases in the cost of production *push up* the price level. If prices increase and real GDP decreases, this combination is called *stagflation*, which will be discussed later in this chapter. Again, to generate sustained and continuous cost-push inflation, the aggregate supply curve would have to keep shifting to the left along a given aggregate demand curve.

## An Historical Look at Inflation and the Price Level

The consumer price index is the price measure you most often encounter, so it gets more attention here. As you have already learned, the *consumer price index (CPI)* measures the cost of a "market basket" of consumer goods and services over time. Figure 13.5 shows prices in the United States since 1913, using the consumer price index. The price *level* is measured by an index relative to the base period of 1982 to 1984. As you can see, the price level actually was lower in 1940 than in 1920. Since 1940, however, the price level has risen steadily, especially during the 1970s.

Ask the Xpert!
econxtra.swlearning.com

*Which is worse: demand-pull inflation or cost-push inflation?*

**cost-push inflation**

Inflation resulting from a leftward shift of the aggregate supply curve

✔ **CHECKPOINT**
Name the types of inflation and two sources of inflation.

---

**Consumer Price Index Since 1913**

Figure **13.5**

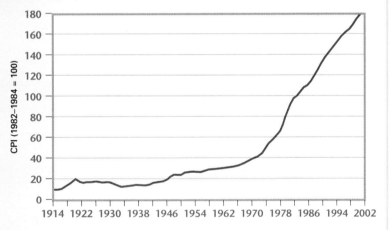

Despite fluctuations, the price level, as measured by the consumer price index, was lower in 1940 than in 1920. Since 1940, the price level has risen almost every year.

Source: U.S. Bureau of Labor Statistics.

---

### Inflation Basics

Sketch a graph of demand and supply on the board. Tell students that it represents aggregate demand and supply, and the average price level for the entire economy. Read the following descriptions of events to the class and ask students to describe how each would affect the curves on the graph and average price levels. Which of these events cause demand-pull inflation and which cause cost-push inflation?

- There is an increase in the cost of imported aluminum ore (supply curve shifts left, causing cost-push inflation).
- There is a cut in federal income tax rates (demand curve shifts right, causing demand-pull inflation).
- There is an improvement in consumer confidence (demand curve shifts right, causing demand-pull inflation).
- There is a drought that reduces farm production in many nations (supply curve shifts left, causing cost-push inflation).
- There is a shortage of skilled labor that forces employers to pay these workers higher wages (supply curve shifts left, causing cost-push inflation).

### *Think Critically Through Visuals*

Direct students to focus their attention on **Figure 13.5—Consumer Price Index Since 1913**. Point out that people are generally less concerned about the price level and more concerned about year-to-year changes in that level.

✔ **CHECKPOINT**
Invite a student to answer the checkpoint that appears on this page.

### Answer

The types of inflation include hyperinflation, disinflation, and deflation. The two sources of inflation are demand-pull inflation and cost-push inflation. Demand-pull inflation results from increases in the aggregate demand. Cost-push inflation results from decreases in aggregate supply.

## Impact of Inflation

Business owners and labor unions can increase prices or negotiate higher wages to compensate for expected inflation. When inflation is not expected, people are more likely to be harmed by the higher prices. Ask students to imagine that they rely on rent from ownership of an apartment building for their income. They receive $7,500 each month in rent. This amount covers their costs and gives them enough to live on. Then, to their surprise, the prices of the things they buy go up 10 percent. But, their tenants have leases that prevent the students from increasing their rents for one year. How would the students be harmed? How could the tenants benefit from the higher prices? (If their wages go up 10 percent, it will be easier for them to pay their rent.) What would the students have done if they had known prices would go up?

### Ethics in Action

Have students work in pairs to discuss this ethical issue and develop an answer to the question presented in the **Ethics in Action** feature on this page.

### Answers to Think Critically

Answers will vary. Possible answer: The economy can benefit from a price gouge because it can raise the national GDP, especially when the gouge is on a necessary good such as gasoline. The government should interfere with price gouging because it is not the fair market price determined by supply and demand.

### CHECKPOINT

Invite a student to answer the checkpoint that appears on page 401.

### Answer

Unexpected inflation creates economic winners and losers within the economy because prices are not what individuals expected or prepared for them to be. It creates arbitrary gains and losses, redistributing income and wealth from one group to another.

---

# Ethics in Action

### Rising Gasoline Prices: Market Economics or Price Gouging?
On August 14, 2003, parts of the United States and Canada were hit by a widespread power outage that shut down businesses and left some people in the dark for days. Shortly after that, gasoline prices nationwide jumped dramatically. From August 18 to 25, the average price of gasoline jumped 12 cents per gallon—the biggest one-week increase ever. By the end of that week, gasoline prices were at a record average high of $1.75 per gallon. The Energy Department immediately launched an investigation. It wanted to determine whether this increase was due to real market economics or to price gouging, an illegal practice of charging unreasonably high prices. This practice usually occurs by taking advantage of public anxiety during times of crisis. The price of gasoline often fluctuates greatly, depending on supply and demand. For example, gasoline prices generally go up during the summer, when more people are traveling and using more gas. However, there have been several occasions when gasoline prices have shot up dramatically after some kind of crisis that has had no real effect on gasoline supplies. These events have led some people to accuse gasoline suppliers of price gouging. Widespread reports of gouging appeared in the days following the September 11, 2001, terrorist attacks on the United States. In some cases, gasoline stations more than doubled their prices within hours of the attacks. Local authorities acted to stop these practices as quickly as possible and to fine those who engaged in price gouging.

### Think Critically

From an economic perspective, how could the economy benefit from price increases immediately after a crisis? From an ethical perspective, should the government be concerned about price gouging? Why or why not?

---

# Impact of Inflation

Changes in the price level are nothing new. Prior to World War II, periods of inflation and deflation balanced out over the long run. Therefore, people had good reason to think the dollar would retain its purchasing power over the long term. Since the end of World War II, however, the CPI has increased by an average of 3.9 percent per year. That may not sound like much, but it translates into a *nine-fold* increase in the consumer price index since 1946. Thus, it now takes $9 to purchase what $1 would buy in 1946. *Inflation reduces the value of the dollar and takes away confidence in the value of the dollar over the long term.*

### Expected Versus Unexpected Inflation

What is the effect of inflation on the economy's performance? *Unexpected* inflation creates more problems for the economy than does *expected* inflation. To the extent that inflation is higher or lower than expected, it arbitrarily creates economic winners and losers. If inflation is higher than expected, the winners are the people who had agreed to pay a price that anticipates lower inflation. The losers are those who agreed to sell at that price.

If inflation is lower than expected, the situation is reversed: The winners are the people who contracted to sell at a price that anticipates higher inflation, and the losers are all those who contracted to buy at that price.

Suppose inflation next year is expected to be 3 percent, and you

**400**   **CHAPTER 13**   Economic Challenges

---

During the last years of World War II, it was illegal for members of unions to call strikes that could harm the national interests. This prohibition ended in February 1946. In the months that followed, hundreds of thousands of U.S. workers went on strike to try to increase their wage rates to make up for what they felt were excessive amounts of inflation that had taken place during the war. Ask students what this did to prices in the United States and how wage increases would lead to greater inflation in the following years. (It was easy to see that prices would have to increase to pay higher wages. This led other businesses and groups to seek higher income, too. This resulted in even more inflation in later years. Once started and expected, inflation can be difficult to stop.)

agree to work next year for a wage that is 4 percent higher than your wage this year. In this case, you expect your *real* wage—that is, your wage measured in dollars of constant purchasing power—to increase by 1 percent. If inflation turns out to be 3 percent, you and your employer will both be satisfied with your nominal wage increase of 4 percent.

If, however, inflation turns out to be 5 percent, your real wage will fall. You will be a loser and your employer will be a winner. If inflation turns out to be only 1 percent, your real wage will increase by 3 percent. In this case, you will be a winner and your employer, a loser.

The arbitrary gains and losses arising from unexpected inflation are one reason that inflation is so unpopular. To the extent that inflation is fully expected by market participants, it is of less concern than unexpected inflation. Unexpected inflation arbitrarily redistributes income and wealth from one group to another.

## The Transaction Costs of Unexpected Inflation

During long periods of price stability, people correctly think that they can predict future prices and can, therefore, plan accordingly. If inflation changes unexpectedly, the future is cloudier and planning gets harder.

Firms that deal with the rest of the world face added complications. These firms must not only plan for U.S. inflation. They also must anticipate how the value of the dollar might change relative to foreign currencies. Inflation uncertainty and the resulting exchange-rate uncertainty increase the difficulty of making international business decisions.

As inflation becomes less predictable, firms must spend more time coping with the effects of inflation. This reduces productivity. The transaction costs of market exchange increase. *High and variable inflation interferes with the ability to make long-term plans. It also forces buyers and sellers to pay more attention to prices.* For example, high and variable inflation rates in the United States during the 1970s and early 1980s slowed economic growth during that period.

## Inflation and Interest Rates

No discussion of inflation would be complete without some mention of the interest rate. *Interest* is the cost of borrowing and the reward for saving. As noted in Chapter 10, the *interest rate* is the interest per year as a percentage of the amount loaned.

The **nominal interest rate** measures interest in terms of current dollars. The nominal rate is the one that appears on the borrowing agreement and the rate discussed in the news media. In contrast, the **real interest rate** equals the nominal interest rate minus the inflation rate:

Real interest rate =
    Nominal interest rate − Inflation rate

With no inflation, the nominal interest rate and the real interest rate would be identical. But with inflation, the real interest rate is less than the nominal interest rate. For example, if the nominal interest rate is 5 percent and the inflation rate is 3 percent, then the real interest rate is 2 percent. Lenders and borrowers are concerned more about the real rate than the nominal rate. The real interest rate, however, is known only after the fact—that is, only after inflation actually occurs.

Because the future is uncertain, lenders and borrowers must form expectations about inflation. They base their willingness to lend and to borrow on these expectations. Lenders and borrowers base their decisions on the *expected* real interest rate, which equals the nominal rate of interest minus the expected inflation rate. Other things constant, the higher the expected inflation rate, the higher the nominal rate of interest that lenders require and that borrowers are willing to pay.

**nominal interest rate**

The interest rate expressed in current dollars as a percentage of the amount loaned; the interest rate on the loan agreement

**real interest rate**

The interest rate expressed in dollars of constant purchasing power as a percentage of the amount loaned; the nominal interest rate minus the inflation rate

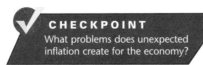

### CHECKPOINT
What problems does unexpected inflation create for the economy?

## APPLY

Assign Lesson 13.2 from the Contemporary Economics Workbook.

### e-con @pps

Encourage students to apply their knowledge of concepts presented in this lesson as they explore economic news stories, policy debates, and data available at **econxtra.swlearning.com.** A sampling of the titles for this lesson appears below.

### EconData
● Consumer Price Index

### EconNews
● The ABC's of Counting
● CPI Might Spell Less Inflation
● Economic Report Card—Inflation Is an A
● German Joblessness Grows
● Inflation Dips and the Economy Smiles
● Less Firing, More Hiring
● Looking and Not Liking
● More Mixed Messages
● Passing the Trough
● A Sign of Recovery
● Some News Is Good

## ASSESS

Assign all or part of Lesson 13.2 Assessment on page 402 as homework or an in-class activity.

### Xtra! Study Tools

Direct students to the online study tools for Lesson 13.2 at **econxtra.swlearning.com.**

## CLOSE

**Revisit** the In the News feature on the first page of the lesson. Ask students to review their preliminary answers and discuss the questions, now that they have completed this lesson.

**Review** the objectives for Lesson 13.2. Students should be able to:
● Describe the types of inflation, and identify two sources of inflation.
● Identify the problems that unexpected inflation creates.

## RETEACH

Tell half of your students to imagine they have $1,000 to lend at a fair interest rate. Tell the other half they would like to borrow $1,000 at a fair interest rate. Inform them that the rate of inflation has been 3 percent per year for each of the last five years. What interest rate would they agree on? Then place slips of paper in a box with the following rates written on different slips, (1%, 2%, 4%, 5%, 6%, 7% 8%, 9% and 10%). Have a student choose a slip of paper and read it. This is the rate of inflation that actually took place in the year. Who gained and who lost from the unexpected rate of inflation? What would this do to the interest rate that would be demanded in following years?

## Key Concepts

1. Students may point out that their family buys about the same amount of gasoline each week, regardless of its price (the de-mand for gasoline is inelastic). When there are higher gasoline prices, most people give up buying some other goods and services. When gasoline prices are lower, most people are able to purchase greater amounts of other goods and services.

2. Students may point out that if they expected inflation to take place, they would buy more products now to avoid higher prices in the future. Expectations of higher inflation tend to increase current demand and reduce future demand.

3. Possible answer: Both of these decisions would increase the amount of money consumers have to spend. This would shift aggregate demand to the right and cause an increase in consumer prices. This would be an example of demand-pull inflation.

4. Possible answer: Unexpected inflation hurts people because they have not been able to prepare for it. Workers who have agreed to labor contracts that give them a 2 percent wage increase will suffer an 8 percent loss in real income when prices go up by 10 percent.

## Graphing Exercise

5. ● Many more foreign consumers choosing to buy products made in the United States would shift aggregate demand curve to the right, the aggregate supply curve would not shift, the average price level would grow, and the amount of production would increase. This would be an example of demand-pull inflation.

● A 20 percent increase in the cost of crude oil would shift the aggregate supply curve to the left, the aggregate demand curve would not shift, the average price level would grow, and the amount of production would decline. This would be an example of cost-push inflation.

● Invention of a new technology that allows automobiles and trucks to be driven 100 miles per gallon of gasoline would shift the aggregate supply curve to the right, the aggregate demand curve would not shift, the average price level would fall, and the amount of production would

---

Xtra!
Study Tools
*econxtra.swlearning.com*

## Key Concepts

1. How have recent changes in gasoline prices affected your family?

2. If you thought that prices would be 10 percent higher one year from now, how would your current demand for goods and services be affected?

3. Suppose that the government reduced personal income taxes by 10 percent. At the same time, it increased social insurance payments by 10 percent. Why would these changes tend to cause inflation? Would this inflation be demand-pull or cost-push inflation?

4. Why would a 10 percent increase in prices be bad for an economy if most people expected prices to go up by only 2 percent?

## Graphing Exercise

5. Consider this graph of the aggregate demand and aggregate supply curves. What would happen to the location of each of these curves, the average price level, and the amount of production as a result of each of the following events? Would the change in the price level be the result of a demand-pull or cost-push in the economy?

• Many more foreign consumers choose to buy products made in the United States.

• There is a 20 percent increase in the cost of crude oil.

• A new technology is invented that allows automobiles and trucks to be driven 100 miles per gallon of gasoline.

• Federal income taxes are increased by 10 percent.

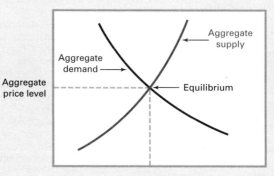

Amount of production (GDP)

## Think Critically

6. **Management** Suppose there was a 3 percent rate of inflation last year. This year the rate of inflation is 5 percent. You are the manager of a large business. It is your job to set the prices your firm will charge next year. How much will you choose to increase prices? Why will you make this choice?

---

increase. This would be an example of deflation resulting from lower costs of production.

● A 10 percent increase in federal income taxes would shift the aggregate demand curve to the left, the aggregate supply curve would not shift, prices would fall, and the amount of production would decline. This would be an example of deflation resulting from reduced demand for production.

## Think Critically

6. Answers will vary. Students may point out that with a trend toward higher rates of inflation, many businesses increase their prices even more (such as 7 percent) to protect themselves from higher costs of production. Once inflation starts, it tends to grow faster as people and businesses try to protect the purchasing power of their income.

## 13.3 Economic Instability

## Objectives

> Use aggregate demand and aggregate supply to analyze the Great Depression.

> Use aggregate demand and aggregate supply to analyze demand-side economics.

> Use aggregate demand and aggregate supply to analyze stagflation.

> Use aggregate demand and aggregate supply to analyze supply-side economics.

## Overview

The recent history of the U.S. economy can be divided into four economic eras: (1) before and during the Great Depression; (2) after the Great Depression to the early 1970s; (3) from the early 1970s to the early 1980s; and (4) since the early 1980s. The first era was marked by recessions and depressions, ending in the Great Depression of the 1930s. The second era was one of strong economic growth, with only moderate increases in the price level. The third era saw high unemployment combined with high inflation. The fourth era showed good growth on average with only moderate increases in the price level. Government leaders in all four eras had to deal with the challenge of economic instability.

## Key Terms

laissez-faire

demand-side economics

stagflation

supply-side economics

Remind students that levels of production and employment fluctuate over time. Economists often call these fluctuations the business cycle. When the economy is growing, businesses often invest in greater productive capacity and employ more workers. This causes the expansion to be even greater than it otherwise would have been. When the economy is in decline, they do the opposite. This tends to make recessions even deeper.

### Objectives

Remind students to read the lesson objectives to help focus their attention before reading the lesson.

### Key Terms

Direct students to write each key term on a separate index card. Then write the matching definition and page reference on the back of the appropriate card. Encourage students to use the cards to study for quizzes and tests.

## [ In the News ]

### ● Global Crisis and Economic Uncertainty

As war with Iraq loomed in the spring of 2003, many people were nervous and uncertain about how the war might affect the U.S. economy. Such feelings are very common in the face of global crises. Some crises, such as the SARS epidemic that struck much of Asia and other parts of the world in 2003, can have a serious impact on global markets as well as the U.S. economy. Yet it is often difficult to tell how much a crisis is going to affect the economy. In uncertain times, is it better to play it safe and avoid large investments? Or should you take advantage of the uncertainty to build for the future? When a foreseeable crisis like a war is looming, most people plan for the worst by cutting spending and saving as much as they can. However, such action actually can make the economy worse off. Some economists suggest that when faced with economic uncertainty, it is better be optimistic about the future and to take bold risks.

### Think About It

Suppose there is significant uncertainty regarding next year's economic conditions. What actions might be good for a typical individual to take that would be bad for the economy as a whole?

**403**

## [ In the News ]

Instruct students to read the passage and write down their answers. Point out that their answers might change after they finish studying Lesson 13.3.

### Answers to Think About It

Answers will vary. Possible answer: With significant uncertainty about next year's economic conditions, it might be wise for a typical individual to curb his or her investments and save. This same action would be bad for an economy as a whole because it would make the economy worse than what is already projected.

### Visual Presentation

Use the PowerPoint presentation on the Instructor's Resource CD as an adjunct to your lecture. The presentation also can be used for review.

### National Content Standards in Economics

A complete list of the NCEE Standards appears on pages xxiv–xxv of this book. The following standards are addressed in Lesson 13.3.

Standard 15: Growth

Standard 16: Role of Government

Standard 17: Using Cost/Benefit Analysis to Evaluate Government Programs

Standard 20: Monetary and Fiscal Policy

## The Great Depression and Before

Tell students that they understand economic principles that were a mystery to most economists 100 years ago. Before the 1930s, most economists believed the economy would take care of itself-that it was self-regulating. If the government would leave the economy alone and allow the market forces of demand and supply free play, no recession could last for very long. When the Great Depression occurred following 1929 and dragged on for many years, it became apparent that there were flaws in the classical theory.

### Think Critically Through Visuals

Direct students to focus their attention on **Figure 13.6—The Decrease in Aggregate Demand Between 1929 and 1933**. Point out that the aggregate supply curve probably also shifted somewhat during this period but, for simplicity, we assume it was unchanged. Most economists agree that the shift in the aggregate demand curve was the dominant factor.

### Think Critically Through Visuals

Direct students to focus their attention on the photograph on page 405. Ask for a volunteer to answer the question posed in the caption.

### Answer

Answers will vary. Possible answer: Because of the decline in aggregate demand, both the price level and the real GDP dropped. As GDP declined, the unemployment rate soared.

### CHECKPOINT

Invite a student to answer the checkpoint that appears on page 405.

### Answer

Because of the decline in aggregate demand, both the price level and the real GDP dropped. As GDP declined, the unemployment rate soared. Higher unemployment led to an even larger decline in GDP and price level. The Great Depression resulted from this downward spiraling cycle.

# The Great Depression and Before

Before World War II, the U.S. economy alternated between periods of prosperity and periods of sharp economic decline. The longest contraction on record occurred between 1873 and 1879. During this time, 80 railroads went bankrupt and most of the nation's steel industry shut down. During the depression of the 1890s, the unemployment rate topped 18 percent. In October 1929, the stock market crashed. This began what was to become the deepest—though not the longest—economic contraction in the nation's history. This period is known as the Great Depression of the 1930s.

## Decrease in Aggregate Demand

In terms of aggregate demand and aggregate supply, the Great Depression can be viewed as a leftward shift of the aggregate demand curve, as shown in Figure 13.6. $AD_{1929}$ is the aggregate demand curve in 1929, before the onset of the depression. Real GDP in 1929 was $822 billion, measured in dollars of

**laissez-faire**
The doctrine that the government should not intervene in a market economy beyond the minimum required to maintain peace and property rights

1996 purchasing power. The price level was 12.6, relative to a 1996 base-year price level of 100.

By 1933, aggregate demand had shifted leftward, decreasing to $AD_{1933}$. Why did aggregate demand decline so much? Though the causes are still debated, the list of possibilities is long. It includes the stock market crash of 1929, grim business expectations, a drop in consumer spending, widespread bank failures, a sharp decline in the nation's money supply, and severe restrictions on world trade.

Because of the decline in aggregate demand, both the price level and real GDP dropped. Real GDP fell 27 percent, from $822 billion in 1929 to $603 billion in 1933, and the price level fell 26 percent, from 12.6 to 9.3. As real GDP declined, the unemployment rate soared, climbing from 3 percent in 1929 to 25.2 percent in 1933. This was the highest U.S. unemployment rate ever recorded.

### Laissez-Faire

Before the Great Depression, macroeconomic policy was based primarily on the **laissez-faire** doctrine that said government should not intervene in a market economy beyond the minimum required to maintain peace and property rights. This doctrine dates back at

**The Decrease of Aggregate Demand Between 1929 and 1933**

**Figure 13.6**

The Great Depression of the 1930s can be represented by a leftward shift of the aggregate demand curve, from $AD_{1929}$ to $AD_{1933}$. In the resulting depression, real GDP fell from $822 billion to $603 billion. The price level dropped from 12.6 to 9.3.

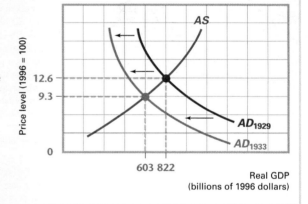

## Outside Resources

**History Web Sites** Many events in history, including the Great Depression, can be investigated at history web sites. Instruct students to find an online resource about the Great Depression. Instruct them to summarize their findings and evaluate the authenticity of the site. Some sites of interest are listed below.

www.newdeal.feri.org

www.memory.loc.gov/ammem/fsowhome.html

www.about.com/history

http://history.searchbeat.com/greatdepression.htm

Day-to-day life during the Great Depression was grim. The unemployment rate reached 25.2 percent in 1933. Many people could not afford to buy food and gathered in "breadlines" to receive free food from charities. How did the sharp drop in aggregate demand from 1929 to 1933 lead to such high unemployment?

least to Adam Smith. In his 1776 book *The Wealth of Nations*, Smith argued that if people were allowed to pursue their self-interest in free markets, resources would be guided as if by an "invisible hand" to produce the greatest, most efficient level of aggregate output.

Although the U.S. economy had suffered several sharp contractions since the beginning of the nineteenth century, most economists of the day viewed these as a natural phase of the economy—unfortunate, but ultimately good for the economy.

**CHECKPOINT**
Use aggregate demand and aggregate supply to analyze the Great Depression.

# From the Great Depression to the Early 1970s

The Great Depression was so severe that it stimulated new thinking about how the economy worked—or didn't

work. In 1936, John Maynard Keynes (1883–1946) published *The General Theory of Employment, Interest, and Money,* the most famous economics book of the twentieth century. In it, Keynes argued that aggregate demand was unstable, in part because investment decisions were often guided by the unpredictable "animal spirits" of business expectations.

If businesses grew pessimistic about the economy, they would cut investment spending. This, in turn, would reduce aggregate demand. This reduction in aggregate demand would cut output and employment. For example, investment dropped more than 80 percent between 1929 and 1933. Keynes saw no natural market forces operating to ensure that the economy would return to a higher level of output and employment.

## Stimulating Aggregate Demand

Keynes proposed that the government shock the economy out of its depression by increasing aggregate demand. The government could achieve this stimulus directly by increasing its own spending, or indirectly by cutting taxes to stimulate consumption and

**TEACH**

**From the Great Depression to the Early 1970s**
Ask students to evaluate the following statement: "Nothing succeeds like success." What do they think it means? If a student is a member of an undefeated football team with many wonderful players, does it mean this particular student is also a wonderful football player? The same can be said for those who make and implement economic policy and the theories that the policies are based on. Following the Great Depression and World War II, many people came to believe that the theories of J. M. Keynes held answers to virtually all economic problems. Simply by adjusting government spending and taxes, aggregate demand could be held at a stable level that would ensure growth in the economy, full employment, and price stability-or so they thought.
In actuality, much of the economic success enjoyed by the United States in the 1950s and 1960s had little to do with government economic policies. The built-up demand from the Great Depression and World War II, the baby boom, increased productivity resulting from investments made during the war, little foreign competition, and a great foreign demand for U.S. products combined to sustain growth with little inflation and relatively full employment in the U.S. economy. During these times, it was easy for economic leaders to look good. They could take credit for successes they might have had little to do with. When significant economic problems appeared in the 1970s, it was quickly discovered that there were limitations on the effectiveness and practicality of these policies.

**ENRICH**

Remind students that unemployment is measured as the share of workers who are without work and who are seeking employment. Official unemployment rates during World War II fell to less than 4 percent. This took place in spite of the fact that many women who would not otherwise have been in the labor force sought and accepted employment because of the labor shortage during the war. Why did this situation change after the war? What was the impact of women leaving the labor force on unemployment rates? Why may this have reinforced the prevailing confidence people had in Keynesian economic theory? (After the war, many women left the labor force to have children. This contributed to low unemployment rates that were credited to Keynesian economic policies.)

### From the Great Depression to the Early 1970s

Divide the class into three groups. Provide each group with one of the situations described below. Ask the groups to write brief explanations of what Keynes would have wanted the government to do in each situation. Ask a spokesperson for each group to share the group's thoughts with the class. Select students to read their answers and discuss the policies they suggest. Point out that Keynesian policies might not fix one or more of the situations.

- Unemployment has grown to 7 percent and production has fallen 2 percent. Prices are stable. (Cut taxes and/or increase government spending to stimulate aggregate demand.)

- Unemployment has fallen to 4 percent, production is growing at 5 percent, and inflation has reached 6 percent. (Increase taxes and/or cut government spending to reduce aggregate demand.)

- Unemployment has grown to 7 percent and production has fallen by 2 percent. Prices are growing at nearly 6 percent. (There is stagflation. Keynesian policies cannot deal with all of these problems. If taxes are cut and spending grows, there will be more jobs and production, but there also will be more inflation. If taxes are increased and spending is cut, there will be more unemployment even if there also is less inflation. The problem is the result of a shift in aggregate supply to the left. Shifting aggregate demand with Keynesian policies will not solve all of these problems.)

**CHECKPOINT**
Invite a student to answer the checkpoint that appears on this page.

### Answer
Demand-side economics suggests that if aggregate demand in the private sector declines, the government should increase government spending to maintain the prior level of aggregate demand. This increase in government spending would shift the aggregate demand curve to the right, which would raise equilibrium real GDP, thus increasing employment.

---

investment. One problem was that either action could create a federal budget deficit. A *federal budget deficit* measures the amount by which total federal spending exceeds total federal revenues.

To understand what Keynes had in mind, imagine federal budget policies that would increase aggregate demand in Figure 13.6. This would shift the aggregate demand curve to the right, back to its original position. Such a shift would raise equilibrium real GDP, which would increase employment.

### Demand-Side Economics

According to Keynes, *fiscal policy*—or changes in government spending and taxes—was needed to compensate for what he viewed as the instability of private spending, especially investment. If demand in the private sector declined, Keynes said the government should pick up the slack.

You can think of the Keynesian approach as **demand-side economics** because it focused on how changes in aggregate demand could promote full employment. Keynes argued that government stimulus could jolt the economy out of its depression and back to health. Once investment returned to normal, the government stimulus would no longer be necessary.

### World War II and Aggregate Demand

World War II boosted demand for tanks, ships, aircraft, and the like. This increased output and employment. It also seemed to confirm the powerful impact that government spending could have on the economy. The increase in government spending, with no increase in tax rates, created federal budget deficits during the war.

Immediately after World War II, memories of the Great Depression were still fresh. Trying to avoid another depression, Congress approved the *Employment Act of 1946*, which imposed a clear responsibility on the federal government to foster "maximum employment, production, and purchasing power." The act also required the president to report annually on the state of the economy and to appoint a

**demand-side economics**
Macroeconomic policy that focuses on shifting the aggregate demand curve as a way of promoting full employment and price stability

*Council of Economic Advisers.* This council is a three-member panel of economists, with a professional staff, to provide the president with economic advice.

### The Golden Age of Keynesian Economics

The economy seemed to prosper during the 1950s, largely without the added stimulus of fiscal policy. The 1960s, however, proved to be the *golden age of Keynesian economics*. During this period, some economists thought they could "fine-tune" the economy to avoid recessions—just as a mechanic could fine-tune a race car to achieve top performance. During the early 1960s, nearly all advanced economies around the world enjoyed low unemployment and healthy growth with only modest inflation. In short, the world economy was booming, and the U.S. economy was on top of the world.

The economy was on such a roll that toward the end of the 1960s, some economists began to think the business cycle was history. In the early 1970s, however, the cycle returned with a fury. Worse yet, the problem of recession was compounded by rising inflation, which increased during the recessions of 1974–1975 and 1979–1980. Until then, inflation was limited primarily to periods of expansion. Confidence in demand-side policies was shaken.

**CHECKPOINT**
Use aggregate demand and aggregate supply to analyze demand-side economics.

## The Great Stagflation: 1973–1980

During the late 1960s, federal spending increased on both the war in Vietnam and social programs at home. This combined stimulus increased aggregate demand enough that in 1968, the inflation rate jumped to 4.4 percent, after

---

*Economic Headlines*

Direct students to find a newspaper or magazine article that describes a government spending program. Be sure to explain that government transfer programs such as welfare or Social Security are not acceptable topics. They should write essays describing the program and evaluating its impact on employment and production in the economy. Ask students to state whether the chosen program is consistent with Keynesian economic theory. If it involves increased spending during a downturn in production, then it is consistent. If it involves increased spending when the economy is growing rapidly, it is not consistent.

averaging only 2.0 percent during the previous decade. Inflation climbed to 4.7 percent in 1969 and to 5.3 percent in 1970.

## Reduction in Aggregate Supply

Inflation rates were so alarming that in 1971, President Richard Nixon tried to put a ceiling on price and wage increases. The ceiling was eliminated in 1973, about the time that crop failures around the world caused grain prices to climb. To compound these problems, OPEC cut its supply of oil, thus increasing oil prices. Decreases in the supplies of grain and oil reduced aggregate supply in the economy.

This reduction in aggregate supply is shown in Figure 13.7 by the leftward shift of the aggregate supply curve from $AS_{1973}$ to $AS_{1975}$. This created the **stagflation** of the 1970s, meaning a *stag*nation, or a contraction, in the economy's aggregate output combined with in*flation*, or a rise, in the economy's price level. Real GDP declined by about $40 billion between 1973 and 1975. At the same time, the price level jumped nearly 20 percent.

The unemployment rate climbed from 4.9 percent in 1973 to 8.5 percent in 1975. Stagflation created higher unemployment and higher inflation.

## Stagflation Repeats in 1980

Stagflation hit again at the end of 1980, fueled partly by another jump in OPEC oil prices. Between 1979 and 1980, real GDP declined and the price level increased by 9.2 percent. Because the problem of stagflation was primarily on the supply side, not on the demand side, Keynesian demand-management solutions seemed ineffective. Increasing aggregate demand might reduce unemployment, but it would worsen inflation.

**CHECKPOINT**
Use aggregate demand and aggregate supply to analyze stagflation.

*stagflation*
A decline, or *stag*nation, of a nation's output accompanied by a rise, or in*flation*, in the price level

**Stagflation Between 1973 and 1975**

**Figure 13.7**

The stagflation of the mid-1970s can be represented as a reduction of aggregate supply from $AS_{1973}$ to $AS_{1975}$. Aggregate output fell from $4.12 trillion to $4.08 trillion (stagnation), and the price level rose from 33.6 to 40.0 (inflation).

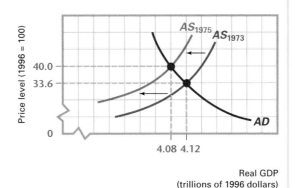

### The Great Stagflation: 1973–1980

Point out that during periods of stagflation, the economy's aggregate supply curve shifts to the left. Such shifts are most often caused by increases in the costs of production. As an example, describe the events that took place in 1974–75. As a result of a war between Israel and its Arab neighbors, the price of imported oil increased by more than 300 percent in 1973. This resulted in a dramatic increase in the cost of energy in the United States. Higher energy prices caused consumers to spend more to heat their homes and operate their automobiles. This reduced the amount of income consumers could devote to buying goods and services. In this situation, aggregate supply was shifted to the left at the same time that aggregate demand for domestic products fell. The result was stagflation. Unemployment grew to almost 10 percent, production fell, and prices grew about 7 percent. Efforts to resolve this situation during the Ford and Carter administrations failed because they were designed to adjust the location of the aggregate demand curve. Only adjustments in the aggregate supply curve could have dealt with unemployment and inflation simultaneously.

### Think Critically Through Visuals

Direct students to focus their attention on Figure 13.7—Stagflation Between 1973 and 1975. Point out that decreases in the supplies of grain and oil reduced aggregate supply. This is shown by the leftward shift of the aggregate supply curve.

**CHECKPOINT**
Invite a student to answer the checkpoint that appears on this page.

### Curriculum Connection—Psychology

Politicians may be motivated to create policies that will help them be reelected as much as by a desire to do what is best for the economy. Ask students to discuss psychological reasons that may motivate the government to "soak the rich" even when it may not make economic sense. Some economists believe that the higher tax rates (36 and 39.6 percent) passed during the Clinton administration did harm to the economy by discouraging people with larger incomes from working to earn even more. Do your students believe this is a valid point of view? What might have been the psychological motivation for passage of this law? (People with limited incomes might resent others who earn much more but who do not pay higher taxes.)

### Answer

An increase in aggregate demand that leads to inflation, combined with decreased aggregate supply, leads to stagflation.

### Since 1980

By encouraging investment and discouraging higher wages during the 1980s, the government was able to help U.S. businesses control their costs of production. At the same time, new technologies contributed to a decline in labor costs. The result was increased growth with falling rates of inflation in most years. These changes caused some individuals economic harm but, as a whole, they improved the competitive position of the United States in the global economy

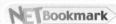

Direct students to **econxtra.swlearning.com**. Remind them to click on the link for Lesson 13.3 to find the appropriate link for the NET Bookmark on this page. In addition to reading the current report, suggest that students skim the reports for several previous months to put the current report in context.

### Answer

Answers will vary. Generally the first sentence of the summary provides the answer to the first question. Students will need to read the entire summary to develop an answer for the second question.

**Try It**

Direct students to the Graphing Workshop for Chapter 13 at **econxtra.swlearning.com**. Instruct students to click on **Try It: Labor Market Effects of Supply-Side Fiscal Policy.**

### Answer

Supply-side economics suggests that lower tax rates will stimulate the economy by creating an incentive to supply labor. Lowering taxes will increase aggregate supply, which will expand the real GDP and reduce the price level.

---

# Since 1980

Increasing aggregate supply, or shifting the aggregate supply curve rightward, seemed an appropriate way to combat stagflation. Such a move would both lower the price level and increase output and employment. Attention thus turned from aggregate demand to aggregate supply.

### Supply-Side Economics

**supply-side economics**
Macroeconomic policy that focuses on a rightward shift of the aggregate supply curve through tax cuts or other changes that increase production incentives

A key idea behind **supply-side economics** was that cutting tax rates would stimulate aggregate supply. Lower tax rates would increase the incentive to supply labor. According to advocates of the supply-side approach, the resulting increase in aggregate supply would expand real GDP and reduce the price level. This, however, was easier said than done.

In 1981, President Ronald Reagan and Congress cut personal income tax rates by an average of 23 percent to be phased in over three years. They hoped the tax cuts would stimulate economic growth enough that the government's smaller share of a bigger pie would exceed what had been its larger share of a smaller pie.

Before the tax cut was fully implemented, recession hit in 1982. The unemployment rate shot up to 10 percent. After the recession, the economy began what at the time was the longest peacetime expansion on record. During the rest of the 1980s,

Review the *Summary of Commentary on Current Economic Conditions by Federal Reserve District,* available through the Federal Reserve System. Access this book, commonly known as "The Beige Book," through econxtra.swlearning.com. Summarize the national economic conditions for the most recent period covered in the report. Overall, is the economy healthy? What problems are there?

**econxtra.swlearning.com**

output grew, unemployment declined, and inflation declined. However, the growth in federal spending exceeded the growth in federal tax revenues during this period. Therefore, federal budget deficits swelled.

### Giant Federal Deficits

Federal budget deficits worsened with the onset of a Gulf War recession in 1990. That recession officially ended in early 1991. However, the deficit continued to grow and topped $290 billion in 1992. Annual deficits accumulated as a huge federal debt. *Government debt* measures the net accumulation of prior deficits. Measured relative to GDP, the federal debt nearly doubled from 33 percent in 1980 to 64 percent in 1992.

During the 1990s, policy makers began to worry more about huge federal deficits. To reduce them, President George H. W. Bush increased taxes in 1990. President Bill Clinton increased taxes on the rich in 1993. A newly elected Republican Congress reduced federal spending growth beginning in 1995. Higher tax rates and a slower growth in federal spending combined with an improving economy to reduce federal deficits. By 1998, the federal budget yielded a surplus.

By early 2001, the U.S. economic expansion became the longest on record. During this stretch, 22 million jobs were added, the unemployment rate dropped from 7.5 percent to 4.2 percent, and inflation remained low.

After achieving this record, the economy softened in 2001. Job losses increased after the terrorist attacks of September 2001. This added to the recession that began in March 2001. Federal deficits then began to grow again. The stock market declined three years in a row. The 2003 war in Iraq to topple Saddam Hussein added to the economic uncertainty of the times.

**CHECKPOINT**
Use aggregate demand and aggregate supply to analyze supply-side economics.

---

Remind students that it is relatively easy to make what appear to be wise investments when times are good. The 1990s were a time of rapid economic growth and increased productivity. Much of this growth resulted from the rapid expansion of the Internet and related industries. Banks, businesses, and individuals were willing to invest billions of dollars in firms with no proven record of earning profits. There was a pervasive fear of being left behind and missing out on the dot-com revolution. After 2000, the fallacy of this became apparent. Many technology-based firms failed, and thousands of their workers became unemployed. Vast fortunes in stock disappeared seemingly overnight. What does this tell students about economic stability? (Periods of rapid growth are often followed by periods of decline.)

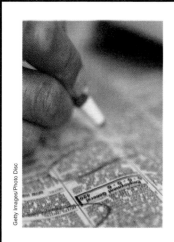

Getty Images/Photo Disc

**Describe the trends in employment since 1980.**

# TEAM WORK

Divide into four groups. Each group should work with a different economic era. Analyze the era by drawing an aggregate supply and aggregate demand graph. A representative from each group should then present and explain their group's graph in class.

# E-CONOMICS

## Layers of the Onion Reveal How to Succeed with an Online Business

During the 1990s, dozens of new companies emerged in an attempt to cash in on the success of the Internet. When the high-tech boom went bust at the end of the decade, most of these firms folded. In the unstable new world of Internet commerce, many companies earned revenues, but few turned a profit. One popular Internet company survived and became more profitable than ever. TheOnion.com, a free online humor magazine, thrived due to a business strategy based on diversification. *The Onion* started out as a satirical humor magazine that poked fun at current news events. When the magazine went online in 1996, it quickly gained a popular following with its bizarre stories and attention-getting

headlines, such as "Clinton Deploys Vowels to Bosnia: Cities of Sjlbvdnzv, Grny to Be First Recipients." As it gained more than one million readers, it kept its spending under control and did not rely entirely on revenues from online advertisers. It continued to publish a print edition, branching out into regional editions mocking local personalities, It also published a series of popular books. Onion leaders expanded the brand into movie deals and a subscription service offering more humor for readers.

### Think Critically

By 2003, TheOnion.com was earning annual profits of $7 million that were expected to grow by 25 percent over the next five years. What assumptions about aggregate demand were made in estimating this growth rate?

Lesson 13.3 • *Economic Instability* **409**

# TEAM WORK

Instruct students to complete the **Team Work** activity. Point out that all the data students need is in this lesson.

# E-CONOMICS

Direct students to read the passage entitled "Layers of the Onion Reveal How to Succeed with an Online Business" on this page.

### Answers to Think Critically

The assumption that was made about aggregate in estimating this growth rate was that aggregate demand for the Onion.com would be increasing over this time period.

## APPLY

Assign Lesson 13.3 from the Contemporary Economics Workbook.

## e-con @pps

Encourage students to apply their knowledge of concepts presented in this lesson as they explore economic news stories, policy debates, and data available at **econxtra.swlearning.com**. A sampling of the titles for this lesson appears below.

### EconData
• Real GDP

### EconDebate
• Is there a new economy?

### EconNews
• The Economy Sputters
• Or, the Landing Ahead May Be Soft

## CLOSE

**Revisit** the In the News feature on the first page of the lesson. Ask students to review their preliminary answers and discuss the questions, now that they have completed this lesson.

**Review** the objectives for Lesson 13.3. Students should be able to:
• Use aggregate demand and aggregate supply to analyze the Great Depression.
• Use aggregate demand and aggregate supply to analyze demand-side economics.
• Use aggregate demand and aggregate supply to analyze stagflation.
• Use aggregate demand and aggregate supply to analyze supply-side economics.

## ASSESS

Assign all or part of Lesson 13.3 Assessment on page 410 as homework or an in-class activity.

## Xtra! Study Tools

Direct students to the online study tools for Lesson 13.3 at **econxtra.swlearning.com**.

## Key Concepts

1. Answers will vary. Possible answer: Most economists recommended that the federal government cut its spending to keep a balanced budget. When this happened, even more workers lost their jobs and the Great Depression became worse.

2. Answers will vary. Possible answer: Keynes would have recommended that the federal government increase its own spending, reduce taxes to give people and businesses more income to spend, or some of both of these policies.

3. Answers will vary. Possible answer: A large increase in the costs of production would cause businesses to earn lower profits and shift the aggregate supply curve to the right. This would cause inflation, a reduced level of production, and more unemployment.

## Graphing Exercise

4. Answers will vary. Possible answer: All of these policies could reduce the costs of production and shift the aggregate supply curve to the right to AS. These are examples of supply-side policies because, if they are successful, they will combat both inflation and unemployment by shifting the supply curve to the right.

## Think Critically

5. Answers will vary. Possible answer: Government spending during World War II eliminated almost all unemployment. This caused many people to conclude that the way to end any recession is simply to increase government spending. Although this idea seemed to make sense at the time, events since 1945 have shown that Keynesian policies are not able to solve all economic problems.

---

Xtra!
**Study Tools**
*econxtra.swlearning.com*

## Key Concepts

1. Before 1929, most economists thought the federal government should always have a balanced budget (government tax revenues = government spending). When the Great Depression began in 1929, government tax revenues fell rapidly. The federal government responded by cutting spending. What was the impact of this policy on the economy?

2. People who support the economic theories of Keynes think that a stable economy will result from a steady increase of aggregate demand. Given this idea, what would Keynes have recommended the federal government do if consumption and investment declined because people and business owners started to worry about the future?

3. How could stagflation result from a large increase in the costs of production throughout the economy?

## Graphing Exercise

4. Study this graph of aggregate demand and supply. The aggregate supply curve has shifted to the left from AS to AS′ because of an increase in the costs of production. This has increased the average price level and reduced the amount of production. Which of the policies listed below might reduce costs of production and cause the aggregate supply curve to return to its original location at AS? Why are these policies examples of supply-side economics?

a. The government reduces taxes for businesses that buy new technology.

b. The government helps pay the wages of newly hired workers.

c. The government lowers taxes on imported raw materials.

d. The government reduces taxes on business profits.

e. The government gives grants to people who carry out applied research.

## Think Critically

5. **History**  The U.S. government borrowed most of the money it used to pay for its military efforts during World War II. The national debt increased by $23.5 billion in 1943, $64.3 billion in 1944, and $10.7 billion in 1945. In these years, the unemployment rate fell from its 1940 level of 14.6 percent, to 4.4 percent in 1942, 1.7 percent in 1943, and 1.0 percent in 1944. Why would these data have supported Keynes's theory that the way to combat a depression is to have more government spending?

# The New Deal and the Deficit

During the early years of the Great Depression, many people—who believed that the economy would correct itself—suggested a laissez-fare approach to the business cycle. They viewed depressions as a helpful and necessary purge of the economy. Budget deficits were feared as inflationary and considered a bad example for the nation's citizens.

Still, from 1929 to 1933, prices dropped severely and the government deficit increased. Early attempts by President Herbert Hoover to balance the budget, such as sharply increasing tariffs on imports, made matters worse. In the face of increasing deficits, Hoover resisted more government intervention in the economy. He continued to advocate spending cuts and tax increases, telling Congress that "nothing is more necessary at this time than balancing the budget."

When Franklin D. Roosevelt swept into office in 1932, he initiated a host of programs known collectively as the New Deal. Although Roosevelt believed in a balanced budget, he was—unlike Hoover—willing to accept deficits in order to pump government money into the economy. The Reconstruction Finance Corporation, first begun under Hoover, was beefed up. New programs—such as the Public Works Administration, the Agricultural Adjustment Administration, National Recovery Administration, and later the Works Progress Administration—were designed to use federal money to stimulate the economy.

Under the New Deal, the economy began a slow recovery until 1937, when Roosevelt, believing that the nation's economy was strong enough to continue on its own, announced a reduction in federal spending and a plan to balance the budget by 1939. Instead, by the fall of 1937, the economy began to falter and the president called for a resumption of deficit spending in April 1938.

By this time, many in the government had become supporters of the ideas of John Maynard Keynes. Keynes himself, however, believed Roosevelt's latest attempts to build up the economy needed far more government spending than the $3 billion prescribed by the president. Before the results of the Second New Deal could be fully judged, World War II intervened and the country was brought back to full employment. The events of the 1930s, however, changed how many Americans viewed fiscal policy. As deficit spending became more accepted, they saw the government as having a crucial role in the nation's economy

© Hulton Archive

**British economist and the founder of 'Keynesian economics', John Maynard Keynes (1883–1946).**

## THINK CRITICALLY

Evaluate and compare the wisdom of deficit spending by the government from an economic perspective, from a social perspective, and from a political perspective.

## Bibliography

Foner, Eric, and John A. Garraty, eds. *The Reader's Companion to American History*. Boston: Houghton Mifflin Company, 1991.

Greider, William. *Secrets of the Temple: How the Federal Reserve Runs the Country*. New York: Simon and Schuster, 1987.

Morris, Richard B., and Jeffrey B. Morris. *Encyclopedia of American History*. New York: Harper Collins, 1996.

Parish, Peter J., ed. *Reader's Guide to American History*. Chicago: Fitzroy Dearborn Publishers, 1997.

Puth, Robert C. *American Economic History*. New York: Dryden Press, 1982.

---

C O N N E C T
*to History*

## FOCUS

Introduce this feature by pointing out that the New Deal was a watershed event in our nation's attitude toward government's responsibility for the economy. Its major components of relief, recovery, and reform were pursued simultaneously. Many of the programs were enacted to put people to work. Others, such as the National Recovery Administration (NRA) and the Agricultural Adjustment Act (AAA), sought the revival of industry. The third part focused on the reform of institutions such as banking and the stock market. Despite a decade of effort, it still took deficit spending on a larger scale (stimulated by World War II) to end the economic crisis. The result is a continuing national debate over the role of government in the economy.

## TEACH

Instruct students to read the **Connect to History** feature and answer the questions.

## ASSESS

Use the questions at the bottom of the page to assess the students' understanding of this feature.

### Answers to **Think Critically**

Deficit spending from an economic perspective is a great thing because it stimulates the economy by increasing employment and real GDP.

Deficit spending from a social perspective is also a great thing because social assistance programs such as Social Security, Medicare and Medicaid, and welfare all benefit.

Deficit spending from a political perspective is not necessarily a great thing. It has long been the source of many heated debates regarding the future state of our country.

## FOCUS

### 13.4 Poverty

Explain that poverty today is different from poverty 100 years ago, and it will be different in the future. Because poverty is relative, there always will be some people who are regarded as living in poverty. Point out that this lesson looks at how poverty is measured in the United States and what steps have been taken to assist those who live in poverty to improve their economic situations.

### Objectives

Remind students to read the lesson objectives to help focus their attention before reading the lesson.

### Key Terms

Direct students use each of the key terms in a separate sentence or short paragraph that helps demonstrate the meaning of the term.

### [ In the News ]

Instruct students to read the passage and write down their answers. Point out that their answers might change after they finish studying Lesson 13.4.

### Answers to Think About It

Answers will vary. Possible answers: Some students will think the position is necessary to lead the government's efforts to help those who are homeless and reduce homelessness. Other students will suggest that the federal government should let local communities and nonprofit organizations deal with homelessness. Steps to prevent homelessness include budgeting, keeping skills current, living within means, reducing consumer debt, saving, and spending wisely.

### Follow-Up Activity

Invite an advocate for the homeless to speak about the problem in your community. Request that the speaker provide statistics about the homeless population and information about services for individuals and families.

### Visual Presentation

Use the PowerPoint presentation on the Instructor's Resource CD as an adjunct to your lecture. The presentation also can be used for review.

## Objectives

> Describe the link between jobs, unmarried motherhood, and poverty.

> Identify some unplanned results of income-assistance programs.

## Overview

In a market economy, your income depends primarily on how much you earn, which depends on the productivity of your resources. The problem with allocating income according to productivity is that some people have difficulty earning income. How should the government respond to the challenge of poverty? Families where the head of household has a job are much more likely to escape poverty than are families with no workers. Thus, the government's first line of defense in fighting poverty is to promote a healthy economy, thereby providing job opportunities for all who want to work.

## Key Terms

cycle of poverty

welfare reform

## [ In the News ]

### ● The Homeless Czar

In the spring of 2002, President George W. Bush named Philip Mangano to be the country's "homeless czar," or head of the government's Interagency Council on Homelessness. This position had been created many years earlier, but no one had filled the position since 1996. Why was this position left empty for so long, and why did President Bush feel the need to fill it in 2002? In 2000, the U.S. poverty rate fell to its lowest levels in two decades. The robust economy of the 1990s had helped ease poverty somewhat. As the economy began to decline in the early 2000s, however, many families only slightly above the brink were among the first to slip back into poverty. By 2001, the poverty rate was on the rise again. With this came a rise in homelessness as people lost their jobs and could not pay their rent or mortgages. Many of these new homeless were families like David and Gina C. and their four children. He was a rental car mechanic, and she worked in a nursing home. When the tourism industry began to decline in late 2001, David lost his job. Gina did not make enough money to support the family. Although David got a new job, that business soon failed, and he had difficulty finding new employment. The family was homeless for 10 months until it received new housing from a charity organization.

### Think About It

Do you think the position of "homeless czar" is needed? What steps can people take to ensure that they will not become homeless in the event of job loss?

412

### National Content Standards in Economics

A complete list of the NCEE Standards appears on pages xxiv–xxv of this book. The following standards are addressed in Lesson 13.4.

Standard 13: Role of Resources in Determining Income

Standard 16: Role of Government

Standard 19: Unemployment and Inflation

# Poverty and the Economy

The best predictor of whether a family is poor is whether someone in that family has a job. Thus the most direct way the government can help reduce poverty is to nurture a healthy economy. The stronger the economy, the greater the job opportunities, and the more likely people will find jobs.

## Poverty and Jobs

The poverty rate is much higher among families with no workers. Figure 13.8 shows the poverty rate based on the type of family and on the number of workers in the family. Overall, the poverty rate is about four times greater in families with no workers than in families with at least one worker. The poverty rate of families headed by a female with no workers is 15 times greater than the rate for married-couple families with at least one worker.

## Poverty and Unemployment

Perhaps the best indicator of whether or not job opportunities are readily available is the unemployment rate. The lower the unemployment rate, the greater the likelihood that someone who wants to work has found a job. The more jobs, the lower the poverty rate.

Figure 13.9 shows poverty rates and unemployment rates in the United States each year since 1969. As you can see, the poverty rate tends to rise when the unemployment rate increases and fall when the unemployment rate declines. For example, between 1979 and 1982 the unemployment rate climbed from 5.8 percent to 9.7 percent. During that time period, the nation's poverty rate rose from 11.7 percent to 15.0 percent.

More recently, the unemployment rate fell from 7.5 percent in 1992 to 4.0 percent in 2000. During that time period, the poverty rate declined from 14.8 percent to 11.3 percent. Both unemployment and poverty increased in the recession year of 2001.

## Unmarried Motherhood and Poverty

Even when the unemployment rate is low, the poverty rate remains stubbornly high. A strong economy with low unemployment is little aid to families with nobody in the labor force. Chapter 3 noted that young, single motherhood is a recipe for poverty. Often the young mother drops out of school, which reduces her future earning possibilities when and if she seeks work outside the home.

---

**U.S. Poverty Rates by Family Type and Number of Workers**

Figure 13.8

Poverty rates in the United States are much higher in families with no workers.

Source: U.S. Census Bureau, *Current Population Survey,* 2002 Annual Demographic Supplement.

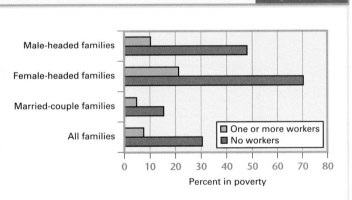

Legend: □ One or more workers ■ No workers

Categories: Male-headed families, Female-headed families, Married-couple families, All families. X-axis: Percent in poverty (0, 10, 20, 30, 40, 50, 60, 70, 80)

---

## Outside Resources

**Joint Center for Poverty Research** Northwestern University and the University of Chicago created the Joint Center for Poverty Research. The center's web site at www.jcpr.org links researchers to sources concerning poverty in the United States. One of the links provides access to *Poverty Research News,* a publication that addresses current issues related to poverty. Ask students to visit this web site and read one of the recent policy briefs posted there. Instruct them to report their findings in a brief report—oral or written. Encourage the appropriate use of graphs and tables.

---

## TEACH

### Poverty and the Economy
Point out that living in poverty is largely the result of having limited income. This implies that those who live in poverty are not able to, or do not chose to, contribute enough value to production to receive what has been called a "living wage." These people are likely to have problems related to their health, education or training, family responsibilities, or personal motivation. People who live in poverty are not only unable to support themselves but also may become a burden on the rest of the economy. People who do not produce are provided with goods and services through a variety of programs. These products are not available to expand production in the economy.

### *Think Critically Through Visuals*
Direct students to focus their attention on **Figure 13.8—U.S. Poverty Rates by Family Type and Number of Workers.** Point out that the poverty rate among families with no workers is four times greater than in families with one worker. The poverty rate of families headed by a female with no workers is 15 times greater than the rate for married-couple families with at least one worker.

### *Think Critically Through Visuals*
Direct students to focus their attention on **Figure 13.9—U.S. Poverty Rates and Unemployment Rates** on page 414. Point out that the poverty rate tends to rise when the unemployment rate increases and fall when the unemployment rate declines.

### *Think Critically Through Visuals*
Direct students to focus their attention on **Figure 13.10—Poverty Rates in the United States** on page 415. Point out the poverty rate for your state and surrounding states.

### ✓ CHECKPOINT
Invite a student to answer the checkpoint that appears on page 414.

**Answer**
The poverty rate is much higher among families with no workers. Additionally, the poverty rate is higher in families headed by a sole female worker.

## Unplanned Results of Income Assistance

Point out that income-assistance programs can alter people's behaviors in ways that are not easy to anticipate. When people are offered the opportunity to receive income, it is reasonable to expect them to adjust their lives in ways that will allow them to take advantage of the situation. This is a question of logic and rational behavior as much as it is one of ethics. Ask students what they would do if they were offered $20 per hour for up to five hours to clean their rooms. Would it be rational for them to take less than five hours to complete the task? Is it rational to expect people who are offered income assistance not to take the greatest possible advantage of what is offered?

### THE WALL STREET JOURNAL

**Reading It Right**

Invite a student to explain the relevance of the statement from *The Wall Street Journal* that appears on page 416.

### Answer

Some argue that welfare states squander money because they take away the incentive to work, while creating a long-term dependency on government assistance and continuing the cycle of poverty.

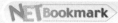

**NET**Bookmark

Direct students to **econxtra.swlearning.com**. Remind them to click on the link for Lesson 13.4 to find the appropriate link for the **NET Bookmark** on page 416. Point out that the link for Temporary Assistance for Needy Families might appear as TANF.

**414     CHAPTER 13**  Economic Challenges

---

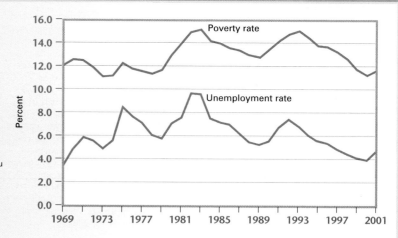

**U.S. Poverty Rates and Unemployment Rates**

Figure **13.9**

The top line shows the percentage of the U.S. population below the official poverty level. The bottom line shows the percentage of the U.S. labor force that is unemployed.

Sources: U.S. Census Bureau and U.S. Bureau of Labor Statistics.

---

Because of a lack of education and limited job skills, most young single mothers go on welfare. Before recently imposed lifetime limits on welfare, the average never-married mother had been on welfare for a decade.

Figure 13.10 shows the poverty rates for each of the 50 states. Those states with a deeper shade of pink have higher poverty rates. States with no shading have lower rates. As you can see, poverty rates are higher across the bottom half of the United States. Poverty rates tend to be higher in states where births to single mothers make up a larger percentage of all births. For example, New Mexico, Louisiana, and Mississippi had the highest poverty rates in 2001. They also had the highest rates of births to unmarried mothers. Nearly half of all births in these three states were to unmarried mothers.

### ✓ CHECKPOINT
What is the link between jobs, unmarried motherhood, and poverty?

## Unplanned Results of Income Assistance

On the plus side, antipoverty programs increase the consumption possibilities of poor families. This is important because children are the largest group living in poverty. However, programs to assist the poor may have other effects that limit their ability to reduce poverty. Consider some unplanned results of these programs.

### Why Work?

Society, through government, tries to provide families with an adequate standard of living, but society also wants to ensure that only the poor receive benefits. As you saw in Chapter 3, income assistance consists of a combination of cash and in-kind transfer programs. Because these programs are designed to help the poor and only the poor, welfare benefits decline as income from other sources increases. This has

---

During the 1990s, the cost of medical insurance increased two to three times faster than the rate of inflation. By 2000, the cost of a basic family medical insurance policy was approaching $10,000 per year in many parts of the country. For people who live in poverty, the government provides basic medical care through its Medicaid program. Ask students to discuss why this benefit may have prevented thousands of poor Americans from accepting employment that did not offer medical coverage as a fringe benefit. Why do some people believe that Medicaid is a drag on productivity in the United States? (People may be hesitant to accept a job that would cost them their Medicaid protection, particularly when many jobs offer no medical coverage. When these people do not work, they do not contribute to production.)

## Poverty Rates in the United States

Figure 13.10

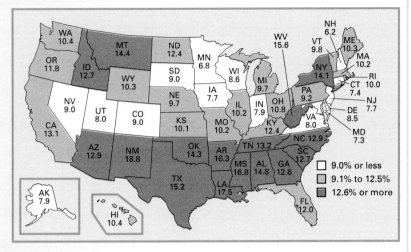

States with a deeper shade of pink have higher poverty rates. States with no shading have lower rates.

Source: U.S. Census Bureau. Rates are averages for 1999, 2000, and 2001.

| | 9.0% or less |
| | 9.1% to 12.5% |
| | 12.6% or more |

resulted in a system in which transfer payments decline sharply as earned income increases.

An increase in earnings reduces benefits from cash assistance, Medicaid, food stamps, housing assistance, energy assistance, and other poverty programs. In some cases, total welfare benefits are cut by $1 or more as earned income increases by $1. Because welfare benefits decline with earnings, this reduces the incentive to find work.

Why work if doing so simply reduces your income and your standard of living? After all, holding even a part-time job involves additional expenses—for transportation and childcare, for instance—not to mention the loss of free time.

In many cases, the value of welfare benefits exceeds the disposable income resulting from full-time employment. Such a system can frustrate people trying to work their way off welfare. *The high tax rate on each additional dollar earned discourages employment and self-sufficiency.*

### Long-Term Dependency

The longer people are out of work, the more their job skills weaken. As a result, when those who have been on welfare for years finally do look for work, their productivity and their pay are lower than when they were last employed. This lowers their expected wage, thus making work even less attractive. Some economists argue that in this way, welfare benefits can lead to long-term dependency on welfare. While welfare seems to be a rational choice in the short run, it has unfavorable long-term consequences for both the family and for society.

By tracking welfare recipients over time, economists have learned that most recipients received welfare for less than a year, but about one third had remained on welfare for at least eight years. Thus there was a core of long-term recipients.

### Cycle of Poverty

A second and more serious concern is that children in welfare families may end up on welfare themselves when they grow up. This is referred to as the **cycle of poverty**. Why might this occur? Children in welfare households may learn the ropes about the welfare system and may come to view welfare

**cycle of poverty**

Children in welfare families may end up on welfare themselves when they grow up

Lesson 13.4 • *Poverty*    **415**

## TEACH
(continued)

### Unplanned Results of Income Assistance

Give several students copies of the following paragraphs. In each case, ask the student whether he or she would accept a job that pays $8 per hour for 40 hours each week ($16,000 per year). The job provides no medical insurance and is located five miles from their home. Ask them to explain their answers. Do other students in the class agree with their choices? (The point is to demonstrate that many people who live in poverty would be economically worse off in the short run to accept any job they are likely to be offered.)

- You are a single parent of three children. You currently receive $280 worth of food stamps and $520 in welfare each month. Your family qualifies for Medicaid, and you have a subsidized apartment that costs $320 each month.

- You are an elderly person who receives Social Security payments of $568 each month. Because you are poor, you also receive $139 worth of food stamps and live in a government-subsidized apartment that costs $210 a month. You receive your medical care through the Medicare program.

- You are single, mildly disabled, and 23 years old. You receive $458 each month from welfare and $150 worth of food stamps. Because you are poor, your medical treatments ($600 per month) are paid by Medicaid. You live rent-free in an apartment that is owned by your uncle.

### Think Critically Through Visuals

Direct students to focus their attention on the photograph on page 416. Ask for a volunteer to answer the question posed in the caption.

### Answer

Answers will vary. Possible answer: It gives individuals an incentive to start working—they can have daycare without having to pay for it. For many single mothers, it was the cost of daycare that forced them to stay on welfare.

## Unplanned Results of Income Assistance

Ask students to make a list of special problems that a single parent of three might experience that would not be experienced by a family with two parents. Ask students why single parents are more likely to live in poverty. (Special problems might include lower income, daycare expenses during work hours, need for assistance with cleaning and laundry, babysitting while shopping, an inability to go out or see friends, or a lack of time to relax and collect one's thoughts. Most of these problems can be reduced by spending, but spending is likely to push families into greater poverty.)

### SPAN THE GLOBE

Direct students to read the short passage "Pro-Poor Tourism" on page 417. Use Think Critically as a starting point for class discussion or have students write a short paragraph to answer the questions.

### Answers to Think Critically

Answers will vary. Possible answer: If environmental effects were taken into consideration when promoting pro-poor tourism, it could be an effective way to help the world's poorest countries. This tourism creates revenue and real GDP where there was none, all through the utilization of the country's natural assets.

### Follow-Up Activity

Invite interested students to learn more about this topic through library and Internet research. Suggest that they report their findings by writing a magazine-style feature including visual images and sidebars.

### ✓ CHECKPOINT

Invite a student to answer the checkpoint that appears on this page.

### Answer

Unplanned results of government assistance include taking away the incentive to work, creating a long-term dependency on assistance, and creating a cycle of poverty throughout generations.

---

**● Reading It Right** What's the relevance of the following editorial statement from *The Wall Street Journal:* "If governments actually knew how to legislate prosperity, we wouldn't have to work. The truth is that welfare states are great excuses for sustaining party political machines, but inevitably, the more they intervene, the more wealth they squander."

**welfare reform**
An overhaul of the welfare system in 1996 that imposed a lifetime welfare limit of five years per recipient and other conditions

as a normal way of life rather than as a temporary bridge over a rough patch.

Research indicates that daughters from welfare families are more likely than daughters in other families to participate in the welfare system themselves. It is difficult to say whether welfare "causes" the link between mother and daughter, because the same factors that contribute to a mother's

### NETBookmark

The U.S. Department of Health and Human Services' Administration for Children and Families (ACF) maintains a web site about welfare reform. Access this site through econxtra.swlearning.com.

Choose one of the links to find out about Temporary Assistance for Needy Families. Write down five facts you learned about this program.

**econxtra.swlearning.com**

**What are the benefits of free or low-cost childcare programs for families trying to work their way out of the welfare system?**

© Getty Images/PhotoDisc

welfare status also can contribute to her daughter's welfare status.

### Welfare Reforms

Concern about welfare dependency and a cycle of poverty prompted **welfare reform**, or an overhaul of the welfare system in 1996. The reform imposed a lifetime welfare limit of five years per recipient. As a condition of receiving welfare, the head of the household also must participate in education and training programs, search for work, or take some paid or unpaid position. The idea is to help people on welfare to learn about the job market. Those who find work are able to maintain some of their welfare benefits, such as free medical care, during a transition period from welfare to work. Those who find jobs also get childcare services. This increases the incentive to work.

Evidence from various states indicates that programs involving mandatory job searches, short-term unpaid work, and training increase employment. Those involved in such programs left welfare rolls sooner. Between 1995 and 2001, the number of welfare recipients fell by more than half.

### ✓ CHECKPOINT
What are some unplanned results of income-assistance programs?

---

## *Economic Headlines*

Ask students to find a newspaper or magazine article that reports on a particular family that is living in poverty. Ask them to prepare a report in which they list the reasons for this family's economic situation. Were they forced into poverty for reasons that were beyond their control, or did they make bad choices? How do government social programs help them? Does there appear to be a cycle of poverty or does it appear that the family (or at least some of its members) will escape poverty in the future? What actions could the family take to escape poverty?

# SPAN THE GLOBE

## Pro-Poor Tourism

For many people in the world's poorest countries, poverty is an ongoing fact of life. About 80 percent of the world's poorest people live in just 12 countries. In many of these countries, a variety of factors make it difficult to build an economic structure that can support the majority of citizens. Recently, though, some economists and developers have begun to promote the idea of building up pro-poor tourism in these countries. This idea involves promoting tourism so as to provide jobs and ongoing economic growth that will allow the majority of the people to rise out of poverty. Because many of these countries have no industry, their undeveloped environments are an attractive draw for tourists. Advocates of pro-poor tourism warn, however, that great care must be taken to ensure that these environments are not harmed by the growth of tourism. In the past, the growth of tourism in some areas has come at the expense of poor people. In Indonesia, for example, land that poor people once used for agriculture was bought up by developers for hotels and golf courses. These projects cut off land and water resources to the poor without providing them with jobs. Pro-poor tourism seeks to minimize these negative results. Development is focused on preserving the natural environment and culture while helping to build a system of public works that can be used by both tourists and local residents. In the Mekong River Basin of Asia, for example, pro-poor tourism loans have been used to help build roads, piers, and better walking paths. These projects improve mobility yet preserve the beauty of the countries in this region and help its residents earn money.

### Think Critically

Do you think pro-poor tourism is an effective way to help the people in the world's poorest countries? Why or why not?

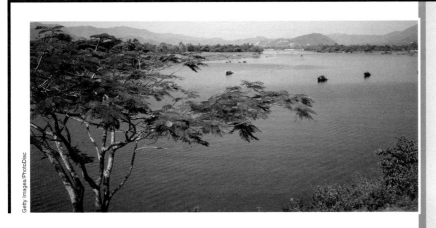

Getty Images/PhotoDisc

Lesson 13.4 • Poverty **417**

## APPLY

Assign Lesson 13.4 from the Contemporary Economics Workbook.

Encourage students to apply their knowledge of concepts presented in this lesson as they explore economic news stories, policy debates, and data available at **econxtra.swlearning.com**. A sampling of the titles for this lesson appears below.

### EconDebate

- Are Americans overworked?
- Does a gender wage gap still exist?
- Does the anti-sweatshop movement help or harm workers in low-wage economies?
- Is a college education a good investment?
- Is workfare working?

### EconNews

- Drawing the Line—Poverty Revisited
- For Richer, for Poorer

## ASSESS

Assign all or part of Lesson 13.4 Assessment on page 418 as homework or an in-class activity.

## Xtra! Study Tools

Direct students to the online study tools for Lesson 13.4 at **econxtra.swlearning.com**.

## CLOSE

**Revisit** the In the News feature on the first page of the lesson. Ask students to review their preliminary answers and discuss the questions, now that they have completed this lesson.

**Review** the objectives for Lesson 13.4. Students should be able to:

- Describe the link between jobs, unmarried motherhood, and poverty.
- Identify some unplanned results of income-assistance programs.

## RETEACH

Remind students that each state has its own welfare system created under federal guidelines. The amount of welfare that is paid, and who qualifies for it, vary widely among states. In some states, able-bodied adults with no children are automatically denied welfare benefits. In other states, they are paid limited amounts. Do students believe this situation is fair? What problems might it create for states that provided more extensive benefits? Would they support a single nationally-funded welfare program? If benefits were identical in every state, why would there still be inequity? (Costs of living vary widely among states and within states.)

### Key Concepts

1. Answers will vary. Possible answer: People who live in poverty in rural areas often are able to raise some of their own food, and rents and other housing costs are typically lower in rural areas. People who live in rural areas, however, may not have access to the types of medical care that are often available to the poor in urban areas.

2. Answers will vary. Possible answer: Growth in production and lower unemployment rates contributed to lower poverty rates in the late 1990s. The fact that fewer people received social benefits may be the result of limitations placed on the length of time people can receive such benefits. Many people may have accepted low-paying jobs to avoid being cut off from social benefit programs.

3. Recent welfare reforms have reduced the number of people receiving social benefits, but this does not mean that these people are no longer living in poverty.

### Graphing Exercise

4. Answers will vary. Students may point out that the relatively small proportion of transfer payments devoted to welfare is less than they would have expected. The largest share of federal transfers is used for Social Security and medical care programs.

   A sample of an acceptable graph appears at the bottom of this page.

### Think Critically

5. Answers will vary. Possible answer: People who live in poverty often believe their situation is the result of circumstances that are beyond their control. This can create a feeling that there is nothing they can do to change their circumstances, which will tend to keep them in poverty.

6. Answers will vary. Possible answer: The firm may not be able to afford to keep all of its workers and stay in business. However, if it does lay off workers, it may have trouble when the recession ends. It may not be able to find qualified workers to fill its job openings, particularly if its former workers have accepted other employment.

**Xtra!**
**Study Tools**
econxtra.swlearning.com

### Key Concepts

1. Why is living in poverty in rural areas often different from living in poverty in an urban area?

2. What reasons can you identify to explain why the number of welfare recipients in the United States fell by more than half between 1995 and 2001?

3. Does the fact that fewer people receive social benefits necessarily mean that fewer people are living in poverty? Explain why or why not.

### Graphing Exercise

4. Many people think the bulk of federal government transfers are used to support the poor. This is not the case. In 2000, the total of all federal government transfer payments to individuals was $1,013 billion. The table shows how these payments were distributed. Use the data in the table to construct a pie graph that shows how federal transfer payments were distributed. Is there any information in the graph that you find surprising? Explain why or why not.

**Federal Transfers by Use, 2000 (in billions of dollars)**

| Type of Spending | Amount | Percent of Total |
|---|---|---|
| Retirement and Disability Insurance (Social Security) | $425.3 | 42.0% |
| Medical Payments (Medicare and Medicaid) | $423.2 | 41.8% |
| Income Maintenance (SSI and Welfare) | $106.4 | 10.5% |
| Unemployment Insurance Benefits | $ 20.7 | 2.0% |
| Veteran's Benefits | $ 24.9 | 2.4% |
| Other transfers to Individuals | $ 12.8 | 1.3% |

### Think Critically

5. **Psychology** Investigate the impact of poverty on people's self-image. Do people who live in poverty feel they are victims of circumstances that are beyond their control? Do they feel there is something that they have done that has caused them to be poor? How might these feelings change the way poor people live and relate to other people in society?

6. **Management** Suppose that you are the owner of a small business that produces precision parts for specialized machines. Your workers are very skilled. If one of your workers were to leave, it would take a long time to find and retrain a replacement. The economy has been in a recession for the past six months, and your firm's sales have fallen by 30 percent. You are having trouble selling enough product to pay your workers and keep them busy. You are thinking of laying off three of your ten workers. What reasons are there for you to do this or not do this? Explain each reason.

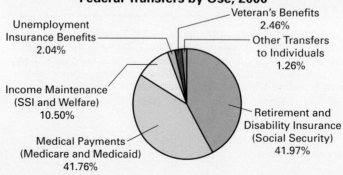

**Federal Transfers by Use, 2000**

- Unemployment Insurance Benefits 2.04%
- Veteran's Benefits 2.46%
- Other Transfers to Individuals 1.26%
- Income Maintenance (SSI and Welfare) 10.50%
- Medical Payments (Medicare and Medicaid) 41.76%
- Retirement and Disability Insurance (Social Security) 41.97%

### Visualizing the Answer— Graphing Exercise

4. The answer includes a graph. Students' graphs should look similar to the one shown here. This graph was constructed using data in the Amount column. An Excel spreadsheet containing this graph, along with supporting data, is available on the Instructor's Resource CD.

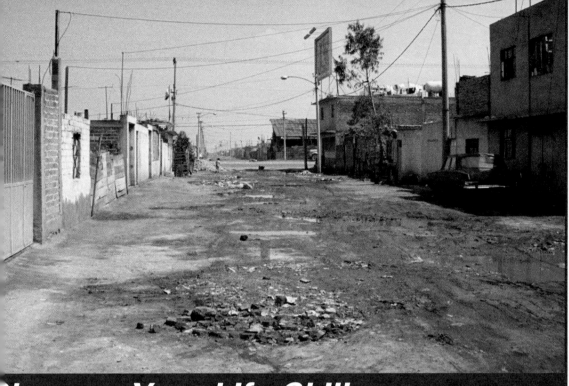

# Sharpen Your Life Skills

## ake Inferences

ple who are unemployed typi-
y experience a reduced standard
iving. It is therefore reasonable to
ect that poverty rates will
ease during times of recession
 fall during times of economic
ansion.

## Apply Your Skill

Study the data in the table and
consider whether they support this
expectation. Write a brief essay that
discusses your findings.

rty and Unemployment Rates, 1992–2000

| ear | Poverty Rate | Unemployment Rate | Year | Poverty Rate | Unemployment Rate |
|---|---|---|---|---|---|
| 92 | 14.8% | 7.5% | 1997 | 13.3% | 4.9% |
| 93 | 15.1% | 6.9% | 1998 | 12.7% | 4.5% |
| 94 | 14.5% | 6.1% | 1999 | 11.8% | 4.2% |
| 95 | 13.8% | 5.6% | 2000 | 11.3% | 4.0% |
| 96 | 13.7% | 5.4% | | | |

## Make Inferences

After studying Lesson 3.4, students
should be able to answer the questions on this page.

## Apply Your Skill

Consider allowing students to work in
pairs for this assignment.

## Answer

Answers will vary. Students may point
out that while the correlation between
unemployment and poverty is not perfect, the two measures do tend to
move together. As unemployment fell
over the last eight years of the 1990s,
the poverty rate also declined in most
years. This seems to indicate a cause-
and-effect relationship.

## *Follow-Up Activity*

Encourage students to use graphs to
illustrate their answers. Suggest that
they use the data to construct two line
graphs similar to the graph that
appears in Figure 13.9. An example of
an acceptable graph appears at the
bottom of this page.

Poverty and Unemployment Rates, 1992 – 2000

## *Visualizing the Answer—*
## *Follow-Up Activity*

Students' graphs should look similar to the one
shown here. An Excel spreadsheet containing
this graph, along with supporting data, is available on the Instructor's Resource CD.

## Summary

### Consider

Ask students to revisit the questions they were asked to consider at the beginning of the chapter. Remind students that they should be able to answer all of the questions after studying Chapter 13.

- Would a high school senior who is not working be considered unemployed? See page 390—Unemployment Rate.

- What type of unemployment might be healthy for the economy? See page 388—Frictional Unemployment.

- What's bad about inflation? See page 400—Impact of Inflation.

- What's stagflation? See page 406—The Great Stagflation: 1973–1980.

- Why don't some families benefit from a strong economy? See page 400—Impact of Inflation.

- How might government transfers change work incentives? See page 414—Unplanned Results of Income Assistance.

### Exam *View*

Use **Exam***View* to assess student learning.

- Create a chapter test using questions from the existing test bank.

- Add your own questions to the existing test bank.

- Generate multiple forms of a chapter test.

### Study Skills

Offer the following study skills suggestions for students as they review this chapter.

- Outline the chapter.
- Review Key Terms.
- Review Checkpoints.
- Work in pairs to quiz each other.
- Use Xtra! Study Tools for each lesson.

 Quiz Prep

Direct students to the online quiz preparation for Chapter 13 at **econxtra.swlearning.com**.

 # Chapter Assessment

## Summary

 **Unemployment**

**a** Unemployment occurs when people who are over 16 are seeking, but unable to find, employment. The *labor force* is made up of all people over 16 who are either employed or seeking work. The *labor force participation rate* is the number of people in the labor force divided by the non-institutionalized adult population.

 **Xtra! Quiz Prep**
econxtra.swlearning.com

**b** Unemployment is more common among individuals who have less education, experience, or training. It also is more likely to affect young people, minorities, and women. In recent years, the differences in unemployment rates among various groups have declined somewhat.

**c** There is always some unemployment in the economy as workers move from job to job. Economists have identified four types of unemployment: *frictional, structural, seasonal,* and *cyclical.* Discouraged workers are not counted as unemployed because they are no longer seeking employment.

**d** Unemployment compensation is paid to workers who lose their jobs through no fault of their own. In general these benefits last for 26 weeks. The benefits may reduce the incentive unemployed workers feel to find new jobs.

**13.2** **Inflation**

**a** *Inflation* is an increase in the economy's general price level. Inflation may be divided into two basic types: *demand-pull* and *cost-push.* Demand-pull inflation results from an increase of aggregate demand. Cost-push inflation is caused by an increase in the costs of production that causes the aggregate supply curve to shift to the left.

**b** Prior to World War II, Inflation in the United States was temporary. Since World War II, there has been sustained inflation that has not been followed by periods of falling prices.

**c** When people do not expect inflation, they often are harmed when prices increase. That is because they made agreements based on a price level that is lower than what actually exists. Higher rates of inflation are associated with higher interest rates.

 **Economic Instability**

**a** Before the Great Depression, most economists held a *laissez-faire* doctrine that said the government should not intervene in a market economy. The economic difficulties of the 1930s convinced many people that government intervention in the economy was necessary for it to work well. Keynes suggested that the government should adjust its own spending and taxing to assure that there is sufficient aggregate demand in the economy to keep production and employment stable.

**b** By the 1970s, it was clear that Keynes's theories could not solve all economic problems. In these years, a combination of high rates of unemployment and inflation called *stagflation* occurred. In the 1980s, some economists suggested that stagflation could be reduced or eliminated by implementing government policies that would reduce the costs of production. The tax cuts of 1981–1983 were intended to stimulate investment in the economy. The most apparent result of these tax cuts, however, was growth in the national debt.

**13.4** **Poverty**

**a** A significant proportion of people in the United States lives in poverty. Poverty is associated with unemployment, single parenthood, and physical or mental disabilities. People with limited education or training also are likely to live in poverty.

**b** Income-assistance programs help people who live in poverty, but they also may cause some people not to seek employment. This has caused a long-term dependency on social programs that lead to what has been called a *cycle of poverty. Welfare reforms* passed in 1996 attempted to eliminate this cycle.

420        **CHAPTER 13**  Economic Challenges

# Review Economic Terms

Choose the term that best fits the definition. On a separate sheet of paper, write the letter of the answer. Some terms may not be used.

_____ 1. Workers who are overqualified for their jobs or who work fewer hours than they would prefer

_____ 2. An increase in the economy's general price level

_____ 3. Macroeconomic policy that focuses on shifting the aggregate demand curve as a way of promoting full employment and price stability

_____ 4. The number of people looking for work divided by the number in the labor force

_____ 5. Macroeconomic policy that focuses on a rightward shift of the aggregate supply curve through tax cuts or other changes that increase production incentives

_____ 6. Doctrine that the government should not intervene in a market economy beyond the minimum required to maintain peace and property rights

_____ 7. Inflation that results from a leftward shift of the aggregate supply curve

_____ 8. A decline of a nation's output accompanied by a rise in the price level

_____ 9. Inflation that results from a rightward shift of the aggregate demand curve

_____ 10. Children in welfare families may end up on welfare themselves when they grow up

_____ 11. The interest rate expressed in current dollars as a percentage of the amount loaned; the interest rate on a loan agreement

_____ 12. Occurs when there is no cyclical employment

a. **cost-push inflation**

b. **cycle of poverty**

c. **demand-pull inflation**

d. **demand-side economics**

e. **full employment**

f. **inflation**

g. **labor force**

h. **labor force participation rate**

i. **laissez-faire**

j. **nominal interest rate**

k. **real interest rate**

l. **stagflation**

m. **supply-side economics**

n. **underemployment**

o. **unemployment benefits**

p. **unemployment rate**

q. **welfare reform**

# Review Economic Concepts

13. Imagine there are 150 million adults in a country. Of these, 45 million adults are not seeking work, and 105 million adults are either working or looking for work. In this case, the labor force participation rate is

a. 40 percent.

b. 70 percent.

c. 30 percent.

d. 60 percent.

14. **True or False** The *labor force* is made up of all the people who would like a job but lack employment.

15. Job seekers who lack skills that are demanded by employers are __?__.

16. **True or False** Interest rates tend to increase when the inflation rate increases.

## Review Economic Terms

1. n. underemployment
2. f. inflation
3. d. demand-side economics
4. p. unemployment rate
5. m. supply-side economics
6. i. laissez-faire
7. a. cost-push inflation
8. l. stagflation
9. c. demand-pull inflation
10. b. cycle of poverty
11. j. nominal interest rate
12. e. full employment

## Review Economic Concepts

13. b. 70 percent
14. False. The labor force is comprised of all those who are working or looking for work.
15. structurally unemployed
16. True

---

 **Assessment**

Continued from page 395.

## Think Critically

8. Answers will vary. Possible answers: The recession of 1837 appears to have been caused by the economic policies of the Jackson administration. Industrial unemployment may have reached 25 percent. The recession of 1873 was caused by bank failures that started in Philadelphia. Industrial unemployment may have reached 15 percent. The recession of 1893 was caused by the inability of many borrowers to repay loans after the failure of several important banks. Industrial unemployment may have reached 18 percent. The recession of 1907 was caused by difficulties related to disputes among large monopolistic businesses. Unemployment may have reached 9 percent. In the nineteenth century, most U.S. residents farmed for a living and therefore could not be laid off or become unemployed. This could happen only to people who worked for others. Their rate of unemployment is sometimes referred to as industrial unemployment.

## Review Economic Concepts

17. a. The price of natural gas increases by 20 percent.
18. Unexpected
19. Stagflation
20. c. try not to intervene in the economy at any time
21. True
22. d. two-parent families

## Apply Economic Concepts

23. D. Functional Unemployment
24. C. Seasonal Unemployment
25. B. Cyclical Unemployment
26. E. Discouraged Worker
27. A. Structural Unemployment
28. The labor force is 5,000 people (7,000 − 2,000 = 5,000).
29. The labor force participation rate is 71.4% (5,000 / 7,000 = 0.714 = 71.4%).
30. The number of people who are unemployed is 250 (5,000 − 4,750 = 250).
31. The unemployment rate is 5% (250 / 5,000 = 0.05 = 5%).
32. Answers will vary but should focus on Nazism, Hitler's rise to power, and World War II.

---

17. Which of the following events would cause *cost-push inflation*?

   a. The price of natural gas increases by 20 percent.
   b. The stock market's value grows by 20 percent.
   c. The federal government cuts income taxes by 20 percent.
   d. The amount of grain produced in the United States grows by 20 percent.

18. __?__ inflation is particularly harmful to people in businesses because they are not able to plan for it.

19. __?__ results in higher unemployment and higher inflation.

20. Before the Great Depression, most economists believed that the government should

   a. intervene in the economy when there was a problem.
   b. intervene in the economy only when the federal government had a large debt.
   c. try not to intervene in the economy at any time.
   d. intervene in the economy at all times to make sure there was full employment.

21. **True or False** Poverty is closely associated with unemployment.

22. Which group is not likely to suffer from higher rates of unemployment and poverty than the average for all people?

   a. single parents
   b. minorities
   c. people with limited education
   d. two-parent families

## Apply Economic Concepts

**Identify Types of Unemployment** Identify each of the following as an example of

   A. Structural Unemployment
   B. Cyclical Unemployment
   C. Seasonal Unemployment
   D. Frictional Unemployment
   E. Discouraged Worker

23. Rosetta quit her job at the public library to look for a job with better pay.
24. Brandon was laid off from his construction job last December.
25. Peter was laid off from his job at Ford when Ford's sales declined.
26. Serena gave up looking for work after she got no job offers in six months of looking.
27. Walter was laid off from his bookkeeping job after his employer installed a new automated inventory control system.

**Calculate the Unemployment Rate** Use the data below to calculate

28. The labor force
29. The labor force participation rate
30. The number of people who are unemployed
31. The unemployment rate for this imaginary economy.

   Total population: 10,000 people

   Non-institutionalized adult population: 7,000 people

   Adults who do not work and are not looking for work: 2,000 people

   People who have employment: 4,750 people

32. **History** Investigate the inflation that took place in Germany after World War I. In 1914, $1 was equal in value to 4.2 marks. By the end of November 1923, $1 had about the same value as 1 trillion marks. What impact did this hyperinflation have on the German economy and German people?

---

 **Assessment**

Continued from page 395.

### Think Critically

9. Answers will vary. Possible answer: When people are unemployed, they are not able to maintain their standard of living. Reduced buying power may lead to family disagreements and to a higher divorce rate.

**33. Sharpen Your Life Skills: Make Inferences**
In 1996, U.S. government public-assistance programs were reformed, and limits were placed on the length of time over which people could receive such assistance. How do you think this change has affected single mothers with young children? Do you think that more of these women would have looked for employment after 1996? What impact might this have on the environment in which their children live? Do the data in the table support your answers?

**Labor Force Participation Rates for All Adults and for Single Mothers of Children through Six Years of Age, 1980–2000**

| Year | Labor Force Participation Rate for All Adults | Labor Force Participation Rate for Single Mothers with Children |
|------|------|------|
| 1980 | 63.8% | 44.1% |
| 1985 | 64.8% | 46.5% |
| 1990 | 66.5% | 48.7% |
| 1995 | 66.6% | 53.0% |
| 2000 | 67.2% | 70.5% |

**34. Graphing Inflation** Use data in the table to construct a line graph that shows the rate of inflation in the United States as measured by the Consumer Price Index (CPI). In 1989 and 1990, prices went up more quickly because the cost of energy increased when Iraq invaded Kuwait. Why were interest rates high in 1989 and 1990?

**Rates of Inflation as Measured by the CPI, 1985–2001**

| Year | Inflation | Year | Inflation | Year | Inflation |
|------|-----------|------|-----------|------|-----------|
| 1985 | 3.6% | 1991 | 4.2% | 1997 | 2.3% |
| 1986 | 1.9% | 1992 | 3.0% | 1998 | 1.6% |
| 1987 | 3.6% | 1993 | 3.0% | 1999 | 2.2% |
| 1988 | 4.1% | 1994 | 2.6% | 2000 | 3.4% |
| 1989 | 4.8% | 1995 | 2.8% | 2001 | 2.8% |
| 1990 | 5.4% | 1996 | 3.0% | 2002 | 1.6% |

*e*-con @pps    econxtra.swlearning.com

**35. Access EconDebate Online** at econxtra.swlearning.com. Read the policy debate entitled "Do technological advances result in higher unemployment?" Analyze this issue from both points of view, and write a paragraph summarizing each side.

## Apply Economic Concepts

33. Answers will vary. Students may point out that the labor force participation rate for single mothers with young children went up dramatically after the law limiting the time people may receive public assistance was passed. This means that more young children were staying in daycare facilities or with relatives while their mothers worked. Whether this trend is good, bad, or unimportant is a matter of personal opinion.

34. Answers will vary. Students may point out that the increased cost of energy caused cost-push inflation. Interest rates tend to be higher when inflation is high because lenders want to protect the purchasing power of the funds they lend.

A sample of an acceptable graph appears at the bottom of this page.

*e*-con @pps

35. Answers will vary. Possible answers for each point of view appear below.

No. Even though technological change may adversely affect the demand for labor in some markets, the overall effect of technological change on total employment can be positive. Technological change tends to increase the rate of economic growth.

Yes. Technological advances take away lower-wage and lower-productivity jobs. The employment security of unskilled workers is threatened when technology can replace the worker.

**Rate of Inflation Measured by the CPI**

*Visualizing the Answer—*
*Apply Economic Concepts*

34. The answer includes a graph. Students' graphs should look similar to the one shown here. An Excel spreadsheet containing this graph, along with supporting data, is available on the Instructor's Resource CD.

This project can be completed in the classroom or as an outside assignment. The activities call for students to work in teams, but students also can complete the assignment working alone. If you organize the class into teams, consider identifying specific roles for team members such as recorder, discussion leader, researcher, etc.

#### The Situation

The emphasis of this project centers more on the business than the personal side of Aleesha's life. Nonetheless, the consequences of her involvement in her enterprise with regard to her relationship with her husband and children also need to be addressed. As far as the business development is concerned, emphasis should be placed on Aleesha's preparation for her life's work by taking college courses in zoology *and* business.

#### The Decision

The decision pattern that confronts Aleesha actually is an enviable one. Her business is going very well, and she has several new products to market. In addition, the patent on her mainstay product still has over a decade to run. The problems that she confronts are environmental rather than of her own creation. Unemployment, social problems, and economic downturns all burden her future, regardless of her preparation and managerial abilities. Nonetheless, these problems are as real as worn-out machinery and could render all her preparation and her life-long dreams worthless.

# Investing In Your Future

| Project 4 | KEEPING THE FAITH |

## The Situation

It was the end of a long day. Shortly, Aleesha would get up and drive to her home a few miles away in the suburbs. There her two children, Tomas, four, and Aleece, two, would come bubbling up to her with stories of what they had done today with their daddy. First, though, Aleesha needed some quiet time to sort things out. She knew how lucky she was. Just seven years ago, she was a struggling college student trying to finance her education and guide the small company she founded into profitability. The company was anchored by a patent Aleesha had received on her invention of a new type of animal-restraint muzzle.

While she was in college, she ran the business out of her parents' garage. After graduation, she devoted her full energies to the enterprise, and sales increased dramatically. Aleesha then bought a small building in the downtown area, and the company had been there ever since. She now had 24 employees, most of whom were single mothers. These women valued not only their chance to work but also the day-care center Aleesha provided as an employee benefit. Aleesha met her husband Tom during a trip to Kenya to observe gorillas. They married four months later and, with the arrival of Tomas, their first child, Tom elected to stay home and care for him.

## The Decision

Now Aleesha faced some vital decisions about which direction to take the company. Demand for its basic products—based on the patent and tailored to each species of animal—continued to increase dramatically. As a consequence, however, the present building was too small, even with the three shifts currently running. Also, the company's machinery now was depreciated fully, and the breakdown rate was increasing, due to its heavy use. The company's small research and development group, comprised of two ex-zookeepers and a mechanical engineer, had several products ready for market. These included more "humane"

Encourage students to use Internet and library resources to learn more about the price of leasing or building commercial real estate and the price ranges of industrial machines. Students might also consult trade journals targeted toward these areas.

animal-restraint devices than the cage and a better means for capturing animals. Regrettably, the country's economy as a whole was having problems. Governmental expenditures on zoos were very low. Some economic forecasters predicted that the economic cycle would reverse and a recovery would follow.

## Activities

**Divide into teams or work individually, as directed by your teacher, to perform the following tasks.**

Apply the steps in the following decision-making process to Aleesha's current situation:

**1.** *Define the problem.* Define Aleesha's problem in a way that will allow a clear solution. Should Aleesha invest in new equipment and a new location?

**2.** *Identify her choices.* List the various alternatives among which Aleesha must choose.

**a.** If the company must move to a distant new location, how should Aleesha provide for her current employees?

**b.** How should a new factory and equipment be financed? What are the risks of using debt to do so? What about selling stock instead?

**c.** Should Aleesha bring out the new products? What would be good way to determine if the new products will sell?

**3.** *Evaluate the pluses and minuses of each choice.* Carefully weigh the value Aleesha puts on each alternative and the opportunity cost(s) for each. Consider what problems each choice might pose for her personal life.

**4.** *Make a choice.* Which course of action should she choose? Be prepared to present and defend your selection to the class.

**5.** *Provide "action" steps that are appropriate to the decision.* Make sure these are realistic and timely to ensure the necessary actions are taken to resolve the problem.

**6.** *Critique the decision.* The class will assist in the review and evaluation of your plan of action. In real life, you should review not only the decision and its result, but also the process by which you make it.

## Research

Research for the information needed to effectively make the decision, such as financing the new factory with debt versus stock and techniques available to assess the marketability of new products.

## Present

Arrive at a decision. Then prepare a presentation for the class on the six steps you took to achieve this decision.

*Project 4* **425**

### APPLY

#### Activities

**Step 2:** There are several alternatives that Aleesha must consider. First of all, she could choose to do nothing and trust that her present situation will not deteriorate and that the same opportunities will be available tomorrow. Second, she could choose to outsource her manufacturing to an offshore site or license production to another factory in the United States. Third, she could choose to invest solely in new machines in an effort to increase productivity and thereby keep pace with new orders. Or, fourth, she could buy/lease a new plant and equipment. **(a)** Treatment of employees who have been loyal and doing an excellent job yet see their employment sent elsewhere is a tricky problem. Is it enough merely to lock the door, or must the employees be retrained and placed in other jobs? The answer to these questions lies in the conscience and social attitudes of the company ownership. **(b)** The new equipment and factory can be financed through the issuance of stock or debt instruments. However, a sale of stock means bringing in new partial owners and, consequently, Aleesha will not be able to act as independently as she has. Issuing debt in the form of bonds or other obligations is probably a better solution at the current time, given the low interest rates. However, debt must be paid on time, and failure to do so may cause the loss of the company. **(c)** Whether or not to bring out new products at this time depends on whether the new products can be copied and sold by a competitor and on the feasibility and results of test marketing the products.

**Step 3:** The time demands and stress levels involved in the carrying out of any of the new ventures will be more damaging to Aleesha's home life than any encountered before. She should assess her relationship with Tom as to its strength, as well as to the children in terms of their mental health, before progressing.

### ASSESS

**Presentation** Consider using a rubric or evaluation form for student presentations. Make sure you share the rubric or form with students before they start working on the project. A sample evaluation form appears on the Instructor's Resource CD. The categories to be evaluated include: **Content** (organization, specific content, and accurate information); **Presentation Skills** (eye contact, grammar and pronunciation, volume, and pitch); **Audiovisual Aids** (appropriate content, style, and spelling); and **Handouts** (appropriate content; grammar, punctuation, and spelling).

*National Content Standards in Economics*

The following NCEE Standards are addressed in Unit 5:

| | |
|---|---|
| **Standard 2** | Marginal Cost/Benefit |
| **Standard 4** | Role of Incentives |
| **Standard 5** | Gain from Trade |
| **Standard 6** | Specialization and Trade |
| **Standard 10** | Role of Economic Institutions |
| **Standard 11** | Role of Money |
| **Standard 12** | Role of Interest Rates |
| **Standard 13** | Role of Resources in Determining Income |
| **Standard 15** | Growth |
| **Standard 16** | Role of Government |
| **Standard 17** | Using Cost/Benefit Analysis to Evaluate Government Programs |
| **Standard 18** | Macroeconomy— Income, Employment, Prices |
| **Standard 19** | Unemployment and Inflation |
| **Standard 20** | Monetary and Fiscal Policy |

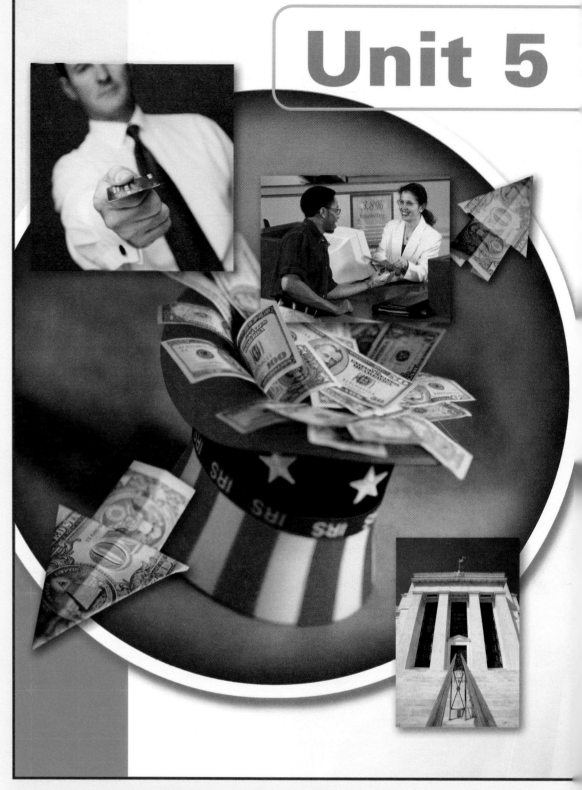

# Unit 5

| Pacing Guide | One-Semester Days of Study | Two-Semesters Days of Study | Block Schedule 90-Minute Blocks |
|---|---|---|---|
| **UNIT 5: PUBLIC POLICY AND THE NATIONAL ECONOMY** | | | |
| Chapter 14: Government Spending, Revenue, and Public Choice | | | |
| **14.1** Public Goods and Taxation | 1 | 2 | 1 |
| **14.2** Federal, State, and Local Budgets | 1 | 3 | 1 |
| **14.3** Economics of Public Choice | 2 | 3 | 2 |
| Chapter 15: Fiscal Policy, Deficit, and Debt | | | |
| **15.1** The Evolution of Fiscal Policy | 1 | 2 | 1 |
| **15.2** Fiscal Policy Reconsidered | 1 | 3 | 1 |
| **15.3** Federal Deficits and Federal Debt | 2 | 3 | 2 |
| Chapter 16: Money and Banking | | | |
| **16.1** Origins of Money | 1 | 2 | 1 |
| **16.2** Origins of Banking and the Federal Reserve System | 1 | 3 | 1 |
| **16.3** Money, Near Money, and Credit Cards | 2 | 3 | 2 |

# Public Policy and the National Economy

**14** Government Spending, Revenue, and Public Choice

**15** Fiscal Policy, Deficits, and Debt

**16** Money and Banking

**17** Money Creation, the Federal Reserve System, and Monetary Policy

Does the economy function pretty well on its own, or does it need government intervention to keep on track? According to one view, the economy can get off track quite easily, resulting in falling output and rising unemployment. To get the economy moving again, government must step in to boost employment and output. According to another view, the economy is fairly stable on its own. Even when things do go wrong, the economy can bounce back pretty quickly. If this second view is true, not only is government intervention unnecessary, it could do more harm than good.

427

## Unit 5 Overview

Unit 5 explores the national economy from a public policy perspective.

Students explore the sources and uses of government revenue as well as the tools of monetary and fiscal policy. The role of banking and the Federal Reserve System in the national economy also is presented.

## Group Activity

Organize students into small groups and ask them to discuss the passage that appears on this page. Instruct students to discuss what they know about public policy as it relates to the economy. Allow about 10 minutes for discussion. Ask a representative of each group to briefly summarize the discussion for the class.

## Think Critically Through Visuals

Direct students study the images on the opposite page and think about how each image relates to public policy and the national economy. Ask them to work with a partner to create their own collage to illustrate public policy and the national economy. Display the finished collages in the classroom while studying Unit 5.

## Look Beyond the Classroom

Every community has some economic challenges. These may include inflation, high tax rates, unemployment, a decline in business production, or a large number of people who live in poverty. A good way to move beyond the classroom is to ask students to identify and investigate economic problems faced by their community. Help them compile and share a list of these challenges.

Instruct students to identify the single economic problem that they believe is most important to people in their community. They should write an essay that explains why they believe this problem is most important and describes steps the government could take to help resolve the problem. If they believe the government should not become involved in the problem, they should explain why they believe this is the better choice.

| Pacing Guide *continued* | One-Semester Days of Study | Two-Semesters Days of Study | Block Schedule 90-Minute Blocks |
|---|---|---|---|
| **UNIT 5: Public Policy and the National Economy** | | | |
| Chapter 17: Money Creation, the Federal Reserve System, and Monetary Policy | | | |
| **17.1** How Banks Work | 1 | 2 | 1 |
| **17.2** Monetary Policy in the Short Run | 1 | 3 | 1 |
| **17.3** Monetary Policy in the Long Run | 2 | 3 | 2 |

### Consider

Ask students to consider the questions posed on this page as they study Chapter 14. After studying all three lessons, students should be able to answer the questions. The content related to each question can be found on the pages indicated below.

- How does the demand for public goods differ from the demand for private goods? See page 430—Public Goods.

- How are responsibilities divided among levels of government? See page 437—Federal, State, and Local Budgets.

- How big is the federal budget, and where does the money go? See page 438—Federal Budgets

- Why do politicians need to deal with special interest groups? See page 448—Role of Special Interest.

- Why do most people remain largely ignorant about what's happening in the public sector? See page 450—Customer Feedback.

> **POINT YOUR BROWSER**

Remind students that they can find additional resources for this chapter at **econxtra.swlearning.com**.

- Xtra! Study Tools
- Net Bookmarks
- Xtra! Quiz Prep
- econ@pps
- Ask the Xpert!
- Graphing Workshop

# 14 Government Spending, Revenue, and Public Choice

### Consider

How does the demand for public goods differ from the demand for private goods?

How are responsibilities divided among levels of government?

How big is the federal budget, and where does the money go?

Why do politicians need to deal with special interest groups?

Why do most people remain largely ignorant about what's happening in the public sector?

© Getty Images/PhotoDisc

> **POINT YOUR BROWSER**

*econxtra.swlearning.com*

---

### Teaching Resources for Chapter 14

- Activities and Projects Masters
- Spanish Resources
- Econ Connection Interactive Tutorial CD
- **Exam***View*® CD
- Workbook Teacher's Edition
- Chapter Test Teacher's Edition
- NCEE Standards and Correlation
- Personal Finance Guide

- Social Studies Skills Review
- Instructor's Resource CD
  - PowerPoint Presentations
  - Lesson Plans
  - Video Discussion Guide
  - Answers to Graphing Exercises
- **econxtra.swlearning.com**

## Objectives

> Calculate the optimal quantity of a public good.

> Distinguish between the two principles of taxation.

> Identify other government revenue sources besides taxes.

## Overview

Markets are marvelous devices, but they are not perfect. They have limitations and short-comings. For example, firms have little incentive to supply public goods because such goods, once produced, are available to all, regardless of who pays and who doesn't. Because a firm cannot limit the good just to those who pay for it, firms can't earn a profit selling public goods. Governments attempt to compensate for this market failure by supplying public goods and paying for them with taxes. People who don't pay their taxes could go to prison.

## Key Terms

**benefits-received tax principle**

**ability-to-pay tax principle**

**tax incidence**

**proportional taxation**

**progressive taxation**

**regressive taxation**

**marginal tax rate**

Remind students that they routinely use goods and services provided by the government. Most people could not afford to purchase these products on their own; therefore, the government must purchase them with tax or other types of revenue.

### Objectives

Remind students to read the lesson objectives to help focus their attention before reading the lesson.

### Key Terms

Direct students to create a database using the key terms for this lesson. The database fields should include terms, definitions, and page numbers. Point out that the process of keying the data is an effective way to study key terms.

## [ In the News ]

### • Will a Heavier Beer Tax Combat Underage Drinking?

A recent National Academy of Sciences report has proposed that the excise tax on alcohol, in particular beer, be raised to help curtail the $53 billion that underage drinking costs taxpayers each year. Alcohol-related traffic accidents involving minors cost almost $20 billion alone. The federal excise tax on beer, currently about 33 cents per six-pack, was last raised in 1991 from around 16 cents. This tax increase resulted in a reported drop of nearly 10 percent in beer sales, according to a spokesperson for beer wholesalers. However, the same spokesperson also commented, "To try to engineer a social problem out of existence [through taxation] is unfair to people who use a product responsibly."

### Think About It

Do you think a tax increase on beer would be effective in reducing underage drinking? Why or why not?

◀ | ▶

**429**

## [ In the News ]

Instruct students to read the passage and write down their answers. Point out that their answers might change after they finish studying Lesson 14.1.

### Answers to Think About It

Answers will vary. Possible answer: I do think a tax increase on beer would be effective in reducing underage drinking. Underage individuals, on average, have a lower income than those who are of age. Therefore, a higher tax will curtail drinking more in their population group than in any other.

### Visual Presentation

Use the PowerPoint presentation on the Instructor's Resource CD as an adjunct to your lecture. The presentation also can be used for review.

---

**NCEE**

### National Content Standards in Economics

A complete list of the NCEE Standards appears on pages xxiv–xxv of this book. The following standards are addressed in Lesson 14.1.

Standard 16: Role of Government

Standard 17: Using Cost/Benefit Analysis to Evaluate Government Programs

## TEACH

### Public Goods

Remind students that many of the goods and services provided by the government are provided at no direct cost to the public or at a reduced cost. This makes it difficult to determine the optimal level of a public good. This task is relatively easy to accomplish in markets for private goods and services, where the efficient level of production occurs at the equilibrium price. But when no price is charged, or when the government sets the price arbitrarily, this allocation method cannot be used.

### Think Critically Through Visuals

Direct students to focus their attention on **Figure 14.1—Market Demand for a Public Good** on page 431. Point out the relationship between the neighborhood demand curve and the individual demand curves.

Direct students to the Graphing Workshop for Chapter 14 at **econxtra.swlearning.com**. Instruct students to click on **See It: Optimal Provision of a Public Good** to view the graph and listen to an explanation.

## Ask the Xpert!

Direct students to **econxtra.swlearning.com** to hear an expert answer the question "What is the meaning of public goods?"

 **CHECKPOINT**

Invite a student to answer the checkpoint that appears on this page.

### Answer

The optimal quantity of a public good may be defined in this way: The efficient level of the public good is found where the sum of the marginal benefits equals the marginal cost of providing the good.

---

# Public Goods

You already learned about the market demand for a private good. For example, the market quantity of pizza demanded when the price is $10 is the quantity demanded by Alan plus the quantity demanded by Maria plus the quantity demanded by all other consumers in the pizza market. Because private goods are rival in consumption, the market quantity demanded of a private good is the sum of the quantities demanded by each consumer.

## The Demand for Public Goods

A public good is different because it is nonrival in consumption. A public good is available to all consumers in an identical amount. For example, if the town sprays a neighborhood for mosquitoes for two hours a week, each resident benefits from the two hours of spraying. The spraying is a public good that spreads through the neighborhood.

The market demand for the spraying reflects the marginal benefit that Alan gets from each hour of spraying plus the marginal benefit that Maria gets from each hour plus the marginal benefit that all others in the community get from each hour.

For simplicity, suppose the neighborhood consists of only two households, one headed by Alan and the other by Maria. Alan spends a lot more time in the yard and therefore values a mosquito-free environment more than Maria does. Maria spends more time away from home. Alan's demand curve, $D_a$, is shown in the bottom panel of Figure 14.1. Maria's demand curve, $D_m$, appears in the middle panel. These demand curves reflect the marginal benefits that each person enjoys from each additional hour of spraying.

For example, when the town sprays two hours a week, Maria values the second hour at $5 and Alan values it at $10. To derive the sum of the marginal benefits for the neighborhood, simply add up the marginal benefit to get $15, as identified by point $e$ in the top panel. By vertically summing up marginal

## Ask the Xpert!

**econxtra.swlearning.com**

*What is the meaning of public goods?*

---

valuations at each rate of output, you derive the neighborhood demand curve, $D$, for mosquito spraying.

Note again that the demand for private goods is found by summing quantities *across* consumers at each price. Pizza and other private goods are rival in consumption. A pizza sold to Alan cannot also be sold to Maria. But public goods are nonrival, so any given quantity of mosquito spraying benefits both Alan and Maria. They may value that public good differently, but the same quantity is available to each.

## Optimal Quantity of the Public Good

How much mosquito spraying should the town government provide? To determine the optimal level of a public good, compare the sum of the marginal benefits of the good with the marginal cost. Suppose the marginal cost of spraying for mosquitoes is a constant $15 an hour, as shown in the top panel of Figure 14.1.

*The efficient level of the public good is found where the sum of the marginal benefits equals the marginal cost of providing the good.* This occurs where the neighborhood demand curve intersects the marginal cost curve. These curves intersect at two hours per week. Thus, two hours is the efficient amount of spraying. That's where the marginal benefit enjoyed by the community just equals the marginal cost. If the town sprayed three or more hours per week, the marginal cost would exceed the marginal benefit.

 **CHECKPOINT**

What is the optimal quantity of a public good?

# Tax Principles

Two hours per week is the efficient, or optimal, level of the public good. How should the government pay for it? Taxes are the source of most government revenue. The way a tax is imposed often is justified on the basis of one of two general principles: the benefits received or the ability to pay.

**430** CHAPTER 14 Government Spending, Revenue, and Public Choice

---

### Outside Resources

**Office of Management and Budget** Recent articles regarding the federal budget can be found at the Office of Management and Budget's website. Have students find *A Citizen's Guide to the Federal Budget* located at www.whitehouse.gov/omb. Have them explore one of the links and summarize their findings in a short report. Some of the links they might choose include "Where the Money Comes From—and Where It Goes," "How Does the Government Create a Budget?" and "The Budget Surplus and Fiscal Discipline."

**430** CHAPTER 14 Government Spending, Revenue, and Public Choice

## Market Demand for a Public Good

Figure **14.1**

Neighborhood demand curve

Marginal cost

15 — e

D

0

2   Hours of mosquito spraying per week

Maria's demand curve

5 —

$D_m$

0

2   Hours of mosquito spraying per week

Alan's demand curve

10 —

$D_a$

0

2   Hours of mosquito spraying per week

Because public goods, once produced, are available to all in identical amounts, the market demand for a public good sums up each person's demand at each quantity. In this example, the neighborhood demand for mosquito spraying sums up Alan's demand, $D_a$, and Maria's demand, $D_m$. The efficient level is found where the marginal cost of mosquito spraying equals the sum of the marginal benefits. This occurs where the marginal cost curve intersects the neighborhood demand curve, resulting in point *e* in the top panel. The optimal output is two hours of mosquito spraying per week.

## Benefits-Received Taxation

The **benefits-received tax principle** relates taxes to the benefits taxpayers receive from a public good. In the mosquito-spray example, the government would impose a tax on each resident equal to his or her marginal benefit from the good. In this case Alan would pay $10 per hour of spraying, or $20 in all. Maria would pay $5 per hour of spraying, or $10 in all. This seems simple enough, but there are at least two problems with it.

First, once people realize that their taxes are based on how much the government thinks they value the good, they tend to understate their true valuation. Why admit how much you value the good if, as a result, you get hit with a higher tax bill? Therefore, taxpayers are reluctant to offer information about their true valuation of public goods. This creates the *free-rider* problem, which occurs because people try to benefit from the public good without paying for it or by paying less than they think it's worth.

Even if the government has accurate information about how much people value the good, the resulting tax may not seem fair if those who value the good more highly have lower incomes. In this example, Alan values mosquito control more than Maria does because he spends more time in the yard than she does. What if Alan is around more because he can't find a job? Maria is around less because she has a job. Should Alan's taxes be double those of Maria? Taxing people according to their marginal benefit may seem reasonable, but it may not be fair if the ability to pay differs sharply across taxpayers.

## Ability-to-Pay Tax Principle

The second approach to taxes is based on the **ability-to-pay tax principle**. Those with a greater ability to pay are taxed more. In the mosquito-spray example, Maria would pay more taxes because she has the greater ability to pay. For example, Maria might pay twice

**benefits-received tax principle**

Those who receive more benefits from the government program funded by a tax should pay more of that tax

**ability-to-pay tax principle**

Those with a greater ability to pay, such as those with a higher income, should pay more of a tax

**Lesson 14.1** • *Public Goods and Taxation*   **431**

## TEACH

### Tax Principles

Remind students that no one likes to pay taxes. Although it is necessary to impose taxes to pay for public goods and services, there are two basic principles that are often used to justify the manner in which taxes are imposed: benefits-received and ability-to-pay. The benefits-received principle of taxation suggests that taxes should be imposed in proportion to the benefit taxpayers receive from the public good or service the tax supports. A toll to cross a bridge is a good example of this type of tax. Those who pay the toll benefit from crossing the bridge. The ability-to-pay principle of taxation suggests that taxes should be imposed disproportionately on those who receive greater incomes, regardless of the benefit they receive from the public good or service the tax supports. Tax rates that increase as incomes grow are a good example of this type of tax. People who receive larger incomes pay a higher rate of income tax than those who receive smaller incomes.

### ✓ CHECKPOINT

Invite a student to answer the checkpoint that appears on page 432.

### Answer

The two principles of taxation are the benefits-received tax principle and the ability-to-pay tax principle.

## ENRICH

In the first years of the twenty-first century, many state governments found their budgets deep in red ink. An economic downturn had increased the need for social programs that were funded by the states at the same time that state tax receipts declined. Furthermore, most states have constitutional or statutory prohibitions against running deficit budgets. State leaders were forced to cut spending, increase taxes, or both. Ask students to discuss what this says about the idea that spending for public goods should be equal to the sum of the marginal benefits received by the people. If there is no money to spend, does it matter how great the benefit will be?

## Other Revenue Issues

Explain that tax incidence can sometimes be related to the principles of taxation, but that these two concepts are not the same. Tax incidence is exclusively a matter of the relative share or percent of income that is paid at different levels of income. It implies no value judgment about who should or should not pay the tax. A proportional tax takes the same percent of income, regardless of how much income is received. There are no perfect examples of proportional taxes in the United States. A progressive tax takes a larger percentage of income as amounts of income received grow. The federal and most state income taxes are progressive. Ability-to-pay principle taxes are almost always progressive. A regressive tax takes a smaller percentage of income as amounts of income received grow. Most state and local taxes are regressive. A tax that is paid on a gallon of gasoline is a greater share of smaller incomes than it is of larger incomes. Progressive and regressive taxes also can be recognized by changes in marginal tax rates that take place as incomes change. When higher incomes result in higher marginal tax rates, the tax is progressive. When higher incomes result in lower marginal tax rates, the tax is regressive.

## E–CONOMICS

Direct students to read the passage entitled "Library Internet Access for Some but Not All?" on this page.

### Answers to Think Critically

Internet service, whether provided to an individual or to a public library, does not meet the economist's definition of a public good because it is both rival in consumption and excludable. The question about availability to adults and minors will vary. Some students may feel the government is justified in excluding minors from viewing material of questionable morality; others may feel that denying minors access to the entire Internet keeps them from reaping its full educational benefits.

# E–CONOMICS

## Library Internet Access for Some but Not All? You

head for the nearest public library to do research on human anatomy for your science project. Sitting down at a computer Internet station, you type in a search request. Unfortunately, when you try to access a useful site, the download is blocked by the library's pornography filtering system. You talk to a librarian about getting the material but the librarian responds that, unlike adults, minors are not empowered by federal law to have the filters removed at their request. Your situation reflects a choice that was made by the library under the Children's Internet Protection Act. Under the Act, if the library wanted to receive federal money supporting Internet access for its patrons, it had to agree to install the filters and

to enforce the rules surrounding their use. The Supreme Court upheld the Act over a challenge by libraries, their patrons, web-site publishers, and the like. These groups maintained that the software filters blocked a great deal of useful, non-offending information on topics such as health issues. Other recipients of federal subsidies—for example, publicly supported radio and TV stations and the National Endowment for the Arts—worry that, as a consequence of the Court's decision, the material they present may be censored by the government.

### Think Critically

Is Internet access at the library a public good? Do you think Internet access at the library should be available to adults and minors alike with no restrictions? Why or why not?

---

as much as Alan. Income and property taxes usually rely on the ability-to-pay approach. The ability-to-pay tax principle focuses more on taxpayer's income than on the taxpayer's benefit from the public good. Maria might not think the tax is fair, because she is paying twice as much as Alan even though she values the good only half as much as he does. Fairness is not necessarily an issue when it comes to taxation.

Public goods are more complicated than private goods in terms of what goods should be produced, in what quantities, and who should pay. These decisions are sorted out through public choices, which are examined later in the chapter.

**tax incidence**
Indicates who actually bears the burden of a tax

**proportional taxation**
The tax as a percentage of income remains constant as income increases; also called a *flat tax*

 **CHECKPOINT**
What are the two principles of taxation?

## Other Revenue Issues

Taxes provide most revenue at all levels of government. The federal government relies primarily on the individual income tax. State governments rely on income and sales taxes. Local governments rely on the property tax. In addition to taxes, other revenue sources include (1) aid from higher levels of government; (2) user fees, such as highway tolls; (3) fines, such as speeding tickets; and in some states (4) monopoly profits from having the exclusive right to sell certain goods, such as lottery tickets and liquor. If revenues fall short of expenditures, governments cover the resulting deficit by borrowing from the public.

### Tax Incidence

**Tax incidence** indicates who actually bears the burden of the tax. One way to

**432**   **CHAPTER 14**   Government Spending, Revenue, and Public Choice

---

### Economic Headlines

Instruct students to locate an article in a current magazine or newspaper that relates to one of the topics in this lesson. For example, they might find articles about taxation. Instruct students to read the article, write a brief summary, and include a reference citation. Identify the style you want them to use for the citation.

As an alternative, you might locate several articles of interest and provide citations for students to use in locating one of the articles. Direct students to read the article they have chosen and write a brief explanation of how it relates to this lesson.

evaluate tax incidence is by measuring the tax as a percentage of income. Under **proportional taxation**, taxpayers at all income levels pay the same percentage of their income toward that tax. A proportional income tax is called a *flat tax,* because the tax as a percentage of income remains constant, or flat, as income increases.

Under **progressive taxation**, the percentage of income paid in taxes increases as income increases. The federal income tax and most state income taxes are progressive, because tax rates increase as taxable income increases.

Finally, under **regressive taxation**, the percentage of income paid in taxes decreases as income increases, so the tax rate declines as income increases. For example, Social Security taxes in 2003 collected 6.2 percent of the first $87,000 of a workers' earnings. The tax rate imposed on income above that level dropped to zero. The average tax rate declines as income increases above $87,000.

## Marginal Tax Rate

The **marginal tax rate** indicates the percentage of each additional dollar of a taxpayer's income that goes to taxes. High marginal rates reduce the after-tax income from working, saving, and investing. Therefore, high rates can reduce people's incentives to work, save, and invest. As of 2003, there were six marginal rates for those who pay federal income taxes, ranging from 10 percent to 35 percent, depending on income. Millions of low-income households pay no income taxes. Many with low earnings receive tax refunds that exceed the amount paid in.

Income tax rates are, therefore, progressive. Figure 14.2 shows the top marginal tax rate on federal personal income taxes since the tax was introduced in 1913. Note that most recently the highest rate was relatively low by historical standards. Still, the top 10 percent of tax filers, based on income, pay about two-thirds of all federal income taxes collected.

## Pollution Taxes and Sin Taxes

At times, taxes and fines are imposed to discourage some activities. For example, government may impose a tax or a fine on pollution emissions. Fines for littering, disturbing the peace, and having a defective muffler are designed to reduce these externalities. To discourage activities deemed socially undesirable, governments also impose *sin taxes* on cigarettes, liquor, and legal gambling.

## User Fees

Sometimes the government can easily exclude those who don't pay for a good and so can charge a user fee. For example, states charge entrance fees to state parks and tuition to state colleges.

*progressive taxation*
The tax as a percentage of income increases as income increases

*regressive taxation*
The tax as a percentage of income decreases as income increases

*marginal tax rate*
The percentage of each additional dollar of income that goes to pay the tax

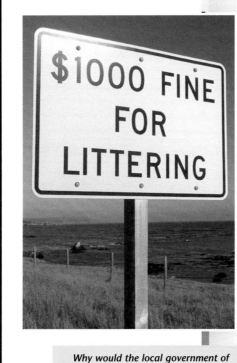

**Why would the local government of this beach town impose a $1,000 fine for littering?**

## CHECKPOINT

Invite a student to answer the checkpoint that appears on this page.

**Answer**

Other sources of revenue besides taxes include user fees and borrowing.

### APPLY

Assign Lesson 14.1 from the Contemporary Economics Workbook.

### ASSESS

Assign all or part of Lesson 14.1 Assessment on page 435 as homework or an in-class activity.

## Xtra! Study Tools

Direct students to the online study tools for Lesson 14.1 at **econxtra.swlearning.com**.

### CLOSE

**Revisit** the In the News feature on the first page of the lesson. Ask students to review their preliminary answers and discuss the questions, now that they have completed this lesson.

**Review** the objectives for Lesson 14.1. Students should be able to:

• Calculate the optimal quantity of a public good.

• Distinguish between the two principles of taxation.

• Identify other revenue sources besides taxes.

---

Those unwilling to pay are not admitted. User fees are just like prices for private goods except that the fees often do not cover the cost.

### Borrowing

Governments sometimes borrow from households and firms to fund public programs. Borrowing by the public sector can be justified for capital projects that increase the economy's productivity—investments such as highways, airports, and schools. The cost of these capital projects should be borne in part by future taxpayers, who also will benefit from these investments. Governments also borrow when revenues fall short of expenditures. Borrowing by the federal government will be examined in the next chapter.

## CHECKPOINT

What are the other revenue sources besides taxes?

---

## THE WALL STREET JOURNAL

**Reading It Right** What's the relevance of the following statement from *The Wall Street Journal:* "Simply put, the IRS data demonstrate once again that the income tax system is steeply progressive . . . The top 10% of taxpayers [in 2001] continued to cough up well over half of all tax revenues—about 65%."

## TEAM WORK

Working in groups of three, brainstorm a list of user fees—other than those listed in the text—that you might have to pay. Share your results with the rest of the class.

---

**Top Marginal Tax Rate on Personal Income, 1913–2003**                                    **Figure 14.2**

The top 10 percent of tax filers, based on income, pay about two-thirds of all federal income taxes collected.

Source: U.S. Internal Revenue Service.

---

### RETEACH

Remind students that the marginal tax rate is one of the primary considerations people take into account when they decide what to do with their time and resources. Ask students how much they would expect to pay a worker to cook hamburgers at a fast-food restaurant they own. How much more would they be forced to offer if the marginal tax rate the worker had to pay was 50 percent, 75 percent, or 90 percent of the amount of pay? Why do higher personal tax rates result in higher labor costs for businesses?

## Key Concepts

1. Why isn't a campsite you rent in a national park a perfect example of a public good?

2. Suppose your town council has determined that it would need to spend $1 million to repave and widen the road that leads to your school. How should the members of the town council decide whether to undertake this project?

3. Why isn't it logical for the government to try to pay for a welfare program by imposing a *benefits-received principle* tax?

4. Why aren't property taxes, particularly for older people, always examples of *ability-to-pay principle* taxes?

5. Why is it difficult for people to agree on a tax structure that is fair for all?

6. How willing would you be to work 10 hours next week at a local store to earn $100? If $25 of your earnings were taken to pay taxes, what would happen to your willingness to work? What if $50 or $75 were taken? How does this example demonstrate the importance of the marginal tax rate to production in the economy?

## Graphing Exercise

7. Many residents of Oakwood, a small town, have asked to have the town's swimming pool kept open for eight hours each day during the summer instead of only six hours. The cost of operating the pool is $80 per hour. Draw a graph that shows the efficient level of swimming-pool hours per day to be eight hours. The marginal cost should be shown by a horizontal line that hits the vertical axis at $80. The sum of the marginal benefit or demand curve should slope downward from left to right and intersect the marginal cost above eight hours of daily operation. Explain how your graph demonstrates that this is the optimal quantity of this public good.

## Think Critically

8. **Math** Patty is a loan officer for a bank. She earns $60,000 per year and drives a new Jaguar. Tony is a night janitor who works for the same bank. He earns $20,000 per year and drives an old Ford. Both Patty and Tony buy 1,000 gallons of gasoline for their cars each year. The tax per gallon of gasoline is $.50. How much does each person pay in gasoline tax? What percent is this payment of each person's income? Is the tax on gasoline proportional, progressive, or regressive? Explain how you know.

**Xtra!**
**Study Tools**
econxtra.swlearning.com

### Optimal Hours of Swimming Pool Operation

Marginal cost for an additional hour
Efficient level of hours
Sum of the marginal benefit for an additional hour (Demand Curve)

Cost — Daily Hours of Operation

## Visualizing the Answer— Graphing Exercise

7. The answer includes a graph. Students' graphs should look similar to the one shown here. An Excel spreadsheet containing this graph, along with supporting data, is available on the Instructor's Resource CD.

---

## Key Concepts

1. Answers will vary. Possible answer: The campsite has rivals for consumption. While you rent it, no one else is able to use the campsite.

2. Answers will vary. Possible answer: The town council should undertake the project if it believes the value of the sum of its marginal benefits is greater than $1 million.

3. Answers will vary. Possible answer: People who receive welfare are economically disadvantaged and therefore unable to pay for such a program.

4. Answers will vary. Possible answer: Many people who own property have little income that would give them the ability to pay a tax.

5. Answers will vary. Possible answer: Most people would rather have others pay a greater portion of the tax burden while they pay less. There is no tax structure that can accomplish this for all taxpayers.

6. Answers will vary. Possible answer: The higher the marginal tax rate, the less willing people are to work to earn income. People who work less also produce less.

## Graphing Exercise

7. Answers will vary. Possible answer: The efficient level of a public good is when the value of the sum of its marginal benefits is equal to its marginal cost. The efficient level of a public good is demonstrated by the intersection on the graph.

   An example of an acceptable graph appears at the bottom of this page.

## Think Critically

8. Answers will vary. Students should point out that both Patty and Tony pay $500 in gasoline tax per year ($.50 ? 1,000 = $500). The $500 is 0.833 percent of Patty's income ($500 / $60,000 = 0.00833 = 0.833%), while it is 2.5 percent of Tony's income ($500 / $20,000 = 0.025 = 2.5%). The tax is regressive because the person with the smaller income pays a larger percent in tax.

### Apply Math Skills

After studying Lesson 14.1, students should be able to answer the questions on this page.

### Apply Your Skill

Some students will benefit from creating a table to help them compare Job A and Job B. A sample table appears at the bottom of this page.

### Answers

1. $0 in Florida

   $1,400 in New York (0.05 × $28,000 = $1,400)

2. $560 in Florida ($8,000 × 0.07 = $560)

   $660 in New York ($8,000 × 0.0825 = $660)

3. $6,600 in Florida ($550 × 12 = $6,600)

   $8,100 in New York ($675 × 12 = $8,100)

4. $1,200 in Florida ($200 × 6 = $1,200)

   $690 in New York (($75 × 6) + ($40 × 6) = $690)

5. ($1,400 + $100 + $1,500 − $510 = $2,490)

6. Answers will vary. Possible answer: The amount people earn is less important than the amount they are able to take home after taxes. The amount they must pay to live is also important. More people have moved to states with relatively lower tax rates and costs of living. This has caused rates of economic growth to be higher in these states.

# Sharpen Your Life Skills

### Apply Math Skills

To make rational decisions, people need to quantify and evaluate the costs and benefits of alternative choices they might make. This can be seen in choosing among job offers you might receive when you finish your education. Taking a job that pays a high wage may not be your best financial choice if it is located in a city that has high taxes and costs of living. A lower wage could provide you a better standard of living in a different community. Study the two job offers described below. Then use your math skills to answer the questions that follow.

**Job A in Florida**

- You would work as an assistant manager in a retail clothing store.

- Your salary would begin at $23,000 per year.

- There is no state income tax in Florida.

- The sales tax in Florida is 7%.

- You can rent an apartment you like for $550 per month.

- You won't need to pay high heating costs, but your air conditioning could cost as much as $200 per month during the six months of summer.

**Job B in New York State**

- You would work as an assistant manager in a jewelry store.

- Your salary would begin at $28,000 per year.

- You would pay state income tax at an average rate of 5 percent.

- The sales tax in New York is 8.25%.

- You can rent an apartment you like for $675 per month.

- You would expect to pay an average of $75 per month to heat your apartment during the six months of winter and $40 per month to air condition it in summer.

### Apply Your Skill

1. How much state income tax would you pay in each state?

2. If you spent $8,000 buying products that are subject to sales tax, how much would you pay in tax in each state?

3. How much would you pay per year to rent an apartment in each state?

4. How much would you pay per year to heat or cool your apartment in each state?

5. How much more per year would taxes and costs of living be in New York than in Florida?

6. Why do you think many people have moved from higher-tax states to lower-tax states in recent years?

**436**   **CHAPTER 14**   Government Spending, Revenue, and Public Choice

### Visualizing the Answer

| Job A: Florida | | | Job B: New York State | | |
|---|---|---|---|---|---|
| Salary | Income Tax Rate | Income Tax | Salary | Income Tax Rate | Income Tax |
| $23,000 | 0% | $0 | $28,000 | 5% | $1,400 |
| Purchases | Sales Tax Rate | Sales Tax | Purchases | Sales Tax Rate | Sales Tax |
| $8,000 | 7% | $560 | $8,000 | 8,25% | $660 |
| Monthly Rent | Months | Yearly Rent | Monthly Rent | Months | Yearly Rent |
| $550 | 12 | $6,600 | 675 | 12 | $8,100 |
| Heating Rate | Months | Heating Cost | Heating Rate | Months | Heating Cost |
| $0 | 6 | $0 | 75 | 6 | $450 |
| AC Rate | Months | AC Cost | AC Rate | Months | AC Cost |
| $200 | 6 | $1,200 | 40 | 6 | $240 |
| | | $8,360 | | | $10,850 |

## 14.2 Federal, State, and Local Budgets

## Objectives

> Identify the top spending category in the federal budget and the top source of revenue.

> Identify the top spending category in state budgets and the top source of revenue.

> Identify the top spending category in local budgets and the top source of revenue.

> Compare the relative size of the U.S. government during the last decade with other major economies.

## Overview

The United States has a federal system of government, meaning that responsibilities are shared across levels of government. State governments grant some powers to local governments and surrender some powers to the national, or federal, government. As the system has evolved, the federal government has assumed primary responsibility for national security and the stability of the economy. State governments fund public higher education, most prisons, and—with grants from the federal government—highways and welfare. Local governments are responsible mainly for local schools, though some funding for this comes from the state.

## Key Terms

**government budget**

**payroll taxes**

**FOCUS**

Tell students that all governments are required to create budgets, including expected revenues and expected spending. In this lesson, students will learn how the federal, state, and local governments typically receive revenues and then either spend them or transfer them to others. They will learn that budget decisions are sometimes a reflection of the values held by society and expressed through decisions made by their elected leaders. In other cases, budget decisions are made to preserve the political power of current government leaders.

### Objectives

Remind students to read the lesson objectives to help focus their attention before reading the lesson.

### Key Terms

Direct students to write each of the key terms on a separate index card. Instruct students to write the complete definition of each key term on the back of the appropriate card along with the page number where the definition is located. Encourage students to use the cards to study for quizzes and tests.

## [ In the News ]

### ● Which Way Does the Tax Cut Cut?

Recent reports on the effect of the $350 billion income tax cut of 2003 have given it mixed reviews. As a result of the tax cut, a typical middle-income family with two children had approximately $1,200 extra to spend. However, some analysts believed that families would spend this windfall in the same way they spent the 2001 tax cut funds—on foreign-made consumer goods. As a consequence, sales of domestic manufacturers would not increase, nor would these manufacturers spend money on machinery or hire new employees. The decreased taxes on stock dividends and other investments, however, had positive effects. They encouraged more people to buy stock, which sent stock prices higher. This came at a good time for baby boomers and others whose savings and retirement plans, dependent on stock prices, gained back much of the value lost in the market decline of the previous years. Finally, the loss of federal revenue from the tax cut contributed to massive actual and projected budget deficits. In fact, in a little more than three years, a federal budget surplus of more than $230 billion dollars in 2000 became a deficit of $374 billion for 2003.

### Think About It

What are the benefits and downsides of income tax cuts?

◀ ▮ ▶

**437**

## [ In the News ]

Instruct students to read the passage and write down their answers. Point out that their answers might change after they finish studying Lesson 14.2.

### Answers to Think About It

Answers will vary. Possible answers: Consumers benefit from a tax cut because they pay less tax and have more money to spend or save. If consumers spend the extra money on domestic goods, it will result in an increase in jobs and production. On the downside, if the money is spent on foreign goods, there is very little effect on jobs and production and no real benefit to the U.S. economy. In addition, an income tax cut increases the federal deficit.

### Visual Presentation

Use the PowerPoint presentation on the Instructor's Resource CD as an adjunct to your lecture. The presentation also can be used for review.

**NCEE**

### National Content Standards in Economics

A complete list of the NCEE Standards appears on pages xxiv–xxv of this book. The following standards are addressed in Lesson 14.2.

Standard 16: Role of Government          Standard 20: Monetary and Fiscal Policy

Standard 17: Using Cost/Benefit Analysis to Evaluate Government Programs

## Federal Budgets

Remind students that governments are able to provide public goods and services only when they receive revenues from taxing, borrowing, or other sources. Recent changes in sources of federal revenues and types of federal spending or transfers reflect a change in the priorities of the federal government and the role it plays in the U.S. economy. In the past 80 years, the share of GDP that flows through all levels of government has grown from roughly 10 percent to more than 30 percent. This is an indication of the larger role that government plays in the U.S. economy today.

### *Think Critically Through Visuals*

Direct students to focus their attention on **Figure 14.3—Defense Spending as a Share of the Federal Budget**. Point out that this graph illustrates the share of federal spending by major category since 1960.

---

**government budget**
A plan for government outlays and revenues for a specified period, usually a year

# Federal Budgets

A **government budget** is a plan for outlays and revenues for a specified period, usually a year. The word *budget* derives from the Old French word *bougette*, meaning "little bag." The federal budget is now more than $2,300,000,000,000—$2.3 trillion a year. If this "little bag" contained $100 bills, it would weigh more than 25,000 *tons*! These $100 bills could cover a 14-lane highway stretching from northern Maine to southern California.

## Federal Spending

One way to track the impact of government spending over time is to compare that spending to the U.S. gross domestic product, or GDP. In 1929, the year the Great Depression began, government spending at all levels totaled about 10 percent of GDP. Local government spending accounted for about half that total. The federal government played a minor role in the economy. In fact, during the nation's first 150 years, federal spending, except during war years, never exceeded 3 percent relative to GDP.

The Great Depression, World War II, and a change in economic thinking

have boosted government spending, particularly at the federal level, to 32 percent of GDP most recently. The federal portion totals 20 percent and state and local governments, 12 percent. Thus, since 1929, government spending has more than tripled as a share of GDP, and the federal portion has increased more than six times.

Figure 14.3 shows the share of federal spending by major category since 1960. The share of the budget going to national defense fell from 52 percent in 1960 to only 18 percent in 2004. Redistribution, which consists largely of Social Security, Medicare, and welfare, grew steadily as a share of the total, climbing from 21 percent in 1960 to 49 percent in 2004. In 1960, the federal government focused primarily on national defense. By 2004, spending had shifted to income redistribution.

Interest payments on the federal debt stood at 8 percent of the budget in 1960, grew during the middle years, and then returned to 8 percent by 2004 (thanks to record-low interest rates). Spending on all other programs, from federal prisons to the environment, went from 20 percent in 1960 to 26 percent in 2004.

---

**Defense Spending as a Share of the Federal Budget**     **Figure 14.3**

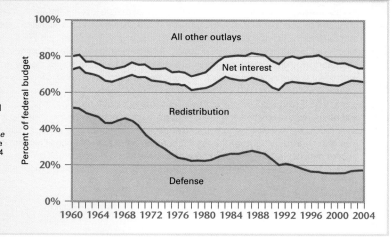

As a share of the federal budget, defense spending has declined and redistribution has increased since 1960.

Source: *Economic Report of the President,* February 2003, Table B-80. Figures for 2003 and 2004 are estimates.

---

**438**     **CHAPTER 14**   Government Spending, Revenue, and Public Choice

---

## *Outside Resources*

**State Budget Web Sites** Every state has an office that is in charge of its budget. In California, for example, it is the California Department of Finance. This office maintains a web site at www.dof.ca.gov. Direct students to search the Internet to find the equivalent office in your state. Ask students to investigate information that is available at the web site and write a brief summary of their findings.

## Federal Revenue

During its first century, the federal government raised most of its revenue from taxes on imports, taxes on specific goods, and property taxes. All that changed with the Sixteenth Amendment to the U.S. Constitution. This empowered Congress to levy a tax on personal income. The personal income tax was introduced in 1913. The tax originally affected only the top 10 percent of households based on income. Rates were raised to help pay for World War II. Since then the personal income tax has remained the primary source of federal revenue.

Figure 14.4 shows the composition of federal revenue since 1960. The individual income tax fluctuated from 42 percent to 50 percent of the total during the period. In part because of income tax cuts in 2001 and 2003 and in part because the economy remained weak, income taxes made up 44 percent of total revenue in 2004, the same as in 1960.

The share from payroll taxes more than doubled from 15 percent in 1960 to 40 percent. **Payroll taxes** are deducted from paychecks to support Social Security, which is a retirement

Access the current fiscal year's federal budget document through econxtra.swlearning.com. Click on the link to the current year's budget. Choose one topic in the Table of Contents for the budget. Click on that link, read the document, and then write a paragraph explaining how the topic relates to the budget.

*econxtra.swlearning.com*

program, and Medicare, which funds medical care for the elderly. The abbreviation *FICA* on your paycheck stub refers to these payroll taxes. FICA stands for the Federal Insurance Contributions Act. Corporate income taxes and revenue from other taxes and user fees have declined as a share of the total from 40 percent in 1960 to 16 percent in 2004.

Note that Figure 14.4 shows the composition of revenue sources and ignores borrowed funds. Most years the federal government spends more than it takes in and makes up the difference by borrowing

**payroll taxes**
Taxes deducted from paychecks to support Social Security and Medicare

**Ask the Xpert!**
*econxtra.swlearning.com*

*Why do we keep the income tax if it is so unpopular?*

---

**Payroll Taxes as a Share of Federal Revenue**

**Figure 14.4**

**Payroll taxes have grown as a share of federal revenue since 1960.**

Source: Based on fiscal year revenue figures from the *Economic Report of the President*, February 2003. Figures for 2003 and 2004 are projections.

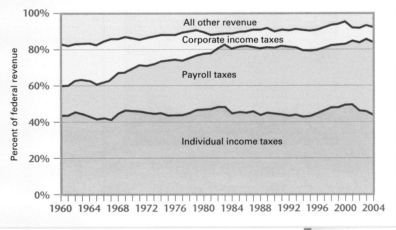

---

## ENRICH

Remind students that federal income taxes are collected through a system that requires taxpayers to calculate and pay their own tax liabilities. Each person who receives any substantial amount of income in the United States is required to complete and submit an individual tax return. Although the IRS reviews each tax return, less than 1 percent of them are actually audited in any given year. This means that some people do not pay the full amount of taxes they owe. It has been estimated that the federal government may fail to collect as much as $100 billion in tax revenue that it is owed each year. This places a greater burden on those individuals who do pay. What, if anything, do students believe should be done about this situation?

---

## TEACH (continued)

### Federal Budgets

Ask students to identify types of federal spending or transfers. Compile their lists on the board. Then designate each type of spending or transfer according to the classifications used in Figure 14.3 on page 438. Spending for the military would be part of defense, welfare and Social Security would fall into redistribution, and so on. When this is finished, ask students to consider how important federal spending and transfers are to the American way of life. What would happen if the federal government had only 3 percent of GDP to spend, as it did in most of the nineteenth century?

### Ask the Xpert!

Direct students to **econxtra.swlearning.com** to hear an expert answer the question "Why do we keep the income tax if it is so unpopular?"

### NETBookmark

Direct students to **econxtra.swlearning.com**. Remind them to click on the link for Lesson 14.2 to find the appropriate link for the **NET Bookmark** on this page. Consider asking students to select topics so that each student is focused on a different section of the budget.

### *Think Critically Through Visuals*

Direct students to focus their attention on **Figure 14.4—Payroll Taxes as a Share of Federal Revenue**. Point out that this graph illustrates the composition of federal revenue by category since 1960.

### ✓ CHECKPOINT

Invite a student to answer the checkpoint that appears at the top of page 440.

### Answer

Redistribution, in the form of Social Security, Medicare, and welfare, is the top spending category in the federal budget. The income tax is the primary source of revenue for the federal government.

## State Budgets

Point out that state spending is likely to have a more direct impact on students' daily lives than are federal spending and transfers. Although Social Security is federally funded and administered, state governments administer welfare, unemployment compensation, Medicaid, and worker's compensation programs. A large proportion of the costs of public schools, law enforcement, and highway construction and maintenance are state funded. To pay for these goods and services, state governments impose taxes that are often regressive. States also receive a significant share of their revenue in the form of aid from the federal government. Although federal spending declined as a share of GDP in the 1990s, state spending grew as a share of GDP in these years. Ask students to discuss ways in which state spending affects their lives.

### *Think Critically Through Visuals*

Direct students to focus their attention on the photograph on this page. Ask for a volunteer to answer the question posed in the caption.

### Answer

The top two spending categories for state government are grants to local governments, mostly to pay for schools, and welfare payments.

### *Think Critically Through Visuals*

Direct students to focus their attention on Figure 14.5—Composition of State Spending and State Revenue on page 441. Point out that this is a composite of all the states. A pie chart for any particular state would look different. For example, a chart for the state of Washington would not show any revenue from income tax, and Oregon's chart would not include revenue from sales tax.

### CHECKPOINT

Invite a student to answer the checkpoint that appears at the bottom of page 440.

### Answer

Top spending for the state government is assistance to schools. The biggest revenue for the state is aid from the federal government.

---

from the public. This is discussed in the next chapter.

### ✓ CHECKPOINT
What is the top spending category in the federal budget and the top source of revenue?

## State Budgets

You already know something about state government. You travel on state roads, visit state parks, and may be planning to attend a state college. State regulations dictate how old you must be to get a driver's license, how fast you may drive on most roads, and how many days a year school is in session. You pay state excise taxes on certain items, including gasoline and movie tickets. If you earn a paycheck, you

© Getty Images/PhotoDisc

**A small portion of a state's budget goes to fund the prison system. What are the top two spending categories for state government?**

**440**      **CHAPTER 14**   Government Spending, Revenue, and Public Choice

may pay state income taxes. You also may pay state sales taxes on most purchases. From the department of motor vehicles to the department of education, state government affects your life in many ways.

### State Spending

The pie chart on the left of Figure 14.5 shows the composition of state spending. The biggest outlay, 34 percent of the total, goes toward grants to local governments, mostly to help pay for schools. The next biggest share, 20 percent, consists of welfare payments, most of which go toward medical care for the poor, especially elderly in nursing homes. Higher education ranks third at 14 percent of the total. The remaining 32 percent pays for highways, state police, prisons, interest on state debt, administration, and other state activities.

### State Revenue

The right pie chart in Figure 14.5 lays out the sources of state revenue. The largest source, 28 percent of the total, is aid from the federal government, which covers more than half of state welfare costs. The second biggest source, sales and excise taxes, makes up 25 percent of state revenue. Sales taxes apply to broad categories of goods. All but five states impose a general sales tax, with rates ranging from 3 percent to 7 percent of the purchase price. Does your state have a general sales tax? If so, what's the tax rate? Excise taxes apply to specific goods such as cigarettes and gasoline.

The state income tax ranks third, accounting for 19 percent of state revenue. The fourth greatest source of state revenue is user fees, making up 17 percent of the total. Examples include admissions to state campgrounds and tuition at state colleges.

### ✓ CHECKPOINT

What is the top spending category in state budgets and the top source of revenue?

---

### *Economic Headlines*

Instruct students to locate an article in a current magazine or newspaper that relates to one of the topics in this lesson. For example, they might find articles about a current state budget issue. Instruct students to read the article, write a brief summary, and include a reference citation. Identify the style you want them to use for the citation.

As an alternative, you might locate several articles of interest and provide citations for students to use in locating one of the articles. Direct students to read the article they have chosen and write a brief explanation of how it relates to this lesson.

## Composition of State Spending and State Revenue

Figure 14.5

### Composition of State Spending

Administration and interest 6%
Other spending 15%
Police and prisons 5%
Highways 6%
Higher education 14%
Aid to local government 34%
Welfare 20%

### Composition of State Revenue

Other revenue 8%
User charges 17%
Corporate income tax 3%
Individual income tax 19%
Federal aid 28%
Sales and excise taxes 25%

The biggest portion of state spending goes toward grants to local governments. The largest source of state revenue is aid from the federal government.

Source: Based on general expenditure figures for fiscal year 2000 from the U.S. Census Bureau.

# Local Budgets

Of all government levels, you may be most familiar with the local one. You may be attending a public school. You may get to school in a government-funded bus on roads maintained by local government and patrolled by local police. Local schools decide school hours, what you may wear to school, and when you eat lunch. You may stroll on city sidewalks to visit city parks or the local library. Your family pays property taxes either directly as property owners or as part of the rent. Your family also may pay user fees for water, garbage collection, and other local services.

## Local Spending

Before the Great Depression, local government accounted for half of all government spending. However, the growing importance of the federal government has decreased the local share to one-sixth of the total. The left pie chart in Figure 14.6 shows the composition of local spending. No other spending category comes close to education, which accounts for 47 percent of the total. Police and fire protection combine for 11 percent of local spending.

Environment and housing issues also combine for 11 percent.

## Local Revenue

As the right-hand pie chart in Figure 14.6 shows, state and federal aid make up 40 percent of local revenue, by far the largest source. Most of this aid goes toward local schools. Local governments raise from their own sources only $6 out of every $10 they spend. The property tax accounts for 27 percent of

**Investigate Your Local Economy**

Research to find out the size of your local government's budget and how much of this budget is spent on local schools. What are the other items in the budget, and how much is spent on each item? Present your findings in a pie chart.

## Local Budgets

Point out that most local government spending is devoted to paying for public education. Other types of local spending include police and fire protection, highways, environment, and housing. None of these other areas amount to more than 11 percent of total local government spending. The greatest source of local revenue is aid from the federal and state governments. This is closely followed by property taxes and then by user fees. Other sources of local revenue are much less significant. Ask students to discuss ways in which local government spending affects their lives.

 **Investigate Your Local Economy** Pie charts created by students should look similar to the chart on the left side of Figure 14.6. Encourage interested students to extend this activity by creating a pie chart for local revenue.

### *Think Critically Through Visuals*

Direct students to focus their attention on **Figure 14.6—Composition of Local Spending and Local Revenue** on page 442. Point out that this is a composite of all localities. A pie chart for any particular local government might look significantly different.

---

## *Group Activity*

Organize students into small groups and provide the scenario shown below, without the information in parentheses. Ask each group to report its decision, including a rationale, to the class. Ask each group to identify the principle of taxation involved in the chosen alternative.

Each group represents the town council for a community of 10,000 residents. The town budget is in the red, and the council has decided to impose a new tax to balance the budget. The council wants to impose this tax in the most equitable way. There are only four viable options available:

- Place a 2-cent per gallon tax on gasoline sold in the community and use the money to maintain the roads (benefits-received principle).
- Increase property taxes on businesses by 5 percent (ability-to-pay principle).
- Charge a $10-per-car fee for plowing snow off town roads (benefits-received principle).
- Impose a 2 percent tax on the sale of luxury items in the community (ability-to-pay principle).

## Local Budgets

Obtain copies of budgets for your community. There are likely to be separate budgets for the school district and local government. Ask students to combine these budgets and use them to create pie graphs similar to the ones in Figure 14.6. Discuss how the graphs in Figure 14.6 compare with the revenue and spending proportions that exist in your community. Can students think of explanations for any differences in how revenues are received or spending is allocated?

### Think Critically Through Visuals

Direct students to focus their attention on the photograph on this page. Ask for a volunteer to answer the question posed in the caption.

### Answer

Answers will vary. Possible answer: Some spending categories in a local school's budget are building maintenance, utilities, textbooks, bus transportation, teacher salaries, and funding for extracurricular activities.

### ✓ CHECKPOINT

Invite a student to answer the checkpoint that appears on this page.

### Answer

The top of spending category for local governments is education, while the top source of revenue is federal and state aid.

---

**Composition of Local Spending and Local Revenue** | **Figure 14.6**

**Composition of Local Spending**

- Administration and interest 8%
- Other spending 8%
- Environment and housing 11%
- Education 47%
- Highways 7%
- Health and hospitals 8%
- Police and fire 11%

**Composition of Local Revenue**

- Other revenue 12%
- User charges 15%
- State and federal aid 40%
- Sales and excise taxes 6%
- Property taxes 27%

The largest category of local spending is education. State and federal aid make up the largest percent of local revenue.

Source: Based on general expenditure figures for fiscal year 2000 from the U.S. Census Bureau.

the total. User fees rank third at 15 percent. Examples include fees for water usage and school lunches.

### ✓ CHECKPOINT

What is the top spending category in the local budget and the top source of revenue?

## Relative Size and Growth of Government

So far, the focus has been on each level of government, but a fuller picture includes all three levels. How has the size of government in America changed

Nearly half of local spending goes to schools. What spending categories might be included in a local school district's budget?

© Getty Images/PhotoDisc

**442** **CHAPTER 14** Government Spending, Revenue, and Public Choice

---

### Curriculum Connection—Business

Many communities impose two different property tax rates. One is for residential property and the other is for business property. In some communities, the business property tax rate is more than twice as high as the residential rate. Small business owners often complain that they are being required to pay an unfair portion of the local government's costs. Others argue that the firms earn their profit from doing business in the community and therefore should pay a larger share of the cost of government. Ask students to choose a side on this issue and prepare a presentation to support their point of view.

in the last decade, and how does that size compare with what's been going on in other major economies around the world?

## An International Comparison

Figure 14.7 shows government outlays at all levels relative to GDP in 10 industrial economies for 1993 and 2003. Government outlays in the United States in 2003 were 32 percent relative to GDP, the smallest share in the group. This is down slightly from 34 percent in 1993, a year when only Japan among the 10 industrial economies had a smaller government share.

Between 1993 and 2003, government outlays relative to GDP decreased in 9 of the 10 industrial economies. The average dropped from 44 percent to 40 percent. Why the drop? The breakup of the Soviet Union in the early 1990s reduced defense outlays in major economies. The

poor performance of most socialist economies around the world shifted attitudes more toward private markets, thus lessening the role of government. Growing prosperity of market economies during most of the period made it less important for governments to spend funds to stimulate their economies or provide social services to their people.

The world economy began to sour beginning in 2001. The terrorist attacks on America temporarily stalled the trend toward a shrinking government. Government stepped up spending to fight terrorism and help revive the economy.

### CHECKPOINT

How did the relative size of government change between 1993 and 2003 compared with other major economies?

---

**Government Outlays as Percentage of GDP**

Figure **14.7**

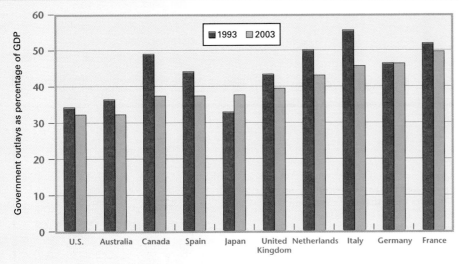

Government outlays as percentage of GDP declined between 1993 and 2003 in major industrial economies except Japan.

Source: Based on outlays at all government levels as reported in *OECD Economic Outlook,* June 2003. Figures for 2003 are projections.

---

## TEACH

### Relative Size and Growth of Government

Many governments around the world have reduced their spending for social programs. At the same time, they have experienced significant growth in their GDPs. These conditions led to a reduced proportion of their GDP being allocated to government spending. Japan is an exception. Historically, Japan experienced low unemployment and spent little on social benefit programs. During the 1990s, however, the Japanese government began to spend a greater proportion of that nation's GDP on social benefit programs in response to higher unemployment rates and the needs of an aging population. Do students believe the trend toward smaller proportions of GDP being spent by governments is likely to continue? What will happen as the baby-boom generation reaches retirement age and begins to collect Social Security benefits? Point out that the baby boom took place throughout the world. It was not exclusively a U.S. event.

### *Think Critically Through Visuals*

Direct students to focus their attention on **Figure 14.7—Government Outlays as Percentage of GDP**. Point out that government outlays in the United States in 2003 were the smallest share in the group.

### SPAN THE GLOBE

Direct students to read the short passage "Why Japan Is Different" on page 444. Use Think Critically as a starting point for class discussion or have students prepare written answers.

### Answers to **Think Critically**

Answers will vary. Possible answer: This statement suggests that Japan's citizens must be willing to spend and invest for the situation to improve. Citizens may need to take some risks in order to bolster confidence in the economy. At this point, there is little else the Japanese government can do to improve the situation.

### *Think Critically Through Visuals*

Use the photograph and caption on page 444 to augment the **Span the Globe** feature on the same page.

---

## RETEACH

Remind students that many large corporations operate in many countries as multinationals. Different countries have different tax burdens. Some of the highest tax rates can be found in the nations of northern Europe. Some of the lowest are found in South America, Africa, and Asia. Ask students to speculate on the relationship between tax burdens and where multinational corporations choose to produce goods or services. If taxes in one country are lower than in other countries, what does this suggest about the share of GDP that passes through the hands of the government? How might this be related to the rate of growth and productivity in that nation? (Businesses in countries with lower tax rates may be able to allocate more resources to investments that would increase their production and productivity.)

## CHECKPOINT

Invite a student to answer the checkpoint that appears on page 443.

**Answer**

Government outlays in 9 out of the 10 industrial economies decreased from 1993 to 2003. The average dropped from 44 percent to 40 percent. Only Japan experienced an increase. Government outlays for the United States decreased from 34 percent in 1993 to 32 percent in 2003

## APPLY

Assign Lesson 14.2 from the Contemporary Economics Workbook.

## e-con @pps

Encourage students to apply their knowledge of concepts presented in this lesson as they explore economic news stories, policy debates, and data available at **econxtra.swlearning.com**.

## ASSESS

Assign all or part of Lesson 14.2 Assessment on page 445 as homework or an in-class activity.

## Xtra! Study Tools

Direct students to the online study tools for Lesson 14.2 at **econxtra.swlearning.com**.

## CLOSE

**Revisit** the In the News feature on the first page of the lesson. Ask students to review their preliminary answers and discuss the questions.

**Review** the objectives for Lesson 14.2. Students should be able to:

• Identify the top spending category in the federal budget and the top source of revenue.

• Identify the top spending category in state budgets and the top source of revenue.

• Identify the top spending category in local budgets and the top source of revenue.

• Compare the relative size of the U.S. government during the last decade with other major economies.

# SPAN THE GLOBE

## Why Japan Is Different

The exception to the trend toward a smaller GDP share for government outlays is Japan, where the economy has been suffering for more than a decade. The troubles began with a collapse in real estate values and stock prices in 1990. The crash of these two sources of wealth crushed consumer confidence. With consumers unwilling to spend as much, the government tried to stimulate aggregate demand by increasing its spending for government projects. Government outlays relative to GDP in Japan rose from 33 percent in 1993 to 38 percent in 2003. Despite the stepped-up role for government, the unemployment rate in Japan more than doubled from 2.5 percent in 1993 to 5.4 percent in 2003. Japan remains one of the most troubled economies in the world.

### Think Critically

According to a *Wall Street Journal* editorial, "Japan is stuck in an awkward stage of development between two worlds....The government can no longer solve Japan's problems, but effective market mechanisms have yet to take over." What does this statement suggest must happen in Japan in order for its economy to improve?

Japan's growth in the 1980s was driven by government-directed industrial policies. Some politicians in Japan think that these economic policies, mired in bureaucracy, need to be reformed and the country moved toward a more entrepreneurial system. One area where reform is needed is the Japan Highway Corporation, which spends trillions of yen on wasteful projects.

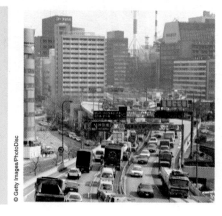

© Getty Images/PhotoDisc

## Key Concepts

1. Why were most Americans willing to accept a larger role for the government in the economy during the Great Depression and World War II?

2. Why does the share of federal tax revenue that comes from personal income taxes change from year to year even when the tax rates remain unchanged?

3. What has made it possible for state spending to grow more rapidly than state tax collection in many recent years?

4. Why have some state courts ruled that funding public schools from local property tax receipts results in unequal educational opportunities for school children?

5. Why do governments in countries that experience rapid economic growth often spend smaller portions of GDP?

## Graphing Exercise

6. Since its creation in 1967, the Medicare program that provides medical coverage for our nation's elderly population has accounted for a growing proportion of our GDP in most years. Use data in the table to construct a double line graph that shows the rates of growth of federal Medicare payments and GDP from 1995 through 1999. What does your graph show about the relative rates of growth in these amounts in these years? Given the large number of people born in the baby boom from 1946 through 1964, what will happen to the relationship between these amounts in future years?

**Growth in Federal Medicare Payments and GDP, 1995–1999**

| Year | Growth in Medicare Payments | Growth in GDP |
|------|------------------------------|----------------|
| 1995 | 9.5% | 4.9% |
| 1996 | 7.1% | 5.6% |
| 1997 | 5.1% | 6.7% |
| 1998 | 1.4% | 5.7% |
| 1999 | 3.7% | 5.8% |

## Think Critically

7. **Government** An important part of state government spending is governed by federal laws that require these governments to provide Medicaid programs for people who are unable to pay for their own medical care. Investigate Medicaid spending in your state. Have these payments grown more rapidly than other types of government spending? What reasons can you think of that could explain the growth in your state's Medicaid payments?

**Xtra!**
**Study Tools**
econxtra.swlearning.com

**Growth in Federal Medicare Payments and GDP, 1995 to 1999**
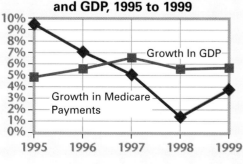

### Visualizing the Answer— Graphing Exercise

6. The answer includes a graph. Students' graphs should look similar to the one shown here. An Excel spreadsheet containing this graph, along with supporting data, is available on the Instructor's Resource CD.

---

### *Key Concepts*

1. Answers will vary. Possible answer: During these difficult economic times, many Americans felt powerless to look out for their own financial interests and so turned to the government to protect them from unemployment, poverty, and inflation.

2. Answers will vary. Possible answer: Individuals pay income taxes based on the amount of income they receive. When the economy is expanding, people earn more and pay more income tax. When the economy is in recession, people earn less and pay less income tax.

3. Answers will vary. Possible answer: State spending has been able to grow more rapidly because of increased aid from the federal government.

4. Answers will vary. Possible answer: School districts in economically disadvantaged areas have less property tax revenue and are therefore less able to provide quality education for students than more wealthy districts.

5. Answers will vary. Possible answer: With rapid economic growth, these governments will need a smaller portion of GDP to maintain their current services, while their people will have less need for government social programs because they can easily find employment.

### *Graphing Exercise*

6. Answers will vary. Possible answer: Over these years, the total growth in GDP was slightly greater than payments for Medicare. This situation is likely to change because a larger proportion of the U.S. population soon will be over 65 and qualified to receive Medicare benefits. This will cause Medicare spending to grow much more rapidly than GDP.

An example of an acceptable graph appears at the bottom of this page.

### *Think Critically*

7. Answers will vary. Possible answer: A growth in Medicaid spending could result from an increased number of poor people, an increase in the cost of medical care, or an increase in the proportion of poor people who require care.

Remind students that the personal income tax was introduced in 1913, but taxes have been an issue throughout American history.

Instruct students to read the **Connect to History** feature and answer the questions.

Use the questions at the bottom of the page to assess the students' understanding of this feature.

**Answers to Think Critically**

It would be difficult for the United States to revert to funding government by relying on high tariffs because the U.S. economy has become much more dependent on international goods in the last 100 years. In addition, foreign countries have become much more dependent on U.S. goods. An alternative form of taxation that the United States could employ is an excise tax on alcohol, cigarettes, gasoline, etc.

C O N N E C T
*to History*

# The Evolution of the Income Tax

One trigger for the American Revolution was a tax revolt. It was through trade that England lightly taxed its American colonies. When England attempted to impose an internal tax through the Stamp Act, the American colonists reacted against the government's attempt to impose taxes on them. They saw it as a violation of the British Bill of Rights, which historically had held that taxes could not be imposed without the approval of Parliament. Because the colonies had no direct representation in Parliament, they rejected the government's right to tax them directly.

Following the Revolution, the first American constitution, the Articles of Confederation, did not give the central government the power to levy taxes. Therefore, taxation was one of the problems addressed at the Constitutional Convention held in Philadelphia. Through the U.S. Constitution, the new government was given the power to "lay and collect Taxes, Duties, imports, and Excises."

During the nation's early days, the federal government relied primarily on tariffs (taxes on imports) and land sales to fund its operations. An early attempt to increase revenue by levying excise taxes on items such as carriages, sugar, salt, and distilled spirits met with armed resistance in Western Pennsylvania. The "Whisky Rebellion" was quickly put down. However, with the election of Thomas Jefferson in 1800, most of the excise taxes were repealed.

The government returned to relying on tariffs for revenue until the demands of the Civil War led to a need for new sources of revenue. The nation's first income tax was imposed during the conflict, as well as taxes on many commodities. Following the war, the high tariffs imposed during the war remained.

However, the income tax was first cut and then allowed to expire by 1872.

In the 1890s, the idea of an income tax resurfaced, and a new income tax was passed in 1894. The following year, the Supreme Court declared it unconstitutional. A decade later, following the Panic of 1907, a federal income tax once again emerged as an issue. President William Howard Taft, not wanting to directly challenge a Supreme Court decision, suggested a constitutional amendment permitting an income tax. He also suggested a tax on corporate profits. The corporate profits tax passed a Supreme Court challenge, and Congress and the states passed the Sixteenth Amendment, which was adopted in 1913. Later that year, President Woodrow Wilson signed the personal income tax into law.

The tax burden from the income tax fell on the wealthy. In its first year, only 357,598 tax forms were filed. In 1910, the tariff on imported goods supplied 90 percent of the government's revenues. Today that figure is about one percent. Where previously the debate over tariffs pitted regions of the country against each other, today the argument is between economic classes.

**THINK CRITICALLY**

A century ago the United States underwent a fundamental change in how it funds the government—from relying on tariffs to relying on personal and corporate income taxes. Could the country undergo such a change today? What alternate forms of taxation could it employ?

*Bibliography*

Allen, Larry. *Encyclopedia of Money.* Santa Barbara: Checkmark Books, 2001.

Engerman, Stanley L., and Robert E. Gallman. *The Cambridge Economic History of the United States: The Long Nineteenth Century.* Vol. II. Cambridge, England: Cambridge University Press, 2000.

Foner, Eric, and John A Garraty, eds. *The Reader's Companion to American History.* New York: Houghton Mifflin, 1991.

Gordon, John Steele. "American Taxation." *American Heritage* (May/June 1996).

Puth, Robert C. *American Economic History.* Fort Worth: Dryden Press, 1988.

Rosenbaum, Robert A., ed. *The Penguin Encyclopedia of American History.* New York: Penguin Reference, 2003.

Weisman, Steven R. *The Great Tax Wars: Lincoln to Wilson—The Fierce Battles over Money and Power that Transformed the Nation.* New York: Simon and Schuster, 2002.

## Objectives

> Discuss how representative democracy may favor special interests at the expense of the public interest.

> Distinguish between bureaus and firms, and explain why bureaus might be less responsive to customers than firms are.

## Overview

This book, for the most part, has assumed that governments make optimal adjustments to the shortcomings of the private sector. In other words, when confronted with market failure, governments adopt just the right program to address the problem. However, there are limits to government's effectiveness, just as there are limits to the market's effectiveness. For example, elected officials may side more with special interests than with the public interest. Government bureaus get less consumer feedback and face less competition than private firms do.

## Key Terms

**maximizing political support**

**rational ignorance**

**bureaus**

Remind students that many people are motivated by forces other than money. In this lesson, they will learn about motivations that affect the political process and that help determine government taxing, borrowing, and spending decisions. They will discover that decisions made by the government often are designed more to achieve political objectives than economic ones. It is possible that politically motivated decisions may not be appropriate for the economy.

### Objectives

Remind students to read the lesson objectives to help focus their attention before reading the lesson.

### Key Terms

Direct students use each of the key terms in a separate sentence or short paragraph that helps demonstrate the meaning of the term.

## [ In the News ]

### • Special Interests vs. the Interests of Seniors

Congress has set aside $400 billion dollars to be spent between now and 2010 on prescription drug benefits for seniors. However, tens of billions of dollars of that money are being redirected, thanks to the lobbying efforts of healthcare providers such as HMOs, ambulance companies, hospitals in rural areas, kidney dialysis providers, psychologists, and others. Each of these special interests has lobbied successfully for a spending provision for their cause to be added to the main bill. Taken together, these provisions reduce the benefits seniors were intended to receive. One of the authors of the Senate bill said that these "add-ons" for healthcare providers are being paid for with cuts in other parts of the Medicare program. Seniors' organizations point out that these resulting cuts bring on costs for their members to cover the "add-on" expenditures. These costs include a provision that seniors pay 20 percent of the cost for important diagnostic tests performed at hospital or doctors' office laboratories. Currently there is no charge to beneficiaries for these tests, and many lower-income patients could not afford to pay even such a small percentage.

### Think About It

What types of activities do you think the lobbying groups engage in to see that their special interests are addressed? In this specific case, who wins and who loses?

◀ | ▶

**447**

## [ In the News ]

Instruct students to read the passage and write down their answers. Point out that their answers might change after they finish studying Lesson 14.3.

**Answers to Think About It**

Answers will vary. Possible answers: Lobbying groups engage in talking to the general public and their local government representatives about why their cause needs to be taken into consideration and the benefits to be attained if they were given assistance. If the lobbying group wins, those who lose must fund the assistance. In this case, it was the seniors.

### *Visual Presentation*

Use the PowerPoint presentation on the Instructor's Resource CD as an adjunct to your lecture. The presentation also can be used for review.

### *National Content Standards in Economics*

A complete list of the NCEE Standards appears on pages xxiv–xxv of this book. The following standards are addressed in Lesson 14.3.

Standard 2: Marginal Cost/Benefit

Standard 16: Role of Government

Standard 17: Using Cost/Benefit Analysis to Evaluate Government Programs

## Representative Democracy

Remind students that few politicians would run for office on a platform that advocated higher taxes and reduced government spending, even if this was clearly the best alternative for the long-run health of the economy. Political campaign speeches often include phrases intended to make people believe that the politician will accomplish the economically impossible: spending more while taxing less and balancing the budget all at the same time. They talk of cutting the fat, enhancing efficiency, making government more responsive, and having smarter government. These phrases often have little meaning and may be used to mislead the voting public.

### Ethics in Action

Have students work in pairs to discuss the ethical issue featured on page 449, and develop an answer to the questions presented.

### Answers to Think Critically

Answers will vary. Possible answers: I do not support this particular prohibition because I do feel minors should be allowed to contribute financially to election campaigns. I do feel, however, that some form of campaign finance reform is needed.

---

*maximizing political support*

Objective assumed to guide the behavior of elected officials; comparable to profit maximization by firms and utility maximization by households

---

# Representative Democracy

In market choice, each person votes for what should be produced with dollars. The rule is: one dollar, one vote. People with more to spend get more votes. In public choice, each person has a single vote to decide what should be produced. The rule is: one person, one vote, regardless of income. People vote directly on public choices at New England town meetings and on the occasional referendum, but direct democracy is unusual. When you consider the thousands of public choices required to run a government, it would be impractical for voters to make all those choices. Instead, voters elect representatives, who—at least in theory—make public choices that reflect constituent views. Delegating choices to representatives involves complications, however.

## Maximizing Political Support

Economists assume that households try to maximize their utility and firms try to maximize profit, but what about governments—or, more specifically, what about elected representatives? What do they try to maximize? One problem is that the U.S. system of federal, state, and local governments consists of not one government but more than 87,000 separate governments in all. These range from a local school district to the federal government.

What's more, even a particular government does not act as a single, consistent decision maker. For example, the federal government relies on a system of checks and balances to limit the executive, legislative, and judicial branches.

Even within the federal executive branch, there are so many agencies and bureaus that at times they seem to work at cross-purposes. For example, for decades the U.S. Surgeon General has required health warnings on cigarette packages. During that same time,

however, the U.S. Department of Agriculture has been subsidizing tobacco farmers.

Economists assume that elected representatives try to maximize their political support, including votes and campaign contributions. In this theory, **maximizing political support** guides the decisions of elected officials who, in turn, direct government employees.

## Role of Special Interest

Elected representatives often appear to cater to special interests rather than the public interest. Consider only one of the thousands of decisions made by elected representatives: funding an obscure federal program that subsidizes U.S. wool production. Under the wool-subsidy program, the federal government guarantees sheep farmers a certain price for each pound of wool they produce. This subsidy costs taxpayers more than $75 million per year. During deliberations to renew the program, the only person to testify before Congress was a representative of the National Wool Growers Association, who claimed that the subsidy was vital to the nation's economic welfare. Why didn't a single taxpayer challenge the subsidy?

As a consumer, you do not specialize in woolen goods. You buy thousands of different goods and services, from software to underwear. You have no special interest in wool legislation. Wool producers do have a special interest, because that's how they earn a living. As a result of this mismatch of interest, legislation often favors producers rather than consumers. Well-organized producer groups, as squeaky wheels in the legislative machinery, get the most grease in the form of favorable legislation.

Special interest groups expend abundant resources to secure these advantages. For example, political action committees, known more popularly as PACs, contribute millions to congressional campaigns. More than 4,000 PACs try to shape federal legislation. Top contributors recently included tobacco companies and the American Trial Lawyers

---

**448**  **CHAPTER 14**  Government Spending, Revenue, and Public Choice

---

*Outside Resources*

**U.S. Government Printing Office** GPOAccess is the official web site of the U.S. Government Printing Office. The GPO uses this web site to disseminate official information from all three branches of the federal government.
This web site is an excellent resource for research. Ask students to click on the A–Z Resource List and choose one of the links. After students explore the contents of the link, have them prepare a short presentation of their findings.

Association. Tobacco interests want to influence cigarette legislation, and lawyers fear reforms that would limit liability suits.

## Rational Ignorance

How do elected officials get away with serving special interests? Why don't voters elect someone else? Sometimes voters do. However, some people don't bother to vote and even those who do vote consume so many different goods and services that they have neither the time nor the incentive to keep up with public choices that affect any particular product. For example, the $75 million subsidy for wool growers amounts to only about 30 cents per U.S. citizen. Would you make the effort to protest passage of this law to save 30 cents?

Therefore, unless voters have a special interest in the legislation, they adopt a stance of **rational ignorance**. This means the costs and benefits of the thousands of proposals considered by elected officials remain largely unknown

to voters. The cost to the typical voter of acquiring and acting on such information usually is greater than any possible benefit.

In contrast, consumers have much more incentive to gather and act on information about market choices. For example, a consumer in the market for a new car has an incentive to examine the performance records of different models, test-drive a few, and check prices at dealerships and on the Internet. That person has complete control over the choice of a new car. *Because information and the time required to acquire and digest it are scarce, consumers focus more on private choices than on public choices. The payoff in making wise private choices usually is more direct, more immediate, and more substantial.*

**rational ignorance**

A stance adopted by voters when they find that the cost of understanding and voting on a particular issue exceeds the benefit expected from doing so

**CHECKPOINT**
Why does representative democracy favor special interests?

# Ethics in Action

### Minors Banned from Making Political Contributions
A lawsuit argued before the U.S. Supreme Court affects both political campaign reform and the rights of minors. The Bipartisan Campaign Reform Act, known popularly as the McCain-Feingold bill, includes a provision that bans political campaign contributions by minors. Evidently, such donations made in the name of the actual donor's children were a means used to avoid donation limits imposed on individuals. These limits previously were set at $2,000 but have now been boosted to $4,000. The result was a prohibition (or ban) on such donations in the new campaign finance law that closed the loophole. However, it also eliminated the

potential for legitimate contributions by minors. A lawsuit was brought against the bill by a group of minors along with other plaintiffs—including the National Rifle Association *and* the American Civil Liberties Union— versus the Federal Election Commission. The Court heard the case in September of 2003 on appeal from a 1,600-page decision of a three-judge federal appeals court that threw out numerous sections of the law as unconstitutional.

### Think Critically

What ethical balance is being struck by the law? Do you support the prohibition? Why or why not?

Lesson 14.3 • *Economics of Public Choice*    **449**

**TEACH** (continued)

### Representative Democracy

Identify one or more current political issues in your community that involve a potential increase in government spending. Ask students to work in groups of three to write a campaign speech for a politician who is taking a stand on the issue. Have each group select a member to deliver their speech to the class. Ask the class to evaluate each speech. Is it honest? Did it provide useful information? Does it reflect what would be best for the community?

**NET**Bookmark

Direct students to **econxtra.swlearning.com**. Remind them to click on the link for Lesson 14.3 to find the appropriate link for the **NET Bookmark** on page 450. Consider having students print the home page for the site they select and attach it to their work.

**CHECKPOINT**
Invite a student to answer the checkpoint that appears on this page.

### Answer

A representative democracy might favor special interests because they contribute millions to campaigns to secure favorable legislation.

The tax law of 1981 allowed owners of racehorses to depreciate the value of horses they owned as if they were pieces of industrial machinery. This law saved owners thousands of dollars in federal income tax. Some people believed this law made sense, but others thought it was little more than a political payoff for campaign contributions to elected officials. Most U.S. citizens knew absolutely nothing about this part of the tax law. Ask students to explain why most people neither knew nor cared about the tax write-off for racehorses. (It was a clear example of rational ignorance. The cost of learning about this part of the law far exceeded any benefit that might be received from gaining such knowledge.)

## Bureaus Versus Firms

Remind students that most people desire stability and safety in their lives. People who are employed in private industry achieve security by helping the firm to earn a profit. Workers who are employed by government bureaus may be better able to ensure their job stability by working to achieve political objectives rather than by serving people. It is difficult to determine the efficiency of a government bureau that is not designed to earn a profit.

### Think Critically Through Visuals

Direct students to focus their attention on the photograph on page 451. Ask for a volunteer to answer the question posed in the caption.

### Answer

Answers will vary. Possible answer: Using cost/benefit analysis to evaluate hazardous waste clean-up programs would start with analyzing the costs to society of the specific hazardous waste problem. These costs might involve health care for those who are sick due to the problem or the costs of cleaning up a specific location tainted with waste. These costs would then be compared to the cost involved in the clean-up program. If the program costs are less than the costs to the public for the problem, the program can be considered effective.

Main Idea

### NCEE Standard 17: Using Cost/Benefit Analysis to Evaluate Government Programs

Costs of government policies sometimes exceed benefits. This may occur because of incentives facing voters, government officials, and government employees; because of actions by special interest groups that can impose costs on the general public; or because social goals other than economic efficiency are being pursued.

---

## NETBookmark

Access the Campaign Finance Reform Special issue of the American Prospect Online web site through econxtra.swlearning.com. You will find a comprehensive list of web sites on campaign reform. Choose one of these links and write a paragraph describing the web site's message.

*econxtra.swlearning.com*

## Bureaus Versus Firms

Elected representatives approve legislation, but the task of implementing that legislation typically is delegated to **bureaus**. These are government departments and agencies whose activities are financed through legislative bodies. Examples include the FBI, FDA, FCC, EPA, the Pentagon, your state's department of motor vehicles, and your public school system.

**bureaus**
Government agencies charged with implementing legislation and financed through legislative bodies

### Voluntary Exchange Versus Coercion

Market exchange relies on the voluntary behavior of buyers and sellers making private choices. Don't like tofu? No problem—don't buy any. Nobody can force you to buy something you don't want. In political markets the situation is different. Any voting rule except for unanimous consent will involve some government influence. Even if you object to certain government programs, you must still pay the taxes that ultimately fund those programs. Public choices are enforced by the police power of the state. If you fail to pay your taxes, you could go to jail.

### Product Prices

For-profit firms sell products for prices that at least cover the cost of production. Bureaus usually offer products for either a zero price or some price below cost. For example, if you plan to attend a public college or university in your

---

state, your tuition will probably cover only about half the cost of providing your education.

Because the revenue side of the government budget usually is separate from the expenditure side, there is no necessary link between the cost of a public program and the benefit. Contrast this with the private sector, in which the marginal benefit of a good is at least as great as its marginal cost. Otherwise, people wouldn't buy it.

### Customer Feedback

Markets offer firms a steady stream of consumer feedback. If prices are too high or too low, surpluses or shortages become obvious. Not only is consumer feedback abundant in markets, but firms have a profit incentive to act on that feedback. The firm's owners stand to gain from any improvement in customer satisfaction or any reduction in the cost of production.

Because public goods and services are not sold in markets, government bureaus receive less consumer feedback. There usually are no prices for public goods and no obvious shortages or surpluses. For example, how would you know whether there was a shortage or a surplus of police protection in your community?

### Voter Incentives

Voters can move from a jurisdiction if they think the government there is inefficient. This mechanism, whereby people "vote with their feet," promotes some efficiency at the state and local levels. Voters who are not satisfied with the federal government, however, cannot easily vote with their feet.

In the private sector, competition makes firms more responsive to customers. If a firm does not know consumer preferences, it will either have to shape up or go out of business. Bureaus that do not know about public preferences do not necessarily go out of business. A bureau that is inefficient may continue to be funded and waste resources indefinitely. Thus, bureaus face less pressure to satisfy consumer demand or to minimize costs. A variety

---

---

### Economic Headlines

Instruct students to locate the transcript of a broadcast segment from a news magazine program such as "20/20," "48 Hours," "60 Minutes," "Dateline," or "Primetime" that relates to one of the topics in this lesson. For example, they might find a segment related to government inefficiency. Instruct students to read the transcript and write a brief summary along with a reference citation. Identify the style you want them to use for the citation.

of studies compares costs for products that are provided by both public bureaus and private firms, such as garbage collection. Of those studies that show a difference, most find private firms are more efficient. A competitive private firm that is inefficient will earn no profit and go out of business.

### Private Versus Public Production

Just because some goods and services are *financed* by the government does not mean they must be *produced* by the government. Elected officials may contract directly with private firms to produce public output. This could introduce more competition and more efficiency. For example, a city council may contract with a firm to handle garbage collection for the city. Profit-making firms now provide everything from fire protection to prisons to schools in certain jurisdictions.

Elected officials also may use some combination of bureaus and firms to produce the desired output. For example, the Pentagon, a giant bureau, hires and trains military personnel. Yet the Pentagon contracts with private firms to develop and produce weapons systems. State governments typically hire private contractors to build roads but employ state workers to maintain them.

The mix of firms and bureaus varies over time and across jurisdictions. However, the trend is toward greater production by the private sector. These goods and services are still financed by government, usually with taxes.

When governments produce public goods and services, they are using *the internal organization of the government*—the bureaucracy—to supply the product. When governments contract with private firms to produce public goods and services, they are using *the market* to supply the product. Legislators may prefer dealing with bureaus rather than with firms for two reasons. First, in situations where it is difficult to specify in a contract just what is being produced, as with education or social work, bureaus may be more responsive to the legislature's concerns. Second, bureaus provide legislators with more opportunities to reward political supporters with government jobs.

**CHECKPOINT**
Why might bureaus be less responsive to customers than firms are?

 **Main Idea**

**Cost/Benefit Analysis for Government Programs**

*Government policies are carried out through bureaus. The costs of carrying out policies sometimes exceed the benefits derived from them. This may occur due to the following factors: incentives facing voters, government officials, and government employees; actions by special interest groups; or other social goals. The EPA is a government bureau that, among other activities, oversees programs that control the cleanup of hazardous wastes. How could the costs versus the benefits of the hazardous waste cleanup programs be evaluated?*

© Getty Images/PhotoDisc

Lesson 14.3 • *Economics of Public Choice*     **451**

**Answer**
Bureaus offer a public good. Because public goods are not sold in markets, government bureaus receive less consumer feedback than do firms. Bureaus therefore are less responsive to consumers than are firms.

**APPLY**

Assign Lesson 14.3 from the Contemporary Economics Workbook.

 *e*-con @pps

Encourage students to apply their knowledge of concepts presented in this lesson as they explore economic news stories, policy debates, and data available at **econxtra.swlearning.com**.

**ASSESS**

Assign all or part of Lesson 14.3 Assessment on page 452 as homework or an in-class activity

**Xtra!** Study Tools

Direct students to the online study tools for Lesson 14.3 at **econxtra.swlearning.com**.

**CLOSE**

**Revisit** the In the News feature on the first page of the lesson.

**Review** the objectives for Lesson 14.3. Students should be able to:

● Discuss how representative democracy may favor special interests at the expense of the public interest.

● Distinguish between bureaus and firms, and explain why bureaus might be less responsive to customers than firms are.

## RETEACH

In recent years, many schools and school districts have contracted with private companies to provide food services or janitorial services. Ask students to investigate this situation for several school districts or individual schools. Ask students to compare a district that has a contract with a private company with one that does not. Suggest that students use the Internet to find the information needed. Ask students to explain why many school districts have chosen to outsource food services or cleaning services to private industry.

## Key Concepts

1. Answers will vary. Possible answer: A vote could be taken in which each student would have an equal say, or a representative body of students could be given the power to make the decision, similar to what takes place in our different levels of government.

2. Answers will vary. Possible answer: Most students don't participate in sports and won't care whether other teams receive new equipment. Their lack of concern about the situation is rational, given their lack of interest in sports.

3. Answers will vary. Possible answer: Government decisions often are made by politicians whose primary concern is being reelected. They are likely to spend money to satisfy voters who care enough about government programs to complain about the way funds are spent.

4. Answers will vary. Possible answer: Government bureaucracies often have monopolies on the services they provide and therefore may not need to be responsive to constituents, particularly when these people are not organized to exert political pressure.

5. Answers will vary. Possible answer: Public schools are funded by taxes that are imposed on the population in general. Therefore, many parents regard the schools as free, or paid for by others. This may cause them to demand services that they would be unwilling or unable to pay for themselves.

## Graphing Exercise

6. Answers will vary. Possible answer: Spending differences could be accounted for in terms of differences in the cost of living, employment alternatives available to teachers, or political power of teacher organizations. High funding does not guarantee high quality education, although low funding may prevent it.

   An example of an acceptable graph appears at the bottom of this page.

## Think Critically

7. Answers will vary. Possible answer: Politicians are likely to be responsive to their own constituents. A group of constituents is more likely to be successful in having its wishes acted on because it could mean the difference between the politician's being reelected or turned out of office in the future.

---

**Xtra!**
**Study Tools**
econxtra.swlearning.com

## Key Concepts

1. Imagine that your class has decided to earn money to take a class trip in their senior year. The big question is deciding where the class should go. Some students want to visit Washington, D.C., some would prefer New York City, others would choose Disney World or other well-known destinations. Describe how this decision might be made and why this decision-making process is similar to the way in which choices are made by government.

2. Suppose a school's sports director decided to spend $15,000 to purchase new equipment for the football team. Although this decision left only $5,000 to pay for equipment for all of the school's other teams, most of the students at the school didn't complain. Explain how this situation demonstrates the idea of *rational ignorance.*

3. Why does the saying "the squeaky wheel gets the grease" often describe how government decisions are made?

4. What would happen to a private firm that employed clerks who were rude or unresponsive to customer requests? Why may bureaucracies employ such workers and still continue to exist over many years?

5. Why might parents demand fewer services from public schools if they were required to pay for these services directly from their own funds?

## Graphing Exercise

6. Use data in the table to construct a bar graph that shows the per-student spending in selected states for public schools. What might explain the difference in the levels of funding among states? Do you think that there is a direct relationship between the amount spent and the quality of education provided? Explain your answer.

**Per-Student Public School Spending in Selected States, 2000**

| State | Per-Student Spending | State | Per-Student Spending |
|---|---|---|---|
| Connecticut | $10,711 | Texas | $ 6,588 |
| Rhode Island | $ 8,773 | Nevada | $ 6,283 |
| Indiana | $ 7,254 | Mississippi | $ 4,905 |
| Ohio | $ 7,152 | North Dakota | $ 4,621 |

Source: *Statistical Abstract of the United States, 2001,* p. 154.

## Think Critically

7. **Government** Identify and describe a current public policy issue that is important to you. Explain how you could work to influence legislation that would affect government policy toward this issue. Why might you be more successful acting as a member of a group rather than as an individual voter?

---

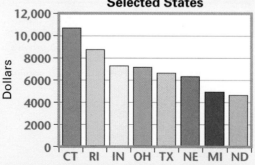

**Per Student Spending in 2000 Selected States**

(Bar graph: Dollars on vertical axis from 0 to 12,000; states CT, RI, IN, OH, TX, NE, MI, ND on horizontal axis)

## Visualizing the Answer— Graphing Exercise

6. The answer includes a graph. Students' graphs should look similar to the one shown here. An Excel spreadsheet containing this graph, along with supporting data, is available on the Instructor's Resource CD.

# movers & shakers

## Kathleen Sebelius *Governor of Kansas*

You might say that politics is in Kathleen Sebelius's blood. When she was young, her father John J. Gilligan served as a councilman in Cincinnati, Ohio; a U.S. Representative; and Governor of Ohio. Kathleen decided to pursue a political science degree from Trinity College in Washington, D.C. Later she earned a master's degree in public administration from the University of Kansas. Along the way she met and married Gary Sebelius, the son of a former congressman from Kansas.

Sebelius won a seat in the Kansas House of Representatives, where she served from 1987 to 1994. She then was elected Insurance Commissioner for Kansas and earned a reputation as a tough, innovative, and tight-fisted leader. She was named one of America's Top Ten Public Officials in 2001 by *Governing Magazine.* In 2003, Kathleen Sebelius began her first term as Governor of Kansas.

In her campaign for the governorship, Sebelius promoted her ability to rid the government of wasteful spending, indicating that "I know firsthand you find waste in state government." She added, "As Insurance Commissioner, I reduced the department's budget by 19 percent while vastly improving department services." During her tenure she fired two state attorneys, who she believed "were double-billing the state and charging exorbitant fees." She lowered the fees paid to other state attorneys and, in all, saved the state more than $4 million.

Throughout her campaign, she called for a strict accounting of where Kansas was spending its money, something not done for more than 20 years. She promised voters she would begin "an in-depth look at government operations and initiate an extensive review of state government, looking for waste and inefficiency."

As Sebelius took over as Governor, the Kansas sales tax was designed to tax only tangible goods such as groceries, cars, and clothing. Service providers, such as accountants, beauticians and veterinarians, were not taxed. Asked if she thought such a tax structure was fair, she replied, "I will fight to make sure that no single sector of our economy or group of our citizens bears a disproportionate share of our tax burden."

Throughout her campaign for governor, Sebelius declared her commitment to education. "Education is the key to our children's future and Kansas' economic prosperity," she told voters. She promised she would "fight to see that Kansas schools will have the funds they need." This promise helped her win the hearts of many Kansans who were unhappy with statements made by her opponent, state Treasurer Tim Shallenburger. He maintained that the schools in Kansas "can make it with 1 or 2 or 3 percent" less funding." Although a Democrat in a state where only 28 percent of voters are registered Democrats, Sebelius easily beat Shallenburger, a Republican.

### SOURCE READING
Kathleen Sebelius promised "to fight to make sure that no single sector of our economy or group of our citizens bears a disproportionate share of our tax burden." Does this statement support the benefits-received principle of taxation or the ability-to-pay principle? Explain your answer.

### ENTREPRENEURS IN ACTION
In small groups, discuss the pros and cons of running for political office and serving the public as an elected official. How might the need to maximize political support conflict with the elected official's ability to follow through with his or her political goals?

---

# movers & shakers

## FOCUS

Ask students what motivates people to run for political office. In most cases, it isn't money. Most politicians could earn more in private industry than they do from political office. Further, the cost of running a campaign can result in personal expenses that far exceed the income that could ever be earned in political office. Point out that Malcolm Forbes spent more than $60 million of his own money in his failed presidential campaigns of 1996 and 2000. Are politicians motivated by a desire to serve the public, to have power over people's lives, to be remembered in history, or is there something else that motivates them? More specifically, what do students believe motivates Kathleen Sebelius?

## TEACH

Instruct students to read the **Movers & Shakers** feature about Kathleen Sebelius. Point out that some students may find it helpful to read the article, read the questions at the bottom of the page, and then reread the article.

## ASSESS

Use the questions in Source Reading and Entrepreneurs in Action at the bottom of the profile to assess the students' understanding of this **Movers & Shakers** feature.

### Answers to Source Reading

Answer: This form of taxation follows the benefits-received taxation principle. Under this principle, everyone pays for the services that they receive; no one is charged a disproportionate amount— they pay only for what they use.

### Answers to Entrepreneurs in Action

One pro of running for political office is that the winner can implement changes in government. The cons are that it is a very stressful job and one that is scrutinized from the outside. In order to gain political support, one might have to appeal to certain populations of voters (seniors, minorities, etc.) and change his or her stance on certain issues (Social Security and affirmative action, etc.) in order to gain their support.

## Summary
### Consider

Ask students to revisit the questions they were asked to consider at the beginning of the chapter. Remind students that they should be able to answer all of the questions after studying Chapter 14.

- How does the demand for public goods differ from the demand for private goods? See page 430—Public Goods.
- How are responsibilities divided among levels of government? See page 437—Federal, State, and Local Budgets.
- How big is the federal budget, and where does the money go? See page 438—Federal Budgets.
- Why do politicians need to deal with special interest groups? See page 448—Role of Special Interest.
- Why do most people remain largely ignorant about what's happening in the public sector? See page 450—Customer Feedback.

### Exam*View*

Use **Exam***View* to assess students' learning.

- Create a chapter test using questions from the existing test bank.
- Add your own questions to the existing test bank.
- Generate multiple forms of a chapter test.

### Study Skills

Offer the following study skills suggestions for students as they review this chapter.

- Outline the chapter.
- Review Key Terms.
- Review Checkpoints.
- Work in pairs to quiz each other.
- Use Xtra! Study Tools for each lesson.

Direct students to the online quiz preparation for Chapter 14 at **econxtra.swlearning.com**.

## Summary

 **14.1** *Public Goods and Taxation*

a Public goods are different from private goods in that they are nonrival in consumption. The market demand for public goods is equal to  the sum of the marginal benefit for all members of a community. The efficient level of a public good is found where the sum of the marginal benefits is equal to its marginal cost.

*Xtra! Quiz Prep*
*econxtra.swlearning.com*

b There are two generally recognized principles of taxation: the *benefits-received principle* and *the ability-to-pay principle.* According to the benefits-received principle, taxpayers should pay in proportion to the benefit they receive from the service the tax supports. According to the ability-to-pay principle, people should be taxed at higher rates as their ability to pay in terms of income or wealth grows.

c *Tax incidence* indicates who actually bears the burden of a tax. Under a *proportional tax,* all people would pay the same percent of their incomes in tax. When there are *progressive taxes,* people pay a greater share of their incomes in tax as their incomes grow. This is true of personal income taxes. When there are *regressive taxes,* people pay a smaller share of their income in tax as their incomes grow. This is true of most excise taxes such as the tax on tobacco products or gasoline.

d The *marginal tax rate* is the percentage of each additional dollar of a taxpayer's income that is paid in taxes. High marginal tax rates reduce a person's after-tax income and can discourage people from working to earn additional income. The government gathers additional revenue by imposing sin taxes to discourage certain types of behavior, user fees, and by borrowing funds.

 **14.2** *Federal, State, and Local Budgets*

a Through the first 150 years of U.S. history, federal spending amounted to about 3 percent of GDP except during times of war. In the past 70 years, however, this share has grown to roughly 20 percent of GDP, or more than $2.3 trillion in 2004. The largest share of federal spending goes to income redistribution (49 percent). The largest source of federal revenue is the personal income tax (44 percent).

b The largest share of state spending is devoted to aid to local government (34 percent). The largest source of state revenue is aid received from the federal government (28 percent).

c Local governments spend the largest share of their incomes for education (47 percent). The greatest source of local government revenue is received as aid payments form the state and federal governments (40 percent).

d On average, at 32 percent, the United States takes a smaller share of GDP than governments in any other major industrial nation. The average share of GDP taken by governments in most industrial nations fell between 1993 and 2003.

**14.3** *Economics of Public Choice*

a When government leaders make decisions, they do not necessarily try to bring about economic efficiency. They may instead work to optimize their political support and chances of being reelected. Special interest groups often work to influence governments to make choices beneficial to their interests. Many voters are not concerned or even aware of these efforts to influence legislation. They adopt a stance of *rational ignorance* because the cost of learning about legislation exceeds any benefits they might receive from working to influence the legislation.

b Many laws are implemented or enforced by government *bureaus* that are not always responsive to interests of the population as a whole. Bureaus administer government programs that often have little link between costs and the value of benefits provided by the programs. Inefficient use of government funds and resources may result from this situation.

c Some governmental units have attempted to supply services more efficiently by contracting with private firms to provide them.

454    **CHAPTER 14**  Government Spending, Revenue, and Public Choice

# Review Economic Terms

Choose the term that best fits the definition. On a separate sheet of paper, write the letter of the answer. Some terms may not be used.

1. A tax as a percentage of income increases as income increases

2. Government agencies charged with implementing legislation and financed through legislative bodies

3. A plan for government outlays and revenues for a specified period, usually a year

_____ 4. Those who receive more benefits from a government program funded by a tax should pay more of that tax

_____ 5. A tax as a percentage of income decreases as income increases

_____ 6. Those with a greater ability to pay should pay more of a tax

_____ 7. The percentage of each additional dollar of income that goes to pay a tax

_____ 8. A tax as a percentage of income remains constant as income increases

_____ 9. Taxes deducted from paychecks to support Social Security and Medicare

10. A stance adopted by voters when they find that the cost of understanding and voting on a particular issue exceeds the benefit expected from doing so

a. **ability-to-pay tax principle**

b. **benefits-received tax principle**

c. **bureaus**

d. **government budget**

e. **marginal tax rate**

f. **maximizing political support**

g. **payroll taxes**

h. **progressive taxation**

i. **proportional taxation**

j. **rational ignorance**

k. **regressive taxation**

l. **tax incidence**

# Review Economic Concepts

11. Public goods are __?__ in consumption.

12. **True or False** The efficient level of production of a public good is found where the marginal benefit of additional units of that good is zero.

13. Which of the following is an example of the *benefits-received tax principle*?

   a. the excise tax on cigarettes

   b. a tariff on imported automobiles

   c. a sales tax on purchases of new clothing

   d. the toll that is paid to cross a bridge

14. **True or False** Taxes that fall more heavily on people who earn larger incomes represent the *ability-to-pay principle of taxation*.

15. An *ability-to-pay tax* also is likely to be

   a. regressive.

   b. progressive.

   c. proportional.

   d. reactionary.

16. If a tax structure is *progressive* and we know that Tom pays $1,000 on his $10,000 income, then Alicia, who earns $30,000, must pay

   a. more than $3,000 in tax.

   b. exactly $3,000 in tax.

   c. less than $3,000 in tax.

   d. more than $4,000 in tax.

## Review Economic Terms

1. h. progressive taxation
2. c. bureaus
3. d. government budget
4. b. benefits-received tax principle
5. k. regressive taxation
6. a. ability-to-pay tax principle
7. e. marginal tax rate
8. i. proportional taxation
9. g. payroll taxes
10. j. rational ignorance

## Review Economic Concepts

11. nonrival
12. False. The efficient level of production for a public good is where the marginal benefits equal the marginal cost.
13. d. the toll that is paid to cross a bridge
14. True
15. b. progressive
16. a. more than $3,000 in tax

## Review Economic Concepts

17. marginal tax rate

18. False. High marginal tax rates discourage people from working to earn additional income.

19. b. income redistribution

20. False. The largest source of government revenue is the income tax.

21. grants to local governments

22. a. tariffs on imported goods

23. True

24. c. 32

25. True

26. d. they think the cost of learning about how tax money is spent is greater than the benefits of working to influence legislation

27. rational ignorance

28. c. a firm that has been hired to collect garbage in your community

29. True

## Apply Economic Concepts

30. Answers will vary. Possible answer: The break wall will be a waste of money unless the community spends $1.8 million to build the entire 1800 yards at $100,000 per 100 yards. Since the community has voted to spend only $1 million, then none of it should be spent.

31. Answers will vary. Possible answer: The tax on water used is a benefits-received principle tax. The more water people use, the more tax they pay and the more they benefit from the new sewage system. The income tax is an ability-to-pay principle tax. People with greater incomes would pay a larger share of their income in tax. Most communities facing this problem have chosen to impose a tax on water usage.

---

17. The part of the next dollar you earn that is taken in tax is your __?__.

18. **True or False** High *marginal tax rates* encourage people to work and earn additional income.

19. The largest share of federal spending is allocated to
    a. national defense.
    b. income redistribution.
    c. interest on the national debt.
    d. government employee salaries.

20. **True or False** The largest source of federal government revenue is borrowing.

21. The biggest type of outlay for state governments is __?__.

22. Which of the following is not a source of revenue for state or local governments?
    a. tariffs on imported goods
    b. aid from the federal government
    c. income taxes
    d. sales taxes

23. **True or False** The largest part of local government spending is used for schools.

24. Government spending in the United States accounts for roughly ____ percent of the nation's GDP.
    a. 21
    b. 27
    c. 32
    d. 36

25. **True or False** Some political leaders appear to be more interested in whether they are reelected than in how efficiently the economy works.

26. Voters sometimes choose not to learn about how their taxes are spent because
    a. they are not able to influence government decisions.
    b. there is little information available to them about how their tax money is spent.
    c. they are not affected by how the government spends tax money.
    d. they think the cost of learning about how tax money is spent is greater than the benefits of working to influence legislation.

27. One theory states that unless voters have a special interest in a piece of legislation, they are likely to adopt a stance of __?__.

28. Which of the following is not an example of a government *bureau*?
    a. your community's public school system
    b. the state highway department
    c. a firm that has been hired to collect garbage in your community
    d. the federal court system

29. **True or False** *Bureaus* usually offer products for either a zero price or some price below cost.

# Apply Economic Concepts

30. **Identify the Optimal Quantity of a Public Good** Imagine that many residents of a riverside community wish to have a break wall built around their town to protect their homes when the river floods. The cost of construction is $100,000 per 100 yards. The break wall will have no value unless it is 1,800 yards long to surround the entire community. The people of the community have voted to spend up to $1,000,000 for the break wall. How much of this amount should they spend? How does this situation demonstrate a problem of achieving an efficient level of public goods?

31. **Decide Which Tax Is Best** Suppose that the Environmental Protection Agency (EPA) has determined that the sewer system in your town is inadequate and must be replaced. Your community will need to borrow $20,000,000 to build a new system. This loan must be repaid from tax revenues over the next 20 years. There is a debate over the type of tax that should be imposed to collect the needed money. One idea is to charge people an extra $1 for each thousand gallons of water they use. The other is to impose a city income tax and charge people 5 percent of their annual federal income tax payment. What principle of taxation is each of these proposals based on, and which would you support? Explain your answer.

**32. Evaluate the Marginal Tax Rate** Members of Congress often have debated the importance of the marginal income tax rate to the economy. Suppose that your marginal federal income tax rate is 30 percent. You pay Social Security and Medicare taxes at a rate of 7.65 percent, and your state income tax will take 6 percent of any additional income you earn. Your boss has asked you to go on a sales trip to Chicago next weekend. She has offered to pay you an extra $1,000 if you agree to go. Would you accept this offer? If you did, how much of the $1,000 will you keep?

**33. Petition Your Congressional Representative** The national debt is growing rapidly, and you are concerned that you will grow up to owe debts that have been taken on by older generations. Write a letter to your congressional representative expressing your concern and listing steps you think the government should take to reduce the size of the deficit. Explain why the representative may pay only limited attention to what you have to say.

**34. Assess a Proportional Income Tax** Some politicians believe that high marginal tax rates discourage people from working. They have suggested that it would be better to charge all taxpayers the same percent of their income so that the lower marginal tax rates for many people would encourage them to work and earn more. It has been estimated that the same amount of tax revenue could be collected if all taxpayers paid roughly 23 percent of what they earn in tax. This would mean that a person who earns $10,000 per year would pay $2,300 in tax while a person who earns $100,000 would pay $23,000. Decide whether you believe this is a good or a bad idea. Then write several paragraphs that identify and explain reasons for your point of view. Be

careful to discuss the impact of such a tax structure on the economy as well as your opinion of its fairness.

**35. Calculate Historical Tax Liabilities** In the past, maximum federal income tax rates have been much higher than they are today. In 1944, for example, those who had taxable incomes of $1,000,000 or more paid a marginal tax rate of 90 percent. If a person's taxable income increased from $1 million to $1.1 million in that year, how much of the additional income would he or she have been able to keep? What might have justified such a high tax rate at that time? What impact do you think such a high tax rate would have on the U.S. economy today?

**36. Construct a Bar Graph to Show Marginal Income Tax Rates** The federal marginal income tax rates for single individuals in 2003 are shown in the table. Construct a bar graph to show these rates. What has happened to these rates since 2003? Why have changes been made in these rates or why have they remained unchanged?

**Federal Income Tax Rates For Single Filers**

| Taxable Income In 2003 | Marginal Tax Rate |
|---|---|
| $0 – $14,000 | 10% |
| $7,001 – $28,400 | 15% |
| $28,401 – $68,800 | 25% |
| $68,801 – $143,500 | 28% |
| $143,501 – $311,950 | 33% |
| $311,951 or more | 35% |

e-con @pps    econxtra.swlearning.com ▶ ▪ ▪ ▪

**37. Access the Policy** Debate entitled "How should we reform the current tax system?" in the **EconDebate Online** at econxtra.swlearning.com. Read the Issues and Background. Write a paragraph summarizing both sides of this

debate. Then choose one of the links listed under "Different Perspectives in the Debate." Write another paragraph that explains which side of the debate the writer of the article is on and summarizes the writer's basic argument.

*Chapter Assessment*    **457**

## Apply Economic Concepts

32. Answers will vary. Possible answer: Their marginal tax rate could be as high as 43.65 percent (30% + 7.65% + 6% = 43.65%). Therefore, they could keep only $566.35 of the extra $1,000. This might discourage many people from accepting the extra work.

33. Answers will vary. Possible answer: High school students do not have the right to vote until they are 18 years of age and, even then, relatively few of them choose to exercise this power. Representatives are less likely to respond to the wishes of a single non-voter than to those of current voters who do not want to see cuts in programs that benefit them or increases in the taxes they pay.

34. Answers will vary. Answers should express a point of view and should be supported by logical reasons.

35. This person would have paid $90,000 more in tax and kept $10,000. In 1944, the government was paying for our involvement in World War II. Today many people would react to such high tax rates by refusing to work to earn additional income. They would probably take more time off and earn less.

36. The answers for this item will vary depending on when students answer this question. An example of an acceptable bar graph appears at the bottom of this page.

e-con @pps

37. Answers should include a reference to the article and reflect an understanding of the issue. Some of the issues addressed are listed below.

- Flat tax
- Internet tax
- Marriage and the federal income tax
- National sales tax
- Phaseouts
- Tax reform

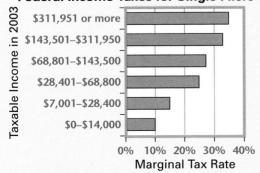

**Federal Income Taxes for Single Filers**

*Taxable Income in 2003* — $311,951 or more; $143,501–$311,950; $68,801–$143,500; $28,401–$68,800; $7,001–$28,400; $0–$14,000. *Marginal Tax Rate* — 0% 10% 20% 30% 40%

*Visualizing the Answer—Apply Economic Concepts*

36. The answer includes a graph. Students' graphs should look similar to the one shown here. An Excel spreadsheet containing this graph, along with supporting data, is available on the Instructor's Resource CD.

## Chapter Overview

**LESSON 15.1** *The Evolution of Fiscal Policy:* This lesson explains the economy's potential output and distinguishes between fiscal policy before and after the Great Depression.

**LESSON 15.2** *Fiscal Policy Reconsidered:* This lesson focuses on the two tools of fiscal policy: discretionary fiscal policy and automatic stabilizers. It also identifies problems with discretionary fiscal policy.

**LESSON 15.3** *Federal Deficits and Federal Debt:* This lesson looks at federal deficits from an historic perspective. It also looks at the effect of federal deficits on interest rates. Federal debt and its impact also are discussed.

### Consider

Ask students to consider the questions posed on this page as they study Chapter 15. After studying all three lessons, students should be able to answer the questions. The content related to each question can be found on the pages indicated below.

- What is your normal capacity for academic work, and when do you usually exceed that effort? See page 460—Potential Output.

- If the economy is already operating at full employment, how can it produce more? See page 461—Output Exceeding Potential.

- Can fiscal policy reduce swings in the business cycle? See page 464—The Multiplier Effect.

- Why has the federal budget been in deficit most years? See page 477—Why Is the Budget Usually in a Deficit?

- How is a strong economy like a crowded restaurant? See page 478—Crowding Out.

- What did President George W. Bush mean when he proposed a tax cut to "get the economy moving again"? See page 469—Fiscal Policy Tools.

### ▶ POINT YOUR BROWSER

Remind students that they can find additional resources for this chapter at **econxtra.swlearning.com**.

- Xtra! Study Tools
- Net Bookmarks
- Xtra! Quiz Prep
- econ@pps
- Ask the Xpert!
- Graphing Workshop

# 15 Fiscal Policy, Deficits, and Debt

The Evolution of Fiscal Policy **15.1**

Fiscal Policy Reconsidered **15.2**

Federal Deficits and Federal Debt **15.3**

### Consider

What is your normal capacity for academic work, and when do you usually exceed that effort?

If the economy is already operating at full employment, how can it produce more?

Can fiscal policy reduce swings in the business cycle?

Why has the federal budget been in deficit most years?

How is a strong economy like a crowded restaurant?

What did President George W. Bush mean when he proposed a tax cut to "get the economy moving again"?

© Reuters NewMedia Inc./CORBIS

### ▶ POINT YOUR BROWSER

*econxtra.swlearning.com*

---

### *Teaching Resources for Chapter 15*

- Activities and Projects Masters
- Spanish Resources
- Econ Connection Interactive Tutorial CD
- **Exam**View® CD
- Workbook Teacher's Edition
- Chapter Test Teacher's Edition
- NCEE Standards and Correlation

- Personal Finance Guide
- Social Studies Skills Review
- Instructor's Resource CD
  – PowerPoint Presentations
  – Lesson Plans
  – Video Discussion Guide
  – Answers to Graphing Exercises
- **econxtra.swlearning.com**

**15.1** *The Evolution of Fiscal Policy*

## Objectives

> Identify the economy's potential output level.

> Distinguish between fiscal policy before and after the Great Depression.

## Overview

Government spending for national defense, education, the environment, and other programs aims to achieve specific objectives, such as national security, a more educated work force, cleaner air, and the like. Fiscal policy has a broader focus. Fiscal policy considers the overall impact of the government's budget on the economy, especially on employment, output, and prices. Fiscal policy tries to promote full employment and price stability by targeting changes in aggregate demand.

## Key Terms

**potential output**

**natural rate of unemployment**

**classical economists**

**annually balanced budget**

**multiplier effect**

Remind students that taxes and government spending are more than ways for the government to receive income and provide public goods. They are also ways to influence people's behavior. The government's efforts to stabilize the economy by adjusting its taxing and spending is called fiscal policy.

### Objectives

Remind students to read the lesson objectives to help focus their attention before reading the lesson.

### Key Terms

Direct students to create a database using the key terms for this lesson. The database fields should include terms, definitions, and page numbers. Point out that the process of keying the data is an effective way to study key terms.

### [ In the News ]

Instruct students to read the passage and write down their answers. Point out that their answers might change after they finish studying Lesson 15.1.

### Answers to Think About It

Answers will vary. Possible answer: I do feel it is important for the government to continue to fund the Social Security system because many of the baby boomers have been giving part of their paycheck to the system, and they deserve to reap some of the benefits of the program when they retire.

### Visual Presentation

Use the PowerPoint presentation on the Instructor's Resource CD as an adjunct to your lecture. The presentation also can be used for review.

## [ In the News ]

### ● The Challenge of Protecting Social Security

One of the greatest fiscal policy challenges political leaders have faced in recent years is what to do about the future of Social Security. This program was created in the 1930s to help make sure that older Americans received an income after retirement. Payroll taxes from current workers pay for the program. For many years, whenever tax revenues exceeded the cost of the program, Congress raised benefits, expanded eligibility, or spent the surplus on something else. By the 1980s, however, lawmakers began to realize that the retirement of baby boomers—persons born between 1946 and 1964—would place a heavy burden on the system. In 1983, Congress passed reforms to save money for the future baby-boomer retirement era. These reforms included raising payroll taxes, expanding the tax base by the rate of inflation, gradually increasing the retirement age from 65 to 67, increasing penalties for early retirement, and offering incentives to delay retirement. Congress also called for any surpluses to be saved in trust funds. Despite these reforms, experts expect Social Security to be bankrupt by 2039, when payroll taxes will cover only about 73 percent of payments to retirees. Saving the system is a difficult challenge. Both of the ideas of cutting benefits to retirees or raising payroll taxes are unpopular. President George W. Bush proposed allowing younger workers to direct part of their Social Security payroll taxes to private investments, such as the stock market. While such investments usually provide larger returns over the long run, the stock market crash raised concerns about the plan. Also, Bush's plan would have taken away funds needed to pay current retirees. Recognizing the need to help the system, in 2002 President Bush proposed spending an extra $600 billion over 10 years to help support Social Security.

### Think About It

Do you think it's important for government to continue to fund the Social Security system? Why or why not?

◀ I ▶

**459**

 **National Content Standards in Economics**

A complete list of the NCEE Standards appears on pages xxiv–xxv of this book. The following standards are addressed in Lesson 15.1.

Standard 13: Role of Resources in Determining Income

Standard 16: Role of Government

Standard 19: Unemployment and Inflation

Standard 20: Monetary and Fiscal Policy

## Fiscal Policy and Potential Output

Use the following example to illustrate the concept of potential output. The setting is the sixteenth century, and Rose lives on a small farm where she keeps sheep. Her sheep grow enough wool for her to make 15 sweaters each winter. Over the years, she has accumulated enough wool to produce 25 sweaters in a single winter if she works very long hours. What is her potential output of sweaters? How can she make more than this amount? Why isn't this higher level of production sustainable in the long run? (Her potential output is 15 sweaters per winter. She can make more than 15 sweaters by using accumulated wool and working long hours. However, this higher level of production is not sustainable in the long run because once she uses the accumulated wool, she will have enough to make only 15 sweaters each year.)

### *Think Critically Through Visuals*

Direct students to focus their attention on **Figure 15.1—Fiscal Policy and Potential Output.** Point out that potential output is the vertical line, where real GDP is $12 trillion.

**NCEE Standard 20: Monetary and Fiscal Policy**

Federal government budgetary policy and the Federal Reserve System's monetary policy influence the overall levels of employment, output, and prices.

**The Graphing Workshop** — See It · Try It

Direct students to the Graphing Workshop for Chapter 15 at **econxtra.swlearning.com.** Instruct students to click on **See It: Tracing Potential Output.** As an enrichment exercise, students may complete **Try It: The Self-Correction Process.** This enrichment exercise presents concepts more advanced than those discussed in the textbook.

---

*The Graphing Workshop*

**natural rate of unemployment**

The unemployment rate when the economy is producing its potential level of output

**potential output**

The economy's maximum sustainable output in the long run

*Main Idea*

---

# Fiscal Policy and Potential Output

Fiscal policy uses government taxing and spending to move the economy toward full employment with price stability. It focuses mainly on shifts of the aggregate demand curve. If unemployment is high, fiscal policy aims to increase aggregate demand as a way of boosting output and employment. If aggregate demand is already so strong that it threatens to trigger higher inflation, fiscal policy tries to relieve that pressure by reducing aggregate demand.

## Potential Output

Fiscal policy tries to move the economy to its potential output. **Potential output** is the economy's maximum sustainable output in the long run, given the supply of resources, the state of technology, and the rules of the game that nurture production and exchange. Potential output also is referred to as the full-employment output. When the economy produces its potential output,

it is operating on its production possibilities frontier.

Suppose potential output equals a real GDP of $12 trillion. Potential output in Figure 15.1 is the vertical line where real GDP is $12 trillion. If potential output is achieved, the economy reaches full employment with no inflationary pressure. At full employment, the economy is doing as well as possible in the long run. In theory, fiscal policy can be used to ensure the economy achieves its potential, with full employment and price stability.

The unemployment rate that occurs when the economy is producing its potential GDP is called the **natural rate of unemployment**. At this rate, there is no cyclical unemployment. Generally accepted estimates of the natural rate of unemployment are in the range of 4 percent to 5 percent of the labor force.

## Output Below Potential

If the aggregate demand curve and aggregate supply curve intersect in the pink-shaded area of Figure 15.1, then output falls short of the economy's potential. The economy is not producing

---

**Main Idea** | Fiscal Policy and Potential Output | **Figure 15.1**

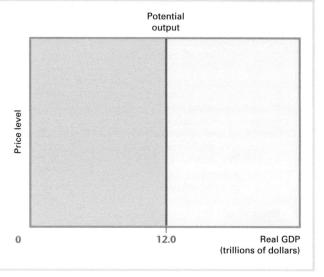

Potential output is the economy's maximum sustainable output in the long run. The pink-shaded area indicates real GDP below the economy's potential. The blue-shaded area indicates real GDP exceeding the economy's potential. *When the economy, through federal fiscal policy, reaches potential output, there is full employment and price stability.*

---

**Outside Resources**

**Labor Library** The U.S. Department of Labor provides online access to its Labor Library at www.dol.gov/dol/library.htm. One of the reports that can be found through this web site is *Report on the American Workforce.* This report, updated periodically, describes trends and changes in U.S. employment and the jobs workers hold. It indicates where job growth is likely to occur and where there may be declines in the future. Ask students to investigate this web site and describe their findings in a short report.

as much as it can. Unemployment exceeds its natural rate. The amount by which short-run output falls below the economy's potential output is called a *contractionary gap*. If output is below the economy's potential, policy makers often decide to reduce taxes or increase government spending. The idea is to stimulate aggregate demand as a way of increasing output to its potential. Figure 15.2 illustrates this situation.

## Output Exceeding Potential

If the aggregate demand curve and aggregate supply curve intersect in the blue-shaded area of Figure 15.1, then output exceeds the economy's potential. Unemployment is below its natural rate. The amount by which actual output in the short run exceeds the economy's potential output is called the *expansionary gap*.

This seems like a good outcome. However, production beyond the economy's potential creates inflationary pressure in the economy. Production exceeding the economy's potential is not sustainable in the long run. The result is higher inflation and a return to the economy's potential output. To head off this higher inflation, policy makers sometimes increase taxes or reduce government spending to reduce aggregate demand.

## How Can Output Exceed the Economy's Potential?

You probably have no problem understanding that output may fall below its potential. But how can the economy produce more than its potential? Remember, potential output means not zero unemployment, but the natural rate of unemployment. Even in an economy producing its potential

### Fiscal Policy and Potential Output

Return to the example of Rose and her sweater business. Explain that Rose produced 15 sweaters between December 1550 and March 1551. During 1551, she was able to sell only 10 sweaters because the economy in her village was weak and many people had little money to spend. As a result, she plans to produce only five sweaters between December 1551 and March 1552. During 1552, she will have 10 sweaters to sell—five each from her last two production periods. Rose will produce below her potential. If many other entrepreneurs in her village do the same, there will be a contractionary gap in the local economy. Many people will not be able to find work, so unemployment will exceed the natural rate. This contractionary gap could be closed by an increase in aggregate demand. Perhaps the local nobility could decide to purchase more goods and services from the community to stimulate the local economy.

### Think Critically Through Visuals

Direct students to focus their attention on **Figure 15.2—Discretionary Fiscal Policy to Close a Contractionary Gap**. Point out that if the aggregate demand curve and the aggregate supply curve intersect in the pink-shaded area, then output falls short of the economy's potential.

 **See It**

Direct students to the Graphing Workshop for Chapter 15 at **econxtra.swlearning.com**. Instruct students to click on **See It: Discretionary Policy and a Contractionary Gap**.

---

*The Graphing Workshop*
**Discretionary Fiscal Policy to Close a Contractionary Gap**     **Figure 15.2**

*econxtra.swlearning.com*

The aggregate demand curve *AD* and the aggregate supply curve *AS* intersect at point *e*. Output of $11.5 trillion falls short of the economy's potential of $12.0 trillion. The result is a contractionary gap of $0.5 trillion. This gap could be closed by discretionary fiscal policy that increases aggregate demand by just the right amount. An increase in government spending, a decrease in taxes, or some combination of the two could shift aggregate demand to *AD\**, moving the economy to its potential level of output at *e\**.

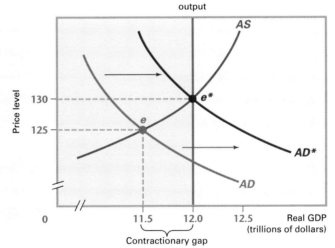

Lesson 15.1 • *The Evolution of Fiscal Policy*     **461**

---

Explain that during much of the 1960s, output in the U.S. economy exceeded its potential, and unemployment fell below the natural rate. Many reasons brought about this condition. One was the war in Vietnam. Hundreds of thousands of U.S. citizens either joined or were conscripted into the military, thereby leaving the civilian labor force. The war also required the allocation of billions of dollars worth of resources. At the same time, Congress passed laws that expanded government transfers for social programs and spending for the new Medicare program. Unemployment fell to less than 5 percent at a time when economists estimated that the natural rate exceeded 6 percent. What do students believe would have happened to prices during this expansionary gap? (Inflation did increase from roughly 4 percent in the early 1960s to more than 7 percent by 1968.)

## Fiscal Policy and Potential Output

Once more, return to the example of Rose and her sweater business. Imagine that the local nobles decided to organize a regional spring fair. They invited people to visit their community and shop for the many products produced there. To prepare for the fair, local entrepreneurs (including Rose) expanded production, using most of their accumulated resources and staying up late at night to work. As it turned out, the fair was a great success. Many businesses sold all the products they had at prices higher than they had expected to receive. Unfortunately, they could not have another fair soon because they had used up most of their resources. They had experienced an expansionary gap.

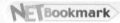

Direct students to **econxtra.swlearning.com**. Remind them to click on the link for Lesson 15.1 to find the appropriate link for the **NET Bookmark** on this page.

### Answer

Answers will vary, depending on when students access the web site.

### Think Critically Through Visuals

Direct students to focus their attention on the photograph on this page. Ask for a volunteer to answer the question posed in the caption.

### Answer

Answers will vary. Possible answer: Potential output would be the highest grades you could receive by using all of your abilities and time to the fullest.

 **CHECKPOINT**

Invite a student to answer the checkpoint that appears on this page.

### Answer

The economy's potential output is the maximum sustainable output in the long run, given the supply of resources, the state of technology, and the rules of the game that nurture production and exchange. This also is referred to as full-employment output.

---

 **NETBookmark**

The University of Washington's Fiscal Policy Center provides an extensive list of links about U.S. fiscal policy. Access that site through econxtra.swlearning.com and use the links to determine what tax and spending proposals have been made in Congress during the past six months. Choose one of those proposals and use aggregate demand and aggregate supply to explain its likely impact.

**econxtra.swlearning.com**

output, there is still some unemployed labor and some unused production capacity.

If you think of potential output as the economy's *normal production capacity,* you get a better idea of how the economy can temporarily exceed that capacity. Consider your own study habits. During most of the school year, you display your normal capacity for academic work. As the end of a grading period draws near, however, you may step it up a notch to finish long-standing

assignments. You may study more than usual and make an extra push trying to pull things together. During these brief stretches, you study beyond your normal capacity, beyond the schedule you follow on a regular or sustained basis.

Producers, too, can exceed their normal capacity in the short run to push output beyond the economy's potential. For example, during World War II, businesses pulled out all the stops to win the war. The unemployment rate fell below 2 percent. However, in the long run, the economy does not exceed its potential, just as you don't boost your study effort permanently. Output in the long run gravitates back to the economy's potential. Production beyond the economy's potential usually leads only to inflation in the long run. For example, despite price controls put in place during World War II, inflation was still relatively high.

 **CHECKPOINT**
What is the economy's potential output?

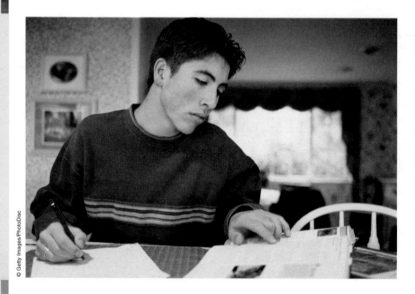

**How does the concept of potential output relate to your study habits?**

© Getty Images/PhotoDisc

**462**      **CHAPTER 15**   Fiscal Policy, Deficits, and Debt

---

### Economic Headlines

Instruct students to obtain an article in a current magazine or newspaper that relates to one of the topics in this lesson. For example, they might find articles about a business that is having trouble finding workers to fill job openings. Instruct students to read the article, write a brief summary, and include a reference citation. Identify the style you want them to use for the citation.

As an alternative, you might locate several articles of interest and provide citations for students to use in locating one of the articles. Direct students to read the article they have chosen and write a brief explanation of how it relates to this lesson.

# The Rise of Fiscal Policy

Before the Great Depression, most policy makers believed that an economy producing less than its potential in the short run would move to its potential in the long run without intervention from the federal government. They thought the government should just balance its budget and forget about trying to stabilize the economy in the short run. Besides, before the Great Depression, the federal government itself played a minor role in the economy. At the onset of the Great Depression, for example, federal outlays were less than 3 percent of GDP, compared to about 20 percent today.

## View of Classical Economists

Before the 1930s, fiscal policy was seldom used to influence the overall performance of the economy. Prior to the Great Depression, public policy was shaped by the views of **classical economists**. They advocated *laissez-faire*, the belief that free markets without government intervention were the best way to achieve the economy's potential output.

Classical economists did not deny the existence of depressions and high unemployment. They argued, however, that the sources of such crises lay outside the market system, in the effects of wars, tax increases, poor growing seasons, and the like. Such external events could shock the economy, reducing output and employment in the short run. Classical economists believed, however, that natural market forces, such as declining prices, wages, and interest rates, would end any recession in a relatively short time by encouraging people and businesses to spend more.

Simply put, classical economists argued that if the economy's average price level was too high to sell all that was produced, prices would fall until the quantity supplied equaled the quantity demanded. If wages were too high to employ all who wanted to work, wages would fall until the quantity of labor supplied equaled the quantity demanded. If interest rates were too high to invest all that had been saved, they would fall until the amount invested equaled the amount saved.

The classical approach claimed that natural market forces, through flexible

> **classical economists**
> A group of laissez-faire economists, who believed that economic downturns corrected themselves in the long run through natural market forces

# SPAN THE GLOBE

## Laissez-Faire Policies in France

The French term laissez-faire literally means "allow to do." The exact origins of the term are unknown. It was first associated with a group of French economists called the Physiocrats. This group was popular in the late 1700s and is generally considered the founders of a scientific school of economic thought. Physiocrats believed that economies worked best if grounded in agriculture and allowed to run freely based on natural laws, not regulation by the government. Physiocrats strongly opposed the growing European policies of mercantilism, in which governments heavily regulated trade and manufacturing more for their own good than that of individual property owners. Physiocrats also believed that land and the products grown from it were the basis of wealth. Mercantilists believed that hard currency and precious metals were the basis of wealth. In the end, the mercantilists' theories of wealth became more widely accepted than those of the Physiocrats. Nevertheless, the Physiocrats' laissez-faire ideas were embraced by many people. When the French Revolution was launched in 1789, the new government instituted a number of reforms aimed at easing regulations on trade. The French government today is far from laissez-faire. Modern France has a mixed economy, which includes heavy regulation over the economy but not complete control of private property.

### Think Critically

Why do you think the French government moved away from applying the ideas of the Physiocrats to its economy? With which philosophy regarding wealth—the mercantilist or the Physiocrat—do you most agree? Justify your answer.

## The Rise of Fiscal Policy

Give one student 100 pennies. Write $1.00 on the board. Tell this student to keep 10 pennies and give (spend) the other 90 to another student. Write $.90 on the board. The second student should keep 9 pennies, and give (spend) the other 81 to another student. Write $.81 on the board. The third student should keep 8 pennies and give (spend) the remaining 73 to another student. Write $.73 on the board. Continue this process, having each student save roughly 10 percent of the money received and spend the rest. Total the amount of money that is spent. Point out that the total amount of spending that took place far exceeds the original 100 pennies you provided. This activity can be used to illustrate the multiplier effect of fiscal policy.

### TEAM WORK

For the **Team Work** activity on page 465, organize students into pairs and allow them to choose their role. Allow five minutes for the classical economists to explain the classical approach and then five minutes for the Keynesian economists to explain Keynesian approach. Have students share their lists with the class.

### Think Critically Through Visuals

Direct students to focus their attention on the photograph on page 465. Ask for a volunteer to answer the question posed in the caption.

### Answer

Answers will vary. Possible answer: One tool of fiscal policy is increasing government spending. Government spending increased at the start of World War II to support the war effort. This spending resulted in increased production and employment, thus ending the Depression.

---

**annually balanced budget**

Matching annual spending with annual revenue, except during war years; approach to the federal budget prior to the Great Depression

**multiplier effect**

Any change in fiscal policy affects aggregate demand by more than the original change in spending or taxing

---

prices, wages, and interest rates, would move the economy toward its potential GDP in the long run. Classical economists saw no need for changes in spending or taxing to "correct" the economy.

Instead, fiscal policy prior to the Great Depression aimed to maintain an **annually balanced budget**, except during wartime. Tax revenues tend to rise during expansions and fall during recessions. Therefore, an annually balanced budget means that spending increased during expansions and declined during recessions. However, such a pattern magnified fluctuations in the business cycle. This overheated the economy during expansions and increased unemployment during recessions.

### The Great Depression and Keynes

Classical economists acknowledged that market economies could produce less than potential in the short run. The prolonged depression of the 1930s strained belief in the economy's ability to correct itself. The Great Depression was marked by unemployment reaching 25 percent and much unused plant capacity. With vast unemployed resources, output and income fell far short of the economy's potential for many years.

The market adjustments predicted by classical theory and the years of unemployment experienced during the Great Depression represented a clash between theory and fact. In 1936, John Maynard Keynes of Cambridge University, England, published *The General Theory of Employment, Interest, and Money.* This book challenged the classical view and touched off what would later come to be called the Keynesian revolution. *Keynesian theory and policy were developed to address the problem of unemployment during the Great Depression.*

Keynes's main quarrel with the classical economists was that prices and wages did not appear flexible enough even in the long run to ensure the full employment of resources. According to Keynes, prices and wages were relatively inflexible—they were "sticky." So if unemployment was high, natural

market forces would not return the economy to full employment in a timely fashion. Keynes also believed business expectations might at times become so grim that even very low interest rates would not encourage fir to invest.

### The Multiplier Effect

Keynes also argued that any change in taxing or government spending had a magnified effect on aggregate demand For example, suppose the government spends $100 million on a new presidential plane, Air Force One. Workers and suppliers at Boeing, the manufacturer the 747, see their incomes rise by $100 million. These people will spend at lea part of that higher income on product such as food, clothing, housing, cars, appliances, and the like. As a result, t people who make all those products will have more income. They will spe some of that higher income on yet more stuff.

Each round of income and spendin increases aggregate demand a little more. This is called the **multiplier effect** of fiscal policy, which says that any change in fiscal policy affects aggregate demand by more than the original change in spending or taxing.

The multiplier effect also could resu from a change in business investment and even a change in consumption. However, Keynes focused on changes in government spending and taxing.

### The Rise of Fiscal Policy

Three developments in the years following the Great Depression support the use of fiscal policy in the United States. The first was the influence of Keynes's *General Theory.* Keynes thoug the economy could get stuck at a leve of output that was well below its pote tial, well below the full-employment level. He argued that increasing gover ment spending or cutting taxes could have a multiplier effect on aggregate demand. According to Keynes, fiscal policy should be used in times of hig unemployment to increase aggregate demand enough to boost output and employment.

The second development giving credibility to fiscal policy was the powerful impact World War II had on output and employment. The demands of war greatly increased production and cut unemployment sharply, ending the depression.

The third development, largely a consequence of the first two, was the passage of the Employment Act of 1946, which gave the federal government the responsibility for promoting full employment and price stability.

Again, prior to the Great Depression, the dominant fiscal policy was pursuit of a balanced budget. Indeed, in 1932, when the economy was in the depths of the Depression, federal taxes were increased to head off a budget deficit. This made things worse. In the wake of Keynes's *General Theory* and World War II, however, policy makers grew more receptive to the idea that fiscal policy could improve economic performance. The objective of fiscal policy was no longer to balance the budget but to promote full employment with price stability, even if this resulted in budget deficits.

 **CHECKPOINT**
How did the Great Depression change fiscal policy?

 **TEAM WORK**

Working with a partner, perform a role play. Acting as a classical economist, one partner will explain that economic approach to the partner. Acting as a Keynesian economist, the other partner will explain that approach. Make a list of the issues about which these two schools of thought disagree.

© Time Life Pictures

**What role did fiscal policy play in ending the Great Depression?**

Lesson 15.1 • *The Evolution of Fiscal Policy* **465**

## RETEACH

Ask students to imagine it is 1929 and they are government leaders who believe in the classical economic theory: that the government should always have a balanced budget. At the end of October, the stock market starts to fall and many people lose their investments. Some banks that lent money to people to buy stock fail when the loans are not repaid. There is no deposit insurance, so many people lose their savings. People cut back on spending and sales fall. Workers are laid off and cannot buy products or make payments on those they have already purchased. Government tax revenues plummet. What would the students do? Remind them of their belief in the classical theory. (In actuality, the government cut spending to try to balance the budget. This caused the Depression to become even worse.

 **CHECKPOINT**
Invite a student to answer the checkpoint that appears on this page.

**Answer**
Prior to the Great Depression, the dominant fiscal policy was the pursuit of a balanced budget. After the Great Depression, the objective of fiscal policy was to promote full employment with price stability, even if it resulted in larger deficits.

## APPLY

Assign Lesson 15.1 from the Contemporary Economics Workbook.

## *e*-con @pps

Encourage students to apply their knowledge of concepts presented in this lesson as they explore economic news stories, policy debates, and data available at **econxtra.swlearning.com**. A sampling of the titles for this lesson appears below.

**EconNews**
- And the Award for Best Director Goes to . . .
- Economy Spotting

## ASSESS

Assign all or part of Lesson 15.1 Assessment on page 466 as homework or an in-class activity.

## Xtra! Study Tools

Direct students to the online study tools for Lesson 15.1 at **econxtra.swlearning.com**.

## CLOSE

**Revisit** the In the News feature on the first page of the lesson. Ask students to review their preliminary answers and discuss the questions.

**Review** the objectives for Lesson 15.1. Students should be able to:
- Identify the economy's potential output level.
- Distinguish between fiscal policy before and after the Great Depression.

## Key Concepts

1. Answers will vary. Possible answer: Low rates of unemployment, high production, and increases in price levels could indicate that the economy has reached, or possibly temporarily exceeded, its potential output.

2. Answers will vary. Possible answer: The natural rate of unemployment occurs when no workers are cyclically unemployed because the economy is producing below its potential rate. However, some workers are between jobs, out of work because of the season of the year, or in need of additional training to qualify for job openings that exist.

3. Answers will vary. Possible answer: Classical economists believed that in a recession, prices, wages, and interest rates would fall until people would buy all products offered for sale, all workers would find employment, and banks would lend all the funds that were available to borrow. When this happened, the economy would have recovered.

4. Answers will vary. Possible answer: An additional $5 billion in spending will result in $5 billion in additional income. This added income causes additional spending, which then results in even more income. This process of spending, causing income that leads to additional spending, ripples through the economy in repeated cycles.

## Graphing Exercise

5. Answers will vary. Possible answer: The additional $10 million in government spending has the potential to increase income and spending in the economy by as much as $100 million. This total will not be achieved in reality, though, because some people will hold cash rather than spend additional income. Additional spending can have a powerful effect on income and therefore on production in the economy.

An example of an acceptable graph appears at the bottom of this page.

The Answer Key is continued on page 484.

Xtra!
Study Tools
econxtra.swlearning.com

## Key Concepts

1. How close do you think the U.S. economy is currently to its potential output? Explain your answer.

2. Why can the economy have a 4 to 5 percent rate of unemployment when it is at its natural rate of unemployment?

3. In 2001, the U.S. economy was in recession. Why would classical economists have believed that this downturn in the economy would not last very long?

4. If the federal government borrows and spends an additional $5 billion, why are aggregate demand, production and income likely to grow by more than $5 billion?

## Graphing Exercise

5. Draw a bar graph to show five rounds of the multiplier effect on spending when the federal government implements fiscal policy by borrowing and spending an additional $10 million. Remember that all money that is spent becomes someone else's income. Assume that each person who receives additional income saves 10 percent and spends 90 percent of these funds, as shown in the table below. How does your graph demonstrate the power of government spending?

**Five Rounds of the Multiplier Effect**

| Round | Additional Spending | Additional Income | Amount Saved |
|-------|---------------------|-------------------|--------------|
| 1 | $10,000,000 | $10,000,000 | $1,000,000 |
| 2 | $ 9,000,000 | $ 9,000,000 | $ 900,000 |
| 3 | $ 8,100,000 | $ 8,100,000 | $ 810,000 |
| 4 | $ 7,290,000 | $ 7,290,000 | $ 729,000 |
| 5 | $ 6,561,000 | $ 6,561,000 | $ 656,100 |

## Think Critically

6. **History** When Keynes first asserted that the government could stabilize the economy by adjusting its spending and taxing, his ideas were met with skepticism from many economists and politicians. Events during World War II, however, caused most people to change their minds and come to believe that his ideas were correct. Investigate government borrowing and spending that took place during World War II and explain how they supported Keynes's ideas.

**Impact of an Additional $10 Million in Government Spending**

## Visualizing the Answer— Graphing Exercise

5. The answer includes a graph. Students' graphs should look similar to the one shown here. An Excel spreadsheet containing this graph, along with supporting data, is available on the Instructor's Resource CD.

# Sharpen Your Life Skills

## Evaluate and Construct Pie Graphs

... its 2002–2003 budget, the state of ... w York anticipated revenues and ...penditures that are shown in ...se pie graphs. Study the graphs ...d then answer the four questions ... Apply Your Skill.

## Apply Your Skill

Which of New York state's sources of tax revenue would you expect to have fallen the most below expectations because of the economic downturn in 2003?

Which type of government spending would have been easiest to cut when New York leaders found that their tax revenues fell below expectations in 2003?

3. Why were cuts in aid to local governments an important issue in preparing the budget for 2003–2004 in New York state?

4. Find the budgeted revenue and spending in your state's current budget. Use these data to construct similar pie graphs for your state. What might explain differences between sources of revenue and types of spending between your state and New York state?

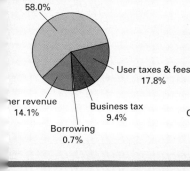

...w York State Sources of Revenue, 2002–2003 Budget

...sonal income tax 58.0%
...er revenue 14.1%
Borrowing 0.7%
Business tax 9.4%
User taxes & fees 17.8%

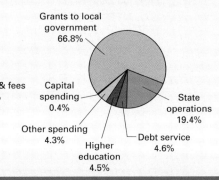

New York State Expenditures, 2002–2003 Budget

Grants to local government 66.8%
Capital spending 0.4%
Other spending 4.3%
Higher education 4.5%
Debt service 4.6%
State operations 19.4%

## Federal Aid as a Percent of State and Local Spending 1980

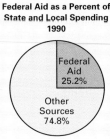

Other Sources 60.1%
Federal Aid 39.9%

## Federal Aid as a Percent of State and Local Spending 1990

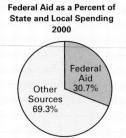

Federal Aid 25.2%
Other Sources 74.8%

## Federal Aid as a Percent of State and Local Spending 2000

Other Sources 69.3%
Federal Aid 30.7%

---

## Evaluate and Construct Pie Graphs

After studying Lesson 15.1, students should be able to answer the questions on this page.

## Apply Your Skill

Consider allowing students to work in pairs for this assignment.

### Answers

1. Answers will vary. Students may point out that the economic downturn would probably have caused personal income tax and business tax revenues to fall.

2. Answers will vary. Students may point out that spending for state operations would have been relatively easy to cut by not hiring replacement workers when state employees retired.

3. Answers will vary. Students may point out that aid to local governments accounted for about two-thirds of budgeted spending in the 2003 budget. It would be difficult to reduce spending significantly in 2004 without cutting this aid.

4. Answers will vary. Students should demonstrate their ability to construct pie graphs and provide reasonable explanations for differences in sources of revenue and allocation of spending.

### Follow-Up Activity

Although federal aid is an important source of revenue for state and local governments, it has not been a steady source of revenue over extended periods of time. The proportions that federal aid represented in state and local government spending in 1980, 1990, and 2000 appear in the table below. Use these data to construct three pie graphs showing the proportions of state and local government spending that was funded through federal aid, and from other sources, in these years.

### Visualizing the Answer— Follow-Up Activity

The answer includes three pie graphs. Students' graphs should look similar to those shown here.

| Federal Aid as a Percent of State and Local Spending: 1980, 1990, and 2000 | | |
|---|---|---|
| Year | Federal Aid | Other Sources |
| 1980 | 39.9% | 60.1% |
| 1990 | 25.2% | 74.8% |
| 2000 | 30.7% | 69.3% |
| Source: Statistical Abstract of the United States, 2002, p. 264. | | |

An example of acceptable pie graphs appears at the bottom of this page.

## FOCUS

### 15.2 Fiscal Policy Reconsidered

Although Keynesian theory came to be widely accepted after World War II, events during and after the 1970s demonstrated that there are limitations on the ability of these fiscal policies to resolve many economic problems. Point out that alternative economic theories may be more useful in resolving some economic difficulties.

### Objectives

Remind students to read the lesson objectives to help focus their attention before reading the lesson.

### Key Terms

Direct students to look up key terms in a business or economics dictionary. Some students will find it helpful to read another definition. In addition to a definition, many entries will include a brief explanation and an example.

### [ In the News ]

Instruct students to read the passage and write down their answers. Point out that their answers might change after they finish studying Lesson 15.2.

### Answers to Think About It

Answers will vary. Possible answer: Yes, it does make more sense to plan budgets on a year-to-year basis rather than a 10-year basis. It is difficult to predict all the recessions and growths that the economy might experience in 10 years. It is easier to predict what recessions and growths might occur in one year.

### Visual Presentation

Use the PowerPoint presentation on the Instructor's Resource CD as an adjunct to your lecture. The presentation also can be used for review.

## Objectives

> Identify the two tools of fiscal policy.

> Evaluate discretionary fiscal policy in light of the time lags involved.

## Overview

From the Great Depression through the 1960s, fiscal policy appeared to be the miracle drug to cure what ailed the economy. Policy makers would adopt the necessary spending and tax policies to move the economy to its potential. The 1970s brought a new set of problems—problems that seemed beyond the reach of fiscal policy. Policy makers face the challenge of lags between the time they select and implement a policy and when it actually has an effect on the economy.

## Key Terms

**discretionary fiscal policy**

**automatic stabilizers**

**recognition lag**

**decision-making lag**

**implementation lag**

**effectiveness lag**

## [ In the News ]

### ● Requiring a Balanced Budget

By the early 1980s, the U.S. national debt had reached more than $2 trillion. To force the government to curb spending and balance the budget, Congress in 1985 passed the Gramm-Rudman-Hollings Act. This act required automatic cuts if government spending exceeded income. In its first year, the law cut the deficit by $70 billion. However, the Supreme Court struck down the automatic spending cuts as unconstitutional. Congress responded by passing several new versions of the law, the most significant being the Budget Enforcement Act of 1990. This new law tried to control the budget by limiting discretionary spending. It also required that any attempt to increase spending or reduce revenues had to be offset by other actions to provide money for those changes. By the end of the 1990s, it looked as if this legislation was working, as the federal government experienced budget surpluses for the first time in years. This was during an era of widespread economic growth, however. Many lawmakers feared that an economic downturn would lead to more deficits, despite the laws in place. In 2001, Senator Fritz Hollings, one of the original sponsors of the Gramm-Rudman-Hollings Act, argued that the only way to secure a balanced budget was to abandon the practice of writing budgets based on projected ten-year economic forecasts. Hollings called for both federal and state governments to return to the tradition of planning budgets one year at a time based on current situations.

### Think About It

Do you agree with Hollings that planning budgets one year at a time would be more effective than planning budgets based on ten-year forecasts? Why or why not?

◀ ❘ ▶

### National Content Standards in Economics

A complete list of the NCEE Standards appears on pages xxiv–xxv of this book. The following standards are addressed in Lesson 15.2.

Standard 4: Role of Incentives

Standard 16: Role of Government

Standard 18: Macroeconomy—Income, Employment, Prices

Standard 19: Unemployment and Inflation

Standard 20: Monetary and Fiscal Policy

# Fiscal Policy Tools

The tools of fiscal policy sort into two broad categories: discretionary fiscal policy and automatic stabilizers.

## Discretionary Fiscal Policy

This chapter so far has focused mostly on discretionary fiscal policy. **Discretionary fiscal policy** requires congressional action to change government spending or taxing. These actions are designed to promote macroeconomic goals such as full employment and price stability. President Bush used discretionary fiscal policy in proposed plans for tax cuts in 2001 and 2003.

## Automatic Stabilizers

Once adopted, a discretionary fiscal policy measure usually becomes an ongoing part of the federal budget. Most taxing and spending programs, once implemented, become **automatic stabilizers**. They automatically change with the ups and downs of the economy to stabilize *disposable income*, the income available after taxes. By smoothing fluctuations in disposable income, automatic stabilizers also smooth fluctuations in consumption and in aggregate demand.

One automatic stabilizer is unemployment insurance. During a recession, unemployment benefits automatically flow to the unemployed. This increases disposable income and props up consumption and aggregate demand. Likewise, welfare spending automatically increases as more people become eligible during hard times.

As another example of an automatic stabilizer, the federal income tax takes a bigger bite out of income as income increases. During an economic expansion, income taxes claim a growing percentage of income. This slows the growth in disposable income, which slows the growth in consumption. Therefore, the progressive income tax relieves some of the inflationary pres-

sure that might otherwise arise when output increases during an economic expansion.

On the other hand, when the economy goes into a recession, real GDP declines, but taxes decline faster. Therefore disposable income does not fall as much as real GDP does. This props up consumption and aggregate demand during recessions. The progressive income tax protects against declines in disposable income, in consumption, and in aggregate demand.

*Automatic stabilizers smooth fluctuations in disposable income over the business cycle. They boost aggregate demand during periods of recession and dampen aggregate demand during periods of expansion.*

Automatic stabilizers do not eliminate economic fluctuations, but they do reduce their magnitude. The stronger and more effective the automatic stabilizers, the less need there is for discretionary fiscal policy. Because of automatic stabilizers introduced during the Great Depression, *the economy is more stable today than it was during the Great Depression and before.* Without much fanfare, automatic stabilizers have been quietly doing their work, keeping the economy on a more even keel.

**CHECKPOINT**
What are the two tools of fiscal policy?

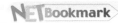
*econxtra.swlearning.com*

In theory, how does a tax cut work to stimulate the economy?

**discretionary fiscal policy**
Congressional changes in spending or taxing to promote macroeconomic goals

**automatic stabilizers**
Government spending and taxing programs that year after year automatically reduce fluctuations in disposable income, and thus in consumption, over the business cycle

## NETBookmark

In the United States, fiscal policy is determined jointly by the president and Congress. The Congressional Budget Office provides analysis to Congress. The Office of Management and Budget does the same for the executive branch. Access the web sites for these offices to get a sense of the kinds of analysis being done and how they might be used in determining fiscal policy. Write a one-page paper describing your findings.

*econxtra.swlearning.com*

---

## TEACH

### Fiscal Policy Tools

Point out that many government services are provided without the need for any new decisions. For example, if it snows in Chicago, the city's snowplows are put into action; no new laws or decisions need to be made. However, when a new or unexpected problem arises, new legislation may need to be passed to deal with the situation. There were no laws, for example, that limited unsolicited mass e-mail before Internet use became commonplace. Explain that some types of fiscal policy are automatic because they deal with problems that can be anticipated. Other fiscal policy issues are discretionary because they require the government to take action.

### Ask the Xpert!

Direct students to **econxtra.swlearning.com** to hear an expert answer the question "In theory, how does a tax cut work to stimulate the economy?"

### NETBookmark

Direct students to the **econxtra.swlearning.com** Remind them to click on the link for Lesson 15.2 to find the appropriate link for the **NET Bookmark** on this page.

### CHECKPOINT

Invite a student to answer the checkpoint that appears on this page.

### Answer

The two tools of fiscal policy are discretionary fiscal policy and automatic stabilizers. Discretionary fiscal policy involves congressional changes in spending or taxing to promote macroeconomic goals. Automatic stabilizers are government spending and taxing programs that year after year automatically reduce fluctuations in disposable income and thus in consumption, over the business cycle.

---

## Outside Resources

**Tax Foundation** According to its own web site, "As a nonpartisan educational organization, the Tax Foundation does not represent any particular economic sector's point of view. Through the years, the organization has earned a reputation for independence and credibility." Yet, the Foundation is not void of perspective. Instruct students to visit the foundation's web site at www.taxfoundation.org. Ask them to review several of the articles about taxes or government spending and choose an article to summarize. In addition, ask them to answer the following question: Do you agree that this article does not represent any particular economic sector's point of view?

# Problems with Discretionary Fiscal Policy

Discretionary fiscal policy is a type of demand-management policy. The idea is to increase or decrease aggregate demand to smooth economic fluctuations and move the economy toward its potential output. This seemed to work between the Great Depression and the 1960s. The 1970s, however, turned out to be different.

## Stagflation

The problem during the 1970s was stagflation. A decrease in aggregate supply created the double trouble of higher inflation and higher unemployment. The aggregate supply curve shifted left because of crop failures around the world, sharply higher oil prices, and other adverse supply shocks. Demand-management policies are not suited to solving the problem of stagflation. This is because in the short run, it is impossible to fight unemployment and inflation at the same time with fiscal policy. An increase in aggregate demand would worsen inflation, whereas a decrease in aggregate demand resulting from reduced government spending or higher taxes would worsen unemployment.

## Calculating the Natural Rate of Unemployment

The unemployment rate that occurs when the economy is producing its potential output is called *the natural rate of unemployment.* Before adopting discretionary fiscal policies, public officials must correctly estimate this natural rate. That's no easy task, and they may get it wrong.

For example, suppose the economy is producing its potential output of $12.0 trillion, as shown in Figure 15.3, where the natural rate of unemployment is 5 percent. Also suppose that public officials mistakenly think the natural rate of unemployment is 4 percent. They then attempt to increase output and reduce unemployment through discretionary fiscal policy. This attempt would only lead to inflation in the long run.

**When Discretionary Fiscal Policy Underestimates the Natural Rate of Unemployment** | **Figure 15.3**

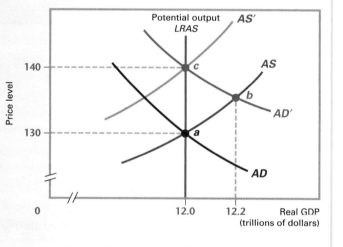

If public officials underestimate the natural rate of unemployment, they may attempt to stimulate aggregate demand even if the economy is producing its potential output, as at point *a*. In the short run, this expansionary policy yields a short-run equilibrium at point *b*. At this point the price level and output are higher and unemployment is lower. The policy appears to be working. Thus, attempts to increase production beyond potential GDP lead only to inflation in the long run.

## The Problem of Lags

So far, the discussion has ignored the time required to implement discretionary fiscal policy. The assumption has been that the desired policy is selected and implemented instantaneously. The presentation also has assumed that, once implemented, the policy works fast. Actually, there may be long, sometimes unpredictable, lags at several stages in the process. These lags reduce the effectiveness of discretionary fiscal policies.

### Recognition Lag

First, there is a **recognition lag**, which is the time it takes to identify a problem and determine how serious it is. Because a recession is not identified until more than six months after it begins and the average recession lasts only about 11 months, a typical recession will be more than half over before it is officially recognized as such.

### Decision-Making Lag

Even after it becomes clear that the economy is in trouble, Congress and the president must develop and agree on an appropriate course of action. Because policy makers usually take time deciding what to do, there is a **decision-making lag**. Changes in fiscal policy usually take months to approve, but they could take more than a year.

### Implementation Lag

Once a decision has been made, the new policy must be introduced. This often involves an **implementation lag**. For example, in early 2001, President Bush proposed a tax cut to stimulate the economy. Although Congress passed the measure relatively quickly, tax rebate checks were not mailed until six months after Bush introduced the legislation.

### Effectiveness Lag

Once a policy has been implemented, there is an **effectiveness lag** before the full impact of the policy registers on the economy. Fiscal policy, once implemented, takes between 9 and 18 months to register its full effect.

© Getty Images/PhotoDisc

**Once government decision makers implement a policy, there is a lag before the full impact of the policy registers on the economy. What is this lag called, and how long does it usually last?**

*recognition lag*
The time needed to identify a macroeconomic problem

*decision-making lag*
The time needed to decide what to do once the problem has been identified

*implementation lag*
The time needed to execute a change in policy

*effectiveness lag*
The time needed for changes in policy to affect the economy

These lags make it difficult to carry out discretionary fiscal policy. Discretionary fiscal policy to address a recession could take hold only after the economy has recovered on its own. Thus, discretionary fiscal policy aimed at increasing output and employment may end up just fueling inflation. These lags are reasons why policy makers need to be careful with dscretionary fiscal policy.

### THE WALL STREET JOURNAL

**Reading It Right** What's the relevance of the following statement from *The Wall Street Journal:* "Inevitably, there is a big, long lag between the time spending is ordered by Congress and the time spending actually shows up in the economy."

### Problems with Discretionary Fiscal Policy

Hand the following note to a student: "Unemployment has just hit 8 percent. It's time for the government to do something." Have this student write the message on the board. Give the class five minutes to agree on exactly what needs to be done. Don't help them—let them work on their own. They are unlikely to agree in the amount of time provided. Point out that the 535 members of Congress also have trouble agreeing on what should be done when an economic problem needs to be addressed.

### ➤ E-CONOMICS

Direct students to read the passage entitled "Using Technology to Make Economic Forecasts" on page 472.

### Answers to Think Critically

Economic forecasts before computer technology were not nearly as accurate as those after computer technology. Computer technology has allowed economists to handle significantly larger amounts of data, which, in turn, enables them to predict more accurately economic outcomes.

 **CHECKPOINT**

Invite a student to answer the checkpoint that appears on page 472.

### Answer

The various lags involved with discretionary fiscal policy are the recognition lag, the decision-making lag, the implementation lag, and the effectiveness lag.
The recognition lag is the time needed to identify a macroeconomic problem. The decision-making lag is the time needed to decide what to do once the problem has been identified. The implementation lag is the time needed to execute a change in policy. The effectiveness lag is the time needed for changes in policy to affect the economy.

---

## Group Activity ✎

This activity is to be completed outside class, over a week's time. Assign groups of students to meet on their own time to write a single report on issues involving proposed spending changes that are being discussed in Congress. They are to choose one type of spending that they think is most likely to be changed, and explain the reasons for their choice. Once the assignment is given, say nothing more about it. When the assignment is due, ask how many groups completed their work. Ask the groups whether they ran into any of the time lags that occur when discretionary fiscal policy decisions are made. Did they encounter a decision-making lag or an implementation lag? Why does it often take a long time for work to be done when it requires cooperation among many people?

### Fiscal Policy and Aggregate Supply

So far the discussion of fiscal policy has been limited to effects on aggregate demand. Fiscal policy also can affect aggregate supply, although often that effect is unintentional. For example, suppose the government increases unemployment benefits by imposing higher taxes on the employed. This redistributes income from workers to the unemployed. These offsetting effects may leave aggregate demand unchanged.

What about the possible effects of these changes on aggregate supply? Those who receive higher unemployment benefits have less incentive to find work, so they may search at a more leisurely pace. On the other hand, the higher marginal tax rate makes work less attractive. In short, the supply of labor could decrease as a result of offsetting changes in taxes and transfers. A decrease in the supply of labor would decrease aggregate supply, reducing output and employment.

*Both automatic stabilizers, such as unemployment insurance and the progressive income tax, and discretionary fiscal policies, such as changes in tax rates, may affect individual incentives to work, spend, save, and invest, although these effects are usually unintended.* Policy makers should keep these secondary effects in mind when they evaluate fiscal policies.

**CHECKPOINT**
What are the various lags involved with discretionary fiscal policy?

## E-CONOMICS

### Using Technology to Make Economic Forecasts

Predicting economic developments can be as tricky as predicting the weather. It is based on a number of factors and calculations involving current and past economic data. Computer technology has aided economists greatly in their ability to recognize and predict economic trends. One economic forecasting tool using computers is input-output analysis. This method looks at the interdependence of all the various productive sectors in an economy by analyzing each product as both a commodity to be consumed and as an input in the production of other goods. The method is used to predict the total amount of various goods that are affected by a given amount of spending. As an example, economists might be trying to project the future development of the shipping industry. They must figure out the distribution of the total production of ships, broken down into the quantity of ships used in different parts of the economy. The purpose of such a chart is to foresee how a change in one part of the economy would affect other parts of the economy. For example, if the amount of food the United States exported to other countries increased by a certain amount, then the number of ships needed to transport that food would increase as well. Economic forecasters use methods like this to predict "economic ripples" that can have far-reaching effects. However, input-output analysis requires an enormous amount of data from countries throughout the world. Computer programs can help economists quickly compile this data and predict outcomes.

#### Think Critically

How do you think making economic forecasts before computer technology differed from economic forecasting today?

## RETEACH

A change in government spending does not always cause the expected change in aggregate demand or aggregate supply. During the late 1970s, Congress expanded funding for the Comprehensive Employment and Training Act (CETA) by billions of dollars. This program was intended to pay for job training for unemployed workers. The objective was to increase income, demand, and production in the economy. Much of the funding was sent to local governments that sometimes used the money to pay the wages of people who were already working, or to replace current workers with new workers who qualified for training under the CETA program. A large part of these funds was wasted, and aggregate demand and supply grew by much less than had been expected. Can students think of other government programs that were less effective than it was hoped they would be?

# 15.2 Assessment

## Key Concepts

1. Why is the unemployment compensation program an example of an automatic stabilizer for the economy?

2. Inflation often results when the economy is growing rapidly. Why is it politically difficult for Congress to use discretionary fiscal policy by passing tax increases that could slow economic growth and reduce inflation?

3. If the government decided to extend unemployment compensation payments for an extra 13 weeks beyond the 26 that normally are paid, what would happen to the incentive unemployed people have to find work? How might this affect the economy?

4. Why do many economists believe that the decision-making lag is the longest of the lags that reduce the effectiveness of discretionary fiscal policy?

5. Suppose that the federal government borrowed and spent an additional $10 billion to stimulate the economy. Because of this extra government borrowing, interest rates increased by 1 percent on average. How might this increase affect the willingness of people and businesses to borrow and spend? What could this do to the effectiveness of the government's attempt to stimulate the economy?

## Graphing Exercise

6. The so-called *misery index* is found by summing the unemployment rate and the inflation rate by year. Construct a line graph of the misery index based on data in the table. How does the misery index appear to be related to the economic conditions of the country? What would you expect to happen to the misery index if the economy began to grow rapidly?

## Think Critically

7. **History** In 1980 and 1981, there was a deep recession in the U.S. economy. Unemployment exceeded 10 percent. To try to help the economy recover, Congress passed a law in 1982 that increased federal excise taxes on gasoline. The funds collected were intended to create additional jobs when they were spent to repair roads and highways throughout the nation. The tax increase went into effect on April 1, 1983. The first contracts were awarded to construction companies in the fall of that year. Actual construction began early in 1984, when the economy was already well on its way to recovery. Explain how this situation demonstrates a problem with using discretionary fiscal policy.

**Xtra!**
Study Tools
econxtra.swlearning.com

**Inflation, Unemployment, and Misery Index, 1993–2003**

| Year | Unemployment | Inflation | Misery index |
|------|------|------|------|
| 1993 | 6.9% | 2.7% | 9.6% |
| 1994 | 6.1 | 2.7 | 8.6 |
| 1995 | 5.6 | 2.5 | 8.1 |
| 1996 | 5.4 | 3.3 | 8.7 |
| 1997 | 4.9 | 1.7 | 6.6 |
| 1998 | 4.5 | 1.6 | 6.1 |
| 1999 | 4.2 | 2.7 | 6.9 |
| 2000 | 4.0 | 3.4 | 7.4 |
| 2001 | 4.7 | 1.6 | 6.3 |
| 2002 | 5.8 | 2.4 | 8.2 |
| 2003* | 6.1 | 3.6 | 9.7 |

*Projections based on first four months of 2003.

Lesson 15.2 • *Fiscal Policy Reconsidered* 473

---

# 15.2 Assessment

## Key Concepts

1. Answers will vary. Possible answer: When the economy is doing well, few workers are unemployed and so do not apply for compensation. When the economy turns down, more workers become unemployed and receive unemployment compensation payments that allow them to continue to spend. This takes place without the need for further legislation and helps create spending, income, and jobs in the economy.

2. Answers will vary. Possible answer: Politicians never want to be remembered by voters as having supported tax increases. Even when tax increases are clearly needed, politicians would rather wait to support them until after they have been reelected.

3. Answers will vary. Possible answer: The additional weeks of compensation may encourage some unemployed workers to continue to be unemployed. If their benefits were cut off, they might work harder to find employment, and the unemployment rate might fall.

4. Answers will vary. Possible answer: Politicians often disagree with each other because of their political party or interests of their elective districts. Even when decisions are made, the process is likely to be slow and done to try to please many people. This often prevents legislators from taking strong or effective steps.

5. Answers will vary. Possible answer: The higher interest rates could discourage people and businesses from borrowing and spending as much. This could reduce the effectiveness of the additional government spending in stimulating the economy.

## Graphing Exercise

6. Answers will vary. Possible answer: The misery index seems to fall when the economy is growing, while it seems to be higher when the economy is in, or emerging from, a recession. This was the case in 1993 and 2003.

An example of an acceptable graph appears at the bottom of this page.

## Think Critically

7. Answers will vary. Students may point out that time lags kept this discretionary policy from being implemented when it was most needed. By the time additional jobs were actually created, they were no longer needed.

---

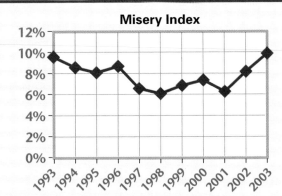

### Misery Index

### Visualizing the Answer— Graphing Exercise

6. The answer includes a graph. Students' graphs should look similar to the one shown here. An Excel spreadsheet containing this graph, along with supporting data, is available on the Instructor's Resource CD.

Lesson 15.2 • *Fiscal Policy Reconsidered* **473**

# movers & shakers

## FOCUS

Ask students whether they believe large businesses are better off than small businesses. Does big business have a downside? Do the students prefer to shop at mega-retailers, such as Wal-Mart or Target, or at a smaller, locally owned stores? What are their reasons for their shopping preferences? If they were starting a business, would they dream of becoming the biggest firm in their market? Do they believe Philip Knight was right to lead NIKE so far? Did he lose anything by his quest?

## TEACH

Instruct students to read the **Movers & Shakers** feature about Philip Knight. Point out that some students may find it helpful to read the article, read the questions at the bottom of the page, and then reread the article.

## ASSESS

Use the questions in Source Reading and Entrepreneurs in Action at the bottom of the profile to assess the students' understanding of this **Movers & Shakers** feature.

### Answers to Source Reading

Answer: Mr. Knight was not afraid to make mistakes, which allowed him to take risks. These risks resulted in his business success.

### Answers to Entrepreneurs in Action

Answers will vary. Possible answer: Some of the choices you will likely encounter in starting your business are when and where to advertise, what products to develop, and knowing into which markets to expand. Two good decisions are to learn from your mistakes and to offer great incentives to keep good employees. Two bad decisions are to expand beyond your means and to exploit your workers.

# movers & shakers

## Philip Knight *Chairman, President, CEO, and Co-Founder, NIKE, Inc.*

Philip Hampson Knight grew up in Portland, Oregon. He attended the University of Oregon, majoring in accounting. Knight was a member of the school's track team— at the time, one of the best college teams in the country. His coach, Bill Bowerman, was always experimenting with running shoes in order to make his team faster. Not happy with the shoes available at that time, Bowerman began making his own shoes. "Since I wasn't the best guy on the team, I was the logical one to test the shoes," Knight explains.

After graduation and a year in the army, Knight enrolled in Stanford University's Graduate School of Business. It was there, as an assignment for one of his business classes, that Knight came up with the idea for Blue Ribbon Sports, later named NIKE. Once up and running, Blue Ribbon Sports operated by selling shoes from a van at high-school track meets and other athletic events. Within a few years, a retail site was secured, and the company was renamed NIKE. A local designer was paid $35 to come up with a logo, and the NIKE "swoosh" was born. The new shoe, with its new logo, debuted at the 1972 U.S. Olympic trials in Eugene, Oregon. The launch was a success. That year, $3.2 million worth of NIKE shoes were sold. Profits doubled each of the next 10 years. In 1980, NIKE passed Adidas to become the industry leader.

Astronomical growth in the 1980s and 1990s was a result of Knight's idea to sign 21-year-old Michael Jordan to endorse a basketball shoe. It wasn't long before Air Jordans were must-have shoes among American youths. Later, athletes including Tiger Woods, Bo Jackson, Gabrielle Reese, and Andre Agassi kept NIKE sneakers in the minds of aspiring athletes, and the company's success continued. When speaking of his company's advertising campaigns, Knight stated, "We didn't invent it [advertising], but we ratcheted it up several notches." The company typically budgets $200 million each year for advertising and celebrity endorsements.

In fiscal year 2003, NIKE—still the world's number-one shoemaker—had sales of $10.7 billion, with net income of just over $1 billion. The company employs 23,300 and manufactures and sells shoes for baseball, cheerleading, golf, volleyball and other sports. The company also sells Cole Haan dress and casual shoes, manufactures a line of athletic apparel and equipment, and operates numerous retail outlets. NIKE products are sold throughout the United States and in 200 other countries. The company's "swoosh" is recognizable today even without the name.

Although shy and aloof, Knight is known as one of the smartest brand builders ever. He inspires employees with the "NIKE Spirit" and motivates them to help take the company to the next level time after time. In addition to his trademark sunglasses—he is rarely seen without them—and wrinkled, casual wardrobe, one of Knight's trademark sayings is: "The trouble in America is not that we are making too many mistakes, but that we are making too few." His belief in making mistakes clearly has served him well.

### SOURCE READING

Knight is fond of saying: "The trouble in America is not that we are making too many mistakes, but that we are making too few." Explain what you think he means by this. How did his belief in making mistakes serve him—and NIKE—well?

### ENTREPRENEURS IN ACTION

Imagine you are an entrepreneur building your own company. What are some of the choices you likely will face in the process of helping your company grow? Explain what you would consider to be two good decisions regarding company growth and two bad decisions regarding company growth.

**474**   **CHAPTER 15**   Fiscal Policy, Deficits, and Debt

## 15.3 Federal Deficits and Federal Debt

### Objectives

> Discuss why federal deficits have been common since the Great Depression.

> Distinguish between crowding out and crowding in.

> Discuss changes in the relative size of federal debt since World War II.

> Explain who bears the burden of the federal debt.

### Overview

When governments spend more than they take in, budget deficits result. These deficits can have their own effect on the economy, beyond the stimulus provided by changes in spending and taxing. These deficits add up to the federal debt, which also can have its own effect on the economy. Policy makers usually focus on the immediate impact of a policy and ignore the long-term effects.

### Key Terms

**crowding out**

**crowding in**

## [ In the News ]

### ● The National Debt Clock

The old saying "time is money" usually refers to someone wasting money by wasting time. The phrase also could be applied to the U.S. National Debt Clock, which literally ticks out how much the U.S. national debt is increasing every second, down to the penny. The clock is located in New York City and was the brainchild of real estate developer Seymour Durst. In 1989, Durst funded the building of the National Debt Clock in Times Square to draw public attention to how much the debt was growing. At the time the clock started, the national debt was increasing by $13,000 per second. By the mid-1990s, the national debt was rising so fast that it crashed the computer used to run the clock. By the end of 1999, however, as budget surpluses were able to help pay down some of the national debt, the clock started to reverse itself. This caused some confusion for observers and led the clock's owners to shut it down on September 7, 2000. At the time it shut down, the clock read, "Our national debt: $5,676,989,904,887. Your family share: $73,733." Less than two years later, however, the debt was rising again, and the National Debt Clock restarted on July 11, 2002, showing a debt of $6,126,597,702,503, or about $66,800 per family.

#### Think About It

Do you think the display of a National Debt Clock is a good idea? Why or why not?

475

### National Content Standards in Economics

A complete list of the NCEE Standards appears on pages xxiv–xxv of this book. The following standards are addressed in Lesson 15.3.

Standard 10: Role of Economic Institutions

Standard 12: Role of Interest Rates

Standard 15: Growth

Standard 20: Monetary and Fiscal Policy

## Budget Deficits

Remind students that the government decision-making process is not guaranteed to make choices that are best for the economy because it may be intended to achieve political objectives instead of economic ones. Politicians are reluctant to increase taxes or cut government programs that could anger their constituents. When tax revenues fall in an economic decline, it is easier for politicians to borrow funds than to accept other alternatives. The fact that the individuals who will ultimately bear the burden of the debt are not current voters is a political advantage of deficit financing.

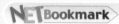

Direct students to **econxtra.swlearning.com**. Remind them to click on the link for Lesson 15.3 to find the appropriate link for the **NET Bookmark** on this page.

### *Think Critically Through Visuals*

Direct students to focus their attention on **Figure 15.4—Federal Deficits and Surpluses as Percent of GDP**. Point out that this graph illustrates the federal deficits and surpluses as a percentage of GDP during the last 70 years.

---

## NETBookmark

The Office of Management and Budget prepares *A Citizen's Guide to the Federal Budget* each year. This publication contains numerous easy-to-read charts and graphs indicating sources of revenue and the types of spending. Access these guides and other budget documents for the current year and previous years through econxtra.swlearning.com. Choose one of the links in the Table of Contents, and write a one-paragraph summary of web page you access.

**econxtra.swlearning.com**

## Budget Deficits

When government spending exceeds government revenue, the result is a *budget deficit*. The federal budget deficit measures the amount by which total federal spending exceeds total federal revenues. The federal government finances a deficit by selling U.S. government securities, such as bonds. People and businesses buy them because the bonds earn interest.

## Federal Deficits Over the Years

Between 1789, when the U.S. Constitution was officially adopted, and 1930, the first full year of the Great Depression, the federal budget was in deficit 33 percent of the time. Federal deficits during that stretch occurred primarily during war years. Because wars involved much personal hardship, public officials were understandably reluctant to increase taxes much to finance war-related spending. After a war, government spending dropped more than government revenue. Thus, deficits arising during a war were largely self-correcting once the war ended.

Since the Great Depression, the federal budget has been in deficit 85 percent of the time. Figure 15.4 shows federal deficits and surpluses as a percentage of GDP during the last 70 years. Unmistakable are the huge deficits during World War II.

The federal budget experienced a surplus from 1998 to 2001. However, before that it had been in deficit every year but one since 1960 and in all but eight years since 1930. The average annual deficit grew from less than 1 percent of GDP in the 1960s to an

---

**Federal Deficits and Surpluses as Percent of GDP**  |  **Figure 15.4**

Between 1934 and 2004, the federal budget has been in deficit 85 percent of the time.

Source: Fiscal-year figures from *Economic Report of the President,* February 2003. Figures for 2003 and 2004 are projections based on the President's 2004 budget proposal and estimates from the Congressional Budget Office.

**476**  **CHAPTER 15**  Fiscal Policy, Deficits, and Debt

---

### *Outside Resources*

**Public Debt** The amount of the federal debt at any given time is available online. Have students view the two web sites mentioned below to get different perspectives on the national debt.
The U.S. National Debt Clock web site at www.brillig.com/debt_clock is privately maintained. In addition to displaying the current amount of the debt, it provides links to recent articles that concern the national debt.
The Bureau of the Public Debt web site at www.publicdebt.treas.gov includes information about the amount of the national debt and a page of frequently asked questions.

average of about 4 percent during the 1980s, during the first half of the 1990s, and in 2003 and 2004.

## Why Is the Budget Usually in a Deficit?

Why has the federal budget been in deficit for all but 12 years since 1930? One obvious reason is that, unlike legislatures in 49 states, Congress is not required to balance the budget. Why does Congress approve budgets with deficits most years?

One widely accepted model of the public sector discussed in the previous chapter argues that elected officials try to maximize their political support. Voters like public spending programs but hate paying taxes. Therefore, spending programs win voters' support and taxes lose it. Public officials try to maximize their political support by spending more than they tax. This results in chronic deficits. Why were deficits more common after the Great Depression? The answer can be traced back to Keynes and his followers, who thought deficits were a justifiable result of fiscal policy. They were less worried about the long-run consequences. As Keynes once said, "In the long run we are all dead."

## The Surplus of 1998–2001

What about the budget surpluses from 1998 to 2001? Where did they come from? Concern about rising deficits during the 1980s led to two tax hikes in the early 1990s. The Republican Congress elected in 1994 imposed more discipline on federal spending. Meanwhile, the economy experienced a healthy recovery resulting from technological innovation, market globalization, and the strongest stock market in history.

As a result of tax increases and a strengthening economy, revenues gushed into Washington, growing an average of 8.3 percent per year between 1993 and 1998. Meanwhile, federal spending was held in check, growing by an average of only 3.2 percent per year. By 1998, that one-two punch

knocked out the federal deficit, a deficit that only six years earlier had reached $290 billion, a record to that point. The federal surplus grew from $69 billion in 1998 to $236 billion in 2000, the highest ever.

The economy entered a recession in March 2001. In the spring of 2001, the newly elected President George W. Bush pushed through an across-the-board tax cut in income tax rates to, in his words, "get the economy moving again." On September 11, 2001, 19 men in four hijacked airplanes ended thousands of lives and squelched chances of a quick rebound from the recession. The attacks grounded commercial flights across the country for weeks, and knocked down the travel industry for months. Stock markets and insurance markets also suffered.

Since peaking in early 2001, job totals fell 2.5 million by May 2003. The stock market went into a three-year funk. As the economy softened, automatic stabilizers reduced federal revenues and increased federal spending. All this fueled the federal deficit, which reached $374 billion by 2003. The federal surpluses seemed at that point like ancient history.

 **CHECKPOINT**
Why have federal deficits been so common since the Great Depression?

## Deficits and Interest Rates

What effect do federal deficits have on interest rates? Recall that interest rates affect investment, a critical component of economic growth. In fact, year-to-year fluctuations in investment are the primary source of shifts in aggregate demand and in GDP. Figure 15.5 compares the percent change in real investment and the percent change in real GDP since 1960. As you can see, investment fluctuates much more than GDP.

### Budget Deficits

Ask students to imagine they are members of Congress, and it has been decided that $10 billion will be spent to rebuild the nation's railroads and stimulate the economy. These funds can be obtained by imposing a new tax on gasoline, cutting spending for highway maintenance, or through borrowing. Which alternative would students choose? How might their choice influence their chance of being reelected next year? Is their choice the best choice for the economy? (If the economy is truly in a recession, borrowing may be a good alternative. If it is not, borrowing is likely to lead to increased interest rates. This might discourage people and businesses from borrowing. An increased debt burden will be borne by future generations.)

 **CHECKPOINT**
Invite a student to answer the checkpoint that appears on page 477.

### Answer

Reasons why federal deficits have been so common since the Great Depression are:

- Congress is not required to balance the budget.
- Elected officials want to maximize the political support of voters by spending more than the tax.
- The Keynesian philosophy that deficits are a justifiable result of fiscal policy is still popular.

Direct students to the Graphing Workshop for Chapter 15 at **econxtra.swlearning.com**. As an enrichment exercise, students may complete **Apply It: Analyzing the Impact of Deficit Spending on Interest Rates**. This enrichment exercise presents concepts more advanced than those discussed in the textbook.

## ENRICH

In the twentieth century, budget surpluses were fairly rare events. The longest period of time during which the federal government had surplus budgets was from 1919 to 1930. Ask students to identify differences in the role of the federal government that made it easier to have a surplus budget in those years than it is today. (At that time, the federal government did not provide social benefits nor did it impose large taxes on most people. Federal spending was largely for road construction, the military, and maintaining the federal government itself. Most people were not significantly affected by federal budgetary decisions. Today, many people rely on federally funded transfer programs and pay significant federal taxes. They are very interested in changes in the federal budget and generally oppose tax increases or spending cuts for programs that serve them.)

## Deficits and Interest Rates

Remind students that at any given time, only so much money is available for loans. If the government borrows large amounts of additional money, less will be available for people and businesses to borrow (assuming nothing else changes). Increased government borrowing is likely to lead to higher interest rates that may crowd others out of the credit market. In other cases, it is possible that additional government spending will improve business conditions and encourage others to borrow and spend additional funds, even if interest rates are higher. This is called crowding in. In either case, additional government borrowing results in higher interest rates.

### Ask the Xpert!

Direct students to **econxtra.swlearning.com** to hear an expert answer the question "What is fiscal policy, and what is it supposed to accomplish?"

### Think Critically Through Visuals

Direct students to focus their attention on **Figure 15.5—Investment Fluctuations**. Point out that this graph compares the percent change in real investment and the percent change in real GDP between 1960 and 2002.

### CHECKPOINT

Invite a student to answer the checkpoint that appears on this page.

### Answer

Crowding out involves private investment that falls when higher government deficits drive up interest rates. Crowding in is when government spending stimulates private investment in an otherwise stagnant economy.

---

**crowding in**
Government spending stimulates private investment in an otherwise stagnant economy

**crowding out**
Private investment falls when higher government deficits drive up interest rates

### Ask the Xpert!

*econxtra.swlearning.com*

*What is fiscal policy, and what is it supposed to accomplish?*

---

## Crowding Out

How do federal deficits affect investment? Here's a way of looking at the question. Were you ever unwilling to go to a particular restaurant because it was too crowded? You simply did not want to put up with the hassle and long wait. You were "crowded out." Some version of this also can result from federal deficits.

The higher the deficit, the more that must be borrowed. This increased demand for borrowed funds drives up the market rate of interest. Higher interest rates discourage, or *crowd out*, some private investment. **Crowding out** occurs when higher government deficits drive up interest rates and thereby reduce private investment. Decreased investment spending reduces the effectiveness of federal deficits that are intended to stimulate aggregate demand.

## Crowding In

Did you ever pass up an unfamiliar restaurant because the place had few customers? If you had seen just a few more customers, you might have stopped in—you might have been willing to "crowd in." Similarly, businesses may hesitate to invest in a seemingly lifeless economy.

If government stimulates a weak economy, the business outlook may improve. As expectations grow more favorable, firms become more willing to invest. This ability of government deficits to stimulate private investment is sometimes called **crowding in**.

### CHECKPOINT
What's the difference between crowding out and crowding in?

## Federal Debt

Federal deficits add up. It took 39 presidents, six wars, the Great Depression, and more than 200 years for the federal debt to reach $1 trillion, as it did in 1981. It took only three presidents and another 15 years for that debt to triple in real terms, as it did by 1996. The federal deficit measures the amount by which annual spending exceeds annual revenue. The *federal debt* measures the accumulation of past deficits, the total amount owed by the federal government. Federal debt adds up all federal deficits and subtracts federal surpluses.

---

**Investment Fluctuations**

**Figure 15.5**

**Investment fluctuates much more from year to year than does GDP.**

Source: U.S. Department of Commerce. Investment and GDP are in real terms—that is, adjusted for changes in the price level.

[Line graph showing Annual percent change (y-axis from -30 to 40) versus years from 1960 to 2002 (x-axis). Two lines plotted: "Investment" (dashed) and "GDP" (solid).]

**478**      **CHAPTER 15** Fiscal Policy, Deficits, and Debt

---

### Economic Headlines

Instruct students to locate an article in a current magazine or newspaper that relates to one of the topics in this lesson. For example, they might find articles about growth in the national debt and how it may affect the economy. Instruct students to read the article, write a brief summary, and include a reference citation. Identify the style you want them to use for the citation.

As an alternative, you might find several articles of interest and provide citations for students to use in locating one of the articles. Direct students to read the article they have chosen, and write a brief explanation of how it relates to this lesson.

## Gross Debt Versus Debt Held by the Public

In talking about the federal debt, economists often distinguish between gross debt and debt held by the public. The gross debt includes U.S. Treasury securities purchased by various federal agencies. Since this is debt the federal government owes to itself, economists often ignore it and focus instead on debt held by the public. Debt held by the public includes debt held by households, firms, non-profit institutions, and foreign entities. As of 2003, gross federal debt totaled $6.8 trillion, and debt held by the public totaled $4.0 trillion. Public debt amounted to about $14,000 per capita.

## Debt Relative to GDP

One way to measure debt over time is relative to the economy's production and income, or GDP. In a sense, GDP shows the economy's ability to carry debt, just as household income shows that family's ability to carry a mortgage.

Figure 15.6 shows federal debt held by the public relative to GDP. The cost of World War II increased the debt to more than 100 percent relative to GDP in 1946. *Despite recent setbacks, the federal debt held by the public relative to GDP dropped nearly two-thirds between 1946 and 2004.*

Note that usual measures of the federal debt do not capture all future liabilities. The Social Security programs and other retirement programs promise benefits that must be paid from taxes or further borrowing.

> **✓ CHECKPOINT**
> What has happened to federal debt levels relative to GDP since World War II?

*Credit card debt accounts for much of the debt held by the public. What types of expenditures does the $14,000 in debt per capita represent?*

## Federal Debt Held by the Public as Percent of GDP, 1940 to 2004 — Figure 15.6

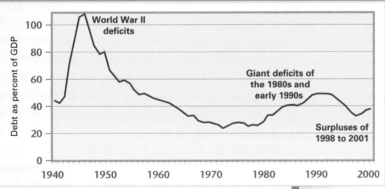

The federal debt held by the public relative to GDP dropped nearly two-thirds between 1946 and 2004.

Source: Fiscal year figures from *Economic Report of the President,* February 2003, Table 79. Figures for 2003 and 2004 are projections.

(Graph labels: World War II deficits; Giant deficits of the 1980s and early 1990s; Surpluses of 1998 to 2001. Y-axis: Debt as percent of GDP, 0 to 100. X-axis: 1940 to 2000.)

## Group Activity

Before class, write the following information on five separate sheets of paper. Organize the class into five groups and have each group choose one piece of paper.

| Group 1 | Group 2 | Group 3 | Group 4 | Group 5 |
|---|---|---|---|---|
| Income $50 | Income $500 | Income $5,000 | Income $50,000 | Income $500,000 |
| Debt $5,000 | Debt $5,000 | Debt $5,000 | Debt $5,000 | Debt $5,000 |

Instruct students to discuss how important the debt is to the group, based on its current income and debt. Following the group discussion, have each group summarize its discussion for the class. Students should realize the size of the debt is less important than the ability to carry the debt. This is true of the federal government as much as it is of individuals.

## TEACH

### Federal Debt

Ask students whether they think borrowing $500 from a parent is different from borrowing $500 from a bank. In both cases, they owe the same amount of money. But when they owe money to a parent, the money they repay remains within the family spending unit. Money they repay to a bank leaves their family spending unit. Tell students they will learn in this lesson that the federal debt is much the same. A significant portion of the federal debt "stays in the family." For example, the largest single holder of the federal debt in 2003 was the Social Security system, which had invested excess tax receipts in federal securities. When these securities are paid off, the money will flow from one part of the government to another. Do students believe this type of debt is as important as debt owed to non-government institutions or to people who live in other countries?

### Think Critically Through Visuals

Direct students to focus their attention on the photograph on this page. Ask for a volunteer to answer the question posed in the caption.

**Answer**

Answers will vary. Possible answers: Households use debt to pay for everything they purchase and their homes, cars, furniture, clothing, and food.

### Think Critically Through Visuals

Direct students to focus their attention on **Figure 15.6—Federal Debt Held by the Public as Percent of GDP, 1940 to 2004**. Point out that the cost of World War II increased the debt to more than 100 percent relative to GDP in 1946.

> **✓ CHECKPOINT**
> Invite a student to answer the checkpoint that appears on this page.

**Answer**

Since 1946, the federal debt held by the public relative to the GDP dropped by nearly two-thirds.

## Economic Impact of the Debt

Remind students that the interest on the national debt has been in the range of $220 to $240 billion per year over the past few years. Roughly 20 percent of this payment is made to people or institutions located in other nations. This $44 to $48 billion leaves the United States and creates purchasing power in other countries. Most economists believe this flow of funds out of the country is a greater concern to the economy of the United States than is the absolute size of the national debt or the amount that is paid to carry it. Interest payments that are made to U.S. institutions or individuals stay within the U.S. economy to increase aggregate demand and encourage production and employment here. Interest payments that leave the country do not increase our aggregate demand or supply.

 Direct students to complete the activity described in the **Investigate Your Local Economy** feature on this page. Suggest that students collect basic demographic information about the adults they interview. This information might include age, occupation, and education level.

### Ethics in Action

Have students work in pairs to discuss the ethical issue featured on page 481, and develop answers to the questions presented.

**Answers to Think Critically**

Answers will vary. Students' opinions should be supported by logical reasons.

### Think Critically Through Visuals

Direct students to focus their attention on the photograph on page 481. Ask for a volunteer to answer the question posed in the caption.

### Answer

Answers will vary. Possible answer: I do not feel it is responsible to pass along our debt to future generations. There is no guarantee that these future generations will benefit from some of the programs that are in place today.

# Economic Impact of the Debt

What is the impact of a large federal debt on the economy?

## Debt and Interest Rates

The federal government seldom pays off any debt. When bonds mature, the federal government simply sells more to pay off maturing bondholders. Nearly half the debt is refinanced every year. With nearly $200 billion in bonds coming due each month, debt service payments are quite sensitive to changes in interest rates. Based on a $4.0 trillion debt held by the public in 2003, a one-percentage point increase in the interest rate raises annual interest costs by about $40 billion.

Interest payments on the federal debt were about 8 percent of the federal budget in 1978. Thanks to record-low interest rates, interest payments in 2003 were also about 8 percent of the federal budget. When interest rates rise from their low levels, so will the cost of servicing the debt.

## Who Bears the Burden of the Debt?

Deficit spending is a way of billing future taxpayers for current spending. The federal debt raises questions about the right of one generation to pass on to the next generation the burden of its borrowing. To what extent do budget deficits shift the burden to future generations?

### We Owe It to Ourselves

It is often argued that the debt is not a burden to future generations because, although future generations must service the debt, those same generations will receive the debt service payments. In that sense, the debt is not a burden on future generations. It's all in the family, so to speak.

### Foreign Ownership of Debt

But the "we-owe-it-to-ourselves" argument does not apply to that portion of the federal debt purchased by foreigners. Foreigners who buy U.S. government bonds forgo present consumption. *As foreigners buy more government bonds, this increases the burden of the debt on future generations because future debt service payments no longer remain in the country.* Foreigners owned about 20 percent of all federal debt in 2003, compared to 14 percent in 1991.

**CHECKPOINT**
Who bears the burden of the federal debt?

Interview three or four adults about the federal budget deficit. Ask if they know the size of the federal deficit. Ask if they think having a budget deficit is a good idea or a bad idea for the economy, and why. Then compare the answers you receive with the answers your classmates receive. Did you uncover any trends? If so, what are they?

### Curriculum Connection—Mathematics

Ask students to calculate how many years it would take to pay off the national debt at a rate of $1,000 per second. Have students look up the national debt or provide the amount for a specific day. The debt amount on December 1, 2003, is used for the example below.

| Hours in a day | 24 | Current debt | $6,914,406,243,287.65 |
|---|---|---|---|
| Minutes in an hour | 60 | Paid off per day | $86,400,000.00 |
| Seconds in an hour | 60 | Days to pay off debt | $80,027.85 |
| Seconds in a day | 86,400 | Days in a year | 365 |
| Paid off per second | $1,000.00 | Years to pay off debt | 219.25 |
| Paid off per day | $86,400,000.00 | | |

# Ethics in Action

**Preventing Deficits from Harming Future Generations** One common concern about deficit spending is that it will place an unfair burden on future generations. One economist argued that people can prevent this from happening by saving more and spending less now. Harvard economist Robert Barro argued that when governments increase deficits, they generally keep taxes low. Eventually, however, taxes on future generations will have to be raised to make up for this deficit. If no one cared about future generations, then adults today would support deficit spending because they would be dead before the tax bills would come due. Barro argued that people concerned about the well-being of their children and grandchildren will offset the future harm of deficits by spending less and saving more today. This saved money will be passed along to their children and grandchildren, who can use it to pay the higher taxes that will come due when they are adults. Many economists disagree that Barro's idea

really works, however. Many point out that during the 1980s, when deficits were very high, people's tendency to save money was very low. Barro's supporters argue that this may have been because people in the 1980s were optimistic about the future growth of the economy and believed that the deficits would be offset by lower government spending, not by future higher taxes. Barro's critics also argue that the growing number of people with no children may be less concerned about the welfare of future generations. Also, his theory assumes a great deal of public knowledge and understanding about the national debt and its effects on the future. One survey found that few adults had any idea about the size of the federal deficit. This would make it very difficult for them to plan ahead and spend with the idea of protecting future generations in mind.

### Think Critically

Do you agree with Barro's supporters or his critics? Explain your reasons.

**Do you think the federal government is acting responsibly in passing debt on to future generations? Why or why not?**

## RETEACH

There was a time when children could inherit their parents' debts as easily as their parents' property. In sixteenth-century England, for example, when a tenant farmer died, his children were expected to pay his debts. If they could not, they were required to remain on the rented land and continue to farm it until they could pay the debts. Thus, debts were sometimes passed from one generation to the next, and to the next, and so on. Ask your students whether they believe the national debt they will inherit is similar to this old English system. Do they see a better way to resolve this situation?

 **CHECKPOINT**
Invite a student to answer the checkpoint that appears on page 480.

### Answer
The domestic portion of the federal debt is not a burden to future generations because, although they must service the debt, they also will receive the debt service payments. However, the burden of federal debt purchased by foreigners does fall on future generations because debt service payments do not remain in the country.

### APPLY
Assign Lesson 15.3 from the Contemporary Economics Workbook.

### *e*-con @pps

Encourage students to apply their knowledge of concepts presented in this lesson as they explore economic news stories, policy debates, and data available at **econxtra.swlearning.com**.

### ASSESS
Assign all or part of Lesson 15.3 Assessment on page 482 as homework or an in-class activity.

### Xtra! Study Tools
Direct students to the online study tools for Lesson 15.3 at **econxtra.swlearning.com**.

### CLOSE
**Revisit** the In the News feature on the first page of the lesson. Ask students to review their preliminary answers and discuss the questions, now that they have completed this lesson.

**Review** the objectives for Lesson 15.3. Students should be able to:
- Discuss why federal deficits have been common since the Great Depression.
- Distinguish between crowding out and crowding in.
- Discuss changes in the relative size of federal debt since World War II.
- Explain who bears the burden of the federal debt.

## Key Concepts

1. Answers will vary. Students may point out that there is nothing to which this debt can be compared. If the amount of GDP for 1930 were provided, then this number would have meaning because there would be a way to measure the nation's ability to carry this debt.

2. Answers will vary. Students may point out that world events caused people to worry about the future and to hesitate to spend or invest, regardless of lower tax rates.

3. Answers will vary. Students may point out that the money used to pay off the bonds held by the Social Security system will come from general tax revenues in the future. This is why some economists believe these bonds represent a financial responsibility for the government, no less than bonds held by the public.

4. Answers will vary. Students may point out that with the $6.8+ trillion debt, a 3 percent increase in rates would cost the federal government as much as $20.4 billion more each year as old bonds matured and new bonds that paid higher rates of interest were sold ($6.8 trillion × 0.03 = $20.4 billion).

## Graphing Exercise

5. Answers will vary. Students may point out that as the people born during the baby boom of 1946–1964 age and retire, the balance in the Social Security Trust Fund will be drawn down as benefits paid exceed tax revenue collected.

   An example of an acceptable graph appears at the bottom of this page.

## Think Critically

6. Answers will vary. Students may point out that the total deficit would grow to $9.14 trillion by 2013. Whether this amount should concern U.S. citizens depends on whether the U.S. GDP has grown as quickly. If it has grown more, the added debt will be easier for the United States to carry. If the GDP has grown less, this debt will represent an increased financial burden for the nation.

Xtra!
Study Tools
econxtra.swlearning.com

## Key Concepts

1. In 1930, the national debt was just over $16.8 billion. Why doesn't this fact provide much information about the size or importance of this debt? What other information would you need in order to evaluate the debt's importance?

2. Why didn't the across-the-board income tax cut of 2001 immediately cause people to spend more and get the economy moving?

3. The Social Security system has invested many billions of dollars by purchasing bonds from the U.S. treasury. Some economists believe this is simply a matter of taking money from one of the government's pockets and putting it in another. Others do not agree. When the Social Security system cashes in its bonds to pay benefits to retired workers in the future, where will the funds come from? Are these bonds really less of a financial responsibility than other bonds held by the public?

4. If interest rates increased by 3 percent across the board, what would happen to interest payments on the debt over a period of several years?

## Graphing Exercise

5. During the 1980s and 1990s, tax payments received by the Social Security system far exceeded the amount paid to beneficiaries. Money that the system accumulated was invested in government bonds and held in the Social Security Trust Fund to be used to make future payments. Use the data in the table to construct a line graph that shows the growth in this trust fund. Why will this trend toward larger balances in the Social Security Trust Fund be reversed in the future?

Social Security Trust Fund Balance, 1980–2000
(in billions of dollars)

| Year | Balance |
| --- | --- |
| 1980 | $ 22.8 |
| 1985 | 35.8 |
| 1990 | 214.2 |
| 1995 | 458.5 |
| 2000 | 931.8 |

## Think Critically

6. **Math** The federal debt was approximately $6.8 trillion dollars in 2003. If this debt grew at a rate of 3 percent per year in each of the following 10 years, how much would the debt total be in 2013? Should such an increase in the debt be a concern for U.S. citizens? Why or why not?

**Social Security Trust Fund Balance**

Billions

$1,000
$800
$600
$400
$200
$0

1980  1985  1990  1995  2000

## Visualizing the Answer— Graphing Exercise

5. The answer includes a graph. Students' graphs should look similar to the one shown here. An Excel spreadsheet containing this graph, along with supporting data, is available on the Instructor's Resource CD.

# Alexander Hamilton
## and the Question of the National Debt

Economic issues played a major role in causing the American Revolution, and the United States emerged from the struggle in poor financial shape. It had fought the war on borrowed money. It stopped paying interest on its bonds. It was behind in paying the army. It also had issued more than $200 million in near worthless money, or "continentals." When representatives from the various states met in Philadelphia during the summer of 1787 to correct these problems, the result was a new constitution. The new U.S. Constitution gave the government powers to tax, borrow, and spend.

President George Washington appointed Alexander Hamilton as the first secretary of the treasury in 1789. Hamilton was not the first choice. Robert Morris, the "financier of the Revolution," turned Washington down and recommended Hamilton. Hamilton realized he needed to establish the country's credit by resolving the problems of the nation's debt. The United States and its credit were held in low esteem, and no one was willing to lend money. Hamilton realized that establishing the nation's credit would set the conditions for its future prosperity and economic success. It also would provide an incentive for individuals and nations to invest in the United States. For Hamilton, the prospect of a federal debt was desirable, as he felt it would bind the moneyed class to the new government. Hamilton had written to Morris, "A national debt, if not excessive, will be to us a national blessing."

Three types of debt arose from the Revolution: (1) federal debt owed to foreigners, (2) federal debt owed to Americans, and (3) state debts. There was no question about paying the foreign debt at face value. Domestic debt had depreciated to about 25 cents on the dollar, but Hamilton proposed to pay it at face value as well. Because many speculators who had purchased the depreciated certificates would stand to profit, some in Congress resisted this solution. They felt it would enrich speculators rather than those who originally had purchased the debt. Despite the opposition, Hamilton's solution prevailed. He proposed to repay the debt by issuing new bonds for the full amount of the old debts. The new debt would be repaid over time from tariff revenues.

Hamilton also proposed that the federal government assume state debts. Much of the debt had been incurred during the Revolution for the benefit of all the states. In addition, wealthy residents held many state bonds. If their investments could be shifted from the states to the federal government, he believed their long-term interests in the nation's success would be ensured. Southern states defeated these proposals four times, putting Hamilton's entire financial plan in danger. It was only when he gained Thomas Jefferson's support by agreeing to locate the capital to the south—in the area of Washington, D.C.—that Hamilton was able to gain enough votes to pass his plan.

Hamilton was successful, and the nation's credit was insured. By 1794, the United States had a high credit rating and its bonds were highly sought.

## THINK CRITICALLY

The perfect solution at one time in history may not be the proper solution in another. Hamilton saw that the national debt could be a positive factor in the nation's economy. How does that differ from attitudes today?

### FOCUS

Ask students whether they have ever borrowed money they felt they should not have to repay. Tell them to imagine they had borrowed $500 from a parent to buy a home computer. Although they use it, everyone else in the household does, too, including the parent who lent them the $500. Still, the parent expects the student to repay the loan. The student knows that the money must be repaid, but he or she really doesn't think it's fair. Ask students why it is important for people to do what they say they will do, even if it seems unjust. If they fail to repay the loan, will they ever be able to borrow from this parent in the future? How does this situation parallel that faced by the U.S. government in the 1790s?

### TEACH

Instruct students to read the **Connect to History** feature and answer the questions.

### ASSESS

Use the questions at the bottom of the page to assess the students' understanding of this feature.

**Answers to Think Critically**

Today, some people believe the national debt can be a positive factor in the economy. Other people are concerned about the burden that will be passed on to future generations.

## Bibliography

Faragher, John Mack, ed. *The American Heritage Encyclopedia of American History*. New York: Henry Holt and Company, 1998.

Gordon, John Steele. *Hamilton's Blessing*. New York: Walker & Company, 1997

Gordon, John Steele. "The Founding Wizard." *American Heritage*, July/August 1990, pp. 41–51.

Spalding, Matthew, ed. *The Founders' Almanac*. Washington, D.C.: The Heritage Foundation, 2002.

## Consider

Ask students to revisit the questions they were asked to consider at the beginning of the chapter. Remind students that they should be able to answer all of the questions after studying Chapter 15.

- What is your normal capacity for academic work, and when do you usually exceed that effort? See page 460—Potential Output.

- If the economy is already operating at full employment, how can it produce more? See page 461—Output Exceeding Potential.

- Can fiscal policy reduce swings in the business cycle? See page 464—The Multiplier Effect.

- Why has the federal budget been in deficit most years? See page 477—Why Is the Budget Usually in a Deficit?

- How is a strong economy like a crowded restaurant? See page 478—Crowding Out.

- What did President George W. Bush mean when he proposed a tax cut to "get the economy moving again"? See page 469—Fiscal Policy Tools.

## Exam*View*

Use Exam*View* to assess students' learning.

- Create a chapter test using questions from the existing test bank.
- Add your own questions to the existing test bank.
- Generate multiple forms of a chapter test.

## Study Skills

Offer the following study skills suggestions for students as they review this chapter.

- Outline the chapter.
- Review Key Terms.
- Review Checkpoints.
- Work in pairs to quiz each other.
- Use Xtra! Study Tools for each lesson.

 Quiz Prep

Direct students to the online quiz preparation for Chapter 15 at **econxtra.swlearning.com**.

---

 **Chapter Assessment**

# Summary

 **15.1** *The Evolution of Fiscal Policy*

**a** Fiscal policy is intended to move the economy toward full employment at its potential output with price stability. It does this primarily by working to shift aggregate demand. The *potential output* is the level of production that that is sustainable in the long run. Some unemployment will occur at the potential output. This level of unemployment is called the *natural rate of unemployment*.

Xtra! Quiz Prep
econxtra.swlearning.com

**b** When output is below its potential, government may use fiscal policy to stimulate production by increasing its spending or cutting taxes. If output exceeds its potential, government may use fiscal policy to reduce production by cutting its spending or increasing taxes.

**c** Before the Great Depression of the 1930s, *classical economists* believed that natural market forces would cause the economy to automatically recover from recessions without government intervention. During the Great Depression, it became apparent the classical economic theory had some problems.

**d** Keynes developed a theory in the 1930s that argued prices, wages, and interest rates were "sticky" and would not quickly fall in a recession to bring about economic growth. Keynes argued that it is the responsibility of the government to get the economy moving again by adjusting government spending and taxes.

**15.2** *Fiscal Policy Reconsidered*

**a** Fiscal policy may either be automatic or *discretionary*. Automatic fiscal policy takes place without passage of new legislation. An example of automatic fiscal policy is the progressive federal income tax. When the economy is in recession, people pay a smaller share of their reduced incomes in tax while in an expansion their greater incomes force them into higher tax brackets.

**b** There are a number of limitations on the effectiveness of fiscal policy. Because fiscal policy is designed to adjust aggregate demand, it is not effective in fighting stagflation, when there is both unemployment and inflation. Time lags that slow the carrying out and impact of fiscal policy reduce its effectiveness.

**c** Changes in aggregate demand that result from fiscal policy decisions may have unforeseen results on aggregate supply. When unemployed workers are provided with additional weeks of unemployment compensation, for example, the result may be that they choose not to look for work. This would reduce production and aggregate supply from what it might have been if they had looked for work aggressively and succeeded in finding it.

**15.3** *Federal Deficits and Federal Debt*

**a** Before the Great Depression, the federal government normally spent only as much money as it collected in taxes, except in time of war. Since the 1930s the government has spent more than it received from taxes in most years. These annual deficits have accumulated over time to create a federal debt that totaled $6.8 trillion by 2003.

**b** In most years in the 1980s and 1990s, the federal deficit averaged about 4 percent of GDP. This trend was reversed between 1998 and 2001, when tax hikes of the early 1990s and reduced spending increases temporarily eliminated the annual deficits. A recession in 2001 triggered automatic stabilizers that increased the federal deficit. Bush's tax cuts to revive the economy also worsened the deficit after 2001.

**c** Deficit spending often has been linked to higher interest rates. When the federal government borrows additional money to fund a deficit, interest rates often have increased. These higher interest rates can discourage borrowing and spending by business and consumers.

**d** Some economists argue that the importance of the federal debt should be evaluated in terms of our nation's ability to carry it.

484     **CHAPTER 15**   Fiscal Policy, Deficits, and Debt

---

**15.1** Assessment

Continued from page 466.

## Think Critically

6. Answers will vary. Possible answer: During World War II, government borrowing and spending increased the total federal debt from less than $50 billion in 1941 to about $280 billion at a time when the total U.S. GDP was only about $213 billion. This enor- mous amount of government spending helped to reduce unemployment to about 2 percent and brought about a growth in production that exceeded 10 percent per year. These events convinced many people that Keynes was right.

# Review Economic Terms

Choose the term that best fits the definition. On separate paper, write the letter of the answer.

1. Private investment falls when higher government deficits drive up interest rates

2. The unemployment rate when the economy is producing its potential level of output

3. Congressional changes in spending or taxing to promote macroeconomic goals

_____ 4. The economy's maximum sustainable output in the long run

_____ 5. The time needed for changes in government policy to affect the economy

_____ 6. A group of laissez-faire economists, who believed that economic downturns were short-run problems that corrected themselves in the long run through natural market forces

_____ 7. The time needed to execute a change in government policy

_____ 8. Matching annual spending with annual revenue, except during war years

_____ 9. The time needed for the government to decide what to do once an economic problem has been identified

10. Any change in fiscal policy affects aggregate demand by more than the original change in spending or taxing

11. Government spending and taxing programs that, year after year, automatically reduce fluctuations in disposable income and thus in consumption over the business cycle

_____ 12. The time needed to identify a macroeconomic problem

_____ 13. Government spending stimulates private investment in an otherwise lifeless economy

a. **annually balanced budget**

b. **automatic stabilizers**

c. **classical economists**

d. **crowding in**

e. **crowding out**

f. **decision-making lag**

g. **discretionary fiscal policy**

h. **effectiveness lag**

i. **implementation lag**

j. **multiplier effect**

k. **natural rate of unemployment**

l. **potential output**

m. **recognition lag**

# Review Economic Concepts

14. An economy's *potential output* is reached

   a. when there is no unemployment.

   b. at the natural rate of unemployment.

   c. when there is only cyclical unemployment.

   d. at the frictional rate of unemployment.

15. **True or False** Output can only exceed the potential rate in the short run.

16. When output is less than the potential rate, there is a(n) __?__ gap in the economy.

17. The *natural rate of unemployment* in the United States is estimated to fall between

   a. 2 and 3 percent.

   b. 3 and 4 percent.

   c. 4 and 5 percent.

   d. 5 and 6 percent.

## Review Economic Terms

1. e. crowding out
2. k. natural rate of unemployment
3. g. discretionary fiscal policy
4. l. potential output
5. h. effectiveness lag
6. c. classical economists
7. i. implementation lag
8. a. annually balanced budget
9. f. decision-making lag
10. j. multiplier effect
11. b. automatic stabilizers
12. m. recognition lag
13. d. crowding in

## Review Economic Concepts

14. b. at the natural rate of unemployment
15. True
16. contractionary
17. c. 4 and 5 percent

## Review Economic Concepts

18. annually balanced
19. True
20. a. unemployment
21. multiplier effect
22. c. More welfare compensation is paid because more people are unemployed in a recession.
23. True
24. b. Congress spends an extra $2 billion to provide jobs for unemployed workers.
25. False. Keynes believed it was necessary for the government to increase fiscal policy to stimulate the economy, even it if meant developing a federal deficit.
26. Stagflation
27. True
28. a. Many workers have been laid off because of a decline in sales.
29. recognition lag
30. d. 1980
31. True
32. True
33. d. all of the above

## Apply Economic Concepts

34. Answers will vary. Students may point out that this expansion of CETA was an example of discretionary fiscal policy because it required new legislation to allocate additional funds to the program. Students should discover that relatively few of these workers were able to find permanent employment. Most of their jobs lasted only as long as CETA funding continued. Some economists argued that the program made it more difficult for businesses to hire workers because CETA jobs paid higher wages.

35. Answers will vary. Students may point out that workers have many fixed expenses they must pay. They are hesitant to accept pay cuts that could lower their standard of living or push them into personal bankruptcy, particularly if they have a union contract that entitles them to a higher wage rate. This will cause them to resist wage reductions, making wage rates "sticky" when the economy turns down.

18. *Classical economists* believed that the federal government should always have a(n) __?__ budget.

19. **True or False** *Classical economists* believed that in a recession prices, wages, and interest rates would fall, and this would bring the recession to an end.

20. Keynes developed a theory that was intended to address which problem during the Great Depression?

    a. unemployment

    b. inflation

    c. government deficits

    d. high interest rates

21. Keynes believed that the __?__ would cause an increase in government spending or reduction in taxes to have a larger impact on aggregate demand.

22. Which of the following is an automatic stabilizer for the economy?

    a. Congress decides to increase welfare benefits during a recession.

    b. An increase in income tax rates is passed by Congress during a period of inflation.

    c. More welfare compensation is paid because more people are unemployed in a recession.

    d. Congress decides to require people to work until they are 68 years old to collect their full Social Security benefit.

23. **True or False** According to Keynes, prices and wages are quite inflexible—they are "sticky."

24. Which of the following is an example of *discretionary fiscal policy*?

    a. Income tax payments grow during an economic expansion.

    b. Congress spends an extra $2 billion to provide jobs for unemployed workers.

    c. Fewer workers receive unemployment compensation payments in an expansion.

    d. More people apply for and receive welfare benefits in a recession.

25. **True or False** Keynes believed that it was necessary for the government to balance its budget in every year.

26. __?__ takes place when there are both high rates of inflation and high unemployment.

27. **True or False** Because of lags, it is difficult for the government to implement *discretionary fiscal policy* effectively.

28. Which of the following situations would indicate that the economy is below its *potential output*?

    a. Many workers have been laid off because of a decline in sales.

    b. A large number of construction workers are unemployed each February.

    c. In June, many graduating students spend several months looking for a job.

    d. There are many people who need to be trained to qualify for job openings.

29. The time that it takes the government to realize that there is a problem in the economy is called the __?__

30. The federal government accumulated most of its debt during the 20 years following

    a. 1920.

    b. 1940.

    c. 1960.

    d. 1980.

31. **True or False** Between 1946 and 2002, the federal debt held by the public as a percentage of GDP declined by about 10 percent.

32. **True or False** *Crowding out* refers to people and businesses choosing to borrow and spend less money because of higher interest rates that result from greater federal borrowing.

33. Gross debt refers to debt the federal government owes to itself, whereas debt held by the public refers to debt held by

    a. households and firms.

    b. non-profit institutions.

    c. foreign entities.

    d. all of the above.

486      **CHAPTER 15**  Fiscal Policy, Deficits, and Debt

# Apply Economic Concepts

**34. Evaluate Government Policy** In the late 1970s, President Jimmy Carter and Congress expanded spending under the Comprehensive Employment and Training Act (CETA) to provide temporary employment to as many as 500,000 unemployed workers. Most of this money was made available to state and local governments that were supposed to hire and train workers so that they would eventually be able to find permanent employment working for private industry. Explain why this was an example of discretionary fiscal policy. How successful do you imagine this program was? Investigate the program at your library or online to find out whether your expectations were correct.

**35. "Sticky" Wages** Imagine that you are 20 years older and married with two children. You have purchased a car, a house, and furniture on credit. Most of your income goes to pay bills. You work for a business where you are a member of a union. Your contract states that you will be paid $13.50 per hour. Yesterday your employer announced that its sales have declined 30 percent and that if workers don't agree to a 15 percent pay cut, the business will lay off 10 percent of its employees and may fail in the next year. Would you agree to the pay cut? Explain your answer. Why are wages "sticky"?

**36. Calculate the Impact of the Multiplier Effect** In 1993, President Bill Clinton asked Congress to approve an additional $15 billion in spending to repair and upgrade the nation's highways. In addition to improving the nation's roads, President Clinton argued that this spending would increase output and employment in the economy. Assume that each person who received any of this extra spending as income would have spent 80 percent of it. Describe how the multiplier effect would have increased the total increase in spending to far more than the original $15 billion President Clinton wanted to spend. What does this show about the importance of changes in government spending?

**37. Explain the Benefits of Unemployment Compensation** When there is a downturn in the economy, unemployment grows and more workers receive unemployment compensation. How do these payments benefit workers who have not lost their jobs?

**38. Evaluate a Proposed Constitutional Amendment** Members of Congress have from time to time argued in favor of a constitutional amendment that would require the federal government to maintain a balanced budget except in times of war. Discuss whether you think this would be a good idea. Be sure to explain the reasons for your point of view.

**39. Sharpen Your Life Skills: Graphs of Interest on the National Debt** Interest on the national debt is an important part of the federal budget. The amount of this cost depends on the size of the federal debt and the interest rate the government pays on the debt. Use the data in the table to construct three pie graphs showing the part of the federal budget that was devoted to paying interest in 1950, 1980, and 2000. Why did this proportion of the budget first decline and then grow?

**Payments on the National Debt as a Percent of the Federal Budget 1950, 1980, and 2000**

| Year | Interest Payment as a Percent of the Federal Budget |
|------|-----------------------------------------------------|
| 1950 | 14.51% |
| 1980 | 8.89% |
| 2000 | 12.47% |

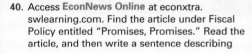
econxtra.swlearning.com

**40. Access EconNews Online** at econxtra. swlearning.com. Find the article under Fiscal Policy entitled "Promises, Promises." Read the article, and then write a sentence describing what the article says is the problem with Social Security. What did President Bush propose as a solution to this problem?

---

**Interest Payment as a Percent of the Federal Budget 1950**
Interest 14.51%
Other Spending 85.49%

**Interest Payment as a Percent of the Federal Budget 1980**
Interest 8.89%
Other Spending 91.11%

**Interest Payment as a Percent of the Federal Budget 2000**
Interest 12.47%
Other Spending 87.53%

## Visualizing the Answer—Apply Economic Concepts

**39.** The answer includes three pie graphs. Students' graphs should look similar to those shown here. An Excel spreadsheet containing graphs along with supporting data is available on the Instructor's Resource CD.

---

## Apply Economic Concepts

**36.** Answers will vary. Students may point out that in the first round, income and spending resulting from the extra federal spending would have totaled $12 billion, creating an equal amount of additional income. This income would have led to another $9.6 billion in income and spending, then $7.68 billion, and so on. This shows that changes in government spending (or taxing) have much larger impacts on aggregate demand in the economy.

**37.** Answers will vary. Students may point out that unemployment compensation payments allow laid-off workers to continue to spend. This helps maintain aggregate demand that allows many employed workers to keep their jobs. Without unemployment compensation, unemployed workers could not continue to spend, aggregate demand would fall even more, and more workers would lose their jobs.

**38.** Answers will vary. Students may point out that forcing the federal government to always have a balanced budget would prevent Congress and the president from implementing fiscal policy in times of recession or inflation. Further, if the economy fell into a recession, government tax revenue would decline. This type of amendment would force the government to cut its spending, making the situation even worse.

**39.** Answers will vary. Students may point out that the debt was very large, relative to the federal budget in 1950 because of the debt that was accumulated during World War II. By 1980, the economy and the budget had grown so much that the interest payment was a smaller proportion of the total. By 2000, the debt had again increased rapidly while the budget had grown more slowly. As a result, the interest payment was a larger part of the total budget.

**e-con @pps**

**40.** Over the next 20 years, as baby boomers retire, there will be fewer workers for each Social Security recipient, and tax receipts will fall. This will cause the Social Security program to operate at a deficit. President Bush proposed not raising taxes or lowering benefits to solve the problem. He believed that economic growth would solve the problem.

**LESSON 16.1** *Origins of Money:* This lesson traces the evolution from barter to money and describes the three functions of money. The properties of ideal commodity money are identified.

**LESSON 16.2** *Origins of Banking and the Federal Reserve System:* This lesson describes the earliest banks and how they operated. It also describes modern depository institutions. The history and purpose of the Federal Reserve System is described.

**LESSON 16.3** *Money, Near Money, and Credit Cards:* This lesson includes both the narrow and broad definitions of money. It explains M1, M2, and M3.

### Consider

Ask students to consider the questions posed on this page as they study Chapter 16. After studying all three lessons, students should be able to answer the questions. The content related to each question can be found on the pages indicated below.

- Why are you willing to exchange a piece of paper bearing Alexander Hamilton's portrait and the number 10 in each corner for a pepperoni pizza? See page 490—Three Functions of Money.
- Why is paper money more efficient than gold coins? See page 490—Medium of Exchange.
- Why was a Montana bank willing to cash a check written on a clean but frayed pair of underpants? See page 497—Bank Checks.
- How do banks create money? See page 497—Bank Notes.
- When were thousands of different currencies circulating in the U.S. economy? See page 504—Connect to History.
- Why is there so much fascination with money, anyway? See page 490—Medium of Exchange.

# 16 Money and Banking

Origins of Money **16.1**

Origins of Banking and the Federal Reserve System **16.2**

Money, Near Money, and Credit Cards **16.3**

### Consider

Why are you willing to exchange a piece of paper bearing Alexander Hamilton's portrait and the number 10 in each corner for a pepperoni pizza?

Why is paper money more efficient than gold coins?

Why was a Montana bank willing to cash a check written on a clean but frayed pair of underpants?

How do banks create money?

When were thousands of different currencies circulating in the U.S. economy?

Why is there so much fascination with money, anyway?

© Getty Images/PhotoDisc

**POINT YOUR BROWSER**

> *econxtra.swlearning.com*

**POINT YOUR BROWSER**

Remind students that they can find additional resources for this chapter at **econxtra.swlearning.com**.

Xtra! Study Tools

Net Bookmarks

Xtra! Quiz Prep

econ@pps

Ask the Xpert!

*Teaching Resources for Chapter 16*

- Activities and Projects Masters
- Spanish Resources
- Econ Connection Interactive Tutorial CD
- **Exam***View*® CD
- Workbook Teacher's Edition
- Chapter Test Teacher's Edition
- NCEE Standards and Correlation

- Personal Finance Guide
- Social Studies Skills Review
- Instructor's Resource CD
  - PowerPoint Presentations
  - Lesson Plans
  - Video Discussion Guide
  - Answers to Graphing Exercises
- **econxtra.swlearning.com**

## 16.1 Origins of Money

## Objectives

› Trace the evolution from barter to money.

› Describe the three functions of money.

› Identify the properties of ideal commodity money.

## Overview

The word *money* comes from the name of the goddess in whose temple Rome's money was coined. Money has come to symbolize all personal and business finance. You can read *Money* magazine and the "Money" section of *USA Today*. You can watch TV shows such as *Moneyline* and visit hundreds of web sites about money, such as the web site of the federal agency that prints money (www.moneyfactory.com). With money, you can express your preferences—after all, money talks. When it talks, it says a lot, as in "Put your money where your mouth is" and "Show me the money."

## Key Terms

medium of exchange

commodity money

## [ In the News ]

### ● The Price of Admission to the Barter

Can you imagine Kevin Spacey, Meg Ryan, and Quentin Tarantino walking around with signs reading "Will work for food"? Well, many famous actors, actresses, and directors did just that during the Great Depression at the Barter Theatre in Abingdon, Virginia. Created in 1933 under the Depression-era "Will Work for Food" program, the Barter was founded by a troupe of unemployed actors who headed south from New York to offer live theater in exchange for produce. With an original admission price equivalent to 35 cents in barter, the first ticket was purchased with a pig. Community members, including a local barber, provided services as well in return for tickets. Tradition has it that the first season ended with a net profit of $4.35 and a total weight gain among the players of some 300 pounds. Today, cash generally has replaced produce as the medium of exchange at the Barter. Nonetheless, in a recent season, non-perishable food items were accepted as payment of admission for several performances and donated to a local food bank.

### Think About It

Why was barter originally used at the Barter Theatre? Why do you think cash eventually replaced barter as the main admission medium?

◄ | ►

489

## National Content Standards in Economics

A complete list of the NCEE Standards appears on pages xxiv–xxv of this book. The following standards are addressed in Lesson 16.1.

Standard 4: Role of Incentives

Standard 5: Gain from Trade

Standard 6: Specialization and Trade

Standard 10: Role of Economic Institutions

Standard 11: Role of Money

## The Evolution of Money

Remind students that it can be difficult to trade goods they own or services they can provide for other goods or services they want. In order to do this, a condition called a double coincidence of wants must exist. This condition exists when two parties want what each other has and values them equally. Then, they can simply trade what they have, and both will gain. In the real world, this does not happen often. Even when people want to trade or barter items, it is unlikely that they will value them equally. Suppose one of your students owns a bicycle and another owns a CD player. They would like to trade these items, but they both agree that the bicycle is worth at least twice as much as the CD player. How can they complete the trade? Unless the owner of the CD player has something else to trade that will make up for the difference in value, the trade is not likely to be completed. The use of money can eliminate this problem.

### TEAM WORK

Organize students into pairs. Instruct students to complete the **Team Work** activity shown on this page. Set a timer for five minutes. When the timer goes off, invite students to compare their results with those of other students.

### CHECKPOINT

Invite a student to answer the checkpoint that appears on this page.

### Answer

Money evolved from the high transaction costs of the barter system. In the barter system, traders began to accept certain goods because other people readily accepted the goods, so they could be held for exchange. As one good became generally accepted in return for all other goods, that good began to function as money.

---

# The Evolution of Money

In the beginning, there was no money. The earliest families were self-sufficient. Each produced all it consumed and consumed all it produced, so there was no need for exchange. Without exchange, there was no need for money. When specialization first emerged, as some families farmed the land and others went hunting, farmers and hunters began to trade. Thus, the specialization of labor resulted in exchange. The kinds of goods people traded were limited enough that they easily could exchange their products directly for other products. This is a system called *barter,* which you read about in Chapter 2.

## Problems with Barter

As long as specialization was limited to just a few goods, mutually beneficial trades were relatively easy to discover. As the economy developed, however, greater specialization increased the kinds of goods produced. As the variety of goods increased, so did the difficulty of finding mutually beneficial trades. For example, a heart surgeon in a barter economy would have to find people willing to accept a heart operation in exchange for what the surgeon wanted. Barterers also had to agree on an exchange rate. Negotiating such exchanges every time the surgeon

### TEAM WORK

Working with a partner, role-play a barter situation. One partner will have a portable radio to barter. The other student will barter another item or items for the radio. After completing your role-play barter, compare your results with those of other students. Were the items bartered for the radios of comparable value?

---

needed to buy something would prove difficult and time consuming. *Greater specialization increased the transaction costs of barter.*

A huge difference in the values of the units to be exchanged also made barter difficult. For example, suppose a hunter wanted to buy a home that exchanged for 2,000 hides. A hunter would be hard-pressed to find a home seller in need of that many hides.

### The Birth of Money

*The high transaction costs of barter gave birth to money.* Nobody actually recorded the emergence of money, so we can only speculate about how it developed. Through barter experience, traders may have found that certain goods always had ready buyers. If a trader could not find a good that he or she desired, some good with a ready market could be accepted instead.

Thus, traders began to accept certain goods not for personal use but because the goods were readily accepted by others and so could be held for exchange later. For example, corn might become accepted because traders knew that corn was always in demand. As one good became generally accepted in return for all other goods, that good began to function as money. *Money* is anything that is widely accepted in exchange for goods and services.

### CHECKPOINT

How did money evolve from barter?

# Three Functions of Money

Money fulfills three important functions: it is a *medium of exchange,* a *unit of account,* and a *store of value.*

### Medium of Exchange

If a society, by luck or by design, can find one good that everyone will accept in exchange for whatever is sold,

---

*Outside Resources*

**Barter Web Sites** Thousands of web sites on the Internet offer to help people or businesses trade goods or services. Their main advertising point is that they will help people preserve cash that they can then use for other purposes. Ask students to search the Internet and investigate several of these sites, using the keyword *barter*. One site you can suggest is www.web-barter.com. Invite students to share their findings during a class discussion. Ask what limitations still exist on the barter process, even when online trading takes place. (You still need to find someone who has what you want and wants what you have.)

traders can save time, disappointment, and sheer aggravation. Suppose corn plays this role—a role that clearly goes beyond its role as food. Corn becomes a medium of exchange because it is accepted in exchange by all buyers and sellers, whether or not they want corn to eat. A **medium of exchange** is anything that is generally accepted in payment for goods and services sold. The person who accepts corn in exchange for some product believes corn can be used later to purchase whatever is desired.

In this example, corn is both a *commodity* and *money*, so corn is called **commodity money**. The earliest money was commodity money. Gold and silver have served as money for at least 4,000 years. Cattle were used as money, first by the Greeks, and then by the Romans. In fact, the word *pecuniary* (meaning "of or relating to money") derives from the Latin word for cattle, *pecus*. Salt also served as money. Roman soldiers received part of their pay in salt. The salt portion was called the *salarium*, the origin of the word *salary*.

Commodity money used at various times included wampum (polished shells strung together) and tobacco in colonial America, tea pressed into small cakes in Russia, and palm dates in North Africa.

### Unit of Account

As one commodity, such as corn, became widely accepted, it also served as a *unit of account*, a standard on which to base prices. The price of shoes or pots or hides could be measured in bushels of corn. Thus, corn became a common denominator, a yardstick, for measuring the value of all goods and services. Rather than having to determine the exchange rate between each good and every other good, as was the case in a barter economy, buyers and sellers could price everything using a common measure, such as corn.

### Store of Value

Because people do not want to buy something every time they sell something, the purchasing power acquired

**Ask the Xpert!**
econxtra.swlearning.com

*What are the functions of money?*

***medium of exchange***
Anything generally accepted by all parties in payment for goods or services

***commodity money***
Anything that serves both as money and as a commodity, such as gold

© Getty Images/PhotoDisc

**Why were cattle, salt, and corn all useful as commodity money?**

---

## TEACH

### Three Functions of Money

Money carries out three functions in the economy. It serves as a medium of exchange, a unit of account, and a store of value. Show your class a $10 bill. Ask students whether if they would be willing to help you sort books after school in exchange for the bill. Many students will be willing to trade their labor for the money. Then ask them why they are willing to accept your money for their labor. Why does it have value? How is it serving as a medium of exchange?

## Ask the Xpert!

Direct students to **econxtra.swlearning.com** to hear an expert answer the question "What are the functions of money?"

### *Think Critically Through Visuals*

Direct students to focus their attention on the photographs on this page. Ask for a volunteer to answer the question posed in the caption.

#### Answer

Answers will vary. Possible answer: Cattle, salt, and corn were all useful as commodity money because they were accepted in exchange by all buyers and sellers.

### ✓ CHECKPOINT

Invite a student to answer the checkpoint that appears on page 492.

#### Answer

Money functions as a medium of exchange, which is anything generally accepted by all parties in payment for goods or services; a unit of account, which is a standard on which to base prices; and a store of value, which is something that retains purchasing power over time.

---

## ENRICH

During the American Civil War, the Confederacy attempted to pay the expenses of the war by printing money. Between 1862 and 1864, more than 1.5 billion Confederate dollars were placed in circulation. When it became apparent that the South would lose the war, these dollars became worthless. Ask students to explain why Confederate dollars ceased to function as money in that economy. (When people realized that Confederate dollars would not be backed by a functioning government after the Civil War, they stopped accepting them as a medium of exchange. With no value, these dollars could not be used as a unit of account. And, they could not be a store of value when they had no value to store.)

## Commodity Money

Before there was either paper money or coins, people often used products, or commodities, that could hold a stable value over time. In the United States in the late 1700s, whiskey often was used this way. It could be distilled from grain and stored or shipped relatively easily. It had a value that could last for years and was recognized even by people who had no interest in drinking it. Someone always was willing to trade something else of value for the whiskey. Even the federal government recognized the value of whiskey when it imposed a special tax on its production. This tax led to the "Whiskey Rebellion" in 1794.

### Think Critically Through Visuals

Direct students to focus their attention on **Figure 16.1—Qualities of the Ideal Money** on page 493. Invite students to explain each quality of the ideal money.

through a sale must somehow be preserved. Money serves as a *store of value* when it retains purchasing power over time. The better it preserves its purchasing power, the better money serves as a store of value.

To understand the store-of-value function of money, consider the distinction between a stock and a flow. A *stock* is an amount measured at a particular point in time, such as the amount of food in your refrigerator this morning, or the amount of money you have with you right now. In contrast, a *flow* is an amount received or expended within a period of time, such as the calories you consume per day, or the income you earn per week.

Income has little meaning unless the period is specified. For example, you would not know whether to be impressed that a friend earns $300 unless you know whether this is earnings per week, per day, or per hour. Don't confuse money with income. *Money* is a stock measure, and *income* is a flow measure.

**✓ CHECKPOINT**
What are three functions of money?

# Commodity Money

The introduction of commodity money reduced the transaction costs of exchange compared with barter. Commodity money does involve some transaction costs, however.

## Limitations of Commodity Money

*The ideal money is durable, portable, divisible, of uniform quality, has a low opportunity cost, does not fluctuate wildly in value, and is in limited supply.* The ideals are brought to life in Figure 16.1. As you will see, most commodity money falls short of these ideals.

**492**    **CHAPTER 16**    Money and Banking

### Durable
If the commodity money is perishable, as is corn, it must be properly stored or its quality deteriorates. Even then, it won't last long. The ideal money is *durable*.

### Portable
If the commodity money is bulky, exchanges for major purchases can become unwieldy. For example, if a new home cost 5,000 bushels of corn, many cartloads of corn would be needed to purchase that home. The ideal money is *portable*.

### Divisible
Some commodity money is not easily divisible into smaller units. For example, when cattle served as money, any price involving a fraction of a cow posed an exchange problem. The ideal money is *divisible*.

### Uniform Quality
If commodity money like corn is valued equally in exchange, regardless of quality, people will keep the best corn and trade away the rest. Over time, the quality remaining in circulation deteriorates and becomes less acceptable. The ideal money is of *uniform quality*.

### Low Opportunity Cost
Commodity money usually ties up valuable resources, so it has a relatively high opportunity cost compared with, say, paper money. For example, corn that is used for money cannot at the same time be used as food. The ideal money has a *low opportunity cost*.

### Supply or Demand Must Not Fluctuate Erratically
The supply and demand of commodity money determine the prices of all other goods. A record harvest would increase the supply of corn. An increase in the popularity of corn as food would increase the demand for corn. Each would alter the price level measured in corn. Erratic fluctuations in the supply or demand for corn limit its usefulness as money, particularly as a unit of account and as a store of value.

## Qualities of the Ideal Money

Figure **16.1**

The ideal money is durable, portable, divisible, of uniform quality, has a low opportunity cost, does not fluctuate wildly in value, and is in limited supply.

Durable

Portable

Divisible

Uniform Quality

Low Opportunity Cost

Supply or Demand Must Not Fluctuate Erratically

Limited Supply

---

The supply or demand for the ideal money *should not fluctuate wildly.*

### Limited Supply

Because the value of money depends on its limited supply, anything that can be gathered or produced easily would not serve well as commodity money. For example, tree leaves or common rocks would not serve well as commodity money. The ideal money should be in *limited supply.*

### Coins

Measuring a unit of commodity money often was quite natural, as in a bushel of corn or a head of cattle. When rock salt served as money, it was cut into bricks. Because salt was usually of consistent quality, a trader could simply count the bricks to determine the amount of money. However, when silver and gold were used as money, both their quantity and quality were open to question. When these precious

Lesson 16.1 • *Origins of Money* **493**

---

---

## *Curriculum Connection—Mathematics*

Gold is sometimes thought of as the ultimate store of value. For generations, nations defined the value of their paper money in terms of gold. Still, gold has its disadvantages. In 1930, a twenty-dollar gold piece weighed approximately 0.667 ounces. At that weight, how much would a $1 million payment made in gold pieces weigh? Was gold truly portable? Why are paper money or checks a better alternative to gold in making large transactions? ($1 million worth of $20 gold pieces would weigh 2,084.4 pounds. That's more than a ton of gold to make the $1 million payment. A check could transfer the same value and weigh less than 1 ounce.)

Assign Lesson 16.1 from the Contemporary Economics Workbook.

## e-con @pps

Encourage students to apply their knowledge of concepts presented in this lesson as they explore economic news stories, policy debates, and data available at **econxtra.swlearning.com**. A sampling of the titles for this lesson appears below.

### EconNews

- Making It Tough on Counterfeiters
- The Midas Factor

Assign all or part of Lesson 16.1 Assessment on page 495 as homework or an in-class activity.

## Xtra! Study Tools

Direct students to the online study tools for Lesson 16.1 at **econxtra.swlearning.com**.

**Revisit** the In the News feature on the first page of the lesson. Ask students to review their preliminary answers and discuss the questions, now that they have completed this lesson.

**Review** the objectives for Lesson 16.1. Students should be able to:

- Trace the evolution from barter to money.
- Describe the three functions of money.
- Identify the properties of ideal commodity money.

## NETBookmark

Access the web site for the Identity Theft Resource Center through econxtra.swlearning.com. Spend about five minutes reading the various web pages on the site. Then write down five things you and your family can do to avoid becoming a victim of identity theft.

**econxtra.swlearning.com**

metals were combined with cheaper metals, their quality lessened. Thus, the quantity and the quality of the metal had to be determined with each exchange.

This quality-control problem was solved by coining silver and gold. *Coinage determined both the amount and quality of the metal.* The earliest known coins appeared in the seventh century B.C. in Asia Minor to assist sea trade. The use of coins allowed payment by count rather than by weight. Coins were attractive because they were durable and easy to carry. They also contained precious metals, so they were intrinsically valuable. The table on which money was counted during this era came to be called the *counter*, a term still used today.

Originally, the power to coin was vested in the feudal lord, or *seignior*. If the exchange value of the coin exceeded the cost of making it, minting coins became a source of revenue to the seignior. Revenue earned from coinage is called *seigniorage* (pronounced "seen´-your-edge").

*Token money* is money whose exchange value exceeds the cost of production. Coins and paper money now in circulation in the United States are token money. For example, a quarter (a 25-cent coin) costs the U.S. Mint only about 4 cents to make. Coin production alone nets the federal government more than $500 million per year in seigniorage. Paper money is a far greater source of seigniorage, as you will learn later.

### ✓ CHECKPOINT
What seven properties would the ideal commodity money exhibit?

## Ethics in Action

**Identity Theft—Revisited** People who steal the identities of others basically have one motive—that is, to steal money. This crime can be carried out in a variety of ways. One common means is someone pulling the mail from your unlocked mailbox and sending in for a credit card in your name to be sent to a "new" address. You are eventually sued for nonpayment of the bills that result. Your credit standing may suffer, perhaps permanently. According to the FTC, more than 10 million instances of such identify theft occurred during a recent year. Much of the increase in these numbers is due to the use of the Internet and fraudulent phone solicitations. What's to be done? One avenue of approach for the victims is to contact the Identity Theft Resource Center

(ITRC), a nationally recognized business operated by the Foley family of San Diego, California. The Foleys feel a moral duty to assist those who call or read the warnings posted on their web site. They have organized former victims into a volunteer support and legislative lobbying network. The Foleys also serve as a resource for legislation intended to curtail this "fastest-growing crime in the United States."

### Think Critically

According to the ITRC web site, "the burden of proving innocence rests on the shoulders of the victim." Why do you think this is so? What can you do to keep your identity from being stolen? How can you help others from being victimized?

**494**     CHAPTER 16 Money and Banking

Paper money has the advantage of being relatively inexpensive to print and put in circulation. Unfortunately, it does not last forever. A typical $1 bill can be expected to last from six to eight months before it needs to be replaced. It may cost only a few pennies to print a new bill, but over time, this cost adds up. Coins, on the other hand, last for many years. What does this have to do with why the U.S. government has repeatedly tried to replace the $1 bill with a $1 coin? Why have Americans resisted these efforts in most cases? (The government is convinced that it would cost less to use $1 coins in the long run, even if they cost a little more to make in the first place.)

## Key Concepts

1. Why could it be difficult for you to exchange your collection of 500 CDs for a good-quality used car in a world with no money?

2. Why have wheat and corn been used as commodity money in the past while strawberries and lettuce have not?

3. On the Pacific island of Yap, commodity money took the form of donut-shaped pieces of stone that could weigh one ton or more. In what ways did these stones fall short of being ideal forms of money?

4. At times in history the value of the gold or silver in coins has been greater than the face value of the coins themselves. What did this give people an incentive to do? How would this have affected the economy?

5. What would happen if there were more than one type of commodity money in use—one that people trusted to hold its value and one that they did not? If you had some of both types of money, which would you spend and which would you save? How would this affect the economy?

Xtra!
Study Tools
econxtra.swlearning.com

## Graphing Exercise

6. Fred has an electric saw he would like to trade for a tire for his boat trailer. Mary has a tire for a boat trailer that she would be willing to trade for an electric lawn mower. Rachel has an electric lawn mower she would like to trade for a portable TV. Tony has a portable TV he would be willing to trade for an electric saw. Draw a chart that shows the trades that must take place for each of these people to obtain the product he or she wants. Explain why barter is not an efficient way to carry out complicated transactions.

## Think Critically

7. **History** When gold and silver coins were the primary type of money in circulation, merchants often weighed the coins before accepting them. Why do you think they did this? What problem of using gold or silver coins as money does this situation demonstrate?

8. **English** You probably have either read or seen a televison production of *A Christmas Carol,* a short novel written by Charles Dickens, published in 1843. In his book, Dickens told the story of Ebenezer Scrooge, a miser who accumulated wealth more for the sake of having money than to be able to use it to buy goods or services. Scrooge was regarded by all who knew him as a sour old man who hated everything about Christmas. His lack of charity kept even the poorest of the poor from asking him for help. However, after being visited by the ghosts of Christmas Past, Christmas Present, and Christmas Yet to Come, Scrooge came to view his wealth in a different way. Write an essay in which you identify and explain Scrooge's original point of view about the three functions of money (medium of exchange, unit of account, and store of value). How did the the three Christmas ghosts change his perspective on money? If you have never read this publication, it can be found in almost every library or online, and it is only 124 pages long.

Lesson 16.1 • *Origins of Money* **495**

## Key Concepts

1. Possible answer: It would be difficult and time consuming to locate someone who owns a good-quality used car and is willing to trade it for 500 CDs.

2. Possible answer: Strawberries and lettuce are not durable and therefore are not good stores of value.

3. Possible answer: These stones were neither portable nor divisible.

4. Possible answer: People could melt the coins and sell the metal. This would reduce the amount of money in the economy.

5. Possible answer: People would spend the money they did not trust and save the money they did trust. Transaction would be difficult to complete because people would be trying to spend money with doubtful value.

## Graphing Exercise

6. Possible answer: (1) Fred trades his saw for Tony's portable TV. (2) Mary trades her tire for the portable TV. (3) Rachel trades her electric lawn mower for the portable TV. Organizing these trades will be complicated, and it assumes each person values each item equally. If these people do not place equal values on these items, the exchanges may become impossible.

   A chart diagramming the transactions appears at the bottom of this page.

## Think Critically

7. Possible answer: Merchants weighed the coins to make sure they were getting the appropriate amount of the precious metal. For example, people might reduce the value of coins by shaving small slivers of metal from the coins to sell.

8. Possible answer: At first, Scrooge saw money as only a unit of account. Although his money could have been regarded as a store of value, he had no intention of spending it. After the ghosts of Christmas visited him, he saw that by spending money, he could bring joy and happiness to those who had little wealth of their own, and to himself by sharing in the benefits that his money could buy. Using money as a medium of exchange then became the most important purpose of his wealth.

## Visualizing the Answer— Graphing Exercise

6. The answer includes a diagram. Students' diagrams will vary. This is an example of an acceptable diagram.

## FOCUS

###  16.2 Origins of Banking and the Federal Reserve System

Remind students that banks are businesses that are designed to earn a profit by providing a service to savers and borrowers. They improve the working of the economy by facilitating the flow of funds from people and institutions that save to other people and institutions that want to borrow. For this process to work effectively, the people involved must be confident that the financial transactions are being carried out in an honest way. The Federal Reserve System works to provide this assurance and therefore helps the economy function more efficiently.

### Objectives

Remind students to read the lesson objectives to help focus their attention before reading the lesson.

### Key Terms

Direct students to look up key terms in a business or economics dictionary. Some students will find it helpful to read another definition. In addition to a definition, many entries will include a brief explanation and an example.

### [ In the News ]

Instruct students to read the passage and write down their answers. Point out that their answers might change after they finish studying Lesson 16.2.

### Answers to Think About It

Answers will vary. Possible answer: If all paper currencies were replaced by precious metals like gold or silver, there would be a probable shortage of these precious metals, and there would not be enough currency to go around.

### Visual Presentation

Use the PowerPoint presentation on the Instructor's Resource CD as an adjunct to your lecture. The presentation also can be used for review.

## Objectives

> Describe how the earliest banks made loans.

> Based on whom they lend to, identify two types of depository institutions.

> Explain when and why the Federal Reserve System was created.

## Overview

The word *bank* comes from the Italian word for bench, *banca*. Italian moneychangers originally conducted their business on benches. Banking spread from Italy to England, where London goldsmiths offered people "safekeeping" for their gold, or money. When people needed to make purchases, they would visit the goldsmith to withdraw some money. Deposits by some people tended to offset withdrawals by others, so the amount of money in the goldsmith's vault remained relatively constant over time. Goldsmiths found they could earn interest by lending some of these idle deposits. Today's banks still earn a profit by lending some of the money deposited with them.

## Key Terms

**check**

**fractional reserve banking system**

**representative money**

**fiat money**

**commercial banks**

**Federal Reserve System (the Fed)**

**reserves**

**discount rate**

**Federal Open Market Committee (FOMC)**

**open-market operations**

## [ In the News ]

### ● Will Gold Return as a World Currency?

After three quarters of a century without it, the Muslim world and its bankers are considering creating a currency of their own to rival the dollar and the euro. The currency would be in the form of the gold *dinar,* a coin that had been used for almost 1,500 years but then dropped from circulation in 1924. National paper currencies would still be allowed. However, the central banks of the various Muslim countries on the gold standard would settle the differences in their trade accounts by shifting gold from the debtor to the creditor country's account in a bank. Currently such settling of accounts is done in either dollars or euros. The return to gold is being advocated by many countries that believe the United States has an unfair advantage when the dollar is used for such purposes. The change also may protect against problems like the 1997 currency crisis that swept Asia, seemingly as a result of currency speculation. The potential for such speculation would be reduced greatly by tying paper currencies to something with real value—like gold. Paper currency has value only if its users believe it will continue to be accepted for trade in goods and services.

### Think About It

What practical problems might occur if all paper currencies were replaced with precious metals like gold and silver?

496

### *National Content Standards in Economics*

A complete list of the NCEE Standards appears on pages xxiv–xxv of this book. The following standards are addressed in Lesson 16.2.

Standard 4: Role of Incentives

Standard 10: Role of Economic Institutions

Standard 11: Role of Money

Standard 12: Role of Interest Rates

Standard 16: Role of Government

Standard 20: Monetary and Fiscal Policy

# The Earliest Banks

Keeping money, such as gold coins, on deposit with a goldsmith was safer than carrying it around or leaving it at home, where it could be easily stolen. Still, visiting the goldsmith every time one needed money was a nuisance. For example, a farmer might visit the goldsmith to withdraw enough gold to buy a horse. The farmer would then pay the horse trader, who would promptly deposit the receipts with the goldsmith. Thus, money made a round trip from goldsmith to farmer to horse trader, back to goldsmith.

## Bank Checks

Depositors eventually grew tired of visiting the goldsmith every time they needed cash. They began writing notes instructing the goldsmith to pay someone, such as the horse trader, a given amount from the depositor's account. This payment amounted to moving gold from one stack (the farmer's) to another (the horse trader's). These written instructions to the goldsmith were the first bank checks. A **check** is a written order for the bank to pay money from amounts deposited.

Checks have since become official-looking instruction forms. However, they need not be, as evidenced by the actions of a Montana man who paid his speeding fine by writing a payment instruction on a clean but frayed pair of underpants. The Western Federal Savings and Loan of Missoula cashed the check.

## Bank Loans

By combining the ideas of cash loans and checks, the goldsmith soon discovered how to make loans by check. Rather than lend idle cash, the goldsmith could simply create a checking account for the borrower. *The goldsmith could extend a loan by creating an account against which the borrower could write checks. In this way goldsmiths, or banks, were able to create a medium of exchange—to*

*"create money."* This money, based only on an entry in the bank's ledger, was accepted because of the public's confidence that the bank would honor these checks.

The total claims against the bank consisted of claims by people who had deposited their gold plus claims by people for whom the bank had created deposits. So both groups were depositors. Because the claims by those with deposits at the bank exceeded the value of gold on reserve, this was the beginning of a **fractional reserve banking system**. In this system, the goldsmith's reserves amounted to just a fraction of the claims by depositors.

The *reserve ratio* measures bank reserves as a share of deposits. For example, if the goldsmith had gold reserves valued at $40,000 but deposits totaling $100,000, the reserve ratio would be 40 percent.

## Bank Notes

Another way early banks could create money was by issuing bank notes. *Bank notes* were pieces of paper promising the bearer a specific amount of gold or silver when the notes were redeemed at the issuing bank. In London, goldsmiths introduced bank notes about the same time they introduced checks. *Checks could be redeemed for gold only if endorsed by the payee. Bank notes, however, could be redeemed for gold by anyone who presented them to the issuing bank.*

A bank note was "as good as gold," because the bearer could redeem it for gold. In fact, this paper money was more convenient than gold because it was more portable. Bank notes that exchanged for a specific commodity, such as gold, were called **representative money**. The paper money *represented* gold in the bank's vault. Initially, these promises to pay were issued by banks. Over time, governments took a larger role in printing and circulating bank notes.

## Fiat Money

Once representative money became widely accepted, governments began issuing **fiat money** (pronounced "fee´at"). Fiat money is not redeemable

---

**fractional reserve banking system**
Only a portion of bank deposits is backed by reserves

**check**
A written order instructing the bank to pay someone from an amount deposited

**representative money**
Bank notes that exchange for a specific commodity, such as gold

**fiat money**
Money not redeemable for anything of intrinsic value; declared money by government decree

---

---

### The Earliest Banks

Explain that the government did not effectively regulate early banks. Although many were run in an honest and responsible way, some were not. During much of the early nineteenth century, there was not enough gold to coin money to meet the needs of the economy. To deal with this shortage, many banks printed bank notes that they promised to redeem for gold or silver at some time in the future. These notes circulated as money as long as people trusted the banks that had issued them. Unfortunately, some banks issued many more notes than they had gold or silver to back. As a result, many bank notes were of doubtful value and could not serve the functions of money in the economy—mediums of exchange, units of account, or stores of value. After the Civil War, the government began to regulate banks more carefully and created new types of money that replaced the private bank notes. Banks were required to operate under a fractional reserve system, and Treasury notes that were backed by federal securities were placed in circulation. These steps strengthened the banking system in the United States but could not prevent the panic in 1907, which lead to the creation of the Federal Reserve System in 1913.

### CHECKPOINT

Invite a student to answer the checkpoint that appears on page 498.

### Answer

The earliest banks made loans by creating an account against which a borrower could write checks, much the same way as it is done today.

---

## Outside Resources

**Federal Reserve System** The Fed web site at www.federalreserve.gov provides a brief history of the Federal Reserve System and describes its organization and functions within the economy. Direct students to visit this web site and create a 10-point bulleted list describing the contents of the site.

## Depository Institutions

There are several types of depository institutions in the United States, including commercial banks, saving banks, saving and loan associations, and credit unions. Although most of these institutions are quite similar, they were fairly different when they were first created. These institutions all share at least one essential function in the economy—they accept deposits from savers and help move these funds to people and businesses that want to borrow.

### *Think Critically Through Visuals*

Direct students to focus their attention on the photograph on this page. Ask students to think of other images that could be used to illustrate the role of economic institutions in their lives.

### NCEE Standard 10: Role of Economic Institutions

Institutions evolve in market economies to help individuals and groups accomplish their goals. Banks, labor unions, corporations, legal systems, and not-for-profit organizations are examples of important institutions. A different kind of institution—clearly defined and enforced property rights—is essential to a market economy.

## E-CONOMICS

Direct students to read the passage entitled "Internet Banking: Full Service or Self-Help?" on page 499.

### Think Critically

Other services could be fraud alerts, transfers between accounts, stock market updates, detailed statement updates, and automatically filled-out loan applications.

---

for anything of intrinsic value, such as silver or gold. Fiat money is money because the government says it is. People came to accept fiat money because they believed that others would accept it as well. You can think of fiat money as mere paper money. The currency issued by the U.S government and nearly all other governments throughout world today is fiat money.

A well-regulated system of fiat money is more efficient than commodity money or even representative money. Fiat money requires only some paper and a printing press. (Both $1 notes and $100 notes cost about 5 cents each to print). Commodity money and representative money, however, tie up more valuable resources, such as gold.

**commercial banks**
Depository institutions that make loans primarily to businesses

### CHECKPOINT
How did the earliest banks make loans?

**Main Idea**
Role of Economic Institutions

Banks evolved from London goldsmiths into a wide variety of institutions that help individuals and groups accomplish their financial goals. What are the two broad classifications of depository institutions?

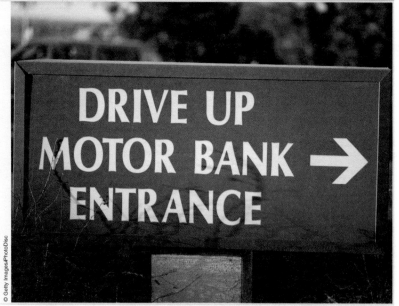

© Getty Images/PhotoDisc

**498**    CHAPTER 16   Money and Banking

---

## Depository Institutions

Banks evolved from London goldsmiths into a wide variety of institutions that respond to the economy's demand for financial services. *Depository institutions* accept deposits from the public and make loans from these deposits. These institutions, modern-day versions of the London goldsmith, are classified broadly into commercial banks and thrift institutions.

### Commercial Banks

Commercial banks are the oldest, largest, and most diversified of depository institutions. They are called **commercial banks** because historically they lent primarily to *commercial* ventures, or businesses, rather than to households. There are about 8,000 commercial banks in the United States, holding more than two-thirds of all

---

Savings and loan associations (S&Ls) were once quite different from commercial banks. They were created to serve the needs of small savers and people who wanted to borrow to purchase homes. Before the 1980s, they were not allowed to make consumer or commercial loans. However, during that decade, S&Ls found themselves paying high interest rates for deposits and receiving low interest rates from fixed rate mortgages. In an effort to help S&Ls, Congress passed laws during the 1980s that allowed them to do most of the same things commercial banks were allowed to do. This change came too late for many S&Ls that failed during the 1980s and were eventually closed or merged with other banking institutions.

# E-CONOMICS

## Internet Banking: Full Service or Self-Help?

Consumers would be well advised to comparison shop before choosing an Internet bank. A recent study indicated that Internet banking service providers know that their users often do not have a chance to compare services and ease of use before setting up their accounts. As a result, some banks offer only the bare necessities, such as account history statements and fund transfers between accounts. However, the top sites in the survey were found to offer much more. For example, those on the cutting edge provide the customer not only with bill-payment services but also with a system of account alerts to warn the depositor of upcoming financial deadlines, loan deals, and potential overdrafts. Other features typically offered at no additional charge include online statements, automatically filled-out loan applications, and document image archives so you can download a copy of that disputed check. In short, consumers can receive a lot of enhancements that both aid and protect them—if they do their homework.

### Think Critically

Can you think of some other services that banks might offer online? Would the services mentioned above make a difference to you in choosing an online bank? Why or why not?

---

bank deposits. Until 1980, commercial banks were the only depository institutions that offered demand deposits, or checking accounts. *Demand deposits* are so named because a depositor with such an account can write a check *demanding* those deposits.

### Thrifts

*Thrift institutions,* or *thrifts,* include savings and loan associations, mutual savings banks, and credit unions. Historically, savings and loan associations and mutual savings banks specialized in making home mortgage loans. Credit unions, which tend to be small, account for most thrifts. They extend loans only to their "members" to finance homes or other major consumer purchases, such as new cars.

### Dual Banking System

Before 1863, commercial banks in the United States were chartered, or authorized, by the states in which they operated, so they were called *state banks.* These banks, like the English gold-smiths, issued bank notes. Thousands of different notes circulated at the same time, and nearly all were redeemable for gold.

The National Banking Act of 1863 and its later amendments created a new system of federally chartered banks

Research a depository institution in your area to learn something about its history. When was it established, and by whom? In which category of depository institution does it fit now? Write a one-page report explaining your findings.

---

### Depository Institutions

Choose three students to help with this demonstration. Give one student a piece of paper that is labeled $1,000. Tell the class that the paper represents money this student has saved. Tell the second student that he would like to borrow $1,000 to buy a new oven for a restaurant he owns. The second student and the first student do not know each other and have no idea whether they are trustworthy or honorable people. The third student represents a bank. This person will accept deposits and make loans. She is specially skilled and qualified to evaluate credit risks and a borrower's character. Ask the class to discuss how this third student can help funds flow from the saver to the borrower and therefore allow the economy to work better.

### *Investigate Your Local Economy*

Suggest that students contact the depository institution directly to learn about the history of the institution. You also can suggest contacting the local historical society. Consider allowing students to work in pairs.

 **CHECKPOINT**

Invite a student to answer the checkpoint that appears on page 500.

### Answer

The two types of depository institutions are commercial banks, which make loans primarily to businesses, and thrift institutions, which specialize in mortgage loans.

---

## *Group Activity*

Organize students into small groups. Have each group find the current mortgage rates for several lenders. This information is available in the Sunday edition of many newspapers and online at bank and realtor web sites. Have students determine the monthly payments and total interest cost of loans for several rates, and terms for a $100,000 home with a $25,000 down payment. Ask them to report their findings in a table. Encourage students to use online calculators to determine payments and interest costs. Calculators are available at many bank and realtor sites, as well as at www.interest.com. A sample table appears below.

| Loan Amount | Rate | Years | Monthly Payment | Total Interest Cost |
|---|---|---|---|---|
| $75,000 | 6 | 30 | $449.66 | $86,880.51 |
| $75,000 | 5 | 30 | $402.62 | $69,940.05 |
| $75,000 | 5 | 20 | $444.97 | $43,791.49 |
| $75,000 | 4 | 20 | $454.49 | $34,075.86 |

## The Federal Reserve System

Point out that the Federal Reserve System is much like a bank for bankers. It stands ready to lend money to commercial banks that are in need of cash and oversees banks to assure the public that banks make responsible decisions. Although individuals do not deal with the Fed directly, the economy—and therefore their financial well-being—are closely tied to the policies and decisions of the Fed.

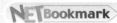

Direct students to **econxtra.swlearning.com**. Remind them to click on the link for Lesson 16.2 to find the appropriate link for the NET Bookmark on page 501.

### Answer

Answers will vary. Possible answer: The Federal Reserve Bank of New York is the only regional bank that buys and sells U.S. Treasury securities, carries out foreign exchange market intervention, examines the U.S. operations of foreign banks, and offers banking and financial services to foreign central banks, foreign governments, and international official institutions. In addition to these activities, the New York Fed operation has two other unique aspects. It is where most Fedwire transfers originate, and the New York Fed's president is the only regional Bank president with a permanent vote on the Federal Open Market Committee.

### Think Critically Through Visuals

Direct students to focus their attention on **Figure 16.2—The Twelve Federal Reserve Districts** on page 501. Ask for a volunteer to answer the question posed in the caption.

### Answer

Answers will vary, depending on the location of your school. Point out that the districts cross state lines and that some states fall into more than one district. Suggest that students visit the Federal Reserve web site at www.federalreserve.gov to see an interactive map with links to the district web sites.

---

called *national banks*. Only national banks were authorized to issue notes and were regulated by the Office of the Comptroller of the Currency, part of the U.S. Treasury. The state banks survived by substituting checks for notes. To this day, the United States has a *dual banking system* consisting of both state banks and national banks.

### CHECKPOINT
Based on whom they lend to, what are the two types of depository institutions?

## The Federal Reserve System

During the nineteenth century, the economy experienced a number of panic "runs" on banks by depositors seeking to withdraw their funds. A panic was usually set off by the failure of some prominent bank. As depositors became alarmed, they tried to withdraw their money. But they couldn't because each bank held only a fraction of its deposits as reserves, using the rest to earn interest, as in making loans.

### Birth of the Federal Reserve System

The failure of a large New York City bank set off the Panic of 1907. During this banking calamity, thousands of depositors lost their savings and many businesses failed. The situation so aroused public wrath that Congress began developing what would become the **Federal Reserve System**, or **the Fed** for short. The Fed was established in 1913 as the central bank and monetary authority of the United States.

By that time nearly all industrialized countries had established central banks, such as the Bundesbank in Germany, the Bank of Japan, and the Bank of England. The American public's suspicion of monopolies initially led to the

**Federal Reserve System (Fed)**

Established in 1913 as the central bank and monetary authority of the United States

**reserves**

Cash that banks have on hand in their vaults or on deposit with the Federal Reserve

---

establishment of 12 separate banks in 12 Federal Reserve districts around the country. The banks were named after the cities in which they were located—the Federal Reserve Banks of Boston, New York, Chicago, San Francisco, and so on, as shown in Figure 16.2. Later legislation passed during the Great Depression left the 12 Reserve Banks in place but centralized the power of the Federal Reserve System with a Board of Governors in Washington.

All national banks became members of the Federal Reserve System and were thus subject to new regulations. For state banks, membership was voluntary. Most state banks did not join the Federal Reserve System because they did not want to face tighter regulations.

### Powers of the Federal Reserve System

The founding legislation directed the Federal Reserve Board of Governors "to exercise general supervision" over the Federal Reserve System to ensure sufficient money and credit in the banking system. The power to issue bank notes was taken away from national banks and turned over to the Federal Reserve Banks. (Take a look at paper currency and you will read "FEDERAL RESERVE NOTE" across the top.) These notes actually are printed by the U.S. Bureau of Printing and Engraving, which is part of the U.S. Treasury. The Treasury prints the notes, but the Fed has responsibility for putting them into circulation.

Federal Reserve Banks do not deal with the public directly. Each may be thought of as a bankers' bank. Reserve Banks hold deposits for member banks, just as commercial banks and thrifts hold deposits for the public. The name "Reserve Bank" comes from the responsibility to hold member-bank *reserves* on deposit.

**Reserves** consist of cash that banks have on hand in their vaults or on deposit with Reserve Banks. By holding reserves of member banks, a Reserve Bank can clear a check written by a depositor at one bank, such as Citibank, and deposited in another bank, such as your bank. This check-clearance process

**500**     **CHAPTER 16**   Money and Banking

is, on a larger scale, much like the goldsmith's moving gold from the farmer's pile to the horse trader's pile.

Reserve Banks also extend loans to member banks. The interest rate charged for these loans is called the **discount rate**. By making loans to banks, the Fed can increase reserves in the banking system.

## Directing Monetary Policy

The Federal Reserve's Board of Governors is responsible for setting and carrying out the nation's monetary policy. *Monetary policy,* as you will recall, is the regulation of the economy's money supply and interest rates to promote macroeconomic objectives such as full employment, price stability, and economic growth.

The Board of Governors consists of seven members appointed by the president and confirmed by the Senate. Each governor serves one 14-year nonrenewable term, with one member appointed every two years. One is also appointed to chair the Board of Governors for a four-year renewable term. Board members tend to be economists. In 2003, six of the seven Governors, including Chairman Alan Greenspan, held Ph.D.s in economics.

For an online introduction to the Federal Reserve System, access the New York Federal Reserve Bank web site through econxtra.swlearning.com. This site provides a very readable overview of the Fed's structure and operations. Read the article under "About the Fed." Then make a list of activities that sets the New York Federal Reserve Bank apart from the other district banks in the system.

**econxtra.swlearning.com**

Board membership is relatively stable because a new U.S. president can be sure of appointing or reappointing only two members in a presidential term. *The Board structure is designed to insulate monetary authorities from pressure by elected officials.*

## Federal Open Market Committee

Originally, the power of the Federal Reserve System was vested in each of the 12 Reserve Banks. Later reforms established the **Federal Open Market Committee (FOMC)** to consolidate decisions regarding the most important

**discount rate**
Interest rate the Fed charges banks that borrow reserves

**Federal Open Market Committee (FOMC)**
Twelve-member group that makes decisions about open-market operations

---

**The Twelve Federal Reserve Districts**

**Figure 16.2**

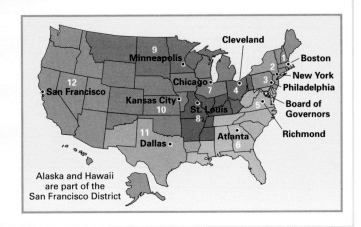

The twelve Federal Reserve districts are named after the cities in which they are located. Which district are you in?
Source: Federal Reserve Board.

Alaska and Hawaii are part of the San Francisco District

---

## Curriculum Connection—Government

In the past 50 years, there have been only six chairmen of the Fed's Board of Governors. Direct students to choose one of these people to investigate. What qualifications did this person bring with him to the office? What did he accomplish as chairman? What issues did he deal with? The names and the years each served as chairman are shown below.

Thomas B. McCabe (1948–51)

William Martin, Jr. (1951–70)

Arthur F. Burns (1970–78)

G. William Miller (1978–79)

Paul A. Volcker (1979–87)

Alan Greenspan (1987–2004)

---

## TEACH (continued)

### The Federal Reserve System

Choose three students to help with this demonstration. Student 1 represents the Federal Reserve System, Student 2 represents ABC Commercial Bank, and Student 3 represents XYZ, Inc. The ABC Commercial Bank has extended a line of credit for $10 million to XYZ, Inc. This means XYZ can borrow up to $10 million at any time with no warning. Tell Student 3 that XYZ has decided to invest $10 million and will use the line of credit to obtain the needed funds. Ask Student 2 where ABC Commercial Bank will get the $10 million to lend XYZ, and what interest rate ABC will pay its lender. (Student 2 should borrow the money from Student 1 at the discount rate.) Ask Student 2 what interest rate ABC will charge XYZ. (XYZ will pay the prime interest rate when it borrows against this line of credit.) Ask Student 1 why the prime interest rate is normally about 2 to 3 percent higher than the discount rate. (The difference is where the bank earns its profit. In reality, banks borrow from each other more often than they borrow from the Fed.)

### *Think Critically Through Visuals*

Direct students to focus their attention on the photograph on page 502. Ask students to explain what FOMC stands for and describe the main function of the FOMC. (The Federal Open Market Committee makes decisions about buying or selling U.S. government securities to influence the money supply and interest rate in the economy.)

### *Think Critically Through Visuals*

Direct students to focus their attention on **Figure 16.3—Organization Chart for the Federal Reserve System** on page 502. Point out that although the President of the United States appoints members of the Board of Governors, any one President has limited influence because each member's term is 14 years.

Explain that it is possible for someone to serve more than 14 years if that person is first appointed to fill an unexpired term and then appointed to serve a full term. For example, Alan Greenspan became a member of the board in 1987 and was appointed to a full term in 1992.

## CHECKPOINT

Invite a student to answer the checkpoint that appears on page 502.

### Answer

The Federal Reserve Bank was established in 1913 to serve as the central bank and monetary authority of the United States. The Federal Bank ensures that there is sufficient money and credit in the banking system.

## APPLY

Assign Lesson 16.2 from the Contemporary Economics Workbook.

## e-con @pps

Encourage students to apply their knowledge of concepts presented in this lesson as they explore economic news stories, policy debates, and data available at **econxtra.swlearning.com**.

## ASSESS

Assign all or part of Lesson 16.2 Assessment on page 503 as homework or an in-class activity.

## Xtra! Study Tools

Direct students to the online study tools for Lesson 16.2 at **econxtra.swlearning.com**.

## CLOSE

**Revisit** the In the News feature on the first page of the lesson. Ask students to review their preliminary answers and discuss the questions, now that they have completed this lesson.

**Review** the objectives for Lesson 16.2. Students should be able to:

- Describe how the earliest banks made loans.
- Based on whom they lend to, identify two types of depository institutions.
- Explain when and why the Federal Reserve System was created.

**open-market operations**

Buying or selling U.S. government securities as a way of regulating the money supply

© Getty Images/PhotoDisc

The FOMC is required to meet at least four times each year in Washington, D.C. What tool of monetary policy is this group responsible for implementing?

tool of monetary policy—open-market operations. **Open-market operations** consist of buying or selling U.S. government securities to influence the money supply and interest rates in the economy.

The FOMC consists of the seven Board Governors plus 5 of the 12 presidents of the Reserve Banks. The chair of the Board of Governors heads the FOMC. The organizational structure of the Federal Reserve System as it now stands is presented in Figure 16.3. The FOMC and, less significantly, the Federal Advisory Committee advise the Board of Governors. The Federal Advisory Committee consists of one commercial banker from each of the 12 Reserve Bank districts.

## CHECKPOINT

When and why was the Federal Reserve System created?

**Organization Chart for the Federal Reserve System**

**Figure 16.3**

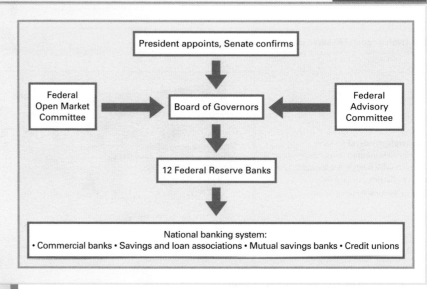

The Federal Reserve's Board of Governors is responsible for setting and carrying out the nation's monetary policy.

President appoints, Senate confirms

Federal Open Market Committee → Board of Governors ← Federal Advisory Committee

12 Federal Reserve Banks

National banking system:
• Commercial banks • Savings and loan associations • Mutual savings banks • Credit unions

**502** CHAPTER 16 Money and Banking

## RETEACH

The chairman of the Federal Reserve's Board of Governors is required to appear before committees of both houses of Congress to testify at least two times each year. The chairman's testimony most often deals with the Fed's understanding of trends in the economy and the general direction that the Fed's monetary policy will push the economy in the future. It almost never includes specific information about what the Fed will do or when it will do it. Ask students why the Fed's chairman is usually rather vague when he makes public statements. (If he is too specific, his statements may cause people and businesses to alter their plans, which could affect the economy. If everyone knows what the Fed is about to do, it comes as no surprise when the Fed does it. Then, there is no reaction to the Fed policy.)

## Key Concepts

1. How would you feel about taking $10,000 in cash to an automobile dealership to purchase a used car? Why might you prefer to complete this type of transaction with a bank check instead?

2. Why are banks able to keep only 10 percent of checking deposits on reserve and still be reasonably sure that they will be able to pay all checks presented for payment?

3. Why are you willing to accept Federal Reserve Notes (fiat money) in payment for your labor? Remember, these notes are backed by nothing other than the government's statement that they are money.

4. Why is it important to the economy that people who save and deposit money in banks can be sure that they will be able to withdraw their savings at anytime in the future without suffering a loss?

5. How may banks obtain extra cash on short notice if the need arises?

## Graphing Exercise

6. Although there were more than 8,000 commercial banks in the United States at the beginning of the twenty-first century, most of these banks were relatively small. Most of the business in the banking industry was dominated by a few large banks. Use data in the table to construct a double bar graph that shows the number of commercial banks of different sizes and the amount of assets held by each-size group in 2001. Do you think the smaller banks could compete successfully with the larger banks? Why might some of these banks merge in the future?

**Xtra!**
Study Tools
econxtra.swlearning.com

**Commercial Banks by Asset Size, 2001**

| Asset Size of Banks | Number of Banks in Group | Total Assets for Group in Billions of Dollars |
|---|---|---|
| Less than $5.0 million | 30 | $ 0.1 |
| $5.0 – $9.9 million | 98 | $ 0.8 |
| $10.0 – $24.9 million | 746 | $ 13.6 |
| $25.0 – $49.9 million | 1,548 | $ 58.2 |
| $50.0 – $99.9 million | 2,062 | $ 148.8 |
| $100.0 – $499.9 million | 2,861 | $ 592.0 |
| $500.0 – $999.9 million | 335 | $ 227.6 |
| $1.0 – $2.9 billion | 219 | $ 362.8 |
| $3.0 billion and more | 181 | $5,165.4 |

Source: *Statistical Abstract of the United States,* 2002, p. 722.

## Think Critically

7. **Government** Investigate the Banking Act of 1935 to find out how the creation of the Board of Governors changed the nature of the Federal Reserve System. Why do you think the government was willing to concentrate so much economic power in the hands of only seven people?

**Commercial Banks by Asset Size, 2001**

Less than $5 million
$5 – $9.9 million
$10 – $24.9 million
$25 – $49.9 million
$50 – $99.9 million
$100 – $499.9 million
$500 – $999.9 million
$1 – $2.9 billion
$3 billion and more

Number of Banks in Group
in Billions of Dollars

0   1,000  2,000  3,000  4,000  5,000

### Visualizing the Answer— Graphing Exercise

6. The answer includes a graph. Students' graphs should look similar to the one shown here. An Excel spreadsheet containing this graph, along with supporting data, is available on the Instructor's Resource CD.

---

## Key Concepts

1. Answers will vary. Possible answer: Carrying a large amount of cash can be risky; it could be lost or stolen. Using a bank check can solve these problems. If lost or stolen, a check cannot legally be cashed by anyone other than the payee. A check also provides positive proof that a payment has been made.

2. Answers will vary. Possible answer: In addition to paying all checks presented for payment, banks also receive deposits. On any given day, the flow of funds in and out of banks is likely to be about equal. The 10-percent reserve will more than cover any short-term inequality.

3. Answers will vary. Possible answer: I am willing to accept Federal Reserve Notes because I believe that others will also accept the notes when I wish to spend them. It is a matter of trust.

4. Answers will vary. Possible answer: If people did not believe they could withdraw deposits when they chose to, they would not place their savings in banks. This would reduce or eliminate banks' ability to make loans to others and therefore others' ability to spend or invest in the economy.

5. Answers will vary. Possible answer: Banks can ask the Federal Reserve System for loans. If a loan is granted, the bank will pay interest to the Fed at the discount rate.

### Graphing Exercise

6. Answer will vary. Possible answer: Smaller banks might have difficulty competing with larger banks because they have less income to purchase the new equipment so important in the banking industry. This may cause smaller banks to merge in the future.

   An example of an acceptable graph appears at the bottom of this page.

### Think Critically

7. Answers will vary. Possible answer: The Fed lacked the leadership and power to prevent the Great Depression, or to effectively fight it once it had begun. Members of Congress and the President were willing to give a great deal of economic power to the Board of Governors in the hope that it would be able to create policies and take decisive actions that would prevent similar economic disasters in the future.

CONNECT
*to History*

## FOCUS

The debate over the constitutionality of the creation of the Bank of the United States is what most students remember from their history classes. Point out that underlying the arguments about the Bank is a fundamental debate over the role of government. The creation of the Bank of the United States brought together two conflicting views that remain with us today.

## TEACH

Instruct students to read the **Connect to History** feature and answer the questions.

## ASSESS

Use the questions at the bottom of the page to assess the students' understanding of this feature.

### Answers to Think Critically

Jackson's fear was that the Second Bank of America would become a monopoly of sorts and control too much of the nation's economic activity. However, by not having a centralized bank, Jackson allowed thousands of currencies to develop, each useless and worthless to those outside its immediate region. At that time, gold or "hard money" was the only common denominator that could be traded among people of a different region. Jackson's initial suspicions of a monopoly bank were understandable, but not justified. The same concerns about our centralized banking system today are not valid because checks and balances are in place to make sure it does not become a monopoly. Additionally, today we do have a common currency that is stabilized and able to be traded around the world so we do not need to use hard money such as gold and silver.

# Early Banking in the United States

When Alexander Hamilton approved the charter of the First Bank of the United States, there were only three commercial banks in the country. The Bank was 20 percent owned by the government. It immediately functioned as a central bank with a stabilizing influence on the nation's economy, especially in controlling the over-issuance of private bank notes. Still, many distrusted such a large institution. In 1811, its charter failed to be renewed by only one vote. The lapse was short lived, as the War of 1812 demonstrated to many in government the need for a strong central bank. In 1816, the Second Bank of the United States, chartered under the same basic rules, was formed.

The Second Bank of the United States also was unpopular in some parts of the country. For many, the bank seemed to serve the wealthy Eastern establishment at the expense of the Southern and Western parts of the country. When Andrew Jackson became president in 1829, he brought with him a dislike of banks in general and the Second Bank of the United States in particular. Rather than wait for the Bank's charter to expire in 1836, supporters of the bank pushed for renewal in 1832. It passed Congress, but Jackson vetoed the bill. Wanting to "kill the monster" (the bank), he ordered the government to begin to deposit its funds into various state-chartered banks, or "pet banks." The Second Bank of the United States, devoid of government deposits, limped along until 1849, when it finally went out of business.

Without the restraint imposed by a central bank, banks began to issue too much currency, and so the value of each piece of currency fell. By 1836, Jackson had become alarmed that government debts were being paid in currency of declining value. He ordered the Specie Circular,

which stated that government debts could be paid only in hard currency—or in gold or silver coins. The result was a contraction of the money supply and the "Panic of 1837."

Nationally, Jackson's actions marked the beginning of what is called the "free banking era." Hundreds of state-chartered banks sprang up around the country. Many of these banks were established in such out-of-the-way places that they were called "wildcat banks." Each loosely controlled bank issued its own currency, thus flooding the nation with more than 9,000 denominations and types. People had no way of telling if a particular currency was sound or not. They resorted to "note detectors," which rated the currency according to the soundness of the bank that issued it. This caused many merchants to refuse to accept currency coming from outside their state or region.

The banking and currency problems were left unaddressed until the Civil War forced the passage of the National Banking Act. It wasn't until 1913, with the passage of the Glass-Stegall Act, that the country formed a new central bank, The Federal Reserve.

## THINK CRITICALLY

Even today, historians debate Jackson's actions. Based on your understanding of banks and banking, examine Jackson's opposition to the Second Bank of the United States and his support for "hard money." Were his concerns valid and his veto justified? Are the same concerns about central banking and currency relevant today? Why or why not?

## Bibliography

Allen, Larry. *Encyclopedia of Money.* New York: Checkmark Books, 2001.

Carson, Thomas, ed. *Gale Encyclopedia of United States Economic History.* Detroit: Gale Group, 1999.

Faragher, John Mack, ed. *The American Heritage Encyclopedia of American History.* New York: Henry Holt and Company, 1998.

Froner, Eric, and John A. Garraty, eds. *The Reader's Companion to American History.* Boston: Houghton Mifflin Company, 1991.

Mokyr, Joel, ed. *The Oxford Encyclopedia of Economic History.* New York: Oxford University Press, 2003.

Morris, Richard B., and Jeffery B. Morris, eds. *Encyclopedia of American History.* New York: Harper Collins, 1996.

Parish, Peter J., ed. *Reader's Guide to American History.* Chicago: Fitzroy Dearborn Publishers, 1997.

Puth, Robert C. *American Economic History.* New York: Harcourt Brace Jovanovich College Publishers, 1988.

Raeski, Thomas G., ed. *Economics and the Historian.* Los Angeles: University of California Press, 1996.

Rosenbaum, Robert A., ed. *The Penguin Encyclopedia of American History.* New York: Penguin Reference, 2003.

# 16.3 Money, Near Money, and Credit Cards

## Objectives

> Describe the narrow definition of money.

> Explain why distinctions among definitions of money have become less meaningful over time.

## Overview

When you think of money, what comes to mind is currency—notes and coins. Notes and coins, however, are only part of the money supply. If you deposit this currency in a checking account or a bank extends you a loan by creating a checking account deposit, the amount in that checking account also is money. Currency and checking accounts are money because each serves as a medium of exchange, a unit of account, and a store of value. Some other bank accounts also perform the store-of-value function and sometimes can be readily converted into cash. These bank accounts are viewed as money, based on a broader definition.

## Key Terms

M1

checkable deposits

M2

## FOCUS

### 16.3 Money, Near Money, and Credit Cards

A number of measures of the money supply are used in the U.S. economy. Every year, the Federal Reserve System spends many millions of dollars to gather and tabulate data about the money supply that is reported at the end of business on each Thursday (unless it is a holiday). Bankers, politicians, entrepreneurs, and ordinary people watch for these data and often make economic decisions based on what they learn.

### Objectives

Remind students to read the lesson objectives to help focus their attention before reading the lesson.

### Key Terms

Direct students to create a database using the key terms for this lesson. The database fields should include terms, definitions, and page numbers. Point out that the process of keying the data is an effective way to study key terms.

## [ In the News ]

### • Traveler's Checks Go Electronic

As of October 2003, American Express, the largest and most well known issuer of traveler's checks, began issuing traveler's cards. The result of extensive focus-group research, the cards combine the safety of traveler's checks with the convenience of plastic. Unlike debit or credit cards, the new cards are not tied to an individual's bank or credit card account. Instead they are similar to a phone card; but in place of user minutes, the travel card is loaded with a particular amount of cash. It can then be reloaded from American Express locations around the world. Thus, currency you receive in a transaction overseas can be placed in a safe travel-card account and be accessible for later transactions without the risk of personally carrying the cash. In addition, and unlike regular credit or debit cards, the cards will be replaced in 24 hours if lost or stolen.

### Think About It

With traveler's cards available, would you still want to carry traveler's checks on a trip overseas? Why or why not?

◀ ▮ ▶

**505**

## [ In the News ]

Instruct students to read the passage and write down their answers. Point out that their answers might change after they finish studying Lesson 16.3.

### Answers to Think About It

Answers will vary. Possible answer: Traveler's cards combine the safety of traveler's checks with the convenience of credit cards. If stolen, the cards can be easily replaced, and the cards are not tied to a bank account or credit card account.

### Visual Presentation

Use the PowerPoint presentation on the Instructor's Resource CD as an adjunct to your lecture. The presentation also can be used for review.

## National Content Standards in Economics

**NCEE**

A complete list of the NCEE Standards appears on pages xxiv–xxv of this book. The following standards are addressed in Lesson 16.3.

Standard 4: Role of Incentives

Standard 10: Role of Economic Institutions

Standard 11: Role of Money

Standard 12: Role of Interest Rates

## TEACH

## Narrow Definition of Money: M1

Tell students that the measure of the money supply most often considered by economists is M1. In this lesson, students will learn how M1 is measured, what it contains, and why it is less reliable than it once was thought to be. M1 is the narrowest measure of the money supply in use today. It is thought to be the amount of money that is ready to be spent immediately. It includes cash, checkable deposits, and traveler's checks. At one time, this was a good measure of the money that could be spent immediately, but banking practices have changed to make M1 less accurate than it once was. One limitation on the accuracy of M1 involves the more than $1 trillion deposited in money market accounts. Almost all money market accounts provide check-writing privileges to depositors. This means the depositor can write a check against these funds and spend them immediately. Money market account deposits are not included in M1.

Direct students to **econxtra.swlearning.com**. Remind them to click on the link for Lesson 16.3 to find the appropriate link for the NET Bookmark on this page.

Extend the assignment for this feature by asking students to search the archives of a daily newspaper to see how, or whether, the information in the press release was reported.

### SPAN THE GLOBE

Direct students to read the short passage "Show Me the Dollar." Use the questions as a starting point for class discussion or have students write a short essay to answer the questions.

### Answers to Think Critically

Answers will vary. Possible answer: The dollar is a popular currency around the world because it holds its value extremely well against other currencies. Unlike the euro, the dollar has been in existence for a long time, and unlike the yen, it has proven to fluctuate very little in its stability.

---

# Narrow Definition of Money: M1

**M1**

The narrowest definition of the money supply; consists of currency (including coins) held by the nonbanking public, checkable deposits, and traveler's checks

*Money aggregates* are various measures of the money supply. The narrowest definition, called **M1**, consists of currency (including coins) held by the nonbanking public, checkable deposits, and traveler's checks. The money supply at any given time is a stock measure, just as is the amount of cash you have with you right now.

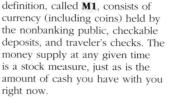

## SPAN THE GLOBE

### Show Me the Dollar

Most Americans do not realize that more than half the dollars in circulation are held overseas. According to recent Federal Reserve figures, the amount of U.S. currency available for use around the world, including in the United States itself, was approximately $1,288 billion. Of that amount, about $620 billion was in general circulation in private hands outside banks and other financial institutions. Between $340 billion and $370 billion of the $620 billion was in use overseas. The number of dollars held outside the United States is approximately 15 to 20 times the number of Japanese yen held outside Japan and about 5 times the number of euros held outside Europe. The rate of counterfeiting, approximately one in every 10,000 bills, was approximately the same whether held in the United States or outside the country.

### Think Critically

Why do you think the dollar is such a popular currency around the world? Do you think this helps the United States? Why or why not?

---

## NETBookmark

Visit the U.S. Treasury Department web site for information about currency through econxtra.swlearning.com. Click on one of the "Latest Press Releases" links. Write a paragraph about the currency-related news reported in the press release.

*econxtra.swlearning.com*

### Currency in Circulation

Dollar bills and coins in circulation are part of the money supply as narrowly defined. Money in bank vaults or on deposit at the Fed is not being used as a medium of exchange and so is not counted in the money supply. Currency makes up about half of M1.

The paper currency circulating in the United States consists of Federal Reserve notes. These notes are issued by, and are liabilities of, the Federal Reserve System. Because Federal Reserve notes are redeemable for nothing other than more Federal Reserve notes, they are fiat money. The other component of currency is coins. Like paper money, U.S. coins are token money because their intrinsic value is less than their exchange value.

### U.S. Currency Abroad

More than half of all Federal Reserve notes, particularly $100 notes, are in foreign hands. Wealthy people around the world, particularly in relatively unstable countries, often hoard U.S. currency as insurance against hard times. Some countries, such as Panama, Ecuador, and El Salvador, even use U.S. dollars as their own currency.

It's actually a good deal for Americans to have U.S. currency held abroad. Think about it this way: A $100 note that costs only about 5 cents to print can be "sold" to foreigners for $100 worth of their goods and services. It's as if these foreigners were granting the United States essentially free goods or services as long as that currency remains abroad, usually for years.

---

### Outside Resources

**Money Supply** Many web sites provide information about the money supply. The BullandBearWise web site includes a five-year graph of the money supply. Have students visit www.bullandbearwise.com/ and write a brief summary of their findings.

## Counterfeiting

Improvements in copy machines, computers, and printers allow even amateurs to make passable counterfeits of U.S. currency. Of the fake notes found in the United States in 2002, about 40 percent were produced with computers, copiers, and printers.

U.S. currency is being redesigned to make it harder to copy. You may have noticed the new $20 note, issued in late 2003. The major difference is the subtle introduction of color, a feature hard to reproduce. A new $50 note is being issued in 2004, and a new $100 note, in 2005.

The Fed and the Treasury have announced plans to redesign the currency every 7 to 10 years. Their idea is to stay one step ahead of counterfeiters.

## Checkable Deposits

Currency, or cash, makes up a little more than half of M1, the money supply narrowly defined. Suppose you have some cash with you right now—notes and coins. If you deposit this cash in a checking account, you can then write checks directing your bank to pay someone from your account. **Checkable deposits**, or deposits against which

THE WALL STREET JOURNAL

**Reading It Right** What's the relevance of the following statement from *The Wall Street Journal:* "The Bank of Mexico will begin issuing new high-denomination bills next week that include improved security features to dissuade counterfeiters. New counterfeit techniques allow for the mass production of false bills."

checks can be written, are part of the narrow definition of money.

Checkable deposits also can be tapped with an ATM card or debit card. Banks hold a variety of checkable deposits. About half of checkable deposits are *demand deposits.* These are held mostly at commercial banks and earn no interest. In recent years, banks have developed other types of accounts, such as negotiable order of withdrawal, or NOW, accounts, which carry check-writing privileges but also earn interest. Checkable deposits make up nearly half of M1.

## Traveler's Checks

If you ever planned a vacation, you may have visited the bank to buy traveler's checks. You signed the checks at the bank, and then signed them again

**checkable deposits**

Deposits in financial institutions against which checks can be written and ATM or debit cards can be applied

Using an ATM is a convenient way to access your checking account. Can you think of any disadvantages of using ATMs?

© Getty Images/PhotoDisc

Lesson 16.3 • *Money, Near Money, and Credit Cards*    **507**

## TEACH    (continued)

### Narrow Definition of Money: M1

Illustrate M1 using the following demonstration. Write different amounts on pieces of paper to represent the items listed below, and give each student a piece of paper.

• cash in wallets

• monthly balances in checking accounts

• traveler's checks

• savings deposits

• money market account deposits

Instruct students to work together to tabulate the amounts of money they have and calculate M1. (They should exclude the savings and money market deposits that are not part of M1.)

THE WALL STREET JOURNAL

**Reading It Right**

Invite a student to explain the relevance of the statement from *The Wall Street Journal* that appears on this page.

**Answer**

The relevance of this statement is that improved security features make counterfeiting more difficult.

✓ **CHECKPOINT**

Invite a student to answer the checkpoint that appears on page 508.

**Answer**

The narrow definition of money is that it consists of currency held by the non-banking public, checkable deposits, and traveler's checks.

## ENRICH

The United States Secret Service oversees federal efforts to eliminate counterfeit money for the economy and to prosecute those who create or use it. The Secret Service maintains a web site at www.ustreas.gov/usss/ that provides information about how to recognize counterfeit money and what to do if you receive a counterfeit bill. Ask students to visit this web site and write a summary of their findings, including the seven steps for what to do if you do receive a counterfeit bill.

## Broader Definitions of Money

Point out that M2 is a broader measure of money than M1. It is made up of funds that are ready to be spent now (M1) and deposits that can easily and quickly be converted to cash to be spent. M2 includes all of M1 plus savings deposits, small denomination time deposits, and most money market account deposits. Tell students that the word "small," when used to describe time deposits, means anything less than $100,000. Most people would regard $99,999 as large. Why does the government define it as small? This was originally an attempt to differentiate between commercial deposits and individual deposits. The thought was that most individuals would not have $100,000 to deposit. Businesses, however, might have millions of dollars to deposit. Today, it is less clear that this distinction makes sense. Many individuals have more than $99,999 to deposit, thanks in part to the inflation that has pushed up incomes as well as prices.

### *Think Critically Through Visuals*

Direct students to focus their attention on the photograph on page 509. Ask for a volunteer to answer the question posed in the caption.

### Answer

A credit card is a convenient way of obtaining a short-term loan from the card issuer

---

*M2*

A broader definition of the money supply, consisting of M1 plus savings deposits, small-denomination time deposits, and money market mutual fund accounts

---

when you spent them. This allowed a merchant to compare your two signatures as the rightful owner of these checks.

If your cash is stolen, you are out of luck. However, if your traveler's checks are stolen, you can get them replaced. Therefore, traveler's checks are safer than cash. Traveler's checks are a tiny part of the money supply, accounting for only about 1 percent of M1.

**✓ CHECKPOINT**
What is the narrow definition of money?

## Broader Definitions of Money

M1 serves as a medium of exchange, a unit of account, and a store of value. Some can be converted readily into M1. Because these other accounts are so close to M1, they are considered to be money, using a broader definition. Here are those bank accounts.

### Savings Deposits

*Savings deposits* earn interest but have no specific maturity date. This means that you can withdraw them any time without a penalty. Banks often allow depositors to shift funds from savings accounts to checking accounts by using a phone, an ATM, or online banking. Because savings can be converted so easily into checkable deposits and cash, distinctions between narrow and broad definitions of money have become blurred. Savings deposits total more than twice the size of M1.

### Time Deposits

*Time deposits* earn a fixed rate of interest if held for a specified period. The holding period ranges from several months to several years. Holders of time deposits are issued certificates of deposit, or CDs

for short. Early withdrawals are penalized by forfeiture of several months' interest. Neither savings deposits nor time deposits serve directly as media of exchange, so they are not included in M1, the narrowest definition of money.

Time deposits are sorted into two categories: Those of less than $100,000, called small-denomination time deposits, account for about half of all time deposits. Those in excess of $100,000 are called large-denomination time deposits and make up the other half.

### Money Market Mutual Fund Accounts

*Money market mutual fund accounts* are another component of the money supply more broadly defined. Funds deposited in these accounts are used to purchase a collection of short-term interest-earning assets by the financial institution that administers the fund. Depositors are then able to write checks against the value of their deposited funds. Because of restrictions on the minimum balance, on the number of checks that can be written per month, or on the minimum amount of each check, these popular accounts are not viewed as money when narrowly defined.

### M2 and M3

Recall that M1 consists of cash held by the nonbanking public, checkable deposits, and traveler's checks. **M2** includes M1 as well as savings deposits, small-denomination time deposits, and money market mutual fund accounts. *M3* includes M2 plus large-denomination time deposits. M3 is less liquid than M2, which is less liquid than M1.

The size and the relative importance of each of the three definitions of money are presented in Figure 16.4. As you can see, compared to M1, M2 is nearly five times larger, and M3 is nearly seven times larger. Distinctions between M1 and M2 become less meaningful as banks make it easier for depositors to transfer funds from one account to another.

---

508

**CHAPTER 16** Money and Banking

---

## *Economic Headlines*

Instruct students to locate an article in a current magazine or newspaper that relates to one of the topics in this lesson. For example, they might find articles about money market deposit accounts. Instruct students to read the article, write a brief summary, and include a reference citation. Identify the style you want them to use for the citation.
As an alternative, you might find several articles of interest and provide citations for students to use in locating one of the articles. Direct students to read the article they have chosen, and write a brief explanation of how it relates to this lesson.

## Debit Cards but Not Credit Cards

Why does the definition of money include funds accessible by debit (or ATM) cards but not include credit cards, such as VISA and MasterCard? After all, credit cards account for about 20 percent of all consumer spending in the United States. Most sellers accept credit cards as readily as they accept cash or checks. Online purchases and mail orders usually require credit cards.

A credit card itself is not money. Using a credit card, however, is a convenient way of obtaining a short-term loan from the card issuer. If you buy an airline ticket with a credit card, the card issuer lends you the money to pay for the ticket. You don't use money until you pay your credit card bill. The credit card has not eliminated your use of money. It has merely delayed it. On the other hand, when you use a debit card at a grocery store, a drugstore, or any of hun-

dreds of other retailers, you draw down your checking account—part of M1.

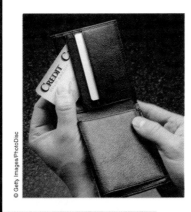

© Getty Images/PhotoDisc

**If a credit card itself is not money, what is it?**

**Think Critically Through Visuals**

Direct students to focus their attention on **Figure 16.4—Alternative Measure of the Money Supply, April 2003**. Point out that this figure illustrates the relationships of M1, M2, and M3. M1 is included in M2, and M1 and M2 are included in M3.

**Think Critically Through Visuals**

Direct students to focus their attention on **Figure 16.5—The Evolution of Money** on page 510. Ask students to give examples of commodity money, representative money, fiat money, and electronic money.

✓ **CHECKPOINT**
Invite a student to answer the checkpoint that appears on page 510.

**Answer**
Distinctions between the broad aggregates of money have become less meaningful over time because depositors have made it easier to transfer funds from one account to another.

**Alternative Measure of the Money Supply, April 2003**      **Figure 16.4**

**M2 is nearly five times larger than M1, and M3 is nearly seven times larger.**

Source: Based on monthly estimates from the Federal Reserve Board.

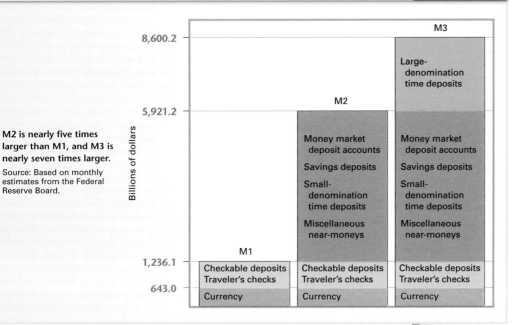

## Curriculum Connection—English

Many documents related to financial matters are written in such a way that the average American cannot understand them. In an effort to remedy this situation, some government agencies have promoted an initiative to use "plain English." The Securities and Exchange Commission published *A Plain English Handbook: How to Create Clear SEC Disclosure Documents*. The handbook is available online at www.sec.gov/. Have students visit the web site and read the Introduction and Chapter 1. Instruct students to create an outline of the key points of the four assigned pages.

Encourage students to apply their
knowledge of concepts presented in
this lesson as they explore economic
news stories, policy debates, and data
available at
**econxtra.swlearning.com**.
A sampling of the titles for this lesson
appears below.

### EconData
- Money Supply

### EconNews
- Banks Behaving Badly?
- Will Cash Become Scarce?
- Default With the Economy

## ASSESS

Assign all or part of Lesson 16.3
Assessment on page 511 as homework or an in-class activity.

### Xtra! Study Tools

Direct students to the online study
tools for Lesson 16.3 at
**econxtra.swlearning.com**.

## CLOSE

**Revisit** the **In the News** feature on the
first page of the lesson. Ask students
to review their preliminary answers
and discuss the questions, now that
they have completed this lesson.

**Review** the objectives for Lesson 16.3.
Students should be able to:
- Describe the narrow definition of
money.
- Explain why distinctions among definitions of money have become less
meaningful over time.

## Electronic Money

Money has grown increasingly more
abstract over time, moving from commodity money to paper money that represented a claim on some commodity
such as gold, to paper money with no
intrinsic value, to an electronic entry at
a bank that can be tapped with a debit
card. Much of modern money consists
of electronic entries in bank computers.
So, money has evolved from a physical
commodity to an electronic entry. This
evolution is depicted in Figure 16.5.
Money today not so much changes
hands as it changes computer accounts.

**CHECKPOINT**
Why have distinctions among the
broad aggregates of money
become less meaningful over
time?

**The Evolution of Money**                                    Figure **16.5**

Money has evolved from a
physical commodity to an
electronic entry.

Commodity Money

Representative Money

Fiat Money

Electronic Money

**510**          **CHAPTER 16**  Money and Banking

## RETEACH

The money supply is not the only factor that can influence prices and interest rates in the economy.
The speed or velocity at which money moves through the economy is also important. After all, it
makes little difference to the economy whether a $10 bill is spent 10 times, or a $100 bill is spent
once. Ask students to discuss what the electronic banking revolution has done to the speed at
which money circulates in the economy. Why do we use money more efficiently now than we did
20 or 50 years ago?

## Key Concepts

1. Why can't the Fed be sure of exactly how much currency is in circulation at any specific time? Why does it have a much better idea of the amount deposited in checkable accounts?

2. If you had $100, would you be more likely to spend it if you held it in cash, had it deposited in a checking account, or had a traveler's check in that amount? Are these forms of money all equally easy to spend?

3. How would the effect of buying a $50 shirt with a credit card be different from buying the same shirt with a debit card from your bank?

4. Before electronic fund transfers became common, it could take days or weeks for checks to be presented to banks for payment. During this time, banks could use funds deposited in checking accounts even though they had already been spent by the depositor. This time was called *float time.* What do you imagine has happened to float time in recent years? Do you think this has had an important impact on the economy? Why or why not?

**Xtra!**
**Study Tools**
econxtra.swlearning.com

## Graphing Exercise

5. Use data in the table to construct two bar graphs to show the components of M-1 and M-2 in May 2003. Calculate the percent each component represented of the total for these two measures of the money supply. Do any of these percentages surprise you? Why or why not?

**Components of M-1 and M-2 in May 2003**
**Values in Billions of Dollars**

| M-1 | | | M-2 | | |
|---|---|---|---|---|---|
| Currency | $645.7 | 51.3% | M-1 | $1,258.3 | 21.0% |
| Traveler's Checks | 7.5 | 0.6% | Savings Deposits | 2,981.0 | 49.7% |
| Checkable Deposits | 605.1 | 48.1% | Small Time Deposits | 864.3 | 14.4% |
| Total | $1,258.3 | | Money Market Funds | 896.3 | 14.9% |
| | | | Total | $5,999.9 | |

Source: Federal Reserve web site, July 21, 2003.

## Think Critically

6. **Mathematics** Calculate the changes in M-1 and M-2 that would result from each of the following. Explain how you found your answers. Why don't the values of M-1 and M-2 always change when the value of their components change?

   a. The Fed buys a $10,000 bond from a person who then deposits the funds in her checking account.

   b. A depositor has $500 transferred from his checking account to his savings account.

   c. A depositor withdraws $1,000 from her savings account in cash.

   d. A depositor transfers $2,000 from her savings account to a time deposit.

## Key Concepts

1. Answers will vary. Possible answer: Cash that is saved by individuals is not truly in circulation. Some cash is taken to other countries each day and is, therefore, no longer in circulation in the United States Banks, however, know and report to the Fed the amount deposited in checkable accounts.

2. Answers will vary. Possible answer: Cash is the easiest of these forms of money to spend, followed by checking deposits, and then traveler's checks.

3. Answers will vary. Possible answer: When the shirt is purchased with a debit card, the bank immediately takes it from my account and puts the purchase amount in the store's account. (The transaction may actually involve multiple banks—my bank, the store's bank, and the banks used by state and local tax authorities.) When I use a credit card, a loan is extended. Money does not flow out of my bank until I pay the credit card bill and the check clears my bank.

4. Answers will vary. Possible answer: Electronic fund transfers have reduced float time to a matter of hours or, at the most, days. This change has increased money's speed of circulation in the economy and increased the number of transactions that take place.

## Graphing Exercise

5. The percentage of each component of M2 is shown in the table below.

| Components of M-1 & M-2 in May 2003 | | |
|---|---|---|
| **Values in billions of dollars** | | |
| Currency | $645.7 | 10.8% |
| Traveler's Checks | 7.5 | 0.1% |
| Checkable Deposits | 605.1 | 10.1% |
| Savings Deposits | 2,981.0 | 49.7% |
| Small Time Deposits | 864.3 | 14.4% |
| Non Institutional Money Market Funds | 896.3 | 14.9% |
| Total | $5,999.9 | 100.0% |

## Visualizing the Answer— Graphing Exercise

5. The answer includes two graphs. Students' graphs should look similar to those shown here. An Excel spreadsheet containing these graphs, along with supporting data, is available on the Instructor's Resource CD.

Answers will vary. Possible answer: The amount of money held in saving deposits that pay relatively lower interest rates is surprising. This may indicate that many individuals value being able to spend their deposits on short notice.

Example of acceptable graphs appear at the bottom of this page.

*The Answer Key is continued on page 514.*

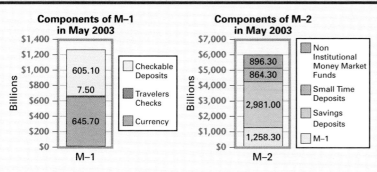

**Components of M–1 in May 2003**

Billions: $1,400 / $1,200 / $1,000 / $800 / $600 / $400 / $200 / $0

605.10 — Checkable Deposits
7.50 — Travelers Checks
645.70 — Currency

M–1

**Components of M–2 in May 2003**

Billions: $7,000 / $6,000 / $5,000 / $4,000 / $3,000 / $2,000 / $1,000 / $0

896.30 — Non Institutional Money Market Funds
864.30 — Small Time Deposits
2,981.00 — Savings Deposits
1,258.30 — M–1

M–2

Ask students whether they believe the government should help people obtain credit who would not be eligible for loans under normal circumstances. The point has often been made that credit is most easily available to those who don't need it. In other words, if you already have lots of assets, cash, and property, then banks are happy to lend you more money. But if you have little money, assets, or property, banks don't want to talk to you. How does this practice perpetuate the existing distribution of wealth in the U.S. economy? Is it a legitimate role for the government to help people obtain credit to start a business? What would students do if they were in Tony Brown's shoes? Would they be concerned if they helped someone obtain credit who was unable to repay the loan?

## TEACH

Instruct students to read the **Movers & Shakers** feature about Tony Brown. Point out that some students may find it helpful to read the article, read the questions at the bottom of the page, and then reread the article.

## ASSESS

Use the questions in Source Reading and Think Critically at the bottom of the profile to assess the students' understanding of this **Movers & Shakers** feature.

### Answers to Source Reading

Answers will vary. Possible answer: In addition to the businesses that receive the new-markets tax credits, others who benefit include customers, employees, and investors. The community where the businesses are located also benefit from the tax credits.

### Answers to Entrepreneurs in Action

The CDFI does not lend money directly to individuals. It invests in and supports community development financial institutions through three programs: the Bank Enterprise Awards (BEA) Program, the Financial Assistance (FA) Component of the CDFI Program, and the Technical Assistance (TA) Component of the CDFI Program.

# movers & shakers

**Tony Brown** *Director, Community Development Financial Institutions (CDFI), U.S. Department of the Treasury*

Tony Brown began his career in banking in 1982 after earning a Bachelor of Arts degree in International Affairs and Business and a Master of Business Administration degree in Finance from Xavier University in Cincinnati. In 1985, he joined Bank of America in Florida, serving as Senior Vice President of Community Development from 1990 to 2001. His work included community development lending and other financial services, resulting in more than $2 billion in annual loan production.

In August 2001, Brown was nominated by President George W. Bush as Director of the Community Development Financial Institutions (CDFI) Fund within the U.S. Department of Treasury. The purpose of the Fund, and Brown's overall role, is to expand the availability of credit, investment capital, and financial services in distressed communities. Since the Fund's creation in 1994, more than $534 million has been awarded to community development organizations and financial institutions.

Vicki and Maurice Marchman are shining examples of the impact CDFI Funds can have on a community. The Marchmans operate a small childcare business in an economically distressed neighborhood of Louisville, Kentucky. They wanted to expand their business, but they lacked the necessary collateral to qualify for a traditional bank loan. The couple found the necessary funding,

$112,000, through a loan from the Louisville Community Development Bank, a CDFI bank. Within the next few years, the business underwent several expansions, again receiving CDFI loans when traditional banks didn't find them eligible. Today the Marchman Learning Centers serve 300 children and provide jobs to 35 people. One of the centers is located in the Marchman Plaza, also home to a Social Security office, a county clerk's office, a laundromat, and a discount store. Once an eyesore, the Marchman Plaza now is a series of clean, well-maintained buildings, surrounded by attractive landscaping—all made possible through CDFI funds.

Success stories like this fuel Tony Brown's passion for serving as director of the CDFI Fund. His desire is to help Americans like the Marchmans, in economically distressed communities, realize a dream by providing better access to credit, capital, and financial services. The overall goal for Brown and his staff is to measurably improve the economic conditions of the residents of low-income communities by spurring economic growth and jobs through community development finance. To reach that goal, Brown requested a $51 million appropriation for the CDFI Fund from President Bush's fiscal year 2004 budget.

"We also have responsibility for administering the $15 billion new-markets tax credit program. These tax credits are provided to investors who invest in companies that in turn invest in businesses in low-income areas," Brown explains.

## SOURCE READING

Analyze Brown's quote, above, about the new-markets tax credit program. Who benefits from the tax credit program he describes?

## ENTREPRENEURS IN ACTION

In small groups, research the CDFI to find out if a small business owner could become eligible to receive one of these loans. Access the CDFI web site through econxtra.swlearning.com for information to use in completing this assignment.

512    **CHAPTER 16** Money and Banking

# Sharpen Your Life Skills

## Decision-Making Skills

Banks use part of the money they receive from deposits in checking, savings, money market funds, and certificates of deposit (CDs) to make loans to their customers. The percent of interest they are willing to pay depositors depends on the type of account in which deposits are made. In general, the longer a bank expects to have a deposit, the greater the interest rate it pays. The reason for this relationship is the interest income banks are able to earn from loans they make. With a few exceptions, banks earn higher rates of interest from long-term loans than from short-term loans. This is why they are willing to pay more for long-term deposits. By carefully evaluating their situations, savers can make optimal decisions when they deposit their funds in banks.

The table below lists average interest rates paid for different types of deposits on July 22, 2003. Study this table, and use the information it contains to answer the questions that follow.

**Interest Paid on Deposits, July 22, 2003**

| Type of Deposit | Interest Rate Paid |
| --- | --- |
| Small Checking Accounts | 0.0% |
| Savings Accounts | 1.2% |
| Money Market Deposits ($500 minimum deposit) | 2.1% |
| 1-Year CD ($500 minimum deposit) | 2.2% |
| 2-Year CD ($1,000 minimum deposit) | 2.5% |
| 5-Year CD ($1,000 minimum deposit) | 3.8% |

## Apply Your Skill

In which type of account would you choose to deposit your funds in each of the following situations? Explain each of your choices.

1. You have $250 in cash that you must spend to pay your rent next Friday.

2. You have $1,000 in cash that you intend to spend sometime in the next few months when a new racing bicycle you have ordered arrives at a bike shop. You do not know precisely when it will arrive.

3. You have decided to start to save by setting aside $20 from each of your weekly paychecks.

4. You were given $2,000 by your uncle, who told you to set it aside for your college tuition after you graduate from high school in two years.

5. You inherit $10,000 and decide to set it aside to help you make a down payment on a house after you graduate from college and get settled in a career.

### Sharpen Your Life Skills

**Decision-Making Skills**

After studying Lesson 16.3, students should be able to answer the questions on this page.

**Apply Your Skill**

Consider allowing students to work in pairs for this assignment.

**Answers**

1. Answers will vary. Students may choose to deposit these funds in a checking account because they intend to spend them in only a few days.

2. Answers will vary. Students may choose to deposit these funds in a money market deposit that pays a relatively high rate of interest but allows them to withdraw their funds at any time with no penalty.

3. Answers will vary. Students may choose to deposit these funds in a savings account because they do not have enough yet to open an account that would pay them a higher rate of interest.

4. Answers will vary. Students may choose to deposit these funds in a two-year CD to earn a higher rate of interest than savings or money market accounts pay.

5. Answers will vary. Students may choose to deposit these funds in a five-year CD to maximize the long-term return on their money.

### Consider

Ask students to revisit the questions they were asked to consider at the beginning of the chapter. Remind students that they should be able to answer all of the questions after studying Chapter 16.

- Why are you willing to exchange a piece of paper bearing Alexander Hamilton's portrait and the number 10 in each corner for a pepperoni pizza? See page 490—Three Functions of Money.

- Why is paper money more efficient than gold coins? See page 490—Medium of Exchange.

- Why was a Montana bank willing to cash a check written on a clean but frayed pair of underpants? See page 497—Bank Checks.

- How do banks create money? See page 497—Bank Notes.

- When were thousands of different currencies circulating in the U.S. economy? See page 504—Connect to History.

- Why is there so much fascination with money, anyway? See page 490—Medium of Exchange.

### Exam*View*

Use Exam*View* to assess students' learning

- Create a chapter test using questions from the existing test bank.

- Add your own questions to the existing test bank.

- Generate multiple forms of a chapter test.

### Study Skills

Offer the following study skills suggestions for students as they review this chapter.

- Outline the chapter.
- Review Key Terms.
- Review Checkpoints.
- Work in pairs to quiz each other.
- Use Xtra! Study Tools for each lesson.

Direct students to the online quiz preparation for Chapter 16 at **econxtra.swlearning.com**.

---

# 16 Chapter Assessment

## Summary

 **Origins of Money**

**a** The earliest families were self-sufficient and did not need money. When people began to specialize, transactions were carried out through barter at first. Problems with using barter centered on the difficulty of finding mutually beneficial trades of products with equal values. Making these exchanges involved large transaction costs that gave birth to money. People began to accept goods that they did not expect to use for themselves but rather to trade later for other products they wished to own. The goods that were used as money became known as *commodity money*.

**b** Money must fulfill three functions. (1) It must be accepted as a *medium of exchange*. (2) It must serve as a *unit of account*. (3) It must provide a *store of value* over time. An ideal form of money would be durable, portable, divisible, of uniform quality, have a low opportunity cost of use, have a supply and demand that does not fluctuate wildly, and exist in limited quantity.

**c** Coins often replaced other types of commodity money in early commerce. They offered the advantages of being more portable, durable, and divisible than most types of commodity money. To assure that the precious metals they contained were pure, coins were stamped with an official seal by the issuing institution. Most coins were *token money*, which means that the value stamped on them was greater than the value of the gold or silver they contained.

 **Origins of Banking and the Federal Reserve System**

**a** The earliest businesses that served as banks were goldsmiths who stored gold for their customers. Depositors often wrote checks to have gold transferred from one account to another. Goldsmiths learned that they could loan part of these funds to earn income and pay depositors a small return for their deposits. They came to operate under the *fractional reserve banking system*.

**b** Paper money was first issued in the form of notes printed by banks. Soon, governments also issued paper money that often was backed by nothing other than the government's statement that it was money. This *fiat money* is accepted because people trust the government and expect others to accept the money as well.

**c** Depository institutions are classified broadly into *commercial banks,* which hold more than two-thirds of bank deposits, and thrift institutions, which include mutual savings banks and credit unions. Banks may be chartered by either state or the federal government in the United States.

**d** The *Federal Reserve System*, or *Fed*, was established in 1913 to stop runs on banks. The Fed is responsible for supervising banking in the United States and for making and implementing monetary policy. The Fed may lend money to banks at the *discount rate*.

 **Money, Near Money and Credit Cards**

**a** The Fed measures the money supply in the U.S. economy through several categories called money aggregates. *M1* includes currency in circulation, checkable deposits, and traveler's checks. The measurement of M1 is complicated by U.S. currency that has been sent abroad, and by counterfeiting.

**b** *M2* is a broader definition of the money supply. It includes M1 plus savings and time deposits, as well as funds placed in money market mutual fund accounts. Another, even broader measure of money is M3, which includes M2 and other less-liquid deposits.

**c** Electronic fund transfers carried out through debit cards have made it easier for people to spend their money. When people use credit cards to purchase goods or services, they are effectively taking out short-term loans.

---

 **Assessment**

Continued from page 511.

### Think Critically

6. Answers will vary. Possible answer: Changes in the components of M-1 and M-2 often result in the same values being added to and subtracted from their total values, leaving these total values unchanged.

a. The amount deposited in checkable accounts will grow by $10,000, as will the total amount in M-1 and M-2.

b. Checking deposits and M-1 will decline by $500. Savings deposits will increase by $500, but M-2 will remain unchanged because M-1 is $500 smaller.

# Review Economic Terms

Choose the term that best fits the definition. On a separate sheet of paper, write the letter of the answer. Some terms may not be used.

_____ 1. Money not redeemable for anything of intrinsic value; declared money by government decree

_____ 2. Anything generally accepted by all parties in payment for goods or services

_____ 3. Buying or selling U.S. government securities as a way of regulating the money supply

_____ 4. Depository institutions that make loans primarily to businesses

_____ 5. A written order instructing a bank to pay someone from the amount deposited

_____ 6. Bank notes that exchange for a specific commodity, such as gold

_____ 7. Interest rate the Fed charges to banks that borrow reserves

_____ 8. Cash that banks have on hand in their vaults or on deposit with the Federal Reserve System

_____ 9. Deposits in financial institutions against which checks can be written

_____10. Anything that serves both as money and as a commodity, such as gold

a. **check**

b. **checkable deposits**

c. **commercial banks**

d. **commodity money**

e. **discount rate**

f. **Federal Open Market Committee (FOMC)**

g. **Federal Reserve System**

h. **fiat money**

i. **fractional reserve banking system**

j. **M1**

k. **M2**

l. **medium of exchange**

m. **open-market operations**

n. **representative money**

o. **reserves**

# Review Economic Concepts

11. Without __?__ there is no need for money.

12. **True or False** The high transaction cost of money gave birth to barter.

13. Which of the following is not a function of money?

   a. medium of exchange

   b. unit of account

   c. standard of deposit

   d. store of value

14. Gold, silver, wheat, and tobacco have all served as __?__ at some time in the past.

15. **True or False** *Fiat money* is accepted when people trust the issuing agency.

16. Which of the following is probably the greatest limitation on the usefulness of diamonds as *commodity money*?

   a. They are not durable.

   b. They are not portable.

   c. They do not have value.

   d. They are not easily divisable.

17. Paper documents issued by banks that promised the bearer a specific amount of gold or silver were called __?__.

18. Goats or sheep make poor money because they

   a. are not portable.

   b. are not divisible.

   c. have no intrinsic value.

   d. exist in almost unlimited quantities.

19. **True or False** Money is a stock while income is a flow.

*Chapter Assessment*     **515**

## Review Economic Terms

1. h. fiat money
2. l. medium of exchange
3. m. open-market operations
4. c. commercial banks
5. a. check
6. n. representative money
7. e. discount rate
8. o. reserves
9. b. checkable deposits
10. d. commodity money

## Review Economic Concepts

11. exchange
12. False. It was the other way around: The high transaction cost of barter gave birth to money.
13. c. standard of deposit
14. commodity money
15. True
16. d. They are not easily divisible.
17. bank notes
18. b. are not divisible
19. True

---

 **Assessment**

Continued from page 514.

### *Think Critically*

c. The amount in currency and M-1 will grow by $1,000. The amount in savings deposits will decline by $1,000, but M-2 will remain unchanged because M-1 will be $1,000 larger.

d. M-1 will remain unchanged. The amount in savings deposits will fall by $2,000, while the amount in time deposits will grow by $2,000. The total amount in M-2 will remain unchanged.

## Review Economic Concepts

20 a. fiat money

21. False. U.S. banks may be chartered by the federal or state governments.

22. d. making home mortgage loans

23. discount rate

24. b. Its members are elected by commercial bank presidents.

25. True

26. c. small savings account deposits

27. money market mutual fund deposit

28. True

29. Electronic fund transfers

## Apply Economic Concepts

30. Answers will vary. A possible answer for each situation is shown below.

    *Rent:* It is important to have a record that this payment was made. The bank will supply such a record with your monthly statement. Also, few people would want to have this much cash on hand.

    *Movie tickets:* Most people would pay cash for such a small purchase that requires no lasting record of having been made.

    *Car loan payment:* Most people make this payment with a check to provide them with a record of the transaction.

    *Lunch:* Answers will vary. Most people would pay cash for such a small purchase that requires no lasting record of having been made.

    *Repay your uncle:* Many people would make this payment with a check to provide them with a record that the payment was made, even if they trusted their uncle.

    *Generalization:* Most small transactions are made in cash while larger payments, or those that require a permanent record of having been made, are made with checks.

31. Answers will vary. Students may point out that these pieces of paper are similar to money because they do have value and are transferable within the resort. However, they have no value outside the resort, cannot be used to store value, and are not a unit of account in any other place.

32. M1 includes currency, checkable deposits, and traveler's checks, for a total of $1,183.3 billion. M2 includes M1 plus savings deposits, small denomination time deposits, and noninstitutional money market funds, for a total of $5,506.5 billion.

---

20. *Federal Reserve* notes are examples of

    a. fiat money.

    b. representative money.

    c. commodity money.

    d. full-bodied money.

21. **True or False** Banks in the United States may be chartered only by state governments.

22. In the past, savings and loans and mutual savings banks specialized in

    a. issuing credit cards.

    b. extending credit to businesses.

    c. maintaining checking accounts.

    d. making home mortgage loans.

23. When the Fed lends money to banks, it charges them the __?__.

24. Which of the following statements about the Federal Reserve's Board of Governors is not true?

    a. Its members are responsible for setting monetary policy.

    b. Its members are elected by commercial bank presidents.

    c. Its members also serve on the Federal Open Market Committee.

    d. Its members serve 14-year terms.

25. **True or False** The *FOMC* was established to coordinate the Fed's *open-market operations*.

26. *M1* includes each of the following except

    a. checkable deposits.

    b. currency.

    c. small savings account deposits.

    d. traveler's checks.

27. A part of a collection of short-term interest-earning assets that individuals are able to purchase is called a __?__.

28. **True or False** The use of a debit card will immediately impact the money supply while the use of a credit card will not.

29. __?__ carried out through debit cards make it easier for people to spend their money.

# Apply Economic Concepts

30. **Decide When to Use Cash** Which of the following transactions would you complete with cash and for which would you write a check? Explain each of your choices. What generalizations can you make about when people choose to use cash to make their payments?

    • Pay your $850 rent.

    • Buy two $8 movie tickets for your friend and yourself.

    • Make a $199 monthly payment for your car loan.

    • Purchase your lunch for $5.99 at a fast-food restaurant.

    • Repay your uncle the $300 he loaned you last year.

31. **Assess What Makes a Piece of Paper Money** Some resort communities issue guests special pieces of paper that may be used to purchase goods or services within the resort. Guests may spend 50 credits to rent a small sailboat, 75 credits to purchase a meal, or 100 credits to play a round of golf or take a tennis lesson. In what ways are these pieces of paper similar to money and in what ways are they different from money?

32. **Calculate the Money Supply** The following table lists amounts of money held in a variety of forms in May 2002. Use these values to calculate the amount in M1 and M2 at that time.

**Money Held in May 2002**
**Values in Billions of Dollars**

| | |
|---|---|
| Currency | $605.0 |
| Checkable Deposits | 570.5 |
| Savings Deposits | $2,499.2 |
| Small Time Deposits | 927.7 |
| Money Market Mutual Funds | 896.3 |
| Traveler's Checks | 7.8 |

33. **Describe What Happens When the Fed Lends Money** Banks that are short on cash may ask to borrow funds from the Federal Reserve System. This sometimes happens when banks located in rural areas need money to make loans to farmers in the spring when they are preparing to plant crops. These loans are repaid the following fall, after farmers have harvested and sold their crops. Write an essay that describes what would happen in the economy if a bank borrowed $10 million from the Fed and used this money to make loans to farmers.

34. **Identify Depository Institutions** Make a list of all the depository institutions that have offices in your community. Identify them as commercial banks, savings and loans, mutual savings banks, credit unions, or other. How much difference is there in the services that they offer typical consumers?

35. **Diagram the Check-Clearing Process** When you deposit your paycheck in your bank, it must have the check cleared to obtain the funds it credits to your account. Here are the steps that take place.

- You deposit your check for $250 in Bank ABC. The check was drawn on Bank XYZ, which is located in a different community in your state.

- Your bank credits your account for $250 and sends the check to the nearest Federal Reserve Bank.

- The Federal Reserve Bank credits Bank

ABC's account for $250 and deducts this amount from Bank XYZ's account.

- The Federal Reserve Bank sends the cancelled check to Bank XYZ, which will draw down your employer's checkable deposits by the amount of the check, keep a record of the check and possibly send the cancelled check to your employer.

Draw and label a diagram to show this process.

36. **Sharpen Your Life Skills** Imagine that you have decided to save $5,000 over the next two years to make the down payment on a used car. You work 20 hours each week after school and take home $127.35 after taxes. You believe you could save $30 each week during the 42 weeks of the school year. In the summer, you plan to work 40 hours each week and take home about $250. During this time you could save more. Use this information to create a savings plan to reach your goal. Which of the following types of savings accounts would you open? How much could you save during each school year? How much would you need to save during each of two summers to reach your goal? Explain your plan in several paragraphs.

**Possible Ways to Save**

- a checking account that pays no interest

- a savings account that pays 1 percent interest

- a one-year certificate of deposit that pays 1.75 percent interest and has a minimum deposit of $500

*e*-con @pps     econxtra.swlearning.com

37. Access **EconNews Online** at econxtra. swlearning.com. Find the article entitled "Making It Tough on Counterfeiters." Read the article, and then answer this question: Why do you think the government is changing the $20 and $100 bills, but not the $1, $5, and $10 bills?

## Apply Economic Concepts

33. Answers will vary. Students may point out that this new money will be used by farmers to purchase seed, fertilizer, and farm equipment. This would increase their demand for these products and their ability to produce food. The result would be an increase in economic activity that will make it easier for these loans to be repaid in the fall.

34. Answers will vary. Students should correctly list and identify local depository institutions. They probably will see little difference among the services most of them offer consumers.

35. Answers will vary. Students may construct a diagram similar to the one shown at the bottom of this page.

36. Answers will vary. The maximum that could be saved during one school year is $1,260 ($30 × 42). If $2,520 is saved in during two school years, an additional $2,480 must come from summer savings and interest.

*e*-con @pps

37. The United States government is changing the $20 bill because it is the most counterfeited bill inside the U. S. The $100 bill is being changed because it is the most counterfeited bill outside the U. S. Additionally, the impact of counterfeit $20 or $100 bills is significantly more costly to our government than is the impact of counterfeit $1, $5, or $10 bills.

| Student | ABC Bank | Federal Reserve Bank | XYZ Bank |
|---|---|---|---|
| • Deposits payroll check for $250 in account at ABC. (Check is drawn on XYZ Bank.) | • Credits student's account for $250. <br> • Sends check to Federal Reserve Bank. | • Credits ABC account for $250. <br> • Debits XYZ account for $250. <br> • Sends check to XYZ. | • Draws down my employer's account by $250. <br> • Returns check to student's employer. |

**Student's Employer**

### Visualizing the Answer—Apply Economic Concepts

35. The answer includes a diagram. Students' diagrams will vary. This is an example of an acceptable diagram.

## Chapter Overview

**LESSON 17.1** *How Banks Work:* This lesson outlines the steps in starting a bank and describes how the banking system can expand the money supply by a multiple of excess reserves.

**LESSON 17.2** *Monetary Policy in the Short Run:* This lesson illustrates the shape of the money demand curve. It also provides an explanation of how changes in the money supply affect interest rates and real GDP in the short run. The federal funds rate is also addressed.

**LESSON 17.3** *Monetary Policy in the Long Run:* This lesson explains why changes in the money supply affect only prices in the long run, not real GDP. It also examines the historical link between money supply growth and inflation. Lower inflation as a result of political independence of central banks is explained.

### Consider

Ask students to consider the questions posed on this page as they study Chapter 17. After studying all three lessons, students should be able to answer the questions. The content related to each question can be found on the pages indicated below.

- How does the Fed create money? See page 521—The Fed Makes a Move.

- Why don't you demand all the money you can get your hands on? See page 526—Money Demand.

- What's the price of holding money? See page 526—The Cost of Holding Money.

- How does the supply of money in the economy affect your chances of finding a job, your ability to finance a new car, and the interest rate you pay on credit cards? See page 528—Money Supply and the Market Interest Rate.

- What's the impact of changes in the money supply on the economy in the short run and in the long run? See page 528—Money Supply.

### POINT YOUR BROWSER

Remind students that they can find additional resources for this chapter at **econxtra.swlearning.com.**

# Money Creation, the Federal Reserve System, and Monetary Policy

© Getty Images/PhotoDisc

### Consider

How does the Fed create money?

Why don't you demand all the money you can get your hands on?

What's the price of holding money?

How does the supply of money in the economy affect your chances of finding a job, your ability to finance a new car, and the interest rate you pay on credit cards?

What's the impact of changes in the money supply on the economy in the short run and in the long run?

### POINT YOUR BROWSER

*econxtra.swlearning.com*

---

## *Teaching Resources for Chapter 17*

- Activities and Projects Masters
- Spanish Resources
- Econ Connection Interactive Tutorial CD
- **Exam***View*® CD
- Workbook Teacher's Edition
- Chapter and Unit Test Teacher's Edition
- NCEE Standards and Correlation

- Personal Finance Guide
- Social Studies Skills Review
- Instructor's Resource CD
  - PowerPoint Presentation
  - Lesson Plans
  - Video Discussion Guide
  - Answers to Graphing Exercises
- econxtra.swlearning.com

## 17.1 How Banks Work

## Objectives

> Discuss what's involved in getting a new banking operation up and running.

> Describe how the banking system can expand the money supply by a multiple of excess reserves.

## Overview

Coins and paper money notes account for only a part of money supply in the U.S. economy. The narrow definition of money also includes checking accounts, which consist mostly of electronic entries in bank computers. The Federal Reserve System creates money not so much by circulating more Federal Reserve notes, but by having banks do what they do best—accept deposits and lend out some of them to borrowers. Bank reserves provide the raw material banks use to make loans, and these loans are how the banks add to the money supply.

## Key Terms

net worth

asset

liability

balance sheet

required reserve ratio

required reserves

excess reserves

money multiplier

Point out that banks are among the most closely regulated businesses in the United States. Banks must be chartered by the government and are subject to spot checks by government regulators. These regulators may appear at any time to review a bank's books and check for compliance with accounting rules and regulations.

### Objectives

Remind students to read the lesson objectives to help focus their attention before reading the lesson.

### Key Terms

Direct students to look up key terms in a business or economics dictionary. Some students will find it helpful to read another definition. In addition to a definition, many entries will include a brief explanation and an example.

### [ In the News ]

Instruct students to read the passage and write down their answers. Point out that their answers might change after they finish studying Lesson 17.1.

**Answers to Think About It**

Answers will vary. Possible answer: Yes, the strength and security of a country's banking system is important to a country's political stability because one cannot exist without the other. Citizens will have no confidence in a weak banking system, and lack of security leads to crime. Both of these situations can undermine the political stability of a country.

### Visual Presentation

Use the PowerPoint presentation on the Instructor's Resource CD as an adjunct to your lecture. The presentation also can be used for review.

## [ In the News ]

### • Stealing the People's Money

Almost from the moment the first banks went into business, there have been bank robbers. Popular fiction and films often have portrayed bank robbers as daring outlaws who are able to gain large sums of money in a single heist. Several famous American outlaws, such as Jesse James, John Dillinger, and Bonnie and Clyde, became well known for their attempts to steal from banks. Some Americans sympathized with these thieves because they saw banks as tools of the rich, whose lending practices often hurt the poorest people. Although usually better guarded than local banks, central banks also can be robbed. These banks often hold billions of dollars in reserve currency and gold. The people of Iraq learned this in the aftermath of the 2003 U.S. war in Iraq. Fleeing dictator Saddam Hussein was discovered to have taken more than $1 billion in U.S. dollars from Iraq's central bank. In addition to raising fears that this money might be used to fund terrorist operations, it further weakened an already unstable Iraqi economy that needed to rebuild after the war.

### Think About It

Do you think the security and strength of a country's banking system is important to a country's political stability? Why or why not?

519

### National Content Standards in Economics

A complete list of the NCEE Standards appears on pages xxiv–xxv of this book. The following standards are addressed in Lesson 17.1.

Standard 10: Role of Economic Institutions

Standard 11: Role of Money

Standard 16: Role of Government

Standard 20: Monetary and Fiscal Policy

## Operating a Bank

Remind students that banks provide savers and borrowers with important services, but they do not do this for free. Point out that there is a relationship between risk and rate of return. In general, the greater the return offered by an investment, the greater the risk associated with that investment. Banks manage their assets and liabilities to reduce their risks. A bank would be wrong to make nothing but automobile loans. If something happened that caused many of these loans to go bad, the bank could be in deep trouble. It would be equally wrong to offer only certificates of deposits to savers. By diversifying, banks are able to control their risk and improve the probability that they will earn a profit.

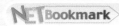

Direct students to **econxtra.swlearning.com.** Remind them to click on the link for Lesson 17.1 to find the appropriate link for the **NET Bookmark** on this page.

### Answer

An application for a savings bank charter granted in South Carolina must contain: (1) A copy of the proposed articles of incorporation, which must be signed by the original incorporators; (2) the names and addresses of the incorporators, the names and addresses of the initial members of the board of directors, and the number of shares they plan to subscribe to; (3) statements of the anticipated receipts, expenditures, earnings, and financial condition of the state savings bank for its first three years of operation, or a longer period as the board may require; (4) a showing satisfactory to the board that (a) the public convenience and advantage are served by the establishment of the proposed state savings bank; (b) there are reasonable demand and necessity in the community that is served by the establishment of the proposed state savings bank; (c) the proposed state savings bank has a reasonable probability of sustaining profitable and beneficial operations within a reasonable time in the community in which the proposed state savings bank intends to locate; (5) the proposed bylaws; and (6) statements, exhibits, maps, and other data that may be prescribed or requested by the board, and which are sufficiently detailed and comprehensive so as to enable the board to pass upon the criteria in this article.

**asset**

Any physical property or financial claim that is owned

**liability**

An amount owed

**balance sheet**

A financial statement showing assets, liabilities, and net worth at a given time; assets must equal liabilities plus net worth, so the statement is in balance

**net worth**

Assets minus liabilities; also called owners' equity

**required reserve ratio**

A Fed regulation that dictates the minimum percentage of deposits each bank must keep in reserve

# Operating a Bank

Suppose some business leaders in your hometown want to establish a bank. The following section discusses what they would need to do and consider to get their new banking operation up and running. These things would apply to the operation of any depository institution, such as a commercial bank, a savings and loan, a mutual savings bank, or a credit union.

## Getting a Charter

The bank founders first need to obtain a *charter*, or the right to operate. They would apply to the state banking authority to start up a state bank or to the U.S. Comptroller of the Currency to start up a national bank. In considering the application, the chartering agency would review the quality of management, the need for another bank in the community, the initial investment, and the likelihood of success.

The founders plan to invest $1,000,000 in the bank, and they indicate this on their charter application. Once their charter is granted, they incorporate, issuing themselves shares of stock, or certificates of ownership. Thus, they exchange $1,000,000 for shares of stock in a bank they name Home Bank. These shares are called the *owners' equity*, and represent the **net worth** of the bank.

The process of obtaining a bank charter in South Carolina is described in its Code of Laws, Title 34 - Banking, Financial Institutions, and Money. Access this document through econxtra.swlearning.com. What six items must an application for a savings bank charter granted in South Carolina contain? (Hint: See Section 34-30-70, B, 1-6.)

**econxtra.swlearning.com**

The owners invest this $1,000,000 buying, furnishing, and building the bank. These become the bank's assets. An **asset** is any physical property or financial claim owned by the bank. The bank is now ready for business.

### Bank Balance Sheet

Opening day is a lucky one for Home Bank because the first customer opens a checking account and deposits $100,000 in cash. The cash becomes the bank's asset. In accepting this deposit, the bank promises to repay the depositor that amount. That bank's promise becomes the bank's **liability**, which is an amount the bank owes.

As a result of this deposit, the bank's assets increase by $100,000 in cash and its liabilities increase by $100,000 in checkable deposits. At this point the money supply has not changed. The depositor simply converted $100,000 in cash to $100,000 in checkable deposits, which become part of the money supply. The bank's vault now holds the cash, which is no longer considered part of the money supply.

Look at the bank's **balance sheet**, presented in Figure 17.1. As the name implies, a balance sheet shows an equality, or a balance, between the two sides of the bank's account. The left side lists the bank's assets. At this stage, assets include the $1,000,000 in building and furnishings owned by Home Bank and the $100,000 in vault cash.

The right side shows two claims on the banks assets: claims by the owners, or net worth, amounting to $1,000,000, and claims by nonowners, or liabilities, which at this point consist of checkable deposits of $100,000. The two sides of the ledger must always be equal, or be in *balance*, which is why it's called a *balance sheet*. Assets must equal liabilities plus net worth.

Assets = Liabilities + Net Worth

### Reserve Accounts

The Fed requires Home Bank to set aside, or to hold in reserve, a percentage of checkable deposits. The **required reserve ratio** dictates the minimum proportion of deposits the

---

### Outside Resources

**How Banks Work** *How Stuff Works* is a commercial web site that provides basic information about a wide variety of businesses and organizations. It is designed to provide an overview of how American institutions function. A number of pages at this web site are devoted to banking and the Federal Reserve System. Direct students to visit this site and investigate the types of information about banking it has to offer. The URL is www.money.howstuffworks.com/bank.htm.

## Home Bank's Balance Sheet After $100,000 Deposit

Figure 17.1

The two sides of a balance sheet—assets and liabilities plus net worth—are always equal, or "in balance."

| Assets | | Liabilities and Net Worth | |
|---|---|---|---|
| Cash | $ 100,000 | Checkable Deposits | $ 100,000 |
| Building and Furniture | 1,000,000 | Net Worth | 1,000,000 |
| Total | $1,100,000 | Total | $1,100,000 |

bank must keep in reserve. The dollar amount that must be held in reserve is called **required reserves**—checkable deposits multiplied by the required reserve ratio.

All banks and thrifts are subject to the Fed's reserve requirement. Reserves are either held as cash in the bank's vault or put on deposit at the Fed. In neither case are those reserves in circulation, so they are not counted as part of the money supply. Neither earns Home Bank any interest. If the reserve requirement on checkable deposits is 10 percent, as it has been in recent years, Home Bank must hold $10,000 as required reserves. That equals 10 percent times $100,000.

Home Bank's reserves now consist of $10,000 in required reserves and $90,000 in **excess reserves**, which are reserves that exceed required reserves.

So far Home Bank has not earned a dime. Excess reserves, however, can be used to acquire interest-earning assets. By law, a bank's interest-bearing assets are limited primarily to loans and to government securities. Suppose Home Bank uses the $90,000 excess reserves to make loans and buy government securities.

### ✓ CHECKPOINT
What needs to be done to get a new banking operation up and running?

# Money Multiplier

Home Bank has used all its excess reserves to make loans and buy U.S. government securities, assets that will

earn interest. The bank now has no excess reserves. What if, in addition to Home Bank having no excess reserves, there are no excess reserves in the entire banking system? In this setting, how can the Fed increase the money supply?

### The Fed Makes a Move

To get the ball rolling, suppose the Fed buys a $10,000 U.S. government bond from Home Bank. This is called an open-market operation, and it's the primary way the Fed can alter the money supply. To pay for the bond, the Fed increases Home Bank's reserve account by $10,000. Where does the Fed get these reserves? It makes them up—creates them out of thin air, out of electronic ether!

In the process, Home Bank has exchanged one asset, a U.S. bond, for another asset, reserves held at the Fed. A U.S. bond is not money, nor are reserves, so the money supply has not yet changed. But Home Bank now has $10,000 in excess reserves, and excess reserves are the fuel for money creation.

### Round One

What will Home Bank do with those excess reserves? Suppose Megan comes in and applies for a $10,000 car loan. Home Bank approves her loan and increases her checking account by $10,000. Home Bank has converted her promise to repay, her IOU, into a

**required reserves**
The dollar amount that must be held in reserve; checkable deposits multiplied by the required reserve ratio

**excess reserves**
Bank reserves in excess of required reserves

---

---

## Money Multiplier

Point out that the money supply changes by much more than any increase or decrease in the amount of money the Fed chooses to place in circulation, because of what is called the money multiplier. Although economists know there is a money multiplier, they also realize it is not always the same. When the economy is growing, the multiplier is likely to be greater than when the economy is in decline. The importance of this fact is that the Fed never knows exactly what will happen to the total money supply when it places more money into, or removes some money from, circulation. Monetary policy is not a precise science.

## E-CONOMICS

Direct students to read the passage entitled "Banking from the Big Rig" on page 523.

## Answers to Think Critically

Answers will vary. Possible answer: Targeting a depository institution to a particular consumer group could be effective if the group demands specialized services and is large enough to support the institution. Online banks can use the Internet to advertise and target particular groups who are already computer-savvy.

## CHECKPOINT

Invite a student to answer the checkpoint that appears on page 523.

## Answer

The banking system can expand the money supply by a multiple of excess reserves under the following circumstances: (1) the banks do not allow excess reserves to sit; (2) borrowed funds do not idle in checking accounts but are spent; and (3) the public does not choose to hold some of the newly created money as cash.

---

**money multiplier**
The multiple by which the money supply increases as a result of an increase in excess reserves in the banking system

$10,000 checkable deposit. *Because her newly created checkable deposit is money, this loan increases the money supply by $10,000.*

She writes a $10,000 check for the car, and the dealer promptly deposits it in the company's checking account at Fidelity Bank. Fidelity Bank increases the car dealer's account by $10,000, and sends Megan's check to the Fed. The Fed transfers $10,000 in reserves from Home Bank's account to Fidelity Bank's account. The Fed then sends the check to Home Bank, which reduces Megan's checkable deposits by $10,000. The Fed has thus "cleared" her check by settling the claim that Fidelity Bank had on Home Bank.

At this point, the $10,000 in checkable deposits has simply shifted from Megan's account at Home Bank to the car dealer's account at Fidelity Bank. The increase in the money supply in this first round remains at $10,000.

### Round Two and Beyond

Because the reserve requirement is 10 percent, Fidelity Bank sets aside $1,000 of the new deposit as reserves and lends the remaining $9,000 for a computer purchase by increasing the borrower's checking account. Thus, the money supply has increased by an additional $9,000, and the cumulative increase is $19,000 to this point.

An individual bank can lend no more than its excess reserves. When the borrower spends the amount loaned, reserves at one bank usually fall. However, total reserves in the banking system do not fall because the money that is spent is most often deposited in a bank by the person who received it. The recipient bank can use most of the new deposit to extend more loans, creating more checkable deposits. The potential expansion of checkable deposits in the banking system equals some multiple of the initial increase in reserves.

This cycle of borrowing, spending, and depositing continues round after round. As a result of the Fed buying this $10,000 bond, the money supply can eventually increase by a multiple of the excess reserves created by the Fed.

Because this money-creation process began with the Fed's open-market operation, the Fed can rightfully claim, "The buck starts here." This slogan appears on a large plaque in the Federal Reserve chairman's office.

### Reserve Requirements and Money Expansion

The banking system as a whole eliminates excess reserves by expanding the money supply. With a 10 percent reserve requirement, the Fed's initial injection of $10,000 in fresh reserves could support up to $100,000 in new checkable deposits.

The **money multiplier** is the maximum multiple by which the money supply increases as a result of an increase in the banking system's excess reserves. The money multiplier equals 1 divided by the required reserve ratio. If $r$ stands for the required reserve ratio, then the money multiplier is $1/r$. In this example, the required reserve ratio is 10 percent, or 0.1, so the money multiplier is $1/0.1$, which equals 10. The formula for the multiple expansion of checkable deposits can be written as:

Change in checkable deposits
= Change in excess reserves $\times\ 1/r$

The higher the reserve requirement, the greater the fraction of deposits that must be held as reserves, so the smaller the money multiplier. A reserve requirement of 20 percent instead of 10 percent would require each bank to set aside twice as much in required reserves. The money multiplier in this case would be $1/0.2$, which equals 5. The maximum possible increase in checkable deposits resulting from an initial $10,000 increase in fresh reserves would be $10,000 $\times$ 5, or $50,000.

*Excess reserves fuel the expansion of checkable deposits. A higher reserve requirement drains this fuel from the banking system, thereby reducing the amount of new money that can be created.* The fractional reserve requirement is the key to the multiple expansion of checkable deposits. If each $1 deposit had to be backed by $1 in required reserves, the money multiplier would be cut to 1.

---

### *Economic Headlines*

Instruct students to locate an article in a current magazine or newspaper that relates to one of the topics in this lesson. For example, they might find articles about changes in the money supply that have made it easier or more difficult for people or businesses to borrow funds. Instruct students to read the article, write a brief summary, and include a reference citation. Identify the style you want them to use for the citation.

As an alternative, you might find several articles of interest and provide citations for students to use in locating one of the articles. Direct students to read the article they have chosen, and write a brief explanation of how it relates to this lesson.

Contraction of the money supply works in the same way, but in reverse. It begins with the Fed *selling* a $10,000 U.S. bond to Home Bank. Therefore, the Fed increases the money supply by buying bonds and decreases it by selling bonds.

## Limitations on the Multiplier

For a given required reserve ratio, the multiplier is greatest if

1. banks do not allow excess reserves to sit idle

2. borrowed funds do not sit idle in checking accounts but are spent

3. the public does not choose to hold some of the newly created money as cash.

If excess reserves remain idle or if borrowed funds sit around in checking accounts, they are less able to fuel an expansion of the money supply. If people stash away some of the newly created money as cash rather than spend it or leave it in checking accounts, then that portion of borrowed funds held as cash cannot provide additional reserves in the banking system.

For the money multiplier to operate, a particular bank need not use excess reserves just to make loans. It could just as well use them to pay all its employees a Christmas bonus. As long as that spending ends up as checkable deposits in the banking system, the money multiplier can operate.

### CHECKPOINT
How can the banking system expand the money supply by a multiple of excess reserves?

## E-CONOMICS

### Banking from the Big Rig

An unexpected development with the rise of online banking technology has been the growth of "specialty banks" created to serve particular types of customers. Most of these banks target members of a specific workforce who would be likely to use online banking. For example, in 2000 NationalInterbank formed a partnership with PNV Inc., a web site company aimed at truckers, to operate an online bank for truckers. Because truckers spend so much of their time on the road, traditional banking is not convenient for them. Truckers "are on the road, not at home, and probably not near a (bank) branch," notes online banking expert Richard Bell. "And most of these guys are sitting on a quarter of a million dollars worth of truck, so they either have money or owe money." With the creation of this specialty bank, a trucker can now do his or her

banking from the seat of a big rig. In some ways, this trend in specialty banks is a throwback to credit unions, which originally were created to serve only members of particular groups, usually particular professions. Ironically, in recent years changes in banking laws have allowed many credit unions to expand their client base beyond the groups they originally were designed to serve. Some credit unions claimed that they had to broaden their client base in order to stay in business. The online specialty banks mark a reversal of this trend.

### Think Critically

Do you think targeting a particular type of customer group would be effective? Why or why not? Would this strategy make more sense for online banking than it does for traditional depository institutions? Explain your answer.

## APPLY

Assign Lesson 17.1 from the Contemporary Economics Workbook.

## *e*-con @pps

Encourage students to apply their knowledge of concepts presented in this lesson as they explore economic news stories, policy debates, and data available at **econxtra.swlearning.com.** A sampling of the titles for this lesson appears below.

### EconNews
● Mortgage Rates and the Fed?

## ASSESS

Assign all or part of Lesson 17.1 Assessment on page 524 as homework or an in-class activity.

## Xtra! Study Tools

Direct students to the online study tools for Lesson 17.1 at **econxtra.swlearning.com.**

## CLOSE

**Revisit** the In the News feature on the first page of the lesson. Ask students to review their preliminary answers and discuss the questions, now that they have completed this lesson.

**Review** the objectives for Lesson 17.1. Students should be able to:

● Discuss what's involved in getting a new banking operation up and running.

● Describe how the banking system can expand the money supply by a multiple of excess reserves.

## RETEACH

The deposit multiplier depends on the willingness of people and businesses to either spend or deposit funds they receive. Suppose the Fed purchased $10 million in government securities, thus increasing banks' excess reserves. Banks would lend the majority of these funds. Borrowers would spend the $10 million, so some other person or institution would receive these funds as additional income. If these funds are then re-spent or deposited in a bank that will use them to make loans, all is well. But some of these funds will be held in cash and not re-spent. Point out that any cash students have in their pockets, purses, piggy banks, or at home in a drawer might just as well not exist from the point of view of the economy. At any given time, about one-third of all cash is being held out of circulation and cannot be multiplied. This is the biggest reason why the multiplier does not work to increase the money supply to its fullest theoretical potential.

## Key Concepts

1. Answers will vary. Possible answer: Requiring the people who organize banks to invest their own money creates a financial "cushion" for depositors. If the bank loses money, it will lose the owners' equity first.

2. Answers will vary. Possible answer: The homeowner will make regular payments to the bank to pay off the mortgage over a period of many years. Thus, the mortgage is a source of income to the bank. Deposits in the bank, on the other hand, must be repaid to the depositor in the future and are therefore a liability to the bank.

3. Answers will vary. Possible answer: The bank has $2 million in excess reserves, upon which it earns no return. It will want to invest or lend these funds as quickly as possible to earn a return on them.

4. Answers will vary. Possible answer: Money held in cash is not part of any bank's excess reserves and cannot be lent to others. The more cash people hold, the smaller the increase in the money supply will be.

## Graphing Exercise

5. Answers will vary. Possible answer: The banks would be required to keep larger reserves and therefore could not lend as much money. This would reduce the total amount of money that could be added to the economy through the expansion process.

   An example of an acceptable graph appears at the bottom of this page.

## Think Critically

6. Answers will vary. Possible answer: Money that people hold in cash and do not spend cannot be lent. This effectively reduces the impact of the expansion process.

**Expansion of a New $2,000 Deposit**

| | New Deposit | Required Reserve | New Loan |
|---|---|---|---|
| Round 1 | $2,000.00 | $240.00 | $1,760.00 |
| Round 2 | $1,760.00 | $211.00 | $1,548.80 |
| Round 3 | $1,548.80 | $185.86 | $1,362.90 |
| Round 4 | $1,362.94 | $163.55 | $1,199.39 |

---

## Key Concepts

1. Why are people who organize a bank required to invest their own funds as owner's equity in the new business? How does this help to protect the bank's depositors?

2. Why is a loan made to help a consumer purchase a house an asset to the bank, while any funds the homeowner deposits in the same bank a liability?

3. Bank ABC holds $100 million in deposits upon which it must maintain a required reserve of 10 percent. The bank currently has $12 million on reserve. How much excess reserves does the bank hold? Why would it want to invest or loan these reserves as quickly as possible?

4. Why doesn't the money multiplier work as effectively if people decide to hold additional funds they receive in cash?

## Graphing Exercise

5. Construct a bar graph to show four rounds of the money-creation process that would result from a new deposit of $2,000 in a checking account when the required reserve is 10 percent.

**Expansion of a New $2,000 Deposit**

| | New Deposit | Required Reserve | New Loan |
|---|---|---|---|
| Round 1 | $2,000.00 | $200.00 | $1,800.00 |
| Round 2 | $1,800.00 | $180.00 | $1,620.00 |
| Round 3 | $1,620.00 | $162.00 | $1,458.00 |
| Round 4 | $1,458.00 | $145.80 | $1,312.20 |

## Think Critically

6. **Math** Recalculate the table in exercise 5 above, assuming that the Fed increased the required reserve ratio from 10 to 12 percent. Why is the required reserve an important factor in determining the amount of money that banks are able to lend? What would happen to consumers' ability to borrow funds from banks if the required reserve was increased?

---

**Expansion of a New $2,000 Deposit**

(bar graph)
New deposits
- $2,500
- $2,000 — Round 1: 2,000
- $1,500 — Round 2: 1,800; Round 3: 1,620
- $1,000 — Round 4: 1,458
- $500
- $0

Round 1   Round 2   Round 3   Round 4

## Visualizing the Answer— Graphing Exercise

5. The answer includes a graph. Students' graphs should look similar to the one shown here. An Excel spreadsheet containing this graph, along with supporting data, is available on the Instructor's Resource CD.

## Objectives

> Explain the shape of the money demand curve.

> Explain how changes in the money supply affect interest rates and real GDP in the short run.

> Discuss the federal funds rate and why the Fed uses this rate to set monetary policy goals.

## Overview

So far the focus has been on how the banking system creates money. A more fundamental question is how the money supply affects the economy as a whole. When the Fed expands the money supply, this drives down interest rates in the short run. Because the cost of borrowing falls, firms borrow more to buy capital goods and households borrow more to buy cars, homes, and other "big ticket" items. Thus, an increase in the supply of money increases aggregate demand, output, and employment in the short run.

## Key Terms

**money demand**

**money supply**

**federal funds market**

**federal funds rate**

## [ In the News ]

### ● Cutting the Federal Funds Rate

In December 2001, the Federal Reserve announced that it was cutting the federal funds rate—the interest rate that banks charge to each other for overnight loans—to 1.75 percent. This was the lowest federal funds rate since 1958, and it marked the eleventh time that the Fed had lowered this rate in 2001. The idea is that lowering the rate reduces the cost of covering any reserve shortfalls, making banks more willing to lend money. For nearly four decades, the Fed has focused its monetary policy on this interest rate. Banks use this rate to help set their prime lending rates for other items. For example, the lowering of the federal funds rate in 2001 helped keep mortgage rates low, boosting the housing market. The Fed lowered its rates so much in 2001 because of rising unemployment and consumer uncertainty caused by the war on terrorism. In 2002, the economy had mixed results, with continuing unemployment but gains in automobile and housing loans thanks to lower interest rates. As a result, the Fed left its federal funds rate alone for more than a year.

### Think About It

Why do you think lower interest rates boost consumers' willingness to make major purchases?

**525**

### National Content Standards in Economics

A complete list of the NCEE Standards appears on pages xxiv–xxv of this book. The following standards are addressed in Lesson 17.2.

Standard 4: Role of Incentives

Standard 10: Role of Economic Institutions

Standard 11: Role of Money

Standard 12: Role of Interest Rates

Standard 15: Growth

Standard 16: Role of Government

Standard 20: Monetary and Fiscal Policy

## Money Demand

Remind students that businesses borrow money when they expect to be able to use that money to earn a profit. If a business believes it can earn a 12 percent return from a machine it might buy with borrowed funds, it will be willing to pay a bank 8 percent interest for a loan. If it expects to earn only 6 percent from the machine, it will not borrow and pay the bank 8 percent. To a large extent, a business's borrowing is determined by its expectation of investment returns. When businesses expect the economy and profits to grow, they demand more money. When they believe the economy and their profits well decline, they demand less money.

People's willingness to borrow is similar but less easy to quantify. When people are confident of their job and future earning power, they are more likely to demand money to spend. When they are worried about the future, they are less willing to demand money. By studying the demand for money in the economy and making appropriate adjustments in the money supply, the Fed is able to adjust interest rates and affect the amount of money that will be borrowed and spent. Monetary policy is reasonably effective in adjusting aggregate demand in the short run.

### *Think Critically Through Visuals*

Direct students to focus their attention on the photographs on this page. Ask for a volunteer to answer the question posed in the caption.

### Answer

Answers will vary. Possible answer: Most people regularly withdraw money and regularly purchase food.

### NCEE Standard 11: Role of Money

Money makes it easier to trade, borrow, save, invest, and compare the value of goods and services.

# Money Demand

Recall the distinction between a *stock* and a *flow*. A stock measures something at a point in time, such as the amount of money you have with you right now. A flow measures something over an interval of time, such as your income per week. It may seem odd to even talk about the demand for money. You might think people would demand all the money they could get their hands on. Remember, however, that *money*, the stock, is not the same as *income*, the flow. People express their demand for money by holding some of their wealth as money rather than holding other assets. People express their demand for income by selling their labor and other resources to earn income.

## A Medium of Exchange

Why do people demand money? Why do people maintain checking accounts and have cash in their pockets, purses, wallets, desk drawers, lockers, and coffee cans? The reason is obvious. *People demand money to carry out market transactions.* Money is a convenient medium of exchange.

Your demand for money is based on your expected spending. If you plan to buy lunch tomorrow, you will carry enough money to pay for it. You may also have extra money on hand in case of an emergency or in case you come across something else you want to buy. You may have a little extra cash with you right now for who knows what. Even you don't know.

## A Store of Value

The demand for money is related to money's role as a medium of exchange. However, money also is a store of value. People save for a new home, for college, for retirement. People can store their purchasing power as money or as other financial assets, such as corporate and government bonds. When people purchase bonds and other financial assets, they are lending their money and earning interest for doing so. The interest rate indicates the cost of borrowing and the reward for lending.

## The Cost of Holding Money

The demand for any asset is based on the flow of services it provides. The big advantage of money is its general acceptance in market exchange. In contrast, other financial assets, such as corporate bonds, government bonds, and some bank accounts, must first be liqui-

 Main Idea

**Role of Money**

As a medium of exchange, *money makes it easier to trade, borrow, save, invest, and compare the value of goods and services.* Which of these activities do you regularly do?

© Getty Images/PhotoDisc
© Getty Images/PhotoDisc

**526**   CHAPTER 17   Money Creation, Federal Reserve, Monetary Policy

### *Outside Resources*

**District Federal Reserve Banks** Each of the 12 District Federal Reserve Banks maintain public education programs. Meetings are held with educators, seminars are provided for business leaders, and the public is invited to visit their web sites to learn about the work the Federal Reserve accomplishes. The San Francisco District Federal Reserve Bank, for example, has a series of web pages that describe and explain the Fed's use of monetary policy. Ask students to visit this web page at www.frbsf.org/publications/federalreserve/monetary and summarize their findings.

dated, or exchanged for money, before they can fund market transactions.

Money, however, has one major drawback when compared with other financial assets. Money in the form of currency, demand deposits, and travelers checks earns no interest. Checkable deposits that do earn interest earn less than other financial assets.

Holding wealth in the form of money means passing up some interest that could be earned by holding some other financial asset. For example, suppose a business could earn 4 percent more interest by holding some financial asset other than money. Holding $1 million in money would have an opportunity cost of $40,000 per year. *The interest given up is the opportunity cost of holding money.*

### Money Demand and Interest Rates

**Money demand** is the relationship between how much money people want to hold and the interest rate. The interest earnings that are given up are the cost of holding money. When the interest rate is low, other things constant, the cost of holding money is low. People hold more of their wealth as money. When the interest rate is high, the cost of holding money is high. People hold less money and more

**Investigate Your Local Economy**

Research interest rates offered on savings accounts at local banks or online banks. Would these rates motivate people to deposit their money in these accounts? Record the interest rates you find, and write a paragraph to explain your answer to the question.

assets that pay higher interest. Thus, *other things constant, the quantity of money demanded varies inversely with the market interest rate.*

The money demand curve, $D_m$, in Figure 17.2 shows the quantity of money people in the economy demand at alternative interest rates, other things constant. *The quantity of money demanded is inversely related to the price of holding money, which is the interest rate.* Movements along the curve reflect the effects of changes

**money demand**
The relationship between how much money people want to hold and the interest rate

**The Graphing Workshop**

**Demand for Money**
econxtra.swlearning.com

**Figure 17.2**

The money demand curve, $D_m$, slopes downward. As the interest rate falls, so does the opportunity cost of holding money. The quantity of money demanded increases.

*Lesson 17.2 • Monetary Policy in the Short Run* **527**

### TEACH (continued)

### Money Demand

Ask one student to represent a bank with the objective of earning as much interest as possible. The bank has $10 million to lend. Ask five other students to represent borrowers. Write the following messages on separate cards and provide a card to each borrower.

- You know of an investment that will earn an 8 percent return if you invest $5 million.
- You know of an investment that will earn a 9 percent return if you invest $5 million.
- You know of an investment that will earn a 10 percent return if you invest $5 million.
- You know of an investment that will earn an 11 percent return if you invest $5 million.
- You know of an investment that will earn a 12 percent return if you invest $5 million.

Instruct the borrowers and bank to negotiate interest rates and loans. They should end up with an interest rate between 10 and 11 percent. Three potential borrowers will not take out a loan because the interest rate they must pay is greater than their expected return.

**Investigate Your Local Economy**
Suggest that students check the interest rates at five or more banks. Point out that the required information can be obtained by telephoning the banks or visiting their web sites. Suggest that students create a table to accompany their paragraph.

### Think Critically Through Visuals

Direct students to focus their attention on **Figure 17.2—Demand for Money.** Point out that movement along the curve reflects the effects of changes in the interest rate on the quantity of money demanded, other things constant.

**The Graphing Workshop** ——— See It

Direct students to the Graphing Workshop for Chapter 17 at **econxtra .swlearning.com.** Instruct students to click on **See It: Money Market Equilibrium** to view the graph and listen to an explanation.

### ENRICH

During the final years of the twentieth century, the U.S. economy experienced rapid growth that was fueled in part by what was called the dot-com revolution. Vast amounts of money were invested in fiber optic networks to carry Internet messages. At the same time, thousands of new web-based businesses were initiated. Another source of spending was generated from individuals, businesses, and government agencies that replaced their computer systems to avoid potential Y2K problems. Much of this investment was financed by borrowed funds. Ask students to investigate what happened to interest rates in the late 1990s. How does this demonstrate that increased demand for money leads to higher interest rates?

**CHECKPOINT**
Invite a student to answer the checkpoint that appears on this page.

**Answer**

Other things constant, the quantity of money demanded varies inversely with the market interest rate. This explains the downward sloping demand curve.

## TEACH

### Money Supply and the Market Interest Rate

Remind students that interest rates are a function of the interaction of the demand for money and the supply of money. Most adjustments in the money supply made by the Fed are the result of the Fed buying either more or fewer government securities. Because the economy is usually growing, there is normally a steady increase in the demand for money. If the Fed allows the money supply to grow, but at a rate that is slower than production's growth, the demand for money will exceed the supply and interest rates will increase. In most cases, it is not necessary for the Fed to sell government securities to force interest rates to increase. All it needs to do is to buy securities at a slower rate. The Fed is likely to sell securities only when it wants to reduce the money supply and force interest rates up quickly.

### Think Critically Through Visuals 👁

Direct students to focus their attention on **Figure 17.3—Effect of an Increase in the Money Supply**. Point out that the money supply curve does not have the usual upward sloping shape of other supply curves.

Direct students to the Graphing Workshop for Chapter 17 at **econxtra. swlearning.com.** Instruct students to click on **See It: Monetary Policy with Aggregate Supply** to view the graph and listen to an explanation.

---

in the interest rate on the quantity of money demanded, other things constant.

**CHECKPOINT**
What explains the shape of the money demand curve?

# Money Supply and the Market Interest Rate

The money demand curve has the usual downward sloping shape of other demand curves. The only difference is that the price is measured not by dollars but by an interest rate. What about money supply?

### Money Supply

**money supply**
The stock of money available in the economy at a particular time

**Money supply** is the stock of money available in the economy at a particular time. Money supply is determined primarily by the Fed through its control over currency and excess reserves in the banking system. The *money supply curve* does not have the usual upward

sloping shape of other supply curves. The supply of money, $S_m$, is depicted as a vertical line in Figure 17.3. A vertical supply curve indicates that the quantity of money in the economy is fixed by the Fed at any given time and is therefore independent of the interest rate. The assumption is that the Fed determines the money supply.

### Market Interest Rate

The intersection in Figure 17.3 of the money demand curve, $D_m$, with the money supply curve, $S_m$, determines the market interest rate, $i$. That rate equates the quantity of money demanded in the economy with the quantity of money supplied by the Fed. At interest rates above the equilibrium level, the opportunity cost of holding money is higher, so the quantity people demand is less than the quantity supplied. At interest rates below the equilibrium level, the opportunity cost of holding money is lower, so the quantity of money people demand exceeds the quantity supplied.

### An Increase in the Money Supply

If the Fed increases the money supply, by, for example, purchasing U.S. bonds, the money supply curve shifts to the

 **Effect of an Increase in the Money Supply**    **Figure 17.3**

*econxtra.swlearning.com*

Because the supply of money is determined by the Federal Reserve, money supply can be represented by a vertical line. The intersection of the supply of money, $S_m$, and the demand for money $D_m$, determines the equilibrium interest rate, $i$. Following an increase in the money supply to $S'_m$, the quantity of money supplied exceeds the quantity demanded at the original interest rate, $i$. People who are holding more money than they would like attempt to exchange money for bonds or other financial assets. In doing so, they drive the interest rate down to $i'$, where quantity demanded equals the new quantity supplied.

**528**    **CHAPTER 17**    Money Creation, Federal Reserve, Monetary Policy right, as shown by the movement from $S_m$ to $S'_m$ in Figure 17.3. The interest rate must fall to encourage people to hold the increased supply of money. The interest rate falls until the quantity of money demanded just equals the quantity supplied. With the decline in the interest rate to $i'$ in Figure 17.3, the opportunity cost of holding money falls enough that the public is willing to hold the now-larger supply of money. *For a given money demand curve, an increase in money supply pushes down the market interest rate, and a decrease in the supply of money pushes up the market interest rate.*

Now that you have some idea how money demand and supply determine the market interest rate, you are ready to see how money fits into the economy in the short run. Specifically, how do changes in the supply of money affect aggregate demand and real GDP?

### Effect of Lower Interest Rates

Suppose the Federal Reserve believes that the economy is operating below its potential and decides to stimulate

output and employment by increasing the money supply. The Fed can expand the money supply by

1. purchasing U.S. government securities

2. reducing the *discount rate* (the rate at which banks can borrow from the Fed), or

3. lowering the required reserve ratio to create excess reserves.

An increase in the money supply reduces the market interest rate. A lower interest rate encourages consumers to save less and borrow more. A lower rate also encourages businesses to invest more in capital goods. Thus, a lower interest rate stimulates consumption and investment. This greater aggregate demand will increase real GDP in the short run, as shown by the movement from $Y$ to $Y'$ in Figure 17.4. Note that the price level also increases.

Thus, monetary policy in the short run influences the market interest rate, which in turn stimulates aggregate demand and increases real GDP. *In the short run, changes in the money supply affect*

## Ask the Xpert!
econxtra.swlearning.com

*Why should we care how fast the money supply grows?*

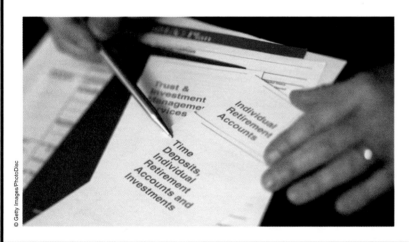

**What effect would lower interest rates have on each of the three topics explained in the brochure—time deposits (checking accounts), individual retirement accounts, and investments?**

© Getty Images/PhotoDisc

## TEACH (continued)

### Money Supply and the Market Interest Rate

Return to the example of the five businesses (students) that are considering borrowing $5 million to make an investment. Give the student who represents a bank a piece of paper that is labeled "$10 million government bond." Explain that you are the Fed and offer to purchase this bond from the student for $10.1 million in additional cash. The student will agree to take advantage of the $.1 million profit. Then have the bank and businesses negotiate new loans and interest rates. This time, the interest rate should fall between 8 and 9 percent because of the increase in the money supply. Four of the businesses will take out loans and invest the money in the economy. This will cause greater economic activity and increased employment.

## Ask the Xpert!

Direct students to **econxtra.swlearning.com** to hear an expert answer the question "Why should we care how fast the money supply grows?"

### *Think Critically Through Visuals*

Direct students to focus their attention on the photograph on this page. Ask for a volunteer to answer the question posed in the caption.

### Answer

Answers will vary. Possible answer: Time deposits would decrease. Individual retirement accounts would decrease. Investments would increase.

---

## *Curriculum Connection—Psychology*

Once a leader's credibility has been lost it, becomes almost impossible for that person to lead successfully. During much of the 1970s, for example, Arthur Burns was Chairman of the Fed's Board of Governors. During that time, he repeatedly stated that the Fed would take steps to fight inflation. At the same time, the Fed increased the money supply and kept interest rates relatively low. This contributed to growing rates of inflation. Many people stopped believing what they were told by the Fed, and the Fed's policies became less relevant to what was happening in the economy. Ask students what this has to do with consumer psychology.

## Money Supply and the Market Interest Rate

Choose two students to help with this demonstration. Each student will represent a commercial bank. One has $5 million in excess reserves. The other is $5 million short of meeting its required reserve ratio. Ask students to explain why each bank is displeased by the situation. (The bank with the excess reserves is earning nothing from these funds. The bank that is not meeting its reserve ratio is in danger of being penalized by the Fed.) Ask students what the logical answer is to each bank's problems. (The bank with the excess reserves should lend $5 million at the federal funds rate to the bank that is short of reserves.)

### Think Critically Through Visuals

Direct students to focus their attention on **Figure 17.4—Effects of a Lower Interest Rate**. Point out that a lower interest rate shifts the aggregate demand curve to the right.

 **CHECKPOINT**
Invite a student to answer the checkpoint that appears on this page.

### Answer

An increase in the money supply pushes the market interest rate down and increases the real GDP, while a decrease in the money supply increases the market interest rate and decreases the real GDP.

---

**Effects of a Lower Interest Rate**

Figure 17.4

A lower interest rate encourages households to spend more and save less. It also encourages businesses to invest more. More consumption and investment increases aggregate demand. Therefore, a lower interest rate shifts the aggregate demand curve to the right, thereby increasing employment and output in the short run. In the short run, this increases real GDP and the price level.

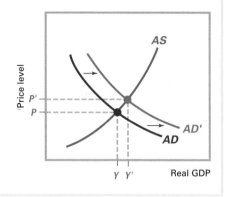

---

the economy through changes in the interest rate.

### Increasing Interest Rates

Now consider the effect of an increase in the interest rate. Suppose Fed officials decide to reduce the money supply to cool down an overheated economy. The Fed can reduce the money supply by

1. selling U.S. government securities

2. increasing the discount rate, or

3. raising the required reserve ratio.

A decrease in the money supply would increase the equilibrium interest rate. At the higher interest rate, businesses find it more costly to finance plants and equipment. Households find it more costly to finance new homes and other major purchases. Thus a higher interest rate reduces aggregate demand, and this reduction in aggregate demand will reduce real GDP in the short run.

**federal funds market**
A market for overnight lending and borrowing of reserves held by the Fed for banks

 **CHECKPOINT**
How do changes in the money supply affect interest rates and real GDP in the short run?

---

## The Federal Funds Rate

At 2:15 P.M. on June 25, 2003, immediately following a meeting, the Federal Open Market Committee (FOMC) announced that it would lower its target for the federal funds rate by one quarter of a percentage point to 1 percent, the lowest rate since 1958. What is the federal funds rate, and how did the Fed's action affect the economy?

### Federal Funds Market

*Because reserves earn no interest, banks usually try to keep excess reserves to a minimum.* Banks continuously "sweep" their accounts to find excess reserves that can be put to some interest-bearing use. They do not let excess reserves remain idle even overnight. The **federal funds market** provides for overnight lending and borrowing among banks of excess reserves on account at the Fed.

For example, suppose that at the end of the business day, Home Bank has excess reserves of $10,000 on account with the Fed and wants to lend that amount to another bank that finished the day requiring reserves of $10,000. These two banks make a deal in the federal funds market—that is, the

**530** CHAPTER 17 Money Creation, Federal Reserve, Monetary Policy

---

### Group Activity

Organize students into five groups.

Group 1: *Local Bank.* Your bank is short on excess reserves. You can't make additional loans unless you receive more deposits.

Group 2: *Business A.* Sales are low for your business. You won't borrow money at any interest rate.

Group 3: *Business B.* Sales are high for your business. You will borrow even if interest rates go up 5%.

Group 4: *Business C.* Your business is doing okay but not great. You would borrow funds if interest rates fell by 3%.

Group 5: *The Fed.* Make each of the following policy decisions one at a time. Give the other groups time to react to each decision.

*Continued on the bottom of page 531.*

market for borrowing and lending reserves at the Fed. The interest rate paid on such loans is called the **federal funds rate** or the *interbank loan rate*. This is the interest rate targeted by the Fed's monetary policy.

### Aggressive Rate Cuts

Between early 2001 and June 2003, the Fed cut the federal funds rate 5.5 percentage points in 13 steps. This was the most aggressive effort to stimulate the economy ever. In cutting the target rate on that June afternoon, the FOMC said the series of cuts was "providing important ongoing support to economic activity." Yet the economy "has yet to exhibit sustained growth."

To lower the federal funds rate, the FOMC made open-market purchases of government securities, increasing reserves in the banking system until the rate fell to the target level.

### Why Target This Rate?

For nearly four decades, the Fed has influenced the money supply by focusing mostly on changes in the federal funds rate. There are many interest rates in the economy—for credit cards, new car sales, mortgages, home equity loans, personal loans, and so on. Why does the Fed choose to focus on the federal funds rate? First, by changing bank reserves through open-market operations, the Fed has a direct lever on this rate. The Fed's ability to influence this rate is stronger than it is for any other market rate. Second, the federal funds rate serves as a benchmark in the economy for determining many other interest rates. For example, after the Fed announces a change in its target federal funds rate, major banks around the country often change by the same amount their prime interest rate—the interest rate they charge their best corporate customers.

**federal funds rate**
The interest rate charged in the federal funds market; the Fed's target interest rate

### The Federal Funds Rate

Point out that a bank has several options when it needs to raise cash on short notice. Each option has a downside:

- Reduce the amount of new loans. (presents problems for customers)
- Sell government securities. (takes time and might have to sell at a loss)
- Borrow funds from the Fed at the discount rate. (Fed can refuse or charge rate higher than the current discount rate.)
- Borrow funds from another bank and pay the federal funds rate. (federal funds rate is high)

## Ethics in Action

**Interest Rates and Risky Lending** In the 1930s, government regulators put a ceiling on the interest rates that banks could pay depositors. This ceiling was designed to reduce what was viewed as harmful competition among banks that had led to bank failures during the Great Depression. For decades after that, savings and loans (S&Ls) paid 2 or 3 percent interest to depositors and turned around and lent the money to homebuyers for 4 or 5 percent interest. All this worked well in a low-interest environment. In the 1970s, however, interest rates started rising. Depositors found they could earn more interest elsewhere, so they began withdrawing their money from S&Ls and buying money market mutual funds and other assets that paid more interest. S&Ls needed to attract deposits to cover their loans, which would remain on their books for years to come. In an effort to help the situation, Congress eliminated the ceiling on interest rates that S&Ls could pay depositors. However, getting more deposits didn't do the S&Ls much good because they had to pay more for deposits than they were making on the loans those deposits supported. They were on a collision course, and many of them failed. S&Ls began looking to make loans that would pay more interest. Many were too eager to lend money to customers who turned out to be poor credit risks. There was questionable behavior on both sides—S&L operators who were willing to go for broke in making loans and borrowers who misrepresented the potential success of their projects. Ultimately the taxpayers paid for much of the mess left in the wake of these questionable practices.

### Think Critically

What was the ethical problem in this scenario?

### Ethics in Action

Have students work in pairs to discuss the ethical issue featured on this page and develop answers to the questions presented.

### Answers to Think Critically

Answers will vary. Possible answer: There are two ethical problems in this scenario. The S&L operators made risky loans, and borrowers misrepresented the potential success of their projects.

**NET Bookmark**

Direct students to **econxtra.swlearning.com.** Remind them to click on the link for Lesson 17.2 to find the appropriate link for the **NET Bookmark** on page 532.

*Think Critically Through Visuals*

Direct students to focus their attention on **Figure 17.5—Recent Ups and Downs in the Federal Funds Rate** on page 532. Point out the reasons for the dramatic drop in interest rates during 2001.

Continued from the bottom of page 530.

### Group Activity

Direct the group that represents the Fed's Board of Governors to announce policy changes one at a time. How do the other groups react? The point to make is that businesses do not always respond to the Fed's actions.

1. Sell bonds to reduce the money supply and raise interest rates by 2%.

2. Buy bonds to increase the money supply and lower interest rates by 2%.
3. Increase the reserve ratio by 1% so banks are less able to lend funds.
4. Lower the discount rate by 1% to pressure banks to lower the prime rate.

**TEAM WORK**

Instruct students to reproduce the graph shown in Figure 17.5 and add information that they gather from their research. Each team should produce a single graph.

CHECKPOINT

Invite a student to answer the checkpoint that appears on this page.

## Answer

The federal funds rate is the interest rate charged in the federal funds market. The Fed uses it to set monetary policy because it serves as a benchmark in the economy of determining many other interest rates.

### APPLY

Assign Lesson 17.2 from the Contemporary Economics Workbook.

## e-con @pps

Encourage students to apply their knowledge of concepts presented in this lesson as they explore economic news stories, policy debates, and data available at **econxtra.swlearning. com.** A sampling of the titles for this lesson appears below.

### EconData

• 10-Year Treasury Bond Yield
• Money Supply

### ASSESS

Assign all or part of Lesson 17.2 Assessment on page 533 as homework or an in-class activity.

## Xtra! Study Tools

Direct students to the online study tools for Lesson 17.2 at **econxtra.swlearning.com.**

### CLOSE

**Revisit** the In the News feature on the first page of the lesson. Ask students to review their preliminary answers and discuss the questions, now that they have completed this lesson.

**Review** the objectives for Lesson 17.2. Students should be able to:

• Explain the shape of the money demand curve.
• Explain how changes in the money supply affect interest rates and real GDP in the short run.
• Discuss the federal funds rate and why the Fed uses this rate to set monetary policy goals.

## NETBookmark

Access the web page for the Federal Open Market Committee through econxtra.swlearning.com. Under the heading "Meetings and Proceedings of the FOMC," you will find a calendar of meetings. Choose one of the years, and click on "Statement" for all of the meetings in that year. Write a paragraph summarizing the decisions the FOMC made regarding the federal funds rate for that year.

*econxtra.swlearning.com*

## TEAM WORK

Work in groups of three to four students to research the federal funds rate on the Federal Open Market Committee web page, as directed in the Net Bookmark activity. Each group member should choose a different year to research. Compare and discuss your findings as a group, referring to the line graph in Figure 17.5.

**Recent Ups and Downs in the Federal Funds Rate**

To understand the fluctuations of the federal funds rate, consider what was going on in the economy during the periods shown here.

Source: Based on monthly averages from the Federal Reserve Bank.

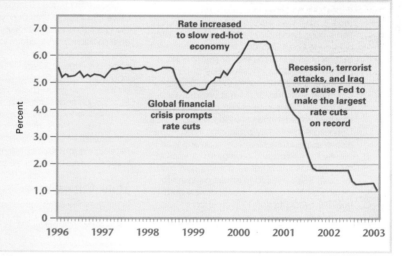

**Figure 17.5**

## Recent History of Federal Funds Rate

Figure 17.5 shows the federal funds rate since early 1996. Consider what was going on in the economy during the period. Between early 1996 and late 1998, the economy grew nicely with low inflation, so the FOMC kept the federal funds rate relatively stable in a range of 5.25 percent to 5.5 percent. In late 1998, fears of a global financial crisis prompted the FOMC to drop its target rate to 4.75 percent.

By the summer of 1999, those fears had subsided, and the FOMC became concerned that robust economic growth would trigger higher inflation. In a series of six steps, the FOMC raised the federal funds rate from 4.75 percent to 6.5 percent. In early 2001, concerns about declining consumer confidence, weaker capital spending, falling manufacturing output, and a sinking stock market prompted the FOMC to reverse course. That began the series of rate cuts into 2003.

### CHECKPOINT

What is the federal funds rate, and why does the Fed use it to set monetary policy?

### RETEACH

In 1979, Paul Volcker was appointed Chairman of the Fed's Board of Governors. At his confirmation hearing, Mr. Volcker said he would lead the Fed to allow the money supply to grow at a rate of 6 to 7 percent per year. He was confirmed, and the average rate of growth in M1 over the next three years was almost exactly 7 percent. Interest rates, however, leaped from less than 10 percent to as much as 20 percent by 1982. This happened because the rate of inflation was about 10 percent in these years. Although the nominal money supply grew by 7 percent, when it was adjusted for inflation, the *real* money supply fell by roughly 3 percent per year. This helped cause high interest rates, resulting in the recession of 1980-82. In that recession, the rate of inflation was cut by around half. Some people believe that this is exactly what Mr. Volcker had intended.

## Key Concepts

1. The demand for money normally grows when there is economic growth. What effect does this growth in the demand for money have on interest rates? Explain your answer.

2. If something happened to cause savers to lose faith in the safety of banks, what might happen to the economy? Explain your answer.

3. People tend to spend, deposit, or invest their cash quickly when interest rates are high. This increases the speed at which financial transactions take place. What then would happen if interest rates are low? How would this affect the economy?

4. If the Fed purchased $2 billion in government bonds, what would happen to the money supply and interest rates in the economy? Why might the Fed implement such a policy?

5. Why might the Fed set a target rate for the federal funds rate that is 1 percent higher than its current rate? What steps would the Fed be likely to take to accomplish its goal?

## Graphing Exercise

6. Use data in the table to construct a double line graph to show changes in the federal funds rate and the prime interest rate over the years from 1993 through 2003. Does there appear to be a relationship between these interest rates? Would you expect to find similar relationships between the federal funds rate and other interest rates? Why or why not?

## Think Critically

7. **Government** Investigate the policies of the Reagan administration that were intended to stimulate the economy in 1981 and 1982. Compare these policies with the monetary policy implemented at the same time under the Federal Reserve's Chairman Paul Volcker. How does this show that government policies are not always coordinated?

**Xtra!**
**Study Tools**
*econxtra.swlearning.com*

**Average Annual Federal Funds Rate and Prime Interest Rate, 1993–2003**

| Year | Federal Funds Rate | Prime Interest Rate |
|------|--------------------|--------------------|
| 1993 | 3.02% | 6.00% |
| 1994 | 4.21 | 7.15 |
| 1995 | 5.83 | 8.83 |
| 1996 | 5.30 | 8.27 |
| 1997 | 5.46 | 8.44 |
| 1998 | 5.35 | 8.35 |
| 1999 | 4.97 | 8.00 |
| 2000 | 6.24 | 9.23 |
| 2001 | 3.88 | 6.91 |
| 2002 | 1.67 | 4.67 |
| 2003 | 1.26 * | 4.25 * |

\* 2003 interest rates based on first six months of that year.

Source: *Economic Indicators,* June 2003.

## Key Concepts

1. Answers will vary. Possible answer: With economic growth, people will want to carry out more transactions and will need more money to do this. As a result of this increased demand for money, there will be more people who want to borrow. The result will be higher interest rates.

2. Answers will vary. Possible answer: If savers became worried that money they deposited in banks might not be safe, they would be more likely to hold cash. This would reduce banks' ability to make loans and would reduce economic activity.

3. Answers will vary. Possible answer: When interest rates are low, people feel less pressure to spend, deposit, or invest their cash quickly. This tends to decrease the speed at which financial transactions take place. As a result, the economy might be less likely to change.

4. Answers will vary. Possible answer: By purchasing $2 billion in government bonds, the Fed would add this amount of money to the economy that would then be increased by the expansion process. These additional funds would force interest rates down and cause greater activity in the economy. The Fed might do this to encourage growth in the economy.

5. Answers will vary. Possible answer: The Fed would be trying to discourage borrowing and spending with higher interest rates. It would do this when the economy or prices were growing too rapidly. The Fed could accomplish this by selling government bonds to reduce the amount of money in circulation.

## Graphing Exercise

6. Answers will vary. Possible answer: The prime interest rate is generally approximately 3 percentage points higher than the federal funds rate. Other interest rates tend to move with the federal funds rate, although short-term consumer credit rates do not move as quickly or as much.

   An example of an acceptable graph appears at the bottom of this page.

*The Answer Key is continued on page 544.*

## Visualizing the Answer— Graphing Exercise

6. The answer includes a graph. Students' graphs should look similar to the one shown here. An Excel spreadsheet containing this graph, along with supporting data, is available on the Instructor's Resource CD.

**Average Annual Federal Funds and Prime Interest Rate, 1993 to 2003**

### Sharpen Your Life Skills

## Make Predictions

After studying Lesson 17.2, students should be able to answer the questions on this page.

## Apply Your Skill

Consider allowing students to work in pairs for this assignment.

## Answers

1. Answers will vary. Possible answer: With increasing inflation, the Fed is likely to raise interest rates that would cause the flexible rate on mortgages to increase by more than one-half percent. Students might choose to refinance at a higher rate to avoid an even greater increase in interest later.

2. Answers will vary. Possible answer: The Fed is likely to increase interest rates soon. This would make it harder for potential customers to obtain a mortgage and therefore for the house to be sold. However, by waiting, inflation might cause the value of the house to increase, so a decision not to place the home on the market might be in order.

3. Answers will vary. Possible answer: With a declining economy and higher unemployment rates, the Fed is likely to soon cut interest rates. This would make the rate on the flexible mortgage even lower than its current 6.5 percent. If rates look as if they will increase in the future, the mortgage could be refinanced at a fixed rate then.

# Sharpen Your Life Skills

## Make Predictions

In general, people are pretty smart. They tend to know what's happening in the world by keeping up with the news. Government decisions often come as no surprise to them, including decisions of the Federal Reserve System. In fact, many people think they know what the Fed is going to do long before it does it. If this is true, can the Fed make decisions that surprise people and cause them to change their plans? Or, put more simply, would an interest-rate increase have any impact on your plans if you had been sure for weeks it would take place? Making predictions about the future of the economy is important to ordinary consumers and business managers alike.

What do you think the Fed would do in each of the situations described below? How would your expectations affect your own choices? Explain the reasons for your choice.

## Apply Your Skill

1. You have a $100,000 mortgage on a house that has a flexible interest rate of 6.0 percent that could change at any time. The economy has been growing rapidly for the past six months, and the rate of inflation has been going up steadily. You can refinance your mortgage at a fixed rate of 6.5 percent if you do it now. Would you refinance your mortgage now?

2. You plan to sell your home at some time in the next year or two. Right now, mortgages can be obtained at an interest rate of 6.0 percent. The economy has been growing rapidly for the past six months, and the rate of inflation has been going up steadily. Would your choose to put your home on the market right now, or would you wait awhile?

3. You have found a home you wish to buy. You need to take out a $100,000 mortgage to make this purchase. Your bank offers to lend you the money at either a 7 percent fixed rate or at a flexible rate that currently is 6.5 percent. On one hand, you like the idea of having a fixed rate that you know won't change in the future. On the other, you would like to pay the lower rate now. The economy has been in decline for six months, and the unemployment rate has reached 7 percent. Which mortgage would you choose?

# movers & shakers

**Howard Schultz** *Chairman, Chief Global Strategist, Starbucks Corporation*

Howard Schultz's family lived in a Brooklyn, New York, housing project. Thanks to a football scholarship, Howard was able to attend Northern Michigan University. After graduating he worked a variety of jobs until becoming the manager of U.S. operations for Hammarplast, a Swedish maker of stylish kitchen equipment.

While at Hammarplast, Schultz noticed that a company in Seattle, Washington, seemed to be purchasing an unusual number of specialty coffee makers. So in 1981 he traveled there to see what the company, called Starbucks, was doing with them. He fell in love with the rich aroma of the Starbucks store and with the extraordinary care the owners of the store put into selecting and roasting coffee beans. "I walked away...saying, 'What a great company, what a great city. I'd love to be a part of that.'"

Schultz convinced the Starbucks owners to hire him, and he became director of marketing and operations. During a trip to Italy, Schultz noticed the popularity of Italian coffee bars. There were, in fact, 200,000 such coffee bars in Italy at that time. Unlike his bosses, Schultz couldn't shake his enthusiasm for opening coffee bars in the United States, so he opened one of his own, called "Il Giornale." A year later, with the backing of local investors, he bought Starbucks for $3.8 million. By year's end, 17 Starbucks coffee bars were established. Within five years, 165 Starbucks were open, in such cities as San Francisco, San Diego and Denver.

By 1995, the company began opening Starbucks in Barnes & Noble and in Canada's Chapters bookstores. It finalized deals to have Starbucks served to all United Airlines customers and to guests of some of the finest U.S. hotels. It also opened a second roasting plant. By the end of 1995, Starbucks operated 676 coffee bars. The next five years saw growth into foreign markets, the introduction of Starbucks ice cream, and Starbucks coffee being sold in grocery stores.

"Our first priority is to take care of our people (employees), because they are the ones responsible for communicating our passion to our customers. If we do that, we accomplish our second priority, taking care of our customers," Schultz believes. He is true to his word, offering stock options to all employees and comprehensive health insurance for any employee working 20 or more hours a week.

Starbucks began to sell its common stock in 1992 under the trading symbol SBUX. The trend has been upward ever since. "Our stock market listing provided the liquidity that has allowed many people at Starbucks, including me, to cash in stock options and buy things we need or have long wished for. It has likewise served as a great incentive to attract talented people, who join us not only because of the excitement of building a fast-growing company but also because of the value we are creating."

Today there are more than 6,200 Starbucks throughout the world. Revenues for fiscal year 2003 were $4.1 billion, which represented a 24 percent increase from fiscal year 2002 and marked 12 consecutive years of growth.

## SOURCE READING
Is it more beneficial for Starbucks employees to receive stock options instead of cash bonuses? Why or why not? Find the passage in Lesson 17.2 of this textbook that supports your answer.

## ENTREPRENEURS IN ACTION
What traits does Howard Schultz possess that have helped him be successful in business? If you were starting your own business, which of these traits would you want to have, and why?

---

## movers & shakers

### FOCUS

Point out that this feature proves that success breeds success. Ask students to imagine what would happen if they went to a bank and asked to borrow $250,000 to open a coffee shop. Or, what would happen if they tried to find investors who would be willing to buy $250,000 worth of stock in a corporation they were forming that would sell coffee at a local shop. Would anyone take them seriously? Would the get the funds they need? Then consider what would happen if Howard Schultz did the same. Why is it important for people to develop a record of success if they hope to expand in the business world?

### TEACH

Instruct students to read the **Movers & Shakers** feature about Howard Schultz. Point out that some students may find it helpful to read the article, read the questions at the bottom of the page, and then reread the article.

### ASSESS

Use the questions in Source Reading and Entrepreneurs in Action at the bottom of the profile to assess the students' understanding of this **Movers & Shakers** feature.

**Answers to Source Reading**
Answers will vary. Possible answer: Given the overwhelming success of Starbucks, stock in this company is growing at a much faster pace than the average interest rate, making stock worth more than cash.

**Answers to Entrepreneurs in Action**
Answers will vary. Possible answers: Traits that have helped Schultz be successful include: efforts to keep his employees happy; recognizing employees as ambassadors for his company; willingness to take risks by introducing new products; and willingness to trade Starbucks on the NASDAQ to provide funding for growth.
Answers to the question regarding which traits students would want to have will vary.

---

## Extend the Content

Sometimes good ideas don't work. In 1991, Hollywood producer Keith Barish founded the Planet Hollywood restaurant chain. His business relied on people being willing to pay high prices for meals while they were surrounded by memorabilia from Hollywood stars and movies. At first the restaurants were successful, but soon people learned that sitting in the front seat of a 1959 pink Cadillac didn't make food taste any better. The Planet Hollywood chain filed for bankruptcy in 2001, when the economy went into recession and it became unable to pay its bills. Ask students to contrast the NIKE experience with that of the Planet Hollywood restaurant chain.

Remind students that there is a potential level of production at which an economy's resources are being fully utilized. An increase in the money supply can reduce interest rates and increase aggregate demand in the short run. This also can lead to increased production in the short run as accumulated resources are used up. In the long run, however, production cannot be sustained at a level that exceeds the economy's potential. If the Fed puts progressively larger amounts of money into circulation, the impact in the long run is likely to be only higher prices. Higher prices diminish the value of savings and are likely to foster uncertainty, which can lead to lower levels of production over time. Most economists believe that in the long run, the money supply should not be allowed to grow at a rate that exceeds the rate of growth in production.

## Objectives

Remind students to read the lesson objectives to help focus their attention before reading the lesson.

## Key Term

Direct students use the key term in a short paragraph that demonstrates the meaning of the term.

## [ In the News ]

Instruct students to read the passage and write down their answers. Point out that their answers might change after they finish studying Lesson 17.3.

## Answers to Think About It

Answers will vary. Possible answer: GDP is reliant on consumers purchasing goods. If consumers are hoarding money, they are not putting it back into the economy and real GDP falls.

## Visual Presentation

Use the PowerPoint presentation on the Instructor's Resource CD as an adjunct to your lecture. The presentation also can be used for review.

## Objectives

> Understand why changes in the money supply affect only prices in the long run, not real GDP.

> Examine the historical link between money supply growth and inflation.

> Determine why political independence of central banks results in lower inflation.

## Overview

In the short run, money influences aggregate demand and real GDP through its effect on interest rates. In the long run, the impact of money on aggregate demand is more direct. If the Fed increases the money supply, people will try to spend more. However, because the economy's potential output remains fixed from one year to the next, this greater spending simply increases the price level—there is more money chasing the same output. Thus, in the long run, increases in the money supply result only in inflation.

## Key Term

euro

## [ In the News ]

### ● The Problems of Too Much or Too Little Money

What happens when there is too much money in circulation? In the 1990s, extremely high inflation in Russia following the breakup of the Soviet Union increased Russian demand for so-called hard currencies, including the U.S. dollar. As a result, Russians traded their rubles and hoarded their dollars. In 1995, a Russian central banker claimed that the value of Russians' dollar holdings exceeded the value of their ruble holdings. What about the opposite problem when there is not enough money to go around? This happened a few years ago to Panama, a country that relies on the U.S. dollar as its currency. In 1988, in response to charges that Panama's leader was involved in drug dealing, U.S. officials froze Panamanian assets in the United States. This touched off a panic in Panama as bank customers tried to withdraw their deposits. Banks were forced to close for nine weeks. Dollars were hoarded, and people resorted to barter. Because barter is less efficient than a smoothly functioning monetary system, Panama's GDP fell by 30 percent in 1988. Both of these examples show that when a country has too much or too little of its currency available, people will come to rely on another mechanism for exchange. This alternative is seldom as efficient as a smoothly functioning monetary system, however. It has been said that no machine increases the economy's productivity as much as properly functioning money.

### Think About It

Why did Panama's GDP decrease as a result of people hoarding their money?

### National Content Standards in Economics

A complete list of the NCEE Standards appears on pages xxiv–xxv of this book. The following standards are addressed in Lesson 17.3.

Standard 11: Role of Money

Standard 12: Role of Interest Rates

Standard 16: Role of Government

Standard 19: Unemployment and Inflation

Standard 20: Monetary and Fiscal Policy

# Long-Run Effect of Money Supply Changes

Monetary authorities try to keep the economy on an even keel by smoothing fluctuations in the economy over the business cycle. These are based mostly on short-run adjustments in the federal funds rate. What happens in the long run?

## Production in the Long Run

In the short run, the aggregate supply curve slopes upward. Thus, an increase in aggregate demand increases both real GDP and the price level, as was shown in Figure 17.4. In the long run, the economy produces its potential level of output, which is the economy's maximum sustainable output. Potential output is determined by the supply of resources in the economy, the state of technology, and the rules of the game that nurture production and exchange. Potential output is the economy's normal capability on a regular or sus-tained basis. The economy can't produce any more than potential output in the long run.

An increase in the money supply doesn't change potential output. An increase in the money supply means only that there is more money chasing the same potential output.

## Changes in Aggregate Demand

The economy cannot produce more than its potential output in the long run. You could think of the economy's long-run supply curve as a vertical line drawn at the economy's potential level of output, as shown in Figure 17.6. That figure also shows the long-run effect of an increase in the money supply. An increase in the money supply causes a rightward shift of the aggregate demand curve from *AD* to *AD'*. Because output in the long run is fixed at the economy's potential output, the rightward shift of the aggregate demand curve leads only to a higher price level. Output remains unchanged at its potential level. The economy's potential output level is not affected by changes in the money supply. In the long run,

---

**An Increase in the Money Supply in the Long Run**

Figure 17.6

An increase in the supply of money in the long run results in a higher price level, or inflation. Because the long-run aggregate supply curve is fixed, increases in the money supply affect only the price level, not real output.

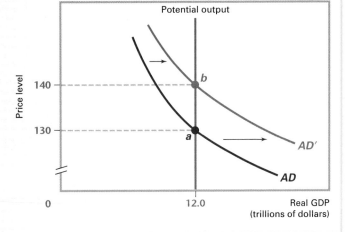

---

---

## TEACH

### Long-Run Effect of Money Supply Changes

Ask students to imagine they own a firm that manufactures desk lamps. They employ 100 workers and are earning a fair profit. Then one day the Fed puts $100 billion more into the economy. Interest rates fall, and demand for lamps skyrockets as people borrow to buy new products. As a result, students decide to expand production by hiring additional workers. To attract 20 more workers, they must raise wage rates for all their workers by 10 percent. When these new employees come to work, they have fewer tools to use, are less experienced, and are less motivated to do good work than are the people who have been with the firm longer. To meet production schedules, the workers are asked to work 10 hours of overtime each week. All of these events add to the firm's costs, so it raises its prices by 15 percent. Other businesses are having the same experience, so they raise their prices, too. The higher prices cause many people to decide not to buy desk lamps or other products, so sales fall and the business returns to the same level of production it used to have. Workers are laid off until there are again 100 employees. Everything seems to be the same, but prices are higher than they used to be. In the long run, the Fed's effort to stimulate the economy only added to inflation and did nothing to change the level of production and employment.

### *Think Critically Through Visuals*

Direct students to focus their attention on **Figure 17.6–An Increase in the Money Supply in the Long Run**. Point out that the economy's long-run supply curve is a vertical line drawn at the economy's potential level of output.

## ✓ CHECKPOINT

Invite a student to answer the checkpoint that appears on page 538.

### Answer

A change in money supply does not change potential output. An increase or decrease in the money supply means only that there is more or less money chasing the potential same output.

### Long-Run Evidence

Point out that there have been times when governments were unable to tax to obtain the revenues they needed to function. In other cases, they may have deliberately set out to lessen the value of their money. This was true of the German government after World War I. Under the Treaty of Versailles that ended the war, Germany was to pay reparations to the Allied powers that would have totaled 132 billion marks, or $33 billion. There was no way the German government could possibly have paid this amount. It was unable to even collect enough money to pay its own bills. Therefore, it started printing money. The result was hyperinflation. In 1914, it took 4.2 marks to purchase one U.S. dollar. By the end of 1924, it required 4.2 trillion marks to trade for one U.S. dollar. The German mark became worthless, and the German economy's production fell sharply. This is an extreme example, but it shows what can happen when too much money is put into circulation.

### *Think Critically Through Visuals*

Direct students to focus their attention on **Figure 17.7—Inflation and Money Growth Worldwide**. Point out that the graph illustrates the situation between 1980 and 1990.

**Apply It**

Direct students to the Graphing Workshop for Chapter 17 at **econxtra.swlearning.com.** As an enrichment exercise, students may complete **Apply It: Analyzing the Impact of Restrictive Monetary Policy**. This enrichment exercise presents concepts more advanced than those discussed in the textbook.

---

increases in the money supply result only in higher prices, or inflation.

**CHECKPOINT**

Why do changes in the money supply affect only the price level in the long run, not real GDP?

## Long-Run Evidence

In the United States and around the world, what has been the long-run relationship between increases in the money supply and inflation?

### Money Supply Growth and Inflation in U.S. History

Since the Federal Reserve System was established in 1913, the United States has suffered three bouts of high infla-

tion. These periods occurred from 1913 to 1920, 1939 to 1948, and 1967 to 1980. Each was preceded and accompanied by a corresponding growth in the money supply. Each U.S. episode of high inflation was related to a rapid growth in the money supply.

### Money Supply Growth and Inflation Around the World

What has been the link around the world between changes in the money supply and inflation in the long run? Again, monetary theory points to a relationship in the long run between the percentage change in the money supply and the percentage change in the price level. Figure 17.7 illustrates this using the average annual growth rate in M2 over a 10-year period and the average annual inflation rate during that period for 85 countries around the world. As you can see, the points fall rather neatly along the line, showing a positive relation between money growth, measured

**Inflation and Money Growth Worldwide**

**Figure 17.7**

**Inflation is higher in countries where the money supply grows faster.**

Source: The World Bank, *World Development Report 1992* (New York: Oxford University Press, 1992), Table 13. Figures are annual averages for 85 countries between 1980 and 1990.

---

Current data regarding inflation and growth in the money supply can be found in *Economic Indicators.* Issues of this publication can be found online at www.access.gpo.gov/. Ask students to compare growth in prices and growth in M2 over several years. Do they see any correlation between these two measures of financial conditions in the economy? How do they imagine these measures have influenced people's willingness to borrow?

**CHECKPOINT**

Invite a student to answer the checkpoint that appears on page 539.

### Answer

As money growth increases, so does inflation.

along the horizontal axis, and inflation, measured along the vertical axis.

Extremely high inflation, or *hyperinflation,* became a problem for some countries in the twentieth century. In every case, hyperinflation has been accompanied by extremely rapid growth in the supply of paper money. For example, Argentina—which had the highest average annual inflation rate over the 10-year period in the sample, at 395 percent—also had the highest average annual rate of growth in the money supply, at 369 percent.

Argentina, Bolivia, and Israel all managed to tame inflation. Households in all three countries, perhaps mindful of their experience with hyperinflation, still hoard a lot of U.S. currency.

The most famous hyperinflation during the last century was in Germany between August 1922 and November 1923, when inflation averaged 322 percent *per month.* Inflation was halted when the German government created an independent central bank that issued a limited supply of new currency convertible on demand into gold.

### CHECKPOINT
What has been the link between money growth and inflation in the United States and around the world?

# Other Issues in Monetary Policy

Three issues remain with regard to monetary policy:

1. the relationship between inflation and the central bank's independence from political pressure,

2. the problem of deflation, and

3. the lags involved with monetary policy.

### Fed Independence

Some economists argue that the Fed would do better in the long run if it were committed to the single goal of

---

price stability. To focus on price stability, a central bank would have to remain insulated from political pressure. Elected officials usually urge the Fed to

## SPAN THE GLOBE

### Hyperinflation and Political Instability

Incidents of hyperinflation have often been accompanied by political upheaval. Almost every country that has experienced hyperinflation has had subsequent political instability as desperate citizens looked for ways to protect themselves. In Germany, the hyperinflation following World War I led many people to lose faith in the democratic government. Both the Communist Party and the rising Nazi Party thought they could use this uncertainty to gain control of the country. The democratic government was able to remain in power by undertaking currency reform, but the memories of hyperinflation played a role in the eventual rise of the Nazis in the 1930s. More recently, hyperinflation in Bolivia resulted in no less than ten different governments ruling the country between 1978 and 1982. These included several military governments as the result of numerous overthrow attempts. Not until after a democratically elected government issued reforms to stop the inflation did political stability begin to emerge in Bolivia. The same kind of situation happened in Argentina. Hyperinflation in that country sparked a massive economic crisis, which ended in the country having four different presidents during one two-week period in 2001. After weeks of public rioting and looting, it looked as if democracy might be dead in Argentina. However, a caretaker president then instituted a series of reforms that helped ease the economic crisis. The violence stopped, and people were willing to give the government another chance. Argentineans finally went to the polls in the spring of 2003 to elect a new president.

### Think Critically

Why do you think a country tends to experience political instability when hyperinflation occurs in its economy?

---

### Other Issues in Monetary Policy

Remind students that members of the Fed's Board of Governors are appointed to serve 14-year terms. They cannot be fired or replaced unless they are impeached and convicted. This has never happened. Essentially, once a person is confirmed to be on the Board of Governors, he or she will remain there for many years. This gives these men and women a degree of independence to do what they think is best for the economy. They do not need to worry about appealing to voters so they can be reelected in a few years. This may have something to do with why the Fed has been more decisive in its actions than has the Congress.

### SPAN THE GLOBE

Direct students to read the short passage "Hyperinflation and Political Instability." Use the questions as a starting point for class discussion or have students write a paragraph to answer the questions.

### Answers to Think Critically

Answers will vary. Possible answer: Hyperinflation is a sign of economic instability. Economic instability brings unrest among the people, who most often blame the current government.

### NETBookmark

Direct students to **econxtra.swlearning.com.** Remind them to click on the link for Lesson 17.3 to find the appropriate link for the **NET Bookmark** on page 540.

### Answer

Advantages include economic credibility, low inflation, and lower interest rates. Disadvantages include problems related to financial policies and banks in financial trouble. When a currency board controls the money supply, a central bank can no longer be an unlimited lender of last resort to banks in financial trouble. The use of currency boards also limits the national authorities' ability to use financial polices, such as adjustments of interest and exchange rates, to stimulate the economy.

---

## *Economic Headlines*

Instruct students to locate an article in a current magazine or newspaper that relates to one of the topics in this lesson. For example, they might find articles about money policy, the Fed, or the euro. Instruct students to read the article, write a brief summary, and include a reference citation. Identify the style you want them to use for the citation.

As an alternative, you might find several articles of interest and provide citations for students to use in locating one of the articles. Direct students to read the article they have chosen, and write a brief explanation of how it relates to this lesson.

## Other Issues in Monetary Policy

Choose a student to represent the Chairman of the Fed's Board of Governors. Choose several other students to be the Senate Banking Committee. Tell them that the economy is suffering from stagflation. Unemployment rates are high and production is down while inflation has reached a rate of 10 percent. The Fed has decided to increase interest rates to slow borrowing and fight inflation. This has made unemployment worse and caused production to fall even more. Have these students role play as if a Congressional hearing were taking place, with the senators asking the Chairman what he thinks he is doing. Why don't these people have the same concerns? Why are the senators upset with the Fed's monetary policy? What would they probably like the Fed to do?

### THE WALL STREET JOURNAL

#### Reading It Right

Invite a student to explain the relevance of the statement from *The Wall Street Journal* that appears on page 541.

#### Answer

Answers will vary. Possible answer: This statement points to the link between interest rates, money supply, and inflation. As interest rates decrease, money supply increases and inflation increases.

### Ask the Xpert!

Direct students to **econxtra.swlearning.com** to hear an expert answer the question "Why do so many people listen to Alan Greenspan?"

### Think Critically Through Visuals

Direct students to focus their attention on the photograph on page 541. Ask for a volunteer to answer the question posed in the caption.

#### Answer

Answers will vary. Possible answer: Monetary policy has the advantage over fiscal policy with regard to decision-making lags because the FOMC can make a decision in one meeting and can begin executing open-market operations within minutes.

stimulate the economy whenever it's performing below its potential. All this short-run stimulation, however, can lead to inflation in the long run.

When the Fed was established in 1913, several features insulated it from politics, such as the 14-year terms with staggered appointments for members of its Board of Governors. Also, the Fed does not rely on a Congressional appropriation. The Fed has its own source of income.

Here's how the Fed earns a profit. The Fed, like any other bank, has a balance sheet. More than three-fourths of the Fed's assets are U.S. government securities. The Fed bought them through open-market operations. They are IOUs from the federal government, and they earn interest for the Fed.

More than three-fourths of the Fed's liabilities are Federal Reserve notes in circulation. These notes—U.S. currency—are IOUs from the Fed and are therefore liabilities of the Fed. However, the Fed pays no interest on Federal Reserve notes.

The Fed's primary assets—U.S. government securities—earn interest for the Fed. Its primary liabilities—Federal Reserve notes—require no interest payments by the Fed.

The Fed also earns income from various services it provides member banks. After covering its operating costs,

*euro*
The new European common currency

the Fed turns over any remaining income to the U.S. Treasury. In some years the Fed turns over more than $20 billion. You might think of this as profit resulting from the Fed's ability to issue notes and create bank reserves.

### Central Bank Independence and Inflation

Does a central bank's independence from political pressure affect its performance? In one study, the central banks of 17 advanced industrial countries were ranked from least independent to most independent. It turned out that inflation during the 15-year span studied was lowest in countries with the most independent central banks and highest in countries with the least independent central banks. The U.S. central bank is considered relatively independent, and inflation here averaged about halfway between the most independent and least independent groups of banks.

### Independence Trend

The trend around the world is toward greater central bank independence from political pressure. For example, Australia and New Zealand, two countries that had problems with inflation, have amended laws governing their central banks to make price stability the primary goal. Chile, Colombia, and Argentina—developing countries that have experienced hyperinflation—have legislated more central bank independence.

The framework that established the new European currency, the **euro**, identified price stability as the main objective of the new European Central Bank. That bank announced a policy to keep inflation under 2.0 percent. In fact, the bank came under criticism recently for appearing reluctant to cut its target interest rate even though a recession loomed and the unemployment rate exceeded 8 percent.

### Could Deflation Pose a Problem?

Hyperinflation can bring an economy to its knees. But deflation, a decline in the average price level, is no picnic either.

### NETBookmark

Argentina limited its central bank's ability to issue new currency by creating a currency board. The currency board required that each new peso be backed by one U.S. dollar held in reserve by the bank. Access the article "Are Currency Boards a Cure for All Monetary Problems?" through econxtra.swlearning.com. This article, from the IMF publication *Finance and Development,* explores the use of independent currency boards to control the supply of money in advanced industrial countries. What does the article note as the advantages and disadvantages of having a currency board in a country?

**econxtra.swlearning.com**

**540**     **CHAPTER 17**   Money Creation, Federal Reserve, Monetary Policy

### Group Activity

Divide students into groups of five. In each group, assign students to play the following roles: (1) Chairman of the Fed's Board of Governors, (2) President of the United States, (3) a person who wants to buy a home, (4) a person who wants to sell a home, and (5) a banker who wants to lend money to finance the purchase of a home. Tell them the Fed has pushed up interest rates by 2 percent because there is growing inflation and the federal government has a large budget deficit. This has angered many people. Ask each group to write a description of how each member feels about the increased interest rates and what they think should be done in this situation. Have the groups compare their statements. How does this demonstrate why it is important for the Fed to be independent of the political process?

Falling prices during the Great Depression caused consumers to delay major purchases, waiting for prices to drop even more. This reduced aggregate demand, output, and employment. Investment also tanked because lower prices erased profits. Further, borrowers found it more difficult to pay off their debts as their incomes fell.

In recent years, Japan has suffered from deflation averaging about 1 percent a year. Germany, now the world's third largest economy (behind the United States and Japan) also is facing deflation. Fed Chairman Alan Greenspan has voiced concern about the possibility of deflation here. He said the Fed would fight deflation as fiercely as it fights high inflation. Most economists, including Greenspan, don't think the nation will experience deflation. Regardless, you should know that deflation can create as much havoc in an economy as high inflation.

## Lags and Monetary Policy

One final consideration: How do the lags involved with monetary policy compare with those involved with fiscal policy? Recall that one problem with fiscal policy involves lags at several stages of the process. Does monetary policy face the same problems?

The *recognition lag*, the time required to identify a problem with the economy, is probably about the same for both policies. Monetary and fiscal decision makers are each supported by a competent team of economists tracking the economy.

With regard to the *decision-making lag*, monetary policy has the advantage, since the FOMC can make a decision during one meeting. Once a decision is made, monetary policy also has the advantage because the FOMC can begin executing open-market operations within minutes. Fiscal policy may take months to implement, so the *implementation lag* is shorter for monetary policy.

Finally, with regard to the *effectiveness lag*, it may be a toss-up. Market interest

**Reading It Right** What's the relevance of the following statement from *The Wall Street Journal:* "[The Philadelphia Fed President] has warned about the danger of cutting interest rates too much this year because, given the 6- to 12-month lags with which monetary policy affects the economy, it could lead to the economy growing unsustainably quickly next year, fueling inflation pressure."

rates can move quickly in response to a change in Fed policy, but there is no way to know how long it will take businesses and consumers to react to changed interest rates. The full effect of changes in the money supply may take a year or more, as long as it may take fiscal policy to show its full effects.

### ✓ CHECKPOINT

What is the relationship between inflation and the political independence of central banks?

Ask the Xpert!

econxtra.swlearning.com

*Why do so many people listen to Alan Greenspan?*

**What advantage does monetary policy have over fiscal policy regarding decision-making lags? What role does the FOMC play in this?**

### ✓ CHECKPOINT

Invite a student to answer the checkpoint that appears on this page.

**Answer**

Inflation is lower when the central bank is more politically independent.

### APPLY

Assign Lesson 17.3 from the Contemporary Economics Workbook.

### *e*-con @pps

Encourage students to apply their knowledge of concepts presented in this lesson as they explore economic news stories, policy debates, and data available at **econxtra.swlearning.com**.

### ASSESS

Assign all or part of Lesson 17.3 Assessment on page 524 as homework or an in-class activity.

### Xtra! Study Tools

Direct students to the online study tools for Lesson 17.3 at **econxtra.swlearning.com**.

### CLOSE

**Revisit** the In the News feature on the first page of the lesson. Ask students to review their preliminary answers and discuss the questions, now that they have completed this lesson.

**Review** the objectives for Lesson 17.3. Students should be able to:

- Understand why changes in the money supply affect only prices in the long run, not real GDP.
- Examine the historical link between money supply growth and inflation.
- Determine why political independence of central banks results in lower inflation.

### RETEACH

Remind students that the Fed took action after 2000 to lower interest rates in the United States to their lowest levels in more than 40 years. Even with these very low interest rates, most businesses did not choose to borrow to increase their investments, and they continued to lay off workers as production fell. Ask students to explain how this situation demonstrated the effectiveness lag in carrying out monetary policy. In what way is this situation similar to the old saying, "You can lead a horse to water, but you can't make it drink"? (You can lower interest rates but you can't make people borrow.)

## 17.3 Assessment

### Key Concepts

1. Answers will vary. Possible answer: Three percent unemployment is below the natural rate. Achieving this goal in the short run will cause inflation that will reduce aggregate demand and increase unemployment. The Fed will not be able to achieve its goal in the long run.

2. Answers will vary. Possible answer: Lower prices would lead to lower incomes. This would make it difficult for those who are in debt to repay their loans. Further, businesses would be less inclined to invest in new facilities or machines if they were not able to charge prices that were high enough to cover their costs.

3. Answers will vary. Possible answer: People and businesses consider more than interest rates when they decide whether or not to borrow and spend funds. If business conditions are bad, businesses may be unwilling to borrow and invest, regardless of the interest rate. People also will be hesitant to borrow if they believe they will have difficulty repaying their loans.

### Graphing Exercise

4. Answers will vary. Possible answer: The relationship is not clear, although interest rates may appear to fall as growth in GDP declines. If this is so, it is possible that the Fed is lowering interest rates in an effort to stimulate the economy.

   An example of an acceptable graph appears at the bottom of this page.

### Think Critically

5. Answers will vary. Possible answer: Uncertainty over the Fed's policies might cause businesses to avoid borrowing and investing. This could reduce growth and employment in the economy.

Xtra!
Study Tools
econxtra.swlearning.com

### Key Concepts

1. If the Fed worked to keep the unemployment rate at 3 percent by increasing the money supply year after year, what would happen to prices? Would the Fed be successful in reaching its goal in the long run? Why, or why not?

2. Why would deflation be harmful to the economy?

3. Why might it take many months or possibly more than a year for people and businesses to respond to a changes in the money supply? What does this tell you about the usefulness of monetary policy?

### Graphing Exercise

4. Use data in the table to create a double line graph of interest rates and changes in real (adjusted for inflation) GDP from 1994 through 2002. Does there seem to be a relationship between these values? Which do you think is the cause and which is the effect? Explain your answer.

**Interest Rate on 3-Year Government Bonds and Change in Real GDP, 1994–2002**

| Year | Interest Rate on 3-Year Government Securities | Percentage Growth in Real GDP |
|------|-----------------------------------------------|-------------------------------|
| 1994 | 6.27% | 4.04% |
| 1995 | 6.25 | 2.67 |
| 1996 | 5.99 | 3.57 |
| 1997 | 6.10 | 4.44 |
| 1998 | 5.14 | 4.32 |
| 1999 | 5.49 | 4.11 |
| 2000 | 6.22 | 3.75 |
| 2001 | 4.09 | 0.25 |
| 2002 | 3.10 | 2.43 |

Source: *Economic Indicators*, June 2003, pp. 2, 30.

### Think Critically

5. **Management** Business owners cannot be sure what policy the Fed will follow. When they guess wrong, it can have a devastating effect. In 1978, for example, the owners of a small steel mill in upstate New York borrowed $50 million to purchase new equipment. They agreed to pay a flexible rate of interest set at prime plus 1 percent. (When prime was 8 percent, they were required to pay 9 percent.) When the loan was first taken out, they were paying 9 percent interest, or $4.5 million per year. Three years later, actions of the Federal Reserve System had caused the prime interest rate to grow to 20 percent, forcing the firm to pay 21 percent on its loan. This amounted to $10.5 million in interest per year. The firm was unable to make these payments and failed in 1983. If you owned a firm and were considering borrowing funds, how concerned would you be over what the Fed's future monetary policy might be? Would you avoid borrowing if you could? How might this uncertainty affect the economy?

**542** CHAPTER 17 Money Creation, Federal Reserve, Monetary Policy

**Interest Rate on 3-Year Government Bonds and Change in Real GDP, 1994 to 2002**

### Visualizing the Answer— Graphing Exercise

4. The answer includes a graph. Students' graphs should look similar to the one shown here. An Excel spreadsheet containing this graph, along with supporting data, is available on the Instructor's Resource CD.

# to History

# Deflation in the Nineteenth Century

Following the Civil War, the United States' prices, especially for agricultural products, began to suffer from deflation. In the decade following 1866, wheat prices dropped from $2.06 a bushel to $1.00. Fifteen years later, farmers were receiving 60 cents a bushel for wheat. Over the same period, corn prices dropped from 66 cents a bushel to 30 cents. Some decline in prices was due to the introduction of new techniques and equipment, which helped farmers become more productive, thus increasing supply faster than demand. Farmers, however, wanted inflation. Many had run up debts to buy or expand farms, to buy equipment, or to support themselves after a bad year. While the cost to pay back their loans remained the same, lower prices meant they had to produce more to earn enough money to make the payments.

Farmers saw one solution to their problem in the government's issuance of Greenbacks. This was paper money issued during the Civil War, which had no backing in gold or silver. After the War, the government had been withdrawing Greenbacks, thereby leaving less money in circulation. The effect was that fewer dollars were chasing more goods, thus bringing lower prices. For farmers, the answer seemed to be the government's issuing as many Greenbacks as it took to raise prices. This idea was so strong that a political party—the Greenback Party—was formed around it. Business interests, however, opposed this solution, and most politicians pursued a policy of "sound money."

In 1873, the government passed the Coinage Act. The Act said that the government would no longer buy silver to turn into coins. The cost of silver was more than the government was willing to pay. Farmers were outraged because they believed more silver purchases would increase the money supply, resulting in inflation and higher farm prices. Farmers and

now silver miners, referring to the act as the "Crime of '73," demanded that the government resume the buying and coining of silver. The government responded by passing the Bland Allison Act (1878) and the Sherman Silver Purchase Act (1890). These acts authorized a limited amount of silver to be purchased and turned into coins. Neither created the inflation desired by the farmers and silver miners, however.

In the election of 1896, which pitted William Jennings Bryan for the Democratic and Populist parties against Republican William McKinley, a major issue was the gold standard. Bryan traveled the country, arguing against the government policy and demanding an increased money supply. Despite his defeat, Bryan's "cross of gold" speech stands as one of the most famous in American history. However, by the turn of the century the farmers got their wish, and prices stopped declining. This had nothing to do with their efforts to change government policy, but with the additional deposits of gold that were discovered in Alaska and other parts of the world, which doubled the world's supply of gold.

## THINK CRITICALLY

Write a paragraph to explain the effect deflation had on farmers' income and their ability to meet their fixed costs (mortgages, etc.). Assume that a farmer's income and fixed costs are both $1,000 and that there is 10 percent deflation each year. What would the deflation do with the farmer's ability to meet his debts? Next, assume income and fixed costs of $1,000 and a 10 percent *inflation* rate. What would this do to the farmer's ability to meet his debts? In what way is the homebuyer of today similar to the farmer of the late 1800s?

Lesson 17.3 • *Monetary Policy in the Long Run*    **543**

## Bibliography

Foner, Eric, and John A. Garraty, eds. *The Reader's Companion to American History.* Boston: Houghton Mifflin Company, 1991.

Greider, William. *Secrets of the Temple: How the Federal Reserve Runs the Country.* New York: Simon and Schuster, 1987.

Morris, Richard B., and Jeffrey B. Morris. *Encyclopedia of American History.* New York: Harper Collins, 1996.

Parish, Peter J., ed. *Reader's Guide to American History.* Chicago: Fitzroy Dearborn Publishers, 1997.

Puth, Robert C. *American Economic History.* New York: Dryden Press, 1982.

C O N N E C T

# to History

## FOCUS

Ask students to imagine that they have borrowed to buy a house, a car, and furniture. They owe a total of $150,000 and are required to pay $2,250 each month. This has been no problem in the past because they have a job that pays them $6,000 each month. But there is deflation. Their employer is forced to lower the prices of the product she sells. She tells the students that she can pay them only $4,000 each month. Would the students agree? If they do agree, what will happen to their ability to buy new products? What will happen to sales in the economy? If sales fall, why may prices fall even further? Once deflation takes hold, why is it very difficult to stop?

## TEACH

Instruct students to read the **Connect to History** feature and answer the questions.

## ASSESS

Use the questions at the bottom of the page to assess the students' understanding of this feature.

### Answers to **Think Critically**

Many framers had gone into debt for land and equipment when wheat was earning a high of $2.06 per bushel. Deflation after the Civil War, plus an increase in productively that drove farmers' income down (supply was greater than demand), caused the price earned to drop. Deflation had no effect on fixed prices but it did affect income by reducing it. Farmers wanted inflation because it would bring the price per bushel back up.

If the farmer's income and fixed costs are both $1,000, and there is a 10 percent deflation rate each year, the fixed cost of $1,000 will remain the same while the income will drop by $100 a year. Conversely, if income and fixed costs are both $1,000 and there is a 10 percent inflation rate each year, the farmer will come out a little ahead. The homebuyer of today is similar to the farmer of the late 1800s because costs remain fixed, while deflation or inflation take today's buyer's income up or down.

## Summary

### Consider

Ask students to revisit the questions they were asked to consider at the beginning of the chapter. Remind students that they should be able to answer all of the questions after studying Chapter 17.

- How does the Fed create money? See page 521—The Fed Makes a Move.

- Why don't you demand all the money you can get your hands on? See page 526—Money Demand.

- What's the price of holding money? See page 526—The Cost of Holding Money.

- How does the supply of money in the economy affect your chances of finding a job, your ability to finance a new car, and the interest rate you pay on credit cards? See page 528—Money Supply and the Market Interest Rate.

- What's the impact of changes in the money supply on the economy in the short run and in the long run? See page 528—Money Supply.

### Exam*View*

Use ExamView to assess student learning.

- Create a chapter test using questions from the existing test bank.

- Add your own questions to the existing test bank.

- Generate multiple forms of a chapter test.

### Study Skills

Offer the following study skills suggestions for students as they review this chapter.

- Outline the chapter.
- Review Key Terms.
- Review Checkpoints.
- Work in pairs to quiz each other.
- Use Xtra! Study Tools for each lesson.

- Direct students to the online quiz preparation for Chapter 17 at **econxtra.swlearning.com**.

---

 **Chapter Assessment**

## Summary

 **How Banks Work**

**a** To establish a bank, a group of people must obtain a charter from either the federal or state government. They must agree to invest an amount of money in the new bank. The bank will report its financial status on a *balance sheet,* which lists its *assets* on one side and its *liabilities* and the amount of the owners' equity on the other. The amounts on both sides must be equal. Under the fractional reserve system, banks are required to maintain a portion of deposits on reserve.

**Xtra! Quiz Prep**
econxtra.swlearning.com

**b** New funds deposited in a bank can be multiplied into much larger increases in total deposits over time. When the Fed buys a bond from a bank, the money paid is new to the economy. The bank will have increased reserves that it will loan or spend in some other way. When the money is spent, it is received as income by someone else, who will deposit it back into a bank. The bank then, after holding back its required reserve, will make additional loans or invest these funds in some other way. This cycle of deposits, reserves, loans, spending, and more deposits is repeated many times, causing the amount of money in the economy to grow by much more than the amount of the original bond purchase.

**c** The *money multiplier* is limited by the *required reserve ratio.* When banks are required to keep more deposits on reserve, they are able to make fewer loans and the process will be slowed.

 **Monetary Policy in the Short Run**

**a** People demand money so they can complete financial transactions and to hold as a store of value. The amount they wish to hold at any time depends on many factors, including the interest rate. When interest rates are high, people are willing to hold less money.

**b** The *Money supply* is determined by the amount of money that the Federal Reserve System has placed in the economy. It can be viewed as a vertical line graph. The intersection of a demand for money with the supply of money determines the market interest rate in the economy. An increase in the money supply will lead to a lower interest rate while a decrease in the money supply will cause a higher market interest rate. Lower interest rates stimulate the economy while higher rates slow its growth.

**c** The Fed sets targets for the *federal funds rate,* which is the rate banks charge each other for borrowing bank reserves. The Fed targets this rate because it has tighter control over it than other interest rates. When the Fed changes its target for the federal funds rate, most other interest rates change, too.

**17.3** **Monetary Policy in the Long Run**

**a** Production in the long run cannot be sustained above the economy's potential. Efforts to expand aggregate demand and production beyond its potential can succeed in the short run, but will cause prices to rise and production to fall back to its potential in the long run.

**b** All economically developed nations have a monetary authority similar to the Fed. In some nations, this authority is quite independent of the political process. In others, it is controlled by political figures in the government. In these latter nations, rates of inflation have tended to be higher than in other nations where the monetary authorities are more independent.

**c** Deflation makes it more difficult for those in debt to repay their loans and discourages businesses from investing in new facilities or hiring as many workers. Some people think there is a danger of deflation in the United States and in other developed nations.

**d** There are lags in the effectiveness of monetary policy. It takes time for the Fed to recognize that there is a problem, decide what action to take, implement the policy, and for the economy to react to the changed policy.

**544**   **CHAPTER 17**   Money Creation, Federal Reserve, Monetary Policy

---

**17.2** **Assessment**

Continued from page 533.

### Think Critically

7. Answers will vary. Possible answer: The Reagan administration was successful in having tax cuts passed in Congress that were intended to stimulate demand, production, and employment in the economy. At the same time, Paul Volcker led the Fed to increase interest rates to levels that were higher than they had been for more than 50 years. This discouraged borrowing and spending and reduced demand and employment in the economy. This situation demonstrates that federal economic policies are not always coordinated.

# Review Economic Terms

Choose the term that best fits the definition. On a separate sheet of paper, write the letter of the correct answer. Some terms may not be used.

_____ 1. Bank reserves in excess of required reserves

_____ 2. The stock of money available in the economy at a particular time

_____ 3. Any physical property or financial claim that is owned

_____ 4. The dollar amount that must be held in reserve

_____ 5. The interest rate charged in the federal funds market

_____ 6. The relationship between how much money people want to hold and the interest rate

_____ 7. A Fed regulation that dictates the minimum percentage of deposits each bank must keep in reserve

_____ 8. A financial statement showing assets, liabilities, and net worth at a given time

_____ 9. An amount owed

_____ 10. The multiple by which the money supply increases as a result of an increase in excess reserves in the banking system

a. **asset**

b. **balance sheet**

c. **euro**

d. **excess reserves**

e. **federal funds market**

f. **federal funds rate**

g. **liability**

h. **money demand**

i. **money multiplier**

j. **money supply**

k. **net worth**

l. **required reserve ratio**

m. **required reserves**

# Review Economic Concepts

11. **True or False** Anyone who has enough money has the legal right to start a banking business.

12. A bank's _balance sheet_ lists its _assets_ on one side and its _liabilities_ and the amount of the owner's __?__ on the other.

13. The _required reserve ratio_ is the

 a. amount of money a bank's owners must invest in the bank.

 b. share of its deposits that a bank may lend.

 c. amount of its deposits that a bank must hold on reserve.

 d. share of its deposits that a bank must hold on reserve.

14. **True or False** If the Fed bought a $100,000 government bond from a bank, the money supply would immediately grow by more than $100,000.

15. If the Fed lowered the _required reserve ratio_ from 10 percent to 8 percent, the money __?__ would increase from 10 to 12.5.

16. If people choose to hold a smaller share of income they receive in cash and deposit more of their earnings in checking accounts, the money expansion will be

 a. greater than it was in the past.

 b. the same as it was in the past.

 c. smaller than it was in the past.

 d. carried out more slowly than it was in the past.

17. **True or False** The demand for money is a measure of a stock. It is the amount of money people wish to hold at a particular time.

18. Which of the following events would reduce the impact of the _money multiplier_?

 a. The Fed purchases additional government bonds.

 b. People choose to hold more of their money in cash.

 c. The Fed lowers the required reserve ratio.

 d. The federal government borrows and spends more money.

## Review Economic Terms

1. d.  excess reserves
2. j.  money supply
3. a.  asset
4. m. required reserves
5. f.  federal funds rate
6. h.  money demand
7. l.  required reserve ratio
8. b.  balance sheet
9. g.  liability
10. i.  money multiplier

## Review Economic Concepts

11. False. A charter is also needed to start a bank.
12. equity
13. d.  share of its deposits that a bank must hold on reserve
14. False. The bank is required to keep some money on reserve.
15. multiplier
16. a.  greater than it was in the past
17. True
18. b.  People choose to hold more of their money in cash.

546

## Review Economic Concepts

19. a. remain unchanged
20. True
21. growth
22. d. selling some of its government bonds
23. federal funds rate
24. True
25. a. increase output to its potential in the short run
26. c. rapid growth in their money supplies
27. Deflation

## Apply Economic Concepts

28. Answers will vary. Possible answer: In theory, the multiplier would change from 10 to 8 ($\frac{1}{0.10} = 10$, $\frac{1}{0.125} = 8$). This would reduce the amount of each checking deposit banks could lend by 2.5 percent and cause the money supply to fall and interest rates to increase. These higher interest rates would discourage people from borrowing and spending and therefore slow the economy.

29. Answers will vary. Possible answer: With the savings account paying only 2 percent interest, there is little cost to keeping extra money in cash in their checking account. If the interest rate increased to 10 percent, there would be a large cost to holding cash or placing money in a checking account that pays no interest. In this case, they would be more likely to deposit a larger share of their income in a savings account.

30. Answers will vary. Possible answer: If they wait, they will not have the use of the new car for a period of time, even if they are able to borrow at a lower interest rate. They should also be concerned over the state of the economy. If they are laid off in a few months, they could have a hard time repaying their loan, whether the interest rate is 9 or 7 percent.

19. If the Fed increases the *money supply,* the demand curve for money will

    a. remain unchanged.
    b. immediately shift to the right.
    c. immediately shift to the left.
    d. eventually shift to the left.

20. **True or False** The opportunity cost of holding cash is the interest that could have been earned but is forgone.

21. Lower interest rates stimulate the economy, while higher rates slow its __?__.

22. The Fed could increase interest rates by

    a. buying additional government bonds.
    b. lowering the required reserve ratio.
    c. lowering the discount rate.
    d. selling some of its government bonds.

23. The Fed sets interest rate targets for the __?__.

24. **True or False** Inflation is likely to occur if the Fed increases the *money supply* when the economy is already at its potential level of output.

25. By increasing the *money supply,* the Fed can

    a. increase output to its potential in the short run.
    b. increase output beyond its potential in the long run.
    c. decrease output to its potential in the short run.
    d. decrease output below its potential in the long run.

26. Countries that have experienced high rates of inflation also have usually had

    a. totalitarian forms of government.
    b. independent monetary authorities.
    c. rapid growth in their money supplies.
    d. large government budget surpluses.

27. __?__ may result from a decline in aggregate demand that forces the price level to fall.

# Apply Economic Concepts

28. **Calculate the Impact of a Change in the Reserve Ratio** Suppose that the Fed decided to increase the reserve ratio from 10 to 12.5 percent. In theory, how would this change the value of the money multiplier? What would this do to the amount of each checking deposit that banks could lend? How would this decision affect interest rates and the economy? Explain your answer.

29. **Decide How Much Cash to Hold** Imagine that it is 10 years in the future. You are married and have two young children. Every month you pay $800 for your rent, $300 for your car loan, and at least $1,900 in other costs of living. You are trying to save $300 from every paycheck to make a down payment on a house in a few years. You earn a salary that provides you with a take-home pay of $2,000 every two weeks. Your savings account currently pays 2 percent interest. How much of your bi-weekly pay would you take in cash, deposit in your checking account, and put in your saving account? How would your decision change if the interest rate on your saving account increased to 10 percent?

30. **Choose When to Borrow** Imagine that you have a job that pays you a good wage. You have decided to borrow $20,000 to buy a new car. Right now the interest rate on a new-car loan is 9 percent. You have read in the newspaper that the Fed is likely to lower interest rates soon because many workers are being laid off and unemployment is on the rise. You believe that if you wait a few months, you might be able to borrow the money you need at only 7 percent interest. Would you buy the car now or wait for lower interest rates? What else should concern you? Explain your answers.

31. **Decide Whether to Accept an After-School Job** You spend many hours every week doing school work and helping around your home. You like to go out with your friends on the weekend. You really don't have much spare time. The economy is booming, and interest rates are low. On your way home from school, you notice a sign in the window of a store that promises a $10 per-hour wage for anyone who accepts a job as a sales clerk. When you ask about the job, the store owner says she will hire you only if you agree to work 16 hours each week. You accept the job, but you're not happy with the number of hours you must work. After you receive your first paycheck, you go shopping and find that because of taxes and inflation your money doesn't go very far. You decide you really don't want the job so you hand in your resignation and go back to asking your parents for money. Explain how this story is related to economic problems that take place when the Fed tries to move production in the economy to exceed its potential.

32. **Sharpen Your Life Skills: Make Predictions** On October 28, 2003, the Fed announced that it had left the target federal funds rate at 1.0 percent and that there was no expectation that this rate would be increased at any time in the near future. This was the lowest rate that had been targeted by the Fed in more than 40 years. The Fed chose to keep interest rates low at that time because the economy was suffering from a relatively high unemployment rate of more than 6 percent and a low rate of economic growth of about 2.5 percent. Inflation

was of little concern because it was running at only about 2.0 percent. What if two years later the economy had recovered with unemployment down to 4.0 percent, production growing at a rate of more than 6 percent per year, and inflation up to a rate of 5.2 percent? Predict what the Fed would do to its target for the federal funds rate under these circumstances. Explain what the likely results would be for the economy.

33. **Construct a Graph of Demand and Supply for Money** The hypothetical data in the table represents the demand and supply for money in the U.S. economy. Construct a graph from these data. What is the equilibrium interest rate in this example? What are two events that might cause the equilibrium interest rate to increase? What are two events that might cause the equilibrium interest rate to fall?

**Demand and Supply for Money
(in billions of dollars)**

| Amount Demanded | Amount Supplied | Interest Rate |
|---|---|---|
| $ 500 | $1,000 | 12.0% |
| 750 | 1,000 | 10.0% |
| 1,000 | 1,000 | 8.0% |
| 1,250 | 1,000 | 6.0% |
| 1,500 | 1,000 | 4.0% |

e-con @pps   econxtra.swlearning.com

34. Access **EconNews Online** at econxtra. swlearning.com. Find the article entitled "Will the Fed Raise Rates?" Read the article, and then answer this question: What was

the relationship between the lack of inflation in the economy in late 2003 and the large numbers of unemployed and underemployed workers?

## Apply Economic Concepts

31. Answers will vary. Possible answer: The Fed increasing the money supply could have caused the economic growth and low interest rates. This can temporarily increase production beyond its potential, but it will cause inflation. This inflation will cause people and businesses to purchase fewer goods and services and discourage some people from working. In the long run, production will fall back to its potential.

32. Answers will vary. Possible answer: The Fed would probably increase its target for the federal funds rate. This would cause other interest rates to increase as well and discourage borrowing and spending. As a result, there would be less pressure on prices, and inflation should either stabilize or begin to fall.

33. The equilibrium rate is 8.0 percent.

Answers will vary. The following events might cause the equilibrium interest rate to increase:
- decrease in money supply
- increase in growth in income and production in the economy

Answers will vary. The following events might cause the equilibrium interest rate to fall:
- increase in money supply
- decline in growth in income and production in the economy

An example of an acceptable graph appears at the bottom of this page.

e-con @pps

34. Even thought there had been seven straight quarters of economic growth, there was no inflation because the recovery was not robust enough to take up all the "slack" created by the recession. "Slack" refers to the millions of unemployed workers, millions more of underemployed workers, and the large amount of U.S. production equipment that was either idle or under used. If economic growth continued, these idle resources could be brought in line without causing inflation.

## *Visualizing the Answer—
Apply Economic Concepts*

33. The answer includes a graph. Students' graphs should look similar to the one shown here. An Excel spreadsheet containing this graph, along with supporting data, is available on the Instructor's Resource CD.

**Demand and Supply for Money
(in billions of dollars)**

### PREPARE

This project can be completed in the classroom or as an outside assignment. The activities call for students to work in teams, but students also can complete the assignment working alone. If you organize the class into teams, consider identifying specific roles for team members such as recorder, discussion leader, researcher, etc.

### TEACH

### The Situation

The issues here involve a transition in perspective in both Aleesha's personal and public lives. Suddenly, the seemingly unjustifiable actions of the business and propertied classes become not just objects of bewilderment and ridicule but alternatives included, no matter how uncomfortably, in Aleesha's potential range of actions.

### The Decision

The decisions that must be made relate to the economic and personal futures of her business and the people who depend on her. Unfortunately, the business, founded on the love of animals, now acts as a barrier to Aleesha's ability to express that love. It is taking her time and testing her principles. The same is true of her relationship with her children. She must be away developing the business or perhaps just preserving it, while Tom enjoys the day-to-day warmth and love of Tomas and Alcoce in their most wonderful years. In general, the tests keep getting bigger and more stressful as her business grows. Her personal rewards decline, but the positive results for those who depend on her increase with each hurdle she overcomes successfully.

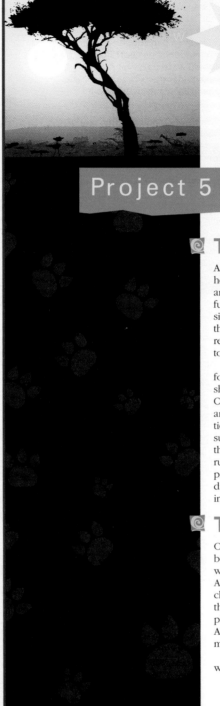

# Investing In Your Future

Project 5 > SHIFTING PERSPECTIVES

## The Situation

As she walked past security at the airport, Aleesha looked back at her family. Aleesha regretted taking this business trip more than anyone. She and Tom recently had been talking about the children's future schooling and needed to make a decision. However, discussions were to begin Monday in Washington with representatives of the Department of Defense about a possible deal to sell animal-restraint devices for use by the military. Later in the week, she was to meet with the law firm of Winston and Bailey on another matter.

So much had changed over the last two years. The sales figures for the new products were increasing monthly and should soon show a profit. The most dramatic success, the company's Capturecare device, had been purchased by several leading animal-control departments throughout the United States. In addition, the company also was test-marketing several spin-off consumer products for use by hunters. The new factory, located near the zoo, had started operations several months ago, and it was running smoothly. Unfortunately, the introduction of the new products and the new factory's financing had been based on predictions for an economic upturn. When the predictions proved incorrect, the future of the entire company was placed in jeopardy.

## The Decision

Once in the air, Aleesha pulled out her laptop, opened a file, and began listing the pros and cons of the children's schooling. Tom wanted to send the children to the local public grade school. Aleesha preferred a nearby private school that would assure the children more individual attention. Thanks to the earlier profits of the business, she and Tom now owned their own home and had plenty in savings to pay the private school tuition for many years. Aleesha worked on the lists for some time. Then she took a moment to reflect on how different her life had become.

Finally, her thoughts turned to the upcoming meetings. The first, with representatives of the Armed Services, resulted from months

### RESEARCH

Encourage students to use Internet and library resources to learn more about the issues in this project. Have them contact local private schools to obtain the costs of an education there. For information about the use of animals in modern warfare, suggest typing "animals and warfare" into an Internet search engine such as ask.com. To learn about the world of Washington lobbyists, suggest typing "Washington lobbyists" into the search engine.

of preparation. Aleesha had been awarded a government contract to supply animal capture, restraint, and other devices to the Army and the Marines. At first Aleesha was elated, as the contract payout would solve most of the company's current financial problems. However, she soon realized that one of the contract provisions could commit her company to develop devices used to capture animals used as weapons by opposing military forces and terrorist organizations. Her animal-capture devices would be used by U.S. forces to capture animals used to carry explosives, and the animals then would be put to death. The thought horrified her, and she knew she would be reluctant to agree to the contract.

The meetings later in the week also concerned her. Over the last two years, because of her factory's location, the company had been given tax breaks. Now, due to the economic downturn, the tax-relief program was about to be eliminated. As there was no national group representing her type of business, Aleesha hired the lobbying firm of Winston and Bailey to try to keep the program alive.

## Activities

**Divide into teams or work individually, as directed by your teacher, to perform the following tasks.**

Apply the steps in the following decision-making process to Aleesha's current situation:

1. *Define the problem.* Aleesha faces multiple decisions this time. Define each problem in a way that will allow a clear solution. The issues involve:

**a.** her children's schooling
**b.** the Department of Defense contract
**c.** the law firm of Winston and Bailey

2. *Identify her choices.*
3. *Evaluate the pluses and minuses of each choice.*
4. *Make a choice.*
5. *Provide "action" steps that are appropriate to the decision.*
6. *Critique the decision.*

## Research

Research for the information needed to make the decision, such as the pros and cons of public versus private school, the use of animals in modern warfare, and the world of Washington lobbyists.

## Present

Arrive at a decision. Then prepare a presentation for the class on the six steps you took to achieve this decision.

6/24

1/5

5/14

### APPLY

#### Activities

**Step 1:** The factors listed by individual students will reflect their perspectives on life and what is important to them at the current time. **(a)** The economics of the schooling situation should be noted but, as mentioned in the narrative, they are secondary given the level of affluence of Aleesha and Tom. Other factors should include the diversity of a public school vs. the sameness/elitism of the private; the relative safety of each; carryover to higher educational opportunities, etc. **(b)** Aleesha should use her leverage of having the most cost-effective solution to the military's problems to fully investigate the potential uses for her products being considered by the military. Then, should they prove to be as feared, it becomes a question of her ethical system: Is she able to rationalize that the good done by the contractual remuneration outweighs the potential harm done to the animals she loves, using her products? Or does she turn down the contract upon learning of any improper harmful use of her products? **(c)** The justification for employing lobbyists lies with open competition for scarce resources. Anyone can lobby, but some have more clout through money and power. Aleesha's efforts through the lobbyists will compete with others trying to feed at the same governmental trough.

### ASSESS

**Presentation** Consider using a rubric or evaluation form for student presentations. Make sure you share the rubric or form with students before they start working on the project. A sample evaluation form appears on the Instructor's Resource CD. The categories to be evaluated include: **Content** (organization, specific content, and accurate information); **Presentation Skills** (eye contact, grammar and pronunciation, volume, and pitch); **Audiovisual Aids** (appropriate content, style, and spelling); and **Handouts** (appropriate content; grammar, punctuation, and spelling).

### National Content Standards in Economics

The following NCEE Standards are addressed in Unit 6:

| | |
|---|---|
| **Standard 1** | Scarcity |
| **Standard 3** | Allocation of Goods and Services |
| **Standard 4** | Role of Incentives |
| **Standard 5** | Gain from Trade |
| **Standard 6** | Specialization and Trade |
| **Standard 7** | Markets—Price and Quantity Determination |
| **Standard 10** | Role of Economic Institutions |
| **Standard 11** | Role of Money |
| **Standard 13** | Role of Resources in Determining Income |
| **Standard 14** | Profit and the Entrepreneur |
| **Standard 15** | Growth |
| **Standard 16** | Role of Government |
| **Standard 17** | Using Cost/Benefit Analysis to Evaluate Government Programs |
| **Standard 18** | Macroeconomy—Income, Employment, Prices |
| **Standard 19** | Unemployment and Inflation |
| **Standard 20** | Monetary and Fiscal Policy |

# Unit 6

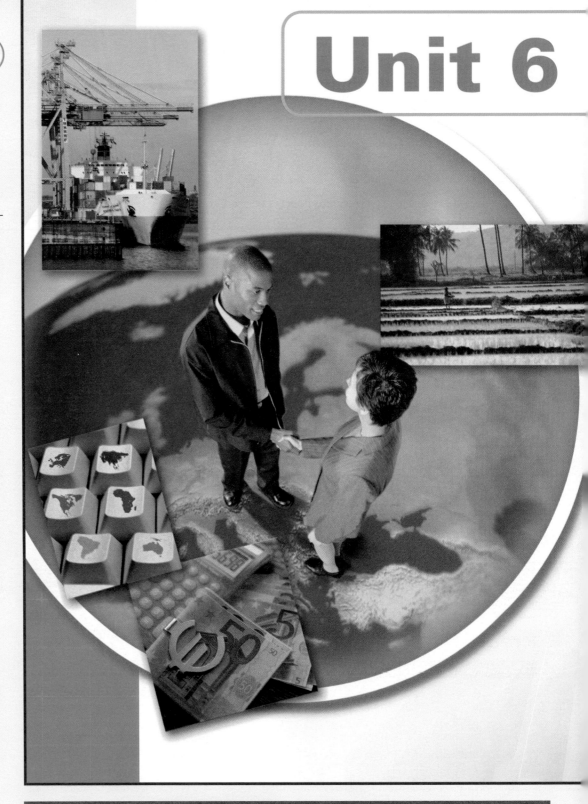

| Pacing Guide | One-Semester Days of Study | Two-Semesters Days of Study | Block Schedule 90-Minute Blocks |
|---|---|---|---|
| **UNIT 6: THE INTERNATIONAL ECONOMY** | | | |
| Chapter 18: International Trade | | | |
| **18.1** Benefits of Trade | 1 | 2 | 1 |
| **18.2** Trade Restrictions and Free-Trade Agreements | 1 | 2 | 1 |
| **18.3** Balance of Payments | 1 | 3 | 1 |
| **18.4** Foreign Exchange Rates | 2 | 3 | 2 |
| Chapter 19: Economic Development | | | |
| **19.1** Developing Economies and Industrial Market Economies | 1 | 2 | 1 |
| **19.2** Foreign Trade, Foreign Aid, and Economic Development | 1 | 3 | 1 |
| **19.3** Rules of the Game, Transition Economies, and Convergence | 2 | 3 | 2 |

# The International Economy

 **18** International Trade

 **19** Economic Development

Comparative advantage, specialization, and exchange help people get the most from their scarce resources. Despite the clear benefits from free international trade, trade restrictions date back centuries. Pressure from producers on governments to impose trade barriers continues to this day. Still, the United States plays a major role in the world economy, not only as the largest importer but also as the largest exporter. While the U.S. dollar remains the currency of choice in world trade, all nations face the challenge of achieving greater stability in their global finances.

551

## Chapter Overview

**LESSON 18.1** *Benefits of Trade:* This lesson identifies sources of comparative advantage and discusses the gains from international trade. U.S. exports and imports are also described.

**LESSON 18.2** *Trade Restrictions and Free-Trade Agreements:* This lesson identifies trade restrictions and evaluates their impact. An explanation of the rationale behind free-trade agreements is provided.

**LESSON 18.3** *Balance of Payments:* This lesson describes the components of a nation's current accounts and financial accounts.

**LESSON 18.4** *Foreign Exchange Rates:* This lesson analyzes the market for foreign exchange and identifies participants. It also distinguishes between flexible and fixed exchange rates.

### Consider

Ask students to consider the questions posed on this page as they study Chapter 18. After studying all three lessons, students should be able to answer the questions. The content related to each question can be found on the pages indicated below.

- If the United States is such a rich and productive nation, why are so many goods and services imported? See page 554—Comparative Advantage.
- Why isn't the United States self-sufficient? See page 556—U.S. Exports and Imports.
- If free trade is such a good idea, why do some producers try to restrict foreign trade? See page 560—Trade Restrictions.
- What's up with the euro? See page 575—The Euro.
- Is a growing U.S. trade deficit a growing worry? See page 568—The Merchandise Trade Balance.

### POINT YOUR BROWSER

Remind students that they can find additional resources for this chapter at **econxtra.swlearning.com**.

- Xtra! Study Tools
- Net Bookmarks
- Xtra! Quiz Prep
- econ@pps
- Ask the Xpert!
- Graphing Workshop

# 18 International Trade

*Benefits of Trade* **18.1**

*Trade Restrictions and Free-Trade Agreements* **18.2**

*Balance of Payments* **18.3**

*Foreign Exchange Rates* **18.4**

### Consider

If the United States is such a rich and productive nation, why are so many goods and services imported?

Why isn't the United States self-sufficient?

If free trade is such a good idea, why do some producers try to restrict foreign trade?

What's up with the euro?

Is a growing U.S. trade deficit a growing worry?

© Getty Images/PhotoDisc

### POINT YOUR BROWSER

*econxtra.swlearning.com*

### *Teaching Resources for Chapter 18*

- Activities and Projects Masters
- Spanish Resources
- Econ Connection Interactive Tutorial CD
- **Exam***View*® CD
- Workbook Teacher's Edition
- Chapter Test Teacher's Edition
- NCEE Standards and Correlation

- Personal Finance Guide
- Social Studies Skills Review
- Instructor's Resource CD
    - PowerPoint Presentation
    - Lesson Plans
    - Video Discussion Guide
    - Answers to Graphing Exercises
- **econxtra.swlearning.com**

## Objectives

> Identify sources of comparative advantage.

> Discuss the gains from international trade even without comparative advantage.

> Describe U.S. exports and imports.

## Overview

This morning you put on your Levi jeans made in Mexico, pulled on your Benetton sweater from Italy, and laced up your Timberland boots from Thailand. After a breakfast that included bananas from Honduras, you headed for school in a Swedish Volvo fueled by Venezuelan oil. The world is a giant shopping mall, and Americans are big spenders. Foreigners buy American products, too—products such as grain, personal computers, aircraft, movies, trips to Disney World, and thousands of other goods and services.

## [ In the News ]

### ● Mexico Bleeds Workers and Jobs

When the North American Free Trade Agreement (NAFTA) took effect January 1, 1994, it was praised as a way to improve economic conditions in the United States, Canada, and Mexico. Mexico immediately benefited from the shifting of manufacturing jobs from the United States into Mexican factories. However, today Mexico is caught in a situation that is bleeding it of its work and workers. The recent downturn in the U.S. economy led U.S. companies to redirect to China the manufacturing jobs it had been sending to Mexico. In China, labor costs are roughly one-third of the $13 a day paid on average in Mexico. In other words, Mexico no longer enjoyed the comparative advantage of providing the lowest-cost labor force for these jobs. Many Mexicans then decided to move north to the United States, where they would receive higher wages than they could in Mexico. Consequently, a river of undocumented workers totaling well over five million people began to flow into the United States, where transplanted Mexicans can make as much in a day as they can in a week in Mexico.

### Think About It

What might motivate these undocumented workers to return to Mexico? Is having these workers in the U. S. a good or bad thing? Explain your answer.

◀ | ▶

553

### National Content Standards in Economics

A complete list of the NCEE Standards appears on pages xxiv–xxv of this book. The following standards are addressed in Lesson 18.1.

Standard 4: Role of Incentives

Standard 5: Gain from Trade

Standard 6: Specialization and Trade

Standard 7: Markets—Price and Quantity Determination

Standard 16: Role of Government

Remind students of the concept of comparative advantage that they studied in Chapter 2. Explain that in this lesson, they will learn how countries benefit from trade because of comparative advantage. Nations have different opportunity costs of producing goods and services because they have different quantities and qualities of resources. When nations specialize in the production of goods and services that have the lowest opportunity costs, and trade with other nations for products that they cannot produce as efficiently, total production grows and all trading partners benefit.

### Objectives

Remind students to read the lesson objectives to help focus their attention before reading the lesson.

### [ In the News ]

Instruct students to read the passage and write down their answers. Point out that their answers might change after they finish studying Lesson 18.1.

### Answers to Think About It

Answers will vary. Possible answer: Undocumented workers might return to Mexico if the job market and wages improve in Mexico. Having these workers in the United States is not a good thing because there is already a shortage of low-skilled jobs in America. These undocumented workers are serving to increase that shortage.

### Follow-Up Activity

Invite interested students to research Mexico's current economy. Has it recovered from losing manufacturing jobs to China? Are undocumented Mexican workers still streaming across the boarder to the United States?

### Visual Presentation

Use the PowerPoint presentation on the Instructor's Resource CD as an adjunct to your lecture. The presentation also can be used for review.

## Comparative Advantage

Point out that labor and capital are two key resources needed for production. Nations with well-educated and trained workers are likely to benefit from specializing in production that requires such talent. Other nations that are able to use advanced technologies to produce goods and services will benefit from specializing in this type of production. The most fortunate nations can benefit because they possess both highly skilled workers and advanced technology. Even nations that lack natural resources, such as Japan, can become valuable trading partners when they possess both highly skilled workers and advanced technology.

### Ethics in Action

Have students work in pairs to discuss the ethical issue featured on page 555, and develop an answer to the question presented there.

#### Answers to Think Critically

Answers will vary. Possible answer: Moving plants that cause pollution to Mexico is unethical because there is a cost to the local society from this pollution. Local health will be adversely affected from the increase in the various wastes brought about by such plants moving into the area.

See It

Direct students to the Graphing Workshop for Chapter 18 at **econx-tra.swlearning.com**. Instruct students to click on **See It: Comparative Advantage** to view the graph and listen to an explanation.

 **CHECKPOINT**
Invite a student to answer the checkpoint that appears on this page.

#### Answer

The resources that lead to a nation's comparative advantage are labor and capital, soil and seasons, and mineral deposits.

---

# Comparative Advantage

Recall the discussion in Chapter 2 about how you and your neighbor could increase output by specializing. The law of comparative advantage says that the individual with the lowest opportunity cost of producing a particular good should specialize in that good. Just as individuals benefit from specialization and exchange, so do businesses, states, and nations.

To reap the gains that arise from specialization, countries engage in international trade. *To maximize the benefits of trade, each country specializes in the goods that it produces at the lowest opportunity cost.* As a result, all countries can become better off than if each tried to go it alone. World output increases when countries specialize.

How does a country decide what to produce? In other words, how does it determine its comparative advantages? Trade based on comparative advantage is usually prompted by differences in the quantity and quality of resources across countries. These resources include labor and capital, soil and seasons, and mineral deposits.

## Labor and Capital

Two key resources are labor and capital. Countries differ not only in their availability of labor and capital but also in the qualities of these resources. Countries with a well-educated and well-trained labor force will specialize in producing goods that require such talent. Similarly, countries with state-of-the-art manufacturing technologies will specialize in producing goods that require high-tech capital.

Some countries, such as the United States and Japan, have an educated labor force and abundant high-tech capital. Both resources result in greater productivity per worker. This makes each nation quite competitive globally in producing goods that require skilled labor and technologically advanced capital.

## Soil and Seasons

Some countries are blessed with fertile land and favorable growing seasons. The United States, for example, has been called the "bread basket of the world." The country's rich farmland is ideal for growing corn, wheat, and other grains. Honduras has the ideal climate for growing bananas. Coffee grows best in the climate and elevation of Colombia, Brazil, and Jamaica. Thus, the United States exports grain and imports coffee and bananas.

Seasonal differences across countries also create gains from trade. For example, during America's winter months, Chileans sell Americans fruit and Canadians travel to Florida for sun and fun. During the summer months, Americans export fruit to Chile and Americans travel to Canada for fishing and camping.

## Mineral Deposits

Mineral resources often are concentrated in particular parts of the world, such as oil in Saudi Arabia, bauxite in Jamaica, and diamonds in South Africa. The United States has abundant coal deposits but not enough oil to satisfy domestic demand. Thus, the United States exports coal and imports oil.

In summary, *countries export what they can produce at a lower opportunity cost and import products that other countries can produce at a lower opportunity cost. As a result of this trade, all countries can produce and consume more.*

 **CHECKPOINT**
What resources lead to a country's comparative advantage?

---

### Outside Resources

**International Trade** Toutor2U is an online educational service that provides free information and instructional materials. Although it is located in the United Kingdom, the basic information it provides is equally applicable to the U.S. economy. It maintains a variety of web pages that deal with international trade and related topics, all of which can be reached from its home page at www.tutor2u.net/default.asp. Ask students to visit this web site and report on what they find about international trade and comparative advantage.

# Ethics in Action

### Should Lax Environmental Laws Be a Comparative Advantage?

When the North American Free Trade Agreement (NAFTA) was negotiated 10 years ago, environmental concerns were addressed by what was called the "green guardian." This phrase referred to a side accord among the signers of NAFTA—Mexico, the United States, and Canada. This accord officially was named the North American Agreement on Environmental Cooperation (NAAEC). It set up a Commission for Environmental Cooperation (CEC) to help coordinate and implement policy solutions to environmental problems. Unfortunately, the creation of the CEC seems to have been the high point of its operations, with things going downhill from there. Critics claim the NAAEC actually aided polluters by allowing the referral of recognized environmental problems to a commission (the CEC) that lacked the powers to take effective corrective action. In a recent self-analysis report, the CEC itself concluded that the free trade allowed by NAFTA had the partial effect of allowing companies to move severely polluting factories to jurisdictions with less-strict anti-pollution laws. In particular, industries such as pulp and paper, mining, iron and steel production, and chemicals all found relatively safe havens in Mexico under the free-trade umbrella. A provision similar to the "green guardian" is being considered for inclusion in the Free Trade Area of the Americas (FTAA) agreement that will create a similar free-trade zone stretching throughout North and South America.

### Think Critically

Do you think moving plants that cause pollution to Mexico is ethical? Why or why not?

## Other Benefits of Trade

If each country had an identical stock of resources and each country combined those resources with equal efficiency, then there would be no comparative advantage. Yet international trade could still benefit both sides. Here are two reasons why.

### Economies of Scale

If a producer experiences *economies of scale*—that is, if the average cost of output declines as a firm expands its scale of production—countries can gain from specialization and trade. Such specialization allows firms in each nation to produce enough to enjoy economies of scale.

As you will see later in the chapter, the primary reason for establishing one single market in Europe was to offer producers there a large, open market of more than 330 million consumers. European producers can increase production, have economies of scale, and sell for less. In the process, these producers also will become more competitive trading outside of Europe.

### Differences in Tastes

Even without comparative advantage, countries can gain from trade as long as tastes and preferences differ across countries. Consumption patterns do differ across countries, and some of these differences likely stem from differences in tastes. For example, the Danes eat twice as much pork as do Americans. Americans eat twice as much chicken as do Hungarians.

Soft drinks are four times more popular in the United States than in Western Europe. The English like tea. Americans like coffee. Algeria has an ideal climate for growing grapes, but its large Muslim population abstains from alcohol. Thus, Algeria exports wine.

Lesson 18.1 • *Benefits of Trade* **555**

## TEACH

### Other Benefits of Trade

Point out that there are other advantages of trade that are not directly related to comparative advantage. In some cases, firms located in small nations would not be able to take advantage of economies of scale if they manufactured products that were sold only within their own nation. Firms that manufacture precision machine tools in Luxemburg, for example, could never sell enough of their products within Luxemburg to justify their extensive investment in this type of production. By selling most of the tools it produces to other nations, Luxemburg's firms have been able to grow and become more efficient. Differences in tastes also support specialization and trade. Most U.S. citizens do not eat sea cucumbers. These sea creatures, considered a delicacy in Asia, are harvested in Hawaii and shipped to other nations.

### *Think Critically Through Visuals* 👁

Direct students to focus their attention on the photographs on page 556. Ask for a volunteer to answer the question posed in the caption.

#### Answer

Answers will vary. Possible answer: Technology improvements in textile machinery exported to Italy might decrease the cost of Italian suits. This decrease might increase consumption and production of Italian suits.

**Main Idea**

### NCEE Standard 6: Specialization and Trade

When individuals, regions, and nations specialize in what they can produce at the lowest cost and then trade with others, both production and consumption increase.

## ENRICH

Remind students that a nation may gain a comparative advantage but end up destroying natural resources in the process. The United States has exploited its natural resources in the past to gain a comparative advantage. In October 1871, there were two huge fires in the United States. Many people are familiar with the Great Chicago Fire, but fewer people know about the Great Peshtigo Fire. This fire occurred in the north woods of Wisconsin and Minnesota when loggers started a forest fire that consumed more than 2,000 square miles of forests and killed approximately 1,200 people. Ask students whether there is any difference between the United States allowing clear-cutting of American forests in the twentieth century and cutting the tropical rain forest in Brazil at the present. Why do countries destroy their natural resources to gain an advantage in trade?

## ✓ CHECKPOINT

Invite a student to answer the checkpoint that appears on page 556.

#### Answer

Nations can benefit from trade even if there is no comparative advantage through economies of scale and from differences in tastes.

## U.S. Exports and Imports

Point out that several categories of production make up the most important U.S. exports and others constitute most U.S. imports. By studying these categories of products, students will be able to tell where the United States has its greatest comparative advantages and where other nations have theirs.

### TEAM WORK

Organize students into groups of four or five. Instruct teams to select a recorder and a spokesperson. Instruct students to complete the **Team Work** activity shown on page 557. Set a timer for 10 minutes. When the timer goes off, invite the spokesperson from each group to take a turn naming an example.

Consider allowing students to move about the classroom and look for products that were manufactured in the nations listed. They should also look at their personal belongings. For example they might discover a box of pens from Japan, a remote control from China, eyeglasses frames from Italy, cosmetics from Great Britain, or computer components from Mexico.

### Think Critically Through Visuals

Use Figure 18.1—Composition of U.S. Exports and Imports in 2002 on page 557 to recap this section.

### CHECKPOINT

Invite a student to answer the checkpoint that appears on page 557.

### Answer

Capital goods are the largest category of U.S. exports. Consumer goods are the largest category of U.S. imports.

---

Comparative advantage stimulates trade, but countries still may benefit from international trade even if all countries have identical resources and even if all countries produce with identical efficiency.

### CHECKPOINT
How might countries benefit from trade even if there is no comparative advantage?

## U.S. Exports and Imports

Countries trade with one another—or, more precisely, people and firms in one country trade with those in another—because each side expects to gain from the exchange. People expect to increase their consumption possibilities.

### U.S. Exports

Just as some states are more involved in interstate trade than others, some nations are more involved in international trade than others. For example,

exports account for about one-quarter of the gross domestic product (GDP) in Canada and the United Kingdom; about one-third of the GDP in Germany, Sweden, and Switzerland; and about half of the GDP in the Netherlands. Despite the perception that Japan has a giant export sector, exports there make up only about one-seventh of GDP.

*In the United States, exports of goods and services amounted to about one-tenth of GDP in 2002.* Although relatively small compared to most other countries, exports play a growing role in the U.S. economy.

The left-hand panel of Figure 18.1 shows the composition of U.S. exports by major category. Capital goods account for nearly half of all exports. Capital goods include high-tech products, such as computers and jet aircraft. Next most important is industrial supplies and materials, at 23 percent of the total. Together, capital goods and industrial supplies and material make up 67 percent, or two-thirds, of U.S. exports. It seems that most U.S. exports help foreign manufacturers make things. Consumer goods account for only 12 percent of exports. This category includes entertainment products, such as movies and recorded music.

 Main Idea

**Specialization and Trade**

*When nations specialize in what they can produce at the lowest cost and then trade with others, both production and consumption increase.* The largest category of U.S. exports is capital goods, such as machinery used in the textile industry. The largest U.S. import category is consumer goods, which inclues men's suits from Italy. How do U.S. exports of textile machinery to Italy boost production and consumption of the men's suits that country produces?

556     **CHAPTER 18**   International Trade

---

### Group Activity

Organize students into small groups. Direct each group to choose a category of products that they commonly use, such as shoes, television sets, computers, or telephones. Instruct them to investigate the international trade of this category of product. Does the United States export or import more of these products? How does trade in this product affect consumers and businesses in the United States? Suggest that students use the *Statistical Abstract of the United States* to start their research. Invite groups to share their findings with the class, and ask students whether there are common factors among the products that are imported and among the products that are exported.

## U.S. Imports

America is a rich country and Americans spend more on imports than foreigners spend on U.S. exports. *U.S. imports of goods and services were one-seventh the size of U.S. GDP in 2002.* The right-hand panel of Figure 18.1 shows the composition of U.S. imports. Whereas consumer goods accounted for only 12 percent of U.S. exports, they are the largest category of imports at 27 percent of the total. Imported consumer goods include consumer electronics from Taiwan, shoes from Brazil, and kitchen gadgets from China.

The next most important category of imports is capital goods, at 25 percent, such as printing presses from Germany. A close third, at 23 percent, is industrial supplies and materials, such as crude oil from the Middle East and raw metals, including lead, zinc, and copper, from around the world. Note that automotive vehicles are only 11 percent of exports but are 17 percent of imports.

To give you some feel for America's trading partners, here are the top 10 destinations for U.S. goods in order of importance: Canada, Mexico, Japan,

**TEAM WORK**

In small groups, brainstorm examples of specific products imported from the top 10 sources of imports: Canada, Mexico, Japan, China, Great Britain, Germany, South Korea, France, Italy, and Taiwan.

Great Britain, Germany, South Korea, France, the Netherlands, China, and Taiwan. The top 10 sources of U.S. imports consist of this same group in the same order, except Italy replaces the Netherlands and China jumps from ninth to fourth.

 **CHECKPOINT**
What are the most important categories of U.S. exports and imports?

---

**Composition of U.S. Exports and Imports in 2002**          Figure **18.1**

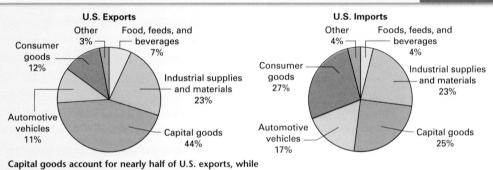

**U.S. Exports**
- Other 3%
- Food, feeds, and beverages 7%
- Consumer goods 12%
- Industrial supplies and materials 23%
- Automotive vehicles 11%
- Capital goods 44%

**U.S. Imports**
- Other 4%
- Foods, feeds, and beverages 4%
- Consumer goods 27%
- Industrial supplies and materials 23%
- Automotive vehicles 17%
- Capital goods 25%

**Capital goods account for nearly half of U.S. exports, while consumer goods are the largest category of imports.**

Source: Developed from export and import estimates in "U.S. International Transactions," *Survey of Current Business*, U.S. Department of Commerce, April 2003, Table E.

Lesson 18.1 • *Benefits of Trade* **557**

---

**APPLY**

Assign Lesson 18.1 from the Contemporary Economics Workbook.

**e-con @pps**

Encourage students to apply their knowledge of concepts presented in this lesson as they explore economic news stories, policy debates, and data available at **econxtra.swlearning.com**. A sampling of the titles for this lesson appears below.

**EconDebate**
- Does the U.S. economy benefit from foreign trade?

**EconNews**
- Germany: You Are the Weakest Link!

**ASSESS**

Assign all or part of Lesson 18.1 Assessment on page 558 as homework or an in-class activity.

**Xtra! Study Tools**

Direct students to the online study tools for Lesson 18.1 at **econxtra.swlearning.com**.

**CLOSE**

**Revisit** the In the News feature on the first page of the lesson. Ask students to review their preliminary answers and discuss the questions, now that they have completed this lesson.

**Review** the objectives for Lesson 18.1. Students should be able to:
- Identify sources of comparative advantage.
- Discuss the gains from international trade even without comparative advantage.
- Describe U.S. exports and imports.

---

**RETEACH**

Remind students that nations import products they are not able to produce efficiently themselves (that have a relatively high opportunity cost of production for them). Ask students to work together to make a list of products the United States is not well suited to produce. What characteristics do these products have in common? Why would it be inefficient for U.S. producers to try to make these products? Can students think of products the United States is well suited to produce with relatively low opportunity costs? Does the United States specialize in producing and exporting these products? Why or why not?

## Key Concepts

1. Answers will vary. Possible answer: Lambs are born in the spring, which occurs during April and May in the northern hemisphere and during October and November in the southern hemisphere.

2. Answers will vary. Possible answer: The latest technology will not increase a nation's productivity or reduce its opportunity costs unless it also has skilled workers who are able to use that technology.

3. Answers will vary. Possible answer: Nations in which people do not share this taste are able to export bats to nations that do, with very low opportunity costs.

4. Answers will vary. Possible answer: People in wealthy nations have more income with which to purchase consumer goods, both domestic and imported. Less wealthy nations often spend their limited income to import capital goods they need to develop their economies.

5. Answers will vary. Possible answer: The climate in the United States is not suited to the production of these crops. The opportunity cost of producing these goods would be very high in the United States.

## Graphing Exercise

6. Answers will vary. Possible answer: Events must have taken place to cause people in other nations to demand fewer U.S. products. This could have been the result of an economic downturn. In reality, it was largely the result of a very strong dollar that made U.S. prices high to foreigners. They had to exchange more of their currencies to obtain the dollars they needed to purchase U.S. goods and services. By 1990, the U.S. dollar had weakened, making U.S. prices more competitive. Fewer exports would have reduced demand for U.S. products and therefore employment in U.S. export industries.

   An example of an acceptable graph appears at the bottom of this page.

## Think Critically

7. Answers will vary. Possible answer: Many nations refuse to import genetically engineered foods. Although the United States is able to produce these products at a lower opportunity cost than can other nations, their unwillingness to purchase them tends to negate the value of our comparative advantage.

---

Xtra!
**Study Tools**
econxtra.swlearning.com

## Key Concepts

1. Why does the United States have a comparative advantage over New Zealand in the production or lamb during April and May, while New Zealand enjoys a similar comparative advantage over the United States during the months of October and November?

2. Why wouldn't the purchase of the most advanced technology necessarily provide a nation with a comparative advantage relative to other nations?

3. In the Far East, some people think that soup made from boiled bats is a special delicacy. How does this give nations in which people who do not share this taste a comparative advantage?

4. Why do wealthy nations import a larger proportion of consumer goods than nations that are not as wealthy?

5. Why doesn't it make sense for the United States to try to export coffee or bananas?

## Graphing Exercise

6. Although exports have accounted for roughly 10 percent of U.S. production in recent years, there have been periods of time when these sales have been smaller. Construct a line graph that shows the value of U.S. exports as a percent of U.S. GDP in recent years using data in the table. What happened in 1985 to cause U.S. exports to decline as a percent of GDP? How did this affect the U.S. economy?

**U.S. Exports of Goods and Services as a Percent of U.S. GDP, 1980–2000**

| Year | Percentage |
|------|------------|
| 1980 | 9.76% |
| 1985 | 6.92% |
| 1990 | 9.32% |
| 1995 | 10.93% |
| 2000 | 10.79% |

## Think Critically

7. **Biology** In recent years, many genetically engineered foods have been developed and marketed in the United States. These products include tomatoes that are firm and easy to ship, corn and wheat that resist fungus diseases, and fruit that can be stored for long periods of time without spoiling. It would be reasonable to assume that the development of these products would give the U.S. a comparative advantage over nations that do not grow genetically engineered foods. Investigate these products to see whether this assumption is accurate. What do you find? Why does a comparative advantage benefit a nation only when there is a willingness by potential customers to purchase the product?

---

**U.S. Exports as a Percent of GDP**

## Visualizing the Answer— Graphing Exercise

6. The answer includes a graph. Students' graphs should look similar to the one shown here. An Excel spreadsheet containing this graph, along with supporting data, is available on the Instructor's Resource CD.

## Objectives

> Identify trade restrictions and evaluate their impact.

> Explain why nations seek free-trade agreements.

## Overview

International trade expands the consumption possibilities of trading nations. Despite the benefits of such trade, nearly all countries at one time or another have erected trade barriers across national borders. Trade restrictions usually benefit domestic producers but harm domestic consumers. The losses to domestic consumers typically exceed the gains to domestic producers. If free trade is such a good deal, why do most countries impose trade restrictions? Producer groups are well organized and are able to encourage governments to restrict imports. Consumers are disorganized and seldom even make the connection between trade restrictions and higher prices. The good news is that trade restrictions are diminishing around the world.

## Key Terms

**world price**

**tariff**

**quota**

**General Agreement on Tariffs and Trade (GATT)**

**Uruguay Round**

**World Trade Organization (WTO)**

### FOCUS

**Trade Restrictions and Free-Trade Agreements**

Point out that all nations have established at least some barriers to trade. Often, these barriers take the form of tariffs or quotas. In other cases, nations join together in associations to reduce barriers to trade within the group while maintaining barriers to other nations that are not members of the group. Nations also have established organizations that set rules for international trade to reduce the possibility of a trade war that could harm all trading partners in the global economy.

#### Objectives

Remind students to read the lesson objectives to help focus their attention before reading the lesson.

#### Key Terms

Direct students to create a database using the key terms for this lesson. The database fields should include terms, definitions, and page numbers. Point out that the process of keying the data is an effective way to study key terms.

### [ In the News ]

Instruct students to read the passage and write down their answers. Point out that their answers might change after they finish studying Lesson 18.2.

#### Answers to Think About It

Answers will vary. Possible answer: No, the government should not impose tariffs because tariffs prevent its citizens from purchasing a good at the lowest cost possible. If a nation doesn't have a comparative advantage in an industry, it is not right to establish a pseudo-comparative advantage by creating a tariff.

#### Follow-Up Activity

Invite interested students to investigate the current situation regarding tariffs on steel imports.

#### Visual Presentation

Use the PowerPoint presentation on the Instructor's Resource CD as an adjunct to your lecture. The presentation also can be used for review.

## [ In the News ]

### ● Tariffs on Steel Trigger Conflict Among American Industries

In 2002, the U.S. government imposed tariffs on steel imports in order to save the domestic steel industry from what might have been a deadly slump. Since then, a lobbying war has been waged over the tariffs' effect and continuation. In a little more than a year, the tariff added more than $600 million to the cost of imported steel and allowed domestic steel producers to profit from higher prices. Touting this success, representatives of the steel companies that benefited told of plant upgrades and consolidations that will, they say, better prepare the industry for competition. Countering this viewpoint, two dozen members of the Automotive Coalition met with U.S. government officials to detail the damage done to manufacturers of automotive parts and components. Plant closings, layoffs and permanent job losses, transfers of business to overseas suppliers, and other extremely negative effects were attributed to the tariffs. Consequently, on its behalf and the behalf of other users of steel products who were losing business and jobs, the Coalition begged the government to end the tariff.

#### Think About It

When should a government impose a tariff? Is it reasonable to expect a tariff to have a totally positive or negative impact? Why or why not?

◀ I ▶

**559**

### National Content Standards in Economics

A complete list of the NCEE Standards appears on pages xxiv–xxv of this book. The following standards are addressed in Lesson 18.2.

Standard 4: Role of Incentives

Standard 5: Gain from Trade

Standard 6: Specialization and Trade

Standard 16: Role of Government

Standard 17: Using Cost/Benefit Analysis to Evaluate Government Programs

## Trade Restrictions

Explain the different types of barriers nations have established to restrict free trade. A tariff is a tax on imported goods that makes these products more expensive to consumers in the nation that imposes the tariffs. Quotas are a restriction on the amount of a product that may be imported into a nation within a period of time. Quotas may or may not be imposed in conjunction with a tariff. A final type of barrier is restrictions that might be called "rules of the game." By establishing rules that shippers of imported products cannot easily follow, many nations discourage trade.

Direct students to **econxtra.swlearning.com** to hear an expert answer the question "What are some arguments for restricting trade with other nations?"

Direct students to the Graphing Workshop for Chapter 18 at **econxtra.swlearning.com**. Instruct students to click on **See It: Effect of a Quota** to view the graph and listen to an explanation. In addition, instruct students to click on **Apply It: Illustrating the Effects of a Quota in the Market for Wheat.**

Direct students to the Graphing Workshop for Chapter 18 at **econxtra.swlearning.com**. Instruct students to click on **See It: Effect of a Tariff** to view the graph and listen to an explanation. In addition, instruct students to click on **Try It: The Effects of a Tariff.**

---

**Ask the Xpert!**
*econxtra.swlearning.com*

*What are some arguments for restricting trade with other nations?*

**world price**
The price at which a good is traded internationally; determined by the world supply and world demand for the good

*The Graphing Workshop*

**tariff**
A tax on imports

**quota**
A legal limit on the quantity of a particular product that can be imported

*The Graphing Workshop*

---

# Trade Restrictions

For internationally traded goods, such as wheat, oil, or steel, a price is established on the world market. The **world price** is determined by world supply and world demand for the product. With free trade, U.S. consumers can buy any amount desired at the world price.

## Tariffs

U.S. producers would like to be able to sell their product in the United States for more than the world price. To achieve this, they often try to persuade legislators to restrict competition from abroad. One way the government can put foreign producers at a disadvantage is to impose a tariff on imports. Simply put, a **tariff** is a tax on imports. The tariff reduces the quantity of imports supplied. With fewer imports, the supply of goods in the U.S. market declines, so the price of the goods goes up. As a result, U.S. producers get to sell their products for more on the U.S. market. A tariff on U.S. imports benefits U.S. producers. However, a tariff harms U.S consumers, who must pay that higher price. The revenue from tariffs goes to the government.

## Quotas

Another way domestic producers try to limit foreign competition is by getting the government to impose import quotas. A **quota** is a legal limit on the amount of a particular commodity that can be imported. Quotas usually target imports from particular countries. For example, a quota may limit automobiles from Japan or shoes from Brazil. *By limiting imports, a quota reduces the supply in the U.S. market, which raises the U.S. price above the world price.* Again, this helps U.S. producers but harms U.S. consumers. Foreign producers who get to sell their goods for the higher U.S. price also benefit.

Producer support for quotas, coupled with a lack of opposition from consumers (who remain mostly unaware of all this), has resulted in quotas that

---

have lasted for decades. For example, apparel quotas have been in effect for more than 30 years and sugar quotas for more than 50 years.

## Tariffs and Quotas Compared

Consider the similarities and differences between a tariff and a quota. Both restrict supply, thereby increasing the price, which hurts U.S. consumers and helps U.S. producers. The primary difference is that the revenue from a tariff goes to the U.S. government, whereas the revenue from the quota goes to whoever has the right under the quota to sell foreign goods in the U.S. market. Usually the beneficiary of a quota is a foreign exporter.

Perhaps the worst part about tariffs and quotas is that foreign governments typically respond with tariffs and quotas of their own. This shrinks the U.S. export market, reducing specialization and exchange around the world.

## Other Trade Restrictions

Besides tariffs and quotas, a variety of other measures restricts free trade. To promote exports, a country may provide subsidies to exporters or low-interest loans to foreign buyers. Some countries impose *domestic content requirements* specifying that at least a certain portion of a final good must be produced domestically.

Other requirements concerning health, safety, or technical standards often discriminate against foreign goods. For example, European countries prohibit beef from hormone-fed cattle, a measure aimed at U.S. beef. Food purity laws in Germany bar many non-German beers.

Until the European Community adopted uniform standards, differing technical requirements forced manufacturers to offer as many as seven different models of the same TV set for that market. Sometimes exporters will voluntarily limit exports, as when Japanese automakers agreed to cut auto exports to the United States. *The point is that tariffs and quotas are only two of many tools that restrict imports and reduce the benefits of comparative advantage.*

---

## Outside Resources

**World Trade Organization** Because the World Trade Organization (WTO), along with some of its policies, has been the subject of protests in recent years, suggest that students learn more about this organization by visiting the WTO web site at www.wto.org. Instruct students to read the overview that can be found by clicking on the link "What is the WTO?" Interested students should be encouraged to learn more about current controversies that inspire protests. Invite students to discuss their findings in class.

## Problems with Trade Restrictions

Trade restrictions raise a number of problems. The biggest problem is that other countries often respond with tariffs and quotas of their own, thus shrinking the gains from trade. This can trigger still greater trade restrictions, and lead to an outright trade war.

Second, protecting one stage of production from international competition often requires protecting other stages of production. For example, protecting the U.S. textile industry from foreign competition raises the cost of cloth to U.S. garment makers. This reduces the competitiveness of U.S. garments compared to foreign ones. As a result, the domestic garment industry might need protection as well.

Third, the cost of protection also includes spending for lobbying fees, propaganda, and legal actions to secure and maintain this favorable treatment. All these outlays are, for the most part, a social waste for they reduce competition but produce nothing besides trade restrictions.

A fourth problem with trade restrictions is the high transaction costs of enforcing quotas, tariffs, and other restrictions. The U.S. Customs Service operates 24 hours a day, 365 days a year, inspecting the luggage of the 500 million people who enter the country each year via air, sea, and more than 300 border crossings. On highway I-35 in Laredo, Texas, for example, more than 6,000 18-wheeler trucks roll in from Mexico every day. Policing and enforcement costs add up.

Finally, research indicates that trade barriers slow the introduction of new goods and better technologies. So, rather than simply raising domestic prices and reducing the gains from specialization, trade restrictions also slow economic progress.

**CHECKPOINT**

What are the two main trade restrictions and how do they affect U.S. prices?

# Free Trade by Multilateral Agreement

International trade arises from voluntary exchange among buyers and sellers pursuing their self-interest. Since 1950, world output has risen seven-fold, but world trade has increased seventeen-fold. World trade offers many advantages to the trading countries. These include increased consumption possibilities, access to markets around the world, lower costs through economies of scale, improved quality from competitive pressure, and lower prices. Because of these advantages, the trend around the world is toward freer trade.

## General Agreement on Tariffs and Trade (GATT)

Trade restrictions introduced during the Great Depression contributed to that economic disaster. To avoid a return to such dark times, after World War II the United States invited its trading partners to negotiate lower tariffs and quotas. The result was the **General Agreement on Tariffs and Trade (GATT)**, an international trade agreement adopted in 1947 by the United States and 22 other countries. Each signer of GATT agreed to reduce tariffs through multinational negotiations; reduce quotas; and treat all member nations equally with respect to trade.

Since then, a series of trade negotiations among many countries, called *trade rounds,* has continued to lower trade barriers. Trade rounds offer a package approach to trade negotiations rather than an issue-by-issue approach. A particular industry might not object to freer trade when it sees that other industries also agree to freer trade.

The most recent round of negotiations was completed in Uruguay in 1994. More than 140 countries have signed this agreement, called the **Uruguay Round**. This was the most

**General Agreement on Tariffs and Trade (GATT)**

An international tariff-reduction treaty adopted in 1947 that resulted in a series of negotiated "rounds" aimed at freer trade

**Uruguay Round**

The most recent and most comprehensive of the eight postwar multilateral trade negotiations under GATT; created the World Trade Organization

**CHECKPOINT**

Invite a student to answer the checkpoint that appears on this page.

### Answer

The two main trade restrictions are tariffs and quotas. Quotas, by limiting imports, reduce the supply in the U.S. market, which raises the U.S. price above the world price. Tariffs also limit the amount of imports supplied and, as a result, raise U.S. prices above the world price.

## TEACH

### Free Trade by Multilateral Agreement

Explain several multilateral agreements that have been made by groups of nations to facilitate trade among participants. The General Agreement on Tariffs and Trade (GATT) was formed for the purpose of reducing tariffs and quotas and to ensure that all trading partners within GATT were treated equally. The World Trade Organization (WTO) replaced GATT and expanded its powers beyond the trade of merchandise. Common markets and free-trade agreements have also been formed by groups of nations to increase trade within these groups. The best known of these are the European Common Market, and the North American Free Trade Agreement (NAFTA).

Try It

Direct students to the Graphing Workshop for Chapter 18 at **econxtra.swlearning.com**. Instruct students to click on **Try It: Free Trade Equilibrium Using Supply and Demand Analysis.**

**NET Bookmark**

Direct students to **econxtra.swlearning.com**. Remind them to click on the link for Lesson 18.2 to find the appropriate link for the **NET Bookmark** on page 562.
Point out that students will find many interesting topics at this site. Suggest that they look for a link to "trade topics" to start their exploration.

## Free Trade by Multilateral Agreement

On the board, draw one large circle and next to it, draw a group of 10 small circles of different sizes. Explain that these circles represent nations and that the larger the circle, the larger the nation's population. Explain that each nation has tariffs to protect its own industries. Ask why production in the large nation is likely to be more efficient than production in any of the smaller nations. (It can take advantage of economies of scale.) Ask why the smaller nations might choose to form a free-trade association and exclude the larger nation. (Their businesses could then grow by selling to each other and become as efficient as the businesses in the larger nation.)

### Think Critically Through Visuals

Direct students to focus their attention on **Figure 18.2—U.S. Tariff Revenue as a Percentage of Merchandise Imports**. Point out that the current low tariffs are a result of globalization and the Uruguay Round.

### SPAN THE GLOBE

Direct students to read the short passage "Proposal to Create World's Largest Free-Trade Area Under Attack" that appears on page 563. Use the Think Critically as a starting point for class discussion or have students create a table to answer the questions.

### Answers to Think Critically

Answers will vary. Possible answer: The advantages of free trade are higher quality from competitive pressure and lower prices. The disadvantages are losing jobs to nations with lower labor costs and losing exports to nations that have more of a comparative advantage in that industry.

### Follow-Up Activity

Invite interested students to research the outcome of the November 2003 meeting. Instruct students to write a short paper about their findings, including answers to these questions: What happened in Miami? Was the agreement put into effect?

---

**World Trade Organization (WTO)**
The legal and institutional foundation of the multilateral trading system that succeeded GATT in 1995

comprehensive of the eight postwar multilateral trade rounds. The Uruguay Round phased in tariff reductions on 85 percent of world trade and will eventually eliminate quotas.

Figure 18.2 shows tariff revenue as a percentage of the value of merchandise imports since 1821. You can see that tariffs have been up and down. Note that during the Great Depression of the 1930s, tariffs spiked. These high tariffs were contributing factors to the global economic troubles of that

**NETBookmark**

The World Trade Organization's web site describes its role and functions and explains the value of reducing trade barriers. Browse the web site through econxtra.swlearning.com and choose a topic that interests you. Prepare a two-minute oral presentation explaining the topic you chose to your classmates.

**econxtra.swlearning.com**

period. Thanks to trade agreements, average tariffs are lower now than at any time in history. When the Uruguay Round is fully implemented, the average tariff will fall from 6 percent to 4 percent.

### World Trade Organization

The Uruguay Round also created the World Trade Organization (WTO) as the successor to GATT. The **World Trade Organization (WTO)** now provides the legal and institutional foundation for world trade. Whereas GATT was a multilateral agreement with no staff or permanent location, the WTO is a permanent institution in Geneva, Switzerland, staffed mostly by economists. Whereas GATT involved only merchandise trade, the WTO deals with services and trade-related aspects of intellectual property, such as books, movies, and computer programs.

### Common Markets

Some countries have looked to the success of the U.S. economy, which is

---

**U.S. Tariff Revenue as a Percentage of Merchandise Imports**   **Figure 18.2**

**Over the years, tariffs have been up and down, spiking during the Great Depression.**

Source: 1821–1970: U.S. Dept. of Commerce, Bureau of Census, *Historical Statistics of the United States,* Part 2, 1976, and *Economic Report of the President,* February 2003, Table B-81.

**562**   **CHAPTER 18**   International Trade

---

**ENRICH**

"European Union in the U.S." is the title of the web site for the European Union's Delegation of the European Commission to the United States. The URL is www.eurunion.org. This web site provides a wide variety of information about the structure and organization of the EU, as well as its policies and objectives that can affect U.S. residents and businesses. Ask students to investigate a particular topic at this web site that involves trade and report on their findings. Why do they believe the EU has taken the time and gone to the expense of creating and maintaining this web site? As an alternative, consider asking students to investigate "The European Union: A Guide for Americans" which also can be found by searching www.eurunion.org. This site includes a self-scoring quiz where students can test their understanding of the European Union.

essentially a free-trade zone across 50 states, and have tried to develop free-trade zones of their own. The largest and best known is the European Union, which began in 1958 with six countries and has expanded to 15. The idea was to create a barrier-free European market in which goods, services, people, and capital flow freely to their highest-valued use. Twelve members of the European Union have adopted a common currency, the *euro*, which replaced national currencies in 2002.

The United States, Canada, and Mexico also have developed a free-trade pact called the North American Free Trade Agreement (NAFTA). Around the world, the trend is toward free-trade agreements.

 **CHECKPOINT**
Why have nations signed free-trade agreements?

# SPAN THE GLOBE

## Proposal to Create World's Largest Free-Trade Area Under Attack

The North American Free Trade Agreement (NAFTA) was signed and put into effect by Mexico, Canada, and the United States in 1994 in order to lower tariffs and create economic prosperity in those three nations. In November 2003, the leaders of the 34 democracies of the Western Hemisphere met in Miami, Florida, to work out the details of a new trade agreement called the Free Trade Area of the Americas (FTAA). The FTAA would create the world's largest free-trade area—a tariff-free trade zone stretching from Canada to the tip of South America. The FTAA is touted as the logical successor to NAFTA, and it has many supporters. However, some governments and anti-globalization groups from the various countries involved oppose the creation of this free-trade area. Brazil, for example, is reluctant to enter the agreement due to issues involving import quotas, tariffs, and agricultural subsidies. Groups representing U.S. workers also oppose the free-trade area. Labor organizations blame NAFTA for hundreds of thousands of lost manufacturing jobs. These groups are concerned that an FTAA agreement will only increase this job loss. Manufacturers, on the other hand, argue that to survive they must be able to reduce costs.

### Think Critically

What advantage is there in having a free-trade area such as FTAA? What are the disadvantages?

 **CHECKPOINT**
Invite a student to answer the checkpoint that appears on page 563.

### Answer

Nations have signed free-trade agreements to have access to markets around the world, lower costs through economies of scale, improved quality from competitive pressure, and lower prices.

## APPLY

Assign Lesson 18.2 from the Contemporary Economics Workbook.

## ASSESS

Assign all or part of Lesson 18.2 Assessment on page 564 as homework or an in-class activity.

## Xtra! Study Tools

Direct students to the online study tools for Lesson 18.2 at **econxtra.swlearning.com**.

## CLOSE

**Revisit** the **In the News** feature on the first page of the lesson. Ask students to review their preliminary answers and discuss the questions, now that they have completed this lesson.

**Review** the objectives for Lesson 18.2. Students should be able to:

- Identify trade restrictions and evaluate their impact.
- Explain why nations seek free-trade agreements.

## RETEACH

The World Trade Organization is designed to help nations settle trade disputes equitably and peacefully. The WTO's dispute-settlement procedures are described on its web site at www.wto.org (use the site map to locate information on "dispute settlement"). Ask students to investigate how this system works and report on their findings. Suggest that they view the video "Introduction to WTO Dispute Settlement" available at the web site. Invite students to discuss their findings in class.

**18.2** *Assessment*

## Key Concepts

1. Answers will vary. Possible answer: Many U.S. farmers believe they face unfair competition from nations that have much lower wage rates for agricultural workers. Tariffs on imported fruit would benefit U.S. fruit farmers but harm U.S. consumers by forcing them to pay higher prices for fruit.

2. Answers will vary. Possible answer: A quota on imported automobiles would reduce the quantity of the products supplied, causing an increase in the equilibrium prices for automobiles in the United States. This would benefit U.S. producers and their employees. It would force U.S. consumers to pay higher prices and prevent some individuals from obtaining an automobile at all.

3. Answers will vary. Possible answer: The cost of completing such tests might prevent firms from importing cars. Consumers in these nations have fewer choices in automobiles than they otherwise would have and will pay higher prices.

4. Answers will vary. Possible answer: New businesses in these nations often are not able to produce products as efficiently as established firms in developed nations. By discouraging tariffs and quotas, they believe GATT and then the WTO have made it more difficult for their industries to develop and become competitive over time.

5. Answers will vary. Possible answer: Many businesses have moved production from states with higher taxes and wage rates to other states that have lower taxes and wage rates. This movement has contributed to lower costs of production and prices. It has also caused an economic downturn in parts of the Northeast and Midwest. Similar problems can occur when free-trade organizations are created.

## Graphing Exercise

6. Answers will vary. Possible answer: U.S. producers of soybeans, airplanes, and scientific instruments are not as likely to ask for tariff or quota protection as are producers of footwear or fruits and vegetables because they were able to export more products than were imported in 2000.

   An example of an acceptable graph appears at the bottom of this page.

*The Answer Key is continued on page 582.*

---

**Xtra!**
**Study Tools**
*econxtra.swlearning.com*

## Key Concepts

1. Why do many fruit farmers in the United States think tariffs should be placed on fruit imported from South America and China? Whom would such tariffs benefit, and whom would they harm?

2. If a quota was placed on the number of automobiles that could be imported into the United States, how would U.S. consumers be affected?

3. Many nations require imported car models to be crash-tested before they can be marketed to consumers. They refuse to accept the results of crash tests performed in other countries. This process is expensive for firms involved in trade. How is such a requirement a barrier to trade? How are consumers in these nations affected by such laws?

4. Why have some less-developed nations argued that they have been discriminated against by first GATT and then the WTO rules that discourage tariffs and quotas?

5. What problems and benefits that might result from the creation of a free-trade organization can be seen within the U.S. economy?

## Graphing Exercise

6. Nations are most likely to impose either tariffs or quotas on trade for products for which they do not have a comparative advantage. Study the data in the table, and use it to construct a double bar graph that shows the value of U.S. imports and exports for these classifications of goods in 2000. In which types of production would there have been the greatest pressure from U.S. businesses and labor organizations for the imposition of either tariffs or quotas? Explain your answer.

**U.S. Exports and Imports of Selected Commodity Groups, 2000**
**(Values in billions of dollars)**

| Commodity Group | Exports | Imports |
|---|---|---|
| 1. Soybeans | $ 5,284 | $ 31 |
| 2. Fruits and Vegetables | $ 7,477 | $ 9,286 |
| 3. Airplanes | $24,777 | $ 12,412 |
| 4. Footwear | $ 663 | $ 14,842 |
| 5. Scientific Instruments | $30,984 | $ 22,007 |

Source: *Statistical Abstract of the United States,* 2002, p. 800.

## Think Critically

7. **Government** The creation of a free-trade organization requires a formal international treaty. Approval of such treaties often involves political issues that go beyond economic considerations. The treaty that created the European Union, for example, was debated by governments in Europe for many years. Some nations, such as Norway and Switzerland, chose not to join the organization. What possible reasons could these nations have had for their choice? Why might they change their decision in the future?

**U.S. Exports and Imports, 2000**

## Visualizing the Answer— Graphing Exercise

6. The answer includes a graph. Students' graphs should look similar to the one shown here. An Excel spreadsheet containing this graph, along with supporting data, is available on the Instructor's Resource CD.

# movers & shakers

**Yoshimi Inaba** *Toyota Motor Sales*

When it comes to selling vehicles in the United States, Toyota is not eager to be the number one supplier. As president and chief executive officer of Toyota Motor Sales, U.S.A., Yoshimi Inaba didn't like the possibility that Toyota sales in the United States might exceed those of Ford, DaimlerChrysler, or General Motors. "I don't want to see any of them go into difficulty," Inaba said about the "Big Three" U.S. automakers. "If that happens, public sentiment will change," he explained.

Nearly all the vehicles Toyota sells in the United States come from the Japanese automaker's 11 manufacturing and parts facilities located in the United States. Together these facilities provide employment to more than 30,000 Americans.

In 2001, for the first time, more Toyotas were sold in the United States than in Japan, thus inching Toyota closer to overtaking the number-three U.S. carmaker, DaimlerChrysler. In spite of his company's success, Inaba wasn't celebrating. He worried that should DaimlerChrysler or another of the Big Three automakers face serious financial losses, many Americans would be forced out of a job, and Toyota could suffer as a result. Here's why:

The rise of foreign automakers has been a huge blow to the United Automobile Workers (UAW). The union has never succeeded in organizing a plant owned by a foreign manufacturer, including Toyota. Decreasing membership in a powerful labor union, combined with the loss of jobs should a U.S. automaker fail, could easily raise sentiment among Americans to buy only American-made vehicles. So, in spite of the 30,000 U.S. citizens that Toyota employs, and the money those employees churn back into the U.S. economy, the fact that Toyota is Japanese-owned could be enough to cause a backlash.

In spite of his concerns, Inaba continues to infuse Toyota with his innovative ideas.

Working for Toyota since graduating from Kyoto University with a degree in economics, Inaba has spent many years outside his homeland. After earning a master's degree from Northwestern University's Kellogg School of Business, he worked for three years at Toyota's German sales company. Later he returned to Japan but concentrated his efforts on the company's European division. In 1993, he moved to Toyota's U.S. sales company and within three years was named senior vice president.

Later, as president and chief executive officer of Toyota Motor Sales U.S.A. Inc., Inaba worked to develop direct web-based connections to Toyota's U.S. auto dealers and to Toyota's supply chain. He also was involved in developing technology in the navigation system of Toyota vehicles that will pay tolls and make payments at gas stations, parking lots, and restaurants.

In July 2003, Inaba returned to Toyota in Japan. He now serves as senior managing director and chief officer for the Americas, Oceania, Middle East and Southwest Asia Operations Group.

## SOURCE READING

Why did Inaba say, "I don't want to see any [U.S. auto manufacturers] go into difficulty. If that happens, public sentiment will change." Why should he be concerned about this?

## ENTREPRENEURS IN ACTION

In small groups, discuss the pros and cons of Toyota's success in the United States. Which groups benefit from its success? Which groups might suffer from this success?

# movers & shakers

## FOCUS

Remind students of the risks a firm faces if it becomes a monopoly. The U.S. government might prosecute such firms under antitrust laws. Even if the firm wins its case, the damage it may suffer in terms of legal fees and public image can be devastating. It makes little difference whether the firm is based in the United States, whether it exports goods to the United States, or manufactures them here. Ask students to imagine they manage firm that produces television sets in some other nation. They could export their television sets to the United States and sell them at a price that would be lower than the price any other producer could afford to charge. Would they choose to do this? What risks might they take for following such a policy? How long do they imagine U.S. government officials would let their decision go unchallenged?

## TEACH

Instruct students to read the **Movers & Shakers** feature about Yoshimi Inaba. Point out that some students may find it helpful to read the article, read the questions at the bottom of the page, and then reread the article.

## ASSESS

Use the questions in Source Reading and Entrepreneurs in Action at the bottom of the profile to assess the students' understanding of this **Movers & Shakers** feature.

### Answers to Source Reading

If an American car industry faces financial difficulty and goes out of business, American sentiment might shift to buying only American-made cars to protect American businesses. This would severely hurt foreign-owned car industries such as Toyota.

### Answers to Entrepreneurs in Action

On the positive side, Toyota's success in the United States provides jobs for American workers. On the negative side, the popularity of Toyota products among American drivers means fewer sales for U.S.-owned automakers and fewer jobs.

---

### Extend the Content

Remind students that Toyota is not the only foreign-based firm to produce products in the United States. Just a few of the others are SONY, Honda, Nestlé, Royal Dutch Shell, and BASF. Ask students to investigate a foreign-based firm that produces goods or services in the United States. Ask them to explain why the chosen firm produces goods or services in the United States.

## Sharpen Your Life Skills

### Critical Thinking

After studying Lesson 18.2, students should be able to answer the questions on this page.

### Apply Your Skill

Consider allowing students to work in pairs for this assignment.

## Answers

1. Answers will vary. Possible answer: Most jobs in the United States related to the production of footwear have already been lost to foreign competition, and there is little chance they will return. Foreign producers have lower opportunity costs for producing footwear than do U.S. firms. It would make more sense to devote U.S. resources to production that will give this nation a comparative advantage. This decision is most consistent with the second point of view.

2. Answers will vary. Possible answer: It is difficult or impossible to ignore the results of the technological revolution. If it is less costly for businesses to provide services in other nations, it is unlikely they will choose to provide them here. This would harm their competitive position in the global market and could ultimately lead to their failure. There is little chance that an attempt to avoid dealing with firms that outsource services would succeed in changing those firms' decisions. It would make more sense to devote U.S. resources to production that will give this nation a comparative advantage. This decision is most consistent with the second point of view.

3. Answers will vary. Possible answer: Buying one of these hybrid cars would send U.S. dollars to Japan even if it would reduce the amount of imported oil they would consume. It is not clear with which of the two points of view this type of purchase is consistent. Students might also consider what impact reducing their consumption of fuel might have on the environment.

# Sharpen Your Life Skills

## Critical Thinking

Some people think it is a wise and patriotic choice to pay higher prices to buy goods and services manufactured in the United States rather than to purchase similar products that have been imported from foreign countries. They point out that dollars spent on imported products deprive U.S. workers of employment and U.S. firms of profits.

Other people argue that consumers should look only for the best price and highest quality in the products they buy, regardless of where they were produced. They argue that paying more to buy American-made goods and services allows inefficient firms to stay in business and use scarce resources in ways that do not take advantage of our nation's comparative advantage.

Which of these two points of view seems most logical to you? Is it always possible to make choices that clearly support one side or the other? Use your critical thinking skills to evaluate each of the following situations and decide what you would do in each case. Explain your choice, and describe how it is consistent with the point of view you think is most logical.

## Apply Your Skill

1. In 2003, more than 90 percent of athletic shoes (tennis, running, basketball, etc.) sold in the United States were imported from other countries. The relatively few athletic shoes produced in this country most often were designed for special uses and were more expensive than similar imported footwear. Suppose you needed a new pair of athletic shoes for a school team you joined. You could buy an imported pair for $80 or a similar pair made in the United States for $120. Which pair of shoes would you purchase?

2. In 2003, advancements in communications technology made it possible for U.S. manufacturers to provide "help lines" and technical support to their customers from people located in almost any nation of the world. When U.S. consumers called the toll-free number to ask for assistance in operating their new appliance, they were likely to end up talking with a person located in India or Pakistan. These workers were paid much less than workers in the United States. Would you try to avoid purchasing products from firms that outsourced their consumer support services to other nations? Why or why not?

3. In 2003, more than 60 percent of the petroleum consumed in the United States was imported from other nations. Some consumers chose to conserve gasoline by purchasing hybrid automobiles imported from Japan that were powered by both electric motors and gasoline engines. These vehicles could go 50 miles or more on each gallon of gasoline. Would you buy this type of vehicle if you were ready to purchase an automobile? Why or why not?

## Objectives

> Describe the components of a nation's current account.

> Describe the components of a nation's financial account.

## Overview

Money doesn't grow on trees. In the course of a week, a month, or a year, the amount you spend, save, and give away must equal the amount you earn, borrow, or are given. You, like everyone else in the world, face a budget constraint. Your outflow of money must not exceed your inflow. Just as you must make sure ends meet, so too must families, businesses, governments, and even countries. For example, the flow of receipts into the United States from the rest of the world must equal the outflow of payments to the rest of the world. There's no getting around it.

## Key Terms

**balance of payments**

**current account**

**merchandise trade balance**

**trade surplus**

**trade deficit**

**financial account**

Point out that more than goods and services flow among nations; there is also a flow of funds that can result in a positive or negative balance of payments. Explain that there are many reasons for money to flow among nations and that making payments for traded merchandise is only one of these. When a nation has a negative or positive balance of merchandise trade, there will be a flow of funds to balance out the difference in the value of that nation's imports and exports. In fact, flows of funds can inhibit flows of goods and services by impacting exchange rates. The value of the U.S. dollar grew in the early 1980s because many foreign businesses and individuals chose to send their money here. The increased value of the dollar made it difficult for U.S. businesses to compete in the global economy and U.S. exports fell.

### Objectives

Remind students to read the lesson objectives to help focus their attention before reading the lesson.

### Key Terms

Direct students to look up key terms in a business or economics dictionary. Some students will find it helpful to read another definition. In addition to a definition, many entries will include a brief explanation and an example.

## [ In the News ]

### ● Illegal Foreign Workers Make Dollars and Jobs Disappear

One significant source of inaccuracy in the balance of payments is the amount of money earned and transferred home by the millions of illegal workers in the United States. These workers may send this money home to family members by various means during the workers' stays in the United States. Or, they might keep it in an international account as a nest egg they will use once they return home. In either case, the dollars they earn but don't spend in the United States total in the hundreds of millions of dollars. The jobs lost to U.S. workers because of their presence here totals in the tens of thousands. Many of these illegal workers learn of work opportunities in the United States from web sites such as AmericaGo.biz, which advertises work in American stores such as Target, K-Mart, Home Depot, T.J. Maxx, and Wal-Mart. Once in this country, the workers are contacted and hired by firms who contract such services as housekeeping and domestic help to American firms.

#### Think About It

What effects do these workers and international transfers of dollars have on the U.S. economy?

◄ | ►

### [ In the News ]

Instruct students to read the passage and write down their answers. Point out that their answers might change after they finish studying Lesson 18.3.

#### Answers to Think About It

Answers will vary. Possible answer: Many Americans lose their jobs to these workers. The international transfer of dollars pulls money out the American economy and therefore decreases consumer spending in the economy.

### Visual Presentation

Use the PowerPoint presentation on the Instructor's Resource CD as an adjunct to your lecture. The presentation also can be used for review.

567

 **National Content Standards in Economics**

A complete list of the NCEE Standards appears on pages xxiv–xxv of this book. The following standards are addressed in Lesson 18.3.

Standard 4: Role of Incentives

Standard 5: Gain from Trade

Standard 6: Specialization and Trade

Standard 7: Markets—Price and Quantity Determination

Standard 10: Role of Economic Institutions

Standard 16: Role of Government

## Current Account

Point out that the current account is used to measure the flow of goods and services in and out of the United States. When the value of exports is greater than the value of imports in the current account, there is trade surplus. When the value of exports is less than the value of imports in the current account, there is a trade deficit. Whether a nation has a trade surplus or trade deficit is probably less important than why this trade position exists. A nation that imports many machines to increase its production may have a trade deficit, but this can be good in the long run if it becomes more productive. A trade deficit that results from the importation of luxury consumer goods, however, is a sign of impending economic difficulties.

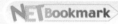

Direct students to **econxtra.swlearning.com**. Remind them to click on the link for Lesson 18.3 to find the appropriate link for the NET Bookmark on this page. Routine releases cover a variety of topics including the following:

- Foreign Investors' Spending to Acquire or Establish U.S. Businesses
- Gross Domestic Product by Industry
- Gross Domestic Product (quarterly)
- International Investment Position of the United States
- Local Area Personal Income
- Personal Income and Outlays (monthly)
- State Personal Income (quarterly)
- State Per Capita Personal Income
- Tourism Satellite Accounts (quarterly)
- U.S. International Trade in Goods and Services (monthly)
- U.S. International Transactions (quarterly)

### Think Critically Through Visuals

Direct students to focus their attention on **Figure 18.3—U.S. Imports and Exports Since 1960** on page 569. Point out that, since 1976, imports have exceeded exports every year, resulting in trade deficits (shaded in pink).

---

**balance of payments**
A record of all economic transactions between residents of one country and residents of the rest of the world during a given period

**trade surplus**
The amount by which the value of merchandise exports exceeds the value of merchandise imports during a given period

**trade deficit**
The amount by which the value of merchandise imports exceeds the value of merchandise exports during a given period

**current account**
That portion of the balance of payments that records exports and imports of goods and services, net investment income, and net transfers

**merchandise trade balance**
The value of a country's exported goods minus the value of its imported goods during a given period

---

# Current Account

The U.S. **balance of payments** is the record of all economic transactions between U.S. residents and residents of the rest of the world. Because it reflects all the transactions that occur during a particular period, usually a year, the balance of payments is a *flow* measure. Balance-of-payments accounts are maintained according to the principles of *double-entry bookkeeping*, in which entries on one side of the ledger are called *credits*, and entries on the other side are called *debits*. Because total credits must equal total debits, there must be a *balance* of payments when all the separate accounts are added together.

The balance of payments is divided into two broad accounts: the current account and the financial account. The **current account** keeps track of trade in goods and services, the flow of interest and profits across international borders, and the flow of foreign aid and cash gifts. The most important of these is the trade in goods, also called *merchandise trade*.

## The Merchandise Trade Balance

The **merchandise trade balance** equals the value of merchandise exports minus the value of merchandise imports. Merchandise trade reflects trade in goods, or tangible products, such as Irish sweaters and U.S. computers. The merchandise trade balance usually is referred to in the media as simply the *trade balance*.

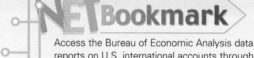

Access the Bureau of Economic Analysis data reports on U.S. international accounts through econxtra.swlearning.com. Click on the "Latest news release," and then write a paragraph summarizing the information in the release.

*econxtra.swlearning.com*

---

The value of U.S. merchandise exports is listed as a credit in the U.S. balance-of-payments account because U.S. residents must *be paid* for the exported goods. The value of U.S. merchandise imports is listed as a debit in the balance-of-payments account because U.S. residents must *pay* foreigners for imported goods.

If the value of merchandise exports exceeds the value of merchandise imports, there is a *surplus* in the merchandise trade balance, or a **trade surplus**. If the value of merchandise imports exceeds the value of merchandise exports, there is a *deficit* in the merchandise trade balance, or a **trade deficit**. The merchandise trade balance, which is reported monthly, influences the stock market, currency exchange rates, and other financial markets.

The trade balance depends on a variety of factors, including the relative strength and competitiveness of the U.S. economy compared with other economies and the value of the dollar compared with other currencies. The U.S. merchandise trade balance since 1960 is depicted in Figure 18.3, where exports (the blue line) and imports (the red line) are expressed as a percentage of GDP. In the 1960s, exports exceeded imports, so there were trade surpluses, shaded in blue. Since 1976, imports have exceeded exports every year, resulting in trade deficits, shaded in pink. Trade deficits as a percentage of GDP have increased steadily in recent years, growing from 1.3 percent in 1991 to an all time high of 4.7 percent in 2002, when the U.S. trade deficit reached a record $484.3 billion.

The United States imports more from each of the world's major economies than it exports to them. Figure 18.4 shows the U.S. trade deficit with major economies or regions of the world in 2002. The $103 billion trade deficit with China was the largest. China bought $22 billion in U.S. goods, but Americans bought $125 billion in Chinese goods, including $82 billion in nonfood consumer goods. Chances are, most of the utensils in your kitchen were made in China.

---

### Outside Resources

**Survey of Current Business** Each year, the April edition of the *Survey of Current Business*, published by the U.S. Department of Commerce Bureau of Economic Analysis, includes a regular feature entitled "U.S. International Transactions, Fourth Quarter and Year." Traditionally, this article includes "Table K. U.S. Trade in Goods by Major End-Use Category for Selected Areas and Countries." Data for 2002 was used to create the graph that appears in Figure 18.4 on page 570. Instruct students to locate this information for the most recent full year and create a graph similar to the one shown in Figure 18.4. To begin this activity, direct students to www.bea.doc.gov/bea/pubs.htm#subject.

## U.S. Imports and Exports Since 1960

Figure 18.3

U.S. imports of goods have exceeded U.S. exports of goods since 1976, and the trade deficit has widened.

Source: Developed from merchandise trade data in the *Economic Report of the President,* February 2003, and the U.S. Bureau of Economic Analysis. Imports and exports are shown relative to GDP.

## The Balance on Goods and Services

The merchandise trade balance focuses on the flow of goods, but some services also are traded internationally. *Services*

Research to find an example of a good or service produced in your local economy that is exported. If possible, find out the annual dollar value of the exported good or service. Share your results in class.

are intangible products, such as transportation, insurance, banking, consulting, and tourism. Services also include the income earned from foreign investments less the income earned by foreigners from their investment in the U.S. economy.

The value of U.S. service exports, such as when an Italian visits Chicago, is a credit in the U.S. balance-of-payments account because U.S. residents receive payments for these services. The value of U.S. service imports, such as when a computer specialist in India enters data for a Connecticut insurance company, is a debit in the balance-of-payments account because U.S. residents must pay for the imported services. Because the United States exports more services than it imports, the balance on services has been in surplus for the last three decades.

The *balance on goods and services* is the value of exports of goods and services minus the value of imports of goods and services. Because the service account

## TEACH (continued)

### Current Account

Point out that the flow of services is also an important part of the current account. Since World War II, the United States has consistently enjoyed a positive flow of funds from its trade in services. Among these are the funds generated by the U.S. entertainment industry. The United States exports more music, movies, and other media than any other nation in the world. American software programs, in particular Microsoft's Windows, dominate computer applications in most of the world. This has been a major source of foreign income to the U.S. economy and continues as one of the bright spots in the United States' position within the global market.

### Think Critically Through Visuals

Direct students to focus their attention on **Figure 18.4—U.S. Trade Deficit in 2002 by Country or Region** on page 570. Point out the $103 billion dollar trade deficit with China. To emphasize the point, create a display of things in your classroom that were made in China. Likely examples are:

binder clips      remote control

computer mouse      staples

electrical power cords      telephone

 Point out that the business section of the local newspaper might be a good place to start this activity. Stories about local companies might provide leads for more targeted research, including contacting a local company.

Consider allowing students to work in pairs and encourage creativity in the way they present their findings to the class. Copies of advertisements, product brochures, or a sample of the product could be used.

Lesson 18.3 • *Balance of Payments*      **569**

## Current Account

Point out that there is no reliable measurement of the number of illegal aliens who live and work in the United States, but that the number is probably well into the millions. Many, if not most, of these people send U.S. dollars earned here to their family and friends in other nations. This flow of money has been estimated to range from as little as $10 billion to as much as $50 billion per year. U.S. citizens also give billions of dollars to charities each year that send substantial amounts to other nations. Regardless of its absolute size, unilateral transfers of money are an important reason that funds flow from the United States to other nations.

## *Think Critically Through Visuals*

Direct students to focus their attention on the photograph on this page. Ask for a volunteer to answer the question posed in the caption.

## Answer

Answers will vary. Possible answer: The money spent by Europeans in America is considered a credit instead of a debit because the money was made in a foreign country but is being spent in America.

## ► E-CONOMICS

Direct students to read the passage entitled "U.S. Foreign Aid for Internet Use in Uzbekistan?" on page 571.

## Answers to Think Critically

The Uzbek program enhances economic freedom because it provides business opportunities for workers and companies located within that nation. This money is being invested in human capital, which is probably the best investment that can be made. Another good investment would be physical capital.

---

### U.S. Trade Deficit in 2002 by Country or Region

Figure 18.4

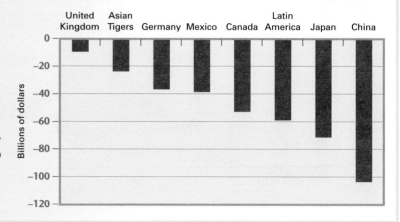

The United States has a trade deficit with each of the world's major economies because it imports more from them than it exports to them.

Source: U.S. Department of Commerce, *Survey of Current Business,* April 2003, Table K. The so-called Asian Tigers are Hong Kong, South Korea, Singapore, and Taiwan.

---

has been in surplus, the balance on goods and services has not been as negative as the merchandise trade balance.

### Unilateral Transfers

Unilateral transfers consist of government transfers to foreign residents, foreign aid, personal gifts to friends and relatives abroad, personal and institutional charitable donations, and other

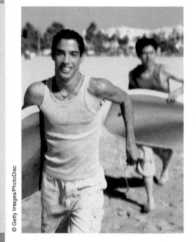

When Europeans visit U.S. beaches, is the money they spend considered a debit or a credit in the U.S. balance-of-payments account? Explain your answer.

© Getty Images/PhotoDisc

transfers. Money sent abroad by a U.S. resident to friends or relatives would be included in U.S. unilateral transfers and would be a debit in the balance-of-payments account. For example, immigrants to the United States often send money to families back home.

*Net unilateral transfers* equal the unilateral transfers received from abroad by U.S. residents minus unilateral transfers sent to foreign residents by U.S. residents. Included are U.S. government grants to foreign governments. U.S. net unilateral transfers have been negative each year since World War II, except for 1991, when the U.S. government received sizable transfers from foreign governments to help pay their share of the Persian Gulf War. In 2002, the U.S. net unilateral transfer was a negative $56 billion. To give you some feel for that amount, the net transfer abroad averaged about $500 for each U.S. household. These transfers represent an important source of spending power for many poor countries.

When net unilateral transfers are combined with the balance on goods and services, the result is the *current account balance,* a figure reported quarterly by the federal government. *The current account includes all international transactions in currently produced goods and services, flows of interest and profit, plus unilateral*

---

**ENRICH**

Much of the foreign aid granted by the United States since World War II has been *tied.* This means that money provided by the grant had to be spent in the United States even if needed goods or services could be purchased for less from other nations. A large part of U.S. assistance has also been given in the form of matching funds. In this case, recipient nations were required to match the value of the U.S. aid either in funds or other products. As a result of these rules, many recipient nations spent the aid they received, as well as a share of the matching funds they put up, in the United States. It is possible that U.S. foreign aid ended up increasing the flow of money into this country from less developed nations.

# E-CONOMICS

## U.S. Foreign Aid for Internet Use in Uzbekistan?

Foreign aid, the unilateral transfer payments by the United States to other countries that are intended to raise living standards and spur economic development, has gone through many changes over the years. The progression began with the post-World War II Marshall Plan, generally credited with helping to rebuild a Europe devastated by conflict. It then moved through the Alliance for Progress, aimed at increasing the standard of living in Latin America in the 1960s. Foreign aid during the 1980s was aimed at supporting governments in Latin America threatened by revolutionary movements. The George W. Bush administration planned to increase the size of foreign aid by half again, to help countries that are "ruling justly, investing in their people, and establishing economic freedom." Through it all, however, the actual good done by the programs has been difficult to see, due to the sheer size of the amounts paid out in these programs and the political motives behind them. This may be changing, however. The Bush administration placed great emphasis on accountability for the use of the funds. The aid agencies, as proof of their undertakings, have begun publishing stories about their programs. A case in point is the foreign aid targeted at developing e-commerce in Uzbekistan. A central Asian country founded in 1991, Uzbekistan has some 22.5 million people and a literacy rate of 99 percent. To help boost the country's economic activity and the well-being of its people, seminars and training sessions about the Internet and how to use it as a marketing device recently have been held throughout the country. These seminars, sponsored by USAID, have been responsible for several millions of dollars of business being transacted.

### Think Critically

How does the Uzbek program enhance economic freedom? Can you think of better uses for the money?

---

*transfers.* It can be negative, reflecting a current account deficit; positive, reflecting a current account surplus; or zero.

### CHECKPOINT
What is included in a nation's current account?

## Financial Account

The United States has been running a current account deficit for years. How can it pay for all the imports and all the transfers? The United States gets the money from selling financial assets, such as stocks and bonds, and from selling real assets such as land, housing, factories, and other property. When the current account comes up short, asset sales make up the difference.

The **financial account** tracks the flow of financial capital by recording international transactions involving financial and real assets. For example, if U.S. residents buy foreign assets, money flows from the United States to pay for these assets. Money flows into the United States when foreigners buy U.S. assets, such as U.S. stocks and bonds, an office building in New York City, or a ski chalet in Colorado. The financial account deals with buying and selling assets across international borders.

**financial account**
That portion of the balance of payments that records international transactions involving financial assets, such as stocks and bonds, and real assets, such as factories and office buildings

Lesson 8.3 • *Balance of Payments*

**571**

---

---

## Curriculum Connection—Mathematics

Many Americans contribute to private charities that serve people in other nations. U.S. law requires charities to disclose how they use the funds they collect. Instruct students to investigate a charity to find out how much money it has spent to send goods and services abroad. Ask students how this has affected the flow of funds from the United States to other countries. Have students calculate the percentage of the charity's budget spent on goods or services in other countries. CARE, for example, reported that it received just over $100 million from the U.S. public in 2003 and spent just over 90 percent of these funds providing goods and services to people in developing nations.

### Record of the Financial Account

Between 1917 and 1982, the United States ran a deficit in the financial account, meaning that U.S. residents purchased more foreign assets than foreigners purchased assets in the United States. Since 1983, however, the financial account has been in surplus nearly every year. This means foreigners have been buying more U.S. assets than Americans have been buying foreign assets. Foreign purchases of assets in the United States contribute to America's productive capacity and promote employment. However, the return on these investments flows to foreigners, not to Americans.

### Statistical Discrepancy

Again, the U.S. balance of payments records all transactions between U.S. residents and foreign residents during a specified period. It is easier to describe the balance of payments than to compile it. Despite efforts to capture all international transactions, some are nearly impossible to trace. For example, the government can't easily monitor cross-border shopping or illegal drug trafficking. But as the name *balance of payments* suggests, the entire balance-of-payments account must by definition be in balance—debits must equal credits.

To ensure that the two sides balance, the *statistical discrepancy* was created. An excess of credits in all other accounts is offset by an equivalent debit in the statistical discrepancy, or an excess of debits in all other accounts is offset by an equivalent credit in the statistical discrepancy.

You might think of the statistical discrepancy as the official "fudge factor." The statistical discrepancy provides analysts with both a measure of the error in the balance-of-payments data and a means of satisfying the double-entry bookkeeping requirement that total debits equal total credits. In 2002, the current account and the financial account combined for a deficit of $29.2 billion. To offset that deficit, the statistical discrepancy added $29.2 billion back into the balance. Thus, the balance of payments for all accounts, including the statistical discrepancy, sums to zero.

 **CHECKPOINT**
What is included in a nation's financial account?

The government has difficulty tracking cross-border transactions, such as when an American visiting Italy purchases gold jewelry. How does the government try to measure such purchases?

## Key Concepts

1. A large part of the U.S. national debt is owned by people who live in other nations. How is the U.S. current account affected by interest payments made by the federal government on its debt?

2. Would the merchandise trade balance be affected by millions of people in foreign nations choosing to pay to see a recent Hollywood action movie? Why or why not? If not, what measure of trade would this affect?

3. Why must the total value of all nations' trade surpluses and deficits be balanced?

4. If you received a gift of 100 euros from a relative who lives in Germany, how would this gift affect the U.S. balance of payments?

5. Suppose the value of stocks in the United States increased, causing many foreigners to sell their U.S. stock to earn a profit. They then have their funds sent to them in their own nations. What would this do to the U.S. financial account?

## Graphing Exercise

6. When foreigners purchase or build businesses in the United States, their payments for these investments flow into this country. Construct a line graph from the data in the table that shows the growth in foreign investment in U.S. businesses from 1995 through 2000. What does your graph tell you about this investment? How would this investment affect the U.S. economy?

**Value of U.S. Businesses Acquired or Established by Foreign Investors, 1995–2000 (Values in millions of dollars)**

| 1995 | $57,195 | 1998 | $215,256 |
|------|---------|------|----------|
| 1996 | $79,929 | 1999 | $274,956 |
| 1997 | $69,708 | 2000 | $320,858 |

Source: *Statistical Abstract of the United States*, 2002, p. 787.

## Think Critically

7. **Accounting** Keeping track of a nation's balance of payments is a major accounting problem that is never totally accurate. Determine whether each of the following would be a credit or a debit for a nation's balance of payments and how each would affect the nation's economy. Why is it difficult for government officials to keep track of some of these flows of value?

- There is a $500 million increase in the nation's exports of computers.
- People send $30 million more to their relatives in other countries.
- Foreigners invest an additional $450 million in that nation's businesses.
- There is an $800 million increase in the nation's imports of automobiles.
- Residents of the nation spend $40 million more on travel in other nations.
- Businesses in that nation pay $25 million more in dividends to foreigners.

**Xtra!**
**Study Tools**
econxtra.swlearning.com

Lesson 8.3 ○ *Balance of Payments* 573

## Key Concepts

1. Answers will vary. Possible answer: The current account includes flows of interest across international borders. Therefore, the interest paid to foreigners by the federal government appears as a debit in the U.S. current account.

2. Answers will vary. Possible answer: People purchase a service when they buy a movie ticket. Services are not included in the merchandise trade balance. This would affect the balance of goods and services.

3. Answers will vary. Possible answer: Every trade surplus for a nation is also a trade deficit to one or more other nations. These amounts must therefore be the same.

4. Answers will vary. Possible answer: This flow of funds would be included in the U.S. balance of payments as a credit.

5. Answers will vary. Possible answer: The flow of money from the United States to pay for stock that was sold in this nation would appear as a debit in the U.S. financial account.

## Graphing Exercises

6. Answers will vary. Possible answer: The growth in investment after 1997 may reflect confidence in the U.S. economy by foreign investors. This investment increased the amount of capital in the U.S. economy that helped production and employment in the U.S. grow. At the same time, a flow of profits from these U.S. investments went from this nation to people in other nations.

An example of an acceptable graph appears at the bottom of this page.

*The Answer Key is continued on page 583.*

**Value of U.S. Businesses Acquired or Established by Foreign Investors, 1995 to 2000**

## Visualizing the Answer— Graphing Exercise

6. The answer includes a graph. Students' graphs should look similar to the one shown here. An Excel spreadsheet containing this graph, along with supporting data, is available on the Instructor's Resource CD.

### FOCUS

**18.4 Foreign Exchange Rates**

Explain that when goods or services are traded, there is a corresponding flow of value in money to pay for these products. This most often requires the exchange of one type of currency for another. The exchange rate among currencies can be as important to international trade as the actual price of the products that are traded. If, for example, the value of the U.S. dollar falls relative to other currencies, it will make all U.S. products appear to be less expensive to foreign buyers and all foreign products more expensive to U.S. buyers. This type of change is sure to affect the nation's balance of trade as well as its balance of payments.

### Objectives

Remind students to read the lesson objectives to help focus their attention before reading the lesson.

### Key Terms

Direct students use each of the key terms in a separate sentence or short paragraph that helps demonstrate the meaning of the term.

### [ In the News ]

Instruct students to read the passage and write down their answers. Point out that their answers might change after they finish studying Lesson 18.4.

### Answers to Think About It

Answers will vary. Possible answer: American industries, where there is steep competition with similar Chinese industries, would benefit from the imposition of a tariff on Chinese goods.

### Follow-Up Activity

Invite interested students to investigate the current exchange rate of the yuan to the U.S. dollar. Also have students determine whether the current rate of exchange is fixed or flexible.

### Visual Presentation

Use the PowerPoint presentation on the Instructor's Resource CD as an adjunct to your lecture. The presentation also can be used for review.

## Objectives

> Analyze the market for foreign exchange.

> Identify the participants in the market for foreign exchange.

> Distinguish between flexible and fixed exchange rates.

## Overview

Now that you have some idea about international trade and the balance of payments, you can take a closer look at the forces that determine the rate of exchange between the U.S. dollar and other currencies. When Americans buy foreign goods or travel abroad, these transactions involve two currencies—the U.S. dollar and the foreign currency. What is the dollar cost of a British pound, a Mexican peso, a Japanese yen, or a European euro? As you will see, the exchange rates between the dollar and other currencies usually are determined just like other prices—by the forces of supply and demand.

## Key Terms

foreign exchange

exchange rate

flexible exchange rates

### [ In the News ]

#### • China Not Cited for Foreign Exchange Manipulation

In late 2003, the Chinese currency exchange rate was 8.3 yuan to the dollar, where it had been pegged for nine years. At the time, the Chinese were enjoying a more than $100 billion dollar trade surplus with the United States, with this figure rising by more than 20 percent annually. Some members of Congress called for imposing steep tariffs on Chinese goods. They also accused the Chinese government of manipulating its foreign exchange rate to improve its trading position. However, in testimony before the Senate Banking Committee, the U.S. Secretary of the Treasury announced that the Chinese government was not guilty of doing this. In their defense, the Chinese said that the pegging at 8.3 was a result of the last trade imbalance outcry by the United States almost 10 years before. The Chinese also pointed out that if the yuan was allowed to float, it might even drop in value against the dollar because the Chinese overall trade balance is far smaller than its surplus with the United States. This is because the Chinese have to import the raw materials and the unassembled parts for the goods they manufacture for sale in the United States. A cheaper yuan would cause an even greater trade imbalance with the United States in China's favor. Other analysts pointed out that the trade imbalance may be just a natural occurrence of a marketplace where China, with its overwhelming supply of labor, has a wide comparative advantage in producing toys, shoes, textiles, and other labor-intensive goods. More than 70 percent of the trade imbalance falls within this range of products. Therefore, these analysts believe the market should be left alone to make its own ultimate correction.

#### Think About It

Who would benefit from the imposition of a tariff on Chinese goods?

**National Content Standards in Economics**

A complete list of the NCEE Standards appears on pages xxiv–xxv of this book. The following standards are addressed in Lesson 18.4.

Standard 4: Role of Incentives

Standard 5: Gain from Trade

Standard 7: Markets—Price and Quantity Determination

Standard 10: Role of Economic Institutions

Standard 11: Role of Money

Standard 16: Role of Government

Standard 20: Monetary and Fiscal Policy

# The Market for Foreign Exchange

**Foreign exchange** is foreign money people need to carry out international transactions. Typically, foreign exchange is made up of bank deposits in the foreign currency. When foreign travel is involved, foreign exchange may consist of foreign paper money. The **exchange rate** is the dollar price of purchasing a unit of another currency. The exchange rate, or price of another currency, is determined by the interaction of all those who buy and sell foreign exchange. The exchange rate between two currencies is set through the interaction of demand and supply for these currencies.

## The Euro

The foreign exchange market involves all the arrangements used to carry out international transactions. This market is not so much a physical place as it is a network of telephones and computers connecting large financial institutions worldwide. The foreign exchange market is like an all-night diner—it never closes. A trading center is always open somewhere in the world.

Consider the market for a particular foreign currency, the euro. For decades the nations of Western Europe have tried to increase their economic cooperation and trade. These countries believed they would be more productive and more competitive with the United States if they acted more like the 50 United States and less like separate economies, each with its own trade regulations, trade barriers, and currency. Imagine the hassle involved if each of the 50 states had its own currency, which you had to exchange every time you wanted to buy something in another state.

In January 2002, *euro* notes and coins entered circulation in the 12 European countries that adopted the new common currency. The euro is now the common currency in the *euro area*, as the dozen countries are now called. The price, or exchange rate, of the euro is the dollar price of one euro. Because the exchange rate

*foreign exchange*

Foreign money needed to carry out international transactions

*exchange rate*

The price of one country's currency measured in terms of another country's currency

© Getty Images/PhotoDisc

Why do you think adoption of the euro as a common currency in Europe has increased trade among the 12 countries in the euro area?

Direct students to focus their attention on **Figure 18.5—The Foreign Exchange Market**. Point out that the horizontal axis shows the quantity of foreign exchange and the vertical axis indicates the dollar price of one euro.

Direct students to **econxtra.swlearning.com**. Remind them to click on the link for Lesson 18.4 to find the appropriate link for the **NET Bookmark** on page 577. Students should be able to explain their findings. Before assigning this activity, offer the following examples using data from early 2004:

| Currency | Bid | Ask |
|---|---|---|
| EUR/USD | 1.25 | 1.2505 |
| USD/JPY | 106.95 | 107.0 |
| USD/CAD | 1.2895 | 1.2911 |

According to the above information, euro buyers are willing to pay $1.25 (in U.S. dollars) for 1 euro. Euro sellers are willing to accept $1.2505 (in U.S. dollars) for 1 euro. This means that 100 euros are worth approximately $125. It also means that $100 is worth approximately 80 euros.

## CHECKPOINT

Invite a student to answer the checkpoint that appears on page 577.

## Answer

The exchange rate between the euro and the dollar is determined by the respective demands worldwide for the euro and the dollar. The higher the demand for the euro, the higher the price of the euro and the higher the exchange rate for the euro.

---

is a price, it is determined using supply and demand. *The equilibrium price of foreign exchange is the one that equates quantity demanded with quantity supplied.*

## Demand for Euros

U.S. residents need euros to pay for goods and services from the euro area, to buy assets from there, to make loans to the euro area, or simply to send cash gifts to friends or relatives there. Whenever U.S. residents need euros, they must buy them in the foreign exchange market, which could be as near as the local bank, paying for them with dollars.

Figure 18.5 depicts a market for foreign exchange—in this case, euros. The horizontal axis shows the quantity of foreign exchange, measured here in millions of euros. The vertical axis indicates the dollar price of one euro. The demand curve $D$ for foreign exchange shows the relationship between the dollar price of the euro and the quantity of euros demanded, other things assumed constant. Some of the factors assumed constant along the demand curve are the incomes and preferences of U.S. consumers, the expected inflation rates in the United States and the

euro area, and interest rates in the United States and the euro area.

People have many reasons for demanding foreign exchange; but in the aggregate, the lower the dollar price of foreign exchange, the greater the quantity demanded. The cheaper it is to buy euros, the lower the dollar price of euro area products, so the greater the quantity of euros demanded by U.S. residents. For example, a cheap-enough euro might persuade you to tour Rome, climb the Austrian Alps, or wander the museums of Paris.

## Supply of Foreign Exchange

The supply of foreign exchange is generated by the desire of foreign residents to acquire dollars—that is, to exchange euros for dollars. Residents of the euro area want dollars to buy U.S. goods and services, to buy U.S. assets, to make loans in dollars, or to make cash gifts in dollars to their U.S. friends and relatives. Europeans supply euros in the foreign exchange market to acquire the dollars they need.

An increase in the dollar-per-euro exchange rate, other things constant, makes U.S. products cheaper for

**The Foreign Exchange Market**

**Figure 18.5**

The fewer dollars needed to purchase one unit of foreign exchange, the lower the price of foreign goods and the greater the quantity of foreign goods demanded. The greater the demand for foreign goods, the greater the amount of foreign exchange demanded. The demand curve for foreign exchange slopes downward. An increase in the exchange rate makes U.S. products cheaper for foreigners. The increased demand for U.S. goods implies an increase in the quantity of foreign exchange supplied. The supply curve of foreign exchange slopes upward.

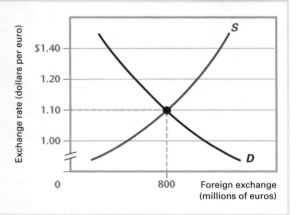

---

## Outside Resources

**Online Exchange Rate Calculator** Create a list of items that can be purchased at a grocery store or mass merchandise store and include current prices. Ask students to visit an online exchange rate calculator to convert the prices to another currency. Exchange rate calculators can be found at the web sites listed below.
www.xe.com/ucc
www.bankofcanada.ca/en/exchform.htm
www.finance.yahoo.com/m3?u
www.exchangerate.com/
www.money.cnn.com/markets/currencies/

foreigners, because foreign residents need fewer euros to get the same number of dollars. More euros will be supplied on the foreign exchange market to buy dollars. Figure 18.5 shows the upward-sloping supply curve for foreign exchange (again, euros in this example).

The supply curve is drawn assuming other things remain constant. These include the euro area's incomes and preferences, inflation expectations in the euro area and the United States, and interest rates in the euro area and the United States.

### Determining the Exchange Rate

Figure 18.5 brings together the supply and demand for foreign exchange to determine the exchange rate. At a rate of $1.10 per euro, the quantity of euros demanded equals the quantity supplied—in this example, 800 million euros.

What if this equilibrium exchange rate is upset by a change in one of the underlying forces that affect supply or demand? For example, suppose an increase in U.S. income causes Americans to increase their demand for all normal goods, including those from the euro area. An increase in U.S. income will shift the U.S. demand curve for euros to the right, as Americans seek euros to buy more German automobiles and European vacations.

This increased demand for euros is shown in Figure 18.6 by a rightward shift of the demand curve for euros. The supply curve does not change, because an increase in U.S. income should not affect the euro area's willingness to supply euros. The rightward shift of the demand curve from *D* to *D'* leads to an increase in the exchange rate from $1.10 per euro to $1.12 per euro. Thus, the euro increases in value, while the dollar falls in value. The higher exchange value of the euro prompts some people in the euro area to purchase more American products, which are now cheaper in terms of the euro.

An increase in the dollar price of a euro indicates a weakening of the

### NETBookmark

Access the Forex-Markets web site for "Tools and Information for Online Currency Traders" through econxtra.swlearning.com. Browse the site to find the current value of the U.S. dollar compared with the euro, the yen, and the Canadian dollar. Also find out whether the U.S. dollar is trending up or down as compared to these currencies. Record your answers.

**econxtra.swlearning.com**

dollar, or *currency depreciation*. A decrease in the dollar price of a euro indicates a strengthening of the dollar, or a *currency appreciation*.

 **CHECKPOINT**
What determines the rate of exchange between the dollar and the euro?

## Who Buys Foreign Exchange?

Foreign exchange is purchased mainly by those who buy foreign goods or invest abroad, such as importers and exporters, investors in foreign assets, central banks, and tourists. Other groups also regularly participate in foreign exchange markets as well, including speculators, arbitrageurs, and people seeking a safe haven.

### Speculators

*Speculators* buy or sell foreign exchange in hopes of profiting later by trading the currency at a more favorable exchange rate. By taking risks, speculators aim to profit from market fluctuations—that is, they try to buy low and sell high.

Lesson 18.4 ∘ *Foreign Exchange Rates* **577**

### TEACH

**Who Buys Foreign Exchange?**
Point out that different types of people and institutions are involved in buying and selling foreign currencies. There are individuals and international businesses that are very wealthy and hold large amounts of different types of money in cash or bank accounts. These people have the ability to influence exchange rates through speculation.

*Think Critically Through Visuals*

Direct students to focus their attention on **Figure 18.6—Effect on the Foreign Exchange Market of an Increase in Demand for Euros** on page 578. Point out that the rightward shift of the demand curve indicates an increased demand for euros.

**The Graphing Workshop — Try It · Apply It**

Direct students to the Graphing Workshop for Chapter 18 at **econxtra.swlearning.com**. Instruct students to click on **Apply It: The Impact of a Change in Relative Interest Rates on the Value of the Euro**. As an enrichment exercise, students may complete **Try It: The Foreign Exchange Market** and **Try It: Intervention in the Foreign Exchange Market**. These enrichment exercises present concepts more advanced than those discussed in the textbook.

**CHECKPOINT**
Invite a student to answer the checkpoint that appears on page 578.

**Answer**
Foreign exchange is purchased mainly by those who buy foreign goods or invest abroad. Other groups who routinely participate in foreign exchange markets include speculators, arbitrageurs, and people seeking a safe haven.

### ENRICH

In the years from 2000 through 2003, the Federal Reserve System took steps to force interest rates in the United States to their lowest levels in many years. Although it did not happen immediately, these low interest rates eventually contributed to a depreciation of the U.S. dollar relative to other currencies. Ask students why this happened and what its impact was on the ability of U.S. producers to sell their products to other nations. (The lower interest rates helped cause the value of the dollar to fall because fewer foreigners wished to deposit their funds in U.S. banks. The reduced value of the dollar caused U.S. products to appear less expensive to foreign buyers.)

## TEACH

### Exchange Rate Systems

When there is a free float, governments do not intervene in currency markets in any way. They allow demand and supply the unfettered power to set exchange rates. Today currency markets are not completely free. There is a "managed" float in which governments buy or sell currencies in an effort to balance out buying and selling by currency speculators.

### Think Critically Through Visuals

Direct students to focus their attention on the photograph on page 579. Ask a volunteer to answer the question.

**Answer**

Answers will vary. Possible answer: Individuals gain from trade among countries because there are more goods available to them and some goods are available at lower prices.

### NCEE Standard 5: Gain from Trade

Voluntary exchange occurs only when all parties expect to gain. This is true for trade among individuals or organizations within a nation, and usually among individuals or organizations in different nations.

### THE WALL STREET JOURNAL

**Reading It Right**

Invite a student to explain the relevance of the statement from *The Wall Street Journal* that appears on page 579.

**Answer**

Many believe an exchange rate is better off being determined by the market and not by central banks.

### CHECKPOINT

Invite a student to answer the checkpoint that appears on page 579.

**Answer**

Flexible exchange rates are determined by the forces of supply and demand without government intervention. Fixed exchange rates are fixed within a narrow range of values and are maintained by central banks' ongoing purchases of sales and currencies.

---

### Arbitrageurs

Exchange rates between specific currencies are nearly identical at any given time in markets around the world. For example, the dollar price of a euro is nearly the same in New York, Frankfurt, Tokyo, London, Zurich, Hong Kong, Istanbul, and other financial centers. *Arbitrageurs* are money dealers who take advantage of tiny differences in exchange rates between markets. Their actions help to equalize exchange rates across markets. For example, if one euro trades for $1.10 in New York but for $1.11 in Paris, an arbitrageur could buy, say, $10,000,000 worth of euros in New York and at the same time sell them in Paris for $10,090,909, thereby earning $90,909 minus the transaction costs of the trades.

Abitrageurs take less risk than speculators because they *simultaneously* buy currency in one market and sell it in another. In this example, the arbitrageur increases the demand for euros in New York and increases the supply of euros in Paris. These actions increase the dollar price of euros in New York and decrease it in Paris.

### Those Seeking a Safe Haven

Finally, people in countries suffering from economic and political turmoil may buy more stable currencies as a hedge against the depreciation and instability of their own currency. For example, the dollar has long been accepted as an international medium of exchange. It is also the currency of choice in world markets for oil and illegal drugs.

The euro may eventually challenge that dollar as the key world currency, in part because the largest euro denomination, the 500 euro note, is worth about five times a 100 dollar note, the top U.S. note. So it would be five times easier to smuggle currency or conduct cash transactions using euros rather than dollars.

### CHECKPOINT

Who participates in the market for foreign exchange?

**The Graphing Workshop**

**Effect on the Foreign Exchange Market of an Increase in Demand for Euros**   **Figure 18.6**

The intersection of supply curve *S* and demand curve *D* determines the exchange rate. At an exchange rate of $1.10 per euro, the quantity of euros demanded equals the quantity supplied. An increase in the demand for euros from *D* to *D'* leads to an increase in the exchange rate from $1.10 to $1.12 per euro.

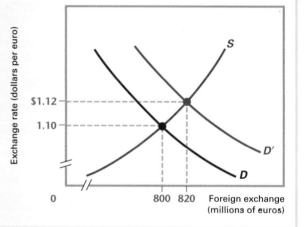

---

### Curriculum Connection—History

During World War II, the United States government transferred vast quantities of funds to other nations to help them fight the war. These amounts totaled more than $40 billion during the four years of the war. This was a time when the total U.S. GDP was in a range between $140 and $210 billion. The U.S. government neither asked nor expected the bulk of these funds to be repaid. Ask students to discuss how U.S. foreign commitments contribute to our current negative balance of payments.

# Exchange Rate Systems

So far the discussion has been about **flexible exchange rates**, with the rate determined by supply and demand. A flexible, or *floating*, exchange rate adjusts continually to the many forces that affect the foreign exchange market. When the exchange rate is flexible, government officials usually have little direct role in foreign exchange markets.

However, if government officials try to set, or fix, the exchange rate, active and ongoing central bank intervention is often necessary to establish and maintain this **fixed exchange rate**. For example, prior to World War II, the value of each major currency was fixed in relation to gold. This was called the *gold standard*. Because currencies were fixed in relation to gold, they also were fixed in relation to each other.

From the end of World War II until 1971, other nations could redeem dollars for gold at a fixed exchange rate. The dollar during that period was tied to gold. The U.S. Treasury was by law required to sell foreigners gold at $35 per ounce. The values of other currencies were fixed in relation to the dollar, which was fixed in relation to gold.

In 1971, the United States developed a serious trade deficit and stopped selling gold to foreigners with dollars. No longer tied to gold, the value of the dollar began to float. Exchange rates among major world currencies became flexible, and they remain so today. Some smaller economies choose to fix the value of their currency in terms of dollars.

> **✓ CHECKPOINT**
> Compare a system of flexible exchange rates to one of fixed exchange rates.

**flexible exchange rate**
Exchange rate determined by the forces of supply and demand without government intervention

**fixed exchange rate**
Exchange rate fixed within a narrow range of values and maintained by central banks' ongoing purchases and sales of currencies

## THE WALL STREET JOURNAL

**Reading It Right** What's the relevance of the following statement from *The Wall Street Journal:* "U.S. Treasury Secretary John Snow repeated his view that exchange rates are best determined by market forces. He also repeated his desire to see China free the yuan from its close peg to the dollar 'as soon as possible' in order that the world see China isn't 'rigging' its exchange rate."

**Main Idea** 💡 **Gain from Trade**

Exchange rate systems allow trade among nations to take place. *How do individuals gain from trade among nations?*

© Getty Images/PhotoDisc

Assign Lesson 18.4 from the Contemporary Economics Workbook.

### e-con @pps

Encourage students to apply their knowledge of concepts presented in this lesson as they explore economic news stories, policy debates, and data available at **econxtra.swlearning.com**. A sampling of the titles for this lesson appears below.

**EconDebate**
- Does dollarization benefit developing nations?
- Does foreign direct investment hinder or help economic development?

**EconNews**
- Talking Down the Yen
- Russia Gushing with Oil Dollars
- Like a Good Neighbor
- Inciting Inflation
- Germany's Troubles Bubble Up
- Problems in Euro Land
- Lula's Problem

## ASSESS

Assign all or part of Lesson 18.4 Assessment on page 580 as homework or an in-class activity

### Xtra! Study Tools

Direct students to the online study tools for Lesson 18.4 at **econxtra.swlearning.com**.

## CLOSE

**Revisit** the In the News feature on the first page of the lesson. Ask students to review their preliminary answers and discuss the questions, now that they have completed this lesson.

**Review** the objectives for Lesson 18.4. Students should be able to:
- Analyze the market for foreign exchange.
- Identify the participants in the market for foreign exchange.
- Distinguish between flexible and fixed exchange rates.

## RETEACH

In the months following the 2003 U.S. invasion of Iraq, the value of the U.S. dollar fell relative to most other currencies in the world. There is a variety of possible reasons for this depreciation of the U.S. currency. For one, U.S. spending for the war on terror and the war in Iraq, coupled with tax cuts, caused the federal deficit to increase to more than $300 billion in fiscal 2002-2003. Ask students to discuss why a large federal deficit would contribute to a lower value for the U.S. dollar. (There are many possible answers. One would be that the extra borrowing by the U.S. government caused investors in other countries to suspect that inflation would re-emerge as a problem in the U.S. economy. This would lower the value of the dollars they would receive when any U.S. securities they held were sold or came due. This reduced their demand for dollars to buy U.S. securities.)

## Key Concepts

1. *Sports car*—The demand for the Japanese car will cause an increased demand for Japanese yen that will cause the value of the dollar to fall and the value of the yen to increase.

   *Interest rates*—Foreigners will convert their currencies to U.S. dollars to deposit in U.S. banks. This will cause the value of U.S. dollars to increase and the value of other currencies to fall.

   *Investment in businesses in other nations*—U.S. businesses will exchange U.S. dollars for other currencies to pay for investments they make in other nations. This will cause the value of U.S. dollars to fall and the value of other currencies to increase.

2. Although a single currency may eliminate exchange problems among currencies, it will not eliminate differences between product standards and units of measure.

3. It is easier for U.S. firms to compare prices among European nations. The firms no longer have to convert multiple currencies into U.S. dollars to find the best price.

4. When arbitrageurs either buy or sell large amounts of currencies, they change the exchange rates for these currencies. If arbitrageurs think the value of the euro is about to go up and buy many millions of euros, then the value of the euro will increase because of the added demand for the currency.

5. When the exchange rates among currencies were fixed for long periods of time by governments, nations with higher rates to inflation found it difficult to sell their products to other nations that had lower prices. This often caused production in their economies to fall.

## Graphing Exercise

6. *Trip to Canada*—$1,200

   *Trip to Japan*—$2,000

   *Trip to Germany*—$1,600

   *Trip to Mexico*—$1,400

   The length of time spent traveling and the quality of the hotel would have an impact on their choice.

   An example of an acceptable graph appears at the bottom of this page.

*The Answer Key is continued on page 585.*

**Xtra!**
Study Tools
econxtra.swlearning.com

## Key Concepts

1. What effect would each of the following events have on the exchange rate for the U.S. dollar relative to other currencies? Explain each of your answers.

   • A new sports car is produced in Japan that many U.S. consumers choose to purchase.

   • U.S. banks offer higher interest rates for deposits. This causes many people in other nations to deposit funds in U.S. banks.

   • Many U.S. businesses choose to invest in businesses in other nations.

2. Why didn't the conversion by many European nations to the euro at the start of 2002 eliminate all trade problems between these nations?

3. How may the conversion by many European nations to the euro have helped U.S. firms that trade with these nations?

4. How are arbitrageurs able to change the exchange rates for different currencies?

5. Why did the fixed exchange rate system often result in imbalances in trade among nations?

## Graphing Exercise

6. In August 2003, exchange rates for the U.S. dollar in other currencies varied widely. Suppose you were considering taking a package vacation in one of the nations listed below. Divide each price by the appropriate exchange rate to calculate the number of U.S. dollars you would have to pay for each trip. Construct a bar graph to show the relative cost of each trip. What other factors would you consider when choosing among these trips?

   **Exchange Rate for U.S. Dollar in Selected Currencies, 2003**

   $1 = 1.385 Canadian dollars     $1 = 119.25 Japanese yen

   $1 = 0.888 euros     $1 = 10.730 Mexican pesos

   • A one-week trip to Canada costs 1,662 Canadian dollars.

   • A one-week trip to Japan costs 238,500 Japanese yen.

   • A one-week trip to Germany costs 1,420.80 euros.

   • A one-week trip to Mexico costs 15,022 Mexican pesos.

## Think Critically

7. **Math** Toward the end of 2000, the exchange rate for the euro fell to 0.90 euros to the U.S. dollar. By the summer of 2003, the euro had appreciated to 1.125 euros per dollar. What percentage increase was this in the value of the euro? How did this appreciation affect the ability of U.S. firms to sell their products to European Union member nations?

**Cost of Different Vacations in U.S. Dollars**

| | |
|---|---|
| $2,500 | |
| $2,000 | $2,000 |
| $1,500 | $1,600 |
| $1,000 | $1,200   $1,400 |
| $500 | |
| 0 | One Week Trip to Canada   One Week Trip to Japan   One Week Trip to Germany   One Week Trip to Mexico |

### Visualizing the Answer—
### Graphing Exercise

6. The answer includes a graph. Students' graphs should look similar to the one shown here. An Excel spreadsheet containing this graph, along with supporting data, is available on the Instructor's Resource CD.

# Tariffs and Trade, Part I

Alexander Hamilton's vision of the United States included manufacturing. To protect the nation's young industries, he proposed a protective tariff. Because most Americans were doing well at agriculture, there was little incentive in the United States to engage in manufacturing. Therefore, Congress, which had passed a modest tariff in 1789 for revenue purposes, did not support Hamilton's proposal. Still, the tariff became the federal government's chief source of revenue until 1913.

The Napoleonic Wars provided the spark for American manufacturing and a move toward protective tariffs. This pattern, repeated during each war in the country's early history, would trigger protectionism. Tariff rates were increased for revenue purposes during the War of 1812, and they were not reduced when the war ended.

Throughout the nineteenth century, the tariff was the most important economic policy and became a huge political issue. The South supported low tariffs, and the North favored higher, more protective rates. Tariff rates inched up until the crisis caused by the 1828 "Tariff of Abominations" led to some rollback of duties. The South, believing the tariff favored the more industrial North, claimed the theory of "nullification," by which it could invalidate federal laws within its borders. President Jackson threatened to collect the tariff duties by force. Henry Clay defused the situation by negotiating a reduction of rates. The South did not renounce the theory of nullification, and the rift between it and the North was open.

When the split between the two sections of the nation erupted into the Civil War, the United States' tariff policy changed. Strapped for money, the government raised tariff rates by passing the 1861 Morrill Tariff, and tariffs were kept high until 1913. Following the Civil War, the South's political power diminished. As the United States began a period of rapid industrialization and became more self-sufficient, the importance of international trade declined. The nation's industrialists, supported by the Republican Party, were able to maintain high tariffs. Advocates of low tariffs feared that protective tariffs would cause manufacturing to grow, giving that sector more political power.

When tariff rates finally were reduced in 1913, they were replaced by an income tax so as to maintain (and shift the burden of) revenues. Still, the reductions of 1913 had less effect than predicted, primarily because of World War I. The return of higher tariffs reached a peak with the Smoot-Hawley Tariff. This tariff, enacted in 1930 during the beginning of the Great Depression, further decreased world trade.

## THINK CRITICALLY

Imagine you are a member of Congress immediately after the Civil War. Take a position for or against keeping tariffs high. Then write a paragraph justifying your point of view.

### FOCUS

Point out that many economic decisions have political considerations. United States tariff policy in the nineteenth century was highly politicized. Prior to the Civil War, it was one cause of the rift between the North and South. Following the war, it remained a major political issue until it began to be replaced by the income tax.

### TEACH

Instruct students to read the **Connect to History** feature and answer the questions. Invite students to role play and debate the question. They could take roles as legislators representing some of the constituency they identified.

### ASSESS

Use the questions at the bottom of the page to assess the students' understanding of this feature.

#### Answers to Think Critically

A possible answer is: Tariffs are important to us as a nation for several reasons. First and foremost, they protect American business from foreign companies that will try to sell their products cheaply here. These foreign products at a lower price will not match the quality of American-made products. Also, purchasing these cheaper foreign goods will take away American jobs and give them to individuals overseas. Another reason tariffs are good is that they are the largest source of revenue for the American government.

## Bibliography

Carnes, Marc C. *MacMillan Information Now Encyclopedia: U.S. History.* New York: MacMillan Library Reference, 1996.

Schwarz, Frederic. "1828: Abominations." *American Heritage*, November/December 2003, page 12.

## Summary

### Consider

Ask students to revisit the questions they were asked to consider at the beginning of the chapter. Remind students that they should be able to answer all of the questions after studying Chapter 18.

- If the United States is such a rich and productive nation, why are so many goods and services imported? See page 554—Comparative Advantage.

- Why isn't the United States self-sufficient? See page 556—U.S. Exports and Imports.

- If free trade is such a good idea, why do some producers try to restrict foreign trade? See page 560—Trade Restrictions.

- What's up with the euro? See page 575—The Euro.

- Is a growing U.S. trade deficit a growing worry? See page 568—The Merchandise Trade Balance.

### Exam*View*

Use Exam*View* to assess students' learning

- Create a chapter test using questions from the existing test bank.

- Add your own questions to the existing test bank.

- Generate multiple forms of a chapter test.

### Study Skills

Offer the following study skills suggestions for students as they review this chapter.

- Outline the chapter.
- Review Key Terms.
- Review Checkpoints.
- Work in pairs to quiz each other.
- Use Xtra! Study Tools for each lesson.

 Quiz Prep

Direct students to the online quiz preparation for Chapter 18 at **econxtra.swlearning.com**.

## Summary

###  18.1 *Benefits of Trade*

**a** Countries trade to improve the average standard of living of their people. Each country benefits from comparative advantage by specializing in the production of goods and services it is able to produce with the lowest opportunity cost.

**b** Trade can benefit nations even when they do not enjoy a comparative advantage. When nations trade, they produce larger quantities of goods and services and are able to take advantage of economies of scale.

econxtra.swlearning.com

**c** The United States exports many products, including capital goods, industrial supplies, services, and some consumer goods. The most important U.S. imports are consumer goods, capital goods, industrial supplies, and automobiles.

###  18.2 *Trade Restrictions and Free-Trade Agreements*

**a** The flow of trade in the global economy is restricted by barriers that take the form of *tariffs, quotas,* and other measures. Tariffs are taxes placed on imported goods. Quotas are legal limits on amounts of goods that may be imported.

**b** All barriers to trade reduce supplies of goods and services and increase prices consumers pay for them. When one nation sets trade restrictions, other nations are likely to respond with their own restrictions. Resources are wasted when firms and groups pressure governments to impose trade restrictions.

**c** The *General Agreement on Tariffs and Trade (GATT)* encouraged the reduction of tariffs and quotas. Its members agreed to treat all other member nations equally. The *Uruguay Round* of trade agreements, which took place between 1986 and 1994, set the goals of

reducing tariffs by 85 percent and eliminating all quotas. The agreement also established the *World Trade Organization (WTO),* which provides the foundation for the world's multilateral trading system. Common markets or free-trade zones have been established worldwide to allow a free flow of goods, services, people, and capital among the member nations.

###  18.3 *Balance of Payments*

**a** The *balance of payments* is the record of all economic transactions between U.S. residents and residents of the rest of the world. Two broad accounts are included in each nation's balance of payments: the *current account* and the *financial account*. Trade of goods is measured by the *merchandise trade balance*.

**b** Individuals may make unilateral transfers of funds to people in other countries. This flow of money is a debit in the balance-of-payments account. Net unilateral transfers combined with the balance of goods and services results in the current account balance.

**c** The financial account tracks the flow of capital resulting from international transactions. It is impossible to keep track of every international transaction, so any discrepancy between credits and debits in the current account and the financial account is "balanced" by including an offsetting statistical discrepancy.

###  18.4 *Foreign Exchange Rates*

**a** *Foreign exchange* is the money used to carry out international transactions. The *exchange rate* is the amount of a foreign currency that can be purchased with one U.S. dollar.

**b** Twelve European nations have agreed to use a single currency, the euro.

**c** Foreign exchange is most often purchased to buy foreign goods or invest abroad.

**d** Before 1971, many nations fixed exchange rates for their currencies in terms of gold. This system was replaced in 1971 with a floating exchange rate system.

###  18.2 *Assessment*

#### Think Critically

7. Answers will vary. Possible answer: These nations may have felt that joining the EU might cause them to give up some of their economic independence. They might also have been worried about their businesses being forced to compete with businesses in other nations without tariff protection. It is possible that political pressure was put on leaders by groups that felt they could be

Continued from page 564.

harmed by membership in the EU. These nations may change their decisions if they find themselves at an economic disadvantage in the future.

# Review Economic Terms

Choose the term that best fits the definition. On a separate sheet of paper, write the letter of the answer. Some terms may not be used.

_____ 1. The amount by which the value of merchandise exports exceeds the value of merchandise imports during a given period

_____ 2. A tax on imports

_____ 3. A record of all economic transactions between residents of one country and residents of the rest of the world during a given period

_____ 4. Foreign money needed to carry out international transactions

_____ 5. The portion of the balance of payments that records exports and imports of goods and services, net investment income, and net transfers

_____ 6. An exchange rate determined by the forces of supply and demand without government intervention

_____ 7. The amount by which the value of merchandise imports exceeds the value of merchandise exports during a given period of time

_____ 8. A legal limit on the quantity of a particular product that can be imported

_____ 9. An exchange rate fixed within a narrow range of values and maintained by central banks' ongoing purchases and sales of currencies

_____ 10. The portion of the balance of payments that records international transactions involving financial assets

a. balance of payments
b. current account
c. exchange rate
d. financial account
e. fixed exchange rate
f. flexible exchange rate
g. foreign exchange
h. General Agreement on Tariffs and Trade (GATT)
i. merchandise trade balance
j. quota
k. tariff
l. trade deficit
m. trade surplus
n. Uruguay Round
o. world price
p. World Trade Organization (WTO)

# Review Economic Concepts

11. **True or False** The law of comparative advantage states that the individual or firm with the lowest opportunity cost of producing a particular good should specialize in that good.

12. A nation may enjoy a comparative advantage as a result of possessing each of the following except

   a. superior labor.

   b. superior resources

   c. superior capital.

   d. superior consumers.

13. Countries can gain from specialization and trade if that trade results in __?__ for producers in that country. That is, the producers' average costs of output decline as they expand their scale of production to meet the increased demand.

14. **True or False** Without comparative advantage, there is no reason for a nation to trade.

15. The category of exports from the United States that has the greatest value is

   a. capital goods.

   b. consumer goods.

   c. industrial supplies.

   d. agricultural products.

16. The __?__ for a good or service is determined by world supply and world demand for the product.

## Review Economic Terms

1. m. trade surplus
2. k. tariff
3. a. balance of payments
4. g. foreign exchange
5. b. current account
6. f. flexible exchange rate
7. l. trade deficit
8. j. quota
9. e. fixed exchange rate
10. d. financial account

## Review Economic Concepts

11. True
12. d. superior consumers
13. economies of scales
14. False. Nations also trade because of differences in tastes and economies of scale.
15. a. capital goods
16. world price

---

 **Assessment**

### Think Critically

Continued from page 573.

7. *$500 million increase in the nation's exports of computers*—This will be a credit for the nation's balance of payments. It will contribute to production and employment. *People send $30 million more to their relatives in other nations*—This will be a debit for the nation's balance of payments. It will detract from production and employment.

*Foreigners invest an additional $450 million in that nation's businesses*—This will be a credit for the nation's balance of payments. It will contribute to production and employment. *$800 million increase in the nation's imports of automobiles*—This will be a debit for the nation's balance of payments. It will detract from production and employment.

## Review Economic Concepts

17. b. consumer goods

18. b. harm consumers and benefits producers

19. False. A tariff will raise the price of products made in that nation.

20. quota

21. d. the number of people employed in export industries to decline

22. World Trade Organization (WTO)

23. False. When one nation seeks trade restrictions, other nations are likely to respond with their own restrictions.

24. c. the value of a nation's exports less the value of its imports

25. True

26. c. farmers in that country sell grain to firms in other countries

27. current account balance

28. False. The exchange rate for the U.S. dollar is flexible. When an exchange rate is flexible, or floating, government officials usually have little direct role in foreign exchange markets.

29. d. according to the value of gold

30. flexible (or floating)

## Apply Economic Concepts

31. The camera would cost $250.25 (275 ? 0.91 = 250.25).

    Answers will vary. Possible answer: Students should also consider taxes (generally value-added taxes or VATs), which can be quite substantial in Europe.

32. Answers will vary. Possible answer: Country A can produce a chair at a cost of $47.50 while Country B must spend $56.20 to produce a similar chair. This means that Country A has a comparative advantage in the production of chairs. Country B should shift its production to other goods or services where it has a lower opportunity cost.

---

17. The category of imports to the United States that has the greatest value is

    a. capital goods.

    b. consumer goods.

    c. industrial supplies.

    d. agricultural products.

18. A *tariff* that is placed on an imported good will __?__ of the taxed product.

    a. harm consumers and producers

    b. harm consumers and benefit producers

    c. benefit consumers and producers

    d. benefit consumers and harm producers

19. **True or False** A *tariff* on imported goods will have no affect on the price of products made in that country.

20. A(n) __?__ is a legal limit on the amount of a product that may be imported into a nation.

21. Trade restrictions cause

    a. the value of international trade to grow.

    b. the price of products consumers purchase to decline.

    c. the selection of products from which consumers may choose to grow.

    d. the number of people employed in export industries to decline.

22. The __?__ provides the legal and institutional foundation for the world's multilateral trading system.

23. **True or False** When one nation sets trade restrictions, other nations are unlikely to respond with their own restrictions.

24. Trade of goods is measured by the *merchandise trade balance* that is equal to

    a. the value of a nation's exports plus the value of its imports.

    b. the value of a nation's imports less the value of its exports.

    c. the value of a nation's exports less the value of its imports.

    d. the value of a nation's exports.

25. **True or False** The *current account* keeps track of trade in goods and services, the flow of interest and profits across international borders, and the flow of foreign aid and cash gifts.

26. Which of the following would appear as a credit in a nation's *balance of payments*?

    a. Businesses in that country purchase resources from other nations.

    b. Banks in that country lend money to people in other nations.

    c. Farmers in that country sell grain to firms in other countries.

    d. Residents of that country send cash to their relatives in other countries.

27. When the unilateral transfers are combined with the balance of goods and services, the result is the __?__.

28. **True or False** The *exchange rate* for the U.S. dollar relative to other currencies is set and controlled by the U.S. government.

29. Before 1971, many nations fixed *exchange rates* for their currencies

    a. according to the value of crude oil.

    b. according to the value of a group of European currencies.

    c. according to the value of the Japanese yen.

    d. according to the value of gold.

30. A __?__ *exchange rate* system was created in 1971 under which exchange rates for major currencies are determined by demand and supply.

# Apply Economic Concepts

31. **Determine the Price of an Imported Good** You have decided to buy a new camera while you are traveling in Germany. Its price is 275 euros. If the exchange rate for euros is 0.91 per one U.S. dollar, how many dollars will the camera cost? What other costs should you consider?

32. **Determine Comparative Advantage** In the following table, countries A and B are able to produce similar chairs from the resources

---

 **Assessment**

### Think Critically

*Residents of the nation spend $40 million more on travel in other nations*—This will be a debit for the nation's balance of payments. It will detract from production and employment in the economy.

*Businesses in that nation pay $25 million more in dividends to foreigners*—This will be a debit for the nation's balance of payments.

Continued from page 583.

It will detract from production and employment. Answers will vary. Possible answer: It is difficult for a nation to keep track of flows of funds that result from tourism and people sending money to individuals in other nations.

shown. Determine which nation has a comparative advantage in this type of production.

What should the other nation do to maximize the value of its production?

| Type of Resource | Amount of Resource Required | | Cost of Resource | |
|---|---|---|---|---|
| | A | B | A | B |
| Labor | 2 hours | 6 hours | $10 per hour | $6 per hour |
| Raw materials | 20 lbs | 20 lbs | $1.00 per lb | $.80 per lb |
| Power | 150 kwh | 80 kwh | $.03 per kwh | $.04 per kwh |
| Tools | 1 robot system | 20 hand tools | $3 per chair | $1 per chair |

**33. Impose a Barrier to Trade?** Assume you are the prime minister of a poor nation that is located in another part of the world. Your government has been working to encourage economic growth by investing in new technology and training in modern skills for its workers. Although some progress has been made, there is a long way to go before your nation's businesses can compete successfully with those in other countries. Decide what type of barrier to trade (tariff or quota) you would impose in the following situations. You also may choose to impose no barrier at all. Explain each of your choices.

a. Your nation has invested in firms that produce kitchen appliances. These firms' costs are about 25 percent higher than the cost of buying imported appliances from producers in other nations. The firms are selling few of their products and are in danger of failing. What barrier would you place on the importation of appliances?

b. Your nation has no known oil reserves. It imports all the oil it uses from other nations. More money is spent paying for oil than is spent for any other imported product. A large part of the imported oil is used by consumers who like to take long weekend drives in the country. You would like to see more of your nation's money spent importing tools and machinery. What barriers would you place on the importation of oil?

c. Your nation has fertile land that could be used to grow fruits it might export. Unfortunately, it lacks the ability to produce fertilizer, which the production of these crops requires. What barriers would you place on the importation of fertilizer?

**34. Sharpen Your Life Skills: Critical Thinking** Because of fears of terrorism and a general decline in economic activity in 2003, many airlines and hotels suffered from a reduced demand for their services. U.S. consumers were able to take discounted vacations either in the United States or in foreign nations. One New York City travel agency offered consumers a one-week vacation in London for $699 or a one-week vacation in California for the same price. If you had been looking for a vacation destination, which of these alternatives would you have chosen? What role would a desire to support the U.S. economy have played in your decision-making process?

 **e-con @pps**   econxtra.swlearning.com

**35. Access EconDebate Online** at econxtra.swlearning.com. Read the policy debate entitled "Does the U.S. economy benefit from foreign trade?"

Choose one side of this issue (for or against foreign trade) and write a paragraph arguing for that point of view.

*Chapter Assessment*   **585**

---

## Apply Economic Concepts

33. Answers will vary. Possible answers:

a. Applying a 25 percent tariff to imported appliances would allow the domestic firms to sell more products. The domestic firms might eventually become more efficient.

b. Placing a quota or tariff on imported oil would reduce importation of oil and leave more money for purchasing machinery and tools.

c. No barriers should be placed on the importation of fertilizer. This will result in increased production of fruit for exportation and bring foreign currency into the economy.

34. Answers will vary. Possible answer: A decision to vacation in the United States would support employment and production in this nation. This may help support the U.S. economy, but it precludes students from enjoying the many sights and events offered to tourists in London.

**e-con @pps**

35. Answers will vary. Possible answers: Yes, the United States does benefit from foreign trade. The total consumption possibilities increase for the United States. Because foreign trade encourages specialization and division of labor, the United States is able to import goods at a cheaper cost than it could produce them. Consumers benefit from lower prices resulting from foreign trade. In addition, foreign trade encourages American firms to engage in innovation.

No, the United States does not benefit from foreign trade. Industries important to national security are not protected. Jobs are lost overseas as a result of foreign trade. Companies move operations to nations with less strict environmental laws, thus hurting the environment. Infant industries are not protected and cannot compete effectively in their formative years.

---

**18.4** *Assessment*

Continued from page 580.

### Think Critically

7. Answers will vary. Possible answer: The euro appreciated 25 percent relative to the U.S. dollar between 2000 and 2003. This made U.S. products appear to be 25 percent less expensive to EU member nations and contributed to an increase in U.S. exports to them.

## Chapter Overview

**LESSON 19.1** *Developing Economies and Industrial Market Economies:* This lesson distinguishes between developing countries and industrial market countries, and it explains why labor productivity is so low in developing countries.

**LESSON 19.2** *Foreign Trade, Foreign Aid, and Economic Development:* This lesson identifies two foreign-trade strategies. It also assesses the impact of trade and foreign aid on economic development.

**LESSON 19.3** *Rules of the Game, Transition Economies, and Convergence:* This lesson assesses the impact of a nation's physical infrastructure and rules of the game on its economic development. The difficulty of introducing market forces in centrally planned economies is addressed. In addition, convergence theory is explained and discussed.

### Consider

Ask students to consider the questions posed on this page as they study Chapter 19. After studying all three lessons, students should be able to answer the questions. The content related to each question can be found on the pages indicated below.

- Why are some countries poor while others are rich? See page 588—Developing and Industrial Market Countries.
- What determines the wealth of nations? See page 591—Productivity and Economic Development.
- How much does foreign aid help poorer countries? See page 600—Foreign Aid.
- How does terrorism affect economic development? See page 604—Physical Infrastructure.
- What's the "brain drain," and how does it affect poorer countries? See page 599—International Migration.
- Why are birth rates higher in poorer countries? See page 589—High Birth Rates.
- Are poorer countries catching up with the rest of the world? See page 607—Are the World's Economies Converging?

 **POINT YOUR BROWSER**

Remind students that they can find additional resources for this chapter at **econxtra.swlearning.com**

---

# 19 Economic Development

### Consider

Why are some countries poor while others are rich?

What determines the wealth of nations?

How much does foreign aid help poorer countries?

How does terrorism affect economic development?

What's the "brain drain," and how does it affect poorer countries?

Why are birth rates higher in poorer countries?

Are poorer countries catching up with the rest of the world?

© Getty Images/PhotoDisc

 **POINT YOUR BROWSER**

*econxtra.swlearning.com*

---

*Teaching Resources for Chapter 19*

- Activities and Projects Masters
- Spanish Resources
- Econ Connection Interactive Tutorial CD
- **Exam***View*® CD
- Workbook Teacher's Edition
- Chapter and Unit Test Teacher's Edition
- NCEE Standards and Correlation

- Personal Finance Guide
- Social Studies Skills Review
- Instructor's Resource CD
  – PowerPoint Presentation
  – Lesson Plans
  – Video Discussion Guide
  – Answers to Graphing Exercises
- **econxtra.swlearning.com**

# Developing Economies and Industrial Market Economies

## Objectives

> Distinguish between developing countries and industrial market countries.

> Explain why labor productivity is so low in developing countries.

## Overview

People around the world face the day under very different circumstances. Many Americans rise from a comfortable bed in their own home, select the day's clothing from a wardrobe, choose from a variety of breakfast foods, and ride to school or to work in one of the family's automobiles. In contrast, most of the world's 6.5 billion people have little housing, clothing, or food. They own no automobile, and many have no real job. Their health is poor, as is their education. Many cannot read or write. Rich nations are very different from poor ones.

## Key Terms

developing countries

industrial market countries

fertility rate

## [ In the News ]

### • Longevity Differences Among Nations

On September 17, 2003, the world's oldest woman celebrated her 116th birthday. Kamato Hongo was born and raised on a small island in Japan. Her island also was home to the oldest confirmed person ever known to have lived—a woman who died at the age of 120. Less than two weeks after Hongo's 116th birthday party, the world's oldest man at that time died at the age of 114. Yukichi Chuganji also was from Japan. Coincidence? Not really. Japan, an industrial market economy, has a higher percentage of people over the age of 100 than any country in the world. It also has the highest average life expectancy (ALE)—85 years for women and 78 years for men. During the 1900s, Japan saw its ALE rate more than double. Why do the Japanese live so long? It's partly because their culture promotes a healthy lifestyle with a fish-based, low-fat diet. Even more important, the country has been able to nearly wipe out most infectious diseases. Eliminating tuberculosis and gastroenteritis accounted for nearly 40 percent of the ALE increase. The Japanese experience shows the positive effects of good medical care and a healthy lifestyle. Many developing countries do not have either, and so also have a low ALE. The African country of Sierra Leone has a low life expectancy of about 43 years for both men and women. Infectious diseases account for much of this difference. In Sierra Leone, AIDS, malaria, tuberculosis, even pneumonia and diarrhea are major causes of death. The country also has suffered through a civil war in which 50,000 people were killed. Not surprisingly, the countries that have the lowest ALEs also are among the poorest in the world.

### Think About It

Based on the information in this article, what do you think is the relationship between average life expectancy and a country's economy?

587

### National Content Standards in Economics

A complete list of the NCEE Standards appears on pages xxiv–xxv of this book. The following standards are addressed in Lesson 19.1.

Standard 1: Scarcity

Standard 4: Role of Incentives

Standard 13: Role of Resources in Determining Income

Standard 14: Profit and the Entrepreneur

Standard 15: Growth

Standard 18: Macroeconomy—Income, Employment, Prices

Standard 19: Unemployment and Inflation

## FOCUS

### 19.1 Developing Economies and Industrial Market Economies

Point out that the world's economic systems can be divided into two basic groups: developing countries and industrial market economies. Developing countries are those that are relatively poor and are unable to expand their production rapidly. Industrial market economies are those that are wealthy and are growing at a relatively high rate. Growth requires national savings that can support investment in greater human and physical capital. Savings can occur when a country's production is not entirely devoted to current consumption as it is in most developing countries. Lack of savings also renders developing countries unable to invest to expand their production rapidly.

### Objectives

Remind students to read the lesson objectives to help focus their attention before reading the lesson.

### Key Terms

Direct students to look up key terms in a business or economics dictionary. Some students will find it helpful to read another definition. In addition to a definition, many entries will include a brief explanation and an example.

### [ In the News ]

Instruct students to read the passage and write down their answers. Point out that their answers might change after they finish studying Lesson 19.1.

### Answers to Think About It

Answers will vary. Possible answer: The stronger a country's economy and the wealthier a country, the higher the average life expectancy of its citizens.

### Visual Presentation

Use the PowerPoint presentation on the Instructor's Resource CD as an adjunct to your lecture. The presentation also can be used for review.

## Worlds Apart

Point out that developing economies share some common problems that prevent them from achieving rapid rates of growth or, in some cases, even maintaining their current per capita GDP. Industrial market economies either do not share these problems or are able to cope with them.

## Ask the Xpert!

Direct students to **econxtra.swlearning.com** to hear an expert answer the question "Why are some nations rich but others are poor?"

### Think Critically Through Visuals

Direct students to focus their attention on the photograph on this page. Ask for a volunteer to answer the question posed in the caption.

### Answer

Answers will vary. Possible answer: The conditions appear primitive.

---

## Ask the Xpert!

econxtra.swlearning.com

*Why are some nations rich but others are poor?*

**industrial market countries**
Economically advanced market countries of Western Europe, North America, Australia, New Zealand, and Japan

**developing countries**
Nations with low GDP per capita, high rates of illiteracy, high unemployment, and high fertility rates

---

# Worlds Apart

Countries can be classified in a variety of ways, based on their level of economic development. The yardstick used most often is to compare living standards across nations. The most common measure of living standards is a nation's *GDP per capita*. Recall that GDP per capita measures how much an economy produces on average per resident. Based on that measure, countries can be sorted into two broad categories:

1. developing countries, which have lower levels of GDP per capita income, and

2. industrial market countries, which have higher levels of GDP per capita.

## Developing and Industrial Market Countries

**Developing countries** not only have lower GDP per capita. They also usually have higher rates of illiteracy, higher unemployment rates, extensive under-

**How does this photograph suggest that the woman lives in a developing country?**

© Getty Images/PhotoDisc

employment, and rapid population growth. On average, more than half the labor force in developing countries works in agriculture. Because farming methods are relatively primitive there, farm productivity is low, and most people barely subsist.

About 5 billion of the world's 6.5 billion people live in developing countries. China and India, the two population giants, are developing countries that together account for half the developing world's population.

**Industrial market countries** not only have higher GDP per capita. They also have lower illiteracy rates, lower unemployment, and slower population growth. Industrial market countries consist of the economically advanced nations of Western Europe, North America, Australia, New Zealand, and Japan. They were the first countries to experience long-term economic growth during the nineteenth century. About 1.5 billion of the world's 6.5 billion population live in industrial market countries.

Figure 19.1 shows 10 representative countries based on GDP per capita. GDP has been adjusted to reflect the actual buying power of currency in each respective economy. The United States, Canada, Japan, and the United Kingdom are industrial market economies. The rest are developing economies.

The United States had a GDP per capita in 2001 that was about five times that of Brazil, a developing country. But GDP per capita in Brazil, in turn, was about 15 times that of Sierra Leone, one of the poorest countries on Earth. Thus, developing countries are not uniformly poor. Residents of Brazil likely feel poor relative to industrial market countries such as the United States, but they are well off compared to the poorest developing countries. Per capita GDP in the United States was 70 times greater than in Sierra Leone. Thus, there is a wide range of productive performance around the world.

---

### Outside Resources

**OneWorld United States** OneWorld, according to its web site, is a network of people and groups around the world dedicated to human rights and sustainable development. OneWorld United States, based in Washington, D.C., is one of 12 regional and country centers. It is devoted to disseminating information about problems facing developing countries. Instruct students to visit the OneWorld United States web site at http://us.oneworld.net, click on "About One World," and summarize their findings in a bulleted list of five to ten key points. Discuss the lists in class and ask students whether this organization provides balanced reporting or promotes a particular agenda.

Figure 19.1

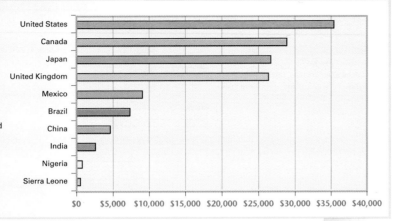

**There is a wide range of productive performance around the world.**

Source: The Central Intelligence Agency's *World Factbook 2002* and OECD estimates. Figures reflect the purchasing power of currencies in each country.

## Life Expectancy

Differences in stages of development among countries are reflected in a number of ways besides GDP per capita. For example, many people in developing countries suffer from poor health as a result of malnutrition and disease. HIV/AIDS is devastating some developing countries, particularly those in Africa and the Caribbean. About 5,000 Haitian children are born with the HIV/AIDS virus each year.

The average life expectancy around the world ranges from about 43 years in the poor African country of Sierra Leone to 81 years in the industrial market economy of Japan. The world average is 67 years. Countries with the shortest life expectancies also have the highest infant mortality. *Infant mortality* refers to the death of a baby before its first birthday. For example, the infant mortality rate in Sierra Leone is about 35 times higher than the rate in Japan. Among industrialized nations in the world, the United States ranks 23rd in infant mortality.

Malnutrition is a primary or contributing factor in most deaths among young children in poor countries. Diseases that are easily controlled in industrial

economies—malaria, whooping cough, polio, dysentery, typhoid, and cholera—can become epidemics in poor countries, where clean drinking water often is hard to find.

## High Birth Rates

Developing countries also are identified by their high birth rates. This year, about 65 million of the 75 million people added to the world's population will be born in developing countries. In fact, the **fertility rate**, which is the average number of births during a woman's lifetime, is an easy way of distinguishing between developing and industrial countries. Few developing countries have a fertility rate of less than 2.2 births per woman, but no industrial country has a fertility rate above that level.

Figure 19.2 presents the average fertility rate for the 10 countries introduced in Figure 19.1. As you can see, fertility rates are lower in industrial countries and higher in developing countries. Sub-Saharan African countries are the poorest in the world and have the fastest-growing populations.

Fertility rates are higher in developing countries for a variety of reasons.

*fertility rate*
The average number of births during each woman's lifetime

**Worlds Apart**

Recruit eight students to help with this demonstration. Three of the students represent a family in an industrial market economy (two adults and one child). The other five represent a family in a developing country (two adults and three children). The first family earns $500 per week. The second family's income totals $50 per month. The cost of supporting a person in the industrial market economy is $100 per week. The cost in the developing country is $10 per month. Which family will be able to save and therefore invest in advanced education for children, open a business, or purchase shares of corporate stock? Use this example to foster a discussion about the differences in the standards of living these two families would enjoy. Many basic costs in the developing country would be lower, but the family would still have difficulty paying them. How does the larger size of the second family contribute to its economic difficulties? Why would the family in the developing country be harmed more by a downturn in that country's economy?

### Think Critically Through Visuals

Direct students to focus their attention on **Figure 19.1—GDP Per Capita for Selected Countries in 2001**. Point out that there is wide disparity between the industrial market economies and the developing countries.

Lesson 19.1 • *Developing Economies and Industrial Market Economics*

**589**

During the late nineteenth and early twentieth centuries, when the United States was undergoing rapid industrial expansion, the fertility rate was high compared with the current rate. In 1880, for example, fertility was 4; today, the rate is less than 2.2. Ask students why the high rate did not hinder U.S. development in the same ways that high rates in today's developing countries negatively impact development. (At that time, the United States had vast lands that could be farmed, many natural resources that could be exploited, foreign markets for its products, and a high rate of investment by both U.S. and foreign citizens.)

## Worlds Apart

Ask students to consider the following situation. A young couple in a poor country recently married. They are discussing how many children to have. They own a small farm but have no power-driven tools. Their water buffalo pulls their plow, and they plant and weed by hand. There is no public health system in their country and no government-sponsored retirement benefits. Everyone must look out for himself or herself. How many children would this couple want to have? Why would they make this choice? (They might choose to have a large family so their children could help them with the farm and take care of them if they become sick or need assistance in their old age.)

### *Think Critically Through Visuals*

Direct students to focus their attention on **Figure 19.2—Fertility Rates for Selected Countries in 2001**. Explain that fertility rate is the average number of births during a woman's lifetime. Point out that no industrial county has a fertility rate above 2.2.

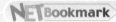

Direct students to **econxtra.swlearning.com**. Remind them to click on the link for Lesson 19.1 to find the appropriate link for the **NET Bookmark** on this page. Extend this activity by asking students to complete the activity for a second country, perhaps one they know little about.

 **CHECKPOINT**

Invite a student to answer the checkpoint that appears on this page.

### Answer

Industrial economies have an increased GDP per capita, decreased illiteracy rates, decreased unemployment, and decreased population growth. Developing economies have the reverse of all of these.

---

**Fertility Rates for Selected Countries in 2001**  **Figure 19.2**

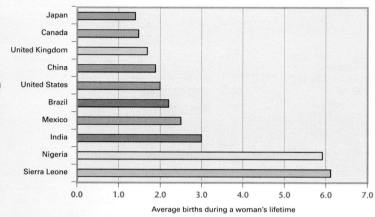

**Fertility rates are lower in industrial countries and higher in developing countries.**

Source: Estimates from the World Bank in *World Development Report 2003*, which can be found at econ.worldbank.org/wdr/wdr2003/.

Among these is that parents there view children as a source of farm labor. Also, most developing countries have no pension or social security systems so parents want children to support them in old age. The higher infant mortality rates in poorer countries also lead to higher birth rates, as parents strive to achieve sufficiently large families.

Attitudes about family size are changing, however, even in the poorest countries. According to the United Nations, the birth rate during a typical woman's lifetime in a developing country has fallen from six in 1965 to less than three children today. As women become better educated, they earn more. Women who are pregnant or who have young children are less able to work. Thus, because their opportunity cost of child bearing has increased, women have chosen to have fewer children.

 **NET Bookmark**

The CIA World Factbook web site is a great source for information about the populations and economic situations of countries throughout the world. Access this site through econxtra.swlearning.com. Select a country that interests you. Find the following facts about that country's people: infant mortality rate, life expectancy at birth, and total fertility rate. Then examine the information about the country's economy. Read the "Economy—Overview" paragraph and the statistics given about the country's economy. Compare the facts you found about the country's people with the information about the economy. Write a paragraph that explains the relationship between the two sets of information.

*econxtra.swlearning.com*

✓ **CHECKPOINT**
What are some clear differences between developing economies and industrial market economies?

---

### *Economic Headlines*

Instruct students to locate an article in a current magazine or newspaper that relates to one of the topics in this lesson. For example, they might find articles about conditions in a specific developing country. Instruct students to read the article, write a brief summary, and include a reference citation. Identify the style you want them to use for the citation.

As an alternative, you might find several articles of interest and provide citations for students to use in locating one of the articles. Direct students to read the article they have chosen and write a brief explanation of how it relates to this lesson.

# Productivity and Economic Development

You have examined some symptoms of poverty in developing countries. However, you have yet to explore why poor countries are poor. Simply put, poor countries are poor because they do not produce many goods and services.

## Low Labor Productivity

Labor productivity, measured as output per worker, is low in developing countries. Why? Labor productivity depends on the quality of the labor and on the amount of capital, natural resources, and other resources that combine with labor to create production. For example, a farmer who has abundant land and uses modern techniques and equipment, healthy seeds, and proper irrigation can grow more than a hundred farmers trying to scratch out a living on smaller plots using primitive tools.

One way a country raises its productivity is by investing more in human and physical capital. National savings usually finance this investment. Income per capita often is too low in developing countries to allow for much national saving or investment. In poor countries with unstable governments, the wealthy who can afford to save and invest in their nation's economy often send their savings abroad to invest in more stable economies.

What about foreign investments in developing countries? Governments of developing countries heavily regulate private international borrowing and lending. These countries are therefore less attractive for foreign investors. For example, some developing countries, such as China, have required foreign investors to find a local partner who must be granted controlling interest in the business.

Thus, in developing countries there is less financial capital available for investment in either human or physical capital. With less physical and human capital, workers produce less, so labor productivity is lower.

## Less Education

Education enables workers to use modern production techniques and technology. Education also makes people more receptive to new ideas and methods. Countries with the most advanced educational systems also were the first to develop economically. For example, the United States has been a world leader in free public education and in economic development.

In the poorest countries, most adults can't read or write. For example, 70 percent of adults in Sierra Leone are illiterate. When knowledge is lacking, other resources are not used as efficiently. For

The literacy rate in the United States is 97 percent. This means that 97 percent of the U.S. population over the age of 15 can read and write. Why do you think that countries with the most advanced educational systems also have the most highly developed economies?

## Productivity and Economic Development

Remind students that a worker's productivity depends on the skills he or she brings to the job and the tools that are available to use. Many developing countries lack the resources to create a comprehensive system of education and training for all their children. This shortage is aggravated by high birth rates. The more children there are, the greater is the need for educational facilities. Teachers do not add much to current production. The time and effort they spend instructing young people is time and effort that cannot be used to produce additional goods and services. An economy must be productive enough that it can afford to allocate a significant amount of labor to teaching and still be able to produce enough goods and services to satisfy current needs and invest for the future. Much the same can be said for the creation of physical capital. While a worker is building a new machine or installing a new technology, she or he is not adding to current production of consumer goods. When countries need to devote all of their current productive capacity to the creation of consumer goods, they will not be able to increase their capital goods. Without capital goods, workers cannot be as productive as other workers who do have capital goods to use.

### Think Critically Through Visuals

Direct students to focus their attention on the photograph on this page. Ask for a volunteer to answer the question posed in the caption.

### Answer

Answers will vary. Possible answer: Countries with the most advanced educational system have the most highly developed economies because their workers can use modern production techniques and technologies. Education also makes individuals more receptive to new ideas. When education is lacking, resources are not used as efficiently.

## Group Activity

Organize students into small groups. Tell each group that it represents government leaders of a developing country. Their country has enough resources to provide training for 10,000 people in only one of the following skills or professions. Their job is to choose the type of training that would be most useful to the country in the long run. Ask them report on their decisions. Compare choices made by the different groups.

- Train nurses to provide better medical care for the country's population.
- Train engineers who could design and assemble electronic products.
- Train people to teach math, writing, and reading to 300,000 students each year.
- Train people in basic entrepreneurial skills such as accounting and small business management.
- Train farmers in ways to increase production of food and other crops.

**TEACH**

## Productivity and Economic Development

Explain that during the 1960s, nearly 50,000 students graduated each year with degrees in economics from universities in India. At that time, the Indian government and Indian businesses had job openings for roughly 10,000 new economists each year. Ask several students what they would have done if they had been one of the 40,000 graduates who had been unable to find employment as an economist. What do they believe these people did for a living? Why were so many professionals trying to emigrate from India to Europe or North America at that time?

 **E-CONOMICS**

Direct students to read the passage entitled "Technology Outsourcing to Developing Countries" on this page.

### Answers to Think Critically

Answers will vary. Possible answer: (a) Advantages include lower labor costs. Disadvantages include possible political unrest in developing countries. (b) Advantages include holding down prices for goods and services. Disadvantages include increased unemployment. (c) Advantages include decreased unemployment and increased real GDP. Disadvantages include strong American influence that might result in unwanted social and cultural changes.

### *Think Critically Through Visuals*

Direct students to focus their attention on the photograph on page 593. Ask for a volunteer to answer the question posed in the caption.

#### Answer

Productivity is lower than if modern farming equipment were used.

 **CHECKPOINT**

Invite a student to answer the checkpoint that appears on page 593.

#### Answer

Labor productivity is low in developing countries because it is dependent on capital and education, both of which are low in developing countries.

---

example, a country may be endowed with fertile land, but farmers may not understand irrigation and fertilization techniques. Farmers also may not know how to rotate crops to avoid soil depletion. Rates of illiteracy are much lower in industrial economies, where fewer than 5 percent of adults can't read or write.

Child labor in developing countries reduces educational opportunities. In Pakistan, for example, there are enough classrooms and teachers for only one-third of the country's school-age children. More than 10 million Pakistani children work full-time, usually in agriculture.

### Inefficient Use of Labor

Another feature of developing countries is that they use labor less efficiently than do industrial nations. Unemployment and underemployment reflect inefficient uses of labor. Recall that underemployment occurs when skilled workers are employed in low-skill jobs or when people are working less than they would like—such as working only part time when a full-time job is preferred. Only a small proportion of the work force in developing countries have what you would call a regular job with normal hours and a steady paycheck. Most work as day laborers in the informal economy or scratch out a living in agriculture.

### Few Entrepreneurs

In order to develop, an economy must have entrepreneurs who are able to bring together resources and take the risk of profit or loss. Many developing

---

 **E-CONOMICS**

## Technology Outsourcing to Developing Countries

American businesses have taken advantage of unemployment and underemployment in developing countries by outsourcing work to these countries. For many years, such outsourcing mainly involved moving factory work to developing countries, where the company could hire workers for a much lower pay rate than in the United States. The ability to outsource has only increased with the advent of the Internet. "With advancements in communications and the Internet," says Chris Kizzier, an offshore outsourcing consultant, "the world has shrunk to the size of a pea, and the fact that you might be 9,000 miles away is irrelevant." In recent years, many companies have saved as much as 60 percent in labor costs by moving information technology (IT) work to developing countries. India has been one of the primary beneficiaries of such outsourcing. An American company that outsources only a portion of its work can save huge amounts of money. For example, in 1999 an IT team that had 25 percent of its workers in the United States and

75 percent in India could average a combined hourly labor rate of $37 per worker. If 100 percent of the team was in the United States, the hourly labor costs would have averaged about $75 to $100 per worker. Companies as diverse as Amazon.com, DirectTV, and Delta Airlines have outsourced many of their customer service and telemarketing operations to India. The downside to this trend is that it moves jobs out of the United States. It also can leave those jobs vulnerable to political crises in the developing countries. The threat of war between India and Pakistan, for example, has concerned some American business leaders. Some experts also worry that outsourcing and the electronic communications it requires may make information less secure.

### Think Critically

What are the advantages and disadvantages of U.S. firms outsourcing jobs to developing countries to (a) the firms themselves, (b) the U.S. economy in general, and (c) the economy to which the jobs are outsourced?

**592**     **CHAPTER 19**   Economic Development

---

*Curriculum Connection—Business*

Ask students to make a list of values, aptitudes, skills, and types of training that are likely to make a person a successful entrepreneur in the United States. Then ask them to write an essay in which they explain why there is likely to be a short supply of people with these aptitudes, skills, and training in many developing countries. Ask students whether they believe sending retired U.S. entrepreneurs to developing countries as mentors is a good way to help these countries. Why might these mentors have difficulty creating successful businesses in a developing country? (They may not understand the language, customs, or social values that exist in these lands. Their own values may prevent them from transferring much useful knowledge.)

countries, particularly those in Africa, were once under colonial rule, where a foreign country governed. Under this system, the local population had few opportunities to develop leadership or entrepreneurial skills.

### Reliance on Agriculture

In some developing countries, the average farm is as small as two acres, so the average farmer does not produce much. Even where more land is available, a lack of physical capital limits the amount of land that can be farmed. More than half the labor force in developing countries works in agriculture. However, because farm productivity is low, less than a third of GDP in those countries stems from agriculture.

In contrast, modern equipment helps a U.S. farmer to work hundreds of acres. Though only 2 percent of the U.S. labor force, American farmers grow enough to feed the nation and lead the world in agricultural exports.

### Vicious Cycle of Low Income and Low Productivity

Low productivity obviously results in low income, but low income, in turn, affects worker productivity. Low income means less saving, and less saving means less investment in human and physical capital. These difficult beginnings are made even worse by poor diet and insufficient health care. Therefore, as children grow into adults, they are not well suited for regular employment. Thus, *low income and low productivity may reinforce each other in a vicious cycle of poverty.*

**CHECKPOINT**
Why is labor productivity low in developing countries?

**On rice plantations in Indonesia, much of the labor is performed by people rather than by modern farming equipment. How does this affect the productivity of Indonesian agriculture?**

Lesson 19.1 • *Developing Economies and Industrial Market Economies* **593**

### APPLY

Assign Lesson 19.1 from the Contemporary Economics Workbook.

### e-con @pps

Encourage students to apply their knowledge of concepts presented in this lesson as they explore economic news stories, policy debates, and data available at **econxtra.swlearning.com**. A sampling of the titles for this lesson appears below.

### EconDebate

- Does dollarization benefit developing countries?
- Does foreign direct investment hinder or help economic development?
- Does international trade harm the environment?
- What are the pros and cons of IMF involvement with global economies?

### ASSESS

Assign all or part of Lesson 19.1 Assessment on page 594 as homework or an in-class activity.

### Xtra! Study Tools

Direct students to the online study tools for Lesson 19.1 at **econxtra.swlearning.com**.

### CLOSE

**Revisit** the In the News feature on the first page of the lesson. Ask students to review their preliminary answers and discuss the questions, now that they have completed this lesson.

**Review** the objectives for Lesson 19.1. Students should be able to:

- Distinguish between developing countries and industrial market countries.
- Identify why labor productivity is so low in developing countries.

### RETEACH

Remind students that efficient production is not the result of a single resource but of a combination of many resources. American farmers, for example, can be efficient if they know how to use modern farm machinery, which crops to plant, when to irrigate and fertilize, how to control pests and diseases, when to harvest, and how to store or distribute their crops. Ask students to explain why a program that sends only tractors or only irrigation equipment to farmers in a developing country is not likely to have much success.

## Key Concepts

1. Answers will vary. Possible answer: Yes. In the nineteenth century, there were vast lands that additional people could farm, ready markets in other countries for U.S. products, and few other countries that were significantly more industrialized than the United States.

2. Answers will vary. Possible answer: Lower infant mortality rates lead to even more rapid population growth so that production must be shared among a larger number of people.

3. Answers will vary. Possible answer: High rates of population growth require a greater investment in education, which many developing countries are often unable to make from their limited production.

4. Answers will vary. Possible answer: When parents teach children how to produce goods and services, they pass on their inefficient techniques. Greater production often requires new skills that can be learned only from other people.

5. Answers will vary. Possible answer: U.S. farmers are better trained, have larger farms, and are able to use capital (tractors, irrigation systems, etc.) and advanced farming technology that is neither available nor understood in many developing countries.

## Graphing Exercise

6. Answers will vary. Possible answer: The ownership of personal computers shows that residents are wealthy enough to buy these items, that they are well-educated so they can use them, and that there are likely to be many people using personal computers to help them operate productive businesses.

   An example of an acceptable graph appears at the bottom of this page.

## Think Critically

7. Answers will vary. Possible answer: Without skilled workers, there is little advantage in buying the machine. In fact, unskilled workers could destroy the machine. The owner may have no alternative other than to save more money over time to both purchase the machine and train the workers. This is one reason that production in developing countries often grows slowly.

---

*Xtra! Study Tools*
econxtra.swlearning.com

## Key Concepts

1. Do you think it was easier for the United States to become an industrialized market economy in the nineteenth century than it is for developing countries today? Why or why not?

2. Why don't reductions in infant mortality rates necessarily cause an improvement in the standard of living in developing countries?

3. Why is labor productivity likely to be relatively low in nations that have rapid population growth?

4. Many developing countries rely on parents to teach their children how to produce goods and services. How does this contribute to their limited ability to increase production?

5. Why are 2 percent of U.S. residents able to produce more food than our nation needs while other nations cannot grow enough food for themselves with nearly 90 percent of their population working in agriculture?

## Graphing Exercise

6. There are many indicators of a nation's economic wealth and development. One of these is the number of personal computers per 1,000 residents. In 2000, residents of the United States owned more computers than people in any other nation. In the same year, this rate was 3 computers per 1,000 people in Ghana. Use data in the table to construct a bar graph that shows the computer ownership rates in the identified nations. Why is computer ownership a good indicator of a nation's economic wealth and development?

**Personal Computer Ownership Per 1,000 Residents in 2000**

| Country | PC Ownership | Country | PC Ownership |
|---------|--------------|---------|--------------|
| Switzerland | 502 | Norway | 491 |
| Australia | 465 | Belgium | 344 |
| Malaysia | 105 | Mexico | 51 |
| Turkey | 38 | Indonesia | 10 |

Source: *Statistical Abstract of the United States*, 2002, p. 852.

## Think Critically

7. **Management** Assume that you own a small business in a developing country that produces aluminum cooking pots. Through hard work and thrift, you have been able to save enough money to purchase a machine that can be used to produce cooking pots twice as fast as your business has in the past. In order to use this machine, you would need to hire someone to train your workers. This training would cost almost as much as the machine itself. Under these conditions, would it make sense for you to purchase the machine? What alternatives do you have if you really want your business to become more efficient and grow?

---

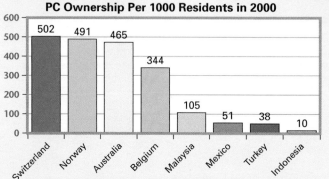

PC Ownership Per 1000 Residents in 2000

## Visualizing the Answer— Graphing Exercise

6. The answer includes a graph. Students' graphs should look similar to the one shown here. An Excel spreadsheet containing this graph, along with supporting data, is available on the Instructor's Resource CD.

# Sharpen Your Life Skills

## Analyze Visuals

You can quickly compare economic conditions in different nations by constructing graphs that demonstrate different attributes of their population.

## Apply Your Skill

Study the bar graph below and evaluate the information it provides about the economic conditions in each nation.

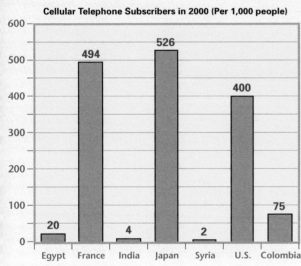

**Cellular Telephone Subscribers in 2000 (Per 1,000 people)**

- Egypt: 20
- France: 494
- India: 4
- Japan: 526
- Syria: 2
- U.S.: 400
- Colombia: 75

Source: *Statistical Abstract of the United States*, 2002, p. 852.

Lesson 19.1 • *Developing Economies and Industrial Market Economies*     **595**

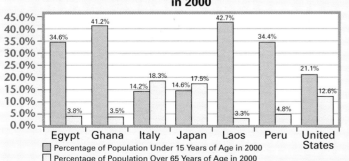

**Percent of Population Under 15 and Over 65 Years of Age in 2000**

- Egypt: 34.6% / 3.8%
- Ghana: 41.2% / 3.5%
- Italy: 14.2% / 18.3%
- Japan: 14.6% / 17.5%
- Laos: 42.7% / 3.3%
- Peru: 34.4% / 4.8%
- United States: 21.1% / 12.6%

☐ Percentage of Population Under 15 Years of Age in 2000
☐ Percentage of Population Over 65 Years of Age in 2000

## movers & shakers

Remind students of Adam Smith's invisible hand of market forces. The electronic age has brought this concept to new extremes. Consumers are able to compare goods, services, and prices in a matter of moments over the Internet. eBay is not the only online auction service; it is just the most successful one. By continually trying new ideas and expanding those that worked while discarding those that did not, Meg Whitman led eBay to serve its customers more effectively. Her firm was rewarded for its superior service by becoming the most successful online auction service in the world.

### TEACH

Instruct students to read the **Movers & Shakers** feature about Meg Whitman. Point out that some students may find it helpful to read the article, read the questions at the bottom of the page, and then reread the article.

### ASSESS

Use the questions in Source Reading and Entrepreneurs in Action at the bottom of the profile to assess the students' understanding of this **Movers & Shakers** feature.

### Answers to Source Reading

Whitman's mission serves developing countries because it brings to them a marketplace through which to trade their goods where a marketplace previously was not available. Whitman's passion to see the customer succeed ensures that she will try to serve every customer she can.

### Answers to Entrepreneurs in Action

Whitman's businesses practices are similar to those of other entrepreneurs because she is willing to take risks and to explore expanding into every market niche possible. There are several ways in which eBay is different from the more traditional firms. It is not limited to selling one type of good, and its customers both supply and purchase the goods.

# movers & shakers

## Meg Whitman *CEO, eBay Inc.*

Meg Whitman had not planned to become a business executive. Growing up in Long Island, New York, she longed for a career in the medical field and entered college with medicine on her mind. However, a summer job selling advertising sparked an interest in business, and she returned to college after summer break, declaring herself an economics major. Two years after earning her economics degree from Princeton University, she graduated from Harvard Business School with an MBA. The next 20 years included stints at some of the most prestigious companies in the world: Procter & Gamble, Walt Disney Company, Stride Rite Corporation, Florists Transworld Delivery (FTD), and Hasbro Inc.

In 1998, while overseeing global marketing for Mr. Potato Head and Playskool brands at Hasbro, Whitman received an offer that would change her life. Would she be interested in running a tiny online auction company? She eventually said "yes" and has been CEO of eBay Inc. ever since. When she began her new position, eBay was a haven for Beanie Baby buyers and collectors. Today, eBay is on track to host more than $20 billion in gross annual sales of everything from cars to laptops to farm equipment.

Whitman considers eBay "a small economy," meaning it's a place where 62 million registered members meet each day to do business. These members, not eBay, control pricing for the items for sale on the web site. "If prices go up in a category, then sellers automatically bring more product to the marketplace. If prices are headed down, then sellers automatically reduce the amount of product they have because they're only willing to sell products at a certain price."

Although she's CEO, in some respects Whitman feels totally powerless over her company. "It's not something we can manage," she explains. "Our users are on to the next idea, the next hot thing, faster than we could ever be as a company. It's the millions of entrepreneurs who maximize their own business on eBay, which in turn maximizes the economy."

Whitman's passion for her customers drives the company's success. Some make their living on eBay. She refers to eBay customers as her partners and is eager for their feedback, which comes in the form of 100 to 500 e-mails a day. This feedback drives her decision making. For example, when a group of craftswomen in Guatemala wanted to trade their products on eBay, Whitman traveled to the country to meet with them. She also arranged to help install the technology needed in their village to make trading possible. This gesture demonstrates Whitman's belief in the company's stated mission "to provide a global trading platform where practically anyone can trade practically anything." She has further spread this mission by establishing global sites in 21 countries including Korea, Argentina, Singapore, and Taiwan.

### SOURCE READING

Meg Whitman indicates eBay's stated mission is "to provide a global trading platform where practically anyone can trade practically anything." How does this mission serve developing countries? How does Whitman's passion for the customer help carry out this mission?

### ENTREPRENEURS IN ACTION

In what ways are Meg Whitman's business practices and philosophy similar to those of other entrepreneurs? In what ways is eBay different from a more traditional firm that produces and sells goods and services?

**596**    **CHAPTER 19**   Economic Development

## Extend the Content

Late in 2003, eBay found a new product—information about the selling prices of goods and services actually purchased through its site. People want to know the value of items, even when they have no intention of selling. For example, suppose you inherited an antique silver tray and you want to know the value for insurance purposes. By paying eBay a small fee, you can find out the selling prices of similar trays in recent online auctions. Or, if you decided to donate an heirloom clock to a museum, how would you know how much to deduct on your income tax return? Again, you can check with eBay. Businesses that find new ways to serve consumers' needs are likely to be successful.

# Foreign Trade, Foreign Aid, and Economic Development

## Objectives

> Identify two foreign-trade strategies and assess their impact on economic development.

> Assess the impact of foreign aid on economic development.

## Overview

Higher labor productivity and a higher standard of living go hand in hand. To boost labor productivity, developing countries must trade with developed countries to acquire the best capital and the latest technology. This deepening of capital will increase labor productivity on the farm, in the factory, in the office, and in the home. To import capital and technology, developing countries first must acquire the foreign exchange needed to pay for them. Exports usually generate more than half of the annual flow of foreign exchange in developing countries. Foreign aid and private investment make up the rest.

## Key Terms

import substitution

export promotion

brain drain

foreign aid

bilateral aid

multilateral aid

U.S. Agency for International Development (USAID)

## FOCUS

**Foreign Trade, Foreign Aid, and Economic Development**

Point out that industrial market economies support efforts to help developing countries increase production and improve the standards of living. In addition, governments of developing countries have implemented policies intended to speed their growth. Many of the efforts that have been made in the past have not been particularly successful, for a variety of reasons.

### Objectives

Remind students to read the lesson objectives to help focus their attention before reading the lesson.

### Key Terms

Direct students to create a database using the key terms for this lesson. The database fields should include terms, definitions, and page numbers. Point out that the process of keying the data is an effective way to study key terms.

### [ In the News ]

Instruct students to read the passage and write down their answers. Point out that their answers might change after they finish studying Lesson 19.2.

### Answers to Think About It

Answers will vary. Possible answer: The leaders of developing countries are reluctant to discuss the rights of workers because they need the employment opportunities in their country regardless of the labor wage and labor rights that are offered. If the labor does not go to their country, it will end up in some other developing country.

### Visual Presentation

Use the PowerPoint presentation on the Instructor's Resource CD as an adjunct to your lecture. The presentation also can be used for review.

## [ In the News ]

### ● Protests Against the WTO

In recent years, most major meetings of World Trade Organization (WTO) leaders have been met with angry protests. One of the most violent clashes occurred at the 1999 WTO meeting in Seattle, Washington. More than 50,000 protestors disrupted the city, more than 500 were arrested, and about $3 million in property was damaged. The violent protestors mainly targeted multinational corporations, smashing windows at Starbucks, McDonald's, Nike Town, and Old Navy, and burning khakis in front of the Gap. The Seattle protests marked the largest demonstration against free trade ever held in the United States. It brought together protestors with a variety of worries. Many expressed concerns that industrialized nations were exploiting workers and the environment in developing countries. Yet, the United States and European WTO members have pushed the hardest to protect workers around the world. In contrast, the leaders of many developing countries, including Mexico, Egypt, India, and Pakistan, have objected even to discussing labor rights. These poorer nations are most concerned that the tradable items they produce are not getting onto the markets of richer countries quickly enough. Many developing countries view attempts to impose labor and environmental standards as efforts to keep them poor. International groups like the WTO provide a forum for discussing labor and environmental issues around the world. The reality is that working conditions, especially in poor countries, are improving, thanks to trade opportunities along with pressure for labor rights from the WTO and other international groups.

### Think About It

Why do you think the leaders of developing countries are reluctant to discuss the rights of workers?

◄ | ▶

597

## National Content Standards in Economics

A complete list of the NCEE Standards appears on pages xxiv–xxv of this book. The following standards are addressed in Lesson 19.2.

Standard 3: Allocation of Goods and Services

Standard 4: Role of Incentives

Standard 5: Gain from Trade

Standard 6: Specialization and Trade

Standard 10: Role of Economic Institutions

Standard 15: Growth

Standard 16: Role of Government

Standard 17: Using Cost/Benefit Analysis to Evaluate Government Programs

Standard 19: Unemployment and Inflation

## Foreign Trade and Migration

Point out that import substitution and export promotion are programs that have been implemented by developing countries to try to speed economic growth. Import substitution takes place when a country places trade barriers against specific types of imports that it then works to produce itself. This has the advantage of offering a chance to produce in a proven market. It does not earn foreign exchange and can lead to retaliation by other countries. Export promotion is a policy that is intended to expand production in areas where a country is likely to possess a natural or potential comparative advantage. By assisting firms in these areas with investment in physical and human capital, the governments attempt to compete with foreign producers. This policy has the advantage of earning foreign exchange that can then be invested in other forms of production. In general, the record has shown export promotion has enjoyed greater success than import substitution.

### SPAN THE GLOBE

Direct students to read the short passage "Enforcing Trade Restrictions" on page 601. Use the Think Critically as a starting point for class discussion.

### Answers to Think Critically

Answers will vary. Possible answer: It is difficult to enforce the quotas or tariffs they impose on imports from certain countries because these imports can go through intermediary countries to get around the restrictions.

### TEAM WORK

Instruct students to complete the **Team Work** assignment on this page.

---

# Foreign Trade and Migration

What is the role of international trade in economic development? The least-developed economies rely on farming and on natural resources, such as wild game, timber, and mining. Economic development usually involves a shift from agricultural products and raw materials to manufacturing more complex products. If a country is fortunate, this transformation occurs gradually through natural market forces. Sometimes government pushes along the shift. How quickly an economy develops a manufacturing base depends on its trade relations with the rest of the world.

## Import Substitution

Many developing countries, including Argentina and India, have pursued a trade policy called **import substitution**, whereby the country manufactured products that until then had been imported. Often the packaging and even the name of the product were quite similar to the import, such as "Crust" toothpaste instead of "Crest" toothpaste. To insulate domestic producers from foreign competition, the

**import substitution**

A development strategy that emphasizes domestic manufacturing of products that are currently imported

**export promotion**

A development strategy that concentrates on producing for the export market

### TEAM WORK

In groups of six or eight students, debate the pros and cons of the import substitution trade strategy versus the export promotion strategy. Divide the group into two smaller groups. One group will represent import substitution and the other, export promotion. Spend about 10 minutes in your small groups, studying the textbook in preparation for the debate. Start the debate by presenting your group's strategy to the other group. Then debate the effectiveness of the strategies.

government usually imposed tariffs, import quotas, or other trade restrictions.

Import substitution became a popular development strategy for several reasons.

**1.** Demand already existed for these products, so the "what to produce" question was easily answered.

**2.** By reducing imports, the approach addressed a common problem among developing countries—the shortage of foreign exchange.

**3.** Import substitution was popular with those who supplied labor, capital, and other resources to the protected domestic industries.

Like all protection measures, however, import substitution wiped out the gains from specialization and comparative advantage among countries. Often the developing country replaced low-cost foreign goods with high-cost domestic goods. Domestic producers, insulated from foreign competition, usually failed to become efficient. They often produced goods of inferior quality, compared to the imports they replaced.

Even the balance-of-payments picture did not improve, because other countries typically retaliated with their own trade restrictions. Import substitution protected some domestic industries but hurt consumers with higher prices and lower quality.

## Export Promotion

Critics of the import-substitution approach claim that export promotion is a surer path to economic development. **Export promotion** is a development strategy that focuses on producing for the export market. This approach begins with relatively simple products, such as textiles. As a developing country builds its educational and technological base, producers can then export more complex products.

Economists favor export promotion over import substitution because the emphasis is on comparative advantage and trade expansion, rather than trade

---

### Outside Resources

**U.S. Agency for International Development (USAID)** This agency provides economic and humanitarian assistance throughout the world. The USAID web site provides descriptions of major programs and answers to frequently asked questions. It explains how various USAID programs work and includes links to related web sites. Direct students to visit the web site at www.usaid.gov and click on one of the features. Instruct students to read the selected feature and create a sentence outline of the contents.

restriction. Export promotion also forces producers to become more efficient in order to compete in world markets. Research shows that global competition increases domestic efficiency. What's more, export promotion requires less government intervention in the market than does import substitution.

Export promotion has been the more successful development strategy. For example, the newly industrialized "Asian Tigers" (Taiwan, South Korea, Hong Kong, and Singapore) have grown much more quickly than import-substituting countries such as Argentina, India, and Peru.

Most Latin American nations, which for decades favored import substitution, are now pursuing free-trade agreements with the United States. Even India is in the process of dismantling trade barriers, especially for high-technology capital goods such as computer chips. Trade barriers in India still are in place for many consumer goods. When it comes to imports, one slogan of Indian trade officials is "Microchips, yes! Potato chips, no!"

## International Migration

International migration also affects developing economies. Because unemployment and underemployment are high in developing countries, job opportunities are better in industrial economies. This is a big reason why people in poorer countries try to move to richer countries. Some Mexicans, for example, risk their lives trying to get to the United States.

A major source of foreign exchange in some developing countries is the money sent home by migrants who find jobs in industrial countries. For example, Salvadorans working in the United States account for a significant chunk of spending power in El Salvador. In fact, the Salvadoran economy now uses the U.S. dollar as legal tender alongside its own currency. Thus, migration provides a valuable safety valve for poor countries.

There is a downside to migration, however. Sometimes the best and the brightest professionals, such as doctors, nurses, and engineers, migrate from developing to industrial countries. Because human capital is such a key resource, this **brain drain** hurts the developing economy in the long run.

**brain drain**
A developing country's loss of educated migrants to industrial market countries

### CHECKPOINT
What are two foreign trade strategies, and what is the impact of each on economic development?

Nearly 30 million of the 105 million people of Mexico live in Mexico City. Since 1980, the population of that city has just about doubled. Many of these people have come to Mexico City from rural areas in Mexico. What, if anything, do you think this has to do with the migration of Mexicans to the United States?

© Getty Images/PhotoDisc

## Foreign Trade and Migration

Provide the information in the table shown below.

### Indexes of Hourly Compensation for Production Workers

|  | 1980 | 1990 | 2000 |
|---|---|---|---|
| United States | 100 | 100 | 100 |
| Canada | 88 | 107 | 81 |
| Mexico | 22 | 11 | 12 |
| Hong Kong | 15 | 22 | 28 |
| Japan | 56 | 86 | 111 |
| South Korea | 10 | 25 | 41 |
| Taiwan | 10 | 26 | 30 |

*Source: Statistical Abstract of the United States, 2002, p. 850, Table No. 1354.*

Using the data for 2000, explain that for every $100 earned by a production worker in the United States, a similar worker in the Canada earns $81. Ask students where they would live if they had a choice. What other information should they consider before they make this choice? (They should consider the costs of living in these countries.)

### *Think Critically Through Visuals*

Direct students to focus their attention on the photograph on this page. Ask for a volunteer to answer the question posed in the caption.

### Answer

Answers will vary. Possible answers: People in rural Mexico seemed to be interested in moving to cities and towns in hopes of finding employment. Some people seek employment within Mexico's borders, and others come to the United States.

### CHECKPOINT
Invite a student to answer the checkpoint that appears on this page.

### Answer

Two foreign trade strategies are import substitution and export promotion. Import substitution is where the country manufactures products that had previously been imported. Import substitution wipes out the gains that are attained from specialization and comparative advantage. Export promotion focuses on producing for the export market. Here, the focus is on comparative advantage and trade expansion.

## ENRICH

Many developing countries spend a large part of the foreign currencies they earn for imported luxury goods and services. Swiss watchmakers, for example, reported in 2003 that more than 10 percent of their world sales of expensive watches (priced at over $2,000 each) were made to individuals who live in Middle Eastern countries. The population of these countries constitute just over 2 percent of the world's total population. These sales were only slightly less than sales of expensive imported watches in the United States. Why do students believe many luxury items are sold to people in developing countries? What impact may these sales have on these countries' ability to grow? (Funds spent on luxury goods and services cannot be spent on imported tools that could be used to expand production.)

## Foreign Aid

Point out that foreign aid takes many forms, including money, capital goods, technical assistance, and food. In theory, providing these things to developing countries should be helpful but, in reality, it is some times difficult to extend aid that only helps and does no harm. Another problem with foreign aid efforts involves the diversion of aid by government officials and others away from the people and businesses most in need.

### THE WALL STREET JOURNAL

**Reading It Right**

Invite a student to explain the relevance of the statement from *The Wall Street Journal* that appears on this page.

**Answer**

Answers will vary. Possible answer: The improvement of Brazil's economy offers proof that IMF policies are effective and may help that institution's reputation in the South American region.

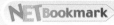

Direct students to **econxtra.swlearning.com**. Remind them to click on the link for Lesson 19.2 to find the appropriate link for the **NET Bookmark** on this page. Consider asking students to create a tabletop display using the information they have gathered about a country. Have half the students stand by their displays and act as economics experts while the other students tour the displays as if on an economic fact-finding mission. Switch roles and repeat the display activities.

### CHECKPOINT

Invite a student to answer the checkpoint that appears on page 601.

**Answer**

It is not clear whether foreign aid adds to national savings, thus increasing investment, or simply substitutes for national savings, thereby increasing consumption rather than investment. What is clear is that foreign aid often benefits not so much the poor, but government officials who decide how to allocate the funds.

---

*multilateral aid*
Development aid from an organization, such as the World Bank, that gets funds from a group of countries

*foreign aid*
An international grant or a loan made on especially favorable terms to promote economic development

*U.S. Agency for International Development (USAID)*
The federal agency that coordinates foreign aid to the developing world

*bilateral aid*
Development aid from one country to another

---

# Foreign Aid

Because poor countries do not generate enough savings to fund an adequate level of investment, these countries often rely on foreign sources of financial capital. What is the role of foreign aid in economic development?

## What Is Foreign Aid?

**Foreign aid** is any international transfer made on especially favorable terms, for the purposes of promoting economic development. Foreign aid includes grants, which need not be repaid. It also includes loans extended on more favorable terms than the recipient could receive otherwise. These loans have lower interest rates, longer repayment periods, and sometimes are wiped off the books entirely. Foreign aid can take the form of money, capital goods, technical assistance, food, and others.

Some foreign aid is granted by one country, such as the United States, to another country, such as the Philippines. Country-to-country aid is called **bilateral aid**. Other foreign aid goes through inter-national bodies, such as the World Bank. Assistance provided by organizations that get funds from a number of countries is called **multilateral aid**. For example, the *World Bank* provides grants and loans to benefit development. This includes aid for health and education programs or for basic infrastructure projects like dams, roads, and communications networks. The *International Monetary Fund* extends loans to countries that have trouble with their balance of payments.

During the last four decades, the United States has provided more than $400 billion to aid developing countries. Most U.S. aid has been coordinated by the **U.S. Agency for International Development (USAID)**, which is part of the U.S. State Department. Its mission is

1. to further America's foreign policy interests in expanding democracy and free markets, and

2. to improve living standards in the developing world.

USAID concentrates primarily on health, education, and agriculture. It provides both technical assistance and loans.

Foreign aid is a controversial, though relatively small, part of the federal budget. In the last decade, official U.S. aid has been less than 0.2 percent of U.S. GDP, compared to an average of 0.3 percent of GDP in aid given by other advanced industrial nations.

## Does Foreign Aid Promote Economic Development?

In general, foreign aid provides additional purchasing power to the country that receives it. It's not clear whether foreign aid *adds* to national saving, thus increasing investment, or simply *substitutes* for national saving, thereby increasing consumption rather than investment.

What is clear is that foreign aid often benefits not so much the poor as government officials, who decide how to allocate the funds. More than 90 percent of the funds distributed by USAID has been dispersed by local governments. There is reason to believe that much

### THE WALL STREET JOURNAL

**Reading It Right** What's the relevance of the following statement from *The Wall Street Journal*: "The prospect of Brazil emerging from economic recession offers a bright spot for the IMF in a troubled region that largely resents the fund's traditional prescription of budget austerity and free markets."

Access the International Monetary Fund's web site through econxtra.swlearning.com. Click on Country Info, and then click on the same country you researched for Net Bookmark in Lesson 19.1. Read several articles about the IMF's involvement in that country. Then write a paragraph describing that involvement.

*econxtra.swlearning.com*

---

*Economic Headlines*

Instruct students to locate an article in a current magazine or newspaper that relates to one of the topics in this lesson. For example, they might find articles about "brain drain" or foreign aid. Instruct students to read the article, write a brief summary, and include a reference citation. Identify the style you want them to use for the citation.

As an alternative, you might find several articles of interest and provide citations for students to use in locating one of the articles. Direct students to read the article they have chosen and write a brief explanation of how it relates to this lesson.

of this aid has been diverted from its intended purpose by government officials in recipient nations.

Much bilateral funding is tied to purchases of goods and services from the donor nation, and such programs can sometimes be counterproductive. For example, in the 1950s, the United States began the Food for Peace program, which required recipient nations to purchase food from the United States. Although this helped sell U.S. farm products abroad, it did little to help these nations develop their own agricultures. It also did not help them to become less dependent on imported food. Worse yet, the availability of low-priced food drove down farm prices in the developing countries, hurting farmers there.

Foreign aid may have raised the standard of living in some developing countries. However, it has not necessarily increased their ability to become self-supporting at that higher standard of living. Many countries that receive aid are doing less of what they had done well. Their agricultural sectors have suffered. For example, per capita food production in Africa has fallen since 1960. Much of this decline is the result of civil wars, the HIV/AIDs epidemic, and the end of colonization.

Because of disappointment with the results of government aid, the trend is now toward channeling funds through private nonprofit agencies such as CARE. More than half of all foreign aid now goes through private channels. The privatization of foreign aid matches a larger trend toward privatization of state enterprises around the world. This important development is discussed later in this chapter.

**CHECKPOINT**
What has been the impact of foreign aid on economic development?

# SPAN THE GLOBE

## Enforcing Trade Restrictions

Many countries impose trade restrictions in the form of quotas or tariffs on goods that come into their country. These restrictions usually serve to prevent foreign countries from flooding their markets with cheap goods that compete with domestic producers of the same goods. Sometimes this can lead to a trade war, in which one country responds to another's trade restrictions by imposing restrictions of its own. In 2000, Korea and China engaged in a trade war after Korea imposed a tariff on Chinese garlic. The Chinese responded by banning the importation of Korean-made mobile telephones and petrochemicals. A year later, Japan and China entered into a similar conflict when Japan imposed quotas on three Chinese farm products—string onions, shiitake mushrooms, and the grass used to make a popular Japanese mat. Two months later, China cut Japanese car imports by half. In addition to the dangers of trade wars, enforcing trade restrictions can be very time consuming and expensive. Many countries try to find creative ways to get around those restrictions. For instance, if Country A allows a more generous quota to some countries than to others, exporters in countries under tight controls sometimes will ship their goods through Country A. For example, because Nepal is not subject to a U.S. clothing quota but India is, India ships clothing to the United States through Nepal. To get around U.S. quotas on sugar imports, Brazil exports molasses to Canada, from where it is then brought into the United States without a quota.

### Think Critically

Why is it difficult for countries to enforce the quotas or tariffs they impose on imports from certain countries?

## APPLY

Assign Lesson 19.2 from the Contemporary Economics Workbook.

## e-con @pps

Encourage students to apply their knowledge of concepts presented in this lesson as they explore economic news stories, policy debates, and data available at **econxtra.swlearning.com**. A sampling of the titles for this lesson appears below.

### EconDebate
- Do slave redemption programs reduce the problem of slavery?
- Does dollarization benefit developing countries?
- Does the anti-sweatshop movement help or harm workers in low-wage economies?

### EconNews
- Bad Czech Banks
- Banking on Big Trouble in China
- China, Communist or Capitalistic?
- Grading the IMF and World Bank
- How Do Some Spell Relief? Lower Debt

## ASSESS

Assign all or part of Lesson 19.2 Assessment on page 602 as homework or an in-class activity.

## Xtra! Study Tools

Direct students to the online study tools for Lesson 19.2 at **econxtra.swlearning.com**.

## CLOSE

**Revisit** the In the News feature on the first page of the lesson. Ask students to review their preliminary answers and discuss the questions, now that they have completed this lesson.

**Review** the objectives for Lesson 19.2. Students should be able to:
- Identify two foreign-trade strategies and assess their impact on economic development.
- Assess the impact of foreign aid on economic development.

## RETEACH

Remind students that even well-intentioned foreign aid programs can be a mixed blessing for people who live in developing countries. During the 1960s and 1970s, for example, some U.S. foreign assistance was spent helping countries in Southeast Asia construct roads. While this might seem to be a positive act for development, it facilitated the cutting of rain forests in many countries. Ask students to try to imagine aid programs that would bring about only good results. Can they come up with any examples? Why is it often hard to help countries develop?

## Key Concepts

1. Answers will vary. Possible answer: This was not an example of import substitution because the U.S. government did not impose restrictive tariffs or quotas to prevent Japanese automobiles from being imported to this country.

2. Answers will vary. Possible answer: Although these people will not be available to work in their home economies, they will probably send money to their relatives. This will improve their standards of living and may help them become more productive.

3. Answers will vary. Possible answer: If all people were provided with enough food for free, they would have little reason to purchase additional food from local farmers, who would then have no reason to produce. Foreign aid can harm a developing country's economy if it drives entrepreneurs in that country out of business.

4. Answers will vary. Possible answer: Guaranteed prices would assure producers in developing countries that they can earn a profit and encourage them to take the risk to increase their production of goods and services.

## Graphing Exercise

5. Answers will vary. Possible answer: The amount of assistance sent to the Near East and South Asia includes support provided by the United States to Israel, Egypt, and other countries that are working to achieve a peaceful settlement to issues in that region. The steady decline in assistance to Africa may reflect an end to apartheid in South Africa and an increase in military conflicts. The decline in assistance to Eastern Europe may have been caused by the success of these countries in shifting from socialist to market economies that required less aid.

   An example of an acceptable graph appears at the bottom of this page.

*The Answer Key is continued on page 612.*

---

Xtra!
**Study Tools**
*econxtra.swlearning.com*

## Key Concepts

1. In the 1980s, many U.S. automobile manufacturers introduced smaller, more fuel-efficient cars to compete with the flood of small Japanese cars that many consumers were buying. Was this an example of import substitution? Explain your answer.

2. How may developing countries be both harmed and helped when their people migrate to industrial market economies to obtain employment?

3. If the United States sent every person in a developing country enough food to eat for free, what would happen to farmers in that country? Why can foreign aid be a mixed blessing?

4. Why do some leaders in developing countries argue that the most effective aid they could receive would be a guarantee from industrial market economies that they will purchase imports from these countries at prices that allow their producers to earn a profit?

## Graphing Exercise

5. The United States provides foreign aid though grants and loans to many developing countries. The amount given, however, is not constant or equally distributed among nations or regions. Construct a multiple bar graph using data in the table to show how U.S. foreign assistance was provided between 1994 and 2000. What reasons can you think of that might explain changes in how this aid was awarded?

**U.S. Foreign Assistance Provided Through Grants and Loans, 1994–2000 (Values in Millions of Dollars)**

| Region | 1994 | 1996 | 1998 | 2000 |
|---|---|---|---|---|
| Africa | $2,031 | $1,957 | $1,366 | $1,033 |
| Near East & South Asia | $7,042 | $7,666 | $5,045 | $7,669 |
| Eastern Europe | $2,910 | $1,957 | $1,790 | $1,818 |
| Western Hemisphere | $1,005 | $ 511 | $1,033 | $1,167 |

Source: *Statistical Abstract of the United States*, 2002, pp. 788–790.

## Think Critically

6. **History** After World War II, the United States provided nearly $12 billion worth of assistance through the Marshall Plan to help the nations of Western Europe rebuild from the war. This effort was a great success. Between 1948 and the end of 1952, the nations of Western Europe increased their collective GDPs by well over 100 percent. What advantages did these nations have in rebuilding that are not shared by developing countries today?

**602** CHAPTER 19 Economic Development

---

**U.S. Foreign Assistance Provided Through Grants and Loans, 1994 to 2000**

Millions

| | |
|---|---|
| $8,000 | |
| $7,000 | |
| $6,000 | |
| $5,000 | |
| $4,000 | |
| $3,000 | |
| $2,000 | |
| $1,000 | |
| 0 | |

1994    1996    1998    2000

■ Africa    ■ Near East & South Asia    □ East Europe    ■ Western Hemisphere

## Visualizing the Answer— Graphing Exercise

5. The answer includes a graph. Students' graphs should look similar to the one shown here. An Excel spreadsheet containing this graph, along with supporting data, is available on the Instructor's Resource CD.

# Rules of the Game, Transition Economies, and Convergence

## Objectives

> Assess the impact of a nation's physical infrastructure and rules of the game on its economic development.

> Discuss why many centrally planned economies are trying, with difficulty, to introduce market forces.

> Explain convergence theory, and discuss why the reality has not yet matched the theory's prediction.

## Overview

Economic systems are classified based on the ownership of resources, the way resources are allocated to produce goods and services, and the incentives used to motivate people. Laws regarding resource ownership and the role of government in resource allocation determine the "rules of the game"—the incentives and constraints that guide the behavior of individual decision makers. Resources in centrally planned economies are owned mostly by the government and are allocated by central planners. Resources in market economies are owned mostly by individuals and are allocated through market coordination. Regardless of the economic system, economic development depends on establishing a trusted, reliable, and fair framework for productive activity.

## Key Terms

**physical infrastructure**

**soft budget constraint**

**privatization**

**convergence theory**

Explain that many developing countries lack basic infrastructure that is needed for rapid economic growth. They also often lack political stability that would encourage people to invest in greater production. Political instability encourages people to take rather than produce. In this environment, those who possess resources, financial or otherwise, are likely to try to move them to other countries that offer greater stability—most often countries that have industrial market economies. And yet, there is movement throughout the world toward allowing markets to operate more freely to allocate resources. Efforts are being made that may one day result in a convergence of economies.

### Objectives

Remind students to read the lesson objectives to help focus their attention before reading the lesson.

### Key Terms

Direct students use each of the key terms in a separate sentence or short paragraph that helps demonstrate the meaning of the term.

## [ In the News ]

### ● Africa Reaches Out to the Internet

In June 2000, African business leaders met in Sun City, South Africa, for their annual African Computing and Telecom Summit (ACT). In 1994, only one country in sub-Saharan Africa had Internet access. Now virtually all African countries are connected. During the annual ACT conferences, African leaders discuss such challenges as how to expand networking capabilities throughout Africa, protect technology, and encourage new business enterprises. Many African leaders believe the future of their economies depends on the ability to educate students in technology. In the late 1990s, the country of Ghana launched a major effort to expand technology training in schools. In some areas, they even bus students from rural schools to computer centers in central areas. In 1998, Ghana had only about 100,000 telephone lines for 18 million people. The government privatized the telecommunications industry in order to encourage the creation of more lines. To encourage Internet use, the government set up free Internet centers at post offices and other public places.

### Think About It

Why do you think African leaders believe technology training will lead to economic development in their countries?

◀ ▮ ▶

**603**

### [ In the News ]

Instruct students to read the passage and write down their answers. Point out that their answers might change after they finish studying Lesson 19.3.

### Answers to Think About It

Answers will vary. Possible answer: African leaders believe that technology training will lead to economic development because it provides business opportunities and resources for knowledge growth.

### Visual Presentation

Use the PowerPoint presentation on the Instructor's Resource CD as an adjunct to your lecture. The presentation also can be used for review.

### National Content Standards in Economics

**NCEE** A complete list of the NCEE Standards appears on pages xxiv–xxv of this book. The following standards are addressed in Lesson 19.3.

Standard 1: Scarcity

Standard 3: Allocation of Goods and Services

Standard 5: Gain from Trade

Standard 7: Markets—Price and Quantity Determination

Standard 10: Role of Economic Institutions

Standard 13: Role of Resources in Determining Income

Standard 15: Growth

Standard 16: Role of Government

Standard 17: Using Cost/Benefit Analysis to Evaluate Government Programs

Standard 18: Macroeconomy—Income, Employment, Prices

## Infrastructure and Rules of the Game

Remind students that efficient production requires easy access to physical and human capital. This implies that countries must have good roads, reliable power, navigable rivers and ports, healthy living areas for workers, adequate schools—and the list goes on and on. Before a factory that produces computer microchips can be built and operated, an electric power system must be built. The investment needed to create a basic infrastructure is beyond the capacity of many developing countries. Furthermore, many of these countries have suffered from political instability and internal wars that have destroyed much of the infrastructure they once possessed. This problem will have to be resolved if these countries are to ever escape their cycle of poverty.

 Consider allowing students to work in small groups to complete this assignment. For example, each group could focus on one of the infrastructure categories mentioned in the book. In addition to looking at the infrastructure in your local community, you might ask students to investigate a rural community where infrastructure concerns are different. Other areas to investigate include the small communities surrounding urban areas where growth is putting a strain on the existing infrastructure.

### Think Critically Through Visuals

Direct students to focus their attention on **Figure 19.3—Fixed and Mobile Telephone Lines Per 1,000 Population by Country in 2001**. Point out that in the industrial market economies, there are more phone lines than there are people. For example, in the United States, there are more than 1,100 telephone lines for every 1,000 people.

# Infrastructure and Rules of the Game

Key ingredients for economic development that have not yet been discussed are the physical infrastructure and rules of the game that support the economic system. Whether the system involves central planning or competitive markets, all economies rely on a stable and supportive institutional framework.

## Physical Infrastructure

**physical infrastructure**
Transportation, communication, energy, water, and sanitation systems provided by or regulated by government

Production and exchange rely on the economy's **physical infrastructure**, which are transportation, communication, energy, water, and sanitation systems provided by or regulated by government. Roads, bridges, airports, harbors, and other transportation facilities are vital to production. Reliable mail and phone service along with a steady supply of electricity and water also are essential for advanced production techniques. Imagine how difficult it would be to run even a personal computer if the supply of electricity and phone service was continually interrupted, as is often the case in developing countries.

Think about the physical infrastructure in your area. List the infrastructure categories mentioned in this section of the book on the left side of a sheet of paper. On the right side, place a plus sign (+) next to the categories that seem to be working efficiently and a minus sign (−) next to those that seem to need some attention. For the categories you think need attention, research to find out if the local, state, or federal government has any plans underway for improvement. If they do, write a paragraph describing these plans. If not, write a letter to a political leader describing the problem and asking for their office's help in solving it.

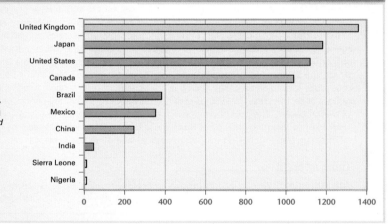

**Fixed and Mobile Telephone Lines Per 1,000 Population by Country in 2001** — **Figure 19.3**

**Many developing countries have serious deficiencies in their physical infrastructures.**

Source: Estimates reported by the World Bank in *World Development Report 2003*, which can be found at econ.worldbank.org/wdr/wdr2003/.

**604**     CHAPTER 19   Economic Development

### Outside Resources

**United Nations** The UN Department of Economic and Social Affairs, Division for Sustainable Development works with developing countries to plan projects and investments that will help them grow without destroying or using an unreasonable amount of their resources. No funds are provided to developing countries, but technical expertise is available at no cost or little cost. This division of the UN also encourages countries to cooperate in development projects. Instruct students to visit the Division for Sustainable Development web site at www.un.org/esa/sustdev to learn about recent development projects that have been facilitated by this organization. Invite students to share their findings with the class.

Many developing countries have serious deficiencies in their physical infrastructures. As just one measure of that infrastructure, Figure 19.3 shows the number of fixed and mobile telephone lines per 1,000 population in 2001 for the 10 countries examined earlier. Note how much greater is the number in the top four countries—which are industrial market economies—compared with the bottom six countries, which are developing economies. The United Kingdom, the top rated in this category, had 1,358 phone lines per 1,000 population. Compared this to only 10 phones lines per 1,000 in Sierra Leone and only 9 per 1,000 in bottom-rated Nigeria.

Worse still for the infrastructure, some of the poorest countries in Africa have been ravaged by internal political strife. For example, civil war raged in Sierra Leone for more than a decade. In Sudan, civil war has been going on for two decades. Wars destroy bridges, roads, electrical systems, water works, and other vital infrastructure. Without these things, efficient production will not take place.

## Rules of the Game

Reliable and trusted rules of the game also are important for economic development. Recall that the rules of the game are the formal and informal institutions that promote production incentives and economic activity. They include the laws, customs, conventions, and other social and political elements that encourage people to undertake productive activity.

On the *formal* end of the spectrum, rules of the game include a country's codified rules and laws, along with the system for establishing and enforcing those rules and laws. On the *informal* end of the spectrum, rules of the game include the customs and informal mechanisms that help coordinate production.

Rules of the game are vital for economic development. When operating properly, they allow people to work, spend, and save to build a better future for themselves and their families. When they are weak, corrupt, or operate

**In the past four years, Egypt has been spending much of its budget on national infrastructure projects. What types of physical infrastructure do you think might be needed in this Egyptian farmers' village?**

unfairly, people lack confidence in the economic system. Weak or corrupt rules of the game also encourage people to "take" rather than "make." This means they may find it easier to steal what others have, rather than to produce something of value themselves. When taking becomes more attractive than making, production declines and incomes fall.

Better incentives can boost productivity and improve the standard of living. For example, a more stable political climate promotes investment in the economy. Conversely, destabilizing events such as wars and terrorist attacks discourage investment, harm productivity, and reduce the standard of living.

 **CHECKPOINT**
What is the impact of a nation's physical infrastructure and rules of the game on its economic development?

## Infrastructure and Rules of the Game

Describe a situation where a dictator has total control in a small developing country. The dictator is rich, and everyone else is poor. Taxes are high, and the dictator uses the funds to build palaces and swimming pools for his family. Ask students to explain why this dictator would work to prevent economic growth. Why might he oppose construction of roads and installation of electric power for the average people? What might happen if a middle class of successful merchants developed? What does this have to do with the seeming inability of some developing countries to actually develop?

*Think Critically Through Visuals*

Direct students to focus their attention on the photograph on this page. Ask for a volunteer to answer the question posed in the caption.

### Answer

Answers will vary. Possible answer: Physical infrastructure needed by Egyptian farmers includes roads, bridges, and water and sanitation systems.

**CHECKPOINT**
Invite a student to answer the checkpoint that appears on this page.

### Answer

Poor physical infrastructure impedes economic development. Rules of the game, a country's codified rules and customs, are vital for economic development. When operating properly, rules of the game allow people to work, spend, and save to build a better future for themselves and their families.

## ENRICH

Many developing countries have asked for a guaranteed market for goods they produce rather than for foreign aid. Coffee growers, for example, argue that the most useful help they could receive would be a guarantee that they could sell their coffee beans at a set price that would allow them to earn a living. It takes seven years for a coffee tree to mature and bear beans. Farmers in developing countries worry that after seven years of work and investment, they won't be able to sell their beans for a profit. As a result, they may choose to grow some other crop instead. Do students believe guaranteed prices would be a reasonable way to extend foreign assistance? What problems might such a program cause? (There could be a giant surplus of coffee beans with this price floor.)

## Economies in Transition

Point out that most countries trying to shift to a market economy share at least one important obstacle—a lack of people who have experience in operating businesses in free market economies. This can be seen in many countries but particularly in the countries that make up the former Soviet Union.

### Ethics in Action

Have students work in pairs to discuss this ethical issue and develop an answer to the question presented in the **Ethics in Action** feature on this page.

#### Answers to **Think Critically**

Answers will vary. Possible answer: The rules of the game that prevented Haiti from achieving economic growth were the corruption of the government and the embezzlement of government funds.

### CHECKPOINT

Invite a student to answer the checkpoint that appears on page 607.

#### Answer

Centrally planned economies are trying to introduce market forces because prices did not allocate products very well in a centrally planned economy. The process has been slow because the centrally planned economies have no history of market interaction. They have no established record of codified law or rules of conduct for market participants.

# Ethics in Action

## When Political Leaders Steal a Country's Money: The Case of Haiti

Developing countries face many difficulties in transitioning into a strong economy. Their ability to succeed depends largely on the strength and stability of their political leadership. In some countries, political leadership has been corrupt to the point that leaders have weakened the economy by stealing from the national treasury. One of the worst cases of such corruption was the experience of Haiti. Haiti had never been a rich country, but it had enjoyed some economic growth in the 1940s and 1950s, thanks to rising prices for the goods it exported. Then, in the 1950s, François Duvalier established a dictatorship. He imposed heavy taxes on the population to fund a powerful army and his own lavish lifestyle. Under his rule, government officials openly stole money from the public treasury for their own use. The harsh regime drove the most talented and skilled people out of the country, leaving only the very poor to suffer under heavy taxes and a draining economy. Haiti soon became the poorest country in the Western Hemisphere, and it fell far behind the rest of the world in economic growth. After Jean-Claude Duvalier took over from his father in 1971, some countries, including the United States, began to give aid money to Haiti. Much of this money was stolen as well. Fed up with government corruption and facing desperate poverty, the Haitian people staged a successful revolt to oust Duvalier in the mid-1980s. Slowly Haiti has started to build a more stable political structure. However, it remains one of the world's poorest countries as a result of years of political greed and economic neglect.

### Think Critically

What "rules of the game" in Haiti under the Duvaliers prevented the country from achieving economic growth?

# Economies in Transition

From the breakup of the Soviet Union to China's move toward freer markets, markets are replacing central plans in countries around the world The attempt to replace central planning with markets is one of the greatest economic experiments in history.

## Prices and Profit in Centrally Planned Economies

Most prices in centrally planned economies are established not by market forces but by central planners. Once set, prices tend to be inflexible. As a result, consumers have less say in what's produced. Consumer goods often are priced below the market-clearing level, so shortages are common. For example, just prior to the collapse of the Soviet Union in 1991, the price of bread had not changed since 1954. That price amounted to only 7 percent of bread's production cost. Some rents had not changed in 60 years. Thus, prices had little relation to supply and demand, and shortages were common.

Evidence of shortages of consumer goods included long waiting lines at retail stores. Shoppers in the former Soviet Union sometimes would wait in line all night and into the next day. Consumers often relied on "connections" through acquaintances to obtain many goods and services. Scarce goods were frequently diverted to the black market, where prices were much higher.

Prices did not allocate products very well in centrally planned economies. To make matters worse, state enterprises faced little pressure to cover costs. With central planning, any "profit" earned by a state enterprise was appropriated by the state. Any "loss" was covered by a state subsidy. Thus, covering costs was not important for a state enterprise. Such enterprises face what has been

**606**     **CHAPTER 19**   Economic Development

### *Economic Headlines*

Instruct students to locate an article in a current magazine or newspaper that relates to one of the topics in this lesson. For example, they might find articles about infrastructure or convergence. Instruct students to read the article, write a brief summary, and include a reference citation. Identify the style you want them to use for the citation.

As an alternative, you might find several articles of interest and provide citations for students to use in locating one of the articles. Direct students to read the article they have chosen and write a brief explanation of how it relates to this lesson.

called a **soft budget constraint**. Managers could ignore market forces, could allocate resources inefficiently, and could make poor investment decisions—yet still survive.

## Privatization

One necessary step in the move from central planning to a market economy is **privatization**, which is the process of turning government enterprises into private enterprises. It is the opposite of *nationalization*, which is turning private enterprises into government enterprises.

The problem is that most centrally planned economies that are trying to privatize have no history of market interaction. They also have no established record of codified law or rules of conduct for market participants. For example, Russian privatization began in 1992 with the sale of municipally owned shops. Most property in countries of the former Soviet Union was owned by the state. Thus, it often remained unclear who had the authority to sell the property and who should receive the proceeds from the sale. This uncertainty resulted in cases in which different buyers purchased the same property from different officials. Yet there was no clear legal process for resolving title disputes to establish property rights. Russia did not have a reliable legal system.

Worse still, self-serving managers stripped some enterprises of their assets. The process of privatization does not work well when the general population perceives it to be unfair.

Thus, establishing a market system is easier said that done. Economists involved in structuring the transition from central planning to market systems are learning as they go. Many centrally planned economies have little experience with laws and customs that are trusted, reliable, and fair.

### CHECKPOINT
Why are centrally planned economies trying to introduce market forces, and what has been slowing down the process?

# Are the World's Economies Converging?

Given enough time, will poor countries eventually catch up with rich ones? The **convergence theory** argues that developing countries can grow faster than advanced ones and should eventually close the gap.

## Reasons for Convergence

Countries that are far behind economically can grow faster by copying existing technology. It is easier to copy new technology once it is developed than to develop that technology in the first place. Advanced economies, which are already using the latest technology, can boost productivity only with a steady stream of technological breakthroughs.

Advanced countries, such as the United States, find their growth limited by the rate of creation of new knowledge and improved technology. Follower countries can grow more quickly by, for instance, adding computers where they previously had none. For example, the United States makes up just 5 percent of the world's population. But in 1995, Americans owned most of the world's personal computers. By 2001, most PC purchases were outside the United States.

## Not Much Convergence

What is the evidence for convergence? Some poor countries have begun to catch up with richer ones. For example, the newly industrialized Asian economies of Hong Kong, Singapore, South Korea, and Taiwan have invested heavily in technology and in education. These Asian Tigers have moved from the ranks of developing countries to the ranks of industrial market economies.

The Asian Tigers are more the exception than the rule. Among the nations that make up the poorest third of the world's population, consumption per capita has grown by an average of only about 1.0 percent per year during the last two decades, compared with a 2.5

**soft budget constraint**
In centrally planned economies, the budget condition faced by state enterprises that are subsidized when they lose money

**privatization**
The process of turning public enterprises into private enterprises

**convergence theory**
A theory predicting that the standard of living in economies around the world will grow more similar over time, with poorer countries gradually closing the gap with richer ones

### Are the World's Economies Converging?

Point out that many countries have experienced difficulties when they tried to privatize enterprises that were once owned by the state. A major problem has been an inability to find a buyer. In the former Soviet Union, the government actually gave all adults 10,000 rubles each that could be used only to invest in businesses. This did little good as people sold these rubles to others for small amounts of money that could be used to purchase food and clothing that were in short supply. The individuals who speculated in these special rubles were able to purchase some of the government facilities, but the process was so flawed and corrupt that many people turned against the system. A modern competitive market economy does not just happen. It is developed over many years and is something that needs the support of its people. There hasn't been much successful convergence of economic systems in the world to date.

## *Group Activity*

Organize students into groups of four or five. Instruct the groups to spend 15 minutes setting up rules and policies for employees of the enterprise described below. After 15 minutes, have a spokesperson for each group explain the rules and policies developed by the group. Have the class decide on a final set of rules. Ask students why they can't they be sure of success.

You are the owners of a furniture factory in the former Soviet Union that has recently been privatized. You have 500 employees who know how to make quality furniture, but the quality of current output is unacceptable. In addition to poor quality, other areas of concern are insubordination, absenteeism, tardiness, substance abuse, breakage, and theft. There is no pool of skilled workers that could replace the current employees. Workers argue that they are not being paid a living wage and that no one pays attention to their concerns.

**Growth**

Singapore, one of the so-called Asian Tigers, is a highly developed and successful free market economy. *Due to investments in factories, machinery, new technology, and in the health, education, and training of people, the population of Singapore enjoys a high standard of living.* The country boasts one of the highest per capita GDPs in the world. Singapore is an island country. How has this helped Singapore to successfully develop its economy?

percent average growth in the rest of the world. Therefore, while the standard of living in the poorest third of the world has improved, that living standard has fallen further behind the rest of the world.

### Higher Birth Rates and Less Human Capital

One reason per-capita consumption has grown so slowly in the poorest economies is that birth rates there are double those in richer countries. Therefore, poor economies must produce still more just to keep up with a growing population. Another reason why convergence has not taken hold, particularly for the poorest third of the world, is the vast difference in the amount of human capital across countries. Whereas

technology is indeed portable from industrial economies to developing economies, the knowledge, skill, and training usually required to take advantage of that technology are not portable.

Some poor countries, such as most of those in Africa, simply do not have the human capital needed to identify and absorb new technology. Consider personal computers. Figure 19.4 shows the number of personal computers per 1,000 people in 2001 for the 10 nations examined earlier. Notice how many more PCs the top four countries, which are industrial market economies, have than the bottom six, which are developing economies. The United States had 625 PCs per 1,000 people. Sierra Leone had only one PC per 1,000 people.

As already noted, poor economies tend to have low education levels and

## Curriculum Connection—Social Studies

Demography is the study of population trends. As the U.S. population ages, there will be a growing need for labor that can be supplied by people who live in developing countries or who immigrate to the United States. Current demographics indicate there will be fewer than three people working for each person who is retired in the United States by 2030. Remember, these people must produce enough goods and services to support themselves as well as the retired population. Do students believe this situation will contribute to a convergence of economies over time? Why or why not?

high illiteracy rates. Those persons who do become well educated often migrate to richer economies. This is part of the brain drain, discussed earlier.

Most developing countries lack the stable institutions needed to nurture economic development. Many developing countries have serious problems with their infrastructures. For example, they may lack a reliable source of electricity needed to power new technologies. Some of the poorest nations have been ravaged by civil war for years.

### Reasons for Optimism

Despite all that, working conditions in most poor countries are improving, thanks to greater trade opportunities and pressure from international bodies such as the World Trade Organization. For example, Cambodia is extremely poor, but the highest wages in the country are earned by the 1 percent of the population working in the export sector. This tiny group makes products for companies such as Nike and Gap. Though pay is low by U.S. standards, workers in the export sector earn more than twice what judges and doctors average in Cambodia. Child labor is still a problem in poor countries, but most children work on family farms. Because of world pressure on manufacturers, fewer and fewer children are working in factories.

The reduction in trade barriers resulting from the Uruguay Round, the latest round of trade negotiations, is projected to boost world income by more than $500 billion in 2005, the target date for full implementation. This amounts to an increase of about $400 for each household on Earth. That payoff may not impress those who object to greater globalization through freer trade, but for households in some poor countries, it can be a lifesaver.

**CHECKPOINT**
What does the convergence theory predict, and why hasn't the reality yet matched that prediction?

---

**Personal Computers Per 1,000 Population by Country in 2001**　　　**Figure 19.4**

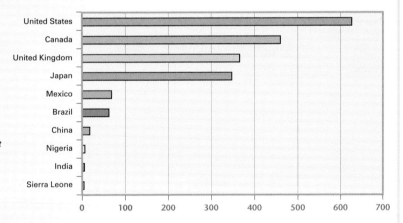

Some poor countries simply do not have the human capital needed to identify and absorb new technology.

Source: Estimates from the *World Bank in World Development Report 2003*, which can be found at econ.worldbank.org/wdr/wdr2003/.

Lesson 19.3 • *Rules of the Game, Transition Economies, and Convergence*　　　**609**

---

**APPLY**

Assign Lesson 19.3 from the Contemporary Economics Workbook.

### e-con @pps

Encourage students to apply their knowledge of concepts presented in this lesson as they explore economic news stories, policy debates, and data available at **econxtra.swlearning.com**. A sampling of the titles for this lesson appears below.

#### EconDebate
- Does globalization require a change in antitrust policy?
- Will the European monetary union succeed?

#### EconNews
- Trouble Ahead?

**ASSESS**

Assign all or part of Lesson 19.3 Assessment on page 610 as homework or an in-class activity.

### Xtra! Study Tools

Direct students to the online study tools for Lesson 19.3 at **econxtra.swlearning.com**.

**CLOSE**

**Revisit** the In the News feature on the first page of the lesson. Ask students to review their preliminary answers and discuss the questions, now that they have completed this lesson.

**Review** the objectives for Lesson 19.3. Students should be able to:
- Assess the impact of a nation's physical infrastructure and rules of the game on its economic development.
- Discuss why many centrally planned economies are trying, with difficulty, to introduce market forces.
- Explain convergence theory, and discuss why the reality has not yet matched the theory's prediction.

---

**RETEACH**

Many U.S. residents have complained in recent years that more and more U.S. jobs are being outsourced to people who live and work in developing countries. Workers who live in India often answer telephone calls made by Americans seeking tech support. Workers in Indonesia assemble air conditioners used to cool American homes. Cents-off coupons redeemed in grocery stores in the United States are sorted in countries of the Caribbean. Although this situation can look bad for U.S. workers, from the perspective of foreign workers, it represents a great improvement in their lives. Ask students whether they believe the flow of jobs to developing countries is a sign of economic convergence. Why or why not?

## Key Concepts

1. The firm would find it much more costly to produce and deliver its products, and it might be forced to close. Countries that lack basic physical infrastructure are not able to use resources efficiently to produce manufactured products and therefore are not likely to have a comparative advantage.

2. Having a civil code provides little benefit if there is no justice system to apprehend, try, and punish those who break the laws. Entrepreneurs in countries that lack an efficient justice system are less likely to invest resources to create greater production.

3. People who grew up seeing little relationship between an effort to increase production and personal rewards are unlikely to quickly change their work ethic in a competitive market economy. It will be difficult for entrepreneurs to encourage their employees to make efficient use of resources or to become competitive with businesses in other countries.

4. Letting people own and operate businesses without government interference does not give them the capital or skills needed to be successful. These people require a source of funds and training.

5. These investments have more benefits than costs for people who live in developing countries. Many people in these countries are happy to take jobs offered by businesses owned by wealthy foreign countries because they pay more than other types of employment they could accept. These jobs often provide workers with experience and knowledge that they can then apply to other types of production. At the same time, the funds they earn can be used to purchase capital for new local businesses.

## Graphing Exercise

6. U.S. businesses invest in developing countries because they expect these investments to help them earn a profit. These investments provide jobs and income for workers in these countries and help them earn foreign exchange that can be used to make investments in other productive facilities.
   An example of an acceptable graph appears at the bottom of this page.

*The Answer Key is continued on page 613.*

---

Xtra!
Study Tools
*econxtra.swlearning.com*

## Key Concepts

1. Choose a business in your community that employs many workers. How would this business be affected if suddenly there were no local roads and bridges, electric power, telephone service, water supplies, and waste removal services? Why is a country that lacks basic physical infrastructure unlikely to have a comparative advantage in manufacturing?

2. Many developing countries have created laws to regulate the production of goods and services. Regardless of this fact, many businesses in these nations largely ignore these laws and carry out production as they choose. What do these nations need in addition to their laws? Explain your answer.

3. Why do people who live in nations that once had government ownership and control of businesses often find it difficult to operate in a competitive market economic system?

4. Will giving individuals the right to own and operate businesses without government interference guarantee a nation's smooth transition from a centrally planned to a free market economy? Why or why not? What other conditions need to be created for this to take place?

5. Some people think that investments made in developing countries by businesses from industrial market economies help these nations improve in terms of their production and standards of living. Others think that this investment will not lead to a material improvement in the lives of these people. Which of these points of view do you think is nearest to the truth? Explain your answer.

## Graphing Exercise

6. U.S. businesses invest billions of dollars every year in developing countries. Construct a line graph showing the total accumulated value of U.S. investments in Latin America in the years from 1994 through 2000. Why do businesses make these investments? How do such investments benefit people in Latin America?

**Value of Total U.S. Direct Investments in Latin America, 1994–2000 (Values in Millions of Dollars)**

| Year | Investment | Year | Investment |
|------|-----------|------|-----------|
| 1994 | $116,478 | 1998 | $196,755 |
| 1995 | $131,377 | 1999 | $220,705 |
| 1996 | $155,925 | 2000 | $239,388 |
| 1997 | $180,818 | | |

Source: *Statistical Abstract of the United States,* 2002, p. 788.

## Think Critically

7. **Sociology** You have learned that poverty in the United States is frequently found in households led by single parents. These households often include many young children. In what ways are the problems of these households in the United States similar to those faced by people who live in developing countries? In what ways are their problems different?

---

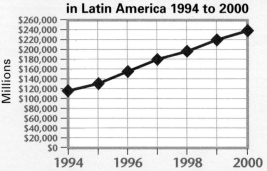

**Value of Total U.S. Direct Investments in Latin America 1994 to 2000**

## Visualizing the Answer— Graphing Exercise

6. The answer includes a graph. Students' graphs should look similar to the one shown here. An Excel spreadsheet containing this graph, along with supporting data, is available on the Instructor's Resource CD.

# CONNECT *to History*

## Tariffs and Trade, Part II

The Reciprocal Trade Agreement Act of 1934 and its 12 extensions through 1962 ushered in an era of tariff reduction worldwide. The Act authorized the U.S. president to negotiate tariffs and give nations "most favored nation status."

In 1947, following World War II, 23 nations negotiated the General Agreement on Tariffs and Trade (GATT). The goal of this agreement was to encourage nations to lower tariffs and other trade barriers. For the United States, lowering tariffs also had a foreign-policy component in helping to rebuild Europe and develop poor nations. While the general principle is for a country to treat all members equally, some exceptions were allowed for developing countries to protect necessary industries. These reductions were tied to a "no injury" clause, which limited the impact of tariff reductions if they were determined to have a negative effect on domestic industries. It also allowed for free-trade areas to be created, such as the European Community and the North American Free Trade Agreement (NAFTA). The first five agreements, or "rounds," were characterized primarily by countries negotiating an agreement on a product for tariff reductions. They would then apply the agreement to all members on a "most favored nation" basis.

During the 1964 Kennedy Round, the United States proposed across-the-board reductions to the 62 member nations. The negotiations, which lasted three years, focused primarily on deciding what items to include. Success was obvious as average tariff rates, which were at 47 percent in 1947, dropped to 9 percent in 1972, and reached 4 percent in 2003. Following the Kennedy Round, discussions began to focus more on non-tariff barriers, such as dumping, subsidized exports, and other exclusionary practices. Most industrialized nations agreed to the provisions that were resisted by developing countries.

By the Uruguay Round (1986–1994), membership in GATT had grown to 123 countries. This round led to the creation of the World Trade Organization (WTO). The WTO now has nearly 150 members, accounting for more than 97 percent of the world's trade. Fifty additional nations are now negotiating membership in the organization.

The WTO operates principally under the rules formed by GATT. Documentation of those rules runs to 50,000 pages and incorporates 30 agreements, called schedules. WTO decisions are not put to a vote. In fact, voting rarely is used under GATT. Decisions typically are made by consensus, and then agreements are ratified by member parliaments.

The system allows countries to bring disputes to the WTO if they believe that their rights or agreements are being infringed. The organization encourages disagreements to be settled by consultation. In the eight years from 1995 to 2003, the WTO had about 300 cases before it. This was about the same number dealt with by GATT from 1947 to 1994.

With 75 percent of its membership consisting of developing countries, the WTO faces huge challenges. The latest round of negotiations (the Doha round, 2001) is scheduled to end in 2005. In the current round of negotiations, developing countries, which typically depend on agriculture for a large portion of their exports, are asking for the elimination of export subsidies. The agricultural sectors in industrialized nations, however, rely on these subsidies to stay afloat. Therefore, ending export subsidies on agricultural goods is difficult for industrialized countries.

### THINK CRITICALLY

Given a world economy, do you think a country can both promote free trade and protect its domestic industries at the same time? What would be the advantages to a country of doing both?

## Bibliography

Carnes, Marc C. *MacMillan Information Now Encyclopedia: U.S. History*. New York: MacMillan Library Reference, 1996.

"The Past, Present and Future of the Multilateral Trading System." *WT Conference Daily*, September 10, 2003.

## CONNECT *to History*

### FOCUS

Remind students that in addition to being domestic political issues, trade and tariffs are often the focus of foreign policy. The international struggle between the "haves" and the "have-nots" manifests itself in trade policy. Many countries must juggle political considerations at home with international considerations. They should understand that although the specifics may change the tension between rich and poor, domestic and international issues will remain.

### TEACH

Instruct students to read the **Connect to History** feature and answer the questions. Encourage students to draw upon their knowledge of American history and what they have learned in this class as they think about any obligations the United States has in dealing with less developed countries. Have them consider the advantages and disadvantages for both countries of the United States opening markets with a developing country.

### ASSESS

Use the questions at the bottom of the page to assess the students' understanding of this feature.

### Answers to Think Critically

Answers will vary. Possible answer: No, a country cannot promote free trade and protect its domestic industries at the same time. If all countries acted in this way, there would be no free trade. Many countries suggest that they do this, although they cannot. President Bush, for example, said he supported free trade in 2002—the same year he imposed a 30 percent tariff on steel imported to the United States. Many countries would like to have free trade for the goods and services through which they enjoy a comparative advantage in production. They would also choose to have barriers to trade to protect domestic firms that produce goods and services that are not competitive in the global market. These positions are fundamentally inconsistent.

## Summary

### Consider

Ask students to revisit the questions they were asked to consider at the beginning of the chapter. Remind students that they should be able to answer all of the questions after studying Chapter 19.

- Why are some countries poor while others are rich? See page 588—Developing and Industrial Market Countries.

- What determines the wealth of nations? See page 591—Productivity and Economic Development.

- How much does foreign aid help poorer countries? See page 600—Foreign Aid.

- How does terrorism affect economic development? See page 604—Physical Infrastructure.

- What's the "brain drain," and how does it affect poorer countries? See page 599—International Migration.

- Why are birth rates higher in poorer countries? See page 589—High Birth Rates.

- Are poorer countries catching up with the rest of the world? See page 607—Are the World's Economies Converging?

### Exam *View*

Use ExamView to assess students' learning.

- Create a chapter test using questions from the existing test bank.

- Add your own questions to the existing test bank.

- Generate multiple forms of a chapter test.

### Study Skills

Offer the following study skills suggestions for students as they review this chapter.

- Outline the chapter.
- Review Key Terms.
- Review Checkpoints.
- Work in pairs to quiz each other.
- Use Xtra! Study Tools for each lesson.

Direct students to the online quiz preparation for Chapter 19 at **econxtra.swlearning.com**.

---

 # **19** Chapter Assessment

## Summary

 ### 19.1 *Developing Economies and Industrial Market Economies*

**a** Countries may be classified in a variety of ways based on their levels of economic development. *Developing countries* have lower levels of GDP per capita income and higher rates of illiteracy, unemployment, underemployment, and rapid population growth than *industrial market countries*. They also have relatively short average life expectancies and high birth rates.

**b** Developing countries suffer from low labor productivity. Their workers often lack skills and basic education. Income per capita is low and does not allow individuals to save to make investments in physical capital.

**c** Developing countries have few entrepreneurs who are able to bring together resources and take the risks necessary to develop new and more efficient means of production.

### 19.2 *Foreign Trade, Foreign Aid and Economic Development*

**a** Developing countries have used many techniques to try to speed their economic growth. One method is *import substitution*. This policy places barriers on specific types of imported products that are targeted to be replaced with domestic production. Domestic producers then are able to sell products in a proven market without foreign competition. Another method used to speed growth is *export promotion*. Under this policy, a government provides assistance to businesses targeted for export expansion.

**b** Many people who live in developing countries move to *industrial market economies* each year. This allows them to earn greater incomes, some of which they send home to their friends and relatives. When skilled workers migrate, however, they are no longer able to contribute to production in their native

lands. This movement of skilled workers has been called the *brain drain*.

**c** Countries with industrial markets have attempted to assist developing countries through various programs that encourage investment in human and physical capital. *Foreign aid* has been extended through *bilateral* agreements between individual countries and *multilateral* organizations. Over the past 40 years, the United States has extended more than $400 billion in assistance to developing countries. Most of this aid was coordinated by the *U.S. Agency for International Development (USAID)*. Foreign aid provides additional purchasing power in developing countries. There is, however, a question about its effectiveness.

 ### 19.3 *Rules of the Game, Transition Economies, and Convergence*

**a** For a country to produce goods and services efficiently and to experience economic growth, its economy must provide businesses with both a *physical infrastructure* and a stable environment in which to operate. Many developing countries lack sufficient roads, bridges, airports, harbors, and other transportation facilities. They do not have reliable mail, phone service, or steady supplies of electricity, water, and other necessary services.

**b** Political stability is a necessary component for production and growth in many developing countries. Entrepreneurs will not work to expand production if they are not convinced they will benefit from that production.

**c** Inefficiencies in centrally planned economic systems led most to move to market-based economies. However, *privatization*, transferring ownership of businesses to private individuals, does not mean that these people have the entrepreneurial skills needed to run them efficiently.

**d** Some economists and politicians believe that the world's economies are gradually converging into one global system. A reduction in trade barriers, increased international investments, and a spread of technology and education may allow many people to escape poverty in the future.

**612** **CHAPTER 19** Economic Development

---

 ### 19.2 Assessment

Continued from page 602.

#### *Think Critically*

6. Answers will vary. Possible answer: The countries of Western Europe had a trained workforce that was able to produce goods and services as soon as it had the tools and resources it needed. The countries also benefited from having many entrepreneurs who were able to bring resources together to create production.

# Review Economic Terms

Choose the term that best fits the definition. On separate paper, write the letter of the answer. Some terms may not be used.

1. The process of turning public enterprises into private enterprises

2. Development aid from one country to another

3. Nations with low GDP per capita, high rates of illiteracy, high unemployment, and high fertility rates

_____ 4. Transportation, communication, energy, water, and sanitation systems provided by or regulated by government

_____ 5. Development aid from an organization, such as the World Bank, that gets funds from a group of countries

_____ 6. A developing country's loss of educated migrants to industrial market countries

_____ 7. The average number of births during each woman's lifetime

_____ 8. Economically advanced market countries of Western Europe, North America, Australia, New Zealand, and Japan

_____ 9. A development strategy that concentrates on producing for the export market

10. A development strategy that emphasizes domestic manufacturing of products that are currently imported

a. bilateral aid

b. brain drain

c. convergence theory

d. developing countries

e. export promotion

f. fertility rate

g. foreign aid

h. import substitution

i. industrial market countries

j. multilateral aid

k. physical infrastructure

l. privatization

m. soft budget constraint

n. U.S. Agency for International Development (USAID)

# Review Economic Concepts

11. **True or False** *Developing countries* typically have low GDP per capita, high rates of illiteracy, high unemployment rates, and rapid population growth.

12. *Developing countries* are likely to have each of the following except

    a. a limited physical infrastructure.

    b. few educational opportunities for students.

    c. easy access to high-quality medical care.

    d. a low savings rate.

13. A country's __?__ is the average number of children born during each woman's lifetime.

14. **True or False** Countries with low life expectancies also have high infant mortality rates.

15. People in *developing countries*

    a. are all equally poor.

    b. vary in their degree of poverty.

    c. are able to support their families because their prices are much lower.

    d. are provided with free medical care by their governments.

16. Countries that use tariffs or quotas to encourage the production of products that were formerly imported are following a policy of __?__.

*Chapter Assessment* **613**

## Review Economic Terms

1. l. privatization
2. a. bilateral aid
3. d. developing countries
4. k. physical infrastructure
5. j. multilateral aid
6. b. brain drain
7. f. fertility rate
8. i. industrial market countries
9. e. export promotion
10. h. import substitution

## Review Economic Concepts

11. True
12. c. easy access to high-quality medical care
13. fertility rate
14. True
15. b. vary in their degree of poverty
16. import substitution

**Assessment**

Continued from page 610

## *Think Critically*

7. Answers will vary. Possible answer: Any group that has many young and unproductive people will have difficulty providing for all its members. The group is likely to have fewer resources to invest in anything other than current consumption. This is true of poor families and poor countries. The household in the United States may have a better opportunity for improvement because there is an established infrastructure, including schools and programs for occupational training. In the United States and all over the world, people living in single-parent households are more likely to live in poverty.

## Review Economic Concepts

17. False. The export promotion strategy emphasizes specialization and comparative advantage in producing for the export market.

18. c. the farmers do not work hard enough to be efficient

19. brain drain

20. a. bilateral aid

21. U.S. Agency for International Development

22. c. roads upon which products are moved

23. False. There are many effective informal rules that affect production, including the customs and mechanisms that help coordinate production.

24. Soft budget constraints

25. b. little evidence that the world's economies are converging

## Apply Economic Concepts

26. Answers will vary. Possible answer: These young people are probably needed to work at the present to produce food so they may survive. The cost of training them to be more productive is so great that such a poor country cannot afford to provide this education to more than a very few of these young people.

27. Answers will vary. Answers should include a logical explanation for the choice.

---

17. **True or False** Like all protection measures, *export promotion* reduces the gains from specialization and comparative advantage.

18. Farms in *developing countries* are often inefficient for each of the following reasons except

    a. they are too small to be efficient.

    b. they lack tools and fertilizer that could make them more efficient.

    c. the farmers do not work hard enough to be efficient.

    d. the farmers do not understand modern farming techniques.

19. When skilled workers leave developing countries to find employment in industrial market countries, there is a(n) __?__.

20. Foreign assistance extended by one nation to another nation is called

    a. bilateral aid.

    b. unilateral aid.

    c. multilateral aid.

    d. quadrilateral aid.

21. Most U.S. assistance provided to developing countries in the past 40 years has been coordinated by the __?__.

22. Which of the following is an example of *physical infrastructure*?

    a. savings used to purchase machinery

    b. land upon which crops are grown

    c. roads upon which products are moved

    d. good weather that helps crops to grow

23. **True or False** For rules to be effective in regulating production, they must be written into laws.

24. __?__ in centrally planned economies allows inefficient producers to continue to operate over long periods of time, even when their costs were greater than the income they received from products they sold.

25. In the past decade, there has been

    a. a steady convergence of the world's economies.

    b. little evidence that the world's economies are converging.

    c. a narrowing of gaps in productivity among all the world's countries.

    d. no growth in productivity by any of the world's developing countries.

# Apply Economic Concepts

26. **Evaluate the Cost of Education** In many of the world's poorest countries, nearly 50 percent of the population is under 15 years of age. If these people are to help improve the productivity of their economies, they must be trained in modern methods of production. In 2000, just over 4 million of the 8.8 million people of Chad were under 15. Explain why it would be difficult for many of these children to be educated and become productive members of a growing economy.

27. **Determine the Best Type of Aid** Imagine that you have been given control of the USAID program. You have the power to decide how to use the funds provided to this organization by the U.S. government. Unfortunately, there is a limit to what you can spend, and there are many nations that need assistance. You have allocated $20,000,000 to a developing country. These funds may be spent to do any of the following. How would you spend this money to do the most good? Explain your choice.

    - Spend the money to provide better education for 20,000 students.

    - Spend the money to provide better health care for 200,000 people.

    - Spend the money to purchase better farm equipment for 10,000 farmers.

    - Spend the money to build a highway that leads to the country's only port.

    - Spend the money to provide 1,000,000 people with better nutrition.

28. **Encourage Foreign Investment** Imagine you have been put in charge of a developing country's Office of Economic Growth. Your job includes setting policies intended to encourage foreign businesses to invest in your

country and provide jobs to your people. Which of the following policies would you support? Which would you oppose? Explain your answers.

- Allow foreign firms to pay any wage rate that your people are willing to accept. Have no required minimum wage, overtime pay, or days off.

- Assure foreign firms that their investment will not be nationalized by the government.

- Provide foreign firms with reduced tax rates

- Allow foreign firms to ignore pollution control laws

- Pass laws that make it illegal for workers to go on strike against foreign firms

**29. Sharpen Your Life Skills: Analyze Visuals** Study the graph below and evaluate the information it provides about newspaper sales. How does it show which countries are still developing and which are established industrial market economies?

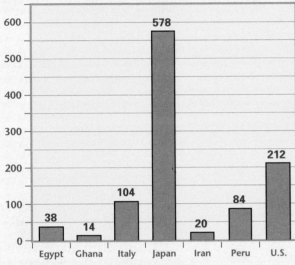

**Daily Newspaper Circulation Per 1,000 Residents**

Source: *Statistical Abstract of the United States*, 2002, p. 852

  econxtra.swlearning.com

**30.** Access **EconNews Online** at econxtra. swlearning.com. Read the article entitled "Grading the IMF and World Bank." Also reread the Ethics in Action feature on page 606 of this chapter. What political and economic circumstances in Haiti might explain why critics of the World Bank point to this country "as an example of the failure of the World Bank"? Do you think this criticism is wholly justified? Why or why not?

## Apply Economic Concepts

28. Answers will vary. Possible answer: The first, fourth, and last policies would harm residents of the country. Giving foreign investors tax breaks or assuring them that their investment will not be nationalized by the government are likely to be seen as more acceptable policies.

29. Answers will vary. Possible answer: People who are not able to read are not likely to buy newspapers. Therefore, the more newspapers sold the more educated the people are and the more productive they are likely to be. Buying a newspaper also shows a desire to learn more and sufficient income to be able to pay for the newspaper.

*e*-con @pps

30. Answers will vary. Possible answer: The critics of the World Bank may not have considered the political circumstances that led to Haiti's economic disaster.

# Investing In Your Future

## PREPARE

This project can be completed in the classroom or as an outside assignment. The activities call for students to work in teams, but students also can complete the assignment working alone. If you organize the class into teams, consider identifying specific roles for team members such as recorder, discussion leader, researcher, etc.

## TEACH

### The Situation

The natural development of her company has slowly moved Aleesha's focus from her own development, to the development of her products, to the development of her company at first nation- and then worldwide.

### The Decision

Decisions that need to be made to maintain a certain level of sales—and thereby keep the business productive and the workers employed—become more and more subject to the level of influence Aleesha can bring to bear on the government. Tax credits and other government programs lobbied out of Congress are only part of the cooperation Aleesha needs from her elected officials. She also needs protective tariffs, stronger treaties protecting intellectual property (her patents), a currency policy more favorable to marketing American products worldwide, etc. Her political contributions now probably encompass money flows to liberal as well as to conservative business-oriented candidates. She is now part and parcel of the American tradition of economically motivated compromise that is at the heart of our country's ability to meld all backgrounds, religions, colors, and creeds into a well-functioning whole.

## The Situation

Aleesha stared at herself in the bathroom mirror. That couldn't be a gray hair! The stress of the last few years had taken its toll. At least the children were okay. Tomas and Aleece had adjusted well to private school. Even Tom had to agree that the education was first class, and it opened all kinds of possibilities for their college education and beyond.

As for the business, there were new challenges. The lobbyists Aleesha hired a few years ago had earned their money. They had kept the tax credits for the inner-city factory in each tax bill that rolled through Congress. In addition, they had managed to get other credits to apply to Aleesha's new program that allowed employees to do pre-assembly piecework in their homes. The lobbying firm even used its media contacts to bring national television attention to the innovative approach. A similar campaign by Winston and Bailey brought media interest to the wartime use of animals as weapons carriers. As a consequence, Aleesha was able to get the worrisome term on such potential use of her products dropped from her Defense Department contract and had signed the result. The contract kept both factories at near full production.

## The Decision

The government contract would not last forever, however. To keep up the current level of production, new markets would have to be found and developed. In addition, new problems in the United States consumer market recently had arisen. Funding for zoos and similar institutions around the country continued to dry up, due to decreasing tax revenues as a result of the economic downturn. Further, just last Monday Aleesha's vice-president for sales had discovered nearly identical rip-offs of two of the company's most important consumer products. The rip-offs, made in China, were of decent quality. They were now being sold by

## RESEARCH

Encourage students to use Internet and library resources to learn more about the issues in this project. They may research the issue of rip-off products from China by typing "rip-off products and China" into an Internet search engine such as ask.com. Typing "trade and Japan" and "trade and Africa" will lead them to web sites about ways U.S. companies can trade with Japan and countries in Africa. Students can consult the USAID web site (www.usaid.gov) for information about loans and grants the United States makes available to other nations.

two discount chains around the country at half the price. Something had to be done about the situation.

Another problem surfaced, involving international trade. Japan, one of the most lucrative potential markets for Aleesha's pet consumer products, would allow only a small number of the products to be imported. Also on the international front, many nations in Africa represented wide-open markets for the company's products, in particular the Capturecare line. However, customers in these countries were unable to buy the products, due to the strength of the dollar against their currencies and the resulting higher prices than the competition was offering on its outmoded (and far less animal-friendly) devices. Aleesha wondered how she could change these situations to benefit her company.

## Activities

**Divide into teams or work individually, as directed by your teacher, to perform the following tasks.**

Apply the steps in the following decision-making process to Aleesha's current situation:

**1.** *Define the problem.* Again, Aleesha faces multiple decisions. Define each problem in a way that will allow a clear solution.

**2.** *Identify her choices.* List the various alternatives among which Aleesha must choose for each problem.

**3.** *Evaluate the pluses and minuses of each choice.* Carefully weigh the value Aleesha puts on each alternative and the opportunity cost(s) for each.

**4.** *Make a choice.* Which course of action should she choose? Be prepared to present and defend your selection to the class.

**5.** *Provide "action" steps that are appropriate to the decision.* Make sure these are realistic and timely to ensure the necessary actions are taken to resolve the problem.

**6.** *Critique the decision.* The class will assist in the review and evaluation of your plan of action.

## Research

Research for the information needed, such as the funding of zoos through taxation, rip-off products from nations such as China, and the trade situation with Japan and countries in Africa.

## Present

Arrive at a decision. Then prepare a presentation for the class on the six steps you took to achieve this decision.

### APPLY

#### Activities

**Step 1:** The problem statements should touch on the following issues: (1) Finding and developing new markets; (2) economic downturn decreasing customers' ability to purchase Aleesha's products; (3) imported rip-off products from China; and (4) entering the Japanese and African markets.

**Step 2:** (2) Aleesha could lobby politicians to direct funds to zoos and similar institutions; her company could make loans or sales on credit to the zoos on generous terms. (3) Possible solutions include lobbying for the imposing of tariffs on all Chinese goods imported into the United States (such a proposal was before Congress in 2003); potential patent infringement suits (however, enforcement of international laws against piracy of intellectual property has been lax in China, to say the least); and shifting production of Aleesha's products to Mexico or China to cut her own costs. (4) Aleesha could have the lobbyists work to get U.S. trade representatives to bargain for the lowering of the Japanese trade barriers at the next round of world trade talks; she also could enter into business deals with Japanese firms. For example, she could license the products to a Japanese firm for manufacture and sale in that country. Of course, that would not enhance production at her American plants. Aleesha could bring political pressure to bear through the representatives and senators whose campaigns she has backed to get the United States' monetary policy changed so as to weaken the dollar relative to other currencies. She also could work for increased foreign aid in the form of grants and loans from the U.S. Aid bank to the prospective customer nations so that they would be able to buy her products. She can also directly offer business loans and favorable sales terms to (hopefully solvent) institutions and nations to allow the purchase of her goods.

### ASSESS

**Presentation** Consider using a rubric or evaluation form for student presentations. Make sure you share the rubric or form with students before they start working on the project. A sample evaluation form appears on the Instructor's Resource CD. The categories to be evaluated include: **Content** (organization, specific content, and accurate information); **Presentation Skills** (eye contact, grammar and pronunciation, volume, and pitch); **Audiovisual Aids** (appropriate content, style, and spelling); and **Handouts** (appropriate content; grammar, punctuation, and spelling).

## Economic Indicators

**Consumer Price Index Since 1913**

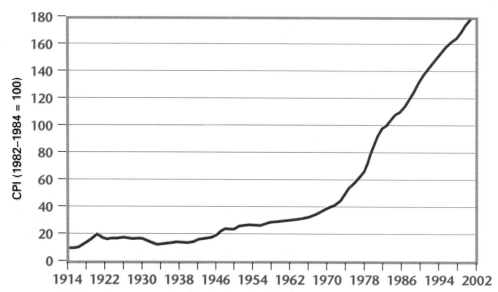

Despite fluctuations, the price level, as measured by the consumer price index, was lower in 1940 than in 1920. Since 1940, the price level has risen almost every year.

Source: U.S. Bureau of Labor Statistics.

**U.S. Real GDP and Price Level Since 1929**

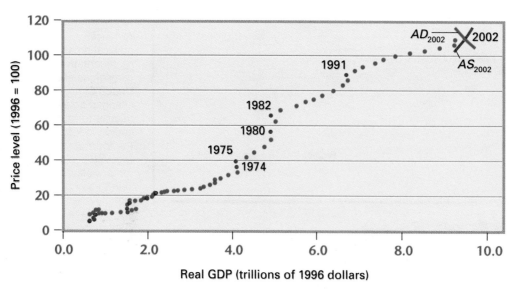

Both real GDP and the price level increased since 1929. Blue points indicate years of growing real GDP, and red points are years of declining real GDP. Real GDP in 2002 was more than 11 times greater than it was in 1929. The price level was more than 8 times greater.

Source: Based on annual estimates from the U.S. Department of Commerce.

## U.S. Spending Components as Percentages of GDP Since 1960

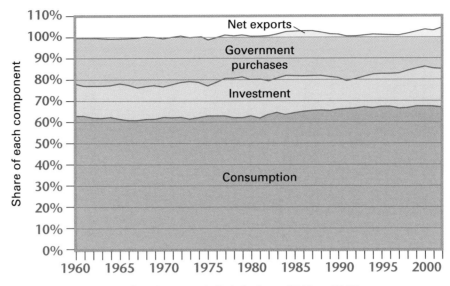

Consumption's share of total U.S. spending increased slightly from 1960 to 2002. Most recently, it accounted for about 67 percent of the total.

Source: Computed from annual estimates from the U.S. Department of Commerce.

## Annual Percentage Change in U.S. Real GDP Since 1929

Since the end of World War II in 1945, the economy has gone through 10 business cycles. Expansions averaged just under five years. Recessions averaged just under one year. Note: In this chart, declines are shown in red and increases, in blue.

Source: Based on annual estimates from the U.S. Department of Commerce.

# Labor and Employment Data

## The U.S. Unemployment Rate Since 1900

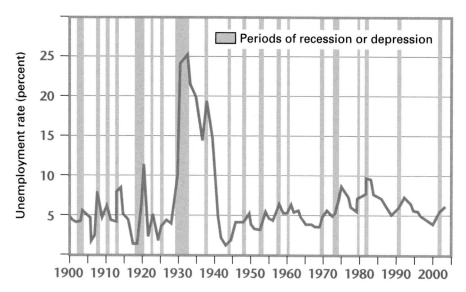

Since 1900, the unemployment rate has fluctuated widely, rising during recessions and falling during expansions. During the Great Depression of the 1930s, the rate rose as high as 25.2 percent.

Sources: U.S. Census Bureau, *Historical Statistics of the United States: Colonial Times to 1970* (Washington, D.C.: U.S. Government Printing Office, 1975); *Economic Report of the President,* February 2003; and U.S. Bureau of Labor Statistics.

## Education Pays More for Every Age Group

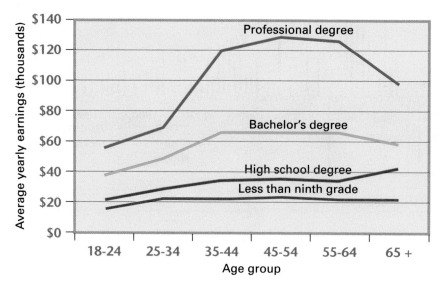

At every age, those with more education earned more. Earnings increased as workers gained more job experience and became more productive.

Source: U.S. Bureau of Labor Statistics. Figures are average earnings for all full-time, year-round workers in 2001.

## U.S. Union Membership for Men and Women by Age

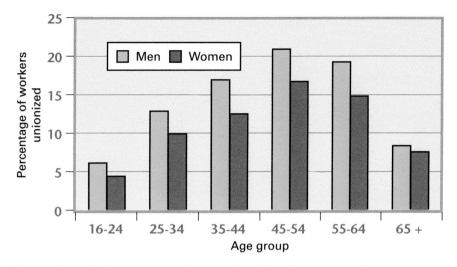

Men in the United States have higher rates of union membership than women, due to the nature of the work each group typically performs.

Source: U.S. Bureau of Labor Statistics. Percentages are for 2001.

## Long-Term Trend in U.S. Labor Productivity Growth: Annual Average by Decade

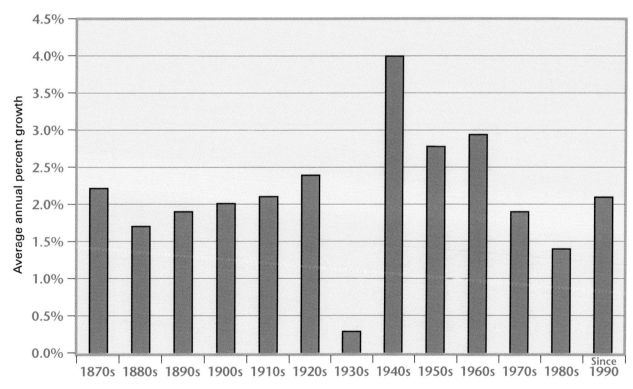

For the entire period since 1870, productivity growth averaged 2.1 percent per year.

Sources: Angus Maddison, *Phases of Capitalist Development* (New York: Oxford University Press, 1982) and U.S. Bureau of Labor Statistics.

## Income Redistribution—Composition of Federal Outlays

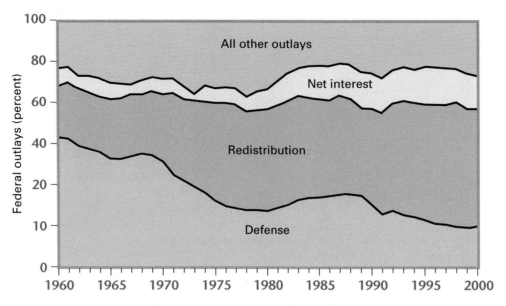

Since 1960, spending on income redistribution has increased and spending on defense has decreased as a share of federal outlays.

Source: Computed based on figures from the *Economic Report of the President,* January 2001, Table B-80. Access the most current report through econxtra.swlearning.com.

## Defense Spending as a Share of the Federal Budget

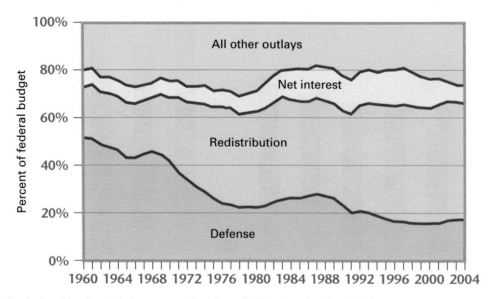

As a share of the federal budget, defense spending has declined and redistribution has increased since 1960.

Source: *Economic Report of the President,* February 2003, Table B-80. Figures for 2003 and 2004 are estimates.

## Payroll Taxes as a Share of Federal Revenue

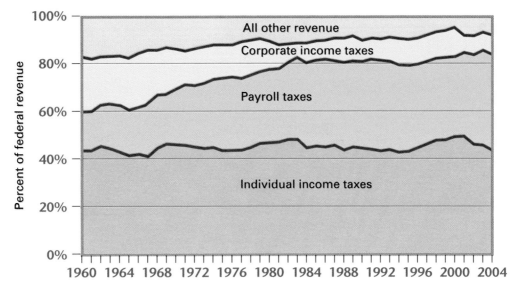

Payroll taxes have grown as a share of federal revenue since 1960.

Source: Based on fiscal year revenue figures from the *Economic Report of the President,* February 2003. Figures for 2003 and 2004 are projections.

## Federal Debt Held by the Public as Percent of GDP, 1940 to 2004

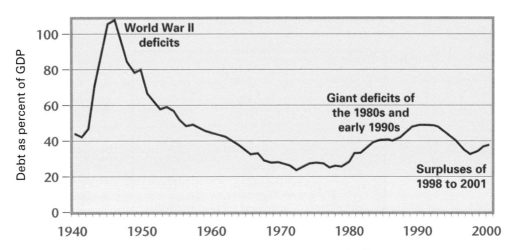

The federal debt held by the public relative to GDP dropped nearly two-thirds between 1946 and 2004.

Source: Fiscal year figures from *Economic Report of the President,* February 2003, Table 79. Figures for 2003 and 2004 are projections.

## Recent Ups and Downs in the Federal Funds Rate

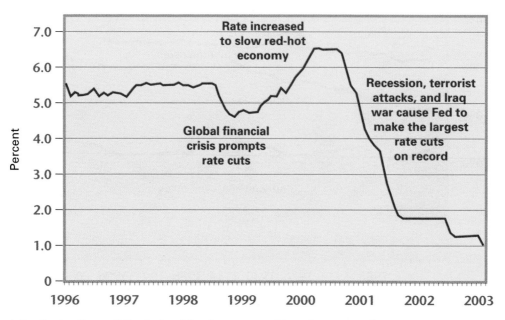

To understand the fluctuations of the federal funds rate, consider what was going on in the economy during the periods shown here.

Source: Based on monthly averages from the Federal Reserve Bank.

## Source of U.S. Patents Awarded for Inventions by Year

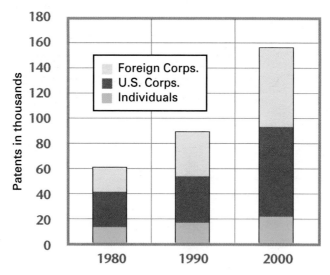

The number of patents grew from 61,800 in 1980 to 157,500 in 2000. In 1980, 22 percent of all patents were awarded to individuals. By 2000, only 14 percent went to individuals.

Source: U.S. Bureau of the Census, *Statistical Abstract of the United States,* 2001.

## Composition of State Spending and State Revenue

### Composition of State Spending

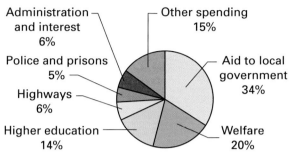

Administration and interest 6%

Police and prisons 5%

Highways 6%

Higher education 14%

Other spending 15%

Aid to local government 34%

Welfare 20%

### Composition of State Revenue

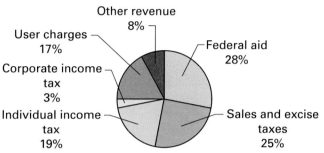

Other revenue 8%

User charges 17%

Corporate income tax 3%

Individual income tax 19%

Federal aid 28%

Sales and excise taxes 25%

The biggest portion of state spending goes toward grants to local governments. The largest source of state revenue is aid from the federal government.

Source: Based on general expenditure figures for fiscal year 2000 from the U.S. Census Bureau.

## Composition of Local Spending and Local Revenue

### Composition of Local Spending

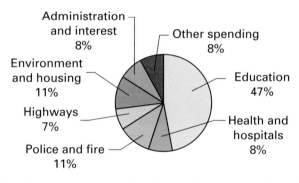

Administration and interest 8%

Environment and housing 11%

Highways 7%

Police and fire 11%

Other spending 8%

Education 47%

Health and hospitals 8%

### Composition of Local Revenue

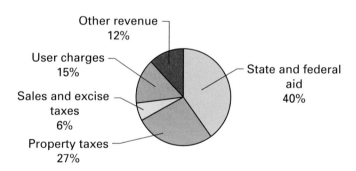

Other revenue 12%

User charges 15%

Sales and excise taxes 6%

Property taxes 27%

State and federal aid 40%

The largest category of local spending is education. State and federal aid make up the largest percent of local revenue.

Source: Based on general expenditure figures for fiscal year 2000 from the U.S. Census Bureau.

# Business Data

## Distribution of Sole Proprietorships Based on Annual Sales and by Industry

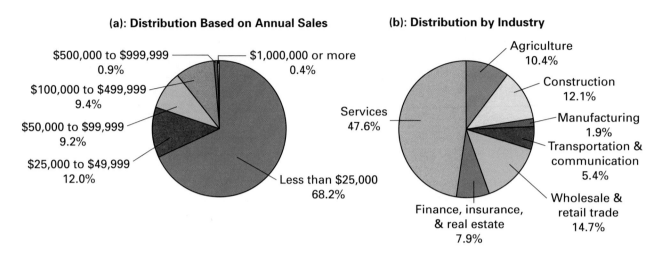

### (a): Distribution Based on Annual Sales

$500,000 to $999,999
0.9%

$1,000,000 or more
0.4%

$100,000 to $499,999
9.4%

$50,000 to $99,999
9.2%

$25,000 to $49,999
12.0%

Services
47.6%

Less than $25,000
68.2%

### (b): Distribution by Industry

Agriculture
10.4%

Construction
12.1%

Manufacturing
1.9%

Transportation &
communication
5.4%

Wholesale &
retail trade
14.7%

Finance, insurance,
& real estate
7.9%

More than half of all sole proprietors earn $25,000 or less a year. Most sole proprietorships are service businesses.

Source: U.S. Bureau of the Census, *Statistical Abstract of the United States*, 2002.

## Distribution of Partnerships Based on Annual Sales and Industry

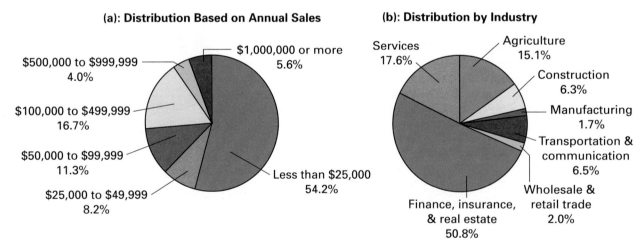

### (a): Distribution Based on Annual Sales

$500,000 to $999,999
4.0%

$1,000,000 or more
5.6%

$100,000 to $499,999
16.7%

$50,000 to $99,999
11.3%

$25,000 to $49,999
8.2%

Less than $25,000
54.2%

### (b): Distribution by Industry

Services
17.6%

Agriculture
15.1%

Construction
6.3%

Manufacturing
1.7%

Transportation &
communication
6.5%

Wholesale &
retail trade
2.0%

Finance, insurance,
& real estate
50.8%

Most partnerships had annual sales of less than $25,000. About half of all partnerships are in finance, insurance, or real estate.

Source: U.S. Bureau of the Census, *Statistical Abstract of the United States*, 2002.

## Distribution of Corporations by Annual Sales and by Industry

### (a): By Annual Sales

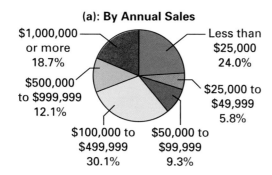

$1,000,000 or more 18.7%
Less than $25,000 24.0%
$500,000 to $999,999 12.1%
$25,000 to $49,999 5.8%
$100,000 to $499,999 30.1%
$50,000 to $99,999 9.3%

### (b): By Industry

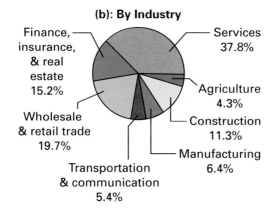

Finance, insurance, & real estate 15.2%
Services 37.8%
Agriculture 4.3%
Wholesale & retail trade 19.7%
Construction 11.3%
Manufacturing 6.4%
Transportation & communication 5.4%

Nearly one in five corporations had annual sales of $1 million or more. About four in ten corporations are in services, such as health care.

Source: U.S. Bureau of the Census, *Statistical Abstract of the United States,* 2002.

## Comparing Corporations with Sole Proprietorships and Partnerships

### (a): As a Share of All Businesses

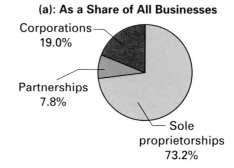

Corporations 19.0%
Partnerships 7.8%
Sole proprietorships 73.2%

### (b): As a Share of Business Sales

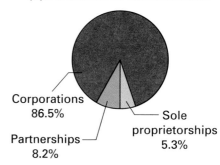

Corporations 86.5%
Sole proprietorships 5.3%
Partnerships 8.2%

Sole proprietorships account for nearly three quarters of all U.S. businesses, but corporations account for most business sales.

Source: U.S. Bureau of the Census, *Statistical Abstract of the United States,* 2002.

## Value of Business Structures and Equipment in the United States

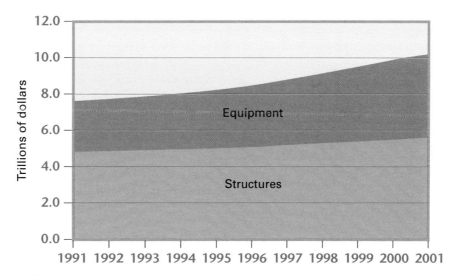

The combined value of business equipment and business structures increased nearly $3 trillion from 1991 to 2001.

Source: Developed from estimates in the U.S. Department of Commerce, *Survey of Current Business,* September 2002, Table 15. Structures include factories, buildings, and other permanent business fixtures. Figures are adjusted to eliminate the effects of inflation.

# Glossary

## A

**ability-to-pay tax principle** Those with a greater ability to pay, such as those with a higher income, should pay more of the tax (p. 431)

**absolute advantage** To be able to make something using fewer resources than other producers require (p. 51)

**aggregate demand** The relationship between the economy's price level and the quantity of aggregate output demanded, with other things constant (p. 344)

**aggregate demand curve** A curve representing the relationship between the economy's price level and real GDP demanded per period, with other things constant (p. 344)

**aggregate expenditure** Total spending on all final goods and services produced in the economy during the year (p. 325)

**aggregate income** The sum of all the income earned by resource suppliers in the economy during a given year (p. 326)

**aggregate output** A composite measure of all final goods and services produced in an economy during a given period; real GDP (p. 344)

**aggregate supply curve** A curve representing the relationship between the economy's price level and real GDP supplied per period, with other things constant (p. 346)

**allocative efficiency** Achieved when the firm produces the output most preferred by consumers (p. 179)

**American Federation of Labor (AFL)** An organization of national craft unions founded in 1886; not a union itself but a collection of independent unions (p. 274)

**annual inflation rate** The percentage increase in the economy's general price level from one year to the next (p. 398)

**annually balanced budget** Matching annual spending with annual revenue, except during war years; approach to the federal budget prior to the Great Depression (p. 464)

**antitrust activity** Government efforts aimed at preventing monopoly and promoting competition in markets where competition is desirable (p. 209)

**antitrust laws** Laws that prohibit anticompetitive behavior and promote competition in markets where competition is desirable (p. 71)

**applied research** Research that seeks answers to particular questions or applies scientific discoveries to develop specific products (p. 375)

**arbitrageur** Someone who profits from temporary geographic differences in the exchange rate by simultaneously purchasing a currency in one market and selling it in another market (p. 578)

**articles of partnership** A legal agreement spelling out each partner's rights and responsibilities (p. 243)

**asset** Any physical property or financial claim that is owned (p. 520)

**automatic stabilizers** Government spending and taxing programs that year after year automatically reduce fluctuations in disposable income, and thus in consumption, over the business cycle (p. 469)

**average cost** Total cost divided by output (p. 154)

## B

**balance of payments** A record of all economic transactions between residents of one country and residents of the rest of the world during a given period (p. 568)

**balance sheet** A financial statement showing assets, liabilities, and net worth at a given point in time; since assets must equal liabilities plus net worth, the statement is in balance (p. 520)

**bank note** A piece of paper promising gold or silver to whoever presented it to the issuing bank for redemption; an early form of money (p. 497)

**barriers to entry** Anything that prevents new firms from competing on an equal footing with existing firms in an industry (p. 194)

**barter** A system of exchange in which products are traded directly for other products (p. 52)

**basic research** The search for knowledge without regard to how that knowledge will be used; a first step toward technological advancement (p. 375)

**behavioral assumption** The simplifying assumption about what motivates people, such as rational self interest (p. 11)

**benefits-received tax principle** Those who receive more benefits from the government program funded by the tax should pay more of that tax (p. 431)

**bilateral aid** Development aid from one country to another (p. 600)

**binding arbitration** When labor negotiations have broken down and the public interest is involved, a neutral third party is brought in to impose a settlement that both sides must accept (p. 274)

**bond** A contract promising to repay borrowed money on a designated date and pay interest along the way (p. 299)

**brain drain** A developing country's loss of educated migrants to industrial market countries (p. 599)

**bureaus** Government agencies charged with implementing legislation and financed by appropriations from legislative bodies (p. 450)

**business cycle** Fluctuations reflecting the rise and fall of economic activity relative to the long-term growth trend of the economy (pp. 72, 336)

## C

**capital deepening** An increase in the quantity and quality of capital per worker; one source of rising labor productivity (p. 360)

**capital goods** all human creations used to produce goods and services; for example, factories, trucks, and machines (p. 8)

**cartel** A group of firms that agree to coordinate and pricing decisions to maximize group profits by behaving as a monopolist (p. 204)

**charter** The legal authorization to organize a business as a corporation (p. 243)

**check** A written order instructing the bank to pay someone from the amount deposited (p. 497)

**checkable deposits** Deposits in financial institutions against which checks can be written and ATM, or debit, cards can be applied; part of the narrow definition of money (p. 507)

**circular-flow model** A figure that describes the flow of resources, products, income, and revenue among economic decision makers (p. 15)

**classical economists** A group of laissez-faire economists, who believed that economic downturns were short-run problems that corrected themselves in the long run through natural market forces (p. 463)

**cluster** Firms in the same industry or in related industries that group together in a region, such as Wall Street, Hollywood, or Silicon Valley (p. 379)

**coincident economic indicators** Measures that reflect recessions or expansions as they occur (p. 339)

**collateral** An asset owned by the borrower that can be sold to pay off the loan in the event the loan is not repaid (p. 297)

**collective bargaining** The process by which representatives of the union and the employer negotiate wages, employee benefits, and working conditions (p. 274)

**collusion** An price-fixing agreement among firms to reduce competition and increase profit (p. 204)

**commercial banks** Depository institutions that make loans primarily to businesses (p. 498)

**commodity money** Anything that serves both as money and as a commodity, such as gold (p. 491)

**commodity** A product that is identical across sellers, such a bushel of wheat (p. 192)

**common-pool problem** People use an open-access resource until the benefit of additional use drops to zero, so open access resources are overused (p. 76)

**competitive firm's supply curve** The rising portion of a firm's marginal cost curve at or above the price that will allow the firm to cover variable cost (p. 153)

**complements** Goods, such as milk and cookies, that relate in such a way that a decrease in the price of one shifts the demand for the other rightward (p. 120)

**conglomerate merger** One firm combines with another firm in a different industry, such as a merger between a plastics maker and an electronics firm (p. 305)

**Congress of Industrial Organizations (CIO)** A national organization of unions in mass-production industries formed in 1935 (p. 274)

**constant returns to scale** Over a range of production in the long run, long-run average cost neither increases nor decreases with changes in the firm size (p. 154)

**consumer cooperative** A retail business owned and operated by some of all of its customers in order to reduce costs (p. 246)

**consumer price index,** or **CPI** Measure of inflation based on the cost of a fixed "market basket" of goods and services purchased by a typical family (p. 333)

**consumer surplus** The difference between the maximum amount that consumers are willing to pay for a given quantity of a good and what they actually pay (p. 181)

**consumption** Household purchases of final goods and services except for new residences, which count as investment (p. 323)

**convergence theory** A theory predicting that the standard of living in economies around the world will grow more similar over time, with poorer countries gradually closing the gap with richer ones (p. 607)

**cooperative** An organization consisting of people who pool their resources to buy and sell more efficiently than they could independently (p. 245)

**copyright** Assigns property rights to original expressions of an author, artist, composer, or computer programmer (p. 63)

**corporation** A legal entity with an existence that is distinct from the real people who organize, own, and run it (p. 245)

**cost-push inflation** Inflation resulting from a leftward shift of the aggregate supply curve (p. 399)

**cottage industry system** Entrepreneurs hired rural households to turn raw materials into finished goods (p. 64)

**craft union** A union whose membership is limited to workers with a particular skill, or craft—such as carpenters or plumbers (p. 274)

**credit** The ability to borrow now based on the promise of repayment in the future (p. 295)

**crowding in** Government spending stimulates private investment in an otherwise dead economy (p. 478)

**crowding out** Private investment falls when higher government deficits drive up interest rates (p. 478)

**currency appreciation** A decrease in the dollar price of a unit of foreign exchange in a flexible exchange rate system (p. 577)

**currency depreciation** An increase in the dollar price of a unit of foreign exchange in a flexible exchange rate system (p. 577)

**current account** That portion of the balance of payment that records exports and imports of goods and services, net investment income, and net transfers (p. 568)

**current dollars** Dollar values at the time the output is produced (p. 331)

**cycle of poverty** Children in welfare families may end up on welfare themselves when they grow up (p. 415)

**cyclical unemployment** Occurs because of the jobs lost during the recession phase of the business cycle (p. 388)

## D

**decision-making lag** The time needed to decide what to do once the problem has been identified (p. 471)

**decrease in demand** Consumers are less willing and able to buy the product at every price (p. 171)

**decrease in supply** Producers are less willing and able to supply the product at every price (p. 173)

**default** To not pay back a loan (p. 297)

**deflation** A *decrease* in the general price level (p. 398)

**demand** A relation showing the quantities of a good that consumers are willing and able to buy at various prices per period, other things constant (p. 102)

**demand curve** A curve or line showing the quantities of a particular good demanded at various prices during a given time period, other things constant (p. 105)

**demand deposits** Originally, the only type of checking accounts (p. 499, 507)

**demand for loans curve** A downward sloping curve showing the negative relationship between the interest rate and the quantity of loans demanded, other things constant (p. 290)

**demand-pull inflation** Inflation resulting from a rightward shift of the aggregate demand curve (p. 398)

**demand schedule** Columns of numbers showing the quantities of a particular good demanded at various possible prices during a given period, other things constant (p. 105)

**demand-side economics** Macroeconomic policy that focuses on shifting the aggregate demand curve as a way of promoting full employment and price stability (p. 406)

**depository institutions** Financial institutions that accept deposits from the public and lend out a portion of those deposits (p. 498)

**depreciation** The value of the capital stock that is used up or becomes obsolete to produce GDP during the year (p. 330)

**depression** A sharp reduction in the nation's total production lasting more than a year and accompanied by high unemployment (p. 336)

**deregulation** A reduction in government control over prices and firm entry in previously regulated markets, such as airlines and trucking (p. 212)

**derived demand** The demand for a resource is derived from the demand for the product that resource produces (p. 256)

**developing countries** Countries with a lower standard of living because they have relatively little human and physical capital; also called Third-World countries (p. 367); nations with low GDP per capita, high rates of illiteracy, high unemployment, and high fertility rates (p. 588)

**differentiated oligopoly** Oligopoly market where firms sell products that differ across producers, such as Ford versus Toyota (p. 203)

**discount rate** Interest rate the Fed charges banks that borrow reserves (p. 501)

**discouraged workers** Someone who, unable to find a job, drops out of the labor force (p. 389)

**discretionary fiscal policy** Congressional changes in spending or taxing to promote macroeconomic goals (p. 469)

**diseconomies of scale** In some industries, forces that eventually increase a firm's average cost as the scale of operation increases in the long run (p. 154)

**disequilibrium** A mismatch between quantity demanded and quantity supplied as the market seeks equilibrium; usually temporary, except where government intervenes and sets the price (p. 180)

**disinflation** A reduction in the rate of inflation (p. 398)

**dividend** That portion of after-tax corporate profit paid out to shareholders (p. 299)

**division of labor** Sorting the production process into separate tasks to be carried out by separate workers (p. 53)

**domestic content requirements** Regulations specifying that a certain portion of a final good must be produced domestically (p. 560)

**double counting** The mistake of including the value of intermediate goods plus the value of final goods in computing gross domestic product; counting an item's value more than once (p. 322)

**dual banking system** The U.S. banking system, which consists of both state banks and national banks (p. 500)

**durable goods** Goods expected to last at least three years, such as televisions and furniture (p. 323)

## E

**earned-income tax credit** A federal program that supplements wages of the working poor (p. 87)

**economic growth** An expansion in the economy's production possibilities or ability to produce (p. 45)

**economic system** The set of mechanisms and institutions that resolve the *what, how,* and *for whom* questions for an economy (p. 34)

**economic theory, economic model** A simplification of economic reality used to make predictions about the real world (p. 11)

**economics** The study of how people use their scarce resources to satisfy their unlimited wants (p. 6)

**economies of scale** Forces that reduce a firm's average cost as the firm's size, or scale, increases in the long run (p. 154)

**economy** The structure of economic activity in a locality, a region, a country, a group of countries, or the world (p. 322)

**effectiveness lag** The time needed for changes in policy to affect the economy (p. 471)

**efficiency** Producing the maximum possible output from available resources (pp. 42, 46)

**elastic demand** A change in the price has a relatively large effect on quantity demanded; the percentage change in quantity demanded exceeds the percentage change in price; the resulting elasticity is greater than 1.0 (p. 109)

**elastic supply** A change in the price has a relatively large effect on quantity supplied; the percentage change in quantity supplied exceeds the percentage change in price; the resulting elasticity is greater than 1.0 (p. 136)

**elasticity of demand** Measures how responsive quantity demanded is to a price change; the percentage change in quantity demanded divided by the percentage change in price (p. 110)

**elasticity of supply** A measure of the responsiveness of quantity supplied to a price change; the percentage change in quantity supplied divided by the percentage change in price (p. 135)

**entrepreneur** A profit-seeker who develops a new product or process and assumes the risk of profit or loss (p. 7)

**equilibrium** The quantity consumers are willing and able to buy equals the quantity producers are willing and able to sell (p. 164)

**equilibrium interest rate** The only interest rate at which the quantity of loans demanded equals the quantity of loans supplied (p. 292)

**equilibrium point** The point of intersection between the demand curve and the supply curve (p. 165)

**equilibrium price** The price that equates quantity demanded with quantity supplied; the market-clearing price (p. 165)

**equilibrium quantity** The quantity demanded and the quantity supplied when the market is in equilibrium (p. 165)

**equilibrium wage** The wage at which there is neither an excess quantity of labor demanded nor an excess quantity of labor supplied (p. 258)

**euro** The common currency put into circulation in 2002 by 12 European countries (pp. 540, 563)

**excess capacity** The amount by which a firm's actual production falls short of the firm's capacity; increasing output would reduce per unit cost (p. 203)

**excess reserves** Bank reserves in excess of required reserves (p. 521)

**exchange rate** The price of one country's currency measured in terms of another country's currency (p. 575)

**exclusive** Those who fail to pay for a good can be easily excluded from its consumption (p. 77)

**exhaustible resource** A natural resource that does not renew itself and so is available in a finite amount, such as oil or copper ore (p. 7)

**expansion** The phase of economic activity during which the economy's total output increases (p. 337)

**expenditure approach to GDP** A method of calculating GDP by adding up the spending on all final goods and services produced during the year (p. 323)

**export promotion** A development strategy that concentrates on producing for the export market (p. 598)

## F

**featherbedding** Union efforts to force employers to hire more workers than demanded for the task (p. 276)

**federal budget deficit** The amount by which total federal outlays exceed total federal revenues (p. 408)

**federal funds market** A market for overnight lending and borrowing of reserves held by the Fed for banks (p. 531)

**federal funds rate** The interest rate charged in the federal funds market; the Fed's target interest rate (p. 531)

**Federal Open Market Committee (FOMC)** Twelve-member group that makes decisions about open-market operations (p. 501)

**Federal Reserve System, or Fed** Established in 1913 as the central bank and monetary authority of the United States (p. 500)

**fertility rate** The average number of births during each woman's lifetime (p. 589)

**fiat money** Money not redeemable for anything of intrinsic value; declared money by government decree (p. 497)

**final goods and services** Goods and services sold to the final, or end, users (p. 322)

**financial account** That portion of the balance of payments that records international transactions involving financial assets, such as stocks and bonds, and real assets, such as factories and office buildings (p. 571)

**financial capital** Money needed to start or expand a business (p. 229)

**financial intermediaries** Banks and other institutions that serve as go-betweens, accepting funds from savers and lending them to borrowers (p. 295)

**firm** A business unit or enterprise formed by a profit-seeking entrepreneur who combines resources to produce goods and services (p. 63)

**fiscal policy** The federal government's use of taxing and public spending to influence the national economy (p. 72)

**fixed cost** Any production cost that is independent of the firms output (p. 150)

**fixed exchange rate** Exchange rate fixed within a narrow range of values and maintained by central banks' ongoing purchases and sales of currencies (p. 579)

**fixed resource** Any resource that cannot be varied in the short run (p. 148)

**flexible exchange rate** Exchange rate determined by the forces of supply and demand without government intervention (p. 579)

**foreign aid** An international grant or a loan made on especially favorable terms to promote economic development (p. 600)

**foreign exchange** Foreign money needed to carry out international transactions (p. 575)

**fractional reserve banking system** Only a portion of bank deposits is backed by reserves (p. 497)

**free-riders** Those who consume a public good without paying for it (p. 76)

**frictional unemployment** Occurs because of the time required to match qualified job seekers with available openings (p. 388)

**full employment** Occurs when there is no cyclical unemployment; relatively low unemployment (p. 388)

## G

**GDP price index** A comprehensive measure of inflation based on all goods and services included in GDP (p. 336)

**General Agreement on Tariffs and Trade (GATT)** An international tariff-reduction treaty adopted in 1947 that resulted in a series of negotiated "rounds" aimed at freer trade (p. 561)

**general partnership** Partners share both in the responsibility for running the business and in any liability from its operation (p. 237)

**golden age of Keynesian economics** The 1960s, when some economists thought they could "fine-tune" the economy to avoid recessions (p. 406)

**good** An item you can see feel and touch that requires scarce resources and satisfies human wants (p. 8)

**government budget** A plan for government outlays and revenues for a specified period, usually a year (p. 438)

**government purchases** Spending by all levels of government for goods and services; does not include transfer payments (p. 324)

**green accounting** Reflects the impact of production on air pollution, water pollution, lost trees, soil depletion, and the loss of other natural resources (p. 331)

**gross domestic product (GDP)** The market value of all final goods and services produced in the United States during a given period, usually a year (p. 322)

**gross investment** The value of all investment during a year; used to compute GDP (p. 330)

**Group of Seven (G-7)** The seven leading industrial market economies, including the United States, United Kingdom, France, Germany, Italy, Japan, and Canada (p. 368)

## H

**horizontal merger** One firm combines with another that produces the same product, such as Exxon and Mobil (p. 209)

**hostile takeovers** One firm buys control of another firm against the wishes of the purchased firm's management; a common merger strategy during the 1980s (p. 300)

**household** The most important economic decision maker, consisting of all those who live under one roof (p. 62)

**human capital** The accumulated knowledge, skill, and experience of the labor force (p. 360)

**human resources** The broad category of human efforts, both physical and mental, used to produce goods and services (p. 7)

**hyperinflation** Extremely high inflation (p. 398)

## I

**implementation lag** The time needed to execute a change in policy (p. 471)

**import substitution** A development strategy that emphasizes domestic manufacturing of products that are currently imported (p. 598)

**income approach to GDP** A method of calculating GDP by adding up all payments to owners of resources used to produce output during the year (p. 323)

**income effect of a price change** A fall in the price of a good increases consumers' real income, making consumers more able to purchase the good; for normal goods, the quantity demanded increases (p. 103)

**income-assistance programs** Government programs that provide money and in-kind assistance to poor people (p. 86)

**increase in demand** Consumers are more willing and able to buy the product at every price (p. 170)

**increase in supply** Producers are more willing and able to supply the product at every price (p. 172)

**increasing returns** The marginal product of a variable resource increases as each additional unit of the resource is employed, other resources assumed constant (p. 148)

**index number** Compares the value of some variable in a particular year to its value in a base year, or reference year (p. 333)

**individual demand** The demand of an individual consumer (p. 107)

**industrial market countries** Economically advanced market countries of Western Europe, North America, Australia, New Zealand, and Japan (p. 588)

**industrial market countries** The advanced market economies of Western Europe, North America, Australia, New Zealand, and Japan; also called developed countries (p. 367)

**industrial policy** The view that government—using taxes, subsidies, and regulations—should nurture the industries and technologies of the future, thereby giving domestic industries an advantage over foreign competition (p. 378)

**Industrial Revolution** Development of large-scale production under one roof during the eighteenth century (p. 64)

**industrial union** A union whose membership includes all workers in an industry, such as all autoworkers and all steelworkers (p. 274)

**industry** All firms that supply output to a particular market, such as the market for autos, shoes, or wheat (p. 191)

**inelastic demand** A change in price has relatively little effect on quantity demanded; the percentage change in quantity demanded is less than the percentage change in price; the resulting elasticity is less than 1.0 (p. 111)

**inelastic supply** A change in price has relatively little effect on quantity supplied; the percentage change in quantity supplied is less than the percentage change in price; the resulting elasticity is less than 1.0 (p. 136)

**inferior good** A good for which demand decreases, or shifts leftward, as consumer incomes rise (p. 119)

**inflation** An increase in the economy's general price level (p. 398)

**initial public offering (IPO)** The initial sale of corporate stock to the public (p. 299)

**innovation** The process of turning an invention into a marketable product (p. 229)

**institutional investors** Banks, insurance companies, mutual funds, and other businesses that buy, sell, and own securities (p. 300)

**interest rate** Annual interest as a percentage of the amount borrowed or saved (p. 289)

**intermediate goods and services** Goods and services purchased for additional processing and resale (p. 322)

**inventories** Stocks of goods in process, such as computer parts, and stocks of finished goods, such as new computers awaiting sale (p. 324)

**investment** The purchase of new plants, new equipment, new buildings, new residences, and net additions to inventories (p. 324)

## L

**labor force** Those in the adult population who are either working or looking for work (p. 390)

**labor force participation rate** The number in the labor force divided by the adult population (p. 391)

**labor productivity** Output per unit of labor; measured as total output divided by the hours of labor employed to produce that output (p. 359)

**labor union** A group of workers who join together to seek higher pay and better working conditions by negotiating a labor contract with their employers (p. 273)

**labor** The physical and mental effort used to produce goods and services (p. 7)

**lagging economic indicators** Measures that follow, or trail, recessions or expansions (p. 340)

**laissez-faire** The doctrine that the government should not intervene in a market economy beyond the minimum required to maintain peace and property rights (p. 404)

**law of comparative advantage** The worker, firm, region, or country with the lowest opportunity cost of producing an output should specialize in that output (p. 51)

**law of demand** The quantity of a good demanded per period relates inversely to its price, other things constant (p. 102)

**law of diminishing marginal utility** The more of a good a person consumes per period, the smaller the increase in total utility from consuming one more unit, other things constant (p. 103)

**law of diminishing returns** As more of a variable resource is added to a given amount of fixed resources, marginal product eventually declines and could become negative (p. 148)

**law of increasing opportunity cost** Each additional increment of one good requires the economy to give up successively larger increments of the other good (p. 44)

**law of supply** The quantity of a good supplied in a given time period is usually directly related to its price, other things constant (p. 132)

**leading economic indicators** Measures that usually predict, or *lead to,* recessions or expansions (p. 339)

**liability** The legal obligation to pay any debts the business encounters (p. 235); An amount owed (p. 520)

**limited liability company (LLC)** Business with limited liability for some owners, single taxation of business income, and no ownership restrictions (p. 245)

**limited liability partnership (LLP)** Like a limited liability company but more easily converted from an existing partnership (p. 245)

**limited partnership** At least one general partner runs the business and bears unlimited personal liability; other partners provide financial capital but have limited liability (p. 245)

**line of credit** An arrangement with a bank through which a business can quickly borrow needed cash (p. 296)

**liquidity** The ability of any asset to be exchanged for cash (p. 300)

**long run** A period during which all resources can be varied (p. 148)

**long-run average cost** the lowest average cost of production at each rate of output when the firm's size is allowed to vary (p. 154)

**long-run average cost curve** A curve that indicates the lowest average cost of production at each rate of output when the firm's size is allowed to vary (p. 154)

## M

**M1** The narrowest definition of the money supply; consists of currency (including coins) held by the nonbanking public, checkable deposits, and traveler's checks (p. 506)

**M2** A broader definition of the money supply consisting of M1 plus savings deposits, small-denomination time deposits, and money market mutual fund accounts (p. 508)

**marginal** Incremental, additional, or extra; refers to a change in an economic variable, a change in the status quo (p. 13)

**marginal cost** The change in total cost resulting from a one-unit change in output; the change in total cost divided by the change in output (p. 152)

**marginal product** The change in total product resulting from a one-unit change in a particular resource, all other resources constant (p. 148)

**marginal revenue** The change in total revenue from selling another unit of the good (p. 152)

**marginal tax rate** The percentage of each additional dollar of income that goes to pay the tax (p. 433)

**marginal utility** The change in total utility resulting a one-unit change in consumption of a good (p. 103)

**market** The means by which people buy and sell something (p. 15); an arrangement that allows buyers and sellers to exchange things for a market price (p. 163)

**market-clearing price** The price that equates quantity demanded with quantity supplied; the equilibrium price (p. 165)

**market demand** The sum of the individual demands of all consumers in the market (p. 107)

**market economics** Study of economic behavior in particular markets, such as the market for computers or for unskilled labor (p. 14)

**market economy** Describes the U.S. economic system, where markets plays a relatively large role (p. 38)

**market for loans** The market that brings together borrowers (the demanders of loans) and savers (the suppliers of loans) to determine the market interest rate (p. 291)

**market power** The ability of a firm to raise its price without losing all its customers to rivals (p. 193)

**market structure** Important features of a market such as the number of buyers and sellers, product uniformity across sellers, ease of entering the market, and forms of competition (p. 192)

**maturity date** The date when the money borrowed by issuing a bond must be repaid (p. 299)

**maximizing political support** Objective that guides the behavior of elected officials; comparable to profit maximization by firms and utility maximization by households (p. 448)

**means-tested program** To qualify for welfare benefits, a household's income and assets must fall below a certain amount (p. 87)

**median income** The middle income when a group of incomes is ranked from lowest to highest (p. 83)

**mediator** An impartial observer brought in when labor negotiations break down to suggest how to resolve differences (p. 274)

**Medicaid** A program that funds medical care for those with incomes below a certain level who are elderly, blind, disabled, or are living in families with dependent children (p. 87)

**medium of exchange** Anything generally accepted by all parties in payment for goods or services (p. 491)

**merchandise trade balance** The value of a country's exported goods minus the value of its imported goods during a given period (p. 568)

**merger** The combination of two or more firms to form a single firm (p. 209)

**minimum acceptable price** The lowest price that will allow the firm's total revenue to cover variable cost; the minimum price the firm needs to produce in the short run rather than shut down (p. 153)

**minimum efficient scale** The smallest size that allows the firm to take full advantage of economies of scale; the smallest output that minimizes long run average cost (p. 154)

**minimum wage law** Establishes a minimum price that an employer can pay a worker for an hour of labor (p. 270)

**mixed economy** Economic systems that mix central planning with competitive markets (p. 37)

**monetary policy** The central bank's attempts to control the money supply to influence the national economy (p. 72)

**money** Anything that everyone is willing to accept in exchange for goods and services (p. 53)

**money demand** The relationship between how much money people want to hold and the interest rate (p. 527)

**money income** The number of dollars received per period, such as $100 per week (p. 103)

**money market mutual fund** A collection of short-term interest-earning assets (p. 508)

**money multiplier** The multiple by which the money supply increases as a result of an increase in excess reserves in the banking system (p. 522)

**money price** The dollar price of the good (p. 122)

**money supply** The stock of money available in the economy at a particular time (p. 528)

**monopolistic competition** A market structure with no entry barriers and many firms selling products differentiated enough that each firm's demand curve slopes downward (p. 202)

**monopoly** A sole supplier of a product with no close substitutes (p. 193)

**movement along a given demand curve** Change in quantity demanded resulting from a change in the price of the good, other things constant (p. 122)

**movement along a given supply curve** Change in quantity supplied resulting from a change in the price of the good, other things constant (p. 143)

**multilateral aid** Development aid from an organization, such as the World Bank, that gets funds from a group of countries (p. 600)

**multinational corporation (MNC)** A large corporation that makes and sells its products around the world (p. 307)

**multiplier effect** Any change in fiscal policy affects aggregate demand by more than the original change in spending or taxing (p. 464)

**mutual fund** A financial institution that issues its own stock and with the proceeds buys a portfolio of securities (p. 300)

**N**

**national banks** Banks chartered, or authorized by the federal government (p. 500)

**national economics** Study of the economic behavior of the economy as a whole, especially the national economy (p. 14)

**national income accounts** System that organizes huge quantities of data collected from a variety of sources across America (p. 322)

**natural monopoly** One firm that can serve the entire market at a lower per-unit cost than can two or more firms (p. 71)

**natural rate of unemployment** The unemployment rate when the economy is producing its potential level of output (p. 460)

**natural resources** So-called "gifts of nature" used to produce goods and services; includes renewable and exhaustible resources (p. 7)

**negative externalities** By-products of production or consumption that impose costs on third parties, neither buyers nor sellers (p. 78)

**net domestic product** Gross domestic product minus depreciation (p. 324)

**net exports** The value of a country's exports minus the value of its imports (p. 325)

**net investment** Gross investment minus depreciation; used to compute net domestic product

**net unilateral transfers** Grants and gifts of cash received from abroad by U.S. residents minus grants and gifts of cash sent to foreign residents by U.S. residents (p. 570)

**net worth** Assets minus liabilities; also called owners' equity (p. 520)

**nominal GDP** GDP based on prices prevailing at the time of the transaction; current-dollar GDP (p. 331)

**nominal interest rate** The interest rate expressed in current dollars as a percentage of the amount loaned; the interest rate on the loan agreement (p. 401)

**nondurable goods** Goods expected to last less than three years, such as soap and soup (p. 323)

**nonhorizontal merger** One firm combines with another that does not produces the same product, such as Ford and U.S. Steel (p. 209)

**noninstitutional adult population** All those 16 years of age and older, expect people in the military, prisons, or mental hospitals; used to determine the unemployment rate (p. 390)

**normal good** A good for which demand increases or shifts rightward, as consumer incomes rise (p. 119)

**normative economic statement** An opinion, which cannot be shown to be true or false by reference to the facts (p. 13)

**not-for-profit organizations** Groups that do not pursue profit as a goal; they engage in charitable, educational, humanitarian, cultural, professional, or other activities often with a social purpose (p. 246)

**O**

**oligopoly** A market structure with a small number of firms whose behavior is interdependent (p. 203)

**open-access good** A good that is rival in consumption but exclusion is costly (p. 76)

**open-market operations** Buying or selling U.S. government securities as a way of regulating the money supply (p. 502)

**opportunity cost** The value of the best alternative passed up for the chosen item or activity (p. 20)

**other-things-constant assumption** The simplifying assumption that nothing else of importance changes except the variables in question (p. 11)

**overhead** Another word for fixed cost (p. 150)

## P

**partnership** Two or more people agree to contribute resources to the business in return for a share of the profit (p. 236)

**patent** The exclusive right an inventor receives to sell that invention for up to 20 years (p. 70)

**payroll taxes** Taxes deducted from paychecks to support Social Security and Medicare (p. 439)

**perfect competition** A market structure with many fully informed buyers and sellers of an identical product with no barriers to entry (p. 192)

**physical capital** The machines, buildings, roads, airports, communications networks, and other manufactured creations used to produce goods and services; also called capital goods (pp 324, 360)

**physical infrastructure** Transportation, communication, energy, water, and sanitation systems provided by or regulated by government (p. 604)

**positive economic statement** An assertion about economic reality that can be supported or rejected by reference to the facts (p. 13)

**positive externalities** By-products of consumption or production that benefit third parties, neither buyers nor sellers (p. 79)

**potential output** The economy's maximum sustainable output in the long run (p. 460)

**price** What you pay when you buy something, and what you receive when you sell it (p. 164)

**price ceiling** A maximum legal price above which a product cannot be sold; to have an impact, a price floor must be set below the equilibrium price (p. 180)

**price floor** A minimum legal price below which a product cannot be sold; to have an impact, a price floor must be set above the equilibrium price (p. 180)

**price level** A composite measure reflecting the prices of all goods and services in the economy relative to prices in a base year (p. 344)

**prime rate** The interest rate banks charge for loans to their most trustworthy business borrowers (p. 297)

**private good** A good with two features: (1) the amount consumed by one person is unavailable for others and (2) nonpayers can easily be excluded (p. 76)

**private property rights** Legal claim that guarantees an owner the right to use a resource or to charge others for its use (p. 69)

**privatization** The process in transition economies of converting state-owned enterprises into private enterprises (p. 40, 607)

**producer cooperative** Producers join forces to reduce their costs by purchasing supplies and equipment as a group and selling their output as a group (p. 246)

**product market** A set of arrangements by which goods and services are bought and sold (p. 15)

**production possibilities frontier (PPF)** Shows the possible combinations of the two types of goods that can be produced when available resources are employed fully and efficiently (p. 42)

**productive efficiency** Achieved when a firm produces at the lowest possible cost per unit (p. 179)

**productive resources** The inputs, or factors of production, used to produce the goods and services that people want (p. 6)

**productivity** The value of output produced by each additional unit of a resource (p. 257); the ratio of output to a specific measure of input; usually reflects an average, such as bushels of grain per acre of farm land (p. 359)

**profit** Equals the revenue from sales minus the cost of production (p. 5)

**progressive taxation** The tax as a percentage of income increases as income increases (p. 433)

**proportional taxation** The tax as a percentage of income remains constant as income increases; also called a flat tax (p. 433)

**public good** A good that, once produced, is available for all to consume, but the producer cannot easily exclude nonpayers (p. 76)

**public utility** A government-owned or government-regulated monopoly (p. 63)

**publicly traded corporation** Owned by many shareholders; shares can be bought or sold (p. 243)

**pure centrally planned economy** An economic system in which all resources are government-owned and production is coordinated by the central plans of government (p. 37)

**pure market economy** An economic system with no government involvement so private firms account for all production (p. 35)

## Q

**quantity demanded** The amount demanded at a particular price (p. 106)

**quantity supplied** The amount supplied at a particular price (p. 134)

**quasi-public good** A good that, once produced, is available to all, but nonpayers are easily excluded (p. 76)

**quota** A legal limit on the quantity of a particular product that can be imported (p. 560)

## R

**ration** To allocate goods, not by markets, but based on a certain amount per household (p. 37)

**rational** Making the best choices one can based on the information available (p. 11)

**rational ignorance** A stance adopted by voters when they find that the cost of understanding and voting on a particular issue exceeds the benefit expected from doing so (p. 449)

**real GDP** The economy's aggregate output measured in dollars of constant purchasing power; GDP measured in terms of the goods and services produced (p. 331)

**real GDP per capita** Real GDP divided by the population; the best measure of an economy's standard of living (p. 348)

**real income** Income measured in terms of the goods and services it will buy (p. 103)

**real interest rate** The interest rate expressed in dollars of constant purchasing power as a percentage of the amount loaned; the nominal interest rate minus the inflation rate (p. 401)

**recession** A decline in total production lasting at least two consecutive quarters, or at least six months (p. 336)

**recognition lag** The time needed to identify a macroeconomic problem (p. 471)

**regressive taxation** The tax as a percentage of income decreases as income increases (p. 433)

**renewable resource** A natural resource that can be drawn on indefinitely if used conservatively, such as the atmosphere or water supply (p. 7)

**representative money** Bank notes that exchange for a specific commodity, such as gold (p. 497)

**required reserve ratio** A Fed regulation that dictates the minimum percentage of deposits each bank must keep in reserve (p. 520)

**required reserves** The dollar amount that must be held in reserve; checkable deposits multiplied by the required reserve ratio (p. 521)

**reserve ratio** Bank reserves as a share of bank deposits (p. 497)

**reserves** Cash that banks have on hand in their vaults or on deposit with the Federal Reserve (p. 500)

**resource complements** One resource works with the other in production; a decrease in the price of one increases the demand for the other (p. 260)

**resource market** A set of arrangements by which productive resources are bought and sold (p. 15)

**resource substitutes** One resource can replace another in production; an increase in the price of one resource increases the demand for the other (p. 260)

**rest of the world** Economic decision makers formed by households, firms, and governments in the more than 200 sovereign nations throughout the world (p. 65)

**retained earnings** That portion of after-tax corporate profit reinvested in the firm (p. 299)

**right-to-work law** State law that says a worker at a union company does not have to join the union or pay union dues to hold a job there (p. 274)

**rival in consumption** The amount consumed by one person is unavailable for others to consume; a feature of private goods (p. 76)

**rules of the game** The formal and informal institutions that provide production incentives and promote economic activity, such as laws, customs, and conventions (p. 360)

## S

**savings deposits** Deposits that earn interest but have no specific maturity date (p. 507)

**scarce** The amount people want exceeds the amount available at a zero price (p. 9)

**scarcity** A condition facing all societies because there are not enough productive resources to satisfy people's unlimited wants (p. 6)

**S corporation** Limited liability combined with the single taxation of business income; must have no more than 75 stockholders with no foreign stockholders (p. 245)

**seasonal unemployment** Occurs because of seasonal changes in labor demand during the year (p. 388)

**secondary markets** Securities markets where stocks and bonds already sold by the corporation can be exchanged (p. 300)

**secondhand securities** Stocks and bonds that have already been sold by the corporation (p. 300)

**securities** Corporate stock and corporate bonds (p. 299)

**security exchanges** Markets where stocks and bonds can be traded, or bought and sold (p. 299)

**seigniorage** The difference between the exchange value of money and the cost of supplying it; the "profit" from issuing money (p. 494)

**service** Something not physical that requires scarce resources and satisfies human wants (p. 8)

**shares of stock** Proof of corporate ownership; owners are entitled to profits and to vote on directors of the corporation (p. 243)

**shift of a demand curve** Increase or decrease in demand resulting from a change in one of the determinants of demand other than the price of the good (p. 122)

**shift of a supply curve** Increase or decrease in supply resulting from a change in one of the determinants of supply other than the price of the good (p. 144)

**short run** A period during which at least one of a firm's resources is fixed (p. 148)

**shortage** At a given price, the amount by which quantity demanded exceeds quantity supplied; a shortage usually forces the price up (p. 164)

**sin tax** A tax on products that are deemed socially undesirable, such as cigarettes, liquor, and legal gambling (p. 432)

**social insurance** Cash transfers for retirees, the unemployed, and others with a work history and a record of contributions to the program (p. 86)

**soft budget constraint** In centrally planned economies, the budget condition faced by state enterprises that are subsidized when they lose money (p. 607)

**sole proprietorship** The simplest form of business organization; a firm is owned and run by one person (p. 234)

**specialization** Occurs when individual workers focus on single tasks, enabling each one to be more efficient and productive (p. 51)

**speculator** Someone who buys or sells foreign exchange in hopes of profiting from fluctuations in the exchange rate over time (p. 577)

**stagflation** A decline, or *stag*nation, of a nation's output accompanied by in*flation* in the price level (p. 407)

**standard of living** An economy's level of economic prosperity; best measured by the value of goods and services produced per capita (p. 359)

**state banks** Banks chartered, or authorized, by the states in which they operated (p. 499)

**store of value** Anything that retains its purchasing power over time (p. 492)

**strike** A labor union's attempt to withhold labor from the firm (p. 274)

**structural unemployment** Occurs because job seekers do not have the skills demanded (p. 388)

**substitutes** Goods, such as pizza and tacos, that relate in such a way that an increase in the price of one shifts the demand for the other rightward (p. 120)

**substitution effect of a price change** When the price of a good falls, consumers substitute that good for other goods, which are now relatively more expensive (p. 103)

**sunk cost** A cost you have already incurred and cannot recover, regardless of what you do now (p. 22)

**Supplemental Security Income (SSI)** Provides cash to the elderly poor and the disabled (p. 87)

**supply** A relation showing the quantities of a good producers are willing and able to sell at various prices during a given period, other things constant (p. 132)

**supply curve** A curve or line showing the quantities or a particular good supplied at various prices during a given time period, other things constant (p. 132)

**supply of loans curve** An upward sloping curve showing the positive relationship between the interest rate and the quantity of loans supplied, other things constant (p. 291)

**supply schedule** Columns of numbers showing the quantities of a particular good supplied at various possible prices during a given period, other things constant (p. 132)

**supply-side economics** Macroeconomic policy that focuses on a rightward shift of the aggregate supply curve through tax cuts or other changes that increase production incentives (p. 408)

**surplus** At a given price, the amount by which quantity supplied exceeds quantity demanded; a surplus usually forces the price down (p. 164)

## T

**Taft-Hartley Act** Federal legislation approved in 1947 authorizing states to approve right-to-work laws (p. 274)

**tariff** A tax on imports (p. 560)

**tastes** Consumer preferences; likes and dislikes in consumption; assumed to be constant along a given demand curve (p. 122)

**tax incidence** Those who bear the burden of the tax (p. 432)

**technology** Knowledge about how best to combine resources to make goods and services (p. 42)

**Temporary Assistance for Needy Families (TANF)** Provides cash to poor families with dependent children (p. 87)

**thrift institutions, or thrifts** Depository institutions that make long-term loans primarily to households; savings and loan institutions, mutual savings banks, and credit unions (p. 499)

**time deposits** Deposits that earn a fixed rate of interest if held for a specified period (p. 508)

**time price** The time required for a good or service to provide its benefits (p. 122)

**token money** Money whose exchange value exceeds its intrinsic value (p. 497)

**total cost** Fixed cost plus variable cost; the cost of all resources used by the firm (p. 150)

**total product** A firm's total output (p. 148)

**total revenue** Price multiplied by the quantity demanded at that price (p. 111)

**trade deficit** The amount by which the value of merchandise imports exceeds the value of merchandise exports during a given period (p. 568)

**trade surplus** The amount by which the value of merchandise exports exceeds the value of merchandise imports during a given period (p. 568)

**trademark** Establishes property rights to unique commercial marks and symbols, such as McDonald's golden arches (p. 70)

**traditional economy** Economic system shaped largely by custom or religion (p. 40)

**transaction cost** The cost of time and information needed to carry out market exchange (pp. 63, 167)

**transition economy** Economic system in the process of shifting from central planning to competitive markets (p. 39)

## U

**U.S. Agency for International Development (USAID)** The federal agency that coordinates foreign aid to the developing world (p. 600)

**underemployment** Workers are overqualified for their jobs or work fewer hours than they would prefer (p. 389)

**underground economy** Market exchange that goes unreported either because it is illegal or because those involved want to evade taxes; also called the black market (p. 329)

**undifferentiated oligopoly** Oligopoly market where firms sell an identical product, such as a barrel of oil (p. 203)

**unemployment benefits** Cash transfers to unemployed workers who actively seek work and who meet other qualifications (p. 394)

**unemployment rate** The number looking for work divided by the number in the labor force (p. 390)

**Uniform Partnership Act (UPA)** In most states, governs partnerships lacking their own agreement (p. 245)

**unit of account** A common unit for measuring the value of every good or service (p. 491)

**unit-elastic demand** The percentage change in quantity demanded equals the percentage change in price; the resulting elasticity equals 1.0 (p. 110)

**unit-elastic supply** The percentage change in quantity supplied equals the percentage change in price; the resulting elasticity equals 1.0 (p. 136)

**Uruguay Round** The most recent and most comprehensive of the eight postwar multilateral trade negotiations under GATT; created the World Trade Organization (p. 562)

**utility** The satisfaction from consumption; sense of well-being (p. 63)

## V

**value added** At each stage of production, the value of a product minus the cost of intermediate goods used to produce it (p. 326)

**variable cost** Any production cost that changes as output changes (p. 150)

**variable resource** Any resource that can be varied in the short run to change output (p. 148)

**vertical merger** One firm combines with another from which it buys inputs or to which it sells output, such as a merger between a steel producer and an automaker (p. 305)

## W

**wages** Payment to resource owners for their labor (p. 7)

**welfare reform** An overhaul of the welfare system in 1996 that imposed a lifetime welfare limit of five years per recipient and other conditions (p. 416)

**world price** The price at which a good is traded internationally; determined by the world supply and world demand for the good (p. 560)

**World Trade Organization (WTO)** The legal and institutional foundation of the multilateral trading system that succeeded GATT in 1995 (p. 562)

## A

**ability-to-pay tax principle** *principio de la habilidad de pagar el impuesto* Aquellos con más habilidad de pagar, tal como aquellos que tienen más ingresos, deben pagar más del impuesto (p. 434)

**absolute advantage** *ventaja absoluta* El poder hacer algo usando menos recursos que lo que requieren otros productores (p. 51)

**aggregate demand** *demanda total* La relación entre el nivel del precio de la economía y la cantidad de producción total exigida, otras cosas constantes (p. 344)

**aggregate demand curve** *curva de demanda total* Una curva que representa la relación entre el nivel del precio de la economía y el verdadero PIB exigido por periodo, otras cosas constantes (p. 344)

**aggregate expenditure** *gastos totales* Gasto total en todo bien y servicio terminado y producido en la economía durante el año (p. 325)

**aggregate income** *ingresos totales* La suma de todo el ingreso ganado por proveedores de recursos en la economía durante un año asignado (p. 326)

**aggregate output** *producción total* Una combinación de medidas de todos los bienes y servicios producidos en una economía durante un periodo asignado; PIB verdadero (p. 344)

**aggregate supply curve** *curva de oferta total* Una curva que representa la relación entre el nivel del precio de la economía y el verdadero PIB ofrecido por periodo, otras cosas constantes (p. 346)

**allocative efficiency** *eficiencia de asignar* Se logra cuando una empresa produce el producto más preferido por los consumidores (p. 179)

**annually balanced budget** *presupuesto anual ajustado* Igualando gastos anuales con ingresos anuales, excepto durante años de guerra; aproximación al presupuesto federal antes de la Gran Depresión (p. 466)

**antitrust activity** *actividad de antimonopolio* Esfuerzos del gobierno dirigidos a prevenir monopolios y promover competencia en mercados donde competencia se desea (p. 209)

**antitrust laws** *leyes de antimonopolio* Leyes que prohiben comportamiento anticompetitivo y promueve competencia en mercados donde se desea la competencia (p. 71)

**applied research** *investigación aplicada* Investigación que busca respuestas a preguntas en particular o aplica descubrimientos científicos para desarrollar productos específicos (p. 375)

**asset** *activo* Cualquier propiedad física o reclamo financiero que sea propio (p. 520)

**automatic stabilizers** *estabilizadores automáticos* Programas de gastos e impuestos por el gobierno que año tras año automáticamente reducen fluctuaciones en poder adquisitivo, y por lo tanto en consumo, durante el ciclo de negocios (p. 471)

## B

**balance of payments** *ajuste de pagos* Una constancia de todas las transacciones económicas entre residentes de un país y residentes del resto del mundo durante un tiempo asignado (p. 568)

**balance sheet** *balance* Un estado de cuentas que muestra los activos, los pasivos y el valor neto en una fecha asignada; como los activos tienen que igualar a los pasivos más el valor neto, el estado de cuentas está ajustado (p. 520)

**barriers to entry** *obstáculos al entrar* Cualquier cosa que previene nuevas empresas de competir en forma igual con empresas que existen en una industria (p. 194)

**barter** *intercambiar* Un sistema de comercio en el cual productos se intercambian directamente por otros productos (p. 52)

**basic research** *investigación básica* La búsqueda por conocimiento sin prestar atención a como se usará ese conocimiento; un primer paso hacia avances tecnológicos (p. 375)

**benefits-received tax principle** *beneficios recibidos principio de impuesto* Aquellos que reciben más beneficios del program de gobierno financiado por el impuesto debe pagar más de ese impuesto (p. 434)

**bilateral aid** *ayuda bilateral* Ayuda de desarrollo de un país a otro (p. 600)

**binding arbitration** *arbitraje fijo* Cuando negociaciones de trabajo se han quebrado y el interés del público está involucrado, un tercer partidiario neutro se trae para imponer un acuerdo que los dos lados deben aceptar (p. 274)

**bond** *bono* Un contrato prometiendo pagar dinero prestado en una fecha designada y pagar interés en el proceso (p. 299)

**brain drain** *drenaje cerebral* La perdida de migrantes educados de un país en desarrollo a paises con mercados industriales (p. 598)

**bureaus** *departamentos* Agencias del gobierno encargadas de implementar legislación y que son financiadas por apropiaciones de cuerpos legislativos (p. 452)

**business cycle** *ciclo de negocio* Cambios que reflejan aumentos y reducciónes de actividad económica en relación con la tendencia de crecimiento de largo plazo de la economía (p. 336)

## C

**capital deepening** *profundizando en capital* Un aumento en la cantidad y la calidad del capital por trabajador; una fuente para aumentar productividad en el trabajo (p. 360)

**capital goods** *bienes de capital* Toda creación humana usada para producir bienes y servicios; por ejemplo, fábricas, camiones y máquinas (p. 8)

**cartel** *cartel* Un grupo de empresas que acuerda coordinar decisiones de precio para maximar beneficios del grupo al comportarse como un monopolista (p. 204)

**check** *cheque* Una orden escrita instruyendo al banco de pagarle a alguien del monto depositado (p. 497)

**checkable deposits** *depositos verificables* Depositos en instituciones financieras contra los cuales se puede escribir cheques y/o tarjetas de cajero automático o de débito se pueden aplicar (p. 507)

**classical economists** *economistas clásicos* Un grupo de laissez-faire economistas, que creían que fases de bajas en la economía eran problemas a corto plazo que se corregían por ellos mismos a largo plazo por fuerzas naturales del mercado (p. 465)

**cluster** *conjunto* Empresas en la misma industria o en industrias relacionadas que se agrupan en una región, tal como Wall Street (La Bolsa), Hollywood o Silicon Valley (p. 379)

**collateral** *garantía* Una propiedad del prestatario que se puede vender para pagar el prestamo en caso de que el prestamo no se pague (p. 297)

**collective bargaining** *negociación colectiva* El proceso por el cual representantes del sindicato y

del empresario negocean salarios, beneficios de empleados y condiciones de trabajo (p. 274)

**commercial banks** *bancos comerciales* Instituciones de deposito que hacen prestamos primariamente a negocios (p. 498)

**commodity** *bien de consumo* Un producto que es idéntico entre vendedores, tal como una medida de áridos de trigo (p. 192)

**commodity money** *dinero de producto* Cualquier cosa que sirve tanto como dinero que como producto, tal como el oro (p. 491)

**competitive firm's supply curve** *curva de oferta de una empresa competitiva* La porción de la curva de costo marginal de una empresa que aumenta al precio o más del precio que permitirá que la empresa cubra el costo variable (p. 153)

**conglomerate merger** *fusión de conglomeración* Una empresa combina con otra empresa en una industria diferente, tal como la fusión entre un productor de plásticos y una empresa de electrónicos (p. 305)

**consumer price index (CPI)** *índice del precio del consumidor* Medida de inflación basada en el costo de un canasto fijo de bienes y servicios que se compran por una típica familia (p. 333)

**consumer surplus** *excedente de consumidor* La diferencia entre la máxima cantidad que consumidores quieren pagar por una cantidad determinada de un bien y lo que en realidad pagan (p. 181)

**consumption** *consumo* Compras por un hogar de un bien o servicio terminado excepto por nuevas residencias, las cuales cuentan como inversiones (p. 323)

**convergence theory** *teoría de convergencia* Una teoría que predice que el nivel de vida en economías por todo el mundo crecera más similar sobre el tiempo, con los paises más pobres gradualmente cerrando el espacio con los paises más ricos (p. 607)

**cooperative** *cooperativa* Una organización que consiste de personas que unen sus recursos para comprar y vender más eficientemente que lo que pudieran hacer en forma independiente (p. 245)

**corporation** *corporación* Una entidad legal con una existencia que es distinta de las verdaderas personas que la organizan, la poséen y la dirigen (p. 245)

**cost-push inflation** *inflación de costo y empuje* Inflación que resulta de un cambio hacia la izquierda de la curva de oferta total (p. 399)

**credit** *crédito* La habilidad de prestar ahora basada en la promesa de pagar en el futuro (p. 295)

**crowding in** *alojamiento* Gastos del gobierno estimulan inversión privada en una economía muerta (p. 480)

**crowding out** *desplazamiento* Inversión privada cae cuando déficits más altos del gobierno hacen subir los intereses (p. 480)

**current account** *cuenta actual* La porción del estado de pagos que da constancia a exportaciones e importaciones de bienes y servicios, ingresos netos de inversión, y transferencias netas (p. 568)

**cycle of poverty** *ciclo de pobreza* Niños en familias de bienestar pueden terminar en bienestar ellos mismos cuando crezcan (p. 415)

**cyclical unemployment** *desempleo cíclico* Ocurre por los empleos perdidos durante la fase de recesión del ciclo de negocio (p. 388)

### D

**decision-making lag** *lapso para hacer una decisión* El tiempo necesitado para decidir que hacer cuando el problema se ha identificado (p. 473)

**decrease in demand** *reducción en demanda* Los consumidores mucho menos quieren y pueden comprar el producto a cualquier precio (p. 171)

**decrease in supply** *reducción en oferta* Los productores mucho menos quieren y pueden ofrecer el producto a cualquier precio (p. 173)

**demand** *demanda* Una relación que muestra las cantidades de un bien que los consumidores quieren y pueden comprar a diferentes precios por periodo, otras cosas constantes (p. 102)

**demand curve** *curva de demanda* Una curva o linea que muestra las cantidades de un bien en particular en demanda a varios precios durante un periodo específico, otras cosas constantes (p. 105)

**demand for loans curve** *curva de demanda por prestamos* Una curva con inclinación hacia abajo mostrando una relación negativa entre el índice de interés y la cantidad de prestamos exigidos, otras cosas constantes (p. 290)

**demand-pull inflation** *inflación de demanda y hala* Inflación que resulta por cambios hacia la derecha de la curva de demanda total (p. 398)

**demand-side economics** *economía de lado de demanda* Póliza de macroeconomía que enfoca en cambiar la curva de demanda total como forma de promover empleo total y estabilidad de precio (p. 406)

**depreciation** *depreciación* El valor de la acción capital que se usa o se vuelve obsoleto al producir PIB durante el año (p. 330)

**deregulation** *deregulación* Una reducción en el control del gobierno sobre los precios y entradas de empresas en mercados previamente regulados, tal como las aerolineas y el transporte por carretera (p. 212)

**derived demand** *demanda derivada* La demanda por un recurso se deriva de la demanda por el producto que ese recurso produce (p. 256)

**developing countries** *paises en desarrollo* Paises con un nivel de vida más bajo porque tienen relativamente poco capital humano y físico; también se llaman paises del Tercer Mundo (p. 367, 588)

**discount rate** *taza de descuento* Taza de interés que el gobierno federal le cobra a los bancos que prestan reservas (p. 501)

**discouraged workers** *trabajadores desilucionados* Alguien que no ha podido encontrar trabajo, se sale de la fuerza de trabajo (p. 389)

**discretionary fiscal policy** *póliza fiscal discrecional* Cambios a gastos o impuestos por el Congreso para promover metas macroeconómicas (p. 471)

**disequilibrium** *desequilibrio* Algo desigual entre la cantidad exigida y la cantidad ofrecida al paso que el mercado busca equilibrio; usualmente temporal, excepto donde el gobierno interviene y fija el precio (p. 180)

**dividend** *dividendo* La porción que se paga a los accionistas, del beneficio de una corporación después de impuestos (p. 299)

**division of labor** *división de trabajo* Clasificación del proceso de producción en diferentes tareas que se llevan a cabo por diferentes trabajadores (p. 53)

### E

**economic growth** *crecimiento económico* Una expansión en las posibilidades de producción en la economía o en la habilidad de producir (p. 45)

**economic system** *sistema económico* Un conjunto de mecanismos e instituciones que resuelven las preguntas del qué, cómo y para quién para una economía (p. 34)

**economic theory, economic model** *teoría de economía, modelo de economía* Una simplificación de la realidad de la economía usada para hacer predicciones sobre el mundo verdadero (p. 11)

**economics** *economía* El estudio de como la gente usa sus recursos escasos para satisfacer sus deseos ilimitados (p. 6)

**economies of scale** *economías de escala* Fuerzas que reducen el costo promedio al paso que el tamaño, o escala de la empresa aumenta a largo plazo (p. 154)

**economy** *economía* La estructura de actividad económica en una localidad, región, país, un grupo de paises, o el mundo (p. 322)

**effectiveness lag** *lapso en eficacia* El tiempo necesitado para cambios en póliza para afectar la economía (p. 473)

**efficiency** *eficiencia* Producir el máximo producto posible de los recursos disponibles (pp. 42, 46)

**elasticity of demand** *elasticidad de demanda* Mide como la cantidad receptiva exigida es al cambio del precio; el cambio de porcentaje en cantidad exigida dividida por el cambio de porcentaje en precio (p. 110)

**elasticity of supply** *elasticidad de oferta* Una medida de receptividad de la cantidad ofrecida a un cambio de precio; el cambio de porcentaje en la cantidad dividido por el cambio de porcentaje en el precio (p. 135)

**entrepreneur** *empresario* Un buscador de beneficio que desarrolla un nuevo producto o proceso y asume el riesgo de beneficio o perdida (p. 7)

**equilibrium** *equilibrio* La cantidad que los consumidores quieren y pueden comprar es igual a la cantidad que productores quieren y pueden vender (p. 164)

**equilibrium interest rate** *índice de interés en equilibrio* El único índice de interés al cual la cantidad de prestamos exigidos es igual a la cantidad de prestamos ofrecidos (p. 292)

**equilibrium wage** *salario de equilibrio* El salario al cual no hay ni un exceso en la cantidad de trabajo en demanda ni un exceso en la cantidad de trabajo en oferta (p. 258)

**euro** *euro* La nueva moneda común europea (p. 540)

**excess reserves** *reservas en exceso* Reservas del banco en exceso de las reservas requeridas (p. 521)

**exchange rate** *taza de cambio* El precio de la moneda de un país medido en términos de la moneda de otro país (p. 575)

**expansion** *expansión* La fase de actividad económica durante la cual la producción total de la economía aumenta (p. 337)

**expenditure approach to GDP** *método de gastos al PIB* Un método de calcular el PIB al sumar los gastos en todos los bienes y servicios terminados producidos durante un año (p. 323)

**export promotion** *promoción de exportaciones* Una estrategia de desarrollo que se concentra en producir para el mercado de exportación (p. 598)

## F

**featherbedding** *prebendaje (contratar mano de obra que no es necesaria)* Esfuerzos de un sindicato de forzar a un empresario para emplear a más trabajadores que los que se necesitan para la tarea (p. 274)

**federal funds market** *mercado de fondos federales* Un mercado para hacer prestamos y prestar de un día para el otro de las reservas que mantiene el gobierno federal para los bancos (p. 531)

**federal funds rate** *taza de fondos federales* La taza de interés que se cobra en el mercado de fondos federales; el objetivo de la taza de interés que tiene el gobierno federal

**Federal Open Market Committee (FOMC)** *Comité Federal de Mercado Abierto* Un grupo de doce miembros que hacen decisiones sobre operaciones de mercado abierto (p. 501)

**Federal Reserve System (the Fed)** *Sistema Federal de Reserva* Establecido en 1913 como el banco central y autoridad monetaria de los Estados Unidos (p. 500)

**fertility rate** *nivel de fertilidad* El promedio en número de nacimientos durante la vida de cada mujer (p. 589)

**fiat money** *dinero fiat* Dinero que no se puede cambiar por nada de valor intrínsico; declarado dinero por decreto de gobierno (p. 497)

**financial account** *cuenta financiera* La porción del ajuste de pagos que da constancia a transacciones internacionales que tiene activos financieros, como acciones y bonos, y activos verdaderos, tal como fábricas y edificios de oficinas (p. 571)

**financial capital** *capital financiero* Dinero necesitado para comenzar o expandir un negocio (p. 229)

**financial intermediaries** *intermediarios financieros* Bancos y otras instituciones que sirven como intermediarios, aceptando fondos de ahorradores y prestandolos a los prestatarios (p. 295)

**firm** *empresa* Unidad de negocio o empresa formada por un empresario que busca beneficio el cual combina recursos para producir bienes y servicios (p. 63)

**fixed cost** *costo fijo* Cualquier costo de producción que es independiente de la producción de una empresa (p. 150)

**fixed exchange rate** *taza de cambio fija* Taza de cambio fija dentro de un estrecho rango de valores y mantenida por las continuas compras y ventas de la moneda de un banco central (p. 579)

**flexible exchange rate** *taza de cambio flexible* Taza de cambio determinada por las fuerzas de oferta y demanda sin que el gobierno intervenga (p. 579)

**foreign aid** *ayuda extranjera* Una beca internacional o un prestamo hecho en términos favorables para promover desarrollo económico (p. 599)

**foreign exchange** *cambio extranjero* Dinero extranjero necesitado para hacer transacciones internacionales (p. 575)

**fractional reserve banking system** *sistema bancario de reserva fraccional* Solo una porción de los depositos del banco se respalda por las reservas (p. 497)

**frictional unemployment** *desempleo friccional* Ocurre por el tiempo requerido de emparejar buscadores de trabajo calificados con puestos disponibles (p. 388)

**full employment** *empleo completo* Ocurre cuando no hay nada de desempleo cíclico; relativamente bajo desempleo (p. 388)

## G

**General Agreement on Tariffs and Trade (GATT)** *Acuerdo general a tarifas y comercio* Un tratado internacional de reducción de tarifas adoptado en 1947 que resultó en una serie de "vueltas" negociadas con la meta a un comercio más libre (p. 561)

**general partnership** *sociedad colectiva general* Los socios comparten en la responsabilidad de mantener el negocio y en cualquier responsabilidad legal de su operación (p. 237)

**good** *bien* Algo que se puede ver, sentir y tocar que requiere recursos escasos y satisface deseos humanos (p. 8)

**government budget** *presupuesto del gobierno* Un plan para desembolsos e ingresos del gobierno por un periodo específico, usualmente un año (p. 440)

**government purchases** *compras de gobierno* Gastos por todos los niveles de gobierno por bienes y servicios; no incluye transferencia de pagos (p. 324)

**gross domestic product (GDP)** *producto interno bruto (PIB)* El valor del mercado de todos los bienes y servicios terminados y producidos en los Estados Unidos durante un periodo asignado, usualmente un año (p. 322)

**Group of Seven (G-7)** *el grupo de siete of G-7* Los siete mercados de economía industrial principales, incluyendo los Estados Unidos, el Reino Unido, Francia, Alemania, Italia, el Japón y el Canada (p. 368)

## H

**hostile takeovers** *toma de poder hostil* Una empresa compra el control de otra empresa contra los deseos de la gerencia de la empresa que se compra; una estrategia común de fusión en los años de 1980 (p. 300)

**household** *hogar* El más importante determinador de decisiones económicas, consistiendo en todos aquellos que viven bajo un techo (p. 62)

**human capital** *capital humano* El conocimiento, habilidad, y experiencia de una fuerza de trabajo aculumado (p. 360)

**human resources** *recursos humanos* La amplia categoría de esfuerzos humanos, tanto físicos como mentales, usada para producir bienes y servicios (p. 7)

## I

**implementation lag** *lapso de implementación* El tiempo necesitado para ejecutar un cambio en póliza (p. 473)

**import substitution** *sustitución de importaciones* Una estrategia de desarrollo que enfatiza fabricación doméstica de productos que actualmente son importados (p. 598)

**income approach to GDP** *método de ingresos al PIB* Un método de calcular PIB al sumar todos los pagos a los dueños de los recursos usados para producir productos durante el año (p. 323)

**income-assistance programs** *programas de asistencia de ingresos* Programas del gobierno que ofrecen dinero y ayuda en-especie a los pobres (p. 86)

**income effect of a price change** *el efecto de ingresos a un cambio de precio* Una caida en el precio de un bien aumenta los verdaderos ingresos de un consumidor, haciendo que los consumidores puedan comprar el bien; para bienes normales, la cantidad exigida aumenta (p. 103)

**increase in demand** *aumento en demanda* Los consumidores mucho más quieren y pueden comprar el producto a cualquier precio (p. 170)

**increase in supply** *aumento en oferta* Los productores mucho más quieren y pueden ofrecer el producto a cualquier precio (p. 172)

**individual demand** *demanda individual* La exigencia de un consumidor individual (p. 107)

**industrial market countries** *paises de mercado industrial* Los mercados de economías avanzados del Oeste de Europa, Norteamérica, Australia, Nueva Zelanda y el Japón; también se llaman paises desarrollados (pp. 367, 588)

**industrial policy** *póliza industrial* La vista que el gobierno usando impuestos, subsidios y regulaciones debe nutrir las industrias y tecnologías del futuro, al darle a las industrias domésticas una ventaja sobre la competencia extranjera (p. 378)

**Industrial Revolution** *Revolución Industrial* Desarrollo de producción de grande escala bajo un techo durante el siglo 18 (p. 64)

**inflation** *inflación* Un aumento en el nivel del precio general de la economía (p. 398)

**initial public offering (IPO)** *oferta inicial pública* La venta inicial de acciones de una corporación al público (p. 299)

**innovation** *innovación* El proceso de cambiar una invención a un producto comercializable (p. 229)

**institutional investors** *inversionistas institucionales* Bancos, compañías de seguros, fondos mutuales, y otros negocios que compran, venden y son dueños de valores (p. 300)

**interest rate** *índice de interés* Interés anual como porcentaje de la cantidad prestada o ahorrada (p. 289)

**investment** *inversión* La compra de nuevas plantas, nuevo equipo, nuevos edificios, nuevas residencias, y adiciones netas al inventario (p. 324)

**L**

**labor** *trabajo* El esfuerzo físico y mental usado para producir bienes y servicios (p. 7)

**labor force** *fuerza de trabajo* Aquellos en la población adulta que están trabajando o buscando empleo (p. 390)

**labor productivity** *productividad de trabajo* Producción por unidad de trabajo; medida como el total de producción dividido por las horas de trabajo empleadas para producir ese producto (p. 359)

**labor union** *sindicato de trabajo* Un grupo de trabajadores que se juntan para obtener más pago y mejores condiciones de trabajo al negociar un contrato de trabajo con sus empresarios (p. 273)

**laissez-faire** *laissez-faire (política de mínima interferencia)* La doctrina que el gobierno no debe intervenir en una economía de mercado más allá de lo mínimo requerido para mantener paz y derechos de propiedad (p. 404)

**law of comparative advantage** *ley de ventaja comparativa* El trabajador, empresa, región, o país con el costo de oportunidad más bajo de producir un producto debe especializarse en ese producto (p. 51)

**law of demand** *la ley de demanda* La cantidad de un bien exigido por periodo se relaciona a la inversa con su precio, otras constantes (p. 102)

**law of diminishing marginal utility** *ley de utilidad marginal disminuida* Entre más consuma una persona un bien por periodo, el aumento en utilidad total por consumir otra unidad más será más pequeño, otras cosas constantes (p. 103)

**law of diminishing returns** *ley de rendimientos reducidos* Al añadir más de un recurso variable a una cantidad específica de unos recursos fijos, el producto marginal eventualmente declina y puede ser negativo (p. 148)

**law of increasing opportunity cost** *ley del aumento de la oportunidad del costo* Cada aumento adicional de un bien requiere que la economía abandone sucesivamente aumentos más grandes del otro bien (p. 44)

**law of supply** *ley de oferta* La cantidad de un bien ofrecido en un periodo específico es usualmente relacionado en directo a su precio, otras cosas constantes (p. 132)

**leading economic indicators** *indicadores principales de la economía* Medidas que usualmente predicen, o llevan a recesiones o expansiones (p. 339)

**liability** *responsabilidad legal* La obligación legal de pagar cualquier deuda que el negocio encuentre (p. 235)

**liability** *pasivo* Una cantidad que se debe (p. 520)

**limited liability company (LLC)** *compañía con responsabilidad legal limitada* Un negocio con responsabilidad legal limitada para algunos dueños, el sistema de impuestos sencillo de los ingresos de negocio, y no tiene restricciones de propietarios (p. 245)

**limited liability partnership (LLP)** *sociedad colectiva con responsabilidad legal limitada* Tal como una compañía con responsabilidad limitada pero más facilmente convertida de una sociedad colectiva que exista (p. 245)

**limited partnership** *sociedad colectiva limitada* Por lo menos un socio general dirige el negocio y carga con la responsabilidad legal personal sin limite; otros socios suministran capital financiero pero tienen responsabilidad legal limitada (p. 245)

**line of credit** *línea de crédito* Un arreglo con un banco por el cual un negocio puede prestar dinero necesitado rapidamente (p. 296)

**liquidity** *liquidez* La habilidad que cualquier propiedad se pueda cambiar por efectivo (p. 300)

**long run** *a largo plazo* Un periodo durante el cual todos los recursos se pueden variar (p. 148)

**long-run average cost curve** *curva de promedio de largo plazo* Una curva que indica el más mínimo promedio de costo de producción a cada índice de producción cuando el tamaño de una empresa se le permite variar (p. 154)

## M

**M1** *M1* La más estrecha definición del abastecimiento de dinero; consiste en moneda (lo que incluye monedas) que el público no bancario tiene, depositos veríficables, y cheques de viajero (p. 506)

**M2** *M2* Una definición más ancha del abastecimiento de dinero que consiste del M1 más los depósitos de ahorros, depósitos de denominación de poco tiempo, y cuentas de fondo comúm de inversiones (p. 508)

**marginal** *marginal* Incremental, adicional o extra; se refiere a un cambio en un variable de la economía, un cambio en el statu quo (p. 13)

**marginal cost** *costo marginal* El cambio en costo total resultando de una unidad de cambio en la producción; el cambio del costo total divido por el cambio en producción (p. 152)

**marginal product** *producto marginal* El cambio en producto total resultando de un cambio de una unidad en un recurso en particular, otros recursos constantes (p. 148)

**marginal revenue** *ingreso marginal* El cambio en ingreso total al vender otra unidad de un bien (p. 152)

**marginal tax rate** *índice de impuesto marginal* El porcentaje de cada dólar adicional de ingresos que va a pagar el impuesto (p. 435)

**marginal utility** *utilidad marginal* El cambio en servicio total resultando en una unidad de cambio en el consumo de un bien (p. 103)

**market** *mercado* Los medios por los cuales la gente compra y vende algo (p. 15); un acuerdo que permite compradores y vendedores intercambiar cosas por un precio de mercado (p. 163)

**market demand** *demanda del mercado* La suma de las exigencias individuales de todos los consumidores en el mercado (p. 107)

**market economics** *economía de mercado* Estudio del comportamiento de la economía en mercados particulares, tal como el mercado de computadores o por trabajo no cualificado (p. 14)

**market economy** *economía de mercado* Describe el sistema de economía de los Estados Unidos, donde los mercados juegan un papel relativamente grande (p. 38)

**market for loans** *mercado para prestamos* El mercado que trae junto a los prestadores (los que exigen los prestamos) y los ahorradores (los que ofrecen los prestamos) para determinar el índice de interés del mercado (p. 291)

**market power** *poder del mercado* La habilidad de una empresa de subir su precio sin perder todos sus clientes a la competencia (p. 193)

**market structure** *estructura de mercado* Características importantes de un mercado tal como el número de compradores y vendedores, productos uniformes entre vendedores, facilidad de entrar al mercado, y formas de competencia (p. 192)

**maximizing political support** *maximizar apoyo político* Objetivo que guía el comportamiento de oficiales elegidos; comparable a maximizar un beneficio por empresas y maximizar servicios por hogar (p. 450)

**mediator** *mediador* Un observador imparcial que se lleva cuando las negociaciones de trabajo se quiebran, para sugerir como resolver las diferencias (p. 274)

**medium of exchange** *medio de intercambio* Cualquier cosa generalmente aceptada por todos los partidiarios a pago de bienes y servicios (p. 491)

**merchandise trade balance** *ajuste de mercancia de comercio* El valor de los bienes exportados por un país menos el valor de los bienes importados durante un perıdo asignado (p. 568)

**merger** *fusión* La combinación de dos o más empresas que forman una sola empresa (p. 209)

**minimum wage law** *ley de salario mínimo* Establece un precio mínimo que un empresario le puede pagar a un trabajador por una hora de trabajo (p. 270)

**mixed economy** *economía mixta* Sistemas económicos que mezclan planificación central con mercados competitivos (p. 37)

**money** *dinero* Cualquier cosa que todo el mundo está dispuesto a aceptar a cambio de bienes y servicios (p. 53)

**money demand** *demanda de dinero* La relación entre cuánto dinero la gente desea mantener y la taza de interés (p. 522)

**money multiplier** *multiplicador de dinero* El múltiple por el cual el abastecimiento de dinero aumenta como resultado de un aumento en las reservas de exceso en el sistema bancario (p. 522)

**money supply** *abastecimiento de dinero* La reserva de dinero disponible en la economía en un tiempo asignado (p. 527)

**monopolistic competition** *competencia monopolística* Una estructura de mercado sin obstáculos para entrar y muchas empresas vendiendo productos que son lo suficientemente diferentes que la curva de demanda de cada empresa se inclina hacia abajo (p. 202)

**monopoly** *monopolio* Un solo proveedor de un producto sin sustitutos cercanos (p. 193)

**movement along a given demand curve** *movimiento por una cierta curva de demanda* Cambio en cantidad exigida resultando de un cambio en el precio de un bien, otras cosas constantes (p. 122)

**movement along a given supply curve** *movimiento por una curva de oferta determinada* Cambio en cantidad ofrecida resultando de un cambio en el precio del bien, otras cosas constantes (p. 143)

**multilateral aid** *ayuda multilateral* Ayuda de desarrollo de una organización, tal como el Banco Mundial, que obtiene fondos de un grupo de países (p. 600)

**multinational corporation (MNC)** *corporación multinacional* Una corporación grande que hace y vende sus productos en todo el mundo (p. 307)

**multiplier effect** *efecto multiplicador* Cualquier cambio en la póliza fiscal afecta la demanda total por más del cambio original en gastos o impuestos (p. 466)

**mutual fund** *fondo mutual* Una institución financiera que emite sus propias acciones y con sus ganancias compra un portofolio de valores (p. 300)

## N

**national economics** *economía nacional* Estudio del comportamiento de la economía en su totalidad, especialmente la economía nacional (p. 14)

**natural monopoly** *monopolio natural* Una empresa que puede servir al mercado entero a un costo por unidad más bajo de lo que pueden dos o más empresas (p. 71)

**natural rate of unemployment** *desempleo a un índice natural* El índice de desempleo cuando la economía está produciendo su nivel potencial de producto (p. 462)

**natural resources** *recursos naturales* Llamados "regalos de la naturaleza", usados para producir bienes y servicios; incluye recursos renovables y agotables (p. 7)

**negative externalities** *externalidades negativas* Biproductos de producción o consumo que imponen costos a terceros participantes que no son ni compradores ni vendedores (p. 78)

**net exports** *exportación neta* El valor de las exportaciones de un país menos el valor de sus importaciones (p. 325)

**net worth** *valor neto* Activos menos pasivos; también llamado como el capital del dueño (p. 520)

**nominal GDP** *PIB nominal* PIB basado en precios que predominan en el momento de la transacción; PIB del dólar actual (p. 331)

**nominal interest rate** *índice de interés nominal* El índice de interés expresado en dólares actuales como porcentaje de la cantidad prestada; el índice de interés en el acuerdo del prestamo (p. 401)

**not-for-profit organizations** *organizaciones sin fin de lucro* Grupos que no persiguen beneficio como su objetivo; estos se dedican a actividades de caridad, educación, humanitarias, culturales, profesionales u otras con razón social (p. 246)

## O

**oligopoly** *oligopolio* Una estructura de mercado con un pequeño número de empresas cuyo comportamiento es interdependiente (p. 203)

**open-access good** *bien con acceso abierto* Un bien que es un rival en el consumo pero costoso en la exclusión (p. 76)

**open-market operations** *operaciones de mercado abierto* Comprar y vender valores del gobierno de los Estados Unidos como forma de regular el abastecimiento de dinero (p. 502)

**opportunity cost** *costo de oportunidad* El valor de la mejor alternativa que se deja pasar por alguna actividad o algo elegida (p. 20)

## P

**partnership** *sociedad colectiva* Dos o más personas acuerdan de contribuir recursos al negocio por una cantidad del beneficio (p. 236)

**payroll taxes** *impuestos de nómina* Impuestos deducidos de los sueldos para apoyar al Seguro Social y Medicare (p. 441)

**perfect competition** *competencia perfecta* Una estructura de mercado con muchos compradores y vendedores, bien informados, de un producto idéntico sin obstáculos para entrar (p. 192)

**physical capital** *capital físico* Las máquinas, los edificios, carreteras, aeropuertos, redes de comunicación, y otras creaciones fabricadas que se usan para producir bienes y servicios; también se llaman bienes capitales (p. 360)

**physical infrastructure** *infraestructura física* Transportación, comunicación, energía, agua, y sistemas de sanidad que el gobierno facilita y regula (p. 604)

**positive externalities** *externalidades positivas* Biproductos de consumo o producción que benefician a terceros participantes que no son ni compradores ni vendedores (p. 79)

**potential output** *producción potencial* La producción máxima de la economía sostenible a largo plazo (p. 462)

**price** *precio* Lo que se paga cuando se compra algo, y lo que se recibe cuando se vende (p. 164)

**price ceiling** *precio máximo* Un precio máximo legal alto del cual un producto no se puede vender; para tener impacto, un precio máximo debe fijarse abajo del precio de equilibrio (p. 180)

**price floor** *precio mínimo* Un precio mínimo legal más bajo del cual un producto no se puede vender; para tener impacto, un precio mínimo debe fijarse más alto del precio de equilibrio (p. 180)

**price level** *nivel del precio* Una medida de combinación que refleja los precios de los bienes y servicios de la economía en relación a precios en un año de base (p. 344)

**prime rate** *índice de interés preferencial* El interés que cobran los bancos por prestamos a sus más fiables prestatarios de negocio (p. 297)

**private good** *bien privado* Un bien con dos características: (1) la cantidad consumida por una persona no está disponible para otros y (2) los que no pagan pueden ser facilmente excluidos (p. 76)

**private property rights** *derechos de propiedad privada* Reclamo legal que le garantiza a un dueño el derecho de usar un recurso o de cobrarle a otros por su uso (p. 69)

**privatization** *privatización* El proceso de cambiar empresas públicas a empresas privadas (p. 607)

**production possibilities frontier (PPF)** *límites de posibilidades de producción* Muestra las posibles combinaciones de los dos tipos de bienes que se pueden producir cuando recursos disponibles se emplean completa y eficientemente (p. 42)

**productive efficiency** *eficiencia productiva* Se logra cuando una empresa produce al costo más mínimo posible por unidad (p. 179)

**productive resources** *recursos productivos* Materias primas o factores de producción, usados para producir los bienes y servicios que quiere la gente (p. 5)

**productivity** *productividad* El valor de producción por cada unidad adicional de un recurso (p. 257); la proporción de producción a una medida específica de producto; usualmente refleja un promedio, tal como medidas de áridos de grano por hectarea de terreno cultivado (p. 359)

**progressive taxation** *impuestos progresivos* El impuesto como porcentaje de ingresos aumenta al paso que los ingresos aumentan (p. 435)

**proportional taxation** *impuestos proporcionales* El impuesto como porcentaje de ingresos se mantiene constante al paso que los ingresos aumentan; también llamado un impuesto fijo (p. 435)

**public good** *bien público* Un bien que, al producirse, está disponible para que todos lo consuman, pero que el productor no puede excluir facilmente a los que no pagan (p. 76)

**publicly traded corporation** *corporación publicamente comercializada* Propiedad de varios accionistas; las acciones se pueden comprar y vender (p. 243)

**pure centrally planned economy** *economía pura planificada centralmente* Un sistema económico en el cual todos los recursos son del gobierno y la producción es coordinada por los planes centrales del gobierno (p. 37)

**pure market economy** *economía de mercado puro* Un sistema económico sin participación del gobierno para que las firmas privadas den cuenta de toda la producción (p. 37)

## Q

**quantity demanded** *cantidad exigida* La cantidad exigida a un precio en particular (p. 106)

**quasi-public good** *bien cuasi-público* Un bien que, al producirse, está disponible para todos, pero los que no pagan son facilmente excluidos (p. 76)

**quota** *cuota* Un límite legal de la cantidad de un producto en particular que se puede importar (p. 560)

# R

**rational ignorance** *ignorancia racional* Una postura adoptada por votadores cuando ellos encuentran que el costo de comprender y votar sobre un tema en particular excede el beneficio esperado de hacerlo (p. 451)

**real GDP** *verdadero PIB* El total producto de una economía medido en dólares de constante poder de compra; PIB medido en términos de bienes y servicios producidos (p. 331)

**real interest rate** *índice de interés real* El índice de interés expresado en dólares de poder constante de comprar como porcentaje de la cantidad prestada; el índice de interés nominal menos el índice de inflación (p. 401)

**recession** *recesión* Un descenso en producción total que dura por lo menos dos trimestres consecutivos, o por lo menos seis meses (p. 336)

**recognition lag** *lapso de reconocimiento* El tiempo necesitado para identificar un problema macroeconómico (p. 473)

**regressive taxation** *impuestos regresivos* El impuesto como porcentaje de ingresos reduce al paso que los ingresos aumentan (p. 435)

**representative money** *dinero representativo* Notas bancarias que se intercambian por un productor específico, tal como el oro (p. 497)

**required reserve ratio** *proporción de reserva requerida* Una regulación federal que dicta el mínimo porcentaje de depósitos que cada banco debe mantener en reserva (p. 520)

**required reserves** *reservas requeridas* El equivalente del dólar que debe mantenerse en reserva; depósitos verificables multiplicado por la proporción de la reserva requerida (p. 521)

**reserves** *reservas* Efectivo que bancos tienen a la mano en sus cámaras de seguridad o en deposito con la Reserva Federal (p. 500)

**resource complements** *complementos de recursos* Un recurso trabaja con el otro en producción; una reducción en el precio de uno aumenta la demanda por el otro (p. 260)

**resource substitutes** *sustitutos de recurso* Un recurso puede remplazar otro en producción; un aumento en el precio de un recurso aumenta la demanda por el otro (p. 260)

**retained earnings** *ganancias retenidas* La porción del beneficio de una corporación depués de impuestos que se reinvierte en la empresa (p. 299)

**right-to-work law** *ley de derecho de trabajo* Ley estatal que dice que un trabajador en una compañía con sindicato no tiene que unirse al sindicato o pagar cuotas del sindicato para tener un trabajo allí (p. 274)

**rules of the game** *reglas del juego* Las instituciones formales e informales que dan incentivos de producción y promueven actividad económica; tal como las leyes, costumbres y convenciones (p. 360)

# S

**scarcity** *escasez* Una condición en todas las sociedades porque no hay suficientes recursos productivos para satisfacer los deseos ilimitados de la gente (p. 6)

**S corporation** *corporación S* Obligación legal limitada que se combina con el sistema de impuestos sencillo de los ingresos del negocio; no puede tener más de 75 accionistas sin accionistas extranjeros (p. 245)

**seasonal unemployment** *desempleo estacional* Ocurre por cambios en la demanda de trabajo de una estación durante el año (p. 388)

**secondary markets** *mercados secundarios* Mercados de valores donde acciones y bonos que ya se vendieron por la corporación se pueden intercambiar (p. 300)

**secondhand securities** *valores de segunda mano* Acciones y bonos que ya se han vendido por la corporación (p. 300)

**securities** *seguridades* Acciones y bonos de corporación (p. 299)

**service** *servicio* Algo no físico que requiere recursos escasos y satisface deseos humanos (p. 8)

**shift of a demand curve** *cambio de una curva de demanda* Aumento o reducción en demanda resultando de un cambio en uno de los determinantes de demanda fuera del precio del bien (p. 122)

**shift of a supply curve** *cambio en una curva de oferta* Aumento o rebaja en oferta resultando de un cambio en uno de los determinantes de oferta fuera del precio del bien (p. 144)

**short run** *a corto plazo* Un periodo durante el cual por lo menos uno de los recursos de la empresa es fijo (p. 148)

**shortage** *escasez* A un precio determinado, la cantidad por la cual la cantidad exigida excede la cantidad ofrecida; una escasez usualmente forza que el precio suba (p. 164)

**social insurance** *seguro social* Transferencias de efectivo para los retirados, los desempleados y otros con una historia de trabajo y un historial de contribuciones al programa (p. 86)

**soft budget constraint** *restricción de presupuesto temporal* En economías planeadas centralmente, la condición del presupuesto que se enfrenta por empresas estatales que son subvencionadas cuando pierden dinero (p. 607)

**sole proprietorship** *negocio propio* La más sencilla forma de organización de un negocio; una sola persona es dueña y dirige la empresa (p. 234)

**specialization** *especialización* Ocurre cuando trabajadores individuales enfocan en tasks individuales, permitiendo que cada uno sea más eficaz y productivo (p. 51)

**stagflation** *estanflación* Una caída o estancamiento, del producto de una nación acompañado por inflación en el nivel de precio (p. 407)

**standard of living** *nivel de vida* El nivel de una economía de prosperidad económica; mejor medida por el valor de bienes y servicios producidos por cápita (p. 359)

**strike** *huelga* El intento de un sindicato de trabajo de retener trabajo de una empresa (p. 274)

**structural unemployment** *desempleo estructural* Ocurre porque los que buscan trabajo no tienen las habilidades exigidas (p. 388)

**substitution effect on a price change** *el efecto de sustituir a un cambio de precio* Cuando el precio de un bien cae, los consumidores sustituyen ese bien por otros bienes, los cuales son ahora relativamente más caros (p. 103)

**supply curve** *curva de oferta* Una curva o linea que muestra las cantidades o un bien en particular ofrecido a varios precios durante un periodo específico, otras cosas constantes (p. 132)

**supply of loans curve** *curva de oferta de prestamos* Una curva con inclinación hacia arriba mostrando la relación positiva entre el índice de interés y la cantidad de prestamos ofrecidos, otras cosas constantes (p. 291)

**supply** *oferta* Una relación mostrando las cantidades de un bien que productores quieren y pueden vender a varios precios durante un periodo específico, otras cosas constantes (p. 132)

**supply-side economics** *economía de oferta de lado* Póliza de macroeconomía que enfoca en el cambio hacia la derecha de la curva de oferta total por medio de una reducción de impuesto u otros cambios que aumenten incentivos de producción (p. 408)

**surplus** *excedente* A un precio determinado, la cantidad por la cual la cantidad ofrecida excede la cantidad exigida; un excedente usualmente forza que el precio baje (p. 164)

## T

**tariff** *trifa* Un impuesto a importaciones (p. 560)

**tastes** *gustos* Preferencias del consumidor; preferencias y aversiones en cosumo; se asume que son constantes por una cierta curva de demanda (p. 122)

**tax incidence** *incidencia de impuesto* Aquellos que soportan la carga del impuesto (p. 435)

**total cost** *costo total* Costo fijo más costo variable; el costo de todos los recursos usados por una empresa (p. 150)

**total product** *producto total* La producción total de una empresa (p. 148)

**total revenue** *ingresos totales* El precio multiplicado por la cantidad exigida a ese precio (p. 111)

**trade deficit** *déficit de comercio* La cantidad por la cual el valor de mercansias de importación excede el valor de mercansias de exportación durante un periodo asignado (p. 568)

**trade surplus** *exceso de comercio* La cantidad por la cual el valor de mercansias de exportación excede el valor de mercansias de importación durante un periodo asignado (p. 568)

**traditional economy** *economía tradicional* Sistema económico formado en su mayor parte por costumbre o religión (p. 40)

**transaction cost** *costo de transacción* El costo de tiempo e información requerido para realizar intercambio (p. 167)

**transition economy** *economía en transición* Sistema económico en proceso de cambio de planificación central a mercados competitivos (p. 39)

## U

**U.S. Agency for International Development (USAID)** *Agencia de los Estados Unidos para Desarrollo Internacional* La agencia federal que coordina ayuda extranjera al mundo en desarrollo (p. 600)

**underemployment** *subempleo* Trabajadores están sobre calificados para sus trabajos o trabajan menos horas que lo que prefieren (p. 389)

**unemployment benefits** *beneficios de desempleo* Transferencias de dinero a trabajadores desempleados que buscan trabajo activamente y que llenan otros requisitos (p. 394)

**unemployment rate** *índice de desempleo* El número buscando trabajo divido por el número en la fuerza de trabajo (p. 390)

**Uruguay Round** *La vuelta de Uruguay* La más reciente y la más completa de las ocho negociaciones de comercio multilaterales después de la guerra bajo GATT; creó la (WTO) Organización Mundial de Comercio (OMC) (p. 562)

**utility** *servicio* La satisfacción de consumo; sensación del bienestar (p. 63)

## V

**value added** *valor adicional* A cada etapa de producción, el valor de un producto menos el costo de bienes intermediarios usado para producirlo (p. 326)

**variable cost** *costo variable* Cualquier costo de producción que cambia al paso que cambia la producción (p. 150)

**vertical merger** *fusión vertical* Una empresa combina con otra de la cual compra aportaciones o a la cual vende productos, tal como una fusión entre un productor de acero y un productor de autos (p. 305)

## W

**welfare reform** *reforma de bienestar* Una revisión del sistema de bienestar en 1996 que impuso un límite de bienestar de por vida de cinco años por recipiente y otras condiciones (p. 416)

**world price** *pecio mundial* El precio al cual un bien se intercambia internacionalmente; determinado por la oferta mundial y la demanda mundial por el bien (p. 560)

**World Trade Organization (WTO)** *Organización Mundial de Comercio* La fundación legal e institucional del sistema multilateral de comercio que siguió a GATT en 1995 (p. 562)

# Index

# Acknowledgements

**Chapter 1   p. 5**, In the News: The Gallup Business Monitor, "Many Americans have dreams of wealth," *Las Vegas Review Journal,* February 17, 2003, 1D **p. 8,** Span the Globe: Peter Hadfield, "Public Sold on Ugly, Wasteful Vending Machines," *South China Morning Post,* February 14, 2001; "Coke Testing Vending Unit That Can Hike Prices in Hot Weather," *New York Times,* October 28, 1999; "Sales Per Vending Machine Accelerates in Japan," *Beverage Digest,* August 29, 1999 **p. 10,** In the News: The Gallup Business Monitor, "As the Dow average goes, so goes Americans' economic confidence," *Las Vegas Review Journal,* October 28, 2002, 1D **p. 11,** E-conomics: May Wong, The Associated Press, "More businesses feeling right at home," *Las Vegas Review Journal,* June 24, 2002, 3D **p. 18,** Movers & Shakers: *USA Today Magazine,* www.randomhouse.com **p. 19,** In the News: Rebecca Gomez, The Associated Press, "Women continue moves into top jobs," *Las Vegas Review Journal,* November 19, 2002, 6D **p. 27,** Connect to History: Cotton, Lee. (July 15, 2002). The Virginia Company of London: Success or Failure? *Colonial National Historical Park, National Park Service, Jamestown Historic Briefs.* Retrieved February 7, 2003 from the World Wide Web: http://www.nps.gov/colo/Jthanout/VACompany.html; Fishwick, Marshall W. (1974) *Jamestown: First English Colony.* New York: American Heritage Publishing Company; Harrington, J.C. (1952) *Glassmaking at Jamestown.* Richmond: Dietz Press; Lieberman, Jethro K. (1999). *Companion to the Constitution: How the Supreme Court Has Ruled on Issues from Abortion to Zoning.* Los Angeles: University of California Press; Short, John. (February, 1994). *Glassmaking at Jamestown. Colonial National Historical Park, National Park Service, Jamestown Historic Briefs.* Retrieved February 7, 2003 from the World Wide Web: http://www.nps.gov/colo/Jthanout/Glassmak.html

**Chapter 2   p. 33,** In the News: Peter Landers, "Westerners Profit As Japan Opens Its Drug Market," *Wall Street Journal,* December 2, 2002, p.1 **p. 39,** Ethics in Action: Chris Jones, Gaming Wire, "COMDEX, 'Star Wars' creator pushes for better prevention of digital piracy," *Las Vegas Review Journal,* November 20, 2002, 4D **p. 41,** In the News: Joel Millman, "U.S. Chile to Meet for Final Round of Talks Over Free-Trade Pact," *The Wall Street Journal,* October 02, 2002, A2 **p. 44,** E-conomics: Jon Swartz, *USA Today,* November 18, 2002, 2C **p. 49,** Connect to History, Fishwick, Marshall W. (1974) *Jamestown:*

*First English Colony.* New York: American Heritage Publishing Company; Lieberman, Jethro K. (1999). *Companion to the Constitution: How the Supreme Court Has Ruled on Issues from Abortion to Zoning.* Los Angeles: University of California Press. Middletown, Arthur Pierce. (1953). *Tobacco Coast.* Newport News, Virginia: Mariners' Museum; Scharf, J. Thomas. (1967) *History of Maryland: From the Earliest Periods to the Present Day.* Hatboro, Pennsylvania: Tradition Press; *Tobacco News and Information.* (1998). A Brief History of Jamestown, Virginia. http://tobacco.org/History/Jamestown.html, February 10, 2003; *Tobacco News and Information.* (1998). Economic Aspects of Tobacco during the Colonial Period, 1612–1776; http://tobacco.org/History/Jamestown.html. February 10, 2003 **p. 50,** In the News: The Associated Press, "Heart patients do better with specialized outpatient care," *Las Vegas Review Journal,* November 21, 2002, 10B **p. 52,** Span the Globe: Julie Watson, The Associated Press, "Mexican inmates making furniture bound for Texas," *Las Vegas Review Journal,* December 2, 2002, 22A **p. 55,** Movers & Shakers: Interview via email; www.scripps.com/annrpt/99/nofrills/mess/mmain.html, and www.cablecenter.org/library/collections/oral_histories/history_detail.cfm?Selected History=183 (This is the Cable Center Library/Special Collections/Oral Histories)

**Chapter 3   p. 61,** In the News: Genaro C. Armas, The Associated Press, "Working parents finding more child care options," *Las Vegas Review Journal,* May 22, 2002, 1D **p. 65,** Span the Globe: Ted Anthony, The Associated Press, "China still trying to embrace global economy," *Las Vegas Review Journal,* December 11, 2002, 27A and *The New York Times,* April 28, 2003 **p. 68,** In the News: Neil King, Jr., "New Dumping Law Lines the Pockets of Manufacturers," *Wall Street Journal,* December 5, 2002, p. 1 **p. 69,** E-conomics: Bob Porterfield, The Associated Press, "Opening statements aired in copyright case," *Las Vegas Review Journal,* December 4, 2002, 8D and Electronic Frontier Foundation web site, http://www.eef.org/, "Jury Acquits Elcomsoft" press release **p. 74,** Movers & Shakers: *Reno Gazette-Journal:* www.rgj.com/news/stories/html/2003/01/09/31670.php, United States Hispanic Chamber of Commerce: www.ushcc.com **p. 75,** In the News: Sharon Theimer, The Associated Press, "Lobbyists push for new lawsuit limits," *Las Vegas Review Journal,* December 6, 2002, 24A **p. 79,** Ethics in Action: H. Josef Heber, The Associated Press,

"Support grows for arctic oil plan," *Las Vegas Review Journal,* March 13, 2003, 13A  **p. 82,** In the News: Laura Meckler, The Associated Press, "encouraging statistics cited in new report," *Las Vegas Review Journal,* July 12, 2002, 5B  **p. 91,** Connect to History: Hall, Kermit L. (Ed.). (1992). *The Oxford Companion to the Supreme Court of the United States.* New York: Oxford University Press; Lieberman, Jethro K. (1999). *Companion to the Constitution: How the Supreme Court Has Ruled on Issues from Abortion to Zoning.* Los Angles: University of California Press; Puth, Robert C. (1988). *American Economic History.* New York: The Dryden Press, Harcourt Brace Jovanovich College Publishers

**Chapter 4  p. 101,** In the News: Chris Jones, Gaming Wire, "HDTV coming slowly into view," *Las Vegas Review Journal,* April 11, 2003, p. D-1  **p. 106,** Ethics in Action: Pavel Rahman, The Associated Press, "Stampede for free clothes leaves at least 30 dead," *Las Vegas Review Journal,* December 2, 2002, p. 20A  **p. 109,** In the News: Michelle Morgante, The Associated Press, "U.S. avocado capital cheers annual Super Bowl boost," *Las Vegas Review Journal,* Janurary 21, 2003, p. 10B  **p. 111,** Span the Globe: Kenneth R. Weiss, Los Angeles Times, "Study finds industrial fleets have stripped oceans of big fish," *Las Vegas Review Journal,* May 15, 2003, p. 7-A  **p. 117,** Movers & Shakers: Interview via email and www.awib.org  **p. 118,** In the News: Scott McCartney, "Airlines Try Business-Fare Cuts, Find They Don't Lose Revenue," *The Wall Street Journal,* November 22, 2001, p. A-1  **p. 121,** E-conomics: Chris Jones, Gaming Wire, "Electronics experts tout power of women consumers," *Las Vegas Review Journal/Gaming Wire,* January 11, 2003, p. 3-D  **p. 125,** Connect to History: *Gale Encyclopedia of U.S. History.* Thomas Carson & Mary Bonk, ed. Detroit, Gale Group. 1999; Michl, H.E. *The Textile Industries.* Washington, the Textile Foundation. 1938; *Oxford Companion to British History.* John Cannon, ed. New York, Oxford University Press. 1997; Puth, Robert C. *American Economic History.* New York, The Dryden Press. 1988; Watkins, James L. *King Cotton: A Historical and Statistical Review.* New York, Negro University Press. 1969

**Chapter 5  p. 131,** In the News: Yuki Noguchi, The Washington Post, "Wrong numbers: Dwindling profits kill off pay phones," *Las Vegas Review Journal,* January 1, 2003, p. 3D  **p. 136,** Span the Globe: *Las Vegas Review Journal,* "Goats: Love for cashmere grows into affection for flock," February 3, 2003, pp. 1B and 7B; and http://www.bharattextile.com/newsitems/1974934  **p. 140,** In the News: The Office of International Information Programs, U.S. Department of State. http://usinfo.state.gov

**p. 144,** E-conomics: Shirley Leung and Ron Lieber, "The New Menu Option At McDonald's: Plastic," The *Wall Street Journal,* December 16, 2002, B1  **p. 146,** Movers and Shakers: http://www.pmqnews.com/papa_johns_quality_initiative.htm; http://louisville.bizjournals.com/louisville/stories/2001/11/26/story2.html; www.papajohns.com; http://www.louisville.com/voice/schnat113.shtml; http://www.forbes.com/finance/mktguideapps/personinfo/FromPersonIdPersonTearsheet/jhtml?passedPersonId=170010  **p. 147,** In the News: Sources: Joahn Tagliabue, "Now Playing Europe: Invasion of Multiplex," *The New York Times,* January 27, 2000; Bruce Orwall and Gregory Zuckerman, "After Joining the Megaplex Frenzy, Regal Gets the Box-Office Blues," *The Wall Street Journal,* September 27, 2000; Kenneth Gosselin, "State's Cinema Building Boom Fading to Black," *Hartford Courant,* October 26, 2000; and U.S. Census Bureau, *Statistical Abstract of the United States: 2000*  **p. 155,** Ethics in Action: http://www.nytimes.com/2003/06/23/business/23COMP.html?th  **p. 157,** Connect to History: *Gale Encyclopedia of U.S. History.* Thomas Carson & Mary Bonk, ed. Detroit, Gale Group. 1999; Michl, H.E. *The Textile Industries.* Washington, the Textile Foundation. 1938; Oxford Companion to British History. John Cannon, ed. New York, Oxford University Press. 1997; Puth, Robert C. *American Economic History.* New York, The Dryden Press. 1988; Watkins, James L. *King Cotton: A Historical and Statistical Review.* New York, Negro University Press. 1969

**Chapter 6  p. 163,** In the News: Raymond Gorman and James Kehr, "Fairness as a Constraint on Profit Seeking," *American Economic Review,* 82 (March, 1992), pp. 355–58, Joe Pereira, "Hasbro Trims 5% of Work Force," *The Wall Street Journal,* October 13, 2000. "Retailers Predict Hot Toys," Associated Press, October 17, 2000. The Toy Industry Association web site http://www.toy-tma.com/index.html and Pokemon World http:///www.pokemon.com/  **p. 166,** E-conomics: http://wifinetnews.com/  **p. 168,** Movers & Shakers: http://www.maryengelbreit.com; http://sbm.sbmin.com/asp/DisplayArticles.asp?ArticleId=827&CatId=78  **p. 169,** In the News: Thomas A. Fogarty, "Many consumers gasp at February gas bills," *USA Today,* March 12, 2003, p. B-1  **p. 174,** Ethics in Action: The Associated Press, "Price of Recordings Fixed, Judge Rules," June 28, 2002, http://www.nytimes.com  **p. 178,** In the News: Amy Dockser Marcus, "Blood Supply Hits Lowest Level in Years; Surgeries Canceled," *The Wall Street Journal,* June 26, 2002  **p. 185,** Connect to History: Carlos, Ann M. *The North American Fur Trade,* 1804–1821: *A Study in the Life-Cycle of a Duopoly.* New York: Garland Publishing, Inc. 1986; Chittenden, Hiram Martin. *American Fur Trade of the Far West,* vol. 1 & 2. University of Nebraska. Press. 1987; Fuchs, Victor R.

*The Economics of The Fur Industry*. New York: Columbia University Press 1957; Lewis, Jon E. *The Mammoth Book of the West*. New York: Carrol & Graf Publishers, Inc.; 1996; *Oxford History of the American West*. Milner, Clyde A, O'Connor, Carol A., Sandweiss, Martha A., eds. New York: Oxford University Press. 1994

**Chapter 7   p. 191**, In the News: Bruce Stanley, The Associate Press, "War concerns push gold to six-year high," *Las Vegas Review Journal,* December 6, 2002, p. 2D   **p. 194,** Span the Globe: Steve Frank, "Ebay's Stock Charges Ahead," *The Wall Street Journal,* July 8, 2001; Michelle Slatalla, "At a Virtual Garage Sale, It Frequently Pays to Wait," *The New York Times,* November 2, 2000; "The Heyday of the Auction," *Economist,* July 24, 1999   **p. 198,** Ethics in Action: The Associated Press, "States await court ruling on drug case," *Las Vegas Review Journal,* January 23, 2003, p. B-1   **p. 201,** In the News: Martha Brannigan, "Congress's Removal of 'Slots' Opens a Flood of New York Airports Gates," *The Wall Street Journal,* December 4, 2000; "Air Travel, Air Trouble," *Economist,* July 7, 2001; Rafer Guzman and Jane Costello, "Weather, La Guardia Flight Reductions Lift Airlines' On-Time Arrival Records," *The Wall Street Journal,* July 20, 2001; and Steven Morrison and Clifford Winston, *The Evolution of the Airline Industry* (Washington, D.C.: Brookings Institution, 1995) **p. 207,** Movers & Shakers: interview with Dwight Cooper   **p. 208,** In the News: *The New York Times,* August 19, 21, and 23, 2003   **p. 211,** E-conomics: James Grimaldi, "Judge Orders Microsoft Split in 2," *Washington Post,* June 8, 2000; Ted Bridis, "Microsoft Ruling Sets High Standard for Proving Antitrust-Law Violations," *The Wall Street Journal,* July 2, 2001; Paul Krugman, "The Smell Test," *The New York Times,* July 1, 2001; John Wilke et al., "Ruling Sends Case to Lower Court, Denounces Judge Jackson's Findings," *The Wall Street Journal,* June 29, 2001; John Wilke and Ted Bridis, "Justice Department Says It Won't Seek Court-Ordered Breakup of Microsoft," *The Wall Street Journal,* September 7, 2001; Microsoft Announces Concessions on Licensing Deals with PC Makers, *The Wall Street Journal,* July 11, 2001; Steven Levy, Shooting with Live Ammo," *Newsweek,* August 13, 2001 and http://www.msnbc.com/news/COMJUSTICEVSMS_front.asp   **p. 215,** Connect to History: Carlos, Ann M. *The North American Fur Trade, 1804–1821: A Study in the Life-Cycle of a Duopoly*. New York: Garland Publishing, Inc. 1986; Chittenden, Hiram Martin. *American Fur Trade of the Far West,* vol. 1 & 2. University of Nebraska. Press. 1987; Fuchs, Victor R. *The Economics of The Fur Industry*. New York: Columbia University Press 1957; Lewis, Jon E. *The Mammoth Book of the West*. New York: Carrol & Graf Publishers, Inc. 1996; *Oxford History of the American*

*West*. Milner, Clyde A, O'Connor, Carol A., Sandweiss, Martha A., eds. New York: Oxford University Press. 1994

**Chapter 8   p. 225,** In the News: Frappa Stout, *USA Weekend Magazine,* March 7, 2003, p. 17   **p. 230,** Span the Globe: *Fast Company,* January, 2003, p. 104   **p. 232,** Movers & Shakers: www.boomercareer.com/public/127_4.cfm?sd=41 "Roxanne Quimby Mines Her Own Beeswax for Millions" by Denise Lang; www.burtsbees.com   **p. 233,** In the News: Tony Batt, Stephens Washington Bureau, "House votes 315-113 to toughen bankruptcy laws," *Las Vegas Review Journal,* February 23, 2003, p. 3B   **p. 241,** In the News: James F. Peltz, Los Angeles times, "CEOs upset over reputations," *Las Vegas Review Journal,* July 19, 2003   **p. 244,** Ethics in Action: The Gallup Business Monitor, "Americans distrust corporate CEOs, poll shows," *Las Vegas Review Journal,* July 24, 2002, p. 7D and "Execs discuss ethics in U.S. businesses," *Las Vegas Review Journal,* March 17, 2003, p. 2D   **p. 249,** Connect to History: Engerman, Stanley L. & Gallman, Robert E. *The Cambridge Economic History of the United States: The Long Nineteenth Century, volume II*. Cambridge, England: Cambridge University Press. 2000; Foner, Eric & Garraty, John A. eds. *The Readers Companion to American History*. New York: Houghton Mifflin. 1991; Heilbroner, Robert L. "Carnegie & Rockefeller" *A Sense of History: The Best Writing from the Pages of American Heritage*. New York: American Heritage. 1985; Puth, Robert C. *American Economic History*. Fort Worth: Dryden Press. 1988; Wall, J.F. *Andrew Carnegie*. New York: Oxford University Press. 1970; Warren, Kenneth. *Big Steel: The First Century of the United States Steel Corporation, 1901-2001*. University of Pittsburgh Press. 2001

**Chapter 9   p. 255,** In the News: Productivity and Costs report for second quarter 2003, revised, U.S. Department of Labor, Bureau of Labor Statistics, September 4, 2003   **p. 258,** Span the Globe: Frank Davies, Knight Ridder Newspapers, "Survey shows officials and the public at odds regarding immigration," *Las Vegas Review Journal,* February 18, 2002, p.18A   **p. 265,** Movers & Shakers: interview with Dr. Tim Kremchek   **p. 266,** In the News: Stefan Fatsis, "Thanks to Tiger's Roar, PGA Tour Signs Record TV Deal Through 2007," *The Wall Street Journal,* July 17, 2001. "Executive Pay," *Economist,* September 30, 2000. Robert H. Frank and Philip J. Cook, *The Winner-Take-All Society* (New York: Free Press, 1995). Barbara Whitaker, "Producers and Actors Reach Accord," *New York Times,* July 5, 2001. *Economic Report of the President,* January 2001, at http://w3.access.gpo.gov/eop/   **p. 270,** Ethics in Action: Genaro C. Armas, The Associated Press, "Census: Women still trail men at

highest salary levels," *Las Vegas Review Journal,* March 25, 2003, p. 9A   **p. 273,** In the News: Troy Wolverton, "Labor pains," CNET News.com, January 16, 2001, http://www.news.com   **p. 280,** E-conomics: John Miano, "Do High-Tech Firms Really Need Imported Workers?" *USA Today,* September 21, 2000. Scott Thurm, "Cisco Systems Helps to Train Union Workers in Web's Ways," *The Wall Street Journal,* July 3, 2001. Mark Boslet, "Lighting the Labor Fuse," *The Standard.com,* August 20, 2000. Steven Greenhouse, "Amazon Fights Union Activity," *New York Times,* November 29, 2000. Keith Ervin, "Microsoft Temps Group Joins Union," *Seattle Times,* June 4, 1999, and the CWA web site at http://www.cwa-union.org/
**p. 281,** Connect to History: Engerman, Stanley L. & Gallman, Robert E. *The Cambridge Economic History of the United States: The Long Nineteenth Century, volume II.* Cambridge, England: Cambridge University Press. 2000; Foner, Eric & Garraty, John A. eds. *The Readers Companion to American History.* New York: Houghton Mifflin. 1991; Puth, Robert C. American Economic History. Fort Worth: Dryden Press. 1988.

**Chapter 10   p. 287,** In the News: Paraphrase of actual pop-up ad for Mortgage Marketing On Line, September 11, 2003 and "Re-fi boom waning for mortgage lenders," *Milwaukee Business Journal,* September 11, 2003   **p. 292,** Ethics In Action: Christopher J. Gearon, "Tug of War Over Predatory Lending," *AARP Bulletin,* April 2003   **p. 294,** In the News: Stacy Forster, "Web Banks Seek Better Way to Take Customer Deposits," *The Wall Street Journal,* November 20, 2000. Pat Maio, "Wells Fargo CEO Sees Online Unit Profitable by April '02," Dow Jones Newswire, April 29, 2001. Juniper Bank's web address is http://www.juniper.com   **p. 296,** E-conomics: Purva Patel, South Florida Sun-Sentinel, "Credit fraud cases growing nationally," *Las Vegas Review Journal,* December 18, 2003, p. 9D   **p. 303,** In the News: "Banking Mergers," http:biggovernment.com/banking%20mergers.htm, April 15, 2003   **p. 307,** Span the Globe: James Hall and Nina Stechler Hayes, Dow Jones Newswires, "Krispy Kreme, Two Other Parties Plan to open 25 Stores in U.K.," *The Wall Street Journal,* November 20, 2002, p. B5D
**p. 310,** Movers & Shakers: Interview with Paul Gbodi, interview with franchise director at Jani-King, http://www.janiking.com   **p. 311,** Connect to History: Engerman, Stanley L. & Gallman, Robert E. *The Cambridge Economic History of the United States: The Long Nineteenth Century, volume II.* Cambridge, England: Cambridge University Press. 2000. Foner, Eric & Garraty, John A. eds. T*he Readers Companion to American History.* New York: Houghton Mifflin. 1991. Heilbroner, Robert L. "Carnegie & Rockefeler" *A Sense of History: The Best Writing from the Pages of American*

*Heritage.* New York: American Heritage. 1985. Puth, Robert C. *American Economic History.* Fort Worth: Dryden Press. 1988. Wall, J.F. *Andrew Carnegie.* New York: Oxford University Press. 1970. Warren, Kenneth. *Big Steel: The First Century of the United States Steel Corporation, 1901–2001.* University of Pittsburgh Press. 2001

**Chapter 11   p. 321,** In the News: "The U.S. Statistical System and a Rapidly Changing Economy," *Brookings Policy Brief,* no. 63 (July 2000): 2–8. Leonard Nakamura, "Is the U.S. Economy Really Growing Too Slowly? Maybe We're Measuring Growth Wrong," *Federal Reserve Bank of Philadelphia Business Review* (March–April 1997): 1–12 and Economic Report of the President, January 2001   **p. 325,** Span the Globe: Hans Greimel, The Associated Press, "Japan unveils reforms to stimulate economy," *Las Vegas Review Journal,* October 31, 2002, p. 24A   **p. 328,** In the News: *Daily Policy Digest* article, National Center for Policy Analysis, June 27, 2001. D.A. Barber, "The 'New' Economy?," *Tucson Weekly,* January 8, 2003
**p. 332,** E-conomics: Gary McWilliams, "Dell Fine-Tunes Its PC Pricing to Gain an Edge in Slow Market," *The Wall Street Journal,* June 8, 2001. "Improved Estimates of the National Income and Product Accounts for 1959–95; Results of the Comprehensive Revision," *Survey of Current Business* 76 (January/February 1996); *Survey of Current Business* 81 (August 2001); and "From Investment Boom to Bust," *Economist,* March 1, 2001   **p. 335,** In the News: Jon E. Hilsenrath, "Real-Time Data Show Economy Reacting Positively to Iraq News," *The Wall Street Journal,* April 15, 2003, p. D-2   **p. 342,** Movers & Shakers: Interview with Norman Mayne; www.dorothylane.com and http://www.fastcompany.com/magazine/25/dorothy.html
**p. 343,** In the News: John D. McKinnon and Anne Marie Squeo, "Shaky Economic Times Limit Bang of New Defense Spending," *The Wall Street Journal,* April 15, 2003, p. A1   **p. 351,** Connect to History: Chernow, Ron. *The House of Morgan.* New York: Atlantic Monthly Press. 1990; Foner, Eric & Garraty, John A. ed. *The Readers Companion to American History.* Boston: Houghton Mifflin Company. 1991; Greider, William. *Secrets of the Temple: How the Federal Reserve Runs the Country.* New York: Simon and Schuster. 1987; Morris, Richard B. and Morris, Jeffrey B. *Encyclopedia of American History.* New York: Harper Collins. 1996; Parish, Peter J. ed. *Reader's Guide to American History.* Chicago: Fitzroy Dearborn Publishers. 1997; Puth, Robert C. *American Economic History.* New York: the Dryden Press, 1982

**Chapter 12   p. 357,** In the News: "China economic growth seen accelerating in 2004,"Reuters, September 25, 2003. Martin Crutsinger, Associated

Press, "2Q Economic Growth Revised Upward," September 26, 2003. World Bank (National GDP Totals for 2002). "German government casts doubt on own 2003, 2004 growth forecasts," *French Weekly Economic Report,* September 24, 2003   **p. 361,** Ethics in Action: BusinessWeek Online, http://biz.yahoo.com/bizwk/030812/ca200308120184_ca004_1.html
**p. 365,** Movers & Shakers: http://www.govtech.net/magazine/visions/feb99vision/yang/yang.phtml, http://docs.yahoo.com/info/misc/history.html
**p. 366,** In the News: Gordon M. Fisher, "The Development and History of the Poverty Thresholds," *Social Security Bulletin,* Vol. 55, No. 4, Winter 1992, pp. 3–14. U.S. Census Bureau Historical Poverty Tables. U. S. Census Bureau 2003 Poverty Guideline. World Bank report, "Two Years of Intifada, Closures and Palestinian Economic Crisis." *Lusaka Zambia Post,* August 28, 2003. Aneel Salman, "Breaking the cycle of poverty," *Talking Global News*   **p. 372,** E-conomics, "Solving the Paradox," *Economist,* September 23, 2000; David Morgan, "Dot-Coms May Play Sleeper Role in U.S. Slowdown," Reuters, January 17, 2001; Leila Jason, "Software Lets Managers Watch Their Business from a Distance," *The Wall Street Journal,* August 30, 2001; Stephen Oliner and Daniel Sichel, "The Resurgence of Growth in the Late 1990s: Is Information Technology the Story?" Working Paper (May 2000), Federal Reserve Board   **p. 374,** In the News: Center for Defense Information; Hon. Claude Bolton's (Assistant Secretary of the Army) keynote address to Conference on the Acquisition of Software Intensive Systems; "Spending on Homeland Security," Reuters, September 30, 2003; Department of Commerce figures on GDP/GNP
**p. 378,** Span the Globe: http://www.airbus.com/about/history.asp and William A. McEachern, *Economics: A Contemporary Introduction,* 6th edition, p. 463   **p. 381,** Connect to History: Bryant, Keith L. & Dethloff, Henry C. *A History of American Business.* Edgewood Cliffs: Prentice Hall. 1990; Chandler, Jr., A. *Giant Enterprise: Ford General Motors and the Automobile Industry.* New York: Harcourt, Brace, and World; Foner, Eric & Garraty, John A. ed. *The Readers Companion to American History.* Boston: Houghton Mifflin Company. 1991; Hurley, Daniel, *Cincinnati, the Queen City.* Cincinnati: The Cincinnati Historical Society. 1982; Kross, Herman E. and Gilbert, Charles. *American Business History.* Edgewood Cliffs: Prentice Hall, 1972; Morris, Richard B. and Morris, Jeffrey B. *Encyclopedia of American History.* New York: Harper Collins. 1996; Murdock, Eugene. *The Buckeye Empire: an Illustrated History of Ohio Enterprise.* Northbridge: Windsor Publications. 1988; Parish, Peter J. ed. *Reader's Guide to American History.* Chicago: Fitzroy Dearborn Publishers. 1997; Puth, Robert C. *American Economic History.* New York: The Dryden Press, 1982

**Chapter 13   p. 387,** In the News: "No picnic for millions this Labor Day," Associated Press story, August 30, 2003, http://www.cnn.com/2003/US/08/30/labor.day.ap/index.html; "Tarnished Gold," *Newsweek,* July 28, 2003, online archives http://archives.newsbank.com/ar-search/we/Archives?p_action=doc&p_docid=0FC9981EF35…; "Layoff Rose Sharply Last Month, Report Says," *New York Times,* September 5, 2003, http://www.nytimes.com/2003/09/05/business/05CND-JOBS.html?hp=&pagewanted=print&p…   **p. 396,** Movers & Shakers: www.umassalumni.com/special_events/Bateman/taylor_bio.htm; www.pka.com/wjeff.html; www.monster.com
**p. 397,** In the News: "The South Rises Again," *Economist,* March 7, 1998, p. 89, http://www.reelclassics.com/Articles/General/topten-article.htm Checked update on all-time box office champs NOT adjusted for inflation, from Exhibitor Relations Co., 9/2/03, published online at http://movieweb.com/movie/alltime.html   **p. 400,** Ethics in Action: "Energy Dept. probes high gas prices," Associated Press story, http://www.cnn.com/2003/US/South/09/03/gas.price.probe.ap/index/html "Gasoline prices skyrocket in some parts of the country," CNN report, http://www.cnn.com/2001/US/09/12/gas.prices/index.html "Gregg calls for an investigation into gas price gouging," September 12, 2001, Indiana state government press release, http://www.state.in.us/legislative/hdpr/R45_09132001.html "Soaring Gas Prices in Missouri Under Investigation," September 12, 2001, Missouri Digital News, http://www.mdn.org/2001/STORIES/GAS1.HTM   **p. 403,** In the News: http://www.umich.edu/news/Releases/2003/Feb03/r020303.html   http://www.post-gazette.com/localnews/20030408top50psychp8.asp   **p. 409,** E-conomics: "The Onion: Funny site is no joke," from Business 2.0, http://www.cnn.com/2203/TECH/ptech/08/28/bus2.feat.onion.site/index.html
**p. 411,** Connect to History: Allen, Larry, *Encyclopedia of Money.* Santa Barbara: Checkmark Books, 2001; Engerman, Stanley L. & Gallman, Robert E. The *Cambridge Economic History of the United States: The Long Nineteenth Century, Volume II.* Cambridge, England: Cambridge: University Press. 2000; Foner, Eric & Garraty, John A. eds. *The Readers Companion to American History.* New York: Houghton Mifflin. 1991; Gordon, John Steele. "American Taxation," *American Heritage,* May/June, 1996; Puth, Robert C. *American Economic History.* Fort Worth: Dryden Press. 1988; Rosenbaum, Robert A., ed. *The Penguin Encyclopedia of American History.* New York: Penguin Reference, 2003; Engerman, Stanley L & Gallman, Robert E. The Cambridge History of the United States. New York: Cambridge University Press, 1996; Carson, Thomas, ed. Gale Encyclopedia of United States History. Detroit: Gale Group, 1999   **p. 412,** In the News: "The real

face of homelessness," from TIME.COM, January 13, 2003, reprinted online at http://www.cnn.com/2003/ALLPOLITICS/01.13.timep.homelessness.tm/index.html "Census Bureau: U.S. poverty rate lowest in 20 years," CNN report, online http://www.cnn.com/2000/US/09/26/census.poverty.02/index.html 2003 *World Almanac and Book of Facts,* pp. 408–409 **p. 417,** Span the Globe: "Pro-Poor Tourism: Harnessing the World's Largest Industry for the World's Poor," International Institute for Environment and Development, May 2001. "Pro-poor Tourism: Opportunities for Sustainable Local Development," D&C Development and Cooperation (No. 5, September/October 2000, pp. 12–14), reprinted online at http://www.dse.de/zeitschr/de500-3.htm "Developing Tourism in Lower Mekong River Basin Countries," Asian Development Fund news release, December 12, 2002. http://www.adb.org/Documents/News/2002/nr2002250.asp

**Chapter 14   p. 429,** In the News: *Cavalier Daily,* September 18, 2003; United Press International Wire Story: "Nation called on to cut teen drinking," September 11, 2003   **p. 432,** E-conomics: "What Can Government Demand for Its Money?" *The Chronicle of Philanthropy,* July 24, 2003   **p. 437,** In the News: The Boston Globe, August 27, 2003; "On the Economy," *Industry Week,* August, 2003, p. 64; *The Washington Times,* July 21, 2003, Commentary: "Those tax cuts beginning to work," p. A20   **p. 444,** Span the Globe: Emily Parker, "Japan Needs an Exit Strategy," October 15, 2003, *Wall Street Journal* **p. 447,** In the News: "Medicare privatization language softens," United Press International, October 9, 2003; "Medicare Drugs: Fast-Moving Bill Gathers Special Interest Add-Ons," Newhouse News Service, June 20, 2003; "House Republicans fear weakened Medicare bill; Conservatives pledge to vote against measure that lacks reforms," *The Washington Times,* September 15, 2003   **p. 449,** Ethics in Action: "Oral arguments before U.S. Supreme Court," *Minnesota Daily,* September 16, 2003   **p. 453,** Movers & Shakers: http://www.usatoday.com/news/politicselections/2002-11-06-sebelius_x.htm   http://www.ksgovernor.com/meetkathleen.php   http://www.ksgovernor.org/cabinet.html

**Chapter 15   p. 459,** In the News: John Schwartz, "Social Security Checks to Rise 2.6%," *New York Times,* October 20, 2001; David Rosenbaum, "The President's Budget: Putting Faith in Discipline," *New York Times,* April 10, 2001; Charles Zwick and Peter Lewis, "Apocalypse Not: Social Security Crisis Is Overblown," *The Wall Street Journal,* April 11, 2001; "Status of the Social Security and Medicare Programs: A Summary of the 2001 Annual Report," Social Security and Medicare Boards of Trustees, March 19, 2001   **p. 463,** Span the

Globe: "laissez-faire," *Encyclopedia Britannica online,* http://search.eb.com/eb/print?eu=47953; "physiocrats," *Encyclopedia Britannica online,* http:search.eb.com/eb/print?eu=61379; "France," *Encyclopedia Britannica online,* http://search.eb.com/eb/print?eu=119330 **p. 468,** In the News: "Gramm-Rudman-Hollings," *Encyclopedia Britannica online,* http://search.eb.com/ebi/article?eu=335534&query=gramm-rudmann&ct= "Deficit-Focused Budget Reforms," http://www.house.gov/rules/jcoc2z.htm "The Budget Enforcement Act: Its Operation Under a Budget Surplus," CRS Report for Congress, http://www.house.gov/rules/98-97.htm; "BUDGET: Eliminating the National Debt is Priority #1," Fritz Hollings's Newsroom   **p. 472,** E-conomics: "input-output analysis," *Encyclopedia Britannica online,* http://search.eb.com/eb/print?eu=43439; "economic forecasting," *Encyclopedia Britannica online,* http://search.eb.com/eb/article?query=economic+forecasting&ct=&eu=109000&tocid=25804   **p. 474,** Movers & Shakers: http://www.askmen.com/men/business_politics/29c_philip_knight.html www.nike.com http://www.stanfordalumni.org/news/magazine/1997/janfeb/articles/knight.html http://www.hoovers.com/free/co/factsheet.xhtml?COID=14254   **p. 475,** In the News: Department of Treasury Bureau of Public Debt, http://www.publicdebt.treas.gov/cgi-bin/cgiwrap/~www/opdpnhis.cgi http://www.publicdebt.treas.gov/opd/opdpenny.htm; "National Debt clock stops, despite trillions of dollars in red ink," CNN, online report, http://www.cnn.com/2000/US/09/07/debt.clock/index.html "Stopping the Clock: National Debt Clock to be Unplugged as Debt Shrinks," Associated Press story, reprinted on http://abcnews.go.com/sections/business/DailyNews/debtclock000515.html "National Debt Clock restarted," Associated Press story, reprinted on http://www.tallahassee.com/mld/tallahasee/business/3643411.htm?template=contentModule... and on http://abcnews.go.com/sections/business/DailyNews/debtclock020711.html   **p. 481,** Ethics in Action, Robert J. Barro, "The Ricardian Approach to Budget Deficits," *Journal of Economic Perspectives* 3 (Spring 1989); Jay Mathews, "How High Is the Deficit, the Dow? Most in Survey Didn't Know," *Hartford Courant,* October 19, 1995, and David Rosenbaum, "Congress Agrees on Final Details of Tax-Cut Bill," *New York Times,* May 26, 2001 **p. 483,** Connect to History: *The American Heritage Encyclopedia of American History,* John Mack Faragher, ed., New York: Henry Holt and Company, 1998; Gordon, John Steele, Hamilton's Blessing, New York: Walker & Company, 1997; Gordon, John Steele, "The Founding Wizard" American Heritage, v. 41, no.5, July/August, 1990; Owens, Mackubin, "Alexander Hamilton," *The Founders Almanac*

**Chapter 16   p. 489,** In the News: *Knoxville News-*

*Sentinel,* June 22, 2003 **p. 494,** Ethics in Action: "Getting your life back; Locally based resource center supports victims of identity theft," *The San Diego Union-Tribune,* October 20, 2003 **p. 496,** In the News: "Gold could become Islamic euro," The Times (London), October 8, 2003 **p. 499,** E-conomics: "Review of Top US Online Banking Sites Finds Many Common Features, but Significant Gaps in Functionality and Usability," PR Newswire Association, Inc., October 6, 2003 **p. 504,** Connect to History: Allen, Larry. *Encyclopedia of Money.* New York: Checkmark Books, 2001; Carson, Thomas, ed. *Gale Encyclopedia of United States Economic History.* Detroit: Gale Group, 1999; *Economics and the Historian,* Berkeley & Los Angles: University of California Press, 1996; "Evolution of Money and Banking in the United States," *Business Review.* Federal Reserve Bank of Dallas (December, 1975); Faragher, John Mack, ed. *The American Heritage Encyclopedia of American History.* New York: Henry Holt and Company, 1998; Froner, Eric & Garraty, John A. The Reader's Companion to American History. Boston: Houghton Mifflin Company, 1991; Mokyr, Joel, ed. *The Oxford Encyclopedia of Economic History.* New York: Oxford University Press, 2003; Morris, Richard B. & Morris, Jeffery B., ed. Encyclopedia of American History. New York: Harper Collins, 1996; Parish, Peter J. ed. *Reader's Guide to American History.* Chicago: Fitzroy Dearborn Publishers, 1997; Puth, Robert C. *American Economic History.* New York: Harcourt Brace Jovanovich College Publishers, 1988; Rosenbaum, Robert A, ed. *The Penguin Encyclopedia of American History.* New York, Penguin Reference, 2003 **p. 505,** In the News: Copyright 2003, American Banker-Bond Buyer, a division of Thomson, CardLine, October 3, 2003 **p. 506,** Span the Globe: Board of Governors of the Federal Reserve System, October 17, 2003 report on M1; Cincinnati Post Online Service: In US They Trust, September 19, 2000, "U.S. Anti-Counterfeiting Efforts Effective, Says Treasury," U.S. Embassy Report, Tokyo, Japan 2003 **p. 512,** Movers & Shakers: E-mail correspondence with Tony Brown; www.cdfifund.gov; www.morethanabank.com/kimsHouseFY04testimony040903.doc

**Chapter 17 p. 519,** In the News: "U.S.: Saddam's family took $1 billion from bank," CNN report, reprinted on http://www.cnn.com/2003/WORLD/meast/05/06/sprj.irq.main/index.html; "Jesse James," *Encyclopedia Britannica online,* http://search.eb.com/ebi/print?eu=297080; "Bonnie and Clyde," *Encyclopedia Britannica online,* http://search.eb.com/eb/print?eu=13655 **p. 523,** E-conomics: "Online bank aimed at truck drivers debuts," *Computerworld,* August 15, 2000, reprinted on http://www.cnn.com/2000/TECH/computing/08/15/ebank.for.truckers.idg/index.html;

"credit unions," Encyclopedia Britannica online, http://search.eb.com/eb/print?eu=27263 **p. 525,** In the News: Greg Ip, "U.S. Federal Reserve Cuts Funds Rate by Half a Point to 40-Year Low Level," *The Wall Street Journal,* November 7, 2001; "How Low Can They Go?," *Economist,* October 6, 2001; "Minutes of the Federal Open Market Committee" and "FOMC Statement on Interest Rates," January 3, 2001, March 20, 2001, April 18, 2001, May 15, 2001, October 2, 2001, and November 6, 2001; "Fed cuts rates a quarter point," CNN report, http://www.cnn.com/2001/BUSINESS/12/11/fed.rate.cut/index.html; "U.S. Fed leaves rates on hold," CNN report, http://www.cnn.com/2002/BUSINESS/asia/09/24/US.fed.biz/index.html **p. 531,** Ethics in Action: "Enron Collapse stirs echoes of '80s Savings and loan woes," *St. Petersburg Times,* January 13, 2002. Reprinted on http://www.sptimes.com/2002/01/13/news_pf/Columns/Enron_collapse_stirs_shtml **p. 535,** Movers & Shakers: http://www.myprimetime.com/work/ge/schultzbio/index.shtml; www.starbucks.com; Howard Schultz, *Pour Your Heart Into It: How Starbucks Built a Company One Cup at a Time, Hyperion,* 1997 **p. 536,** In the News: Peter White, "The Power of Money," *National Geographic,* January 1993; Frederic Dannen and Ira Silverman, : "The Supernote," *New Yorker,* October 23, 1995; "Russia Official Nods to Money Boost," *New York Times,* September 30, 1998; Michael Bryan et al. "Who Is That Guy on the $10 Bill?" *Economic Commentary: Federal Reserve Bank of Cleveland,* July 2000 **p. 539,** Span the Globe: "Close race in Argentina election," CNN report, reprinted on http://www.cnn.com/2003/WORLD/americas/04/27/argentina.poll/index.html; "Germany," *Encyclopedia Britannica online,* http://search.eb.com/eb/article?eu=109160&tocid=58204&query=hyperinflation&ct=; "Bolivia," *Encyclopedia Britannica online,* http://search.eb.com/eb/article?eu=108670&tocid=218814&query=hyperinflation&ct= **p. 543,** Connect to History: Foner, Eric & Garraty, John A. ed. *The Readers Companion to American History.* Boston: Houghton Mifflin Company. 1991; Greider, William. *Secrets of the Temple: How the Federal Reserve Runs the Country.* New York: Simon and Schuster. 1987; Morris, Richard B. and Morris, Jeffrey B. *Encyclopedia of American History.* New York: Harper Collins. 1996; Parish, Peter J. ed. *Reader's Guide to American History.* Chicago: Fitzroy Dearborn Publishers. 1997; Puth, Robert C. *American Economic History.* New York: the Dryden Press, 1982

**Chapter 18 p. 553,** In the News: "Paying the price of free trade: Shattered dreams," *Edmonton Journal* (Alberta), August 31, 2003 **p. 555,** Ethics in Action: "FTAA Environmental Outlook Bleak, Experts Say," Inter Press Service, Inter Press Service, October

14, 2003; "Pollution Intensive Industry In Mexico Under Nafta: Model And Empirical Evidence," The Fletcher Journal of Development Studies VOLUME XV, 1999  **p. 559,** In the News: "Automotive Coalition Company Executives Travel to Washington to Urge Bush Administration to End Steel Tariffs," PR Newswire Association, Inc., October 8, 2003; "End the Steel Tariffs," *The Washington Post,* September 26, 2003, p. A26  **p. 563,** Span the Globe: "Free Trade Area Of The Americas: Big stumbling blocks remain," *The Atlanta Journal and Constitution,* October 30, 2003; "NAFTA and Workers' Rights and Jobs," Public Citizen; "North American Free Trade Agreement," Wikipedia, the free encyclopedia  **p. 565,** Movers & Shakers, Information from Toyota's communications department. http://www.toyota.com/about/community/ education/mx_auto_training.html; http://archive. infoworld.com/articles/hn/xml/00/10/09/001009hn planettoyota.xml; http://www.jsonline.com/wheels/ peak/feb02/23136.asp  **p. 567,** In the News: "Czech couple says they paid middlemen for Wal-Mart jobs," *The Tuscaloosa News* (Alabama), October 27, 2003; "Controversy surrounds employees on L-1 Visas," *The Dallas Morning News,* July 23, 2003  **p. 571,** E-conomics: "US Aid Agency-Backed Project To Develop E-Commerce In Uzbekistan,"BBC Monitoring International Reports, June 20, 2003; Council on Foreign Relations, Inc., Foreign Affairs, September 2003–October 2003; "Bush and Foreign Aid," Copyright 2003 Scripps Howard, Inc., Scripps Howard News Service; "U.S. stingy, says new index method," Scripps Howard News Service, June 13, 2003  **p. 574,** In the News: "Trade imbalance not China's choice," *China Daily,* August 25, 2003; The Main Wire, October 31, 2003; "U.S. Try FX Report Finds No FX Manipulation," AFX News Limited, October 26, 2003  **p. 581,** Connect to History: Carnes, Marc C. MacMillan Information Now Encyclopedia: U.S. History. New York. MacMillan Library Reference, 1996; Schwarz, Frederick D. "Abominations," *American Heritage* (November/ December, 2003)

**Chapter 19   p. 587,** In the News: "Okinawan Longevity: Demographic and Epidemiological Perspectives," a study by Drs. D. Craig Willcox and Bradley J. Willcox, http://www.oic-longevity.wwma. net/Abstracts/Drs._Willcox_willcox.html; "World's oldest turns 116 in Japan," Associated Press Story, September 17, 2003, http://www.cnn.com/2003/ WORLD/asiapcf/east/09/16/japan.oldster.ap/index.html; "World's oldest man dies at 114," Associated Press story, September 29, 2003, http://www.cnn.com/2003/ WORLD/asiapcf/east/09/28/japan.oldest.ap/index.html; "Living Longer: Study: Japanese, Australians Live Longest," ABC news story, http://abcnews.go.com/

sections/world/DailyNews/lifeexpectancy000604.html; "Life is short in Sierra Leone," BBC News story, June 5, 2000, http://news.bbc.co.uk/2/hi/africa/778027.stm  **p. 592,** E-conomics: "Exporting Jobs Saves IT Money," from Computerworld magazine, March 23, 1999, http://www.cnn.com/TECH/computing/9903/23/ exportjobs.idg/index.html; "Finally a Productivity payoff from IT?," Fortune.Com, online version of Fortune Magazine, December 18, 2002, http://cnn.technology. printthis.clickability.com/pt/cpt?action=cpt&expire=- 1&urlID=489270…; "There's More to Consider than Cheap Labor," Computerworld magazine, April 28, 2003, http://www.computerworld.com/printthis/ 2003/0,4814,80662,00.html  **p. 596,** Movers & Shakers: www.ebay.com; http://yahoo.businessweek. com:/print/bwdaily/dnflash/aug2003/nf20030818_ 1844_db049.htm?pi  **p. 597,** In the News: Gina Chon, "Dropped Stitches," *Asiaweek,* December 22, 2000; Naomi Koppel, "Bush Policy May Break WTO Deadlock," Associate Pres, December 27, 2000; David Postman and Linda Mapes, "Why WTO Unified So Many Foes," *Seattle Times,* December 6, 1999; Leslie Kaufman and David Gonzalez, "Labor Standards Clash with Global Reality, New York Times, April 24, 2001; World Trade Organization web site, http://www.wto.org  **p. 601,** Span the Globe: Michael Fletcher, "Fewer People Searched by Customers in Past Year," *Washington Post,* October 19, 2000; Alex Keto, "White House Watch: Bush Put on Notice on Trade," Dow Jones Newswire, August 2, 2001; Daniel Machulaba, "U.S. Ports Are Losing the Battle to Keep Up with Overseas Trade," *The Wall Street Journal,* July 9, 2001; Jim Yardley, "Truck-Choked Border City Fears Being Bypassed," *New York Times,* March 15, 2001; U.S. Customs Service home page, http://www.customs. treas.gov/; "China-Japan trade war worsens," CNN report 6/5/01, http://www.cnn.com/2001/BUSINESS/ asia/06/05/china.tradewar/index.html  **p. 603,** In the News: "African Leaders Prepare for summit," IDG story, June 20, 2000, http://edition.cnn.com/2000/ TECH/computing/06/20/african.it.idg/; "Ghana tries to bridge computer-technology gap," *Computing* magazine, February 17, 1998, http://www.cnn.com/TECH/ computing/9802/17/ghana.internet/index.html  **p. 606,** Ethics in Action: "Haiti: Growth and Structure of the Economy," Library of Congress information online, http://countrystudies.us/haiti/45.htm; "Jean- Claude Duvalier," Library of Congress information online, http://countrystudies.us/haiti/18.htm  **p. 611,** Connect to History: Carnes, Marc C. *MacMillan Information Now Encyclopedia: U.S. History.* New York. MacMillan Library Reference, 1996; "The Past, Present and Future of the Multilateral Trading System," *WT Conference Daily,* September 10, 2003